OZ CLARKE
WINE
BUYING
GUIDE
2000

SIXTEENTH EDITION

'WEBSTER'S'
THE COMPLETE WINE
BUYER'S HANDBOOK

TED SMART

The information and prices contained in the Guide
were correct to the best of our knowledge when we
went to press, and the impression of relative price
and relative value is almost certainly still accurate,
even if a particular price has changed.

Although every care has been taken in the
preparation of the guide, neither the publishers nor
the editors can accept any liability for any
consequences arising from the use of information
contained herein.

Oz Clarke's Wine Buying Guide is an
annual publication. We welcome any suggestions
you might have for the next edition.

Editor Bill Evans
Wine Editor Margaret Rand
Database Managing Editor Loma Bateson
Price Guides Editor Julie Ross
Editorial Assistants Rebecca Khan, Oliver
Robinson, Sarah Cooke
Design Assistants Keith Bambury, Jane Wallker
Indexer Naomi Good
Database Consultants Cognitive Applications,
Brighton
Production Kåren Smith
Publishing Director Claire Harcup
Art Director Nigel O'Gorman
Photography for Millennium Party Guide Stephen
Bartholomew

Advertising Sales
Logie Bradshaw Media Limited.
Strathallan House, Fernville Lane,
Midland Road, Hemel Hempstead,
Herts HP2 4LS
tel 0144 2233331, fax 0144 2231131

A LITTLE, BROWN/WEBSTERS BOOK

First published in 1999 by
Little, Brown and Company (UK)
Brettenham House
Lancaster Place
LONDON WC2E 7EN

This edition produced for
The Book People Ltd
Hall Wood Avenue
Haydock
St Helens WA11 QU2

Created and designed by
Websters International Publishers Limited
Axe and Bottle Court
70 Newcomen Street
LONDON SE1 1YT

Oz Clarke's Wine Buying Guide 2000 Edition
Copyright © 1999 Webster's International
Publishers

A CIP catalogue for this book is available from
the British Library.

ISBN 0-316-85165-5

Printed and bound in the UK by
Clays Ltd, St Ives plc

CONTENTS

Oz Clarke's Millennium Party Guide: *centre pages*

INTRODUCTION

I don't know which I find more shocking. That 30 years ago the average price of a bottle of wine (in 1999 terms) was £15? That 15 years ago I was able to talk to the wine buyer for one of the big supermarket groups and he could say 'Australian wine? No, it won't catch on. Doesn't taste good and doesn't offer value for money'? That Piat d'Or was £3.79 in 1983 and is still £3.79 today? That we still drink Piat d'Or? That Piat d'Or is still in the lists of top wine brands?

And what about other old chestnuts like Lutomer Rizling? Well, to my amazement, in bars and restaurants Lutomer Rizling is still one of the most popular brands. And if it's sherry you're talking about, Harvey's Bristol Cream still outsells the lot. Port? Cockburn's Special Reserve walks over the opposition. Just as it always did.

So have we really made any progress in the 16 years since I first wrote this *Guide*? Have we really changed at all? Oh yes we have. Don't be fooled by the statistics. We live in a different wine world now, and in nearly every way, a better one.

I mean, take the average price of a bottle. If, today, we had to shell out 15 quid for an average bottle every time we wanted a glass of wine…well, no wonder the wine culture was an elitist, minority interest that most people dismissed as 'not for folk like us'. The average price of a bottle of wine is now less than £4, and as our tastings show, you can still drink well and interestingly at £2.99 a bottle. So the wine revolution is a reality, and millions upon millions of British people can, and do, enjoy wine on a regular basis.

And what about that Australian wine? When I look at the 1985 edition of this *Guide* I find I was having to exhort readers to buy any sort of New World wine. Not just readers, merchants too – because there were virtually no examples of the wines over here. I gave Australia four pages in that *Guide*. This year it has 31 pages. (Oh, and that supermarket? It went on to become the biggest seller of Aussie wine in the UK.) Chile has gone from 1½ pages to 9; NZ from 1½ to 11. But Bordeaux has dropped from 84 to 63; Germany from 25 to14.

So the upstarts have leapt ahead. Bordeaux is still immensely important to those of us who like to read about wine, but less and less relevant to those of us who drink it. Germany has never recovered from its suicidal charge towards cheaper and cheaper wine, usually labelled Liebfraumilch. I have to say, 16 years ago it all seemed a bit obvious to me, but then I had just returned from a theatre trip to Australia gobsmacked at how tasty and ripe cheap wines could be over there. And not just there. California could do it just as well, and South Africa had the potential, as did New Zealand, Chile and Argentina. What some of them already had, and what they all gradually acquired, was a 'New World' attitude: make nice wine, please the customer and charge a fair price.

Now, I'd have said that surely every wine producer should have that attitude. Surely that's what a successful business should be based on. Indeed it is. But wine, only 16 years ago, wasn't a business like others, aiming to please and satisfy. With a few noble exceptions, mystification, snobbery and complacency were the order of the day for producers and merchants alike.

What we have experienced in the 16 years since this *Guide* first saw light of day is an explosion of consumer power in this country, and we should be proud. British consumers, by voting with their wallets and forcing producers to start giving them – well, surprise, surprise – a nice wine at a fair price, have changed forever the balance of power.

But for this to happen, we wine drinkers needed allies. And we found two. First, the supermarkets got in on the act. Once they had decided they were missing a trick with wine, it became possible to democratize it.

They all took a leaf out of Sainsbury's book by learning to trade on a touch of wine's mystique to upgrade their corporate images, at the very same time as starting to demand control over the kinds of flavours they wished to supply to their customers – and of course, the prices they wished to charge. Befuddling claptrap designed to exclude rather than include the average punter wouldn't wash as soon as you could pick up a bottle of wine as easily as a pack of lamb chops and a bag of potatoes.

But this still wouldn't work if the product wasn't right. It's all very well avoiding the condescending patter of the worst sort of old-style wine merchant, but at least he might have given you some small germ of self-confidence that the wine you served was the *right* one, even though you thought it tasted horrid. If you were going to have to make the judgement yourself, in a self-service aisle, then you were going to have to rely on a concept that was only just rearing its beautiful head back then – that wine should taste nice, so *you* could say, 'I'll have that *because* it tastes nice.'

In which case we needed our second ally, one who had the New World attitude (nice wine, fair price, etc…), and we found it in Australia. At last, we could make our own decisions because the flavours were so clear and ripe. Either we did or we didn't like them. And New World labels were just so simple – the country of origin, the people who made the wine, and the grape variety.

Above all, the grape variety. It sounds a bit simplistic, but a little thing like labelling the wine according to the grape variety, the factor that most clearly indicates its flavour, was one of the most revolutionary changes in our wine world. Because it put the power of choice in our hands for the first time.

The unstoppable march of varietally labelled wines forced the old-fashioned countries to reconsider their positions. Of course, the top-level wines disdained the practice, saying it demeaned their geographical birthright, their *terroir*, but the vast majority of Europe's vineyards had no cachet attached to their place of origin. The idea of being able to label according to grape variety was seized upon in what had been the wastelands of southern Portugal, central Spain, southern Italy, Eastern Europe – but above all in the South of France. Producers found they could massage the region-based vin de pays – or 'country wine' – regulations and plaster the grape variety prominently across the label. Suddenly, the New World could be found with a French accent bubbling with excitement on the shores of the Med. And if you look at statistics to find out what is the biggest, most successful category of wines in the British market, it's French vin de pays, usually with a grape variety like Cabernet, Merlot, Syrah, Sauvignon or Chardonnay on the label. More than one bottle in ten of wine sold in Britain is now vin de pays. And if you wonder how on earth we're still drinking Piat d'Or when all the other plonk brands of yore have sunk without trace into the sewers of history, well, Piat d'Or is a vin de pays nowadays, and not a bad glass of grog.

Sixteen years ago I was virtually blackballed by large sections of the more traditional wine world. I was regarded as a dangerous hooligan, a radical, spewing revolutionary ideas and dissent. There wasn't much discussion available for me and the small band of similarly minded wine fans who wanted to lead a movement that had as its first and only real maxim the desire for wine to be pleasant, affordable and available to as many people as possible.

Now, I look around and I worry that I'm almost mainstream. Well, if mainstream means searching out the best flavours, encouraging producers round the world to produce wines I think you'll like, and to charge prices that we can all afford, so be it. I leave the 20th century in the mainstream. I never thought I'd hear myself saying that.

As for the 21st century, there'll be new battles to wage. But I won't be on my own this time: I'll have an army of wine drinkers behind me all searching for nice wines at a fair price – and if you follow, I'll lead.

HOW TO USE THIS BOOK

The first part of the *Guide* features specific wine recommendations. The Best Buys are the pick of the crop from the UK's top merchants; the Supermarket Selection has been chosen from a huge array of own-brand and exclusive wines to help you take advantage of their low prices and ready availability. Then we've let five wine merchants have their say, dreaming up their Ideal Cellars alongside my own.

In most of the wine region chapters you'll find further specific recommendations in the form of an Instant Cellar: a selection of wines to help you acquaint yourself with the region in greater depth, without breaking the bank. And there are wine recommendations in the Merchant Directory at the back of the book, too.

If you are looking for specific wines, turn straight to the Price Guides. These are the pages on which we have collated the current retail prices of the thousands of wines we hold on our computer database. Just a glance at the price of the same wine from one merchant to another can show why this information is so valuable – the difference can be dramatic.

In addition, many wines are in limited distribution: it is therefore of crucial importance to find out where the wines are stocked, and whether they'll sell by mail order. And that's where the Merchant Directory comes in: it gives you the low-down on over 100 of the UK's top wine merchants, chosen on the basis of the quality and interest of their lists. If you want to find local suppliers, merchants are listed by region in the Who's Where directory on page 450; if you want to find a specialist in a particular country's wines, you'll find a list of these at the beginning of each country's Price Guides.

But buying wine can feel like a lucky dip when you are faced with shelves or lists full of unfamiliar names. The chapters on the wine-producing countries of the world will help you to develop a nose for the wines that suit your palate. They provide a quick introduction and a guide to the grapes, wines styles, regions and producer names, plus a review of recent vintages – in other words, a complete run-down of what's on the bottle label.

To get the most out of the Price Guides in the book, please remember that they are not meant to replace up-to-date merchants' lists. What they *do*, however, is give you a unique opportunity to compare prices; to develop a sense of what you can expect to pay for any given wine; to spot a bargain; to work out what you can afford – *and to find it*. This book is an invaluable reference whenever you are ordering or buying wine.

It is our aim to make sure this *Guide* improves every year. For this edition we have made the Price Guides easier to use than ever before, with all the prices for each wine listed *together* for the first time. We hope you find the *Guide* easy and rewarding to use. Please let us know what you think: that way we can produce an even better *Guide* next year.

SYMBOLS AND ABBREVIATIONS

In the Price Guides, the letters in brackets are abbreviations for the names of the stockists for each of the wines listed. The key to these abbreviations is on page 8 and full details of these and other merchants appear in the Merchant Directory on pages 413–49.

★–★★★★★ These star ratings appear in the Producers Who's Who sections, and apply to the quality of wine currently being made by a producer, ranging from good to world class. A star in brackets (★) indicates that the producer can attain that quality but does not always do so.

£ This symbol is used in the Bordeaux chapter to denote producers that are particularly good value – though that's not the same as saying that they're cheap.

EC and **IB** *See Red Bordeaux Price Guides.*

NV This abbreviation is used in the Champagne Price Guides to denote Non-vintage wines.

HOW THE PRICE GUIDES WORK

We hope you find the Price Guides fairly self explanatory, but to make full use of them you should be aware of the following:

● All prices listed are *per bottle inclusive of VAT*, unless otherwise stated. The prices we list are those which applied in the late spring/early summer of 1999. When comparing prices remember that some wine merchants sell only by the case. In this instance, we have arrived at a bottle price by dividing by 12 the VAT-inclusive price of a single case. Where merchants who sell by the case will sell cases of mixed bottles, we have used the bottle price that would apply in a mixed case.

● Wines are listed in price bands – under £5, £5 to £5.99, and so on. Price bands run from the lowest to the highest. Within each band the wines are listed in alphabetical order. If more than one vintage of the same wine appears within one price band, these run from the most recent to the oldest.

● Stockists are listed using the abbreviations shown over the page. All stockists for a particular wine are shown after its entry in ascending order of price. The wines are placed in bands according to the lowest price for which each is available. This means that the highest prices for a wine may overstep the upper limit of the price band in which the wine is featured. Before you get too agitated about variations in price, remember that wine warehouses,

for example, often come out much cheaper than individual merchants because you have to buy by the case, they do not deliver, they do not have smart high street premises to maintain, and so on. Equally, there's no getting away from the fact that the price of a given wine sometimes varies wildly for no good reason.

● When clubs have both member and non-member prices we have used the *non-member* prices.

RED BORDEAUX PRICE GUIDES

The Red Bordeaux Price Guides are a special case. The châteaux are listed alphabetically regardless of appellation or class, with prices for each château given in order of vintage from the most recent to the oldest. There are some dramatic price variations here. Note that while most of the prices are per bottle, inclusive of all duty and VAT charges, others are per case, with extra to pay on top before you can have the wine delivered.

A wine quoted **EC** (ex-cellars) is offered on an *en primeur* basis (i.e. as a young wine) in Bordeaux or at the château in the summer following the vintage; one quoted **IB** (in bond) is offered in bond in the UK. All EC and IB prices are **per case**.

The EC price simply includes the price of the wine in the bottle and excludes shipping, duties and taxes such as VAT. The IB price includes shipping, but still excludes duties and taxes.

The EC price is usually payable when the wine is offered *en primeur*. Other costs (including VAT on both invoices) become payable when the wine is shipped. The *crus classés* and better *bourgeois* are shipped two years after the wine is offered, the *petits châteaux* and the lesser *bourgeois* after a year. You should check beforehand the exact terms of sale with your merchant who will give you a projection of the final 'duty paid delivered' price at current rates of shipping, duty and VAT.

MERCHANT NAME CODES

These are the merchants whose prices are featured in the Price Guides. The abbreviations
are shown in brackets after the price of each of the listed wines they stock.

AD	Adnams		MORR	William Morrison Supermarkets
AME	Amey's Wines		MV	Morris & Verdin
AS	Ashley Scott		NA	Nadder Wines Ltd
ASD	ASDA		NEZ	Le Nez Rouge
AUS	Australian Wine Club		NI	James Nicholson
AV	Averys of Bristol		NLW	New London Wine
BAL	Ballantynes of Cowbridge		NO	The Nobody Inn
BALL	Balls Brothers		NZW	New Zealand Wines Direct
BAN	Adam Bancroft		OD	Oddbins
BEN	Bennetts		PEN	Penistone Court Wine Cellars
BER	Berry Bros. & Rudd		PHI	Philglas & Swiggot
BIB	Bibendum		PIP	Christopher Piper Wines
BOT	Bottoms Up		PLA	Terry Platt
BO	Booths		PLAY	Playford Ros
BU	Butlers Wine Cellar		POR	Portland Wine Co
BY	Anthony Byrne		RAE	Raeburn Fine Wines
CAP	Cape Province Wines		REI	Reid Wines (1992) Ltd
CAV	Cave Cru Classé		RES	La Réserve
CB	Corney & Barrow		RIP	Howard Ripley
CHA	Châteaux Wines		ROB	Roberson
CO	CWS (Co-op)		ROS	Rose Tree Wine Company
COC	Cockburns of Leith		RSJ	RSJ Wine Company
CON	Connolly's		SAF	Safeway
CRO	Croque-en-Bouche		SAI	Sainsbury's
DI	Direct Wine Shipments		SAT	Satchells
DOM	Domaine Direct		SAV	Savage Selection
ELL	Ben Ellis Wines		SO	Somerfield
FA	Farr Vintners		SOM	Sommelier Wine Co
FLE	Le Fleming Wines		STA	Frank Stainton Wines
FORT	Fortnum & Mason		STE	Stevens Garnier Wine Merchants
FRI	Friarwood		TAN	Tanners
FUL	Fuller's		TES	Tesco
GAU	Gauntleys		THR	Thresher
GW	Great Western Wine		TW	T & W Wines
HA	John Harvey & Sons		UB	The Ubiquitous Chip
HAH	Haynes Hanson & Clark		UN	Unwins
HAW	Roger Harris Wines		VA	Valvona & Crolla
HED	Hedley Wright		VIC	Victoria Wine
HIG	High Breck Vintners		VIN	Vintage Wines Ltd
JER	Jeroboams		WAI	Waitrose
JON	S H Jones		WAT	Waterloo Wine Co
JU	Justerini & Brooks		WHI	Whitesides of Clitheroe
LAY	Lay & Wheeler		WIW	Wines of Westhorpe Ltd
LEA	Lea & Sandeman		WR	Wine Rack
LIB	Liberty Wines		WRI	Wright Wine Co
MAJ	Majestic		WS	Wine Society
MAR	Marks & Spencer plc		WT	Wine Treasury
MI	Millésima		WY	Peter Wylie Fine Wines
MON	Montrachet		YAP	Yapp Brothers
MOR	Moreno Wines		YOU	Noel Young Wines

BEST BUYS

Merchants from every corner of the British Isles sent in the pick of their wines for us to taste this year, and the result was our biggest-ever selection to choose from, and a reassuring sign that homogenization of flavour in retail outlets is still being held at bay. For now, at least

The British drinks industry is indulging in an orgy of consolidation at the moment, mostly involving breweries, pubs and spirits companies. But wine retailers are affected too, and the usual result of consolidation is less choice and worse quality. Well, tell that to individualistic outfits of overachievers, like Waterloo Wine Company, Great Western Wines and the Australian Wine Club, and tell that to the buyers of giant organizations like Somerfield, Safeway and Tesco, because both large and small have triumphed this year in our tastings.

In general, large companies have been best in the under-£4 and under-£5 categories, and smaller companies have excelled at the very top end of the Best Buys and in our 'Magnificent Misfits' section. But big companies *have* scored amongst the top selections, and independents *do* figure at under a fiver.

Please bear in mind that wines are not made in infinite quantities – some of these may well sell out, but the following year's vintage should then become available

MY 2000 TOP DOZEN

What an encouraging show of strength from the world's most diverse and imaginative wine scene – as we enter a very challenging period at the start of the new Millennium

1 **1998 Chardonnay, Allandale, Hunter Valley, £7.99, Australian Wine Club (white, Australia)**
Oh wow! I remember wines like this! This is a throwback to the great old days of Aussie Chardonnay. Banish all thoughts of delicacy and restraint, and get set for a rollercoaster ride of Australia's answer to great Burgundy, offering all the oatmeal and cashew nut and dripping buttered toast of a great Burgundy – then doubling the concentration and halving the price!

2 **1997 The Fergus, Tim Adams, Clare Valley, £9.50, Australian Wine Club (red, Australia)**
The Fergus won our tasting two years ago, and any of you who tried the wine cannot have forgotten its astonishing, scurrilous, irreverent Judgement Day cauldron of self-indulgent delights. Well, 1997 is a leaner year for the Fergus than that magical 1995, so it flirts briefly with the mainstream before throwing itself somersaulting backwards into a millrace of mulberries, sweet baked apples, plums and cracked black pepper which gobble up handful after handful of dill, eucalyptus and mint.
also at Bottoms Up, Thresher, Victoria Wine, Wine Rack

3 **1997 Alsace Gewürztraminer Kaefferkopf Cuvée Catherine, Martin Schaetzel, £13.99, Great Western Wine (white)**
Time for a little European restraint? Don't bank on it. This is another self-indulgent smasher. Gewürztraminer as a grape is a hedonist's delight when it's properly made, and this bundles peaches, pears and lychees into a nectar of honey, rose petals and the smooth skincare fragrance of Nivea Crême.

4 **1997 Shiraz, Water Wheel, Bendigo, £8.50, Australian Wine Club (red, Australia)**
You want a red wine that oozes flavour? Step right on to the Water Wheel, where chocolate and Fowlers Black Treacle bubble away contentedly in the company of blackcurrant, liquorice, eucalyptus, toffee and mint.

5 **1995 Walker Zinfandel, Boeger, El Dorado Walker Vineyards, £10.99, Great Western Wine (red, United States)**
We can't let Australia have it all its own way in the OTT stakes. This is the kind of brilliant, brash red that catapulted the Golden West to fame years ago. Loads of old-style overripe fruit, loads of dates and figs and chewing tobacco, all mixed up with cedar and bitter-sweet peppery prunes.

6 **1996 The Custodian Grenache, d'Arenberg, McLaren Vale, £7.99, Oddbins (red, Australia)**
A ghettoblaster of a wine, a wall-shaking, eardrum-numbing and juddering, jiving Mother of a wine. A flood of sweet strawberry sauce, laced with runny toffee and liquorice, but peppered with herbs and the bitter bite of bark.

7 **1997 Crozes-Hermitage Cuvée Alberic Bouvet, Gilles Robin, £9.69, Great Western Wine (red, Rhône)**
Again, if you think we're clambering back on to the saner shores of France, you're only half-right because this red is steaming with dark rich loganberry fruit, dollops of cream sullied by coal smoke and the haunting memory of violets.

8 **1998 Riesling, Tim Adams, Clare Valley, £7.99, Australian Wine Club (white, Australia)**
At last, something restrained from Australia: a full, dry white from the woefully underrated Riesling grape. Yet in the Boris Karloff-like hands of red wine supremo Tim Adams, the delicate Riesling becomes assertive and imperious, its hard, lean, pithy core wrapped about with apple blossom scent and the flesh of super-ripe Bramley apple – all tangled with cloves and nutmeg. *also at Tesco*

9 **1994 Côtes du Rhône, Domaine de St-Georges, André Vignal, £6.10, Christopher Piper Wines (red)**
The Côtes du Rhône can produce memorable wines at seriously affordable prices, but it takes a passionate Francophile like Christopher Piper to winkle out the best. This is full, rich, perfumed with violets and lilies and the manly scent of Imperial Leather soap, and thick with the sweet summer ripeness of cherries and damsons.

10 **1996 Shiraz, Pikes, Clare Valley, £9.95, Lea & Sandeman (red, Australia)**
Is there such a thing as 'restrained' Shiraz? Almost, nearly, but never quite. This starts out serious, demanding a bit more cerebral attention than usual, but the effect doesn't last long, as the wine courses down your throat and the roaring richness of chocolate and prunes – kept just this side of pure indulgence by the herb scrape of eucalyptus and mint – rapidly takes over.

11 **1998 Verdelho, Fox Creek, McLaren Vale, £7.99, Noel Young (white, Australia)**
Fascinating wine at an irresistible price. A heavenly flavour of banana and nectarine, soft, but exotic and pushed nearer the kasbah by the scent of clove and cinnamon.

12 **1998 Sauvignon Blanc, Palliser Estate, Martinborough, £8.05, Anthony Byrne (white, New Zealand)**
Amazingly 1998 was almost too hot for Sauvignon in the traditional cool climate of New Zealand. But Palliser is a brilliant estate, and has produced a white that is a little richer, more syrupy even, than usual, but piled full of pear and green melon fruit, and still prickling with grapefruit acidity. *also at Bottoms Up, Le Fleming, Philglas & Swiggot, Thresher, Victoria Wine, Wine Rack*

THE RUNNERS UP

Twenty more palate-pleasers with a range of flavours as wide-reaching as the most demanding wine lover could want

1 1995 Valpolicella Superiore Ripassa, Zenato, £7.99, Bottoms Up, Wine Rack (red, Italy)
One of the great oddball taste experiences: this remarkable red has a slight sourness almost like sherry, and a bitterness like almond skins, but a pulsing heart pumped full of plums and cherries and cedar.

2 1998 Unwooded Chardonnay, Chapel Hill, South Australia, £6.99, Tesco (white)
Delightfully fresh, with gentle peach and pineapple fruit that will go honeyed over the months and gradually dissolve its shroud of mineral dust.
also at Australian Wine Club

3 1996 Vacqueyras, Château de Roques, £7.10, Haynes, Hanson & Clark (red, Rhône)
Lovely Rhône red – gentle but weighty, not at all frivolous, perfectly balancing sweet cherry and raspberry fruit with the heady scent of bayleaf and Angostura.

4 1998 Riesling, St Hallett, Eden Valley, £7.99, Australian Wine Club (white, Australia)
Wonderfully refreshing Riesling, once again in the burly hands of a Shiraz expert. There's a fairly aggressive acid heart to the wine, with grapefruit, lime and kumquat all squabbling for ascendancy, but there's also a lovely windblown lime blossom and honeysuckle scent that revives the senses and freshens the appetite.
also at Bottoms Up, Wine Rack

5 1996 Chardonnay, Waipara West, Waipara, £9.99, Waterloo Wine Co. (white, New Zealand)
All the New World weight and ripeness that NZ Chardies do so well, with a calm, mellow cream-and-hazelnuts flavour and gentle apple acidity that's pure Burgundy.

6 1997 Crozes-Hermitage, Cave des Clairmonts, £6.99, Waitrose (red, France)
Classic northern Rhône loganberry, damson and cream flavours, seasoned with coal dust and violets at a seriously affordable price.

7 1998 Chardonnay, Longridge, Stellenbosch, £8.99, Oddbins (white, South Africa)
Big, powerful Chardonnay from the Cape blending a toasty-smoke oak scent with softer oatmeal and hazelnut mellowness. It's full, it's fat, but it's balanced.

8 1997 Overlook Chardonnay, Landmark, California, £12.99, Oddbins (white, United States)
Is this too much of a good thing? Is it a bit too oaky and domineering? Is that rich butter and crème fraiche and positively syrupy sumptuous nutty fatness too much? Well, what are good things for if they can't go OTT now and then?

9 1997 Douro, Quinta do Crasto, £6.76, Savage Selection (red, Portugal)
Beautiful, classy, perfumed red that has become a little more reserved than before. Hmm…. It's still got that beguiling scent of violets and wisteria, and a juicy damson fruit that oozes perfumed ripeness – don't let it get any more serious than this, please.
also at Adnams, Sommelier, T&W, Valvona & Crolla, Noel Young

10 1997 Semillon, Peter Lehmann, Barossa, £5.49, ASDA (white, Australia)
Australian Semillon can be rather haughty and stand-offish in its youth. But that's not Peter Lehmann's way. He's an openhearted kind of a guy and this wine has a lovely perfume like custard creams and hot cross buns to counter the snappy zest of grapefruit and lime.
also at Fuller's

⓫ 1997 Rully 'La Chaume', Chartron et Trébuchet, £12.24, Jeroboams (white, Burgundy)

Classy white Burgundy to drink now or for aging a bit. Either way, you'll enjoy the gentle oatmeal and hazelnut mellowness and a slightly meaty, but typically Burgundian, 'sauvage' scent.

⓬ 1997 Elston Chardonnay, Te Mata, Hawkes Bay, £13.69, Bottoms Up, Thresher, Victoria Wine, Wine Rack (white, New Zealand)

This used to be more Meursault than Meursault itself in its cashew-and-oatmeal understated dry yet luscious style. It's still a lovely wine and still has some Meursault character, but now also some peachy fruit and a rather candyish, sugary perfume.
also at Balls Brothers, Portland, T&W

⓭ 1997 Cabernet/Malbec, Tatachilla, South Australia, £6.99, Bottoms Up, Wine Rack (red)

This bursts with black cherry and juicy plum fruit, but also shows a strange Malbec character of raw grape skins and eelskin leather that is inexplicably but unquestionably attractive.

⓮ 1997 Pinot Noir, Palliser Estate, Martinborough, £11.05, Anthony Byrne (red, New Zealand)

Palliser Pinot usually has a little more floral aroma and a little more sweet summer fruit than this, but it's still good stuff, and rather Burgundian in its strange blend of stewed cherries and plums with dried apricot and the crumbs of a chocolate brownie.
also at Bottoms Up, Thresher, Victoria Wine, Wine Rack

⓯ 1997 Anjou-Villages Brissac, Domaine des Rochelles, J-Y LeBreton, £7.35, RSJ (red, Loire)

How refreshing that this overlooked Loire red style can still poke its nose through the assembled heavyweights. '97 produced lovely reds in the Loire Valley, and this is richer than usual, with deep raspberry and blackcurrant fruit and enjoyable mineral dryness, like pebbles washed by a stream.
also at Tanners

⓰ 1997 Riesling, Pewsey Vale, Eden Valley, £5.99, Bottoms Up, Thresher, Victoria Wine, Wine Rack (white, Australia)

Another example of why we should look to less fashionable grape varieties for top value: Riesling from red wine experts Yalumba that's full and richly ripe – the honey almost losing the battle with lemon sherbet, lime cordial and a whiff of petrol.
also at Oddbins

⓱ 1998 Verdelho, David Traeger, Victoria, £8.50, Australian Wine Club (white, Australia)

The same story again. Unknown grape, great flavour, great value. Lovely angelica and goldengage fruit teased and tantalized by parsley scent and the sting of nettles.
also at Bottoms Up, Wine Rack

⓲ 1996 Cabernet Sauvignon, Castillo de Molina Reserva, Viña San Pedro, Lontue, £5.95, Roberson (red, Chile)

Chile's inability to shine this year has been dispiriting, but here at last is a warming rich stew of blackcurrant and chunky plums seasoned with soft, warm oak.
also at Morrisons

⓳ 1997 Shiraz, Tim Adams, Clare Valley, £8.99, Tesco (red, Australia)

This needs a year or two to throw off its slightly nervous cloak of red fruit and tannin and emerge pumping us full of blackberries, black plums, chocolate and eucalyptus.
also at Australian Wine Club

⓴ 1997 Montes Alpha Chardonnay, Montes, Curicó, £8.99, Morrisons (white, Chile)

Good gentle Chardonnay, slightly syrupy in texture, with attractively fleshy fruit and a vaguely briny undertow of seashells.

THE ECONOMY DOZEN

It really does pay to trade up a quid. Despite our encouraging discoveries at £3.99, you're far more likely to get really interesting wines at up to £4.99

❶ 1997 Riesling, Stoneleigh Vineyard, Marlborough, £4.99, Bottoms Up, Thresher, Victoria Wine, Wine Rack (white, New Zealand)
Lovely rich but dry wine, awash with honey yet sharpened to rapier keenness by lemon, lime and grapefruit.
also at Oddbins

❷ 1998 Baga, Bela Fonte, Beiras, £4.99, Unwins (red, Portugal)
A stunning and unlikely mix of savoury black pepper and clove spice with the gooey richness of cherry cake and sweet red plums.

❸ 1998 Vin de Pays d'Oc Viognier, Domaine de la Ferrandière, £4.95, Waterloo Wine (white, southern France)
Bright, ripe apricot flavour, flecked with honey and mint, and streaked with the acidity of a juicy Bramley apple.

❹ 1998 Basa, Rueda, £4.95, Adnams (white, Spain)
You don't think of Spain as a place capable of producing tangy, tingling, aggressively dry whites. But this wine has a real zip of lemon and grapefruit zest, a whiff of anis and some reassuring glycerine ripeness too.
also at Bennetts, Croque-en-Bouche, Le Fleming

❺ 1998 Rioja Valdemar, Martínez Bujanda, £4.99, Bottoms Up, Thresher, Victoria Wine, Wine Rack (red, Spain)
It's rare to find a really tasty bargain Rioja. This one's soft, fresh, with a bright, happy-faced raspberry and apple fruit to soothe the slightly earthy undertow.

❻ 1998 Bin 65 Chardonnay, Lindemans, South Eastern Australia, £4.99, Somerfield (white)
This is the Aussie Chardonnay that led our white wine revolution. Lindemans now makes nearly 20 million bottles of this lovely soft pineapple, peaches 'n' cream white each year, and it's never been better.
widely available elsewhere

❼ 1998 Alsace Pinot Blanc Réserve, Turckheim, £4.99, Bottoms Up, Thresher, Victoria Wine, Wine Rack (white, Alsace)
Fresh, but full Pinot Blanc with a soft, honeyed texture, a nice apple and lemon freshness, and a twist of spice.

❽ 1998 Cabernet Sauvignon Rosé 'Doña Paula', Santa Rita, Maipo, £4.99, Le Nez Rouge (rosé, Chile)
This is lovely stuff, bursting with Cabernet flavours of blackcurrant and leaves, yet with a ripe New World syrupy nuttiness too.

❾ 1998 Pinot Grigio, La Vis, Trentino, £4.99, Valvona & Crolla (white, Italy)
Bright, fluffy apple flesh flavour, the scent of an orchard bower, and a refreshing streak of lemon acidity. Perfect picnic white.

❿ 1996 Verdejo/Chardonnay, Albacora, £4.99, CWS (white, Spain)
Half-price Burgundy from northern Spain! Soft oatmeal and hazelnut texture, a lemony zing and a truly Burgundian smell that resembles a really good pork sausage!

⓫ 1997 Vacqueyras, Vignerons de Beaumes-de-Venise, £4.99, Majestic (red, Rhône)
A very attractive gentle Rhône red with a meandering strawberry fruit-gum ripeness stroked lightly with herbs.

⓬ 1997 Merlot, Valdivieso, Central Valley, £4.99, Bottoms Up, Thresher, Victoria Wine, Wine Rack (red, Chile)
Good and plummy, if a touch stewy, and the oak is sweet. I'd prefer a fuller, fresher fruit and less oak, but there you go.

BARGAINS UNDER £4

Maybe the strong pound is beginning to have an effect after all, because the selection of wine we tried at the crucial £3.99 price point was very strong this year – and the wines came from all kinds of places, not just the usual suspects

1 1998 Tempranillo, Santa Julia, Mendoza, £3.99, Somerfield (red, Argentina)
So soft, so utterly easy to drink and enjoy, with a gentle pudding fruit, a twist of pepper and the scent of apple blossom.

2 1998 Vin de Pays d'Oc Syrah, £3.49, Safeway (red, southern France)
This is what Vin de Pays d'Oc is supposed to be like, but so rarely is – full of the ripe, rich fruit of France's far South, scented with the hillside herbs. Oh, and affordable.

3 1998 Chardonnay Sur Lie, Danie de Wet, Robertson, £3.99, Oddbins (white, South Africa)
Fresh, bright and simple: beautifully balanced with a bright apple and green melon fruit, a spoon of honey and sprinkle of mineral dust.

4 1997 Bulgarian Oaked Chardonnay, Rousse Region, £3.69, Safeway (white)
There should be dozens of attractive, affordable Bulgarian Chardonnays, but there's just one – this one – a most individual wine, soft, well-made but hardly recognizable as Chardonnay with its pear and peach fruit and its perfume of Pink Camay and Oil of Ulay.

5 1997 Montepulciano d'Abruzzo, Miglanico, £3.99, Unwins (red, Italy)
Pretty powerful stuff, this, and definitely not mainstream. A good, sturdy mouthful, with chunky stewed plum and strawberry fruit and a splash of raspberry vinegar.

6 1997 Nanya Estate Malbec/Ruby Cabernet, Angove's, South Australia, £3.99, Bottoms Up, Thresher, Victoria Wine, Wine Rack (red)
A bit coarse – but so what? Solid, fresh red fruit given a semi-serious veneer by a swatch of leather and a handful of earth.

7 Vin de Pays d'Oc Grenache Prestige, £3.69, Tesco (red, southern France)
Praise be! Another tasty Vin de Pays d'Oc. Enjoyably direct strawberry fruit-gum ripeness tempered by Mediterranean herbs.

8 1998 Barrel Fermented Chenin Blanc, Ryland's Grove, Stellenbosch, £3.99, Tesco (white, South Africa)
This has become an extremely dependable and enjoyable label, showing just how delightful Chenin can be when it's fully ripe, with a beguiling honey and greengage fruit and just a hint of toast.

9 1997 Vin de Pays du Gers, Jean des Vignes, £3.75, Savage Selection (white, southern France)
Gers is a name to look out for if you like really snappy, zesty French dry whites. This has a lemon and lime zest, green apple style that cuts like a surgeon's scalpel.

10 1998 Australian Shiraz/Ruby Cabernet, £3.99, Safeway (red)
More good, gutsy Aussie red – this one's surprisingly fresh and grassy – not a common Aussie trait – but there's also a fair slug of toasty richness to bring it within the Aussie sphere again.

11 1997 Vin de Pays d'Oc Syrah/Mourvèdre, Goûts et Couleurs, £3.99, Somerfield (red, southern France)
Pretty dry, with a bit of tannic firmness, but the fruit is good enough to cope and there's a nice glow of bayleaf scent as well.

12 1998 Chardonnay, Tollana, South East Australia, £3.99, Bottoms Up, Thresher, Victoria Wine, Wine Rack (white)
Good, full flavours of pineapple and pear swathed in coconut and vanilla. Subtle? Who wants it to be?

SWEETIES AND FORTIFIEDS

In the run-up to Millennium madness, we have quaint old celebrations like Christmas, when a few glasses of something sweet and succulent will be very welcome – and this year we'll be spoilt for choice

1 D.P.63 Show Muscat 1998 bottling, Seppelt, Rutherglen, £7.49 (half bottle), Oddbins (Australia)

Wonderful, riproaring lovin' spoonful of gorgeous grog. A sensuous goo of syrup and chocolate, coffee and ultra-juicy Muscat sweetness with a great big splat of thyme.
also at Noel Young

2 1996 Botrytis Affected Riesling, Heggies, Eden Valley, £7.99 (half bottle), Fuller's (Australia)

Fat, unctuous stuff, oozing the sweetness of crystallized honey and the brilliant acid fruit of a juicy baked apple packed full of sultanas and dates.

3 1997 Coteaux du Layon St-Aubin de Luigné Cuvée des Forges, Domaine des Forges, £10.80, Tanners (Loire)

Thick, rich, full of sweet candy and peach syrup, all charmingly held in check by acid.
also at Wright Wines

4 1995 Saussignac, Clos d'Yvigne, £13.95, Justerini & Brooks (southern France)

Exciting, powerful wine from near Bergerac, which piles up a super-sweet stack of barley sugar and pineapple chunks then souses them in a delicious tingling acidity.

5 1995 Saussignac Cuvée Flavie, Château des Eyssards, £6.95 (50cl), Adnams (southern France)

Softer and not quite so rich. Still a lovely sweet mouthful of lanolin and thick peach jam muddled up with a whiff of putty.

6 1997 Elysium Black Muscat, Quady, £5.99 (half bottle), Averys (United States)

Thrilling, original stuff, scented with rosehip and apple blossom and packed with the sweetness of morello cherries in syrup.
widely available elsewhere

7 1996 Coteaux du Layon Beaulieu 'L'Anclaie', Château Pierre-Bise, £10.95 (50cl), Lea & Sandeman (Loire)

Another fine Loire sweetie, with a bright orchard freshness of goldengages sweetened with honey from the hive.

8 1996 Dulce Monastrell, Olivares, £16.99, Moreno (Spain)

A cross between Portuguese and Aussie versions of Vintage Port, lacking quite the grip and spiritous fire of Portugal, but with the classic berry and leather flavours of Oz.

9 1995 Ruster Ausbruch, Heidi Schröck, Neusiedlersee-Hügelland, £16.60 (50cl), Savage Selection (Austria)

Austria makes some of the richest wines in Europe. They're no bargain, but for deep, rich, almost syrupy wines (though some just lack a little freshness) they're hard to beat.

10 10-year-old Tawny Port, Cálem, £13.99, Unwins (Portugal)

A classic tawny, with the familiar sweet smell of manila envelopes (sniff one – you'll see what I mean) and a lovely restrained richness of dates, raisins and hazelnuts.

11 Fine Vintage Character Port, £6.85, CWS (Portugal)

Powerful, peppery, streaked with liquorice, but heartwarmingly rich.

12 1997 Kirchheimer Schwarzerde Beerenauslese, Zimmermann-Graeff, Pfalz, £4.29 (half bottle), CWS (Germany)

A big, sweet mouthful of barley sugar and pineapple at a seriously attractive price.

13 Moscatel de Valencia, Vicente Gandia, £3.29, ASDA (Spain)

Bargain basement gobful of orange sherbet, glycerine and sweet grapy syrup.

MAGNIFICENT MISFITS

Some more reserved styles are overshadowed by big, bouncy New World babes; some flavours demand a certain amount of reflection and gradual evaluation; and some wines have marvellously dotty characters that just don't fit the mainstream. Well, here they all are...

1 1997 Marsanne, Chateau Tahbilk, Victoria, £6.99, Waitrose (white, Australia)

Intense, but not too oaky, fat as lanolin, eager as tanned leather and come-hither as orchard apples, honeysuckle and quince.

2 1996 Ram Paddock Red, Waipara West, Waipara, £8.59, Waterloo Wine Co. (New Zealand)

Like a good-quality Bordeaux, this is strong and deep with excellent black cherry and black plum fruit and a grassy streak of acid.

3 1997 St-Nicolas-de-Bourgueil Cuvée Estelle, Cognard-Taluau, £7.80, Haynes, Hanson & Clark (red, Loire)

Lovely raspberries and cream fruit and an earthiness like a summer meadow after rain, with a texture that floats across the tongue like a deb's taffeta evening gown.

4 1997 Incredible Red Zinfandel, Peachy Canyon, California, £9.95, Berry Bros. (United States)

Bursting with rich bramble and date and toffee, then there's a dollop of crab apple purée, and a ladleful of sun-dried tomatoes.

5 1997 St-Véran Tête de Cuvée, Verget, £9.96, Lay & Wheeler (white, Burgundy)

Maybe it's the stylish aroma of freshly made pork sausage that keeps this out of the mainstream, but this is a classic Burgundy smell. Combine it with buttered nuts and a good fat texture, and you've got lovely Burgundy, to drink or to keep.

6 1996 Bandol, Château de Pibarnon, £13.06, Anthony Byrne (red, southern France)

Herbs are the dominant flavour – the almost sweet perfume of bayleaf, some fresh pepper-tree scent – plus wild, mellow fruit. Then it lingers on your palate with the austere scent of fresh thyme.

7 1997 Alsace Pinot Auxerrois Vieilles Vignes, Albert Mann, £7.89, Lay & Wheeler (white)

Lovely, bright, fresh apple and honey fruit kept well this side of indulgent by a dryness like chalk bleached by the summer sun.

8 1997 Douro, Quinta de la Rosa, £6.50, Morris & Verdin (red, Portugal)

Delicious, oaky, spicy, with a fairly good splash of stewed damson skins.

9 1998 Langhe 'Il Fiore', Serra dei Fiori, £9.90, Tanners (white, Italy)

Redolent of lemon blossom and anis, an apple sliced open and glistening, a sprig of mint laid carefully on the glass's rim...

10 1996 Givry Premier Cru, Clos Jus, Gérard Mouton, £10.50, Tanners (red, Burgundy)

Ripe soft red fruit, fruitcaky texture and a strictly controlled measure of beef tea: excellent-value Burgundy.
also at Sommelier

11 1997 Juliénas, Domaine Claude & Michelle Joubert, £7.30, Tanners (red, Burgundy)

Smart Beaujolais – but it's still bright, breezy and gluggable, with the happy flavours of raspberry and earth, so drink it now.

12 1995 Corbières Cuvée Hélène de Troie, Château Hélène, £8.15, Waterloo Wine Co. (red, southern France)

Tastes as if Imperial Leather soap and a bottle of Angostura have been thrown into the vat – with a satisfying soft, dry red fruit.

SUPERMARKET SELECTION

In the third year of our supermarkets-only tasting it looks like we've finally penetrated their corporate shields – none of them sent in tired old rubbish or flash-in-the-pan special offers, just loads of tasty wines at all price levels

Well done the supermarkets on choosing wines that really competed for my attention instead of driving me to despair. Even the wines we didn't choose were rarely horrid: a certain saminess – drinkable but unmemorable – was likely to be our complaint.

Some supermarkets, Morrisons to name one, are clearly happier further down the price scale – which is great! You know where to go for your bargains. Others are able to straddle the various levels of quality with impressive care. Tesco, Safeway, Somerfield and Waitrose stand out here. Sainsbury's entered mostly its more expensive wines, so had to be judged on that basis. Well, it certainly has some good stuff in the upper echelons!

One terrible concern, however, and it's something I'm going to keep banging on about, is the incidence of cork taint. Frankly, it's a disgrace, and there is little sign so far that cork producers are honestly addressing the problem. In one section of the tasting we had 11 corked bottles out of 39! No, your eyes don't deceive you: 11 out of 39. Nearly a quarter of the bottles. Natural cork may or may not be the best closure for wine – when the cork is healthy and clean – but until the cork producers start supplying consistent quality, I implore you to drop all prejudices you may have had against plastic corks and screwtops: they're both excellent, reliable, modern closures that ensure a clean, fresh glass of wine every time you open a bottle.

Please bear in mind that wines are not made in infinite quantities – some of these may well sell out, but the following year's vintage should then become available.

SUPERMARKET SUPERSTARS

This was a case of what to leave out rather than what to put in – so we've got a baker's dozen of outstanding supermarket buys here – and only two of the table wines over £6.99. South Africa and Australia are dominating the scene, because that's where the flavour is.

1 1998 Andrew's Hope Merlot/Cabernet, Spice Route, Swartland, £5.99, Waitrose (red, South Africa)
Fantastic stuff, and a fantastic story. Spice Route is a company set up by some of South Africa's most talented winemakers and a black wine merchant. Profits are used to help black integration and involvement in the Cape winelands. If the wine was no good, you could be excused for saying 'so what?'. But the wine is good – it's a great big brawny boy bulging with blackcurrant and black plum fruit and streaked though with lava and coal smoke. Do yourself and the Cape a favour. Buy it.

2 Old Oloroso, £3.49 (half bottle), Sainsbury's (sherry, Spain)
This is one of the great wine styles of the world – yet hardly anyone drinks it nowadays. Old, amber-brown Oloroso sherry. And it's dry, bone-dry, with flavours of nut husks and dried out chocolate brownies, everything the sepia tone of an ancient college library full of leather-bound books not opened for decades.

③ 1997 Chardonnay, Warwick Estate, Stellenbosch, £6.99, Waitrose (white, South Africa)

Back to the modern world, out into the sunlight of the South with a splendid, serious Cape Chardonnay full of butter and nuts and perfumed leather.

④ 1995 Shiraz, McLaren Vale, £6.99, Tesco (red, Australia)

An old favourite still delivering the goods, a lovely rich mix of big black plums and loganberries, mint, chocolate and liquorice. Wonderful mouthful at a keen price.

⑤ 1997 Riesling, Clare Valley, £4.99, Tesco (white, Australia)

The people at Tesco really have done some brilliant work on their own-labels, because this Riesling is seriously classy stuff. Made by leading Clare Valley producer Mitchell, it has really zippy lemon acid, yet it's almost soft like the lemon peel left in a hot punch. That and a taste of loft apples and biscuits make this a delight to drink now, or to keep for years.

⑥ 1983 Traditional Late Bottled Vintage Port, Fonseca, £14.55, Waitrose (Portugal)

A deep, rich, plummy style of port, that isn't massively concentrated – after all, it's 16 years old! – but beautifully combines its brooding dark fruit with a stern peppery bite.

⑦ 1997 Grenache, McLaren Vale, £5.99, Tesco (red, Australia)

Tesco own-label Aussies again! This time the ultra-gluggable Grenache grape, full of jelly baby, marshmallow and Turkish delight fruit slapped about with fresh-ground pepper and chalk dust.

⑧ 1996 Chardonnay, Hardy's, Padthaway, £7.99, Sainsbury's (white, Australia)

Hardy's made this for Sainsbury's – it's a producer famous for a sumptuous, almost rich style of Chardonnay, packed with peach and banana fruit and laced with oatmeal, coffee smoke and grilled cashews.

⑨ 1998 Gran Reserva Merlot, La Palmeria, Rapel, £7.99, Sainsbury's (red, Chile)

I'd hoped to see a bigger presence from Chile in our Superstars selection – I'm worried they are starting to make too lean a European style. Don't they realise we all drink Chilean wines to get away from European styles? At least this one is deep, dark, packed with black plums and blackcurrant, softened a little with fruit cake.

⑩ 1998 Barrel Fermented Chenin Blanc, Fairview, Paarl, £4.99, Waitrose (white, South Africa)

Lovely example of how good Chenin can be if made by a top-notch outfit like Fairview. Still young and showing greengage fruit, mint and dusty nuts, it'll taste of honey and caramel-coated almonds in a year.

⑪ 1996 Château Carsin, Premières Côtes de Bordeaux, £6.99, Sainsbury's (red)

A rare sighting of classy, affordable red Bordeaux – inky dark red fruit to start, almost peppery, but gradually opening out to delicious dry blackcurrant if you give it time.

⑫ 1996 Mâcon Chardonnay, Domaine les Ecuyers, £6.99, Sainsbury's (white, Burgundy)

This domaine is one of the best in southern Burgundy and the wine mixes oatmeal and stewed apple fruit with a delightful touch of late-night Horlicks!

⑬ 1997 Australian Shiraz, South Eastern Australia, £4.99, Sainsbury's (red)

Sainsbury's showing it also knows how to buy Australian Shiraz with this unrepentantly indulgent soup of cooked blackberries and prunes, chocolate, toffee and spice.

HIGH-STREET HEROES

Two dozen excellent mouthfuls that just lacked the class for our top dozen, with Chile and France leading the way.

1 1998 Classic Selection Australian Chardonnay, £5.99, Sainsbury's (white)
Excellent, traditional Aussie Chardie – full of peaches-and-cream ripeness, with a good whallop of toast and grilled nuts as well. I wish there were more Aussie Chardonnays like this.

2 1997 Chardonnay, McLaren Vale, £5.99, Tesco (white, Australia)
Or you can try the Tesco version – also weighty and ripe, but with more pineapple and melon fruit, and a mouth-coating waxy texture.

3 1997 St-Chinian Cuvée des Fées, Château Cazal-Viel, £6.49, Somerfield (red, southern France)
This still needs a little time, but is full, broad-beamed meaty red, still a little minerally, but just starting to reveal a creamy texture and ripe cherry fruit.

4 Solera Jerezana Rich Cream Sherry, £5.49, Waitrose (Spain)
Wow. This is rich! But it's old as well and consequently full of fascinating flavours like caramelized blackberries, Christmas cake and dates, and a haunting hint of decay, reminiscent of an old British Railways waiting room. Carnforth, perhaps?

5 1998 Viognier, Cono Sur, Casablanca, £4.99, Somerfield (white, Chile)
Very attractive and unusual white that matches an exotic yet not really rich fruit, like dried apricots, with a perfume blending both may blossom and Havana cigar tobacco.

6 1998 Oaked Cabernet Sauvignon, South Eastern Australia, £4.99, Safeway (red)
Another really tasty own-label from Australia – this time a massive macho pudding of rich black plums and blackcurrants, mixed with handfuls of nutmeg and clove.

7 1997 Gran Reserva Chardonnay, La Palmeria, £7.99, Sainsbury's (white, Chile)
Good, broad Chardonnay with deep, ripe pear and pineapple fruit and an attractive syrupy weight; but from a Gran Reserva, I want a little more character.

8 1997 Lugana, Villa Flora Zenato, £5.25, Waitrose (white, Italy)
A delightful white for those of you who are a bit tired of oak flavours and Chardonnay. This wine is all about nuance, with hints of mint, nut husks and pears all peeping out – and as you swallow, a whisper, just a whisper of honey.

9 1998 Alsace Gewürztraminer, £5.99, Safeway, Somerfield (white)
Quite full and assertive, the rose petal and talcum powder perfume having to share the limelight with a whoosh of men's pomade, but a nice sappy greenness, like a broken twig in springtime, keeps it nicely refreshing.

10 1997 Alentejo, Sinfonia, £4.99, Waitrose (red, Portugal)
Full, deep and baked like an earthen oven full of overripe fruit. This rich date and raisin stew almost tastes like port – but it's dry, good and unusual.

11 1997 Sangiovese Tenuta di Corbara, Bigi, Umbria, £4.99, Sainsbury's (red, Italy)
Moustachio'd Aussie Geoff Merrill has got his hands on the unforgiving Sangiovese grape and produced an original blend of redcurrant fruit, pine needle and orange zest perfume, and some toffeed oak to go with the rasping Italian tannin. Good job, Blue.

12 1998 Côtes du Rhône, Domaine Clavel, £4.99, Marks & Spencer (red)
I was disappointed not to see more Côtes du Rhône reds in the tasting, but at least M&S came up with this typically brusque but tasty mix of strawberry, bayleaf and dust.

13 1997 Vin de Pays d'Oc Blanc Tête de Cuvée, La Domeque, £5.49, ASDA (white, southern France)
Interesting mix of Marsanne, Rousanne and Muscat that gives a pleasantly perfumed dry white with a fruit like crystallized greengages.

14 1997 Chablis Cuvée D. Y. Pautre, £7.99, Safeway (white, Burgundy)
This is so gentle and mild that I'm not sure I'd recognize it as Chablis in a blind tasting. It's more like a soft, honeyed white Burgundy with a handful of hazelnuts thrown in. Not typical Chablis, but a very agreeable drink.

15 1996 Monastrell/Cabernet Sauvignon/Merlot, Hécula, Yecla, £4.99, ASDA (red, Spain)
This is a bit too tannic, unless you're getting stuck into a big beef casserole, but its black plum fruit and perfume of peppercorn, bayleaf and Elastoplast would make it a pretty interesting drinking partner.

16 Zinfandel, Stratford, California, £5.99, Tesco (red, United States)
Wild and whacky combination of dates and Garibaldi biscuits with plums stewed in raspberry vinegar and a sprig of rosemary. Weird? Sure. Try it.

17 1997 Reserve Merlot, La Palmeria, Rapel, £5.99, Waitrose (red, Chile)
This is a bit tannic for Chilean Merlot – a problem that I've been coming across frequently this year – and should have more juicy fruit. But there's some black cherry and blackcurrant, along with some pleasantly perfumed oak.

18 1998 Chilean Merlot Reserve, Lontue/Curico, £5.49, Tesco (red)
The same story – where's the fruit gone? There's a reasonable fistful of blackcurrant and black cherry there, but the sawmill oak is now too strong. Less oak and more fruit would suit me.

19 1997 Pinot Noir, Cono Sur, Rapel, £4.99, Tesco (red, Chile)
This also needs to be less oaky – it's still good, there's still some nice strawberry fruit there, but there's now more tannin, and more oak that tastes like savoury corn chips.

20 1998 Young Vatted Pinotage, Kleinbosch, Paarl, £4.99, Safeway (red, South Africa)
This is fairly aggressive stuff with a prickly rasp halfway between pepper and chilli flakes. There's decent damson fruit, but – the same old litany – there used to be more.

21 1998 Malbec, Valdivieso, £4.99, Sainsbury's (red, Chile)
This has a slightly milky nose that I don't really want, but it does show the come-hither softness of Malbec, with a little, but not enough, stewed plum fruit.

22 Rioja Alavesa, Viña Mara, £5.49, Tesco (red, Spain)
This is a bit more rugged than a traditional Rioja, but there's a suggestion of strawberry and violet and a touch of savoury oak.

23 1998 Reserve Selection South African Pinotage, Stellenbosch, £5.49, Sainsbury's (red)
Too tannic, but a pretty individual firework display of damsons, toasted marshmallows and coal smoke just about balances it out.

24 1996 Château Saint Robert, Graves, £6.75, Somerfield (red, Bordeaux)
Good, direct, old-style claret. Not very fruity, meaty rather, with a definite undertow of earth and tannin – but that's claret!

VINOPOLIS
CITY OF WINE

EXPLORE
THE WHOLE WORLD OF WINE AT
VINOPOLIS
CITY OF WINE

EXPLORE a whole world of wine on The Wine Odyssey with your personal audio guide. **TASTE** five wines of your choice from over 200 on offer – it's all included with your entry ticket. **ENJOY** all that goes with wine: restaurant, wine bar, works of art and gift shopping for wine lovers. BOOK NOW AND AVOID THE QUEUES **0870 4444 777**

www.evinopolis.com

ON LONDON'S BANKSIDE, BETWEEN
SOUTHWARK CATHEDRAL AND SHAKESPEARE'S GLOBE.

THE ECONOMY CLASS

We shifted our price limit to £4.49 from £3.99 last year, and though the majority of the wines still hit the £3.99 barrier, we've swept in a whole tide of quite classy bottles. Our only complaint here would be a slight homogeneity, but at least it's a highly drinkable homogeneity

1 1998 Bin 381 Semillon, South Eastern Australia, £4.49, Marks & Spencer (white)
Really big, broad Aussie white, with loads of custard cream richness and burnt rice pudding toastiness, and a kind of nutty syrup laced with lemon.

2 1997 California Carignane, Arius, £4.29, ASDA (red, United States)
This is refreshingly drier than most Californian reds, but makes up for lack of richness with a really interesting John Steinbeck blend of fish skin and metal with redcurrant jelly, toffee and fresh mint leaves. Perfect for *Cannery Row* soirées.

3 1997 Primitivo, Terrale, Puglia, £3.99, Somerfield (red, Italy)
Proudly Italian, splattering a gobful of black cherry fruit all over the taste buds, followed by tobacco leaf, lavender, and limy acidity.

4 Winemaker South African Cabernet/Merlot, £4.49, Tesco (red)
Muscular stuff, stained with coal dust and lava, but luckily pumped full of blackcurrant and black cherry fruit to balance it out.

5 1997 Vin de Pays d'Oc Mourvèdre/Syrah, L'Enclos Domeque, £3.99, Waitrose (red, southern France)
Good stuff, really showing the wild but fascinating Syrah flavours of raw potato, cream and smoke mixed in with dark dry loganberry fruit – and a handful or two of local herbs provided by the Mourvèdre.

6 1997 Cabernet Sauvignon, Casa Leona, Rapel, £4.49, Marks & Spencer (red, Chile)
Bright, juicy blackcurrant throat pastille fruit, and a little wisp of coal smoke. Not as ripe as it usually is, but a very nice glass of red.

7 1998 Cinsaut/Shiraz Estate Wine, Landskroon, Paarl, £4.29, Safeway (red, South Africa)
We're certainly going through a patch of smoky reds here – this has that appetizing aroma of grilling meat, while the fruit is all soft marshmallows, red cherry juice and pink icing sugar.

8 1997 California Zinfandel, Arius, £3.99, ASDA (red, United States)
No smoke this time, but loads of almost overripe dates and raisins and stewed blackberries. It's got a tannic bite, but with this richness, who's complaining?

9 1997 Atlantic Vines Baga, Bright Brothers, Beiras, £4.49, Somerfield (red, Portugal)
Are you brave enough for this? You'll never know if you don't try it – a remarkable red from a whacky Portuguese variety that smells of petrol and tastes of raw tomatoes, red cherries, sour Korean pickled plums and a wad of chewing tobacco.

10 1998 Vin de Pays d'Oc Sauvignon Blanc Reserve, Saint Marc, £4.29, Sainsbury's (white, southern France)
After eight reds in a row I was beginning to wonder if we'd ever get to another white. Well, this is ultra-white, icy cold grapefruit, lemon zest and anis leaves white, to revive the most jaded palate.

11 1998 Vin de Pays du Gard Counoise, Domaine Jeune, £4.49, Marks & Spencer (red, southern France)
It couldn't last! Back to red. This M&S special has been better, but it still has a lovely lavender and violet perfume, and some damson softness, though it's leaner than usual.

VINOPOLIS
CITY OF WINE

WINE KNOWLEDGE. IT'S ALL ABOUT GOING TO THE RIGHT SCHOOL.

Looking to develop your wine knowledge? The right school is now Vinopolis Academy.

At Vinopolis on London's Bankside, we'll be offering courses at all levels of learning, from newcomers to ambitious sommeliers.

Our courses have been devised with some of the world's leading wine gurus, including Michael Broadbent MW, Oz Clarke, Hugh Johnson, Jancis Robinson MW and Steven Spurrier.

For full details of all the courses on offer at Vinopolis Academy, please call the number below and ask for our prospectus.

FOR OUR PROSPECTUS, CALL: 0171 645 3700

Ask for Pierre Mansour at Vinopolis Academy.

⑫ 1997 Nero d'Avola/Syrah, Firriato, Sicily, £3.99, Waitrose (red, Italy)
Almost coarse with its windfallen fruit of bruised plum and scrumped apples, but chocolate and spice bring it back into line.

⑬ 1997 'Gold Label' Vin de Pays d'Oc Cabernet Sauvignon, £4.49, Marks & Spencer (red, southern France)
There's far too much feeble Cabernet from the South of France, but this has good juicy blackcurrant fruit, some soft buttery oak and a nice streak of green-leaf acidity.

⑭ Australian Chardonnay, South Eastern Australia, £3.99, Sainsbury's (white)
Most tasty Aussie Chardonnay is now nearer £4.99 in price, so this soft, spicy number with its gentle banana and pear fruit is quite a bargain at £3.99.

⑮ 1998 Chilean Cabernet Sauvignon, Lontue, £3.99, Safeway (red)
More grassy than usual, but still a fair splash of blackcurrant and a coffee-bean, chalky undertow – European rather than Chilean.

⑯ Viognier, Picajuan Peak, Mendoza £4.49, Tesco (white, Argentina)
Viognier at £3.99 is almost unheard of, and Argentina hardly has any Viognier in any case – so let's enjoy it's peach blossom and roses drinkability while we can.

⑰ 1998 Malbec/Ruby Cabernet, Nanya Vineyard, South Eastern Australia, £3.99, Waitrose (red)
An unusual combination for Australia, and so no surprises in it's unusual flavour of eelskin leather, sweet plums and dates that will go chocolaty and pruny in a year or so.

⑱ Chilean Old Vines Carignan, £3.99, CWS (red)
Carignan is a grape variety widely despised in Europe, but if you ripen it perfectly, the wine can be good. This is dry and austere, but with a rather prune-skin and baked apple fruit and a whiff of clove spice.

⑲ 1997 Portada, Estremadura, £3.99, Somerfield (red, Portugal)
Excellent chunky glugger, with coarse-cut rich red fruit, blended with sawmill fumes and half-cooked sponge cake.

⑳ 1998 Bin No. 121 Merlot/Ruby Cabernet, Western Cape, £4.49, Marks & Spencer (red, South Africa)
Good, weighty, brawn-before-beauty stuff, with the typical South African coal dust and Ruby Cabernet earthiness, but enough beef to make it a good glass of grog.

FOR MORE WINE RECOMMENDATIONS SEE:

OZ CLARKE'S
MILLENNIUM PARTY GUIDE

• **Best Buy Fizz for the Millennium and beyond** • **How to make your party go with a big, big bang** • **How to get through the morning after**
on the centre pages

*See also Ideal Cellars on pages 26–35
and the Merchant Directory on pages 413–49.
Look out for the Instant Cellar lists in the wine region chapters, too.*

BARGAIN BASEMENT

We upped our Bargain Basement price point from £2.99 to £3.49 this year – and virtually doubled the numbers as well as netting some seriously interesting wines

1 1998 Australian Oaked Colombard, South Eastern Australia £3.49, Safeway (white)
The oak gives it a luscious clove, nutmeg and custard apple excitement to go with the tangy orange-zest fruit.

2 1998 Argentinian Bonarda, Mendoza, £3.49, ASDA (red)
'98 was not a good year in Argentina, but this delightful juicy red – all cherries, rosehip and lilac leaves – still bounces through.

3 1998 Corbières, £3.19, Safeway (red, southern France)
Corbières is supposed to be gutsy stuff, but it must have fruit too, and this big bruiser is full of black plums and bayleaf scent.

4 Portuguese Red, Terras do Sado, £2.99, Somerfield
Similar but a bit rougher, a bit wilder, full of forest-floor red fruit and damson skins.

5 1998 Woodcutter's White, £2.99, Safeway (Hungary)
Made from some unpronounceable grape variety, this is a dead easy to drink white blend of nice apple-peel and lemon-zest acidity with the perfume of vines in flower.

6 1998 Hungarian Irsai Olivér, Neszmély Region £2.99, ASDA, Safeway (white)
Pretty dry for a wine that simply swamps the room with a perfume like the blossom of orange, grapefruit and nectarine bushes.

7 1998 Vin de Pays du Gers, £2.99, Marks & Spencer (white, southern France)
Good aggressive white. Loads of green-apple and nettle acidity, but flecked with mint, and actually pleasantly ripe.

8 Côtes du Roussillon, £2.99, Morrisons (red, southern France)
This is a pretty burly mouthful, but there's some pleasant bright fruit there and a little spice to sweeten up the monster.

9 1998 Cabernet Sauvignon Rosé, Nagyrede, £3.49, Waitrose (Hungary)
Excellent tobacco, apple and straw scent in a good dry rosé, that manages a little of the gruffness of a red.

10 1997 Chardonnay, Tolna Region, £3.49, Somerfield (white, Hungary)
Really good bargain Chardie – fresh apple and grapefruit zinged up by lemon and a flicker of flowers.

11 Ideal with Friends Sauvignon Blanc, Mór, £3.49, Morrisons (white, Hungary)
I'm not sure about the name but the wine is good, snappy gooseberry and nettle Sauvignon from a go-ahead producer.

12 1998 Karalta Oak Aged Dry Red, South Eastern Australia, £3.29, ASDA
Good, tasty basic Aussie red: redcurrant jelly fruit spiced up with toffee and cloves.

13 Californian Red, £3.49, Morrisons (United States)
Not subtle, but it's good, juicy, rich, caky red.

14 Ideal with Friends Vin de Pays d'Oc Merlot, £3.49, Morrisons (red, southern France)
Pretty good grassy plummy Merlot. What Bordeaux should be doing, but isn't.

15 1997 Semillon/Chardonnay, South Eastern Australia, £3.49, Morrisons (white)
Nice, straight dry white with a soft custard-creams flavour wrapped around a slice of dried apricot.

IDEAL CELLARS

For a Millennium treat we've offered our contributors a mighty £2000 to put together a cellar of everything from day-to-day drinking to dream bottles

The offer of £2000 set our five guest writers – all independent-minded wine merchants – to work with a sense of mission to produce beautifully balanced cellars of classic wines and modern wines, wines for the year ahead and wines for many more to come. Me it just sent mad, like a no-restrictions ticket to fly around the world gathering up a huge haul of superbly flavoursome bottles.

SIMON LOFTUS
CHAIRMAN OF ADNAMS

My usual pattern of wine purchases is much like everyone else's – hand to mouth – but every now and then I am spurred to extravagance by a great vintage or an unexpected windfall, and I splurge on a few splendid wines

For my Millennium selection I have chosen to use up my budget of £2000 on a few cases of truly exceptional wines, and I intend to keep them for at least a decade. All the wines are red, and three out of the seven are from women winemakers. These are modern classics, of exhilarating splendour.

1994 Clos des Cistes, Domaine Peyre Rose, Coteaux du Languedoc (southern France)
Marlène Soria's wine is amazing, concentrated, wildly individual and complex. Fully justifies its startling price.
£238.20 for 12

1995 Chambolle-Musigny 'La Combe d' Orveau', Domaine Anne Gros (Burgundy)
Still closed, secretive. Burgundy of guts and elegance from one of the best winemakers of the Côte d'Or.
£306 for 12

1995 Domaine de Chevalier, Pessac-Léognan (Bordeaux)
A wine to justify all the hype about Bordeaux. Classic Graves from a wonderful vintage. A bargain!
£334.20 for 12

1993 Barolo Riserva, Vigna San Giuseppe 'Bricco Boschis', Cavalotto (Italy)
Perfect expression of Nebbiolo at its best, from an exceptional producer in a fine vintage. Truly grand.
£226.20 for 12

1996 Cabernet/Merlot, Cullen, Margaret River (Australia)
Vanya Cullen is a winemaker of genius and this is a triumph. Intense and elegant, subtle and strong.
£388.80 for 6 magnums

1996 Santa Cruz Mountains Cabernet, Ridge (United States)
A classic bargain – beautifully balanced Cabernet from California's finest winemaker, Paul Draper.
£238.20 for 12

1997 Colomé, Vinos de Davalos, Molinos (Argentina)
Mighty stuff from the world's highest vineyard. A rich, gamey blend of old vine Malbec and Cabernet.
£190.20 for 12

Total £1921.80

LUCY FAULKNER
MORRIS & VERDIN

It is no coincidence that my collection contains not a drop of Chardonnay, Merlot or Cabernet, the world's three most predictable grape varieties

An Ideal Cellar should be a place of refuge for the world's more mysterious vinous treasures. Besides which, less obvious varieties tend to offer better value for money, and you will be able to chart the maturation of your Rieslings, Chenins and Syrahs for decades to come.

1996 Scheurebe Spätlese, Lingenfelder (white, Germany)
Lingenfelder is a genius at Scheurebe. He brings out all its delicate varietal aromas to perfection: grapefruit, lemon meringue and a lovely floral character. A perfect apéritif.
£117.48 for 12, Charles Taylor

1996 Coteaux du Layon Chaume Sélection de Grains Nobles, Branchereau (sweet white, Loire)
Truly one of the most stunning wines I have ever tasted. Golden colour, unbelievable concentration and complexity of flavour, with classic sweet-sour Chenin character.
£151.20 for 12, Morris & Verdin

1996 Hermitage Blanc, Chave (white, Rhône)
Peachy, lemon fruit with a hint of vanilla oak and an almondy tang. Very lush palate that feels almost sweet due to the glycerol.
£210 for 6, Yapp Brothers

1997 Viognier, Jade Mountain (white, California)
Classically delicate Viognier, bearing more than a passing resemblance to its northern Rhône counterparts. Apricot aromas and a blossom-infused and rich (but dry) palate.
£138 for 6, Morris & Verdin

1996 Alsace Riesling Muenchberg, Ostertag (white, Alsace)
Smoky, aromatic and deeply mineral; one of the world's most elegant wines.
£83.70 for 6, Morris & Verdin

1997 Zeltinger Sonnenuhr Riesling Auslese, Selbach-Oster (white, Germany)
A wine so beautiful you want to kiss it not drink it. Lightly floral, with berry fruits and elderflower, bursting open on the palate with an exotic sweetness.
£65.94 for 6 half bottles, Morris & Verdin

1998 Sauvignon Blanc, Isabel Estate, Marlborough (white, New Zealand)
All the gooseberry you could possibly want from a Sauvignon, and a racy acidity.
£101.52 for 12, Morris & Verdin

1997 Graciano, Viña Ijalba, Rioja (red, Spain)
A rare opportunity to taste a single-varietal Graciano, usually used to give grace to Tempranillo. Deep red colour, spicy, plummy flavours and lovely round ripeness.
£105 for 12, Vintage Roots

1997 Geyserville, Ridge Vineyards (red, United States)
A blend of Zinfandel (almost 80%), Carignan and Petite Sirah. Delicious sweet fruit, lots of herbs and spices. Lovely now or in about ten years' time.
£99.90 for 6, Morris & Verdin

1997 Le Cigare Volant, Bonny Doon (red, United States)
A delicious, spicy, soft-fruited southern Rhône blend. The wine pays homage to a decree passed in 1954 in the village of Châteauneuf forbidding flying saucers from landing amongst the vines.
£102 for 6, Morris & Verdin

1995 Chianti Rufina Riserva, Fattoria Selvapiana (red, Italy)
Densely coloured, with chocolaty, liquoricy aromas and cherry fruit. Perfect Chianti.
£71.70 for 6, Liberty Wines

1998 Crozes-Hermitage, Graillot (red, Rhône)

Superb concentration for a Crozes, with lots of Syrah pepper and spice. Lovely ripe blackberry fruit, chunky tannins and crisp acidity. Enjoy over the next few years.

£131.40 for 12, Yapp Brothers

1997 Vosne-Romanée, Engel (red, Burgundy)

Engel typically makes Pinot Noir on the deeper, darker side. This village wine has lovely purity of fruit and a soft perfume.

£237.60 for 12, Morris & Verdin

NV Amontillado del Puerto, Almacenista José Luis Gonzalez Obregon (sherry, Spain)

Amber colour, a smoky nose reminiscent of hazelnuts. It is an intensely dry wine, although the alcohol may give a slight hint of sweetness.

£97.20 for 12 halves, Morris & Verdin

1993 Tokaji 5 Puttonyos, Oremus (sweet white, Hungary)

A magical sugar-acid balance which prevents it from becoming cloying; delicate honeyed, orange-peel flavours with lots of exotic fruits. A wine that will keep improving for decades.

£172.80 for 12 50cl bottles, Morris & Verdin

1995 Vintage Port, Quinta de la Rosa (fortified, Portugal)

Complex pruny nose with tobacco flavours and a herbal intensity. Delicious dark sweet fruits and firm wood tannins. Will develop and broaden over the next 50-odd years.

£113.94 for 6, Morris & Verdin

Total cost: £1999.38

Stockists not featured in this book:
Vintage Roots: tel 0118-976 1999
Charles Taylor: tel 0207-928 8151

ROGER HIGGS
FULLER'S

My aim was to choose wines rather than labels. This does not rule out famous names but does not mean that just because I've got two grand to spend the cellar has got to be full of claret and white Burgundy

I also wanted a combination of wines for immediate drinking and wines that can be drunk now but will develop over the next few years. I'd like to mention a few wines that I'd love to have in my cellar but just cannot get hold of: any Merlot (or Cabernet for that matter) from Leonetti in the Columbia Valley, Niellon's white Burgundies, Etude's Pinot Noirs, the Burgundies of Jayer-Gilles (especially his 1996 Échézeaux du Dessus, but his Hautes-Côtes de Nuits red and white will do just fine). Finally, anything from Kistler!

1997 Explorer Pinot Noir, Concha y Toro, Maipo (red, Chile)

Something for everyday drinking. Chile seems to be particularly successful with Pinot Noir, a grape that can be very difficult to get right. This is a great example,

produced using Burgundian winemaking techniques. It has classic Pinot Noir characters – delicious and a real bargain.

£53.89 for 12, Fuller's

1998 Viognier, Fairview, Paarl (white, South Africa)

The first Viognier I've ever tasted from South Africa and what a cracker. Peaches, apricots and everything Viognier should be.

£89.88 for 12, Fuller's Brewery Store, Oddbins Fine Wine

1997 Vin de Pays de l'Aude 'les Aurièges', Domaine de Clovallon (white, southern France)

An eclectic blend of Viognier, Chardonnay, Petit Manseng and Clairette in equal amounts. Fermented in oak, producing

RIEDEL

since 1756

The key to flavor !

Indispensable for those who
care for the true sensual enjoyment of wine.

I recommend using our instruments
to make your wine taste even finer!

Riedel stemware is tailored to the character
of the grape - it is the key to flavor!

For details of stockists please contact Michael Johnson Ceramics, 81 Kingsgate Road,
London NW 6 4 JY, Tel. 44-(0)171-624 2493, Fax: 44-(0)171-625 7639, or Riedel Glas,
A-6330 Kufstein/Austria, Tel. 0043-5372-64896, Fax: 0043-5372-63225
http://www.riedelcrystal.com

excellent fruit/oak balance, great concentration and a long, clean finish. A top effort from the South of France.

£97.09 for 12, Fuller's

1996 Old Vine Shiraz, Grant Burge, Barossa Valley (red, Australia)

Known as the 'black monster', this archetypal Barossa Valley Shiraz is big and brooding yet with lots of sweet fruit. Delicious now but will age well over the next five to ten years.

£80.91 for 9, Fuller's, Unwins

1997 Pic St-Loup, Gausselm de Guilhem (red, southern France)

For me Pic St-Loup is one of the most exciting grape growing regions in the world. This blend of 95 per cent Syrah and 5 per cent Grenache aged in new oak is probably the finest wine to come out of the region to date. A Côte-Rôtie or Hermitage of this quality would cost at least twice the price.

£119.88 for 12, Fuller's

1997 Reserve Chardonnay, Vergelegen, Stellenbosch (white, South Africa)

Combines New World fruit concentration with elegance and finesse. A top-quality South African Chardonnay. Its only negative aspect is there isn't enough to go round!

£59.94 for 6, Waitrose

1996 Pinot Noir, Rippon Estate, Central Otago (red, New Zealand)

Another New World Pinot Noir that is particularly successful. From one of the most beautiful vineyards in the world. This is a delicious New Zealand Pinot Noir that offers excellent quality compared to Burgundy at the same price level and it's organic.

£71.94 for 6, Fuller's

1997 Merlot, Broken Stone, Hawke's Bay (red, New Zealand)

I'm not a big claret fan. I just don't get enough pleasure for my money so here's a New World alternative. Loads of soft,

plummy fruit balanced by good structure with nice acidity and oak integration. Pomerol eat your heart out.

£65.94 for 6, Fuller's

1996 Pouilly-Vinzelles, Domaine Valette (white, Burgundy)

Not one of Burgundy's most famous regions but a wine from one of its most quality-conscious producers. Hand-picked grapes are fermented with natural yeasts to produce a white Burgundy of stunning complexity.

£83.94 for 6, Fuller's

1995 Eileen Hardy Shiraz, Hardy's (red, Australia)

The 1995 Eileen Hardy Shiraz won the prestigious Jimmy Watson Trophy, Australia's most coveted wine prize. The wine is massively concentrated with black fruit flavours and deliciously spicy undertones. One to keep for a few years, though.

£167.94 for 6, Fuller's

1990 Champagne Dom Pérignon

There seems to be a bit of snobbery about Dom Pérignon due to its connections with Moët & Chandon. I'm not sure why, as Moët is one of the most consistent Grande Marque Champagnes around. Dom Pérignon in my opinion is simply the finest Champagne available and the 1990 is one of the best vintages I've tasted – stunning – the perfect celebration wine for now and for years to come.

£389.94 for 6, Tesco

1996 Meursault-Perrières, Comtes Lafon (white, Burgundy)

Total self indulgence. Meursault is not usually my favourite white Burgundy but the wines of Comtes Lafon are for me some of the most exciting in the world. Silly money – but I'm not paying!

£720 for 6, Farr Vintners

Total: £2001.29

SEBASTIAN PAYNE
THE WINE SOCIETY
I am tempted to blow my £2000 windfall on the three most consistently delicious clarets I know: Cheval Blanc, Palmer and Haut Bailly

dozen each of the 1998 vintage en primeur would cost about £1500. But my wife and our guests like mature claret and it would be a long wait, so I have plumped for a more balanced selection of wines, some of which I can start right away. First, we need good house wines, a red and a white to open at the end of a long day or when extra youngsters turn up unexpectedly for lunch.

1998 Sauvignon de Touraine, Bougrier (white, Loire)
This year's bargain Sauvignon. Last year it came from New Zealand.
£46 for 12, Wine Society

1996 Lirac La Fermade, Domaine Maby (red, Rhône)
Village Rhône is another household essential and this is excellent value.
£63 for 12, Wine Society

We like fruity, dry, whistle-clean Riesling on summer weekend evenings. They keep their youthful freshness remarkably for many years, if stored in a cold place.

1997 Saarburger Rausch Riesling Kabinett, Milliken (white, Germany)
I am not sure six bottles is enough of this.
£47.70 for 6, Wine Society

We drink less Chardonnay than we used to. Top-class Côte d'Or is not cheap so must be the real thing.

1996 Chassagne-Montrachet Les Caillerets, Jean-Noël Gagnard (white, Burgundy)
£204 for 6, Wine Society

Neither of us likes white wine that smells and tastes more of oak than wine, which rules out a lot of New World whites. Chablis, Alsace

Riesling and that rare animal real Vouvray can be excellent value and seem often to match our mood and the food we enjoy.

1996 Chablis Montmains, Brocard (white, Burgundy)
A perfect year for Chablis: clean and long. Louis Michel's wines would also be ideal.
£63 for 6, Wine Society

1995 Alsace Riesling, Trimbach (white, Alsace)
The Alsace Riesling specialist par excellence makes lovely wine at every level.
£47.70 for 6, Wine Society

1996 Vouvray Le Haut Lieu, Huet (dry white, Loire)
Of course, great Vouvrays are sweet, but Huet's biodynamically grown dry wines do you nothing but good and go well with food.
£41.70 for 6, Wine Society

Champagnes for achievements and anniversaries for us come usually from the marvellous traditional house of Alfred Gratien.

The Wine Society's Champagne Brut NV
£89 for 6, Wine Society

1989 Champagne Alfred Gratien
Perfect for the Millennium. It's still a bit early for the best 1990s.
£328 for 6 magnums, Wine Society

Now the reds. We both adore good Chianti and the estates we like best are getting better and better every year, it seems.

1995 Chianti Rufina Riserva Bucerchiale, Giuntini (red, Italy)
Beautifully balanced wine from the Selvapiana estate.
£83.70 for 6, Wine Society

1996 Chianti Classico Fontodi, Manetti (red, Italy)
Or the superb but pricier Flaccianello.
£51 for 6, Wine Society

1995 Chianti Classico Riserva Vigneto Rancia, Felsina Berardenga (red, Italy)
This would be a first growth if the Italians were stupid enough to classify Chianti.
£99 for 6, Wine Society

You have to move fast to buy the best red Burgundy. My wife loves good Chambolle and Volnay for their fragrance and silkiness.

1998 Chambolle-Musigny Les Fuées, Ghislaine Barthod (red, Burgundy)
From J&B's well-chosen Burgundy list.
£192 for 6, Justerini & Brooks

1993 Volnay les Caillerets Clos des 60 Ouvrées, Domaine de la Pousse d'Or (red, Burgundy)
To replace the wonderful bottles of 1990 we drank for our 25th wedding anniversary.
£180 for 6, Wine Society

1996 Médocs, with their well-ripened Cabernet, good balance and length of flavour, will give claret lovers enormous pleasure. Mercifully the Americans seem to prefer 1995 in general and Merlots in particular.

1996 Château Pontet-Canet, Pauillac (red, Bordeaux)
Right back on form with this vintage.
£162 for 6, Justerini & Brooks

1996 Château Marquis-de-Terme, Margaux (red, Bordeaux)
A star in this vintage.
£129 for 6, Wine Society

1990 was truly remarkable for sweet white Bordeaux.

1990 Château Climens, Barsac
My favourite sweet white Bordeaux
£135 for 6 half bottles, Wine Society

…and I've got just over £38 left to spend on that bargain of the wine world, dry sherry.

Manzanilla Pasada, San Leon, Herederos de Argüeso (sherry, Spain)
£38.70 for 6, Wine Society

Total cost £2000.50

HEW BLAIR
JUSTERINI & BROOKS
A change of residence to the Borders of Scotland where entertaining is de rigeur – and a thirsty clutch of teenagers and their friends – has, by economic necessity, defined the amount I wish to spend per bottle

Rather than labels that easily impress I have chosen domaine-bottled wines that deliver quality and variety at all levels, that do not break the bank but stimulate the palate. So, some less expensive but interesting cases and a fair amount for the grown-ups.

1998 Vin de Pays de l'Hérault Chardonnay, Domaine Montrose (white, southern France)
There is so much boring Chardonnay about. This is most definitely not one of them. Made by genius Michel Le Goec it is fresh with stacks of butter and blossom fruit.
£54 for 12

1996 Côtes du Rhône, Cuvée des Capucines, Domaine du Vieux Chêne (red)
A moreish Côtes du Rhône with crunchy, wild strawberry fruit and delicious explosive tannins.
£65.40 for 12

1997 Mâcon-Uchizy, Domaine Gérald & Philibert Talmard (white, Burgundy)

The Mâcon that keeps your interest glass after glass – indeed case after case. The freshness of the fruit and richness of flavour makes this Justerini & Brooks' fastest-selling white wine.

£78 for 12

1996 Riesling, Fritz Haag (white, Germany)

Fritz Haag is the master of Riesling. The exquisite floral fruits and intense refreshing mineral flavour make this as moreish as they come.

£95.40 for 12

1995 Château la Chenade, Lalande de Pomerol (red, Bordeaux)

A real crowd-pleaser. Sumptuous, rich, velvety fruit is complemented by ripe stylish tannins.

£150 for 12

1998 Marsannay Les Longeroies, Domaine Bruno Clair (red, Burgundy)

The class of the Côtes de Nuits is clearly shown in this high-toned, beautifully polished Pinot Noir. The 1996 is bursting with sloe and damson fruit and is highly concentrated and focused.

£156 for 12

1996 Chardonnay, Dalwhinnie Estate, Moonambel (white, Australia)

I drink this Chardonnay because of its balance. There is no problem with ripeness of fruit in this part of Australia. The interest lies in the complex and mineral qualities that accompany its richness.

£167.40 for 12

NV Champagne Premier Cru Brut, Forget-Brimont

A complex, graceful Pinot-based Champagne from the Montagne de Reims. A slow élévage brings extra richness to intense lemon and floral aromas.

£179.40 for 12

1997 Chablis Premier Cru, Fôrest, Domaine Dauvissat-Camus (white, Burgundy)

This is true Chablis. Although delicious, showing true vivacity and chalky character, it does improve with keeping for 3–4 years. Treating it like a red wine by opening the bottle a few hours before drinking and decanting will allow its intense complex flavours to be released.

£190.80 for 12

1995 Chinon Clos de la Dioterie, Charles Jaquet (red, Loire)

Great Cabernet Franc is hard to find. However the old vines planted some 80 years ago in the great Dioterie vineyard deliver wonderful, profound, fully ripe and complex examples. This 1995 is a top-rate vintage.

£192 for 12

1997 Pinot Noir, Dry River, Martinborough (red, New Zealand)

Quite simply the New World's premier Pinot. It has a purity of flavour, great intensity and haunting length.

£240 for 12

1997 Condrieu, Coteau de Cherry, André Perret (white, Rhône)

Truly hedonistic – violets, greengages, honey – yet with exquisite mineral complexity and delicious acidity to balance the natural richness of the Viognier grape.

£264 for 12

1995 Barbaresco Ronchi, Albino Rocca

Barbaresco is the more feminine neighbour of Barolo – it is elegant and fruity yet with lovely ripe sloe and damson fruit and all-singing, all-dancing tannins.

£264 for 12

Total cost: £2096.40

A shade over the budget, Hew, but you can borrow the leftover cash from Simon Loftus's cellar to square things up. [Ed.]

OZ CLARKE

What's my brief? £2000 to splash on a dozen cases of glitzy bottles from the classic regions? Sorry, Ed., I just can't bring myself to

I've got lots of friends thirsty for jugs full of decent grog and not many friends only interested in the superstar stuff. So, I'm off around the world to heap up some bargain bottles before I branch out into the glorious self-indulgence of some really smart kit.

Some of the wines I've chosen haven't yet made it into UK shops, but I make no apologies: we deserve these great flavours and it's down to the wine trade to get them to us. If you see them – buy them!

Well, I have to start with Argentina. This rapidly awakening South American giant has given so much pleasure in the last year with gorgeous, juicy reds and fragrant, floral whites: **1998 Bonarda/Barbera, Caballo de Plata (red) and Torrontés, Caballo de Plata (white), £41.88 for 6 of each, Safeway**

Hungary has shown fantastic form with whites in the last few years – and at really keen prices. But has anyone out there ever tasted an Austrian red? Well, try this one: **1997 Hárslevelü, Deer Leap, £17.94 for 6, Waitrose (white, Hungary) and Blauer Zweigelt, Lenz Moser, £23.94 for 6, Tesco (red, Austria)**

A quick flip back to South America – Chile – and a pair of stunningly fruity wines: **1998 Sauvignon Blanc Reserva, Antu Mapu, £23.94 for 6, Waitrose (white) and 1998 Merlot, Carta Vieja, £23.94 for 6, Oddbins (red)**

And while I'm down South – on to Australia for two of the most brilliant cheap wine inventions the world has yet seen: **1998 Bin 202 Riesling, Penfolds and 1999 Bin 65 Chardonnay, Lindemans, widely available, c.£54 for 6 of each (both white)**

Back in Europe I've found a stunning Mediterranean sticky: **Muscat, Samos, £17.94 for 6 halves, Somerfield (Greece)**

Now, fizz. Lovely soft, creamy Prosecco: **NV Prosecco, La Marca, £31.74 for 6, Waitrose (Italy)**

So that's what, £235 or so? Okay, that's the bargain basement well filled – I'm off up-market! Well, not too far up-market. There's such fantastic stuff around at between five and six pounds a bottle that I think I'll stick there for a little longer, mixing some more bargains with wines that are just a little more expensive.

Portugal has got a whole gaggle of fascinating reds and some of the best are being made by ex-pats from the southern seas. So I'll have two sumptuous, rich-flavoured reds from resident Aussie, Peter Bright: **1998 Cepa Torta, Bright Brothers, £23.94 for 6, Tesco; 1998 Palmela, Bright Brothers, not yet in UK, c.£30 for 6**

Want to trade up? Portuguese reds get even more exciting for another couple of quid. These you must taste one day: **1998 Pegos Claros, not yet in UK** – but Oddbins have the very good 1994 for £8.29 per bottle; **1998 Touriga Nacional, Esporão, not yet in UK; 1998 Touriga Nacional, Quinta da Boavista, not yet in UK; c.£148 for 6 of each**

Hell, I'm in Portugal, let's pop over to Spain. There have been some silly price rises recently, but the quality coming out of Spain gets more exciting every year. **1998 Unwooded Chardonnay, Valonga, 6 for £40.50, Roberson (white); 1997 Albariño, Pazo de Senorans, £48 for 6, Liberty Wines (white)** – but Albariño is so fashionable in Spain that I'm afraid the 1998 vintage will be twice the price; **1996 Muruve Crianza, Toro, £38.94 for 6, Tesco (red)**

Right, time for the New World again – and let's go up-market in Argentina. There are some stunning top-line wines being made – and you can afford them! **1999 Tempranillo, Finca el Retiro, Mendoza, £32.94 for 6, Waitrose (red); 1998 Malbec, Diego Murillo, Patagonia, £35.94 for 6, Safeway (red); 1997 Tempranillo, 'Q', £47.94 for 6, Tesco (red)**

You see, I just can't force the prices up: the wines are too good. Okay, maybe I can spend more on South Africa. Well, not if I stick with Fairview, the Cape's greatest quality/value producer:

1998 Malbec, £35.94 for 6, Waitrose (red); 1998 Viognier, £44.94 for 6, Fuller's Brewery Store (white); 1998 Shiraz/Mourvèdre, £41.94 for 6, Oddbins (red); 1998 Zinfandel…

…actually the Zinfandel is so good – and so potent – that the EU won't allow it to be sold to us poor wine lovers! So I'll estimate the price at £42 for 6.

Still not expensive enough, this stuff. What about a great South African Chardonnay and a great Pinotage?

1996 Chardonnay Reserve, Constantia Uitsig, £50.94 for 6, Parisa (tel: 01925 754545); 1998 Pinotage, Clos Malverne, Stellenbosch, £41.94 for 6, Waitrose (red)

Sorry, that only came to £93. But believe me – I am trying. And I'm close to £1000 already, at £939.22. And there's still Chile. How on earth did I forget Chile? Okay, here goes:

1998 La Escultura Sauvignon Blanc, Errázuriz, £29.94 for 6, Oddbins (white); 1998 El Descanso Merlot, Errázuriz, £35.94 for 6, Oddbins (red)

two marvellous, affordable new wines

1997 Santa Isabel Merlot, Viña Casablanca, £53.94 for 6, Moreno; 1997 Santa Isabel Cabernet Sauvignon, Viña Casablanca, £53.94 for 6, Oddbins

two unbelievably good reds from Ignacio Recabarren

1999 Carmenère, Viña Gracia (red) and 1999 Montes Alpha Syrah, Montes, (red), not in UK, c.£252 for 6 of each

if '99 is Chile's best vintage yet – here's why. I'm finding it so difficult to trade up because there's so much wonderful stuff at these prices. Oh, did I forget Greece? I forgot Greece. These you gotta have:

1997 Barrique Chardonnay, Tselepos, £35.94 for 6, Oddbins (white); 1997 Chardonnay, Antonopoulos, £65.94 for 6, Oddbins (white)

…and, don't laugh, a stunning sweet red:

NYX Mavrodaphne, 'Spiliopoulos, £41.94 for 6 50cl bottles, Oddbins

Well, that's another £144. So, at last, I really am trading up, but not before I've snatched these Aussies:

1997 The Footbolt Shiraz, d'Arenberg, McLaren Vale, £41.94 for 6, Oddbins (red); 1997 Semillon, Amberley Estate, Margaret River, £60.60 for 6, C. Piper (white); 1996 Cabernet Sauvignon, Sevenhills, Clare, not yet in UK, c.£60 for 6 (red)

Now, at last, the big leap…whoops, I forgot Italy. Just a couple from the super '98 vintage:

1998 Dolcetto d'Alba, Altare, £53.70 for 6, Justerini & Brooks (red); 1998 Dolcetto d'Alba, Albino Rocca, £52.50 for 6, Justerini & Brooks (red)

Er, sorry, but those 12 only cost me just over £106. Still, that's, that's…£1777.54. Where did the money go? On luscious, affordable, world-beating reds and whites – that's where. But if I'm down to my last 220-odd quid, I promise I will start to indulge:

1996 Louis Semillon, Henschke, Eden Valley, £65.70 for 6, Lay & Wheeler (white, Australia); 1996 Alsace Pinot Gris Réserve St-Urbain, Meyer-Fonné, £65.46 for 6, Lay & Wheeler (white); 1996 Patriarch Shiraz, David Wynn, £25.98 for 2, Philglas & Swiggot (red, Australia)

See? It's easy. And now – I will go mad. To The Classics. Well, my sort of classics:

1996 Cuvée Sauvage Chardonnay, Franciscan Estates, £15.49, Oddbins (white, United States); 1995 Cabernet Sauvignon, Thelema Mountain Vineyards, £15.95, Waitrose (red, South Africa); 1997 Condrieu, La Côte, Cuilleron, £19.99, Oddbins (white, Rhône); 1995 Taurasi, Caggiano, £23, Justerini & Brooks (red, Italy)

– four fascinating wines: old classics, new classics. A couple more…?

…sorry, Oz: you're out of space, out of time and out of money. [Ed.]

Total cost £2009.11

AUSTRALIA

The most interesting Australian wines are not the cheapest, but they don't have to be the most expensive, either. And do look beyond Chardonnay

Right, here's how to get the best out of Australia. First, go to the Australian section of your best local wine merchant. (By 'best' I mean most enterprising, most varied – and that might be a high street chain or a supermarket, or it might be an independent. 'Best' doesn't automatically mean most expensive, but neither does it automatically mean cheapest.) Look for the Chardonnays. And then look along the shelf for the Rieslings, the Semillons, perhaps a Verdelho or two; the Cabernets, yes, but also the Cabernet blends, the Shirazes, the blends of Mourvèdre and Grenache and a bit of this, a bit of that.

The point I'm trying to make is that we've all got so stuck on Australian Chardonnay as being so easy, so reliable, so everlastingly drinkable, that we can forget that Australia is actually much more than just Chardonnay. At first, when good Aussie wines started appearing here, we lacked a bit of confidence and it took that lovely reassuring word on the label – Chardonnay – to make us realise that actually we were in safe territory. Well, now we know more. And the Aussies have gained confidence, too. (Is that possible? I hear you ask.) Confidence in us, I mean: they know now that we're prepared to experiment, and if they send us some whacky blend or some complex, subtle single-vineyard number we'll give it a go. Well, provided that the price is right.

It's true that prices have risen, and to be honest they probably won't ever come down again at the top level. People who produce top-class wines reckon they should get top-class prices for them, and I'm the last person to say that's wrong. And the very cheapest wines are likely to lack character. But at the £5 to £8 range there are some wonderful, characterful wines to be had, perhaps from producers you've never heard of or grapes and regions you've never heard of. But all of them worth risking a few quid on. And after all, wasn't Australia built by pioneers?

GRAPE VARIETIES

CABERNET SAUVIGNON (red) This can be rich and chocolaty in the Barossa, austere and minty in Victoria's Pyrenees, full of moss, tobacco and cedar flavours in the Eden Valley, and dense, phenolic and black in the Hunter. Sometimes it can be all of these, sometimes it can taste of nothing more than simple blackcurrant jelly. It's an Aussie staple these days, and even cheaper ones generally have clear fruit, without the muddiness that can mar cheap claret. And when it's good, it's breathtaking. It's also often blended with other grapes, particularly Shiraz or the Bordeaux varieties Cabernet Franc and/or Merlot. Best: *Clancy's Shiraz/ Cabernet, Greenock Creek, Peter Lehmann, Rockford, St Hallett Cabernet/Merlot, Seppelt's Dorrien, Yalumba The Menzies* and *The Signature* (Barossa); *Grosset, Knappstein Cabernet/Merlot* (also a good Cabernet Franc), *Leasingham Cabernet/Malbec* and *Classic, Wendouree* (Clare); *Bowen Estate, Hollick's Ravenswood, Katnook Odyssey, Leconfield, Lindemans Pyrus, Lindemans Limestone Ridge* and *Lindemans St George, Orlando, Parker, Penley Estate, Petaluma, Wynns Coonawarra* and *John Riddoch, Yalumba* (Coonawarra); *Heggies, Henschke Cyril Henschke, Hill-Smith Estate, Mountadam The Red, Seppelt's Partalunga* (Eden Valley);

Chateau Tahbilk (Goulburn Valley); *Mt Langi Ghiran* (Grampians); *Frankland Estate, Goundrey, Howard Park, Plantagenet* (Great Southern); *Brokenwood, Lake's Folly, Rothbury Shiraz/Cabernet* (Hunter); *Cape Mentelle, Capel Vale, Chateau Xanadu, Cullen, Devil's Lair, Leeuwin Estate, Lenton Brae, Moss Wood, Sandstone, Vasse Felix The Heytesbury* (Margaret River); *Chapel Hill The Vicar, Chateau Reynella, Coriole Shiraz/Cabernet, d'Arenberg Coppermine Road, Mount Hurtle, Reynella Basket Press, Shottesbrooke, Simon Hackett Foggo Road, Wirra Wirra* (McLaren Vale); *Dromana Estate* (Mornington); *Taltarni* (Pyrenees); *Domaine A, Freycinet* (Tasmania); *Seppelt's Drumborg, Tisdall Mt Helen* (Victoria); *Coldstream Hills, Mount Mary, Seville Estate, St Huberts, Yarra Yering* (Yarra); *Kangaroo Island* (South Eyre Peninsula); *Geoff Merrill, Penfolds* (various).

CHARDONNAY (white) Australia has done more than most to give this grape mass appeal with its rich, fruity wines. Most are now far more restrained than they were, but the fruit is still there. The best have gained complexity while not losing their original appeal. Best: *Ashton Hills, Bridgewater Mill, Petaluma, Shaw & Smith Reserve* (Adelaide Hills); *Andrew Garrett, Basedow, St Hallett, Greenock Creek, Peter Lehmann* (Barossa); *Giaconda* (Beechworth); *Grosset* (Clare); *Katnook* (Coonawarra); *Richmond Grove* (Cowra); *Henschke, Hill-Smith Estate, Mountadam, Seppelt's Partalunga* (Eden Valley); *Bannockburn* (Geelong); *Michelton Preece* (Goulburn); *Frankland Estate, Howard Park, Plantagenet, Wignalls* (Great Southern); *Allandale, Allanmere, Brokenwood, Glenguin, McWilliams' Mount Pleasant, Rosemount, Scarborough* (Hunter); *Knappstein, Stafford Ridge* (Lenswood); *Chateau Reynella, Geoff Merrill, Wirra Wirra* (McLaren Vale); *Cape Mentelle, Chateau Xanadu, Cullen, Evans & Tate, Leeuwin Estate, Lenton Brae, Moss Wood, Pierro* (Margaret River); *Dromana Estate* (Mornington); *Goundry* (Mount Barker); *Eileen Hardy, Lindemans* (Padthaway); *Pipers Brook* (Tasmania);

Tisdall Mt Helen (Victoria), *Coldstream Hills* (Yarra); *Koonunga Hill* (various).

CHENIN BLANC (white) The Australian incarnation of this grape ripens to a much fuller, fruitier and blander style than its steely Loire counterpart. *Moondah Brook* (Swan Valley) does a good example; *Sandalford* (Western Australia) blends it with the Madeira grape Verdelho.

FORTIFIEDS Shiraz and other Rhône-type grapes are often used to make port styles. Vintage is wonderful. Best: *Chateau Reynella, Lindemans, Montara, Penfolds, Saltram, Seppelt, Stanton & Killeen, Yalumba.*

GEWÜRZTRAMINER (white) Decent, faintly spicy examples smelling of lychees and honeydew melon are made by *Brown Brothers, Delatite* and *Lillydale* (Victoria), and *Tim Knappstein* (Clare). *Orlando-Wyndham Flaxman's* (Eden Valley) and *Tolleys* (Barossa) are always good. *Rymill*'s botrytis version (Coonawarra) is intense.

GRENACHE (red) The Southern Vales around Adelaide are the heartland of this Mediterranean variety, and the rediscovery of old vines sitting there squeezing out more and more concentrated grapes has resulted in a range of wonderful wines; the *Turkey Flat* vines have been in constant production since 1847. Best: *Charles Melton, RBJ, Rockford, St Hallett Gamekeeper's Reserve, Turkey Flat, Whitmore Old Vineyard, Yaldara Reserve, Yalumba Bush Vine Grenache* and *The Reserve* (Barossa); *James Halliday Shiraz/Grenache, Mitchelton III* (Goulburn); *d'Arenberg Ironstone Pressings, Tim Gramp* (McLaren Vale).

MARSANNE (white) In Central Victoria, both *Chateau Tahbilk* and *Mitchelton* have made big, broad, ripe Marsanne.

MUSCAT (white) There are two types of Muscat in Australia: first, the bag-in-box Fruity Gordo or Muscat of Alexandria –

fruity, sweetish, swigging wine, from a heavy-cropping lowish-quality grape grown along the Murray River; second, liqueur Muscat, made from the Brown Muscat, a strain of the top quality Muscat à Petits Grains, grown in Victoria. It is a sensation: dark, treacly even, with a perfume of strawberry and honeyed raisins. Best producers include *All Saints, Baileys, Bullers, Campbells, Chambers, Morris, Stanton & Killeen* and *Yalumba*.

PINOT NOIR (red) It looks increasingly as if New Zealand is Pinot Noir's Southern Hemisphere heartland. But Australia makes a few decent ones. Best: *Ashton Hills, Hillstowe, Pibbin* (Adelaide Hills); *Giaconda* (Beechworth); *Mountadam* (Eden Valley); *Bannockburn* (Geelong); *Wignall's* (Great Southern); *Tyrrell Vat 6* (Hunter); *Ashton Hills, Henschke, Tim Knappstein, Lenswood* (Lenswood); *Moss Wood* (Margaret River); *Freycinet, Spring Vale, Pipers Brook, Tasmania Wine Co* (Tasmania); *Coldstream Hills, Mt Mary, St Huberts, Tarrawarra, Yarra Yering* (Yarra).

RIESLING (white) Australia makes highly individual Rieslings, all sharing a lime aroma: some are clean and crisp (*Ashton Hills, Pewsey Vale, Leeuwin Estate*), some softer and more rounded (*Heritage, Skillogalee*), and others beg to be aged (*Orlando Steingarten, Mount Langhi Ghiran*). It's a wonderful apéritif and the perfect partner for Thai and Pacific Rim cooking: not many white wines could stand up to those flavours, but Australian Riesling sails through them. Other good ones: *Rockford* (Barossa); *Tim Adams, Jim Barry, Grosset, Tim Knappstein, Mitchell, Petaluma, Pikes* (Clare); *Heggies, Hill-Smith Estate, Lindemans Leo Buring, Orlando St Helga, Seppelt's Partalunga* (Eden Valley); *Frankland Estate, Howard Park* (Great Southern); *Henschke* (Lenswood or Eden Valley); *Pipers Brook* (Tasmania); *Delatite* (Victoria), *Tim Gramp* (McLaren Vale). Botrytis-affected wines: *Mt Horrocks, Petaluma* and *St Huberts.*

SAUVIGNON BLANC (white) Here too New Zealand is leading the field in the southern hemisphere, though cool Adelaide Hills is proving its worth, with *Shaw & Smith, Stafford Ridge* and *Lenswood*, while Margaret River's richer styles are like southern hemisphere Graves (*Cullen, Evans & Tate*). Best: *Jim Barry, Pikes* (Clare); *Katnook, Riddoch* (Coonawarra); *Hill-Smith Estate* (Eden Valley); *Bannockburn, Scotchmans Hill* (Geelong); *Frankland Estate, Wignalls* (Great Southern); *Amberley Estate, Ribbon Vale* (Margaret River); *Mount Hurtle, Wirra Wirra* (McLaren Vale); *Hardy, Lindemans* (Padthaway); *Yarra Valley Hills* (Yarra); *Brown Brothers, Mitchelton Preece* (Victoria); *Bridgewater Mill* (various).

SEMILLON (white) Unoaked Aussie Semillon is rare and great; lean and grassy when young, and needing years for its flavours of toast and honey to emerge. That makes it hopelessly uncommercial: you can hardly blame the producers for opting for oak and a quick sale. *Glenguin, McWilliams Elizabeth* and *Tyrrell's Vat 1* are the unoaked versions to look for. But oaked Semillon is delicious as well, waxy and toasty, and the best will age. Try: *Heritage, Peter Lehmann, Rockford, Grant Burge* (Barossa); *Grosset, Mitchell, Mount Horrocks* (Clare); *Henschke, Hill-Smith Estate* (Eden Valley); *Cassegrain* (Hastings Valley); *Brokenwood, Lindemans, Petersen, Rothbury* (Hunter); *Knappstein* (Lenswood); *Evans & Tate, Moss Wood, Sandstone* (Margaret River); *Simon Hackett* (McLaren Vale); *Brown Bros* (Milawa). Best blends with Sauvignon: *St Hallett* (Barossa); *Brokenwood* (Hunter); *Cape Mentelle, Pierro, Xanadu Secession, Cullen* (Margaret River); *Wirra Wirra* (McLaren Vale). *Geoff Merrill* blends with Chardonnay. Best sweet wines: *Peter Lehmann, Tim Adams, de Bortoli, Fern Hill, Cranswick.*

SHIRAZ (red) The most widely planted red vine in Oz, but look for wine from old vines for greatest depth of flavour. There's the dense, black iron intensity of Clare, the chocolate, earth and moss of the Barossa, the black pepper of the cooler bits of Victoria and Western Australia, or the simple red berry sweetness of the hot Murray Valley. Try: *Basedow, Grant Burge Meshach, Greenock Creek, Peter Lehmann, Charles Melton, Rockford, St Hallett Old Block, Yalumba Octavius* (Barossa); *McWilliams* (Barwang); *Jasper Hill, Passing Clouds* (Bendigo); *Tim Adams, Jim Barry The Armagh, Mitchell, Pikes, Wendouree* (Clare); *Bowen, Majella, Wynns, Zema* (Coonawarra); *Craneford, Henschke, David Wynn Patriarch* (Eden); *Bannockburn* (Geelong); *Ch. Tahbilk* (Goulburn); *Mt Langi Ghiran* (Grampians); *Plantagenet* (Great Southern); *Allandale Matthew, Brokenwood, McWilliams Old Paddock* and *Old Hill, Rothbury, Tulloch Hector, Tyrrell's Vat 9* (Hunter); *Craiglee* (Macedon); *Cape Mentelle* (Margaret River); *Chapel Hill, Chateau Reynella, d'Arenberg Old Vine* and *Dead Arm, Hardy* (McLaren Vale); *Goundrey* (Mount Barker); *Dalwhinnie, Taltarni* (Pyrenees); *Baileys* (Rutherglen); *Baileys 1920s Block* (Victoria); *Yarra Yering* (Yarra Valley); *Hardy, Penfolds, Yaldara Reserve* (various).

SPARKLING WINES In the lead for quality are *Croser, Green Point, Yalumba D, Salinger* and *Jansz*. Cheaper ones include: *Seaview, Angas Brut, Orlando Carrington*. Upmarket: *Seppelt's Blanc de Blancs* and *Pinot Noir/Chardonnay*. And try *Yalumba's Cabernet* and *Seppelt's Shiraz* (sparkling red).

OTHER GRAPES *Heggies* is increasing plantings of Viognier, and very good it is too. Verdelho makes rich, lime-flavoured wines (*Richmond Grove, Pendarves Estate, Rothbury Estate, Broke Fordwich Wine Co, Moondah Brook, Hill of Hope*). Look too for Rhône grapes like Mourvèdre and Grenache, and blends of these from *St Hallett, d'Arenberg, Basedow, Grant Burge* and *Tim Gramp*.

WINE REGIONS

The Australian Geographical Indication system aims to identify areas that produce wines with their own distinct character. But it also has to accommodate the widespread system of inter-regional blending: that is, trucking grapes from several different regions, possibly in different states, to a central winery for blending together. Some of Australia's most famous wines *(Grange,* for example) are blended like this.

The most general designation is Produce of Australia. The next most general is South-Eastern Australia, an appellation which already exists and is much seen; it covers most of the wine-producing area. Then there is the more specific State of Origin, and then there are zones, regions and sub-regions. In all there will be about 400 Geographical Indications.

ADELAIDE HILLS (South Australia)
This cool area was pioneered by *Petaluma*, which has been joined by firms such as *Shaw & Smith, Stafford Ridge, Henschke* and *Lenswood*, making classically pure Sauvignon Blanc, Chardonnays with great length and some classy Pinot Noir.

BAROSSA VALLEY (South Australia)
This is the heart of the Australian wine industry, planted originally by immigrants from Silesia. Most of Australia's wine passes through the Barossa Valley, if only for bottling or aging. It's also a source of wonderful old-vine Grenache and Shiraz. Best: *Penfolds, Orlando-Wyndham, Peter Lehmann, Mildara-Blass, Rockford, Greenock Creek, Charles Melton, Grant Burge, St Hallett, Basedow*.

INSTANT CELLAR:
LIFE BEYOND CHARDONNAY

• 1996 Semillon/Sauvignon, Cullen, Margaret River, £12.75, Adnams All the complexity and finesse one expects of this grower.
• 1997 Riesling, St Hallett, Eden Valley, £7.99, Australian Wine Club Lime-lemon fruit with a swirl of flowers. It'll age, too.
• 1996 Semillon, Willows Vineyard, £8.50, Australian Wine Club Classic lemony Semillon that seems light now but that will age to lovely toastiness.
• 1998 Verdelho, David Traeger, £8.50, Australian Wine Club Limes and herbs, full fruit and very good balance.
• 1998 Sauvignon Blanc, Geoff Weaver, £9.99, Ballantynes Zingy Sauvignon of the type seldom found in Oz.
• 1997 Viognier, Heggies, Eden Valley, £11.95, Balls Brothers One of the best Viogniers around, it ages to a rich waxiness.
• 1993 Mount Pleasant Elizabeth Semillon, McWilliams, Hunter Valley, £9.25, Cockburns of Leith Classic unoaked Semillon with waxy, lemony fruit.

BENDIGO (Victoria) This 19th-century region, destroyed by phylloxera, has been replanted with excellent Cabernet, good Shiraz and some Pinot Noir. *Balgownie* is the leader, with *Chateau Leamon, Craiglee, Harcourt Valley, Heathcote, Mount Ida, Passing Clouds* and *Yellowglen* important.

CANBERRA DISTRICT (ACT) In the Australian Capital Territory, with some modest wineries producing wines to match.

CLARE VALLEY (South Australia) An upland complex of four valleys (Skillogalee, Clare, Watervale and Polish River), Clare is all things to many grapes: cool and dry enough for steely, limy Riesling (*Leo Buring, Tim Knappstein, Jim Barry, Pikes, Grosset*) and soft, light Chardonnay (*Penfolds*), but warm enough for rounded Semillon (*Mitchell*) and long-living reds (*Wendouree, Knappstein, Skillogalee, Leasingham* and *Watervale*).

COONAWARRA (South Australia) A big, flat, wide open landscape with the famous cigar-shaped strip of *terra rossa* soil at its heart. It is Australia's most profitable red wine vineyard, and its incredibly expensive land is jam-packed with great names. Coonawarra is best at Cabernet and unirrigated Shiraz. Try: *Bowen, Brand's Laira, BRL Hardy, Hollick, Katnook, Lindemans, Majella, Mildara, Orlando, Penfolds, Penley, Petaluma, Rouge Homme, Rosemount, Rymill, Wynns* and *Zema*. Other similar limestone ridges nearby – so new they hardly have names yet – are currently being planted, with promising results.

EDEN VALLEY (South Australia) Home to some of Australia's oldest vineyards, like *Henschke*'s 120-year-old Hill of Grace, and some of the newest and most high-tech (*Mountadam* and *Seppelt's Partalunga*). Most of the major Barossa companies take fruit from these rolling uplands. *Yalumba* is here, with *Heggies* and *Hill-Smith Estate* vineyards.

GEELONG (Victoria) Best are intense Cabernets from vineyards like *Idyll* and *Bannockburn*, Pinot Noir from *Prince Albert* and *Bannockburn*, and whites from *Idyll*.

GLENROWAN (Victoria) Famous for *Baileys*' torrid, palate-blasting reds from Cabernet and Shiraz and (more importantly) Muscats. These are intensely sweet, the very essence of the overripe brown Muscat grape, full of an exotic tangle of orange and honey. *Brown Brothers* makes a wide range, but its best are from the *Koombahla* and *Whitlands* sites.

GOULBURN VALLEY (Victoria) This houses *Mitchelton*, a medium-sized modern winery, and *Chateau Tahbilk*, one of the nation's oldest, still making traditional intense reds and long-lived Marsanne. Tiny, high-tech *Delatite* is nearby.

GRAMPIANS (Victoria) The new name for Great Western; still the source of base wine for *Seppelt's Great Western* fizz, but more exciting for its reds. Shiraz is full of chocolate, coconut and cream at *Cathcart Ridge*, or liquorice and pepper at *Mount Langi Ghiran*. *Best's*, *Montara* and *Seppelt* are other top names. Excellent Chardonnay from *Best's* and *Seppelt*, Cabernet from *Mount Langi Ghiran*, fortified from *Montara*.

GRANITE BELT (Queensland) The vines are planted high up in what is otherwise a banana and mango belt. Most wines serve the local market and some (*Ballandean, Kominos Wines, Rumbalara, Robinsons Family* and *Stone Ridge*) are good. *Ironbark Ridge* is one to watch.

GREAT SOUTHERN (Western Australia) One of Australia's most promising wine areas, good for Riesling, limy Chardonnay, peppery Shiraz and magnificent Cabernet. Try *Goundrey, Alkoomi, Plantagenet, Frankland Estate* and *Howard Park*, home of *Madfish Bay* blends.

HUNTER VALLEY (New South Wales) This old-established region is home to wonderfully individual Semillons that will last for decades, and great leathery Shiraz. Best producers include: *McWilliams Mount Pleasant, Tyrrell's, Rosemount* and its *Roxburgh* vineyard, *Reynolds, Rothbury, Allandale* and *Glenguin*.

LOWER GREAT SOUTHERN (Western Australia) A vast, rambling area of great promise, especially round Mount Barker. *Alkoomi, Forest Hill, Goundrey, Howard Park* and *Plantagenet* are good. The whites are fragrant and appetizing, with zesty Riesling and Sauvignon, but the reds are best, with spicy, tobaccoey Cabernets.

MARGARET RIVER (Western Australia) A source of increasingly poised wines that reek of a sense of place, combining richness of fruit with elegance of structure. *Moss Wood, Cape Mentelle, Cullen, Pierro, Vasse Felix* and *Leeuwin Estate* are the

names to watch, and while Semillon and Sauvignon (as varietals and blends), Cabernet and Chardonnay are the most common wines, there is a scattering of other grapes like Zinfandel, Malbec, Sangiovese and Nebbiolo.

MCLAREN VALE (South Australia) Some wonderful old Shiraz vineyards are now under tarmac, thanks to the spread of Adelaide suburbia. The building has been slowed by a revival of interest in the singular quality of the area's fruit, in particular the boldness of the black pepper Shiraz and the sweet concentration of Grenache. Recommended are *Four Sisters, Chateau Reynella Basket Pressed Shiraz, Coriole Redstone Shiraz/Cabernet, d'Arenberg Ironstone Pressings, Twentyeight Road, Custodian* and *Coppermine Road, Geoff Merrill, Mount Hurtle*.

MORNINGTON PENINSULA (Victoria) One of the coolest Aussie wine zones, this is a weekend playground for the Melbourne rich. Good for light Chardonnay, sparkling wine and sometimes Pinot Noir. Among the best wineries are *Dromana, Stonier's* and *Moorooduc Estate*.

MUDGEE (New South Wales) Though Mudgee was established on Shiraz (*Montrose* is outstanding), the best reds have been tarry, plummy Cabernets. But Chardonnay is even better, usually rich, soft and full of fruit-salad flavours. Best: *Montrose, Craigmoor, Huntington, Miramar*.

ORANGE (New South Wales) A new cool-climate region already making intense Loire-style Sauvignon Blanc (*Highland Heritage*) and cashew nut Chardonnay (*Rosemount*), while the reds, notably Shiraz Cabernet and Merlot (from *Bloodwood, Reynolds* and *Rosemount*) are outstanding.

PADTHAWAY (South Australia) High quality whites, notably Chardonnay, Riesling and Sauvignon Blanc. Grapes for sparkling wine are grown here, and there is some excellent sweet Riesling. Best: *Hardy, Lindemans, Seppelt*; major names like *Orlando* and *Penfolds* also use the grapes.

PEMBERTON (Western Australia) New region achieving promising results with Pinot Noir.

PYRENEES (Victoria) Very dry Shiraz and Cabernet reds, and mostly Sauvignon whites. Tops: *Dalwhinnie, Mount Avoca, Redbank, Taltarni, Warrenmang*, and for fizz, *Chateau Remy* (also stylish Cabernet and Chardonnay) and *Taltarni*.

RIVERINA (New South Wales) The vast irrigated Riverina (which used to be called Murrumbidgee Irrigation Area) provides ten to 15 per cent of the total Australian crop. Most is bulk wine, but *McWilliams* makes some attractive wines, as does *de Bortoli*, including a Sauternes-style Semillon and marmalady Rare Dry Botrytis Semillon.

RIVERLAND (South Australia) A vast irrigation project on the Murray River providing a large chunk of the national crop. Dominated by the huge *Angove's* winery, and the even bigger *Berri-Renmano-Loxton* group (part of BRL Hardy), it makes huge amounts of bag-in-box wines of consistently good quality. But it also yields fresh, fruity Riesling, Chardonnay, Chenin, Sauvignon, Colombard, Cabernet and Shiraz.

RUTHERGLEN (Victoria) The centre of the fortified wine tradition. The white table wines are generally dull, except for the reliably fine *St Leonards*. The reds are rich and robust. The fortifieds, either as solera-method 'sherries', as 'vintage ports', or as intense, brown sugar-sweet Tokays, are all memorable. The true heights are achieved by sweet Muscats, unbearably rich but irresistible with it. Best: *Bullers, Campbells, Chambers, Morris, Stanton & Killeen*.

SWAN VALLEY (Western Australia) This hot region made its reputation on big, rich reds and whites, but even the famous *Houghton Supreme* is now much lighter and fresher. Good names: *Bassendean, Evans & Tate, Houghton, Moondah Brook, Sandalford*.

TASMANIA Only tiny amounts, but there is some remarkable Chardonnay from *Pipers Brook* and *Tasmanian Wine Co.*, and Cabernet from *Freycinet* and *Domaine A*. Pinot Noir can be terrific.

YARRA VALLEY (Victoria) Victoria's superstar. It suits the Champagne grapes, Pinot Noir and Chardonnay, for fizz, plus Cabernet and Pinot for superb reds. Best producers include: *Coldstream Hills, de Bortoli, Diamond Valley, Lillydale, Mount Mary, St Huberts, Seville, Tarrawarra, Yarra Burn, Yarra Ridge, Yarra Yering* and *Yeringberg*. Lots of big names are moving in, so expect more Yarra wines on the shelves.

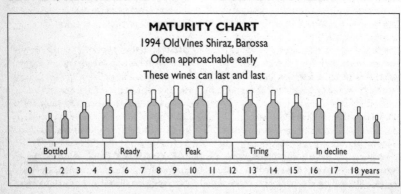

MATURITY CHART
1994 Old Vines Shiraz, Barossa
Often approachable early
These wines can last and last

| Bottled | Ready | Peak | Tiring | In decline |

| 0 | 1 | 2 | 3 | 4 | 5 | 6 | 7 | 8 | 9 | 10 | 11 | 12 | 13 | 14 | 15 | 16 | 17 | 18 years |

PRODUCERS WHO'S WHO

TIM ADAMS ★★★★(★) (South Australia) Spellbinding Semillon and a dense, full-flavoured Shiraz.

ALLANDALE ★★★(★) (New South Wales) One of the best Hunter Semillons; also complex, slightly honeyed Chardonnay and the excellent Matthew Shiraz.

BAILEYS OF GLENROWAN ★★★(★) (Victoria) Traditional winery famous for stunning sweet Muscats and Tokays, which are reassuringly rich. Red table wines are full and correct, though lacking the sense of history.

BANNOCKBURN ★★★★ (Victoria) Some of cool-climate Geelong's best wines: a rich Pinot Noir, full-bodied Chardonnay and Shiraz.

BAROSSA VALLEY ESTATES ★★(★) (South Australia) BRL Hardy-owned, this specializes in good quality, cheap wine.

JIM BARRY ★★★★ (South Australia) Clare Valley winery; outstanding unwooded Chardonnay, Rhine Riesling, Sauvignon Blanc and a splendidly rich Shiraz, The Armagh.

BASEDOW ★★★★ (South Australia) Barossa winery with big, toasty, oaky Chardonnay and Semillon, fine Watervale Riesling, chocolaty Shiraz and Cabernet. Old fashioned in the best way.

WOLF BLASS ★★★(★) (South Australia) The wines are decent at this Mildara-owned winery – modern, well plumped out with fruit and oak – but rarely match the silky, come-hither brilliance of the old days. Voluptuous Chardonnay, good Riesling and five styles of red which are, in rising price order, red, yellow, grey, brown and black labels.

BOWEN ESTATE ★★★★ (South Australia) The best value in Coonawarra: elegant Cabernet/Merlot and razor-fine Shiraz renowned for consistency and quality. Very good Riesling and Chardonnay.

BRL HARDY★★★★ (South Australia) Huge company making both high-standard, cheap own-labels and Hardy's impressive range from Nottage Hill to Chateau Reynella and Eileen Hardy. Look out, too, for Hardy's rich, sweet Botrytized Riesling.

BROKENWOOD ★★★★(★) (New South Wales) Small, high-class Hunter Valley winery noted for eclectic blends such as Hunter/Coonawarra Cabernet and latterly Hunter/McLaren Vale Semillon/Sauvignon Blanc. Low-yielding Graveyard vineyard produces one of Australia's best Shirazes: concentrated, profound and long-living.

BROWN BROTHERS ★★★ (Victoria) A huge range of good wine. The best vineyards are the cool Koombahla and even cooler Whitlands; look for Muscat, Semillon, Chardonnay, Koombahla Cabernet, Whitlands Gewürz and Riesling, the last in every style up to sweet and botrytized.

CAPE MENTELLE ★★★★(★) (Western Australia) Excellent Cabernet and variations on the Semillon/Sauvignon theme as well as Shiraz – and Zinfandel.

CHAPEL HILL ★★★★ (South Australia) Impressive wines with restraint and style include toasty Eden Valley Riesling, unwooded Chardonnay and chocolaty, blackberry-flavoured The Vicar, a blend of Cabernet and Shiraz.

CHATEAU TAHBILK ★★★★ (Victoria) Historic Goulburn Valley winery with great traditional Shiraz and Cabernet Sauvignon, and excellent Marsanne.

COLDSTREAM HILLS ★★★★
(Victoria) World-class Pinot Noir, exciting
Chardonnay and Cabernet-Merlot blend,
Briarston. Now owned by giant Southcorp,
which seems to want to maintain quality.

CULLEN ★★★★(★) (Western
Australia) Cullen has made consistently
intense wines from the word go, and gets
better with each vintage. Releases include a
benchmark Sauvignon Blanc, a richly elegant
Cabernet and good Pinot Noir.

D'ARENBERG ★★★★ (South
Australia) Firmly traditional winemaking
produces powerfully rich Shiraz capable of
almost infinite aging, sweetly fruity
Custodian Grenache and densely structured
Ironstone Pressings Grenache/Shiraz. Dead
Arm is Cabernet and Shiraz; The Other
Side is Chardonnay; Twentyeight Road is
Mourvèdre and Nostalgia is 12-year-old
fortified.

DE BORTOLI ★★★(★) (New South
Wales) Rich sweet Noble One Botrytis
Semillon, plus a string of well-priced basics.
Rare Dry Botrytis Semillon has bags of
marmalade flavour but little subtlety. De
Bortoli's Yarra Valley property makes good
Chardonnay, Cabernet and Shiraz.

DELATITE ★★★★ (Victoria) Wines
with individuality of style plus superb wine-
making which puts them in the top class.
Dry Riesling is delicious, the sweet version
superb, while Pinot Noir, Gewürztraminer,
Cabernet and Shiraz are brilliant.

DROMANA ★★★(★) (Victoria)
Excellent Chardonnay, promising Pinot Noir
and Cabernet/Merlot in the Mornington
Peninsula, as well as the good-value
Schinus-Molle label.

EVANS & TATE ★★★(★) (Western
Australia) Beautifully crafted, stylish wines; in
particular weighty Semillon (straight and
blended with Sauvignon), Merlot and Shiraz.

GOUNDREY ★★★(★) (Western
Australia) Wines of real concentration,
including the Windy Hill pairing of
Chardonnay and Cabernet, and the soft,
coffee bean aromas of Shiraz from Mount
Barker.

GREEN POINT ★★★★ (Victoria) Moët
& Chandon's Australian outpost, making
possibly Australia's best sparklers from
Champagne grape varieties.

HENSCHKE ★★★★★ (South Australia)
Old red vines, some of them 100 years old,
that yield deep, dark, curranty wines of top
class. Cyril Henschke Cabernet Sauvignon is
terrifically rich. Whites are equally stunning
– Riesling, Semillon and Chardonnay.

HERITAGE ★★★(★) (South Australia)
Among Barossa's boisterous winemakers,
Heritage is a hidden gem, quietly producing
classic wines from a wide range of varieties
– limy Riesling, softly honeyed Semillon and
an elegant Cabernet Franc.

HILL-SMITH/YALUMBA ★★★★
(South Australia) A large Barossa company
producing good wines under the Yalumba
and Hill-Smith labels, and exceptional ones
under the Signature, Heggies and Pewsey
Vale Vineyard labels, where dry and sweet
Rieslings are some of the finest in Australia.
Yalumba D is very good fizz. Look out for
The Octavius Shiraz and Antipodean –
Sauvignon Blanc, Semillon and Viognier –
from Yalumba.

HOLLICK ★★★ (South Australia) Some
of Coonawarra's suavest reds; rich Wilgha
Shiraz/Cabernet and an outstanding
Cabernet cuvée, Ravenswood. There is also
fine Pinot and Chardonnay fizz and the
district's most successful Riesling.

HOWARD PARK ★★★(★) (Western
Australia) Expensive but superb, long-living
wines. Intense, structured Chardonnay and
rich Cabernet/Merlot. Both need cellaring.

KNAPPSTEIN ★★★ (South Australia) Ageworthy Riesling, spicy, restrained Traminer, nutty, long Chardonnay and ripe, grassy Cabernet Franc.

LAKE'S FOLLY ★★★★ (New South Wales) Tiny Hunter Valley winery making highly idiosyncratic Chardonnay and Cabernet Sauvignon that become very exciting with age.

LEEUWIN ESTATE ★★★★ (Western Australia) Ultra-high profile, ultra-high prices for exciting Chardonnay and Pinot Noir, blackcurrant-and-leather Cabernet Sauvignon, good Riesling and Sauvignon. Prelude Cabernet Sauvignon is tops.

LINDEMANS ★★★★ (Victoria) Exceptionally good basic varietals, while Coonawarras, Padthaways and Hunters are among Australia's finest. Coonawarra reds Limestone Ridge and St George are tip-top, as is the Bordeaux blend, Pyrus. New is smoky, leafy Bin 70: Semillon, Verdelho, Sauvignon and Chardonnay.

MCWILLIAMS ★★(★) (New South Wales) Blends like the Hillside Colombard/ Chardonnay show what can be done with fairly basic fruit. Unoaked Elizabeth Semillon repays aging.

CHARLES MELTON ★★★★ (South Australia) A small Barossa winery with Grenache-based Nine Popes and a Shiraz of exceptional concentration and character.

GEOFF MERRILL ★★★(★) (South Australia) Wines here include worthy Cabernet, full Chardonnay, crisp Sauvignon/ Semillon and thirst-quenching Grenache rosé at Mount Hurtle.

MILDARA-BLASS ★★★ (South Australia) Own labels include Jamieson's Run and Robertson's Well and the Coonawarra reds are beginning to live up to their potential. Chardonnay is also improving, but Sauvignon and Pinot Noir need a bit of work yet. Umpteen subsidiaries: see also entries for Baileys of Glenrowan, Wolf Blass, Rothbury, St Huberts and Tisdall.

MITCHELTON ★★★(★) (Victoria) Wide range of styles, notably fine, full-flavoured Rieslings, good Chardonnay under the Preece label and the speciality of the house, Marsanne. Also interesting Rhône blends: Mitchelton III white is Marsanne, Roussanne and Viognier; Mitchelton III red is Shiraz, Grenache and Mourvèdre.

MOORILLA ESTATE ★★(★) (Tasmania) A polished range of crisp, cool-climate wines. Pinot Noir is a speciality; aromatic Riesling, Chardonnay and Gewürztraminer are also good.

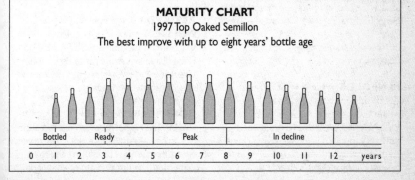

MATURITY CHART
1997 Top Oaked Semillon
The best improve with up to eight years' bottle age

| Bottled | Ready | | Peak | | In decline | |

0 1 2 3 4 5 6 7 8 9 10 11 12 years

MORRIS ★★★★(★) (Victoria) The leading producer of sweet liqueur Muscat and Tokay which give a new meaning to the words 'intense' and 'concentrated'.

MOSS WOOD ★★★★ (Western Australia) Superbly original wines. Semillon, with and without wood-aging, is some of the best in Australia. Pinot Noir is daring and delicious, Chardonnay less daring but just as delicious, Cabernet rich and structured. All have lots of polished fruit.

MOUNTADAM ★★★★(★) (South Australia) French-trained Adam Wynn makes complex, Burgundian Chardonnay, substantial Pinot Noir, idiosyncratic Riesling and lean Cabernet. The Red is a Cabernet/Merlot blend, and there's good rosé fizz, too.

MOUNT LANGI GHIRAN ★★★★ (Victoria) Grampians winery making richly flavoured, dry, intense Shiraz, long-lived Cabernet Sauvignon and properly spicy Pinot Grigio.

MOUNT MARY ★★★★ (Victoria) Finely structured Cabernet-based Bordeaux blend and a Pinot Noir improving with age. Tiny production, much sought-after.

ORLANDO ★★★ (South Australia) Barossa winery with fine quality at every level. Its boxed wine is outstanding, its RF Cabernet, Riesling and Chardonnay are usually the best in the price bracket, and St Helga Riesling, St Hilary Chardonnay and St Hugo Cabernet are among the best. Excellent Jacaranda Ridge Cabernet from Coonawarra.

PENFOLDS ★★★★★ (South Australia) Great red wine producer, and now good in whites too, particularly Old Vine Barossa Valley Semillon. Its basics are clean and tasty, its varietals packed with flavour, and its special selection reds, culminating in the deservedly legendary Grange, are

superlative, hugely structured wines of world class. Reserve Bin 94A Chardonnay is supposed to be the white equivalent of Grange.

PENLEY ESTATE ★★★★ (South Australia) There's rich, concentrated Shiraz/Cabernet from here as well as ageworthy Cabernet Sauvignon, supple Phoenix Cabernet and elegant Chardonnay.

PETALUMA ★★★★(★) (South Australia) Brian Croser's fizz is always correct, and his tip-top Chardonnay deserves aging. Riesling is limy and elegant. Coonawarra red is good, but the whites are even better.

PIPERS BROOK ★★★★ (Tasmania) Steely aromatic Riesling, classically reserved Chardonnay, serious Pinot Noir and tasty, barrel-fermented Sauvignon Blanc are joined by elegant Tamar Cabernet and rounder Bordeaux blend Opimian.

PLANTAGENET ★★★(★) (Western Australia) Noted for peppery Shiraz, melony/nutty Chardonnay, fine limy Riesling and elegant Cabernet Sauvignon. Sparkling wine is good too, as is Pinot Noir.

REYNOLDS ★★★★ (New South Wales) This recently established Upper Hunter estate has already built a reputation with its chocolaty Cabernet, powerful Shiraz and well-structured Semillon.

ROCKFORD ★★★★(★) (South Australia) The individuality of Rocky O'Callaghan's wines, especially his Basket Press Shiraz, has made him a Barossa cult. Grenache and Riesling are marvellous, too, and all improve with aging.

ROSEMOUNT ★★★(★) (New South Wales) The company which did more than any to help Australia take Britain by storm with Chardonnay, Fumé Blanc and Cabernet. The last two are no longer so good, though Chardonnay is on the way back and the single-vineyard Roxburgh and Show Reserve Chardonnays are impressive. Also surprising Pinot Noir and excellent Semillon and Shiraz.

ROTHBURY ★★★★ (New South Wales) Idiosyncratic but successful when it was under Len Evans' obsessive control; now owned by Mildara-Blass. Capable of producing the Hunter's greatest Semillon and juicy, fat crowd-pleasing Chardonnays. Some great Shiraz and Pinot Noir on occasion, too.

ST HALLETT ★★★★ (South Australia) Full, oaky Semillon and Chardonnay and a rich Shiraz, Old Block, from old vines. Gamekeeper's Reserve is Shiraz, Grenache, Mourvèdre and Touriga Nacional, brambly and spicy. One of the leading names in the Barossa revival.

ST HUBERTS ★★★(★) (Victoria) At best produces superb Chardonnays, exciting Cabernets and Pinots plus the odd thrilling sweetie, but has never settled into a totally reliable groove and some vintages fail to convince.

SEPPELT ★★★ (Victoria) Leading makers of quality fizz from Champagne grapes, peaking with Salinger. Also fruity, easy-drinking styles, and blackberryish sparkling red Shiraz.

SHAW & SMITH ★★★★ (South Australia) Fine Sauvignon Blanc and Chardonnay – including an unoaked version.

STAFFORD RIDGE ★★★★(★) (South Australia) Adelaide Hills winery with crisply intense and pure Sauvignon Blanc and delicate but long Chardonnay.

STONIER'S ★★★ (Victoria) Good cool-climate Chardonnay and Cabernet from this Mornington Peninsula winery.

TALTARNI ★★★ (Victoria) Remarkable bone-dry, grassy-sharp Fumé Blanc; fine Cabernet and Shiraz which soften (after about a decade) into classy, if austere reds.

TISDALL ★★★ (Victoria) Mildara-Blass-owned winery with excellent grape sources, but has never quite lived up to its exceptional potential. If less oak were used the fruit would sing through. That said, there's good Chardonnay here and Mount Ida Reserve Shiraz is a cracker.

TYRRELL'S ★★★(★) (New South Wales) Eccentrically brilliant Hunter winery which sells 'port' and 'blackberry nip' to tourists through the front door while making some classic wines out the back. Vat 1 Semillon is excellent, as is the 'plonk' – Long Flat Red and White, named after the vineyard. Vat 9 is supple, leathery Shiraz.

VASSE FELIX ★★★★ (Western Australia) One of the original Margaret River wineries, producing a classic regional style of rich, leafy, curranty Cabernet and spicy, fleshy Shiraz. Classic Dry White is a blend of Chardonnay, Semillon and Sauvignon Blanc.

WIRRA WIRRA★★★★ (South Australia) Fine, concentrated reds, whites and sparkling wine, and exceptional Angelus Cabernet.

WYNNS ★★★★ (South Australia) Big, oaky Chardonnay, refined Cabernet and Shiraz from this Coonawarra company. Top-line John Riddoch Cabernet is expensive but worth every penny.

YARRA YERING ★★★★★ (Victoria) Wonderful Yarra Valley winery, where Bailey Carrodus labels his Cabernet-based wine Dry Red No.1 and his Shiraz-based wine Dry Red No. 2: exceptional, powerful and concentrated yet fragrant reds. Fine Pinot Noir and Chardonnay as well, in a very personal style.

AUSTRALIA PRICES

RED

Under £4.00

Dry Red Lindemans Cawarra 1996 £3.99 (FUL)

Dry Red Rolleston Vale **Non-vintage** £3.99 (CON) £4.03 (GW)

★ Malbec/Ruby Cabernet Angove's Nanya Estate 1998 £3.99 (VIC) £3.99 (THR) £3.99 (WR) £3.99 (BOT)

Shiraz/Cabernet Sauvignon Hardys Stamp 1998 £3.99 (WAI) £4.99 (MORR) £4.99 (SAF) £4.99 (THR) £4.99 (WR) £4.99 (BOT)

Shiraz/Merlot Barramundi **Non-vintage** £3.95 (MORR) £3.99 (ASD) £4.29 (CO)

£4.00 → £4.99

Cabernet Sauvignon Deakin Estate 1998 £4.99 (DI) £4.99 (YOU)

Cabernet Sauvignon McWilliams Hanwood 1997 £4.99 (MORR) £5.99 (NLW)

Cabernet Sauvignon Red Cliffs Coonawarra 1997 £4.95 (BALL) £4.99 (VIC) £4.99 (THR) £4.99 (WR) £4.99 (BOT)

Cabernet Sauvignon Sunnycliff 1997 £4.95 (HAH) £5.49 (POR) £5.59 (JON)

Grenache Peter Lehmann 1998 £4.99 (SAF) £4.99 (ASD)

Grenache Peter Lehmann 1997 £4.85 (FUL)

Grenache/Shiraz Mount Hurtle 1997 £4.99 (ASD)

Rawson's Retreat Bin 35 Penfolds 1997 £4.80 (SOM) £5.29 (POR) £5.49 (SAF)

Shiraz/Cabernet Sauvignon Aldridge Estate 1996 £4.89 (CON)

Shiraz/Cabernet Sauvignon Lindemans Cawarra 1998 £4.69 (ASD) £4.99 (UN) £4.99 (MAJ)

Shiraz/Cabernet Sauvignon Lonsdale Ridge 1997 £4.89 (YOU)

Shiraz/Cabernet Sauvignon Rolleston Vale 1996 £4.49 (CON) £4.50 (GW)

Shiraz/Mourvèdre Canoe Tree 1997 £4.92 (FLE)

Tarrango Brown Brothers 1998 £4.99 (WAI) £5.27 (STE) £5.29 (POR) £5.85 (PIP)

Tarrango Brown Brothers 1997 £4.99 (BO) £5.49 (CON) £5.69 (JON) £5.70 (PLA) £5.78 (NO) £5.95 (DI) £6.03 (GW) £6.10 (UB)

£5.00 → £5.99

Cabernet Sauvignon Hardy Nottage Hill 1996 £5.49 (CO)

Cabernet Sauvignon Lindemans Bin 45 1997 £5.99 (MORR) £5.99 (MAJ)

Cabernet Sauvignon Lindemans Bin 45 1996 £5.98 (PEN) £5.99 (FUL) £5.99 (UN)

Cabernet Sauvignon Lindemans Bin 45 1995 £5.99 (JON)

Cabernet Sauvignon Salisbury Estate 1997 £5.99 (YOU) £7.25 (FORT)

Cabernet Sauvignon Salisbury Estate 1996 £5.64 (ROS)

Cabernet Sauvignon David Wynn 1998 £5.70 (SOM) £7.75 (AD)

Cabernet Sauvignon/Mourvèdre Grant Burge Oakland 1996 £5.49 (FUL) £5.99 (CON)

Cabernet Sauvignon/Shiraz Hardy Collection 1996 £5.99 (ASD)

Cabernet Sauvignon/Shiraz Hardy Nottage Hill 1998 £5.49 (THR) £5.49 (WR)

Cabernet Sauvignon/Shiraz Hardy Nottage Hill 1997 £5.49 (FUL) £5.49 (SAI) £5.49 (SAF)

Cabernet Sauvignon/Shiraz Ironstone 1996 £5.99 (NI)

MERCHANTS SPECIALIZING IN AUSTRALIA
see Merchant Directory (page 413) for details

Virtually every merchant will be able to sell you some Australian wines. But for more than the usual names, try: Adnams (AD), Australian Wine Club (AUS), Averys of Bristol (AV), Ballantynes (BAL), Bennetts (BEN), Bibendum (BIB), Anthony Byrne (BY), Direct Wine Shipments (DI), First Quench Group (BOT, THR, VIC, WR), Lay & Wheeler (LAY), James Nicholson (NI), The Nobody Inn (NO), Oddbins (OD), Terry Platt (PLA), Philglas & Swiggot (PHI), Raeburn Fine Wines (RAE), Roberson (ROB), Sainsbury's (SAI), Safeway (SAF), Sommelier Wine Co (SOM), Tanners (TAN), The Ubiquitous Chip (UB), Wine Society (WS), Wine Treasury (WT), Noel Young (YOU).

Cabernet Sauvignon/Shiraz Penfolds
Koonunga Hill 1996 £5.99 (SOM) £6.95
(COC) £6.99 (UN)

Cabernet Sauvignon/Shiraz Penfolds
Private Bin 1995 £5.49 (GW)

Cabernet Sauvignon/Shiraz Riddoch 1996
£5.99 (SAF) £6.99 (VIC) £6.99 (THR) £6.99
(WR) £6.99 (BOT) £7.29 (BO)

Cabernet Sauvignon/Shiraz Rosemount
1998 £5.49 (ASD)

Cabernet Sauvignon/Shiraz Yalumba
Oxford Landing 1997 £5.49 (FUL) £5.49
(CO) £5.49 (THR) £5.49 (WR) £5.49 (BOT)

Cabernet Sauvignon/Shiraz Yalumba
Oxford Landing 1996 £5.59 (JON)

Cabernet Sauvignon/Shiraz/Merlot
Woolshed 1996 £5.99 (FUL)

Grenache/Shiraz Rosemount 1998 £5.99
(WHI) £6.49 (SAF) £6.49 (VIC) £6.49 (THR)
£6.49 (WR) £6.49 (BOT) £6.49 (ASD)

Jacob's Creek Red Orlando Non-
vintage £5.49 (ASD)

Jacob's Creek Red Orlando 1997 £5.05
(COC) £5.49 (SO)

Jacob's Creek Red Orlando 1996 £5.49
(UN)

Long Flat Red Tyrrell's 1996 £5.99 (JON)

Pinot Noir David Wynn 1998 £5.70
(SOM) £6.99 (NI) £6.99 (YOU) £7.03 (GW)

Rawson's Retreat Bin 35 Penfolds 1996
£5.49 (FUL) £5.49 (JON) £5.49 (CO) £5.49
(VIC) £5.49 (THR) £5.49 (WR) £5.49 (BOT)

Shiraz Peter Lehmann Vine Vale 1996
£5.25 (BO)

Shiraz Lindemans Bin 50 1997 £5.00
(MORR) £5.99 (UN) £5.99 (MAJ) £5.99
(YOU) £6.66 (BY)

Shiraz Rothbury 1996 £5.99 (DI)

Shiraz Yaldara Reserve 1997 £5.65 (SOM)
£7.03 (GW) £7.04 (PLA) £7.61 (PLAY)

Shiraz/Cabernet Sauvignon Orlando
Jacob's Creek 1997 £5.49 (MORR) £5.49
(FUL) £5.49 (SAF)

Shiraz/Cabernet Sauvignon Orlando
Jacob's Creek 1996 £5.49 (VIC) £5.49
(THR) £5.49 (WR) £5.49 (BOT)

Shiraz/Cabernet Sauvignon Penfolds
Rowlands Brook 1995 £5.00 (HAH)

Shiraz/Mourvèdre Penfolds Bin 2 1997
£5.60 (SOM) £5.79 (POR) £5.95 (WS) £6.29
(YOU) £6.49 (VIC) £6.49 (THR) £6.75 (FORT)

Shiraz/Mourvèdre Penfolds Bin 2 1996
£5.49 (WAI) £5.78 (NO) £5.98 (PEN)

Tarrango Brown Brothers 1996 £5.10
(ROS) £5.29 (GW)

£6.00 → £6.99

Barbera Brown Bros King Valley 1996
£6.95 (PIP)

Cabernet Sauvignon Berri 1994 £6.40 (CRO)

Cabernet Sauvignon Best's Victoria 1994
£6.50 (CRO) £7.50 (FLE)

Cabernet Sauvignon Brown Bros 1996
£7.76 (PEN) £8.40 (PIP) £8.50 (TAN)

Cabernet Sauvignon McWilliams
Hanwood 1996 £6.19 (COC)

Cabernet Sauvignon Mitchelton Preece
1996 £6.74 (NO)

Cabernet Sauvignon Wakefield Clare
Valley 1996 £6.75 (BO) £6.99 (BAL)
£6.99 (RAE) £7.63 (PLA)

Cabernet Sauvignon Wolf Blass Yellow
Label 1997 £6.99 (PHI) £7.49 (MORR)
£7.49 (SAI) £7.49 (MAJ) £7.49 (SAF) £7.49
(ASD) £7.78 (BY) £8.19 (NLW)

Cabernet Sauvignon Wolf Blass Yellow
Label 1996 £6.99 (FUL) £7.45 (COC)

Cabernet Sauvignon David Wynn 1997
£6.74 (FLE) £6.99 (YOU) £7.03 (GW)

Cabernet Sauvignon/Cabernet
Franc/Merlot St Hallett 1996 £6.99 (SOM)

★ Cabernet Sauvignon/Malbec Tatachilla
1997 £6.99 (BOT)

Cabernet Sauvignon/Merlot Tyrrell's Old
Winery 1997 £6.99 (SAI) £6.99 (UN)
£7.48 (PLAY)

Cabernet Sauvignon/Merlot Yaldara
Reserve 1995 £6.49 (FLE) £6.75 (GW)
£9.55 (VIN)

Cabernet Sauvignon/Mourvèdre Grant
Burge Oakland 1997 £6.25 (STA)

Cabernet Sauvignon/Mourvèdre
Marienberg 1995 £6.85 (JER)

Cabernet Sauvignon/Shiraz Penfolds
Koonunga Hill 1997 £6.75 (POR) £6.99
(OD)

Gamekeeper's Reserve St Hallett 1998
£6.99 (AUS)

Grenache/Shiraz d'Arenberg d'Arry's
Original 1996 £6.99 (OD) £6.99 (YOU)

Long Flat Red Tyrrell's 1998 £6.25 (AME)

Mourvèdre/Grenache Magpie Estate The
Thief 1998 £6.99 (YOU)

*Stars (★) indicate wines
selected by Oz Clarke in the
Best Buys section which begins
on page 9.*

Pinot Noir Tyrrell's **1997** £6.20 (COC)
Pinot Noir Tyrrell's **1996** £6.58 (PEN)
Pinot Noir David Wynn **1995** £6.99 (GW)
£7.80 (MV)
Pinot Noir/Shiraz Montara 'M' **1997**
£6.20 (SOM) £7.99 (YOU)
Pinot Noir/Shiraz Montara 'M' **1996**
£6.90 (CRO)
Shiraz Baileys **1996** £6.39 (YOU) £7.49 (AME)
Shiraz Best's Victoria **1996** £6.95 (GW)
£6.99 (FUL)
Shiraz Brown Bros **1995** £6.85 (ROS)
£7.65 (GW) £7.75 (CON)
Shiraz Hardy Bankside **1997** £6.99 (SAI)
£6.99 (SAF)
Shiraz Houghton Wildflower Ridge **1995**
£6.49 (CON)
Shiraz Peter Lehmann **1997** £6.99 (WAI)
Shiraz Riddoch Limited Release **1996**
£6.99 (VIC) £6.99 (THR) £6.99 (BOT)
Shiraz Rosemount **1997** £6.90 (CRO) £6.99
(ASD) £7.49 (MORR) £7.49 (FUL) £7.49 (SO)
£7.49 (SAF) £7.49 (THR) £7.49 (BOT)
Shiraz Wyndham's Bin 555 **1996** £6.99
(NLW) £6.99 (COC) £6.99 (MAJ)
Shiraz Wynns Coonawarra Estate **1996**
£6.99 (MAJ) £6.99 (YOU)
Shiraz/Cabernet Sauvignon Krondorf
1996 £6.95 (HED)
Shiraz/Cabernet Sauvignon Penfolds
Koonunga Hill **1997** £6.99 (FUL) £6.99
(SO) £6.99 (VIC) £6.99 (THR) £6.99 (WR)
Shiraz/Cabernet Sauvignon Penfolds
Koonunga Hill **1996** £6.95 (WS) £6.99
(TES) £6.99 (JON) £6.99 (PEN) £6.99 (SAF)
£6.99 (YOU) £7.95 (FORT)
Shiraz/Cabernet Sauvignon Rouge
Homme **1994** £6.99 (BAL) £7.70 (HA)
Shiraz/Cabernet Sauvignon Saltram
Stonyfell Metala **1997** £6.99 (SAF) £7.49
(BO)
Shiraz/Mourvèdre Penfolds Bin 2 **1994**
£6.45 (COC)

£7.00 → £7.99

Cabernet Franc Tim Knappstein **1996**
£7.99 (SAF) £8.49 (BO) £9.50 (PIP)
Cabernet Sauvignon Brown Bros **1995**
£7.69 (CON) £7.99 (CO)
Cabernet Sauvignon Brown Bros Milawa
1996 £7.99 (JON)
Cabernet Sauvignon Grant Burge **1996**
£7.75 (BALL) £9.65 (CON) £9.80 (AS)
Cabernet Sauvignon Richard Hamilton
Hut Block **1995** £7.95 (JU)

Cabernet Sauvignon Rosemount **1997**
£7.49 (SO) £7.49 (SAI) £7.49 (BO) £7.49
(THR) £7.49 (WR) £7.49 (ASD) £7.99 (UN)
Cabernet Sauvignon Rosemount **1996**
£7.49 (FUL)
Cabernet Sauvignon Simon Hackett Foggo
Road **1995** £7.45 (PIP) £11.55 (NO)
Cabernet Sauvignon David Traeger **1996**
£7.99 (AUS)
Cabernet Sauvignon/Merlot Goundrey
Mount Barker **1994** £7.89 (WHI)
Cabernet Sauvignon/Merlot Tim
Knappstein **1996** £7.99 (SAF)
Cabernet Sauvignon/Merlot Koppamurra
1996 £7.99 (AUS)
Cabernet Sauvignon/Merlot Tisdall **1995**
£7.50 (HED)
Cabernet Sauvignon/Shiraz Riddoch **1997**
£7.14 (BIB)
Cabernet Sauvignon/Shiraz/Merlot Wynns
Coonawarra Estate **1996** £7.99 (POR)
Clancy's Red Peter Lehmann **1996** £7.99
(FUL) £7.99 (SAI) £9.45 (HAH)
Coonawarra Red Jamiesons Run **1996**
£7.99 (SAF)
★ Grenache d'Arenberg The Custodian
1996 £7.99 (OD)
Grenache Simon Hackett **1996** £7.25
(CON) £7.29 (YOU)
Grenache Yalumba Bush Vine **1997** £7.99
(NI) £8.99 (BEN)
Merlot Brown Bros **1996** £7.11 (STE)
£7.49 (DI) £7.99 (YOU) £8.95 (AD)
Pinot Noir Rosemount **1997** £7.99 (ASD)
Shiraz Basedow **1997** £7.99 (SAF) £8.20 (BIB)
Shiraz Best's Victoria **1997** £7.03 (GW)
£7.39 (NI) £7.46 (PLA)
Shiraz Brown Bros **1996** £7.49 (DI) £7.56
(STE) £7.69 (YOU) £7.99 (POR) £8.25
(WHI) £8.40 (PIP) £8.40 (NA) £8.50 (TAN)
Shiraz Houghton Wildflower Ridge **1997**
£7.49 (POR)
Shiraz Mitchell Peppertree **1996** £7.95
(BALL) £9.99 (PHI) £11.10 (PIP)
Shiraz Mitchelton **1995** £7.95 (POR) £8.99
(AME) £9.50 (WS)

- *All prices for each wine are listed together in ascending order.*
- *Price bands refer to the lowest price for which the wine is available.*

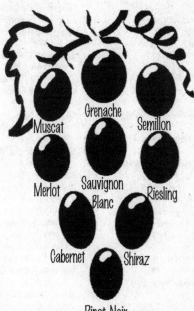

Shiraz Neil Paulett **1995** £7.90 (JU)

Shiraz Penfolds Kalimna Bin 28 **1995** £7.80 (SOM) £8.75 (POR) £8.95 (COC) £8.99 (FUL) £8.99 (JON) £8.99 (PEN) £8.99 (YOU) £9.20 (TAN) £9.39 (BO) £9.65 (PIP) £9.99 (PHI)

Shiraz St Hallett **1997** £7.99 (AUS) £7.99 (VIC) £7.99 (THR) £7.99 (WR) £7.99 (BOT)

★ Shiraz Water Wheel **1997** £7.99 (AUS)

Shiraz/Cabernet Sauvignon Wolf Blass Red Label **1996** £7.39 (NLW)

Shiraz/Grenache Veritas Christa-Rolf **1998** £7.99 (YOU) £8.35 (LAY)

Shiraz/Malbec/Cabernet Sauvignon Hollick Wilga **1996** £7.96 (LAY)

£8.00 → £8.99

Cabernet Sauvignon Jim Barry **1996** £8.95 (TAN) £9.40 (BEN)

Cabernet Sauvignon Eldredge **1996** £8.99 (AUS)

Cabernet Sauvignon Peter Lehmann **1995** £8.75 (BALL)

Cabernet Sauvignon Marienberg **1994** £8.71 (JER)

Cabernet Sauvignon Mitchell **1995** £8.20 (HAH) £8.25 (BALL) £8.45 (AD) £8.95 (POR)

Cabernet Sauvignon Rouge Homme **1994** £8.99 (WAI) £8.99 (AME) £10.99 (YOU)

Cabernet Sauvignon Rymill **1995** £8.25 (HAH) £8.25 (BALL)

Cabernet Sauvignon Stonier's **1995** £8.99 (WAT)

Cabernet Sauvignon Vasse Felix **1987** £8.81 (REI)

Cabernet Sauvignon/Malbec Galah **1995** £8.99 (AUS)

Cabernet Sauvignon/Malbec Leasingham Bin 56 **1992** £8.99 (CO)

Cabernet Sauvignon/Merlot Cape Mentelle **1996** £8.95 (STA) £8.99 (NI)

Cabernet Sauvignon/Merlot Cape Mentelle **1995** £8.30 (NO) £8.35 (CON) £8.99 (REI) £8.99 (YOU) £9.75 (ROB)

Cabernet Sauvignon/Merlot Cape Mentelle **1993** £8.90 (CRO)

> • Wines are listed in A–Z order within each price band.
> • For each wine, vintages are listed in descending order.
> • Each vintage of any wine appears only once.

Cabernet Sauvignon/Merlot Hollick Coonawarra **1993** £8.20 (SOM)

Cabernet Sauvignon/Shiraz Ironstone **1995** £8.50 (CRO)

Cabernet Sauvignon/Shiraz Wirra Wirra Church Block **1997** £8.95 (WS) £8.99 (PHI)

Cabernet Sauvignon/Shiraz Wirra Wirra Church Block **1996** £8.99 (NO)

Grenache Bethany **1995** £8.67 (NO)

Grenache Simon Hackett **1998** £8.50 (BER)

Grenache Rockford Dry Country **1997** £8.13 (FLE)

Grenache Rockford Dry Country **1996** £8.80 (PIP) £8.95 (WS) £8.99 (FUL) £8.99 (YOU) £9.10 (TAN) £9.25 (ELL) £9.75 (PHI)

Grenache Rockford Dry Country **1995** £8.99 (REI)

Grenache Yalumba Bush Vine **1996** £8.25 (SOM) £8.99 (VIC) £8.99 (THR) £8.99 (WR) £8.99 (BOT)

Grenache/Shiraz Wirra Wirra Original Blend **1997** £8.99 (OD)

Pinot Noir Hollick **1995** £8.99 (NI)

Richardsons Red Block Rouge Homme **1995** £8.99 (FUL) £9.49 (POR) £9.95 (AME) £11.20 (AV)

Sangiovese Coriole **1994** £8.10 (NO) £8.90 (CRO)

★ Shiraz Tim Adams **1997** £8.99 (AUS)

Shiraz Tim Adams **1996** £8.99 (TES)

Shiraz Beresford Longhorne Creek **1996** £8.50 (ROB)

Shiraz Grant Burge Old Vine **1996** £8.99 (FUL)

Shiraz Campbells Bobbie Burns **1996** £8.99 (YOU) £10.10 (PIP)

Shiraz Goundrey **1992** £8.50 (CRO)

Shiraz Mitchell Peppertree **1997** £8.30 (TAN) £8.50 (HAH) £8.69 (JON) £8.85 (AD) £8.95 (POR) £9.65 (AV)

Shiraz Montara Estate **1995** £8.50 (FLE) £9.95 (AD)

Shiraz Penfolds Coonawarra Bin 128 **1995** £8.20 (SOM) £8.99 (MORR) £9.49 (UN) £9.49 (BO) £10.26 (BY)

Shiraz Penfolds Kalimna Bin 28 **1996** £8.99 (THR) £8.99 (WR) £8.99 (BOT) £8.99 (ASD)

Shiraz Petaluma Bridgewater Mill **1995** £8.68 (PEN)

Shiraz St Hallett Faith **1997** £8.99 (AUS)

Shiraz Taltarni **1995** £8.29 (CON) £8.85 (AV) £8.99 (AME) £9.40 (PEN)

Shiraz/Cabernet Sauvignon/Merlot Bremerton **1995** £8.86 (NO)

£9.00 → £9.99

Cabernet Franc Tim Knappstein 1994 £9.00 (CRO)

Cabernet Sauvignon Jim Barry 1995 £9.95 (DI)

Cabernet Sauvignon Best's Great Western 1996 £9.99 (UN)

Cabernet Sauvignon Best's Great Western 1993 £9.50 (CRO) £10.90 (GAU)

Cabernet Sauvignon Bremerton 1994 £9.63 (NO)

Cabernet Sauvignon Cape Mentelle 1994 £9.73 (PLAY) £9.95 (AD) £14.20 (TAN) £16.27 (PLA) £16.50 (PHI) £16.50 (RAE)

Cabernet Sauvignon Leconfield 1995 £9.95 (JU)

Cabernet Sauvignon Mitchell 1997 £9.09 (JON)

Cabernet Sauvignon Pikes 1996 £9.95 (LEA)

Cabernet Sauvignon Robertson's Well Coonawarra 1995 £9.99 (FUL)

Cabernet Sauvignon Rymill 1994 £9.95 (RAE)

Cabernet Sauvignon Stonier's 1994 £9.99 (DI)

Cabernet Sauvignon Wynns Coonawarra 1995 £9.95 (POR) £9.99 (MAJ)

Cabernet Sauvignon Wynns Coonawarra 1994 £9.99 (PEN) £9.99 (AME)

Cabernet Sauvignon/Malbec Galah 1996 £9.50 (AUS)

Cabernet Sauvignon/Malbec Leasingham Bin 56 1996 £9.99 (THR) £11.25 (BALL)

Cabernet Sauvignon/Merlot Hollick Coonawarra 1994 £9.99 (YOU) £10.95 (BALL) £12.57 (TW)

Cabernet Sauvignon/Merlot Pipers Brook Ninth Island 1995 £9.50 (ROB)

Cabernet Sauvignon/Merlot Reynolds Yarraman 1996 £9.75 (LAY)

Cabernet Sauvignon/Merlot Tisdall 1994 £9.80 (AS)

Durif Morris 1994 £9.65 (SOM)

★ The Fergus Tim Adams 1997 £9.49 (VIC) £9.49 (THR) £9.49 (WR) £9.49 (BOT) £9.50 (AUS)

Grenache Tim Gramp 1996 £9.49 (YOU)

Grenache/Shiraz d'Arenberg Ironstone Pressings 1996 £9.95 (WS) £11.25 (FORT)

Grenache/Shiraz Wirra Wirra Original Blend 1995 £9.50 (WS)

Grenache/Shiraz/Mourvèdre Cornerstone 1997 £9.99 (AUS)

Merlot Charles Cimicky 1994 £9.45 (JU)

Nine Popes Charles Melton 1996 £9.90 (SOM) £15.39 (NO) £17.75 (ROB)

Shiraz Baileys 1920 Block 1995 £9.95 (AME)

Shiraz Cape Mentelle 1994 £9.80 (JU)

Shiraz Coriole 1996 £9.50 (TAN) £9.75 (WS) £10.99 (YOU) £14.00 (CRO)

Shiraz Leasingham 1994 £9.99 (TES)

Shiraz Mitchell Peppertree 1995 £9.19 (YOU)

Shiraz Penfolds Coonawarra Bin 128 1994 £9.18 (NO) £9.45 (COC) £9.79 (BY)

Shiraz Penfolds Kalimna Bin 28 1994 £9.15 (WHI)

Shiraz Penley Estate Hyland 1996 £9.22 (LAY) £10.13 (WT)

★ Shiraz Pikes Polish Hill River 1996 £9.95 (LEA)

Shiraz Plantagenet 1996 £9.86 (STE) £10.95 (NA) £12.99 (LIB) £14.80 (HAH)

Shiraz Primo Estate 1995 £9.34 (REI)

Shiraz Rothbury Reserve 1995 £9.95 (DI)

Shiraz Tatachilla Foundation 1996 £9.45 (BAN) £12.99 (YOU)

Shiraz The Willows Vineyard 1996 £9.99 (AUS)

Shiraz/Grenache Veritas Christa-Rolf 1996 £9.50 (ROB)

Shiraz/Grenache/Mourvèdre Penfolds Old Vine 1995 £9.10 (SOM) £11.00 (PEN)

Zinfandel Cape Mentelle 1994 £9.25 (CON) £9.95 (JU)

£10.00 → £10.99

Cabernet Sauvignon Bowen Estate 1992 £10.75 (PHI)

Cabernet Sauvignon Katnook 1996 £10.96 (BIB) £10.99 (DI)

Cabernet Sauvignon Lindemans Bin 45 1987 £10.50 (CRO)

Cabernet Sauvignon Penfolds Bin 407 1996 £10.99 (BO)

Cabernet Sauvignon/Merlot Chateau Reynella Basket Pressed 1994 £10.99 (CO) £11.13 (NO)

Cabernet Sauvignon/Merlot Voyager Estate 1993 £10.95 (JU)

Cabernet Sauvignon/Shiraz Penfolds Bin 389 1995 £10.40 (SOM) £11.99 (YOU) £12.99 (FUL) £12.99 (SAF) £14.00 (CRO)

Pinot Noir Cullen 1994 £10.49 (AME)

Pinot Noir Pipers Brook 1996 £10.35 (SOM) £13.50 (STA)

Pinot Noir Yarra Valley Hills 1996 £10.94 (STE) £12.15 (NA)

Shiraz Balgownie 1986 £10.50 (CRO)
Shiraz Bowen Estate 1997 £10.99 (AUS)
Shiraz Grant Burge 60-year-old vines
  1995 £10.50 (CON)
Shiraz Grant Burge Old Vine 1997 £10.75
  (AS) £10.75 (BU)
Shiraz Tim Gramp 1996 £10.75 (SOM)
Shiraz David Wynn Patriarch 1996
  £10.60 (SOM) £11.57 (FLE) £12.75 (WRI)
  £12.99 (NI) £12.99 (PHI)
Shiraz/Malbec/Cabernet Sauvignon
  Hollick Wilga 1995 £10.28 (TW)

£11.00 → £11.99

Cabernet Sauvignon Balgownie 1996
  £11.49 (YOU)
Cabernet Sauvignon Cape Jaffa 1996
  £11.00 (ELL) £11.95 (LLO)
Cabernet Sauvignon Cape Mentelle 1992
  £11.95 (CON) £12.34 (REI) £14.99 (NI)
Cabernet Sauvignon McGuigan Personal
  Reserve 1997 £11.59 (WHI)
Cabernet Sauvignon Plantagenet 1996
  £11.99 (LIB) £12.95 (VA)
Cabernet Sauvignon Rockford 1994
  £11.99 (YOU)
Cabernet Sauvignon Simon Hackett Foggo
  Road 1996 £11.75 (WRI) £13.65 (CON)
Cabernet Sauvignon Stonier's Reserve
  1993 £11.99 (WAT)
Cabernet Sauvignon Wolf Blass President's
  Selection 1996 £11.40 (COC)
Durif Morris 1993 £11.21 (NO)
'Mary Kathleen' Coriole 1994 £11.29 (YOU)
Obliqua Ashton Hills 1996 £11.99 (AUS)
Pellion Pipers Brook 1996 £11.94 (ROS)
  £12.71 (PEN)
Pinot Noir Scotchman's Hill 1996 £11.50
  (JU) £13.95 (UB)
Shiraz Balgownie 1996 £11.49 (AME)
Shiraz Jim Barry Macrae Wood 1995
  £11.95 (SOM) £13.30 (TAN) £13.61 (NO)
  £14.59 (YOU) £14.95 (PIP) £14.99 (BAL)
  £14.99 (OD) £15.70 (AD) £15.95 (RES)
  £15.95 (DI) £15.99 (PHI)
Shiraz Brokenwood Graveyard 1996
  £11.29 (YOU)
Shiraz Grant Burge Old Vine 1994 £11.75
  (ROB)
Shiraz Chateau Reynella 1995 £11.99 (SAF)
Shiraz Chateau Reynella Basket Pressed
  1995 £11.99 (WAI)
Shiraz Tim Gramp 1997 £11.53 (NO)
Shiraz St Hallett Old Block 1995 £11.99
  (SOM) £13.99 (AUS) £13.99 (THR)

£12.00 → £12.99

Cabernet Sauvignon Cape Mentelle 1993
  £12.99 (RAE) £14.86 (REI) £16.09 (NO)
Cabernet Sauvignon Vasse Felix 1997
  £12.99 (YOU) £13.55 (BEN)
Cabernet Sauvignon Wolf Blass
  President's Selection 1993 £12.99 (PHI)
Cabernet Sauvignon/Merlot Voyager
  Estate 1994 £12.99 (YOU)
Cabernet Sauvignon/Shiraz Penfolds Bin
  389 1996 £12.95 (POR) £12.99 (OD)
Cabernet Sauvignon/Shiraz Penfolds Bin
  389 1994 £12.90 (COC) £13.09 (NO)
Pellion Pipers Brook 1995 £12.99 (AME)
Pinot Noir Cullen 1995 £12.03 (NO)
Pinot Noir Lenswood Knappstein 1997
  £12.80 (NEZ)
Pinot Noir Mountadam 1997 £12.99 (VIC)
  £12.99 (THR) £12.99 (BOT) £13.29 (FLE)
Pinot Noir Mountadam 1996 £12.99 (YOU)
  £13.52 (GW) £15.25 (FORT) £15.95 (AD)
Pinot Noir Mountadam 1995 £12.87
  (GW) £12.95 (CON)
Pinot Noir Pipers Brook 1997 £12.50 (POR)
St George Lindemans 1994 £12.93 (PEN)
  £12.99 (OD) £12.99 (YOU)
Shiraz Best's Victoria 1994 £12.99 (PHI)
Shiraz De Bortoli Yarra Valley 1995
  £12.24 (STE) £12.99 (PHI) £13.50 (STA)
Shiraz Charles Melton 1994 £12.95 (ROB)
Shiraz St Hallett Blackwell 1996 £12.49
  (AUS) £12.49 (VIC) £12.49 (THR) £12.49
  (WR) £12.49 (BOT) £12.95 (POR)
Shiraz Vasse Felix 1997 £12.30 (SOM)
  £14.99 (YOU) £15.45 (BEN)
Shiraz/Cabernet Sauvignon Henschke
  Keyneton Estate 1995 £12.20 (SOM)
  £14.49 (YOU) £15.00 (FLE) £15.69 (JON)
  £15.75 (FORT) £15.95 (RES)

£13.00 → £13.99

Angelus Wirra Wirra 1996 £13.99 (PHI)
  £14.50 (WS)
Cabernet Sauvignon De Bortoli 1993
  £13.95 (BAL)
Cabernet Sauvignon Knappstein 1994
  £13.87 (CB)
Cabernet Sauvignon McGuigan Personal
  Reserve 1995 £13.65 (CON)
Cabernet Sauvignon Rouge Homme 1993
  £13.89 (VIN)
Cabernet Sauvignon Vasse Felix 1996
  £13.10 (BEN) £13.50 (BAL) £13.95 (RES)
  £13.95 (ROB)

Coonawarra Petaluma **1996** £13.82 (STE)
£13.99 (YOU) £14.70 (BEN) £15.35 (NA)
Gaia Grosset **1995** £13.51 (DOM) £15.99
(YOU)
Limestone Ridge Lindemans **1994** £13.97
(PEN) £13.95 (POR) £13.99 (YOU) £14.09
(NO) £16.25 (FORT)
Pinot Noir Henschke Giles **1995** £13.50
(NI)
Pinot Noir Pipers Brook **1995** £13.79 (CON)
Pyrus Lindemans **1995** £13.99 (OD)
£13.99 (SAF)
Pyrus Lindemans **1994** £13.97 (PEN)
£13.99 (SAI) £13.99 (UN) £13.99 (JON)
Shiraz De Bortoli Yarra Valley **1994**
£13.50 (BAL)
Shiraz Mount Langi Ghiran **1997** £13.99
(BO) £14.99 (YOU) £19.95 (LIB)
Shiraz St Hallett Old Block **1994** £13.50
(FLE) £13.81 (REI) £14.59 (FA) £15.00
(FORT) £15.50 (CRO)
Shiraz Wirra Wirra R.S.W. **1996** £13.99
(PHI)

£14.00 → £15.99

Cabernet Sauvignon Brown Bros Family
Reserve **1990** £15.92 (PLA) £16.30 (PIP)
£16.92 (PEN)
Cabernet Sauvignon Dalwhinnie **1996**
£14.99 (YOU)
Cabernet Sauvignon Leeuwin Estate Art
Series **1994** £15.90 (SOM) £17.99 (YOU)
Cabernet Sauvignon Mountadam **1996**
£15.49 (NI)
Cabernet Sauvignon Penley Estate
Coonawarra **1994** £14.99 (AUS) £18.00
(WT)
Cabernet Sauvignon Rosemount Show
Reserve **1996** £14.99 (SAF)
Cabernet Sauvignon Seppelt Drumborg
1994 £14.99 (YOU) £15.49 (AME)
Cabernet Sauvignon Yalumba Menzies
1993 £14.50 (FORT)
Cabernet Sauvignon/Merlot Cullen **1996**
£15.50 (FLE) £17.49 (YOU)
Cabernet Sauvignon/Merlot Howard Park
1996 £15.75 (BAN) £19.50 (WS) £20.20
(BAN) £21.99 (YOU)
Coonawarra Petaluma **1995** £14.85 (HAH)
£15.84 (PLAY) £15.95 (ROB)
Gaia Grosset **1996** £14.99 (PHI)
Nine Popes Charles Melton **1997** £14.40
(FLE) £17.95 (VA) £18.49 (LIB) £18.75 (WRI)
Pinot Meunier Best's **1993** £15.99 (NI)
£17.00 (CRO)

Pinot Noir Henschke Giles **1994** £14.26
(NO) £15.55 (BEN) £23.00 (CRO)
Pinot Noir Lenswood Knappstein **1996**
£14.95 (PHI) £16.00 (CRO) £16.40 (HAH)
Pinot Noir Mountadam **1991** £15.95 (WRI)
Pinot Noir Tarrawarra **1995** £14.75 (GW)
Pinot Noir Wignalls **1995** £14.75 (ROB)
Shiraz Jim Barry Macrae Wood **1996**
£15.50 (BEN)
Shiraz Cape Mentelle **1988** £14.00 (CRO)
Shiraz Lengs & Cooter **1994** £14.99
(YOU) £15.25 (CON)
Shiraz Lengs & Cooter Old Vine **1995**
£15.15 (NO)
Shiraz Charles Melton **1997** £14.99 (FLE)
£17.29 (YOU) £17.95 (BEN) £18.50 (AD)
Shiraz Mount Langi Ghiran **1996** £14.43
(NO) £14.50 (CON) £14.99 (NI) £14.99
(FUL) £15.10 (HAH) £15.50 (BAL)
Shiraz Neil Paulett Andreas **1995** £14.50
(JU)
Shiraz Rockford Basket Press **1995**
£14.29 (AME) £15.00 (FLE) £24.00 (CRO)
Shiraz St Hallett Blackwell **1995** £14.45 (AD)
Shiraz Vasse Felix **1996** £14.99 (PHI)
£15.45 (BEN) £15.50 (PIP)
Shiraz Wolf Blass President's Selection
1993 £15.00 (CRO)
Zinfandel Cape Mentelle **1993** £14.50 (CRO)

£16.00 → £19.99

Cabernet Sauvignon Chateau Tahbilk
1985 £17.00 (CRO)
Cabernet Sauvignon Dalwhinnie **1995**
£17.95 (JU)
Cabernet Sauvignon Giaconda **1992**
£17.15 (NO)
Cabernet Sauvignon Howard Park **1995**
£17.50 (WS) £20.99 (PHI) £22.95 (BAL)
Cabernet Sauvignon Leeuwin Estate Art
Series **1995** £17.03 (DOM)
Cabernet Sauvignon Moss Wood **1995**
£19.95 (BAL)
Cabernet Sauvignon Penley Estate
Coonawarra **1993** £16.49 (YOU) £17.48
(WT) £19.50 (RES)
Cabernet Sauvignon Seppelt Black Label
1983 £18.00 (CRO)

> **Oz Clarke's Wine Guide**
> is an annual publication.
> We welcome your suggestions
> for next year's edition.

Cabernet Sauvignon/Merlot Howard Park
1995 £17.10 (SOM) £23.50 (FORT)
Coonawarra Petaluma **1993** £17.04 (REI)
Grenache Clarendon Hills Clarendon
Vineyard Old Vines **1996** £17.50 (JU)
Nine Popes Charles Melton **1991** £19.00
(CRO)
Pinot Noir Bannockburn **1996** £16.80
(TAN) £17.95 (BAL) £17.95 (BEN) £18.95
(RES) £19.58 (JER) £29.95 (UB)
Pinot Noir Coldstream Hills Reserve
1996 £16.99 (OD)
Pinot Noir Moss Wood **1995** £16.50 (PLAY)
Pinot Noir Tyrrell's **1989** £18.51 (REI)
Shiraz Jim Barry Macrae Wood **1992**
£19.50 (CRO)
Shiraz Dalwhinnie **1995** £17.29 (YOU)
£19.90 (JU)
Shiraz d'Arenberg Dead Arm **1996**
£16.50 (FORT)
Shiraz Eileen Hardy **1994** £19.65 (NO)
Shiraz Henschke Mount Edelstone **1994**
£17.95 (SOM) £24.50 (RES) £27.50 (ROB)
Shiraz Jasper Hill Georgia's Paddock **1996**
£19.97 (FA) £30.00 (FORT)
Shiraz Lengs & Cooter Old Vine **1992**
£19.95 (RES)
Shiraz Penfolds Kalimna Bin 28 **1991**
£16.00 (CRO)
Shiraz Yarra Yering Underhill **1996**
£16.50 (SOM) £18.99 (GW) £19.99 (CON)
£21.50 (BEN) £21.99 (NI) £22.25 (AD)
Shiraz/Cabernet Sauvignon Yalumba The
Signature **1993** £19.50 (FORT)
Shiraz/Mourvèdre Leconfield **1997**
£18.00 (JU)

£20.00 → £29.99

Cabernet Sauvignon Chateau Reynella
Basket Pressed **1984** £28.00 (CRO)
Cabernet Sauvignon Chateau Tahbilk
1982 £25.00 (CRO)
Cabernet Sauvignon Henschke Cyril
Henschke **1992** £29.95 (DI) £38.00 (CRO)
Cabernet Sauvignon Hollick Ravenswood
1993 £23.50 (RES) £24.00 (SOM) £26.44
(TW)
Cabernet Sauvignon Moss Wood **1996**
£25.00 (WS)
Cabernet Sauvignon Parker Coonawarra
Estate Terra Rossa **1996** £23.97 (CB)
Cabernet Sauvignon Penfolds Bin 707
1993 £22.47 (COC)
Cabernet Sauvignon Penfolds
Coonawarra **1989** £29.00 (CRO)

Cabernet Sauvignon Rosemount Show
Reserve **1985** £23.00 (CRO)
Cabernet Sauvignon Wolf Blass Black
Label **1992** £26.00 (CRO)
Cabernet Sauvignon Wynns John Riddoch
1994 £28.45 (SOM) £31.99 (YOU) £32.90
(PEN) £32.95 (POR) £36.11 (NO)
Cabernet Sauvignon Yarra Yering Dry
Red No.1 **1984** £27.61 (REI)
Cabernet Sauvignon/Merlot Cullen **1997**
£22.75 (AD)
Cabernet Sauvignon/Merlot/Shiraz Blue
Pyrenees Estate **1982** £24.00 (CRO)
Cabernet Sauvignon/Shiraz Penfolds Bin
389 **1992** £22.00 (CRO)
Grenache Clarendon Hills Blewitt Springs
Vineyard Old Vines **1997** £20.46 (FA)
Limestone Ridge Lindemans **1988** £29.00
(CRO)
Merlot Clarendon Hills **1996** £23.00 (JU)
Meshach Grant Burge **1992** £20.50 (RES)
£24.50 (WRI) £37.72 (PLAY)
Octavius Yalumba **1995** £26.12 (FLE)
Pinot Noir Coldstream Hills Reserve
1993 £20.00 (CRO)
Pinot Noir Yarra Yering **1990** £27.50
(BEN) £27.50 (FORT)
Shiraz Clarendon Hills **1996** £21.00 (JU)
£28.30 (FA)
Shiraz E&E Black Pepper Barossa Valley
Estate **1995** £25.36 (FA) £28.75 (WRI)
Shiraz E&E Black Pepper Barossa Valley
Estate **1993** £29.00 (CRO)
Shiraz Elderton Command **1993** £23.95
(POR)
Shiraz Eileen Hardy **1995** £27.99 (FUL)
Shiraz Henschke Mount Edelstone **1996**
£26.50 (FORT) £27.50 (WS) £27.75 (PHI)
Shiraz Henschke Mount Edelstone **1995**
£22.00 (FLE) £24.95 (LAY) £26.19 (JON)
Shiraz Jasper Hill Georgia's Paddock **1997**
£25.00 (YAP)
Shiraz Jasper Hill Georgia's Paddock **1994**
£22.95 (ROB)
Shiraz Penfolds Magill Estate **1992** £22.33
(PEN)
Shiraz Tyrrell's Vat 9 Winemakers
Selection **1990** £25.00 (CRO)
Shiraz Wynns Michael **1994** £28.45 (SOM)
£31.99 (YOU) £32.90 (PEN) £32.95 (WAI)
£32.99 (POR) £39.95 (ROB) £45.43 (FA)
Shiraz Yarra Yering Dry Red No.2 **1995**
£22.00 (FORT)
Shiraz/Cabernet Sauvignon Henschke
Keyneton Estate **1993** £27.00 (CRO)

£30.00 → £39.99

Cabernet Sauvignon Lake's Folly 1983
£32.00 (CRO)
Cabernet Sauvignon Penfolds Bin 707
1996 £34.99 (BO)
Cabernet Sauvignon Penfolds Bin 707 1994
£32.90 (PEN) £32.95 (POR) £32.99 (UN)
£35.99 (PHI) £48.00 (CRO) £54.43 (NO)
Cabernet Sauvignon Taltarni 1980 £30.00
(CRO)
Cabernet Sauvignon Wynns John Riddoch
1996 £34.95 (WAI)
Cabernets Mount Mary 1989 £30.00 (YOU)
Meshach Grant Burge 1994 £32.50 (CON)
£34.95 (STA) £36.50 (BALL) £40.00 (ROB)
St George Lindemans 1985 £33.00 (CRO)
Shiraz Jim Barry The Armagh 1996 £33.00
(PHI) £34.95 (BEN)
Shiraz Jim Barry The Armagh 1995 £31.99
(YOU) £32.10 (TAN) £34.50 (BAL) £34.99
(OD) £36.50 (RES) £39.95 (DI) £47.00 (CRO)
Shiraz Jim Barry The Armagh 1994 £33.29
(JER) £38.77 (NO)
Shiraz Wynns Michael 1991 £31.67 (REI)
£49.00 (CRO)
Shiraz/Cabernet Sauvignon Rouge
Homme 1976 £32.00 (CRO)

£40.00 → £59.99

Cabernet Sauvignon Parker Coonawarra
Estate Terra Rossa 1988 £40.00 (CRO)
Cabernet Sauvignon Wynns John Riddoch
1995 £47.00 (REI)
Cabernet Sauvignon Wynns John Riddoch
1986 £50.00 (YOU) £110.00 (CRO)
Cabernet Sauvignon Yarra Yering Dry
Red No.1 1987 £52.88 (REI)
Cabernet Sauvignon/Merlot Henschke
Abbott's Prayer 1994 £40.89 (NO)
Cabernet Sauvignon/Shiraz Petaluma
1985 £44.00 (CRO)

£60.00 → £99.99

Cabernet Sauvignon Henschke Cyril
Henschke 1986 £60.00 (CRO)
Cabernet Sauvignon Penfolds Bin 707
1990 £64.63 (REI)
Grange Penfolds 1993 £80.66 (BY) £99.50
(BEN) £109.00 (CRO) £110.00 (YOU)
Grange Penfolds 1991 £60.61 (BY)
£155.00 (YOU) £205.00 (RES)
Shiraz Clarendon Hills Astralis 1996
£75.00 (JU) £93.41 (FA)
Shiraz Henschke Hill of Grace 1992
£75.00 (ROB) £105.75 (NO) £165.87 (FA)

£100.00 → £199.99

Cabernet Sauvignon Wynns John Riddoch
1982 £106.00 (UB)
Grange Penfolds **1992** £102.00 (CRO)
£118.87 (FA) £130.00 (BEN) £135.13 (REI)
Grange Penfolds **1988** £170.00 (YOU)
Grange Penfolds **1982** £193.88 (REI)
Grange Penfolds **1979** £185.00 (YOU)
Shiraz Henschke Hill of Grace **1991**
£156.18 (CAV) £160.00 (CRO)

Over £200.00

Grange Penfolds **1990** £275.00 (BEN)
Grange Penfolds **1980** £201.13 (FA)

WHITE

Under £4.00

Chardonnay Red Cliffs **1997** £3.49 (VIC)
£3.49 (THR) £3.49 (WR) £3.49 (BOT)
Chardonnay Rothbury Cowra **1995**
£3.99 (MORR)
★ Chardonnay Tollana **1998** £3.99 (VIC)
£3.99 (THR) £3.99 (WR) £3.99 (BOT)
Colombard/Chardonnay Lindemans
Cawarra **1998** £3.60 (SOM)
Colombard/Chardonnay Lonsdale Ridge
1997 £3.99 (FUL)
Colombard/Chardonnay Red Cliffs **1997**
£3.49 (VIC) £3.49 (WR) £3.49 (BOT)
Dry White Dalwood **1997** £3.60 (SOM)
Rawson's Retreat Bin 202 Penfolds **1998**
£3.90 (SOM) £3.99 (POR) £3.99 (SAF)
£3.99 (FUL) £3.99 (WAI) £3.99 (VIC)
Rawson's Retreat Bin 21 Penfolds **1998**
£3.99 (YOU) £4.49 (MORR) £4.49 (FUL)
£4.49 (ASD) £4.65 (WS) £4.69 (UN)
Rawson's Retreat Bin 21 Penfolds **1997**
£3.98 (SOM) £4.49 (COC) £4.49 (CO) £4.49
(THR) £4.49 (WR) £4.49 (BOT) £5.24 (BY)
Semillon/Chardonnay Barramundi **Non-
vintage** £3.99 (CO) £3.99 (ASD)
Semillon/Chardonnay Barramundi **1998**
£3.99 (MORR)
Semillon/Chardonnay Penfolds Rowlands
Brook **1997** £3.99 (POR) £4.90 (HAH)
£4.95 (BALL)

£4.00 → £4.99

Autumn Harvest McGuigan Bros **1996**
£4.90 (UB)
Chardonnay Aldridge Estate **1997** £4.96
(NO) £5.69 (YOU)

Chardonnay Cockatoo Ridge **1997** £4.99
(BAL) £5.99 (YOU)
Chardonnay Deakin Estate **1997** £4.99
(MORR) £4.99 (BO) £4.99 (DI)
Chardonnay Deakin Estate Alfred Barrel-
Fermented **1998** £4.99 (OD)
Chardonnay Hardy Nottage Hill **1998**
£4.99 (MORR) £4.99 (FUL) £4.99 (SO)
£4.99 (UN) £4.99 (SAF) £4.99 (ASD)
Chardonnay Hardy Nottage Hill **1997**
£4.99 (CO)
Chardonnay Krondorf **1997** £4.99 (DI)
£6.95 (HED)
★ Chardonnay Lindemans Bin 65 **1998** £4.35
(SOM) £4.79 (POR) £4.95 (WS) £4.99
(MORR) £4.99 (FUL) £4.99 (MAR) £4.99 (SO)
£4.99 (SAI) £4.99 (MAJ) £4.99 (OD) £4.99
(SAF) £4.99 (VIC) £4.99 (THR) £4.99 (ASD)
Chardonnay Lindemans Bin 65 **1997**
£4.99 (PEN) £4.99 (UN) £4.99 (CO)
Chardonnay Lindemans Cawarra
Unoaked **1998** £4.49 (MAJ) £4.49 (ASD)
Chardonnay Orlando Jacob's Creek **1998**
£4.99 (FUL)
Chardonnay Penfolds Koonunga Hill **1998**
£4.80 (SOM) £5.49 (FUL) £5.49 (WAI)
£5.49 (SO) £5.49 (POR) £5.49 (YOU)
Chardonnay Penfolds Rowlands Brook
1997 £4.95 (POR) £5.25 (BALL)
Chardonnay Rolleston Vale **1996** £4.95
(CON)
Chardonnay Sunnycliff **1998** £4.95 (HAH)
Chardonnay Yalumba Oxford Landing
1998 £4.86 (STE) £4.99 (FUL) £4.99 (SAF)
Chenin Blanc Brown Bros **1998** £4.95
(STE) £5.29 (POR) £5.50 (NA) £5.95 (AD)
Chenin Blanc Peter Lehmann **1997** £4.85
(FUL)
Chenin Blanc/Semillon/Sauvignon Blanc
Tatachilla Growers **1998** £4.40 (BAN)
Colombard Deakin Estate **1998** £4.99
(YOU)
Colombard/Chardonnay Lonsdale Ridge
1998 £4.79 (BIB)
Dry White Rolleston Vale **Non-vintage**
£4.03 (GW) £4.14 (PEN)
Dry White Rolleston Vale **1994** £4.25
(CON)

---

*Stars (★) indicate wines
selected by Oz Clarke in the
Best Buys section which begins
on page 9.*

Jacob's Creek White Orlando 1998 £4.99
(SO)
Marsanne Mitchelton Unoaked 1996
£4.99 (OD)
Muscat Brown Bros Dry 1998 £4.50
(POR) £5.40 (PIP) £5.52 (GW) £5.65 (WRI)
Muscat Grant Burge Dry Late Picked
1997 £4.99 (FUL) £5.95 (BU)
Riesling Orlando Jacob's Creek Dry 1997
£4.59 (VIC) £4.59 (THR) £4.59 (BOT)
Riesling David Wynn 1997 £4.99 (MAJ)
£6.35 (FLE)
Riesling Wynns Coonawarra Estate 1997
£4.99 (JON)
Riesling Wynns Rhine 1996 £4.99 (YOU)
Sauvignon Blanc Deakin Estate 1998
£4.99 (BO) £4.99 (DI)
Sauvignon Blanc Yalumba Oxford Landing
1997 £4.99 (CO) £4.99 (VIC) £4.99 (THR)
Sauvignon Blanc Yalumba Oxford Landing
1996 £4.99 (NI)
Semillon/Chardonnay Aldridge Estate
1995 £4.95 (CON)
Semillon/Chardonnay Hardys Stamp 1998
£4.49 (MORR) £4.49 (SO) £4.49 (ASD)
Semillon/Chardonnay Orlando Jacob's
Creek 1997 £4.49 (TES) £4.59 (UN) £4.59
(CO) £4.59 (THR) £4.59 (BOT) £4.89 (NLW)
Semillon/Chardonnay Orlando Jacob's
Creek 1996 £4.45 (COC)
Semillon/Chardonnay Penfolds Rowlands
Brook 1996 £4.69 (JON)
Semillon/Chardonnay Rosemount 1998
£4.49 (ASD) £5.99 (WHI) £5.99 (BO) £5.99
(SAF) £5.99 (THR) £5.99 (WR) £5.99 (BOT)
Semillon/Chardonnay Tatachilla Wattle
Park 1997 £4.95 (BAN) £6.99 (VIC) £6.99
(THR) £6.99 (WR) £6.99 (BOT)

£5.00 → £5.99

Chardonnay Aldridge Estate 1996 £5.95
(CON)
Chardonnay Jim Barry Clare Valley 1996
£5.99 (PHI) £6.45 (JON)
Chardonnay Canoe Tree 1997 £5.99 (YOU)
Chardonnay Deakin Estate Alfred Barrel-
Fermented 1997 £5.99 (YOU)
Chardonnay Houghton Wildflower Ridge
1996 £5.99 (CO) £6.29 (ROS)
Chardonnay Lindemans Limestone Coast
1997 £5.99 (FUL)
Chardonnay Penfolds Koonunga Hill 1997
£5.45 (COC) £5.49 (MORR) £5.49 (PEN)
£5.49 (THR) £5.49 (WR) £5.49 (BOT) £5.99
(JON) £6.07 (BY) £6.45 (FORT) £6.75 (AV)

Chardonnay Penfolds Private Bin 1998
£5.49 (STE) £5.82 (BY) £6.10 (NA)
Chardonnay Penfolds Rowlands Brook
1996 £5.29 (JON)
Chardonnay Riddoch 1996 £5.99 (SAF)
£6.99 (VIC) £6.99 (THR) £7.49 (YOU)
Chardonnay Rosemount 1998 £5.49
(ASD) £6.59 (WHI) £6.99 (TES) £6.99 (BO)
£6.99 (SAF)
Chardonnay Rothbury Cowra 1997
£5.99 (DI)
Chardonnay Sunnycliff 1996 £5.59 (JON)
Chardonnay Woolshed 1996 £5.99 (FUL)
Chardonnay Wyndham's Bin 222 1997
£5.99 (MAJ)
Chardonnay David Wynn 1998 £5.70
(SOM) £6.95 (AD)
Chenin Blanc Brown Bros 1997 £5.29
(YOU) £5.49 (DI) £5.52 (GW) £5.65 (UB)
HWB Houghton 1998 £5.49 (POR)
Long Flat White Tyrrell's 1997 £5.65 (UB)
£6.25 (AME) £6.25 (PIP)
Long Flat White Tyrrell's 1996 £5.99 (JON)
Muscat Brown Bros Dry 1997 £5.29 (YOU)
£5.59 (JON) £5.63 (COC) £5.65 (STA)
Muscat Brown Bros Dry 1996 £5.85 (UB)
Muscat Grant Burge Dry Late Picked
1995 £5.99 (CON)
Poachers Blend St Hallett 1998 £5.99 (AUS)
Poachers Blend St Hallett 1997 £5.40 (SOM)
Poachers Blend St Hallett 1996 £5.46 (REI)
£6.20 (FLE)
Riesling Jim Barry Watervale 1997 £5.99
(YOU) £6.49 (DI) £6.50 (ELL) £6.50 (TAN)
Riesling Brown Bros King Valley 1997
£5.76 (STE) £5.99 (YOU) £6.40 (NA)
Riesling Pewsey Vale 1998 £5.99 (TES) £5.99
(BEN)
★ Riesling Pewsey Vale 1997 £5.99 (OD) £5.99
(VIC) £5.99 (THR) £5.99 (WR) £5.99 (BOT)
Semillon Basedow 1997 £5.99 (SAF)
Semillon Leasingham 1993 £5.99 (CO)
★ Semillon Peter Lehmann 1998 £5.25 (WS)
£5.49 (SAF)
Semillon/Chardonnay Ironstone 1997
£5.73 (NO) £6.49 (NI) £6.95 (ROB) £8.49
(VA)
Semillon/Chardonnay Penfolds Barossa
Valley 1998 £5.49 (ASD)
Semillon/Chardonnay Penfolds Barossa
Valley 1997 £5.20 (SOM) £5.95 (POR)
£5.99 (THR) £5.99 (WR) £5.99 (BOT)
Semillon/Sauvignon Blanc Rosemount
1997 £5.99 (FUL)
Verdelho McGuigan Bros 1995 £5.65 (UB)

£6.00 → £6.99

Chardonnay Basedow 1997 £6.99 (SO) £7.41 (BIB)

Chardonnay Bridgewater Mill 1996 £6.99 (SAI)

★ Chardonnay Chapel Hill Unwooded 1998 £6.99 (TES) £7.99 (AUS)

Chardonnay d'Arenberg Olive Grove 1997 £6.49 (OD) £6.49 (YOU) £6.51 (BIB)

Chardonnay Howard Park Madfish Bay 1997 £6.95 (WS) £7.30 (SOM) £7.99 (FUL) £9.39 (BAN) £9.95 (ROB) £9.99 (YOU)

Chardonnay Penfolds The Valleys 1998 £6.95 (SO)

Chardonnay Penfolds The Valleys 1997 £6.50 (SOM) £6.99 (SAI) £7.49 (FUL) £7.49 (PEN) £7.49 (POR) £7.49 (VIC) £7.49 (THR)

Chardonnay Plantagenet Omrah 1998 £6.99 (LIB)

Chardonnay Rosemount 1997 £6.99 (MORR) £6.99 (UN) £6.99 (CO) £6.99 (VIC) £6.99 (THR) £6.99 (WR) £6.99 (BOT)

Chardonnay Rothbury 1996 £6.99 (JON)

Chardonnay Tyrrell's Old Winery 1997 £6.58 (PEN) £7.45 (PIP)

Chardonnay Wolf Blass 1997 £6.99 (MORR)

Chardonnay Wyndham Estate Oak Cask 1996 £6.99 (MAJ)

Chardonnay David Wynn 1997 £6.99 (PHI) £7.03 (GW)

Chardonnay Wynns Coonawarra Estate 1997 £6.99 (MORR) £7.77 (BY)

Chardonnay Wynns Coonawarra Estate 1996 £6.99 (PEN)

Chardonnay Yaldara Reserve 1996 £6.51 (PLAY)

Colombard Primo 1998 £6.99 (AUS) £6.99 (VIC) £6.99 (THR) £6.99 (WR) £6.99 (BOT)

Fumé Blanc Rosemount 1998 £6.99 (WAI)

★ Marsanne Chateau Tahbilk 1997 £6.95 (AD) £6.99 (WAI)

Marsanne Chateau Tahbilk 1996 £6.99 (UB)

Marsanne Chateau Tahbilk 1995 £6.20 (COC)

Riesling Jim Barry Watervale 1996 £6.29 (PHI)

Riesling Best's 1996 £6.03 (GW)

Riesling Tim Knappstein 1996 £6.50 (CRO)

Riesling Krondorf Rhine 1997 £6.45 (AS) £6.95 (HED)

Riesling Mitchell Watervale 1998 £6.50 (TAN) £6.65 (HAH) £6.81 (LAY) £6.95 (POR)

Riesling Mitchelton Blackwood Park 1994 £6.10 (UB)

Riesling Veritas Christa-Rolf 1996 £6.99 (YOU)

Riesling David Wynn 1998 £6.95 (AD)

Sauvignon Blanc David Wynn 1995 £6.99 (NI) £7.80 (MV)

Semillon Brown Bros 1995 £6.99 (GW) £7.11 (ROS)

Semillon Henschke 1995 £6.99 (SOM) £9.75 (FORT) £10.95 (WRI) £11.50 (ROB)

Semillon Penfolds Barossa Valley Old Vine 1997 £6.92 (NO)

Semillon/Chardonnay Ironstone 1998 £6.26 (STE) £6.49 (FUL) £6.69 (PHI)

Semillon/Chardonnay Penfolds Barossa Valley 1996 £6.15 (WAT)

Verdelho Rothbury Hunter Valley 1998 £6.99 (SAF)

£7.00 → £7.99

★ Chardonnay Allandale 1998 £7.99 (AUS)

Chardonnay Allandale 1997 £7.81 (REI)

Chardonnay Brown Bros 1996 £7.99 (DI) £8.40 (PIP) £8.61 (PEN) £8.70 (TAN)

Chardonnay Brown Bros King Valley 1996 £7.99 (POR) £8.49 (JON) £8.60 (STA)

Chardonnay Brown Bros King Valley 1995 £7.83 (ROS) £8.50 (CON)

Chardonnay Goundrey Reserve Mount Barker 1997 £7.59 (PLAY)

Chardonnay Hardy Padthaway 1998 £7.99 (SO)

Chardonnay Honey Tree Reserve 1998 £7.99 (MAR)

Chardonnay Howard Park Madfish Bay 1998 £7.99 (BAL) £9.99 (VA)

Chardonnay Leasingham 1996 £7.95 (BALL)

Chardonnay Lindemans Padthaway 1996 £7.99 (SAI)

Chardonnay Neil Paulett 1996 £7.90 (JU)

Chardonnay Penfolds Barrel-Fermented 1994 £7.50 (PIP)

Chardonnay Pipers Brook Ninth Island 1998 £7.25 (SOM) £7.99 (BO) £7.99 (YOU) £8.49 (TES) £8.75 (STA) £9.40 (MV)

Chardonnay St Hallett 1996 £7.81 (REI) £8.17 (DOM)

Chardonnay Yaldara Reserve 1997 £7.03 (GW) £7.50 (ROB) £9.55 (VIN)

Fifth Leg Devil's Lair 1997 £7.95 (SOM) £9.73 (GW) £9.74 (FLE) £9.80 (BAN)

Gewürztraminer Tim Knappstein 1997 £7.95 (FORT)

Marsanne Mitchelton 1997 £7.99 (AME)

Mitchelton III 1994 £7.88 (NO)

★ Riesling Tim Adams 1998 £7.99 (AUS) £8.49 (TES)

Riesling Brown Bros Family Reserve 1996 £7.49 (DI)

Riesling Eldredge 1998 £7.99 (AUS)

Riesling Leconfield 1997 £7.20 (JU)

Riesling Mitchell Watervale 1997 £7.99 (YOU)

Riesling Mitchell Watervale 1995 £7.09 (JON)

Riesling Mount Langhi Ghiran 1996 £7.15 (SOM) £7.99 (VA) £8.79 (YOU)

Riesling Neil Paulett 1997 £7.50 (JU) £7.99 (YOU)

Riesling Rockford 1995 £7.70 (FLE)

★ Riesling St Hallett Eden Valley 1998 £7.99 (AUS) £8.99 (WR) £8.99 (BOT)

Riesling David Wynn 1996 £7.80 (MV)

Sauvignon Blanc Katnook 1998 £7.14 (BIB) £8.99 (DI)

Sauvignon Blanc Pikes 1998 £7.95 (LEA)

Sauvignon Blanc Shaw & Smith 1997 £7.95 (SOM) £8.99 (YOU) £9.34 (REI) £9.35 (BEN) £9.50 (WRI) £9.90 (FLE) £10.35 (PIP)

Sauvignon Blanc/Chardonnay/Semillon Vasse Felix 1996 £7.30 (SOM) £8.95 (TAN) £8.99 (BEN) £9.39 (JON) £9.95 (ROB)

Semillon Tim Adams 1997 £7.95 (WS)

Semillon Allandale 1997 £7.50 (AUS)

Semillon Brown Bros 1996 £7.29 (YOU) £7.45 (PIP) £7.75 (WRI) £7.75 (STA) £7.88 (GW) £8.35 (AD)

Semillon Grant Burge Old Vine 1996 £7.95 (CON) £8.25 (BU)

Semillon McWilliams Mount Pleasant Elizabeth 1994 £7.99 (TES)

Semillon/Sauvignon Blanc Cape Mentelle 1996 £7.94 (NO) £8.49 (CON) £8.99 (JON)

Semillon/Sauvignon Blanc Mitchell The Growers 1997 £7.10 (TAN)

Verdelho Chapel Hill 1998 £7.49 (WR) £7.49 (BOT) £7.50 (AUS)

Verdelho Chapel Hill 1997 £7.99 (WAI)

★ Verdelho Fox Creek 1998 £7.99 (YOU)

Verdelho Houghton Gold Reserve 1994 £7.75 (ROB)

★ Verdelho David Traeger 1998 £7.99 (AUS) £8.49 (VIC) £8.49 (THR) £8.49 (WR)

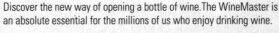

£8.00 → £8.99

Chardonnay Campbells Bobbie Burns
1997 £8.95 (UB)

Chardonnay Campbells Bobbie Burns
1996 £8.99 (YOU)

Chardonnay Capel Vale 1995 £8.63 (FLE)

Chardonnay Chapel Hill Unwooded 1994
£8.52 (REI)

Chardonnay Green Point 1993 £8.99
(RAE) £12.50 (CRO)

Chardonnay Hollick 1994 £8.05 (SOM)

Chardonnay Howard Park Madfish Bay
1996 £8.99 (NI)

Chardonnay Mitchelton Preece 1997
£8.20 (PLAY)

Chardonnay Montara Estate 1996 £8.75
(CON)

Chardonnay Orlando St Hilary 1996
£8.57 (COC)

Chardonnay Pipers Brook Ninth Island
1996 £8.40 (GW) £8.55 (PHI)

Chardonnay Reynolds Yarraman 1996
£8.69 (LAY)

Chardonnay Shaw & Smith Unoaked 1998
£8.99 (LIB) £10.30 (TAN) £12.30 (CON)

Chardonnay Shaw & Smith Unoaked 1997
£8.99 (YOU) £9.40 (HAH) £9.49 (TES)

Chardonnay Stonier's 1996 £8.99 (WAT)

Chardonnay Yarra Valley Hills 1997
£8.99 (OD) £9.86 (STE) £10.95 (NA)

Marsanne Mitchelton Victoria Reserve
1994 £8.46 (PEN) £8.70 (PIP) £8.90 (TAN)

Marsanne Mitchelton Wood-Matured
1993 £8.95 (WRI)

Riesling Tim Adams 1997 £8.20 (SOM)

Riesling Brown Bros Family Reserve 1994
£8.59 (YOU) £9.99 (PEN)

Riesling Henschke Julius Eden Valley 1997
£8.70 (SOM) £10.59 (YOU) £11.95 (ROB)

Riesling Tim Knappstein 1997 £8.48 (NO)

Riesling Leeuwin Estate Art Series 1998
£8.52 (DOM)

Riesling Pikes Polish Hill 1998 £8.95 (LEA)

Riesling Pipers Brook 1998 £8.15 (SOM)
£11.50 (BALL)

Riesling Rockford 1996 £8.99 (FUL) £8.99
(YOU)

Sauvignon Blanc Amberley Estate 1998
£8.49 (THR) £8.49 (WR) £8.49 (BOT)

Sauvignon Blanc Katnook 1997 £8.99
(FUL) £9.99 (WR) £9.99 (BOT)

Sauvignon Blanc Shaw & Smith 1998
£8.99 (LIB) £8.99 (BO) £9.35 (BEN)

Sauvignon Blanc/Semillon Howard Park
Madfish Bay 1997 £8.53 (GW) £9.59 (YOU)

Semillon Tim Adams 1996 £8.99 (AUS)
£8.99 (VIC) £8.99 (THR) £8.99 (WR) £8.99
(BOT) £9.49 (TES) £10.00 (FORT)

Semillon Brokenwood 1997 £8.99 (NO)
£9.39 (YOU)

Semillon Grant Burge Old Vine 1995
£8.75 (WS)

Semillon Henschke 1996 £8.81 (REI)

Semillon Rockford Local Growers 1996
£8.60 (GAU) £8.99 (FUL) £9.49 (YOU)

Semillon St Hallett Select 1998 £8.99 (AUS)

Semillon Willows Vineyard 1996 £8.49
(THR) £8.49 (WR) £8.49 (BOT) £8.50 (AUS)

Semillon/Sauvignon Blanc Cape Mentelle
1998 £8.95 (STA) £8.95 (TAN) £8.99
(PLA) £8.99 (PHI) £9.49 (AME) £9.50 (RAE)

Semillon/Sauvignon Blanc Cape Mentelle
1997 £8.26 (NO) £8.99 (YOU) £9.10 (HAH)
£9.93 (PLAY) £9.95 (AD)

Verdelho David Traeger 1997 £8.50 (ELL)

Verdelho David Traeger 1996 £8.65 (WRI)

£9.00 → £9.99

Chardonnay Jim Barry Clare Valley 1997
£9.40 (BEN)

Chardonnay Best's 1995 £9.95 (GW)
£9.99 (WHI)

Chardonnay Cape Jaffa 1996 £9.50 (ELL)

Chardonnay Cape Jaffa 1995 £9.38 (NO)

Chardonnay Green Point 1996 £9.99 (DI)
£10.50 (FORT)

Chardonnay Hollick 1995 £9.25 (WRI)
£10.95 (RES) £12.57 (TW)

Chardonnay Inglewood Show Reserve
1996 £9.95 (HED) £9.95 (POR)

Chardonnay Penley Estate 1996 £9.50 (AUS)
£10.19 (LAY) £10.63 (WT) £10.95 (YOU)

Chardonnay Pikes 1997 £9.95 (LEA)

Chardonnay Rosemount Show Reserve
1997 £9.99 (MORR) £9.99 (MORR) £9.99
(FUL) £9.99 (WAI) £9.99 (THR) £9.99 (BOT)

Chardonnay Rosemount Show Reserve
1996 £9.45 (HA) £9.99 (CO)

Chardonnay Scotchman's Hill 1995 £9.95
(FUL) £16.70 (UB)

Chardonnay Shaw & Smith Unoaked
1995 £9.60 (NI)
Chardonnay Wirra Wirra **1997** £9.99 (OD)
Chardonnay Wolf Blass President's
Selection **1995** £9.60 (CRO)
Fifth Leg Devil's Lair **1998** £9.49 (YOU)
Riesling Henschke Julius Eden Valley **1998**
£9.95 (WS)
Riesling Howard Park **1996** £9.59 (YOU)
£10.15 (BAN) £10.50 (BAL) £10.99 (NI)
Riesling Leeuwin Estate Art Series **1996**
£9.99 (YOU)
Riesling Mount Langhi Ghiran **1998** £9.21
(FLE)
Riesling Petaluma **1997** £9.60 (TAN) £9.95
(BEN) £10.05 (PIP) £10.50 (FORT)
Riesling Petaluma **1996** £9.69 (YOU) £9.99
(PHI) £10.10 (HAH) £11.57 (REI)
Riesling Pipers Brook **1997** £9.95 (YOU)
£10.95 (PHI)
Riesling Rockford **1997** £9.20 (GAU)
Sauvignon Blanc Amberley Estate **Non-
vintage** £9.65 (CON)
Sauvignon Blanc Lenswood Knappstein
1998 £9.30 (NEZ)
Sauvignon Blanc Scotchman's Hill **1996**
£9.90 (JU)
Sauvignon Blanc Geoff Weaver **1998**
£9.99 (BAL) £9.99 (AUS)
Semillon Amberley Estate **1995** £9.99
(VIC) £9.99 (THR) £9.99 (WR) £9.99 (BOT)
Semillon McWilliams Mount Pleasant
Elizabeth **1993** £9.25 (COC)
Semillon/Chardonnay Henschke Tilly's
Vineyard Eden Valley **1997** £9.40 (NO)
£9.45 (LAY) £9.69 (YOU) £9.95 (FORT)
Semillon/Chardonnay Henschke Tilly's
Vineyard Eden Valley **1996** £9.99 (JON)
Viognier Heggies Estate **1995** £9.99 (NI)

£10.00 → £10.99

Chardonnay Best's **1997** £10.64 (FLE)
Chardonnay Cape Mentelle **1997** £10.50
(CRO) £11.30 (HAH) £11.46 (PLA) £11.99
(VA) £12.50 (AD) £12.57 (PLAY)
Chardonnay Cape Mentelle **1996** £10.26
(NO) £10.99 (PHI) £11.16 (REI)
Chardonnay Chain of Ponds **1997** £10.95
(BAN)
Chardonnay Chapel Hill Reserve **1996**
£10.87 (REI)
Chardonnay De Bortoli Yarra Valley **1995**
£10.95 (BAL) £11.25 (WRI) £11.50 (LEA)
Chardonnay De Bortoli Yarra Valley
1993 £10.01 (NO)

Chardonnay Mountadam **1994** £10.50
(SOM) £14.00 (CRO)
Chardonnay Voyager Estate **1996** £10.95
(JU)
Marsanne Chateau Tahbilk **1990** £10.46
(NO)
Riesling Brown Bros Family Reserve **1991**
£10.50 (NO)
Riesling Grosset Polish Hill **1998** £10.99
(PHI) £11.50 (BEN)
Riesling Henschke Green Hill **1997**
£10.65 (FLE) £10.99 (YOU)
Sauvignon Blanc Lenswood Knappstein
1997 £10.45 (HAH) £11.50 (PHI)
Sauvignon Blanc/Semillon Henschke Eden
Valley **1995** £10.95 (DI)
Semillon Henschke **1993** £16.00 (CRO)
Semillon Moss Wood **1995** £10.75 (NO)
Semillon Voyager Estate **1996** £10.50 (JU)

£11.00 → £12.99

Chardonnay Chateau Xanadu **1996**
£12.95 (DI)
Chardonnay Cullen **1996** £12.99 (YOU)
£13.95 (FORT)
Chardonnay Cullen **1995** £11.30 (FLE)
Chardonnay De Bortoli Yarra Valley
1996 £11.95 (STA)
Chardonnay Grosset Piccadilly **1996**
£12.50 (WS) £14.25 (FORT)
Chardonnay Hollick **1992** £12.57 (TW)
Chardonnay Katnook **1996** £11.75 (BO)
Chardonnay Mountadam **1997** £12.99 (THR)
£12.99 (BOT) £13.50 (WRI) £13.95 (AD)
Chardonnay Mountadam **1996** £11.98 (FLE)
£12.99 (YOU) £13.50 (NI) £13.52 (GW)
Chardonnay Mountadam **1995** £12.95
(CON) £14.25 (FORT)
Chardonnay Mountadam **1993** £11.99 (NI)
£11.99 (AME) £12.84 (NO)
Chardonnay Penfolds Adelaide Hills **1996**
£11.43 (NO) £11.79 (POR) £11.99 (JON)
Chardonnay Penley Estate **1995** £12.50
(RES)
Chardonnay Pipers Brook **1996** £12.71
(PEN) £12.99 (AME) £14.25 (ROB)
Chardonnay Scotchman's Hill **1996**
£11.50 (JU)
Chardonnay Stonier's Reserve **1994**
£11.99 (WAT)
Chardonnay Tarrawarra **1997** £12.95 (WS)
Chardonnay Tyrrell's Vat 47 **1995** £12.75
(REI) £14.73 (NO) £17.50 (PHI)
Chardonnay Voyager Estate **1995** £12.49
(YOU)

Riesling Jasper Hill **1997** £11.75 (YAP)
Riesling David Wynn **1995** £11.85 (UB)
Sauvignon Blanc Cullen **1995** £11.61 (FLE)
Sauvignon Blanc Paracombe **1997** £12.50
(PHI)
Semillon Tyrrell's Vat 1 **1992** £17.50 (BAL)
Viognier Heggies Estate **1997** £11.95 (WRI)
£11.99 (PHI) £13.50 (BALL) £13.92 (PLAY)
Viognier Heggies Estate **1996** £12.49 (YOU)

£13.00 → £15.99

Chardonnay Bannockburn **1996** £15.70
(BEN) £16.95 (RES) £17.33 (JER) £29.95 (UB)
Chardonnay Coldstream Hills Reserve
1996 £14.99 (YOU)
Chardonnay Dalwhinnie **1996** £13.95 (JU)
£14.99 (YOU)
Chardonnay Grosset Piccadilly **1995**
£14.99 (PHI)
Chardonnay Henschke Croft **1996** £15.99
(NI) £15.99 (PHI) £16.95 (BEN) £19.39 (REI)
Chardonnay Henschke Eden Valley **1997**
£14.95 (RES)
Chardonnay Howard Park **1997** £13.02
(GW) £14.20 (BAN) £14.99 (YOU) £16.50
(FORT)
Chardonnay Petaluma **1997** £13.82 (STE)
£13.95 (TAN) £14.70 (BEN) £15.82 (PLAY)
Chardonnay Petaluma **1996** £14.50 (WS)
£15.50 (FORT) £15.50 (BALL) £15.95 (ROB)
Chardonnay Pipers Brook **1995** £13.79
(CON)
Chardonnay Tarrawarra **1995** £15.99 (PHI)
Semillon Moss Wood **1996** £13.49 (PLAY)
Semillon Moss Wood Wooded **1991**
£13.50 (CRO)
Semillon Rosemount Whites Creek **1986**
£13.51 (REI)

£16.00 → £19.99

Chardonnay Chain of Ponds **1996** £16.99
(PHI) £16.99 (VA) £18.95 (ROB)
Chardonnay Dalwhinnie **1993** £19.05 (NO)
Chardonnay Petersons **1991** £19.39 (REI)
Chardonnay Rosemount Roxburgh **1996**
£19.75 (WHI)
Chardonnay Tyrrell's Vat 47 **1996** £16.95
(STA) £16.99 (FUL) £17.35 (NO)
Chardonnay Yarra Yering **1990** £18.88
(NO) £25.00 (FORT)
Semillon Clarendon Hills **1997** £19.00 (JU)
Semillon Lindemans Hunter River **1987**
£18.50 (ROB)
Semillon Tyrrell's Vat 1 **1993** £17.50 (FORT)
Semillon Tyrrell's Vat 1 **1990** £16.75 (RAE)

£20.00 → £24.99

Chardonnay Clarendon Hills Kangarilla
Vineyard **1996** £23.00 (JU)
Chardonnay Lake's Folly **1989** £22.00 (CRO)
Chardonnay Leeuwin Estate **1995** £23.40
(SOM)
Chardonnay Moss Wood **1997** £22.11
(PLAY)
Chardonnay Mountadam **1989** £23.50 (FLE)

Over £25.00

Chardonnay Leeuwin Art Series **1995**
£26.99 (YOU) £30.00 (FORT) £36.50 (ROB)
Chardonnay Leeuwin Estate **1996** £29.95
(PHI)
Chardonnay Rosemount Roxburgh **1995**
£34.99 (UN)
Chardonnay Rosemount Roxburgh **1987**
£38.00 (CRO)
Chardonnay Tyrrell's Vat 47 **1993** £26.00
(CRO)

ROSÉ

£7.00 → £8.99

Rose of Virginia Charles Melton **1999**
£8.99 (LIB)
Rose of Virginia Charles Melton **1998**
£8.10 (SOM) £8.99 (YOU)
Rose of Virginia Charles Melton **1995**
£7.29 (FLE)

SPARKLING

Under £5.00

Killawarra Brut **Non-vintage** £4.30
(SOM) £5.69 (GW)
Seppelt Great Western Brut **Non-vintage**
£4.99 (VIC) £4.99 (THR) £4.99 (WR) £4.99
(BOT) £5.49 (MORR) £5.69 (YOU)
Seppelt Great Western Brut Rosé **Non-
vintage** £4.99 (THR) £5.45 (CON) £5.49
(MORR) £5.69 (YOU) £5.80 (TAN)

£5.00 → £5.99

Angas Brut **Non-vintage** £5.15 (SOM)
£5.99 (VIC) £5.99 (THR) £5.99 (WR) £5.99
(BOT) £6.49 (CO) £6.50 (NA)
Angas Brut Rosé **Non-vintage** £5.75 (NI)
£5.85 (STE) £5.99 (TES) £5.99 (OD)
Barramundi Sparkling **Non-vintage**
£5.29 (MORR) £5.29 (ASD)

Carrington Extra Brut **Non-vintage**
£5.99 (JON) £6.60 (UB)
Carrington Extra Brut **1996** £5.99 (NLW)
Killawarra Rosé **Non-vintage** £5.89 (POR)
Penfolds Rowlands Brook **Non-vintage**
£5.50 (BALL) £5.89 (JON) £5.89 (POR)
Rolleston Vale Brut **Non-vintage** £5.45
(CON) £5.86 (PEN)
Seaview Brut **Non-vintage** £5.00 (MORR)
£5.99 (POR) £6.49 (MAJ) £6.49 (BO) £6.49
(CO) £6.49 (THR) £6.50 (WS) £6.50 (PHI)
Taltarni Brut Taché **Non-vintage** £5.95
(SOM) £8.95 (WS) £8.95 (STA) £8.99
(CON) £8.99 (AME) £8.99 (POR) £9.15 (AV)
£9.18 (COC) £9.28 (PEN) £10.99 (PHI)

£6.00 → £7.99

★ Australian Brut Chardonnay **1995** £6.99
(SO)
Redbank Cuvée Emily **Non-vintage**
£6.95 (ROB)
Seaview Pinot Noir/Chardonnay **1994**
£7.99 (WAI) £8.49 (YOU) £8.99 (SAI)
Tatachilla Brut Non-Vintage **Non-vintage** £6.55 (BAN)
Yalumba Pinot Noir/Chardonnay **Non-vintage** £7.90 (NI) £8.49 (BO) £8.49
(VIC) £8.49 (THR) £8.49 (WR) £8.49 (BOT)
Yalumba Pinot Noir/Chardonnay Cuvée
One Prestige **Non-vintage** £7.30
(SOM) £8.95 (AD)

£8.00 → £9.99

Green Point Brut **1995** £9.90 (SOM) £11.16
(BIB) £11.49 (MAJ) £11.49 (OD) £11.49 (SAF)
£11.49 (THR) £11.49 (YOU) £11.99 (JON)
£12.38 (PLAY) £12.65 (HAH) £12.75 (FORT)
★ Seaview Pinot Noir/Chardonnay **1995**
£8.99 (JON) £8.99 (SAF) £8.99 (OD)
Seppelt Salinger Brut **1992** £8.99 (AME)
£8.99 (OD) £8.99 (YOU)
Seppelt Show Sparkling Shiraz **1993** £8.99
(BO)
Seppelt Sparkling Shiraz **Non-vintage**
£9.39 (JON)
Seppelt Sparkling Shiraz **1993** £8.99 (TES)
Yellowglen Brut **1995** £9.99 (OD)

£10.00 → £11.99

★ Berry's Australian Sparkling Wine,
Taltarni **1992** £10.75 (BER)
Grant Burge Méthode Traditionelle **Non-vintage** £10.45 (CON)
Green Point Blanc de Blancs **1992** £11.95
(WS) £11.99 (DI)

Green Point Brut **1994** £10.99 (COC)
£11.49 (TES) £11.49 (WAI) £11.74 (PLA)
£11.99 (POR) £12.95 (ROB)
Green Point Brut **1993** £11.50 (PHI)
Seppelt Sparkling Shiraz **1994** £10.90 (TAN)

£12.00 → £15.99

Clover Hill **1995** £12.30 (AV) £12.95 (STA)
£12.99 (AME)
Croser **1994** £13.49 (YOU) £13.95 (FORT)
£13.99 (PHI) £18.00 (CRO)
Croser **1993** £13.90 (BEN)
Green Point Brut **Non-vintage** £12.50
(CRO)
Green Point Brut **1996** £13.95 (JU)
Charles Melton Sparkling Red **1995**
£15.99 (YOU)
Mitchell Sparkling Shiraz **Non-vintage**
£14.95 (POR)
Seppelt Show Sparkling Shiraz **1990**
£13.51 (NO)
Seppelt Show Sparkling Shiraz **1987**
£15.99 (PHI)

£16.00 → £19.99

★ Mountadam Chardonnay/Pinot Noir
1992 £18.99 (YOU) £19.95 (AD)
Mountadam Chardonnay/Pinot Noir
1991 £16.75 (FLE) £17.59 (CON)

Over £20.00

Charles Melton Sparkling Red **Non-vintage** £25.95 (LIB)

SWEET & FORTIFIED

Under £5.00

Penfolds Magill Tawny ½ bottle **Non-vintage** £4.99 (SAF) £5.99 (BO) £5.99
(YOU)

£5.00 → £5.99

Brown Bros Muscat Late-Harvest **1997**
£5.99 (TES) £5.99 (JON) £5.99 (DI) £5.99
(YOU) £6.25 (PIP) £6.35 (STA) £6.45 (WRI)
£6.46 (PEN) £6.49 (AME) £6.90 (AD)
Brown Bros Muscat Late-Harvest **1995**
£5.70 (COC) £6.40 (UB) £6.49 (MORR)
Brown Bros Orange Muscat & Flora ½
bottle **Non-vintage** £5.99 (SAI)
Brown Bros Orange Muscat & Flora ½
bottle **1998** £5.99 (POR) £5.99 (VIC)
£5.99 (THR) £5.99 (WR) £5.99 (BOT)
£6.20 (NA) £6.35 (STA) £7.93 (PLAY)

Brown Bros Orange Muscat & Flora ½ bottle **1997** £5.49 (CO) £5.75 (FUL) £5.99 (AME) £5.99 (UN) £5.99 (JON) £5.99 (BO) £5.99 (YOU) £6.20 (PIP) £6.23 (PEN) £6.30 (TAN) £6.35 (WRI) £6.65 (UB)

Brown Bros Orange Muscat & Flora ½ bottle **1996** £5.53 (ROS) £5.85 (DI) £6.20 (GW) £6.45 (JU)

Brown Bros Orange Muscat & Flora ½ bottle **1995** £5.91 (COC) £5.99 (WHI)

Chambers Rutherglen Liqueur Muscat ½ bottle **Non-vintage** £5.99 (PHI) £6.95 (FORT)

Lindemans Coonawarra Botrytis Riesling ½ bottle **1996** £5.90 (SOM) £5.99 (AME) £5.99 (JON)

Morris Liqueur Muscat **Non-vintage** £5.01 (TES)

Morris Liqueur Muscat ½ bottle **Non-vintage** £5.30 (SOM) £5.92 (NO)

Seppelt Show Fino DP117 ½ bottle **Non-vintage** £5.99 (YOU) £6.42 (NO) £6.99 (PHI)

Stanton & Killeen Rutherglen Liqueur Muscat ½ bottle **Non-vintage** £5.85 (WS) £5.99 (FUL) £5.99 (AME) £5.99 (YOU) £6.00 (PHI) £6.25 (CON) £6.90 (GAU)

£6.00 → £6.99

Brown Bros Noble Riesling ½ bottle **1994** £6.99 (YOU) £7.64 (PEN) £8.15 (PIP)

Brown Bros Noble Riesling ½ bottle **1982** £6.80 (UB)

Brown Bros Orange Muscat & Flora **1996** £6.25 (CON)

Campbells Rutherglen Liqueur Muscat **Non-vintage** £6.95 (AD) £11.95 (ROB)

Chambers Rosewood Liqueur Muscat ½ bottle **Non-vintage** £6.50 (LEA) £6.83 (NO)

Peter Lehmann Botrytis Semillon ½ bottle **1996** £6.99 (OD)

Rothbury Museum Reserve Liqueur Muscat **Non-vintage** £6.29 (NO)

£7.00 → £9.99

Brown Bros Muscat Reserve **Non-vintage** £8.99 (YOU) £9.49 (JON) £9.99 (PEN)

Brown Bros Noble Riesling **1995** £9.75 (VIN)

Brown Bros Orange Muscat & Flora **1997** £8.99 (VIN)

Cranswick Estate Botrytis Semillon ½ bottle **1995** £9.99 (OD) £12.00 (WRI) £12.75 (NO)

★ Heggies Botrytis Riesling ½ bottle **1998** £7.99 (FUL)

Primo Joseph La Magia Botrytis Riesling ½ bottle **1996** £9.99 (AUS)

★ Seppelt Show Reserve DP63 ½ bottle **Non-vintage** £7.49 (OD) £7.99 (YOU)

Vasse Felix Noble Riesling ½ bottle **1996** £7.80 (SOM) £8.49 (YOU) £8.95 (BEN) £9.44 (PLAY) £9.50 (ROB)

Veritas Liqueur Tawny **Non-vintage** £9.99 (YOU)

Yalumba Museum Release Rutherglen Muscat **Non-vintage** £7.99 (OD)

Yalumba Pewsey Vale Botrytis Late-Harvest Riesling ½ bottle **1991** £9.25 (NO)

£10.00 → £11.99

Brown Bros Liqueur Muscat **Non-vintage** £11.95 (DI) £11.99 (ROS) £12.95 (POR) £13.52 (GW) £13.59 (JON) £13.89 (WAT) £13.95 (WRI) £14.22 (NO)

Chambers Rutherglen Liqueur Muscat **Non-vintage** £10.47 (NO) £10.59 (YOU) £14.00 (CRO)

Cranswick Estate Botrytis Semillon ½ bottle **1994** £10.93 (CB)

De Bortoli Noble One Botrytis Semillon ½ bottle **1994** £11.66 (STE) £11.99 (AUS) £12.50 (STA) £12.95 (LEA) £12.95 (NA)

De Bortoli Noble One Botrytis Semillon ½ bottle **1993** £10.85 (SOM) £12.25 (WRI) £12.51 (REI) £12.99 (BAL) £13.30 (NO)

£12.00 → £13.99

Chambers Rosewood Liqueur Muscat **Non-vintage** £12.50 (TAN)

Chambers Rutherglen Old Vine ½ bottle **Non-vintage** £13.07 (NO)

Seppelt Old Trafford **Non-vintage** £12.85 (NO)

£14.00 → £19.99

Seppelt Para Port **Non-vintage** £15.99 (AME)

Seppelt Para Port **1976** £19.51 (NO)

Over £20.00

Brown Bros Noble Riesling **1982** £20.00 (CRO)

Campbells Merchant Prince Liqueur Muscat **Non-vintage** £37.99 (NO)

De Bortoli Noble One Botrytis Semillon **Non-vintage** £26.95 (PHI)

De Bortoli Noble One Botrytis Semillon **1995** £28.50 (BEN)

CHILE

**Chile is starting to make super-premium, super-expensive wines.
But are they worth the price?**

Who decides which is a really great wine and which merely a very good one? I'd have thought – but you don't have to agree with me – that it would be a consensus reached over time. Drinkers, merchants and the producers would watch the progress of a wine over a number of vintages and would decide, tentatively at first and then more firmly, that such and such a wine is absolutely top class.

So how far should we believe a producer who launches a new wine – perhaps even from newly planted vineyards – at a sky-high price, with the claim that it's one of the world's great wines? We've seen it happen time and time again in California (Opus One and Dominus are just two of many possible examples), we've seen it in Bordeaux (Le Dôme and others) and in the last couple of years we've seen the same phenomenon beginning in Chile. A couple of £30 reds have already been launched from here, and there'll be others.

Personally I take more convincing. I'd like to see how they stack up against wines half their price – are they really twice as good? – and I'd like to watch their progress over at least a decade. Perhaps I'm too sceptical. But it seems to me that greatness and fashion are different things.

GRAPE VARIETIES

CABERNET SAUVIGNON (red) Characterized by relatively soft, well-rounded tannins; unusually, Chilean Cab often doesn't need Merlot to fill it out. Unoaked versions are best within two years of the vintage. Best unoaked Cabernets: *Monte La Finca, La Rosa, Andes Peak.* Best premium: *Concha y Toro Don Melchor, Canepa Magnificum.*

CARMENÈRE (red) Marvellously spicy wines, sometimes under its alias of Grande Vidure. Try *Carmen, Montes.*

CHARDONNAY (white) Generally light and melony, with or without oak, but some properly complex wines are emerging. Unoaked: *La Rosa, Luis Felipe Edwards, Casa Porta, Santa Monica.* Wild-yeast wines: *Viña Casablanca, Errázuriz, Montes.* As with Cabernet, subtler oaking is increasingly the norm. Cool-climate Casablanca tends to produce a crisper, more citrus-fresh Chardonnay than its Central Valley counterparts.

GEWÜRZTRAMINER (white) The lychee and rose petal packed *Viña Casablanca* version of this grape is still the best. Others seem to lack heart.

MERLOT (red) Ever more fashionable, and bursting with colour and vibrant, plummy fruit. Try *La Rosa, Santa Monica, Carta Vieja, La Fortuna, Canepa* (all for drinking young); *Errázuriz Reserve, Casa Lapostolle, Carmen, Viña Porta, Mont Gras, Montes, Concha y Toro* and *Segu Ollé* (all with aging potential).

PINOT NOIR (red) Chile is a prime source of inexpensive Pinot Noir, but there's still not that much. Try *Concha y Toro Explorer, Villard, Cono Sur.*

RIESLING (white) Only minimal amounts of the great German grape are grown in Chile, and it's not being pursued with any great zeal. Nor are the results terribly exciting. *Miguel Torres* makes a good Gewürztraminer/Riesling blend in the

Curicó Valley, however; try also *Santa Monica* and *Santa Rita*.

SAUVIGNON BLANC (white) The Casablanca region leads and is the only region with a distinct style (ripe gooseberry and asparagus fruit, and firm acidity). *Viña Casablanca's Santa Isabel Estate, Villard, Concha y Toro* and *Caliterra* are the labels to watch. Outside Casablanca, the Curicó Valley is producing some goodies (*Viña Casablanca White Label, Montes, San Pedro*).

SEMILLON (white) Widely planted but rarely used for the domestic market. For exports, *Carmen's* Alvaro Espinoza uses it in a good Chardonnay blend and a rich, oily Late Harvest. *Viña San Carlos* is decent.

WINE REGIONS

Although grapes are grown in the far north and pretty far south, only a 400km strip of the Central Valley is responsible for producing quality wine. Frost and rain limit development further south, searing heat and desert are the problems to the north.

Recent appellation legislation splits the main wine growing region into Aconcagua (incorporating the sub-region of Casablanca), the Central Valley (including Maipo, Rapel, Curicó and Maule) and the Southern Region (including the valleys of Itata and Bío-Bío).

ACONCAGUA VALLEY Dominated by one producer (*Errázuriz*) in Panquehue. The main vine is Cabernet Sauvignon (*Errázuriz' Don Maximiano* is one of the top Cabernets in Chile) and new plantings of Sangiovese, Nebbiolo and Zinfandel add to the red bias.

CASABLANCA VALLEY Chile's premier white wine region, and the only one with an identifiable style (though look out for Limari Valley in years to come). Chardonnay dominates, with Sauvignon Blanc and Gewürztraminer, and small amounts of Cabernet Sauvignon, Merlot and Pinot Noir. Chardonnay tends to be green and citrus-flavoured, often with figgy aromas, and Sauvignons are grassy and crisp with firm acidity. Best: *Viña Casablanca, Caliterra, Concha y Toro, Villard.*

CURICÓ Mainly known for its Chardonnay (*Valdivieso, Montes, San Pedro, Caliterra*). Valdivieso has emerged as the leading producer, also making beautiful Pinot Noir, Merlot and Cabernet.

MAIPO VALLEY Birthplace of the Chilean wine industry and home to some of the biggest and most traditional players (*Santa Rita, Concha y Toro, Santa Carolina*). Alto Maipo (*Aquitania, Cousiño Macul, William Fèvre*) has colder nights, so the grapes keep their acidity better. Cabernet Sauvignon made the valley's name and is still the main grape, although excellent Chardonnay is made here, too. The spread of Santiago's suburbs and smog is creating pressure on some producers. Most innovative: *Carmen, Canepa, Concha y Toro.*

MAULE A handful of producers (*Terra Noble, Domaine Oriental, Carta Vieja, Segu Ollé*) are achieving variable results, with reds (particularly Merlot) so far beating whites hands down on quality.

RAPEL A seedbed of new winery activity, particularly in the Colchagua Valley where new arrivals *Mont Gras, Luis Felipe Edwards* and *Casa Lapostolle* are producing good Chardonnay and Cabernet. Top Pinot Noir comes from *Cono Sur*, and Merlot from *La Rosa* and *Concha y Toro*. *Viña Porta* and *Santa Monica* make top-class Cabernet and Merlot.

SOUTHERN REGION *Concha y Toro* has produced a top-class Gewürztraminer from Mulchen.

PRODUCERS WHO'S WHO

FRANCISCO DE AGUIRRE ★★★
Clean, fresh Chardonnay and Cabernet under the Palo Alto label.

AQUITANIA ★★★ Made by Bordelais duo Bruno Prats of Ch. Cos d'Estournel and Paul Pontallier of Ch. Margaux. It's questionable whether the Domaine Paul Bruno is worth its hefty price tag.

CANEPA ★★★★ The company behind many of the best own-labels here, Canepa also makes the good Montenuevo and Rowan Brook. Merlot, Zinfandel and Magnificum Cabernet are its top reds.

CARMEN ★★★★ State-of-the-art sister operation to Santa Rita. Reds are best; beautiful Merlot Reserve, Grande Vidure/Cabernet and Petite Sirah.

INSTANT CELLAR: GLORIOUS MERLOTS

- 1997 Merlot Echeverría Reserva, Curicó **£7.15, Averys** Soft and juicy, to drink now.
- 1996 Merlot Casa Lapostolle Cuvée Alexandre, Colchagua, £9.99, **Bottoms Up, Wine Rack** Superior stuff full of wild fruit, made by Bordeaux star Michel Rolland.
- 1996 Merlot, Cousiño Macul, Maipo **£6.99, Great Western Wines** Textbook juicy blackberry fruit.
- 1996 Merlot Montes Alpha, Montes, Curicó, £9.95, **Hedley Wright** Vanilla plums – delicious.
- 1996 Unfiltered Merlot , Santa Rita, Maipo, £5.99, **Oddbins** Lots of character and depth.
- 1995 Merlot Villard Reserve, Maipo, £8.99, **Philglas & Swiggot** Single-vineyard wine of good concentration and style.
- 1997 Merlot Mont Gras Reserva, Colchagua, £7.99, **Valvona & Crolla** Modern, fruit-driven style from a state-of-the-art winery.

CARTA VIEJA ★★★ Old Maule Valley winery delivering good value, inexpensive wine. Reds are best. Very good Merlot.

CASA LAPOSTOLLE ★★★(★) No-expense-spared winery making grassy Sauvignon, rich, buttery Chardonnay and spectacular oak-aged Merlot.

CONCHA Y TORO ★★★★ Chile's biggest winery has resources to reach both good value and premium ends. Trio red and white are superb, as is Amelia Chardonnay, a new Syrah, and constantly improving Don Melchor Cabernet. Latest is a joint venture with Ch. Mouton-Rothschild in Bordeaux.

CONO SUR ★★★★ Superb Pinot Noir and Isla Negra red are both excellent value.

COUSIÑO MACUL ★★ Traditionalist making old-style reds under the Santiago smog. A new location and a new wine-making philosophy would help.

ECHEVERRÍA ★★★ Leading boutique winery with vineyards in Curicó Valley. Good reserve Chardonnay and Cabernet.

LUIS FELIPE EDWARDS ★★★(★) Large specialist in Chardonnay and Cabernet.

ERRÁZURIZ ★★★★ Chardonnay and Reserve Merlot have improved; there is also a wild yeast Chardonnay. A joint venture with Robert Mondavi of California has produced Seña, an extremely expensive, lush Cabernet-Merlot-Carmenère blend.

LA FORTUNA ★★★ Malbec is best here, but Merlot and Cabernet are both good. Decent whites.

MONT GRAS ★★★ Go for the reds here: Cabernet and Merlot are both good. Whites are less impressive so far.

ON THE CASE
*Quality in Chile improves each
year – but beware ambitious
pricing. We're looking for value,
not status*

MONTES ★★★ Slightly erratic, but currently on form with intense Malbec, good Merlot and juicy unoaked La Finca and premium Montes Alpha Cabernets.

LOS ROBLES ★★★ Upfront flying winemaker-style Cabernet and Merlot.

LA ROSA ★★★★ Top unwooded Chardonnay and Merlot. Watch out for new Cabernet from Palmeria Estate.

SAN PEDRO ★★★ There have been big improvements in quality here. Best of the Castillo de Milina range is the Chardonnay Reserve.

SANTA CAROLINA ★★★ Reliable producer of reds, particularly Merlot from San Fernando. Whites are dull compared with the vibrant wines of its sister company Viña Casablanca.

SANTA INÉS ★★★ Small company making good quality wines.

SANTA MONICA ★★★ Small family-run winery making excellent Riesling and Merlot.

SANTA RITA ★★★ Erratic quality in recent years. The 120 range is the most reliable, and the latest release of premium Casa Real shows welcome restraint with the new oak.

SEGU OLLÉ ★★★ Merlot is the star turn here, but the Cabernet Sauvignon is also good and worth a punt.

TERRA NOBLE ★★★★ Winery based at Talca in the Maule Valley, where

Touraine wizard Henri Marionnet makes very good Sauvignon Blanc and Merlot.

TORRÉON DE PAREDES ★★★(★) Large winery based in Rapel. Good wines throughout, particularly an award-winning Merlot.

TORRES ★★★ Another piece of foreign investment that hasn't delivered the goods. Whites are above average but not spectacular.

UNDURRAGA ★★★ One of the old camp that needs an injection of inspiration. Merlot and Cabernet are good.

VALDIVIESO ★★★★ Traditional sparkling wine producer, now top of the premium still wine league. Excellent oaked Pinot Noir, Merlot, and red blend (the grapes are a secret) Caballo Loco, which is given a number rather than a vintage.

LOS VASCOS ★★★ Château Lafite-Rothschild of Bordeaux's joint venture in Chile. So far, the Cabernet has not lived up to its potential.

VILLARD ★★★★ Good Sauvignon and Chardonnay from Casablanca, and fruity Merlot.

VIÑA CASABLANCA ★★★★ White label wines come from outside the Casablanca area (good new El Bosque Cabernet is from Maipo). From the valley itself, Santa Isabel Estate Sauvignon, Chardonnay and Gewürztraminer are all excellent.

VIÑA PORTA ★★★★ Boutique winery delivering consistently good oak-aged Chardonnay and Cabernet. A good Merlot here, too.

VIÑA SAN CARLOS ★★★ The blend of Cabernet and Malbec is worth trying; also ripe Semillon.

CHILE PRICES

RED

Under £4.00

Cabernet Sauvignon Viña Porta 1996 £3.99 (MORR)
Cabernet Sauvignon Vistamar Vistasur 1998 £3.99 (MAJ)
Merlot Peteroa 1998 £3.74 (WIW)

£4.00 → £4.49

Cabernet Sauvignon Concha y Toro 1997 £4.49 (POR) £4.99 (CON) £5.10 (UB)
Cabernet Sauvignon Montes 1998 £4.49 (MORR) £5.25 (AS) £5.45 (PIP) £5.50 (HED)
Cabernet Sauvignon Santiago 1997 £4.49 (MOR)
Cabernet Sauvignon Santiago 1996 £4.49 (BAL) £4.59 (NI)
Cabernet Sauvignon Valdivieso 1997 £4.49 (VIC) £4.49 (THR) £4.49 (BOT)
Cabernet Sauvignon Viña San Pedro Sur 35 1998 £4.49 (ASD)
Merlot Concha y Toro 1998 £4.25 (WAI)
Merlot Las Colinas 1998 £4.49 (VIC) £4.49 (THR) £4.49 (WR) £4.49 (BOT)
Merlot Santa Emiliana Andes Peaks 1998 £4.49 (YOU) £4.75 (CON) £4.83 (GW)
Merlot Viña La Rosa La Palma 1997 £4.49 (FUL) £4.49 (WAI) £4.99 (UN)

£4.50 → £4.99

Cabernet Sauvignon Caliterra 1996 £4.99 (VIC) £4.99 (THR) £4.99 (WR) £4.99 (BOT)
Cabernet Sauvignon Carmen 1996 £4.74 (FLE) £4.99 (UN)
Cabernet Sauvignon Concha y Toro 1996 £4.99 (JON)
Cabernet Sauvignon Concha y Toro Casillero del Diablo 1997 £4.99 (SAF)
Cabernet Sauvignon Cono Sur Isla Negra 1997 £4.99 (FUL) £4.99 (TES) £4.99 (OD) £4.99 (WAI)

Cabernet Sauvignon Peteroa Oak Aged 1996 £4.62 (WIW)
Cabernet Sauvignon Santa Carolina Special Reserve 1996 £4.99 (VIC) £4.99 (THR) £4.99 (WR) £4.99 (BOT)
Cabernet Sauvignon Santa Rita 120 1997 £4.99 (WAI) £4.99 (DI)
Cabernet Sauvignon Valdivieso Reserve 1996 £4.99 (FUL)
Cabernet Sauvignon Viña San Pedro Sur 35 1997 £4.95 (ROB)
Cabernet Sauvignon/Merlot Norte Chico 1998 £4.52 (GW)
Merlot Concha y Toro Casillero del Diablo 1996 £4.99 (FUL) £6.25 (ROB)
Merlot Mont Gras 1997 £4.95 (SOM) £5.46 (FLE) £5.99 (VA)
Merlot Santa Inés 1996 £4.99 (VIC) £4.99 (THR) £4.99 (WR) £4.99 (BOT)
★ Merlot Valdivieso 1998 £4.55 (BO) £4.99 (SAI) £4.99 (VIC) £4.99 (THR) £4.99 (WR)
Merlot Viña La Rosa La Palma 1998 £4.99 (OD)
Merlot Viña San Pedro Gato Negro 1998 £4.50 (ROB)
Pinot Noir Cono Sur 1998 £4.95 (WS) £4.99 (TES)
Pinot Noir Undurraga 1998 £4.99 (TES) £6.85 (PLAY)
Zinfandel Canepa 1997 £4.99 (UN)

£5.00 → £5.99

Cabernet Franc Palo Alto 1996 £5.10 (AV)
Cabernet Sauvignon Concha y Toro Trio 1996 £5.99 (VIC) £5.99 (THR) £5.99 (BOT)
Cabernet Sauvignon Errázuriz 1996 £5.49 (FUL) £5.49 (VIC) £5.49 (THR) £5.49 (WR)
Cabernet Sauvignon Los Vascos 1996 £5.90 (CRO) £5.92 (COC) £6.40 (HAH)
Cabernet Sauvignon Jacques Lurton Estate-Bottled 1995 £5.78 (JER)
Cabernet Sauvignon Mont Gras 1997 £5.99 (SAI) £5.99 (VA)

MERCHANTS SPECIALIZING IN CHILE

see Merchant Directory (page 413) for details

Not many merchants stock a long list, but the following have a good choice: First Quench Group (BOT, THR, VIC, WR), Hedley Wright (HED), Lay & Wheeler (LAY),

Oddbins (OD) – few independent merchants have as much variety, Thos. Peatling, Safeway (SAF), Tanners (TAN), The Ubiquitous Chip (UB), Noel Young (YOU).

Cabernet Sauvignon Montes 1996 £5.45 (JU) £5.49 (POR) £6.70 (TAN)

Cabernet Sauvignon Santa Rita Reserva 1997 £5.49 (MAJ) £5.99 (NEZ)

Cabernet Sauvignon Torres Santa Digna 1997 £5.49 (DI) £6.09 (JON)

Cabernet Sauvignon Viña Casablanca Miraflores Estate 1997 £5.50 (WS)

Cabernet Sauvignon Viña Linderos 1998 £5.22 (STE) £5.95 (NA)

Cabernet Sauvignon Viña Portal del Alto 1997 £5.10 (HAH) £5.50 (BALL)

★ Cabernet Sauvignon Viña San Pedro Castillo de Molina Reserva 1996 £5.95 (ROB) £5.99 (MORR)

Malbec Villa Montes 1998 £5.49 (POR)

Merlot Casa Lapostolle 1996 £5.70 (SOM) £6.49 (FUL) £8.23 (PLA) £8.75 (FORT)

Merlot Errázuriz 1997 £5.99 (FUL) £6.70 (HAH) £6.80 (CRO)

Merlot Montes 1997 £5.99 (PHI) £6.10 (AS)

Merlot Morandé Vitisterra 1997 £5.99 (UN)

Merlot Santa Rita Reserva 1997 £5.99 (NEZ) £6.49 (DI)

Merlot Valdivieso Reserve 1998 £5.49 (TES)

Merlot Viña La Rosa Cornellana 1998 £5.00 (AS)

£6.00 → £6.99

Cabernet Sauvignon Caliterra Reserve 1995 £6.99 (THR) £6.99 (WR) £6.99 (BOT)

Cabernet Sauvignon Carmen Reserve 1996 £6.89 (FLE) £7.85 (ELL)

Cabernet Sauvignon Casa Lapostolle 1996 £6.49 (VIC) £6.49 (THR) £6.49 (WR) £6.49 (BOT) £6.50 (WS) £8.05 (PLA)

Cabernet Sauvignon Cousiño Macul Antiguas Reservas 1995 £6.95 (POR) £7.15 (WRI) £7.11 (PEN) £7.25 (BALL)

Cabernet Sauvignon Echeverría Family Reserve 1996 £6.79 (YOU) £11.99 (POR)

Cabernet Sauvignon Luis Felipe Edwards Reserva 1996 £6.49 (MAJ)

Cabernet Sauvignon Montes Oak-Aged Reserve 1996 £6.10 (AS) £6.19 (AME) £6.20 (PIP) £6.74 (PLAY)

Cabernet Sauvignon Torres Curico 1997 £6.29 (AME)

Cabernet Sauvignon Veramonte Valle Central 1997 £6.99 (OD)

Malbec Villa Montes 1997 £6.50 (FORT) £7.70 (TW)

Merlot Carmen Reserve 1997 £6.71 (STE) £6.95 (WS) £7.45 (NA) £8.50 (ELL)

Merlot Casa Lapostolle 1997 £6.50 (WS) £10.74 (NO)

Merlot Domaine Oriental Clos Centenaire 1996 £6.21 (COC)

Merlot Mont Gras Reserva 1997 £6.25 (SOM) £7.23 (FLE) £7.95 (ROB) £7.99 (VA)

Merlot Valdivieso Reserve 1997 £6.99 (SAF)

Merlot Viña Casablanca Santa Isabel Estate 1996 £6.29 (NI) £10.29 (YOU) £10.95 (UB)

Merlot Viña Casablanca White Label 1997 £6.99 (POR) £6.99 (MOR)

Merlot Viña La Rosa La Palma Reserve 1997 £6.99 (FUL)

Pinot Noir Cono Sur Reserve 1996 £6.49 (FUL) £6.99 (OD)

Pinot Noir Undurraga 1996 £6.75 (BALL)

£7.00 → £7.99

Cabernet Sauvignon Los Vascos 1997 £7.47 (PLAY)

Cabernet Sauvignon Marqués de Casa Concha 1996 £7.50 (TAN)

Cabernet Sauvignon Santa Rita Medalla Real 1996 £7.95 (WS) £7.99 (NEZ)

Cabernet Sauvignon Viña Casablanca El Bosque 1997 £7.49 (POR) £7.99 (MOR)

Grande Vidure/Cabernet Sauvignon Carmen Reserve 1996 £7.25 (BO)

Merlot Gracia Reserve 1997 £7.49 (UN)

★ Merlot Viña La Rosa La Palma Gran Reserva 1998 £7.99 (HED)

Pinot Noir Valdivieso Reserve 1996 £7.99·(FUL) £7.99 (WR) £7.99 (YOU)

£8.00 → £9.99

Cabernet Sauvignon Montes Alpha 1996 £8.95 (POR) £9.95 (WRI) £9.99 (HED) £9.99 (OD)

Cabernet Sauvignon Viña Casablanca Santa Isabel Estate 1997 £8.99 (MOR) £8.99 (OD)

Merlot Casa Lapostolle Cuvée Alexandre 1996 £8.99 (FUL) £9.99 (WR) £9.99 (BOT) £12.90 (CRO) £12.95 (FORT)

Merlot Montes Alpha 1996 £8.99 (MORR) £9.95 (AS) £9.95 (HED) £10.65 (AD)

Syrah Errázuriz Reserve 1997 £9.99 (UN) £9.99 (SAF) £10.36 (FLE)

Stars (★) indicate wines selected by Oz Clarke in the Best Buys section which begins on page 9.

£10.00 → £12.99

Caballo Loco Valdivieso **Non-vintage**
£11.95 (WAI) £11.99 (FUL) £11.99 (SAF)
£13.00 (BIB)
Cabernet Sauvignon Mont Gras Ninquen
1996 £10.86 (NO)
Cabernet Sauvignon Torres Manso de
Velasco **1995** £12.34 (PEN) £13.95 (POR)
Syrah Errázuriz Reserve **1998** £10.95 (POR)

Over £13.00

Alpha 'M' Montes **1997** £29.95 (POR)
£30.00 (HED) £33.50 (PLAY)
Cabernet Sauvignon Concha y Toro Don
Melchor **1995** £13.20 (TAN) £14.55 (UB)
Cabernet Sauvignon Errázuriz Don
Maximiano Founders Reserve **1997**
£18.99 (POR)
Finis Terrae Cousiño Macul **1995** £15.85
(WRI) £15.99 (FUL)
Sena Errázuriz **1995** £27.99 (UN)

WHITE

Under £4.00

Chenin Blanc Santa Carolina **1997** £2.99
(VIC) £2.99 (THR) £2.99 (WR) £2.99 (BOT)
Semillon Peteroa Barrel Fermented **1997**
£3.95 (WIW)

£4.00 → £4.99

Chardonnay Carmen **1997** £4.99 (OD)
£5.45 (BER)
Chardonnay Concha y Toro **1997** £4.75
(BALL) £4.89 (JON) £4.99 (CON) £4.99 (POR)
Chardonnay Concha y Toro Casillero del
Diablo **1997** £4.99 (FUL) £4.99 (OD) £4.99
(BOT)
Chardonnay Cono Sur Isla Negra **1997**
£4.99 (WAI) £4.99 (BO) £5.49 (FUL) £5.49
(VIC) £5.49 (THR) £5.49 (WR) £5.49 (BOT)
Chardonnay Domaine Oriental **1997**
£4.99 (UN) £5.00 (COC)
Chardonnay Luis Felipe Edwards **1998**
£4.99 (MAJ)
Chardonnay Mapocho **1998** £4.99 (ASD)
Chardonnay Mont Gras **1998** £4.95 (SOM)
Chardonnay Palomar Estate **1997** £4.95 (JU)
Chardonnay Peteroa Barrel Fermented
1998 £4.62 (WIW)
Chardonnay Santa Carolina **1997** £4.49 (CO)
Chardonnay Santa Emiliana Cordillera
Estate **1998** £4.99 (BO)

Chardonnay Valdivieso **1997** £4.99 (FUL)
£4.99 (WAI)
Chardonnay Viña Casablanca **1997** £4.95
(WS) £4.99 (NI) £5.19 (BAL) £6.29 (YOU)
Chardonnay Viña La Rosa La Palma **1998**
£4.49 (FUL) £4.99 (UN)
Chardonnay Vistamar Vistasur **1998**
£4.49 (MAJ)
Chardonnay/Sauvignon Blanc Norte
Chico **1997** £4.25 (CON)
Chardonnay/Semillon Santiago **1997**
£4.49 (BAL) £4.59 (NI)
Gewürztraminer Cono Sur **1997** £4.95
(WS)
Sauvignon Blanc Canepa **1997** £4.49 (UN)
Sauvignon Blanc Carmen **1997** £4.74 (FLE)
£5.49 (JON)
Sauvignon Blanc Concha y Toro **1998**
£4.29 (WAI) £4.95 (TAN) £4.99 (POR)
Sauvignon Blanc Montes **1998** £4.95 (ELL)
£5.45 (PIP) £5.50 (HED) £5.55 (PLAY)
Sauvignon Blanc Montes **1997** £4.95 (JU)
£4.99 (REI) £6.40 (TW)
Sauvignon Blanc Santa Carolina **1997**
£4.98 (HA)
Sauvignon Blanc Santa Emiliana Andes
Peaks **1997** £4.75 (CON) £5.00 (MV)
Sauvignon Blanc Villa Montes **1997** £4.75
(MORR)
Semillon Canepa Oak-aged **1997** £4.79
(TES)
Semillon Canepa Oak-aged **1996** £4.79
(ASD)

£5.00 → £5.99

Chardonnay Casa Lapostolle **1997** £5.99
(FUL) £8.00 (WRI) £8.75 (FORT) £10.58 (NO)
Chardonnay Concha y Toro Trio **1998**
£5.99 (VIC) £5.99 (THR) £5.99 (WR)
Chardonnay Cono Sur Reserve **1998**
£5.99 (ASD)
Chardonnay Cousiño Macul **1998** £5.90
(TAN) £6.50 (STA)
Chardonnay Cousiño Macul **1997** £5.49
(POR) £5.92 (GW) £5.99 (JON)
Chardonnay Errázuriz **1997** £5.49 (TES)
£5.49 (SAF) £5.49 (VIC) £5.49 (THR) £5.49
(WR) £5.49 (BOT) £6.10 (HAH)
Chardonnay Los Vascos **1997** £5.75 (PEN)
Chardonnay Montes **1997** £5.99 (PHI)
Chardonnay Torres Miguel **1998** £5.99
(POR)
Chardonnay Torres Santa Digna **1997**
£5.99 (DI) £6.79 (JON)
Chardonnay Valdivieso **1998** £5.09 (BIB)

Chardonnay Viña Casablanca White Label
1998 £5.49 (SAI) £5.49 (MOR)
Chardonnay Viña San Pedro Casillo de
Molina Reserva **1997** £5.49 (MORR)
Fumé Blanc Montes **1998** £5.51 (FLA)
£5.95 (HED) £5.95 (FORT)
Fumé Blanc Montes **1997** £5.50 (WRI)
£6.99 (TW)
Gewürztraminer Concha y Toro **1996**
£5.39 (JON) £5.60 (STA)
Gewürztraminer Viña Casablanca Santa
Isabel **1997** £5.99 (POR) £6.49 (OD)
Sauvignon Blanc Casa Lapostolle **1997**
£5.49 (VIC) £5.49 (THR) £6.29 (PLA)
Sauvignon Blanc Concha y Toro Explorer
1997 £5.60 (WRI) £5.75 (CON)
Sauvignon Blanc Errázuriz **1997** £5.49 (FUL)
£5.49 (THR) £5.49 (WR) £5.65 (HAH)
Sauvignon Blanc Jacques Lurton Estate-
Bottled **1997** £5.78 (JER)
Sauvignon Blanc Santa Rita Reserva **1998**
£5.49 (NEZ) £5.49 (MAJ)
Sauvignon Blanc Torres **1998** £5.25 (STA)
£5.39 (PEN)
Sauvignon Blanc Villard Aconcagua **1998**
£5.49 (POR) £5.50 (PHI)
Sauvignon Blanc Viña Casablanca White
Label **1998** £5.49 (MOR)

£6.00 → £6.99

Chardonnay Caliterra Reserve **1996**
£6.99 (SAF) £6.99 (VIC) £6.99 (THR)
Chardonnay Carmen Reserve **1997** £6.26
(STE) £6.95 (NA)
Chardonnay Cousiño Macul Antiguas
Reserva **1996** £6.95 (POR) £7.11 (PEN)
£7.15 (WRI) £7.25 (CON)
Chardonnay Echeverría Family Reserve
1997 £6.79 (YOU)
Chardonnay Marqués de Casa Concha
1996 £6.99 (JON)
Chardonnay Montes Barrel Fermented
1998 £6.25 (HED)
Chardonnay Santa Carolina Reservado
1996 £6.49 (MORR)
Chardonnay Santa Rita Medalla Real **1997**
£6.99 (NEZ) £7.75 (DI)
Chardonnay Valdivieso Reserva **1996**
£6.99 (FUL)
Chardonnay Villiard Reserve **1996** £6.40
(SOM)
Gewürztraminer Viña Casablanca Santa
Isabel **1998** £6.50 (WS) £6.99 (MOR)
Sauvignon Blanc Viña Casablanca Santa
Isabel Estate **1998** £6.49 (NI) £6.95 (WS)

Over £7.00

Chardonnay Casa Lapostolle Cuvée
Alexandre **1996** £10.95 (FORT) £11.25
(WRI)
Chardonnay Errázuriz Reserve **1996**
£7.99 (TES)
Chardonnay Errázuriz Wild Ferment
1997 £8.99 (UN) £9.49 (OD)
Chardonnay Gracia Reserve **1997** £7.49
(UN)
Chardonnay Marqués de Casa Concha
1995 £8.31 (HA)
Chardonnay Mont Gras Ninquen **1997**
£7.99 (FUL)
★ Chardonnay Montes Alpha **1997** £8.99
(MORR)
Chardonnay Villiard Reserve **1997** £7.95
(WS)
Chardonnay Viña Casablanca Barrel-
Fermented **1997** £9.99 (OD)

ROSÉ

Under £5.00

Cabernet Rosé Santa Rita 120 **1997** £4.99
(DI)
★ Chardonnay Santa Rita Doña Paula **1998**
£4.99 (NEZ)
Cabernet Sauvignon Torres Santa Digna
Rosado **1998** £4.99 (POR) £5.03 (GW)
£5.25 (WHI) £5.49 (DI)
Cabernet Sauvignon Torres Santa Digna
Rosado **1997** £4.99 (PEN) £5.09 (JON)

SPARKLING

Under £9.00

Miguel Torres Brut Nature **Non-vintage**
£8.99 (DI)
Santa Carolina Brut Sparkling **Non-
vintage** £5.69 (MORR)
Valdivieso Brut Reserve Methode
Traditionelle **1997** £6.26 (BIB)

> *Please remember that*
> **Oz Clarke's Wine Guide**
> *is a price guide and not a*
> *price list. It is not meant to*
> *replace up-to-date*
> *merchants' lists.*

EASTERN EUROPE

At last we're beginning to see the real changes in the wines of Eastern Europe – it's just that they're not quite the changes we'd expected

It's pretty tough on Eastern Europe, actually. There it was under Communism, producing huge quantities of wine that was sometimes good and sometimes dreadful, but it didn't make much odds because the comrades were not exactly connoisseurs and all that mattered really was the alcohol content. Bulgaria was the shining exception to this, sending good cheap Cabernet by the gallon to the West and establishing what it no doubt hoped would be a lasting fan club in Britain.

Then came the fall of Communism, and hopes ran even higher. Now, we thought, we'll see some real improvements. But privatization was slow and patchy, foreign advice sometimes welcome and sometimes not, and in the meantime the world moved on. Chile took our attention, and South Africa, while Australia has continued to be ever more fashionable. We seem to have forgotten about Eastern Europe.

And yet it's hanging on. And it's coming to the fore again in ways we hadn't quite expected. There are superb quality Tokajis coming from Western investment: yes, they're expensive, but they're a revelation to anyone who's only tasted the oxidized, Communist-era style. I don't have a quarrel with their price: I think they're worth it.

From Hungary and Romania we're seeing modern, fresh wines, often with names and labels that make one think they're Australian – and at prices that would be low for an Aussie wine, but are quite high for a Romanian. And from Bulgaria we're seeing some genuinely good-value inexpensive wines – often from the same wineries we knew and loved in the past. Now that's progress.

GRAPE VARIETIES

ALIGOTÉ (white; Romania, Bulgaria, Moldova) Used for sparkling wine and some passable neutral dry white. Often blended with Chardonnay.

BURGUND MARE (red; Romania) Probably the Blauburgunder grape by another name. Produces a light shadow of Pinot Noir style.

CABERNET FRANC (red; Hungary, Moldova, Bulgaria) Lovely velvety, fruity young reds in Hungary.

CABERNET SAUVIGNON (red; Macedonia, Bulgaria, Romania, Moldova, SW Hungary) Capable of producing ripe, long-lived wines in Romania, Moldova and Bulgaria.

CHARDONNAY (white; Bulgaria, Hungary, Moldova, Romania) Good dry whites, usually fresh nowadays. Sometimes barrel fermented, sometimes overoaked.

DIMIAT (white; Bulgaria) Bulk producer, blended with Muscat and Rhine Riesling.

FETEASCĂ ALBĂ/LEANYKA/ MÄDCHENTRAUBE (white; Romania, Hungary) Rich, floral, short-lived, flabby.

FETEASCĂ NEAGRĂ (red; Romania) At best dark, slightly vegetal with sooty tannins. Can easily become too vegetal.

FURMINT (white; Hungary) The top Tokaji grape; good acidity, concentration, long life, very good quality.

GAMZA (red; Bulgaria) Soft, light, and early maturing. Bulgaria's answer to Beaujolais, sort of.

GEWÜRZTRAMINER (white; everywhere) Usually known as Traminer, and has typical spicy style. Amazing dessert wines in Moldova.

GRÜNER VELTLINER (white; CZ, Slovakia) Intense greengage fruit at best; hard acidity if not ripened properly.

HÁRSLEVELÜ (white; Hungary) Earthy, big, peachy, long-lived.

IRSAI OLIVÉR (white; CZ, Slovakia, Hungary) A Muscat cross, very perfumed.

KADARKA (red; Hungary) Seldom allowed to produce the weight and tannin which made its reputation. Usually small, tough, green wines.

KÉKFRANKOS/FRANKOVKA/ BLAUFRANKISCH (red; Hungary, CZ, Slovakia) Vegetal young reds.

KÉKOPORTO/BLAUER PORTUGUEISER (red; Hungary) Light, ordinary, short-lived reds.

MAVRUD (red; Bulgaria) Hefty dark reds.

MERLOT (red; everywhere except CZ and Slovakia) Very successful in Romania, good in southern Bulgaria.

MISKET (white; Bulgaria) Claims not to be a Muscat, but has a lightly perfumed style, and a tendency to blow over quickly.

MÜLLER-THURGAU (white; CZ, Slovakia, Hungary) Floral, early-drinking Germanic type. Widely cultivated.

MUSCAT OTTONEL (white; everywhere) Good but short-lived, vulgar Muscat styles.

PAMID (red; Romania, Bulgaria) Short-lived, empty, can blend well with Merlot.

PINOT BLANC (white; Hungary, CZ, Slovakia) At its best similar to dry Alsace.

PINOT GRIS (white; Hungary, CZ, Slovakia, Romania, Moldova) Can make outstanding dry and off-dry wines with wonderful spicy aroma.

PINOT NOIR (red; Romania, Hungary, Moldova, Slovakia) Can be true to type and elegant, but often too poorly handled.

RHINE RIESLING (white; everywhere) Can be lemony and true to type; rarely as intense as good German versions.

ST LAURENT/BLAUER LIMBERGER/ SVATOVAVRINECKE (red; CZ, Slovakia) Delicious soft reds with black cherry flavours when allowed to ripen.

SAPERAVI (red; Moldova) Very good spicy wine; lots of potential.

SAUVIGNON (white; everywhere) Needs good technology; grassy and vegetal otherwise.

SMEDEREVKA (white; Macedonia and elsewhere in former Yugoslavia) Can make good, fresh wine; often poorly handled.

TĂMÎIOASĂ ROMANEASCĂ/ TAMIANKA (white; Romania, Bulgaria) Classic noble rot grape. Very sweet, raisiny flavours, long-lived.

VRANAC (red; Macedonia) Good solid performer. Takes well to oak.

WELSCHRIESLING/LASKI RIZLING/ VLASSKY RIZLING/ OLASZ RIZLING/ RIZLING ITALICO (white; everywhere) Nothing to do with Rhine Riesling. Earthy, lowish-acid, but can be good; ages well occasionally.

WINE REGIONS AND PRODUCERS

ASSENOVGRAD (Bulgaria) Quite good rustic reds.

BALATON (Hungary) Region centred on Lake Balaton. Well structured wines.

BALATONBOGLÁR (Hungary) Go-ahead region south of Lake Balaton, source of wines made by flying winemaker Kym Milne.

BOHEMIA (Czech Republic) Region making light whites from Riesling, Traminer and others. Quality is fair.

COTNARI (Romania) Region producing excellent, ageworthy botrytized wines from Tămîioasă, Grasa and Fetească Albă grapes.

DEALUL MARE (Romania) Rich, slightly jammy reds come from this region; also some whites. Tămîioasă can be good.

DISZNÓKÖ (Hungary) Western-owned company in Tokaj. Tremendous dry Furmint of exceptional quality.

DRAVA VALLEY (Slovenia) Delimited wine region, otherwise known as Podravski. Good, well-structured, aromatic whites.

EGER (Hungary) Home of Bull's Blood, a red which these days is a shadow of its former self.

GYÖNGYÖS (Hungary) An estate, and also a region. The estate is the source of Hugh Ryman's pioneering Chardonnay and Sauvignon Blanc.

HASKOVO (Bulgaria) Stick to the young Merlot.

HICKORY RIDGE (Moldova) Wines made by Hugh Ryman. The name goes down well in the US, apparently. Nice smoky, nutty Chardonnay and characterful Merlot.

HUNGAROVIN (Hungary) This used to be the name (in small print) on every bottle of Hungarian wine exported. Now it's German owned. It's still exporting, but these are not Hungary's finest.

IAMBOL (Bulgaria) There are decent fruity reds here, in particular a nice young Merlot.

LITTORAL (Slovenia) Region making northern Italian-style reds, especially Refosco, Barbera, Cabernet and Merlot. Known as Primorski in Slovenia.

LJUTOMER-ORMOZ (Slovenia) Leading white region capable of producing excellent Laski Rizling, the best of which seems to stay *in situ* while the poor stuff comes here.

MASSANDRA (Ukraine) The Tsar's old cellars (or the old Tsar's cellars, if you prefer) made fortified wines in every conceivable style, aping port, sherry, Madeira and a few other things besides. They're still making them, too.

MÓR (Hungary) Good quality region, especially for whites.

EASTERN EUROPEAN CLASSIFICATIONS

Quality wine, equivalent to France's Appellation Contrôlée, is Minöségi bor in Hungary, Controliran in Bulgaria, and in Slovenia Vrhunsko Vino or, below this, Kakovostno Vino. Romania's system is too complicated to give in full, but the best are VSOC, which can be late harvest up to nobly rotten; VSO from specific grapes and regions; VS for quality wine.

MORAVIA (Czech Republic) Region with similar grapes (though not always as good quality) as neighbouring Austria.

MURFATLAR (Romania) Black Sea region producing erratic quality. Botrytized Chardonnay is a speciality, but can lack acidity.

PRESLAV (Bulgaria) Winery making decent whites. To catch them at their best, make sure they're young.

ROUSSE (Bulgaria) Currently one of the best in Bulgaria: good tasty reds and whites. Rocky Valley wines are especially good. Yantra Valley reds are nice in a more old-fashioned way.

ROYAL TOKAJI WINE COMPANY (Hungary) Excellent quality new-style Tokaji from this joint venture between British, Danish and Hungarian investors.

SAVA VALLEY (Slovenia) Region with promising whites from Sauvignon Blanc and Laski Rizling, and light reds.

SHUMEN (Bulgaria) Winery producing good fresh whites, but avoid the Premium Oak range unless you really want wine that tastes of little else. Save trees: drink unoaked Chardonnay.

SLIVEN (Bulgaria) Quite attractive reds and whites. The Chardonnay-Misket blend is nicely aromatic.

SLOVAKIA Most of the former Czechoslovakia's vineyards ended up here: there's even a chunk of Hungary's Tokaj. Good, spicy whites; fair reds.

SOPRON (Hungary) Region just south of Austria's Neuseidlersee, producing mostly red wines.

STARA ZAGORA (Bulgaria) The name sounds far too glamorous to be a mere wine region; but the Cabernets and Merlots are decent.

SUHINDOL (Bulgaria) Fair quality, but not as good as it once was.

SVISHTOV (Bulgaria) Quality seems to be sliding here. Light, tired reds.

TÎRNAVE (Romania) Cool region making promising whites, especially Fetească. Best winery: *Jidvei*.

TOKAJ (Hungary) Tokaj is the region, Tokaji the wine it famously produces. We've all adopted the Hungarian spelling of this luscious sweet white now; the English always used to spell it Tokay. The style has also changed: from being oxidized and tasting like cheap sherry, it is now (as a result of Western investment) fresher and infinitely more delicious. The grapes are Furmint, Muscat Lunel and Hárslevelü. It's made from botrytized grapes (known as *aszú*) which are added to dry base wine in measures known as *puttonyos*. A three-puttonyos Tokaji will be sweet, a four-puttonyos one sweeter, and a five or six-puttonyos one very concentrated and rich. Aszú Eszencia is sweeter again, and Eszencia on its own means juice too sweet to ferment to more than a few per cent alcohol. You could almost stand a spoon up in it; but you almost certainly won't be able to buy it in your local shop. It's used for blending in tiny quantities into lesser wines to pep them up or (according to legend) for reviving dying monarchs. Tokajis of three to six puttonyos are a more practical buy: they have a smokiness to their fruit which sets them apart from all other dessert wines, and they age superbly. Best: *Royal Tokaji Wine Company, Disznókö*.

EASTERN EUROPE PRICES

BULGARIA RED

Under £3.00

Bulgarian Cabernet Sauvignon/Merlot
1997 £2.99 (SAI)
Lovico Suhindol Cabernet Sauvignon
1996 £2.70 (WIW)
Lovico Suhindol Cabernet
Sauvignon/Merlot **Non-vintage** £2.99
(VIC) £2.99 (THR) £2.99 (WR) £2.99 (BOT)
Sliven Merlot/Pinot Noir **Non-vintage**
£2.99 (CO)

£3.00 → £3.99

Bulgarian Cabernet Sauvignon **1997** £3.89
(UN)
Bulgarian Reserve Merlot **1994** £3.79
(MORR) £3.99 (SAI)
Iambol Reserve Cabernet Sauvignon **1995**
£3.79 (THR) £3.79 (WR) £3.79 (BOT)
Lovico Suhindol Cabernet Sauvignon
Reserve **1993** £3.50 (WS)
Lovico Suhindol Cabernet
Sauvignon/Merlot **1995** £3.99 (SAF)
Lovico Suhindol Reserve Merlot **1993**
£3.99 (CO)
Lozitza Cabernet Sauvignon **1991** £3.89
(JON)
Oriahovitza Cabernet Sauvignon **1995**
£3.49 (ASD)
Oriahovitza Cabernet Sauvignon Reserve
1996 £3.99 (SO)
Oriahovitza Cabernet Sauvignon Reserve
1995 £3.07 (WIW)
Plovdiv Cabernet Sauvignon **1993** £3.59
(VIC) £3.59 (THR) £3.59 (WR) £3.59 (BOT)
Rousse Cabernet Sauvignon Reserve
1993 £3.49 (MAJ)
Stambolovo Merlot Reserve **1993** £3.69
(SO)
Yantra Valley Cabernet Sauvignon **1995**
£3.99 (SAI)

Over £4.00

Haskovo Merlot **1995** £4.99 (SAF)
Svischtov Cabernet Sauvignon **1989**
£4.85 (WHI)
Rousse Cabernet Sauvignon/Cinsaut
1992 £5.79 (CO)

BULGARIA WHITE

Under £4.00

Chateau Slaviantzi Chardonnay Special
Reserve **1998** £3.98 (WIW)
Khan Krum Chardonnay Reserve **1996**
£3.07 (WIW)
Preslav Chardonnay **1998** £3.07 (WIW)
Sliven Chardonnay Special Reserve
Barrel-Fermented **1995** £3.70 (WIW)

HUNGARY WHITE

Under £3.00

Chapel Hill Irsai Oliver **Non-vintage**
£2.99 (MORR)
Gyorgy Villa Etyeki Chardonnay **1998**
£2.99 (WIW)
Lellei Chardonnay **1998** £2.73 (WIW)
Lellei Pinot Gris **1998** £2.73 (WIW)
Lellei Tramini **1998** £2.73 (WIW)

£3.00 → £3.99

Chapel Hill Chardonnay **Non-vintage**
£3.29 (MORR)
Chapel Hill Chardonnay **1998** £3.39 (BO)
Chapel Hill Chardonnay **1995** £3.87 (PLA)
Chapel Hill Irsai Oliver **1997** £3.29 (CO)
Chapel Hill Irsai Oliver **1996** £3.39 (OD)
Gyöngyös Estate Chardonnay **1997** £3.69
(CO)
Gyöngyös Estate Chardonnay **1996** £3.75
(VIC) £3.75 (THR) £3.75 (WR) £3.75 (BOT)

MERCHANTS SPECIALIZING IN EASTERN EUROPE
see Merchant Directory (page 413) for details

If you want to look beyond bargain
Cabernet Sauvignon, try the following
merchants: Butlers Wine Cellar (BU) –
good for curiosities, First Quench Group
(BOT, THR, VIC, WR), Morris & Verdin (MV),
Thos. Peatling, Sainsbury's (SAI), Safeway
(SAF), T&W Wines (TW) – good for old
Tokaji, Wines of Westhorpe (WIW).

Gyöngyös Estate Sauvignon Blanc **1996**
£3.75 (THR) £3.75 (WR) £3.75 (BOT)
Nagyréde Dry Muscat **1997** £3.49 (OD)
Nagyréde Pinot Gris Oaked Reserve
1997 £3.59 (OD)

£4.00 → £9.99

Tibor Gal Eger Barrique Chardonnay
1997 £5.41 (WIW)
Tokaji Fordítás Dessewffy **1988** £7.50 (CRO)
Tokaji Szamorodni Dry ½ litre, Château
Megyer **1988** £6.95 (ROB)
Tokaji Szamorodni Sweet ½ litre, Château
Megyer **1991** £6.99 (UN)
Tokaji Szamorodni Sweet ½ litre, Oremus
1989 £5.95 (DI)

£10.00 → £19.99

Tokaji Aszú 4 Putts ½ litre, Château
Pajzos **1991** £18.00 (JU)
Tokaji Aszú 5 Putts ½ litre, Château
Megyer **1988** £17.95 (PHI)
Tokaji Aszú 5 Putts ½ litre, Disznókö **1992**
£15.39 (JON) £15.99 (POR) £15.99 (OD)
Tokaji Aszú 5 Putts ½ litre, Royal Tokaji
Wine Co. **1993** £16.06 (FA) £17.50 (HED)
£18.25 (HIG) £19.09 (REI) £19.15 (HAH)
£20.59 (GW) £21.15 (CB) £21.95 (ROB)
Tokaji Aszú 5 Putts ½ litre, Tokaji
Kereskedöhóz **1990** £11.60 (STA)
Tokaji Aszú 5 Putts ½ litre, Tokaji
Kereskedöhóz **1988** £11.99 (UN)
£12.34 (PLA)

£20.00 → £49.99

Tokaji Aszú 5 Putts ½ litre Birsalmàs 2nd
Class, Royal Tokaji Wine Co. **1991**
£29.38 (REI)
Tokaji Aszú 5 Putts ½ litre Nyulaszo 1st
Class, Royal Tokaji Wine Co. **1993**
£32.20 (TAN) £39.77 (REI) £47.50 (FORT)
Tokaji Aszú 5 Putts ½ litre Nyulaszo 1st
Class, Royal Tokaji Wine Co. **1991**
£36.00 (HIG) £39.50 (LEA)
Tokaji Aszú 5 Putts ½ litre, Royal Tokaji
Wine Co. **1990** £24.95 (BER)
Tokaji Aszú 6 Putts ½ litre Szt Tamas,
Royal Tokaji Wine Co. **1993** £35.00
(JU) £36.62 (FA) £39.95 (LEA)

Over £50.00

Tokaji Aszú Essencia ½ litre, J Monyok
1963 £120.00 (JU)
Tokaji Aszú Essencia ½ litre, Royal Tokaji
Wine Co. **1993** £86.36 (REI)

HUNGARY RED

Under £3.00

Eger Bull's Blood **1997** £2.74 (WIW) £3.49
(SAF)
Lellei Cabernet Sauvignon **1998** £2.81
(WIW)
Szekszardi Kadarka Sweet **1997** £2.85
(WIW)

£3.00 → £4.99

Chapel Hill Cabernet Sauvignon **Non-
vintage** £3.29 (MORR)
Chapel Hill Cabernet Sauvignon **1996**
£3.49 (CO) £3.87 (PLA)
Eger Bull's Blood **1996** £3.39 (MORR)
Szekszardi Merlot Late-Harvested **1997**
£3.95 (WIW)
Tiffans Kekoporto **1997** £4.91 (WIW)

Over £5.00

Tibor Gal Cabernet Sauvignon **1996**
£6.24 (WIW)
Tibor Gal Eger Bikaver **1996** £5.64 (WIW)
Tibor Gal Eger Kekfrankos Blaufrankisch
1996 £5.40 (WIW)
Tiffans Cabernet Sauvignon **1996** £5.73
(WIW)
Tiffans Cuvée Cabernet
Sauvignon/Kekfrankos **1994** £7.93 (REI)

MOLDOVA

c. £25.00

Negrú de Purkar **1978** £25.00 (CRO)

ROMANIA

£3.00 → £4.49

Classic Dealul Mare Merlot **1995** £3.25 (UB)
Classic Murfatlar Cabernet Sauvignon
1995 £3.25 (UB)
Classic Murfatlar Chardonnay **1996** £3.25
(UB)
Classic Pinot Noir **1996** £3.49 (CO)
Classic Tarnave Sauvignon Blanc **1997**
£3.25 (UB)
Pinot Noir Dealul Mare **1996** £3.25 (UB)
Romanian Pinot Noir **1997** £3.19 (MORR)
Romanian Sauvignon Blanc **1997** £3.19
(MORR)
Tamîioasa Pietroasele **1995** £4.35 (UB)

FRANCE

If there's one thing that deters me from buying French wine, it's the price. And most prices keep on rising. So Portugal here I come

If the past year has been notable for anything in French wine, it is price rises. Yes, I know it's not only France that is guilty here: they're all at it. But few French wines could honestly claim to have been undervalued before.

Burgundy is rising, putting paid to the happy situation where for a while it was actually better value than Bordeaux. Bordeaux itself has come down a bit: opening prices for the 1998 vintage dropped at the châteaux by up to 30 per cent: the 1998 vintage is not, frankly, fantastic, but it was better on the right bank, and so Pomerols and St-Émilions have seen smaller price drops than Médocs and Graves. But that is for ex-château prices. What will happen twixt château and shop

shelf is less easy to say. And in any case, the top wines are one thing; basic Bordeaux is a disgrace at any price.

What else is happening in France? Price rises in the southern Rhône. Châteauneuf-du-Pape is leading the way, and I can't believe that the rest of the Rhône will fail to take note.

Overall it's bad news for us, the consumers. It means it's going to be increasingly difficult to find interesting, characterful wines that are good value, as more and more regions and producers chase the wallets of the few. Cheaper wine is increasingly mass produced to keep costs down. So what should we do? Look elsewhere: to Chile, Portugal, Argentina. Luckily, we do have alternatives.

WINE CLASSIFICATIONS

The French have the most far-reaching system of wine control of any nation, even though its adequacy as a form of quality control is now in question. The key factors are the 'origin' of the wine, its historic method of production and the use of the correct grape types. The three defined levels are: AC, VDQS, and vin de pays.

APPELLATION D'ORIGINE CONTROLÉE (AC, AOC)
To qualify for AC a wine must meet specific requirements on seven fronts:
Land: Suitable vineyard land is minutely defined. **Grape**: Only those grapes traditionally regarded as suitable can be used. **Degree of alcohol**: Wines must reach a minimum (or maximum) degree of natural alcohol. **Yield**: A basic permitted yield is set for each AC, but the figure may be increased or decreased year by year after consultation between the growers of

each AC region and the Institut National des Appellations d'Origine (INAO). **Vineyard practice**: AC wines must follow rules about pruning methods and density of planting. **Wine-making practice**: Each AC wine has its own regulations as to what is allowed. Typically, chaptalization – adding sugar during fermentation to increase alcoholic strength – is accepted in the North, but not in the South. **Tasting and analysis**: Since 1979 wines must pass a tasting panel.

VIN DÉLIMITÉ DE QUALITÉ SUPÉRIEURE (VDQS)
This second group is, in general, slightly less reliable in quality. It is in the process of being phased out. No more vins de pays are being upgraded to VDQS but there is still no news on when any of the existing ones will be upgraded to AC status (or downgraded to vin de pays).

VIN DE PAYS The third category gives a regional definition to France's basic blending wines. The rules are similar to AC, but allow a good deal more flexibility and some wonderful cheap wines can be found which may well surprise. Quality can be stunning, and expect fruit, value and competent winemaking. There are also one or two high-priced superstars in this category.

VIN DE TABLE 'Table wine' is the title for the rest. No quality control except as far as basic public health regulations demand. Vins de pays are always available for approximately the same price, and offer a far more interesting drink. Many vins de table here are dull and poorly made, and branded, heavily advertised ones are seldom good value.

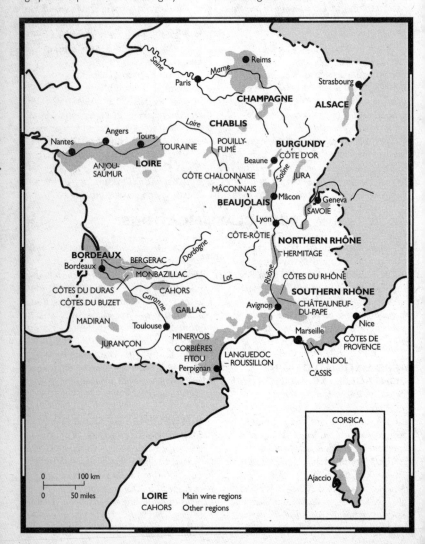

LOIRE   Main wine regions
CAHORS   Other regions

WINE-FINDER: FRANCE

France is packed with famous wine names, but if you don't know whereabouts in the country a wine comes from, life can get confusing. In the following 194 pages we have divided the huge number of appellations in France into eight clearly defined regions: Alsace, Bordeaux, Burgundy, Champagne, Jura & Savoie, Loire, Rhône and Southern France. In Burgundy, we have separated Basic Burgundy and the subregions Beaujolais, Chablis, Côte Chalonnaise, Côte d'Or and Mâconnais. So, if you know the name but are wondering which section to look in, this quick guide to some of the best-known wine names will help.

Aloxe-Corton – *Burgundy, Côte d'Or*
Auxey-Duresses – *Burgundy, Côte d'Or*
Bandol – *Southern France*
Barsac – *Bordeaux (sweet white)*
Beaune – *Burgundy, Côte d'Or*
Blagny – *Burgundy, Côte d'Or*
Bourgueil – *Loire (red)*
Brouilly – *Burgundy, Beaujolais*
Cadillac – *Bordeaux*
Cahors – *Southern France*
Cérons – *Bordeaux*
Chablis – *Burgundy, Chablis*
Chambolle-Musigny – *Burgundy, Côte d'Or*
Chassagne-Montrachet – *Burgundy, Côte d'Or*
Châteauneuf-du-Pape – *Rhône*
Chénas – *Burgundy, Beaujolais*
Chinon – *Loire (red)*
Chiroubles – *Burgundy, Beaujolais*
Chorey-lès-Beaune – *Burgundy, Côte d'Or*
Clairette de Die – *Rhône (sparkling)*
Condrieu – *Rhône (white)*
Corbières – *Southern France*
Cornas – *Rhône (red)*
Coteaux du Tricastin – *Rhône*
Côte-Rôtie – *Rhône (red)*
Côtes de Beaune – *Burgundy, Côte d'Or*
Côtes de Bourg – *Bordeaux*
Côtes de Nuits – *Burgundy, Côte d'Or*
Côtes du Ventoux – *Rhône*
Crozes-Hermitage – *Rhône*
Entre-deux-Mers – *Bordeaux*
Fitou – *Southern France*
Fixin – *Burgundy, Côte d'Or*
Fleurie – *Burgundy, Beaujolais*
Fronsac – *Bordeaux*
Gevrey-Chambertin – *Burgundy, Côte d'Or*
Gigondas – *Rhône (red)*
Givry – *Burgundy, Côte Chalonnaise*
Graves – *Bordeaux (dry white)*
Hautes-Côtes de Beaune – *Burgundy,
    Côte d'Or*
Hautes-Côtes de Nuit – *Burgundy, Côte d'Or*
Haut-Médoc – *Bordeaux*
Hermitage – *Rhône*
Juliénas – *Burgundy, Beaujolais*
Languedoc-Roussillon – *Southern France*
Listrac – *Bordeaux*

Loupiac – *Bordeaux*
Mâcon – *Burgundy, Mâconnais*
Margaux – *Bordeaux*
Marsannay – *Burgundy, Côte d'Or*
Médoc – *Bordeaux*
Mercurey – *Burgundy, Côte Chalonnaise*
Meursault – *Burgundy, Côte d'Or*
Minervois – *Southern France*
Montagny – *Burgundy, Côte Chalonnaise*
Monthelie – *Burgundy, Côte d'Or*
Morey-St-Denis – *Burgundy, Côte d'Or*
Morgon – *Burgundy, Beaujolais*
Moulin-à-Vent – *Burgundy, Beaujolais*
Moulis – *Bordeaux*
Muscadet – *Loire (dry white)*
Muscat de Beaumes-de-Venise –
    Rhône (fortified white)
Nuits-St-Georges – *Burgundy, Côte d'Or*
Pauillac – *Bordeaux*
Pernand-Vergelesses – *Burgundy, Côte d'Or*
Pessac-Léognan – *Bordeaux*
Pomerol – *Bordeaux*
Pommard – *Burgundy, Côte d'Or*
Pouilly-Fuissé – *Burgundy, Mâconnais*
Pouilly-Fumé – *Loire (dry white)*
Provence – *Southern France*
Puligny-Montrachet – *Burgundy, Côte d'Or*
Régnié – *Burgundy, Beaujolais*
Rully – *Burgundy, Côte Chalonnaise*
St-Amour – *Burgundy, Beaujolais*
Ste-Croix-du-Mont – *Bordeaux*
St-Émilion – *Bordeaux*
St-Estèphe – *Bordeaux*
St-Joseph – *Rhône (red)*
St-Julien – *Bordeaux*
St-Véran – *Burgundy, Mâconnais*
Sancerre – *Loire*
Saumur-Champigny – *Loire (red)*
Sauternes – *Bordeaux (sweet white)*
Sauvignon de St-Bris – *Burgundy, Basic*
Savigny-lès-Beaune – *Burgundy, Côte d'Or*
Tavel – *Rhône (rosé)*
Vins de pays – *various*
Volnay – *Burgundy, Côte d'Or*
Vosne-Romanée – *Burgundy, Côte d'Or*
Vougeot – *Burgundy, Côte d'Or*
Vouvray – *Loire*

ALSACE

Imagine if Alsace Riesling or Gewürztraminer were the world's favourite white wine, and Chardonnay were rare and exotic. It's probably a good thing it's the other way round

If it had been possible during the last 50 or so years to grow Riesling, or Pinot Gris, or Gewürztraminer, or Pinot Blanc, anywhere in France except Alsace for Appellation Contrôlée wines, it's my bet that these grapes would be far more fashionable now than they are. Imagine if Riesling were the world's most popular white grape, grown everywhere from Sonoma to Stellenbosch. Imagine asking for a glass of wine in a bar and automatically being poured a glass of Gewürztraminer.

Of course, it won't happen. Couldn't. Chardonnay is a staple for the same reason that potatoes and pasta are staples: they're neutral flavours you can do anything with.

Alsace wines are not like that. They have definite, unmissable character. Their flavours are assertive. And they're resolutely unfashionable in Britain.

In a way I'm rather glad they are. It's not that the Alsaciens can't sell their wines; they can, very easily. The locals lap them up, knowing how well they go with food, how good they are alone. And actually I don't want to drink Alsace wines every day (so I suppose I'm lucky I don't live in Alsace). But when I do want to drink them – with all sorts of spicy food – I want to take them off the shelf knowing that I'm getting the real, uncompromising thing. Not just a me-too, internationally standard flavour.

GRAPE VARIETIES

In Alsace wines are generally labelled according to their grape variety. Cheap blends of two or more varieties are sold as Edelzwicker; go instead for upmarket ones.

AUXERROIS Fatter and more buttery than Pinot Blanc, with a touch of spice and musk. Generally inexpensive, and often blended. Best: *André Kientzler, Marc Kreydenweiss, Jos Meyer, Landmann-Ostholt, Rolly Gassmann, Bruno Sorg*.

CHASSELAS Rare now in Alsace, Chasselas has never been complex, but the few true examples can be vibrantly fruity and must be drunk young. Best: *André Kientzler, Jos Meyer, Schoffit*.

CLASSIC BLENDS These can be superb, and their producers avoid the Edelzwicker designation like the plague. Best: *Hugel Gentil, Marc Kreydenweiss Clos du Val d'Eléon, Co-op de Ribeauvillé Clos du Zahnacker, Schlumberger Réserve, Jean Sipp*

Clos du Schlossberg, Louis Sipp Côtes de Ribeauvillé, Willm Gentil Clos Gaensbrœnnel. They will almost all be best in riper years.

EDELZWICKER Seldom exciting, but *Schlumberger Cristal-Maree* is quite good.

GEWÜRZTRAMINER The least dry of all Alsace, though *Beyer Cuvée des Comtes d'Eguisheim* and *Trimbach Cuvée des Seigneurs de Ribeaupierre* are bone dry. Gewürztraminer is the most voluptuous, upfront and fat of all Alsace wines, overflowing with exotic aromas. In hot years it can lack acidity and turn flabby. Best: *Blanck, Deiss, Hugel, Koehly, Kreydenweiss, Kuentz-Bas, Mure, Ostertag, Rolly Gassmann, Schoffit, Trimbach, Turckheim co-op, Weinbach, Willm Clos Gaensbrœnnel, Zind-Humbrecht*.

MUSCAT Light, fragrant, wonderfully grapy. Imagine crushing a fistful of green grapes and gulping the juice. That's how fresh and grapy a good Muscat should be.

Hotter years give heavy wines that are far from ideal. Seldom made sweet in Alsace. Look for *Becker, Ernest Burn, Joseph Cattin, Dirler, Charles Koehly, Marc Kreydenweiss, Kuentz-Bas, Rolly Gassmann, Pfaffenheim co-op, Schlumberger, Bruno Sorg, Weinbach, Zind-Humbrecht.*

> ## ON THE CASE
> The more expensive Alsace wines generally need some aging, so check the vintage before you buy. Simpler ones can be drunk immediately

PINOT BLANC At its best, this is plump, rich and ripe, with apple or floral overtones and a long creamy finish. Best: *J B Adam, Camille Braun, Théo Cattin, Co-opérative de Cléebourg, Marcel Deiss, Dopff au Moulin, Hugel, Charles Koehly, Kreydenweiss, Albert Mann, Mure, Ostertag, Rolly Gassmann, Schlumberger, Schoffit, Martin Spielmann, Turckheim co-op, Weinbach, Zind-Humbrecht.* Can also be called Klevner.

PINOT NOIR The Burgundy grape makes light reds, perfumed and strawberryish, but lacking in complexity. Most are overpriced for the quality. Best include *J B Adam, Jean Becker, Marcel Deiss, René Fleith, Albert Hertz, Hugel, Jacques Iltis, Albert Mann, Co-opérative de Pfaffenheim, Turckheim co-op, Wolfberger.*

RIESLING Powerful, structured, steely wines that grow 'petrolly' with age. It's with Riesling that the subtleties of *grand cru* soils are most evident. Can be long-lived. Best producers: *Becker, Beyer, Paul Blanck, Deiss,* *Dirler, Dopff au Moulin, Pierre Freudenreich, Pierre Frick, Kreydenweiss, Mader, Frédéric Mallo, Frédéric Mochel, Ostertag, Rolly Gassmann, Edgar Schaller, Schlumberger, Schoffit, Sick-Dreyer, Jean Sipp, Louis Sipp, Bruno Sorg, Trimbach, Weinbach, Wunsch & Mann, Zind-Humbrecht.*

SYLVANER Light, tart, slightly earthy. With age it tastes of tomatoes, for some reason. Best: *Christian Dolder, J Haller, Ostertag* (especially the *Vieilles Vignes*), *Rolly Gassmann, Martin Schaetzel, Schoffit, Albert Seltz, Zind-Humbrecht.*

TOKAY-PINOT GRIS Rich, musky and honeyed, though can run to flab if badly made. Even the lighter ones are luscious behind their dry fruit. The best can age well. Best: *Lucien Albrecht, Barmès-Buecher, Léon Beyer, Ernest Burn, Claude Dietrich, Robert Dietrich, Pierre Frick, Marc Kreydenweiss, Kuentz-Bas, Frédéric Mallo, Schlumberger, Schoffit, Bruno Sorg, Turckheim co-op, Weinbach, Zind-Humbrecht.*

WINE CLASSIFICATIONS

VIN D'ALSACE, AC The simple generic appellation covers the whole Alsace region. It is normally used in conjunction with a grape name, so a wine might be called 'Riesling – Appellation Alsace Contrôlée'.

CRÉMANT, AC White, Champagne-method fizz, made mainly from Pinot Blanc. Usually crisp and decent quality. Look for wines from *Paul Blanck, Robert Dietrich, Dopff & Irion, Dopff au Moulin, Laugel, Co-opérative de Pfaffenheim, Co-opérative de Turckheim, Wolfberger.*

GRAND CRU A decree of 1992 classified 50 historically excellent vineyards as *grands crus*. They can only be planted with Riesling, Tokay-Pinot Gris, Gewürztraminer or Muscat, and notably lower (but still high) yields apply. They can be recognized from the words 'Appellation Alsace Grand Cru Contrôlée' on the label. Grand cru wines should reflect the great variety of soils to be found in Alsace – limestone, schist, granite, clay, sandstone – offering a superb palate of flavours and nuances. The best do when yields are modest.

> **ON THE CASE**
> Everyday wines from the Alsace co-ops are a good buy; you can experiment with flavours for about a fiver

SÉLECTION DE GRAINS NOBLES (SGN)

The higher of two 'super-ripe' legal descriptions, applying to very sweet wines made from botrytized grapes. It applies only to Riesling, Tokay-Pinot Gris, Muscat (very rare) and Gewürztraminer; the wines are not dissimilar to Sauternes in style, though the flavour is different. Acidity levels can be lower, especially from Pinot Gris or from Gewürztraminer. All benefit from aging, for ten years or more. For some of Alsace's top tastes, try producers such as Beyer, Paul Blanck, Bott-Geyl, Hugel, Kuentz-Bas, Meyer, Mure, Ostertag, Schlumberger, Schoffit, Trimbach, Weinbach, Zind-Humbrecht.

VENDANGE TARDIVE

The lesser of the 'super-ripe' categories, made from late-picked grapes, as opposed to the botrytized ones used for sélection de grains nobles. Only applies to Riesling, Tokay-Pinot Gris, Muscat (rare) and Gewürztraminer. They are very full, fairly alcoholic and vary in sweetness from richly dry to dessert-sweet. They, too, can be aged, particularly if from grand cru vineyards. Up to ten years is a good rule of thumb.

ALSACE VINTAGES

1998   A very good year for sweet wines – but don't open them for a while.

1997   Potentially great: beautifully ripe wines of good body and weight.

1996   A mostly good, ripe vintage with nice acidity levels. Small quantities of vendange tardive and even sélection de grains nobles were made.

1995   Similar to 1994, but possibly with lower acidity. Stick to good names.

1994   Mixed: some wines are too light; but conversely other producers made phenomenally rich late-harvest wines.

1993   Good to average, but there is excellent Riesling.

1992   The wines are sound, and range from dilute to excellent. How to tell the difference from the label? Choose good producers only.

1991   Fresh, clean wines, but it is not a late-harvest year. Not one to keep, either.

1990   With healthy grapes and no noble rot, 1990 was a vendange tardive year. Rieslings are powerful and will age well.

1989   Very good but not top quality. The wines have lively fruit, though some are low in acidity. Abundant and superb late-harvest wines.

1988   Pleasant, but hardly inspiring wine. Tokay-Pinot Gris and Riesling are best.

1987   Not great, but better than first thought. Good single-vineyard wines.

1986   The best are at their peak. Good vendange tardive and even some SGN.

1985   An absolute corker – wonderful wines to drink now but they will keep.

ALSACE PRICES

WHITE

Under £5.00

Pinot Blanc Blanck Frères 1997 £4.95 (WAI)
Pinot Blanc Cave Co-op. Turckheim 1998
£4.49 (BO) £4.99 (OD)
Pinot Blanc Cave Co-op. Turckheim 1995
£4.99 (NI)
Pinot Blanc Cave du Roi Dagobert 1998
£4.90 (FRI)
Pinot Blanc Deiss ½ bottle 1996 £3.95
(LEA)
Pinot Blanc Horstein, Cave Vinicole de
Pfaffenheim 1997 £4.99 (POR) £5.40 (HAH)
Pinot Blanc Preiss-Zimmer 1997 £4.39
(MORR)
★ Pinot Blanc Réserve Cave Co-op.
Turckheim 1998 £4.99 (BOT) £4.99 (THR)
£4.99 (WR) £4.99 (VIC)

£5.00 → £5.99

Chevalier d'Alsace, Hügel 1995 £5.95 (JU)
Fleur d'Alsace, Hugel 1996 £5.99 (CON)
£6.65 (VIN)
Gewürztraminer Cave de Turckheim
1998 £5.69 (BO) £5.95 (SO) £5.95 (WS)
£6.49 (AME)
Gewürztraminer Hornstein, Cave
Vinicole de Pfaffenheim 1997 £5.99
(POR) £6.39 (JON) £6.40 (HAH)
Gewürztraminer Preiss-Zimmer 1997
£5.00 (MORR)
Muscat Réserve, Cave Co-op. Turckheim
1997 £5.69 (OD)
Pinot Blanc Cave Co-op. Turckheim 1996
£5.02 (ROS)
Pinot Blanc Cuvée Réservée, Schaetzel
1995 £5.69 (GW)
Pinot Blanc les Vignards, Hugel 1997
£5.95 (WS)
Pinot Blanc Réserve, Seltz 1996 £5.25
(WAT)

Pinot Blanc Schlumberger 1995 £5.99 (NI)
£6.95 (BER) £7.69 (JON) £7.98 (PLA)
Pinot Blanc Tradition, Cave Co-op.
Turckheim 1998 £5.39 (AME)
Riesling Baron de Hoen 1996 £5.99 (WAI)
Riesling Cave Co-op. Turckheim 1997
£5.99 (UN)
Sylvaner Cave Co-op. Turckheim 1997
£5.29 (UN)
Sylvaner Hugel 1997 £5.60 (WS)
Tokay-Pinot Gris Cave Co-op. Turckheim
1997 £5.69 (OD) £6.29 (UN)
Tokay-Pinot Gris Cave de Beblenheim
1997 £5.75 (WAI)

£6.00 → £6.99

Fleur d'Alsace, Hugel 1997 £6.45 (STA)
£6.99 (PLA)
Fruits de Mer, Wiederhirn 1996 £6.50 (HIG)
Gentil Hugel 1997 £6.49 (DI)
Gewürztraminer Cave Co-op. de
Ribeauvillé 1995 £6.99 (FLE)
Gewürztraminer Cave de Turckheim 1996
£6.16 (ROS) £6.35 (CON) £6.49 (UN)
Gewürztraminer Réserve Prestige, Cave
Co-op. Turckheim 1993 £6.99 (NI)
Gewürztraminer Rolly Gassmann ½ bottle
1993 £6.50 (RAE)
Pinot Blanc Béblenheim, Bott-Geyl 1996
£6.99 (BAL)
Pinot Blanc Hugel 1996 £6.95 (CON)
£7.34 (PLA) £7.50 (STA) £7.59 (DI)
Pinot Blanc Muré 1997 £6.55 (NEZ)
Pinot Blanc Rolly Gassmann 1991 £6.99
(RAE)
Pinot Blanc Wiederhirn 1996 £6.50 (HIG)
Riesling Brandluft, Seltz 1986 £6.10 (WAT)
Riesling Tradition, Kuentz-Bas 1996
£6.95 (WS)
Sylvaner Deiss 1994 £6.99 (BAL)
Sylvaner Schleret 1996 £6.75 (YAP)
Tokay-Pinot Gris Tradition, Cave Co-op.
Turckheim 1998 £6.19 (AME)

MERCHANTS SPECIALIZING IN ALSACE

see Merchant Directory (page 413) for details

Adnams (AD), Ballantynes (BAL), Bennetts
(BEN), Berry Bros (BER), Butlers (BU),
Anthony Byrne (BY), Croque-en-Bouche
(CRO), Direct Wine (DI), Cockburns of Leith
(COC), First Quench Group (BOT, THR, VIC,
WR), Lay & Wheeler (LAY), Oddbins (OD),
Reid (REI), T&W (TW), The Ubiquitous Chip
(UB), Wine Society (WS), Noel Young (YOU).

£7.00 → £7.99

Chasselas Cuvée Caroline, Schoffit **1998**
£7.50 (GAU) £8.75 (AD)
Chasselas Vieilles Vignes, Schoffit **1997**
£7.95 (FLE) £8.75 (BER)
Gewürztraminer Cave du Roi Dagobert
1996 £7.34 (FRI)
Gewürztraminer Sipp **1983** £7.50 (BU)
Gewürztraminer Wiederhirn **1994** £7.99
(HIG)
Gewürztraminer Zotzenberg, Seltz **1996**
£7.95 (WAT)
Muscat Albert Mann **1997** £7.99 (OD)
Muscat Réserve, Trimbach **1997** £7.95 (WS)
Muscat Wiederhirn **1996** £7.99 (HIG)
★ Pinot Auxerrois Vielles Vignes, Albert
Mann **1997** £7.89 (LAY)
Pinot Blanc Blanck Frères **1996** £7.25
(JER) £8.00 (FLE)
Pinot Blanc Cattin **1996** £7.52 (CB)
Pinot Blanc Deiss **1994** £7.99 (BAL)
Pinot Blanc Schlumberger **1996** £7.85
(WRI) £7.99 (POR) £8.25 (FORT)
Pinot Blanc Trimbach **1996** £7.20 (COC)
Pinot Blanc Trimbach **1995** £7.34 (REI)
Pinot Blanc Vieilles Vignes, Meyer-Fonné
1996 £7.29 (YOU)
Riesling Cuvée Reservée, Schaetzel **1997**
£7.52 (GW)
Riesling Kuentz-Bas **1996** £7.62 (COC)
Riesling les Faitières, Cave d'Orschwiller-
Kintzheim **1997** £7.33 (CHA)
Riesling Schleret **1994** £7.95 (YAP)
Riesling Trimbach **1995** £7.95 (WS) £8.40
(COC) £11.69 (TW)
Sylvaner Vieilles Vignes, Ostertag **1997**
£7.80 (MV) £7.95 (WRI)
Tokay-Pinot Gris Hornstein, Cave de
Pfaffenheim **1996** £7.19 (JON)
Tokay-Pinot Gris Louis Gisselbrecht
1992 £7.15 (WHI)
Tokay-Pinot Gris Réserve Personnelle,
Seltz **1995** £7.85 (WAT)
Tokay-Pinot Gris Wiederhirn **1994** £7.99
(HIG)

> *Please remember that*
> **Oz Clarke's Wine Guide**
> *is a price guide and not a*
> *price list. It is not meant to*
> *replace up-to-date*
> *merchants' lists.*

£8.00 → £8.99

Gewürztraminer Beyer **1996** £8.75 (WS)
Gewürztraminer Blanck **1998** £8.95 (AD)
Gewürztraminer Blanck **1997** £8.25
(BALL) £9.50 (FLE)
Gewürztraminer Cuvée Réservée,
Schaetzel **1996** £8.34 (GW)
Gewürztraminer Dopff au Moulin **1997**
£8.90 (CRO)
Gewürztraminer Hugel **1996** £8.95 (STA)
£8.99 (WR) £8.99 (BOT) £9.99 (DI)
Gewürztraminer Hugel **1995** £8.99 (OD)
£9.99 (DI) £12.10 (TW) £13.50 (AV)
Gewürztraminer Sipp **1997** £8.25 (WHI)
Gewürztraminer Trimbach **1996** £8.95
(WS) £11.94 (PLAY)
Muscat Albert Mann **1996** £8.50 (BU)
Muscat Blanck **1995** £8.75 (BALL)
Muscat Koehly **1997** £8.30 (HAH)
Muscat Tradition, Hugel **1997** £8.99 (DI)
£11.28 (TW) £12.95 (FORT)
Muscat Tradition, Hugel **1996** £8.95 (STA)
Muscat Trimbach **1993** £8.90 (CRO)
Pinot Blanc Béblenheim, Bott-Geyl **1995**
£8.95 (ROB)
Pinot Blanc Deiss **1996** £8.50 (LEA)
Pinot Blanc Ostertag **1996** £8.49 (YOU)
Pinot Blanc Rolly Gassmann **1996** £8.18
(BIB)
Pinot Blanc Rosenbourg, Blanck **1998**
£8.95 (AD)
Pinot Blanc Rosenbourg, Blanck **1997**
£8.25 (BALL)
Pinot Blanc Schleret **1997** £8.25 (YAP)
Riesling Bennwihr, Deiss **1996** £8.95 (LEA)
£9.49 (BAL)
Riesling Blanck **1996** £8.71 (JER)
Riesling Hugel **1992** £8.99 (CON)
Riesling Hugel **1991** £8.95 (STA) £9.39 (DI)
Riesling Meyer-Fonné **1996** £8.95 (FORT)
Sylvaner Réserve Fut 1, Weinbach **1996**
£8.95 (JU)
Tokay-Pinot Gris Tradition, Kuentz-Bas
1995 £8.99 (UN) £9.05 (COC)

£9.00 → £10.49

Auxerrois Rolly Gassmann **1993** £9.30
(RAE) £9.90 (GAU)
Auxerrois Seefel, Rolly Gassmann **1993**
£9.50 (JU)
Gewürztraminer Albert Mann **1998** £9.15
(WRI)
Gewürztraminer Bollenberg, Cattin **1997**
£10.22 (CB)

Gewürztraminer Cuvée des Evêques,
Hügel 1995 £9.50 (JU)
Gewürztraminer Hugel 1994 £9.85 (CON)
Gewürztraminer Kientzheim, Blanck
1997 £9.60 (JER)
Gewürztraminer Kuentz-Bas 1996 £9.45
(COC)
Gewürztraminer les Princes Abbés,
Schlumberger 1995 £9.69 (REI) £9.99
(JON) £9.99 (POR) £10.40 (TAN) £10.68
(PLA)

Gewürztraminer Réserve Personnelle,
Kuentz-Bas 1995 £9.99 (UN)
Gewürztraminer Réserve Personnelle,
Wiederhirn 1994 £9.99 (HIG)
Muscat Deiss 1991 £9.49 (BAL)
Muscat Réserve, Trimbach 1994 £9.99
(JON) £10.28 (PLA) £10.75 (ROB)
Muscat Schleret 1996 £9.75 (YAP)
Muscat Zind-Humbrecht 1996 £10.40 (BY)
Pinot Blanc Réserve, Weinbach 1996
£9.95 (JU)
Riesling Beyer 1996 £9.75 (AV)
Riesling Herrenweg, Zind-Humbrecht
1990 £9.97 (FLE) £11.37 (BY)
Riesling les Princes Abbés, Schlumberger
1994 £9.39 (PLA)
Riesling Rolly Gassmann 1997 £9.49 (BIB)
Riesling Rosenbourg, Blanck 1997 £9.50
(BALL)
Riesling Wintzenheim, Zind-Humbrecht
1996 £9.99 (NI)
Sylvaner Réserve, Weinbach 1995 £9.45
(JU)
Tokay-Pinot Gris Barriques, Ostertag
1995 £10.35 (SOM)
Tokay-Pinot Gris Cuvée Caroline, Schoffit
1997 £9.95 (GAU)
Tokay-Pinot Gris Patergarten, Blanck
1996 £9.45 (FLE) £9.50 (BALL)
Tokay-Pinot Gris Réserve Personnelle,
Wiederhirn 1993 £9.99 (HIG)
Tokay-Pinot Gris Réserve, Trimbach
1995 £9.85 (WS) £11.40 (GAU)
Tokay-Pinot Gris Tradition, Hugel 1995
£10.49 (CON)

£10.50 → £12.99

Auxerrois 'H' Vieilles Vignes, Josmeyer
1996 £11.75 (GAU)
Gewürztraminer Clos Gaensbroennel, A
Willm 1994 £10.50 (AS)
Gewürztraminer Cuvée Caroline Harth,
Schoffit 1997 £10.95 (AD)
Gewürztraminer les Princes Abbés,
Schlumberger 1994 £11.55 (PHI)
Gewürztraminer Réserve Personnelle,
Kuentz-Bas 1991 £11.59 (COC)
Gewürztraminer Rolly Gassmann 1995
£12.43 (BIB)
Gewürztraminer St Hippolyte, Deiss
1995 £11.50 (BAL) £11.75 (LEA)
Gewürztraminer Schléret 1997 £10.50
(YAP)
Gewürztraminer Tradition, Hugel 1995
£10.99 (OD)
Gewürztraminer Tradition, Hugel 1993
£11.00 (WS)
Muscat Clos St Imer, Burn 1997 £11.29
(YOU)
Muscat Clos St Imer, Burn 1996 £11.95
(BEN)
Muscat Deiss 1996 £10.95 (LEA)
Muscat Herrenweg de Turckheim, Zind-
Humbrecht 1996 £10.99 (NI) £14.00
(CRO)
Muscat Schlumberger 1993 £10.56 (PLA)
Pinot Blanc Domaine Weinbach 1997
£10.95 (TAN)
Pinot Blanc Fuchs 1993 £11.63 (NO)
Pinot Blanc Réserve, Weinbach 1995
£11.50 (JU)
Pinot Blanc Zind-Humbrecht 1995
£10.61 (FLE) £10.69 (NI) £20.00 (CRO)
Riesling Altenberg de Bergheim, Koehly
1997 £10.95 (HAH)
Riesling Clos Haüserer, Zind-Humbrecht
1991 £12.87 (BY)
Riesling Clos St Imer, Burn 1997 £11.50
(BEN)
Riesling Cuvée Caroline Harth, Schoffit
1996 £11.15 (AD)
Riesling Herrenweg, Zind-Humbrecht
1995 £12.81 (BY)
Riesling Herrenweg, Zind-Humbrecht
1991 £11.99 (NI)
Riesling Réserve, Trimbach 1995 £11.60
(GAU) £15.16 (TW)
Riesling Rolly Gassmann 1994 £11.50 (RAE)
Riesling Rosenbourg, Blanck 1995 £10.99
(FLE)

Riesling Saering, Schlumberger **1993**
£12.19 (JON) £14.95 (ROB)
Riesling Saering, Schlumberger **1991**
£11.26 (COC)
Riesling Schoenenbourg, Dopff au Moulin
1995 £12.45 (COC)
Riesling Schoenenbourg, Wiederhirn
1993 £11.55 (HIG)
Riesling Tradition, Hugel **1995** £10.99 (OD)
Riesling Tradition, Hugel **1990** £11.93 (REI)
Riesling Turckheim, Zind-Humbrecht
1996 £10.99 (NI)
Tokay-Pinot Gris Barriques, Ostertag
1996 £12.50 (MV)
Tokay-Pinot Gris Cuvée Caroline, Schoffit
1998 £11.30 (AD)
Tokay-Pinot Gris Hatschbourg, Cattin
1995 £12.28 (CB)
Tokay-Pinot Gris Hugel **1994** £11.85 (DI)
Tokay-Pinot Gris Jubilee, Hugel **1992**
£12.75 (REI)
Tokay-Pinot Gris les Princes Abbés,
Schlumberger **1996** £10.99 (POR)
£11.50 (TAN)
Tokay-Pinot Gris Ostertag **1997** £12.99
(PHI)
Tokay-Pinot Gris Réserve, Trimbach
1996 £12.49 (PLAY)
Tokay-Pinot Gris Schleret **1996** £11.95
(YAP)
Tokay-Pinot Gris Schlumberger **1996**
£11.75 (PLA)
Tokay-Pinot Gris Tradition, Hugel **1996**
£11.75 (STA) £14.39 (TW)
Tokay-Pinot Gris Tradition, Hugel **1992**
£10.87 (REI)
Tokay-Pinot Gris Trimbach **1994** £11.95
(ROB)

£13.00 → £14.99

Gewürztraminer Deiss **1995** £13.50 (LEA)
Gewürztraminer Furstentum Vieilles
Vignes, Blanck **1996** £13.75 (AD)
Gewürztraminer Furstentum Vieilles
Vignes, Blanck **1995** £14.20 (JER) £14.58
(FLE)
Gewürztraminer Herrenweg, Zind-
Humbrecht **1986** £13.48 (BY)
Gewürztraminer Hugel **1990** £14.69 (TW)
★ Gewürztraminer Kaefferkopf Cuvée
Catherine, Schaetzel **1997** £13.99 (GW)
Gewürztraminer Kappelweg, Rolly
Gassmann **1993** £14.95 (RAE)
Gewürztraminer Réserve, Trimbach
1994 £14.17 (MI)

Gewürztraminer Rolly Gassmann **1991**
£13.99 (RAE)
Gewürztraminer Seigneurs de
Ribeaupierre, Trimbach **1990** £14.59
(FA) £18.00 (WS) £18.99 (YOU)
Gewürztraminer Seigneurs de
Ribeaupierre, Trimbach **1988** £14.51
(REI) £17.45 (PLA) £17.50 (MI)
Gewürztraminer Steingrubler, Albert
Mann **1997** £14.79 (YOU)
Gewürztraminer Turckheim, Dopff au
Moulin **1992** £13.00 (COC)
Gewürztraminer Zind-Humbrecht **1997**
£13.68 (BY)
Muscat les Amandiers, Dopff & Irion
1994 £13.50 (UB)
Muscat les Amandiers, Dopff & Irion
1983 £14.50 (CRO)
Muscat Moench Reben, Rolly Gassmann
1996 £14.78 (BIB)
Muscat Moench Reben, Rolly Gassmann
1993 £13.90 (GAU)
Muscat Réserve No 6, Weinbach **1996**
£14.50 (JU)
Muscat Zind-Humbrecht **1990** £13.68 (BY)
Pinot Blanc Zind-Humbrecht **1996**
£13.50 (CRO)
Pinot d'Alsace Zind-Humbrecht **1995**
£14.50 (ROB)
Riesling Clos Haüserer, Zind-Humbrecht
1997 £14.30 (BY) £14.49 (WR)
Riesling Cuvée Théo, Weinbach **1995**
£14.95 (JU)
Riesling Frédéric Émile, Trimbach **1992**
£14.10 (FA) £16.90 (GAU) £17.92 (REI)
£19.95 (ROB) £20.54 (PLAY) £20.74 (TW)
Riesling Heissenberg **1996** £13.00 (MV)
Riesling Jubilee, Hugel **1995** £14.00 (WS)
£16.69 (DI)
Riesling Kappelweg, Rolly Gassmann
1993 £14.50 (JU)
Riesling Silberberg, Rolly Gassmann **1990**
£14.00 (WS)
Riesling Wineck-Schlossberg, Meyer-
Fonné **1995** £13.50 (LAY)
Tokay-Pinot Gris Bergheim, Deiss **1995**
£13.50 (LEA)
Tokay-Pinot Gris Furstentum, Albert
Mann **1995** £14.89 (LAY)
Tokay-Pinot Gris Hengst, Albert Mann
1997 £14.74 (LAY)
Tokay-Pinot Gris Kitterlé, Schlumberger
1994 £14.25 (FORT)
Tokay-Pinot Gris Réserve Millésime, Rolly
Gassman **1994** £14.95 (RAE) £18.90 (JU)

£15.00 → £19.99

Gewürztraminer Cuvée Laurence, Weinbach 1996 £19.00 (JU) £19.99 (YOU)

Gewürztraminer Cuvée Théo, Weinbach 1995 £16.50 (YOU) £16.50 (JU)

Gewürztraminer Herrenweg, Zind-Humbrecht 1997 £16.76 (BY) £21.67 (MI)

Gewürztraminer Jubilee, Hugel 1996 £15.15 (PLA) £15.85 (DI)

Gewürztraminer Jubilee, Hugel 1988 £15.49 (CON)

Gewürztraminer Kessler, Schlumberger 1997 £16.95 (POR)

Gewürztraminer Kitterlé, Schlumberger 1994 £16.50 (NI) £18.95 (PHI)

Gewürztraminer les Sorcières, Dopff & Irion 1996 £15.30 (UB)

Gewürztraminer Seigneurs de Ribeaupierre, Trimbach 1993 £17.99 (GAU)

Gewürztraminer Tradition, Hugel 1996 £15.25 (FORT)

Muscat Goldert, Zind-Humbrecht 1997 £16.00 (WS)

Muscat, Weinbach 1995 £17.95 (JU)

Riesling Brand, Zind-Humbrecht 1991 £17.46 (BY) £25.00 (CRO)

Riesling Clos Haüserer, Zind-Humbrecht 1996 £15.90 (GAU)

Riesling Clos St Imer Cuvée Chapelle, Burn 1995 £16.50 (BAL)

Riesling Cuvée Ste Catherine II, Weinbach 1994 £18.90 (JU)

Riesling Frédéric Émile, Trimbach 1995 £17.50 (GAU) £18.75 (MI) £21.00 (WS)

Riesling Frédéric Émile, Trimbach 1993 £17.95 (FORT) £18.99 (PHI) £19.99 (WR) £19.99 (BOT) £19.99 (YOU) £23.50 (TW)

Riesling Furstentum, Albert Mann 1996 £16.49 (YOU)

Riesling Furstentum Vieilles Vignes, Blanck 1995 £18.11 (JER)

Riesling Herrenweg, Zind-Humbrecht 1996 £18.75 (MI)

Riesling Jubilee Réserve Personnelle, Hugel 1996 £17.50 (STA)

Riesling Kappelweg, Rolly Gassmann 1994 £16.50 (GAU)

Riesling Kitterlé, Schlumberger 1993 £17.50 (POR)

Riesling Kitterlé, Schlumberger 1991 £16.75 (FORT)

Riesling les Pierrets, Josmeyer 1989 £17.50 (GAU)

Riesling Muenchberg, Ostertag 1996 £15.50 (MV)

Riesling Réserve Particulière, Faller 1986 £19.39 (REI)

Riesling Réserve, Trimbach 1989 £18.68 (TW)

Riesling Rosenberg Vendange Tardive, Albert Mann ½ litre 1994 £15.39 (LAY)

Riesling Schlossberg, Blanck 1996 £15.25 (AD)

Riesling Schlossberg II, Weinbach 1996 £18.00 (JU)

Riesling Silberberg, Rolly Gassmann 1993 £15.95 (UB)

Riesling Tradition, Hugel 1996 £15.00 (FORT)

Tokay-Pinot Gris Clos St Imer Cuvée Chapelle, Burn 1997 £15.50 (GAU) £15.99 (YOU) £17.95 (BEN)

Tokay-Pinot Gris Hengst, Albert Mann 1996 £16.49 (YOU)

Tokay-Pinot Gris Jubilee, Hugel 1996 £15.26 (PLA)

Tokay-Pinot Gris Jubilee, Hugel 1994 £16.00 (WS)

Tokay-Pinot Gris Millesime, Rolly Gassmann 1992 £19.50 (UB)

Tokay-Pinot Gris Réserve Personnelle Sigillé de Qualité, Kuentz-Bas 1990 £15.00 (JU)

Tokay-Pinot Gris Réserve Personnelle, Trimbach 1996 £17.50 (MI) £19.20 (GAU)

Tokay-Pinot Gris Réserve, Rolly Gassmann 1989 £18.99 (RAE)

£20.00 → £24.99

Gewürztraminer Altenbourg Cuvée Laurence, Weinbach 1996 £24.00 (JU)

Gewürztraminer Clos Windsbuhl, Zind-Humbrecht 1992 £20.25 (NI)

Gewürztraminer Clos Windsbuhl, Zind-Humbrecht 1991 £22.90 (GAU)

Gewürztraminer Fronholz Vendange Tardive, Ostertag 1994 £23.00 (MV)

Gewürztraminer Goldert, Zind-Humbrecht Non-vintage £22.49 (WR)

Gewürztraminer Hengst, Zind-Humbrecht 1997 £23.31 (BY) £26.67 (MI)

Gewürztraminer Kitterlé, Schlumberger 1989 £22.50 (COC)

Gewürztraminer Réserve Particulière, Faller 1985 £21.74 (REI)

Gewürztraminer Seigneurs de Ribeaupierre, Trimbach 1983 £22.50 (MI) £24.09 (REI) £35.00 (CRO)

Gewürztraminer Seigneurs de Ribeaupierre,
Trimbach 1981 £20.56 (REI)

Gewürztraminer Vendange Tardive,
Wiederhirn 1990 £22.72 (HIG)

Riesling Brand, Zind-Humbrecht 1996
£22.43 (BY)

Riesling Clos Haüserer, Zind-Humbrecht
1994 £23.00 (CRO)

Riesling Clos St Théobald Rangen de
Thann, Schoffit 1997 £22.50 (GAU)

Riesling Cuvée Ste Catherine II,
Weinbach 1996 £21.50 (JU)

Riesling Cuvée Ste Catherine, Weinbach
1995 £22.50 (JU)

Riesling Réserve Personnelle, Hugel 1983
£23.50 (TW) £29.00 (CRO)

Riesling Schoenenbourg Vendange Tardive,
Dopff au Moulin 1981 £22.00 (CRO)

Tokay-Pinot Gris Cuvée Ste Catherine II,
Weinbach 1996 £23.50 (JU)

Tokay-Pinot Gris Heimbourg, Zind-
Humbrecht 1996 £20.00 (FORT) £23.33
(MI)

Tokay-Pinot Gris Heimbourg, Zind-
Humbrecht 1995 £20.95 (FA)

Tokay-Pinot Gris Heimbourg, Zind-
Humbrecht 1993 £21.95 (ROB)

Tokay-Pinot Gris Réserve, Rolly
Gassmann 1983 £22.95 (RAE)

Tokay-Pinot Gris Zind-Humbrecht 1995
£22.00 (CRO)

£25.00 → £29.99

Gewürztraminer Clos St Imer Vendange
Tardive, Burn 1994 £29.95 (BEN)

Gewürztraminer Furstentum Cuvée
Laurence, Weinbach 1996 £29.00 (JU)

Gewürztraminer Vendange Tardive,
Trimbach 1996 £29.58 (MI)

Muscat les Amandiers, Dopff & Irion
1976 £29.00 (CRO)

Riesling Brand, Zind-Humbrecht 1997
£25.97 (BY)

Riesling Clos Ste-Hune, Trimbach 1991
£26.99 (AV) £28.95 (ROB) £33.84 (TW)

Riesling Clos Ste-Hune, Trimbach 1986
£25.85 (FA) £31.14 (REI) £33.00 (GAU)
£38.00 (CRO) £41.71 (PLA) £47.00 (TW)

Riesling Frédéric Émile, Trimbach 1989
£25.00 (CRO) £31.49 (TW)

Riesling Schlossberg Cuvée Ste Catherine,
Weinbach 1995 £28.00 (JU)

Riesling Schoenenbourg Vendange
Tardive, Dopff au Moulin 1983 £29.00
(CRO)

Riesling Vendange Tardive, Faller 1985
£28.79 (REI)

Riesling Vendange Tardive, Hugel 1983
£25.85 (TW) £34.60 (DI) £45.00 (BEN)

Tokay-Pinot Gris Clos St-Urbain, Zind-
Humbrecht 1995 £27.91 (FA)

Tokay-Pinot Gris Clos St Imer Vendange
Tardive, Burn 1995 £29.95 (BEN)

Tokay-Pinot Gris Cuvée Ste Catherine III,
Weinbach 1995 £29.00 (JU)

Tokay-Pinot Gris Rangen Vendange
Tardive, Zind-Humbrecht 1996 £28.83
(BY)

Tokay-Pinot Gris Vendange Tardive,
Hugel 1990 £28.95 (WAI)

Tokay-Pinot Gris Altenbourg, Weinbach
1996 £29.00 (JU)

£30.00 → £39.99

Gewürztraminer Cuvée Christine,
Schlumberger 1994 £34.66 (PLA)

Gewürztraminer Cuvée Christine,
Schlumberger 1989 £38.30 (NO)

Gewürztraminer Cuvée Christine,
Schlumberger 1985 £33.49 (REI) £56.00
(CRO)

Gewürztraminer Vendange Tardive,
Hugel 1989 £32.50 (DI) £35.13 (TW)
£39.99 (JON)

Riesling Clos St-Urbain, Zind-Humbrecht
1997 £32.92 (MI)

Riesling Clos Ste-Hune, Trimbach 1993
£34.99 (AV) £39.00 (BER) £39.99 (YOU)
£42.18 (TW)

Riesling Frédéric Émile, Trimbach 1979
£30.55 (TW)

Riesling Frédéric Émile Vendange Tardive,
Trimbach 1989 £33.68 (FA) £38.99
(YOU) £41.50 (BER) £53.76 (TW)

Riesling Herrenweg, Zind-Humbrecht
1989 £38.00 (CRO)

Riesling Vendange Tardive, Dopff & Irion
1976 £33.00 (CRO)

Riesling Vendange Tardive, Wiederhirn
1983 £31.00 (CRO)

Tokay-Pinot Gris Clos St-Urbain, Zind-
Humbrecht 1996 £32.92 (MI)

Tokay-Pinot Gris Vendange Tardive,
Deiss 1990 £35.25 (REI)

Tokay-Pinot Gris Vendange Tardive,
Hugel 1989 £30.00 (YOU)

Tokay-Pinot Gris Vendange Tardive,
Weinbach 1995 £31.50 (JU) £34.30 (TAN)

Tokay-Pinot Gris Zind-Humbrecht 1990
£37.00 (CRO)

£40.00 → £49.99

Gewürztraminer Cuvée Anne,
Schlumberger 1989 £49.20 (TAN)
£50.00 (FORT) £57.80 (BEN) £70.50 (NO)
Gewürztraminer Cuvée Christine,
Schlumberger 1990 £47.00 (CRO)
Gewürztraminer Herrenweg, Zind-
Humbrecht 1990 £40.00 (CRO)
Gewürztraminer Vendange Tardive,
Trimbach 1989 £45.51 (PLAY)
Riesling Clos Ste-Hune, Trimbach 1994
£45.00 (WS)
Tokay-Pinot Gris Furstentum Sélection de
Grains Nobles, Albert Mann ½ bottle
1994 £48.73 (LAY)
Tokay-Pinot Gris Vendange Tardive,
Faller 1996 £45.00 (WS)

£50.00 → £59.99

Gewürztraminer Seigneurs de
Ribeaupierre, Trimbach 1976 £54.00
(CRO)
Gewürztraminer Sélection de Grains
Nobles, Hugel 1986 £57.00 (WS)
Riesling Clos Ste-Hune, Trimbach 1989
£50.00 (FORT)
Riesling Réserve Personnelle, Hugel 1976
£54.00 (CRO)
Riesling Vendange Tardive, Hugel 1976
£58.16 (REI) £59.00 (CRO) £88.13 (TW)
Riesling Vendange Tardive, Weinbach
1990 £54.00 (JU)
Tokay-Pinot Gris Clos St Imer Sélection
de Grains Nobles, Burn 1994 £59.50
(BEN)
Tokay-Pinot Gris Cuvée Clarisse,
Schlumberger 1989 £58.00 (CRO)
£99.88 (PLA)
Tokay-Pinot Gris Vendange Tardive,
Hugel 1976 £52.29 (FA) £76.38 (TW)

£60.00 → £74.99

Gewürztraminer Clos St Imer Sélection de
Grains Nobles, Burn 1994 £66.00 (BEN)
Gewürztraminer Cuvée Anne Vendange
Tardive, Rolly Gassmann 1985 £65.00
(UB)
Gewürztraminer Furstentum Sélection
des Graines Nobles, Weinbach 1994
£62.00 (JU)
Gewürztraminer Sélection de Grains
Nobles, Hugel 1988 £67.84 (VIN)
Gewürztraminer Sélection de Grains
Nobles, Hugel 1983 £65.51 (REI)

£75.00 → £99.99

Gewürztraminer Cuvée Christine,
Schlumberger 1976 £92.00 (CRO)
Gewürztraminer Sélection de Grains
Nobles, Hugel 1976 £80.00 (CRO)
£83.62 (FA)
Gewürztraminer Sélection de Grains
Nobles, Fuchs 1989 £75.87 (NO)
Riesling Clos Ste-Hune, Trimbach 1976
£99.88 (TW)
Riesling Sélection de Grains Nobles,
Fuchs 1989 £79.58 (NO)
Riesling Sélection de Grains Nobles,
Hugel 1976 £82.25 (REI)
Riesling Vendange Tardive Sélection de
Grains Nobles, Hugel 1976 £82.25 (NO)
Tokay-Pinot Gris Sélection de Grains
Nobles, Hugel 1976 £92.00 (CRO)

Over £100.00

Gewürztraminer Cuvée Anne,
Schlumberger 1976 £120.00 (CRO)
Gewürztraminer Cuvée d'Or
Quintessence Sélection des Grains
Nobles, Weinbach 1994 £138.00 (JU)
Riesling Frédéric Émile, Trimbach 1971
£101.05 (TW)

RED

Under £10.00

Pinot Noir Beyer 1995 £9.90 (AV)
Pinot Noir Hugel 1993 £9.95 (STA) £9.95
(DI)
Pinot Noir Rolly Gassmann 1992 £9.70
(RAE)

£10.00 → £20.00

Pinot Noir Burlenberg, Deiss 1995
£12.95 (LEA)
Pinot Noir Herrenweg, Zind-Humbrecht
1991 £12.14 (BY)
Pinot Noir Réserve, Rolly Gassmann
1990 £19.99 (RAE) £22.69 (BIB)
Pinot Noir Schleret 1996 £10.50 (YAP)

SPARKLING

Under £9.50

Crémant d'Alsace Cuvée Julien, Dopff au
Moulin **Non-vintage** £9.44 (COC)
£10.50 (ROB)

BORDEAUX

Great Bordeaux is glorious; but good cheap red Bordeaux hardly exists any more. If you want good-value Cabernet flavours, look elsewhere

I hardly know what advice to give to a novice of Bordeaux these days. I mean, if you love Australian or Chilean Cabernet Sauvignon and you think it's about time you started a voyage of exploration in Cabernet's homeland, where on earth do you start?

The problem is that there's not much red Bordeaux under £9 that can compete in flavour with what we're used to from the southern hemisphere. That, after many years of extortionate price rises in Bordeaux, is the unhappy truth. Red Bordeaux has priced itself out of the everyday market; anything decent is now around a tenner or more – often much more. There are very few entry-level wines that are good enough to make you want to explore further.

It used to be said of Bordeaux that it had something for everyone: wine of every colour and style, and at every price level, whether you were a millionaire wanting ancient vintages of Château Latour or the rest of us, just looking for something tasty and cedary to go with the lamb chops. (In fact, if you talk to the, shall we say, less young members of the wine trade, they'll reminisce about the days when even they, on their miserable salaries, could afford to buy first growth clarets for high days and holidays. Not now.) Well, I think that view of Bordeaux is outdated. Yes, there are some good inexpensive whites, simply because international demand for Bordeaux's dry whites has never been enough to send blood rushing to the heads of the producers. But everybody, all over the world, from Asia to Germany to the USA, wants to get their hands on the top reds. And so prices rise inexorably, year after year. And the lesser wines, the ones we used to drink, get pulled along in the slipstream.

Quality is another issue: yes, it is there in Bordeaux, at around the £10 level – but so it should be. And given the roller-coaster nature of vintages here, it's not ubiquitous. If you want reliability and flavour at low prices, look to Italy, Portugal, the South of France; Australia at a slightly higher level. But forget about cheap claret.

GRAPE VARIETIES

Fine claret has the most tantalizing and unlikely combination of flavours of any red wine. There's the blast of pure, fragrant blackcurrant fruit, and then the exotic, dry perfumes of lead pencil shavings, fresh-wrapped cigars and cedar to weave an endlessly fascinating balance of sweet and dry tastes with, increasingly, the buttery overlay of new oak barrels.

Bordeaux's vineyards are so poised on the knife-edge of ripening their grapes or failing to do so that every vintage is fascinatingly different. If the year gets too hot, the flavour can be rich, strong and burnt, more like the Californian or Italian attempts at claret. If the summer rains and autumn gales roll in off the Bay of Biscay and the grapes can't ripen, then the taste may be thin and green, resembling the Cabernets of the Loire Valley. But in the years of balance, like 1986, '88, '89 and '90, those astonishing sweet and dry, fruity and tannic flavours mix to produce the glory that is claret.

As for the whites – well, for years the sweet, botrytized wines of Sauternes and Barsac were the only ones which could compete in quality with the reds, and not

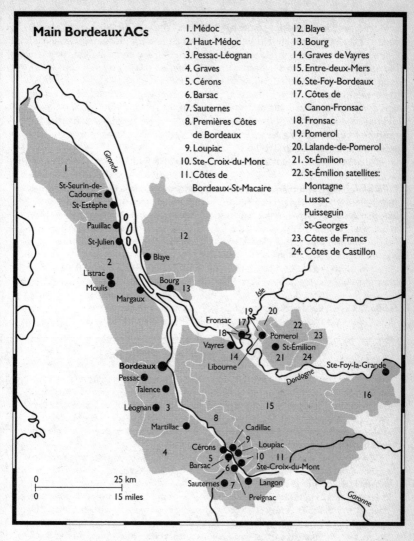

Main Bordeaux ACs

1. Médoc
2. Haut-Médoc
3. Pessac-Léognan
4. Graves
5. Cérons
6. Barsac
7. Sauternes
8. Premières Côtes de Bordeaux
9. Loupiac
10. Ste-Croix-du-Mont
11. Côtes de Bordeaux-St-Macaire
12. Blaye
13. Bourg
14. Graves de Vayres
15. Entre-deux-Mers
16. Ste-Foy-Bordeaux
17. Côtes de Canon-Fronsac
18. Fronsac
19. Pomerol
20. Lalande-de-Pomerol
21. St-Émilion
22. St-Émilion satellites: Montagne Lussac Puisseguin St-Georges
23. Côtes de Francs
24. Côtes de Castillon

always successfully. But recent years have seen a revolution. The sweet whites have improved beyond measure, helped by massive investment and a run of excellent vintages in the 1980s, but so have the dry ones. Inexpensive Bordeaux Blanc, based on Sauvignon, is usually crisp and grassy these days, while fine oak-aged white Graves has taken its place among the greats.

CABERNET FRANC (red) The lesser of the two Cabernets, giving lighter-coloured, softer wines than Cabernet Sauvignon, often slightly earthy but with good, blackcurrant fruit. It's always blended in Bordeaux. In St-Émilion and Pomerol it can give fine flavours and is widely planted. Château Cheval-Blanc in St-Émilion is two-thirds Cabernet Franc.

CABERNET SAUVIGNON (red) This world-famous Bordeaux grape surprisingly covers only a fifth of the vineyard area. Crucially, a wine built to age needs tannin and acidity, and the fruit and extract to keep up with them. Cabernet Sauvignon has all these in abundance. It gives dark, tannic wine with a strong initial acid attack, and stark blackcurrant fruit. When aged in new oak, it can be stunning. It's the main grape of the Haut-Médoc, but other varieties soften it and add complexity.

MALBEC (red) A rather bloated, juicy grape, little seen nowadays in Bordeaux, though it appears in some blends, especially in Bourg and Blaye. In Bordeaux it tastes rather like a feeble version of Merlot, soft and low in acidity. Upriver in Cahors it has real style, which probably explains why there's lots of it there and little in Bordeaux.

MERLOT (red) Bordeaux has more Merlot than Cabernet Sauvignon. It covers almost a third of the vineyard, and is the main grape in St-Émilion and Pomerol, whereas in the Médoc and Graves it's used to soften and enrich the Cabernet. It ripens early and gives a gorgeous, succulent, minty, blackcurranty or plummy wine, which explains why Pomerols and St-Émilions are easier to enjoy than Médocs. It also makes less long-lived wine than Cabernet, and tends to peak and fade sooner.

MUSCADELLE (white) A very little (up to five per cent) of this headily perfumed grape often goes into the Sauternes blend. In dry white blends a few per cent can add a very welcome honeyed softness. It is now being produced in small quantities as a varietal: dry, lean, but perfumed.

PETIT VERDOT (red) A dark, tough grape with a liquorice-and-plums taste, and a violet perfume, used for colour. Little planted in the past but on the increase now because it adds quality in a late, ripe year.

BUYING CLARET EN PRIMEUR

In the spring after the vintage the Bordeaux châteaux make their opening offers. This means that they do not have to sit on very expensive stock for a further two years until the wines are bottled and ready to ship. In theory this also means that you can buy the wine at a preferential price. Traditionally merchants would buy for stock while offering their customers the chance to take advantage of the opening prices as well. In the heady days of the 1980s, however, the market really took off.

There is a lot to be said for buying en primeur. For one thing, you may be able to find the finest and rarest wines far more cheaply than they will ever appear again. This was especially true of the 1990 vintage.

But you should be aware of the risks: as they say in the investment world, prices can go down as well as up. They may easily not increase significantly in the few years after the campaign (witness prices for 1985s and 1989s). The second risk is that the merchant you bought the wine from may not still be around to deliver it to you two years later. Buy from a merchant you can trust, one with a solid trading base in other wines.

Once the wines are shipped you may want your merchant to store the wine for you. If so, you should insist that (1) you receive a stock certificate; (2) your wines are stored separately from the merchant's own stocks; and (3) your cases are identifiable as your property and are labelled accordingly. All good merchants will offer these safeguards as a minimum service. Of course, in an ideal world your house is equipped with its own temperature-controlled cellar, because the best solution is certainly to take possession of your cases yourself.

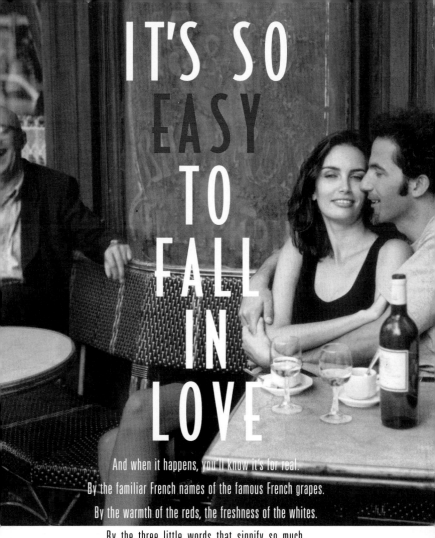

IT'S SO EASY TO FALL IN LOVE

And when it happens, you'll know it's for real.

By the familiar French names of the famous French grapes.

By the warmth of the reds, the freshness of the whites.

By the three little words that signify so much.

VINS DE PAYS

Live from June-http://www.vinsdepays.co.uk

Stony soil creates havoc for farmers but heaven for wine makers. That's why we planted our vineyard in the finest sauvignon blanc region in the world.

Stoneleigh. From stony soil comes stunning New Zealand wine.

ShortBrownWhite 71\6

You don't have to be French to shop in Calais.

The shopping forecast.

Attention all shoppers, especially in areas a short hop from Dover.

Here is the shopping forecast from the English Channel.

Dover to Calais - crossings, frequent.

Shopping prices falling steadily.

Wines plentiful from all regions with bargains, imminent.

Bries moderate. Other cheeses also excellent.

Hotel accommodation - good. Restaurants - fine.

There'll be a few passengers unwinding as the day goes on and we'll see more ferries along shortly.

What are you waiting for? With around 100 crossings a day,

Calais

begins with sea

DOVER/CALAIS. OVER 100 CROSSINGS EVERY DAY.
P&O STENA LINE, SEAFRANCE & HOVERSPEED.

ROSEMOUNT ESTATE

The prestige wine of Australia

SAUVIGNON BLANC (white) There has been a rush to plant more of this fashionable grape in Bordeaux in recent years, but with a couple of exceptions – such as *Couhins-Lurton, Malartic-Lagravière* and *Smith-Haut-Lafitte* – Sauvignon by itself here often gives rather muddy, tough wine. Even so, many dry white Bordeaux are entirely Sauvignon, particularly at the cheaper end, and can be fresh and flowery if from careful winemakers like *Coste, Dourthe, Ginestet* and *Mau*. The best are almost always blended with Sémillon. A little Sauvignon adds acidity to Sauternes and other sweet whites.

SÉMILLON (white) The most important grape of Sauternes, and vital to the best dry wines, too. With modern techniques one can hardly tell a good dry Sémillon from a Sauvignon, except that it's a little fuller. But ideally they should be blended, with Sémillon the main variety. It gives a big, round dry wine, slightly creamy but with an aroma of fresh apples and a lanolin smoothness in the mouth. The result is a wonderful, soft, nutty dry white, often going honeyed and smoky as it ages for seven to 15 years. Like this it produces one of France's great whites, and is an antidote to anyone getting just a little tired of varietals.

WINE REGIONS

BARSAC, AC (sweet white) The only one of the five Sauternes villages with the right to use its own name as an official appellation (it may also call itself Sauternes – or Sauternes-Barsac for that matter). The wines tend to be lighter, and the best combine marvellous richness with a certain delicacy of texture.

BORDEAUX BLANC, AC (dry white) This AC is the catch-all name for all white Bordeaux. Château wines are usually the best and should generally be drunk as young as possible. Recommended names include: *Birot, Grand-Mouëys, du Juge, Lamothe, Reynon*. Good blends are likely from the following merchants: *Coste, Dourthe, Dubroca, Ginestet, Joanne, Lurton, Mau, Sichel* and *Univitis*.

Some classy properties in red areas make good, dry white which is allowed only this AC. *Château Margaux*'s white, for instance, is a simple AC Bordeaux Blanc. Many great Sauternes châteaux make a dry wine from the grapes deemed unsuitable for Sauternes. These also take the Bordeaux Blanc AC and are often named after the initial letter of the château's name – as in 'G' of *Guiraud*, 'R' of *Rieussec* and 'Y' of *Yquem*. They're expensive but complex and unusual. 'Y' can really be spectacular.

BORDEAUX BLANC SUPÉRIEUR, AC (dry white) Rarely used, but requires higher basic strength and lower vineyard yield than Bordeaux Blanc AC.

BORDEAUX ROUGE, AC (red) Unless qualified by one of the other ACs below, this is the everyday red wine of Bordeaux, either from co-ops, from properties in undistinguished localities, or wine disqualified from one of the better ACs. It can come from anywhere in Bordeaux. It is a delicious, appetizing meal-time red when good – and a palate-puckering disappointment when bad. Too many are muddy, coarse and lacking in style.

BORDEAUX SUPÉRIEUR, AC (red) Similar to Bordeaux Rouge but with more alcohol and produced from a slightly lower yield. The same comments on quality apply, but from a good estate the wines can be delicious. Best results are often from properties producing white Entre-Deux-Mers and from the Premières Côtes. Best châteaux: *Brethous, Cayla, Domaine de Terrefort, Fayau, la Gabory, le Gay, Grand-Mouëys, Gromel Bel-Air, Jalousie-Beaulieu, Jonqueyres, du Juge, Lacombe, Méaume, Peyrat, Pierredon, Reynon, la Roche, Tanesse, Thieuley, de Toutigeac, de la Vieille Tour*.

CADILLAC, AC (sweet white) This small region can produce attractive sweet whites, but many properties produce more commercial dry whites and reds – which do *not* qualify for the AC Cadillac. The AC is in any case so involved that few growers bother with it.

CÉRONS, AC (sweet white) Good, fairly sweet whites, but many growers now prefer to produce dry whites instead, which can be sold as Graves. *Château Archambeau* is typical, producing tiny amounts of very good Cérons and larger amounts of good, fresh dry Graves. *Château Cérons* makes splendidly complex sweet whites worthy of the AC of Barsac. Other good names to look out for: *Grand Enclos du Château Cérons, Haura.*

CÔTES DE BOURG, AC (red) The rather full, savoury style of these reds is backed up by sweet Merlot fruit and occasionally a touch of new oak. As Médoc and St-Émilion prices spiral, Bourg wines are slowly coming into their own. Best châteaux: *de Barbe, du Bousquet, Brûle-Sécaille, la Croix, Dupeyrat, Grolet, Guionne, Haut-Guiraud, Haut-Rousset, de Millorit* and wines from the co-op at *Tauriac.*

CÔTES DE CASTILLON, AC (red) and **CÔTES DE FRANCS, AC** (red) Two small regions which are turning out an increasing number of exciting wines. They can be a little too earthy, but at their best they combine a grassy Cabernet Franc freshness with a gorgeous, juicy, minty Merlot sweetness. Several leading Bordeaux proprietors have bought properties here and are leading the way. Best châteaux in the Côtes de Castillon: *Arthus, Beau-Séjour, Belcier, Brisson, Canon-Monségur, La Clarière-Laithwaite, Ferrasses, Fonds Rondes, Grand Taillac, les Hauts-de-Grange, Lessacques, Moulin-Rouge, Parenchère, Peyrou, Pitray, Poupille, Rocher-Bellevue, Vernon.* The Côtes de Francs is increasingly producing fruity, light, delicious wines to drink early, using a

lot of Cabernet Franc. Best châteaux here are *la Claverie, de Francs, Lauriol, Marsau, du Moulin-la-Pitié, la Prade, Puygueraud.*

CÔTES DE FRONSAC, AC (red) with the (in theory) superior **CANON-FRONSAC, AC** (red) Lesser St-Émilion lookalikes, sometimes a bit grassy and tannic, but often supple, balanced clarets of some elegance – even in bad years like 1992. Best: *Barrabaque, Canon-de-Brem, Canon-Moueix, Cassagne Haut-Canon, Dalem, de la Dauphine, Fonteuil, Mayne-Vieil, Mazeris, Moulin Haut-Laroque, Moulin Pey-Labrie, Plain Point, la Rivière, la Truffière, Toumalin, la Valade, La Vieille Cure.*

ENTRE-DEUX-MERS, AC (dry white) Every vintage produces more good, fresh, grassy wines here. Many properties make red, which take the AC of Bordeaux or Bordeaux Supérieur. Best: *Bonnet, Ducla, de Florin, Fondarzac, Moulin-de-Launay, Tertre du Moulin, Thieuley, Union des Producteurs de Rauzan.*

GRAVES, AC (red, dry white) Red Graves run the gamut of claret flavours, and are less easy to sum up than others. Though the Cabernet Sauvignon is the dominant grape in the North, as in the Médoc, there's more stress on Merlot, so the wines are slightly softer. They tend to have some of the blackcurrant and cedar of the Médoc, but without the sheer size of, say, Pauillac; they have some of the full, plummy richness of St-Émilion, yet it never dominates; and there is a slightly gravelly quality in many of them, too. The less well-known châteaux are good value.

Modern white Graves, even at the level of commercial blends, can be sharply fruity and full in style, although too many are overoaked. Best châteaux: *Archambeau, Bouscaut, Cabannieux, Carbonnieux, Domaine de Chevalier, Couhins-Lurton, de Cruzeau, Domaine la Grave, de Fieuzal, la Garance, la Garde, Haut-Brion, Landiras, Laville-Haut-Brion, la Louvière, Malartic-Lagravière,*

Montalivet, Rahoul, Respide, Rochemorin, Roquetaillade-la-Grange, Smith-Haut-Lafitte and la Tour-Martillac.

(Note that in 1987 the prestigious properties in the North were grouped into a separate AC, Pessac-Léognan.)

GRAVES SUPÉRIEURES, AC (sweet or dry white) Graves with a minimum natural alcohol of 12 degrees. Often made sweet. Best property: *Clos St-Georges*.

HAUT-MÉDOC, AC (red) Geographically, the prestigious southern part of the Médoc, nearest Bordeaux. The AC, however, covers the less exciting vineyards because the really juicy business gets done at Margaux, St-Julien, Pauillac, St-Estèphe, Listrac and Moulis, which have their own ACs. Even so, the AC Haut-Médoc has five Classed Growths including two superb ones – *Cantemerle* and *la Lagune* – and an increasing number of fine *bourgeois* properties like *Beaumont, de Castillon, Cissac, Hanteillan, Lamarque, Lanessan, Liversan, Pichon, Sociando-Mallet* and *la Tour-du-Haut-Moulin* – plus lots of lesser properties, such as châteaux *Bernadotte, Cambon-la-Pelouse, Coufran, le Fournas, Grandis, du Junca, Larose-Trintaudon, Malescasse, Maucamps, Moulin de Labarde, Quimper, Sénéjac* and *Verdignan*.

LALANDE-DE-POMEROL, AC (red) Pomerol's equally tiny northern neighbour, is often accused of being overpriced, but since it can produce rich, plummy wines with a distinct resemblance to those of Pomerol at a distinctly less painful price, this criticism is not entirely justified. Best: *Annereaux, Bel-Air, Belles-Graves, Bertineau-St-Vincent, Clos des Moines, Clos des Templiers, la Croix Bellevue, la Fleur St-Georges, Grand Ormeau, Haut-Ballet, les Hauts-Tuileries, Lavaud-la-Maréchaude, Siaurac, les Templiers, Tournefeuille*.

LISTRAC, AC (red) One of the less prestigious communes of the Haut-Médoc.

> **ON THE CASE**
> Inexpensive dry whites are one of the few bargains in Bordeaux: look for Sauvignon Blanc at under £5 a bottle

The wines contain a higher proportion of Merlot than elsewhere, but nevertheless are rather tough and charmless, only lightly perfumed wines. But some properties rise above this, such as *la Bécade, Cap-Léon-Veyrin, Clarke, Fonréaud* (since 1988), *Fourcas-Dupré, Fourcas-Hosten, Fourcaud, Lestage* and the *Grand Listrac* co-op.

LOUPIAC, AC (sweet white) These wines are not as sweet as Sauternes, and most are light, lemony, honeyed Barsac styles. The general improvement in Bordeaux's sweet wines has filtered down here, as well. Best: *Domaine du Noble, Loupiac-Gaudiet, Ricaud*.

MARGAUX, AC (red) Rather sludgy, solid wines at one extreme, and the most fragrant, perfumed red wines France has yet dreamed up at the other. The best include: *d'Angludet, la Gurgue, d'Issan, Labégorce-Zédé, Margaux, Monbrison, Palmer, Prieuré-Lichine, Rauzan-Ségla, du Tertre*. Among the next best are *Durfort-Vivens, Giscours, Lascombes, Marquis d'Alesme-Becker, Marquis de Terme, Siran* and *la Tour-de-Mons*.

MÉDOC, AC (red) This name covers the long tongue of land north of Bordeaux town, between the Gironde river and the sea, including the Haut-Médoc and all its famous communes. As an AC it refers to the less-regarded but important northern part of the area. Médoc reds, with a high proportion of Merlot grapes, are drinkable more quickly than Haut-Médocs and the best have a refreshing, grassy, juicy fruit, backed up by just enough tannin and acidity. Easily the best property is *Potensac*. Other good wines are *le Bernadot, Cardonne, Cassan d'Estevil, David, d'Escot, la Gorce,*

Greysac, Grivière, Haut-Canteloup, Lacombe-Noaillac, Noaillac, Ormes-Sorbet, Patache d'Aux, la Tour-de-By, la Tour-St-Bonnet, Loudenne, Vieux-Château-Landon. Most of the co-ops – especially Bégadan, Ordornac and St-Yzans – make good fruity stuff in the best years.

MOULIS, AC (red) Another lesser commune of the Haut-Médoc next door to, and similar to, Listrac, but with more potentially outstanding properties and a softer, more perfumed style in the best which can equal Classed Growths. Best are Bel-Air-Lagrave, Brillette, Chasse-Spleen, Duplessis-Fabre, Dutruch-Grand-Poujeaux, Grand-Poujeaux, Gressier-Grand-Poujeaux, Maucaillou, Moulin-à-Vent, Poujeaux.

PAUILLAC, AC (red) The most famous of the Haut-Médoc communes, Pauillac has three of the world's greatest red wines sitting inside its boundaries: Latour, Lafite and Mouton-Rothschild. This is where the blackcurrant really comes into its own. The best wines are almost painfully intense, a celestial mixture of blackcurrant and lead pencil sharpenings that sends well-heeled cognoscenti leaping for their cheque books. Best: d'Armailhac (formerly known as Mouton-Baronne-Philippe), Grand-Puy-Lacoste, Haut-Bages-Avérous, Haut-Bages-Libéral, Lafite-Rothschild, Latour, Lynch-Bages, Mouton-Rothschild, Pichon-Baron, Pichon-Lalande. Next best: Batailley, Clerc-Milon-Rothschild, Duhart-Milon, Grand-Puy-Ducasse, Haut-Bages-Monpelou.

PESSAC-LÉOGNAN, AC (red, dry white) Traditionally the Graves' best area, containing all the crus classés. The whites at their best offer a depth surpassed only by the best Burgundies. They start out with a blast of apricot, peach and cream ripeness and slowly mature to a superb nutty richness with a dry savoury finish. The reds have a biscuity, bricky warmth. Best reds: Carbonnieux, Carmes-Haut-Brion, Cruzeau, Domaine de Chevalier, Domaine de Gaillat, Domaine la Grave, Ferrande, de Fieuzal, Haut-Bailly, Haut-Brion, Haut-Portets, la Louvière, Malartic-Lagravière, la Mission-Haut-Brion, Pape-Clément (since 1985), Rahoul, Rochemorin, de St-Pierre, Smith-Haut-Lafitte (since 1988), Roquetaillade-la-Grange, la Tour-Martillac, Tourteau-Chollet. Best whites: Bouscaut, Carbonnieux (from 1988), Couhins-Lurton, Domaine de Chevalier, de Fieuzal, Haut-Brion, la Louvière, Malartic-Lagravière, Rochemorin, Smith-Haut-Lafitte, la Tour-Martillac.

POMEROL, AC (red) The Merlot grape is even more dominant in Pomerol than in St-Émilion, and most Pomerols have a deeper, rounder flavour, the plummy fruit going as dark as prunes in great years, but with the mineral backbone of toughness preserving it for a very long time. Pomerol harbours the Château Pétrus, and the world's (currently) most expensive red wine, Le Pin. Other top names: le Bon Pasteur, Bourgneuf-Vayron, Certan-de-May, Certan-Giraud, Clinet, Clos René, Clos du Clocher, Clos l'Église, la Conseillante, la Croix de Gay, l'Église Clinet, l'Évangile, le Gay, la Grave-Trigant-de-Boisset, Lafleur, Lafleur-Gazin, la Fleur-Pétrus, Lagrange-à-Pomerol, Latour-à-Pomerol, Petit-Village, Pétrus, Le Pin, Trotanoy, Vieux-Château-Certan.

PREMIÈRES CÔTES DE BLAYE, AC (red, dry white) The reds are too often a little 'cooked' in taste and slightly jammy-sweet. They're cheap, but have a lot more improving to do. Good names: Bas Vallon, Bourdieu, Charron, Crusquet-Sabourin, l'Escadre, Fontblanche, Grand Barail, Haut-Sociondo, Jonqueyres, Peybonhomme.

PREMIÈRES CÔTES DE BORDEAUX, AC (red, white) Some very attractive reds and excellent dry whites in the bang-up-to-date, fruit-all-the-way style, plus some reasonable sweetish wines. Best châteaux: de Berbec, Brethous, Cayla, Fayau, Grands-Moüeys, du Juge, Lamothe, de Lucat, Peyrat, la Roche, Reynon, Tanesse.

ST-ÉMILION, AC (red) Soft, round and rather generous wines, because the main grape is the Merlot, aided by Cabernet Franc and Malbec, and only slightly by Cabernet Sauvignon. St-Émilions don't always have Pomerol's minerally backbone, and the sweetness is usually less plummy and more buttery, toffeed or raisiny. Top wines add to this a blackcurranty, minty depth. Basic St-Émilions are seldom exciting, and quality is extremely variable. It's a well-known name, yet with few famous châteaux: the top ones are *Cheval-Blanc* and *Ausone*. Some satellite areas also annex the name, like St-Georges-St-Émilion or Puisseguin-St-Émilion. They're okay, but would be better value if they didn't trade greedily on the St-Émilion handle. Best in satellites: *Montaiguillon, St-Georges, Tour du Pas St-Georges* (St-Georges-St-Émilion); *Haut-Gillet, de Maison Neuve* (Montagne-St-Émilion); *Bel Air, la Croix-de-Berny* (Puisseguin-St-Émilion); *Lyonnat* (Lussac-St-Émilion). Best St-Émilion: *l'Angélus, l'Arrosée, Ausone, Balestard-la-Tonnelle, Beauséjour-Duffau-Lagarosse, Canon, Canon-la-Gaffelière, Cheval-Blanc, Clos des Jacobins, la Dominique, Figeac, Fonroque, Larmande, Magdelaine, Pavie, Pavie-Decesse, Soutard, Tertre-Rôteboeuf, Troplong-Mondot.* Next best: *Belair, Cadet-Piola, Berliquet, Cap-de-Mourlin, Cardinal Villemaurine, Carteau, Clos Fourtet, Corbin-Michotte, Côtes Daugay, Couvent des Jacobins, Destieux, de Ferrand, Fombrauge, Franc-Mayne, la Gaffelière, Grand-Mayne, Gravet, Magnan-la-Gaffelière, Mauvezin, Monbousquet, Pavie-Macquin, Rolland-Maillet, Tour-des-Combes, la-Tour-du-Pin-Figeac, Trappaud, Trottevieille, Villemaurine.* There's a trend towards producing *micro-vins*: take perhaps a single hectare of vines, make a wine of great concentration and oak, then charge a fortune for it. *Valandraud* and *La Mondotte* are leading players; also *Le Dôme*.

ST-ESTÈPHE, AC (red) The northernmost of the great Haut-Médoc communes is a more everyday performer. There are few famous names, and most are relatively cheap. Best: *Calon-Ségur, Chambert-Marbuzet, Cos d'Estournel, Haut-Marbuzet, Lafon-Rochet, Marbuzet, Meyney, Montrose, les Ormes-de-Pez, de Pez, Phélan-Ségur.* Next best: *Andron-Blanquet, Beausite, du Boscq, Cos Labory, le Crock, Lavillotte.*

ST-JULIEN, AC (red) There are two main styles here. One is almost honeyed: gentle, round, wonderfully easy-to-love. The other has glorious cedar-cigar-box fragrance and just enough fruit to make it satisfying as well as exciting. Best: *Beychevelle, Ducru-Beaucaillou, Gruaud-Larose, Lagrange, Lalande-Borie, Langoa-Barton, Léoville-Barton, Léoville-Las-Cases, St-Pierre, Talbot.* Next: *Branaire-Ducru, Gloria, Hortevie, Léoville-Poyferré* and *Terrey-Gros-Caillou.*

STE-CROIX-DU-MONT, AC (sweet white) Very attractive when properly made. *Château Loubens* is the best-known wine, but *Château Lousteau-Vieil* is producing better wine every year, and *Domaine du Tich, la Grave, la Rame, des Tours* and the minuscule *de Tastes* are also good.

SAUTERNES, AC (sweet white) The overall appellation for a group of five villages: Sauternes, Bommes, Fargues, Preignac and Barsac. (Barsac wines may use their own village name, if they wish.) Concentrated by noble rot, the Sémillon, along with Sauvignon and Muscadelle, produces at its best a brilliantly rich and glyceriny wine, combining honey and cream, pineapple and nuts when young; becoming oily and penetrating with age. The sweetness has an intensity of volatile flavours, like a peach, bruised and browned in the sun, then steeped in syrup. These are the fine wines; but the average wines have soared in quality recently, as indeed they ought given their prices. Best include: *Bastor-Lamontagne, Climens, Doisy-Daëne, Doisy-Védrines, de Fargues, Gilette, Guiraud, Lafaurie-Peyraguey, Lamothe-Guignard, Rabaud-Promis, Raymond-Lafon, Rayne-Vigneau, Rieussec, St-Amand, Suduiraut, la Tour Blanche, d'Yquem.*

THE 1855 CLASSIFICATION

This is the most famous and enduring wine classification in the world – but it was intended merely as an impromptu guide to the Bordeaux wines entered for the Great Paris Exhibition of 1855, based on the prices the wines had obtained over the previous century.

Since this classification applies only to the Médoc and one château, Haut-Brion, in the Graves, all the wines are red. The Graves has its own classification, for reds and whites, and Sauternes and St-Émilion are also classified. Pomerol steers clear of any official hierarchy. The only change so far has been the promotion of Mouton-Rothschild to First Growth in 1973.

In general, classified properties do deserve their status, but that's never yet stopped anyone from arguing about it.

CLARET CLASSIFICATIONS

First Growths (1ers crus)
Margaux – *Margaux*; Lafite-Rothschild, Latour, Mouton-Rothschild (promoted in 1973) – *Pauillac*; Haut-Brion – *Pessac-Léognan* (formerly *Graves*).

Second Growths (2èmes crus)
Brane-Cantenac – *Cantenac-Margaux*; Durfort-Vivens, Lascombes, Rauzan-Gassies, Rauzan-Ségla – *Margaux*; Pichon-Longueville, Pichon-Longueville-Lalande (formerly Pichon-Lalande) – *Pauillac*; Cos d'Estournel, Montrose – *St-Estèphe*; Ducru-Beaucaillou, Gruaud-Larose, Léoville-Barton, Léoville-Las-Cases, Léoville-Poyferré – *St-Julien*.

Third Growths (3èmes crus)
Boyd-Cantenac, Cantenac-Brown, d'Issan, Kirwan, Palmer – *Cantenac-Margaux*; Giscours – *Labarde-Margaux*; la Lagune – *Ludon-Haut-Médoc*; Desmirail, Ferrière, Malescot-St-Exupéry, Marquis d'Alesme-Becker – *Margaux*; Calon-Ségur – *St-Estèphe*; Lagrange, Langoa-Barton – *St-Julien*.

Fourth Growths (4èmes crus)
Pouget, Prieuré-Lichine – *Cantenac-Margaux*; Marquis-de-Terme – *Margaux*; Duhart-Milon-Rothschild – *Pauillac*; Lafon-Rochet – *St-Estèphe*; Beychevelle, Branaire (formerly Branaire-Ducru), St-Pierre, Talbot – *St-Julien*; la Tour-Carnet – *St-Laurent-Haut-Médoc*.

Fifth Growths (5èmes crus)
du Tertre – *Arsac-Margaux*; Dauzac – *Labarde-Margaux*; Cantemerle – *Macau-Haut-Médoc*; d'Armailhac (formerly Mouton-Baronne-Philippe), Batailley, Clerc-Milon-Rothschild, Croizet-Bages, Grand-Puy-Ducasse, Grand-Puy-Lacoste, Haut-Bages-Libéral, Haut-Batailley, Lynch-Bages, Lynch-Moussas, Pédesclaux, Pontet-Canet – *Pauillac*; Cos Labory – *St-Estèphe*; Belgrave, de Camensac – *St-Laurent-Haut-Médoc*.

SAUTERNES CLASSIFICATIONS

Grand 1er cru
d'Yquem – *Sauternes*.

1er crus
Climens, Coutet – *Barsac*; Haut-Peyraguey, Lafaurie-Peyraguey, Rabaud-Promis, Rayne-Vigneau, Sigalas-Rabaud, la Tour-Blanche – *Bommes*; Rieussec – *Fargues*; Suduiraut – *Preignac*; Guiraud – *Sauternes*.

2èmes crus
Broustet, Caillou, Doisy-Daëne, Doisy-Dubroca, Doisy-Védrines, Nairac, de Myrat, Suau – *Barsac*; Romer-du-Hayot – *Fargues*; de Malle – *Preignac*; d'Arche, Filhot, Lamothe, Lamothe-Guignard – *Sauternes*.

PRODUCERS WHO'S WHO

L'ANGÉLUS *1er cru cru classé St-Émilion*
★★★★★ Wonderful: gutsy, rich and soft.
New management has brought it to new
heights, and it was excellent even in the
difficult years of the early 1990s. 1996 is
superb, '95 even better and '97 excellent.

D'ANGLUDET *cru bourgeois Margaux*
★★★ £ Tremendous value *bourgeois* red
easily attaining Classed Growth standards.
Much of the perfume of good Margaux
without ever going through the traditional
lean period. 1983 and '90 are the finest *ever*,
'95 and '96 are worthy of their vintages.

D'ARCHE *2ème cru Sauternes* ★★★(★)
A little-known property now increasingly
highly thought of. 1983, '86, '88, '89 and '90
are good but a little over-alcoholic, perhaps.

D'ARMAILHAC *5ème cru classé Pauillac*
★★★ (formerly Mouton-Baronne-Philippe)
A red of very good balance for a Fifth
Growth, with the perfume particularly
marked. 1983 and '86 are very good, as are
'96 and (even better) '95.

AUSONE *1er grand cru classé St-Émilion*
★★★★(★) Between 1976 and 1994 the
wines were made in a very fine, understated
style. A new winemaker was appointed for
the 1995, and it's altogether gutsier. The
1985, '86, '89 and above all the '90, are
especially good, as are the '96 and '97.

BASTOR-LAMONTAGNE *cru
bourgeois Sauternes* ★★★ £ Marvellous,
widely available sweet whites. Pricy, but as
rich as many Classed Growths. 1983, '86,
'88, '89 and '90 epitomize quality Sauternes.
Nice but not thrilling since then.

BATAILLEY *5ème cru classé Pauillac*
★★★ £ The wines have been getting a lot
better. Drinkable young, they age well too.
1990 is excellent, and relatively affordable;
look out for the 1995 and 1997.

BELAIR *1er cru classé St-Émilion* ★★★★
Belair steadfastly ignores the fashion for
ever more richness, concentration and
weight, and focuses instead on seriousness
and finesse. The 1996 has lovely structure.

BEYCHEVELLE *4ème cru classé St-Julien*
★★★★ The most expensive Fourth
Growth, but deservedly so, since traditional
quality puts it alongside the top Seconds. It
takes time to mature to a beautifully
balanced, scented, blackcurranty red. 1989
and '90 are sublime, but there is still
sometimes a tendency to overproduce. '95
and '96 are both worthy of the property.

BRANAIRE *4ème cru classé St-Julien*
★★★ (formerly Branaire-Ducru) Used to
be soft, smooth red with a flavour of plums
and chocolate, achieving a classic, cedary St-
Julien perfume in maturity. The 1980s were
erratic, with dilute flavours and sometimes
unclean fruit, but 1989 and '90 saw a return
to form. Look out for the 1996.

BRANE-CANTENAC *2ème cru classé
Margaux* ★★ A big and famous property
which has been underachieving when most
of the other Second Growths have been
shooting ahead. It has missed chances to
prove itself in the last few years.

BROUSTET *2ème cru classé Barsac* ★★★
A reliable, fairly rich sweet white not often
seen, but worth trying: the 1988 and '90 are
especially good. Dry white is disappointing.

CALON-SÉGUR *3ème cru classé St-
Estèphe* ★★★(★) Intensely traditional claret
that needs time. 1982 is wonderful, if you
can find it, '95 is superb, '96 very good.

CANON *1er grand cru classé St-Émilion*
★★★★(★) Mature Canon reeks of the
soft, buttery Merlot grape as only a top St-
Émilion can. It's marvellously rich stuff,
though the 1995 is less good than the 1996.

CANON-LA-GAFFELIÈRE *1er grand cru classé St-Émilion* ★★★★(★) German owners have invested a fortune here, and everything is of the most modern, including the wine: rich, seductive, luscious. Very good 1990, '93 and '97.

CANTEMERLE *5ème cru classé Haut-Médoc* ★★★(★) Often up to Second Growth standards. Sometimes a little light, as in 1995, but it's always attractive.

CARBONNIEUX *cru classé Pessac-Léognan* ★★★(★) Rich, complex red and oaky whites. The 1996 may have the edge over the 1995, but both are good.

CHASSE-SPLEEN *cru bourgeois Moulis* ★★★(★) A tremendously consistent wine, at the top of the *bourgeois* tree. It sells above the price of many Classed Growths, but it's worth it. Look for the superb 1995 and the very good 1996 and 1997.

CHEVAL-BLANC *1er grand cru classé St-Émilion* ★★★★★ There's some sturdy richness here, but wonderful spice and fruit too, perhaps due to the very high proportion of Cabernet Franc. Good years are succulent. 1995 is as good as claret gets.

CISSAC *cru grand bourgeois Haut-Médoc* ★★★ £ Beautiful, well structured wine made in traditional, slow-maturing style, and one of the best-known *bourgeois* reds. It is best in richly ripe years like 1982 and '85. 1996 is spicy, '95 full of cassis, '97 very good.

CLIMENS *1er cru Barsac* ★★★★★ Undoubtedly the best property in Barsac, making some of the most consistently fine sweet wines in France. 1990 was the best recent year, though '91 is good, too. The delicious second wine, les Cyprès, is well worth seeking out in off vintages.

COS D'ESTOURNEL *2ème cru classé St-Estèphe* ★★★★★ £ The undoubted leader of St-Estèphe. The wines are dark, tannic and oaky: classically made for long aging. Fairly priced, too. 1995 and '96 are both lovely, and '97 looks as good.

COUHINS-LURTON *cru classé Pessac-Léognan* ★★★★ 100 per cent Sauvignon dry white fermented in new oak barrels, producing a blend of grassy fruit and oaky spice. Recent vintages have been excellent.

COUTET *1er cru Barsac* ★★(★) A great sweet wine property making wine second only to Climens in Barsac; also a dry white.

DOISY-DAËNE *2ème cru Barsac* ★★★(★) Very good, consistent, relatively light, but extrèmely attractive sweet wine, plus a particularly good dry white.

DOISY-VÉDRINES *2ème cru Barsac* ★★★★ £ A rich, concentrated sweet white which is usually good value. 1989 and '90 are very good, and '95 is good.

DOMAINE DE CHEVALIER *cru classé Pessac-Léognan* ★★★★(★) The red has a superb balance of fruit and oak, and the white is simply one of France's greatest. Very successful in 1995 and '96. Look also for the refined red and sweetly oaky white second wines, Esprit de Chevalier.

DUCRU-BEAUCAILLOU *2ème cru classé St-Julien* ★★★(★) Great depth and warmth, and lovely balance. Back on form again after a few problematic years in the late '80s: '95, '96 and '97 are excellent.

L'ÉVANGILE *Pomerol* ★★★(★) Topline Pomerol, lacking the sheer intensity of its neighbour Pétrus, but most irresistibly perfumed and rich. Always in huge demand, so it's expensive. 1993 was very good; 1997 also looks terrific.

DE FARGUES *cru bourgeois Sauternes* ★★★★(★) Stunning, rich wines in the best years. Sells at exactly half the price of Yquem, so it ain't cheap.

DE FIEUZAL *cru classé Pessac-Léognan*
★★★★(★) One of the stars of Pessac-Léognan, the white only just behind Domaine de Chevalier. The red starts plum-rich and buttery, but develops earthiness and cedar scent allied to lovely fruit. The 1995 and 1996 are equally good. The unclassified white is scented, complex, deep and exciting. Even the '92 is good.

FIGEAC *1er grand cru classé St-Émilion*
★★★★ Figeac shares many of the qualities of Cheval Blanc but it's always ranked as the ever-reliable star of the second team. A pity, as it's beauty and blackcurranty, minty scent are rare in St-Émilion. Already seductive '89 and '90, tremendous '95, excellent '96.

FILHOT *2ème cru Sauternes* ★★(★) The wines are fairly light, and not particularly complex, although Crème de Tête, made in the best years like 1990, is a winner.

LA FLEUR-PÉTRUS *Pomerol* ★★★★
This red is in the top flight, having some of the mineral roughness of much Pomerol, but also tremendous perfume and length. The 1989 is excellent, as is the 1996, and the 1995 is not far behind.

FOURCAS-DUPRÉ *cru bourgeois Listrac*
★★(★) A top performer in this generally underperforming AC: tough and closed when young, but opening up beautifully into rich fruit and spice. Look for the 1995.

FOURCAS-HOSTEN *cru bourgeois Listrac* ★★(★) Slightly better than its very good neighbour, Fourcas-Dupré, and making wines in a similarly long-lived style. All the nineties vintages have been good.

GAZIN *Pomerol* ★★★★ Lovely perfume and sweetness. 1989 and '90 are really very fine. 1995 is first rate, even better than the very good 1996. 1993 is drinking beautifully.

GILETTE *cru bourgeois Sauternes* ★★★★
Remarkable property which ages its sweet

whites in concrete tanks for 20 to 30 years before releasing them. Usually delicious, with a dry richness unique in Sauternes thanks to long maturation and absence of wood. The wines come in different quality levels, of which Crème de Tête is the top.

GISCOURS *3ème cru classé Margaux*
★★★ Right back on form, with exceedingly nice wines in '91, '92 and '93, and considerable stylishness in 1995 and '96. The eighties were difficult here, but the château seems to have found its old consistency again.

GLORIA *cru bourgeois St-Julien* ★★★
The quality of this quick-maturing red has not always lived up to its hype. But 1995 is super, '96 is very good and '94 is good for the vintage. Gloria is never cheap, though.

GRAND-PUY-DUCASSE *5ème cru classé Pauillac* ★★★ £ Nice, but lagging far behind Grand-Puy-Lacoste in quality.

GRAND-PUY-LACOSTE *5ème cru classé Pauillac* ★★★★ £ Perfume, power and consistency: Pauillac at its brilliant best. Blackcurrant and cigar-box perfumes are rarely in better harmony than here. Consistent even in the poor years of the early nineties. 1989 is gorgeously perfumed with robust fruit, and '90 and '96 are super.

GRUAUD-LAROSE *2ème cru classé St-Julien* ★★★★(★) Often starts rich, chunky and sweetish but will achieve its full cedary glory in time, while still retaining a lovely sweet centre. The early nineties were all good, '90 was almost unnervingly juicy and ripe and '95, '96 and '97 are on form.

GUIRAUD *1er cru Sauternes* ★★★★(★)
The wines are difficult to taste when young but are very special, and the 1983, '86, '88, '89 and '90 are going to be outstanding.

HAUT-BAILLY *cru classé Pessac-Léognan* ★★★★ Haut-Bailly red (there is no white) tastes sweet, rich and perfumed from its youth. But the wines do age well. 1993 was outstanding for the year, and '95 and '96 are both terrific.

HAUT-BATAILLEY *5ème cru classé Pauillac* ★★★ Stylish, relatively light wine, although 1989 is marvellously concentrated. 1986 and '88 are the best of earlier wines; '95 and '96 look very promising.

HAUT-BRION *1er cru classé Pessac-Léognan* ★★★★★ The wines are not big, but are almost creamy in their gorgeous ripe taste, slightly resembling the great Médocs. Although 1982 is insubstantial, the next four vintages are all very fine, and '88 and '89 are outstanding, while '90 could not quite compete. 1996 is outstanding, '95 even better. 1997 is very good. Also makes a little fine, long-lived white (appealing when young, too). '85 and '94 are spectacular.

D'ISSAN *3ème cru classé Margaux* ★★★★ One of the truest Margaux wines, austere when young, but perfumed and deep after ten to 12 years. Fabulous in 1983, '88 and '90, first rate in '85 and '86, with a good '87 too. 1989 has excellent fruit, while '90 is a star, as are '95 and '96.

KIRWAN *3ème cru classé Margaux* ★★★★ Hugely improved, thanks largely to the efforts of oenologist Michel Rolland. Riper, richer – you name it.

LAFAURIE-PEYRAGUEY *1er cru Sauternes* ★★★★(★) Fine sweet wine property back on form. Good in difficult years, and stunning in '83, '86, '88 and '90; 1997 also looks very good.

LAFITE-ROTHSCHILD *1er cru classé Pauillac* ★★★★★ Most difficult of all the great Médocs to get to know. It doesn't stand for power like Latour, or perfume like Mouton, but for the elegant, restrained balance that is the perfection of great claret. 1986, '88, '89, '90, '95 and '96 are the best recent vintages, followed by '82.

LAFLEUR *Pomerol* ★★★★★ The only Pomerol with the potential to be as great as Pétrus. They couldn't be further apart in style, and Lafleur has an astonishing austere concentration of dark fruit and tobacco spice perfume. The 1982 almost knocks you sideways with its naked power, and the '83 and '85 are also remarkable. 1989 is superb, as is '95, and '96 is almost as good.

LAFON-ROCHET *4ème cru classé St-Estèphe* ★★★(★) Much improved, with as much body and a little more perfume than most. 1982, '83 and '85 are all good, though not stunning, while '86, '87, '88, '89 and '90 show real class and a welcome consistency of style. 1995, '96 and '97 are impressive.

LAGRANGE *3ème cru classé St-Julien* ★★★(★) Impressive, but not quite great: the vineyard is not one of St-Julien's best, but there is masses of technical expertise. Look particularly for the 1995 and 1996.

LA LAGUNE *3ème cru classé Haut-Médoc* ★★★★ Making Second Growth-standard red, with a rich, soft intensity. The wine was consistently good, until the disappointing 1994. The 1982 is rich and juicy, with '85 and '88 not far behind, and '83 on their tails. 1986 is burly but brilliant stuff, as is '89. 1987 is more delicate but good. 1995 and '96 are back on form.

LAMOTHE-GUIGNARD *2ème cru Sauternes* ★★★ Recent years have seen dramatic improvements here. 1983, '86, '88, '89 and '90 show how good it can be.

LANESSAN *cru bourgeois Haut-Médoc* ★★★ Ever correct, consistently attractive. 1982, '83 and '88 are exhibiting classic claret flavours now, and '90 is a wine of balance and depth. Very promising 1995 and 1996.

LANGOA-BARTON *3ème cru classé St-Julien* ★★★★ £ Very good, in the dry, cedary style, and sometimes regarded as a lesser version of Léoville-Barton. The wine has character and style, and is reasonably priced. 1982 and '85 are exciting, '86 and '87 typical, but the '88 may be the best for 30 years. The '89 and '96 almost matched Léoville-Barton for elegance and '90 and '95 were its equal. 1997 looks good.

LARRIVET-HAUT-BRION *Pessac-Léognan* ★★★★ The red 1996 here shows a transformation: superb wine, with lots of finesse. Lovely white, too.

LASCOMBES *2ème cru classé Margaux* ★★★ Very attractive early on, but can gain flesh and character with age. 1986 is the most serious effort for a long time. '89, '90 and '95 keep up the good work; '96 doesn't seem quite so good, but '97 is better.

LATOUR *1er cru classé Pauillac* ★★★★★ The easiest of all the First Growths to comprehend. It's a huge, dark, hard brute when young, calming down as it ages and eventually spreading out to a superb, blackcurrant and cedar flavour. It used to take ages to come round, but some recent vintages have seemed a little softer and lighter, whilst retaining their tremendous core of fruit. Let's hope they age as well as the previous ones, because although the '82 is a classic, both '81 and '83 are definitely not. '86 and '88 seem to be back on course, and '89 and '90 look splendidly powerful. The '91 and '92 are the best wines of their years, as is the superb 1996. The second wine, les Forts-de-Latour, is getting better and better. A third wine, Pauillac de Latour, is made in most years.

LAVILLE-HAUT-BRION *cru classé Pessac-Léognan* ★★★★ This should be one of the greatest of all white Pessac-Léognan, since it is owned by Haut-Brion, but despite some great successes, the general effect is patchy. But 1992 and 1993 are wonderful.

LÉOVILLE-BARTON *2ème cru classé St-Julien* ★★★★★ £ Traditionalist's dream. Anthony Barton ignores fashion and simply

goes on making superlative, old-fashioned wine for long aging. All the vintages of the 1980s have been attractive, and '95, '96 and '97 are tremendous. 1991, '92 and '93 are also among the best of their vintages. All the wines are *wonderfully* fairly priced.

LÉOVILLE-LAS-CASES *2ème cru classé St-Julien* ★★★★★ The most brilliant of the St-Juliens, combining all that sweet, honeyed ripeness with strong, dry, cedary perfume. The 1982 is more exciting every time a bottle is broached, and all the vintages of the 1980s are top examples of their year. The 1995 is wonderful, the '96 nearly as good, and prices are startlingly high. The second wine, Clos du Marquis, is better than most Classed Growths.

LÉOVILLE-POYFERRÉ *2ème cru classé St-Julien* ★★★★ Things have been looking up here for some while, and 1995 is wonderful. The 1994 is remarkably good and 1996, too, is extremely attractive.

LILIAN-LADOUYS *cru bourgeois St-Estèphe* ★★(★) A newish property created with huge investment and a degree of hype, but the wines are certainly promising, with a good 1989 and '90. 1995 is good, 1996 seems a bit muddy but '97 is good again.

LOUDENNE *cru bourgeois Médoc* ★(★) Both red and white are fruity and agreeable, and best drunk young.

LA LOUVIÈRE *cru bourgeois Pessac-Léognan* ★★★★ Lovely, modern, oak-aged whites. Reds are also very good, and quite earthy. Quality seems to be on a roll.

LYNCH-BAGES *5ème cru classé Pauillac* ★★★★★ Astonishingly soft and drinkable when very young, yet it ages brilliantly, and has one of the most beautiful scents of minty blackcurrant in all Bordeaux. Most likely to show that character are '83, '86 and '87, but for sheer starry-eyed brilliance '85, '88 and particularly '82, '95 and '96 are the ones. The '89 is unusually big and powerful; the '90 marginally more restrained.

MAGDELAINE *1er grand cru classé St-Émilion* ★★★★ Combines the soft richness of Merlot with the sturdiness needed to age. Expensive, but one of the best. 1982, '85 and '95 are classics, '88, '89 and '96 tremendously good.

MALARTIC-LAGRAVIÈRE *cru classé Pessac-Léognan* ★★★ Improving under its new ownership, but still a tough, traditional style. '95 and '96 show the direction.

MALESCOT-ST-EXUPÉRY *3ème cru classé Margaux* ★★(★) Seemed to have lost its way in the '80s: the wines were becoming too light. Improved in '88, '89 and '90, and continued with a very good 1995.

DE MALLE *2ème cru Sauternes* ★★★ Good, relatively light sweet white. It went through a bad patch in the 1980s, but since '88 the wines have been back on course.

MARGAUX *1er cru classé Margaux* ★★★★★ Refinement and sheer, ravishing perfume: weightier and more consistent than in the past, yet with all its beauty intact. 1982, '83 and '86 are about as brilliant as claret can be, while the '88 may well be the wine of the vintage. The deep, concentrated '89 doesn't seem to match up to the '88, but the '90 is as fragrant and powerful as the '86 – which is saying a lot. In the difficult '91 and '92 vintages the wines were better than most First Growths, and the '95 is stunning.

MEYNEY *cru bourgeois St-Estèphe* ★★★(★) £ This epitomizes St-Estèphe reliability, yet is better than that. It is big, meaty and strong, but never harsh. Recent wines are increasingly impressive, and although it is difficult to taste young, the '82, '83, '85, '86, '88 and '89 are all remarkable, and the '84, '87 and '90 are good. The 1995 is lovely, 1996 seems a touch disappointing.

LA MISSION-HAUT-BRION *cru classé Pessac-Léognan* ★★★★ La Mission likes to put itself in a class apart, between Haut-Brion and the rest. Yet one often feels this red relies more on weight and massive, dark fruit and oak flavours than on any great subtleties. Even so it has considerable richness, and 1982, 1985, 1986, 1989, 1990, 1991 and 1995 are the best of recent vintages.

MONTROSE *2ème cru classé St-Estèphe* ★★★★ Famous for its dark, tannic character, and its slow, ponderous march to maturity. 1989 and '90, and even '91 and '92, saw a return to form after some lightish years. 1995, 1996 and 1997 are excellent.

MOUTON-ROTHSCHILD *1er cru classé Pauillac* ★★★★★ An astonishing flavour, piling intense cigar-box and lead-pencil perfume on to the rich blackcurrant fruit. The 1982 is already a legend, '86 and '89 are likely to join it, and '83, '84 and '85 are well worth the asking price. 1988 and '90 are below par, but the '95 is fabulous.

NENIN *Pomerol* ★★ A thoroughly old-fashioned red, rather chunky and solid with quite a tough core for a Pomerol, which doesn't always attain mellow fruitfulness. The 1985 and '86 aren't bad, but the '82, the '83 and the '88 were pretty feeble here. Recent vintages have improved, though, with a much better 1995 and 1996.

PALMER *3ème cru classé Margaux* ★★★★ Palmer can occasionally out-perform some First Growths in tastings. The 1980s weren't so good, and the '83 lacks some of its neighbours' class. But in 1990 it was better than most of them, and '96 and '97 are very good.

PAPE-CLÉMENT *cru classé Pessac-Léognan* ★★★★(★) Capable of mixing considerable sweetness from ripe fruit and new oak with a good deal of tough structure. Outstanding since 1985, with the 1990 and 1995 both examples of Pessac-Léognan at its best.

PAVIE *1er grand cru St-Émilion* ★★★★ Until recently good but not wonderful, stylish but not grand. But it has the gentle flavours of true St-Émilion and recent releases show a deeper, more passionate style which puts it into the top flight. 1985, '86, '87, '88, '89, '90, '95 and '96 are good examples of the new, '82 of the old.

PETIT-VILLAGE *Pomerol* ★★★★ Not usually one of the softest, most plummy Pomerols. The wine is worth laying down, but the price is always high. 1983, '85 and the juicy '82 are all very good, but the '88, '89, '90 and '95 look likely to be the best yet.

PÉTRUS *Pomerol* ★★★★★ One of the world's most expensive reds, and often one of the greatest. Astonishingly, its fame has only been acquired since 1945. Christian Moueix says his intention is to ensure no bottle of Pétrus ever disappoints. 1982, '89, '90 and '95 were stupendously great. and 1985 and '96 aren't far off.

ON THE CASE
For current drinking, look for the best 1993s and good petits châteaux from 1994; 1995s, 1996s and 1997s still need some time to mature

DE PEZ *cru bourgeois St-Estèphe* ★★★ Famous *bourgeois* châteaux, almost always up to Classed Growth standard: big, reliable, rather plummy and not too harsh. 1982 and '83 and the excellent '86 are the sort of thing. 1995 and 1996 are both successful.

PHÉLAN-SÉGUR *cru bourgeois St-Estèphe* ★★★ £ Classed Growth quality at a *bourgeois* price. Good rich fruit, and it ages well. 1995 and '96 are well worth a punt.

PICHON-LONGUEVILLE *2ème cru classé Pauillac* ★★★★(★) Often described as more masculine than its 'sister', Pichon-Longueville-Lalande, this very correct Pauillac (formerly Pichon-Longueville-Baron) turned out a tremendous 1995, a very good 1996 and '97 and a good 1994. The '87 was very good, the '88 superb, the '89 even better, broodingly intense, while the '90 is one of the Médoc's greatest.

PICHON-LONGUEVILLE-LALANDE *2ème cru classé Pauillac* ★★★★(★) Rich, concentrated red of great quality. Its price has risen inexorably and it wishes to be seen as equal to St-Julien's leading pair, Léoville-Las-Cases and Ducru-Beaucaillou. 1982, '83, '85 and '86 all brim with exciting flavours. '87 and '88 are good, but both '89 and '90 are below par, and outclassed by its neighbour Pichon-Longueville. But since then Lalande has been right back on form, and seems to have the edge on Longueville in '95 and '96.

LE PIN *Pomerol* ★★★★★ This is it: the most expensive red wine in the world. Is it the best? Well, it's very, very good, and utterly seductive. It's tiny — less than two

CLARETS OUT OF THEIR CLASS

One of the great excitements in wine is to catch a château at the beginning of a revival in its fortunes. While reputations are being built or re-built, quality keeps ahead of the price for a while – though some wines have maintained high quality at fair prices year after year. For good value, look out for the names below.

Médoc *Minor châteaux performing like top bourgeois:* Tour-de-By, Tour Haut-Caussan, Tour du Haut-Moulin, Tour-St-Bonnet.

Top bourgeois performing like Classed Growths: d'Angludet, Chasse-Spleen, Citran, Fourcas-Dupré, Fourcas-Hosten, Haut-Marbuzet, Labégorce-Zédé, Lanessan, Meyney, Monbrison, Ormes-de-Pez, Phélan-Ségur, Pibran, Potensac, Poujeaux, Siran, Sociando-Mallet, Tour-de-Mons.

Classed Growths performing above their station: Clerc-Milon-Rothschild, Cos d'Estournel, Ducru-Beaucaillou, Grand-Puy-Lacoste, la Lagune, Léoville-Barton, Léoville-Las-Cases, Lynch-Bages, Montrose, Pichon-Longueville, Pichon-Lalande, Pontet-Canet, Rauzan-Ségla.

Graves and Pessac-Léognan
Outperformers: White: de Fieuzal, Montalivet, Olivier, Smith-Haut-Lafitte. *Red:* de Fieuzal, Haut-Bailly, Larrivet-Haut-Brion, la Tour-Martillac, Pape-Clément, Roquetaillade la Grange.

Pomerol
Outperformers: Beauregard, Bon-Pasteur, Certan-de-May, Clinet, l'Église-Clinet, l'Évangile, Gazin, Vieux Château Certan.

St-Émilion
Outperformers: l'Arrosée, Beau-Séjour-Bécot, Bellefont-Belcier, la Dominique, Grand-Mayne, Larmande, Pavie-Macquin, Tertre Rôteboeuf, Troplong-Mondot.

Sauternes
Outperformers: Bastor-Lamontagne, Chartreuse, Climens, Doisy-Daëne, de Fargues, Gilette, Liot, de Malle, Nairac, Roumieu Lacoste, St-Amand.

Satellites
Outperformers: Canon de Brem, Canon Moueix, Charlemagne, Cassagne-Haut-Canon – *Canon-Fronsac*; Lyonnat – *Lussac-St-Émilion*; Tour-du-Pas-St-Georges – *St-Georges-St-Émilion*; la Prade, de Francs – *Côte de Francs*; des Annereaux, Bertineau-St-Vincent – *Lalande-de-Pomerol*.

---

hectares carved out in the late '70s – and it reached cult status only in the late '80s. If you didn't buy it then you probably can't afford it now. 1997 is lovely, though.

PONTET-CANET *5ème cru classé Pauillac* ★★★ Famous but unpredictable, and still trying to regain its traditionally reliable form. The 1985 and '86 are hopeful, '87 and '88 less so, '90 hopeful again, and '95 and '97 very good.

POTENSAC *cru bourgeois Médoc* ★★★(★) £ Delicious, blackcurrant fruit, greatly improved by a strong taste of oak. Not expensive for the quality. Beats many *crus classés* every year for sheer flavour. Both the 1995 and '96 look good buys.

POUJEAUX *cru bourgeois Moulis* ★★(★) Good spicy, rich wine with plenty of concentration; made to last. 1990, '93, '94, '95 and '97 are all excellent.

PRIEURÉ-LICHINE *4ème cru classé Margaux* ★★★ Reliable, fairly priced and, though not that perfumed, good and sound. 1983, '86, '88 and '89 are good, but '90 was the first real excitement for some time. Further improved in '91 and '92; now on top form with good '94, better '95 and '96.

RABAUD-PROMIS *1er cru Sauternes* ★★★(★) At last! The 1986, '88, '89 and '90 are excellent and show a long-awaited return to First Growth sweet wine quality.

RAHOUL *cru bourgeois Graves* ★★(★) A leader of the modern oak-aged white style, and generally good red. 1988, '89 and '90 were not as special as previous years, but still good. The mid-'90s have been better.

RAUZAN-GASSIES *2ème cru classé Margaux* ★★(★) For years was leagues below most Second and Third Growth reds in quality, but a good 1995 and '96 suggest that attitudes here could be changing.

RAUZAN-SÉGLA *2ème cru classé Margaux* ★★★★(★) 1983, '85 and '86 were triumphs. 1987 was declassified as Château Lamouroux but is still delicious. The '88, '89, '90, '93 and '94 are all very good. 1996 wasn't quite as good as it should have been, but '95 was excellent.

RAYMOND LAFON *cru bourgeois Sauternes* ★★★★ Owned by the former manager of neighbouring d'Yquem, this is fine wine but overpriced.

RIEUSSEC *1er cru Sauternes* ★★★★(★) One of the richest, most exotic Sauternes; the property made particularly good wines during the 1980s. The 1982 is good, the '83, '86 and '88 really special, the '89 and '90 wonderful. 1997 looks good, too.

ST-AMAND *cru bourgeois Sauternes* ★★★(★) **£** Splendid property making truly rich wines that age well, and are affordable. Also seen as Château de la Chartreuse.

> ### ON THE CASE
> With little really good Sauternes made after 1990 until 1996 and 1997, expect high prices for the latter two vintages when they come on stream

ST-PIERRE *4ème cru classé Médoc* ★★★★ Small St-Julien property producing superb, slow-maturing, old-fashioned red. Produced wonderful wines in the 1980s, and judging by 1995 and 1996 is still well on form.

DE SALES *Pomerol* ★★★ **£** A really enormous estate producing a wine which, though it is good round claret, doesn't often excite. 1995 and '96 are, well, respectable.

SÉNÉJAC *cru bourgeois Haut-Médoc* ★★(★) Finesse rather than concentration. It made an excellent 1995 and has in fact been good pretty well every year. The white, made entirely from Sémillon, will age.

SIRAN *cru bourgeois Margaux* ★★★ All vintages have been good lately, and 1995 and 1996 look well worth buying.

SMITH-HAUT-LAFITTE *cru classé Pessac-Léognan* ★★★★ Increasingly concentrated reds and whites that are benefiting from huge investment. All nineties vintages have been terrific.

SUDUIRAUT *1er cru Sauternes* ★★★(★) Rich, exciting Sauternes, frequently deeper and more intense than any except d'Yquem. A remarkable 1982 was followed by a fine '83, a very good '85, but disappointing '86 and '88. '89 and '90 were a leap up again and '95 looks good.

TALBOT *4ème cru classé St-Julien* ★★★ Has seemed in recent years to be lagging behind in quality. The mid- to late 1980s vintages haven't shaped up as well as they should have done, with the 1988 in particular showing poorly (though the '82, '83 and '84 were very good). The '90 seems to lack concentration, and the early '90s are disappointing. 1995 and '96 look better.

DU TERTRE *5ème cru classé Margaux* ★★★(★) Slightly uneven of late. At best it has a lot of body for a Margaux, and the flavour is direct and pure. 1985 is rich and dense but keeps its perfume intact, while '86, '83 and '82 are rich and blackcurranty – already good and sure to improve for ten years more. 1988 was not quite so good, for some reason, but '89 was back to normal. 1995 was a disappointing effort in a very good year; '96 an improvement.

LA TOUR-DE-BY *cru bourgeois Médoc* ★★★ Well-made: plenty of juicy fruit, good structure and a touch of rusticity. Increasingly reliable: look for '95, '96, '97.

TROTANOY *Pomerol* ★★★★ If you didn't know Pétrus existed, you'd say this had to be the perfect Pomerol – rich, plummy, chocolaty fruit, some mineral

hardness, and tremendous fat perfume. The 1982 is brilliant, and although the '85 is also wonderfully good, the mid- and late 1980s weren't quite as thrilling. 1992 and '93 were good in difficult years; '95 is glorious.

VALANDRAUD *St-Émilion* ★★★★ Super-rich wine for the super-rich. The idea at this micro-property is to do everything with extreme care. How the wines will age is unproven, since the first vintage was '91.

VIEUX CHÂTEAU CERTAN *Pomerol* ★★★★★ Practically as good as Pétrus, but more austere in style. 1995 is terrific, 1996 very good, 1997 lovely.

D'YQUEM *grand 1er cru classé Sauternes* ★★★★★ The pinnacle of achievement in great sweet wines. Almost every vintage of d'Yquem is a masterpiece and its outlandish price is almost justified, since d'Yquem at its best is undoubtedly the greatest sweet wine in the world. And it lasts – well, forever, really. There's also a dry white made here, called Ygrec, which can be remarkable.

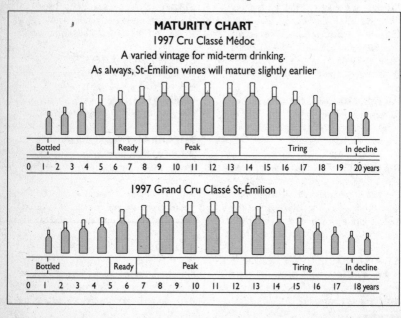

MATURITY CHART
1997 Cru Classé Médoc
A varied vintage for mid-term drinking.
As always, St-Émilion wines will mature slightly earlier

| Bottled | Ready | Peak | Tiring | In decline |

0 1 2 3 4 5 6 7 8 9 10 11 12 13 14 15 16 17 18 19 20 years

1997 Grand Cru Classé St-Émilion

| Bottled | Ready | Peak | Tiring | In decline |

0 1 2 3 4 5 6 7 8 9 10 11 12 13 14 15 16 17 18 years

BORDEAUX VINTAGES

Generic wines like Bordeaux Rouge rarely need any aging. A *petit château* wine from a good vintage might need five years to be at its best, a good *bourgeois* might need ten, and a *premier cru* might need 20. Pomerols and St-Émilions come round faster than Médocs.

1998   A Merlot year rather than a Cabernet one; Pomerol and St-Émilion look very good. There'll be some good Sauternes, too.

1997   A mixed vintage of mostly soft, ripe wines, attractive for relatively early drinking: a good year, but not as good as 1996, which isn't as good as 1995. Being overhyped.

1996   The 1994s were hyped, the 1995s were hyped, and the 1996s too. Increasingly they look good but not great, and they're certainly expensive. Sauternes are good in parts.

1995   Red wines of charm and structure, with a handful of really great wines at the top. Not much noble rot in Sauternes, though the dry whites of the Graves look good.

1994   Most successful in Pomerol, though most regions produced reds with good concentration, but often not much more.

1993   A dilute year, in which the good wines are drinking nicely now. St-Émilion and Pomerol are probably best. Decent dry whites but little of quality in Sauternes.

1992   An unripe vintage: stick to reliable names and drink early. Even better, pick another vintage. Oddly enough there are some nice simple wines in Fronsac.

1991   Wildly variable for reds, and few thrills in Sauternes. Dry whites were good. Most should have been drunk by now.

1990   Excellent quality; the third of a great trio of vintages. Reds are immensely rich, as are Sauternes; lesser regions like Monbazillac and Loupiac also came up trumps. It was a bit too hot for the dry whites, though.

1989   A wonderful Médoc year, although Pomerol and St-Émilion also did well. Graves and Pessac-Léognan were somewhat uneven, as was Sauternes (though good at their best). Dry whites were rather overripe.

1988   Classically balanced reds and very fine Sauternes.

1987   These have proved to be soft, wonderfully drinkable reds – but drink them now: they won't keep. Dry whites were better than sweet; again, they need drinking.

1986   Superb Sauternes, dripping with noble rot, and drinking beautifully now. Reds are good, sometimes very good, but not quite as good as 1988.

1985   Pretty well all the reds are delicious now. Sauternes are pleasant but light.

1984   A fruitless, joyless year in which the Merlot failed.

1983   Classics, especially in Margaux, and delicious now. Superb rich, exciting Sauternes: the beginning of the great 1980s Sauternes revival.

1982   Fabulous fat, ripe, juicy wines. The best still need a year or two; some of the lesser wines are lovely now and shouldn't be kept much longer. Sauternes was mixed in quality.

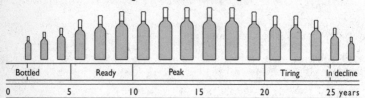

MATURITY CHART
1995 Cru Classé Médoc
A vintage for the medium to long term

| Bottled | | Ready | | Peak | | | Tiring | In decline |

| 0 | 5 | 10 | 15 | 20 | 25 years |

1995 Good Cru Bourgeois Médoc

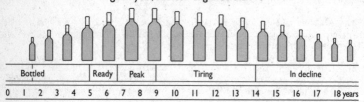

| Bottled | Ready | | Peak | | | Tiring | | In decline |

| 0 | 1 | 2 | 3 | 4 | 5 | 6 | 7 | 8 | 9 | 10 | 11 | 12 | 13 | 14 | 15 | 16 | 17 | 18 years |

1996 Cru Classé Médoc
A good year, but less long-lived than 95

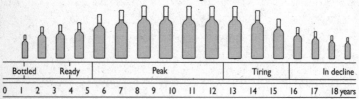

| Bottled | | Ready | Peak | Tiring | | In decline |

| 0 | 1 | 2 | 3 | 4 | 5 | 6 | 7 | 8 | 9 | 10 | 11 | 12 | 13 | 14 | 15 | 16 | 17 | 18 years |

1996 Good Cru Bourgeois Médoc

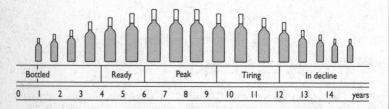

| Bottled | | Ready | | Peak | | Tiring | | In decline |

| 0 | 1 | 2 | 3 | 4 | 5 | 6 | 7 | 8 | 9 | 10 | 11 | 12 | 13 | 14 | years |

EARLIER BORDEAUX VINTAGES

1981 Good but not spectacular. Quite light wines, which need drinking. A slightly graceless year in Sauternes.

1980 Nice light, grassy claret, which should have been drunk by now. The best Sauternes are still drinking well.

1979 All but the very best should be drunk up. There was attractive, mid-weight Sauternes.

1978 All but the top wines are starting to dry out now. Graves and St-Émilion are lovely, and won't improve.

1976 Rather soft and sweet; not inspiring, drink up. Best Sauternes are still fat and rich.

1975 Very tannic wines; frequently they went stale and brown before they had time to soften. The best may yet bloom; I'm not sure when. Nice, well-balanced Sauternes.

1966 All the wines are ready, and some are tipping over the edge.

1961 One of the classic vintages of the century, but now beginning to fade a little. Well, they had an amazing innings.

Most other vintages of the 1960s will now be risky; '64s can still be good, rather solid wines and '62, one of the most gorgeous, fragrant vintages since the war, is showing its age. If your godfather's treating you, and offers '59, '55 or '53, accept with enthusiasm. If he offers you '49, '47 or '45, get it in writing before be begins to change his mind.

MATURITY CHART
1990 Cru Classé Sauternes
May turn out to be one of the greatest vintages of the century

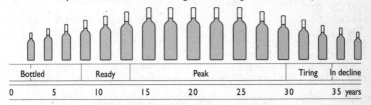

| Bottled | Ready | Peak | Tiring | In decline |

| 0 | 5 | 10 | 15 | 20 | 25 | 30 | 35 years |

1995 Cru Classé White Pessac-Léognan

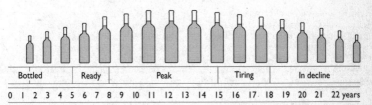

| Bottled | Ready | Peak | Tiring | In decline |

| 0 | 1 | 2 | 3 | 4 | 5 | 6 | 7 | 8 | 9 | 10 | 11 | 12 | 13 | 14 | 15 | 16 | 17 | 18 | 19 | 20 | 21 | 22 years |

RED BORDEAUX PRICES

l'Abbaye *Puisseguin-St-Émilion*
1996 £9.95 (LEA)

d'Aiguilhe *Côtes de Castillon*
1994 £7.69 (NLW) £8.49 (VIC) £8.49 (THR)
   £8.49 (WR) £8.49 (BOT)

Amiral-de-Beychevelle *St-Julien*
1988 £21.85 (WRI)

Angélus *1er grand cru classé St-Émilion*
1997 £70.30 (CB)
1997 IB £500.00 (FA) £594.00 (RAE)
1996 £50.27 (BIB) £60.95 (LAY) £63.33 (MI)
1996 IB £500.00 (BIB) £520.00 (FA)
   £600.00 (FRI) £700.00 (CAV)
1995 IB £650.00 (BIB) £725.00 (FA)
1994 £65.00 (BAL)
1994 IB £480.00 (FA) £695.00 (CAV)
1990 £129.25 (WY) £138.40 (BIB)
1990 IB £1,200.00 (FA) £1,200.00 (CAV)
1989 £84.55 (BIB) £111.63 (CAV)
1989 IB £850.00 (FA) £850.00 (BIB)
1988 £59.09 (BIB) £69.00 (BAL)
1986 IB £380.00 (FA) £380.00 (BIB)
1985 £42.44 (BIB) £93.00 (UB)
1982 £54.19 (BIB)
1959 £146.88 (WY)

d'Angludet *cru bourgeois supérieur*
   exceptionnel Margaux
1997 £119.00 (TAN)
1997 EC £109.90 (HAH)
1996 £15.50 (FLE) £22.10 (TAN)
1995 £19.95 (CON) £20.20 (TAN)
1994 £11.75 (JER) £16.25 (HIG) £16.99
   (AME) £20.00 (FORT) £20.40 (TAN)
1990 £25.00 (WS) £37.70 (JER) £47.00 (UB)

1988 £34.27 (JER)
1986 £31.00 (CRO) £40.00 (FORT)
1983 £44.95 (ROB)
1982 £34.00 (BAL) £34.66 (REI)
1978 £42.00 (CRO)

des Annereaux *Lalande-de-Pomerol*
1996 £12.20 (PLAY)
1995 £9.25 (CON) £10.50 (ROB)
1994 £8.99 (POR)

Anthonic *cru bourgeois supérieur Moulis*
1997 £13.97 (PLA)
1996 £10.80 (CB)
1995 £11.40 (CB)
1990 £18.00 (CRO)

d'Armailhac (was Mouton-Baronne-
   Philippe) *5ème cru classé Pauillac*
1996 £19.17 (MI) £19.30 (TAN) £19.50 (HIG)
1995 IB £180.00 (FA)
1994 £22.95 (AD)
1990 £27.00 (FLE)
1989 £49.00 (UB)
1986 IB £350.00 (CAV)
1961 £135.13 (WY)
1945 £464.13 (WY)

Arnauld *Haut-Médoc*
1996 EC £70.00 (HA)
1995 £11.95 (ROB)

l'Arrosée *grand cru classé St-Émilion*
1996 £30.00 (MI) £34.00 (JU) £35.00 (WS)
1996 IB £280.00 (CAV)
1995 £29.00 (JU)
1994 £20.00 (MI) £21.00 (WS) £23.00 (JU)
1994 IB £180.00 (FA) £192.00 (RAE)

MERCHANTS SPECIALIZING IN BORDEAUX
see Merchant Directory (page 413) for details

Adnams (AD), Averys of Bristol (AV),
Ballantynes (BAL), Bennetts (BEN), Berry
Bros. & Rudd (BER), Bibendum (BIB), Butlers
Wine Cellar (BU), Anthony Byrne (BY), Cave
Cru Classé (CAV), Châteaux Wines (CHA),
Corney & Barrow (CB), Croque-en-Bouche
(CRO), Direct Wine (DI), Farr Vintners (FA),
First Quench Group (BOT, THR, VIC, WR),
Fortnum & Mason (FORT), Friarwood (FRI),
Gelston Castle, Goedhuis, Great Western
(GW), John Harvey (HA), High Breck (HIG),
Justerini & Brooks (JU), Lay & Wheeler (LAY),
Millésima (MI), Montrachet (MON), Oddbins
(OD), Thos. Peatling, Christopher Piper (PIP),
Raeburn Fine Wines (RAE), Reid (REI), T&W
(TW), Tanners (TAN), Ubiquitous Chip (UB),
Wine Society (WS), Peter Wylie (WY), Noel
Young (YOU).

1989 IB £280.00 (FA)
1988 £34.00 (CRO)
1985 £58.75 (WY) £79.50 (BAL)
1982 £82.00 (BAL)

Ausone *1er grand cru classé St-Émilion*
1997 IB £1,320.00 (CB)
1996 £150.40 (CB) £177.50 (MI)
1996 IB £1,200.00 (FA) £1,220.00 (BIB)
1995 £143.30 (BIB) £220.00 (JU)
1995 IB £1,450.00 (BIB) £1,500.00 (FA)
1994 £139.17 (MI)
1994 IB £720.00 (FA)
1990 £118.82 (BIB) £241.67 (MI)
1989 IB £850.00 (FA) £900.00 (BIB)
1988 £64.96 (BIB) £95.00 (CON)
1986 £64.63 (REI) £69.86 (BIB)
1985 £95.96 (FRI) £149.99 (PLAY)
1985 IB £850.00 (FA) £850.00 (BIB)
1983 £87.48 (BIB) £88.00 (CRO)
1982 £185.00 (JU) £223.25 (CAV)
1982 IB £1,600.00 (BIB)
1979 £120.00 (ROB)
1970 IB £1,100.00 (CAV)
1961 IB £3,000.00 (FA)

Bahans-Haut-Brion Graves
1995 £24.00 (JU)
1995 IB £220.00 (WY)
1989 ½ bottle IB £480.00 (FA)

Balestard-la-Tonnelle *grand cru classé St-Émilion*
1995 £22.95 (RES)

Baret *Pessac-Léognan*
1996 £11.75 (HIG)

Barreyres *cru bourgeois Haut-Médoc*
1995 £7.52 (CB)
1959 £41.13 (REI)

Batailley *5ème cru classé Pauillac*
1996 £16.95 (DI) £17.50 (HIG)
1996 EC £165.00 (ELL)
1995 £15.00 (FLE) £16.92 (STE) £18.80 (NA)
    £19.58 (HIG)
1995 IB £187.00 (ELL)
1994 £15.45 (BER) £21.95 (RES)
1989 £30.85 (WRI) £32.72 (PLAY)
1985 £74.00 (UB)
1982 £32.99 (YOU) £33.49 (REI)
1970 £27.50 (BU) £31.00 (CRO) £52.88
    (TW)
1961 £70.50 (WY)

Beau-Séjour-Bécot *1er grand cru classé St-Émilion*
1997 IB £325.00 (CB) £345.00 (TAN)
1996 £49.75 (BER)
1994 £20.60 (TAN)
1986 £44.99 (BO)

Beau-Site *cru grand bourgeois exceptionnel St-Estèphe*
1996 £13.95 (DI)

Beau-Site-Haut-Vignoble *cru bourgeois St-Estèphe*
1986 £16.67 (MI)

Beaumont *cru grand bourgeois Haut-Médoc*
1995 £10.00 (MI) £10.30 (NO) £13.50 (BALL)
1994 £9.50 (WS) £11.06 (HA)
1990 £39.00 (UB)
1986 £24.50 (ROB)

Beausejour *Côtes de Castillon*
1995 £6.55 (HAH)

Beauséjour-Duffau-Lagarrosse *1er grand cru classé St-Émilion*
1997 IB £342.00 (JU)
1996 £35.00 (JU)
1995 £40.00 (JU)
1995 IB £300.00 (FA)
1994 £28.00 (JU)
1990 £223.25 (CAV) £265.00 (BAL)
1990 IB £2,300.00 (FA)
1966 £28.79 (REI)

Bel-Air *Pomerol*
1988 £31.00 (UB)

Bel-Air *Puisseguin-St-Émilion*
1996 £8.75 (HAH)

Bel-Air-Marquis d'Aligre *cru bourgeois supérieur exceptionnel Margaux*
1986 £22.50 (MI)

> **EC** *(ex-cellar) price per dozen, excl shipping, duty and VAT.*
> **IB** *(in bond) price per dozen, excl duty and VAT. All other prices, per bottle incl VAT.*

Bel-Orme-Tronquoy-de-Lalande *cru grand bourgeois Haut-Médoc*
1978 £26.00 (CRO)

de Belcier *Côtes de Francs*
1995 £133.33 (MI)

de Belcier *Côtes de Castillon*
1994 £8.99 (AME)
1992 £7.89 (CON)

Belgrave *5ème cru classé Haut-Médoc*
1996 £16.67 (MI)
1996 IB £100.00 (CAV)
1995 £14.95 (BU) £23.50 (PEN)
1994 £17.63 (JER)

Bellevue *grand cru classé St-Émilion*
1995 £15.75 (NI)

Bertin *Montagne-St-Émilion*
1997 IB £64.00 (CB)
1995 £8.17 (CB)

Bertineau-St-Vincent *Lalande-de-Pomerol*
1996 £9.99 (OD)

Beychevelle *4ème cru classé St-Julien*
1996 £20.90 (BIB) £25.00 (MI) £29.92 (PLAY)
1996 IB £200.00 (FRI) £200.00 (BIB)
1996 magnum £50.00 (MI)
1996 double magnum IB £215.00 (WY)
1995 £25.00 (MI) £25.46 (GW) £29.38 (WY)
£29.50 (UN) £29.95 (CON)
1995 magnum £50.00 (MI)
1995 double magnum IB £315.00 (WY)
1994 £22.50 (BAL) £22.50 (MI) £24.50 (UN)
£31.50 (STA)
1994 magnum £45.00 (MI)
1990 IB £380.00 (FA) £395.00 (BIB)
1989 £57.99 (AV) £70.00 (PLAY) £97.00 (UB)
1989 IB £390.00 (FA) £400.00 (BIB)
1988 £30.69 (BIB) £37.21 (FRI) £49.95 (ROB)
£51.36 (BY)
1986 £42.44 (BIB) £47.00 (FRI) £65.00 (PIP)
1985 £45.38 (BIB)
1983 £40.48 (BIB) £48.95 (ROB)
1982 £49.35 (FA) £96.75 (PLAY)
1982 IB £600.00 (FA)
1981 double magnum £99.88 (FA)
1978 £39.95 (PHI) £41.13 (WY)
1975 £41.13 (PLA)
1959 magnum £334.88 (REI)
1945 £605.13 (WY)

le Bon-Pasteur *Pomerol*
1996 £32.25 (CB)
1996 IB £250.00 (FA) £265.00 (JER)
1995 IB £225.00 (FA) £295.00 (CAV)
1994 £23.95 (BER) £26.67 (MI)
1990 £50.00 (TAN) £57.95 (RES)
1988 £63.00 (POR)

Bonnet *Bordeaux Supérieur*
1996 £6.99 (NI)
1995 £7.49 (VIC) £7.49 (THR) £7.49 (WR)
£7.49 (BOT) £8.37 (NO)

le Boscq *cru bourgeois supérieur St-Estèphe*
1997 IB £132.00 (TAN)
1996 £11.50 (JU) £16.67 (MI)
1995 £13.00 (JU) £15.00 (MI)

Bourgneuf-Vayron *Pomerol*
1990 £37.75 (ROB)
1989 £27.75 (PIP)

de Bourgueneuf *Pomerol*
1994 £17.50 (WS)
1989 £27.50 (ROB)

Bouscaut *cru classé Pessac-Léognan*
1995 £17.49 (UN)
1994 £15.49 (UN)

Boyd-Cantenac *3ème cru classé Margaux*
1982 £28.79 (REI) £35.25 (WY)
1982 IB £280.00 (FA)
1970 £28.79 (REI)

Branaire *4ème cru classé St-Julien*
1997 IB £220.00 (CB) £255.00 (TAN)
1996 £19.92 (BIB) £24.00 (JU) £26.67 (MI)
£27.26 (CB) £27.80 (TAN)
1996 IB £190.00 (BIB) £210.00 (RAE)
1995 £23.35 (BIB) £25.00 (MI) £29.38 (WY)
1995 IB £220.00 (FA) £225.00 (BIB)
1994 £22.20 (TAN)
1990 £34.61 (BIB) £40.00 (FORT) £40.83
(MI) £47.00 (JER)
1989 £32.65 (BIB) £48.70 (GW)
1988 £26.28 (BIB) £37.85 (BY) £46.60 (UB)
1986 £28.73 (BIB)
1985 £30.20 (BIB) £43.80 (JER) £48.69
(GW) 1983 £26.28 (BIB) £26.44 (REI)
1982 £40.48 (BIB) £41.13 (WY) £42.99
(YOU) £52.88 (REI) £52.90 (TAN)
1978 £23.50 (WY)

1970 £29.38 (WY) £38.19 (REI) £48.00
  (CRO)
1966 £47.50 (BU)
1962 £52.88 (REI)
1959 £105.16 (REI) £141.00 (WY)
1959 IB £750.00 (FA)
1934 £141.00 (WY)
1929 £250.00 (CRO)

Brane-Cantenac 2ème cru classé
  Margaux
1996 £24.17 (MI) £26.79 (CB)
1996 magnum £48.33 (MI)
1995 £35.00 (UN)
1994 IB £159.00 (RAE)
1983 £31.99 (YOU)
1970 magnum £75.00 (ROB)
1978 £36.85 (NI)
1966 £52.88 (REI)
1961 £76.38 (WY)
1929 £220.00 (CRO)
1928 £250.00 (JU)
1928 IB £2,150.00 (CAV)

du Breuil *cru bourgeois supérieur Haut-*
  Médoc
1996 £9.95 (DI)
1994 £9.70 (TAN)

Cabannieux *Graves*
1995 £7.75 (CON)
1994 £9.93 (CB)

Cadet-Piola *grand cru classé St-Émilion*
1990 £29.95 (LEA)

Calon-Ségur 3ème cru classé St-Estèphe
1997 IB £135.00 (FA) £176.00 (CB)
  £189.00 (TAN)
1996 £25.80 (BIB) £31.95 (DI) £36.67 (MI)
1996 IB £250.00 (BIB) £265.00 (FA)
  £290.00 (WY) £300.00 (FRI)
1995 £29.50 (UN) £36.57 (BIB) £39.95 (BER)
  £44.06 (FRI) £70.82 (BY)
1995 IB £360.00 (BIB) £395.00 (CAV)
1994 £23.50 (UN) £24.99 (POR) £34.00
  (TAN)
1990 £45.38 (BIB)
1989 £37.50 (ROB) £40.48 (BIB)
1988 £38.52 (BIB) £43.50 (WRI)
1986 £39.50 (ROB) £50.00 (CRO)
1986 IB £330.00 (BIB)
1985 £32.50 (BALL) £41.13 (WY)
1982 £54.19 (BIB) £54.64 (REI)
1982 IB £540.00 (FA) £540.00 (BIB)

1970 £32.90 (WY)
1964 £52.88 (REI)
1955 £88.13 (REI)
1949 £411.25 (CAV)
1947 £290.00 (CRO)
1928 £275.00 (JU)

de Camensac 5ème cru classé Haut-
  Médoc
1995 £12.31 (HA)
1975 £17.04 (REI)

Cana *Côtes de Bourg*
1996 £5.68 (FRI)
1995 £5.68 (FRI)

Canon *1er grand cru classé St-Émilion*
1997 IB £316.00 (CB)
1997 EC £85.40 (HAH)
1996 £28.24 (BIB) £28.33 (MI) £34.37 (CB)
1995 £25.00 (CON) £25.80 (BIB) £27.91
  (FRI) £33.33 (MI)
1994 £23.33 (MI) £24.90 (BER) £35.99 (JON)
1990 £40.48 (BIB) £49.50 (BAL)
1989 £39.50 (BIB) £44.06 (FRI)
1988 £37.21 (FRI) £40.48 (BIB)
1986 £32.00 (UB) £43.42 (BIB) £47.00 (FRI)
1985 £40.48 (BIB) £68.96 (PLAY)
1983 £39.50 (GW) £52.70 (GW)
1982 £81.61 (BIB) £85.00 (JU) £94.50 (BEN)
  £110.00 (BAL)
1982 IB £820.00 (FA) £820.00 (BIB)
1978 £45.24 (REI)
1945 £329.00 (REI)

Canon de Brem *Canon-Fronsac*
1997 IB £100.00 (CB)
1996 £12.46 (CB)
1995 £11.70 (MV) £14.10 (CB)
1994 £11.99 (CB)

Canon-la-Gaffelière *grand cru classé St-*
  Émilion
1997 IB £400.00 (TAN)
1996 £30.83 (MI) £38.48 (CB) £39.00 (JU)
1996 IB £295.00 (CAV) £375.00 (JER)
1995 £29.95 (CON) £33.66 (CB)
1995 IB £275.00 (FA)
1994 £25.00 (JU)

---

*All châteaux are listed
alphabetically
regardless of class.*

1994 IB £210.00 (FA)
1990 £49.35 (CB) £60.00 (FORT)
1985 £32.31 (REI) £41.61 (JER)
1982 £41.13 (REI)

Canon-Moueix *Canon-Fronsac*
1997 IB £102.00 (CB)
1996 £12.63 (CB)
1995 £14.51 (CB)

Cantemerle *5ème cru classé Haut-Médoc*
1997 EC £150.00 (HIG)
1996 £18.33 (MI) £19.95 (DI)
1996 IB £144.00 (RAE) £145.00 (FA)
1995 £15.83 (MI) £19.09 (JER)
1994 £19.50 (UN)
1990 £29.75 (WRI)
1988 £31.95 (DI)
1983 £23.50 (WY) £72.00 (UB)
1970 £28.79 (REI)
1955 £88.13 (REI)

Cantenac-Brown *3ème cru classé Margaux*
1995 £18.33 (MI) £29.50 (UN)
1994 £21.50 (UN)
1993 £30.83 (BY)
1989 £48.00 (UB)
1988 £23.50 (BAL)
1982 £38.19 (REI)

Cap-de-Faugères *Côtes de Castillon*
1996 £8.34 (BIB)
1996 ½ bottle £4.65 (BIB)
1996 ½ bottle IB £95.00 (BIB)
1995 £7.99 (YOU)
1990 £6.67 (HA)

Carbonnieux *cru classé Pessac-Léognan*
1996 £17.50 (MI) £21.44 (CB)
1996 IB £165.00 (JER)
1996 magnum £35.00 (MI) £222.00 (CB)
1995 £15.83 (MI)
1994 £15.83 (MI) £16.29 (YOU) £21.05 (JER)
1982 £27.61 (REI)
1959 £135.13 (WY)

Please remember that
Oz Clarke's Wine Guide
is a price guide and not a
price list. It is not meant to
replace up-to-date
merchants' lists.

---

la Cardonne *cru grand bourgeois Médoc*
1995 £11.75 (PEN) £10.75 (STA) £14.50 (CRO)

les Carmes-Haut-Brion *Pessac-Léognan*
1997 IB £242.00 (CB)
1995 £17.63 (WY)
1982 £29.38 (WY)

Caronne-Ste-Gemme *cru grand bourgeois exceptionnel Haut-Médoc*
1996 IB £90.00 (FA)
1995 £11.40 (NO) £11.95 (SOM)
1995 IB £90.00 (FA)
1994 £8.49 (MORR) £9.90 (TAN) £14.99 (POR)
1994 IB £72.00 (FA)
1989 £14.98 (REI) £16.99 (JON)
1988 IB £100.00 (FA)
1986 IB £145.00 (FA)

Carruades de Lafite (Moulin des Carruades until 1987) *Pauillac*
1997 IB £189.00 (RAE)
1996 £21.00 (JU) £27.50 (MI)
1996 IB £180.00 (RAE) £180.00 (WY) £195.00 (CAV) £200.00 (FA)
1996 EC £300.00 (HA)
1995 £28.33 (MI) £29.50 (BU) £176.25 (WY)
1995 IB £215.00 (FA)
1994 £15.95 (WS) £19.71 (STE) £21.90 (NA) £42.50 (STA)
1986 £62.25 (BER)
1959 £293.75 (REI)
1934 £199.75 (WY)

Carteau-Côtes-Daugay *grand cru St-Émilion*
1995 £9.50 (WS)

Cazebonne *Graves*
1995 £7.83 (JER)

Certan-Giraud *Pomerol*
1991 £21.74 (REI)
1990 £33.19 (REI)
1989 £33.33 (BY)
1988 £30.34 (BY)

Certan-de-May *Pomerol*
1997 IB £517.00 (CB)
1996 £42.95 (LAY) £47.83 (BIB) £53.00 (JU) £54.34 (CB)
1996 IB £475.00 (BIB)
1995 IB £450.00 (BIB) £490.00 (FA)

MILLÉSIMA

Les Vins des Grands Vignobles

THE REFERENCE IN BORDEAUX
FOR EN-PRIMEUR WINES AND WINES AVAILABLE NOW
offers you 4 major guarantees: choice, quality, price and service.

An exceptional choice
2 000 000 bottles age slowly in our cellars
in Bordeaux:
the best vintages in the past 30 years
(including the last En-Primeur vintage) of
the Châteaux, which have made Bordeaux
renowned for its wine, are in our
catalogue.

Absolute quality
All our wines are bought directly from the
Châteaux.

Guaranteed prices
Every year, our Bordeaux prices are valid from 1st January to 31st December
(except the En-Primeur offer).

Service
Should you require any advice, please do not hesitate to contact Christopher Myers
on our free-phone numbers 00800 BORDEAUX (00800 267 33289), or
0800 917 0352, and he will answer any questions that you may have.

 FREE-PHONE NUMBERS
00800 B O R D E A U X
(00800 2 6 7 3 3 2 8 9)
or 0800 917 0352 (UK)

 FAX
00 33 557 808 819

 INTERNET
http://www.millesima.com
E-mail : millesima@millesima.com

---

u can also call us on our free-phone number (00 800 267 33 289) from Austria, Belgium, Germany, Portugal, Switzerland

Return to : MILLESIMA - 87, quai de Paludate - BP 89 - 33038 BORDEAUX CEDEX - FRANCE   GOZ 2

Surname... Forename...

Address..

....

County.. Postcode.......................... Tel..

☐ **Please send me your free catalogue and En-Primeur offer**

1994 £33.78 (CB) £60.00 (JU)
1990 IB £595.00 (BIB) £600.00 (FA)
1989 £40.48 (BIB)
1988 £55.17 (BIB) £95.00 (FORT)
1988 IB £550.00 (FA) £550.00 (BIB)
1986 £50.27 (BIB) £52.88 (REI) £62.00 (RES)
1986 IB £500.00 (BIB) £650.00 (CAV)
1985 £64.96 (BIB)
1983 £40.48 (BIB) £47.00 (WY)
1982 IB £1,800.00 (FA) £1,800.00 (BIB)
1979 £68.50 (BEN)
1975 IB £650.00 (FA)
1966 £105.75 (CAV)

Charmail *cru bourgeois Haut-Médoc*
1995 £11.95 (PHI)

Charron *1ères Côtes de Blaye*
1996 £7.90 (TAN)

Chasse-Spleen *cru grand bourgeois exceptionnel Moulis*
1997 IB £170.00 (TAN)
1996 £17.95 (AD) £18.00 (JU) £18.33 (MI)
£21.15 (CB)
1996 IB £150.00 (FA) £160.00 (FRI)
1996 EC £170.00 (HA) £171.00 (ELL)
1995 £17.95 (CON) £19.58 (FRI)
1994 £17.50 (MI) £22.62 (JER) £22.65 (PIP)
£30.00 (FORT)
1990 £37.50 (ROB) £40.00 (FORT) £40.65
(GW)
1989 £34.35 (NO) £39.95 (DI)
1989 IB £335.00 (WY)
1988 £34.00 (TAN) £35.00 (FORT)
1986 £32.65 (BAL) £33.49 (REI) £36.00
(CRO) £40.00 (FORT)
1985 £42.00 (CRO)
1982 £44.60 (TAN) £47.50 (FORT) £49.95
(RES)
1982 IB £340.00 (FA)
1981 £25.26 (REI)
1975 £44.00 (CRO)

Chauvin *grand cru classé St-Émilion*
1995 £17.00 (JU)

Cheval-Blanc *1er grand cru classé St-Émilion*
1997 IB £990.00 (TAN) £1,075.00 (CB)
1997 EC £995.85 (HAH)
1996 £99.23 (BIB) £105.00 (TAN) £111.21
(CB) £140.00 (JU) £173.33 (MI)
1996 IB £1,000.00 (BIB) £1,200.00 (FRI)
1996 magnum £346.67 (MI)

1995 £146.87 (FRI) £173.33 (MI)
1995 IB £1,170.00 (BIB) £1,535.00 (ELL)
1995 magnum £346.67 (MI)
1994 £69.50 (UN) £85.00 (JU) £121.67 (MI)
£146.88 (PEN)
1990 £260.80 (BIB) £334.88 (CB)
1990 IB £2,400.00 (FA) £2,650.00 (BIB)
1989 £95.00 (BU) £104.13 (BIB) £122.50
(LAY) £130.00 (BEN)
1989 IB £1,050.00 (FA) £1,050.00 (BIB)
1989 magnum IB £1,050.00 (FA)
1988 £89.44 (BIB) £99.50 (BEN)
1988 IB £900.00 (FA) £900.00 (BIB)
1986 £125.00 (CON) £145.00 (ROB) £146.88
(REI) £175.00 (FORT) £210.56 (BY)
1986 IB £1,020.00 (FA) £1,050.00 (BIB)
1986 magnum IB £1,020.00 (FA)
1985 £123.71 (BIB) £146.88 (WY) £159.60
(LAY) £185.65 (REI) £225.00 (ROB)
£284.00 (UB)
1985 IB £1,250.00 (BIB) £1,300.00 (FA)
1983 £141.00 (WY) £230.00 (RES)
1983 IB £1,440.00 (FA) £1,440.00 (BIB)
1982 £295.07 (BIB) £350.00 (JU) £495.00
(RES) £525.00 (FORT) £665.00 (ROB)
1982 IB £3,000.00 (BIB) £3,100.00 (FA)
£3,300.00 (CAV)
1981 £88.13 (WY) £123.49 (BY)
1979 £94.00 (REI)
1978 £130.00 (ROB) £130.00 (JU)
1978 magnum £223.25 (WY)
1975 IB £1,200.00 (FA)
1971 £88.13 (REI)
1970 £146.88 (WY) £195.00 (ROB)
1970 IB £1,100.00 (CAV)
1970 magnum IB £1,000.00 (FA)
1966 £188.00 (WY) £265.00 (RES)
1964 £320.00 (BEN)
1964 IB £3,600.00 (FA)
1955 £199.75 (WY) £217.38 (REI)
1949 £340.75 (WY)
1949 ½ bottle £252.63 (WY)
1947 £2,643.75 (WY)
1947 IB £24,000.00 (FA)
1945 £1,057.50 (WY)
1943 £152.75 (WY)
1939 £229.13 (REI)
1920 £235.00 (FA)

Cheval-Noir *St-Émilion*
1995 £9.75 (WS)

Chicane *Graves*
1996 £8.80 (TAN)
1995 £8.90 (TAN)

Cissac *cru grand bourgeois exceptionnel*
   Haut-Médoc
1997 IB £98.00 (TAN)
1996 £11.95 (JU) £13.95 (DI)
1996 EC £105.00 (HA)
1995 £12.50 (TAN) £12.95 (DI) £13.30
   (PLAY) £13.95 (CON)
1994 £12.44 (PLA) £13.35 (AV)
1990 £18.65 (BER) £19.99 (JON) £25.00
   (TAN)
1989 £22.95 (DI)
1988 £11.29 (CO) £17.04 (REI) £22.50 (BU)
   £23.00 (TAN) £29.95 (VIN)
1986 £25.95 (DI)
1985 £18.95 (BALL)
1982 £31.90 (TAN)
1970 magnum £65.00 (ROB)

Citran *cru grand bourgeois exceptionnel*
   Haut-Médoc
1996 £13.33 (MI)

la Clare *cru bourgeois Médoc*
1996 £8.87 (PLA)

Clarke *cru bourgeois Listrac*
1995 £12.50 (ROB)

la Claverie *Côtes de Francs*
1988 £9.50 (CRO)

Clerc-Milon *5ème cru classé Pauillac*
1996 £24.79 (CB) £24.95 (DI) £33.33 (MI)
1995 IB £330.00 (FA)
1990 £46.00 (BAL)
1989 £32.50 (BAL) £48.30 (UB)
1985 £41.13 (WY)

Clinet *Pomerol*
1997 IB £450.00 (FA)
1996 IB £680.00 (FA)
1995 IB £800.00 (FA) £1,050.00 (CAV)
1994 £58.75 (WY)
1990 £129.25 (WY)
1990 IB £880.00 (FA)
1989 IB £1,850.00 (FA) £1,900.00 (CAV)
1982 £70.50 (WY)

Clos Beauregard *Pomerol*
1995 £11.80 (FLE)

Clos du Clocher *Pomerol*
1995 £18.50 (JU)
1994 £16.90 (AV)
1983 £21.74 (REI)

Clos de l'Eglise *Lalande-de-Pomerol*
1996 IB £159.00 (RAE)
1990 £9.99 (RAE)
1982 £44.30 (NI)

Clos Fourtet *1er grand cru classé St-
   Émilion*
1997 EC £318.00 (JON)
1996 £30.00 (MI)
1996 IB £250.00 (CAV) £285.00 (FA)
1995 £21.67 (MI) £25.95 (FRI)
1995 IB £225.00 (FA)
1962 £37.01 (REI)
1949 £264.38 (WY)

Clos des Jacobins *grand cru classé St-
   Émilion*
1985 ½ bottle £22.50 (RES)
1982 £26.44 (REI)

Clos du Marquis *St-Julien*
1997 IB £253.00 (CB)
1997 EC £249.60 (JON)
1996 IB £220.00 (FA)
1995 £23.00 (JU)
1990 £25.00 (WS)
1989 £35.95 (ROB) £50.00 (FORT)
1983 £34.95 (ROB)

Clos René *Pomerol*
1996 £15.83 (MI)
1995 £19.45 (BER)
1994 £16.67 (MI) £18.00 (JU)
1985 £43.70 (UB)
1983 £19.80 (REI)
1982 £35.25 (WY)
1978 £48.00 (CRO)

du Clos Renon *Bordeaux*
1995 £6.36 (FRI)

Clos des Templiers *Lalande-de-Pomerol*
1996 £9.50 (BALL)

Connétable Talbot *St-Julien*
1994 £12.50 (MI) £13.71 (JER)
1982 £35.25 (REI)

la Conseillante *Pomerol*
1996 £51.67 (MI) £53.00 (JU) £68.15 (CB)
1996 IB £430.00 (BIB) £495.00 (CAV)
1995 £43.42 (BIB) £48.96 (FRI) £60.00 (JU)
   £62.79 (FLE)
1995 IB £410.00 (FA) £435.00 (WY)
1994 £40.83 (MI) £58.75 (PEN)
1990 £118.82 (BIB) £147.50 (MI)
1990 IB £1,200.00 (FA) £1,200.00 (BIB)
1989 £99.23 (BIB) £130.83 (MI)
1989 IB £950.00 (FA) £1,000.00 (BIB)
1988 £38.52 (BIB) £39.30 (AV)
1986 £45.38 (BIB) £70.00 (FORT)
1986 IB £450.00 (FA) £450.00 (BIB)
1985 £110.00 (CRO) £135.00 (RES)
1985 IB £900.00 (FA) £900.00 (BIB)
1983 IB £420.00 (FA) £450.00 (BIB)
1982 IB £1,150.00 (FA) £1,150.00 (BIB)
1982 magnum IB £1,150.00 (FA)
1979 £88.13 (REI)
1978 £35.00 (BU)
1964 IB £1,250.00 (FA)
1961 £229.13 (CAV)
1955 £176.26 (CAV) £246.75 (REI)
1945 £223.25 (WY)

Corbin *grand cru classé St-Émilion*
1995 £17.99 (MAJ)
1994 £15.99 (AME)
1989 £33.00 (UB)

Cormeil-Figeac *grand cru St-Émilion*
1989 £17.04 (REI)

Cos d'Estournel *2ème cru classé St-Estèphe*
1997 IB £492.00 (RAE) £525.00 (TAN)
   £539.00 (CB)
1997 EC £525.00 (ELL)
1996 £52.23 (BIB) £59.22 (CB) £65.00 (MI)
1996 IB £500.00 (FA) £600.00 (FRI)
1996 EC £625.00 (ELL)
1996 magnum IB £500.00 (FA)
1996 double magnum IB £665.00 (WY)
1996 jeroboam £570.00 (MI)
1996 imperial £460.00 (WY) £670.00 (MI)
1995 £49.78 (BIB) £57.77 (FRI) £58.50
   (YOU) £85.00 (FORT)
1995 IB £495.00 (BIB) £530.00 (FA)
1995 jeroboam £580.00 (MI)
1994 £39.50 (BER)
1994 magnum IB £380.00 (FA)
1990 £65.75 (ROB) £67.90 (BIB) £79.00
   (BEN) £89.00 (BAL)
1990 IB £650.00 (FA) £680.00 (BIB)

1989 £50.27 (BIB) £58.75 (FRI) £59.95 (LAY)
   £92.60 (PLAY)
1989 IB £500.00 (BIB) £540.00 (FA)
1989 jeroboam £740.00 (MI)
1988 £45.38 (BIB) £47.50 (CON)
1988 jeroboam £311.38 (FA)
1986 £72.50 (CON) £80.00 (JU) £94.89 (BY)
1986 IB £600.00 (BIB) £650.00 (FA)
1985 £69.86 (BIB) £74.03 (WY) £77.50
   (BEN) £81.03 (PLA) £82.25 (REI) £83.28
   (LAY) £85.15 (TAN) £98.00 (BAL)
1985 IB £700.00 (BIB) £720.00 (FA)
1985 magnum IB £720.00 (FA)
1983 £63.00 (BER) £70.50 (TAN)
1982 £91.40 (BIB) £110.00 (JU) £111.63
   (REI) £120.00 (BEN)
1982 IB £920.00 (FA) £920.00 (BIB)
1982 magnum IB £1,050.00 (CAV)
1975 £82.25 (PEN)
1970 £64.63 (WY) £72.95 (ROB) £75.00 (BU)
1970 IB £480.00 (FA) £720.00 (CAV)
1966 IB £600.00 (FA)
1947 £229.13 (REI)
1945 £217.38 (FA)
1929 £411.25 (CAV)

Cos Labory *5ème cru classé St-Estèphe*
1995 £22.95 (DI)
1986 £49.00 (UB)
1970 £19.39 (REI)

Coufran *cru bourgeois Haut-Médoc*
1994 £11.28 (ROS) £13.10 (BER)
1990 £27.00 (UB)
1975 £17.04 (REI)

la Couspaude *grand cru St-Émilion*
1996 £33.95 (DI)
1995 £18.99 (OD)
1995 IB £195.00 (FA)

Couvent-des-Jacobins *grand cru classé St-Émilion*
1995 £25.95 (STA)
1990 £32.00 (UB)

le Crock *cru grand bourgeois exceptionnel St-Estèphe*
1996 £13.25 (BALL)
1996 IB £111.00 (RAE)
1990 £24.68 (COC) £47.00 (UB)

la Croix *Pomerol*
1996 £5.99 (DI)
1989 £39.60 (NO)

la Croix-Bellevue *Lalande-de-Pomerol*
1989 £21.03 (TW)

la Croix-du-Casse *Pomerol*
1996 £21.00 (JU)
1996 IB £175.00 (JER)
1995 IB £165.00 (CAV)
1994 £19.00 (JU) £19.95 (BAL) £23.50 (STA)
£23.95 (RES)

la Croix-de-Gay *Pomerol*
1995 £19.58 (FRI)
1986 IB £160.00 (FA)
1985 £49.00 (UB)

la Croix-des-Moines *Lalande-de-Pomerol*
1996 £10.77 (BIB)
1995 £11.99 (JON)
1994 £10.40 (TAN) £10.99 (RAE)

Croizet-Bages *5ème cru classé Pauillac*
1995 £11.15 (HA) £22.50 (UN)
1994 £19.50 (UN) £21.67 (BY)
1978 £26.44 (REI)

Croque-Michotte *grand cru classé St-Émilion*
1995 £16.16 (FRI)

la Dame de Montrose *St-Estèphe*
1996 £19.17 (MI) £19.99 (MAJ)
1995 £16.59 (LAY) £17.50 (MI)

Dassault *grand cru classé St-Émilion*
1994 £19.95 (LEA)

de la Dauphine *Fronsac*
1997 IB £84.00 (CB)
1996 £10.69 (CB)
1995 £10.20 (JU) £10.85 (AD) £12.22 (CB)

Dauzac *5ème cru classé Margaux*
1996 £21.95 (DI)
1995 £18.95 (BAL) £21.54 (FRI)
1982 £44.63 (PLAY)

EC (ex-cellar) price per dozen, excl shipping, duty and VAT.
IB (in bond) price per dozen, excl duty and VAT.
All other prices, per bottle incl VAT.

Deyrem-Valentin *cru bourgeois Margaux*
1996 £15.50 (STA)
1995 £13.25 (SOM)

Domaine de Chevalier *cru classé Pessac-Léognan*
1997 IB £228.00 (RAE)
1996 £21.88 (BIB) £27.50 (MI) £29.95 (DI)
1996 IB £200.00 (FRI) £210.00 (BIB)
£228.00 (RAE)
1996 EC £235.00 (HA)
1995 £21.88 (BIB) £22.50 (MI) £25.00 (JU)
£27.61 (CB) £27.95 (AD) £29.29 (NI)
£32.50 (FORT)
1995 IB £210.00 (BIB) £228.00 (RAE)
1994 £22.50 (MI) £24.95 (ROB)
1994 IB £216.00 (RAE)
1990 £40.48 (BIB) £45.00 (ROB) £49.17 (MI)
1990 IB £400.00 (BIB)
1989 £40.48 (BIB) £45.00 (MI) £45.83 (REI)
1989 IB £375.00 (FA) £400.00 (BIB)
1989 ½ bottle £20.99 (RAE)
1988 £24.82 (BIB) £44.17 (MI)
1986 £38.19 (REI) £39.50 (YOU) £53.33 (MI)
1986 IB £360.00 (BIB)
1985 IB £365.00 (BIB)
1983 £34.08 (REI) £42.00 (CRO) £42.44
(BIB) £51.40 (GW)
1983 IB £360.00 (FA) £420.00 (BIB)
1982 £38.19 (REI) £39.99 (BIB) £45.00 (MI)
1981 £55.00 (FORT)
1978 £49.95 (TAN)
1978 IB £460.00 (CAV)
1975 £35.00 (BU)
1970 £85.19 (REI)
1970 IB £680.00 (FA)
1966 £62.00 (CRO)
1964 £60.00 (BU)
1959 £111.63 (REI)
1955 IB £1,000.00 (FA)

Domaine de l'Eglise *Pomerol*
1996 £18.95 (DI) £19.50 (HIG)
1995 £18.95 (DI)
1989 £26.14 (REI) £34.95 (DI)
1982 £95.00 (RES)

Domaine de la Solitude *Pessac-Léognan*
1996 £12.50 (MI)
1995 £9.59 (WAT) £10.83 (MI)
1994 £9.50 (BALL) £10.00 (MI)

Domaine de Terrefort *Bordeaux Supérieur*
1979 £10.75 (BU)

la Dominique *grand cru classé St-Émilion*
1997 IB £329.00 (CB)
1996 £28.33 (MI) £34.00 (JU) £35.00 (AD)
£37.37 (CB)
1996 IB £300.00 (FRI)
1995 £27.91 (FRI) £29.38 (WY) £29.95
(CON) £32.55 (CB) £34.00 (JU)
1994 £35.99 (JON)
1990 IB £420.00 (FA)
1989 IB £850.00 (CAV)

Ducluzeau *cru bourgeois Listrac*
1994 £8.95 (BALL)

Ducru-Beaucaillou *2ème cru classé St-Julien*
1997 IB £400.00 (FA) £429.00 (LAY) £450.00
(RAE) £495.00 (CB) £500.00 (TAN)
1997 EC £475.00 (ELL)
1996 £58.11 (BIB) £65.00 (MI) £70.50 (CB)
1996 IB £580.00 (FA) £580.00 (BIB)
£650.00 (FRI)
1996 EC £795.00 (ELL)
1996 magnum IB £580.00 (FA)
1996 double magnum £290.00 (MI)
1996 double magnum IB £720.00 (WY)
1996 jeroboam £570.00 (MI)
1996 imperial IB £480.00 (WY)
1995 £66.67 (MI) £78.33 (FRI) £79.99 (AV)
1995 IB £720.00 (FA) £750.00 (BIB)
1995 magnum £133.33 (MI)
1995 imperial £690.00 (MI)
1994 £45.00 (BAL)
1994 jeroboam £410.00 (MI)
1990 £45.00 (BU) £45.38 (BIB) £51.70 (WY)
£55.00 (RAE) £57.50 (MI) £68.00 (BER)
1989 £40.48 (BIB) £47.00 (WY) £57.50 (MI)
1989 double magnum £264.38 (WY
1988 £40.48 (BIB) £44.17 (MI) £58.00 (BER)
£59.95 (RES) £69.00 (UB)
1988 magnum IB £360.00 (FA)
1988 imperial £480.00 (MI)
1986 £47.50 (CON) £52.23 (BIB) £55.23
(WY) £57.50 (MI)
1986 IB £520.00 (FA) £520.00 (BIB)
1985 £52.23 (BIB) £59.57 (NO)
1985 magnum IB £520.00 (FA)
1983 £40.48 (BIB) £41.13 (WY) £45.24 (REI)
£52.50 (BALL) £58.40 (PIP)
1982 £77.69 (BIB) £85.00 (JU) £92.70 (TAN)
£94.00 (WY) £94.00 (CAV) £94.50 (BEN)
£100.82 (NO) £110.00 (BAL) £115.00
(RES) £125.00 (FORT)
1982 IB £780.00 (FA) £780.00 (BIB)
1982 double magnum £470.00 (WY)

1981 £48.35 (BY)
1981 imperial £640.00 (MI)
1978 jeroboam £630.00 (MI)
1975 £38.78 (WY) £39.36 (REI)
1975 IB £340.00 (FA)
1975 magnum £145.00 (RES)
1975 magnum IB £340.00 (FA)
1975 double magnum £370.00 (MI)
1975 jeroboam £315.00 (DI)
1970 £76.38 (REI) £85.00 (BEN) £109.00
(CRO)
1970 magnum IB £850.00 (FA)
1970 jeroboam £1,040.00 (MI)
11961 £240.00 (CRO)
1961 ½ bottle £123.38 (REI)
1959 £76.38 (REI) £150.00 (FORT)
1949 £293.75 (REI)
1924 £264.38 (WY)

Duhart-Milon-Rothschild *4ème cru classé Pauillac*
1997 IB £195.00 (CB)
1996 £20.00 (JU) £21.95 (DI) £22.50 (TAN)
£23.33 (MI) £24.38 (CB)
1996 EC £165.00 (NLW)
1995 £25.00 (UN) £25.00 (MI)
1994 £21.50 (UN)
1990 £28.79 (REI) £46.00 (UB)
1989 £28.79 (REI) £33.29 (FRI)
1988 £34.27 (FRI)
1985 £26.44 (REI) £37.21 (FRI)

Duplessis-Fabre *cru bourgeois Moulis*
1982 £19.99 (POR) £21.74 (REI)

Durand-Laplagne *Puisseguin-St-Émilion*
1996 £7.50 (AD)
1995 £6.75 (BALL) £6.95 (TAN)

Durfort-Vivens *2ème cru classé Margaux*
1997 IB £174.00 (RAE)
1996 IB £150.00 (JER) £159.00 (RAE)
1995 £21.54 (FRI) £23.95 (BER)
1995 IB £159.00 (RAE)
1994 £25.50 (STA)
1978 £28.50 (BALL)
1975 £33.50 (BALL)

Dutruch-Grand-Poujeaux *cru grand bourgeois exceptionnel Moulis*
1997 IB £82.00 (CB)
1996 £10.80 (CB)
1995 £11.40 (CB)

l'Église-Clinet *Pomerol*
1996 £81.61 (BIB) £98.00 (JU)
1996 IB £900.00 (FA) £1,350.00 (JER)
1995 £109.02 (BIB) £148.00 (JU)
1995 IB £1,100.00 (BIB) £1,150.00 (FA)
  £1,250.00 (CAV)
1990 £108.05 (BIB)
1990 IB £110.00 (FA) £1,090.00 (BIB)
1989 £31.00 (YOU) £73.77 (BIB)
1989 IB £740.00 (FA) £740.00 (BIB)
1988 £50.27 (BIB)
1986 IB £780.00 (FA) £780.00 (BIB)
1985 £118.82 (BIB) £150.00 (BAL)
1985 IB £1,200.00 (BIB) £1,260.00 (FA)
1983 £45.00 (BAL) £45.38 (BIB)
1982 IB £680.00 (BIB) £720.00 (FA)
1979 IB £480.00 (FA)

l'Enclos *Pomerol*
1994 £18.00 (JU) £18.10 (PIP) £19.95 (STA)
  £19.99 (POR)
1990 £23.00 (CRO)
1983 £29.75 (ROB)

l'Éperon *Bordeaux*
1995 £6.99 (CB)

l'Ermitage de Chasse-Spleen *Haut-Médoc*
1997 EC £81.00 (JON)
1996 £10.83 (MI)
1995 £10.00 (MI)
1994 £10.95 (WRI)

l'Escadre *lères Côtes de Blaye*
1994 £6.20 (COC)

l'Etoile *Graves*
1996 £5.75 (BALL)
1995 £5.95 (BALL)

l'Évangile *Pomerol*
1997 IB £759.00 (LAY) £824.00 (CB)
1996 £75.00 (JU) £79.17 (MI) £88.36 (CB)
1996 IB £500.00 (BIB) £790.00 (JER)
1995 £79.16 (BIB) £160.00 (JU) £165.00 (MI)
1990 IB £1,300.00 (FA) £1,300.00 (BIB)
1989 £52.72 (BIB) £56.99 (REI)
1989 IB £500.00 (FA) £525.00 (BIB)

1986 £40.48 (BIB) £60.00 (FORT)
1985 £89.44 (BIB) £150.00 (RES)
1985 IB £900.00 (FA) £900.00 (BIB)
1983 £85.00 (BAL)
1982 £148.19 (BIB) £176.25 (REI)
1978 £50.00 (BU)
1975 £397.00 (RES)
1975 IB £1,500.00 (FA) £2,250.00 (CAV)

Falfas *Côtes de Bourg*
1997 £8.95 (AD)
1996 £7.52 (GW)

Fayau *lères Côtes de Bordeaux*
1996 £5.94 (MV)

Ferrande *Graves*
1995 £9.75 (BU)
1990 £16.50 (HED)
1989 £14.95 (HED) £18.99 (AME)

Feytit-Clinet *Pomerol*
1997 IB £128.00 (TAN) £155.00 (CB)
1995 £19.56 (CB) £24.95 (BALL)
1989 £42.00 (UB)
1988 £16.95 (BALL)

les Fiefs-de-Lagrange *St-Julien*
1996 £15.00 (MI)
1996 IB £99.00 (JER) £125.00 (FA)
1995 £9.30 (JER) £14.17 (MI) £17.63 (DOM)
  £17.95 (LEA) £20.00 (FORT) £23.50 (ROB)
1995 IB £125.00 (FA)
1990 £30.84 (JER)

de Fieuzal *cru classé Pessac-Léognan*
1997 EC £240.00 (ELL)
1996 £22.50 (MI) £26.44 (CB)
1995 £17.95 (HA) £24.99 (NI) £26.95 (RES)
1995 IB £175.00 (FA)
1994 £18.50 (TAN) £21.95 (BER) £22.95
  (ROB)
1990 £34.95 (ROB) £36.25 (PIP)
1988 £49.00 (UB)
1986 £47.00 (PEN)
1978 £28.79 (REI)

Figeac *1er grand cru classé St-Émilion*
1997 EC £415.20 (JON)
1996 £36.57 (BIB) £46.67 (MI) £64.20 (PLAY)
1996 magnum £93.33 (MI)
1995 £38.00 (JU) £38.03 (BIB) £41.61 (FRI)
  £45.00 (MI)
1995 IB £375.00 (BIB) £390.00 (WY)
1995 magnum £90.00 (MI)

1994 £30.83 (MI) £47.95 (ROB)
1990 IB £600.00 (FA) £600.00 (BIB)
1989 £44.40 (BIB)
1988 £34.61 (BIB) £82.00 (UB)
1986 IB £540.00 (FA) £540.00 (BIB)
1985 £50.27 (BIB) £56.40 (WY)
1985 IB £500.00 (FA) £650.00 (CAV)
1982 £79.65 (BIB) £99.88 (REI)
1982 IB £780.00 (FA) £800.00 (BIB)
1981 £58.75 (GW) £79.99 (POR)
1979 £33.49 (REI) £41.48 (FLE)
1979 IB £390.00 (FA)
1975 £40.54 (REI)
1970 £90.00 (ROB)
1961 IB £2,000.00 (FA)

Fleur Cardinale *grand cru St-Émilion*
1997 EC £95.40 (JON)

la Fleur-Pétrus *Pomerol*
1997 IB £315.00 (TAN) £425.00 (CB)
1996 £29.00 (JU) £34.66 (CB)
1996 EC £270.00 (HA)
1994 £31.73 (CB)
1990 £47.00 (CAV)
1989 £64.63 (CB)
1986 £43.95 (RES)
1983 IB £380.00 (FA)
1970 IB £800.00 (FA) £995.00 (CAV)
1962 IB £900.00 (FA)

Fombrauge *grand cru St-Émilion*
1994 £12.24 (JER)
1966 £17.04 (REI)

Fonpiqueyre *cru bourgeois Haut-Médoc*
1978 £18.50 (CRO)

Fonréaud *cru bourgeois Listrac*
1996 £9.95 (TAN) £10.83 (MI)
1995 £7.66 (HA) £10.00 (MI)

Fonroque *grand cru classé St-Émilion*
1997 IB £115.00 (TAN) £138.00 (CB)
1996 £15.22 (CB)
1995 £17.70 (AD) £17.86 (CB)
1994 £13.98 (CB) £14.50 (WS)

les Forts-de-Latour *Pauillac*
1997 IB £273.00 (LAY) £305.00 (CB)
1996 £38.33 (MI)
1996 IB £300.00 (FA)
1996 EC £265.00 (HA)
1995 £42.30 (WY) £45.00 (MI)
1994 £18.50 (WS) £29.50 (BAL)

1990 £85.00 (BAL)
1990 IB £620.00 (FA)
1989 £43.90 (LAY) £45.00 (BU) £60.00 (FORT)
1988 £46.84 (LAY)
1979 £51.70 (PEN)

Fourcas-Dupré *cru grand bourgeois exceptionnnel Listrac*
1996 £10.95 (WS)
1996 EC £70.00 (HA)
1994 £12.05 (PIP)
1985 £17.04 (REI)
1983 £18.00 (CRO)

Fourcas-Hosten *cru grand bourgeois exceptionnnel Listrac*
1997 EC £68.00 (HIG)
1996 £9.99 (HIG) £12.95 (BER)
1995 £10.50 (STA) £10.95 (DI) £11.70 (TAN)
1994 £9.99 (HIG) £12.06 (AV) £15.99 (POR)
1982 £26.44 (REI)

Franc-Mayne *grand cru classé St-Émilion*
1996 £15.83 (MI)
1996 IB £135.00 (JER)

de Francs *Côtes de Francs*
1995 £7.99 (VIC) £7.99 (THR) £7.99 (WR) £7.99 (BOT)
1989 £18.95 (NI)

la Gaffelière *1er grand cru classé St-Émilion*
1995 £22.73 (HA) £25.00 (MI) £27.91 (FRI)
1994 IB £186.00 (RAE) £190.00 (FA)
1989 £57.00 (UB)
1983 £30.00 (MI)
1966 £38.19 (REI)

la Garde *Pessac-Léognan*
1996 IB £79.00 (CAV)

le Gay *Pomerol*
1996 £20.00 (WS)
1995 IB £220.00 (FA)
1990 £46.00 (BAL)
1986 £41.13 (REI)

Gazin *Pomerol*
1997 IB £372.00 (JU) £440.00 (TAN) £450.00 (CB)
1996 £29.00 (JU)
1995 £6.33 (HA)
1994 £26.26 (CB) £27.50 (YOU)

1990 £76.00 (UB)
1989 £42.50 (MI) £55.00 (BAL)
1982 £52.25 (TAN)
1982 IB £380.00 (FA)
1966 £32.31 (REI)

Giscours *3ème cru classé Margaux*
1996 £18.45 (BIB) £20.00 (MI)
1996 IB £165.00 (JER) £175.00 (BIB)
 £180.00 (FRI)
1995 £18.33 (MI) £19.58 (FRI) £20.90 (BIB)
 £27.50 (UN) £32.59 (PLAY)
1995 magnum £36.67 (MI) £43.08 (FRI)
1990 £24.82 (BIB) £40.83 (MI)
1990 magnum £81.67 (MI)
1989 £38.33 (MI) £39.99 (MI)
1989 magnum £76.67 (MI)
1988 £59.09 (BIB)
1986 £32.65 (BIB)
1983 £30.69 (BIB)
1983 IB £275.00 (FA) £300.00 (BIB)
1982 IB £425.00 (BIB)
1981 £23.00 (CRO)
1975 £65.50 (ROB)
1970 £70.50 (WY)
1970 IB £800.00 (FA)
1966 £52.88 (WY) £61.69 (REI)
1959 £170.04 (WY)

du Glana *cru grand bourgeois exceptionnel
 St-Julien*
1995 £14.49 (JER)
1929 £111.63 (WY)

Gloria *cru bourgeois St-Julien*
1996 £19.17 (MI)
1996 IB £170.00 (FRI)
1996 magnum £38.33 (MI)
1995 £18.33 (MI) £18.60 (FRI) £29.99 (NI)
1995 IB £190.00 (WY)
1994 £15.00 (MI) £17.04 (REI) £21.35 (PIP)
1990 £29.38 (COC)
1989 £33.00 (JON) £57.00 (UB)
1988 £32.50 (NI) £33.95 (ROB)
1983 £26.44 (REI)
1982 IB £300.00 (FA)

la Gorce *cru bourgeois Médoc*
1995 £7.45 (PIP)

> All châteaux are listed
> alphabetically
> regardless of class.

Grand-Barrail-Lamarzelle-Figeac
 grand cru classé St-Émilion
1970 £26.44 (REI)

Grand-Corbin *grand cru classé St-Émilion*
1996 £14.17 (MI)
1994 £17.82 (PLAY)
1988 £12.99 (NI)

Grand-Lartigue *St-Émilion*
1995 £9.99 (UN) £9.99 (RAE) £10.58 (BIB)
1994 £9.99 (RAE)

Grand-Mayne *grand cru classé St-Émilion*
1997 EC £315.00 (ELL)
1996 £26.95 (LAY)
1996 IB £210.00 (CAV)
1995 £21.50 (BAL) £28.00 (JU) £31.95 (RES)
1989 £34.95 (DI)

Grand-Pey-Lescours *St-Émilion*
1996 £8.97 (ROS)

Grand-Pontet *grand cru classé St-Émilion*
1996 £20.00 (JU)
1995 £18.50 (JU)

Grand-Puy-Ducasse *5ème cru classé
 Pauillac*
1996 £20.83 (MI)
1996 IB £140.00 (FA)
1995 £15.83 (MI) £20.00 (BU)
1990 £31.84 (TAN)
1989 £33.00 (COC)
1970 £48.35 (BY)
1961 £58.75 (WY) £97.00 (CRO)

Grand-Puy-Lacoste *5ème cru classé
 Pauillac*
1997 IB £220.00 (FA) £295.00 (TAN)
 £297.00 (CB)
1996 £42.44 (BIB) £47.50 (MI)
1996 IB £450.00 (FA) £500.00 (FRI)
1996 magnum £95.00 (MI)
1996 magnum IB £535.00 (WY)
1995 £32.50 (MI) £35.59 (BIB) £39.75 (BER)
 £44.00 (HIG) £45.53 (FRI) £62.50 (TAN)
1995 IB £350.00 (FA) £350.00 (BIB)
1994 £25.00 (MI) £25.95 (ROB) £31.99
 (POR) £33.21 (STE) £36.90 (NA) £45.00
 (TAN)
1994 IB £210.00 (FA)
1990 £55.17 (BIB) £65.50 (LAY)
1990 IB £550.00 (BIB)
1989 £40.48 (BIB) £45.82 (NO)

1988 £29.22 (BIB) £33.49 (REI)
1986 £46.99 (JON) £47.50 (LAY)
1985 £42.00 (CRO)
1983 £35.59 (BIB) £43.00 (COC)
1982 £72.00 (FLE) £74.75 (BIB) £76.38 (REI)
   £79.00 (POR) £85.50 (BEN)
1982 magnum IB £700.00 (FA)
1979 £28.79 (REI) £38.00 (CRO)
1978 £35.00 (BU)
1975 £28.79 (REI) £35.00 (BU) £77.55 (PEN)
1975 magnum IB £300.00 (FA)
1970 £48.35 (BY) £53.00 (CRO) £89.00 (UB)
1966 £50.00 (YOU) £68.00 (CRO)

de la Grave *Côtes de Bourg*
1996 £4.95 (WS)
1995 £6.25 (WS)

la Grave-Figeac *grand cru St-Émilion*
1995 £19.95 (ELL)

la Grave-Trigant-de-Boisset *Pomerol*
1990 £41.13 (WY)
1986 £26.44 (REI)

Gravet *grand cru St-Émilion*
1989 £14.50 (BU)

Greysac *cru grand bourgeois Médoc*
1995 £9.46 (COC) £11.50 (ROB)
1994 £10.95 (ROB)
1990 £12.34 (TW)

Gruaud-Larose *2ème cru classé St-Julien*
1997 EC £395.00 (ELL)
1996 £29.71 (BIB) £35.00 (WS) £38.00 (JU)
   £38.19 (CB) £38.33 (MI) £43.30 (PLAY)
   £43.50 (TAN)
1996 IB £290.00 (BIB) £295.00 (FA)
   £360.00 (FRI)
1996 EC £358.00 (HAH) £385.00 (ELL)
1996 magnum £76.67 (MI) £76.96 (CB)
1995 £28.73 (BIB) £30.29 (NI) £33.33 (MI)
   £40.00 (UN) £41.12 (FRI)
1995 IB £280.00 (FA) £280.00 (BIB)
1995 magnum £66.67 (MI)
1995 jeroboam £310.00 (MI)
1994 £19.99 (OD) £22.00 (HIG) £26.67 (MI)
   £28.50 (UN) £31.95 (WR) £31.95 (BOT)
1994 IB £230.00 (FA)
1994 magnum £53.33 (MI)
1994 double magnum £160.00 (MI)
1994 jeroboam £250.00 (MI)
1990 £40.48 (BIB) £45.00 (FORT) £49.99
   (OD) £53.33 (MI) £59.00 (BER)

1990 IB £395.00 (FA) £400.00 (BIB)
1990 magnum £106.67 (MI)
1989 £39.99 (BIB) £45.99 (JON) £49.50
   (BAL) £49.69 (VIN)
1989 IB £395.00 (FA) £395.00 (BIB)
1989 magnum £125.00 (FORT)

1988 £39.25 (GW) £39.50 (BIB) £43.50
   (BEN) £47.50 (FORT) £52.88 (TW) £59.95
   (RES) £69.00 (UB)
1986 £69.50 (BEN) £70.50 (WY) £85.00
   (BAL)
1986 IB £580.00 (FA) £580.00 (BIB)
   £695.00 (CAV)
1986 magnum IB £580.00 (FA) £695.00
   (CAV)
1985 £46.50 (BEN) £52.00 (CRO) £52.88
   (WY) £65.00 (FORT) £70.00 (ROB)
1985 IB £500.00 (BIB)
1985 jeroboam £680.00 (MI)
1983 £42.93 (BIB) £49.35 (WY) £53.00
   (ROB) £60.00 (FORT)
1983 IB £425.00 (BIB) £440.00 (FA)
1983 magnum £105.75 (WY)
1982 £76.71 (BIB) £85.00 (BU) £88.13 (WY)
   £89.50 (BEN) £125.00 (FORT)
1982 IB £770.00 (BIB) £795.00 (FA)
1982 magnum IB £995.00 (CAV)
1978 £50.79 (JON) £58.16 (TW) £58.16
   (TW) £59.95 (RES)
1975 IB £250.00 (FA)
1970 £47.00 (WY)
1966 £58.75 (WY) £73.44 (REI) £125.00
   (RES)
1961 £211.50 (REI) £258.50 (WY)
1961 IB £2,400.00 (FA)
1961 magnum £470.00 (FA)
1945 £293.75 (REI)
1928 £317.25 (WY)
1920 £264.38 (WY)

Guillot *Pomerol*
1996 £17.50 (MI)
1995 £15.83 (MI) £18.00 (JU)
1994 £15.83 (MI) £19.00 (JU)
1990 £22.50 (WS)

Guionne *Côtes de Bourg*
1996 £5.99 (COC)

la Gurgue *cru bourgeois supérieur Margaux*
1997 IB £128.00 (TAN)

Haut-Bages-Avérous *cru bourgeois Pauillac*
1996 £16.67 (MI)
1995 £30.88 (BY)
1983 £26.95 (ROB) £39.95 (RES)

Haut-Bages-Libéral *5ème cru classé Pauillac*
1997 IB £172.50 (TAN)
1996 £17.95 (AD) £20.83 (MI)
1996 magnum £41.67 (MI)
1995 £17.50 (MI) £19.95 (RES)
1995 magnum £35.00 (MI)
1994 £34.02 (STE) £37.80 (NA)
1989 £22.50 (WS) £27.90 (PIP) £44.00 (UB)
1982 £38.19 (REI)

Haut-Bages-Monpelou *cru bourgeois Pauillac*
1994 £11.93 (STE) £13.25 (NA)

Haut-Bailly *cru classé Pessac-Léognan*
1997 EC £258.00 (JON)
1996 £27.50 (MI) £28.75 (BALL) £29.00 (JU)
1996 IB £270.00 (JER)
1996 magnum £55.00 (MI)
1995 £21.70 (TAN) £22.15 (JON) £39.95 (AD)
1995 IB £192.00 (RAE) £280.00 (ELL)
1994 £19.50 (WS) £22.50 (STA) £24.50 (BAL)
1994 magnum £45.00 (WS)
1989 £36.50 (BAL)
1982 £33.49 (REI)
1978 IB £220.00 (FA)
1978 magnum £75.67 (PLAY)

Haut-Batailley *5ème cru classé Pauillac*
1997 IB £165.00 (LAY) £180.00 (JU) £187.00 (CB) £195.00 (TAN)
1996 £22.50 (MI) £23.32 (CB)
1996 IB £200.00 (CA)
1996 magnum £45.00 (MI)
1995 £18.33 (MI) £23.50 (WY) £24.00 (UN)
1994 £17.50 (MI) £27.25 (STA)
1994 magnum £35.00 (MI)
1986 £48.60 (BY)
1983 £25.26 (REI)
1982 £34.99 (YOU)

Haut-Bergey *Pessac-Léognan*
1995 £7.99 (OD) £12.50 (JU)

Haut-Beychevelle-Gloria *St-Julien*
1994 £10.49 (NLW) £11.26 (JER)

Haut-Brion *1er cru classé Pessac-Léognan*
1997 £888.00 (LAY)
1997 IB £882.00 (RAE) £990.00 (TAN) £996.00 (JU) £1,040.00 (CB)
1997 EC £995.00 (ELL)
1996 £99.95 (DI) £107.51 (CB) £173.33 (MI)
1996 IB £980.00 (FA) £995.00 (BIB) £1,200.00 (FRI)
1996 magnum £346.67 (MI)
1996 double magnum £880.00 (MI)
1996 imperial IB £825.00 (WY)
1995 £99.23 (BIB) £125.00 (DI) £137.08 (FRI) £173.33 (MI) £230.57 (BY)
1995 IB £1,000.00 (FA) £1,000.00 (BIB)
1995 double magnum £470.00 (FA) £880.00 (MI)
1995 imperial £1,760.00 (MI)
1994 £67.50 (UN) £72.00 (BAL) £79.95 (POR) £82.25 (PEN) £101.59 (JON) £121.67 (MI)
1994 IB £660.00 (FA)
1994 magnum IB £660.00 (FA)
1990 £143.30 (BIB) £165.00 (ROB) £213.85 (CB) £217.38 (REI)
1990 IB £1,450.00 (FA) £1,450.00 (BIB)
1990 magnum IB £1,450.00 (FA)
1990 imperial £1,527.50 (FA)
1989 £216.73 (BIB) £346.63 (CB) £351.52 (JER) £495.00 (CON)
1989 IB £2,200.00 (FA) £2,200.00 (BIB)
1988 £84.55 (BIB) £105.70 (TAN) £135.00 (RES) £199.54 (BY)
1988 imperial £822.50 (WY)
1986 £83.95 (ROB) £85.00 (CON) £88.13 (REI) £94.00 (WY) £105.00 (OD) £109.02 (BIB) £130.83 (MI) £175.00 (FORT)
1985 £110.98 (BIB) £136.10 (VIN) £137.62 (BY) £173.00 (ROB)
1985 IB £1,100.00 (FA) £1,120.00 (BIB)
1983 £63.96 (BY) £76.38 (REI) £82.25 (WY) £87.50 (MI) £93.00 (YOU) £98.89 (JON) £99.50 (STA) £115.00 (FORT)
1983 IB £800.00 (FA) £800.00 (BIB)
1982 £162.88 (BIB) £170.00 (JU) £195.00 (BEN) £230.10 (JER) £258.33 (MI) £275.00 (FORT) £315.00 (RES)
1982 IB £1,650.00 (FA) £1,650.00 (BIB)
1982 magnum IB £1,650.00 (FA)
1982 imperial £2,115.00 (WY)

1981 £60.00 (ROB) £85.00 (BU)
1981 double magnum £282.00 (FA)
1978 £117.44 (BY) £130.00 (ROB)
1975 £95.00 (BU) £105.75 (REI)
1975 IB £995.00 (CAV)
1975 magnum IB £820.00 (FA)
1975 double magnum £311.38 (FA)
1970 £103.40 (WY) £114.73 (BY) £125.00
  (BU) £138.65 (REI) £176.25 (TW)
1970 IB £995.00 (CAV)
1970 magnum £235.00 (WY) £255.00
  (RES)
1966 IB £1,350.00 (FA)
1964 £141.00 (REI) £142.97 (BY)
1964 IB £1,495.00 (FA)
1961 £470.00 (CAV) £587.50 (FA)
1959 £485.00 (CRO) £493.50 (FA) £528.75
  (WY) £699.13 (CAV)
1955 £352.50 (REI)
1949 £558.13 (CAV) £740.25 (WY)
1945 magnum £2,056.25 (WY)
1929 £822.50 (WY)
1928 £495.00 (ROB) £581.63 (CAV)
  £734.38 (WY)
1924 double magnum £2,761.25 (WY)
1920 magnum £1,028.13 (REI)

Haut-Faugères *grand cru St-Émilion*
1990 £11.63 (TW)

Haut-Gaillardet *Bordeaux Supérieur*
  Côtes de Castillon
1990 £8.80 (CRO)

Haut-Gardère *Pessac-Léognan*
1996 EC £89.00 (ELL)

Haut-Guiraud *Côtes de Bourg*
1995 £6.66 (JER)

Haut-Marbuzet *cru grand bourgeois*
  exceptionnel St-Estèphe
1996 £24.00 (JU) £24.17 (MI) £24.31 (NO)
1996 magnum £48.33 (MI)
1995 IB £215.00 (FA) £235.00 (ELL)
1994 £20.50 (WRI) £21.50 (BAL)

Please remember that
Oz Clarke's Wine Guide
*is a price **guide** and not a
price **list**. It is not meant to
replace up-to-date
merchants' lists.*

Haut-Pontet *grand cru St-Émilion*
1996 IB £125.00 (CAV)
1995 £14.49 (JER)

de Haut-Sociondo *1ères Côtes de Blaye*
1997 EC £30.00 (JON)
1994 £9.95 (STA)

Hortevie *cru bourgeois St-Julien*
1995 £12.95 (BAL) £14.49 (JER)
1994 £11.60 (HED) £12.95 (BAL)

d'Issan *3ème cru classé Margaux*
1997 EC £170.00 (HIG)
1996 £20.00 (MI)
1996 magnum £40.00 (MI)
1995 £19.17 (MI) £21.54 (FRI) £25.00 (FLE)
1994 £17.50 (MI)
1990 £32.50 (BAL)
1989 £41.50 (ROB)
1988 £41.00 (UB)
1986 £28.00 (CRO)
1983 £32.31 (REI) £33.00 (CRO)

Jonqueyres *Bordeaux Supérieur*
1995 £7.50 (JU) £9.61 (WT)

Kirwan *3ème cru classé Margaux*
1997 IB £135.00 (FA) £190.00 (TAN)
1997 magnum IB £179.00 (CB)
1996 £20.00 (JU) £21.95 (DI)
1996 IB £150.00 (WY)
1995 £27.50 (UN)
1995 IB £250.00 (WY)
1994 £23.50 (WY) £24.57 (STE) £27.30 (NA)
1989 £53.46 (TW)
1988 £29.50 (BALL) £38.30 (AV) £38.50
  (TAN) £44.99 (POR)
1981 £40.75 (WRI)

Labégorce *cru bourgeois supérieur*
  Margaux
1996 £15.00 (MI) £18.39 (CB)
1994 £10.81 (HA)
1989 £29.38 (COC)

Labégorce-Zédé *cru bourgeois supérieur*
  Margaux
1997 EC £141.00 (JON)
1996 £16.50 (AD) £16.50 (JU) £18.20 (TAN)
1996 IB £144.00 (RAE)
1995 £16.00 (JU) £19.95 (NI)
1990 £43.00 (UB)
1989 £35.92 (NO)
1985 £22.91 (REI) £40.00 (FORT)

Lacombe *Bordeaux Supérieur*
1997 £6.27 (FRI)
1995 £5.49 (CON)

Lacoste-Borie *Pauillac*
1995 £14.75 (WS) £15.00 (MI) £19.00 (CRO)
1995 IB £120.00 (FA)
1994 £12.50 (MI) £20.64 (BY)
1982 £19.59 (YOU) £23.50 (WY)

Lafite-Rothschild *1er cru classé Pauillac*
1997 IB £990.00 (TAN) £996.00 (JU)
 £1,035.00 (CB)
1997 EC £995.00 (ELL)
1996 £99.95 (DI) £129.25 (CB) £148.19
 (BIB) £173.33 (MI)
1996 IB £1,150.00 (FA) £1,350.00 (FRI)
 1996 EC £1,500.00 (ELL)
1996 magnum £346.67 (MI)
1996 double magnum £880.00 (MI)
1995 £109.02 (BIB) £156.67 (FRI) £173.33
 (MI) £258.22 (BY)
1995 IB £1,100.00 (BIB) £1,610.00 (ELL)
1995 double magnum £558.13 (FA)
1994 £67.50 (UN) £85.00 (JU) £104.58
 (PEN) £121.67 (MI) £125.00 (ROB)
1990 £148.19 (BIB) £186.04 (FRI) £215.83
 (MI) £235.00 (ROB)
1990 IB £1,500.00 (FA) £1,700.00 (CAV)
1990 magnum IB £1,500.00 (FA)
1990 double magnum £587.75 (FA)
1989 £118.82 (BIB) £137.08 (FRI) £155.00
 (BAL) £165.00 (MI) £195.00 (FORT)
1989 IB £1,100.00 (FA) £1,200.00 (BIB)
 £1,350.00 (CAV)
1989 imperial £1,660.00 (MI)
1988 £111.63 (WY) £120.00 (YOU) £120.46
 (BY) £122.40 (FRI) £125.50 (BEN)
1988 IB £1,100.00 (FA) £1,100.00 (BIB)
1988 magnum £254.58 (FRI)
1988 double magnum £830.00 (MI)

1986 £152.75 (WY) £157.49 (BIB) £176.25
 (FRI) £207.50 (MI) £275.00 (FORT)
1986 ½ bottle IB £1,550.00 (FA)
1986 magnum £415.00 (MI)

1985 £109.02 (BIB) £130.83 (MI) £132.80
 (AV) £175.00 (JU)
1985 IB £1,100.00 (BIB) £1,150.00 (FA)
1985 ½ bottle £64.63 (REI) £115.00 (UB)
1985 double magnum £434.75 (FA)
1983 £98.25 (BIB) £105.75 (WY) £120.00
 (BEN) £135.00 (POR) £137.00 (BAL)
 £150.00 (FORT) £160.00 (STA)
1983 IB £950.00 (FA) £990.00 (BIB)
1983 magnum £350.00 (FORT)
1982 £205.63 (WY) £241.21 (BIB) £310.00
 (CRO) £320.00 (JU) £323.13 (REI) £386.67
 (MI) £425.00 (FORT) £435.00 (ROB)
 £525.00 (RES)
1982 IB £2,450.00 (FA) £2,950.00 (CAV)
1978 £105.75 (WY) £129.25 (REI) £178.99
 (VIN)
1978 IB £980.00 (FA)
1975 £117.50 (CAV) £141.00 (WY) £145.00
 (BEN)
1975 magnum IB £1,200.00 (FA)
1970 £117.50 (WY) £158.63 (REI) £175.00
 (ROB)
1970 IB £850.00 (FA)
1970 magnum £260.00 (ROB)
1970 magnum IB £995.00 (CAV)
1966 magnum IB £995.00 (FA)
1966 double magnum £650.00 (RES)
1962 £99.88 (FA) £105.75 (WY)
1961 IB £4,200.00 (CAV)
1961 ½ bottle £158.63 (WY)
1961 double magnum £1,821.25 (FA)
1959 £528.75 (FA)
1949 £464.13 (REI) £564.00 (CAV) £705.00
 (WY)
1949 magnum £2,232.50 (WY)
1947 ½ bottle £176.25 (REI)
1945 £1,087.80 (WY)
1934 £340.75 (WY)
1929 £317.25 (WY)
1929 magnum £1,880.00 (WY)
1928 £564.00 (WY)
1918 £340.75 (WY)

Lafleur *Pomerol*
1997 EC £88.70 (HAH)
1996 £133.50 (BIB) £160.38 (CB)
1996 IB £1,250.00 (FA) £1,350.00 (BIB)
1995 £68.54 (FRI) £236.32 (BIB)
1995 IB £2,400.00 (FA) £2,400.00 (BIB)
1994 IB £1,000.00 (FA) £1,900.00 (CAV)
1990 £373.40 (BIB)
1990 IB £3,200.00 (FA) £3,800.00 (BIB)
1989 £216.73 (BIB)
1989 IB £2,200.00 (BIB) £2,300.00 (FA)

1988 £246.75 (REI)
1988 IB £162.88 (BIB) £1,650.00 (BIB)
1986 £177.57 (BIB)
1986 IB £1,800.00 (FA) £1,800.00 (BIB)
    £2,500.00 (CAV)
1985 IB £2,600.00 (FA) £2,600.00 (BIB)
1983 £202.05 (BIB) £235.00 (CAV)
1983 IB £2,050.00 (BIB) £2,250.00 (FA)
1979 IB £3,600.00 (FA)
1978 £352.50 (CAV)

Lafleur-Gazin *Pomerol*
1995 £17.50 (JU)

Lafon-Rochet *4ème cru classé St-Estèphe*
1997 IB £187.00 (CB) £192.00 (TAN)
1996 £23.33 (MI) £23.74 (CB)
1996 IB £170.00 (FRI) £170.00 (FA)
1995 £22.03 (FRI) £25.83 (MI)
1995 IB £290.00 (WY)
1994 £27.00 (STA)
1986 £38.40 (UB)
1982 £38.78 (WY)
1978 £15.00 (CRO)
1975 £20.97 (REI)

Lagrange *Pomerol*
1997 IB £174.00 (CB) £216.00 (LAY)
1995 £19.95 (AD) £22.68 (CB)
1994 £21.74 (CB)
1988 £29.50 (BU)
1978 £26.44 (REI)

Lagrange *3ème cru classé St-Julien*
1997 IB £235.00 (CB)
1996 £28.33 (MI) £28.95 (DI)
1996 IB £230.00 (FA) £235.00 (JER)
    £240.00 (FRI)
1995 £25.00 (CON) £28.20 (WY)
1995 IB £240.00 (FA)
1994 £22.50 (MI)
1990 £39.75 (ROB) £47.00 (WY)
1990 IB £380.00 (FA)
1989 £35.20 (TAN) £41.13 (WY) £41.95
    (ROB) £49.50 (PHI)
1986 £42.95 (ROB)

la Lagune *3ème cru classé Haut-Médoc*
1997 EC £145.00 (HIG) £147.15 (HAH)
1996 £16.00 (BIB) £20.50 (HIG) £21.67 (MI)
1996 IB £150.00 (FRI) £150.00 (BIB)
    £162.00 (RAE)
1996 magnum £43.33 (MI)
1996 imperial £270.00 (MI)
1996 imperial IB £130.00 (WY)

1995 £19.92 (BIB) £21.05 (FRI) £23.33 (MI)
    £29.50 (UN)
1995 IB £190.00 (FA) £190.00 (BIB)
1995 EC £175.00 (ELL)
1995 magnum £46.02 (FRI) £46.67 (MI)
1995 double magnum £140.00 (MI)
1995 double magnum IB £230.00 (WY)
1995 imperial £300.00 (MI)
1995 imperial IB £165.00 (WY)
1994 £21.50 (UN) £23.33 (MI) £34.00 (NO)
1994 magnum £46.67 (MI)
1990 £29.95 (DI) £33.63 (BIB) £45.00 (CRO)
    £50.00 (FORT)
1990 IB £320.00 (FA) £330.00 (BIB)
1989 £32.65 (BIB) £33.29 (FRI) £37.60 (WY)
    £42.50 (BAL) £45.00 (FORT) £46.00 (PIP)
1989 IB £320.00 (BIB)
1988 £29.50 (CON) £33.63 (BIB) £37.85
    (BY) £45.00 (FORT)
1988 IB £275.00 (FA) £330.00 (BIB)
1986 £32.65 (BIB) £38.50 (BAL) £41.50
    (ROB) £45.00 (CON)
1986 IB £320.00 (BIB)
1986 magnum IB £320.00 (FA)
1985 £35.59 (BIB)
1985 IB £350.00 (BIB)
1983 £31.00 (CRO) £35.25 (WY)
1983 IB £320.00 (BIB)
1983 imperial £246.75 (REI)
1982 £42.00 (YOU) £52.23 (BIB) £62.00
    (CRO) £64.60 (TAN) £67.50 (ROB) £76.59
    (BY) £76.85 (GW)
1982 IB £500.00 (FA) £520.00 (BIB)
1982 double magnum £352.50 (WY)
1981 £29.20 (REI) £30.33 (BY)
1979 £26.24 (BY)
1978 £38.19 (REI) £39.00 (CRO) £44.50
    (ROB)
1978 IB £275.00 (FA)
1975 £29.95 (BEN) £32.34 (BY)
1975 IB £190.00 (FA)
1970 £44.00 (CRO) £47.00 (REI) £66.67 (MI)
1970 magnum £102.81 (REI)
1966 £54.64 (REI)
1964 £33.49 (REI)
1924 £152.75 (WY)

Lalande d'Auvion *Médoc*
1995 £7.25 (BALL)

Lalande-Borie *cru bourgeois supérieur St-Julien*
1995 £12.49 (AME)
1994 £13.95 (WS) £14.17 (MI) £15.50 (BALL)
1990 £21.67 (MI)

de Lamarque *cru grand bourgeois Haut-Médoc*
1997 IB £90.00 (CB)
1996 £13.98 (CB)
1988 IB £100.00 (FA)
1975 £20.56 (REI)

Lamothe-Cissac *Haut-Médoc*
1996 £8.49 (DI)

Lanessan *cru bourgeois supérieur Haut-Médoc*
1996 £13.33 (MI)
1995 £11.67 (MI) £13.27 (CHA)
1995 IB £110.00 (FA)
1990 £21.10 (NO) £22.00 (AV)
1988 £20.95 (ROB)
1986 £17.50 (GW)
1982 £31.50 (TAN)

Langoa-Barton *3ème cru classé St-Julien*
1997 IB £204.00 (JU) £240.00 (TAN)
1997 EC £219.60 (JON) £230.00 (HIG)
1996 £25.95 (AD) £26.95 (LAY) £29.95 (DI) £30.32 (CB) £30.60 (TAN)
1995 £21.50 (DI) £22.00 (TAN) £29.99 (AV)
1994 £20.61 (STE) £21.50 (DI) £22.90 (NA) £25.00 (FORT) £28.99 (JON) £35.64 (BY)
1990 £45.69 (JON)
1985 £39.30 (PIP) £39.95 (RES)
1982 £44.06 (REI) £85.00 (RES)
1978 £29.00 (CRO)
1966 £41.13 (REI) £46.50 (YOU)

Larmande *grand cru classé St-Émilion*
1997 IB £240.00 (TAN)
1996 £21.67 (MI) £25.95 (DI)
1995 £19.17 (MI) £21.00 (JU) £26.50 (BAL)
1995 IB £200.00 (FA)
1994 £19.45 (BER)

Laroque *grand cru St-Émilion*
1994 £14.45 (WAI)

Larose-Trintaudon *cru grand bourgeois Haut-Médoc*
1996 IB £85.00 (FRI)
1995 £8.16 (HA) £12.99 (MORR)

Larrivet-Haut-Brion *Pessac-Léognan*
1997 IB £175.00 (TAN)
1996 £15.50 (JU)
1995 £17.98 (CB)
1994 £20.27 (WT)
1983 £25.00 (BU)

Lascombes *2ème cru classé Margaux*
1996 £23.33 (MI)
1996 IB £200.00 (FRI) £230.00 (JER)
1996 magnum £46.67 (MI) £230.00 (JER)
1995 £21.54 (FRI) £22.50 (NI) £40.00 (UN) £57.77 (JER)
1994 £19.50 (HIG) £22.75 (ROB) £28.50 (UN)
1990 £39.00 (COC)
1988 magnum £68.25 (ROB)
1982 IB £380.00 (FA)
1975 £29.50 (BEN) £76.38 (PEN)
1961 £82.25 (WY)

Latour *1er cru classé Pauillac*
1997 IB £750.00 (FA) £886.20 (RAE) £990.00 (TAN) £996.00 (JU) £1,040.00 (CB)
1997 EC £995.00 (ELL)
1996 £134.48 (BIB) £173.33 (MI)
1996 IB £1,360.00 (BIB) £1,400.00 (FA) £1,550.00 (FRI)
1996 magnum £346.67 (WY)
1995 double magnum £880.00 (MI)
1996 double magnum IB £500.00 (WY)
1996 imperial £1,760.00 (MI)
1995 imperial IB £1,000.00 (WY)
1995 £128.61 (BIB) £156.67 (FRI) £173.33 (MI) £410.59 (BY)
1995 IB £1,300.00 (BIB) £1,400.00 (FA)
1995 magnum £346.67 (MI)
1995 imperial £1,760.00 (MI)
1994 IB £820.00 (FA)
1994 double magnum £387.75 (FA)
1993 £79.17 (MI) £79.50 (LAY) £82.25 (AV) £129.19 (BY)
1993 IB £750.00 (FA)
1990 £260.80 (BIB) £450.00 (FORT)
1990 IB £2,650.00 (FA) £2,700.00 (CAV)
1990 magnum IB £2,650.00 (FA)
1989 £99.58 (CB) £107.07 (BIB) £111.63 (REI) £126.46 (LAY) £137.08 (FRI) £175.00 (FORT) £217.60 (PLAY)
1989 IB £1,080.00 (BIB) £1,120.00 (FA)
1989 magnum IB £1,120.00 (FA)

> • Wines are listed in A–Z order within each price band.
> • For each wine, vintages are listed in descending order.
> • Each vintage of any wine appears only once.

1988 £104.13 (BIB) £113.33 (MI) £150.00
(FORT)
1988 IB £980.00 (FA) £1,050.00 (BIB)
1988 magnum £300.00 (FORT)
1988 magnum IB £980.00 (FA)
1988 double magnum £440.63 (WY)
1986 £106.80 (BY) £120.00 (CON) £130.83
(MI) £135.13 (CB) £137.00 (BAL)
1986 IB £1,050.00 (FA) £1,060.00 (BIB)
1986 magnum £261.67 (MI)
1986 magnum IB £1,050.00 (FA)
1985 £108.05 (BIB) £122.50 (LAY) £140.00
(TAN) £169.00 (NI)
1985 magnum IB £1,100.00 (FA)
1983 £88.46 (BIB) £99.99 (POR) £105.00
(MI) £115.79 (JON) £125.00 (STA)
£125.00 (FORT)
1983 magnum IB £900.00 (FA)
1982 £270.59 (BIB) £350.00 (JU) £390.00
(BEN) £450.00 (FORT) £540.00 (ROB)
1982 IB £2,750.00 (BIB) £2,950.00 (FA)
1982 magnum £611.00 (CAV)
1982 double magnum £1,410.00 (WY)
1981 £78.40 (BY) £86.24 (LAY) £99.88 (PLA)
1981 IB £740.00 (FA)
1979 £92.83 (PLA) £110.00 (FORT)
1979 IB £780.00 (FA)
1979 magnum IB £780.00 (FA)
1979 imperial £587.50 (FA) £890.00 (MI)
1978 £120.00 (JU) £150.00 (FORT) £190.00
(ROB)
1975 £285.00 (UB)
1975 IB £1,100.00 (FA)
1970 £311.38 (REI) £450.00 (FORT)
£450.00 (RES)
1970 IB £2,600.00 (FA)
1966 £164.50 (WY) £280.00 (CRO)
£293.75 (CAV) £295.00 (RES) £450.00
(FORT) £465.00 (TAN)
1966 IB £2,650.00 (FA)
1964 £205.63 (CAV) £225.60 (REI) £235.00
(WY) £295.00 (FORT)
1964 IB £1,950.00 (FA)
1964 magnum £464.13 (CAV)
1961 £581.63 (WY) £646.25 (REI)
1961 magnum £2,878.75 (WY)
1961 imperial £24,675.00 (WY)
1959 £470.00 (FA) £500.00 (FORT) £658.00
(WY)
1959 magnum £1,057.50 (TW)
1955 £375.00 (BEN) £376.00 (REI) £445.00
(CRO)
1955 IB £3,600.00 (FA)
1950 £129.25 (REI) £140.00 (BEN) £195.00
(BU) £434.75 (WY)

1949 £199.75 (WY) £934.13 (CAV)
1947 £546.38 (WY)
1945 £1,762.50 (WY)
1944 £299.63 (WY)
1943 £188.00 (WY) £300.00 (JU)
1937 £246.75 (WY) £264.38 (CAV)
1934 £176.25 (REI) £393.63 (WY)
1929 £522.88 (WY)
1920 £323.13 (REI)
1918 £329.00 (WY)
1916 £317.25 (WY)

Latour-à-Pomerol *Pomerol*
1997 IB £330.00 (CB)
1996 £32.55 (CB)
1994 £26.85 (CB)
1982 IB £1,150.00 (FA)
1981 £37.60 (WY)
1970 IB £780.00 (FA) £1,195.00 (CAV)
1955 £229.13 (CAV)

Lavillotte *cru bourgeois Médoc*
1995 £12.50 (FORT)

Léoville-Barton *2ème cru classé St-Julien*
1997 £38.06 (BY)
1997 IB £250.00 (FA) £264.00 (RAE)
£294.00 (JU) £305.00 (TAN) £315.00 (CB)
1997 EC £291.00 (JON) £305.00 (ELL)
£310.00 (HIG)
1996 £34.61 (BIB) £39.17 (MI) £44.59 (CB)
£44.95 (DI)
1996 IB £340.00 (FA) £340.00 (BIB)
£390.00 (FRI) £390.00 (WY)
1996 magnum £78.33 (MI)
1996 double magnum IB £440.00 (WY)
1995 £34.61 (BIB) £39.17 (FRI) £47.00 (WY)
£78.20 (BY)
1995 IB £340.00 (FA) £340.00 (BIB)
1995 double magnum IB £520.00 (WY)
1994 £29.75 (BER) £31.10 (PIP) £35.49 (JON)
1994 IB £260.00 (FA)
1994 magnumIB £315.00 (WY)
1990 £49.30 (BIB) £65.00 (BAL) £65.00 (BU)
1989 £37.50 (CON) £42.44 (BIB) £44.97
(LAY) £47.00 (WY) £54.00 (AV) £64.60
(TAN)

1988 £34.66 (REI) £36.57 (BIB) £39.55 (PLAY) £41.90 (LAY) £43.75 (BAL) £50.00 (FORT) £54.36 (BY)
1986 £45.00 (CON) £45.38 (BIB) £49.50 (BEN) £65.00 (FORT)
1986 IB £450.00 (FA) £450.00 (BIB)
1986 magnum IB £470.00 (WY)
1985 £46.36 (BIB) £49.35 (WY) '£57.28 (JER) £59.57 (NO) £60.00 (FORT) £64.60 (TAN) £69.95 (RES) £450.00 (FA)
1983 £35.00 (COC) £35.25 (WY)
1983 IB £295.00 (FA) £350.00 (BIB)
1982 £60.07 (BIB) £82.25 (CAV) £88.13 (REI) £100.00 (FORT)
1982 IB £600.00 (BIB) £740.00 (CAV)
1982 double magnum £334.88 (WY)
1978 £32.50 (BU)
1970 £42.30 (WY)
1970 magnum £94.00 (WY)
1961 £130.00 (YOU) £152.75 (WY) £165.00 (CRO)
1959 £88.13 (REI)

Léoville-Las-Cases 2ème cru classé St-Julien
1997 IB £774.00 (JU) £880.00 (CB) £900.00 (TAN)
1997 EC £795.00 (ELL)
1996 £93.36 (BIB)
1996 IB £940.00 (BIB) £1,020.00 (FA) £1,050.00 (CAV) £1,100.00 (FRI)
1996 imperial IB £820.00 (WY)
1995 £67.90 (BIB) £76.96 (REI) £78.33 (FRI)
1995 magnum IB £700.00 (FA)
1994 £49.50 (BAL)
1994 IB £420.00 (FA)
1990 £89.44 (BIB) £125.00 (POR) £130.00 (BAL) £135.13 (REI)
1990 IB £900.00 (BIB) £920.00 (FA)
1989 £66.98 (CB) £77.55 (WY) £98.00 (BAL)
1989 IB £680.00 (BIB) £720.00 (FA)
1989 ½ bottle IB £750.00 (WY)
1989 magnum IB £720.00 (FA) £750.00 (WY)
1988 £51.79 (HA) £52.72 (BIB) £93.00 (BER)
1988 IB £525.00 (BIB) £540.00 (FA)
1986 £149.00 (BAL) £151.58 (REI)
1986 IB £900.00 (FA) £900.00 (BIB)
1986 magnum IB £900.00 (FA)
1985 £69.86 (BIB) £74.99 (OD)
1985 IB £680.00 (FA) £795.00 (CAV)
1985 magnum IB £680.00 (FA)
1983 £44.40 (BIB) £49.35 (WY) £49.94 (REI) £62.00 (BER) £80.00 (JU)
1983 IB £440.00 (FA) £440.00 (BIB)

1982 £143.30 (BIB) £158.63 (WY) £159.00 (POR) £165.00 (JU) £170.04 (REI) £195.00 (BEN) £250.00 (FORT)
1982 IB £1,450.00 (BIB) £1,500.00 (FA) £1,795.00 (CAV)
1982 magnum £323.13 (CAV)
1981 £47.95 (ROB) £50.00 (GW) £58.00 (BER) £60.37 (BY)
1979 IB £420.00 (FA)
1979 double magnum £164.50 (FA)
1978 £82.91 (BY) £85.00 (RES)
1978 IB £650.00 (CAV)
1978 magnum IB £695.00 (CAV)
1975 IB £480.00 (FA)
1970 £52.88 (REI)
1966 £99.88 (WY)
1964 magnum IB £550.00 (FA)
1962 £88.13 (REI)
1961 £205.63 (WY) £205.63 (REI) £350.00 (RES)
1945 £493.50 (WY)
1912 £205.63 (REI)

Léoville-Poyferré 2ème cru classé St-Julien
1997 IB £250.00 (FA) £270.00 (RAE) £297.00 (CB) £320.00 (TAN)
1996 £27.26 (BIB) £28.96 (LAY) £30.83 (MI) £32.00 (AD) £37.13 (CB)
1996 IB £265.00 (BIB) £270.00 (RAE) £360.00 (FRI)
1996 magnum £61.67 (MI) £74.85 (CB)
1995 £25.39 (NI) £25.80 (BIB) £27.99 (OD)
1995 IB £250.00 (BIB) £295.00 (CAV) £300.00 (WY)
1994 £25.50 (UN)
1990 £54.19 (BIB)
1990 IB £540.00 (FA) £850.00 (CAV)
1990 magnum IB £795.00 (CAV)
1989 £29.95 (ROB) £30.69 (BIB)
1988 £35.59 (BIB) £56.00 (BER) £60.00 (UB)
1986 £33.14 (BIB) £41.95 (NI)
1985 £27.60 (FLE) £35.59 (BIB)
1985 IB £350.00 (BIB)
1983 £33.63 (BIB) £42.50 (BALL) £42.99 (OD)
1982 £54.50 (BEN) £55.17 (BIB) £89.50 (BER)
1982 IB £540.00 (FA) £550.00 (BIB)
1961 £82.25 (WY)
1961 IB £1,300.00 (FA)
1959 £98.00 (ROB)
1949 £193.88 (WY)
1947 £346.63 (CAV)
1924 £88.13 (WY)
1906 £29.37 (FRI)

Lestage *cru bourgeois supérieur Listrac*
1993 £7.99 (WAT)

Liversan *cru grand bourgeois Haut-Médoc*
1996 £9.95 (DI) £9.99 (SAF)
1995 £10.99 (YOU)
1994 £12.95 (LEA)
1990 £14.55 (AV)
1985 £24.00 (CRO)
1984 £13.51 (REI)

Loudenne *cru grand bourgeois Médoc*
1996 £13.33 (MI)
1995 £10.00 (JU) £11.67 (MI)
1994 £7.49 (MORR)
1989 £13.00 (COC) £15.83 (MI)
1988 £10.50 (FLE)

la Louvière *Pessac-Léognan*
1995 £9.45 (WAI) £16.95 (DI) £22.95 (NI)
1985 £38.00 (PHI)

Lynch-Bages *5ème cru classé Pauillac*
1997 IB £395.00 (TAN) £396.00 (CB)
1997 EC £365.00 (ELL)
1996 £32.65 (BIB) £37.50 (MI) £39.00 (JU)
  £41.54 (CB) £42.50 (TAN) £43.92 (PLAY)
1996 IB £295.00 (CAV) £330.00 (FRI)
1996 EC £395.00 (ELL)
1996 magnum IB £300.00 (FA) £330.00
  (FRI)
1995 £34.12 (BIB) £35.74 (FRI) £36.50 (UN)
  £36.67 (MI) £74.31 (BY)
1995 IB £335.00 (BIB) £350.00 (WY)
1995 magnum £73.33 (MI) £75.40 (FRI)
1995 jeroboam IB £265.00 (WY)
1994 £29.17 (MI) £29.99 (NI) £29.99 (POR)
  £31.50 (UN)
1994 magnum £58.33 (MI) £63.95 (POR)
1994 jeroboam £276.13 (WY) £280.00
  (MI)
1990 £72.66 (NO) £73.44 (FRI) £103.60 (PIP)
1990 IB £650.00 (FA) £680.00 (BIB)
  £700.00 (WY)
1990 magnum £152.75 (FRI)
1989 £74.03 (WY) £100.00 (WAI)
1989 IB £695.00 (FA) £700.00 (BIB)
1988 £50.27 (BIB) £52.88 (WY)
1986 £56.50 (BEN) £85.00 (FORT)
1986 IB £575.00 (FA) £575.00 (BIB)
1985 £76.71 (BIB) £83.50 (BEN) £85.00
  (TAN) £85.00 (BU) £101.00 (BAL) £115.00
  (FORT) £120.00 (RES)
1985 IB £770.00 (BIB) £780.00 (FA)
1985 magnum £170.38 (WY)

1983 £50.27 (BIB) £57.50 (BU) £63.45 (WY)
1983 IB £460.00 (FA) £500.00 (BIB)
1982 £94.34 (BIB) £95.00 (BU) £99.50
  (CON) £99.50 (BEN) £99.88 (WY)
  £150.00 (FORT) £228.00 (UB)
1982 IB £950.00 (FA) £950.00 (BIB)
1979 IB £320.00 (FA)
1978 £51.70 (WY) £64.63 (TW) £70.00
  (ROB) £73.44 (FRI)
1970 £99.50 (BEN) £129.25 (WY) £160.00
  (RES)
1970 IB £1,050.00 (FA)
1966 £70.50 (REI) £135.13 (WY)
1962 £105.75 (REI)
1961 £264.38 (WY) £275.00 (BEN) £300.00
  (FORT) £410.00 (RES)
1961 IB £2,200.00 (FA)
1945 £258.50 (REI) £376.00 (CAV) £628.63
  (WY)

Lynch-Moussas *5ème cru classé Pauillac*
1996 £14.99 (OD) £17.50 (MI) £18.95 (DI)
1995 £15.83 (MI)
1994 £13.33 (MI)

du Lyonnat *Lussac-St-Émilion*
1996 £9.99 (POR) £11.15 (PLAY)
1995 £8.69 (JON) £9.95 (ROB)
1994 £9.75 (ROB)

Macquin-St-Georges *St-Georges-St-Émilion*
1997 IB £69.00 (CB)
1996 £7.50 (HAH) £7.85 (CB) £7.99 (POR)
1995 £6.50 (BALL) £7.50 (TAN) £8.35 (AV)
  £8.50 (CB)
1994 £8.17 (CB)

Magdelaine *1er grand cru classé St-Émilion*
1997 IB £320.00 (CB)
1996 £27.44 (CB)
1996 IB £245.00 (CAV)
1995 £30.69 (BIB) £34.31 (CB)
1994 £26.73 (CB)

EC *(ex-cellar) price per
dozen, excl shipping, duty
and VAT.*
IB *(in bond) price per
dozen, excl duty and VAT.
All other prices,
per bottle incl VAT.*

1990 £32.65 (BIB)
1990 IB £320.00 (BIB)
1989 £38.52 (BIB)
1986 £24.82 (BIB)
1985 £30.69 (BIB)
1983 IB £300.00 (BIB)
1982 IB £600.00 (BIB)
1981 £18.80 (WY) £26.44 (REI)
1978 £45.24 (REI) £57.36 (BY)

Malartic-Lagravière *cru classé Pessac-Léognan*
1983 £26.44 (REI)
1978 £20.56 (REI)
1961 £76.38 (REI)

Malescasse *cru bourgeois Haut-Médoc*
1997 EC £95.00 (HIG)
1996 £13.00 (HIG) £190.00 (MI)
1989 IB £130.00 (FA)
1988 £18.50 (FLE) £18.99 (NI)
1985 £18.00 (CRO) £19.99 (POR)

Malescot-St-Exupéry *3ème cru classé Margaux*
1996 £20.00 (JU)
1994 £29.99 (POR)

de Marbuzet *cru grand bourgeois exceptionnel St-Estèphe*
1996 £19.00 (JU)
1996 IB £158.00 (JER)
1988 £19.95 (CON)
1985 £32.31 (REI)

Margaux *1er cru classé Margaux*
1997 IB £990.00 (TAN) £996.00 (JU) £1,075.00 (CB)
1997 EC £995.00 (ELL)
1996 £10.99 (VIC) £10.99 (THR) £10.99 (WR) £10.99 (BOT) £160.00 (DI) £207.50 (MI)
1996 IB £1,650.00 (FA) £1,720.00 (BIB) £1,800.00 (FRI)
1996 magnum £415.00 (MI)
1995 £162.88 (BIB) £173.33 (MI) £215.42 (FRI)
1994 £128.08 (PEN)
1994 magnum IB £850.00 (FA)
1990 £265.69 (BIB) £287.88 (REI) £320.00 (BEN) £365.00 (BAL)
1990 IB £2,700.00 (BIB) £2,750.00 (FA)
1989 £143.30 (BIB) £182.13 (CB) £198.00 (ROB)
1989 IB £1,250.00 (FA) £1,450.00 (BIB)

1988 £97.27 (BIB) £130.50 (BEN) £150.00 (BAL)
1988 magnum IB £1,100.00 (FA)
1986 £154.07 (BIB) £235.00 (TAN) £250.00 (ROB) £275.00 (BAL) £295.00 (FORT)
1986 magnum IB £1,495.00 (FA)
1985 £160.00 (TAN) £180.00 (BAL) £199.00 (AV) £225.00 (ROB) £250.00 (RES)
1985 IB £1,490.00 (BIB) £1,500.00 (FA)
1983 £148.19 (BIB) £205.63 (REI) £250.00 (FORT) £265.00 (RES) £300.00 (ROB)
1983 magnum IB £1,550.00 (FA)
1982 £265.69 (BIB) £288.00 (BAL) £335.00 (JU) £352.50 (REI) £367.19 (JER) £386.67 (MI) £450.00 (FORT) £475.00 (RES)
1982 IB £2,700.00 (BIB) £2,970.00 (FA)
1982 magnum £611.00 (CAV)
1981 £135.00 (ROB)
1979 £180.00 (ROB)
1979 magnum £378.00 (UB)
1978 £135.13 (WY) £225.00 (ROB)
1978 magnum IB £1,300.00 (FA)
1970 magnum IB £900.00 (FA)
1966 £76.38 (WY) £94.00 (FA) £200.00 (JU)
1962 £95.00 (BU) £164.50 (REI)
1961 £699.13 (CAV)
1961 IB £5,750.00 (FA)
1959 £246.75 (REI) £440.63 (WY)
1959 magnum IB £4,400.00 (FA)
1949 £111.63 (REI) £364.25 (WY)
1945 £470.00 (FA) £699.13 (CAV) £928.25 (WY)
1929 £440.63 (REI) £904.75 (WY)
1928 £787.25 (WY)
1924 £182.13 (WY) £323.13 (REI)
1924 magnum £511.13 (WY)
1908 £810.75 (WY)

Marquis d'Alesme-Becker *3ème cru classé Margaux*
1989 £27.99 (JON)
1989 IB £195.00 (FA)
1982 £35.25 (WY)

Marquis-de-Terme *4ème cru classé Margaux*
1996 £16.50 (JU) £21.50 (WS)
1982 £37.50 (BU)
1959 £75.00 (BU)
1929 £305.50 (WY)
1924 £176.25 (WY)

Marsau *Côtes de Francs*
1997 IB £60.00 (FA)

de Martouret *Bordeaux*
1997 £5.49 (AME)

Maucaillou *cru bourgeois Moulis*
1997 EC £110.00 (HIG)
1996 £14.60 (HIG)
1995 £11.31 (HA)
1990 £22.00 (AV)
1989 £44.00 (UB)

Mayne-Vieil *Fronsac*
1996 £6.54 (NO) £6.85 (BO)

Mazeris *Canon-Fronsac*
1996 £8.95 (JU) £10.99 (CB)
1995 £9.99 (OD) £11.00 (JU) £12.98 (CB)
1994 £9.58 (CB) £9.75 (BALL)
1989 £11.25 (BALL)

Méaume *Bordeaux Supérieur*
1996 £5.99 (MAJ) £6.00 (JU)
1996 EC £34.00 (HA)
1995 £6.95 (JU)
1994 £6.22 (HA) £6.50 (JU)

le Menaudat *Ieres Côtes de Blaye*
1995 £6.60 (AV)

Meyney *cru grand bourgeois exceptionnel*
St-Estèphe
1996 £15.95 (JU) £23.35 (NO)
1996 IB £130.00 (FA)
1996 EC £120.00 (HA) £160.00 (ELL)
1995 £12.64 (HA)
1995 IB £160.00 (FA)
1994 £21.00 (STA)
1990 £30.00 (FORT) £34.95 (DI)
1986 £20.56 (REI)
1982 £50.00 (FORT)
1979 £22.91 (REI)
1978 £20.56 (REI) £29.38 (TW)
1929 IB £1,595.00 (CAV)
1928 IB £1,595.00 (CAV)

Millet *Graves*
1995 £9.60 (FRI) £11.25 (SOM)
1994 £9.20 (FRI)

la Mission-Haut-Brion *cru classé Pessac-*
Léognan
1997 IB £618.00 (RAE) £636.00 (JU)
  £655.00 (CB)
1996 £57.62 (BIB) £66.67 (MI) £70.00 (JU)
1996 IB £550.00 (FA) £575.00 (BIB)
1996 magnum £133.33 (MI)

1995 £55.17 (BIB) £66.67 (MI) £70.50
  (CON) £72.00 (JU)
1995 IB £550.00 (BIB) £600.00 (FA)
1995 double magnum IB £660.00 (WY)
1994 £45.00 (POR) £46.67 (MI) £49.50
  (BAL) £60.00 (JU)
1994 IB £375.00 (FA)
1994 magnum £93.33 (MI)
1990 £88.95 (BIB) £113.33 (MI)
1990 IB £820.00 (FA) £895.00 (BIB)
1989 £177.57 (BIB)
1988 £47.50 (CON) £72.00 (CRO)
1988 IB £520.00 (FA) £520.00 (BIB)
1986 £60.07 (BIB) £64.63 (WY) £72.50
  (CON) £77.00 (BAL) £84.00 (CRO)
1986 IB £600.00 (FA) £600.00 (BIB)
1985 £65.94 (BIB) £69.99 (AV) £150.00 (UB)
1983 £60.07 (BIB) £64.63 (WY)
1983 IB £600.00 (FA) £600.00 (BIB)
1982 £143.30 (BIB) £146.88 (WY) £162.00
  (NI) £225.00 (FORT)
1982 IB £1,320.00 (FA) £1,450.00 (BIB)
1981 £95.00 (RES)
1975 £323.13 (CAV) £346.63 (REI)
1970 IB £1,000.00 (FA) £1,650.00 (CAV)
1966 IB £1,850.00 (FA)
1966 magnum £364.25 (REI)
1964 £170.38 (REI) £1,400.00 (FA)
1964 IB £1,350.00 (CAV)
1962 £170.38 (REI)
1959 £699.13 (CAV)
1945 £1,039.88 (WY)
1920 £499.38 (WY)

Monbousquet *grand cru St-Émilion*
1996 £45.23 (PLAY)
1996 IB £265.00 (FA)
1995 £25.00 (JU)
1995 IB £320.00 (FA)

Monbrison *cru bourgeois Margaux*
1996 £17.95 (JU)
1996 EC £195.00 (HA)
1995 IB £150.00 (FA)
1989 £89.95 (RES)

Monlot-Capet *St-Émilion*
1996 £10.99 (CO)
1995 £12.24 (JER)

Montaiguillon *Montagne-St-Émilion*
1996 £8.90 (TAN)
1995 £8.65 (NEZ) £8.95 (TAN) £9.95 (LEA)
  £10.35 (PIP)
1994 £8.91 (ELL) £9.50 (LEA)

Montbrun *cru bourgeois Margaux*
1945 £99.88 (WY)

Montrose *2ème cru classé St-Estèphe*
1997 IB £445.00 (CB) £480.00 (TAN)
1996 £46.67 (MI) £58.95 (BER) £59.95 (TAN)
1996 IB £390.00 (BIB) £395.00 (FA)
  £500.00 (FRI)
1996 double magnum £250.00 (MI)
1996 imperial £470.00 (MI)
1995 £34.61 (BIB) £35.83 (MI) £44.06 (FRI)
1995 ½ bottle £23.01 (FRI)
1995 double magnum £210.00 (MI)
1995 jeroboam £330.00 (MI)
1994 ½ bottle IB £280.00 (FA)

1990 £128.61 (BIB) £152.75 (CAV)
  £180.00 (BAL) £185.65 (AV)
1990 IB £1,250.00 (FA) £1,300.00 (BIB)
1989 £55.17 (BIB) £63.65 (FRI)
1989 IB £550.00 (FA) £550.00 (BIB)
1989 ½ bottle £33.29 (FRI)
1988 £37.21 (FRI) £39.99 (BIB)
1988 imperial £480.00 (MI)
1986 £40.48 (BIB) £47.00 (FRI) £52.88 (WY)
  £53.33 (MI)
1986 IB £400.00 (FA) £400.00 (BIB)
1985 £39.01 (BIB) £44.06 (FRI) £68.54 (PLAY)
1983 £30.69 (BIB) £69.00 (UB)
1982 £50.27 (BIB) £58.75 (REI) £59.00 (POR)
  £73.44 (FRI) £75.00 (RES) £500.00 (FA)
1982 IB £500.00 (BIB) £650.00 (CAV)
1981 £74.85 (VIN)
1981 double magnum £123.38 (FA)
1981 imperial £275.00 (BEN)
1978 £35.25 (WY)
1970 £84.21 (BY) £99.50 (BEN) £110.00
  (BU) £117.50 (TAN)
1970 IB £850.00 (FA) £900.00 (CAV)
1961 £155.00 (CRO) £204.00 (NI) £229.13
  (REI)
1947 £176.25 (REI) £346.63 (CAV)
1928 £287.88 (REI) £370.13 (WY) £376.00
  (CAV)

Moulin-du-Cadet *grand cru classé St-Émilion*
1996 £15.57 (CB)
1995 £17.86 (CB)
1983 £28.83 (BY)

Moulin Haut-Villars *Fronsac*
1995 £8.62 (JER)

Moulin Pey-Labrie *Canon-Fronsac*
1997 £165.00 (CB)
1995 £11.80 (TAN)
1994 £13.85 (CB)

Moulin-à-Vent *cru grand bourgeois Moulis*
1996 £10.99 (SAF)

Moulinet *Pomerol*
1996 £16.49 (THR) £16.49 (WR) £16.49
  (BOT) £16.49 (VIC)
1959 IB £795.00 (CAV)

Mouton-Rothschild *1er cru classé Pauillac*
1997 IB £750.00 (FA) £888.00 (LAY)
  £990.00 (TAN) £1,040.00 (CB)
1997 EC £995.00 (ELL)
1996 £99.95 (DI) £118.33 (BIB) £173.33 (MI)
1996 IB £1,195.00 (BIB) £1,250.00 (FA)
  £1,350.00 (FRI)
1996 magnum IB £1,250.00 (FA)
1996 double magnum £880.00 (MI)
1996 imperial IB £860.00 (WY)
1995 £125.00 (UN) £126.65 (BIB) £173.33
  (MI) £176.25 (FRI)
1995 jeroboam £1,560.00 (MI)
1994 £72.00 (BAL) £75.00 (DI) £106.93
  (PEN) £121.67 (MI)
1994 magnum £159.00 (POR)
1990 £108.05 (BIB) £117.50 (WY) £122.40
  (FRI) £122.76 (LAY) £139.17 (MI) £139.95
  (DI) £150.00 (ROB) £152.70 (TAN)
  £180.95 (PEN) £185.00 (BAL)
1990 ½ bottle IB £1,020.00 (FA)
1990 jeroboam £646.25 (FA) £1,350.00
  (MI)
1990 imperial £799.00 (FA)
1989 £109.02 (BIB) £117.50 (WY) £141.00
  (REI) £145.00 (BEN) £146.87 (FRI)
  £155.00 (ROB)
1989 IB £1,050.00 (FA) £1,100.00 (BIB)
1989 magnum IB £1,200.00 (CAV)
1989 jeroboam £325.00 (ROB) £1,200.00
  (FORT) £1,450.00 (MI)
1989 imperial £1,660.00 (MI)

1988 £104.13 (BIB) £122.50 (LAY) £125.00 (BU) £130.00 (BAL) £130.50 (BEN) £175.00 (FORT)
1988 double magnum £830.00 (MI)
1988 jeroboam £681.50 (FA)
1986 £216.73 (BIB) £258.50 (WY) £326.50 (BAL) £346.63 (CB) £350.00 (FORT)
1986 IB £2,200.00 (FA) £2,500.00 (CAV)
1986 magnum £558.13 (CAV)
1985 £120.77 (BIB) £146.94 (LAY) £158.00 (BEN) £164.50 (TAN) £175.00 (BAL) £217.60 (PLAY) £220.00 (ROB) £225.00 (FORT) £235.00 (VIN)
1985 IB £1,220.00 (FA) £1,220.00 (BIB)
1985 double magnum £628.63 (WY)
1985 imperial £1,175.00 (FA)
1983 £105.75 (WY) £110.00 (BEN) £130.00 (ROB) £150.00 (FORT) £225.21 (JER)
1983 IB £880.00 (FA) £900.00 (BIB)
1983 magnum IB £880.00 (FA) £1,100.00 (WY)
1983 jeroboam £634.50 (FA) £790.00 (MI)
1982 £304.86 (BIB) £360.00 (JU) £465.10 (JER) £475.00 (FORT) £507.60 (REI) £685.00 (ROB) £695.00 (RES)
1982 IB £3,100.00 (BIB) £3,200.00 (FA) £3,400.00 (CAV)
1982 jeroboam £3,466.25 (WY)
1981 £76.38 (REI) £84.60 (WY)
1981 magnum IB £650.00 (FA)
1979 jeroboam £500.00 (ROB)
1978 IB £850.00 (FA)
1978 double magnum £517.00 (WY)
1978 jeroboam £1,250.00 (MI)
1975 £99.88 (WY)
1975 IB £900.00 (FA)
1975 double magnum £528.75 (WY) £830.00 (MI)
1975 jeroboam £1,250.00 (MI)
1970 £117.50 (FA) £135.00 (CON) £141.00 (WY) £158.63 (REI) £186.00 (ROB) £250.00 (FORT)
1970 magnum IB £1,400.00 (FA)
1966 £276.13 (WY) £295.00 (RES) £395.00 (VIN)

> *Please remember that*
> **Oz Clarke's Wine Guide**
> *is a price **guide** and not a*
> *price **list**. It is not meant to*
> *replace up-to-date*
> *merchants' lists.*

1962 £176.25 (WY) £235.00 (FA) £275.00 (BEN)
1961 £700.00 (FORT) £822.50 (CAV) £881.25 (REI)
1959 IB £7,800.00 (FA)
1955 £323.13 (REI)
1955 IB £4,750.00 (CAV)
1945 £2,820.00 (FA)
1942 £804.88 (WY)
1929 £1,862.38 (WY)
1928 £940.00 (CAV) £1,163.25 (WY)
1926 magnum £3,348.75 (REI)
1920 £581.63 (WY)
1914 £311.38 (WY)
1909 ½ bottle £223.25 (WY)

Nenin *Pomerol*
1995 £21.54 (FRI) £29.50 (UN)
1990 £28.20 (WY)
1989 IB £200.00 (FA)
1982 £44.06 (JER)
1959 £152.75 (WY)
1955 £49.94 (REI)
1949 £358.38 (WY)

les Ormes-de-Pez *cru grand bourgeois St-Estèphe*
1996 £19.17 (MI) £21.00 (STA) £21.74 (CB) £21.95 (BER)
1996 IB £145.00 (JER) £150.00 (FRI)
1995 £17.50 (MI) £18.11 (FRI) £19.39 (JER)
1994 £16.50 (ROB) £16.67 (MI) £19.28 (HA)
1990 £24.48 (FRI) £33.90 (PIP)
1989 £21.00 (ROB)
1986 £43.00 (UB)
1985 £30.00 (FORT)
1983 £26.44 (REI)

Palmer *3ème cru classé Margaux*
1997 IB £495.00 (TAN)
1997 EC £475.00 (ELL)
1996 £20.00 (FLE) £38.03 (BIB) £49.95 (BALL)
1995 £25.95 (BALL) £46.36 (BIB) £49.50 (CON) £50.00 (UN)
1994 £33.50 (UN) £36.89 (LAY)
1994 IB £300.00 (FA)
1990 £58.60 (BIB) £62.28 (WY) £65.00 (BU) £75.00 (CON) £82.20 (TAN) £85.00 (FORT) £98.00 (BER)
1990 IB £585.00 (BIB) £620.00 (FA)
1989 £74.75 (BIB) £88.12 (FRI) £95.00 (CON) £98.00 (BAL) £99.90 (AV) £116.49 (JON) £125.00 (FORT) £134.55 (PLAY)
1988 £45.38 (BIB) £75.00 (CON)

1986 £55.17 (BIB) £58.75 (WY) £69.00
(BAL) £75.00 (CON) £90.00 (FORT)
1985 £55.17 (BIB) £58.75 (WY) £59.50 (BEN)
£75.00 (CON) £77.50 (TAN) £80.00 (FORT)
£84.69 (JON) £89.95 (RES) £93.02 (FRI)
1985 magnum IB £550.00 (FA)
1983 £94.34 (BIB) £99.88 (WY) £120.00
(CRO) £123.38 (REI) £129.99 (AV)
£146.90 (TAN) £175.00 (FORT)
1983 magnum £276.13 (REI) £330.00
(FORT)
1982 £67.41 (BIB) £79.00 (POR) £82.25
(REI) £110.00 (STA)
1982 IB £675.00 (BIB) £720.00 (FA)
1982 magnum £141.00 (WY)
1981 £53.95 (ROB) £60.00 (FORT) £64.60
(TAN) £64.63 (TW)
1979 £60.00 (ROB)
1978 £89.50 (RES) £135.00 (UB)
1978 IB £550.00 (FA)
1975 £68.15 (WY) £69.91 (REI) £95.00
(ROB)
1975 IB £660.00 (FA)
1970 £105.00 (ROB) £140.00 (BU) £147.60
(NI) £175.00 (FORT)
1970 IB £1,200.00 (FA) £1,400.00 (CAV)
1966 £325.00 (FORT)
1966 IB £1,950.00 (FA)
1961 £517.00 (WY) £875.38 (REI)

Panigon *cru bourgeois Médoc*
1990 £8.86 (HA)

Pape-Clément *cru classé Pessac-Léognan*
1997 IB £291.00 (RAE)
1996 £30.69 (BIB) £45.00 (MI)
1996 IB £267.00 (JU) £300.00 (BIB)
1995 £28.50 (JU) £34.61 (BIB) £49.17 (MI)
1995 IB £340.00 (FA) £340.00 (BIB)
1994 £25.45 (BER) £28.00 (JU)
1990 £40.48 (BIB)
1988 £38.03 (BIB) £65.00 (UB)
1986 £38.19 (REI) £45.38 (BIB)
1986 IB £420.00 (FA) £450.00 (BIB)
1985 £38.52 (BIB) £50.50 (AV)
1985 IB £380.00 (FA) £380.00 (BIB)
1983 IB £240.00 (BIB)
1982 £28.73 (BIB)
1975 IB £280.00 (FA)
1970 £38.19 (REI) £38.78 (WY)
1970 IB £390.00 (CAV)
1966 £45.00 (BU)
1961 IB £1,200.00 (FA)
1959 £99.88 (REI)
1934 £110.00 (JU)

Patache d'Aux *cru grand bourgeois
Médoc*
1997 IB £62.50 (TAN)
1997 EC £58.56 (JON)
1996 £8.94 (ROS) £10.50 (HIG)
1995 £9.39 (JON) £9.80 (TAN) £11.99 (POR)
1994 £8.45 (ROB) £8.90 (COC) £8.90 (TAN)
1983 £20.56 (REI)

Pauillac de Château Latour *Pauillac*
1990 £41.13 (REI)

Pavie *1er grand cru classé St-Émilion*
1996 £20.90 (BIB)
1996 IB £200.00 (BIB) £260.00 (FRI)
£264.00 (RAE)
1996 EC £275.00 (HA)
1995 £25.79 (CB) £27.91 (FRI) £29.95 (BAL)
£30.84 (JER) £32.99 (POR) £33.50 (UN)
1995 IB £230.00 (BIB) £240.00 (FA)
1994 £32.50 (UN)
1994 IB £195.00 (RAE)
1990 £35.59 (BIB) £48.96 (FRI) £60.00 (BER)
1989 IB £300.00 (BIB)
1988 £34.61 (BIB) £44.06 (FRI)
1986 £37.06 (BIB) £47.00 (FRI) £70.83 (PLAY)
1983 £30.20 (BIB) £53.85 (JER)
1983 IB £295.00 (FA) £295.00 (BIB)
1983 magnum £217.00 (UB)
1982 £50.27 (BIB) £127.00 (UB)
1978 £33.49 (REI)
1924 £146.88 (WY)

Pavie-Decesse *grand cru classé St-Émilion*
1996 £17.46 (PLAY)
1995 £19.58 (FRI)
1988 £27.42 (FRI) £37.95 (PIP) £38.40 (PLAY)

Pavie-Macquin *grand cru classé St-Émilion*
1997 IB £350.00 (FA)
1996 £32.50 (MI)
1995 £26.00 (JU) £28.33 (MI)

**Pavillon-Rouge-du-Château
Margaux** *Margaux*
1997 IB £180.00 (FA)
1996 £32.50 (MI) £34.37 (CB)
1996 IB £250.00 (CAV)
1995 £23.00 (JU) £41.13 (WY)
1990 IB £480.00 (FA)
1989 £33.49 (REI)
1988 £53.00 (UB)
1986 £32.00 (CRO) £47.00 (WY)
1985 £40.00 (YOU)
1978 £55.75 (ROB)

Pédesclaux 5ème cru classé Pauillac
1996 £18.33 (MI)
1995 £15.00 (MI)

Petit-Village Pomerol
1996 £27.50 (MI)
1996 IB £245.00 (FRI)
1995 £31.82 (FRI) £37.84 (CB) £49.50 (CON)
1994 £26.67 (MI) £32.50 (BER)
1989 £37.00 (JU)
1989 IB £375.00 (FA)
1986 £45.00 (CON)
1982 £80.00 (JU)
1979 £28.79 (REI)
1970 £52.29 (REI) £77.80 (BER)
1961 IB £1,320.00 (FA)
1934 £220.00 (CRO)

la Petite Eglise Pomerol
1996 IB £150.00 (FA)
1995 IB £220.00 (FA)

les Petits Arnauds
1994 £6.20 (COC)

Pétrus Pomerol
1996 £392.98 (BIB)
1996 IB £4,000.00 (BIB) £4,250.00 (FA)
1995 £520.27 (BIB)
1995 IB £5,000.00 (FA) £5,300.00 (BIB)
1990 £693.25 (WY) £701.42 (BIB)
1990 IB £7,150.00 (BIB) £7,250.00 (FA)
1989 £637.77 (BIB) £998.75 (REI)
1989 IB £6,500.00 (BIB) £6,750.00 (FA)
1988 £275.48 (BIB) £550.00 (FORT)
1988 magnum IB £2,800.00 (FA)
1986 £290.17 (BIB)
1985 £334.23 (BIB) £550.00 (JU)
1985 IB £3,400.00 (BIB) £3,500.00 (FA)
1983 £251.00 (BIB) £400.00 (JU)
1983 IB £2,550.00 (FA) £2,550.00 (BIB)
1982 £941.32 (BIB) £969.38 (WY) £1,200.00
(JU) £1,400.00 (FORT) £1,500.00 (ROB)
1981 IB £2,550.00 (FA)
1981 ½ bottle IB £2,550.00 (FA)
1979 £345.69 (BY)
1975 £511.13 (WY)
1975 IB £5,200.00 (FA) £5,500.00 (CAV)
1970 £640.38 (WY) £681.50 (FA) £969.38
(REI) £995.00 (RES) £1,200.00 (FORT)
1970 IB £7,200.00 (FA)
1966 £434.75 (FA) £528.75 (REI)
1955 £699.13 (CAV) £705.00 (FA)
£1,000.00 (JU)
1928 £2,000.00 (JU)

Peybonhomme-les-Tours 1ères Côtes
de Blaye
1997 £6.29 (ASD)
1996 £7.65 (STE) £8.50 (NA)
1995 £8.00 (FORT)

Peyrabon cru grand bourgeois Haut-
Médoc
1996 £11.67 (MI)

de Pez cru bourgeois supérieur St-Estèphe
1996 £15.40 (NO)
1995 £19.95 (WR) £19.95 (BOT)
1982 £20.99 (YOU) £41.13 (REI)
1978 £19.39 (REI)

Phélan-Ségur cru grand bourgeois
exceptionnel St-Estèphe
1997 IB £155.00 (TAN) £170.00 (CB)
1996 £19.95 (BER) £19.95 (DI) £22.56 (CB)
1996 IB £174.00 (JU)
1995 £14.25 (JU) £28.55 (PLAY)
1994 £16.25 (HIG) £17.50 (DI)
1982 £90.00 (UB)
1961 £45.24 (REI)
1959 £45.00 (ROB)

Pibran cru bourgeois Pauillac
1996 £19.17 (MI)
1995 £15.00 (MI)

**Pichon-Longueville (called Pichon-
Baron until 1988)** 2ème cru classé
Pauillac
1997 EC £380.95 (HAH)
1996 £34.61 (BIB) £39.17 (MI)
1996 IB £330.00 (FRI) £335.00 (CAV)
£340.00 (BIB) £369.00 (JU)
1996 EC £495.00 (ELL)
1996 magnum £78.33 (MI)
1995 £27.75 (BIB) £29.95 (CON) £32.00 (JU)
£32.90 (WY) £35.74 (FRI) £45.00 (AD)
1995 IB £270.00 (BIB) £280.00 (FA)
1994 £26.67 (MI) £30.00 (JU) £55.89 (JON)
1990 £64.96 (BIB) £73.44 (FRI) £110.00
(FORT)
1990 IB £650.00 (BIB) £660.00 (FA)
1989 £69.37 (BIB) £75.00 (FORT) £85.00
(CRO)
1989 IB £695.00 (BIB) £700.00 (FA)
1988 £42.30 (REI) £42.44 (BIB)
1988 IB £420.00 (FA) £420.00 (BIB)
1986 £32.65 (BIB) £49.17 (MI) £62.00 (WS)
1985 £36.57 (BIB) £44.50 (BEN)
1985 IB £360.00 (FA) £360.00 (BIB).

1983 £36.57 (BIB) £48.47 (JER)
1982 £54.19 (BIB) £58.75 (CAV) £125.00
  (RES)
1982 IB £540.00 (FA) £540.00 (BIB)
1981 £58.26 (ELL)
1970 £29.38 (WY) £70.50 (TW)
1964 £35.25 (REI)
1961 £88.13 (REI) £100.00 (FORT) £195.83
  (JER)
1955 £99.88 (REI)
1949 £340.75 (WY)
1928 £300.00 (JU)

**Pichon-Longueville-Lalande (called
  Pichon-Lalande until 1993)** *2ème
  cru classé Pauillac*
1997 IB £400.00 (FA) £447.00 (LAY) £459.00
  (RAE) £480.00 (TAN) £500.00 (CB)
1997 EC £475.00 (ELL)
1996 IB £620.00 (BIB) £650.00 (FA)
  £800.00 (FRI) £825.00 (CAV)
1996 imperial IB £545.00 (WY)
1995 £62.51 (BIB) £79.80 (FRI)
1995 IB £625.00 (BIB) £700.00 (FA)
1995 jeroboam IB £590.00 (WY)
1994 £29.50 (BAL) £45.00 (WS) £55.00 (BER)
1990 £62.02 (BIB) £69.99 (OD) £73.44 (FRI)
  £88.13 (WY)
1990 IB £620.00 (BIB) £680.00 (FA)
1990 magnum £152.75 (FRI)
1989 £69.37 (BIB) £70.50 (WY) £72.80
  (LAY) £73.44 (FRI) £75.00 (CON) £78.73
  (CAV) £95.00 (FORT)
1989 magnum IB £650.00 (FA)
1988 £51.25 (BIB) £59.95 (LAY) £63.65 (FRI)
  £65.00 (BAL) £70.00 (FORT) £76.00 (STA)
1988 IB £510.00 (BIB) £520.00 (FA)
1986 £79.16 (BIB) £95.96 (FRI) £99.88 (REI)
  £110.00 (JU) £125.00 (BAL)
1986 IB £795.00 (BIB) £795.00 (FA)
1985 £70.50 (WY) £71.82 (BIB) £75.00 (JU)
  £76.50 (BEN) £78.00 (WS) £82.95 (LAY)
  £94.00 (TAN) £100.00 (FORT)
1985 IB £720.00 (BIB) £750.00 (FA)
1983 £54.17 (FLE) £74.75 (BIB) £75.00 (JU)
  £79.00 (BAL) £79.90 (WY) £115.00 (FORT)
1983 IB £700.00 (FA) £750.00 (BIB)
1983 imperial £740.25 (WY)

1982 £148.19 (BIB) £152.75 (WY) £159.96
  (LAY) £170.00 (BEN) £175.00 (BU)
  £200.00 (JU) £235.00 (REI) £250.00 (RES)
  £275.00 (FORT)
1982 magnum £440.63 (REI)
1981 £58.75 (REI) £70.00 (STA) £70.00
  (FORT) £75.00 (BER)
1981 IB £400.00 (FA)
1979 £61.00 (CRO) £75.00 (FORT)
1979 magnum IB £500.00 (FA)
1978 £85.00 (FORT) £86.39 (JON) £93.02
  (JER)
1975 £84.79 (JON)
1970 £77.55 (WY) £88.00 (CRO) £125.00
  (BER) £146.88 (REI)
1970 IB £750.00 (FA)
1970 magnum IB £750.00 (FA)
1970 jeroboam £804.88 (REI)
1966 £105.75 (WY)
1959 £195.00 (JU) £287.88 (WY)
1916 £230.00 (WY)
1928 £276.13 (REI)
1914 £258.50 (WY)

le Pin *Pomerol*
1996 £386.67 (MI) £412.57 (BIB)
1995 £486.00 (BIB)
1995 IB £4,950.00 (BIB) £5,000.00 (CAV)
1994 £293.75 (CAV)
1990 £602.52 (BIB) £1,000.00 (FORT)
1990 IB £5,800.00 (FA) £6,140.00 (BIB)
1989 £520.27 (BIB) £650.00 (BAL) £875.38
  (REI)
1989 IB £3,600.00 (FA) £5,300.00 (BIB)
1988 £400.82 (BIB) £569.88 (REI) £750.00
  (JU) £775.00 (FORT)
1988 IB £3,000.00 (FA) £4,080.00 (BIB)
1986 £373.40 (BIB) £499.38 (REI) £750.00
  (FORT)
1985 £412.57 (BIB) £464.13 (WY) £900.00
  (FORT)
1983 IB £6,000.00 (FA) £6,000.00 (BIB)
1982 £1,567.98 (BIB)

Pique-Caillou *Pessac-Léognan*
1996 £12.50 (MI) £13.54 (GW)
1995 £10.25 (JU) £12.50 (MI)

Pitray *Bordeaux Supérieur Côtes de
  Castillon*
1997 EC £33.48 (JON)
1996 IB £39.00 (JER) £48.00 (JU)
1995 £6.75 (WS) £6.80 (JU) £6.85 (JER)
  £7.09 (JON) £7.25 (HED)
1994 £8.95 (STA) £9.40 (PIP)

Plaisance *Montagne-St-Émilion*
1996 £8.91 (BIB)
1995 £8.62 (JER)

Plince *Pomerol*
1996 EC £115.00 (HA)
1995 £16.25 (BALL)
1990 £47.00 (UB)
1970 £25.00 (BU)

la Pointe *Pomerol*
1997 EC £162.00 (JON)
1996 £16.67 (MI) £19.98 (CB)
1996 EC £129.00 (NLW)
1995 £17.50 (MI)
1994 £15.83 (MI) £16.99 (JON)
1994 IB £265.00 (WY)
1990 £39.50 (BEN)
1989 £26.00 (CRO)

Pontet-Canet *5ème cru classé Pauillac*
1997 IB £216.00 (RAE) £237.00 (CB)
 £250.00 (TAN)
1997 EC £225.00 (ELL)
1996 £28.79 (CB) £28.95 (DI) £30.00 (MI)
1996 IB £243.00 (JU) £275.00 (CAV)
1996 magnum IB £240.00 (FA)
1995 £20.50 (JU) £21.95 (DI) £32.50 (MI)
1995 IB £295.00 (CAV)
1994 £25.00 (MI) £29.99 (POR)
1994 magnum £50.00 (MI) £59.50 (POR)
1990 £35.83 (MI) £46.51 (JER)
1989 £38.33 (MI)
1983 IB £180.00 (FA)
1982 £57.50 (MI)
1979 £26.44 (REI)
1978 £29.50 (ROB)
1970 £24.32 (BY) £32.31 (REI) £32.90 (TAN)
1959 £76.38 (REI)
1914 £264.38 (WY)

Potensac *cru grand bourgeois Médoc*
1997 IB £154.00 (CB)
1997 EC £137.50 (ELL) £146.40 (JON)
1996 £15.35 (LAY) £159.00 (ELL)
1996 IB £125.00 (JER) £130.00 (FRI)
 £132.00 (RAE) £138.00 (JU)
1996 EC £145.00 (HA) £159.00 (ELL)
1995 £12.00 (JU) £13.22 (JER) £13.72 (CHA)
 £18.40 (TAN) £19.40 (PIP)
1994 £17.99 (POR) £33.00 (FORT)
1990 £27.00 (CRO) £27.91 (JER)
1989 £25.50 (STA) £27.50 (TAN) £64.17 (BY)
1988 £20.07 (PLAY) £38.60 (UB)
1986 £33.00 (FORT)

Poujeaux *cru grand bourgeois exceptionnel
 Moulis*
1997 IB £135.00 (FA) £160.00 (CB)
 £160.00 (TAN)
1997 EC £150.00 (HIG)
1996 £18.33 (MI) £19.95 (DI)
1995 £8.95 (BAL) £15.00 (JU) £16.50 (WS)
 £17.50 (MI) £17.95 (CON)
1995 IB £180.00 (FA)
1988 £53.00 (UB)

de Prade *Bordeaux Supérieur Côtes de
 Castillon*
1994 £8.99 (PHI)

la Prade *Côtes de Francs*
1994 £8.30 (TAN)

le Prieuré *grand cru classé St-Émilion*
1994 £14.50 (AD)

Prieuré-Lichine *4ème cru classé
 Margaux*
1997 IB £215.00 (CB)
1996 EC £200.00 (HA)
1995 £21.50 (HIG) £21.54 (GW)
1985 £39.00 (COC)
1970 £49.00 (CRO)

Puy-Blanquet *grand cru St-Émilion*
1994 £11.95 (BALL)

Puygueraud *Côtes de Francs*
1994 £9.49 (YOU)
1990 £14.95 (DI)
1989 £14.00 (CRO)

Puylazat *Côtes de Castillon*
1995 £5.50 (WS)

Ramage-la-Bâtisse *cru bourgeois Haut-
 Médoc*
1994 £10.95 (VIC) £10.95 (THR) £10.95
 (WR) £10.95 (BOT) £10.99 (BO) £10.99
 (POR) £11.49 (AME) £11.94 (GW)

Rauzan-Gassies *2ème cru classé
 Margaux*
1996 IB £165.00 (JER)
1995 £35.00 (UN)
1982 £95.00 (UB)
1949 £170.38 (REI)
1945 £152.75 (WY)
1928 £276.13 (WY)
1921 IB £1,600.00 (FA)

Rauzan-Ségla *2ème cru classé Margaux*
1997 IB £315.00 (CB)
1996 £31.18 (BIB) £38.48 (CB) £40.83 (MI)
1996 IB £305.00 (BIB) £355.00 (FRI)
1996 magnum £81.67 (MI)
1995 £32.65 (BIB)
1995 IB £300.00 (FA) £320.00 (BIB)
1994 £26.67 (MI)
1990 £35.00 (FLE) £70.50 (PEN) £69.00 (BAL)
1990 IB £495.00 (BIB)
1989 £36.50 (BEN) £40.48 (BIB) £42.50
   (CON)
1988 £42.44 (BIB)
1988 IB £395.00 (FA) £420.00 (BIB)
1986 £47.00 (WY) £54.19 (BIB)
1986 IB £540.00 (BIB)
1985 £34.50 (ROB) £42.44 (BIB)
1985 IB £340.00 (FA) £420.00 (BIB)
1983 £40.48 (BIB)
1983 IB £400.00 (BIB)
1982 £38.03 (BIB) £48.50 (ROB)
1982 IB £375.00 (BIB)
1961 £100.00 (BU)

Réserve de la Comtesse *Pauillac*
1995 £26.00 (WS) £26.40 (TAN) £26.95
   (LAY) £29.70 (STA)
1995 IB £210.00 (FA)
1994 £15.95 (WS) £25.09 (HA) £27.50
   (TAN) £27.99 (RAE)
1982 £47.00 (REI)

la Réserve du Général *Margaux*
1995 £23.97 (CB) £25.49 (JON) £27.45 (NI)
1994 £13.99 (MORR)

Respide-Médeville *Graves*
1995 £17.51 (TW)

Reynier *Bordeaux Supérieur*
1995 £6.03 (STE) £6.70 (NA)

Reynon *1ères Côtes de Bordeaux*
1994 £8.35 (BY)

Reysson *cru bourgeois Haut-Médoc*
1994 £6.91 (HA)

la Rivière *Fronsac*
1995 £10.99 (PHI) £12.49 (AME)
1995 EC £142.80 (TW)
1994 £17.39 (TW)

Roquevieille *Côtes de Castillon*
1995 £6.75 (STA)

Rouget *Pomerol*
1962 £33.49 (REI)

Rozier *grand cru St-Émilion*
1996 £11.70 (MV)
1996 EC £65.00 (HA)
1995 £10.50 (SOM)

Ruat-Petit-Poujeaux *cru bourgeois
   Moulis*
1996 EC £70.00 (HA)
1995 £10.75 (BU)
1994 £8.75 (CON)

St-Georges *St-Georges-St-Émilion*
1996 £13.71 (FRI)
1995 £14.20 (FRI)

St-Pierre *Lussac-St-Émilion*
1989 £28.50 (ROB)

St-Pierre *4ème cru classé St-Julien*
1996 £23.33 (MI)
1996 EC £215.00 (HA)
1994 £21.59 (YOU) £22.50 (MI) £24.99
   (POR)
1989 £40.00 (FORT)
1983 £21.00 (CRO)
1982 £45.00 (MI)
1978 £28.00 (CRO)

St-Saturnin *cru bourgeois Médoc*
1988 £14.50 (BU)

de Sales *Pomerol*
1996 £16.67 (MI)
1995 £15.83 (MI)
1989 £27.14 (BY)
1981 IB £150.00 (FA)

Sarget de Gruaud-Larose *St-Julien*
1996 £15.83 (MI)
1994 £14.99 (MORR) £17.49 (WR) £17.49
   (BOT) £22.00 (STA)
1981 £21.74 (REI)

EC *(ex-cellar) price per
dozen, excl shipping, duty
and VAT.*
IB *(in bond) price per
dozen, excl duty and VAT.
All other prices,
per bottle incl VAT.*

Segonzac *1ères Côtes de Blaye*
1996 £5.25 (WAI)

Sénéjac *cru bourgeois supérieur Haut-Médoc*
1996 EC £81.00 (ELL)
1990 £14.95 (WS)
1985 £27.61 (PLA)

Sénilhac *cru bourgeois Haut-Médoc*
1994 £9.29 (YOU)

la Serre *grand cru classé St-Émilion*
1997 EC £168.60 (JON)
1996 £17.99 (OD)
1994 £16.99 (JON)

Siran *cru bourgeois supérieur Margaux*
1992 £17.20 (GW)
1988 £48.24 (PIP)
1986 £33.50 (ROB)

Sirius *Bordeaux*
1996 £5.95 (WS)
1995 £6.39 (CON) £6.99 (VIC) £6.99 (THR)
£6.99 (WR) £6.99 (BOT)

Smith-Haut-Lafitte *cru classé Pessac-Léognan*
1997 IB £283.00 (CB)
1996 £26.67 (MI) £27.26 (CB)
1996 IB £230.00 (CAV) £255.00 (FA)
1995 £45.00 (FORT)
1994 £23.32 (REI) £23.99 (YOU) £26.99 (POR)
1989 £22.50 (BEN) £35.00 (UB)
1966 £33.49 (REI)
1924 £129.25 (WY)

Sociando-Mallet *cru grand bourgeois Haut-Médoc*
1997 IB £198.00 (RAE)
1996 IB £219.00 (JU) £235.00 (CAV.)
1996 EC £295.00 (HA)
1995 £18.25 (JU) £27.95 (CON)
1994 £22.50 (MI)
1990 IB £480.00 (FA)
1982 £52.95 (RES)

Soutard *grand cru classé St-Émilion*
1996 £16.67 (MI)
1994 £15.83 (MI) £19.50 (ROB)
1990 £20.00 (JU) £26.67 (MI) £41.00 (UB)
1986 £26.44 (PLA)
1982 £35.00 (YOU)

de Tabuteau *Lussac-St-Émilion*
1996 £9.45 (VIN)
1995 £9.14 (NO)

Talbot *4ème cru classé St-Julien*
1997 IB £245.00 (CB)
1997 EC £235.00 (ELL)
1996 £20.90 (BIB) £25.00 (MI) £25.79 (CB)
£219.00 (JU)
1996 IB £195.00 (FA) £200.00 (FRI)
£200.00 (BIB) £225.00 (JER)
1996 EC £195.00 (HA)
1996 magnum IB £225.00 (JER)
1996 double magnum £150.00 (MI)
1996 double magnum IB £235.00 (WY)
1995 £21.00 (JU) £22.52 (FRI) £22.86 (BIB)
£25.00 (UN) £25.00 (MI) £28.20 (WY)
£37.18 (PLAY)
1995 IB £220.00 (FA) £220.00 (BIB)
1995 magnum £50.00 (MI)
1995 double magnum IB £265.00 (WY)
1994 £23.50 (PEN) £22.50 (MI) £29.50
(POR) £32.50 (STA) £38.60 (TAN)
1990 £35.59 (BIB) £39.00 (COC) £40.83 (MI)
£41.13 (REI) £49.50 (PHI) £73.00 (UB)
1990 IB £350.00 (BIB)
1989 £32.65 (BIB) £42.50 (FORT) £44.17 (MI)
£47.00 (WY) £53.00 (ROB) £64.45 (VIN)
1989 ½ bottle £19.98 (WY)
1988 £31.14 (GW) £55.00 (ROB)
1988 double magnum £158.50 (BEN)
1986 £50.27 (BIB) £55.23 (WY) £57.00
(CRO) £79.95 (RES)
1986 IB £500.00 (FA) £500.00 (BIB)
1985 £42.44 (BIB) £42.50 (BEN)
1983 £38.19 (REI) £40.48 (BIB) £45.82 (PLA)
£47.00 (CRO) £47.00 (WY)
1982 £62.02 (BIB) £64.63 (WY)
1982 magnum IB £620.00 (FA)
1978 IB £260.00 (FA)
1970 £66.67 (MI)
1970 magnum £133.33 (MI)
1966 double magnum £352.50 (WY)
1961 £82.25 (WY) £125.00 (CRO) £210.00
(RES)
1945 £296.10 (REI)

> • All prices for each wine are
> listed together in ascending
> order.
> • Price bands refer to the
> lowest price for which the
> wine is available.

Terre Rouge *Médoc*
1997 EC £56.40 (JON)
1995 £6.95 (BALL) £7.25 (CON) £7.99 (JON)
1994 £6.75 (BALL)

du Tertre *5ème cru classé Margaux*
1994 £14.10 (REI) £17.99 (YOU)
1990 £38.95 (ROB)
1986 £24.79 (YOU) £29.95 (PHI)
1985 £47.00 (UB)
1982 £26.44 (REI)

Tertre-Daugay *grand cru classé St-Émilion*
1990 £26.67 (MI)
1924 £188.00 (WY)

Tertre Rôteboeuf *St-Émilion*
1997 IB £605.00 (CB)
1996 £79.90 (CB)
1995 IB £720.00 (FA) £900.00 (CAV)
1989 £158.63 (CAV) £1,200.00 (FA)
1989 IB £1,600.00 (CAV)
1988 £120.00 (CRO)
1986 IB £820.00 (CAV)
1981 £52.88 (REI)

Teyssier *grand cru St-Émilion*
1996 £12.50 (AD) £13.50 (DI)
1995 £12.99 (POR)
1994 £9.49 (MORR)

Thieuley *Bordeaux Supérieur*
1997 £7.95 (BIB)

Toumalin *Canon-Fronsac*
1997 EC £44.40 (JON)
1995 £8.79 (JON)

la Tour-de-By *cru grand bourgeois Médoc*
1996 EC £70.00 (HA)
1995 £9.95 (HED) £10.60 (TAN) £10.79
   (AME) £10.99 (POR) £12.60 (PIP)
1994 £9.29 (JON) £9.50 (WS) £10.79 (AME)
1989 £15.95 (ROB)

la Tour-Carnet *4ème cru classé Haut-Médoc*
1995 £16.29 (HA)
1982 £18.50 (BU)
1978 £15.50 (CRO)

la Tour-Figeac *grand cru classé St-Émilion*
1995 £24.75 (BALL)
1988 IB £150.00 (FA)

la Tour-Haut-Brion *cru classé Pessac-Léognan*
1996 £30.00 (MI)
1982 £99.88 (WY) £110.00 (RES)
1959 £352.50 (CAV)
1955 IB £2,750.00 (CAV)

Tour-Haut-Caussan *cru bourgeois Médoc*
1997 EC £85.80 (JON)
1996 IB £96.00 (RAE) £130.75 (BIB)
1996 EC £99.00 (ELL)
1995 £11.25 (MV) £12.75 (BALL)
1989 £14.50 (WS)

Tour-du-Haut-Moulin *cru grand bourgeois Haut-Médoc*
1994 £12.24 (JER)
1990 £13.25 (DI)

Tour-du-Mirail *cru bourgeois Haut-Médoc*
1990 £11.71 (HA)
1978 £14.50 (BU)

la Tour-de-Mons *cru bourgeois supérieur Margaux*
1996 £14.17 (MI)
1996 IB £138.00 (JU)
1995 £12.50 (MI) £13.50 (BALL)
1990 £21.67 (MI)
1920 £150.00 (CRO)

Tour-du-Pas-St-Georges *St-Georges-St-Émilion*
1996 £8.90 (TAN) £9.69 (BIB)
1995 £9.00 (MV)
1994 £8.46 (MV) £9.31 (BIB)

la Tour-du-Pin-Figeac *grand cru classé St-Émilion*
1978 £23.00 (CRO)
1970 £26.44 (REI)

la Tour-St-Bonnet *cru bourgeois Médoc*
1996 £9.00 (MV)
1996 IB £59.00 (JER) £69.00 (JU)
1995 £8.45 (JU) £9.79 (JON) £10.03 (FLE)
   £10.95 (HED)
1990 £13.95 (ROB)
1970 £19.39 (REI)

la Tour-St-Joseph *cru bourgeois Haut-Médoc*
1985 £13.51 (REI)

les Tourelles de Longueville *Pauillac*
1996 £16.67 (MI) £21.74 (CB)
1996 IB £156.00 (RAE)

Tourteau-Chollet *Graves*
1994 £6.64 (HA)

Tronquoy-Lalande *cru grand bourgeois St-Estèphe*
1996 £10.50 (WS) £15.00 (MI)
1996 IB £85.00 (JER)
1996 ½ bottle IB £85.00 (JER)
1996 magnum IB £85.00 (JER)
1995 £9.50 (JU) £13.33 (MI)
1994 £9.99 (PEN)

Troplong-Mondot *grand cru classé St-Émilion*
1997 IB £250.00 (FA) £358.00 (CB)
1996 £30.79 (LAY) £39.17 (MI) £39.19 (CB)
1996 IB £330.00 (JU)
1995 £49.17 (MI)
1994 £39.50 (WAI)
1990 IB £995.00 (FA)
1989 IB £895.00 (FA)
1988 £55.00 (BAL)
1986 £48.00 (UB)
1985 £75.00 (RES)

Trotanoy *Pomerol*
1997 IB £560.00 (CB)
1996 £30.69 (BIB) £48.18 (CB)
1995 £55.05 (CB) £64.96 (BIB)
1995 IB £640.00 (FA) £650.00 (BIB)
1994 £35.49 (CB)
1990 £58.75 (AV) £61.10 (CB)
1989 £45.38 (BIB) £65.00 (CRO)
1988 IB £360.00 (BIB)
1986 £38.52 (BIB)
1986 IB £380.00 (FA) £380.00 (BIB)
1985 £52.23 (BIB)
1983 £44.40 (BIB) £47.00 (REI)
11982 £162.88 (BIB) £315.00 (ROB) £425.00 (RES)
1982 IB £1,650.00 (BIB) £1,750.00 (FA)
1981 £41.13 (REI) £57.50 (ROB) £59.95 (RES)
1978 £82.25 (REI)
1970 IB £1,850.00 (FA)

Trottevieille *1er grand cru classé St-Émilion*
1996 £24.00 (HIG) £26.95 (DI)
1995 £23.95 (DI)
1989 £34.95 (DI) £55.00 (RES)
1947 £125.00 (ROB)

de Valandraud *grand cru St-Émilion*
1994 IB £2,000.00 (FA)

Verdignan *cru grand bourgeois Haut-Médoc*
1985 £14.50 (ROB)

Victoria *cru bourgeois Haut-Médoc*
1995 £8.54 (ROS)

Vieux-Château-Bourgneuf *Pomerol*
1975 £9.99 (REI)

Vieux-Château-Certan *Pomerol*
1997 IB £420.00 (RAE) £429.00 (LAY) £517.00 (CB) £530.00 (TAN)
1996 £49.17 (MI) £60.81 (CB)
1996 IB £420.00 (FA) £450.00 (FRI) £495.00 (RAE) £495.00 (CAV) £510.00 (JU)
1996 EC £550.00 (ELL)
1995 £48.00 (JU)
1994 £36.50 (RAE) £47.00 (JON) £47.00 (JU)
1990 £75.00 (ROB)
1990 IB £540.00 (FA)
1989 £41.13 (REI) £49.35 (WY) £52.25 (ROB)
1988 £75.00 (FORT)
1986 £56.99 (REI) £75.00 (RES) £149.00 (UB)
1983 £47.00 (CRO)
1982 IB £650.00 (FA) £895.00 (CAV)
1981 £41.50 (ROB) £55.00 (FORT)

Vieux-Château-Landon *cru bourgeois Médoc*
1995 £11.26 (JER)

Villegeorge *cru bourgeois supérieur exceptionnel Médoc*
1995 £12.73 (BIB)
1994 £11.95 (RAE)
1985 £17.04 (REI)
1983 £39.00 (UB)

Villemaurine *grand cru classé St-Émilion*
1993 £19.00 (AV)

Villeneuve de Cantemerle *Haut-Médoc*
1994 £12.95 (WR) £12.95 (BOT)

Yon Figeac *grand cru classé St-Émilion*
1996 £21.03 (NO) £22.27 (PLA)
1995 £14.26 (NO) £17.95 (DI)
1994 £15.99 (VIC) £15.99 (THR) £15.99 (WR) £15.99 (BOT) £17.95 (DI)

WHITE BORDEAUX PRICES

DRY

Under £5.00

Bel Air 1995 £4.49 (CON)
Bonnet 1997 £4.87 (WR) £4.87 (BOT)
 £4.87 (THR)
la Clyde 1997 £4.95 (UB)
Moulin de Launay 1997 £4.95 (AD) £4.95
 (BALL) £5.09 (JON) £5.10 (TAN)
Moulin de Launay 1996 £4.99 (POR)
la Perrière 1998 £4.50 (WS)
Thieuley 1998 £4.95 (SOM) £5.69 (OD)
 £5.95 (WS) £6.52 (GW) £6.60 (AD)
Trois Mouline Sauvignon 1997 £4.50 (BALL)
Trois Mouline Sauvignon 1996 £4.75 (JU)

£5.00 → £6.99

Antonins 1996 £5.99 (RAE)
Bel Air 1998 £5.25 (WS) £5.90 (TAN)
Bonnet 1996 £5.65 (NI)
le Chec 1997 £6.95 (AD)
Civrac Lagrange 1996 £6.76 (JER)
Coucheroy 1995 £6.99 (VIC) £6.99 (THR)
 £6.99 (WR) £6.99 (BOT)
Duchesse de Tutiac 1995 £5.95 (ROB)
l'Étoile 1997 £6.17 (REI) £6.20 (TAN) £6.35
 (AD)
l'Étoile 1996 £5.50 (BALL) £6.49 (JON)
Haut Rian 1997 £5.30 (ELL) £5.30 (PIP)
 £5.49 (YOU) £5.50 (COC) £6.50 (FORT)
Lacroix 1997 £5.49 (NO) £5.99 (DI) £6.50
 (AD)
Maître d'Estournel 1996 £5.99 (OD)
du Moulin 1996 £5.95 (JU)
du Moulin 1994 £5.58 (TW)
Mouton-Cadet 1997 £5.99 (SAI) £5.99
 (THR) £5.99 (WR) £5.99 (BOT) £5.99 (VIC)
Nicot 1997 £5.99 (YOU)
Pierrail 1998 £5.76 (CHA)
Sirius 1995 £5.75 (MORR) £6.39 (CON)
Thieuley 1997 £6.69 (JON)
Thieuley 1996 £5.95 (JU) £6.39 (GW)
Tour de Mirambeau 1996 £6.29 (NI)

£7.00 → £8.99

Cabannieux 1995 £7.99 (CB)
Carbonnieux ½ bottle 1990 £8.81 (REI)
de Castelneau 1996 £8.49 (YOU) £8.99 (RAE)
la Garde ½ bottle 1992 £7.00 (JER)
Hostens-Picant 1997 £8.49 (YOU)
Loudenne 1996 £7.90 (JU)

de Sours 1996 £7.49 (CB)
Thieuley Cuvée Francis Courselle 1996
 £8.95 (BALL) £10.02 (GW)
des Tourtes 1997 £7.45 (SO)

£9.00 → £11.99

Bouscaut 1988 £10.95 (RAE)
Cruzeau 1996 £9.30 (JER)
de Castelneau 1993 £9.85 (RAE) £12.15 (UB)
Doisy-Daëne Grand Vin Sec 1992 £10.60
 (TAN)
Haut Lagrange 1996 £9.49 (JON)
Haut Lagrange 1995 £11.75 (FORT)
Hostens-Picant 1995 £9.49 (ROB)
de Seuil 1997 £9.50 (JU) £9.95 (STA) £9.99
 (DI)
de Seuil 1996 £9.95 (ELL) £9.99 (DI)
Thieuley Cuvée Francis Courselle 1997
 £10.40 (CB)
la Tour Martillac 1987 £9.20 (FA)

£12.00 → £14.99

Bouscaut 1989 £12.95 (RAE)
Carbonnieux 1996 £14.75 (JU) £17.25
 (HAH) £17.95 (BER) £18.33 (MI)
Couhins-Lurton 1994 £13.80 (TAN)
 £14.39 (REI) £14.50 (STA) £15.95 (ROB)
Couhins-Lurton 1993 £13.99 (RAE)
Domaine de la Solitude 1995 £13.33 (MI)
la Garde 1995 £14.49 (JER)
de Landiras 1994 £12.75 (HED)
Larrivet-Haut-Brion 1996 £14.25 (JU)
Laville-Haut-Brion 1980 £12.14 (FA)
la Louvière 1995 £14.90 (JU)
Talbot Caillou Blanc 1996 £13.22 (JER)
Talbot Caillou Blanc 1995 £14.95 (CON)
 £15.83 (MI)

£15.00 → £19.99

Briatte 1992 £17.45 (TW)
Carbonnieux 1997 £17.50 (MI)
Carbonnieux 1995 £15.95 (JU) £17.50 (MI)

- Wines are listed in A–Z order within each price band.
- For each wine, vintages are listed in descending order.
- Each vintage of any wine appears only once.

Carbonnieux **1989** £17.63 (AV)
Couhins-Lurton **1995** £17.99 (NI)
Couhins-Lurton **1981** £16.95 (RAE)
Domaine de la Solitude **1996** £15.00 (MI)
l'Esprit de Chevalier **1995** £16.06 (FA)
l'Esprit de Chevalier **1994** £19.17 (MI)
l'Esprit de Chevalier **1992** £16.95 (RAE)
la Louvière **1996** £15.25 (JU)
la Tour Martillac **1995** £18.33 (MI)
la Tour Martillac **1994** £16.95 (DI)

£20.00 → £29.99

Bouscaut **1967** £29.95 (RAE)
l'Esprit de Chevalier **1990** £26.44 (REI)
de Fieuzal **1996** £26.67 (MI) £32.00 (JU)
de Fieuzal **1995** £24.17 (MI) £27.99 (AV)
de Fieuzal **1993** £24.68 (REI) £39.40 (TAN)
Pavillon Blanc du Château Margaux **1996**
  £26.67 (MI) £33.61 (CB) £37.45 (HAH)
Pavillon Blanc du Château Margaux **1995**
  £24.17 (MI)
Smith-Haut-Lafitte **1996** £22.91 (FA)
  £25.00 (MI) £26.93 (JER) £32.31 (CB)
Smith-Haut-Lafitte **1995** £20.95 (FA)
  £22.50 (MI) £29.67 (CB) £35.00 (FORT)
Smith-Haut-Lafitte **1994** £26.67 (MI)
Smith-Haut-Lafitte **1985** £26.44 (REI)
Talbot Caillou Blanc **1961** £29.38 (REI)
la Tour Martillac **1990** £25.00 (MI)

£30.00 → £39.99

Carbonnieux **1953** £38.99 (YOU)
Domaine de Chevalier **1996** £36.62 (FA)
  £40.83 (MI)
Domaine de Chevalier **1995** £36.67 (MI)
  £43.67 (RAE) £45.00 (JU) £48.00 (CB)
Domaine de Chevalier **1992** £34.17 (MI)
  £55.00 (FORT)
Domaine de Chevalier **1987** £38.58 (FA)
de Fieuzal **1989** £32.99 (NO) £41.13 (REI)
Larrivet-Haut-Brion **1990** £34.00 (JU)
Laville-Haut-Brion **1983** £35.95 (BEN)
  £56.50 (ROB)
Laville-Haut-Brion **1979** £34.50 (YOU)
Pavillon Blanc du Château Margaux **1997**
  £36.62 (CB)

£40.00 → £49.99

Domaine de Chevalier **1990** £43.37 (RAE)
  £49.17 (MI) £58.16 (FA)
Domaine de Chevalier **1989** £48.37 (FA)
Domaine de Chevalier **1988** £49.35 (WY)
Domaine de Chevalier **1986** £45.43 (FA)
  £65.00 (FORT)
Domaine de Chevalier **1977** £45.24 (REI)

Haut-Brion Blanc **1988** £49.50 (RAE)
  £80.49 (REI) £125.00 (FORT)
Larrivet-Haut-Brion **1994** £45.00 (JU)
Laville-Haut-Brion **1996** £47.50 (MI)

£50.00 → £69.99

Haut-Brion Blanc **1981** £58.75 (WY)
Laville-Haut-Brion **1988** £50.00 (ROB)
Laville-Haut-Brion **1982** £50.00 (FORT)
  £56.00 (BAL)
Laville-Haut-Brion **1967** £64.62 (WY)
'Y' d'Yquem **1998** £63.00 (UB)
'Y' d'Yquem **1996** £50.33 (FA) £57.50 (MI)
'Y' d'Yquem **1985** £52.88 (REI) £60.12 (FA)
'Y' d'Yquem **1978** £64.62 (WY)

£70.00 → £99.99

Carbonnieux **1945** £70.50 (REI)
Haut-Brion Blanc **1994** £98.00 (JU)
Haut-Brion Blanc **1989** £88.13 (REI)
  £200.00 (FORT)
'Y' d'Yquem **1972** £76.38 (REI)

Over £100.00

Carbonnieux **1949** £193.87 (WY)
Olivier **1947** £105.75 (WY)
Pavillon Blanc du Château Margaux **1924**
  £111.62 (WY)
'Y' d'Yquem **1964** £111.62 (WY)

SWEET

Under £7.00

Domaine du Noble ½ bottle **1996** £5.50
  (BALL)
Domaine du Noble ½ bottle **1994** £4.99
  (RAE)
Suau **1998** £4.99 (BOT)
Tour Balot **1995** £6.70 (AS)
des Tours **1995** £5.39 (JON) £7.95 (JU)
  £8.95 (AD)

£7.00 → £8.99

des Arroucats **1995** £7.85 (CON)
des Arroucats **1994** £7.64 (REI)
la Caussade **1995** £7.75 (WAI)
Clos Labère ½ bottle **1995** £8.92 (NO)
Domaine du Noble **1993** £8.99 (RAE)
Fayau **1994** £8.10 (MV)
Grand Eclos du Château de Cérons **1996**
  £8.25 (WS)
Liot ½ bottle **1995** £8.90 (TAN)
de Ménota **1995** £7.05 (JER)
des Tours **1994** £8.96 (LAY)

£9.00 → £11.99

d'Arche ½ bottle 1983 £11.75 (WY)
d'Arricaud 1975 £9.95 (RAE)
des Arroucats 1996 £9.28 (CB)
la Chartreuse ½ bottle 1995 £9.75 (HAH)
Doisy-Daëne ½ bottle 1996 £11.26 (JER)
Doisy-Dubroca ½ bottle 1981 £9.34 (REI)
Filhot ½ bottle 1995 £9.99 (MAJ)
Lafaurie-Peyraguey ½ bottle 1994 £11.52
   (STE) £12.80 (NA)
Liot 1990 £10.40 (REI)
Liot ½ bottle 1996 £9.75 (WAI) £9.99 (SAI)
Liot ½ bottle 1994 £11.37 (WT)
Loupiac Gaudiet 1994 £11.69 (TW)
Lousteau-Vieil 1995 £9.40 (COC)
Nairac ½ bottle 1981 £10.46 (REI)
Puy Servain ½ litre 1995 £10.58 (JER)
la Rame 1996 £9.99 (MAJ)
la Rame 1995 £10.35 (NI)
Peter A Sichel 1996 £11.99 (WR) £11.99
   (BOT)
Peter A Sichel 1994 £9.75 (CON)

£12.00 → £14.99

Climens ½ bottle 1985 £13.79 (JON)
   · £20.25 (ROB)
Climens ½ bottle 1982 £14.50 (RAE)
Clos d'Yvigne 1993 £12.95 (JU)
Coutet ½ bottle 1979 £14.10 (WY)
Cyprès de Climens 1992 £12.95 (RAE)
Cyprès de Climens ½ litre 1994 £14.49 (JER)
de Fargues 1995 £13.23 (STE)
Haut-Caplane 1992 £13.95 (ROB)
les Justices ½ bottle 1996 £12.87 (TW)
Lafaurie-Peyraguey ½ bottle 1995 £14.95
   (RES)
Liot 1997 £13.12 (JON)
Nairac ½ bottle 1990 £13.95 (FORT)
   £15.95 (LEA)
Rabaud-Promis ½ bottle 1989 £13.50
   (WS) £17.50 (LEA) £19.95 (RES)
la Rame Reserve du Château 1995 £12.99
   (OD) £14.95 (NI)
Rieussec 1984 £13.95 (ROB)

£15.00 → £19.99

Accabailles de Barréjats 1995 £16.90 (JU)
Bastor-Lamontagne 1997 £16.55 (CB)
Bastor-Lamontagne 1994 £17.90 (JU)
Broustet 1995 £16.16 (FRI) £22.35 (PIP)
Broustet 1989 £19.17 (MI) £22.36 (GW)
Broustet 1988 £18.60 (FRI) £25.70 (PIP)
la Chartreuse 1995 £17.95 (AD) £18.40
   (HAH) £18.95 (CON)

Climens ½ bottle 1990 £18.50 (RAE)
   £22.50 (WS)
Climens ½ bottle 1989 £19.00 (RAE)
   £33.00 (FORT)
Coutet 1978 £18.51 (FA) £21.99 (YOU)
Coutet ½ bottle 1988 £15.27 (WY) £22.95
   (BEN)
Doisy-Daëne ½ bottle 1976 £15.28 (WY)
Doisy-Védrines ½ bottle 1989 £15.65 (WS)
Filhot 1983 £19.00 (FA)
Filhot ½ bottle 1976 £17.62 (WY)
Haura 1976 £15.99 (RAE)
Lafaurie-Peyraguey 1982 £18.02 (FA)
Lafaurie-Peyraguey 1978 £17.04 (REI)
Lafaurie-Peyraguey ½ bottle 1985 £18.00
   (COC)
Liot 1995 £16.47 (STE) £16.75 (ELL)
   £17.92 (CB) £18.30 (NA)
Liot 1989 £17.49 (JON) £17.50 (MI)
Loubens 1994 £15.95 (LAY)
Myrat 1996 £16.16 (JU) £17.50 (MI)
   £18.95 (DI)
Nairac 1988 £19.49 (FA) £22.95 (LEA)
Nairac ½ bottle 1983 £15.00 (CRO)
Rabaud-Promis 1996 £17.82 (RAE) £19.00
   (JU)
Rabaud-Promis 1988 £19.50 (RAE) £47.95
   (ROB)
la Rame Reserve du Château 1990 £18.57
   (NO)
Rayne-Vigneau 1995 £18.33 (MI) £23.40
   (HAH)
Rayne-Vigneau ½ bottle 1988 £15.27 (WY)
de Ricaud 1994 £16.95 (PHI)
Rieussec ½ bottle 1995 £16.45 (CB)
Rieussec ½ bottle 1988 £17.33 (FA)
   £20.95 (FRI) £23.50 (WY) £24.95 (BEN)
Roumieu-Lacoste 1996 £18.95 (WAI)
Suduiraut ½ bottle 1989 £17.29 (BO)
   £17.62 (WY) £21.95 (ROB)
de Veyres 1988 £15.95 (HED)

£20.00 → £29.99

d'Arche 1989 £22.62 (REI) £26.97 (PLA)
la Chartreuse 1990 £20.95 (CON)
la Chartreuse 1989 £20.95 (BALL)
Climens 1995 £27.00 (JU)
Climens 1994 £21.50 (THR) £21.50 (WR)
Climens 1991 £25.95 (RAE) £28.79 (PLA)
Climens 1981 £27.50 (JON)
Climens 1980 £24.95 (RAE)
Coutet 1997 £28.98 (RAE) £31.45 (JON)
   £32.21 (CB)
Coutet 1996 £24.17 (MI) £25.75 (JU)
   £26.95 (LAY) £29.95 (BER) £32.80 (CB)

Coutet **1995** £20.94 (HA) £25.00 (JU)
£29.25 (HAH) £34.38 (PLAY)
Coutet **1989** £28.79 (REI) £30.00 (JU)
£32.00 (CRO) £32.50 (BAL)
Coutet **1986** £29.99 (JON) £31.43 (REI)
£34.50 (ROB)
Doisy-Daëne **1996** £21.93 (JU) £22.52 (JER)
£22.85 (LAY) £25.85 (CB) £25.95 (DI)
Doisy-Daëne **1995** £27.50 (BER)
Doisy-Daëne **1989** £28.99 (JON)

Doisy-Daëne **1971** £28.79 (FA)
Doisy-Védrines **1997** £25.36 (CB)
Doisy-Védrines **1996** £20.83 (MI) £21.99
(OD) £22.52 (JER) £22.85 (LAY)
Doisy-Védrines **1995** £22.99 (OD) £23.99
(LAY)
Doisy-Védrines **1989** £25.83 (MI) £27.50
(WS)
Filhot **1997** £23.89 (CB)
Filhot **1990** £22.99 (OD) £25.60 (TAN)
£25.95 (VIC) £25.95 (THR) £25.95 (WR)
£25.95 (BOT) £27.95 (ROB) £28.00 (JU)
Filhot **1989** £20.00 (WAI) £23.67 (STE)
£26.30 (NA)
Filhot **1988** £26.40 (NO)
Guiraud **1996** £23.33 (MI) £25.75 (JU)
£26.95 (LAY) £29.55 (BER) £31.92 (CB)
Guiraud **1990** £25.85 (FA) £35.00 (CRO)
£35.66 (LAY)
Guiraud **1989** £22.91 (FA) £36.15 (AV)
Guiraud **1988** £26.40 (NO)
Guiraud **1983** £23.40 (FA) £28.33 (MI)
£34.50 (LEA) £45.00 (JU)
les Justices **1995** £25.26 (TW)
Lafaurie-Peyraguey **1995** £29.50 (BER)
de Malle **1997** £22.40 (JON) £23.70 (LAY)
de Malle **1996** £20.00 (MI) £22.45 (BER)
£22.52 (JER)
de Malle **1995** £26.91 (CB)
de Malle **1983** £29.30 (PIP)
de Ménota **1986** £20.00 (SOM)
Nairac ½ bottle **1975** £24.00 (CRO)
Rabaud-Promis **1989** £20.95 (FA) £24.95
(RAE) £31.35 (TAN)
Rayne-Vigneau **1996** £20.00 (MI) £22.85
(LAY) £25.85 (CB)

Rayne-Vigneau **1989** £27.00 (AD)
Rieussec **1996** £27.51 (JU) £29.76 (HA)
£33.19 (CB)
Rieussec **1995** £21.61 (HA) £26.44 (FRI)
£31.95 (LAY)
Rieussec **1970** £28.79 (REI) £47.00 (CAV)
£48.00 (YOU)
Rieussec ½ bottle **1990** £23.99 (CON)
Rieussec ½ bottle **1983** £22.50 (RES)
£30.89 (JON) £42.80 (UB)
Romer du Hayot **1989** £22.50 (AD)
Sigalas-Rabaud **1981** £22.91 (REI)
Suduiraut **1996** £22.91 (FA) £23.33 (MI)
£33.19 (CB) £34.40 (TAN)
Suduiraut **1995** £25.46 (FRI) £31.90 (CB)
Suduiraut **1994** £23.99 (YOU)
Suduiraut **1990** £29.17 (MI)
Suduiraut **1989** £29.38 (CAV) £34.59 (BO)
£35.95 (BEN) £35.95 (DI) £49.99 (POR)
Suduiraut **1988** £26.67 (MI) £29.50 (YOU)
£32.00 (WS) £35.00 (JU) £49.00 (BER)
Suduiraut **1983** £26.83 (FA) £38.95 (ROB)
£39.95 (PIP) £47.00 (WY)
Suduiraut **1982** £29.37 (FRI) £38.50 (ROB)
£88.50 (UB)
Suduiraut ½ bottle **1990** £26.00 (CRO)
la Tour Blanche **1995** £22.27 (HA) £25.46
(FRI)
la Tour Blanche **1989** £28.30 (FA) £28.40
(FRI) £29.50 (WS) £33.00 (JU) £33.25 (AD)
£44.00 (BER)
la Tour Blanche **1983** £27.99 (JON)

£30.00 → £39.99

Climens **1996** £32.50 (MI) £33.40 (RAE)
£37.50 (JU)
Climens **1989** £36.00 (RAE) £49.00 (JU)
£55.00 (FORT)
Climens **1986** £38.58 (FA) £39.17 (MI)
Climens **1983** £30.75 (FA) £39.00 (VA)
£52.90 (BEN) £57.95 (RES) £58.75 (WY)
Climens ½ bottle **1969** £33.46 (PLAY)
Coutet **1990** £31.00 (COC) £31.14 (PLA)
£33.00 (FORT)
Coutet **1983** £31.70 (TAN) £39.95 (ROB)
Coutet **1975** £33.70 (TAN)
Coutet ½ bottle **1990** £39.00 (UB)
Cru Barréjats **1991** £38.00 (JU)
Doisy-Daëne **1988** £36.95 (RES)
Doisy-Dubroca **1975** £31.50 (ROB)
de Fargues **1988** £38.33 (MI) £42.50 (FA)
de Fargues **1985** £35.25 (SOM) £35.83 (MI)
Filhot **1976** £36.72 (REI)
Guiraud **1997** £32.70 (CB)
les Justices **1985** £35.25 (TW)

Lafaurie-Peyraguey 1997 £32.70 (CB)
Lafaurie-Peyraguey 1990 £38.42 (NO)
Lafaurie-Peyraguey 1989 £37.00 (JU)
£38.00 (BER)
Lafaurie-Peyraguey 1988 £34.66 (FA)
£35.25 (SOM) £37.50 (RES) £40.23 (NO)
£47.50 (FORT)
de Malle 1988 £30.50 (ROB) £35.45 (NO)
de Malle 1986 £39.98 (COC)
Nairac 1995 £30.55 (CB)
Raymond-Lafon 1988 £39.50 (BAL) £47.00
(JU)
Raymond-Lafon 1986 £39.95 (RES)
Rayne-Vigneau 1988 £37.50 (RES) £38.95
(ROB)
Rieussec 1989 £35.00 (RAE) £45.82 (NO)
£46.20 (SOM) £55.00 (FORT)
Rieussec 1988 £33.32 (NO) £38.19 (FRI)
£45.45 (STE) £49.99 (POR) £50.50 (NA)
£61.00 (STA)
Rieussec 1986 £32.70 (FA) £37.60 (WY)
£40.80 (TAN) £49.00 (WR) £49.00 (BOT)
£50.00 (FORT)
Sigalas-Rabaud 1989 £32.50 (BEN) £46.50
(BER)
Sigalas-Rabaud 1986 £32.00 (PIP)
Suduiraut 1997 £32.70 (CB)
Suduiraut 1975 £35.64 (FA)
Suduiraut 1971 £32.90 (WY)
la Tour Blanche 1990 £35.66 (LAY) £45.00
(BER)
la Tour Blanche 1935 £35.25 (WY)

£40.00 → £59.99

Climens 1990 £44.17 (MI) £45.00 (WS)
£55.00 (FORT)
Climens 1988 £51.11 (REI) £55.00 (RES)
£60.00 (FORT)
Climens 1976 £58.95 (WY)
Coutet 1967 £52.88 (WY)
Doisy-Daëne 1961 £47.00 (WY)
de Fargues 1990 £45.00 (MI) £49.00 (JU)
£65.00 (RES) £80.00 (FORT)
de Fargues 1989 £42.50 (FA) £45.00 (MI)
Filhot 1975 £47.00 (WY)
Gilette 1962 £58.00 (CRO) £117.50 (TW)

> • All prices for each wine are
> listed together in ascending
> order.
> • Price bands refer to the
> lowest price for which the
> wine is available.

Guiraud 1962 £49.94 (REI)
les Justices 1983 £41.13 (TW)
Lafaurie-Peyraguey 1975 £40.54 (REI)
Lafaurie-Peyraguey 1926 £50.52 (WY)
de Malle 1989 £40.60 (AV)
Raymond-Lafon 1989 £47.50 (RES)
Rayne-Vigneau 1986 £43.00 (CRO)
Rieussec 1983 £44.65 (WY) £50.24 (TAN)
Rieussec 1981 £49.35 (TW)
Rieussec 1979 £44.05 (PLAY)
Rieussec 1976 £41.13 (REI) £47.00 (YOU)
Rieussec 1975 £41.13 (REI) £52.00 (JON)
£54.00 (CRO)
la Tour Blanche 1962 £54.99 (YOU)
£58.75 (WY) £66.00 (CRO)

£60.00 → £99.99

Climens 1967 £64.62 (WY) £69.00 (RAE)
£88.13 (REI)
Climens 1966 £68.74 (REI) £76.38 (WY)
Coutet 1971 £70.00 (CRO)
Coutet 1955 £75.00 (BEN)
Coutet 1942 £82.25 (WY)
Doisy-Daëne 1959 £98.11 (REI)
de Fargues 1959 £82.25 (WY)
Filhot 1955 £68.74 (REI)
Gilette Crème de Tête 1953 £72.00 (CRO)
Guiraud ½ bottle 1924 £88.12 (WY)
Lafaurie-Peyraguey 1938 £64.62 (WY)
Rayne-Vigneau 1941 £94.00 (WY)
Rieussec 1961 £94.00 (WY)
Rieussec 1959 £99.88 (REI)
Sigalas-Rabaud 1962 £64.63 (WY)
Suduiraut 1966 £64.63 (REI)
Suduiraut 1936 £76.37 (WY)
la Tour Blanche 1923 £88.12 (WY)
d'Yquem 1987 £82.23 (CAV) £94.00 (WY)
d'Yquem 1979 £99.29 (FA)
d'Yquem ½ bottle 1990 £74.12 (FA)
£77.92 (MI) £79.99 (OD) £82.25 (WY)
£135.00 (RES)
d'Yquem ½ bottle 1989 £66.78 (FA)
£69.58 (MI) £73.83 (FRI) £74.99 (OD)
£82.25 (WY) £105.00 (ROB)
d'Yquem ½ bottle 1988 £73.75 (MI)
£82.25 (WY) £86.07 (FRI) £100.00 (FORT)
d'Yquem ½ bottle 1986 £95.00 (FORT)
d'Yquem ½ bottle 1981 £82.25 (WY)

£100.00 → £149.99

d'Arche 1945 £117.50 (CAV)
Climens 1962 £116.50 (BEN)
Climens 1953 £135.00 (JU) £180.00 (BEN)
Climens 1952 £112.21 (REI)
Coutet 1934 £141.00 (WY)

Filhot **1949** £108.69 (REI)
Gilette Crème de Tête **1971** £123.96 (TW)
Guiraud **1959** £113.39 (REI)
Guiraud **1921** £141.00 (WY)
Lafaurie-Peyraguey **1953** £141.00 (CAV)
Rayne-Vigneau **1945** £105.75 (WY)
Rayne-Vigneau **1920** £111.63 (REI)
Suduiraut **1948** £146.88 (CAV)
la Tour Blanche **1949** £135.71 (REI)
la Tour Blanche **1920** £111.62 (WY)
d'Yquem **1991** £104.17 (MI) £110.00 (WS)
    £119.68 (LAY) £165.00 (BER)
d'Yquem **1990** £128.66 (FA) £150.00 (JU)
    £152.75 (WY) £155.00 (TAN) £155.83
    (MI) £195.00 (RES)
d'Yquem **1989** £117.50 (HA) £123.77 (FA)
    £130.00 (JU) £139.17 (MI) £141.00 (WY)
    £185.00 (FORT) £197.99 (TW)
d'Yquem **1988** £130.62 (FA) £146.88 (WY)
    £147.50 (MI) £160.00 (JU) £166.46 (FRI)
    £185.00 (FORT)
d'Yquem **1981** £141.00 (WY)
d'Yquem **1963** £135.13 (REI) £395.00 (VA)

£150.00 → £199.99

Caillou **1943** £150.00 (CRO)
Climens **1943** £152.75 (REI)
Coutet **1939** £158.62 (WY)
Filhot **1934** £193.87 (WY)
Gilette **1952** £182.13 (TW)
Gilette **1906** £155.00 (RES)
Lafaurie-Peyraguey **1947** £164.50 (REI)
Rabaud-Promis **1918** £158.62 (WY)
Rayne-Vigneau **1947** £152.75 (WY)
    £275.00 (RES)
Rayne-Vigneau **1939** £164.50 (WY)
Suduiraut **1967** £150.00 (FORT)
la Tour Blanche **1948** £156.28 (REI)
d'Yquem **1986** £152.75 (WY) £156.67
    (CAV) £169.17 (MI) £170.00 (JU) £200.00
    (FORT) £205.00 (BER) £217.38 (TW)
d'Yquem **1985** £152.75 (REI) £160.00 (DI)
d'Yquem **1982** £175.00 (BER)
d'Yquem **1980** £180.00 (ROB) £550.00 (VA)
d'Yquem **1968** £195.00 (POR)
d'Yquem **1966** £164.50 (FA) £346.63 (REI)
d'Yquem ½ bottle **1982** £150.00 (UB)

£200.00 → £299.99

Climens **1947** £205.63 (REI)
Climens **1927** £293.75 (WY) £435.00 (RES)
Gilette **1934** £293.75 (TW)
Guiraud **1945** £210.52 (CAV)
Rayne-Vigneau **1948** £270.25 (WY)
Rayne-Vigneau **1918** £282.00 (WY)

Sigalas-Rabaud **1919** £258.50 (WY)
d'Yquem **1983** £200.00 (JU) £235.00 (FORT)
    £235.00 (VA) £260.00 (RES) £275.00 (ROB)
d'Yquem **1976** £207.00 (FA) £223.25 (WY)
    £264.38 (REI) £325.00 (ROB) £345.00
    (FORT) £360.00 (RES)
d'Yquem **1975** £230.00 (JU) £336.05 (TW)
    £345.00 (BAL)
d'Yquem **1971** £285.00 (BEN)
d'Yquem **1962** £246.75 (FA) £350.00
    (POR) £410.00 (ROB)
d'Yquem **1958** £282.00 (FA) £311.38 (REI)
d'Yquem **1956** £258.50 (REI) £264.38 (WY)
    £282.00 (FA) £435.00 (VA)
d'Yquem **1954** £287.88 (REI)
d'Yquem ½ bottle **1967** £205.63 (REI)

£300.00 → £399.99

Climens **1928** £340.75 (WY)
Coutet **1921** £330.00 (CRO)
Suduiraut **1945** £329.00 (REI)
d'Yquem **1957** £311.38 (REI)
d'Yquem **1953** £399.00 (BEN) £440.63
    (REI) £490.00 (POR) £700.00 (VA)
d'Yquem **1950** £305.50 (FA) £335.00 (BEN)
    £352.50 (REI) £381.88 (WY) £470.00 (TW)
d'Yquem **1944** £323.13 (FA)

£400.00 → £499.99

d'Yquem **1967** £412.62 (FA) £440.63 (REI)
    £495.00 (BEN) £511.12 (WY) £587.50
    (FRI) £750.00 (FORT)
d'Yquem **1955** £495.00 (BEN)
d'Yquem **1919** £499.37 (WY)
d'Yquem **1918** £464.12 (WY) £646.25 (REI)

Over £500.00

d'Yquem **1959** £500.00 (NO) £581.63
    (CAV) £599.25 (REI)
d'Yquem **1949** £528.75 (FA) £810.75 (WY)
d'Yquem **1947** £793.13 (WY)
d'Yquem **1943** £558.12 (WY)
d'Yquem **1926** £593.38 (REI) £975.00 (VA)
d'Yquem **1921** £1,410.00 (FA)

ROSÉ

Under £7.00

Bel Air **1998** £4.95 (WS)
Lacroix **1997** £5.99 (DI)
Lacroix **1996** £5.78 (NO)
de Sours Rosé **1998** £6.99 (MAJ) £9.04
    (PLAY)
Thieuley Clairet **1998** £4.95 (SOM)

BURGUNDY

Beware of Pinot Noir: it's an expensive habit, and people can be hooked after just one taste. If anyone offers you Pinot Noir, Just Say No

Sadly, there's no cheap way of getting the taste of really good Pinot Noir. The same applies to Burgundian Chardonnay, but Chardonnay is always a more obliging grape. Chile, Australia, southern France – you name the region, I'll show you a cheap Chardonnay that packs in the flavour and a stylish one at a decent price. Pinot Noir? Difficult. Much more difficult.

In Burgundy your best bet is simple Bourgogne Rouge from a good producer. You'll get the same careful winemaking he or she applies to top wines; the same thoughtful viticulture, the same pride in attention to detail. Compared to the price of those top wines, a basic Bourgogne Rouge will look dead cheap. Compared to a basic red wine made from almost any other grape it will look pretty pricy.

That's the nature of Pinot Noir. If you compare Burgundy prices to the prices of equal quality Pinot Noir from California or New Zealand they don't look that different.

The obvious answer is never to go near Pinot Noir. Never. Not even once. Why am I so definite? Because once you've tasted that utterly seductive silkiness, that flavour that's a mixture of raspberries and game and undergrowth, you'll want to taste it again. You become hooked incredibly easily. In no time you'll be getting lists from specialist Burgundy merchants ('Well, there's no harm in looking…'). Then you'll go to their tastings ('Just a tiny taste can't hurt'). Then you'll start buying ('Look, it's only a mixed case'). People have been known to start dealing themselves to fund their habit. You have been warned.

GRAPE VARIETIES

ALIGOTÉ (white) Not planted in the best sites – though there are a few vines in Corton-Charlemagne. Aligoté from old vines can produce a lovely, refreshing wine, scented like buttermilk soap yet as sharp and palate-cleansing as a squeeze of lemon juice. *Dujac* and a few others barrique-ferment it with surprising success. *Aubert de Villaine*'s Aligoté de Bouzeron is tops.

CHARDONNAY (white) Burgundy makes the most famous Chardonnay of all. Even in the decidedly dicky Burgundian climate, it produces good to excellent wine almost every year. Chardonnays made without the use of oak barrels for aging will taste very different from barrel-aged wines. A Mâcon produced in stainless steel will have appley fruit; Côte Chalonnaise Chardonnay is generally rather taut and chalky-dry, but given some oak, it can

become delicately nutty. In the North of the Beaujolais region Chardonnay has a stony dryness; in the South it is nearer to the fatter, softer, wines of southern Burgundy. Chablis generally produces lean wine, but in riper years and with some oak aging it can get much rounder. The Côte d'Or is the peak of achievement and top wines from the Côte de Beaune are luscious, creamy and honeyed yet totally dry, the rich, ripe fruit entwined with the scents of oak in a surprisingly powerful wine – from the right producer, the world's greatest dry white.

GAMAY (red) The Gamay has no pretensions: in Beaujolais it can simply make one of the juiciest, most gulpable, gurgling wines the world has to offer. *Can*, I stress: not all Beaujolais is like this. Ideally it is simple, cherry-sharp, with candy-like fruit, sometimes with hints of raspberry or strawberry. The wines from the *crus* go further, but in the main their similarity from the grape is greater than the differences in the places they come from. All but the wines of the top villages should be drunk as young as you can find them.

PINOT BEUROT (white) Known elsewhere as Pinot Gris. Very rare in Burgundy, but it produces rich, buttery wine usually used to soften Chardonnay. There is a little blended Pinot Beurot in the Hautes-Côtes and Aloxe-Corton.

PINOT BLANC (white) There is a little of this in the Côte d'Or – in Aloxe-Corton, for instance, where it makes a soft, quick-maturing wine. Rully in the Côte Chalonnaise has some and it ripens well in the Hautes-Côtes. There is also an odd white mutation of Pinot Noir – found in Nuits-St-Georges where the *premier cru* vineyard la Perrière makes a savoury white, and in the Monts Luisants vineyard in Morey-St-Denis.

PINOT NOIR (red) The sulkiest, trickiest fine-wine grape in the world is the exclusive grape in almost all red Burgundies. It needs a more delicate balance of spring, summer and autumn climate than any other variety to achieve greatness. It used to be true to say that no other part of the world could produce a Pinot Noir to match those of Burgundy, but isolated growers in Oregon, California, New Zealand, Australia and South Africa are now making very fine examples. Even so, Burgundy is still the only place on earth where fine Pinot Noirs are made in any great quantity. The problem is, there are still some awful ones, too: heavy, chewy and sweet-fruited or thin and pallid. But quality is far higher than it used to be. From a good producer it should be light, elegant, intense, and perfumed with raspberry or strawberry fruit and a hint of violets. Oak will add spicier, complex notes. Except for wine from the very top vineyards, Burgundy can be drunk young with pleasure. But a great *cru* from a great vintage really benefits from a decade or more in bottle.

WINE REGIONS

ALOXE-CORTON, AC (Côte de Beaune; red, white) Overwhelmingly a red-wine village, and it has the only red *grand cru* in the Côte de Beaune, le Corton, also sold under various subdivisions like Corton-Bressandes and Corton Clos du Roi and more widely available than the other *grands crus* of Burgundy. If we're talking about village wines, then the reds of Savigny are at least as good, and you're not paying a premium there for the hyphenated Corton. Go for *Chandon de Briailles, Drouhin, Jadot, Jaffelin, Leroy, Daniel Senard* and *Tollot-Beaut.* Also good: *Bouzereau-Gruère, Dubreuil-Fontaine, Faiveley, Juillot, Michel Voarick.*

The village also has one of the Côte's most famous white *grands crus*, Corton-Charlemagne. This can be a magnificent, blasting wall of flavour, not big on nuance, but strong, buttery and ripe, traditionally supposed to require long aging to show its full potential. See Corton-Charlemagne for producers, if you think you can afford it.

AUXEY-DURESSES, AC (Côte de Beaune; red, white) A village with a deservedly high reputation for full, but fairly gentle, nicely fruity reds. Look for *Ampeau, Diconne, Duc de Magenta, Alain Gras, Leroy, Pascal Prunier, Roy, Thévenin.*

The best whites here can be excellent, from producers like *Ampeau, Diconne, Duc de Magenta, Jadot, Leroy* and *Pascal Prunier.* *Leroy's* are probably the best, but prices at that domaine are astronomical.

BÂTARD-MONTRACHET, AC (Côte de Beaune; white) *Grand cru* of Chassagne and Puligny lying just below le Montrachet and, from a good producer, displaying a good deal of its dramatic flavour, almost thick in the mouth, all roast nuts, butter,

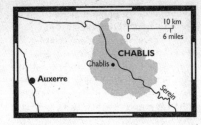

CHABLIS
Auxerre
Chablis
Serein

1. Côte de Nuits ⎤
2. Côte de Beaune ⎦ Côte d'Or
3. Côte Chalonnaise
4. Hautes-Côtes de Beaune
5. Hautes-Côtes de Nuits
6. Mâconnais

Dijon
Marsannay
Fixin
Gevrey-Chambertin
Morey-St-Denis
Chambolle-Musigny
Vougeot
Vosne-Romanée
5
Nuits-St-Georges
Pernand-Vergelesses
Savigny
Aloxe-Corton
4
2
Pommard
Beaune
Volnay
Auxey-Duresses
Meursault
4
Puligny-Montrachet
Santenay
Chassagne-Montrachet
Rully
Mercurey
Givry
Chalon-sur-Saône
3
Montagny
Buxy
Saône
6
Lugny
Viré
Clessé
Prissé
Mâcon
Pouilly
Fuissé
Loché
Vinzelles

CLASSIFICATIONS

Burgundy has five different levels of classification:

Non-specific regional appellations with no geographical definition, e.g. Bourgogne, which may come from inferior land or young vines.

Specific regional appellations, e.g. Côte de Beaune-Villages, generally a blend from one or more villages. Côte de Nuits-Villages is usually better.

Village commune wines Each village has its vineyards legally defined. Vineyards with no special reputation are usually blended together under the village name. But there is a growing move towards even relatively unknown vineyards appearing on the label. These unclassified vineyards are called *lieux-dits* or 'stated places'. They can only appear on the label in letters half the size of the village name.

Premier cru It's typical of Burgundy that *premier cru* or 'First Growth' actually means 'Second Growth', because these are the second-best vineyard sites. Even so, they contain some of Burgundy's finest wines. They are classified by both village and vineyard names, e.g. Gevrey-Chambertin, Combe-aux-Moines. The vineyard name must follow the village name on the label, and it may be in the same size print. Confusingly, some growers use smaller print, but the appellation should make it clear whether it is a *premier cru* or a *lieu-dit*.

Grand cru These are the real top growths. Not every village has one. The reds are mostly in the Côte de Nuits, the whites in the Côte de Beaune. A *grand cru* vineyard name can stand alone on the label without the village – for example, Chambertin from the village of Gevrey-Chambertin. (Note that by tradition, a Burgundy village is allowed to tack on the name of its *grand cru* vineyard, and use the compound name for wines that have nothing to do with the *grand cru*, for instance Puligny-Montrachet.)

toast and honey. Should be wonderfully exciting, if inevitably expensive. Good names: *Blain-Gagnard, Jean-Noël Gagnard, Leflaive, Bernard Morey, Pierre Morey, Michel Niellon, Pernot, Poirier, Ramonet* and *Sauzet*.

BEAUJOLAIS, AC (red) This covers all the basic wines, the produce of the flatter, southern part of Beaujolais. Much of the best is now sold as Nouveau. Run-of-the-mill Beaujolais, apart from Nouveau, can be good, fruity stuff but generally costs too much for the quality. Best: *Blaise, Carron, Charmet, Ch. de la Plume*, the co-op at *Bully, Duboeuf Bouteille Cristal, Garlon, Labruyère, Loron, Paul Sapin, Domaine des Vissoux*.

BEAUJOLAIS BLANC, AC (white) Usually quite expensive, and seldom has much character. At best it should be light and minerally.

BEAUJOLAIS NOUVEAU (or PRIMEUR) (red) The new vintage wine of Beaujolais, released in the November after the harvest. It will normally improve for several months in bottle, and even longer in good Nouveau vintages – a couple of years, maybe. There's seldom much difference in quality between Beaujolais-Villages Nouveau and simple Beaujolais Nouveau.

BEAUJOLAIS ROSÉ, AC (rosé) Usually an apology for a wine, although a good one can be very good indeed. But it's usually too expensive.

BEAUJOLAIS SUPÉRIEUR, AC (red) *Supérieur* means that the basic alcoholic content is higher. It doesn't ensure a better wine, and is rarely seen on the label.

BEAUJOLAIS-VILLAGES, AC (red) Thirty-nine villages can use this title. The wines are certainly better than basic Beaujolais, a little fuller and deeper, and the cherry-sharp fruit of the Gamay is usually more marked. However, always look for a wine bottled in the region, and preferably

one from a single vineyard. *Noël Aucoeur, Château Gaillard, Château des Loges, Château des Vergers, Jacques Dépagneux, Domaine de la Brasse, Domaine de la Chapelle de Vatre (Sarrau), de Flammerécourt, Gutty Père et Fils, André Large, Jean-Charles Pivot, Jean-Luc Tissier* and *Trichard* are good and local, but most domaines are bottled by one of the region's merchants. Labelling by domaine is on the increase.

BEAUNE, AC (Côte de Beaune; red, white) One of the few reliable commune wines, usually quite light, with a soft, 'red fruits' sweetness and a flicker of something minerally to smarten it up nicely. The wines are nearly all red. Beaune has the largest acreage of vines of any Côte d'Or commune, and they are mostly owned by merchants. It has no *grands crus* but many excellent *premiers crus*, for example Grèves, Marconnets, Teurons, Boucherottes, Vignes Franches and Cent Vignes. Prices tend to be reasonable, as Beaune is less fashionable than many. The best producers here are *Morot, Drouhin, Jadot, Lafarge* and *Tollot-Beaut*, but reliable wines are also made by *Besancenot-Mathouillet, Bouley, Germain, Jaffelin* and *Morey*. Drouhin's Clos des Mouches is a cut above the rest.

BIENVENUES-BÂTARD-MONTRACHET, AC (Côte de Beaune; white) A tiny *grand cru* situated in Puligny below le Montrachet, and within the larger Bâtard-Montrachet AC, whose wines are similar. The Bienvenues wines are often lighter and more elegant, although they may lack a tiny bit of Bâtard's drive. Best: *Carillon, Clerc, Leflaive, Pernot, Ramonet*.

BLAGNY, AC (Côte de Beaune; red) The red wines are usually a bit fierce, but then this is the white wine heartland of Burgundy, so I'm a bit surprised they grow any red at all. Best: *Leflaive, Matrot*.

BONNES-MARES, AC (Côte de Nuits; red) Usually one of the most – or should I say one of the very few – reliable *grands crus*, which ages extremely well over ten to 20 years to a lovely smoky, chocolate-and-prunes richness. Best names: *Domaine des Varoilles, Drouhin, Dujac, Groffier, Jadot, Roumier, de Vogüé.*

BOURGOGNE ALIGOTÉ, AC
(white) Usually rather sharp and green except where old vines make exciting wine, but the locals add crème de cassis to it to make kir – which tells you quite a lot about it. Best: *Coche-Dury, Confuron, Devevey, Diconne, Jobard, Rion, Rollin.*

BOURGOGNE ALIGOTÉ DE BOUZERON, AC
(Côte Chalonnaise; white) The white wine pride of the Côte Chalonnaise. The vines are frequently old – this seems to be more crucial for Aligoté than for most other wines – and the buttermilk-soap nose is followed by a very dry, slightly lemony, pepper-sharp wine, too good to mix with cassis. The best Aligoté of all, rich and oaky, comes from *de Villaine.* *Chanzy* and *Bouchard Père et Fils* are also good. Top ones can age for five years or so.

BOURGOGNE BLANC, AC (white)
Anything from a basic Burgundy grown in the less good spots anywhere between Chablis and the Mâconnais to a carefully matured wine from a serious producer, either from young vines or from vineyards that just miss a superior AC, especially on the borders of Meursault. Best: *Boisson-Vadot, Michel Bouzereau, Boyer-Martenot, Boisson-Morey, Coche-Dury, J Deverey, Dussort, Jadot, Javillier, Jobard, Labouré-Roi, Lafon, René Manuel, Millot-Battault* and the *Buxy* co-op (look for *Clos de Chenoves*).

BOURGOGNE GRAND ORDINAIRE, AC
(red) Très ordinaire. Pas très grand. The bottom of the Burgundy barrel, rarely seen outside Burgundy. It may be made from Pinot Noir and Gamay, and even a couple of obscure grapes, the Tressot and César, as well.

BOURGOGNE PASSE-TOUT-GRAINS, AC
(red) Often decent, lightish wine made usually in the Côte d'Or or the Côte Chalonnaise from Gamay blended with a minimum of one-third Pinot Noir. In some years it may be mostly Pinot. *Chanson* and *Rodet* make it well; *Chaley, Cornu, Henri Jayer, Léni-Volpato, Rion* and *Thomas* are also good. But even at its absolute best, true Burgundy it ain't.

BOURGOGNE ROUGE, AC
(red) The basic red AC, stretching from Chablis in the North to the Beaujolais *crus* in the South. Unknown Bourgogne Rouge is best avoided – much of it is very basic indeed. Domaine-bottled Bourgogne Rouge from good growers – and a handful of merchants – can be excellent value. The best wines come from vineyards just outside the village appellations. Look for *Bourgeon, Coche-Dury, Germain, d'Heuilly-Huberdeau, Henri Jayer, Juillot, Lafarge, Mortet, Parent, Pousse d'Or, Rion* and *Rossignol.* Good merchants include *Drouhin, Faiveley, Jadot, Jaffelin, Labouré-Roi, Latour, Olivier Leflaive, Leroy, Rodet, Vallet.* The co-ops at *Buxy* and *Igé* are also good as is the *Caves des Hautes-Côtes.* Most wines should be drunk quite young.

BROUILLY, AC
(Beaujolais; red) Brouilly usually makes one of the lightest *cru* wines, and in general rarely improves much with keeping. In fact, it makes a very good Nouveau. A few properties make a bigger wine to age – but even then, nine months to a year is quite enough. Good names include *Château de la Chaize, Château de Fouilloux, Château de Nevers, Château de Pierreux, Domaine Crêt des Garanches, Domaine de Combillaty (Duboeuf), Domaine de Garanches, Hospices de Belleville* and *André Large. Château des Tours*, although lovely young, can age longer.

CHABLIS, AC
(white) Simple Chablis, mostly soft, sometimes acidic, covers the widest area of the appellation. So it covers a multitude of sins, with a lot of wine going

under négociants' labels, and a lot being sold by the local co-op, *la Chablisienne* – they make most of the négociants' stuff too. Some of the co-op's best *cuvées* are outstandingly good, but many are too bland and soft. New oak, which is lavishly used by growers such as Fèvre and Droin, often smothers the steely and minerally qualities that make top Chablis so exciting. Best: *Adhémar-Boudin, Christian Adine, Pascal Bouchard, Jean-Marc Brocard, la Chablisienne co-op, Jean Collet, René Dauvissat, Defaix, Jean-Paul Droin, Joseph Drouhin, William Fèvre, Alain Geoffroy, Jean-Pierre Grossot, Michel Laroche, Bernard Légland, Long Depaquit, Louis Michel, Dom. des Milandes, Moreau, Guy Mothe, Raveneau, Regnard, Savary, Simmonet-Fèbvre, Robert Vocoret.*

CHABLIS GRAND CRU, AC (white)

The seven *grands crus* (Blanchots, Preuses, Bougros, Grenouilles, Valmur, Vaudésir and les Clos) can be outstanding, though they seldom rival the *grands crus* of the Côte de Beaune. To get the best out of them, you need to age them, preferably after oaking, although *Louis Michel*'s oak-free wines age superbly. Recent vintages have seen a growing use of oak, sometimes giving deeper, richer wines which will benefit from bottle-aging, but some wines are marred by clumsy or excessive use of new oak.

CHABLIS PREMIER CRU, AC (white)

There are some 30 vineyard names in this category, but they have been rationalized into 12 main plots. Expansion mania has meant that many hardly suitable pieces of vineyard are now accorded *premier cru* status, so the difference in quality between basic Chablis and *premier cru* isn't always all that it should be. However, in recent years there has been a definite move towards quality by the better growers and *la Chablisienne* co-op.

CHAMBERTIN, AC (Côte de Nuits;

red) Most famous of the eight *grands crus* of Gevrey-Chambertin, this vineyard should

---

CHABLIS VINEYARDS

Grands Crus

Blanchots, Bougros, les Clos, Grenouilles, Preuses, Valmur, Vaudésir. La Moutonne, considered a *grand cru*, is from a parcel in Preuses and Vaudésir.

Premiers Crus

Fourchaume (including Fourchaume, Vaupulent, Côte de Fontenay, Vaulorent, l'Homme Mort); Montée de Tonnerre (including Montée de Tonnerre, Chapelot, Pied d'Aloup); Monts de Milieu; Vaucoupin; les Fourneaux (including les Fourneaux, Morein, Côte des Prés-Girots); Beauroy (including Beauroy, Troesmes); Côte de Léchet; Vaillons (including Vaillons, Châtains, Séché, Beugnons, les Lys); Mélinots (including Mélinots, Roncières, les Epinottes); Montmains (including Montmains, Forêts, Butteaux); Vosgros (including Vosgros and Vaugiraut); Vaudevey.

---

and can make wines that are big, strong and intense in their youth, mellowing to a complex, perfumed, plummy richness with age – good ones need ten to 15 years. Best: *Drouhin, Faiveley, Leroy, Denis Mortet, Ponsot, Rebourseau, Rousseau, Tortochot.*

CHAMBERTIN CLOS-DE-BÈZE, AC

(Côte de Nuits; red) *Grand cru* in the village of Gevrey-Chambertin next to Chambertin both geographically and in quality. It needs seven to ten years in bottle. May be sold as Chambertin. Best: *Drouhin, Bruno Clair, Faiveley, Gelin, Mugneret-Gibourg, Rousseau, Thomas-Moillard* and *Damoy* since 1992.

CHAMBOLLE-MUSIGNY, AC (Côte

de Nuits; red) This village can make light, cherry-sweet, intensely perfumed Burgundy. Best is *Georges Roumier*, with wonderful wines in every vintage from 1985. The best *premier cru* is les Amoureuses: it deserves to be *grand cru* and is priced accordingly. Top producers: *Barthod-Noëllat, Château de Chambolle-Musigny, Drouhin, Dujac, Groffier, Hudelot-Noëllat, Rion, Serveau, de Vogüé.*

CHAPELLE-CHAMBERTIN, AC

(Côte de Nuits; red) The wines of this *grand cru* are typically lighter and more delicate than the other *grands crus*. But over-lightness – resulting from over-production – is their curse. The best producers are *Damoy* (since 1993), *Louis Jadot* and *Rossignol-Trapet*.

CHARMES-CHAMBERTIN, AC

(Côte de Nuits; red) This is the biggest of the *grands crus* of Gevrey-Chambertin. It can be fine, strong, sensuous wine, but as with all of them, it can also be disgracefully light. Best producers: *Bachelet, Charlopin-Parisot, Drouhin, Dugat, Dujac, Rebourseau, Roty, Rousseau, Tortochot*.

CHASSAGNE-MONTRACHET, AC

(Côte de Beaune; red, white) Its fame lies in its large share of the white *grand cru* vineyard of le Montrachet. The reds are a puzzle. At their best they're good value, if a bit heavy, plummy and earthy. The best names for red are *Amiot, Carillon, Colin, Duc de Magenta, Jean-Noël Gagnard, Gagnard-Delagrange, René Lamy, Albert Morey, Moreau, Jean Pillot, Ramonet*. Of the whites, the *grands crus* are excellent, but the *premiers crus* rarely dazzle quite like those of nearby Puligny-Montrachet. Best: *Blain-Gagnard, Carillon, Colin, Duc de Magenta, Fontaine-Gagnard, Jean-Noël Gagnard, Gagnard-Delagrange, Lamy-Pillot, Laguiche, Château de la Maltroye, Moreau, Albert Morey, Bernard Morey, Niellon, Fernand Pillot* and *Ramonet. Jaffelin* is the top merchant.

CHÉNAS, AC

(Beaujolais; red) This is the second-smallest Beaujolais *cru*, making strong, dark wines, sometimes a bit tough, that can be drunk a year after the harvest, or aged to take on a Pinot Noir-like flavour. Ultra-fashionable in France at the moment. Look out for *Louis Champagnon, Charvet, Château de Chénas, Domaines des Brureaux, Domaine Chassignon, Domaine de la Combe Remont (Duboeuf), Pierre Perrachon* and *Émile Robin*.

CHEVALIER-MONTRACHET, AC

(Côte de Beaune; white) A *grand cru* vineyard of the village of Puligny, giving a leaner wine than le Montrachet itself, but one with a deep flavour as rich and satisfying as a dry white wine can get. Good ones will last 20 years. Best: *Bouchard Père et Fils, Clerc, Jadot, Latour, Leflaive, Niellon*.

CHIROUBLES, AC

(Beaujolais; red) A *cru* for early drinking: naturally light, similar to Beaujolais-Villages in weight, but with a cherry scent that makes it France's favourite Beaujolais *cru*. Look for *Georges Boulon, René Brouillard, Cheysson, Château Javernand, Château de Raousset, Jean-Pierre Desvignes, Duboeuf, Méziat* and *Georges Passot*.

CHOREY-LÈS-BEAUNE, AC

(Côte de Beaune; red) Good value, soft, fruity reds. The village isn't overhyped, so makes some of the few affordable Burgundies. *Drouhin, Germain* and *Tollot-Beaut* are best.

CLOS DES LAMBRAYS, AC

(Côte de Nuits; red) This single-owner *grand cru* in Morey-St-Denis changed hands recently. The estate had become run down and the wines were not only very rare but also not very tasty. Let's hope things change now.

CLOS DE LA ROCHE, AC

(Côte de Nuits; red) Largest and finest *grand cru* of Morey-St-Denis. If not too light, it can be splendid, redcurrant-and-strawberry rich when young, like pretty good Chambertin after ten years. Best: *Amiot, Dujac, Leroy, Hubert* and *Georges Lignier, Ponsot, Rousseau*.

CLOS ST-DENIS, AC

(Côte de Nuits; red) Has rarely achieved great heights and is probably least famous of all the *grands crus*. Best known is *Dujac's*; look for *Charlopin-Parisot, Georges* or *Hubert Lignier, Ponsot*.

CLOS DE TART, AC

(Côte de Nuits; red) *Grand cru* of Morey-St-Denis owned by Beaujolais merchants *Mommessin*. At best it is light but intense wine which lasts.

CLOS DE VOUGEOT, AC (Côte de Nuits; red) Over 80 growers share this *grand cru* and, while the land at the top of the slope is very fine, the land by the road is not. That rare thing, a good bottle of Clos de Vougeot, is fat, rich, strong and thick with the sweetness of perfumed plums and honey, unsubtle but exciting. It is only found in top vintages, and then only from the best producers. Best: *Arnoux, Ch. de la Tour, Jacky Confuron, Drouhin-Laroze, Engel, Grivot, Gros, Hudelot-Noëllat, Jadot, Lamarche, Leroy, Meo-Camuzet, Mugneret, Raphet.*

CORTON, AC (Côte de Beaune; red, white) The only red *grand cru* vineyard in the Côte de Beaune. Ideally, red Corton should have something of the richness and strength of Clos de Vougeot, but it tends to be four-square and unrewarding until it is mature, and then only the top wines are good. Best producers include: *Chandon de Briailles, Dubreuil-Fontaine, Faiveley, Gaunoux, Laleur-Piot, Maldant, Prince de Mérode, Rapet, Daniel Senard, Tollot-Beaut.* The finest white is the *Hospices de Beaune's* Corton-Vergennes, and *Chandon de Briailles* makes Corton-Bressandes that is half Pinot Blanc.

CORTON-CHARLEMAGNE, AC (Côte de Beaune; white) Famous *grand cru* of Aloxe-Corton and Pernand-Vergelesses that occupies the upper half of the dome-shaped hill of Corton. It is planted almost entirely with Chardonnay, but a little Pinot Blanc or Pinot Beurot can add intriguing fatness to the wine. Good names: *Bitouzet, Bonneau du Martray, Chandon de Briailles, Chapuis, Dubreuil-Fontaine, M Juillot, Hospices de Beaune, Jadot, Laleure-Piot, Latour, Rapet.*

CÔTE CHALONNAISE, AC (red, white) Light, usually clean-tasting Chardonnay predominates among the whites – although at long last the idea of oak-aging is catching on. But the Côte Chalonnaise has one star that cannot be overshadowed by the famous Côte d'Or: the village of Bouzeron makes the finest and

---

---

the most famous Aligoté in all France. The top three villages of Rully, Mercurey and Givry all produce good reds, too, with a lovely, simple strawberry-and-cherry fruit.

CÔTE DE BEAUNE (red, white) Wine from the commune of Beaune that doesn't quite rate village status. Not much found.

CÔTE DE BEAUNE-VILLAGES, AC (red) Catch-all red wine appellation for 16 villages on the Côte de Beaune. Only Aloxe-Corton, Beaune, Volnay and Pommard cannot use the appellation. Rarely seen nowadays and rarely exciting. Still, it *is* worth checking out the wines of *Bachelet, Jaffelin* and *Lequin-Roussot.*

CÔTE DE BROUILLY, AC (Beaujolais; red) The Mont de Brouilly, a pyramid-shaped hill in the middle of the *cru* of Brouilly, makes quite different wine to

Brouilly itself. The soil is of volcanic origin, and the slopes lap up the sun. Best: *Château Thivin, Conroy, Domaine de la Pierre Bleue, Jean Sanvers, Lucien Verger, Chanrion.*

CÔTE DE NUITS (red, white) The

northern part of the Côte d'Or, in theory producing the biggest wines. It is almost entirely devoted to Pinot Noir. Standards have risen in recent years. This doesn't mean you won't ever be disappointed, because unpredictability is built into red Burgundy. But your chances are an awful lot better than they used to be.

CÔTE DE NUITS-VILLAGES, AC

(red) Covers the three southernmost villages of Prissey, Comblanchien and Corgoloin, plus Fixin and Brochon in the North. Usually fairly light and dry, it can have good cherry fruit and the delicious vegetal decay taste of good Côte de Nuits red. Often good value. Best producers: *Durand, Rion, Rossignol* and *Tollot-Voarick,* and especially *Chopin-Groffier* and *Domaine de l'Arlot.*

CÔTE D'OR (red, white) The source of

Burgundy's fame – a thin sliver of land worth its weight in gold. It has two halves, the Côte de Nuits in the North and the Côte de Beaune in the South, with a fine crop of illustrious whites.

CRÉMANT DE BOURGOGNE, AC

(white, rosé) Good, quite broad, eminently affordable sparkling wine, made by the Champagne method, from Chardonnay and Pinot Noir. Try *Caves de Lugny* for white and *Caves de Bailly* for lovely fresh, strawberryish pink.

CRIOTS-BÂTARD-MONTRACHET,

AC (Côte de Beaune; white) Tiny *grand cru* in Chassagne-Montrachet nuzzled up against Bâtard-Montrachet. The wines resemble Bâtard's power and concentration but are leaner, more minerally – and rarely seen. Best: *Blain-Gagnard, Fontaine-Gagnard.*

CRU The ten Beaujolais *crus* or growths

(Fleurie, Moulin-à-Vent, Brouilly, Chénas, Côte de Brouilly, Chiroubles, Juliénas, St-Amour, Morgon, Régnié) are the top villages in the steeply hilly, northern part of Beaujolais. All *should* have definable characteristics, but the produce of different vineyards and growers is all too often blended to a mean by merchants elsewhere. There's also a distressing tendency now to age the wines in new oak, which destroys their point. Any old red can taste of new oak; only good Beaujolais has the juiciness of Gamay. Always buy either a single-estate wine, or one from a good local merchant like *Chanut Frères, la Chevalière, Duboeuf, Dépagneux, Ferraud, Loron, Sarrau, Louis Tête,* and *Trenel.* Elsewhere in Burgundy the best vineyards are labelled *grand cru,* and the second-best *premier cru.*

ÉCHÉZEAUX, AC (Côte de Nuits; red)

Large, slightly second-line *grand cru* vineyard in Vosne-Romanée. Best: *Domaine de la Romanée-Conti, Engel, Faiveley, Forey, Louis Gouroux, Grivot, Henri Jayer, Mongeard-Mugneret, Mugneret-Gibourg.*

EPINEUIL, AC (red) Tiny region in the

North of Burgundy, producing light but fragrant styles of Pinot Noir.

FIXIN, AC (Côte de Nuits; red) A suburb

of Dijon, Fixin can make some of Burgundy's sturdiest reds: deep, strong, tough but plummy when young; capable of mellowing with age. Such wines are slowly reappearing. If you want to feel you're drinking Gevrey-Chambertin without shouldering the cost, Fixin from the following producers could fit the bill: *Bordet, Charlopin-Parizot, Bruno Clair, Fougeray, Roger Fournier, Gelin, Guyard, Joliet, Jadot, Moillard, Philippe Rossignol.*

FLAGEY-ÉCHÉZEAUX, AC (Côte de

Nuits; red) A commune that sells its basic wines as Vosne-Romanée but, in Échézeaux and Grands-Échézeaux, has two *grands crus.*

FLEURIE, AC (Beaujolais; red) Often the most delicious of the *crus*, gentle and round, its sweet cherry-and-chocolate fruit just held firm by a touch of tannin and acid. Its deserved popularity in Britain and the US has led to high prices. Look out for: *Château de Fleurie (Loron), Chauvet, Chignard, Colonge, Domaine de la Grand, Grand Pré (Sarrau), Domaine de la Presle, Domaine des Quatre Vents, Duboeuf's la Madone, Bernard Paul, Verpoix,* the *Fleurie* co-op's *cuvées, Cuvée Présidente Marguerite* and *Cuvée Cardinale*.

GEVREY-CHAMBERTIN, AC (Côte de Nuits; red) This village has eight *grands crus*, and two of them, Chambertin and Chambertin Clos-de-Bèze can be some of the world's greatest wines. They should have rough, plumskins and damson strength, fierce when young, but assuming a brilliant, wafting perfume and intense, plummy richness when mature. *Bachelet, Boillot, Burguet, Dugat, Michel Esmonin, Philippe Leclerc, Mortet, Naddef* and *Rossignol-Trapet* are the names to look out for among younger producers. Of the old estates, *Rousseau* is best but *Domaine des Varoilles* is also good. Also look for *Frédéric Esmonin, René Leclerc, Maume* and *Roty,* and for the merchants' bottlings from *Drouhin, Faiveley, Jadot* and *Jaffelin*. Be aware that there are still some overpriced horrors bearing the sacred name.

GIVRY, AC (Côte Chalonnaise; red) Small but important red wine village. At their best, the wines are deliciously warm and cherry-chewy with a slightly smoky fragrance to them, but too many are mediocre, especially from négociants. *Baron Thénard* is best, but *Chofflet, Clos Salomon, Joblot, Laborbe, Lespinasse, Mouton* and *Ragot* are also worth investigating.

LA GRANDE RUE, AC (Côte de Nuits; red) This vineyard is wholly owned by the Lamarche family. Elevated to *grand cru* status in 1990, more because of its potential than because of recent wines.

GRANDS-ÉCHÉZEAUX, AC (Côte de Nuits; red) A *grand cru* capable of delicately scented, plum-and-woodsmoke wine which goes rich and chocolaty with age. Best names: *Domaine de la Romanée-Conti, Drouhin, Engel, Mongeard-Mugneret*.

GRIOTTE-CHAMBERTIN, AC (Côte de Nuits; red) One of the smallest *grands crus* of Gevrey-Chambertin. Best: *Drouhin, Claude Dugat, F Esmonin, Ponsot, Roty*.

HAUTES-CÔTES DE BEAUNE and HAUTES-CÔTES DE NUITS (red, white) A hilly backwater consisting of 28 villages which make fairly good, light, strawberry-like Pinot and a lot of reasonably good, light, dry Chardonnay at a decent price. The red grapes do not always ripen fully every year. Look out for the red Hautes-Côtes de Nuits wines of *Cornu, Domaine des Mouchottes, Jayer-Gilles, Thévenet* and *Verdet* and the red Hautes-Côtes de Beaunes of *Bouley, Capron Manieux, Chalet, Guillemard, Joliot, Mazilly* and *Plait*. The *Caves des Hautes-Côtes* is beginning to produce some of the best-value wines in the whole of Burgundy. Good whites come from *Chaley, Cornu, Devevey, Goubard, Jayer-Gilles, Thévenot-le-Brun, Alain Verdet* (organic).

IRANCY, AC (red) Mostly Pinot Noir from vineyards just to the south-west of Chablis, sometimes with a little of the darker, tougher local grape, César. Rarely deep in colour, but always perfumed, slightly plummy and attractive. Cool years can provide disappointingly thin wines. Best drunk while young and fresh. It must legally be labelled 'Bourgogne Irancy'. Good producers: *Léon & Serge Bienvenu, Bernard Cantin, André & Roger Delaloge, Gabriel Delaloge, Jean Renaud, Simmonet-Fèbvre*.

JULIÉNAS, AC (Beaujolais; red) This *can* be big, with tannin and acidity, but many of the best more closely resemble the mixture of fresh red fruit and soft, chocolaty warmth that makes for good Fleurie. Good: *Château du Bois de la Salle, Château des Capitans, Château de Juliénas, Domaine des Bucherats, Domaine de la Dîme, Domaine de la Vieille Église, Duboeuf, René Monnet, Pelletier.*

LADOIX-SERRIGNY, AC (Côte de Beaune; red) Overshadowed by the more famous Aloxe-Corton next door. It's worth looking out for though: *Capitain, Chevalier, Cornu, Prince de Mérode* and *Ravaut* all make decent, crisp wines at fair prices.

LATRICIÈRES-CHAMBERTIN, AC (Côte de Nuits; red) Small *grand cru* vineyard in Gevrey-Chambertin and very similar in style to Chambertin though without all the power. Best producers: *Leroy, Ponsot, Rossignol-Trapet.*

MÂCON BLANC, AC (Mâconnais; white) This should be good-value, light Chardonnay, but too often it's not. Most Mâcon simply cannot compete with the best-value New World wines.

MÂCON BLANC-VILLAGES, AC (Mâconnais; white) One step up from basic Mâcon Blanc, this must come from the 43 Mâcon communes with the best land. The rare good ones show the signs of honey and fresh apples and some of the nutty, yeasty depth associated with fine Chardonnay. These come from those villages, notably Viré, Clessé, Prissé and Lugny, that add their own village names (Mâcon-Viré, etc): full, buttery yet fresh, sometimes spicy. There is a handful of growers making serious, oak-aged wine from low-yielding vines. *Guffens Heynen,*

Merlin and *Jean Thévenet* are names to look for. Others include: *Bicheron, Bonhomme, Danauchet, Goyard, Guillemot-Michel, Josserand, Lassarat, Manciat-Poncet, Signoret, Talmard* and *Thévenet-Wicart.*

MÂCON ROUGE, AC (Mâconnais; red) There's a lot of red wine made in the Mâconnais but it's usually fairly lean, earthy Gamay without the spark of Beaujolais' fruit. If it appeals, try wines from Igé and Mancey, or *Lafarge*'s wine from Bray. *Lassarat* is improving things by using new oak.

MARANGES, AC (Côte de Beaune; red) An AC created in 1989; previously the wines were sold as Côte de Beaune-Villages but now these sturdy, rustic reds are coming into their own. *Drouhin*'s is good.

MARSANNAY, AC (Côte de Nuits; red, rosé) Used to produce mostly rosé under the name Bourgogne Rosé de Marsannay, but the introduction of an appellation for reds in 1987 has encouraged growers to switch. The first results of this new seriousness are most encouraging and some lovely wines are already emerging, usually quite dry and cherry-perfumed, sometimes more full-blown and exciting. One to watch. Best: *Bouvier, Charlopin-Parizot, Bruno Clair, Collotte, Fougeray, Fournier, Geantet-Pansiot, Huguenot, Jadot, Naddef, Roty.*

MAZIS-CHAMBERTIN, AC (Côte de Nuits; red) This *grand cru* in Gevrey-Chambertin can have a superb deep blackberry-pip, damson-skin and black-currant fruit which gets more exciting after six to 12 years. Best: *Faiveley, Gelin, Hospices de Beaune, Maume, Rebourseau, Roty, Rousseau, Tortochot.*

MAZOYÈRES-CHAMBERTIN, AC (Côte de Nuits; red) *Grand cru* of Gevrey-Chambertin, rarely seen since producers generally take up the option of using the *grand cru* Charmes-Chambertin instead. *Perrot-Minot* produces a fine example.

MERCUREY, AC (Côte Chalonnaise; red, white) The biggest Chalonnais village, producing half the region's wines. Indeed many call the Côte Chalonnaise the 'Région de Mercurey'. It's mostly red wine, often fairly full, with attractive strawberry fruit and a little smoky fragrance. *Faiveley* and *Juillot* make a fine range of red Mercureys, but look out also for *Chandesais, Chanzy, Ch. de Chamirey, Domaine la Marche, Dufouleur, Jacqueson, de Launay, Meix-Foulot, Monette, Saier* and *de Suremain*. Whites have been improving, as rising prices have spurred producers to greater efforts. Good examples come from *Château de Chamirey, Faiveley, M Juillot, Protheau, Rodet.*

MEURSAULT, AC (Côte de Beaune; white) It has by far the largest white production of any commune in the Côte d'Or, and this is one of several reasons why its traditionally high overall standard is gradually being eroded. The wines should be big and nutty and have a delicious, vegetal lusciousness, and sometimes even peachy, honeyed flavours. Try *Ampeau, Pierre Boillot, Boisson-Vadot, Boyer-Martenot, Michel Bouzereau, Buisson-Battault, Coche-Debord, Coche-Dury, Comtes Lafon, Fichet, Gauffroy, Henry Germain, Jean Germain, Grivault, Patrick Javillier, François Jobard, René Manuel, Matrot, Michelot-Buisson, Millot-Battault, Pierre Morey, Prieur, Roulot.*

MONTAGNY, AC (Côte Chalonnaise; white) Quite nice round, ripe wines. Best: *Arnoux,* the co-op at *Buxy, Latour, Olivier Leflaive, B Michel, de Montorge, Rodet, Alain Roy* and *Vache.*

MONTHELIE, AC (Côte de Beaune; red) These wines deserve recognition: they're full, dry, rather herby or piney, but with a satisfying rough fruit. Often a good buy but stick to growers, not négociants. Best: *Boussey, Caves des Hautes-Côtes, Château de Monthelie, Deschamps, Doreau, Garaudet, Monthelie-Douhairet, Potinet-Ampeau, de Suremain, Thévenin-Monthelie.*

LE MONTRACHET, AC (Côte de Beaune; white) This is white Burgundy at its absolute greatest, the finest of fine white *grands crus* in the villages of Puligny and Chassagne. Does it mean most enjoyable, most happy-making? Not really. In fact the flavours can be so intense it's difficult sometimes to know if you're having fun drinking it or merely giving your wine vocabulary an end-of-term examination. So be brave if someone opens a bottle and let the incredible blend of spice and smoke, honey and ripeness flow over you. Best: *Amiot, Comtes Lafon, Domaine de la Romanée-Conti, Drouhin's Laguiche, Jadot, Pierre Morey, Prieur, Thénard* and, since 1991, *Leflaive.*

MOREY-ST-DENIS, AC (Côte de Nuits; red) Expensive, and can suffer from overproduction. At their best they blend the perfume of Chambolle-Musigny with the body of Gevrey-Chambertin, and exhibit a slight savouriness that mellows into a rich chocolaty mouthful. You'll find exciting bottles from *Pierre Amiot, Bryczek, Charloppin, Dujac, Georges* and *Hubert Lignier, Marchand, Perrot-Minot, Ponsot, Serveau* and *Vadey-Castagnier.*

MORGON, AC (Beaujolais; red) The wines of this *cru* can be glorious. They can start thick and dark, and age to a chocolaty, plummy depth with an amazing cherries smell. A sort of reserve category called Morgon Age has to be kept for at least 18 months before release. *Jacky Janodet's* Morgon is intense. Look also for *Aucoeur, Château de Pizay, Château de Raousset, Descombes, Desvignes, Domaine de la Chanaise, Domaine Roche-St-Jean, Domaine de Ruyère, Drouhin, Gobet, Lapierre, Félix Longepierre* and *Georges Vincent.*

MOULIN-À-VENT, AC (Beaujolais; red) Enter the heavy brigade. These *cru* wines should be solid, and should age for three to five years and more from good years. The best of them have a big, plummy, Burgundian style, and their toughness doesn't give you much option but to wait for them to mellow. This is one of the few Beaujolais *crus* that can respond well to discreet oak aging. *Louis Champagnon*'s is good, as is *Brugne, Charvet, Château des Jacques, Château du Moulin-à-Vent, Château Portier, Domaine de la Tour de Bief, Duboeuf, Jacky Janodet, Raymond Siffert* and *Héritiers Maillard* (formerly *Héritiers Tagent*).

MUSIGNY, AC (Côte de Nuits; red, white) Extremely fine *grand cru* which gave its name to Chambolle-Musigny. All but a third of a hectare is planted with Pinot Noir, capable of producing Burgundy's most heavenly scented wine. Look for *Château de Chambolle-Musigny, Jadot, Leroy, Jacques Prieur, Georges Roumier, de Vogüé* (white, too).

NUITS-ST-GEORGES, AC (Côte de Nuits; red) When it's good, this has an enthralling decayed – rotting even – brown richness of chocolate and prunes rising out of a fairly light, plum-sweet fruit – gorgeous, whatever it sounds like. It is expensive but increasingly reliable. *Labouré-Roi* is the most consistent merchant for Nuits, although *Jadot, Jaffelin* and *Moillard* are increasingly good particularly at *premier cru* level. The most famous growers are *Robert Chevillon, Gouges, Michelot* and *Daniel Rion*, but excellent wines are also made by *Ambroise, Jean Chauvenet, Chicotot, Jean-Jacques Confuron, Domaine de l'Arlot*, and then there's the amazingly deep (and amazingly expensive) *Leroy*.

PERNAND-VERGELESSES, AC (Côte de Beaune; red, white) The village whites are generally fairly lean and need time to soften, but can be gently nutty and very enjoyable from a good producer. They can also be quite good value. Best names in white: *Dubreuil-Fontaine, Germain, Laleure-Piot, Pavelot, Rapet, Rollin*. Some quite attractive, softly earthy reds are made. Look for the *premier cru* Île de Vergelesses. Best reds: *Besancenot-Mathouillet, Caves des Hautes-Côtes, Chandon des Briailles, Delarche, Dubreuil-Fontaine, Laleure-Piot, Pavelot, Rapet* and *Rollin*.

PETIT CHABLIS, AC (Chablis; white) There used to be lots of this grown on the least-good slopes. But the growers objected that it made it sound as though their wine was a lesser form of Chablis. Nowadays pretty well the whole lot is called 'Chablis' – so we can't tell what's what, they're all richer, they're happy, we're not… I give up.

POMMARD, AC (Côte de Beaune; red) From good producers, Pommard can have a strong, meaty sturdiness, backed by slightly jammy but attractively plummy fruit. Not subtle, but many people's idea of what red Burgundy should be. They need ten years to show their class. The most consistently fine wines are made by *Comte Armand, de Courcel* and *de Montille*, but also look out for the wines of *Boillot, Château de Pommard, Girardin, Lahaye, Lejeune, Jean Monnier, Parent, Pothier* and *Pousse d'Or*.

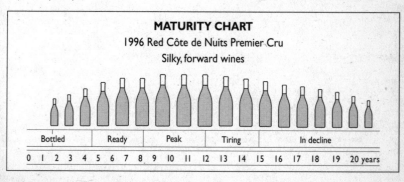

MATURITY CHART
1996 Red Côte de Nuits Premier Cru
Silky, forward wines

Bottled	Ready	Peak	Tiring	In decline

0 1 2 3 4 5 6 7 8 9 10 11 12 13 14 15 16 17 18 19 20 years

POUILLY-FUISSÉ, AC (Mâconnais; white)

Prices here yo-yo according to supply and demand. It is sometimes best in years which are not too rich. Best: *Barraud, Béranger, Cordier, Corsin, Duboeuf*'s top selections, *Ferret, M Forest, Guffens-Heynen, Leger-Plumet, Loron*'s *les Vieux Murs, Manciat-Poncet, Noblet, Roger Saumaize, Valette, Vincent* at *Château Fuissé*. Adjoining villages Pouilly-Loché, AC and Pouilly-Vinzelles, AC are similar at half the price.

PULIGNY-MONTRACHET, AC

(Côte de Beaune; white) The peak of great white pleasure is to be found in the various Montrachet *grands crus*. Le Montrachet is peerless, showing how humble words like honey, nuts, cream, smoke, perfume and all the rest do no honest service to a wine that seems to combine every memory of ripe fruit and scent with a dry, penetrating savouriness. Several other *grands crus* are less intense, but offer the same unrivalled mix. There are *premiers crus* as well. Standards here have risen, and there are many serious producers. Look for *Amiot-Bonfils, Jean-Marc Boillot, Boyer-Devèze, Carillon, Gérard Chavy, Drouhin, Jadot, Labouré-Roi, Laguiche*, both *Domaine Leflaive* and *Olivier Leflaive, Pernot, Ramonet-Prudhon, Antonin Rodet, Sauzet, Thénard*.

RÉGNIÉ, AC (Beaujolais; red)

Beaujolais' tenth *cru*. Quite similar to Brouilly in ripe years but a bit weedy when the sun doesn't shine. *Duboeuf Bouteille Cristal* is best.

RICHEBOURG, AC (Côte de Nuits; red)

Exceptional *grand cru* of Vosne-Romanée. It's a wonderful name for a wine -- Richebourg -- and, at its best, it manages to be fleshy yet filled with spice and perfume and the clinging richness of chocolate and figs. Best producers: *Domaine de la Romanée-Conti, Grivot, Gros, Henri Jayer, Leroy, Méo-Camuzet*.

LA ROMANÉE, AC (Côte de Nuits; red)

This *grand cru* is the smallest AC in France, solely owned by the Liger-Belair family and sold by *Bouchard Père et Fils*. Now that Bouchard is under new and more rigorous ownership, we may see whether Romanée, solid but never sensational hitherto, deserves its status.

LA ROMANÉE-CONTI, AC (Côte de Nuits; red)

This tiny *grand cru* is capable of a more startling brilliance than any other Burgundy. The 7,000 or so bottles it produces per year are instantly seized on by the super-rich before we mortals can even get our tasting sheets out. Wholly owned by the *Domaine de la Romanée-Conti*.

LA ROMANÉE-ST-VIVANT, AC

(Côte de Nuits; red) *Grand cru* in the village of Vosne-Romanée. It is far less easy to taste young than its neighbouring *grands crus* and needs a good 12 years to show what can be a delicious, savoury yet sweet personality. Best names: *Arnoux, Domaine de la Romanée-Conti, Latour, Leroy*.

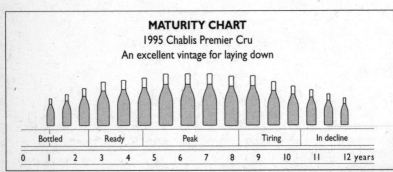

MATURITY CHART
1995 Chablis Premier Cru
An excellent vintage for laying down

| Bottled | Ready | Peak | Tiring | In decline |

| 0 | 1 | 2 | 3 | 4 | 5 | 6 | 7 | 8 | 9 | 10 | 11 | 12 years |

RUCHOTTES-CHAMBERTIN, AC

(Côte de Nuits; red) This is the smallest Gevrey-Chambertin *grand cru*, with wines of deeper colour and longer-lasting perfumed richness than most of the village's other *grands crus*. Best producers: *F Esmonin, Georges Mugneret, Roumier, Rousseau*.

RULLY, AC

(Côte Chalonnaise; red white) This village gets my vote for the most improved white AC in Burgundy. The use of new oak to ferment and age the wine is producing wonderfully soft, spicy Burgundies of good quality – and still at relatively low prices. Relative to the rest of Burgundy, that is. Best whites: *Bêtes, Chanzy, Cogny, Delorme, Domaine de la Folie, Drouhin, Dury, Duvernay, Jacqueson, Jaffelin, Olivier Leflaive, Rodet*. Best for red: *Chanzy, Ch. de Rully, Delorme, Domaine de la Folie, Duvernay, Faiveley, Jacqueson, Jaffelin*.

ST-AMOUR, AC

(Beaujolais; red) Among the most perfect Beaujolais, this pink-red wine usually has freshness and peachy perfume and good, ripe fruit all at once. It isn't that common here (though the French love it), and yet it is frequently the most reliable and most enjoyable *cru*. Look for *Buis, Château de St-Amour, Domaine des Billards (Loron), Domaine des Ducs, Domaine du Paradis, Patissier, André Poitevin, Francis Saillant, Paul Spay*.

ST-AUBIN, AC

(Côte de Beaune; red, white) Some of Burgundy's best-value wines, though the reds are a touch earthy. They are reliable, and can give real pleasure after a few years of aging. Best: *Bachelet, Clergy, Lamy, Prudhon, Gérard Thomas* and *Roux*, but wines from négociants *Jadot* and *Olivier Leflaive* are their equal. Good whites come from *Bachelet, Clerget, Lamy, Olivier Leflaive, Prudhon, Thomas* and *Roux*.

ST-ROMAIN, AC

(Côte de Beaune; red, white) Full, rather broad-flavoured, cherry-stone dry reds, that perform best in very warm years. On the whole sold cheaper

than they deserve. Look for *Bazenet, Buisson, Gras, Thévenin* and *Thévenin-Monthelie*. The flinty, dry whites are often of decent quality and pretty good value. Beware cooler vintages, when the grapes sometimes don't ripen properly. Best are: *Bazenet, Buisson, Germain, Gras, Thévenin, Thévenin-Monthelie*.

ST-VÉRAN, AC

(Mâconnais; white) Pouilly-Fuissé's understudy, capable of simple, soft, quick-maturing but attractive, rather honeyed white Burgundy. Best: *Corsin, Dépardon, Dom. des Deux Roches, Duboeuf, Grégoire, Lassarat, de Montferrand, Saumaize, Thibert, Vincent* – and, above all, *Drouhin*.

SANTENAY, AC

(Côte de Beaune; red) Rough and ready red. At its best it has a strong, savoury flavour and good strawberry fruit, though nowadays is frequently rather lean and mean. Best: *Belland, Drouhin, Girardin, Lequin-Roussot, Morey, Pousse d'Or, Prieur-Bonnet, Roux*. Even these are variable.

SAVIGNY-LÈS-BEAUNE, AC

(Côte de Beaune; red) Gaining in reputation at the expense of Beaune. Light, attractive earthiness and strawberry fruit. Try *Bize, Camus-Bruchon, Capron-Manieux, Chandon de Briailles, Écard-Guyot, Girard-Vollot, Guillemot, Pavelot, Tollot-Beaut*.

SAUVIGNON DE ST-BRIS, VDQS

(white) Wine of AC quality grown south-west of Chablis that languishes as a VDQS because Sauvignon Blanc is not an AC grape in the area. Can be one of the most nettly, most greeny-gooseberryish of all French Sauvignons, but these days it seems less exciting than it used to be. It has not really faced up to the competition from New Zealand – and Bordeaux. Best: *Louis Bersan, Jean-Marc Brocard, Robert & Philippe Defrance, Michel Esclavy, Goisot, André Sorin*.

LA TÂCHE, AC

(Côte de Nuits; red) Another *grand cru* monopoly of the *Domaine de la Romanée-Conti*. The wine is heavenly, so rich and heady that the perfumes are sometimes closer to age-old brandy than table wine and the flavour loaded with spice, dark fruits and the acrid richness of really good black chocolate.

VOLNAY, AC (Côte de Beaune; red) One of the most perfumed red Burgundies, with a memorable cherry-and-strawberry spice, but also, in its *premiers crus*, able to turn on a big, meaty style without losing the perfume. The best are *Comte Lafon, Lafarge, Marquis d'Angerville, de Montille* and *Pousse d'Or*, Other good names: *Ampeau, Blain-Gagnard, Boillot, Bouley, Clerget, Delagrange, Vaudoisey-Mutin, Voillot.*

VOSNE-ROMANÉE, AC (Côte de Nuits; red) The greatest Côte de Nuits village. Its *grands crus* cost more than any red on earth, and, remarkably for Burgundy, they are dominated by a single estate, *Domaine de la Romanée Conti.* These vineyards make wines capable of more startling brilliance than any other, with flavours as disparate yet as intense as the overpowering, creamy savouriness of fresh *foie gras* and the deep, sweet scent of ripe plums and prunes in brandy. There are also fine *premiers crus*, and the village wines can reflect their leaders. The Domaine de la Romanée Conti is by far the most famous estate here, but *Leroy*, owned by a former director of the DRC, is making wines that rival it in both quality and price. Others making terrific wine: *Arnoux, Sylvain Cathiard, Confuron-Coteditot, Engel, Grivot, Jean Gros, Hudelot-Noëllat, Georges Jayer, Henri Jayer, Henri Lamarche, Méo-Camuzet, Mongeard-Mugneret, Georges Mugneret, Pernin-Rossin, Rouget, Daniel Rion* and *Jean Tardy.*

VOUGEOT, AC (Côte de Nuits; red) A village famous only because of its *grand cru,* Clos de Vougeot, which at its best is plummy and broad. However, there are some decent wines made outside the Clos – most notably from *Bertagna* and *Clerget.*

BURGUNDY AND BEAUJOLAIS VINTAGES

Red Burgundy is more subject to vintage fluctuation than white; with the latter, most years can produce a fair amount of pretty good wine. The rule for Beaujolais, drink as young as possible. Only top wines from the best villages will benefit much from aging, although Nouveau may improve with a month or two's rest.

1998 A mixed year. The best will be very good, but there will be a lot of underripe, dilute wines as well, both red and white.

1997 Soft, approachable reds and whites of middling to good quality which should be ready before the 1996s. Prices have risen because quantities were down. It's probably not the greatest value vintage ever, and certainly not one to buy without tasting first.

1996 Excellent, concentrated, classic Chablis; the Côte d'Or whites and reds are also ripe, with good acidity, and should age well. Whites are not as concentrated as in 1995. Beaujolais looks good.

1995 A year of low yields, ripe tannins and good concentration in the reds, and good quality but not greatness in the whites. For once, there is little to choose in quality between the Côte de Beaune and the Côte de Nuits. In Chablis quality is first-rate.

1994 Light wines with attractive, reasonable colours and lowish acidity. The best whites are showing a raciness and vigour that contrasts nicely with the plumper, richer 1992s, which have always overshadowed them. Beaujolais variable.

1993 The reds from the best producers have good depth of colour, power of fruit and well-constructed tannins, though some are a little too tannic or underripe. The whites have turned out far better than at first seemed likely. They have plumped up nicely and have plenty of fruit, but don't count on them making old Beaunes. In Beaujolais there are some good wines among the *crus*.

1992 Acidity is low among the reds, but it's a good year to choose in restaurants, as the wines are fast developers. The whites were far better, with masses of exuberant fruit and seemingly better acidity than their 1991 counterparts.

1991 There were some very good concentrated reds made, but it's a very patchy vintage. The whites are also patchy in quality, though without the reds' occasional brilliance. Beaujolais was excellent, with good colour and relatively high tannin levels.

1990 The 1990 reds are brilliantly fruity, naturally high in sugars. Most producers now consider this the best of the great trio of 1988, 1989 and 1990. Lesser wines are ready now; the best are sumptuously rich. The whites are proving to be inferior to the reds. A good rather than a great vintage for white Burgundy. In Beaujolais it was a corker of a vintage – very good quality and plenty of it. The *crus* are drinking beautifully now.

1989 A lot of good reds, but only a few exceptional ones. They are softer than the 1988s, though some are superbly concentrated, particularly in the Côte de Beaune. Some may prove better than the '88s. It was an outstanding year for white Burgundy, at least in the hands of competent winemakers. Almost all the best growers' wines are beautifully balanced, despite their richness, though some are aging fast. Beaujolais had wonderful colour and pungent fruit, and prices shot up.

1988 Many growers produced firm, concentrated reds, now beginning to emerge from their shells. Some superb wines, but quite a few dour ones, too. Among the whites, Mâconnais wines had a bright, fresh fruit not seen down that way for a few years. Beaujolais was exceptional, with marvellous luscious, clear, ripe fruit, and even the best should be drunk up now.

1987 The best 1987 reds are very good indeed, Côte de Beaune having the edge over Côte de Nuits. The lesser wines aren't as good as those of 1985, but are better than those of 1986. Drink now.

1986 The reds are showing good perfume but need drinking soon, as do most whites. Chablis *grands crus* are drinking well, but there's no hurry to drink up.

1985 The reds have turned out unevenly, though the best are still good. The whites have proper acid balance and an outstanding concentration of fruit. Pity nobody waited to find out because most '85s were consumed long ago. If you do see one from a good producer, go for it – well, perhaps not, I've just remembered the price it'll be. Chablis started out with a lesser reputation, but top Grand Cru wines from good producers can still be good.

1983 The best reds display impressive flavour. Even the top wines are drinking now, and drinking beautifully, although Vosne-Romanée, Chambolle-Musigny and Morey-Saint-Denis didn't have such a good year. The whites are frequently heavy, rather unrefreshing, soggy-flavoured wines (made, all too often, from overripe, rot-affected grapes) which rapidly lost their fruit. Some rare examples may turn out to be wonderful, but if that is the case I have yet to discover them. Even the best should be ready by now, though, and really should be drunk up.

BASIC BURGUNDY PRICES

RED

Under £7.00

Bourgogne Clos de Chenôves, Caves de Buxy 1993 £6.95 (JU)
Bourgogne Rouge, Cave de Lugny 1996 £5.99 (CON)
Bourgogne Rouge, Vallet 1995 £5.00 (MORR)

£7.00 → £7.99

Bourgogne Clos de Chenôves, Caves de Buxy 1997 £7.95 (NA)
Bourgogne Coteaux de St-Bris, Brocard 1997 £7.75 (AD)
Bourgogne Lucien Denizot 1993 £7.95 (JU)
Bourgogne Passe-Tout-Grains, Michel Lafarge 1997 £7.30 (GAU)
Bourgogne Passe-Tout-Grains, Michel Lafarge 1995 £7.95 (CON) £7.99 (RAE)
Bourgogne Rouge, Faiveley 1996 £7.95 (CON) £7.95 (DI)
Bourgogne Rouge Fûts de Chêne, Cave de Buxy 1997 £7.25 (NA)
Bourgogne Rouge, Roger et Joël Remy 1996 £7.50 (LEA)
Bourgogne Rouge Tasteviné, Bichot 1996 £7.35 (UN)

£8.00 → £9.99

Bourgogne Passe-Tout-Grains, Henri Jayer 1995 £9.95 (BAL)
Bourgogne Passe-Tout-Grains, Michel Lafarge 1996 £8.75 (BER)
Bourgogne Rouge, Chevillon 1996 £8.75 (FORT)
Bourgogne Rouge, Domaine Boillot 1997 £8.32 (MON)

Bourgogne Rouge, Domaine de la Pousse d'Or 1996 £8.95 (WS) £9.80 (TAN) £10.49 (CON)
Bourgogne Rouge Ghislaine Barthod 1993 £9.90 (JU) £9.99 (RAE)
Bourgogne Rouge, Parent 1994 £8.00 (NEZ)
Bourgogne Rouge, Rion 1995 £9.40 (MV)

£10.00 → £12.99

Bourgogne Rouge, Bachelet 1996 £11.00 (MV)
Bourgogne Rouge, Domaine de la Pousse d'Or 1995 £10.49 (CON)
Bourgogne Rouge, Georges Roumier 1997 £11.65 (RES)
Bourgogne Rouge, Leroy 1995 £10.95 (JU) £13.50 (BAL)
Bourgogne Rouge, Machard de Gramont 1996 £10.46 (CB)
Bourgogne Rouge, Merlin 1996 £10.01 (NO)
Bourgogne Rouge, Michel Lafarge 1997 £10.80 (GAU)
Bourgogne Rouge, Thierry Mortet 1995 £10.95 (LEA)
Bourgogne Rouge, Mugneret-Gibourg 1996 £11.95 (LEA)

Over £13.00

Bourgogne Rouge, Coche-Dury 1996 £16.16 (CAV)
Bourgogne Rouge, Dugat-Py 1997 £13.50 (LEA)
Bourgogne Rouge, Henri Jayer 1988 £28.79 (REI)
Bourgogne Rouge, Méo-Camuzet 1995 £13.75 (JU)
Bourgogne Rouge, Michel Lafarge 1995 £13.92 (TW)

MERCHANTS SPECIALIZING IN BURGUNDY
see Merchant Directory (page 413) for details

Adnams (AD), Averys (AV), Ballantynes (BAL), Bennetts (BEN), Berry Bros (BER), Bibendum (BIB), Butlers Wine Cellar (BU), Anthony Byrne (BY), Cave Cru Classé (CAV), Châteaux Wines (CHA), Corney & Barrow (CB), Direct Wine (DI), Domaine Direct (DOM), Farr Vintners (FA), Fortnum & Mason (FORT), Goedhuis, Roger Harris (HAW) – for Beaujolais, John Harvey (HA), Haynes Hanson & Clark (HAH), Justerini & Brooks (JU), Lay & Wheeler (LAY), Lea & Sandeman (LEA), Montrachet (MON), Morris & Verdin (MV), Le Nez Rouge (NEZ), James Nicholson (NI), Oddbins (OD), Christopher Piper (PIP), Raeburn (RAE), Reid (REI), Howard Ripley (RIP), T&W (TW), Tanners (TAN), Wine Society (WS), Wine Treasury (WT), Peter Wylie (WY), Noel Young (YOU).

WHITE

Under £6.00

Bourgogne Aligoté, Brocard **1997** £5.99 (POR)

Bourgogne Blanc, A Bichot **1997** £5.99 (UN)

£6.00 → £7.99

Bourgogne Aligoté, Guy Amiot **1996** £7.37 (BIB) £7.75 (BAL)

Bourgogne Aligoté de Bouzeron, Villaine **1996** £7.93 (REI)

Bourgogne Aligoté, Brocard **1996** £6.45 (JU)

Bourgogne Aligoté, Larousse **1997** £6.76 (JER)

Bourgogne Aligoté, Mouton **1995** £6.80 (TAN)

Bourgogne Aligoté, Tollot-Beaut **1995** £6.95 (JU)

Bourgogne Aligoté, Verget **1997** £7.57 (LAY)

Bourgogne Blanc, Cave de Buxy **1996** £7.99 (VA)

Bourgogne Blanc les Champs Perriers, Clerc **1997** £6.50 (BAN)

Bourgogne Blanc, Clos de Chenoves **1995** £6.95 (JU)

Bourgogne Blanc, Cuvée Icarus **1997** £6.50 (BU)

Bourgogne Blanc, Domaine du Bois Guillaume, Devevey **1997** £7.74 (MV)

Bourgogne Blanc la Mouline, Cave de Buxy **1996** £6.50 (BALL)

Bourgogne Blanc les Setilles, Olivier Leflaive **1995** £7.95 (WS)

Bourgogne Blanc Anniversaire, Latour **1996** £6.70 (PEN)

Bourgogne Blanc, Matrot **1995** £7.95 (CON)

Bourgogne Blanc, Verget **1997** £6.76 (FA) £8.80 (LAY) £9.95 (LEA)

£8.00 → £9.99

Bourgogne Aligoté de Bouzeron, Villaine **1997** £8.95 (AD) £9.69 (CB)

Bourgogne Aligoté, Jayer-Gilles **1995** £8.50 (JU)

Bourgogne Aligoté, Olivier Leflaive **1996** £8.20 (PLAY)

Bourgogne Aligoté, Rion **1996** £8.40 (MV)

Bourgogne Aligoté, Rollin **1995** £8.50 (JU)

Bourgogne Blanc, Guy Amiot **1997** £8.95 (BAN)

Bourgogne Blanc, Boyer-Martenot **1997** £9.30 (MON)

Bourgogne Blanc, Clerc **1997** £8.80 (BAN)

Bourgogne Blanc, Faiveley **1996** £8.79 (DI)

Bourgogne Blanc les Setilles, Olivier Leflaive **1996** £8.75 (CB) £10.90 (CRO)

Bourgogne Blanc, Verget **1996** £8.22 (FA) £8.99 (YOU)

£10.00 → £14.99

Bourgogne Blanc, Guy Amiot **1996** £12.50 (BAL)

Bourgogne Blanc Cuvée des Forgets, Patrick Javillier **1996** £10.25 (SOM) £12.10 (BAN)

Bourgogne Blanc, Domaine Leflaive **1993** £14.50 (JU)

Bourgogne Blanc, Jobard **1996** £10.95 (LEA) £13.30 (HAH)

Bourgogne Blanc, Jobard **1992** £13.99 (RAE)

Bourgogne Blanc, Leroy **1996** £13.50 (BAL)

Bourgogne Blanc, Leroy **1995** £11.90 (JU)

Bourgogne Blanc les Setilles, Olivier Leflaive **1993** £12.34 (TW)

Bourgogne Blanc, Michelot **1995** £10.99 (JON) £11.95 (RES)

Bourgogne Blanc Oligocene, Javillier **1995** £12.50 (LAY)

Bourgogne Blanc, Sauzet **1995** £14.50 (RES) £16.00 (JU)

Over £15.00

Bourgogne Aligoté, Coche-Dury **1995** £17.63 (CAV)

Bourgogne Blanc, Clos du Château de Meursault **1994** £19.99 (VIN)

Bourgogne Blanc, Domaine Leflaive **1996** £17.53 (FA)

Bourgogne Blanc Seigneurie de Posanges, Remoissenet **1992** £21.00 (CRO)

ROSÉ

c. £6.50

Bourgogne Rosé de Marsannay, Bruno Clair **1996** £6.30 (SOM)

SPARKLING

Under £7.00

Crémant de Bourgogne Cave de Lugny **Non-vintage** £5.70 (SOM) £6.75 (WAI) £7.80 (HAH)

Crémant de Bourgogne Rosé Cave de Lugny **Non-vintage** £6.95 (WAI)

BEAUJOLAIS PRICES

RED

Under £5.00

Beaujolais Château du Mont 1996 £4.95 (JU)

Beaujolais-Villages Domaine Granjean 1996 £4.99 (CO)

Beaujolais-Villages Duboeuf 1996 £4.99 (UN)

Beaujolais-Villages Duboeuf 1994 £4.99 (TES)

£5.00 → £5.99

Beaujolais Cave de Sain Bel 1998 £5.75 (HAW)

Beaujolais Cave de St-Verand 1998 £5.87 (HAW)

Beaujolais Cave du Bois d'Oingt 1998 £5.95 (HAW)

Beaujolais Château de Pizay 1997 £5.49 (CON)

Beaujolais Cuvée Tradition, Brun 1996 £5.50 (JU)

Beaujolais Loron 1997 £5.75 (TAN)

Beaujolais Loron 1996 £5.95 (DI)

Beaujolais Paul Sapin 1997 £5.50 (MAR)

Beaujolais-Villages Château de Lacarelle 1997 £5.35 (WS) £6.25 (BU)

Beaujolais-Villages Château des Vierres, Duboeuf 1996 £5.99 (NI)

Beaujolais-Villages Château du Basty 1997 £5.69 (OD)

Beaujolais-Villages Colonge 1997 £5.95 (WS) £5.95 (ELL) £6.49 (AME)

Beaujolais-Villages Duboeuf 1997 £5.49 (MAJ) £5.49 (THR) £5.49 (WR) £5.49 (BOT)

Beaujolais-Villages les Champs Bouthier, Sapin 1998 £5.95 (STA)

Beaujolais-Villages Pivot 1997 £5.58 (DOM)

Brouilly Quinson 1997 £5.15 (MORR)

Coteaux du Lyonnais, Cave de Sain Bel 1998 £5.25 (HAW)

Régnié Paul Sapin 1997 £5.49 (MAJ)

£6.00 → £6.99

Beaujolais Blaise Carron 1998 £6.30 (HAW)

Beaujolais Domaine de Milhomme 1998 £6.25 (HAW)

Beaujolais Lantignié, Domaine Joubert 1998 £6.55 (AD)

Beaujolais Père Thomas 1998 £6.20 (HAW)

Beaujolais Vieilles Vignes, Cave de St-Vérand 1998 £6.25 (HAW)

Beaujolais Vieilles Vignes, Garlon 1998 £6.35 (HAW)

Beaujolais-Villages Cave du Château de Chénas 1998 £6.05 (HAW)

Beaujolais-Villages Cave des Producteurs Juliénas 1998 £6.10 (HAW)

Beaujolais-Villages Domaine Aucoeur 1997 £6.35 (RSJ)

Beaujolais-Villages Domaine de Franc-Pierre, Cave Co-op Fleurie 1998 £6.15 (HAW)

Beaujolais-Villages Dumas 1997 £6.95 (LEA)

Beaujolais-Villages Lacondemine 1996 £6.95 (JU)

Beaujolais-Villages Pivot 1998 £6.00 (PIP) £6.65 (HAW)

Chiroubles Loron 1997 £6.85 (SOM)

Juliénas Domaine Joubert 1996 £6.50 (BALL) £6.99 (JON)

Juliénas Loron 1997 £6.99 (UN)

Morgon Château de Pizay 1997 £6.49 (CON)

Morgon Charmes, Domaine Brisson 1995 £6.99 (CO)

Morgon Château Gaillard 1997 £6.99 (NLW) £7.18 (COC)

Morgon Domaine des Arcades 1998 £6.85 (AS)

Morgon Domaine Jean Descombes, Duboeuf 1996 £6.50 (NI)

Morgon Duboeuf 1997 £6.79 (VIC) £6.79 (THR) £6.79 (WR) £6.79 (BOT) £7.90 (CRO)

Morgon Jambon 1997 £6.49 (ASD)

Moulin-à-Vent Domaine des Rosiers, Duboeuf 1997 £6.99 (MAJ)

Régnié Duboeuf 1996 £6.29 (UN)

£7.00 → £7.99

Beaujolais-Villages Château des Vergers 1996 £7.20 (UB)

Beaujolais-Villages les Larmoises Vieilles Vignes, Lacondemine 1996 £7.95 (JU)

Brouilly Château Thivin 1998 £7.52 (GW) £7.95 (AD)

Brouilly Drouhin 1997 £7.64 (PEN)

Brouilly Duboeuf 1996 £7.99 (POR)

Brouilly Large 1997 £7.44 (CHA)

Chénas Château Bonnet 1996 £7.70 (AV)

Chénas Domaine des Vieilles Caves, Charvet 1997 £7.85 (TAN) £8.95 (ROB)

Chénas Domaine Louis Champagnon
1996 £7.81 (NO)

Chiroubles Domaine de la Grosse Pierre
1997 £7.29 (CON)

Chiroubles la Maison des Vignerons **1998**
£7.95 (AD)

Côte de Brouilly Domaine de la Glaciere,
Loron **1996** £7.50 (AV)

Côte de Brouilly Domaine de la Voûte
des Crozes, Chanrion **1997** £7.30 (RSJ)

Côte de Brouilly Domaine de la Voûte
des Crozes, Chanrion **1996** £7.80 (ELL)

Côte de Brouilly Joubert **1997** £7.90 (TAN)

Fleurie Château de Fleurie, Loron **1997**
£7.95 (TAN) £8.37 (PEN) £8.30 (WRI)
£9.50 (AV)

Fleurie Château des Deduits, Duboeuf
1998 £7.99 (WAI)

Fleurie Duboeuf **1996** £7.99 (TES)

Fleurie la Madone, Duboeuf **1996** £7.99
(PHI)

Fleurie Sapin **1997** £7.99 (MAR)

Juliénas Benon **1997** £7.25 (HAW)

Juliénas Cave des Producteurs Juliénas
1998 £7.25 (HAW)

Juliénas Château de Juliénas **1995** £7.64
(PEN)

Juliénas Côte de Bessay **1996** £7.49 (CON)

Juliénas Domaine de Beauvernay, Piat
1997 £7.95 (BU)

Juliénas Domaine de la Bottière, Chanut
1996 £7.17 (NO)

Juliénas Domaine de la Seigneurie **1998**
£7.50 (NEZ)

Juliénas Domaine de la Vieille Église,
Loron **1997** £7.90 (DI)

Juliénas Domaine Joubert **1998** £7.50 (AD)

★ Juliénas Domaine Joubert **1997** £7.30
(TAN) £7.99 (POR)

Juliénas les Envaux, Pelletier **1998** £7.80
(CHA)

Morgon Aucoeur **1997** £7.30 (RSJ)

Morgon Domaine de Lathevalle,
Mommessin **1996** £7.25 (BALL)

Morgon Domaine Jean Descombes,
Duboeuf **1998** £7.60 (NEZ) £7.49 (MAJ)

Morgon Domaine de Leyre-Loup **1996**
£7.99 (YOU) £8.25 (BU)

Morgon Drouhin **1992** £7.64 (REI)

Morgon le Clachet, Brun **1998** £7.44 (CHA)

Morgon les Versauds, Jacques Perrachon
1997 £7.35 (PIP)

Moulin-à-Vent Domaine de la Tour du
Bief, Duboeuf **1996** £7.49 (VIC) £7.49
(THR) £7.49 (WR) £7.49 (BOT)

Moulin-à-Vent Domaine les Fine Graves,
Janodet **1997** £7.25 (SOM) £8.75 (STA)
£10.25 (FORT)

Morgon Domaine des Vieux Cèdres,
Loron **1996** £7.04 (PEN)

Régnié Château Chassantour, Perroud
1997 £7.30 (TAN)

Régnié Roux **1997** £7.61 (FLE)

St-Amour Domaine des Pins, Echallier
1997 £7.99 (AME)

£8.00 → £8.99

Brouilly Château de Pavé, Brac de la
Perrière **1996** £8.90 (JU)

Brouilly Château des Tours **1997** £8.25
(PIP) £8.50 (COC) £8.71 (NO)

Brouilly Domaine Crêts des Garanches,
Bernard Dufaitre **1996** £8.99 (PHI)

Brouilly Domaine du P'tit Baron, Veuve
Marius Carnot **1996** £8.32 (JER)

Brouilly Michaud **1997** £8.90 (MV)

Chénas Domaine de Mongrin, Gaec des
Ducs **1996** £8.25 (WRI)

Chénas Domaine de Mongrin, Gaec des
Ducs **1994** £8.05 (REI)

Chénas Domaine des Vieilles Caves,
Charvet **1995** £8.45 (BER)

Chénas Domaine Louis Champagnon
1995 £8.25 (NO)

Chénas Trenel **1997** £8.99 (BEN)

Chiroubles Château de Raousset **1997**
£8.30 (PIP)

Chiroubles Méziat **1997** £8.03 (GW)

Côte de Brouilly Château Thivin **1997**
£8.03 (GW) £8.99 (DI)

Fleurie Château des Deduits, Duboeuf
1996 £8.66 (NI)

Fleurie Clos de la Chapelle des Bois,
Verpoix **1997** £8.20 (PIP)

Fleurie Colonge **1998** £8.95 (STA) £8.99
(AME)

Fleurie Denojean **1998** £8.69 (WHI)

Fleurie Domaine de la Grand' Cour **1997**
£8.99 (AME)

Fleurie Domaine Paul Bernard **1996**
£8.49 (OD)

Fleurie Duboeuf 1998 £8.49 (VIC) £8.49 (THR) £8.49 (WR) £8.49 (BOT)
Fleurie Grille Midi 1996 £8.29 (CON)
Fleurie la Madone, Duboeuf 1998 £8.50 (NEZ)
Fleurie la Madone, Louis Tête 1997 £8.95 (COC)
Fleurie les Garans, Latour 1997 £8.70 (COC) £9.29 (NLW)
Fleurie Sélection Éventail, Domaine de Montgénas 1997 £8.30 (CHA)
Juliénas Condemine 1998 £8.10 (HAW)
Juliénas Domaine du Clos du Fief, Michel Tête 1997 £8.95 (YOU)
Morgon Cuvée de Py, Château de Pizay 1996 £8.25 (CON)
Morgon Château de Raousset, Duboeuf 1996 £8.45 (JU)
Morgon Domaine de la Chanaise 1997 £8.75 (FORT) £9.02 (PLAY)
Morgon Fontcraine, Loron 1996 £8.45 (UB)
Moulin-à-Vent Brugne 1998 £8.22 (CHA)
Moulin-à-Vent Domaine de la Tour du Bief, Duboeuf 1997 £8.50 (BU)
Moulin-à-Vent Domaine Gay-Coperet 1996 £8.95 (LEA)
Moulin-à-Vent Domaine Lemonon, Loron 1997 £8.50 (WRI)
Moulin-à-Vent Domaine Lemonon, Loron 1996 £8.12 (PEN) £11.10 (UB)
Moulin-à-Vent Drouhin 1997 £8.34 (PEN)
Moulin-à-Vent Grille Midi 1996 £8.29 (CON)
Moulin-à-Vent Janin 1995 £8.70 (PIP)
Régnié Domaine des Pillets 1997 £8.13 (BIB)
St-Amour Domaine des Billards, Loron 1996 £8.60 (UB)
St-Amour Domaine des Duc 1998 £8.80 (HAW)

£9.00 → £10.99

Brouilly Château des Tours 1996 £9.95 (ROB)
Côte de Brouilly Domaine de la Pierre Bleue, Ravier 1997 £9.99 (TW)
Fleurie Château de Fleurie, Loron 1998 £9.50 (DI)
Fleurie Colonge 1996 £9.95 (ROB)

> ### Oz Clarke's Wine Guide
> is an annual publication.
> We welcome your suggestions
> for next year's edition.

Fleurie Drouhin 1997 £10.81 (PEN)
Fleurie Dumas 1997 £9.50 (LEA)
Fleurie Loron 1997 £10.45 (UB)
Fleurie Michel Chignard 1997 £10.25 (FORT)
Fleurie Thévenin 1996 £9.00 (ROS)
Juliénas Monnet 1996 £9.75 (ROB)
Morgon Charmes Château Fuissé, Vincent 1997 £9.65 (UB)
Morgon Charmes Domaine Princesse Lieven, Duboeuf 1993 £9.69 (JER)
Morgon Marcel Lapierre 1998 £10.28 (BIB)
Moulin-à-Vent Domaine Berrod 1997 £9.95 (AD)
Moulin-à-Vent Domaine de Champ de Coeur, Mommessin 1997 £9.87 (PLAY)
Moulin-à-Vent Domaine des Vieilles caves, Charvet 1997 £9.40 (TAN)
Moulin-à-Vent les Hospices, Collin & Bourisset 1995 £10.95 (ROB)
Moulin-à-Vent Le Vieux Domaine 1995 £9.02 (GW)

Over £11.00

Juliénas Cuvée Prestige Domaine du Clos du Fief, Michel Tête 1996 £11.49 (YOU)
Juliénas Domaine du Clos du Fief, Michel Tête 1996 £11.60 (UB)
Moulin-à-Vent Lafond 1988 £15.00 (CRO)

WHITE

Under £9.00

Beaujolais Blanc Cave des Grands Crus Blancs 1998 £6.80 (HAW)
Beaujolais Blanc Château de Chanzé 1997 £6.25 (HAW)
Beaujolais Blanc Château de Pizay 1996 £6.45 (CON)
Beaujolais Blanc Domaine des Terres Dorées 1996 £6.25 (JU)
Beaujolais Blanc Pierre Carron 1998 £6.85 (HAW)
Beaujolais Blanc Paul Sapin 1998 £6.70 (HAW)
Coteaux du Lyonnais, Cave de Sain Bel 1998 £5.45 (HAW)

Over £7.00

Beaujolais Blanc Charmet 1995 £7.90 (HAW)
Beaujolais Blanc Domaine des Terres Dorées 1998 £7.20 (AD)
Beaujolais Blanc Jean-Jacques Martin 1997 £8.40 (HAW)

CHABLIS PRICES

WHITE

Under £6.00

Chablis Domaine de la Conciergerie, Adine ½ bottle **1996** £5.14 (JER)

Chablis Domaine de Vauroux ½ bottle **1995** £4.39 (CON)

Sauvignon de St-Bris, Brocard **1997** £5.95 (AD)

Sauvignon de St-Bris, Brocard **1996** £5.95 (JU)

£6.00 → £7.99

Chablis Alain Geoffroy **1997** £7.49 (OD)

Chablis Domaine de Vauroux **1995** £7.45 (CON) £8.99 (NI)

Chablis Domaine des Manants, Brocard **1997** £7.50 (BALL)

Chablis Domaine des Manants, Brocard **1996** £7.99 (JON) £7.99 (POR)

Chablis Domaine Servin **1998** £7.99 (MAJ)

Chablis Durup **1996** £7.99 (BO)

Chablis J Moreau **1997** £7.99 (WHI)

Chablis la Chablisienne **1997** £7.99 (MAR) £7.99 (WAI) £8.57 (FLE)

Chablis les Ardilles, Vernion **1997** £7.55 (BY)

Chablis Vaillons, Droin ½ bottle **1994** £7.32 (DOM)

Chablis Vocoret **1997** £7.99 (MAJ)

Petit Chablis Brocard **1997** £6.99 (POR)

Petit Chablis Château de Maligny **1996** £7.27 (BY) £7.49 (THR) £7.49 (BOT)

Sauvignon de St-Bris, Defrance **1994** £7.50 (RAE)

Sauvignon de St-Bris, Domaine des Remparts **1996** £6.75 (HIG)

Sauvignon de St-Bris, Goisot **1997** £6.46 (DOM)

Sauvignon de St-Bris, Sorin-Defrance **1996** £6.50 (WRI)

Sauvignon de St-Bris, Verret **1997** £6.95 (BU)

£8.00 → £9.99

Chablis 1er Cru Grand Cuvée, la Chablisienne **1997** £8.95 (NA)

Chablis Domaine de l'Églantière **1996** £8.99 (AME)

Chablis Domaine de Vauroux **1996** £9.33 (ROS)

Chablis Domaine du Valéry, Durup **1996** £8.90 (TAN)

Chablis Domaine Ste-Claire, Brocard **1995** £8.95 (JU)

Chablis Domaine Servin **1996** £9.87 (CB)

Chablis Drouhin **1996** £9.64 (PEN)

Chablis Fèvre **1997** £9.25 (FORT) £9.65 (WRI)

Chablis Gautheron **1996** £8.49 (UN)

Chablis Grossot **1997** £9.23 (LAY)

Chablis Hamelin **1996** £9.50 (ELL)

Chablis Latour **1996** £9.64 (PEN)

Chablis Légland **1997** £9.02 (GW)

Chablis Long-Depaquit **1996** £9.29 (BAL)

Chablis Montée de Tonnerre, Château de Maligny **1996** £9.83 (BY)

Chablis Montmains, Domaine de Vauroux **1995** £9.95 (CON)

Chablis Pautré **1996** £9.99 (HIG)

Chablis Picq **1997** £9.49 (YOU)

Chablis Picq **1996** £9.60 (MV)

Chablis Pinson **1997** £9.25 (PIP)

Chablis Simonnet-Febvre **1997** £8.90 (CHA)

Chablis Vaillons, J Moreau **1995** £9.95 (WS)

Chablis Vau-Ligneau, Alain Geoffroy **1997** £9.99 (OD)

Chablis Vieilles Vignes, Brocard **1996** £8.99 (OD) £9.50 (WS)

Chablis Vieilles Vignes, Château de Maligny **1997** £9.07 (BY)

Petit Chablis Dauvissat-Camus **1995** £9.40 (JU)

Petit Chablis Pautré **1996** £8.25 (HIG)

£10.00 → £11.99

Chablis 1er Cru Grand Cuvée, la Chablisienne **1994** £10.99 (MAR)

Chablis Adhémar Boudin **1996** £10.95 (LEA)

Chablis Chevallier **1996** £10.25 (BEN)

Chablis Cuvée Reserve, Pautré **1996** £10.99 (HIG)

Chablis Daniel Defaix **1996** £10.49 (VIC) £10.49 (THR) £10.49 (WR) £10.49 (BOT)

Chablis Fèvre **1996** £10.52 (REI)

Chablis Fourchaume, Château de Maligny **1996** £11.22 (BY) £13.99 (VIC) £13.99 (THR) £13.99 (WR) £13.99 (BOT)

Chablis Fourchaume, Domaine de Valéry **1996** £11.95 (TAN)

Chablis Fourchaume, Durup **1996** £11.16 (DOM)

Chablis Laroche **1997** £10.90 (DI)

Chablis Montée de Tonnerre, Durup
1995 £11.16 (DOM)
Chablis Montmains, Brocard **1996** £10.50
(WS) £10.95 (BALL)
Chablis Montmains, Domaine de la
Conciergerie **1996** £11.55 (JER)
Chablis Montmains, Domaine de la Tour
Vaubourg **1993** £11.55 (NI)
Chablis Montmains, Légland **1997** £11.02
(GW)
Chablis Montmains, Race **1997** £11.50 (MV)
Chablis Tremblay **1996** £11.30 (VIN)
£11.95 (ROB)
Chablis Tribut **1997** £10.95 (LEA)
Chablis Tribut-Dauvissat **1993** £10.00 (JU)
Chablis Vaillons, Collet **1997** £11.65 (RES)
Chablis Vaillons, J Moreau **1998** £10.99
(VIC) £10.99 (THR) £10.99 (WR) £10.99
(BOT)
Chablis Vaillons, J Moreau **1996** £11.94 (HA)
Chablis Vaillons, Vocoret **1997** £10.49 (MAJ)
Chablis Vau-Ligneau, Hamelin **1997**
£10.50 (NEZ) £12.95 (BEN)
Chablis Vaudevey Domaine des Valéry,
Durup **1996** £11.90 (TAN)
Chablis Vieilles Vignes, Brocard **1995**
£11.90 (JU)
Chablis Vieilles Vignes, Daniel Defaix
1996 £10.95 (CON) £10.99 (BO) £12.24
(LAY) £14.69 (TW)
Chablis Vieilles Vignes, Daniel Defaix
1995 £10.50 (BALL)

£12.00 → £13.99

Chablis 1er Cru, Drouhin **1995** £12.30 (NI)
Chablis Beauregard, Brocard **1996** £12.50
(JU)
Chablis Beauroy, la Chablisienne **1997**
£12.56 (STE) £13.95 (NA)
Chablis Côte de Léchet, Tribut **1996**
£13.95 (LEA) £14.69 (DOM)
Chablis Daniel Defaix **1995** £12.95 (ROB)
Chablis Fourchaume, Boudin **1996** £13.95
(LEA)
Chablis Fourchaume, Brocard **1996**
£12.95 (JU)
Chablis la Forêt, Pinson **1996** £12.55 (PIP)
Chablis Mont de Milieu, Moreau **1997**
£12.62 (COC)
Chablis Mont de Milieu, Pinson **1997**
£12.55 (PIP)
Chablis Montée de Tonnerre, Domaine
Servin **1996** £12.34 (CB)
Chablis Montmains, Louis Michel **1996**
£12.34 (REI)

Chablis Montmains, Race **1996** £12.35 (WRI)
Chablis Vaillons, Collet **1991** £13.12 (JER)
Chablis Vaillons, Long-Depaquit **1996**
£12.95 (BAL) £13.95 (UN)
Chablis Vaillons, Simonnet-Febvre **1997**
£12.42 (CHA)

Chablis Vaudevey, Laroche **1995** £12.90
(CRO)
Chablis Vieilles Vignes, Daniel Defaix
1994 £12.50 (GAU)
Chablis Vosgros, Droin **1996** £13.22 (JER)

£14.00 → £16.99

Chablis 1er Cru, Drouhin **1997** £15.04
(PEN)
Chablis 1er Cru, Domaine Vocoret **1997**
£14.39 (VIN)
Chablis Beauroy, Tribut **1996** £14.50 (LEA)
Chablis Beauroy, Tribut **1995** £14.69 (DOM)
Chablis Côte de Léchet, Etienne et Daniel
Defaix **1994** £15.80 (TAN) £15.95 (CON)
£17.79 (JON)
Chablis Fourchaume, la Chablisienne
1997 £14.99 (COC)
Chablis Fourchaume, Laroche **1995**
£16.55 (DI)
Chablis la Forêt, René Dauvissat **1996**
£16.95 (LEA) £20.46 (FA)
Chablis les Clos, Bouchard Père **1996**
£16.95 (WAT)
Chablis les Clos, J Moreau **1994** £16.63
(HA)
Chablis les Lys, Daniel Defaix **1994**
£15.95 (CON) £16.10 (TAN) £17.99 (YOU)
Chablis les Lys, Daniel Defaix **1993**
£14.95 (BALL)
Chablis les Preuses, la Chablisienne **1992**
£16.90 (FLE)
Chablis Montée de Tonnerre, Louis
Michel **1997** £14.30 (HAH)
Chablis Séchet, Domaine Dauvissat-
Camus **1995** £14.90 (JU)
Chablis Séchet, René Dauvissat **1996**
£16.95 (LEA) £20.95 (FA)
Chablis Vaillons, Daniel Defaix **1994**
£15.95 (CON)

Chablis Vaillons, Domaine Dauvissat-
Camus **1995** £14.90 (JU)

Chablis Vaillons, Droin **1994** £14.04 (DOM)

Chablis Vaillons, Fèvre **1996** £14.25 (WRI)

Chablis Vaillons, Laroche **1998** £14.99
(WHI)

Chablis Vaillons, Laroche **1993** £14.99 (DI)

Chablis Vaillons, René Dauvissat **1994**
£14.69 (DOM)

£17.00 → £19.99

Chablis Blanchots, Servin **1993** £19.51 (CB)

Chablis Bougros, Ancien Domaine Auffray
1992 £17.53 (FA)

Chablis Bougros, Domaine de Colombier,
Mothe **1996** £19.99 (POR)

Chablis Bougros, Domaine de Vauroux
1993 £19.95 (CON)

Chablis Côte de Léchet, Etienne et Daniel
Defaix **1992** £17.15 (GAU) £18.50 (ROB)

Chablis Grenouilles, Domaine de Château
Grenouille **1990** £19.99 (MAR)

Chablis les Clos, Brocard **1995** £19.95
(WAI) £22.59 (JON)

Chablis les Clos, J Moreau **1996** £19.95
(HA) £21.20 (COC)

Chablis Montée de Tonnerre, Verget
1994 £19.00 (FA)

Chablis Pinson **1992** £17.84 (NO)

Chablis Vaillons, Daniel Defaix **1992**
£17.15 (GAU) £21.74 (TW)

Chablis Vaillons, René Dauvissat **1995**
£19.48 (FA)

Chablis Vaudésir, J Moreau **1993** £18.35
(COC)

Chablis Vaudésir, Long-Depaquit **1996**
£19.50 (BAL)

£20.00 → £24.99

Chablis Côte de Léchet, Etienne et Daniel
Defaix **1993** £20.68 (TW)

Chablis Grenouilles, Domaine de Château
Grenouille **1993** £22.32 (RIP)

Chablis Grenouilles, Droin **1996** £23.50
(DOM)

Chablis Grenouilles, Louis Michel **1997**
£22.85 (HAH)

Chablis la Moutonne, Long-Depaquit
1996 £23.95 (BAL)

Chablis la Moutonne, Long-Depaquit
1994 £24.65 (BER)

Chablis les Clos, Brocard **1996** £21.00
(JU) £22.00 (AD)

Chablis les Clos, Brocard **1992** £22.87 (FLE)

Chablis les Clos, Droin **1992** £21.74 (DOM)

Chablis les Clos, Drouhin **1995** £24.43
(PEN) £28.79 (REI)

Chablis les Clos, Pinson **1996** £20.05 (PIP)

Chablis les Clos, Pinson **1995** £21.22 (NO)

Chablis les Clos, René Dauvissat **1994**
£22.91 (DOM)

Chablis les Lys, Daniel Defaix **1990**
£23.44 (TW)

Chablis les Preuses, la Chablisienne **1996**
£22.82 (STE) £25.35 (NA)

Chablis les Preuses, René Dauvissat **1994**
£22.91 (DOM)

Chablis Montée de Tonnerre, Verget
1995 £20.95 (FA)

Chablis Vaillons, Daniel Defaix **1990**
£23.44 (TW)

Chablis Vaillons, René Dauvissat **1996**
£22.42 (FA)

Chablis Valmur, Droin **1995** £21.05 (ELL)

Chablis Valmur, Droin **1994** £23.00 (RAE)
£24.99 (JON)

Chablis Vaudésir, Droin **1996** £22.03 (JER)

Chablis Vaudésir, Drouhin **1995** £22.29 (NI)

£25.00 → £29.99

Chablis Blanchots, Laroche **1995** £25.00
(FORT) £25.50 (WHI)

Chablis Château de Grenouille, la
Chablisienne **1996** £27.54 (STE) £30.60
(NA)

Chablis les Clos, Droin **1995** £25.49 (JON)

Chablis Vaudésir, Drouhin **1997** £26.95
(BEN)

Chablis Vaudésir, Louis Michel **1996**
£26.50 (FORT)

Chablis Vaudésir, Reynier **1996** £25.00
(RES)

Over £30.00

Chablis Blanchots, Daniel Defaix **1992**
£35.00 (ROB)

Chablis Butteaux, Raveneau **1996** £36.62
(FA) £39.75 (WAI)

Chablis les Clos, Domaine Dauvissat-
Camus **1993** £37.95 (ROB)

Chablis les Clos, René Dauvissat **1996**
£36.62 (FA)

Chablis Montée de Tonnerre, Raveneau
1996 £40.05 (FA)

Chablis Vaudésir, Long-Depaquit **1976**
£35.25 (REI)

Chablis Vaudésir, Louis Michel **1988**
£37.00 (CRO)

Chablis Vaulorent, Fèvre **1983** £31.00
(CRO)

CÔTE CHALONNAISE PRICES

RED

Under £9.00

Bourgogne Clos du Liron, Sarrazin **1996** £8.65 (WT)

Givry Clos du Cellier aux Moines, Delorme **1994** £8.09 (WAT)

Givry Latour **1996** £7.99 (PEN) £8.79 (MAJ) £8.88 (JON)

Rully Domaine de la Renarde, Delorme **1996** £8.75 (WAT)

Rully Varot Domaine de la Renarde, Delorme **1995** £7.55 (WAT)

£9.00 → £10.99

Givry Boischevaux, Thenard **1995** £10.28 (JER)

★ Givry Clos Jus, Mouton **1996** £10.50 (TAN) £10.50 (SOM)

Givry le Pied de Clou, Lumpp **1997** £10.95 (LEA)

Givry le Pied de Clou, Lumpp **1996** £10.95 (LEA)

Mercurey Château de Chamilly **1993** £10.95 (CON)

Mercurey Château de Chamirey **1994** £10.70 (HED)

Mercurey Domaine de la Croix Jacquelet, Faiveley **1996** £9.95 (CON) £12.50 (WRI)

Mercurey Domaine de la Croix Jacquelet, Faiveley **1995** £9.95 (CON)

Mercurey la Framboisière, Faiveley **1996** £9.95 (WS)

Mercurey Latour **1995** £9.87 (PEN) £12.50 (BALL)

Mercurey Maréchal **1995** £10.90 (PIP)

Mercurey Myglands, Faiveley **1991** £10.12 (FLE)

Rully Bouchard Père **1996** £9.84 (COC)

Rully Domaine de l'Hermitage, Chanzy **1997** £10.92 (PLA)

Rully Dureuil-Janthial **1995** £10.90 (PIP)

Rully Faiveley **1995** £9.95 (BEN)

£11.00 → £14.99

Givry Clos de la Servoisine, Jean Marc Joblot **1995** £14.00 (AV) £16.00 (JU)

Givry Clos de la Servoisine, Jean Marc Joblot **1994** £14.00 (JU)

Givry Clos Jus, Lumpp **1996** £11.95 (LEA)

Givry Clos Jus, Lumpp **1995** £11.95 (LEA)

Givry Clos Jus, Mouton **1994** £12.95 (ROB)

Givry Gérard Mouton **1995** £12.60 (STA)

Givry la Grande Berge, Ragot **1996** £13.95 (BEN)

Givry le Pied de Clou, Lumpp **1995** £11.95 (LEA)

Givry Remmoissenet **1995** £12.50 (AV)

Mercurey Carillon **1997** £12.24 (MON)

Mercurey Carillon **1996** £12.50 (NA)

Mercurey Château de Chamirey **1996** £13.27 (PLAY) £13.99 (WHI)

Mercurey Domaine de la Croix Jacquelet, Faiveley **1997** £12.40 (PLA)

Mercurey Domaine du Meix-Foulot **1995** £13.95 (ROB)

Mercurey la Framboisière, Faiveley **1997** £13.99 (BEN)

Mercurey la Framboisière, Faiveley **1995** £11.75 (ELL)

Mercurey Juillot **1995** £12.63 (DOM) £16.95 (FORT)

Mercurey Juillot **1994** £11.46 (DOM)

Rully Château de Rully Rodet **1996** £11.69 (WHI)

Rully les Chaponnières, Jacqueson **1996** £11.20 (TAN)

Rully les Chaponnières, Jacqueson **1994** £12.95 (ROB)

Rully Préaux, Eric de Suremain **1995** £14.50 (JU)

Rully Préaux, Eric de Suremain **1994** £12.80 (JU)

Rully Préaux, Eric de Suremain **1993** £12.90 (JU)

Rully Préaux, Eric de Suremain **1992** £13.00 (JU)

£15.00 → £17.99

Givry Clos de la Servoisine, Jean Marc Joblot **1997** £15.76 (RES)

Mercurey Clos des Barraults, Juillot **1996** £15.28 (DOM)

Mercurey Clos des Barraults, Juillot **1993** £17.04 (DOM)

Rully les Chaponnières, Jacqueson **1995** £15.50 (STA)

Over £20.00

Mercurey Juillot **1988** £21.74 (TW)

Mercurey les Combins, Juillot **1992** £22.09 (TW)

WHITE

Under £7.00

Bourgogne les Vignes de la Croix, Cave de Buxy 1997 £5.99 (SAF)
Givry Clos des Vignes Rondes, Lumpp ½ bottle 1997 £6.25 (LEA)
Givry Clos des Vignes Rondes, Lumpp ½ bottle 1996 £6.20 (LEA)
Montagny 1er Cru, Cave de Buxy 1997 £6.99 (MAR) £7.49 (CO) £8.22 (FRI)
Montagny 1er Cru, Cave de Buxy 1996 £5.99 (MAJ)

£7.00 → £8.99

Montagny 1er Cru, Olivier Leflaive 1996 £8.30 (HAH) £9.96 (LAY)
Montagny 1er Cru les Loges, Cave de Buxy 1997 £8.60 (TAN) £8.95 (AD)
Montagny Latour 1994 £7.99 (NLW)
Montagny Bernard Michel 1996 £8.06 (CON)
Rully 1er Cru Meix Cadot, Dury 1996 £8.50 (BALL) £15.50 (ROB)
Rully Jaffelin 1996 £8.99 (MAJ)
Rully la Chaume, Dury 1994 £8.95 (JU)
Rully Olivier Leflaive 1997 £8.96 (LAY) £10.99 (PHI)

£9.00 → £10.99

Bourgogne Blanc les Clous, Villaine 1996 £9.50 (WS)
Givry Clos des Vignes Rondes, Lumpp 1997 £10.95 (LEA)
Givry Clos des Vignes Rondes, Lumpp 1996 £10.95 (LEA)
Givry Thénard 1993 £9.95 (WS)
Mercurey Chartron et Trébuchet 1997 £9.75 (BAN)
Montagny Latour 1997 £10.62 (PLAY)
Montagny Latour 1996 £9.95 (STA)
Montagny Olivier Leflaive 1995 £10.95 (HAH)
Montagny Roy 1996 £10.85 (WRI)
Rully 1er Cru Meix Cadot, Dury 1995 £9.95 (RAE)
Rully Domaine de l'Hermitage, Chanzy 1995 £10.92 (PLA)
Rully Faiveley 1996 £10.99 (DI)
Rully la Chaume, Dury 1996 £9.09 (JON)
Rully les Clous, Olivier Leflaive 1997 £10.49 (LAY)
Rully les Clous, Olivier Leflaive 1996 £10.99 (LAY) £14.03 (PLAY)

Rully Marissou, Dury 1995 £9.75 (JU)
Rully Mont Palais, Olivier Leflaive 1996 £9.64 (CB)
Rully Olivier Leflaive 1996 £9.96 (LAY)

£11.00 → £12.99

Mercurey Chartron et Trébuchet 1996 £11.75 (JER)
Mercurey Clos Rochette, Faiveley 1995 £11.75 (ROB) £13.55 (HAH)
Mercurey Clos Rochette, Faiveley 1993 £12.90 (HAH)
Mercurey Juillot 1996 £12.63 (DOM)
Mercurey Juillot 1995 £11.35 (LAY) £18.95 (FORT)
Montagny 1er Cru, Bertrand et Juillot 1994 £12.16 (TW)
Montagny 1er Cru, Olivier Leflaive 1995 £12.45 (ROB)
Rully Château de Rully Rodet 1995 £11.99 (WHI)
Rully Château de Rully Rodet 1994 £11.16 (REI)
Rully Grésigny, Jacqueson 1997 £11.06 (RES)
Rully la Chaume, Chartron et Trébuchet 1997 £11.82 (BAN)
★ Rully la Chaume, Chartron et Trébuchet 1996 £12.24 (JER)
Rully la Pucelle, Domaine Jacqueson 1997 £12.95 (LEA)
Rully la Pucelle, Domaine Jacqueson 1996 £12.95 (NEZ) £12.95 (LEA) £14.25 (STA)
Rully les St Jacques, Villaine 1996 £11.93 (CB)
Rully les St Jacques, Villaine 1995 £11.81 (CB)
Rully Marissou, Dury 1990 £11.95 (RAE)

£13.00 → £14.99

Mercurey Château de Chamirey, Rodet 1996 £13.99 (WHI)
Mercurey Clos Rochette, Faiveley 1996 £14.95 (ROB) £15.00 (WRI)
Montagny 1er Cru, Bertrand et Juillot 1992 £14.98 (TW)
Rully 1er Cru, de Suremain 1994 £13.90 (JU)
Rully Faiveley 1993 £13.75 (ROB)

Over £15.00

Mercurey Clos Rochette, Faiveley 1997 £15.22 (PLA)
Rully 1er Cru, de Suremain 1995 £15.00 (JU)

CÔTE D'OR PRICES

RED

Under £7.00

Hautes-Côtes de Beaune, Caves des
  Hautes-Côtes 1997 £6.99 (TES)
Hautes-Côtes de Nuits, Caves des
  Hautes-Côtes 1997 £5.99 (TES)
Pernand-Vergelesses Rollin ½ bottle 1993
  £5.75 (BALL)

£7.00 → £7.99

Côte de Beaune-Villages Chanson 1995
  £7.50 (BALL)
Hautes-Côtes de Beaune Bouchard Père
  1996 £7.29 (BY) £7.99 (VIC) £7.99 (THR)
  £7.99 (WR) £7.99 (BOT)
Hautes-Côtes de Beaune Tête de Cuvée,
  Caves des Hautes Côtes 1997 £7.49
  (WAI)
Hautes-Côtes de Nuits Bouchard Père
  1996 £7.99 (MORR) £8.42 (BY)
Savigny-lès-Beaune Vieilles Vignes,
  Camus-Bruchon ½ bottle 1993 £7.99
  (RAE)

£8.00 → £9.99

Auxey-Duresses Bouchard Père 1994
  £8.97 (BY)
Chorey-lès-Beaune Roger et Joël Remy
  1996 £9.95 (LEA)
Côte de Beaune-Villages Chanson 1996
  £8.49 (POR)
Côte de Beaune-Villages Drouhin 1995
  £8.70 (NI) £8.93 (PEN)
Hautes-Côtes de Beaune, Hubert Lamy
  1996 £8.39 (YOU)
Hautes-Côtes de Nuits, Michel Gros
  1993 £9.50 (JU)
Marsannay les Longeroies, Bruno Clair
  1994 £9.90 (JU)
Monthélie Bouchard Père 1994 £8.96 (BY)
Morey-St-Denis Georges Lignier 1993
  £9.99 (RAE) £20.25 (BALL)
St-Aubin les Frionnes, Prudhon 1995
  £8.95 (CON) £12.99 (JON) £13.50 (JU)
St-Aubin Prudhon 1996 £8.50 (WS)
St-Aubin Prudhon 1993 £8.25 (BALL)
  Santenay les Gravières, Roger Belland
  1993 £9.99 (WAT)
Santenay Latour 1995 £9.17 (PEN) £9.92
  (BY)

£10.00 → £11.99

Beaune 1er Cru, Bouchard Père 1995
  £10.40 (BY) £12.99 (VIC) £12.99 (THR)
  £7.99 (WR) £7.99 (BOT)
Chassagne-Montrachet Lamy 1997
  £10.73 (BY)
Chassagne-Montrachet les Chaumes,
  Amiot 1996 £10.50 (BAN) £11.95 (SOM)
  £14.95 (LEA)
Chassagne-Montrachet Vieilles Vignes,
  Amiot 1994 £10.95 (BAL)
Chassagne-Montrachet Vieilles Vignes,
  Bernard Morey 1996 £11.95 (BAN)
  £14.69 (DOM) £17.50 (STA)
Chassagne-Montrachet Villamont 1993
  £11.75 (ROB)
Chorey-lès-Beaune Tollot-Beaut 1995
  £11.49 (VIC) £11.49 (THR) £11.49 (WR)
  £11.49 (BOT) £12.00 (JU)
Côte de Beaune-Villages Bouchard Père
  1996 £10.49 (OD)
Côte de Beaune-Villages Carillon 1995
  £11.07 (STE)
Côte de Nuits-Villages Chopin-Groffier
  1996 £10.99 (YOU) £12.50 (FORT)
Côte de Nuits-Villages Domaine Boillot
  1997 £10.28 (MON)
Côte de Nuits-Villages Faiveley 1996
  £10.95 (CON)
Côte de Nuits-Villages René Durand
  1996 £10.50 (PIP)
Fixin la Croix Blanche, André Geoffroy
  1994 £11.95 (JU)
Hautes-Côtes de Beaune, Caves des
  Hautes-Côtes 1996 £10.99 (VA)
Hautes-Côtes de Nuits, Michel Gros
  1995 £11.57 (REI)
Marsannay les Longeroies, Bruno Clair
  1996 £11.95 (SOM)
Marsannay les Vaudenelles, Bruno Clair
  1995 £10.90 (JU) £11.80 (TAN)
Monthélie Garaudet 1995 £11.80 (PIP)
Monthélie Garaudet 1993 £11.35 (NEZ)
Nuits-St-Georges Faiveley 1992 £10.95
  (DI) £15.95 (CON)
Pernand-Vergelesses Rollin 1996 £11.90
  (TAN)
Pernand-Vergelesses Rollin 1993 £10.75
  (BALL) £12.50 (RAE)
Pernand-Vergelesses Sous le Bois de Noël
  et Belles Filles, Rollin 1994 £11.00 (JU)

St-Aubin les Castets, Lamy **1988** £11.75
(FRI)

St-Aubin les Frionnes, Prudhon **1996**
£10.99 (RAE)

Santenay Bouchard Père **1996** £10.99
(MORR)

Santenay Drouhin **1993** £11.59 (NI)

Santenay la Comme, Adrien Belland **1993**
£11.95 (JU)

Santenay la Maladière, Girardin **1996**
£11.25 (AS)

Savigny-lès-Beaune Girard-Vollot **1997**
£10.77 (MON)

Savigny-lès-Beaune Latour **1995** £11.39
(WHI) £11.46 (PLA) £12.31 (PLAY)

Volnay Jean-Marc Boillot ½ bottle **1993**
£11.75 (ROB)

£12.00 → £13.99

Auxey-Duresses Michel Prunier **1996**
£13.48 (NO)

Beaune Clos du Dessus des Marconnets,
Pernot **1994** £12.65 (NEZ)

Beaune Épenottes, Domaine Boillot **1997**
£13.22 (MON)

Beaune Épenottes, Parent **1996** £13.99
(SAF)

Chassagne-Montrachet Blain-Gagnard
1993 £12.25 (HAH)

Chassagne-Montrachet Clos St Jean,
Blain-Gagnard **1994** £13.00 (HAH)

Chassagne-Montrachet Fontaine-Gagnard
1994 £13.51 (JER)

Chassagne-Montrachet Henri Germain
1995 £12.90 (TAN) £15.95 (LEA)

Chassagne-Montrachet Latour **1996**
£12.40 (PLA)

Chassagne-Montrachet Louis Carillon
1997 £12.24 (MON)

Chassagne-Montrachet Vieilles Vignes,
Bernard Morey **1997** £13.22 (MON)

Chorey-lès-Beaune Tollot-Beaut **1996**
£12.39 (YOU) £12.95 (DI)

Chorey-lès-Beaune Château de Chorey-
lès-Beaune, Jacques Germain **1995**
£12.55 (WHI) £13.25 (AS)

Côte de Beaune-Villages Carillon **1996**
£12.50 (NA)

Côte de Nuits-Villages Clos du Chapeau,
Domaine de l'Arlot **1995** £13.07 (BY)

Fixin la Croix Blanche, André Geoffroy
1991 £12.00 (JU)

Fixin Gelin **1996** £13.40 (PLA)

Marsannay Monchenevoy, Charlopin-
Parizot **1997** £12.24 (MON)

Monthélie Darviot Perrin **1996** £13.22
(JER)

Morey-St-Denis Georges Lignier **1995**
£12.95 (TAN)

Nuits-St-Georges Gouges **1995** £13.95
(SOM) £17.33 (REI)

Nuits-St-Georges Labouré-Roi **1993**
£13.55 (ROS)

Pernand-Vergelesses les Vergelesses,
Pavelot **1996** £13.65 (RES)

Pernand-Vergelesses Sous le Bois de Noël
et Belles Filles, Rollin **1995** £12.50 (JU)

Pommard les Cras, Belland **1993** £13.79
(WAT)

St-Aubin les Castets, Lamy **1996** £12.59
(LAY)

St-Aubin les Frionnes, Prudhon **1989**
£12.50 (CRO)

St-Aubin Pitangerets, Domaine Louis
Carillon **1997** £12.73 (MON) £12.95 (AD)

Santenay les Gravières, Domaine de la
Pousse d'Or **1995** £13.25 (CON)

Savigny-lès-Beaune Domaine Guyon **1996**
£13.71 (FRI)

Savigny-lès-Beaune Latour **1993** £12.92
(WY)

Savigny-lès-Beaune les Lavières, Bouchard
Père **1994** £12.24 (JER)

Savigny-lès-Beaune les Lavières, Camus-
Bruchon **1995** £13.95 (STA) £14.50 (RAE)

Savigny-lès-Beaune Pavelot **1996** £12.34
(DOM)

Volnay Santenots Roger Belland **1995**
£13.85 (WAT)

£14.00 → £15.99

Aloxe-Corton Chandon de Briailles **1995**
£15.57 (REI) £17.15 (HAH)

Aloxe-Corton Latour **1996** £14.50 (TAN)

Aloxe-Corton Latour **1995** £14.69 (PEN)
£14.99 (NLW)

Aloxe-Corton Rollin **1996** £15.47 (RAE)

Aloxe-Corton Rollin **1995** £15.75 (BALL)
£16.99 (RAE)

Auxey-Duresses Michel Prunier **1993**
£15.50 (JU)

Beaune 1er Cru, Bouchard Père **1997**
£15.52 (BY)
Beaune Cent Vignes, Roger et Joël Remy
1995 £15.95 (LEA)
Beaune Clos du Dessus des Marconnets,
Pernot **1996** £15.67 (JER)
Beaune Clos du Roi, Camus-Bruchon
1994 £15.99 (RAE)
Beaune Faiveley **1989** £15.95 (DI)
Beaune les Mariages, Rossignol-Trapet
1995 £15.13 (HA) £15.75 (TW)
Beaune Teurons, Bouchard Père **1995**
£15.95 (COC)
Beaune Teurons, Domaines du Château
de Beaune **1989** £15.90 (COC)
Beaune Teurons, Jadot **1995** £14.59 (FA)
Chassagne-Montrachet Clos de la
Boudriotte, Ramonet **1990** £15.00 (CRO)
Chassagne-Montrachet Gagnard-
Delagrange **1995** £15.67 (JER)
Chassagne-Montrachet Morgeot, Gagnard
1993 £14.90 (JU)
Chassagne-Montrachet Vieilles Vignes,
Amiot **1995** £14.95 (LEA)
Côte de Nuits-Villages Jayer-Gilles **1992**
£15.50 (JU)
Gevrey-Chambertin Alain Burguet **1994**
£15.50 (JU)
Gevrey-Chambertin Chanson **1993**
£14.99 (JON) £15.99 (POR) £16.85 (HA)
Gevrey-Chambertin Perrot-Minot **1995**
£15.95 (BAL) £16.29 (CON) £16.60 (NEZ)
Gevrey-Chambertin Rodet **1996** £15.49
(WHI)
Gevrey-Chambertin Rossignol-Trapet
1997 £14.99 (SAF) £16.75 (PIP)
Gevrey-Chambertin Rossignol-Trapet
1996 £15.73 (BY) £15.86 (TW)
Hautes-Côtes de Nuits, Jayer-Gilles **1994**
£14.90 (JU) £15.00 (WS)
Maranges Clos des Loyères Vieilles
Vignes, Girardin **1996** £15.75 (PHI)
Marsannay Monchenevoy, Charlopin-
Parizot **1994** £14.00 (MV)
Meursault Coche Debord **1982** £15.00
(CRO)

Morey-St-Denis Bouchard Père **1990**
£15.50 (BY)
Morey-St-Denis en la Rue de Vergy,
Bruno Clair **1996** £15.75 (SOM)
Morey-St-Denis en la Rue de Vergy,
Domaine Henri Perrot-Minot **1993**
£15.65 (WAT)
Nuits-St-Georges Bouchard Père **1996**
£14.99 (WR) £14.99 (BOT)
Nuits-St-Georges Bouchard Père **1995**
£15.47 (JER)
Nuits St-Georges Jean Chauvenet **1994**
£14.95 (BALL)
Nuits-St-Georges Labouré-Roi **1996**
£14.99 (SAF)
Nuits-St-Georges les Fleurières, Jean-
Jacques Confuron **1995** £15.95 (BAL)
Nuits-St-Georges Robert Chevillon **1994**
£15.50 (JU)
Nuits-St-Georges Rodet **1994** £14.99 (WHI)
Pernand-Vergelesses Île de Vergelesses,
Rollin **1994** £14.95 (BALL) £16.90 (JU)
£17.95 (RAE)
Pernand-Vergelesses Île de Vergelesses,
Chandon de Briailles **1988** £14.70 (TAN)
Pommard Bouchard Père **1995** £14.40
(COC)
Pommard les Vignots, Coste-Caumartin
1994 £15.93 (GW) £17.50 (JU)
Santenay Clos Tavannes, Domaine de la
Pousse d'Or **1994** £15.95 (DI)
Santenay la Maladière, Girardin **1995**
£14.60 (NEZ)
Santenay la Maladière, Prieur **1995**
£15.95 (NA)
Santeney les Gravières, Girardin **1997**
£15.67 (MON) £18.00 (ELL)
Savigny-lès-Beaune aux Grands Liards,
Javillier **1996** £15.89 (LAY)
Savigny-lès-Beaune Girard-Vollot **1993**
£15.95 (ROB)
Savigny-lès-Beaune les Guettes, Pavelot
1995 £15.86 (DOM)
Savigny-lès-Beaune les Lavières, Bouchard
Père **1996** £15.53 (COC)
Savigny-lès-Beaune les Lavières, Chandon
de Briailles **1996** £15.50 (HAH)
Savigny-lès-Beaune les Lavières, Tollot-
Beaut **1994** £14.95 (JU)
Savigny-lès-Beaune Narbantons, Camus-
Bruchon **1993** £15.99 (JON)
Volnay Blain-Gagnard **1993** £15.80 (HAH)
Volnay Bouchard Père **1993** £14.95 (COC)
Vosne-Romanée Cacheux **1997** £15.67
(MON)

Please remember that
Oz Clarke's Wine Guide
*is a price **guide** and not a*
price list. It is not meant to
replace up-to-date
merchants' lists.

Vosne-Romanée Domaine Mugneret-Gibourg 1997 £14.95 (BAN) £20.95 (LEA)

Vougeot Clos Bertagna, Domaine Bertagna 1995 £15.95 (SAI)

£16.00 → £17.99

Aloxe-Corton Chandon de Briailles 1994 £16.95 (LEA)

Aloxe-Corton les Chaillots, Latour 1993 £17.25 (PLAY)

Aloxe-Corton Rollin 1994 £16.00 (JU)

Aloxe-Corton Tollot-Beaut 1996 £16.39 (DOM)

Aloxe-Corton Tollot-Beaut 1988 £17.92 (REI)

Beaune Bressandes, Henri Germain 1995 £16.60 (TAN) £21.95 (LEA)

Beaune Cent Vignes, Lois Dufouleur 1996 £17.63 (JER)

Beaune Clos du Roi, Camus-Bruchon 1995 £16.95 (BALL) £16.99 (RAE)

Beaune Teurons, Rossignol-Trapet 1995 £16.86 (CB) £17.50 (PIP)

Beaune Toussaints, Albert Morot 1994 £17.00 (WS) £19.30 (AV)

Beaune Vignes Franches, Latour 1995 £16.39 (PLA) £17.50 (STA)

Beaune Vignes Franches, Latour 1992 £17.23 (PLAY)

Bonnes-Mares Drouhin-Laroze 1974 £17.04 (REI)

Chambolle-Musigny Confuron 1996 £16.95 (BAL)

Chambolle-Musigny Ghislaine Barthod 1995 £16.94 (RAE) £21.00 (JU)

Chambolle-Musigny Jadot 1996 £17.53 (FA)

Chambolle-Musigny les Véroilles, Bruno Clair 1995 £17.50 (JU)

Chassagne-Montrachet Champs-Gains, Jean Marc Morey 1995 £17.75 (PIP)

Chassagne-Montrachet Champs-Gains, Jean Marc Morey 1994 £16.95 (RES)

Chassagne-Montrachet Clos St-Jean, J-N Gagnard 1995 £16.00 (JU)

Chassagne-Montrachet la Maltroie, Amiot 1997 £16.95 (BAN)

Corton Pougets, Jadot 1988 £16.45 (REI)

Gevrey-Chambertin Estournelles-St-Jacques, Frédéric Esmonin 1997 £17.50 (BAN)

Gevrey-Chambertin Latour 1995 £17.51 (PEN)

Gevrey-Chambertin Perrot-Minot 1996 £17.50 (CON) £18.50 (BAL)

Gevrey-Chambertin Rossignol-Trapet 1995 £16.22 (CB) £18.05 (NO) £18.74 (TW)

Gevrey-Chambertin Vieilles Vignes, Marchand-Grillot 1995 £17.96 (LAY)

Gevrey-Chambertin Vieilles Vignes, Trapet 1996 £17.04 (FA)

Hautes-Côtes de Nuits, Jayer-Gilles 1995 £17.50 (JU)

Marsannay Longeroies, Denis Mortet 1994 £16.00 (WS)

Monthélie Château de Monthélie, Suremain 1995 £16.50 (JU)

Monthélie les Duresses, Coche-Bizouard 1993 £16.95 (ROB)

Monthélie sur la Velle, Château de Monthélie 1992 £17.60 (RAE) £18.50 (JU)

Morey-St-Denis Bruno Clair 1993 £16.99 (ROS)

Morey-St-Denis Clos des Lambrays, Domaine des Lambrays 1983 £16.06 (FA)

Morey-St-Denis en la Rue de Vergy, Bruno Clair 1994 £16.00 (JU)

Morey-St-Denis en la Rue de Vergy, Domaine Henri Perrot-Minot 1995 £16.50 (BAL)

Nuits-St-Georges Jean Chauvenet 1995 £16.99 (RAE)

Nuits-St-Georges Domaine de l'Arlot 1996 £16.96 (BY) £19.99 (WR) £19.99 (BOT)

Nuits-St-Georges Gouges 1997 £17.17 (MON)

Nuits-St-Georges les Fleurières, Jean-Jacques Confuron 1996 £16.50 (BAL) £23.50 (CAV)

Nuits-St-Georges les Fleurières, Jean-Jacques Confuron 1994 £16.95 (BAL)

Nuits-St-Georges les Porets St-Georges, Faiveley 1992 £16.50 (DI) £19.99 (POR)

Nuits-St-Georges Michelot 1995 £17.25 (NEZ)

Nuits-St-Georges Robert Chevillon 1996 £16.50 (FORT) £20.11 (WT)

Nuits-St-Georges Robert Chevillon 1991 £17.49 (YOU)

Pernand-Vergelesses Île de Vergelesses, Rollin 1991 £17.25 (BALL)

Pernand-Vergelesses Île de Vergelesses, Chandon de Briailles 1995 £16.95 (RES) £17.04 (REI) £18.50 (LEA)

Pommard Jean-Marc Boillot 1994 £16.99 (RAE)

Pommard Clos Blanc, Albert Grivault 1993 £16.50 (JU)

Pommard Clos Blanc, Albert Grivault 1991 £16.50 (JU)

Pommard Coste-Caumartin **1993** £16.90 (JU)

Pommard Clos Blanc, Albert Grivault **1993** £16.50 (JU)

Pommard les Vignots, Coste-Caumartin **1993** £17.99 (GW)

Santenay Clos Tavannes, Gagnard **1995** £16.50 (JU)

Santenay la Maladière, Girardin **1997** £17.04 (RES)

Santeney les Gravières, Girardin **1996** £16.50 (TAN) £19.45 (PHI)

Savigny-lès-Beaune Aux Grands Liards, Bize **1996** £17.39 (YOU)

Savigny-lès-Beaune Aux Grands Liards, Bize **1995** £16.95 (LAY) £21.74 (TW)

Savigny-lès-Beaune la Dominode, Bruno Clair **1996** £17.25 (SOM)

Savigny-lès-Beaune les Lavières, Ampeau **1987** £16.74 (REI) £18.95 (LEA)

Savigny-lès-Beaune les Lavières, Tollot-Beaut **1996** £16.95 (DI)

Savigny-lès-Beaune les Peuillets, Pavelot **1995** £16.74 (DOM)

Savigny-lès-Beaune les Vergelesses, Bize **1994** £17.95 (RES) £22.91 (TW)

Savigny-lès-Beaune Marconnets, Bize **1992** £17.20 (HAH) £27.73 (TW)

Savigny-lès-Beaune Pavelot **1995** £17.50 (FORT)

Volnay Champans, Monthélie-Douhairet **1995** £16.90 (SOM)

Volnay Drouhin **1995** £17.00 (PEN)

Volnay Domaine Leflaive **1994** £17.59 (DI)

Volnay Marquis d'Angerville **1993** £16.50 (JU)

Volnay Michel Lafarge **1994** £16.50 (BALL)

Volnay Santenots Latour **1995** £17.05 (STA)

Volnay Taillepieds, Bouchard Père **1993** £17.74 (COC)

Vosne-Romanée Champs Perdrix, Bruno Clair **1994** £17.50 (JU)

Vosne-Romanée Champs Perdrix, Bruno Clair **1992** £16.50 (JU)

Vosne-Romanée Domaine Mugneret-Gibourg **1994** £16.40 (HAH) £17.95 (LEA)

Vosne-Romanée Engel **1996** £17.75 (BALL) £17.95 (CON) £18.21 (TW) £18.65 (SOM)

Vosne-Romanée Engel **1995** £17.25 (CON) £22.00 (FORT) £22.03 (TW)

Vosne-Romanée Engel **1994** £17.25 (CON)

Vosne-Romanée Gros Frère et Soeur **1993** £16.06 (FA)

Vosne-Romanée Hudelot-Noëllat **1997** £17.53 (RES)

£18.00 → £19.99

Aloxe-Corton les Chaillots, Latour **1996** £18.95 (STA)

Aloxe-Corton les Fournières, Tollot-Beaut **1993** £19.50 (JU)

Aloxe-Corton Tollot-Beaut **1991** £18.50 (STA)

Auxey-Duresses Joseph Matrot **1991** £19.15 (TW)

Beaune Bressandes, Henri Germain **1994** £18.95 (LEA) £19.75 (AD)

Beaune Épenottes, Machard de Gramont **1988** £19.50 (JU)

Beaune Grèves, Tollot-Beaut **1996** £19.00 (RAE) £21.95 (DI) £25.85 (FA)

Beaune Grèves, Tollot-Beaut **1994** £19.50 (JU)

Beaune Grèves, Tollot-Beaut **1993** £19.90 (JU)

Beaune les Mariages, Rossignol-Trapet **1996** £18.25 (WRI)

Beaune Montrevenots, Jean-Marc Boillot **1996** £19.68 (DOM)

Beaune Teurons, Jadot **1993** £19.99 (POR)

Bonnes-Mares Jadot **1987** £19.39 (REI)

Chambolle-Musigny Amiot **1997** £19.09 (MON)

Chambolle-Musigny Ghislaine Barthod **1993** £19.90 (JU)

Chambolle-Musigny Ghislaine Barthod **1988** £18.95 (RAE)

Chambolle-Musigny les Charmes, Hudelot-Noëllat **1996** £18.90 (SOM)

Chapelle-Chambertin Trapet **1983** £19.50 (BU)

Chassagne-Montrachet la Maltroie, Amiot **1993** £18.60 (CAV)

Chassagne-Montrachet Morgeot, Jean Pillot **1997** £19.49 (RES)

Chassagne-Montrachet Morgeot, Jean Pillot **1995** £19.39 (NI)

Corton-Bressandes Michel Voarick **1983** £18.21 (REI)

Corton les Renardes, Delarche **1996** £19.50 (SOM)

In each price band wines are listed in vintage order. Within each vintage they are listed in A–Z order.

Côte de Nuits-Villages Jayer-Gilles **1994**
£18.00 (WS)

Gevrey-Chambertin Bouchard Père **1996**
£19.62 (COC)

Gevrey-Chambertin Clos Prieur, Marc
Roy **1996** £18.99 (OD)

Gevrey-Chambertin Cuvée de l'Abeille,
Ponsot **1996** £19.95 (BAL)

Gevrey-Chambertin Cuvée de l'Abeille,
Ponsot **1995** £19.95 (BAL) £23.99 (YOU)

Gevrey-Chambertin Drouhin **1993**
£18.35 (NI)

Gevrey-Chambertin Latour **1996** £19.50
(STA)

Gevrey-Chambertin Denis Mortet **1994**
£19.99 (RAE)

Gevrey-Chambertin Thierry Mortet **1995**
£18.95 (LEA) £22.00 (JU)

Gevrey-Chambertin Vieilles Vignes,
Dugat-Py **1994** £18.30 (HAH) £22.50
(LEA)

Gevry-Chambertin Vieilles Vignes,
Bachelet **1992** £18.69 (YOU)

Latricières-Chambertin Trapet **1983**
£19.50 (BU)

Monthélie Château de Monthélie,
Suremain **1990** £18.99 (RAE)

Morey-St-Denis Dujac **1994** £18.90 (JU)

Morey-St-Denis en la Rue de Vergy,
Domaine Henri Perrot-Minot **1996**
£19.95 (BAL)

Morey-St-Denis Monts Luisants, Pernin-
Rossin **1996** £19.95 (BAN)

Nuits-St-Georges 1er Cru, Domaine de
l'Arlot **1993** £19.41 (BY)

Nuits-St-Georges Clos de la Maréchale,
Faiveley **1991** £19.90 (HAH) £19.95
(CON) £22.91 (REI)

Nuits-St-Georges Drouhin **1995** £18.97
(PEN)

Nuits-St-Georges Faiveley **1989** £19.95
(DI) £20.95 (WRI)

Nuits-St-Georges les Murgers,
Chauvenet-Chopin **1996** £18.49 (YOU)

Nuits-St-Georges les Chaignots,
Mugneret-Gibourg **1997** £19.75 (BAN)

Nuits-St-Georges les Damodes, Lescure
1995 £18.75 (PIP)

Nuits-St-Georges les Hauts Pruliers,
Machard de Gramont **1996** £18.80 (CB)

Nuits-St-Georges les Pruliers, Gouges
1996 £18.95 (SOM) £25.52 (AV)

Nuits-St-Georges les Pruliers, Grivot
1995 £18.95 (SOM) £23.40 (RAE)

Nuits-St-Georges Robert Chevillon **1995**
£18.00 (JU)

Pommard Jean-Marc Boillot **1995** £18.75
(RAE)

Pommard Clos des Boucherottes, Coste-
Caumartin **1994** £19.65 (GW) £21.90
(JU)

Pommard Clos des Épeneaux, Armand ½
bottle **1995** £18.74 (TW)

Pommard Coste-Caumartin **1990** £19.00
(JU)

Pommard les Épenots, Domaine Mussy
1994 £18.60 (SOM)

Pommard Parent **1992** £19.00 (CRO)

Santenay Clos Tavannes, Domaine de la
Pousse d'Or **1992** £19.39 (TW)

Santenay les Passetemps, Faiveley **1988**
£19.50 (JU)

Savigny-lès-Beaune Champs-Chevrey,
Tollot-Beaut **1996** £19.97 (FA)

Savigny-lès-Beaune la Dominode, Bruno
Clair **1994** £18.50 (JU) £29.00 (CRO)

Savigny-lès-Beaune la Dominode, Pavelot
1995 £18.21 (DOM)

Savigny-lès-Beaune les Fourneaux, Bize
1992 £19.59 (YOU)

Savigny-lès-Beaune les Serpentières,
Drouhin **1993** £18.21 (REI)

Savigny-lès-Beaune les Vergelesses, Bize
1993 £19.38 (RIP)

Volnay Clos d'Audignac, Domaine de la
Pousse d'Or **1996** £19.97 (FA)

Volnay Darviot Perrin **1996** £18.21 (TW)
£19.09 (JER)

Volnay les Caillerets, Clos des 60
Ouvrées, Domaine de la Pousse d'Or
1987 £19.00 (FA)

Volnay Marquis d'Angerville **1995** £18.00
(JU) £25.75 (PHI)

Volnay Vendange Selectionée, Lafarge
1994 £18.95 (HAH) £19.90 (GAU) £28.08
(TW)

Vosne-Romanée Domaine Mugneret-
Gibourg **1996** £19.95 (LEA) £19.95 (HAH)

Vosne-Romanée Engel **1997** £19.20 (GAU)
£23.40 (RES)

Vosne-Romanée Rion **1996** £19.75 (SOM)

£20.00 → £22.49

Aloxe-Corton Drouhin **1995** £20.56 (REI)

Aloxe-Corton les Vercots, Tollot-Beaut **1995** £20.00 (JU) £22.50 (DI)

Auxey-Duresses les Ecusseaux, Ampeau **1985** £22.03 (REI) £24.18 (CHA)

Beaune Bressandes, Henri Germain **1993** £21.95 (LEA)

Beaune Clos des Mouches, Drouhin **1992** £22.03 (REI)

Beaune Clos des Ursules, Jadot **1996** £20.46 (FA) £22.03 (CAV)

Beaune Clos des Ursules, Jadot **1995** £20.00 (BU) £20.56 (REI)

Beaune Clos du Roi, Ampeau **1984** £21.74 (REI) £24.50 (LEA)

Beaune Grèves, Tollot-Beaut **1995** £22.00 (JU) £22.95 (DI)

Beaune Grèves, Tollot-Beaut **1992** £20.89 (JON)

Beaune les Montrevenots, Jean-Marc Boillot **1996** £20.95 (LEA)

Beaune les Montrevenots, Jean-Marc Boillot **1988** £20.91 (RIP)

Blagny la Pièce sous le Bois, Matrot **1993** £22.38 (CB) £22.95 (BALL)

Chambolle-Musigny les Veroilles, Ghislaine Barthod **1992** £22.00 (JU)

Chambolle-Musigny Domaine Roumier **1996** £20.95 (RES) £21.15 (SOM)

Chassagne-Montrachet Clos St Jean, Blain-Gagnard **1996** £21.65 (HAH)

Chassagne-Montrachet Gagnard-Delagrange **1997** £21.54 (MON)

Chassagne-Montrachet Latour **1993** £21.15 (WY)

Gevrey-Chambertin Armand Rousseau **1996** £21.93 (FA) £32.50 (FORT)

Gevrey-Chambertin Bachelet **1993** £21.15 (RIP)

Gevrey-Chambertin Clos de la Justice, Pascal **1993** £21.75 (VIN)

Gevrey-Chambertin Cuvée de l'Abeille, Ponsot **1993** £20.56 (CAV)

Gevrey-Chambertin Drouhin-Laroze **1996** £21.20 (HAH)

Gevrey-Chambertin Jadot **1994** £22.40 (UB)

Oz Clarke's Wine Guide
is an annual publication. We
welcome your suggestions
for next year's edition.

Gevrey-Chambertin la Combe aux Moines, Faiveley **1994** £22.00 (WS) £22.00 (TAN)

Gevrey-Chambertin Denis Mortet **1996** £22.43 (DOM)

Gevrey-Chambertin Vieilles Vignes, Charlopin-Parizot **1997** £21.51 (MON)

Morey-St-Denis Clos des Ormes, Faiveley **1991** £20.56 (REI)

Nuits St-Georges Jean Chauvenet **1988** £21.00 (JU)

Nuits-St-Georges Clos de la Maréchale, Faiveley **1989** £21.40 (COC) £25.00 (FLE)

Nuits-St-Georges Clos de l'Arlot, Domaine de l'Arlot **1991** £20.00 (WS)

Nuits-St-Georges Clos des Forêts St-Georges, Domaine de l'Arlot **1992** £21.87 (BY)

Nuits-St-Georges Domaine de l'Arlot **1991** £21.00 (FLE) £30.30 (DI)

Nuits-St-Georges les Chaignots, Georges Mugneret **1994** £21.35 (HAH) £26.90 (LAY)

Nuits-St-Georges les Chaignots, Robert Chevillon **1993** £22.00 (JU) £33.50 (ROB)

Nuits-St-Georges les Damodes, Jean Chauvenet **1994** £22.00 (WS)

Nuits-St-Georges les Roncières, Robert Chevillon **1994** £21.00 (JU) £23.01 (WT) £27.38 (TW)

Nuits-St-Georges les Roncières, Robert Chevillon **1992** £21.49 (YOU)

Nuits-St-Georges les Vaucrains, Gouges **1993** £20.65 (SOM)

Nuits-St-Georges Richemone, Pernin-Rossin **1996** £21.50 (BAN)

Nuits-St-Georges Richemone, Pernin-Rossin **1992** £21.50 (BAN)

Nuits-St-Georges Robert Chevillon **1992** £21.74 (TW)

Pernand-Vergelesses Île de Vergelesses, Chandon de Briailles **1992** £20.00 (CRO) £22.91 (TW)

Pommard les Bertins, Lescure **1995** £20.50 (PIP)

Pommard les Fremiers, Coste-Caumartin **1993** £21.00 (JU)

Pommard les Saucilles, Jean-Marc Boillot **1993** £21.50 (RAE) £22.50 (NI)

Pommard Pezerolles, Domaine de Montille **1992** £21.85 (HAH)

Ruchottes-Chambertin Frédéric Esmonin **1996** £21.00 (BAN)

Savigny-lès-Beaune aux Grands Liards, Bize **1992** £21.74 (TW)

Savigny-lès-Beaune la Dominode, Pavelot **1994** £22.00 (FORT)

Volnay Jean-Marc Boillot **1997** £21.50 (LEA)

Volnay Carelle sous la Chapelle, Boillot **1996** £21.64 (RAE)

Volnay Clos des Chênes, Domaine Guyon **1993** £21.54 (FRI)

Volnay Clos des Ducs, Marquis d'Angerville **1994** £22.00 (JU)

Volnay Darviot Perrin **1993** £22.09 (TW)

Volnay Frémiets, Marquis d'Angerville **1993** £22.00 (JU) £28.30 (FA)

Volnay les Caillerets, Henri Boillot **1997** £20.07 (MON)

Volnay les Caillerets, Michel Prunier **1993** £21.00 (JU)

Volnay Marquis d'Angerville **1997** £20.86 (RES) £21.05 (MON)

Volnay Michel Lafarge **1993** £20.30 (HAH)

Volnay Santenots Matrot **1993** £21.50 (ELL)

Volnay Santenots Prieur **1992** £21.15 (WHI)

Volnay Vendange Selectionée, Lafarge **1995** £21.74 (REI) £23.50 (HAH) £29.96 (TW)

Volnay Vendange Selectionée, Lafarge **1993** £21.25 (BALL)

Vosne-Romanée Cacheux **1993** £21.95 (ROB)

Vosne-Romanée Michel Gros **1993** £22.00 (JU)

Vosne-Romanée la Montagne, Clavelier **1997** £20.86 (RES)

Vosne-Romanée les Brulées, Engel **1994** £21.75 (CON) £24.75 (ROB) £28.79 (TW)

Vosne-Romanée les Hautes Maizieres, Clavelier **1996** £20.95 (RES)

Vosne-Romanée les Violettes, Georges Clerget **1996** £21.44 (PLA)

£22.50 → £24.99

Aloxe-Corton Tollot-Beaut **1993** £22.99 (JON)

Beaune Bressandes, Morot **1997** £24.38 (RES)

Beaune Champs Pimonts, Lois Dufouleur **1996** £22.95 (VIN)

Beaune Clos des Mouches, Drouhin **1995** £23.24 (PEN) £23.99 (YOU) £29.50 (BEN)

Beaune Clos du Roi, Ampeau **1985** £24.18 (CHA)

Chambolle-Musigny Beaux Bruns, Ghislaine Barthod **1990** £23.95 (RAE)

Chambolle-Musigny Clos du Village Domaine Guyon **1996** £22.52 (FRI)

Chambolle-Musigny Hudelot-Noëllat **1995** £23.50 (ROB)

Chambolle-Musigny Latour **1979** £23.15 (PEN)

Chambolle-Musigny les Cras, Ghislaine Barthod **1995** £22.52 (RAE)

Chambolle-Musigny les Cras, Roumier **1994** £24.45 (HAH) £26.00 (MV)

Chassagne-Montrachet Ramonet **1996** £23.89 (FA)

Clos de la Roche Castagnier **1982** £24.00 (CRO)

Corton Clos de la Vigne au Saint, Latour **1993** £24.98 (HA) £28.00 (WRI)

Corton Pougets, Jadot **1995** £23.40 (FA)

Gevrey-Chambertin Armand Rousseau **1995** £23.50 (RES) £27.42 (JER)

Gevrey-Chambertin Clos Prieur, Thierry Mortet **1997** £23.95 (LEA)

Gevrey-Chambertin Lavaux-St-Jacques, Leclerc **1996** £24.28 (JER)

Gevrey-Chambertin au Vellé, Denis Mortet **1993** £22.95 (RAE)

Gevrey-Chambertin Vieilles Vignes, Alain Burguet **1992** £23.27 (RIP) £27.97 (TW)

Mazis-Chambertin Frédéric Esmonin **1997** £23.00 (BAN)

Morey-St-Denis Clos de la Bussière, Domaine Roumier **1997** £24.38 (RES)

Morey-St-Denis Clos des Ormes, Georges Lignier **1992** £23.25 (PLA)

Morey-St-Denis en la Rue de Vergy, Domaine Henri Perrot-Minot **1997** £23.89 (RES)

Nuits-St-Georges Chopin-Groffier **1994** £24.50 (ROB)

Nuits-St-Georges Clos les Porets St-Georges, Gouges **1997** £23.50 (MON)

Nuits-St-Georges Clos les Porets St-Georges, Gouges **1995** £23.50 (REI)

Nuits-St-Georges Domaine de l'Arlot **1993** £22.50 (CRO)

Nuits-St-Georges Georges & Henri Jayer **1993** £24.00 (JU)

Nuits-St-Georges les Boudots, Grivot **1996** £23.25 (SOM) £23.40 (RAE)

Nuits-St-Georges les Chaignots, Faiveley **1993** £23.00 (DI) £28.40 (HAH)

Nuits-St-Georges les Chaignots, Michelot **1995** £23.50 (DOM)

Nuits-St-Georges les Chaignots, Mugneret-Gibourg **1996** £24.65 (HAH)

Nuits-St-Georges les Chaignots, Robert Chevillon **1995** £23.94 (WT) £24.00 (JU)

Nuits-St-Georges les Damodes, Jean Chauvenet **1993** £24.95 (RAE)

Nuits-St-Georges les Porets St-Georges, Faiveley **1989** £22.75 (WRI)

Nuits-St-Georges les Pruliers, Grivot **1994** £23.50 (RAE) £24.50 (STA)

Nuits-St-Georges les Pruliers, Lucien Boillot **1997** £23.50 (MON)

Nuits-St-Georges les Roncières, Robert Chevillon **1993** £24.00 (JU)

Nuits-St-Georges les St-Georges, Gouges **1996** £22.85 (SOM)

Nuits-St-Georges les St-Georges, Gouges **1983** £22.91 (FA)

Nuits-St-Georges les Vaucrains, Robert Chevillon **1994** £24.40 (WT) £25.00 (JU)

Nuits-St-Georges Rion **1987** £23.95 (ROB)

Pommard Jean-Marc Boillot **1993** £23.95 (ROB)

Pommard Clos des Boucherottes, Coste-Caumartin **1995** £24.00 (JU)

Pommard les Jarollières, Boillot **1991** £23.00 (BALL) £23.95 (RAE) £28.90 (BER)

Savigny-lès-Beaune Ampeau **1985** £24.18 (CHA)

Savigny-lès-Beaune les Lavières, Ampeau **1985** £23.41 (REI)

Volnay Clos d'Audignac, Domaine de la Pousse d'Or **1995** £23.95 (CON)

Volnay Clos de la Bousse d'Or, Domaine de la Pousse d'Or **1992** £23.99 (BO)

Volnay Clos des Chênes, Domaine Guyon **1996** £23.50 (FRI)

Volnay Frémiets, Marquis d'Angerville **1996** £23.15 (CB) £28.30 (FA)

Volnay les Caillerets Cuvée Carnot, Bouchard Père **1996** £23.56 (COC)

Volnay les Caillerets, Domaine de la Pousse d'Or **1995** £22.50 (GAU) £25.50 (CON)

Volnay les Caillerets, Domaine de la Pousse d'Or **1993** £24.50 (BALL) £30.95 (BER)

Volnay Santenots Ampeau **1985** £24.18 (CHA)

Volnay Santenots Ampeau **1981** £22.91 (REI)

Volnay Santenots Matrot **1996** £24.26 (CB)

Volnay Santenots Prieur **1995** £23.76 (STE)

Volnay Vendange Selectionée, Lafarge **1996** £22.50 (CON) £23.95 (HAH)

Vosne-Romanée Cacheux **1996** £24.95 (PHI)

Vosne-Romanée Clos de la Fontaine, Michel Gros **1993** £23.00 (JU)

Vosne-Romanée Hudelot-Noëllat **1995** £23.00 (RES)

Vosne-Romanée les Beaux Monts, Domaine Jean Grivot **1994** £22.90 (BER)

Vosne-Romanée les Suchots, Hudelot-Noëllat **1997** £24.38 (RES)

Vosne-Romanée Remoissenet **1993** £23.65 (AV)

Vosne-Romanée Rion **1995** £23.32 (REI)

£25.00 → £27.49

Beaune Bressandes, Morot **1994** £25.00 (RES)

Beaune Clos des Mouches, Drouhin **1993** £26.95 (NI) £38.19 (REI) £56.99 (TW)

Beaune Cuvée Maurice Drouhin, Hospices de Beaune **1982** £25.26 (REI)

Beaune Grèves Vigne de l'Enfant Jesus, Bouchard Père **1986** £26.44 (REI)

Beaune Toussaints, Albert Morot **1995** £26.00 (RES)

Chambolle-Musigny les Charmes, Ghislaine Barthod **1994** £27.00 (RAE) £29.00 (JU)

Chambolle-Musigny les Cras, Ghislaine Barthod **1993** £26.00 (JU)

Chambolle-Musigny Ponnelle **1996** £27.40 (AV)

Chapelle-Chambertin Jadot **1995** £26.83 (FA)

Charmes-Chambertin Perrot-Minot **1995** £27.05 (WAT) £27.95 (CON)

Clos de la Roche Ponsot **1986** £26.83 (FA)

Corton-Bressandes Dubreuil-Fontaine **1992** £26.95 (RES)

Corton le Rognet, Chevalier **1991** £25.50 (GW)

Corton Clos de la Vigne au Saint, Latour **1988** £27.03 (PEN)

Corton Maréchaudes, Chandon de Briailles **1997** £25.36 (RES)

Corton Maréchaudes, Chandon de Briailles **1996** £26.40 (HAH) £28.00 (RES)

Corton Maréchaudes, Chandon de Briailles **1995** £26.50 (HAH) £26.73 (REI)

Corton Pougets, Jadot **1996** £26.93 (CAV) £27.32 (FA) £29.96 (REI)

Corton Tollot-Beaut **1996** £26.34 (RAE)

Gevrey-Chambertin Bachelet **1994** £27.00 (WS)

Gevrey-Chambertin Cazetiers, Armand
Rousseau **1995** £26.00 (FORT)

Gevrey-Chambertin Clos Prieur,
Rossignol-Trapet **1993** £26.68 (NO)
£31.49 (TW)

Gevrey-Chambertin Coeur du Roy,
Dugat-Py **1993** £26.95 (ROB)

Gevrey-Chambertin Faiveley **1990** £25.85
(PEN) £32.95 (STA)

Gevrey-Chambertin au Vellé, Denis
Mortet **1996** £25.85 (DOM) £27.00
(RES)

Gevry-Chambertin Vieilles Vignes,
Bachelet **1994** £27.00 (MV)

Griotte-Chambertin Ponsot **1994** £25.85
(FA) £44.06 (CAV) £45.00 (BAL)

Morey-St-Denis Clos de la Bussière,
Domaine Roumier **1995** £26.50 (ROB)

Nuits-St-Georges aux Lavières, Leroy
1994 £25.85 (FA)

Nuits-St-Georges Clos de l'Arlot,
Domaine de l'Arlot **1996** £25.77 (BY)

Nuits-St-Georges Clos des Forêts St-
Georges, Domaine de l'Arlot **1995**
£25.00 (FLE) £25.55 (BY)

Nuits-St-Georges Clos des Forêts St-
Georges, Domaine de l'Arlot **1993**
£27.26 (RIP) £27.81 (BY) £38.19 (TW)

Nuits-St-Georges Haut Pruliers, Rion
1991 £25.00 (WS)

Nuits-St-Georges les Cailles, Robert
Chevillon **1992** £26.00 (JU)

Nuits-St-Georges les Chaignots, Chopin-
Groffier **1993** £26.00 (YOU)

Nuits-St-Georges les Chaignots, Georges
Mugneret **1996** £26.95 (LEA)

Nuits-St-Georges les Pruliers, Gouges
1997 £25.46 (MON) £26.73 (RES)

Nuits-St-Georges les Pruliers, Grivot
1992 £25.99 (RAE) £29.00 (BALL)

Nuits-St-Georges les St-Georges, Robert
Chevillon **1994** £25.33 (WT) £26.00 (JU)

Nuits-St-Georges les St-Georges, Robert
Chevillon **1992** £27.00 (JU)

Nuits-St-Georges les Vaucrains, Jean
Chauvenet **1993** £26.95 (RAE)

Pommard Clos Blanc, Machard de
Gramont **1988** £27.00 (JU)

Pommard Clos des Épeneaux, Armand
1996 £27.32 (FA) £32.50 (CON) £32.78
(TW)

Pommard les Argillières, Lejeune **1988**
£26.00 (JU)

Pommard les Épenots, Jean-Luc Joillot
1996 £26.93 (JER)

Pommard les Jarollières, Domaine de la
Pousse d'Or **1995** £26.90 (GAU) £35.13
(TW)

Pommard les Poutures, Lejeune **1988**
£25.00 (JU)

Savigny-lès-Beaune les Vergelesses, Bize
1995 £26.44 (TW)

Volnay 1er Cru, Michel Lafarge **1995**
£26.95 (CON) £28.40 (RAE) £37.01 (TW)

Volnay Champans, Marquis d'Angerville
1997 £26.93 (MON) £29.28 (RES)

Volnay Clos des Ducs, Marquis
d'Angerville **1993** £25.95 (ROB) £35.00
(FORT) £35.25 (CAV)

Volnay Clos des Santenots, Prieur **1995**
£26.40 (NA)

Volnay Cuvée Général Muteau, Hospices
de Beaune **1996** £25.46 (RAE)

Volnay les Angles, Domaine Boillot **1990**
£25.00 (FLE)

Volnay les Caillerets, Marquis d'Angerville
1993 £27.00 (JU) £36.72 (CAV)

Volnay Santenots Lafon **1994** £27.03 (FLE)

Volnay Taillepieds, Marquis d'Angerville
1995 £26.00 (JU) £31.82 (CAV)

Vosne-Romanée Cacheux **1995** £26.95
(PHI)

Vosne-Romanée Gros Frère et Soeur
1988 £26.00 (JU)

Vosne-Romanée Jacqueline Jayer **1987**
£25.50 (GAU)

Vosne-Romanée les Chaumes, Rion **1992**
£25.00 (MV)

£27.50 → £29.99

Beaune Clos des Fèves, Chanson **1990**
£29.95 (DI)

Beaune Clos des Mouches, Drouhin **1991**
£27.95 (ROB)

Beaune Teurons, Leroy **1980** £29.00 (RES)

Blagny la Pièce sous le Bois, Matrot **1991**
£28.08 (TW)

Chambolle-Musigny de Vogüé **1996** £29.95
(DI) £46.41 (TW) £48.47 (CAV) £59.00 (RES)

Chambolle-Musigny les Amoureuses,
Joseph Drouhin **1987** £28.79 (REI)

Please remember that
Oz Clarke's Wine Guide
*is a price guide and not a
price list. It is not meant to
replace up-to-date
merchants' lists.*

Chambolle-Musigny les Feusselottes, Georges Mugneret **1996** £29.00 (LEA)

Chambolle-Musigny Georges Lignier **1983** £28.00 (CRO)

Charmes-Chambertin Perrot-Minot **1996** £29.95 (WAT) £33.50 (CON)

Clos de la Roche Armand Rousseau **1991** £29.38 (RIP) £32.70 (FA) £35.00 (ROB)

Clos de Vougeot Hudelot-Noëllat **1994** £29.20 (SOM)

Corton Clos de la Vigne au Saint, Latour **1989** £28.20 (WY)

Corton Clos du Roi, Dubreuil-Fontaine **1993** £27.81 (BY)

Corton Grancey, Latour **1993** £29.26 (PEN) £33.00 (FORT) £33.50 (STA)

Corton Grancey, Latour **1989** £28.69 (JON)

Corton Viénot **1971** £28.79 (REI)

Échézeaux Engel **1994** £29.50 (CON) £30.00 (MV)

Échézeaux Mugneret **1997** £28.50 (BAN)

Gevrey-Chambertin Armand Rousseau **1993** £28.79 (REI)

Gevrey-Chambertin Cazetiers, Bruno Clair **1994** £28.00 (JU) £31.00 (TAN)

Gevrey-Chambertin Champeaux, Denis Mortet **1994** £27.95 (RAE)

Gevrey-Chambertin Clos St-Jacques, Fourrier **1995** £29.50 (BAL)

Gevrey-Chambertin Claude Dugat **1994** £28.95 (RES)

Gevrey-Chambertin la Combe aux Moines, Faiveley **1993** £29.99 (POR)

Gevrey-Chambertin Lavaux-St-Jacques, Maume **1995** £27.50 (BAL)

Gevrey-Chambertin les Corbeaux, Bachelet **1995** £29.00 (MV)

Morey-St-Denis Clos de la Bussière, Domaine Roumier **1996** £29.77 (FA)

Morey-St-Denis Cuvée des Grives, Ponsot **1993** £29.14 (NO)

Nuits-St-Georges Clos des Argillières, Rion **1988** £29.40 (GAU)

Nuits-St-Georges les Argillières, Dubois **1996** £27.75 (VIN)

Nuits-St-Georges les Cailles, Robert Chevillon **1993** £27.73 (WT)

Nuits-St-Georges les Chaignots, Robert Chevillon **1996** £29.16 (WT)

Nuits-St-Georges les Perrières, Robert Chevillon **1993** £28.05 (WT) £32.95 (ROB)

Nuits-St-Georges les Porets St-Georges, Faiveley **1996** £29.10 (HAH)

Nuits-St-Georges les Roncières, Robert Chevillon **1996** £27.73 (WT)

Nuits-St-Georges les Vaucrains, Robert Chevillon **1996** £27.50 (FORT) £30.51 (WT)

Nuits-St-Georges les Vaucrains, Gouges **1997** £28.89 (MON)

Nuits-St-Georges Vignes Rondes, Rion **1988** £28.50 (GAU)

Pommard Boigelot **1990** £29.95 (ROB)

Pommard Clos des Épeneaux, Armand **1994** £29.00 (MV) £34.66 (TW)

Pommard les Fremiers, Domaine de Courcel **1995** £27.50 (RES)

Pommard les Jarollières, Domaine de la Pousse d'Or **1993** £29.00 (WS)

Pommard les Saucilles, Jean-Marc Boillot **1996** £28.20 (DOM)

Pommard Pezerolles, Domaine de Montille **1993** £28.95 (HAH)

Volnay 1er Cru, Michel Lafarge **1997** £28.95 (GAU)

Volnay Clos de la Bousse d'Or, Domaine de la Pousse d'Or **1996** £28.95 (CON) £29.70 (TAN) £32.70 (FA) £34.02 (TW)

Volnay Clos de la Bousse d'Or, Domaine de la Pousse d'Or **1991** £28.50 (DI)

Volnay Frémiets, Marquis d'Angerville **1995** £28.30 (FA)

Volnay les Caillerets, Clos des 60 Ouvrées, Domaine de la Pousse d'Or **1996** £29.77 (FA) £29.96 (TW)

Volnay les Caillerets, Clos des 60 Ouvrées, Domaine de la Pousse d'Or **1995** £27.95 (CON) £31.49 (TW)

Volnay les Caillerets, Clos des 60 Ouvrées, Domaine de la Pousse d'Or **1993** £28.79 (FA) £30.00 (WS)

Volnay les Caillerets, Domaine de la Pousse d'Or **1996** £27.96 (LAY)

Volnay Michel Lafarge **1995** £28.40 (RAE)

Volnay Santenots Lafon **1996** £29.00 (AD)

Vosne-Romanée Confuron-Cotétidot **1990** £28.79 (YOU)

Vosne-Romanée les Beaux Monts, Domaine Rion **1994** £29.00 (MV)

Vosne-Romanée les Brulées, Clavelier **1996** £29.00 (RES)

Vosne-Romanée les Chaumes, Arnoux **1992** £29.50 (FORT)

Vosne-Romanée les Malconsorts, Lamarche **1996** £27.80 (RAE)

Vosne-Romanée les Orveaux, Mongeard-Mugneret **1996** £28.89 (JER)

Vosne-Romanée Rion **1989** £29.95 (ROB)

£30.00 → £34.99

Beaune Grèves, Michel Lafarge 1993 £32.31 (REI) £32.55 (HAH) £37.50 (RAE)
Beaune Grèves Vigne de l'Enfant Jesus, Bouchard Père 1996 £34.00 (BAL)
Beaune Grèves Vigne de l'Enfant Jesus, Bouchard Père 1988 £32.00 (JU)
Beaune Grèves Vigne de l'Enfant Jesus, Bouchard Père 1971 £30.75 (FA)
Bonnes-Mares Roumier 1994 £34.52 (GW) £44.70 (TAN)

Chambolle-Musigny de Vogüé 1995 £32.37 (REI) £38.58 (FA)
Chambolle-Musigny la Combe d'Orveaux, Clavelier 1997 £34.17 (RES)
Chambolle-Musigny les Cras, Ghislaine Barthod 1997 £30.26 (RES)
Chambolle-Musigny les Fuées, Ghislaine Barthod 1995 £32.00 (JU)
Chambolle-Musigny Domaine Roumier 1993 £33.95 (ROB)
Chambolle-Musigny les Charmes, Christian Clerget 1997 £33.80 (PLAY)
Charmes-Chambertin Armand Rousseau 1994 £34.00 (JU) £55.00 (UB)
Charmes-Chambertin Armand Rousseau 1991 £32.50 (ROB)
Charmes-Chambertin Bachelet 1991 £31.72 (RIP)
Clos de la Roche Ponsot 1992 £30.75 (FA)
Clos de Vougeot Georges Mugneret 1997 £34.50 (BAN)
Clos de Vougeot Grivot 1996 £30.75 (SOM) £44.96 (LAY)
Clos de Vougeot Roumier 1994 £30.53 (GW) £40.40 (TAN)
Corton Bouchard Père 1996 £34.00 (BAL)
Corton Bouchard Père 1995 £33.00 (COC)
Corton Bouchard Père 1971 £33.68 (FA)
Corton-Bressandes Chandon de Briailles 1997 £30.26 (RES)
Corton-Bressandes Chandon de Briailles 1993 £33.49 (REI) £33.60 (HAH)
Corton Clos des Cortons, Faiveley 1991 £30.70 (FLE)

Corton Grancey, Latour 1992 £32.83 (PLAY)
Corton Perrières, Juillot 1995 £32.31 (DOM)
Corton Tollot-Beaut 1995 £32.31 (DOM)
Échézeaux Jacqueline Jayer 1984 £34.66 (REI) £38.50 (BALL)
Échézeaux Lamarche 1996 £30.45 (RAE)
Gevrey-Chambertin Clos de Fonteny, Bruno Clair 1995 £30.00 (JU)
Gevrey-Chambertin Lavaux-St-Jacques, Dugat 1994 £34.50 (ROB)
Gevrey-Chambertin Denis Mortet 1995 £31.82 (CAV)
Mazis-Chambertin Maume 1996 £33.68 (RAE) £43.00 (BAL)
Morey-St-Denis Clos des Lambrays, Domaine des Lambrays 1985 £30.75 (FA)
Morey-St-Denis Dujac 1995 £32.00 (UB) £33.49 (REI)
Nuits-St-Georges aux Cras, Clavelier 1997 £33.19 (RES)
Nuits-St-Georges Clos des Argillières, Rion 1995 £33.00 (MV)
Nuits-St-Georges Haut Pruliers, Rion 1993 £33.00 (MV)
Nuits-St-Georges Georges & Henri Jayer 1995 £30.00 (JU)
Nuits-St-Georges Leroy 1976 £34.66 (REI)
Nuits-St-Georges les Cailles, Robert Chevillon 1996 £30.51 (WT)
Nuits-St-Georges les Chaignots, Michelot 1989 £31.03 (NO)
Nuits-St-Georges les Porets, Michelot 1992 £30.00 (FORT)
Nuits-St-Georges les Pruliers, Gouges 1993 £30.00 (JON)
Nuits-St-Georges les St-Georges, Robert Chevillon 1996 £31.20 (WT)
Nuits-St-Georges les St-Georges, Gouges 1997 £31.82 (MON) £32.70 (RES)
Nuits-St-Georges Vignes Rondes, Rion 1995 £33.00 (MV)
Pommard Clos des Épeneaux, Armand 1995 £30.00 (CON) £35.19 (TW)
Pommard Grand Clos des Épenots, Domaine de Courcel 1996 £32.00 (RES)
Pommard les Épenots, Armand 1997 £32.95 (GAU)
Pommard les Jarollières, Domaine de la Pousse d'Or 1992 £33.95 (ROB)
Pommard Rugiens, Domaine de Courcel 1995 £33.00 (RES)
Ruchottes-Chambertin Domaine Mugneret 1997 £34.50 (BAN)

Ruchottes-Chambertin Domaine
   Mugneret **1994** £31.75 (HAH)
Volnay Ier Cru, Michel Lafarge **1996**
   £30.00 (CON)
Volnay Clos de la Bousse d'Or, Domaine
   de la Pousse d'Or **1995** £30.75 (FA)
   £39.36 (TW)
Volnay Clos des Chênes, Michel Lafarge
   1994 £32.90 (GAU) £34.95 (RAE)
Volnay Clos des Chênes, Michel Lafarge
   1992 £35.95 (BALL) £39.95 (ROB)
Volnay Clos des Chênes, Michel Lafarge
   1991 £34.95 (RAE) £38.77 (RIP)
Volnay Clos des Ducs, Marquis
   d'Angerville **1997** £34.27 (MON)
Volnay Clos du Château des Ducs,
   Lafarge **1995** £34.66 (REI)
Volnay Clos du Château des Ducs,
   Lafarge **1994** £31.55 (HAH) £32.90
   (GAU) £42.07 (TW)
Volnay les Caillerets, Domaine de la
   Pousse d'Or **1991** £32.31 (TW)
Volnay Santenots-du-Milieu, Lafon **1994**
   £30.00 (JU)
Volnay Taillepieds, Marquis d'Angerville
   1997 £31.33 (MON) £33.19 (RES)
Vosne-Romanée Cacheux **1990** £31.00
   (CRO)
Vosne-Romanée les Beaux Monts,
   Clavelier **1995** £31.29 (NI)
Vosne-Romanée les Beaux Monts,
   Domaine Rion **1995** £31.28 (FLE)
Vosne-Romanée les Brulées, Engel **1991**
   £31.14 (TW)
Vosne-Romanée les Chaumes, Arnoux
   1997 £30.84 (MON) £35.64 (RES)
Vosne-Romanée les Suchots, Hudelot-
   Noëllat **1995** £31.50 (ROB)

£35.00 → £39.99

Beaune Cuvée Brunet, Latour **1990**
   £35.25 (PEN)
Beaune Grèves, Michel Lafarge **1996**
   £36.00 (CON)
Bonnes-Mares Drouhin-Laroze **1996**
   £35.50 (HAH)
Chambertin Trapet **1985** £39.00 (YOU)
Chambolle-Musigny les Charmes,
   Georges Clerget **1985** £35.00 (JU)
Chambolle-Musigny les Cras, Roumier
   1996 £35.64 (FA)
Clos de la Roche Armand Rousseau **1996**
   £38.58 (FA) £55.00 (FORT)
Clos de Vougeot Château de la Tour
   1995 £38.38 (HA)

Clos de Vougeot Drouhin **1989** £38.52
   (PEN) £52.88 (REI)
Clos de Vougeot Georges Mugneret
   1994 £36.86 (LAY)
Clos de Vougeot Grand Cru, Prieur **1996**
   £39.99 (YOU)
Clos de Vougeot Méo-Camuzet **1994**
   £36.62 (FA) £42.00 (RAE) £49.50 (NA)
Corton Bonneau du Martray **1995** £36.00
   (JU)
Corton Bouchard Père **1989** £35.00 (ROB)
Corton Maréchaudes, Chandon de
   Briailles **1986** £38.78 (TW)
Corton Viénot **1967** £39.00 (CRO)
Échézeaux Jacqueline Jayer **1987** £38.19
   (REI) £47.75 (BER)
Échézeaux Georges & Henri Jayer **1987**
   £36.00 (JU)
Échézeaux Emmanuel Rouget **1987**
   £36.00 (JU) £54.64 (REI)
Gevrey-Chambertin Combottes, Dujac
   1994 £36.00 (JU) £42.89 (TW)
Gevrey-Chambertin Domaine des
   Varoilles **1969** £39.00 (YOU)
Griotte-Chambertin Esmonin **1994**
   £35.50 (ROB)
Latricières-Chambertin Faiveley **1995**
   £38.95 (DI)
Latricières-Chambertin Trapet **1995**
   £38.68 (HA) £39.56 (FA)
Mazis-Chambertin Armand Rousseau
   1996 £36.62 (FA)
Mazis-Chambertin Faiveley **1992** £36.70
   (HAH)
Morey-St-Denis Clos des Lambrays,
   Domaine des Lambrays **1996** £39.50
   (LEA) £40.70 (HAH)
Nuits-St-Georges Clos de l'Arlot,
   Domaine de l'Arlot **1989** £35.01 (TW)
Nuits-St-Georges Haut-Poiret, Jayer-
   Gilles **1995** £39.00 (JU)
Nuits-St-Georges les Chaignots, Georges
   Mugneret **1993** £38.95 (NO)
Nuits-St-Georges les Murgers, Méo-
   Camuzet **1994** £35.64 (FA) £47.85 (BER)
Nuits-St-Georges les Vaucrains, Gouges
   1985 £37.01 (REI)
Pommard Grand Clos des Épenots,
   Domaine de Courcel **1989** £38.25 (ROB)
Pommard les Jarollières, Domaine de la
   Pousse d'Or **1989** £36.50 (ROB)
Ruchottes-Chambertin Armand Rousseau
   1991 £38.50 (ROB)
Ruchottes-Chambertin Domaine
   Mugneret **1992** £36.50 (LEA)

Ruchottes-Chambertin Roumier 1992
£38.70 (HAH)

Volnay Clos de la Bousse d'Or, Domaine
de la Pousse d'Or 1993 £39.25 (ROB)

Volnay Clos du Château des Ducs,
Lafarge 1996 £38.95 (CON)

Volnay les Caillerets, Domaine de la
Pousse d'Or 1990 £37.99 (YOU)

Volnay Santenots Lafon 1993 £37.01 (REI)
£45.00 (CRO)

Volnay Santenots Matrot 1989 £35.25 (TW)

Vosne-Romanée aux Reignots, Bouchard
Père 1996 £36.50 (BAL)

Vosne-Romanée Rion 1990 £37.00 (CRO)

£40.00 → £49.99

Beaune Clos des Mouches, Drouhin 1985
£40.54 (REI)

Bonnes-Mares de Vogüé 1994 £49.00 (DI)
£70.00 (FORT)

Bonnes-Mares Drouhin 1970 £49.00 (UB)

Bonnes-Mares Drouhin-Laroze 1970
£42.01 (REI)

Bonnes-Mares Dujac 1994 £42.95 (LAY)

Bonnes-Mares Groffier 1992 £46.51 (JER)

Bonnes-Mares Jadot 1996 £42.30 (REI)
£60.12 (FA)

Bonnes-Mares Jadot 1993 £44.06 (CAV)

Bonnes-Mares Georges Lignier 1988
£47.00 (JU)

Bonnes-Mares Roumier 1992 £40.52 (GW)

Chambertin Clos-de-Bèze, Bruno Clair
1996 £46.50 (SOM)

Chambertin Clos-de-Bèze, Faiveley 1992
£49.99 (POR)

Chambertin Clos-de-Bèze, Remoissenet
1992 £44.20 (AV)

Chambertin Trapet 1993 £42.50 (PIP)
Chambertin Trapet 1989 £49.35 (TW)

Chambolle-Musigny les Amoureuses, de
Vogüé 1989 £48.92 (NO)

Chambolle-Musigny les Amoureuses,
Roumier 1997 £48.37 (RES)

Chapelle-Chambertin Ponsot 1996
£46.90 (FA) £62.84 (LAY) £97.43 (CAV)

Chapelle-Chambertin Trapet 1996
£40.54 (FA)

Charmes-Chambertin Armand Rousseau
1995 £42.50 (FA)

Charmes-Chambertin Dujac 1992 £42.89
(REI)

Charmes-Chambertin Faiveley 1988
£43.87 (NO)

Charmes-Chambertin Jean Raphet 1996
£49.50 (BEN)

Clos de la Roche Armand Rousseau 1995
£42.50 (FA) £45.24 (REI)

Clos de la Roche Armand Rousseau 1993
£42.00 (JU)

Clos de la Roche Dujac 1991 £42.30 (RIP)

Clos de la Roche Jean Raphet 1996
£49.50 (BEN)

Clos de Tart Mommessin 1992 £46.86
(PLAY)

Clos de Vougeot Arnoux 1997 £48.47
(MON)

Clos de Vougeot Confuron-Cotétidot
1996 £40.95 (LEA)

Clos de Vougeot Drouhin 1995 £46.00
(BALL)

Clos de Vougeot Engel 1997 £47.88 (RES)

Clos de Vougeot Engel 1995 £45.00
(CON) £52.88 (TW) £55.00 (FORT)

Clos de Vougeot Engel 1991 £48.00
(GAU) £58.75 (TW)

Clos de Vougeot Georges Mugneret
1992 £45.00 (LEA)

Clos de Vougeot Grivot 1997 £40.05 (RES)

Clos de Vougeot Grivot 1990 £42.50 (FA)

Clos de Vougeot Hudelot-Noëllat 1997
£42.99 (RES)

Clos de Vougeot Jean Gros 1997 £49.84
(RES)

Clos de Vougeot Denis Mortet 1993
£42.50 (RAE)

Clos de Vougeot Musigni, Gros Frère et
Soeur 1988 £46.00 (JU)

Corton Bonneau du Martray 1996 £40.05
(HAH)

Corton Bouchard Père 1988 £46.99 (YOU)

Corton-Bressandes Tollot-Beaut 1990
£45.00 (ROB)

Corton-Bressandes Tollot-Beaut 1983
£40.00 (JU)

Corton Clos des Cortons, Faiveley 1995
£45.83 (PEN) £48.25 (HAH)

Corton Clos des Cortons, Faiveley 1989
£47.50 (CON)

Corton Méo-Camuzet 1991 £45.00 (JU)

Corton Tollot-Beaut 1991 £45.00 (RAE)

- Wines are listed in A–Z
  order within each price
  band.
- For each wine, vintages are
  listed in descending order.
- Each vintage of any wine
  appears only once.

Échézeaux Drouhin **1995** £49.50 (BEN)

Échézeaux Engel **1988** £46.00 (CRO)

Échézeaux Gros **1997** £44.94 (RES)

Échézeaux Henri Jayer **1992** £42.00 (RAE)

Échézeaux Georges & Henri Jayer **1991** £43.00 (JU)

Gevrey-Chambertin Bouchard Père **1961** £44.06 (REI)

Gevrey-Chambertin Clos des Varoilles, Domaine des Varoilles **1978** £44.00 (CRO)

Gevrey-Chambertin Clos St-Jacques, Armand Rousseau **1992** £41.00 (JU)

Gevrey-Chambertin Lavaux-St-Jacques, Armand Rousseau **1982** £40.54 (REI)

Grands-Échézeaux Engel **1994** £47.50 (CON)

Grands-Échézeaux Gros Frère et Soeur **1988** £48.00 (JU)

Grands-Échézeaux Mongeard-Mugneret **1994** £43.08 (JER)

Latricières-Chambertin Faiveley **1992** £40.80 (WRI)

Latricières-Chambertin Trapet **1992** £42.89 (TW)

Mazis-Chambertin Armand Rousseau **1993** £47.00 (REI)

Mazis-Chambertin Armand Rousseau **1989** £42.00 (CRO)

Mazis-Chambertin Faiveley **1989** £41.13 (REI)

Mazis-Chambertin Roty **1994** £48.35 (CB)

Morey-St-Denis Clos des Ormes, Faiveley **1976** £41.13 (TW)

Musigny de Vogüé **1976** £43.00 (YOU)

Nuits-St-Georges Clos de l'Arlot, Domaine de l'Arlot **1990** £42.76 (NO)

Nuits-St-Georges Leroy **1985** £43.00 (JU)

Nuits-St-Georges les Chaignots, Robert Chevillon **1989** £43.00 (UB)

Nuits-St-Georges Viénot **1978** £47.00 (TW)

Pommard Ampeau **1978** £47.00 (REI)

Pommard Grands Épenots, Gaunoux **1985** £41.61 (CAV)

Pommard les Vignots, Leroy **1997** £47.88 (RES)

Pommard Pezerolles, Domaine de Montille **1989** £43.95 (ROB)

Pommard Rugiens, Domaine de Courcel **1993** £42.50 (FORT)

Ruchottes-Chambertin Armand Rousseau **1995** £46.41 (FA)

Ruchottes-Chambertin Clos des Ruchottes, Armand Rousseau **1993** £42.00 (JU) £49.94 (REI)

Ruchottes-Chambertin Roumier **1994** £46.00 (MV)

Volnay Clos de la Bousse d'Or, Domaine de la Pousse d'Or **1990** £47.59 (TW)

Volnay Clos de la Bousse d'Or, Domaine de la Pousse d'Or **1989** £41.13 (REI)

Volnay Clos de la Bousse d'Or, Domaine de la Pousse d'Or **1985** £47.00 (REI)

Volnay Clos des Ducs, Marquis d'Angerville **1978** £42.50 (FA)

Volnay Clos du Château des Ducs, Lafarge **1991** £40.83 (TW)

Volnay Santenots Ampeau **1978** £46.41 (REI)

Vosne-Romanée Cros Parantoux Emmanuel Rouget **1994** £48.00 (JU)

Vosne-Romanée Cros Parantoux Emmanuel Rouget **1991** £41.00 (JU)

Vosne-Romanée les Chaumes, Méo-Camuzet **1996** £45.43 (FA)

£50.00 → £59.99

Bonnes-Mares de Vogüé **1992** £56.99 (REI) £59.00 (DI) £72.65 (RAE)

Bonnes-Mares Roumier **1997** £57.67 (RES)

Chambertin Armand Rousseau **1979** £56.99 (REI)

Chambertin Clos-de-Bèze, Armand Rousseau **1992** £52.00 (JU) £60.00 (FORT)

Chambertin Clos-de-Bèze, Bruno Clair **1995** £55.00 (JU)

Chambertin Clos-de-Bèze, Damoy **1997** £55.22 (RES)

Chambertin Clos-de-Bèze, Drouhin **1995** £54.25 (FA) £65.50 (BEN)

Chambertin Clos-de-Bèze, Jadot **1993** £51.11 (REI) £77.84 (CAV)

Chambolle-Musigny les Gruenchers, Dujac **1995** £57.46 (TW)

Clos de la Roche Georges Lignier **1985** £55.00 (JU)

Clos de Vougeot Grivot **1995** £50.00 (YOU)

Clos de Vougeot Grivot **1982** £54.00 (CRO)

Clos de Vougeot Latour **1990** £56.40 (PEN)

Clos de Vougeot Méo-Camuzet **1995** £52.29 (FA)

Clos St-Denis Dujac **1994** £52.29 (TW)

Corton Chandon de Briailles **1992** £58.75 (TW)

Corton Méo-Camuzet **1995** £55.22 (FA)

Échézeaux Arnoux **1997** £50.92 (MON)

Échézeaux Domaine de la Romanée-Conti **1992** £56.99 (REI)

Échézeaux Dujac **1992** £51.41 (REI)

Échézeaux Jayer-Gilles **1994** £54.00 (JU)

Gevrey-Chambertin Clos St-Jacques, Armand Rousseau **1995** £58.16 (FA)

Gevrey-Chambertin Combottes, Dujac **1995** £52.88 (TW)

La Grande Rue François Lamarche **1976** £52.88 (REI)

Grands-Échézeaux Drouhin **1993** £56.99 (REI)

Grands-Échézeaux Engel **1997** £54.74 (RES)

Latricières-Chambertin Faiveley **1982** £52.88 (TW)

Mazis-Chambertin Faiveley **1995** £54.00 (BER)

Musigny Vieilles Vignes, de Vogüé **1987** £56.30 (JER) £67.01 (RAE)

Musigny Vieilles Vignes, de Vogüé **1984** £52.88 (CAV)

Musigny Vieilles Vignes, de Vogüé **1983** £55.88 (NO)

Nuits-St-Georges aux Boudots, Leroy **1992** £50.33 (FA)

Nuits-St-Georges aux Lavières, Leroy **1988** £59.00 (ROB)

Nuits-St-Georges Clos de la Maréchale, Faiveley **1976** £52.88 (TW)

Nuits-St-Georges les St-Georges, Faiveley **1990** £59.90 (DI)

Nuits-St-Georges Richemone, Pernin-Rossin **1985** £59.00 (CRO)

Richebourg Gros Frère et Soeur **1987** £55.00 (JU)

Romanée-St-Vivant Noëllat **1970** £55.81 (REI)

Volnay Champans, Marquis d'Angerville **1988** £58.00 (UB)

Vosne-Romanée Cros Parantoux, Méo-Camuzet **1992** £52.00 (JU)

Vosne-Romanée les Beaux Monts, Leroy **1992** £50.33 (FA) £79.00 (JU)

£60.00 → £79.99

Beaune Clos du Roi, Chanson **1934** £64.63 (REI)

Bonnes-Mares de Vogüé **1996** £72.00 (DI) £90.87 (RAE) £99.29 (FA) £107.22 (CAV)

Bonnes-Mares de Vogüé **1989** £60.00 (CRO)

Chambertin Clos-de-Bèze, Armand Rousseau **1995** £61.00 (TAN) £75.00 (FORT)

Chambertin Clos-de-Bèze, Faiveley **1993** £77.60 (HAH) £82.25 (RIP)

Chambertin Clos-de-Bèze, Jadot **1985** £65.00 (JU)

Chambolle-Musigny de Vogüé **1978** £61.69 (REI)

Chambolle-Musigny les Amoureuses, de Vogüé **1996** £72.00 (DI) £90.87 (RAE)

Chambolle-Musigny les Fremières, Leroy **1997** £67.46 (RES)

Charmes-Chambertin Dujac **1991** £64.63 (TW)

Clos de la Roche Dujac **1988** £76.38 (REI)

Clos de la Roche Faiveley **1985** £60.00 (JU)

Clos de Tart Mommessin **1957** £70.50 (CAV)

Clos de Vougeot Drouhin **1990** £64.63 (PEN)

Clos de Vougeot Faiveley **1979** £70.50 (TW)

Clos de Vougeot Roumier **1996** £65.02 (FA)

Clos St-Denis Georges Lignier **1985** £60.00 (CRO)

Gevrey-Chambertin Clos St-Jacques, Armand Rousseau **1993** £72.00 (NO)

La Grand Rue François Lamarche **1995** £68.05 (JER)

Griotte-Chambertin Domaine des Chezeaux **1995** £74.81 (FA)

Griotte-Chambertin Ponsot **1996** £71.87 (FA) £97.43 (CAV)

Latricières-Chambertin Ponsot **1993** £71.87 (FA)

Mazis-Chambertin Faiveley **1979** £76.38 (TW)

Morey-St-Denis Clos des Lambrays, Domaine des Lambrays **1951** £65.50 (UB)

Musigny Georges Roumier **1997** £78.24 (RES)

Musigny Prieur **1996** £72.99 (YOU)

Musigny Vieilles Vignes, de Vogüé **1994** £61.69 (REI) £73.60 (TAN)

Nuits-St-Georges aux Allots, Leroy **1995** £71.87 (FA)

Nuits-St-Georges Viénot **1949** £67.56 (REI)

Pommard Clos de la Commaraine, Jaboulet-Vercherre **1955** £75.00 (ROB)

Pommard Clos Micault, Parent **1978** £75.00 (CRO)

Richebourg Gros Frère et Soeur **1991** £60.12 (FA)

Richebourg Mongeard-Mugneret 1991
£70.50 (CAV)

Romanée-St-Vivant Domaine de l'Arlot
1992 £64.63 (TW)

Romanée-St-Vivant Domaine de la
Romanée-Conti 1982 £70.00 (CRO)
£146.88 (CAV)

Romanée-St-Vivant les Quatres Journaux,
Latour 1989 £64.63 (WY)

Savigny-lès-Beaune Chauvenet 1996
£67.95 (FA)

Volnay Santenots Lafon 1983 £60.00 (CRO)

Vosne-Romanée Remoissenet 1953
£70.50 (REI)

Vougeot Clos de la Perrière, Bertagna
1978 £65.00 (CRO)

£80.00 → £99.99

Bonnes-Mares de Vogüé 1985 £84.60 (FA)

Chambertin Clos-de-Bèze, Armand
Rousseau 1996 £95.00 (FORT)

Chambertin Clos-de-Bèze, Armand
Rousseau 1989 £88.13 (REI)

Chambertin Clos-de-Bèze, Armand
Rousseau 1972 £88.13 (FA)

Chambertin Clos-de-Bèze, Jadot 1996
£83.62 (FA)

Chambertin Vieilles Vignes, Trapet 1990
£88.13 (TW)

Clos de Vougeot Faiveley 1978 £82.00
(CRO)

Clos de Vougeot Leroy 1994 £84.60 (FA)

Corton Clos de la Vigne au Saint, Latour
1934 £88.13 (REI)

Échézeaux Domaine de la Romanée-
Conti 1993 £84.60 (FA) £120.00 (ROB)

Échézeaux Mongeard-Mugneret 1985
£99.88 (REI)

Grands-Échézeaux Domaine de la
Romanée-Conti 1994 £85.74 (LAY)

Grands-Échézeaux Domaine de la
Romanée-Conti 1992 £81.55 (CB)

Grands-Échézeaux Mongeard-Mugneret
1985 £99.88 (REI)

Nuits-St-Georges aux Vignerondes, Leroy
1988 £85.00 (JU) £126.31 (TW)

Richebourg Domaine Anne Gros 1994
£86.66 (JER)

Richebourg Hudelot-Noëllat 1997 £94.39
(RES)

Richebourg Mongeard-Mugneret 1989
£88.13 (REI)

La Romanée Domaines du Château de
Vosne-Romanée, Bouchard Père 1993
£81.00 (BER)

La Romanée Domaines du Château de
Vosne-Romanée, Bouchard Père 1979
£99.88 (REI)

Romanée-St-Vivant Domaine de la
Romanée-Conti 1994 £98.65 (LAY)
£114.50 (BER) £135.00 (FORT)

Romanée-St-Vivant Domaine de la
Romanée-Conti 1991 £94.00 (CB)

Vosne-Romanée les Beaux Monts, Leroy
1988 £92.00 (JU) £146.88 (TW)

£100.00 → £149.99

Chambertin Bouchard Père 1926
£111.63 (REI)

Chambertin Ponsot 1995 £123.77 (FA)

Charmes-Chambertin Ponnelle 1971
£146.88 (REI)

Clos de la Roche Vieilles Vignes, Ponsot
1995 £111.63 (CAV)

Clos de Tart Mommessin 1945 £105.00
(ROB)

Clos de Vougeot Leroy 1992 £120.00 (JU)
£125.00 (RES) £232.65 (TW)

Clos St-Denis Dujac 1978 £129.25 (REI)

Échézeaux Arnoux 1993 £122.40 (CAV)

Échézeaux Domaine de la Romanée-
Conti 1982 £105.75 (CAV)

Gevrey-Chambertin Combottes, Leroy
1997 £109.08 (RES)

Gevrey-Chambertin Combottes, Leroy
1995 £118.87 (FA)

Grands-Échézeaux Domaine de la
Romanée-Conti 1993 £111.63 (REI)
£118.87 (FA)

Grands-Échézeaux Domaine de la
Romanée-Conti 1986 £140.00 (UB)

Grands-Échézeaux Domaine de la
Romanée-Conti 1981 £117.50 (CAV)

Musigny Vieilles Vignes, de Vogüé 1996
£105.55 (RAE) £152.75 (TW)

Musigny Vieilles Vignes, de Vogüé 1989
£111.62 (WY)

Nuits-St-Georges aux Boudots, Leroy
1997 £109.08 (RES)

Richebourg Domaine Anne Gros 1989
£113.21 (VIN)

Richebourg Domaine de la Romanée-
Conti 1993 £148.25 (FA) £211.50 (CAV)

Richebourg Domaine de la Romanée-
Conti 1992 £120.00 (BER)

Richebourg Domaine de la Romanée-
Conti 1991 £126.70 (FA) £129.25 (CB)
£135.00 (FORT)

Richebourg Domaine de la Romanée-
Conti 1982 £130.00 (JU)

Richebourg Méo-Camuzet 1994 £118.87
(FA) £150.00 (FORT)
La Romanée Domaines du Château de
Vosne-Romanée, Bouchard Père 1989
£125.00 (COC)
Romanée-St-Vivant Domaine de la
Romanée-Conti 1993 £118.87 (FA)
£150.00 (BEN) £170.38 (REI)
Romanée-St-Vivant Hudelot-Noëllat
1993 £135.00 (RES)
La Tâche Domaine de la Romanée-Conti
1992 £146.88 (REI) £203.03 (VIN)
£220.00 (BER)
La Tâche Domaine de la Romanée-Conti
1982 £141.00 (FA)
La Tâche Domaine de la Romanée-Conti
1973 £142.37 (FA)
Vosne-Romanée les Beaux Monts, Leroy
1997 £109.08 (RES)

£150.00 → £199.99

Corton les Renardes, Leroy 1993
£197.20 (FA)
Échézeaux Domaine de la Romanée-
Conti 1969 £176.25 (CAV)
Échézeaux Henri Jayer 1986 £164.50 (REI)
Grands-Échézeaux Domaine de la
Romanée-Conti 1956 £182.13 (REI)
Musigny de Vogüé 1996 £156.28 (CAV)
£190.00 (RES)
Richebourg Domaine de la Romanée-
Conti 1994 £185.00 (FORT)
Richebourg Domaine de la Romanée-
Conti 1989 £162.93 (FA)
Richebourg Gros Frère et Soeur 1990
£176.25 (CAV)
Romanée-St-Vivant Domaine de la
Romanée-Conti 1976 £155.00 (YOU)
La Tâche Domaine de la Romanée-Conti
1986 £162.93 (FA)
Vosne-Romanée les Beaux Monts, Leroy
1995 £177.62 (FA)

£200.00 → £299.99

Chambertin Leroy 1994 £216.79 (FA)
Grands-Échézeaux Domaine de la
Romanée-Conti 1978 £211.50 (FA)

> • All prices for each wine are
>   listed together in ascending
>   order.
> • Price bands refer to the
>   lowest price for which the
>   wine is available.

Musigny Leroy 1994 £207.00 (FA)
Nuits-St-Georges aux Boudots, Leroy
1993 £260.85 (FA)
Richebourg Domaine de la Romanée-
Conti 1988 £219.69 (NO)
Richebourg Leroy 1997 £246.16 (RES)
Romanée-St-Vivant Domaine de la
Romanée-Conti 1990 £285.90 (JER)
Romanée-St-Vivant Leroy 1997 £246.16
(RES)
La Tâche Domaine de la Romanée-Conti
1995 £221.68 (FA)
La Tâche Domaine de la Romanée-Conti
1969 £290.00 (YOU)

£300.00 → £499.99

Bonnes-Mares Leroy 1993 £353.87 (FA)
Clos de Vougeot Leroy 1993 £411.25 (FA)
Musigny Vieilles Vignes, de Vogüé 1949
£334.88 (REI)
Richebourg Domaine de la Romanée-
Conti 1990 £350.00 (BEN)
Richebourg Domaine de la Romanée-
Conti 1985 £381.87 (CAV)
Richebourg Domaine de la Romanée-
Conti 1978 £487.63 (CAV)
Richebourg Domaine de la Romanée-
Conti 1971 £323.13 (FA)
Richebourg Domaine de la Romanée-
Conti 1961 £323.13 (REI)
La Tâche Domaine de la Romanée-Conti
1985 £395.00 (BEN) £450.00 (SOM)
£569.88 (CAV)
La Tâche Domaine de la Romanée-Conti
1966 £464 13(CAV)

Over £500.00

Clos de la Roche Leroy 1993 £622.75 (FA)
Musigny Vieilles Vignes, de Vogüé 1919
£616.88 (CAV)
Nuits-St-Georges aux Boudots, Leroy
1994 £601.21 (FA)
Richebourg Leroy 1993 £646.25 (FA)
Romanée-Conti Domaine de la Romanée-
Conti 1993 £1,176.37 (FA)
Romanée-Conti Domaine de la Romanée-
Conti 1991 £1,057.50 (FA)
Romanée-Conti Domaine de la Romanée-
Conti 1990 £2,115.00 (FA)
Romanée-Conti Domaine de la Romanée-
Conti 1978 £2,937.50 (CAV)
Romanée-Conti Domaine de la Romanée-
Conti 1961 £2,500.00 (FORT)
La Tâche Domaine de la Romanée-Conti
1978 £528.75 (CAV)

WHITE

Under £10.00

Hautes-Côtes de Nuits Chaley **1997**
£7.16 (STE) £7.95 (NA)
Hautes-Côtes de Nuits Clos du Vignon,
Domaine Thévenot-le Brun **1996** £9.95
(RES)
Meursault Jobard ½ bottle **1988** £9.95 (RAE)
St-Aubin Prudhon **1991** £9.95 (BU)
St-Aubin Gérard Thomas **1996** £9.75
(CON) £11.99 (BO)

£10.00 → £11.99

Auxey-Duresses Olivier Leflaive **1997**
£11.95 (LAY)
Auxey-Duresses Olivier Leflaive **1996**
£10.25 (HAH) £10.93 (CB)
Marsannay Bruno Clair **1995** £11.90 (JU)
£19.50 (CRO)
Marsannay Jadot **1996** £10.49 (UN)
Pernand-Vergelesses Olivier Leflaive
1995 £11.28 (CB)
Pernand-Vergelesses Pavelot **1996** £11.95
(RES)
St-Aubin 1er Cru, Bachelet **1993** £11.95
(RAE) £18.40 (UB)
St-Aubin Prudhon **1995** £11.99 (JON)
St-Romain Buisson **1997** £11.75 (DOM)
St-Romain Sous le Château, Coste-
Caumartin **1996** £11.02 (GW)

£12.00 → £13.99

Auxey-Duresses Chartron et Trebuchet
1996 £12.24 (JER)
Auxey-Duresses Coche-Bizouard **1996**
£12.65 (RAE)
Auxey-Duresses Michel Prunier **1996**
£13.50 (TAN)
Bâtard-Montrachet Olivier Leflaive **1989**
£13.75 (DI)
Marsannay Jadot **1995** £12.99 (BOT)
Meursault Clos du Château, Château de
Meursault **1995** £12.99 (POR)
Monthélie le Champ Fulliot, Garaudet
1996 £13.80 (PIP)
Pernand-Vergelesses Dubreuil-Fontaine
1997 £13.61 (RES)
Pernand-Vergelesses Jacques Germain
1995 £13.25 (AS)
Pernand-Vergelesses Rollin **1993** £12.95
(BALL)
St-Aubin en Remilly, Château de Puligny-
Montrachet **1996** £13.49 (OD)

St-Aubin en Remilly, Hubert Lamy **1996**
£13.84 (LAY) £14.50 (LEA)
St-Aubin Jadot **1995** £12.49 (UN)
St-Aubin Jadot **1994** £13.63 (HA)
St-Aubin la Chatenière, Gerard Thomas
1996 £12.90 (PIP)
St-Romain Sous le Château, Coste-
Caumartin **1995** £12.50 (JU)
Santenay Blanc le St-Jean, Girardin **1995**
£13.80 (NI)
Santenay Clos des Champs des Carafe,
Olivier Père et Fils **1993** £13.50 (HIG)
Savigny-lès-Beaune Camus-Bruchon **1995**
£13.59 (JON) £13.65 (RAE)
Savigny-lès-Beaune les Vermots Dessus,
Girardin **1994** £13.80 (NI)

£14.00 → £15.99

Auxey-Duresses Olivier Leflaive **1995**
£14.00 (CRO)
Hautes-Côtes de Beaune Jayer-Gilles
1995 £15.00 (JU)
Meursault Michelot **1997** £14.99 (OD)
Meursault Michelot **1995** £14.95 (TAN)
£16.95 (AD)
Pernand-Vergelesses Rollin **1994** £14.50
(JU) £15.50 (RAE)
Puligny-Montrachet Carillon **1996** £14.75
(SOM) £20.29 (YOU) £20.79 (STE) £21.00
(WAI) £21.25 (FLE) £21.99 (WR)
Puligny-Montrachet Clavoillon, Chavy
1994 £15.75 (SOM)
Puligny-Montrachet Domaine Gérard
Chavy **1996** £15.50 (PIP) £19.95 (PLAY)
Puligny-Montrachet Drouhin **1994** £15.89
(NI) £17.80 (CRO)
St-Aubin la Chatenière, Chartron et
Trébuchet **1995** £14.49 (JER)
St-Aubin la Pucelle, Lamy-Pillot **1996**
£14.82 (BY) £14.99 (WR)
Santenay Blanc le St-Jean, Girardin **1996**
£14.10 (TAN)
Santenay le Biévaux, Olivier Père et Fils
1995 £15.55 (BAN)
Savigny-lès-Beaune Montchenevoy,
Javillier **1996** £15.95 (LAY) £16.70 (BAN)

£16.00 → £17.99

Chassagne-Montrachet Bachelet **1995**
£16.95 (BALL)
Chassagne-Montrachet Colin-Deleger
1996 £17.55 (NEZ)
Chassagne-Montrachet en Pimont,
Château de Chassagne-Montrachet
1995 £17.14 (FRI)

Chassagne-Montrachet Pillot **1997**
£16.95 (LEA) £18.60 (MON)
Hautes-Côtes de Nuits Jayer-Gilles **1995**
£17.50 (JU)
Meursault Clos du Cromin, Javillier **1997**
£17.25 (BAN)
Meursault Coche-Bizouard **1996** £16.65
(RAE)
Meursault Henri Germain **1995** £17.30 (AD)
Meursault Jadot **1995** £17.00 (CRO)
£21.99 (POR)
Meursault les Tillets, Javillier **1997** £17.25
(BAN) £22.91 (RES) £25.95 (ELL)
Meursault Matrot **1994** £17.95 (BALL)
£18.69 (ROS)
Meursault Matrot **1993** £17.14 (ELL)
£20.95 (GAU) £21.75 (BER)
Meursault sous la Velle, Domaine
Michelot **1992** £17.50 (BALL)
Pernand-Vergelesses Rollin **1995** £16.00
(JU)
Puligny-Montrachet Bouchard Père **1996**
£17.59 (BY) £21.98 (COC)
Puligny-Montrachet Clerc **1997** £16.95
(BAN)
Puligny-Montrachet Pillot **1996** £17.50
(LEA) £23.00 (RES)
St-Aubin Combe, Pierre Morey **1996**
£16.50 (TAN)
St-Aubin le Charmois, Jean-Marc Morey
1997 £17.04 (RES)
Santenay le Biévaux, Olivier Père et Fils
1993 £16.50 (HIG)

£18.00 → £19.99

Chassagne-Montrachet Domaine Guy
Amiot **1996** £19.95 (BAL)
Chassagne-Montrachet Latour **1996**
£19.50 (FORT) £19.95 (HED) £21.02 (PLAY)
Chassagne-Montrachet les Baudines,
Bernard Morey **1997** £19.75 (BAN)
Chassagne-Montrachet les Houillères,
Olivier Leflaive **1997** £19.95 (LAY)
Chassagne-Montrachet Sauzet **1993**
£18.95 (BALL)
Meursault-Blagny Latour **1996** £18.51 (FA)
£22.95 (FORT) £25.00 (BU) £25.95 (STA)
Meursault-Blagny Thomas **1996** £18.50
(CON)
Meursault Bouchard Père **1997** £19.95
(WAI)
Meursault Clos de la Barre, Monnier
1997 £18.19 (BY)
Meursault Clos St Felix, Domaine
Michelot **1995** £19.95 (RES)

Meursault Albert Grivault **1995** £18.00 (JU)
Meursault Jobard **1994** £18.47 (HA)
Meursault Latour **1996** £19.99 (MAJ)
£20.62 (PLAY)
Meursault Latour **1995** £18.30 (COC)
£20.99 (NLW)
Meursault les Clous, Javillier **1997** £18.75
(BAN)
Meursault les Grands Charrons, Domaine
Michelot **1995** £18.80 (FLE)
Meursault les Grands Charrons, Domaine
Michelot **1993** £18.50 (BALL)
Meursault les Narvaux, Vincent Girardin
1996 £18.95 (AD) £20.95 (RES)
Meursault les Tillets, Javillier **1996** £18.80
(SOM)
Meursault Michelot-Buisson **1996** £18.63
(STE) £20.70 (NA)
Meursault Olivier Leflaive **1994** £18.55
(DI) £22.91 (TW)
Meursault sous la Velle, Charles et Remi
Jobard **1996** £18.95 (LEA)
Pernand-Vergelesses les Caradeux,
Chanson **1996** £19.95 (DI)
Puligny-Montrachet Carillon **1994** £18.95
(NI)
Puligny-Montrachet Jadot **1995** £18.99
(VIC) £18.99 (THR) £18.99 (BOT)
Puligny-Montrachet la Garenne, Thomas
1996 £19.50 (CON)
Puligny-Montrachet Latour **1995** £18.00
(COC)
Puligny-Montrachet les Charmes, Chavy
1997 £18.50 (MV) £19.50 (BU)
Puligny-Montrachet les Charmes, Chavy
1996 £19.10 (FLE)
Puligny-Montrachet les Folatières, Chavy
1996 £18.85 (SOM) £20.50 (PIP)
Puligny-Montrachet Sous les Puits,
Bachelet **1996** £19.88 (RAE)

£20.00 → £24.99

Chassagne-Montrachet Clos St Jean,
Amiot **1997** £23.50 (BAN) £27.00 (SOM)
Chassagne-Montrachet Colin-Deléger
1995 £21.95 (LAY)

> *Please remember that*
> **Oz Clarke's Wine Guide**
> *is a price **guide** and not a*
> *price **list**. It is not meant to*
> *replace up-to-date*
> *merchants' lists.*

Chassagne-Montrachet Drouhin 1990
£23.00 (VA)

Chassagne-Montrachet en Pimont,
Château de Chassagne-Montrachet
1993 £22.25 (ROB)

Chassagne-Montrachet la Boudriotte,
Gagnard-Delagrange 1997 £24.48 (MON)

Chassagne-Montrachet la Boudriotte,
Gagnard-Delagrange 1995 £24.30 (BAN)

Chassagne-Montrachet la Maltroie,
Fontaine-Gagnard 1996 £23.50 (JER)

Chassagne-Montrachet les Caillerets,
Morey-Coffinet 1996 £21.36 (RAE)

Chassagne-Montrachet les Chenevottes,
Colin-Deleger 1994 £24.48 (CAV)

Chassagne-Montrachet les Macherelles,
Amiot 1996 £24.50 (BAL) £25.50 (LEA)

Chassagne-Montrachet les Masures, Jean
Noël Gagnard 1995 £21.50 (JU)

Chassagne-Montrachet les Vergers,
Fontaine-Gagnard 1996 £23.50 (JER)

Chassagne-Montrachet les Vergers, J-M
Pillot 1995 £24.39 (NI)

Chassagne-Montrachet Morgeot,
Gagnard-Delagrange 1996 £24.10
(HAH) £28.89 (JER)

Chassagne-Montrachet Roux 1996
£22.91 (TW)

Chassagne-Montrachet Verget 1996
£20.99 (YOU) £21.95 (FA)

Chevalier-Montrachet Sauzet 1996
£22.91 (FA)

Meursault-Blagny, Matrot 1995 £24.95
(CON) £27.70 (GAU) £27.97 (CB)

Meursault Charmes, Henri Germain 1995
£23.80 (TAN) £27.95 (LEA)

Meursault Charmes, Matrot 1994 £24.95
(CON)

Meursault Charmes, Monnier 1996
£20.25 (SOM)

Meursault Charmes, Rougeot 1997
£24.50 (BAN)

Meursault Darviot Perrin 1996 £21.05
(JER) £26.09 (TW)

Meursault Goutte d'Or, Latour 1996
£24.79 (JON)

Meursault Jobard 1996 £23.50 (HAH)

Meursault Jobard 1995 £22.50 (BALL)
£22.95 (RAE) £24.00 (MV)

Meursault Jobard 1991 £25.90 (UB)

Meursault Jobard 1990 £27.45 (AD)

Meursault les Luchets, Roulot 1996
£22.91 (DOM)

Meursault les Narvaux, Vincent Girardin
1995 £20.99 (NI)

Meursault les Vireuils, Dupont Fahn 1996
£20.95 (NI)

Meursault l'Ormeau, Coche-Debord
1993 £21.00 (JON)

Meursault Matrot 1995 £21.68 (CB)

Meursault Monatine, Rougeot 1997
£20.15 (BAN) £20.79 (YOU)

Meursault Santenots, Marquis d'Angerville
1997 £24.48 (MON)

Meursault Verget 1996 £22.99 (YOU)
£24.87 (FA)

Morey St-Denis Bruno Clair 1995 £22.50
(JU)

Nuits St-Georges Robert Chevillon 1996
£23.25 (WT)

Pernand-Vergelesses Domaine Chandon
de Briailles 1996 £21.50 (LEA)

Puligny-Montrachet Carillon 1997 £20.07
(MON) £24.71 (STE) £27.45 (NA)

Puligny-Montrachet Champ Canet,
Carillon 1996 £21.75 (SOM) £29.84 (STE)

Puligny-Montrachet Champ Canet,
Latour-Giraud 1997 £23.99 (BIB)

Puligny-Montrachet Chartron et
Trébuchet 1996 £21.54 (JER) £24.95 (DI)

Puligny-Montrachet Clerc 1996 £23.15
(AV) £24.95 (PHI)

Puligny-Montrachet Clos de la Mouchère,
Henri Boillot 1997 £24.48 (CAV) £35.95
(LEA)

Puligny-Montrachet la Garenne, Olivier
Leflaive 1994 £22.95 (ROB)

Puligny-Montrachet Latour 1996 £21.49
(PEN) £22.75 (JON)

Puligny-Montrachet Latour 1992 £23.25
(WHI)

Puligny-Montrachet les Chalumeaux,
Matrot 1992 £24.50 (GAU)

Puligny-Montrachet les Charmes, Chavy
1992 £22.00 (CRO)

Puligny-Montrachet les Combettes, Clerc
1997 £21.95 (BAN)

Puligny-Montrachet les Enseignères,
Olivier Leflaive 1996 £24.99 (PHI)

Puligny-Montrachet les Folatières, Chavy
1997 £23.50 (MON) £24.00 (MV)

Puligny-Montrachet les Folatières, Jadot **1994** £22.03 (CAV) £30.95 (ROB)

Puligny-Montrachet les Folatières, Latour **1996** £22.91 (FA) £25.50 (TAN)

Puligny-Montrachet les Folatières, Remoissenet **1994** £23.80 (AV)

Puligny-Montrachet les Perrières, Carillon **1996** £21.75 (SOM) £30.24 (STE)

Puligny-Montrachet Sauzet **1996** £23.50 (CAV) £24.60 (AD) £25.19 (JON)

£25.00 → £29.99

Beaune Clos des Mouches, Drouhin **1992** £29.95 (DI)

Chassagne-Montrachet Chaumées, Colin-Deléger **1993** £25.95 (CAV)

Chassagne-Montrachet Clos St Jean, Amiot **1994** £25.50 (BAL)

Chassagne-Montrachet Drouhin **1985** £29.38 (WY)

Chassagne-Montrachet les Caillerets, Amiot **1997** £25.00 (BAN) £28.75 (SOM)

Chassagne-Montrachet les Champs Gains, Amiot **1995** £29.95 (LEA)

Chassagne-Montrachet les Maltroie, Colin-Deléger **1996** £25.05 (FA)

Chassagne-Montrachet les Vergers, Colin-Deléger **1995** £28.50 (BER) £28.89 (JON)

Chassagne-Montrachet les Vergers, J-M Pillot **1997** £28.79 (RES)

Chassagne-Montrachet Morgeot, Jean Noël Gagnard **1994** £27.00 (JU)

Chassagne-Montrachet Morgeot, Henri Germain **1996** £29.95 (LEA)

Chassagne-Montrachet Morgeot, Henri Germain **1992** £27.40 (RIP)

Chassagne-Montrachet Sauzet **1997** £27.81 (RES)

Chevalier-Montrachet Sauzet **1994** £26.40 (CRO) £68.05 (CAV) £78.00 (JU)

Meursault Ampeau **1980** £28.68 (CHA)

Meursault-Blagny, Jadot **1992** £28.95 (POR)

Meursault Charmes, Ampeau **1985** £28.68 (CHA)

Meursault Charmes, Jadot **1996** £29.96 (REI)

Meursault Clos de la Barre, Monnier **1993** £25.25 (WT)

Meursault Genevrières, Charles et Remi Jobard **1996** £29.50 (LEA)

Meursault Genevrières, Michelot **1996** £28.95 (BALL)

Meursault la Pièce sous le Bois, Ampeau **1985** £28.20 (CHA)

Meursault le Poruzot Dessus, Charles et Remi Jobard **1996** £28.00 (LEA)

Meursault les Narvaux, Michelot-Buisson **1995** £28.50 (RES)

Meursault les Narvaux, Pierre Morey **1993** £28.00 (CRO)

Meursault les Tessons Clos de Mon Plaisir, Roulot **1994** £27.61 (DOM)

Meursault les Tessons, Pierre Morey **1994** £26.00 (WS) £27.00 (RES)

Meursault les Tillets, Javillier **1995** £29.95 (ROB)

Meursault Olivier Leflaive **1996** £25.97 (TW)

Meursault Pierre Morey **1997** £25.36 (RES)

Meursault Perrières, Albert Grivault **1988** £29.00 (JU)

Meursault Poruzots, Jobard **1994** £29.95 (RAE) £31.50 (JU)

Meursault Poruzots, Roux Père et Fils **1996** £27.50 (BEN)

Nuits-St-Georges Clos de l'Arlot, Domaine de l'Arlot **1994** £29.71 (FLE)

Puligny-Montrachet Champ Canet, Carillon **1995** £27.99 (NI)

Puligny-Montrachet Jean-Marc Boillot **1996** £26.50 (BALL) £28.95 (LEA)

Puligny-Montrachet la Garenne, Sauzet **1991** £29.00 (CRO)

Puligny-Montrachet Domaine Leflaive **1994** £29.96 (REI) £35.65 (PLAY)

Puligny-Montrachet Olivier Leflaive **1996** £29.38 (TW)

Puligny-Montrachet les Chalumeaux, Matrot **1996** £26.50 (CON) £28.50 (GAU)

Puligny-Montrachet les Champs Gains, Michel Bouzereau **1994** £28.20 (FLE)

Puligny-Montrachet les Charmes, Chavy **1995** £25.50 (ROB)

Puligny-Montrachet les Folatières, Chartron **1997** £28.95 (BAN)

Puligny-Montrachet les Folatières, Chartron **1996** £27.91 (JER) £28.99 (YOU)

Puligny-Montrachet les Folatières, ur **1995** £29.38 (WY)

Puligny-Montrachet les Referts, Sauzet **1994** £29.38 (CAV) £33.70 (TAN) £34.08 (DOM) £37.00 (WS) £40.53 (REI)

> ### Oz Clarke's Wine Guide
> *is an annual publication.*
> *We welcome your suggestions*
> *for next year's edition.*

Puligny-Montrachet les Truffières, Colin-Deléger **1994** £25.95 (CAV)

Puligny-Montrachet Sauzet **1994** £25.00 (RES) £31.14 (REI)

Puligny-Montrachet Sous les Puits, Bachelet **1995** £25.95 (STA)

£30.00 → £39.99

Beaune Clos des Mouches, Drouhin **1996** £36.25 (REI) £39.95 (BEN) £44.50 (BAL)

Chassagne-Montrachet la Boudriotte, Blain-Gagnard **1990** £38.00 (CRO)

Chassagne-Montrachet la Boudriotte, Domaine Ramonet **1993** £35.79 (YOU)

Chassagne-Montrachet la Romanée, Olivier Leflaive **1997** £32.90 (CB)

Chassagne-Montrachet Latour **1989** £35.25 (WY)

Chassagne-Montrachet les Caillerets, Amiot **1996** £33.50 (LEA)

Chassagne-Montrachet les Caillerets, Jean-Noël Gagnard **1996** £34.00 (WS)

Chassagne-Montrachet les Vergers, Domaine Ramonet **1995** £32.70 (FA)

Chassagne-Montrachet les Vergers, Olivier Leflaive **1995** £33.49 (TW)

Chassagne-Montrachet Marquis de Laguiche, Drouhin **1996** £36.50 (BEN) £38.50 (BAL)

Chassagne-Montrachet Marquis de Laguiche, Drouhin **1995** £38.19 (REI)

Chassagne-Montrachet Marquis de Laguiche, Drouhin **1994** £30.55 (PEN)

Chassagne-Montrachet Marquis de Laguiche, Drouhin **1976** £38.99 (YOU) £44.65 (REI)

Chassagne-Montrachet Morgeot, Bachelet-Ramonet **1994** £34.95 (ROB)

Chassagne-Montrachet Morgeot, Domaine Ramonet **1993** £38.19 (REI)

Chassagne-Montrachet Morgeot, Jadot **1992** £36.50 (ROB)

Chassagne-Montrachet Morgeot, Verget **1995** £36.69 (NI)

Chassagne-Montrachet Niellon **1995** £30.00 (FORT) £31.33 (CAV)

Chassagne-Montrachet Ramonet **1992** £38.19 (REI)

In each price band wines are listed in vintage order. Within each vintage they are listed in A–Z order.

Corton-Charlemagne Bouchard Père **1990** £35.18 (BY)

Corton-Charlemagne Bouchard Père **1989** £37.15 (HA)

Corton-Charlemagne Chapuis **1997** £39.42 (STE) £43.80 (NA)

Corton-Charlemagne Jadot **1987** £38.19 (REI)

Corton-Charlemagne Latour **1996** £39.99 (MAJ) £42.95 (STA) £44.06 (CAV)

Corton-Charlemagne Latour **1995** £36.50 (COC) £38.58 (FA) £41.12 (CAV) £41.13 (REI) £42.28 (PLAY) £47.00 (WY)

Corton-Charlemagne Latour **1994** £34.66 (FA) £41.13 (PEN)

Corton-Charlemagne Olivier Leflaive **1996** £32.72 (CB)

Corton-Charlemagne Olivier Leflaive **1994** £34.00 (WS)

Corton-Charlemagne Rapet **1982** £38.19 (REI)

Corton-Charlemagne Rollin **1996** £36.62 (RAE) £41.60 (TAN)

Corton Domaine Chandon de Briailles **1994** £38.20 (TAN) £45.00 (RES)

Meursault-Blagny, Jadot **1995** £34.99 (VIC) £34.99 (THR) £34.99 (WR) £34.99 (BOT)

Meursault-Blagny, Jobard **1992** £31.95 (RAE)

Meursault Charmes, Matrot **1997** £30.90 (GAU)

Meursault Charmes, Michelot **1997** £33.99 (OD)

Meursault Charmes, Pierre Morey **1996** £35.90 (TAN) £39.00 (RES)

Meursault Charmes, Pierre Morey **1992** £34.00 (WS)

Meursault Clos de la Barre, Lafon **1994** £30.00 (JU)

Meursault Clos des Perrières, Albert Grivault **1994** £35.00 (JU)

Meursault Genevrières, Charles et Remi Jobard **1997** £33.50 (LEA)

Meursault Genevrières, Henri Boillot **1997** £39.95 (LEA)

Meursault Genevrières, Jobard **1994** £31.50 (JU) £32.50 (RAE)

Meursault Genevrières, Pierre Morey **1995** £39.00 (RES)

Meursault Lafon **1996** £39.00 (YOU) £63.65 (CAV)

Meursault les Vireuils, Roulot **1992** £37.48 (NO)

Meursault Poruzots, Jobard **1995** £30.26 (FA)

Meursault Rougeots, Verget **1995** £34.75 (ROB)

Meursault sous le Dos d'Âne, Henri Clerc **1993** £32.67 (TW)

Nuits-St-Georges Clos de l'Arlot, Domaine de l'Arlot **1997** £33.96 (BY)

Puligny-Montrachet Champ Canet, Carillon **1997** £33.29 (MON) £36.50 (STE) £40.55 (NA)

Puligny-Montrachet Champ Canet, Sauzet **1993** £32.90 (DOM) £40.54 (REI)

Puligny-Montrachet Clavoillon, Domaine Leflaive **1995** £38.58 (FA) £40.49 (JON)

Puligny-Montrachet Clavoillon, Domaine Leflaive **1994** £30.55 (CB) £30.70 (TAN)

Puligny-Montrachet Clos de la Garenne, Drouhin **1988** £32.90 (WY)

Puligny-Montrachet la Garenne, Sauzet **1996** £35.64 (FA) £45.04 (CAV)

Puligny-Montrachet la Garenne, Sauzet **1994** £32.90 (DOM) £34.00 (WS)

Puligny-Montrachet Domaine Leflaive **1993** £38.19 (PLA)

Puligny-Montrachet les Caillerets, Domaine Chartron **1996** £31.33 (JER)

Puligny-Montrachet les Chalumeaux, Matrot **1993** £33.84 (TW)

Puligny-Montrachet les Champs Gains, Michel Bouzereau **1995** £38.50 (ROB)

Puligny-Montrachet les Combettes, Ampeau **1985** £32.67 (CHA)

Puligny-Montrachet les Folatières, Drouhin **1996** £30.26 (REI) £39.95 (LEA)

Puligny-Montrachet les Folatières, Drouhin **1983** £35.25 (WY)

Puligny-Montrachet les Perrières, Carillon **1995** £36.00 (ELL)

Puligny-Montrachet Sous le Puits, Verget **1996** £30.75 (FA)

Puligny-Montrachet Sous le Puits, Verget **1995** £39.50 (ROB)

£40.00 → £49.99

Bâtard-Montrachet Fontaine-Gagnard **1996** £46.50 (SOM)

Bâtard-Montrachet Gagnard-Delagrange **1996** £42.00 (BAN)

Bienvenues-Bâtard-Montrachet Bachelet **1992** £43.50 (RAE)

Chassagne-Montrachet Blanchots Dessus, Darviot-Perrin **1996** £44.42 (TW)

Chassagne-Montrachet Drouhin **1962** £44.06 (REI)

Chassagne-Montrachet les Caillerets, Domaine Ramonet **1996** £40.54 (FA)

Chassagne-Montrachet Marquis de Laguiche, Drouhin **1989** £41.12 (WY)

Chassagne-Montrachet Remilly, Verget **1995** £41.79 (NI)

Chevalier-Montrachet les Desmoiselles, Latour **1994** £49.84 (FA)

Corton-Charlemagne Bonneau du Martray **1994** £41.13 (REI) £63.39 (PLA)

Corton-Charlemagne Bouchard Père **1996** £42.50 (FA) £48.88 (COC)

Corton-Charlemagne Delarche **1992** £45.50 (ROB)

Corton-Charlemagne Drouhin **1995** £48.50 (BEN)

Corton-Charlemagne Drouhin **1989** £40.95 (BO) £88.12 (WY)

Corton-Charlemagne Jadot **1995** £40.05 (FA)

Corton-Charlemagne Jadot **1994** £41.13 (CAV)

Corton-Charlemagne Juillot **1993** £41.13 (DOM)

Corton-Charlemagne Olivier Leflaive **1988** £40.54 (REI)

Corton-Charlemagne Rapet **1997** £40.05 (RES)

Corton-Charlemagne Remoissenet **1995** £41.00 (AV)

Meursault Charmes, Ampeau **1979** £40.54 (FA)

Meursault les Perrières, Pierre Morey **1996** £40.00 (WS)

Meursault Perrières, Michelot **1995** £42.50 (RES)

Meursault Perrières, Roulot **1997** £41.13 (DOM)

Nuits-St-Georges Clos de l'Arlot, Domaine de l'Arlot **1993** £41.13 (TW)

Puligny-Montrachet Champ Canet, Sauzet **1996** £41.99 (BY) £42.50 (FA)

Puligny-Montrachet Champ Canet, Sauzet **1994** £40.53 (REI) £45.00 (RES)

Puligny-Montrachet Clavoillon, Domaine Leflaive **1996** £45.00 (FORT)

Puligny-Montrachet Clavoillon, Domaine Leflaive **1993** £42.00 (CRO)

Puligny-Montrachet les Champs Gains, Domaine Ramonet **1994** £42.89 (REI)

Puligny-Montrachet les Combettes, Domaine Leflaive **1994** £44.65 (CB)

Puligny-Montrachet les Combettes, Sauzet **1994** £41.13 (DOM) £45.00 (JU)

Puligny-Montrachet les Folatières, Domaine Leflaive **1996** £45.50 (BALL)

Puligny-Montrachet les Perrières, Sauzet **1997** £43.47 (RES)

Puligny-Montrachet les Perrières, Sauzet **1994** £44.06 (REI)

Puligny-Montrachet les Pucelles, Domaine Leflaive **1994** £42.50 (FA) £45.71 (CB)

Puligny-Montrachet les Pucelles, Domaine Leflaive **1993** £42.45 (AD)

£50.00 → £69.99

Bâtard-Montrachet Jean-Marc Boillot **1993** £63.00 (RAE)

Bâtard-Montrachet Bouchard Père **1989** £53.04 (BY)

Bâtard-Montrachet Domaine Leflaive **1994** £63.89 (LAY) £69.97 (CB) £70.00 (JU)

Bâtard-Montrachet Domaine Leflaive **1991** £50.00 (FORT)

Bâtard-Montrachet Fontaine-Gagnard **1994** £57.47 (HA)

Bâtard-Montrachet Gagnard-Delagrange **1997** £53.85 (MON)

Bâtard-Montrachet Sauzet **1994** £62.67 (CAV) £65.00 (JU) £70.50 (DOM)

Bienvenues-Bâtard-Montrachet Bachelet-Ramonet **1995** £56.79 (FRI)

Bienvenues-Bâtard-Montrachet Louis Carillon **1997** £63.65 (MON)

Bienvenues-Bâtard-Montrachet Domaine Leflaive **1994** £53.87 (CB) £55.40 (LAY)

Bienvenues-Bâtard-Montrachet Domaine Leflaive **1992** £58.75 (TW)

Bienvenues-Bâtard-Montrachet Sauzet **1994** £58.26 (CAV) £60.00 (JU)

Chassagne-Montrachet les Ruchottes, Domaine Ramonet **1995** £52.29 (FA)

Corton-Charlemagne Bonneau du Martray **1996** £55.00 (BEN)

Corton-Charlemagne Bonneau du Martray **1992** £51.23 (NO) £55.81 (REI) £60.00 (FORT) £60.00 (JU)

Corton-Charlemagne Domaine Chandon de Briailles **1996** £55.00 (LEA)

Corton-Charlemagne Jadot **1990** £65.00 (ROB)

Corton-Charlemagne Olivier Leflaive **1989** £50.00 (CRO)

Corton-Charlemagne Michel Voarick **1992** £68.15 (WY)

Corton-Charlemagne Tollot-Beaut **1986** £50.33 (FA)

Côte de Beaune Villamont **1964** £55.00 (ROB)

Meursault Charmes, Lafon **1996** £63.00 (YOU)

Meursault Poruzots, Jobard **1986** £55.95 (RES)

Puligny-Montrachet Champ Canet, Sauzet **1995** £55.00 (ROB)

Puligny-Montrachet Leroy **1978** £53.85 (CAV)

Puligny-Montrachet les Combettes, Ampeau **1978** £62.00 (CRO)

Puligny-Montrachet les Combettes, Domaine Leflaive **1992** £64.04 (FA)

Puligny-Montrachet les Pucelles, Domaine Leflaive **1997** £59.63 (RES)

Puligny-Montrachet les Pucelles, Domaine Leflaive **1996** £66.00 (FA) £70.00 (FORT)

Puligny-Montrachet les Pucelles, Domaine Leflaive **1991** £51.95 (ROB)

£70.00 → £99.99

Bâtard-Montrachet Domaine Leflaive **1984** £95.00 (ROB)

Bâtard-Montrachet Latour **1995** £70.50 (PEN) £78.00 (STA)

Bâtard-Montrachet Latour **1988** £95.00 (VIN)

Bâtard-Montrachet Latour **1985** £80.49 (REI)

Bâtard-Montrachet Olivier Leflaive **1995** £94.39 (FA)

Bâtard-Montrachet Pierre Morey **1996** £78.20 (TAN)

Bâtard-Montrachet Pierre Morey **1993** £75.00 (RES)

Bâtard-Montrachet Sauzet **1995** £97.33 (FA) £99.88 (REI) £111.63 (CAV)

Bienvenues-Bâtard-Montrachet Louis Carillon **1995** £85.00 (FORT)

Bienvenues-Bâtard-Montrachet Domaine Ramonet **1996** £89.50 (FA)

Bienvenues-Bâtard-Montrachet Domaine Ramonet **1994** £76.38 (REI)

Bienvenues-Bâtard-Montrachet Domaine Leflaive **1997** £94.39 (RES)

Bienvenues-Bâtard-Montrachet Sauzet **1995** £84.60 (FA)

Bienvenues-Bâtard-Montrachet Sauzet **1989** £88.13 (REI)

Chevalier-Montrachet Bouchard Père **1996** £71.88 (FA) £83.23 (CAV)

Chevalier-Montrachet Bouchard Père **1995** £79.00 (COC)

Chevalier-Montrachet Domaine Leflaive **1994** £73.45 (LAY) £82.25 (CB)

Chevalier-Montrachet Domaine Leflaive **1991** £98.00 (ROB)

Chevalier-Montrachet Domaine Leflaive
1986 £88.13 (REI)
Chevalier-Montrachet les Desmoiselles,
Latour **1995** £82.25 (WY) £84.00 (STA)
Chevalier-Montrachet les Desmoiselles,
Latour **1981** £70.50 (PEN)
Chevalier-Montrachet Olivier Leflaive
1992 £76.38 (TW)
Chevalier-Montrachet Sauzet **1993**
£78.00 (JU)
Corton-Charlemagne Bonneau du
Martray **1989** £77.50 (ROB)
Criots-Bâtard-Montrachet Olivier Leflaive
1996 £76.85 (CB)
Meursault Clos de la Barre, Lafon **1995**
£83.62 (FA)
Meursault Perrières, Lafon **1996** £75.00
(YOU)
le Montrachet Jadot **1993** £88.13 (CAV)
£117.50 (ELL)
le Montrachet Marquis de Laguiche,
Drouhin **1991** £82.70 (NI) £94.00 (WY)
£170.38 (REI)
le Montrachet Thénard **1991** £74.00
(CRO)
Musigny de Vogüé **1991** £82.25 (WY)
Puligny-Montrachet la Truffière, Sauzet
1986 £94.00 (CAV)
Puligny-Montrachet les Combettes,
Sauzet **1988** £82.25 (CAV)
Puligny-Montrachet les Pucelles, Domaine
Leflaive **1992** £99.35 (NO)

£100.00 → £199.99

Bâtard-Montrachet Domaine Leflaive
1983 £115.74 (REI)
Bâtard-Montrachet Domaine Ramonet
1996 £113.97 (FA)
Bâtard-Montrachet Domaine Ramonet
1983 £146.88 (CAV)
Bienvenues-Bâtard-Montrachet Domaine
Leflaive **1983** £102.81 (REI)
Chevalier-Montrachet Olivier Leflaive
1986 £111.63 (FA)
Chevalier-Montrachet Sauzet **1997**
£128.17 (RES)
Corton-Charlemagne Latour **1978**
£105.75 (WY)
Meursault Genevrières, Lafon **1994**
£105.75 (CAV)
Meursault Perrières, Lafon **1994** £105.75
(CAV)
Meursault Rougeots, Coche-Dury **1996**
£117.01 (CAV)
le Montrachet Amiot **1996** £165.00 (LEA)

le Montrachet Bouchard Père **1995**
£137.08 (CAV) £157.00 (COC)
le Montrachet Gagnard-Delagrange **1997**
£122.40 (MON)
le Montrachet Jadot **1986** £126.70 (NO)
le Montrachet Latour **1991** £103.40 (PEN)
le Montrachet Latour **1985** £146.87 (WY)
le Montrachet Marquis de Laguiche,
Drouhin **1996** £124.75 (RAE) £143.35
(FA) £170.00 (BEN)
le Montrachet Marquis de Laguiche,
Drouhin **1993** £111.62 (WY) £150.00
(FORT) £170.00 (ROB)
le Montrachet Marquis de Laguiche,
Drouhin **1992** £137.00 (RIP)
le Montrachet Marquis de Laguiche,
Drouhin **1987** £188.00 (TW)
le Montrachet Prieur **1996** £175.00 (YOU)
le Montrachet Sauzet **1994** £103.20 (FA)
£110.00 (JU) £146.87 (CAV)
le Montrachet Sauzet **1993** £125.00 (JU)
£250.00 (RES)
le Montrachet Thénard **1996** £106.70
(AV)
Musigny de Vogüé **1987** £117.50 (TW)

£200.00 → £499.99

le Montrachet Domaine de la Romanée-
Conti **1993** £440.63 (CAV)
le Montrachet Domaine de la Romanée-
Conti **1989** £442.00 (FA)
le Montrachet Domaine de la Romanée-
Conti **1988** £305.50 (WY)
le Montrachet Domaine de la Romanée-
Conti **1974** £236.37 (FA) £346.63 (CAV)
le Montrachet Domaine Leflaive **1994**
£352.50 (CAV) £381.88 (FA)
le Montrachet Lafon **1995** £276.13 (REI)
£387.75 (FA) £581.63 (CAV)
le Montrachet Lafon **1993** £330.00 (BEN)
le Montrachet Marquis de Laguiche,
Drouhin **1971** £293.75 (REI)

Over £500.00

Corton-Charlemagne Coche-Dury **1990**
£528.75 (CAV)
le Montrachet Domaine de la Romanée-
Conti **1986** £881.25 (TW)

> **Oz Clarke's Wine Guide**
> *is an annual publication. We
> welcome your suggestions
> for next year's edition.*

MÂCONNAIS PRICES

WHITE

Under £5.00

Mâcon-Lugny Eugène Blanc, Cave de Lugny 1997 £4.95 (SOM)

Mâcon-Villages Cave Co-op. de Viré 1996 £4.99 (CO)

St-Véran Domaine des Valanges, Paquet ½ bottle 1996 £4.25 (BALL)

£5.00 → £5.99

Mâcon-Lugny les Charmes, Cave de Lugny 1996 £5.99 (UN) £7.75 (BU)

Mâcon-Prissé Duboeuf 1993 £5.85 (NI)

Mâcon-Villages Cave de Lugny 1997 £5.39 (FRI)

Mâcon-Villages Rodet 1998 £5.50 (MAR)

£6.00 → £6.99

Mâcon-Azé Domaine de Rochebin 1997 £6.07 (BIB)

Mâcon Chardonnay Domaine les Ecuyers 1997 £6.49 (SAI)

Mâcon Chardonnay Talmard 1997 £6.80 (HAH) £6.89 (JON) £6.95 (AD) £7.20 (TAN)

Mâcon Chardonnay Talmard 1996 £6.38 (JON) £6.49 (POR) £6.50 (BALL)

Mâcon-Charnay Manciat-Poncet 1998 £6.80 (HAW)

Mâcon-Loché Cave des Grands Crus Blancs 1998 £6.80 (HAW)

Mâcon-Lugny les Genièvres, Latour 1997 £6.49 (POR) £6.90 (TAN) £7.15 (COC) £7.27 (PLA) £7.50 (HIG) £7.69 (WHI)

Mâcon-Lugny les Genièvres, Latour 1996 £6.58 (PEN) £7.25 (BALL) £7.35 (STA) £7.50 (FORT) £7.80 (BEN) £7.99 (VIN) £8.22 (WY)

Mâcon-Prissé Cave Co-op. Prissé 1997 £6.20 (HAH)

Mâcon-Uchizy Raphael Sallet 1997 £6.95 (HAH)

Mâcon-Uchizy Talmard 1998 £6.71 (STE) £8.20 (PLAY)

Mâcon-Uchizy Talmard 1997 £6.99 (YOU) £7.45 (NA)

Mâcon-Uchizy Talmard 1996 £6.95 (JU)

Mâcon-Villages Domaine des Teppes de Chatennay 1996 £6.50 (CON)

Mâcon-Villages Loron 1997 £6.10 (TAN)

Mâcon-Villages Paul Sapin 1998 £6.75 (HAW)

Mâcon-Villages Tête de Cuvée, Verget 1997 £6.76 (FA) £8.95 (LEA)

St-Véran Domaine St-Martin, Duboeuf 1997 £6.40 (NEZ)

St-Véran Drouhin 1995 £7.87 (PEN) £7.80 (CRO)

St-Véran en Crèches, Jacques Saumaize 1997 £6.95 (WS)

£7.00 → £7.99

Mâcon-Charnay Manciat-Poncet 1996 £7.50 (JU)

Mâcon-Clessé Michel 1995 £7.99 (RAE)

Mâcon-Davaye Domaine des Maillettes, Saumaize 1996 £7.64 (JER)

Mâcon-Fuissé la Solutré, Vincent 1996 £7.50 (RES)

Mâcon-Villages Domaine de la Bongran, Thévenet 1998 £7.60 (HAW)

Mâcon-Viré Cuvée Spéciale, Bonhomme 1996 £7.95 (WS) £8.81 (DOM)

St-Véran Caves des Grands Crus 1998 £7.25 (HAW)

St-Véran Corsin 1998 £7.97 (STE) £8.85 (NA)

St-Véran Domaine des Deux Roches 1997 £7.45 (BER) £7.85 (HAH) £8.99 (VIC) £8.99 (THR) £8.99 (WR) £8.99 (BOT)

St-Véran Domaine des Valanges, Paquet 1996 £7.50 (BALL) £8.45 (JU) £8.99 (RAE)

St-Véran Sapin 1998 £7.55 (HAW)

St-Véran Mondange 1996 £7.49 (CON)

£8.00 → £9.99

Mâcon-Clessé Guillemot 1996 £9.40 (HAH) £9.60 (TAN)

Mâcon-Villages Domaine Caveau Lamartine 1995 £8.50 (VIN)

Mâcon-Villages Tête de Cuvée, Verget 1996 £8.22 (FA) £8.96 (LAY) £8.99 (YOU)

Pouilly-Fuissé les Vieux Murs, Loron 1996 £9.95 (BALL) £10.99 (POR)

Pouilly-Fuissé Pascal Renaud 1997 £9.45 (CON)

Pouilly-Loché Cave des Grands Crus Blancs 1998 £8.45 (HAW)

Pouilly-Loché Domaine des Duc 1998 £8.80 (HAW)

Pouilly-Vinzelles Cave des Grands Crus Blancs 1997 £8.21 (PLA)

Pouilly-Vinzelles Bouchard Père et Fils 1995 £9.76 (COC)

Pouilly-Vinzelles Jean-Jacques Martin **1998** £9.40 (HAW)

Pouilly-Vinzelles Mathias **1997** £8.30 (PIP)

St-Véran Château Fuissé, Vincent **1997** £8.13 (RES) £8.52 (DOM) £8.60 (TAN)

St-Véran Domaine de la Collonge, Noblet **1997** £8.60 (LAY)

★ St-Véran Verget **1997** £8.95 (LEA) £9.95 (BEN) £9.96 (LAY)

St-Véran Jean-Jacques Martin **1998** £8.40 (HAW)

£10.00 → £12.49

Mâcon-Clessé Quintaine, Guillemot-Michel **1995** £12.34 (TW)

Mâcon Monbellet, Goyard **1996** £10.99 (RAE) £11.19 (JON)

Mâcon-Viré Quintaine, Jean Thévenet **1996** £11.99 (NI)

Pouilly-Fuissé Cave des Grands Crus Blancs **1998** £10.55 (HAW)

Pouilly-Fuissé Corsin **1997** £11.52 (STE) £12.95 (NA)

Pouilly-Fuissé Domaine Béranger, Duboeuf **1997** £11.10 (NEZ)

Pouilly-Fuissé Domaine de la Collonge **1996** £10.73 (LAY)

Pouilly-Fuissé la Roche, Manciat-Poncet **1996** £10.95 (JU)

Pouilly-Fuissé Latour **1997** £11.36 (COC)

Pouilly-Fuissé Leger-Plumet **1997** £11.65 (RES)

Pouilly-Fuissé Tête de Cuvée, Verget **1997** £11.65 (FA) £15.95 (LAY) £16.95 (LEA) £17.70 (BEN)

St-Véran Cuvée Prestige Lassarat **1996** £10.25 (STA)

St-Véran Vieilles Vignes Domaine des Deux Roches **1996** £10.99 (POR)

£12.50 → £15.99

Mâcon-Clessé Domaine de la Bon Gran, Thévenet **1996** £12.99 (NI) £14.00 (TAN) £14.79 (YOU) £14.95 (BEN) £15.95 (LEA)

Mâcon-Clessé Domaine de la Bon Gran, Thévenet **1995** £14.95 (FORT)

Mâcon-Clessé Quintaine, Guillemot-Michel **1989** £14.69 (TW)

Mâcon-Clessé Quintaine Sélection de Grains Cendrés, Guillemot-Michel **1992** £13.50 (WS) £15.95 (HAH) £29.00 (CRO)

Mâcon-Viré Domaine Emilian Gillet, Thévenet **1996** £13.50 (LEA) £15.51 (TW)

Pouilly-Fuissé Château Fuissé, Vincent **1997** £13.70 (TAN) £14.69 (DOM) £16.95 (LAY)

Pouilly-Fuissé Clos du Bourg, Luquet **1997** £12.95 (FORT)

Pouilly-Fuissé Corsin **1996** £14.69 (REI)

Pouilly-Fuissé la Croix, Denogent **1997** £13.90 (GAU)

Pouilly-Fuissé la Roche, Daniel Barraud **1996** £13.95 (LEA)

Pouilly-Fuissé Latour **1996** £13.61 (PLAY) £13.99 (POR)

Pouilly-Fuissé les Crays, Forest **1994** £15.95 (NI)

Pouilly-Fuissé les Reisses Vieilles Vignes, Denogent **1997** £14.95 (GAU)

Pouilly-Fuissé Manciat-Poncet **1998** £12.90 (HAW)

Pouilly-Fuissé Vieilles Vignes, Daniel Barraud **1996** £15.95 (LEA) £15.99 (YOU)

Pouilly-Fuissé Vieilles Vignes, Manciat-Poncet **1996** £12.50 (JU)

St-Véran en Crèches, Daniel Barraud **1996** £12.95 (LEA)

£16.00 → £19.99

Mâcon-Viré Domaine Emilian Gillet, Thévenet **1992** £17.04 (TW)

Pouilly-Fuissé Château Fuissé, Vincent **1992** £18.50 (DI)

Pouilly-Fuissé Cuvée Claude Vieilles Vignes, Denogent **1997** £17.25 (GAU)

Pouilly-Fuissé le Clos, Château Fuissé **1996** £16.39 (DOM)

Pouilly-Fuissé les Brûlés, Château Fuissé **1997** £17.95 (AD)

Pouilly-Fuissé les Combettes, Château Fuissé **1995** £18.00 (JU)

Pouilly-Fuissé les Crays, Forest **1997** £16.55 (BAN) £16.99 (YOU) £20.00 (FORT)

Pouilly-Fuissé Tête du Cru, Ferret **1996** £17.50 (BAL)

£20.00 → £29.99

Pouilly-Fuissé Château Fuissé Vieilles Vignes, Vincent **1995** £25.77 (PLAY) £26.50 (RES)

Pouilly-Fuissé Hors Classe, Ferret **1996** £21.50 (BAL) £21.54 (JER)

Pouilly-Fuissé les Brûlés, Château Fuissé **1995** £22.75 (BER)

Over £30.00

Mâcon-Clessé Cuvée Botrytis Domaine de la Bon Gran, Thévenet **1983** £79.95 (LEA)

Mâcon-Clessé Domaine de la Bon Gran, Thévenet **1990** £39.95 (LEA)

CHAMPAGNE

**A Millennium just isn't a Millennium without Champagne,
but don't drink the best at parties – you'll need it to see you
through the January blues**

At the time of writing I don't know what Champagne offers there'll be for the Millennium. I don't know whether the shops will be plastering their windows with '20 per cent off' signs, or whether they'll be smugly doling out full-price fizz to queues of thirsty punters. What I do know is what I shall be drinking.

The answer is good non-vintage. No, I'm not mad, and I don't think I'm particularly cheapskate. But for parties (if anyone invites me, that is – I mean, I don't want to appear desperate, but…) I just think non-vintage is better. You need time to appreciate the greater depth of vintage; time to sit over it,

think about it, let it blossom in the glass. How can you do that with 50 people bawling *Auld Lang Syne* in your ear?

I'll keep the vintage for myself. Myself and perhaps one other person, and perhaps I'll keep it for next January when all the fuss has died down and I'm feeling a bit flat and it's raining and my editor's on the telephone demanding my copy with menaces. That's when I'll go to the rack and pull out a bottle of Taittinger 1985, or Roederer, or Veuve Clicquot and watch it fizz gently in the glass. It'll have that lovely golden colour and it'll smell glorious, all toast and nuts and creamy richness. Happy New Millennium.

GRAPE VARIETIES

CHARDONNAY Imparts elegance and freshness to the blend, not to mention acidity and structure. Good Chardonnay from here ages superbly, so just because Blanc de Blancs (which is entirely Chardonnay) has whiplash elegance, don't think you've got to drink it young.

PINOT NOIR Adds weight to the blend, even though it's vinified as a white wine, without the skins: a Champagne relying on Pinot Noir is certain to be heavier than those made from other grapes. It can also

go with food better. And yes, Champagne does make a very little still red wine from Pinot Noir, but it takes a hot year to make it attractive. Most Pinot made as red wine is used to colour rosé.

PINOT MEUNIER Champagne's second black grape, making a softer, fruitier style of wine, important for producing simple wines for drinking young, and useful for lightening the assertive weight of Pinot Noir. Soft, commercial blends are usually heavy on the Pinot Meunier, and none the worse for it.

WINE STYLES AND LABELLING

BLANC DE BLANCS Champagne made only from Chardonnay; it has become more fashionable as drinkers look for a lighter style. Should not only be fresh but creamy and bright as well, and should get deeper and richer as it ages. Some firms, notably *Henriot, Mumm, Joseph Perrier* and *Bruno Paillard* make excellent NV (non-vintage) Blanc de Blancs, and the *Union*

co-operatives at Avize and le Mesnil make the most of their positions at the heart of the Côte des Blancs. Some firms sell vintage Blanc de Blancs (watch out for *Billecart-Salmon, Delamotte, Drappier, Jacquesson, Pol Roger, Roederer, Jacques Sélosse*) and a couple also make luxury cuvées. *Taittinger's Comtes de Champagne, Dom Ruinart, Salon* and *Krug's Clos de Mesnil* are the benchmarks. But with no easy-going Pinot Meunier to fatten out the wine, any fault is glaringly obvious, so stick to good producers.

BLANC DE NOIRS This white style is made from black grapes only. Few have the quality and longevity of *Bollinger's Vieilles Vignes*, but none is even half as expensive. Most are rather solid. *Pierre Vaudon* is an elegant exception, and tremendous value for money; *H Billiot* is fine, and the *Sainsbury's* version is good value, and benefits from extra bottle age.

BRUT Very dry – more so than either 'Sec' or 'Extra Dry'. Most non-vintage Champagne sold in Britain is Brut.

BUYER'S OWN BRAND (BOB) A wine blended to a buyer's specification, or more probably, to a price limit. The grapes are of lesser quality, the wines usually younger, and cheaper. However, *Sainsbury's* and *Waitrose* Champagnes are consistent and good value.

CM Means *co-opérative-manipulant* and shows that the wine comes from a co-op, whatever the brand name implies.

COTEAUX CHAMPENOIS Still wines, red, rosé or white. Overpriced and generally rather acid. A village name, such as Cramant (white) or Bouzy (red) may appear. *Alain Vesselle's* Bouzy and *René* *Geoffroy's* Cumières red can be good, but all producers' still wines are as variable as the climate.

DE LUXE/CUVÉE DE PRESTIGE/ CUVÉE DE LUXE All these terms signify a special highly prized blend, mostly vintage. Some are undeniably great wines and some gaudy coat-tailers. At these prices one's looking for immense complexity and refinement. In general these wines are drunk *far* too young. Most need a good ten years to shine. Some of the best: *Billecart-Salmon Cuvée NF Billecart, Bollinger RD, Cattier Clos du Moulin, Charles Heidsieck Cuvée de Millenaires, Dom Pérignon, Dom Ruinart, Krug Grande Cuvée, Laurent Perrier Grand Siècle, Perrier-Jouët Belle Époque, Philipponnat Clos des Goisses, Pol Roger Cuvée Sir Winston Churchill, Roederer Cristal, Taittinger Comtes de Champagne, Veuve Clicquot la Grande Dame.*

DEMI-SEC Medium-sweet. Rarely very nice, but *Louis Roederer* can be outstanding, and *Veuve Clicquot* is usually the most consistent.

DOUX Sweet. *Louis Roederer's* is an excellent example.

EXTRA DRY Confusingly, this is less dry than 'Brut', but drier than 'Sec'.

GRAND CRU In Champagne it is communes that are classified, not individual

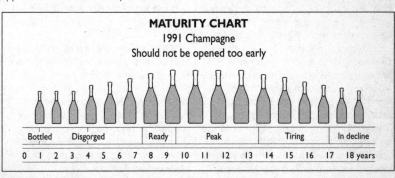

MATURITY CHART
1991 Champagne
Should not be opened too early

Bottled	Disgorged			Ready	Peak			Tiring		In decline

0   1   2   3   4   5   6   7   8   9   10   11   12   13   14   15   16   17   18 years

vineyards, and the 17 *grand cru* communes
in the region are the best. The next best are
the *premiers crus*.

GRANDE MARQUE Ambiguous term
meaning 'great brand', and now officially
defunct, since the Syndicat is disbanded. It
may re-form under a new name, eventually.

NM This means *négociant-manipulant*
(merchant-handler) and shows that the
producer is one of the 265 Champagne
houses operating in the region.

NON-DOSAGE Most Champagne has a
little sweetness – a 'dosage' – added just
before the final cork is put in. A few have
minimal dosage and will have names like
Brut Zero. Best are *Laurent-Perrier, Piper-
Heidsieck,* and *Duval Leroy* has just launched
one. They're designed to show that it's the
wine, not the dosage that provides the
quality. Do they prove their point? Well,
they need to be very ripe to be able to
balance the austerity.

NON-VINTAGE (NV) The flagship of
most houses, and the one by which a
producer should be judged. The wines are
generally based on one vintage and usually
aged for three years. But many of the best
provide greater depth and age, and ensure
consistency by using up to 40 per cent of
vins de réserve (wines from previous years)
thus giving more depth and maturity to the
blend. At the moment quality is generally
pretty good, and of the major names only
Mercier, Mumm, Moët and *Canard-Duchêne*
are seriously disappointing. Rather more
(like *Piper-Heidsieck, Charles Heidsieck*) have
reached a level of good, reliable quality, but

lack personality. For real character try
*Besserat de Bellefon, Billecart-Salmon,
Bollinger, Gosset, Alfred Gratien, Henriot,
Jacquart, Krug, Mailly Grand Cru, Bruno
Paillard, Pol Roger, Pommery, Joseph Perrier,
Roederer, Taittinger* (superb), *Pierre Vaudon,
Veuve Clicquot* and *Vilmart.* All will improve if
you keep them for a few months in bottle
after purchase. A new trend is to feature
the year of bottling on the label, so you can
tell how long the wine has had to mature.
It's a good idea but don't mistake these
wines for vintage Champagne.

PREMIER CRU The 38 *premier cru*
communes are those just below *grand cru* in
quality. All the others are unclassified.

RC *Récoltant-co-opérateur* – or a grower
selling wine made at a co-op. It's supposed
to stop growers from pretending they've
made it themselves, when all they did was
deliver the grapes. Should. Somehow it
doesn't seem to appear on labels that often.

RECENTLY DISGORGED A term for
Champagnes that have been left in the
cellars, drawing flavour from their yeast
deposits, for much longer than usual before
disgorging. The wines can rest for 20 or
perhaps even 30 years on the lees but are
usually released after seven to ten years.
Bollinger RD is the most famous and is still
the best; also good are *Deutz, Alfred Gratien*
and *Laurent-Perrier.* The idea is that you
should drink them as soon as you buy them,
with no further bottle age, at which point
they have freshness balanced by maturity.

RICH The sweetest Champagne. *Roederer*
can be superbly balanced. *Veuve Clicquot* has
a great vintage version.

RM Indicates that a grower, a *récoltant-
manipulant,* made it himself, rather than
taking it to the co-op. Try: *Bara, Billiot,
Bonnaire, Clouet, René Geoffroy, Michel
Gonet, André Jacquart, Lassalle, Legras,
Vesselle, Vilmart.*

ROSÉ Usually made by adding a little still red to white wine before bottling. Only a few companies (like *Laurent-Perrier*) still make it by macerating red grapes on the skins until the right shade of pink is achieved. Ideally rosés are aromatic, fruity wines, with a delicious strawberry or cherry flavour. Sadly, many are indistinguishable from white. Most should be drunk young. Best: *Billecart-Salmon, Bollinger, Dom Ruinart, Alfred Gratien, Jacquart Mosaïque, Lassalle, Laurent-Perrier, Pol Roger, Louise Pommery, Roederer* and *Roederer Cristal. Krug rosé* is way ahead in a class of its own, and at that price so it should be.

SEC Literally 'dry', but any Champagne so labelled will actually be medium dry. 'Extra Dry' and 'Brut' are drier.

SR Société de Récoltants. Label code for a family company of growers.

VINTAGE The wine produced from the grapes of a single, good year. Vintage Champagne should be fuller and deeper than non-vintage, but almost always released too young, so you need to age it yourself. An awful lot of lesser producers make a vintage when they (and we) would be better off if they concentrated on improving their non-vintage. Best names to look for: *Besserat de Bellefon, Billecart-Salmon, Bollinger, Delamotte, Gosset Grande Millésime, Henriot, Krug, Mailly Grand Cru, Bruno Paillard, Joseph Perrier, Laurent-Perrier, Pol Roger, Pommery, Louis Roederer, Ruinart, Salon, Jacques Sélosse, Taittinger, Pierre Vaudon* and *Veuve Clicquot.*

CHAMPAGNE HOUSES WHO'S WHO

BESSERAT DE BELLEFON ★★★★
Makes, elegant, restrained Champagnes of good depth.

BILLECART-SALMON ★★★★(★)
Terrifically elegant Champagne from a family-owned house. Very refined, mature wines and a delicate rosé. Its vintage, Cuvée NF Billecart, is also excellent.

BOLLINGER ★★★★(★) Like Krug, Bollinger makes 'English-style' Champagnes: rich, oaky, but more steely and almost half the price. The NV is excellent. RD is kept on its lees until just before sale.

F BONNET ★★ Inexpensive offshoot of Piper-Heidsieck and Charles Heidsieck, with mature and biscuity non-vintage.

DEUTZ ★★★ This house is back on form again with creamy-rich, biscuity non-vintage and an excellent quality prestige cuvée called William Deutz.

DRAPPIER ★★(★) Consistent quality, although the style bounces between ultra-fruity and rich and biscuity according to how much bottle age the wine has.

DUVAL-LEROY ★★ Fresh, fragrant style in a Chardonnay-dominated Champagne. Good value and consistent decent quality.

ALFRED GRATIEN ★★★★ Serious, oak-fermented wine at a much lower price than Krug. Very long-lived vintage. Even the non-vintage needs extra bottle age.

CHARLES HEIDSIECK ★★★ Good value and reliable; rich, full style and good vanilla finesse.

HENRIOT ★★★★ Good bottle age and unrelenting high quality. Very rich; lovely depth.

KRUG ★★★★★ Classic, mellow, rich. Oak-fermented Grande Cuvée is outstanding. The expensive rosé has incomparable Pinot Noir cherry fruit. Even more expensive Clos de Mesnil is a rich, single-vineyard Blanc de Blancs.

JACQUESSON ★★★ Good quality and finesse in both the elegant, flowery non-vintage or the rich, well-extracted vintage.

LANSON ★★★ Classic, long-maturing vintage. Give the NV extra bottle age, too.

LAURENT-PERRIER ★★★★ One of the most reliable of NVs, with excellent rosé. Prestige brand Grand Siècle is a blend of several vintages, but there is also a more expensive vintage version.

MOËT & CHANDON ★★★ Brut Impérial still seems undistinguished and not worthy of its fame. The 1992 vintage wine is reasonable.

BRUNO PAILLARD ★★★ Fresh, elegant and satisfying Champagne from one of the most consistent producers.

JOSEPH PERRIER ★★★★ The NV is extremely rich and well aged, with biscuity complexity and wonderfully high acidity.

PERRIER-JOUËT ★★★ Light, classic Champagne. Best known for Belle Époque in a pretty bottle, all flowery elegance.

POL ROGER ★★★★ Delicious, delicate Blanc de Blancs. Top class across the board, including prestige cuvée Sir Winston Churchill and vintage Blanc de Chardonnay.

POMMERY ★★★ Currently on good form, with wines of light, flowery elegance. Prestige cuvée Louise Pommery is superb.

LOUIS ROEDERER ★★★★★ Superb quality, lovely depth and finesse. The subtle, ripe NV is hard to beat, and prestige cuvée Cristal is wonderful. Good Demi-sec, too.

RUINART ★★★★ The non-vintage ' R' de Ruinart has lots of bottle age and a style closer to the traditional 'goût anglais' than many. Not for fans of light, young and delicate Champagne. The vintage is rich.

> **INSTANT CELLAR:**
> ## CHAMPAGNE FOR BEYOND 2000
>
> • NV Louis Roederer Brut, c.£24, widely available Perfect elegance and finesse.
> • NV Lanson Black Label, c.£18, widely available Lanson always needs extra time in bottle: drink it straight from the shop shelf and you might be disappointed.
> • 1990 Bollinger, £38.50, Cockburns of Leith One of the richest of all Champagnes, from the richest of all recent vintages: superb.
> • NV Delamotte, £15.92, Corney & Barrow Elegant wine from the house of Salon. The 1988 vintage of the latter is £62.98 and may well be immortal.
> • NV Billecart-Salmon, £19.49, Savage Selection Lovely delicate, complex wine.
> • NV Laurent Perrier Brut 'Extra Aged', £19.95, Lea & Sandeman The stock of Laurent Perrier here has an extra year of landed age compared to that on sale elsewhere, apparently. That's worth having for the richer flavour it gives.
> • NV Gosset Grand Réserve, £28.58, Nadder Wines Lovely rich fizz that keeps brilliantly. Expensive but worth it.
> • NV Le Mesnil Blanc de Blancs Brut, £14.65, Raeburn Fine Wines Elegant Chardonnay from a slow-maturing village.

TAITTINGER ★★★★(★) Splendidly light, modern, Chardonnayish style of great excitement, though its Blanc de Blancs Comtes de Champagne goes sumptuously rich with age.

PIERRE VAUDON ★★★(★) This stands up extremely well against the top Grandes Marques, and it's not expensive. Good weighty, ripe stuff.

VEUVE CLICQUOT ★★★★ The NV has a rich, warm style, and prestige cuvée la Grande Dame is almost chocolate-rich.

VILMART ★★★(★) Rich, full Champagne, more in the Bollinger than the Pommery mode. Plenty of flavour, weight and ripeness. Good vintage.

CHAMPAGNE VINTAGES

In theory Champagne firms only make single-vintage wines in especially fine years. But only a few firms, like Bollinger and Laurent-Perrier, follow the theory. Most either opt too readily for vintage wines in marginal years or, increasingly, release wines after only five years in bottle, which may be okay for French tastes but leaves the average Brit with an acid stomach. Nevertheless, most firms come up with decent vintage.

1998   Ripe wines that promise well. Expect plenty of vintage declarations, and no shortage of good Champagne in the new century.

1997   A ripe vintage with plentiful yields. If we all celebrate the Millenium with the vast quantities of Champagne that the producers are hoping we will, any 1997 wines will be released far too young to make up a shortfall in the market.

1996   Splendidly ripe, balanced wines that are likely to be widely declared. The non-vintage wines should be good, as well, when they start coming on stream.

1995   The wines are significantly superior to those of the previous four years, and this will be the first widely declared vintage since the outstanding 1990.

1994   Of the few reputable producers likely to declare this a vintage, Vilmart's Grand Cellier d'Or will probably be the best.

1993   Roederer managed to produce a vintage Champagne after rejecting no less than half its own crop. Others who will declare this year include A Bonnet, Drappier, Gardet, Gosset, Jacquesson and Vilmart.

1992   The 1992s are appearing on the shelves, and so far they're not impressive. Too many are green and coarse, though Perrier-Jouët might turn out okay.

1991   Coming into the shops now, and looking surprisingly good. Elegance and structure seem to be the keys to this vintage, and it needs time. Taittinger looks good, as do Pommery, Philipponnat's Clos des Goisses, Vilmart's Coeur de Cuvée, Henri Mandois and De Nauroy. Roederer declared a rosé.

1990   Still available at the moment. It was widely declared and many of the wines are superb. Try Jacquart, Lanson, Laurent-Perrier, Perrier-Jouët, Pommery, Roederer, Ruinart, Taittinger, Pierre Vaudon. Some are already sold out, and many are tasting seductive already, though they'll still improve.

1989   Most need a few years yet, though they're coming on beautifully. Look for Besserat de Bellefon, Gosset, Alfred Gratien, Bruno Paillard.

1988   The wines have bite, backbone and fruit, but most are already sold out. Jacques Sélosse, Gauthie and Gardet might still be available, and are worth a punt.

1987   A lot of wine, but even the Champenois are not enthusiastic about its quality. Only Pommery declared a vintage, and any remaining bottles should really be drunk.

1986   Would have made a decent, if slightly hard vintage, but got sold far too young. One or two minor houses have wines available, and they're attractive.

1985   Fine wines, without any of the hardness of some vintages. There's very little still available, but if you've got any it should be delicious now.

CHAMPAGNE PRICES

SPARKLING WHITE

Under £10.00

Georges Gardet Brut Spéciale ½ bottle
NV £8.25 (CON) £9.99 (VIN)
Georges Gardet Guy de St Flavy **NV**
£9.95 (SOM) £11.99 (CON) £12.04 (GW)
£12.95 (NA) £12.99 (BAL) £13.99 (NLW)

£10.00 → £11.99

Billecart-Salmon Brut Réserve ½ bottle
NV £10.75 (LIB)
Deutz Brut Classic ½ bottle **NV** £10.97
(JER)
Devilliers Brut **NV** £11.95 (JU) £12.69 (YOU)
Moët & Chandon Brut Impérial ½ bottle
NV £10.60 (TAN) £10.99 (POR) £11.06
(CB) £11.13 (PLAY) £11.22 (PLA) £11.50
(BALL) £11.61 (STE) £11.75 (WHI) £11.95
(ROB) £11.99 (TES) £11.99 (BO) £11.99
(CO) £12.49 (WR) £12.75 (FORT) £12.75
(OD) £12.90 (NA) £12.95 (VA)
★ Tesco Champagne 1er Cru Brut **NV**
£11.99 (TES)

£12.00 → £13.99

Bauget-Jouette **NV** £13.50 (HIG) £15.49
(AME)
Bauget-Jouette Grande Réserve **NV**
£13.99 (YOU)
Benedick **NV** £12.95 (LEA)
Bollinger ½ bottle **NV** £12.75 (BALL)
£13.22 (REI) £13.45 (CB) £13.65 (CON)
£13.71 (PLAY) £13.79 (YOU) £13.95 (PHI)
£13.95 (STA) £13.95 (ROB) £14.10 (BEN)
£14.22 (TW) £14.99 (VA) £15.25 (FORT)
£16.74 (VIN)
F Bonnet **NV** £13.99 (OD)

Le Brun de Neuville Cuvée Chardonnay
NV £13.75 (WAT)
Bruno Paillard ½ bottle **NV** £12.00 (YAP)
Canard-Duchêne **NV** £13.90 (CRO)
£14.99 (NLW) £14.99 (WHI) £15.22 (PLA)
£15.70 (COC) £16.45 (ROB) £16.49 (UN)
£16.49 (MAJ) £16.49 (SAF) £16.87 (PLAY)
£16.99 (MORR) £16.99 (WAI) £16.99 (BO)
Charles Heidsieck Brut Réserve ½ bottle
NV £13.36 (NO)
Drappier Carte d'Or **NV** £13.90 (BY)
£15.99 (THR) £15.99 (WR) £16.48 (FLE)
Duchâtel **NV** £12.99 (UN)
Ellner **NV** £13.39 (LAY)
Georges Gardet Blanc de Blancs **1990**
£13.95 (SOM) £16.85 (CON)
Georges Gardet Brut Spéciale **NV** £13.95
(CON) £15.24 (ROS) £17.95 (VIN)
Henri Harlin **NV** £13.99 (OD)
Veuve Clicquot ½ bottle **NV** £12.04 (REI)
£12.06 (CB) £12.50 (ROB) £12.75 (CON)

£14.00 → £15.99

★ ASDA 1er Cru Brut **1990** £15.99 (ASD)
Ayala **NV** £15.99 (MAJ)
Baron de Beaupré **NV** £14.99 (POR)
Beerens Brut Réserve **NV** £15.86 (BIB)
Blin **NV** £15.99 (OD)
Camuset Réserve **NV** £14.89 (BIB)
De Castelnau 1er Cru, Blanc de Blancs
NV £14.50 (JU)
★ Drappier Carte d'Or Brut **NV** £15.99
(BY)
Duval Leroy Fleur de Champagne **NV**
£15.16 (PEN) £16.44 (PLA)
★ Forget-Brimont 1er Cru Brut **NV** £14.95
(JU)
★ J M Gremillet Brut Sélection **NV** £14.65
(PIP)

MERCHANTS SPECIALIZING IN CHAMPAGNE
see Merchant Directory (page 413) for details

Most good merchants have a fair variety of Champagnes, and generally list the most popular of the Grandes Marques, plus one or two cheaper ones. Most, too, have a pretty varied list of sparkling wines from other countries, and it is quite hard to single out merchants with exceptionally good lists of Champagne. Nevertheless, for a wider than average choice, try especially: Adnams (AD), Averys of Bristol (AV), Bennetts (BEN), Bibendum (BIB), Farr Vintners (FA), Justerini & Brooks (JU), Lea & Sandeman (LEA), Majestic (MAJ), Oddbins (OD), Roberson (ROB), T&W Wines (TW), Tanners (TAN), Peter Wylie (WY) – a few old vintages.

Heidsieck Dry Monopole **NV** £14.99 (NLW)
£14.99 (JON) £15.49 (WHI) £15.99 (OD)
Lamiable Brut **NV** £15.00 (HIG)
★ Lay & Wheeler Extra Quality Brut **NV**
£15.89 (LAY)
Lenoble **1990** £15.99 (NI)
Louis Roederer Rich ½ bottle **NV** £14.58
(NO) £15.00 (FORT)
Mercier Demi-Sec **NV** £15.99 (MORR)
£17.49 (TES) £17.49 (CO) £17.49 (VIC)
£17.49 (THR) £17.49 (WR) £17.95 (ROB)
Pannier **NV** £15.95 (DI)
Pol Roger White Foil **NV** £15.95 (SOM)
£21.90 (VA) £22.05 (LAY) £22.15 (REI)
£22.17 (PLAY) £22.50 (CON) £22.50 (RES)
£22.50 (WS) £22.79 (ROS) £22.90 (HAH)
£22.90 (COC) £22.91 (PEN) £22.95 (BER)
£22.99 (UN) £22.99 (OD) £22.99 (THR)
£22.99 (BOT) £23.95 (ROB) £23.95 (POR)
£24.00 (MV) £24.25 (WRI) £24.95 (STA)
£24.95 (UB) £25.00 (FORT) £26.65 (VIN)

★ Prince William Blanc de Blancs Grand Cru
Brut **NV** £14.99 (SO)
Le Mesnil Blanc de Blancs **NV** £15.99 (THR)
£15.99 (WR) £15.99 (BOT) £15.99 (YOU)
★ Pierre Vaudon 1er Cru **NV** £15.70 (HAH)

£16.00 → £17.99

Alfred Gratien ½ bottle **1989** £16.00 (WS)
Bauget-Jouette **1990** £17.50 (HIG)
Billecart-Salmon Brut Reserve **NV** £16.67
(MI) £17.95 (NI) £19.39 (VA) £19.51 (CB)
£19.85 (WRI) £19.95 (ELL) £19.95 (LIB)
£19.95 (ROB) £19.99 (OD) £22.00 (JU)
Billecart-Salmon Demi-Sec **NV** £17.95 (NI)
Boizel **NV** £17.00 (WS)
Henri Harlin **1989** £17.49 (OD)
Hurlingham Brut **NV** £17.50 (JU)

*Stars (★) indicate wines
selected by Oz Clarke in the
Best Buys section which begins
on page 9.*

Jacquart Tradition **NV** £16.69 (BO)
Joseph Perrier Cuvée Royal **NV** £16.95
(ROB) £17.06 (STE) £17.95 (BALL) £17.99
(GW) £18.95 (NA)
Laurent-Perrier Brut L.P. **NV** £18.28 (LAY)
£18.75 (GW) £18.79 (PLA) £19.00 (JU)
£19.59 (BIB) £19.74 (CB) £19.95 (ROB)
£20.68 (PLAY) £20.95 (CON) £21.09 (PEN)
£21.99 (WHI) £21.99 (UN) £21.99 (MAJ)
£21.99 (OD) £21.99 (VIC) £21.99 (THR)
£21.99 (WR) £21.99 (BOT) £22.43 (CHA)
£22.75 (AD) £22.95 (HED) £24.00 (MV)
Legras Grand Cru Blanc de Blancs **NV**
£16.95 (LEA)
Mercier **NV** £16.99 (COC) £17.49 (TES)
£17.49 (UN) £17.49 (SAF) £17.49 (VIC)
£17.49 (THR) £17.49 (WR) £17.49 (ASD)
Moët & Chandon Brut Impérial **NV**
£17.99 (POR) £18.79 (PLA) £18.95 (VA)
£19.13 (LAY) £19.49 (MORR) £19.49
(ASD) £19.50 (TAN) £19.95 (CON) £19.95
(BALL) £20.63 (PLAY) £20.75 (WRI) £20.94
(CB) £20.99 (TES) £20.99 (UN) £20.99
(MAJ) £20.99 (BO) £20.99 (CO) £20.99
(SAF) £20.99 (VIC) £20.99 (THR) £20.99
(BOT) £21.50 (WHI) £21.51 (STE) £21.75
(WAT) £21.95 (ROB) £22.00 (JU) £22.50
(FORT) £23.50 (VIN)
Palmer Brut **1990** £16.90 (JU)
Pierre Vaudon 1er Cru **1990** £17.95 (HAH)
Piper Heidsieck **NV** £16.99 (SO) £17.99
(MORR) £17.99 (TES) £17.99 (BO) £17.99
(CO) £17.99 (VIC) £17.99 (THR) £17.99
(WR) £17.99 (BOT) £18.33 (PLAY) £18.99
(SAF) £18.99 (ASD) £20.65 (UB)
de Telmont **1990** £16.99 (MAJ)

£18.00 → £19.99

Alfred Gratien **NV** £19.95 (CON)
Le Brun de Neuville Cuvée du Rois Clovis
NV £18.45 (WAT)
Bruno Paillard **NV** £18.99 (YOU) £19.75
(YAP)
Canard-Duchêne **1990** £19.95 (ROB)
£21.54 (CAV)
Deutz Brut Classic **NV** £19.39 (JER)
£21.99 (NEZ)
Duval Leroy Fleur de Champagne **1988**
£19.92 (PLA)
Georges Gardet **1989** £19.13 (ROS)
Gimonnet **1990** £18.99 (OD)
Lanson **NV** £18.49 (CON) £18.75 (WRI)
£18.99 (MORR) £18.99 (SO) £18.99 (ASD)
£19.99 (TES) £19.99 (WAI) £19.99 (UN)
£19.99 (SAF) £19.99 (THR) £19.99 (WR)

Louis Roederer Brut Premier **NV** £19.90
(NI) £22.05 (LAY) £22.62 (PLA) £22.95
(COC) £22.99 (VA) £23.00 (WS) £23.50
(PEN) £23.50 (CON) £23.95 (LEA) £23.95
(TAN) £23.99 (TES) £23.99 (POR) £23.99
(PHI) £23.99 (BO) £24.08 (STE) £24.25
(WRI) £24.50 (ROB) £24.95 (BALL) £24.99
(VIC) £24.99 (THR) £24.99 (WAI) £24.99
(UN) £24.99 (MAJ) £24.99 (OD) £24.99
(SAF) £25.45 (BER) £25.50 (TW) £25.50
(RES) £25.56 (CB) £25.65 (HAH) £25.95
(STA) £25.95 (BEN) £26.00 (JU) £26.95 (AD)
£27.00 (FORT) £27.99 (VIN) £29.00 (MV)
Louis Roederer Rich **NV** £19.99 (NI)
£23.32 (PLA) £25.00 (CON) £25.16 (STE)
£25.50 (WRI) £25.95 (ROB) £25.99 (MAJ)
£26.00 (JU) £26.80 (HAH) £27.75 (STA)
Mumm Cordon Rouge **NV** £18.50 (ROB)
£19.49 (UN) £19.49 (OD) £19.49 (SAF)
£19.49 (VIC) £19.49 (BOT) £19.49 (ASD)
Perrier-Jouët **NV** £18.95 (ROB) £19.99 (MAJ)
£19.99 (OD) £19.99 (THR) £26.00 (PIP)
Pol Roger **1990** £19.25 (SOM) £29.50 (COC)
£32.31 (CAV) £32.70 (HAH) £33.00 (JU)
£34.50 (LEA) £34.99 (MAJ) £34.99 (BEN)
£34.99 (OD) £34.99 (VIC) £34.99 (THR)
£34.99 (WR) £34.99 (BOT) £35.00 (FORT)
★ Prince William Blanc de Noirs Millennium
Brut **1990** £19.99 (SO)
'R' de Ruinart **NV** £19.51 (LAY) £21.95 (LEA)
£21.99 (WR) £21.99 (BOT) £23.00 (JU)
Taittinger Brut Réserve **NV** £19.68 (PLA)
£20.25 (STE) £20.99 (MORR) £21.00 (PLAY)
£22.04 (GW) £22.90 (VA) £22.95 (LEA)
£22.95 (ROB) £22.99 (POR) £23.99 (TES)
£23.99 (UN) £23.99 (MAJ) £23.99 (OD)
£23.99 (SAF) £23.99 (VIC) £23.99 (WR)
£23.99 (BOT) £24.00 (JU) £25.75 (UB)

£20.00 → £21.99

Bollinger Grande Année ½ bottle **1990**
£20.76 (CB)
Bruno Paillard Blanc de Blancs **NV** £21.90
(GAU) £25.99 (PHI)
Charles Heidsieck Brut Réserve **NV** £21.99
(TES) £23.00 (JU)

Please remember that
Oz Clarke's Wine Guide
*is a price **guide** and not a*
*price **list**. It is not meant to*
replace up-to-date
merchants' lists.

★ Charles Heidsieck Brut Réserve Mis en
Cave 1994 **NV** £21.99 (UN) £23.49 (VIC)
£23.49 (THR) £23.49 (WR) £23.49 (BOT)
Gosset Grande Réserve **NV** £21.95 (SOM)
£26.75 (WRI) £27.95 (LEA) £29.19 (NO)
£29.90 (NA) £29.95 (WR) £30.75 (ROB)
★ Joseph Perrier **1990** £20.66 (STE) £21.98
(GW) £22.95 (NA) £24.99 (NLW)
★ Le Mesnil Blanc de Blancs Réserve
Sélection **1990** £20.99 (YOU) £21.99 (VIC)
£21.99 (THR) £21.99 (WR) £21.99 (BOT)

£22.00 → £23.99

H Billiot Cuvée de Réserve Brut **NV**
£22.71 (BIB)
Bollinger **NV** £22.05 (LAY) £22.90 (CRO)
£23.49 (PLA) £23.60 (TAN) £23.99 (MORR)
£24.03 (REI) £24.75 (WRI) £24.78 (ROS)
£24.89 (STE) £24.95 (COC) £24.95 (DI)
£24.99 (VA) £25.25 (BO) £25.40 (PIP)
£25.70 (BEN) £25.73 (CB) £25.81 (PLAY)
£25.95 (STA) £25.95 (ROB) £25.99 (WAI)
£25.99 (SO) £25.99 (UN) £25.99 (MAJ)
£25.99 (CO) £25.99 (OD) £25.99 (SAF)
£25.99 (THR) £25.99 (BOT) £25.99 (ASD)
£26.00 (YAP) £26.00 (JU) £26.50 (BALL)
£26.85 (HAH) £27.02 (WY) £27.25 (FORT)

Billecart-Salmon ★★★★ (★)

Terrifically elegant Champagne
from a family-owned house.
Very refined, mature wines and
a delicate rosé. It's vintage,
Cuvée NF Billecart is also excellent.

(Oz Clarke's Wine Guide 1999)

For further information on stockists
please contact:

Billecart-Salmon (UK) Ltd

Tel: 0181 405 6345 Fax: 0181 405 6346

Henriot Blanc de Blancs **NV** £23.00 (JU)
Lamiable Le Club **1988** £23.50 (HIG)
Mercier **1993** £22.49 (VIC) £22.49 (THR)
£22.49 (WR) £22.49 (BOT)
Piper Heidsieck **1990** £23.99 (WR) £23.99
(BOT) £24.99 (SAF)
Pol Roger Chardonnay **1990** £22.35
(SOM) £44.00 (BEN) £50.00 (FORT)
Veuve Clicquot **NV** £20.82 (LAY) £21.15
(WY) £21.74 (PLA) £22.15 (REI) £22.73
(STE) £22.90 (FLE) £22.90 (VA) £22.91
(PEN) £22.94 (CB) £22.95 (TAN) £22.95
(BALL) £22.99 (MORR) £23.01 (BIB) £23.25
(COC) £23.35 (PLAY) £23.49 (WHI)
£23.49 (BO) £23.49 (ASD) £23.50 (CON)
£23.60 (HAH) £23.75 (WRI) £23.95 (LEA)
£23.99 (PHI) £23.99 (YOU) £24.49 (NLW)
£24.49 (TES) £24.49 (UN) £24.49 (MAJ)
£24.49 (CO) £24.49 (OD) £24.49 (SAF)
£24.49 (THR) £24.49 (WR) £24.49 (BOT)
£24.95 (STA) £24.95 (ROB) £24.95 (FORT)
£24.99 (VIN) £25.00 (JU) £25.25 (PIP)
£25.25 (NA) £25.95 (AD)
Veuve Clicquot Demi-Sec **NV** £22.99
(YOU) £24.49 (VIC) £24.49 (THR) £24.49
(BOT) £24.95 (STA)

£24.00 → £25.99

★ F Bonnet Cuvée 2000 Brut **1990** £25.00
(WAI)
Deutz Brut **1990** £24.28 (JER)
Hurlingham Brut **1990** £25.00 (JU)
Lanson **1990** £24.99 (JON)
Moët & Chandon Brut Impérial **1995**
£24.99 (ASD)
Moët & Chandon Brut Impérial **1993**
£24.99 (MORR) £26.20 (TAN) £26.30 (HAH)
£26.91 (CB) £26.99 (WHI) £27.49 (WAT)
£27.95 (ROB) £27.99 (TES) £27.99 (SAI)
£27.99 (MAJ) £27.99 (CO) £27.99 (VIC)
£27.99 (THR) £27.99 (WR) £27.99 (BOT)
£28.25 (WRI) £28.65 (PLAY) £30.00 (FORT)
Moët & Chandon Brut Impérial **1992**
£24.99 (POR) £25.00 (CON) £25.26 (PLA)
£25.49 (VA) £26.49 (BO) £26.91 (CB)
£26.95 (BALL) £27.99 (JON) £27.99 (OD)
£27.99 (WR) £27.99 (BOT) £28.00 (JU)
Mumm Cordon Rouge **1990** £24.49 (VIC)
£24.49 (THR) £24.49 (WR) £24.49 (BOT)
Orpale Grand Cru, Blanc de Blancs **1985**
£25.00 (MAR) £25.00 (JU)
Perrier-Jouët **1992** £25.99 (MAJ) £25.99
(OD) £25.99 (VIC) £25.99 (THR) £25.99
(WR) £25.99 (BOT) £32.75 (PIP)
Perrier-Jouët **1990** £25.95 (ROB)

£26.00 → £29.99

Alfred Gratien **1989** £26.00 (WS)
Bauget-Jouette Grande Réserve magnum
NV £29.00 (YOU) £36.00 (HIG)
★ Billecart-Salmon Cuvée N.F. Billecart **1991**
£29.95 (LEA) £29.99 (OD) £30.99 (LIB)
Billecart-Salmon Cuvée N.F. Billecart **1990**
£28.95 (LEA) £29.50 (WS) £30.00 (ELL)
£30.00 (FORT) £30.83 (MI) £30.99 (LIB)
Billecart-Salmon Cuvée N.F. Billecart **1989**
£28.33 (MI) £36.50 (AD)
Billecart-Salmon Cuvée N.F. Billecart **1988**
£28.95 (BER) £29.26 (CB)
Bollinger ½ bottle **1962** £29.38 (REI)
Charles Heidsieck Brut Réserve **1990**
£27.50 (PIP) £29.00 (JU)
Deutz Brut **1993** £26.99 (NEZ)
Krug Grande Cuvée ½ bottle **NV** £29.13
(CAV) £32.99 (VIC) £32.99 (THR) £32.99
(WR) £32.99 (BOT) £34.50 (BEN) £34.95
(STA) £35.04 (CB) £36.50 (FORT) £38.00
(CRO) £38.66 (TW)
Laurent-Perrier Brut **1988** £29.32 (CB)
£31.50 (ROB)
Laurent-Perrier Ultra Brut **NV** £29.99
(WR) £29.99 (BOT) £30.95 (BALL)
Louis Roederer Blanc de Blancs **1988**
£26.30 (NI)
Moët & Chandon Brut Impérial **1990**
£26.73 (COC)
Moët & Chandon Brut Impérial **1988**
£27.99 (UN)
Mumm Crémant de Cramant Blanc de
Blancs **NV** £28.50 (ROB)
Pol Roger **1988** £28.50 (VA) £30.95 (BER)
£32.31 (REI) £32.55 (UB) £33.50 (ROB)
£33.99 (YOU) £60.00 (RES)
'R' de Ruinart **1992** £26.99 (WR) £26.99
(BOT) £28.50 (LEA)
Taittinger **1992** £29.99 (POR) £30.66 (PLAY)
Taittinger **1990** £29.99 (GW) £32.00 (JU)
£34.99 (WR) £34.99 (BOT)
Veuve Clicquot Vintage Réserve **1989**
£28.20 (REI) £29.80 (CRO) £31.50 (ROB)

> • Wines are listed in A–Z
> order within each price
> band.
> • For each wine, vintages are
> listed in descending order.
> • Each vintage of any wine
> appears only once.

THE BEST SELLING C

CHAMPAGNE

MERCIER

Epernay — France

MPAGNE IN FRANCE

£30.00 → £39.99

Billecart-Salmon Brut Réserve 1991
£33.99 (OD)
Billecart-Salmon Blanc de Blancs 1988
£32.08 (MI)
Bollinger 1990 £33.29 (FA) £35.99 (POR)
£36.40 (WAT) £37.70 (PIP) £38.50 (CON)
£38.70 (WRI) £38.95 (COC) £41.95 (HAH)
£41.95 (BEN) £41.99 (TES) £41.99 (THR)
£41.99 (WR) £41.99 (BOT) £46.00 (MV)
Bollinger Grande Année 1990 £33.29 (CAV)
£34.00 (JU) £37.95 (BALL) £38.61 (STE)
£38.90 (VA) £38.95 (DI) £39.95 (LEA)
£40.34 (CB) £40.54 (TW) £41.20 (PLAY)
£41.99 (WAI) £41.99 (MAJ) £41.99 (YOU)
£42.00 (YAP) £42.50 (LAY) £42.50 (FORT)
Bollinger Grande Année 1989 £35.07 (REI)
£35.74 (ROS) £36.00 (CRO) £38.95 (DI)
£40.00 (WS) £41.12 (WY) £41.99 (PHI)
£46.41 (TW) £47.50 (AD) £47.78 (VIN)
Bruno Paillard 1989 £30.00 (YAP)
Charles Heidsieck Brut Réserve 1981
£31.99 (YOU) £32.31 (REI)
Deutz Blanc de Blancs 1993 £34.99 (NEZ)
Dom Ruinart Blanc de Blancs 1990
£39.00 (JU) £54.99 (WR) £54.99 (BOT)
**Duval Leroy Fleur de Champagne
magnum NV** £32.90 (PEN)
**Georges Gardet Brut Spéciale magnum
NV** £31.85 (CON) £38.99 (VIN)
Gosset Grande Millésime 1993 £36.00
(WRI) £39.95 (WR) £39.95 (BOT)
Gosset Grande Millésime 1989 £38.99
(YOU) £39.95 (BAL) £39.95 (BALL) £41.50
(RES)
Heidsieck Diamant Bleu 1989 £39.99 (OD)
Laurent-Perrier 1990 £31.50 (ROB)
£31.70 (AV) £31.95 (LEA) £32.31 (CAV)
£32.54 (PLAY) £32.67 (CB) £33.50 (WHI)
£33.95 (BALL) £33.99 (TES) £34.95 (GW)
£36.00 (HED) £37.95 (AD) £38.55 (CHA)
Laurent-Perrier ½ bottle 1966 £37.01 (REI)
Laurent-Perrier Cuvée Grande Siècle NV
£35.00 (BU) £49.95 (WR) £49.95 (BOT)
£55.00 (AD) £55.00 (WS) £57.05 (CHA)
£61.05 (PEN) £62.50 (BALL)
**Laurent-Perrier Cuvée Grande Siècle
1990** £39.17 (FA) £76.72 (PLAY)
Louis Roederer 1990 £35.00 (JU) £39.36
(PEN) £39.36 (REI) £39.95 (VA) £42.00
(TAN) £42.00 (LEA) £42.50 (LAY) £43.55
(HAH) £44.90 (BER) £45.00 (WAI)
Louis Roederer 1988 £36.90 (COC)
£40.70 (HAH)

Louis Roederer Blanc de Blancs 1990
£38.19 (PLA) £41.45 (GW) £42.30 (PEN)
£42.48 (LAY) £44.50 (STA) £46.00 (BEN)
Louis Roederer Blanc de Blancs 1994
£39.87 (STE) £44.30 (NA)
**Moët & Chandon Brut Impérial magnum
NV** £37.95 (WR) £37.95 (BOT) £38.50
(LAY) £38.99 (MORR) £39.30 (TAN) £40.99
(BO) £41.99 (TES) £41.99 (CO) £42.57 (STE)
£42.75 (WRI) £42.99 (JON) £43.00 (WHI)
£43.05 (CB) £43.95 (ROB) £44.50 (BALL)
£45.50 (VA) £47.30 (NA) £47.50 (FORT)
Pol Roger 1989 £32.31 (REI) £35.00 (BALL)
£39.99 (VIN)
Thienot 1988 £39.50 (UN)

Veuve Clicquot 1990 £31.00 (FLE) £32.00
(JU) £32.75 (WRI) £32.99 (WHI) £33.00
(WS) £33.00 (FORT) £33.95 (ROB) £33.99
(AV) £34.99 (NLW) £35.25 (REI) £35.99
(UN) £35.99 (OD) £36.90 (CB)
Veuve Clicquot Rich 1990 £32.05 (HAH)
£33.95 (LEA) £34.50 (FORT) £35.99 (UN)
Veuve Clicquot Rich 1989 £32.95 (BALL)
Veuve Clicquot Rich 1988 £35.99 (WR)
£35.99 (BOT)
Veuve Clicquot Vintage Réserve 1991
£31.41 (STE) £32.50 (CON) £32.85 (PLAY)
£33.95 (LEA) £33.95 (ROB) £33.99 (AME)
£34.10 (PIP) £34.90 (NA) £34.95 (HAH)
£35.99 (MAJ) £35.99 (SAF) £35.99 (VIC)
£35.99 (THR) £35.99 (WR) £35.99 (BOT)
£36.90 (CB)
Veuve Clicquot Vintage Réserve 1990
£32.95 (BALL) £32.99 (YOU) £33.00 (HAH)
£33.33 (MI) £33.95 (LEA) £35.99 (WAI)

£40.00 → £49.99

Alfred Gratien 1985 £45.00 (FORT)
Billecart-Salmon Blanc de Blancs 1989
£40.00 (FORT)
Billecart-Salmon Grande Cuvée 1988
£44.50 (LEA) £49.50 (VA)
Bollinger magnum NV £44.36 (LAY)
£51.90 (TAN) £51.93 (STE) £52.50 (PHI)
£52.64 (CB) £52.95 (CON) £54.00 (BEN)
£55.00 (WS) £55.61 (WY) £57.70 (NA)

OZ CLARKE'S
MILLENNIUM PARTY GUIDE

**Best Buy Fizz for the Millennium and
beyond • How to make your party go with a big, big
bang • How to get through the morning after**

My one-step plan for a glorious Millennium night goes like this: I'm going to make sure that I'm a guest rather than a host. Since I'm terminally disorganized whenever I invite people round, however enthusiastic and well-intentioned I may be, my friends and family should be grateful that I have taken this decision. In fact I'm hoping that they will be so relieved that they'll repay the favour by laying on something really special. Because, when it comes to a Millennium party the host is going to have to deliver the goods. No second chances with this one.

So, while I'm ducking the organizational responsibilities, I'm rooting for every single one of you, and the least I can do is to help you make a hit with the drink. So. Have a Good One. Welcome, oh Brave New World of Y2K!

WHAT TO DRINK

We have to make one assumption straight off – otherwise we'll agree on nothing. I'm not trying to bully you, but just so as you know, in my book there is no other drink for your Millennium party than thrilling, spilling, frothy, jubilant fizz. It's the sound of popping corks, it's that tantalizing tickle on your tongue and all those bubbles sending the alcohol whooshing round everybody's bloodstream for an instant explosion of joie de vivre – bubbly sets the party alight.

Party fizz wants to be decent stuff that keeps flowing all night, when any subtle nuances of flavour will be swept away in the crazy mayhem of celebration. So don't bother with expensive Vintage or luxury cuvée Champagnes. Then again, skimping on price won't do you any favours. I'd say you want a wine that is not searingly dry (otherwise you'll all have acid stomach ache by 11pm). It must have long-lasting small bubbles and just enough richness of flavour to keep it interesting. A good non-vintage Champagne with a few months of bottle age or a quality New World sparkler will do

the trick. Anything from my Best Buy Fizz recommendations should see you through the night in style.

Tasty wine from New World countries will always beat Champagne on price, though only a few examples match Champagne for sheer style. Australia, New Zealand and California have all mastered the art and South Africa is starting to produce the goods, too. For budget fizz, the choice is no longer limited to Cava from

---

BUBBLY COCKTAILS

The two party classics I love are Kir Royale and Buck's Fizz. For the Kir just add a slop of that wonderful French invention crème de cassis (blackcurrant liqueur) to enjoy an altogether sweeter and fruitier experience (slightly more alcoholic, too – so beware). Buck's Fizz is a mix of two parts Champagne to one of orange juice and it has the advantage that you can pretend it is good for your health. Don't waste expensive fizz on this but do use tasty freshly squeezed orange juice.

Good parties go with a ...

Great parties go with a ...

POP

Once you pop you can't stop.

Spain: you should also consider New World bargains and those neglected Italian classics, sweetish Asti and clean, dry Prosecco.

PRACTICALITIES

As far as quantity is concerned, the only thing you need to worry about is running out. Most wine merchants and supermarkets will let you buy large quantities on a sale-or-return basis, so you can get a refund on any unopened bottles. Seeing as it's such a long party, cater for one bottle per person: it averages out pretty well between enthusiastic drinkers, moderate drinkers and abstainers/drivers.

Now, pay attention, because this is the single most important piece of advice I have to give you. Nobody likes warm bubbly. You absolutely must serve your fizz cold, cold, cold. If your fridge isn't big enough, buy or make large quantities of ice and fill your bath with a decadent display of ice, water and bottles. Immersing a bottle of wine in ice and water is the quickest way to chill it down – it'll be enjoyable in 15 minutes and deliciously crisp-cold in half an hour. A fridge takes four hours to chill a bottle thoroughly. Ideally you should have ice by the sackful and use just enough water to cover the ice. If you add salt to the mixture it will work even faster. This bathtub method is 100 per cent Millennium Bug-proof, too, so you can celebrate in style even if the world is plunged into pre-industrial blackout at midnight.

This is not going to be a night for resorting to coffee mugs and egg-cups, so gather up plenty of glasses in preparation for the party or borrow them from a shop. Go for Champagne flutes. These tall, slender glasses are ideal for bubbly because they make the bubbles last a long time. But even with these glasses, grease and detergent residues can both kill off the bubbles in double-quick time, so give the glasses a rinse in really hot water and air-dry them or polish them with a totally clean linen cloth – even if the shop you borrow them from promises that they're spotless.

Order your wine, glasses and ice in plenty of time, because demand is going to be high. In fact, do it the moment you have finished reading this. Look around for bargains on bulk buys, but most important of all make sure that the wine merchant can guarantee to supply you with everything you need when the time comes. Get a receipt and pay a deposit if necessary.

Well, that's it. All you have to do now is serve the stuff. Open the bottles with care – wounds inflicted by high-velocity Champagne corks will probably be at an all-time high on Millennium night – and with flair: always present a freshly opened, shimmeringly icy bottle just before your guests exhibit that haggard, panicky expression that says, 'Oh God! My glass is empty.'

HOW TO OPEN SPARKLING WINES

The pressure in the bottle does the work, so all you have to do is control it. If you don't, you'll get a loud pop, a rush of foam and a half-empty bottle of rapidly flattening fizz.

Tear off the foil to reveal the wire cage that restrains the cork. Place one thumb over the top of the cork and undo the cage. From the moment the cage is released there is an ever-present danger of the cork shooting off, so point the bottle away from people and breakables. Grasp the cork with one hand and hold the bottle firmly with the other. Now turn the bottle slowly while holding the cork in place. The cork will start to ease out under the pressure. If you want to be doubly sure as the evening wears on and your attention wanders, do the whole thing under a cloth, the weight of which will catch and control any over-enthusiastic corks. But if you think all that rather dampens the party spirit – well, I won't disagree.

the quintessence of Lanson style...

BEST BUY FIZZ

I'll start with the bad news. There is a scandalous amount of faulty cork floating around the world at the moment and far too much is finding its way into bottles of fizz. At our tastings to choose the top drops for the big night, one in eight bottles of fizz was spoiled by a tainted cork. Not one in eighty, one in eight. And if there is ever a time when you absolutely don't want to be offering your friends and loved ones a glass of something that smells like an unwashed football sock left over from last season, Jan 31, 1999 is that time. So, sorry, but I'd advise you to pick up a few extra bottles just in case. At least it makes a good excuse to over-cater, and, looking on the bright side, there's a seven in eight chance that every bottle will be fine! Also, any good wine merchant will give you a refund on a faulty bottle if you take it back.

We also found that it makes good sense to trade up. The cheaper end of the fizz market is tasting rather too cheap at the moment. It's a case of *Millenniumitis* – a quality-impairing ailment caused by the stretching of supplies of decent wine to match the supposedly uncritical demands of over-enthusiastic revellers. Well, it seems to be taking its toll on several New World sparklers that I would have expected to shine, and it is also diminishing the quality of our most reliable budget performer of recent years – Spanish Cava.

And *Millenniumitis* is alive and well and living in Champagne as happily as elsewhere in the world. Any of you who have bought cheap Champagne in the French channel ports recently in the hope of a bargain bootful of frothy delight will probably have had a sour, raw return to reality on opening the first bottle.

But in fact the British Champagne trade seems to have handled the problem reasonably well. Prices have inevitably risen and some famous names and regular supermarket favourites haven't made the grade, but we have found a range of less well-known, smaller producers who have

really hit the mark plus a selection of trusty favourites who haven't compromised their quality in the rush for our Millennium cash.

TOP OF THE POPS

❶ NV Champagne Brut Réserve Mis en Cave 1994, Charles Heidsieck, £23.49, Bottoms Up, Thresher, Victoria Wine, Wine Rack
Ah, if only more of the big names were as resolute and serious about the dedicated pursuit of pleasure as Charles Heidsieck. This specially aged non-vintage shines out above its peers for sheer class and its irresistible marriage of chestnut, cream and chocolate in a foaming cup of fun.
also at Unwins

❷ 1990 Champagne Blanc de Blancs Réserve Sélection Brut, Le Mesnil, £21.99, Bottoms Up, Thresher, Wine Rack, Victoria Wine
This is practically toasty it's so nutty, but it's toffeed too. In fact there's a flavour almost like buttered brazils – and that, from me, is high praise. Add bubbles into the equation and I'm all juiced up and ready to party.

❸ 1991 Champagne Cuvée Nicolas-François Billecart Brut, Billecart-Salmon, £29.99, Oddbins
1991 was a wet, cold, poor year in Champagne. But Billecart-Salmon is one of the region's greats and no-one else could pull this marvellously refined fizz – lean like cedar, yet rich like a hazelnut and Horlicks porridge – out of such a damp fire.
also at Lea & Sandeman, Liberty Wines

❹ 1995 Pinot Noir/Chardonnay Brut, Seaview, £8.99, Oddbins (Australia)
At last – a good foaming, nutty, yeasty delight from the Southern Seas. New

QUESTIONS

(i) Where would you look to find out about an erotic golf course in France or the best place to buy cheese?

(ii) Who would you contact for the best deal on travel insurance and vehicle breakdown cover in France?

(answers below)

Try them & see!

Telephone 0800 136574
Travel Insurance for French Holidays

(ii) RESCUE FRANCE Direct

www.rescuefrance.co.uk

(i) ShareFrance Forum at

ANSWERS

My shoes were squelching,
the bugs were biting and
Joe was being his usual romantic self.

Thank heavens for

HARDYS

www.hardys-wines.com

LUMIÈRE DU
MILLÉNAIRE

RAND SIÈCLE
1990
MILLÉSIME

SIÈCLE

PARTY FOOD

You won't make it through a long party without something to eat. But frankly, fizz is rarely the perfect accompaniment to food – so I'm talking about stomach lining at the basic level here, and the supermarket shelves are full of snacks and nibbles which will do just fine. The best simple snacks with wine are crisps.

If you are planning anything grander, remember to cater for vegetarians and any children. And if you are really splashing out, oysters, caviar and strawberries (presumably imported from the southern hemisphere at vast expense) are the most deliciously luxurious partners for Champagne.

World fizzers were, surprisingly, a big disappointment in this tasting. Thank goodness our trusty old friend Seaview still does the business.
also at S H Jones and Safeway

5 1996 Extra Brut, Warden Vineyard, £11.95, Hedley Wright (UK)
One of the most original sparklers in Britain today. Nothing like Champagne, nothing like Cava, or even New World fizz. Just a brilliant burst of unabashed Englishness – elderflower, hedgerow scent, fresh-tilled earth and the mouthwatering perfume of tomato leaves…

6 1993 Classic Blend Brut, Nyetimber, £17.75, Fortnum & Mason (UK)
…and while we're on the English! This gorgeous, yeasty, nutty fizz, with a tiny suggestion of Horlicks and the savoury crunch of hazelnut is a superb Champagne lookalike – from the depths of greenest, leafiest Sussex.

7 1992 Berrys' Australian Sparkling Wine, Taltarni, £10.75, Berry Bros.
Good stuff, this. Lovely foaming feel in the mouth and a real indulgent splattering of buttered brazils, yeasty cream and a sprig of mint to fill in the gaps in the conversation.

8 NV Champagne Premier Cru Brut, Pierre Vaudon, £15.70, Haynes, Hanson & Clark
The archetypal House Champagne – I don't ever remember a bad bottle. Mild apple fruit, soft bready yeast and lick of cream. Ace party fizz.

9 NV Champagne Brut Rosé, Brossault, £14.99, Fuller's
Brossault Champagnes are always on the mature side, but hey, older people gotta party! – and this delicious, hazelnutty, almost syrupy-ripe wine'll put the rhythm and booze back into your joints.

10 NV Champagne Premier Cru Brut, Forget-Brimont, £14.95, Justerini & Brooks
So ripe that there's a distinct flavour of pineapple – but it works! That pineapple is wrapped with creamy yeast and speared with acid to make a very pleasant sparkler.

BUBBLING UNDER
1 1990 Champagne Blanc de Blancs Cuvée 2000 Brut, £25, Waitrose
Great label – announcing, as if we didn't know, that 'Good wine gladdens the heart of man'. Well this gladdens my heart quite a lot, with its soft yeasty style and almost peppery nuttiness. But there's also quite a rasp of acidity, and I think it'll be better for a party to launch 2001 than this year's bash.

2 1990 Champagne Blanc de Noirs Millennium Brut, Prince William, £19.99, Somerfield
An old favourite, thankfully on fine form, showing a good old-fashioned burly richness and attractive yeast shot through with brisk, brash bubbles.

MARKS & SPENCER
Time to Celebrate™

Oudinot Brut

Cava

Bluff Hill
Sparkling

Asti Spumante

De Saint Gall
Vintage Brut
Champagne

Chablis

Fleurie

Casa Leona
Cabernet
Sauvignon

Chateauneauf
du Pape

Margaux

Marques del
Romeral

Vintage
Character Port

wines beers
&spirits

THE MORNING AFTER

It may feel like the end of the world, but it's the start of a new Millennium. This is no ordinary hangover, it's the hangover of a thousand New Year's Eves rolled into one. Here's how to face it.

The first step is to start rehydrating your body. Drink the occasional glass of water during the party and have more before you go to bed. Have a glass by the bed and take a good slurp every time you become sufficiently conscious. Tea, coffee and soft drinks all make you dehydrate more, so stick to plain still water.

Next, you need to replace all that lost energy and those blitzed nutrients. Fried and sugary food will give an instant rush of comfort, but, for long-term benefits, cereal, bread, pasta and potatoes can't be beaten. Fresh fruit and veg will help restore your vitamin and mineral levels. Limit your ambitions to alternate bouts of eating and sleeping until you feel you can cope with the world.

Don't take aspirin if you have a headache, as it will irritate an already delicate stomach lining. Ibuprofen and paracetamol are both gentler. If you take a painkiller when you go to bed – as a pre-emptive strike before there is any pain to kill – it may make things better in the morning. Something to settle your stomach is a good idea, and many purpose-made hangover cures combine this with a painkiller and a dose of energy-boosting glucose.

And if your energy levels remain resolutely sub-zero, a couple of fizzy vitamin B & C tablets and a couple of Guarana energy tabs should finally kick-start your vital organs. Or of course, you can just write off January 1 altogether. An awful lot of us will.

❸ 1990 Champagne Brut, Joseph Perrier, £21.98, Great Western Wines

This is a famous name which has made a good, but unspectacular, 1990. Already quite mature, it foams along with a pleasing flavour of honey and nuts and a positively intriguing aftertaste of Horlicks.
also at Balls Brothers, Nadder Wines, Roberson, Stevens Garnier

❹ 1992 Pinot Noir/Chardonnay, Mountadam, Eden Valley, £19.95, Adnams (Australia)

Hey, here's an Aussie battler! Packed full of flavours of old strawberry and chocolate and leather, it's an acquired taste but it's a mighty mouthful. It's not a wine that'll keep you dancing till dawn, but it's just the drop for a spot of armchair philosophy.
also at Noel Young Wines

❺ NV Champagne Blanc de Blancs Grand Cru Brut, Prince William, £14.99, Somerfield

Baby brother of the Prince William Blanc de Noirs above, this is good, traditional, nutty Champagne – quite mature and with a soft, shiny elegance like a polished hazelnut shell.

❻ NV Champagne Premier Cru Brut, £11.99, Tesco

Bright, exhilarating modern Champagne from an excellent supplier in the Côte de Blancs, pleasantly nutty with a nice apple acid and a downy quilt of creamy yeast.

❼ 1990 Champagne Premier Cru Brut, £15.99, ASDA

This isn't a classic, gently foaming, biscuity, nutty 1990. In fact it's positively raisiny, almost like a raisin-stuffed baked russet apple. Dry, yes, but it hardly seems so.

❽ NV Champagne Carte d'Or Brut, Drappier, £15.99, Anthony Byrne

Quite full-flavoured and traditional, with a rather attractive nutty butter quality to it and a touch of mushroom. But that's just the bottle maturity. The froth is still fresh, so it works.

❾ NV Champagne Extra Quality Brut, £15.89, Lay & Wheeler

Good-quality youngish fizz with a hint of perfume, a gentle creamy yeast, a flick of leather and the promise that this will be peaking nicely as 2000 starts.

The real taste of California

njoy the new wines of Blossom Hill.
erfect for drinking any time.

Carol A. Thorup
Blossom Hill winemaker

LEFTOVER FIZZ

If you're fortunate enough to have some unopened bottles left over at the end of the party, tuck a few away for a rainy day. Champagne and the best New World fizz will become richer and more delicious for several years. Cava, however, won't improve, so take it back for a refund or drink it up during the winter.

If it's a matter of leftover bottles that have already been opened, the best way to preserve the bubbles and the freshness for a few days is to combine the contents so that you have one or two full bottles to store rather than several half-empty ones. You can buy purpose-made sparkling wine stoppers or alternatively push in an ordinary cork from a bottle of still wine and stand your leftover fizz in the fridge door. If you keep the sealed bottles refrigerated, they should be fine for a few more days.

10 NV Champagne J.M. Gremillet Brut Sélection, £14.65, Christopher Piper Wines

Quite classy stuff. It'll still be fairly young on Millennium night but will mature to gain a depth of chocolate, cream and nuts.

11 NV Marlborough Cuvée Brut, Deutz, £10.99, Oddbins (New Zealand)

This isn't quite the same ultra-reliable classy Champagne lookalike it used to be – partly because pressure on supply is causing them to release the wine too young. But with a few months age this still achieves a marvellously nutty flavour better than much Champagne.

also at Booths, Bottoms Up, Croque-en-Bouche, Tesco, Thresher, Victoria Wine, Wine Rack

12 NV Domaine de l'Aigle Tradition Brut, £8.95, Christopher Piper Wines (France)

It's got just a touch more gooey banana-split perfume about it than I'd like, but it's good, gentle, soft and creamy too and makes a very pleasant glass of fizz.

BARGAIN BIN

1 NV Cava Rosé Brut, £4.99, Somerfield (Spain)

Best of the Cavas, pink or white, and the right price. Loads of pink colour and a really refreshing flavour that mixes strawberry fruit gums, pepper and celery. Smashing pink party pop.

2 Asti, Gianni £4.49, Morrisons (sweet, Italy)

Lovely bright, breezy slightly sweet fizz with the carefree flavours of hedgerow elderflower and orchard apples sprinkled with icing sugar.

3 1998 South African Sparkling Sauvignon Blanc Brut, £4.99, Tesco

Amazing! A fizzer that tastes of nettles and Granny Smiths and green melon flesh. Purely and simply: Sauvignon with bubbles.

4 1995 Australian Chardonnay Brut, £6.99, Somerfield

Good, powerful old-style Aussie Chardie that someone has whacked some bubbles into. Not delicate, not subtle, just a big, buttery, bubbly Aussie gobsmacker.

5 1996 Vintage Cava, £6.49, ASDA (Spain)

Typically peppery Cava taste, with a flash of gunmetal grey, but an extra handful of autumnal fruit makes it worth the money.

6 NV Cava Bonaval, Bodegas Inviosa, £6.95, Adnams (Spain)

Not at all like typical Cava – I even thought there was a touch of sweetness. There's certainly a hint of perfume and a mild pear, lemon sherbet and icing sugar flavour that's pretty easy on the palate and on the skull.

DID YOU KNOW...
There are reputed to be 49 million bubbles in a bottle of Champagne – though I don't personally know anyone who's counted them all

Ordinary days have extraordinary moments!

Bollinger RD 1985 £45.04 (FA) £46.51 (CAV) £49.95 (DI) £53.60 (PIP) £55.00 (WS) £56.95 (BEN) £57.95 (WR) £57.95 (BOT) £58.75 (CB) £59.00 (BAL) £60.00 (MV)

Bollinger RD 1982 £49.50 (WRI) £51.66 (ROS) £59 00(VA) £60.71 (FA) £66.99 (YOU) £70.50 (PEN) £70.50 (REI) £71.50 (BEN) £75.00 (FORT) £84.42 (TW)

Deutz Cuvée de William Deutz 1988 £43.08 (JER)

Dom Ruinart Blanc de Blancs 1988 £48.00 (BER) £54.00 (LEA) £125.00 (FORT)

Georges Lilbert Blanc de Blancs 1976 £44.65 (TW)

Gosset Grande Millésime 1990 £40.00 (FORT)

Lanson magnum NV £41.49 (VIC) £41.49 (THR) £41.49 (WR) £41.49 (BOT)

Laurent-Perrier Brut L.P. magnum NV £40.66 (CB) £43.99 (MAJ) £46.06 (CHA)

Louis Roederer 1993 £43.40 (NA) £45.00 (FORT)

Moët & Chandon Brut Impérial magnum 1988 £41.99 (UN) £59.50 (ROB)

Mumm René Lalou 1985 £47.00 (CRO)

Perrier-Jouët Belle Époque 1990 £49.99 (VIC) £49.99 (THR) £49.99 (WR) £49.99 (BOT) £54.99 (OD) £60.00 (FORT)

Pol Roger Chardonnay 1990 £42.00 (RES) £50.29 (VIN)

Pol Roger Chardonnay 1988 £41.13 (PEN) £42.50 (WRI) £46.00 (LEA)

Pol Roger Cuvée Sir Winston Churchill 1988 £41.95 (SOM) £61.69 (CAV) £70.95 (TAN) £72.15 (HAH) £72.90 (BEN) £75.00 (RES) £75.00 (FORT) £78.95 (VIN)

Pol Roger Cuvée Sir Winston Churchill 1985 £49.95 (VA)

Pol Roger White Foil magnum NV £45.41 (REI) £47.00 (PEN) £50.00 (WRI) £52.50 (FORT) £52.50 (BALL) £55.95 (RES)

Veuve Clicquot magnum NV £45.00 (YOU) £46.99 (PHI) £47.00 (CON) £47.50 (ROB) £48.00 (VA) £49.99 (VIC) £49.99 (THR)

Veuve Clicquot Vintage Réserve 1982 £47.00 (REI)

• *All prices for each wine are listed together in ascending order.*

• *Price bands refer to the lowest price for which the wine is available.*

£50.00 → £59.99

Alfred Gratien magnum 1989 £55.00 (WS)

Billecart-Salmon Grande Cuvée 1989 £54.95 (LIB)

Bollinger Grand Année ½ bottle 1966 £52.29 (REI)

Deutz Cuvée de William Deutz 1990 £54.99 (NEZ)

Dom Pérignon 1992 £58.50 (STE) £59.00 (WHI) £59.50 (TAN) £59.99 (BO) £61.69 (BIB) £64.50 (STA) £64.95 (LEA) £64.99 (UN) £64.99 (MAJ) £64.99 (THR) £64.99 (BOT) £65.00 (NA) £65.89 (PLAY) £69.00 (PHI)

Dom Pérignon 1990 £53.85 (FA) £58.46 (PLA) £58.50 (CON) £58.60 (COC) £58.75 (WY) £59.93 (AV) £59.99 (JON) £60.00 (WRI) £60.00 (VA) £60.34 (TW) £61.34 (CB) £61.99 (WAI) £61.99 (POR) £61.99 (YOU) £62.50 (BALL) £62.75 (HAH) £63.95 (PIP) £64.95 (LEA) £64.99 (TES) £64.99 (OD) £65.00 (FORT) £67.00 (JU) £68.05 (CAV) £75.00 (MI) £79.00 (VIN)

Dom Pérignon 1988 £56.20 (WAT) £58.50 (CON) £75.00 (ROB) £79.00 (LEA)

Krug Grande Cuvée NV £50.92 (FA) £55.00 (BU) £58.26 (CAV) £64.00 (WAT) £64.63 (PLA) £65.00 (VA) £65.50 (COC) £65.95 (THR) £65.95 (WR) £66.50 (CON) £67.75 (BEN) £67.90 (AV) £68.00 (LEA) £68.30 (TAN) £68.54 (BIB) £68.95 (ROB) £69.00 (JU) £69.40 (PLAY) £69.95 (BER) £69.98 (LAY) £70.00 (FORT) £70.00 (BALL) £70.50 (HAH) £71.50 (PIP) £71.85 (REI) £72.00 (CRO) £75.00 (RES) £75.00 (POR) £75.95 (VIN)

Louis Roederer Cristal 1986 £58.74 (NO)

Moët & Chandon Brut Impérial magnum 1992 £55.95 (THR) £55.95 (WR)

Pol Roger Cuvée Sir Winston Churchill 1986 £59.50 (COC) £68.15 (PEN) £68.75 (WRI) £70.00 (BALL) £78.95 (VIN)

Taittinger Collection Artist's Label 1990 £55.81 (FA) £85.00 (FORT)

Taittinger Comtes de Champagne Blanc de Blancs 1993 £57.15 (STE) £63.50 (NA)

Taittinger Comtes de Champagne Blanc de Blancs **1990** £53.85 (CAV) £74.99 (MAJ)

Taittinger Comtes de Champagne Blanc de Blancs **1989** £57.36 (PLAY) £60.00 (FORT) £69.95 (ROB) £75.00 (TES)

Taittinger Comtes de Champagne Blanc de Blancs **1988** £52.00 (LEA) £59.00 (JU) £59.06 (GW) £62.50 (ROB) £75.00 (WR)

Veuve Clicquot Vintage Réserve **1988** £58.16 (TW)

Veuve Clicquot la Grande Dame **1990** £50.92 (FA) £62.50 (CON) £62.94 (PLAY) £63.45 (HAH) £65.00 (FORT) £66.95 (RES)

Veuve Clicquot la Grande Dame **1989** £53.85 (WY) £58.00 (JU) £62.90 (VA) £65.00 (BALL) £65.00 (MI) £65.95 (AD)

£60.00 → £74.99

Bollinger Grand Année **1975** £70.00 (YOU)

Krug **1989** £66.58 (FA) £68.05 (CAV) £74.99 (AV) £76.38 (BIB) £76.99 (THR) £79.00 (LEA) £79.00 (JON) £79.31 (CB) £79.50 (CON) £80.00 (WS) £80.00 (FORT) £82.50 (ROB) £82.80 (PIP) £84.93 (PLAY) £85.00 (OD) £85.10 (HAH) £85.95 (BEN) £87.71 (TW) £89.95 (RES) £89.95 (AD) £93.60 (VIN)

Krug **1981** £65.60 (FA) £82.00 (JU)

Laurent-Perrier Cuvée Grande Siècle **1988** £64.05 (AV) £75.00 (FORT)

Louis Roederer Cristal **1989** £69.33 (REI) £82.48 (NO) £85.00 (ROB) £85.70 (WRI) £87.20 (COC) £95.50 (BEN) £99.00 (VA) £105.75 (TW)

Mercier **1961** £64.63 (REI)

Moët & Chandon Brut Impérial **1976** £65.00 (MI)

Moët & Chandon Brut Impérial ½ bottle **1921** £64.63 (REI)

Perrier-Jouët Belle Époque **1992** £60.75 (PIP)

Perrier-Jouët Belle Époque **1983** £67.00 (VIN)

Pol Roger magnum **1990** £68.50 (RES) £75.00 (FORT)

Pol Roger magnum **1988** £66.27 (PEN)

Louise Pommery Prestige Cuvée **1988** £65.00 (ROB)

Salon **1988** £62.98 (CB) £68.05 (CAV)

Taittinger Comtes de Champagne Blanc de Blancs **1986** £69.99 (VIN) £152.75 (TW)

Veuve Clicquot la Grande Dame **1988** £68.00 (WR) £68.00 (BOT)

Veuve Clicquot Vintage Réserve **1964** £70.00 (YOU)

£75.00 → £99.99

Bauget-Jouette Grande Réserve jeroboam NV £99.88 (HIG)

Bollinger Grande Année magnum 1990 £80.00 (CON) £81.85 (CB) £83.99 (YOU) £84.90 (BEN) £85.00 (NA) £90.00 (FORT)

Bollinger Grande Année magnum 1989 £75.00 (BO) £77.55 (PEN) £81.51 (NO) £106.81 (TW)

Bollinger RD 1979 £79.95 (DI) £85.00 (RES) £87.99 (YOU) £90.00 (FORT) £95.50 (BEN) £96.00 (MV) £98.99 (VIN) £107.04 (TW)

Charles Heidsieck Brut Réserve 1953 £99.88 (REI)

Dom Pérignon 1985 £76.99 (YOU) £84.25 (BER) £85.00 (AV) £90.00 (ROB) £99.50 (RES) £125.00 (MI)

Dom Pérignon 1982 £99.88 (FA) £108.69 (REI)

Dom Pérignon 1980 £94.00 (REI)

Krug 1990 £83.95 (STA)

Krug 1982 £99.88 (FA)

Louis Roederer Cristal 1998 £99.95 (WR) £99.95 (BOT)

Louis Roederer Cristal 1993 £81.59 (STE) £90.65 (NA) £91.20 (PLAY) £99.00 (RES) £99.99 (MAJ) £99.99 (POR)

Louis Roederer Cristal 1990 £75.00 (JU) £80.05 (AV) £81.00 (JON) £81.85 (GW) £84.60 (CB) £85.00 (CON) £85.00 (BALL) £85.80 (TAN) £87.20 (COC) £88.13 (PLA) £88.77 (NO) £92.00 (STA) £92.04 (FA) £95.00 (FORT) £95.15 (HAH) £99.99 (OD) £105.52 (TW) £110.50 (BEN)

Louis Roederer Cristal 1988 £87.20 (COC) £89.50 (NI) £94.95 (VIN)

Louis Roederer Cristal 1983 £82.48 (NO) £105.75 (REI)

Louis Roederer Cristal 1974 £76.38 (REI)

Moët & Chandon Brut Impérial 1978 £95.00 (MI)

Pol Roger 1964 £88.13 (REI)

£100.00 → £129.99

Bollinger jeroboam NV £115.50 (TAN) £123.19 (LAY)

Bollinger Grande Année magnum 1988 £105.00 (RES)

Bollinger RD 1975 £115.00 (RES) £125.50 (BEN) £129.25 (TW) £145.00 (FORT)

Deutz Brut Classic jeroboam NV £103.40 (JER)

Dom Pérignon 1983 £127.96 (TW)

Dom Pérignon 1975 £111.63 (REI) £182.13 (CAV)

Dom Pérignon magnum 1989 £125.00 (BO)

Dom Pérignon magnum 1988 £127.00 (YOU) £150.00 (MI) £159.99 (VIN) £162.74 (TW)

Krug 1979 £102.78 (NO) £160.00 (RES)

Krug magnum 1989 £129.25 (FA) £185.00 (RES)

Krug Clos du Mesnil Blanc de Blancs 1989 £109.67 (FA) £152.75 (CAV) £163.50 (BEN) £170.00 (FORT) £175.00 (YOU) £185.00 (RES)

Krug Clos du Mesnil Blanc de Blancs 1985 £127.29 (FA) £170.65 (HAH)

Laurent-Perrier La Cuvée Grande Siècle magnum NV £115.30 (CHA)

Louis Roederer Cristal 1982 £125.00 (BEN)

Moët & Chandon Brut Impérial jeroboam NV £109.50 (CON) £112.68 (STE) £115.00 (ROB) £120.00 (BALL) £122.40 (COC) £125.20 (NA) £135.00 (WR) £135.00 (BOT)

Perrier-Jouët Belle Époque magnum 1990 £125.00 (FORT)

Perrier-Jouët Belle Époque magnum 1989 £129.25 (TW)

Pol Roger Cuvée Sir Winston Churchill magnum 1988 £127.29 (CAV) £150.00 (FORT) £155.00 (RES)

Pol Roger White Foil jeroboam NV £124.20 (PEN) £130.00 (WRI)

Veuve Clicquot jeroboam NV £125.16 (VIN) £129.00 (WR) £129.00 (BOT)

Veuve Clicquot la Grande Dame 1985 £110.00 (MI)

Veuve Clicquot Vintage Réserve 1970 £103.33 (MI)

£130.00 → £199.99

Bollinger Grand Année magnum 1979 £199.75 (TW)

Bollinger Vieilles Vignes Françaises, Blanc de Noirs 1990 £140.00 (YOU) £153.50 (BEN)

Bollinger Vieilles Vignes Françaises, Blanc de Noirs 1989 £130.00 (FORT) £145.96 (NO) £146.88 (TW)

Dom Pérignon 1978 £152.75 (CAV) £211.50 (TW)

Dom Pérignon 1971 £195.00 (RES)

Dom Pérignon 1964 £146.88 (CAV) £170.38 (REI) £195.00 (ROB)

Dom Pérignon magnum 1990 £135.00 (FORT)

Dom Pérignon magnum **1985** £137.50 (ROB)

Dom Pérignon magnum **1982** £199.00 (BEN)

Krug **1966** £176.25 (REI) £225.00 (YOU)

Krug magnum **1985** £180.16 (FA) £188.00 (WY)

Krug Grand Cuvée magnum **NV** £140.00 (ROB) £155.00 (RES)

Krug Clos du Mesnil Blanc de Blancs **1982** £176.25 (REI)

Lanson **1945** £146.88 (REI)

Louis Roederer Cristal **1975** £141.00 (REI)

Louis Roederer Cristal magnum **1989** £180.00 (ROB)

Moët & Chandon Brut Impérial **1952** £190.00 (MI)

Perrier-Jouët **1959** £135.13 (REI)

Pol Roger **1955** £146.88 (REI)

Pol Roger Cuvée Sir Winston Churchill magnum **1986** £136.30 (PEN) £145.00 (RES) £159.92 (VIN)

Pommery **1945** £146.88 (REI)

Salon magnum **1983** £142.18 (CB)

Veuve Clicquot Vintage Réserve **1955** £176.25 (REI)

£200.00 → £299.99

Dom Pérignon magnum **1978** £293.75 (CAV) £408.90 (TW)

Krug Collection **1979** £225.00 (ROB)

Louis Roederer **1949** £205.63 (REI)

Louis Roederer Cristal magnum **1990** £200.00 (FORT) £219.84 (TW)

Moët & Chandon Brut Impérial magnum **1964** £205.00 (MI)

Moët & Chandon Brut Impérial magnum **1962** £280.00 (MI)

Moët & Chandon Brut Impérial methuselah **NV** £225.00 (CON) £239.00 (COC) £250.00 (ROB) £250.00 (BALL) £259.00 (WR) £259.00 (BOT)

Pol Roger White Foil methuselah **NV** £245.58 (PEN) £247.00 (WRI) £275.00 (FORT)

Over £300.00

Krug **1953** £311.38 (REI)

Krug magnum **1966** £495.00 (VIN)

Moët & Chandon Brut Impérial salmanazar **NV** £359.00 (WR) £359.00 (BOT) £375.00 (BALL)

Perrier-Jouët magnum **1947** £323.13 (REI)

Pol Roger White Foil salmanazar **NV** £367.00 (WRI) £400.00 (FORT)

SPARKLING ROSÉ

Under £15.00

F. Bonnet **NV** £13.99 (OD)

★ Brossault Brut **NV** £14.99 (FUL)

Ellner Brut **NV** £14.50 (BALL)

Georges Gardet **1992** £13.50 (SOM) £17.50 (CON)

Lenoble **NV** £13.99 (NI)

£15.00 → £19.99

Ayala **NV** £17.99 (MAJ)

Bauget-Jouette **NV** £17.50 (HIG) £17.99 (AME)

Beerens **NV** £18.60 (BIB)

Le Brun de Neuville Cuvée Rosé **NV** £15.80 (WAT)

Canard-Duchêne **NV** £16.50 (CRO)

Duval Leroy Brut Rosé **NV** £18.74 (PLA)

Lamiable **NV** £18.00 (HIG)

Mercier **NV** £16.69 (COC) £17.49 (VIC) £17.49 (THR) £17.49 (WR) £17.49 (BOT)

Piper Heidsieck **NV** £17.99 (TES)

Pol Roger **1990** £19.95 (SOM) £35.25 (PEN) £36.23 (CAV) £37.50 (RES) £37.50 (ROB) £38.50 (WY) £38.60 (HAH) £39.00 (WS) £39.99 (OD) £40.00 (FORT)

£20.00 → £29.99

Billecart-Salmon Brut **NV** £24.50 (NI) £25.95 (LEA) £25.95 (ROB) £25.99 (PHI) £25.99 (VA) £26.50 (STA) £27.50 (ELL) £27.50 (FORT) £27.75 (LIB) £27.95 (BER) £27.95 (WRI) £27.99 (OD) £35.13 (TW)

Bruno Paillard **NV** £21.55 (WHI) £22.99 (PHI)

Bruno Paillard 1er Cuvée **NV** £22.71 (BIB)

Charbaut **1990** £21.03 (PEN)

Deutz Brut **1993** £27.99 (NEZ)

Deutz Brut **1990** £26.93 (JER)

Georges Gardet **1989** £26.95 (VIN)

Gosset Grande **NV** £27.81 (STE) £27.95 (LEA) £29.95 (BALL) £30.90 (NA) £31.49 (YOU)

Joseph Perrier **NV** £21.56 (STE) £23.95 (NA)

Lanson **NV** £21.49 (MORR) £23.49 (UN) £23.49 (VIC) £23.49 (THR) £23.49 (WR) £23.49 (BOT) £23.99 (WHI)

Lanson **1993** £25.99 (VIC) £25.99 (THR) £25.99 (WR) £25.99 (BOT)

Laurent-Perrier **NV** £23.20 (REI) £25.00 (WS) £25.07 (LAY) £26.00 (JU) £26.05 (GW) £26.44 (PLA) £26.50 (ROB) £26.91 (CB) £26.95 (LEA) £26.99 (TES) £26.99 (JON) £26.99 (YOU) £27.22 (BIB) £27.61

(PEN) £27.82 (PLAY) £27.95 (BALL) £27.95
(VA) £28.00 (CON) £28.70 (TAN) £28.75
(WHI) £28.75 (FORT) £28.95 (HAH)
£28.95 (WY) £28.99 (UN) £28.99 (MAJ)
£28.99 (CO) £28.99 (OD) £28.99 (VIC)
£28.99 (THR) £28.99 (WR) £28.99 (BOT)
£29.08 (CHA) £29.08 (TW) £29.50 (HED)
£29.99 (NLW) £30.00 (MV) £31.00 (STA)

Moët & Chandon Brut NV £24.99 (JON)
£24.99 (SAF) £25.00 (TAN) £25.64 (PLAY)
£27.99 (VIN)

Moët & Chandon Brut Impérial 1993
£27.99 (UN)

Moët & Chandon Brut Impérial 1988
£29.95 (ROB)

'R' de Ruinart NV £25.99 (BO) £25.99
(WR) £25.99 (BOT) £26.95 (LEA)

Taittinger NV £26.99 (POR) £27.50 (FORT)
£27.94 (PLAY) £29.00 (JU)

£30.00 → £39.99

**Billecart-Salmon Cuvée Elisabeth Salmon
1989** £31.50 (VA)
Bollinger Grande Année 1988 £39.99 (DI)
Gosset Grande 1990 £36.95 (ROB)
Charles Heidsieck 1985 £30.70 (PIP)
Louis Roederer 1994 £39.87 (STE) £44.30
(NA)
Louis Roederer 1991 £38.00 (JU) £39.95
(VA)
Louis Roederer 1986 £39.95 (PEN)
Moët & Chandon Brut Impérial 1992
£33.50 (FORT)
Pol Roger 1988 £30.96 (REI) £35.00 (CON)
£36.72 (CAV) £37.40 (UB) £42.62 (VIN)
Veuve Clicquot 1989 £33.99 (YOU)
£35.25 (WY) £35.25 (CB) £36.50 (FORT)
Veuve Clicquot 1988 £33.50 (ROB) £34.50
(CON) £37.99 (THR) £37.99 (BOT)
Veuve Clicquot 1985 £56.67 (MI)

£40.00 → £99.99

**Billecart-Salmon Cuvée Elisabeth Salmon
1991** £40.00 (FORT)
**Bollinger 1990 Bollinger Grande Année
1990** £41.20 (TAN) £42.50 (BEN) £43.94
(LAY) £45.00 (FORT)
Dom Ruinart 1986 £59.99 (WR) £59.99
(BOT) £66.00 (LEA)
Krug NV £77.84 (CAV) £93.20 (HAH)
£98.00 (JU) £100.00 (FORT) £105.00 (RES)
Laurent-Perrier magnum NV £46.99
(CON) £47.59 (REI) £52.50 (ROB) £54.99
(CB) £55.64 (PLAY) £58.95 (BALL) £59.37
(CHA) £60.00 (FORT)

Moët Hennessy
UK LIMITED

13, GROSVENOR CRESCENT,
LONDON SW1X 7EE
Tel: 0171 235 9411   Fax: 0171 235 6937

Louis Roederer 1993 £44.40 (HAH)
£44.50 (STA)
Louis Roederer 1990 £44.00 (CRO)
Louis Roederer 1989 £42.95 (ROB)
Louis Roederer Cristal 1990 £89.30 (PEN)
Moët & Chandon Brut Impérial 1966
£76.38 (REI)
Perrier-Jouët Belle Époque 1990 £49.99
(VIC) £49.99 (THR) £49.99 (WR) £49.99
(BOT)
Perrier-Jouët Belle Époque 1988 £54.95
(ROB) £60.00 (FORT)
Taittinger Comtes de Champagne 1993
£58.44 (PLAY)
Taittinger Comtes de Champagne 1986
£59.00 (JU) £82.25 (TW)
Veuve Clicquot 1964 £80.49 (REI)

£100.00 → £199.99

Dom Pérignon 1988 £125.33 (CAV) £149.00
(AV) £150.00 (FORT) £160.00 (OD)
Dom Pérignon 1986 £125.33 (CAV)
£149.60 (PLAY) £175.00 (MI)
Dom Pérignon 1985 £160.00 (JU)
Dom Pérignon 1982 £159.00 (VA)
£165.00 (ROB) £205.63 (TW)
Louis Roederer Cristal 1989 £141.00
(REI) £147.11 (CB) £165.00 (RES)

Over £200.00

Louis Roederer Cristal 1988 £209.15
(TW)
Veuve Clicquot 1959 £255.00 (MI)

STILL WHITE

c. £20.00

**Coteaux Champenois Blanc de
Chardonnay, Laurent-Perrier NV**
£19.54 (CHA)

JURA & SAVOIE

There's nothing anonymous about these wines; make the effort to get to know them and you may find you love them. If you can find them

These are mountain wines – and the curious thing about mountain wines is that although we often expect them to be neutral and a bit anonymous, the reverse is often true. And the wines of Jura and Savoie are not short on character. It may not be the most fashionable of characters – the wines tend either to be deliberately oxidized or very fresh and crisp indeed – but nobody can accuse them of being me-toos. That's quite something these days. I'm rather fond of them.

WINES & WINE REGIONS

ARBOIS, AC (red, white, rosé) The reds are thuddingly full of flavour. The Savagnin grape weaves its demonic spell on the whites, though Chardonnay sometimes softens it. There are some attractive light reds and rosés made from Pinot Noir or Poulsard. Best: *Henri Maire, Pupillin co-op.*

BUGEY, VDQS (red, white) Look for the deliciously crisp Chardonnays; they're among the most refreshing (and yes, fruity) in France.

CÔTES DU JURA, AC (red, white, rosé) Virtually indistinguishable in style and flavour (and grape varieties) from Arbois wines, though sometimes a little less weird.

CRÉPY, AC (white) The Chasselas grape here produces an even flimsier version of the already delicate Swiss Fendant, if that's possible. Drink young and fast, or not at all.

L'ÉTOILE, AC (white) Whites from Savagnin and Chardonnay. Also *vins jaunes.*

ROUSSETTE DE SAVOIE, AC (white) Fullest and softest of the Savoie whites.

SEYSSEL, AC and SEYSSEL MOUSSEUX, AC (white) The Roussette (blended with a little Molette) makes quite full, flower-scented but sharp-edged whites. The fizz is light but pepper-pungent. Best: *Varichon et Clerc.*

VIN JAUNE (white) This grows the same yeasty *flor* as dry sherry, and its startlingly, painfully intense flavours from the Savagnin grape just get more and more evident as it matures. In fact it seems virtually indestructible. Château-Chalon AC is the most prized – and most pricy – and is difficult to find even in the region.

VIN DE SAVOIE, AC (red, white) These Alpine vineyards are some of the most beautiful in France and produce fresh, snappy wines. The white, from the Jacquère, Chardonnay or Chasselas, can be excellent, dry, biting, but with lots of tasty fruit. Drink young. The reds from Pinot Noir or Gamay are subtly delicious, while the Mondeuse produces some beefy beauties in hot years. A *cru* name may be on the best. Look for the villages of Abymes, Chignin, Apremont, Cruet, Montmélian, Chautagne and Arbin.

MERCHANTS SPECIALIZING IN JURA AND SAVOIE
see Merchant Directory (page 413) for details

Very few of these wines are available in the UK. Nobody exactly specializes in them, but the following merchants have some: Anthony Byrne (BY), S H Jones (JON), Terry Platt (PLA), Roberson (ROB), Tanners (TAN), Wine Society (WS).

LOIRE

Loire wines are resolutely Old World in style, and you won't find so much as a hint of mango or pineapple in your glass. They're for those days when you just can't face any more mango

If anyone wants a break from the flavour of new oak and from white wines that taste of tropical fruit – all pineapple and mango and banana – the Loire is the spot. Yes, they grow Chardonnay there, but not much, and they find it pretty difficult to sell, mostly because it doesn't taste of pineapple and mango and the rest. More famously, they grow Sauvignon Blanc, which brings us into cut grass and cat's pee territory. They also grow Chenin Blanc, which is one of the most difficult grapes to appreciate and one

of the most rewarding when you do; and they make Anjou Rosé, which is generally a mistake. (To get the best out of Chenin Blanc you have to go to the smaller appellations, like Bonnezeaux or Savennières. There is no way of getting the best out of Anjou Rosé, because there isn't one.)

In the reds, yes, you'll find some new oak. But it's all to the good, and rounds out their cherry-grassy fruit. They don't taste like New World wines. That's their attraction.

GRAPE VARIETIES

CABERNET FRANC (red) The great quality grape of Anjou and Touraine. All the best reds are based on Cabernet Franc, and the styles span the spectrum from the palest, most fleeting of reds to deep, strong and often austerely tannic wines of character and longevity. Often added to (white) sparkling wines, too.

CABERNET SAUVIGNON (red) This doesn't always ripen very well in the Loire, but even so it adds some backbone to the wines. It is really at its best in the warmest, ripest years.

CHARDONNAY (white) Increasingly widespread in the Loire and producing lean, light but tangy results in Haut-Poitou, in Anjou as Vin de Pays du Jardin de la France and in Orléans as Vin de l'Orléanais (where it's called Auvernat) – *Clos St-Fiacre* is terrific. It also occurs in Muscadet (*le Chouan* and *Domaine Couillaud* are good) and adds character and softness to Anjou Blanc.

CHASSELAS (white) Makes adequate but dull wine at Pouilly-sur-Loire; it's actually best as a table grape, in a fruit salad.

CHENIN BLANC (white) A grape that cries out for sun and ripens long after the other varieties. It also performs superbly in the Loire in a few warm and misty mesoclimates (especially in Quarts de Chaume and Bonnezeaux), where noble rot strikes the Chenin with enough frequency to make it worthwhile going through all the pain and passion of producing great sweet wine, with steely acidity and the flavour of honeyed, ripe-apple fruit.

These wines can seem curiously disappointing when young, but fine sweet Chenin manages to put on weight and become sweeter for perhaps 20 years before bursting out into a richness as exciting as all but the very best from Germany or Bordeaux. And then it lasts and lasts…. Because Chenin Blanc is unfashionable, these wines can be remarkably undervalued; but you have to be prepared to tuck them away in the cellar for a long time.

GAMAY (red) In the Loire this rarely achieves the lovely, juicy glugginess of Beaujolais, but when made by a careful modern winemaker it can have a fair amount of fruit, though it always seems to have a tough edge.

MELON DE BOURGOGNE (white) The grape of Muscadet, light and neutral. It's good at producing fresh white, usually quite biting, and with a salty tang. It's usually for drinking young though the odd good domaine-bottled *sur lie* can mature surprisingly well.

PINOT NOIR (red) In and around Sancerre this can, in warm years like the Loire has had lately, produce a lovely, light,

cherry-fragrant wine that will be either a rosé or a light red. It's not Burgundy, but it's very attractive.

SAUVIGNON BLANC (white) The grape of Sancerre and Pouilly, with a whole range of fresh, green, tangy flavours – anything from gooseberries to nettles and fresh-cut grass, and there's sometimes even a whiff of newly roasted coffee. The wines are usually quite tart – but thirst-quenching rather than gum-searing – and have loads of fruit. Sauvignon can age interestingly in bottle, but the odds are against it, except for the high-priced oak-aged cuvées.

WINE REGIONS

ANJOU BLANC SEC, AC (white) France's cheapest AC dry white made mostly from the hard-to-ripen Chenin Blanc. It *can* be good, steely and honeyed, especially from Savennières with its two tiny special ACs, Coulée-de-Serrant and la Roche-aux-Moines, and from names such as *Domaine Richou* which mixes Chardonnay with the Chenin, for extra flavour and fruit. Other good names: *Mark Angeli (Cuvée Christine), Baranger, Château de Valliennes, Domaine de la Haute Perche, Jaudeau.*

ANJOU ROUGE CABERNET, AC (red) This ranges from mostly quite light when from the co-ops, and spicy, strong and capable of aging from the best estates. It can rival Bourgueil. Best: *Mark Angeli (Cuvée Martial), Ch. d'Avrille, Ch. de Chamboureau (Soulez), Ch. d'Épiré, Clos de Coulaine, Dom. de la Petite Croix, Dom. du Petit Val, Dom. de Rochambeau, Dom. des Rochettes (Chauvin), Logis de la Giraudière (Baumard), Vincent Ogereau, Richou, Roussier.*

ANJOU ROUGE GAMAY, AC (red) Rarely more than adequate, but in the hands of someone like *Richou*, the 'rooty' character is replaced by a fresh, creamy fruit that is sharp and soft at once, and *very* good. *Domaine des Quarres* is also worth a try.

ANJOU-VILLAGES, AC (red) Cabernets Franc and Sauvignon from the 46 best villages in Anjou. Some are labelled Anjou-Villages Val-de-Loire. *Domaine de Montgilet, Domaine Ogereau, J-Y & A Lebreton* and *Richou* are good.

BONNEZEAUX, AC (white) One of the most unfairly forgotten great sweet wines of France. Prices for the lovely noble rot-affected wines have risen, but are still low compared to Sauternes – which itself is cheap at the price. Look out for the outstanding wines of *Mark Angeli* (from old vines), *Château de Fesles, Denéchèr, Jean Godineau, Goizil* and *Renou*.

BOURGUEIL, AC (red) Some of the best reds of the Loire. When they are young they can taste a bit harsh and edgy, but give them a few years and they will have a piercing blackcurrant fruit, sharp and thirst-quenching. They can age well, developing complex leathery, meaty flavours. Best: *Audebert* (estate wines), *Pierre Breton, Paul Buisse, Caslot-Galbrun, J-F Demont, Domaine des Forges, Domaine des Ouches, Pierre-Jacques Druet, Lamé-Delisle-Boucard.*

CABERNET D'ANJOU, AC (rosé) There is a reasonable chance of a pleasant drink here, because the Cabernets – mostly Franc, but often with Cabernet Sauvignon too – do give pretty tasty wine, usually less sweet than simple Rosé d'Anjou. Best: *Château de Valliennes, Domaine Baranger, Domaine de Hardières, Domaine Richou.*

CHEVERNY, AC (red, white) This Touraine region is improving fast. Its claim to fame is the teeth-grittingly dry white Romorantin grape, but there is also Chardonnay, Sauvignon Blanc and Chenin. *Dom. des Huards* is delicate and fine, and the *confrérie* at Oisly-et-Thésée is reliable. Others: *Cazin, Gendrier, Gueritte* and *Tessier.* Red Cheverny tends to be light and crisp, with a healthy dollop of Gamay perhaps beefed up with Cabernet Franc. *Oisly-et-Thésée's* is strawberryish with a fair bit of Pinot Noir in it.

CHINON, AC (red) In a ripe year (1995, '96 or '97), Chinon can be delicious, exhibiting a great gush of blackcurrant and raspberry flavours. In poorer vintages it can be unpalatably bitter with surprising levels of green tannin. But wine-making standards have risen. Domaine wines are *far* better than négociant wines, which can be thin. Best: *Bernard Baudry, Jean Baudry, Couly-Dutheil, Domaine du Colombier, Domaine du Roncée, Domaine de la Tour, Druet, Gatien Ferrand, René Gouron, Charles Joguet, Alain Lorieux, Pierre Manzagol, Jean-François Olek, Jean-Maurice Raffault, Julien Raffault, Olga Raffault.*

COTEAUX DE L'AUBANCE, AC (white) Quite cheap, pleasant semi-sweet whites. Best: *Dom. des Rochettes, Dom. Richou* and *Jean-Yves Lebreton.*

COTEAUX DU LAYON, AC (white) A large AC producing varying qualities of sweet white wine, at its best rich and tasty with a taut acidity that allows the wine to age for a long time. *Mark Angeli, Château du Breuil* (from very old vines), *Château de la Guimonière, Château de la Roulerie, Clos Ste-Catherine, Domaine Ambinois, Domaine du Baumard, Domaine du Petit Val, Domaine de la Pierre St-Maurille, Domaine des Quarres, Domaine de la Soucherie* and *Ogereau* are worth trying. There are also six Coteaux du Layon-Villages ACs that usually offer higher quality. Some Anjou growers are now making *sélection de grains nobles*, very sweet, concentrated wines made only from botrytized grapes, and therefore in only the best years.

CRÉMANT DE LOIRE, AC (white) Sparkling wine AC intended to denote higher quality than basic sparkling Saumur. Can be made partly or entirely from Chardonnay; Chenin-based ones are in fact indistinguishable from Saumur. Best include *Ackerman, Bouvet Ladubay, Caves de Grenelle, Cave des Liards, Gratien & Meyer, Langlois-Château, St-Cyr-en-Bourg* co-op.

GROS PLANT, VDQS (white) Gros Plant rejoices in being one of the rawest wines in France, and the prosperity of dentists in Nantes is thanks in no small measure to the locals' predilection for the stuff. That said, it *does* go amazingly well with seafood and seems to suit oysters. *Bossard's* is soft and honeyed. *Métaireau* and *Sauvion* have also tamed its fury. *Clos de la Sénaigerie* and *Clos de la Fine* from *Dom. d'Herbauges* are good.

HAUT-POITOU, VDQS (red, white) Chardonnay and Sauvignon from the *Cave Co-opérative du Haut-Poitou* are good but tend to leaness, for the whites; the reds are fairly 'green' but reasonably enjoyable, and are usually made from Gamay.

MENETOU-SALON, AC (red, white, rosé) The Sauvignon is as good as that of Sancerre, and there are some fair reds and rosés. The *Vignerons Jacques Coeur* co-op produces about half the Sauvignon. *Henry Pellé* makes the best in Menetou, followed by *Henri Bourgeois, Domaine de Chatenoy, Joseph Mellot* and *Jean-Max Roger.*

MONTLOUIS, AC (white) Chenin-based wines similar to Vouvray, but often more robust – which, when it comes to the Chenin grape, isn't always a good idea. *Domaine des Liards, Dominique Moye* and *Jean-Pierre Trouvé* are good, but don't expect the finesse of good Vouvray.

MUSCADET, AC (white) Simple, light, neutral wine from near the coast. Straight Muscadet, without any further regional title, is usually flat and boring. But at least it's light – the Muscadet ACs are the only ones in France to impose a *maximum* alcohol level (12.3 per cent).

MUSCADET CôTES DE GRAND-LIEU, AC (white) Demarcated in 1994, this latest sub-region accounts for nearly half of the area that was basic Muscadet, and quality varies. At least most is *sur lie.*

MUSCADET DE SÈVRE-ET-MAINE, AC (white) The best Muscadet. A good one may taste slightly nutty, peppery or salty, even honeyed, sometimes with creaminess from being left on the lees and sometimes with a slight prickle. It should always have a lemony acidity, and should feel light. Buy domaine-bottled wine only, and check the address, looking out for St-Fiacre and le Pallet, two of the best villages.

MUSCADET DES COTEAUX DE LA LOIRE, AC (white) Quality in this sub-region isn't bad. *Pierre Luneau* is good.

MUSCADET SUR LIE (white) This is the most important thing to look for on a Muscadet label. The French apparently believe it means wine that comes from the banks of the river Lie; in fact it indicates that the wine has been bottled straight off the lees (the yeast sediment from fermentation), thus having more depth than usual and a slight prickle. Best: *Sauvion's Ch. du Cléray* and *Découvertes* range, *Guy Bossard, Dom. de Coursay-Villages, Dom. du Grand Mouton, Pierre Luneau, Dom. de la*

Montaine, Ch. de Chasseloir, Clos de la Sénaigerie, Jean-Louis Hervouet, Dom. du 'Perdson-pain', Louis Métaireau, Huissier, both *Michel* and *Donatien Bahuaud*'s single-domaine wines, *Bonhomme* and *Guilbaud.*

POUILLY-FUMÉ, AC (white) They can be fuller than Sancerre, and the best have a mineral complexity, but there are still too many under-achievers for the price. Best: *Ch. Favray, J C Châtelain, Didier Dagueneau* (Pouilly's most brilliant winemaker), *Serge Dagueneau, André Figeat, Baron de L.*

POUILLY-SUR-LOIRE, AC (white) Made from the dull Chasselas grape which makes good eating but not memorable drinking. *Serge Dagueneau* is good.

QUARTS DE CHAUME, AC (white) Rare and expensive nobly-rotten sweet wines, with high acid stalking the rich apricot-and-honey fruit. Try *Jean Baumard Ch. de Bellerive, Ch. de l'Echarderie*.

QUINCY, AC (white) Crisp Sauvignon Blanc, usually lighter than Sancerre. *Dom. de Maison Blanche, Pierre Mardon, Jacques Rouzé* and *Jacques Coeur* co-op are good.

REUILLY, AC (white) Light, fragrant Sauvignon Blanc. *Gérard Cordier* and *Claude Lafond* are the main growers here. There is also some tasty red and rosé.

ROSÉ D'ANJOU, AC (rosé) The omnipresent and frequently omnihorrid French rosé. It suffers in the main from lack of fruit and excess of sulphur. A few, like the co-op at *Brissac*, can make it fresh.

ROSÉ DE LOIRE, AC (rosé) A little-made dry rosé from Anjou or Touraine, generally much better than Rosé d'Anjou.

ST-NICOLAS-DE-BOURGUEIL, AC (red) These Cabernet reds tend to be lighter and more forward than the reds of nearby Bourgueil. They can be very good, but stick to warm years. Best: *Claude Ammeux, Caslot-Jamet, Couly-Dutheil, Jean-Paul Mabileau* and *Joël Taluau*.

SANCERRE, AC (white) Green, smoky, tangy wine from the Sauvignon Blanc grape. At its best young, it should be super-fresh and fruity, tasting and smelling of gooseberries or cut grass. Look for single-domaine wines – especially from *Archambault, Sylvain Bailly, Balland-Chapuis, Henri Bourgeois, Francis and Paul Cotat, Lucien Crochet, Pierre and Alain Dézat, Gitton, Dom. Laporte, Alphonse Mellot, Paul Millérioux, Henri Natter, Reverdy, Jean-Max Roger, Pierre Riffault, Vacheron* and *André Vatan*.

SANCERRE ROUGE, AC (red) Pinot Noir, and in general overrated, but the best have a lovely cherry fragrance and sweetness of strawberries that can survive a

> ## ON THE CASE
> *If you want Sauvignon Blanc flavour without Sancerre prices, check out Sauvignon de Touraine: fresh as a daisy and light on the wallet*

year or two in bottle. Silly prices, though. *Henri Bourgeois, Pierre & André Dezat* and *Domaine Vacheron* are good and worth a try.

SAUMUR, AC (white) Champagne-method fizz from Chenin Blanc, perhaps with the welcome addition of Chardonnay or Cabernet Franc to round out the acid Chenin. Quality is better than it's been for years, thanks to warm summers and better winemaking. Best: *Ackerman, Bouvet-Ladubay, Gratien & Meyer, Langlois-Château, Jacky Clée, Caves de Grenelle, Dom. Hauts de Sanziers*.

SAUMUR BLANC, AC (white) Usually ultra-dry Chenin Blanc, though it can be sweet, similar to Anjou Blanc.

SAUMUR-CHAMPIGNY, AC (red) Cabernet from the best villages in Saumur. It is way above other Loire reds thanks to a firm structure and velvety softness, fruit that is slightly raw and rasping, yet succulent and rich at the same time. Although the term 'vieilles vignes' is open to interpretation it is always the best bet for quality. *Domaine Filliatreau* makes an outstanding one. Also good: *Château de Chaintres, Château du Hureau, Château de Targé, Domaine Dubois, Domaine Lavigne, Domaine Sauzay-Legrand, Domaine de Nerleux, Domaine des Roches Neuves, Domaine du Val Brun, Denis Duveau*.

SAUMUR ROUGE, AC (red) Usually very light and dry Cabernet Franc from 38 villages round Saumur. Although it's light the fruit is often marked and attractively blackcurrant. The co-op at *St-Cyr-en-Bourg* is good, as is *Château Fouquet*.

SAVENNIÈRES, AC (white) Some of the world's steeliest, longest-living, diamond-dry white wines come from this tiny Anjou AC where the Chenin grape comes into its own. One vineyard, Savennières Coulée-de-Serrant, has its own AC within Savennières, and *Nicolas Joly's Clos de la Coulée-de-Serrant* is excellent. Also: *Yves Soulez* from the *Château de Chamboreau, Château d'Épiré, Clos du Papillon, Jean Baumard (Clos Ste-Catherine), Dom. de la Bizolière, Dom. aux Moines, Dom. du Closel, Mme Laroche.*

TOURAINE, AC (red, white) Everybody sees Touraine Sauvignon, with some justification, as a Sancerre substitute. The *Confrérie des Vignerons d'Oisly-et-Thésée* is good, as are *Paul Buisse, Ch. de l'Aulée, Dom. de la Charmoise (Marionnet), Ch. de Chenonceau, Dom. des Corbillières, Dom. Joël Delaunay* and *Dom. Octavie.* The reds have benefited from a run of warm years, though even at their ripest are seldom terrifically weighty. The *Domaine de la Charmoise (Marionnet),* and the co-op of *Oisly-et-Thésée* produce fair Gamays. *Château de Chenonceau's* is also good.

VIN DE PAYS DU JARDIN DE LA FRANCE (white) The general vin de pays of the Loire. Those based on Sauvignon Blanc and Chardonnay are the ones to go for. *Biotteau's Château d'Avrille* and *Domaine des Hauts de Saulière's* Chardonnays have lovely fruit.

VIN DE PAYS DES MARCHES DE BRETAGNE (red, white) These wines from the mouth of the Loire are usually fairly flimsy, lightweight numbers. *Guy Bossard* makes a good fruity red from Cabernet Franc.

VOUVRAY, AC (white) Sparkling and still whites from tangily dry to richly sweet, though often at its best in the off-dry demi-sec style. From a good producer this Chenin wine, initially all searing acidity and rasping dryness, over many years develops a deep honey-and-cream flavour. Most commercial Vouvray is poor. Best: *Daniel Allias, Bourillon-Dorléans, Brédif, Paul Buisse, Chamalou, Ch. Gaudrelle, Ch. Moncontour, Dom. des Aubuisières, Dom. du Margelleau, Dom. de Vaugoudy, Foreau, Benoît Gautier, Huet, Pierre Mabille, Prince Poniatowski.*

LOIRE VINTAGES

Loire vintages are very variable, and can be radically different along the river length. In poor vintages, Muscadet is most likely to be OK, while in hot vintages Sauvignon goes dull, but the Chenin finally ripens. The red grapes need the warm years.

1998   Less good and more mixed than '96 or '97. Sauvignon and Cabernet Franc look best.

1997   A splendid year for reds and for Chenin, both of which seem forward and round. Good fruity Sauvignon

1996   The reds and the Chenin had a bumper year and should age well, but there's enough acidity to keep the Sauvignon balanced, too.

1995   Some luscious dessert wines as well as fine reds, but quality is not even.

1994   Fair dry whites, but Coteaux du Layon should be best of all. Reds are lightweight.

1993   Good, flinty whites. The best Coteaux du Layon is botrytized and concentrated.

1990   Sweet Chenins, built to last, may beat the '89s. Great reds too.

LOIRE PRICES

DRY WHITE

Under £4.00

Muscadet de Sèvre-et-Maine les Roseaux
1996 £3.99 (CON)

Saumur Domaine de la Paleine 1996
£3.99 (NI)

Sauvignon de Touraine Bougrier 1997
£3.95 (WS)

Sauvignon du Haut Poitou, Cave Co-op. du
Haut Poitou **Non-vintage** £3.99 (MORR)

VdP du Jardin de la France Chenin Blanc
de Blanc, Bougrier 1997 £2.95 (WS)

Vouvray Guery 1997 £3.99 (MORR)

£4.00 → £4.99

Cheverny Domaine Salvard 1998 £4.50
(WS)

Muscadet de Sèvre-et-Maine des Ducs,
Chereau Carré 1997 £4.56 (BIB)

Muscadet de Sèvre-et-Maine Fief de la
Brie, Bonhomme 1997 £4.99 (POR)
£5.20 (TAN)

Muscadet de Sèvre-et-Maine sur lie Carte
d'Or, Sauvion 1998 £4.95 (NEZ)

Muscadet de Sèvre-et-Maine sur lie Château
de Cléray 1997 £4.95 (ROB) £6.25 (PIP)

Muscadet de Sèvre-et-Maine sur lie
Domaine Saupin 1997 £4.99 (NI)

Muscadet de Sèvre-et-Maine sur lie Fief
de la Brie, Bonhomme 1997 £4.75
(BALL) £4.99 (JON)

Muscadet de Sèvre-et-Maine sur lie
Domaine des Ratelles 1998 £4.95 (WS)

Muscadet sur lie Côtes de Grand Lieu,
Clos de la Senaigerie 1998 £4.99 (THR)

Muscadet Vieilles Vignes, Marcel Martin
1997 £4.70 (JER)

Sancerre Côte de Sury, Domaine Pastou
½ bottle 1996 £4.36 (JER)

Saumur Cave des Vignerons de Saumur
1997 £4.75 (AD)

Sauvignon de Touraine Confrérie d'Oisly
et Thésée 1998 £4.29 (MAJ)

Sauvignon de Touraine Domaine de la
Charmoise, Marionnet 1996 £4.95 (BALL)

Sauvignon de Touraine Domaine de
Bellevue, Tijou et Fils 1997 £4.99 (HIG)

Sauvignon de Touraine Domaine de la
Renaudie 1998 £4.99 (OD)

£5.00 → £5.99

Muscadet de Sèvre-et-Maine sur lie
Château de Chasseloir 1996 £5.25 (AV)

Muscadet de Sèvre-et-Maine sur lie
Château de Cléray 1998 £5.85 (NEZ)

Muscadet de Sèvre-et-Maine sur lie
Domaine de Bois Joly 1997 £5.39 (CON)

Muscadet de Sèvre-et-Maine sur lie
Thuaud 1997 £5.88 (CHA)

Muscadet sur lie Château de la
Galissonière 1997 £5.99 (DI)

Muscadet sur lie Côtes de Grand Lieu,
Clos de la Senaigerie 1996 £5.25 (JU)

Muscadet sur lie Domaine de Basseville,
Bossard 1998 £5.04 (STE)

Reuilly Beurdin 1998 £5.99 (MAJ) £6.75 (AD)

St-Pourçain Cuvée Printanière, Union des
Vignerons 1998 £5.75 (YAP)

Saumur Domaine des Hauts de Sanziers
1997 £5.00 (RSJ)

Saumur Domaine de la Paleine 1997
£5.85 (TAN)

Sauvignon de Touraine Domaine de la
Bergerie 1997 £5.03 (GW)

Sauvignon de Touraine Domaine de la
Preslé 1997 £5.49 (YOU) £5.98 (COC)

Touraine Azay-le-Rideau la Basse
Chevrière, Pavy 1996 £5.95 (WS)

Touraine Azay-le-Rideau Pascal Pibaleau
1996 £5.15 (WAT)

MERCHANTS SPECIALIZING IN THE LOIRE

see Merchant Directory (page 413) for details

Unusually imaginative lists can be found at:
Adnams (AD), Averys of Bristol (AV),
Ballantynes (BAL), Bennetts (BEN), Anthony
Byrne (BY), Justerini & Brooks (JU), Lay &
Wheeler (LAY), The Nobody Inn (NO),
Terry Platt (PLA), Raeburn Fine Wines
(RAE), The RSJ Wine Co (RSJ), T&W Wines
(TW), Tanners (TAN), Ubiquitous Chip (UB),
Waterloo Wine (WAT), Wine Society (WS),
Noel Young (YOU).

VdP du Jardin de la France Sauvignon
Blanc Petit Bourgeois, Henri Bourgeois
1997 £5.95 (CON) £6.76 (CB)
Vouvray Domaine les Perruches **1995**
£5.99 (CO)

£6.00 → £6.99

Coteaux du Giennois Gitton **1995** £6.99
(HIG)
Gros Plant Château de la Ragotière **1997**
£6.99 (VIN)
Menetou-Salon Morogues, la Tour St
Martin **1996** £6.45 (NI)
Montlouis Domaine des Liards, Berger
1998 £6.95 (YAP)
Muscadet de Sèvre-et-Maine sur lie
Château de l'Oiselinière de la Ramée
1996 £6.99 (BAL)
Muscadet de Sèvre-et-Maine sur lie
Domaine de la Bretonnière **1997** £6.55
(BAN)
Pouilly-Fumé Chatelain **1997** £6.50 (SOM)
£7.95 (WS)
Quincy Rouzé **1997** £6.90 (HAH)
Sancerre Cuvée Flores, Vincent Pinard
1997 £6.50 (SOM) £8.69 (GW)
Sauvignon de Touraine Caves de Coteaux
Romanais **1994** £6.31 (WT)
Savennières Clos du Papillon, Baumard
1994 £6.75 (SOM) £10.87 (REI)
Vouvray Château Moncontour **1998**
£6.70 (NA)
Vouvray le Haut Lieu, Huet **1996** £6.95
(WS)
Vouvray Spéciale, Saget **1996** £6.99 (VIN)

£7.00 → £7.99

Menetou-Salon Clos des Blanchais, Pellé
1997 £7.49 (OD) £7.75 (SOM) £8.60
(MV) £8.99 (YOU) £11.34 (TW)
Menetou-Salon Domaine du Prieuré **1997**
£7.49 (CON) £7.59 (JON)
Menetou-Salon la Charnivolle, Fournier
1997 £7.75 (STA)
Menetou-Salon Morogues, le Petit Clos
1996 £7.50 (FORT)
Montlouis les Batisses, Délétang **1995**
£7.95 (WS)
Muscadet de Sèvre-et-Maine sur lie
Château de la Ragotière **1997** £7.76 (VIN)
Pouilly-Fumé Chatelain **1998** £7.99 (WAI)
Pouilly Fumé Fine Caillottes, Pabiot **1997**
£7.95 (AD) £7.99 (JON)
Pouilly-Fumé les Griottes, Bailly **1998**
£7.34 (STE) £8.50 (NA)

Pouilly-Fumé Masson-Blondelet **1998**
£7.99 (WAI)
Quincy Jaumier **1998** £7.50 (YAP)
Reuilly Beurdin **1997** £7.10 (ELL) £7.80
(BAN) £9.25 (FORT)
Reuilly Robert & Gérard Cordier **1997**
£7.25 (YAP)
Sancerre Crochet **1996** £7.95 (JU)
Sancerre Daulny **1997** £7.29 (WHI) £7.49
(JON) £7.85 (HAH)
Sancerre Domaine du P'tit Roy **1997**
£7.99 (BO) £9.32 (COC)
Sancerre Domaine Rossignole **1998**
£7.99 (OD)
Sauvignon de Touraine Domaine des
Cabotières **1994** £7.93 (TW)
Savennières Clos de la Coulaine, Château
de Pierre Bise **1997** £7.95 (RSJ) £8.95
(LEA)
Savennières Clos des Maurières, Domaine
des Forges **1996** £7.95 (JU)
Savennières Domaine du Closel, Mme de
Jessey **1996** £7.95 (WS)
Touraine Azay-le-Rideau la Basse
Chevrière, Pavy **1995** £7.25 (YAP)
Vouvray Domaine Peu de la Moriette
1997 £7.75 (PIP)
Vouvray Domaine la Saboterie **1992**
£7.56 (CON)

£8.00 → £9.99

Menetou-Salon Domaine de Chatenoy
1997 £8.75 (BU) £10.50 (ROB)
Menetou-Salon Morogues, Pellé **1997**
£8.79 (YOU)
Menetou-Salon Roger **1996** £8.20 (TAN)
Pouilly-Fumé Château Favray **1998** £8.99
(MAR)
Pouilly-Fumé Château Favray **1997** £9.11
(DOM)
Pouilly-Fumé Chatelain **1996** £9.29 (BAL)
£10.50 (FORT)
Pouilly-Fumé Domaine des Berthiers,
Jean-Claude Dagueneau **1997** £9.69
(REI) £9.85 (WRI)
Pouilly-Fumé Domaine des Rabichattes
1996 £8.99 (RAE)
Pouilly-Fumé Domaine Thibault **1997**
£8.90 (TAN) £9.49 (JON) £9.75 (ELL)
Pouilly Fumé Fine Caillottes, Pabiot **1996**
£8.75 (BU)
Pouilly-Fumé les Bascoins, Masson-
Blondelet **1997** £9.39 (BAN)
Pouilly-Fumé les Berthiers, Claude Michot
1998 £8.72 (BIB)

Pouilly-Fumé les Chantes des Vignes, Mellot **1996** £9.04 (PEN)

Pouilly-Fumé les Logères, Saget **1997** £8.99 (POR) £10.69 (VIN)

Pouilly-Fumé les Loges, Jean-Claude Guyot **1997** £9.75 (YAP)

Pouilly-Fumé Seguin **1998** £8.49 (VIC) £8.49 (THR) £8.49 (BOT)

Pouilly-Fumé Seguin **1997** £8.95 (LEA) £9.75 (RAE)

Sancerre André Dezat **1997** £8.90 (TAN) £8.99 (NI) £9.10 (BER)

Sancerre Balland-Chapuis **1997** £8.95 (BER)

Sancerre Chavignol, Delaporte **1998** £9.95 (LEA)

Sancerre Clos des Roches, Vacheron **1998** £8.96 (STE) £9.95 (NA) £10.99 (UN)

Sancerre Clos du Chêne Marchand, Roger **1997** £8.80 (TAN)

Sancerre Clos du Roy, Millérioux **1997** £8.79 (YOU) £9.60 (COC)

Sancerre Cuvée Flores, Vincent Pinard **1996** £8.95 (JU)

Sancerre Domaine de la Mercy Dieu, Bailly-Reverdy **1996** £9.95 (FORT)

Sancerre Domaine de Montigny, Natter **1997** £8.50 (WS) £9.60 (LAY)

Sancerre Domaine du Nozay, de Benoist **1997** £9.69 (CB)

Sancerre Domaine de la Tonnelerie **1997** £8.99 (POR)

Sancerre Jean Thomas **1997** £8.42 (BIB)

Sancerre la Bourgeoise, Henri Bourgeois **1997** £9.95 (SOM)

Sancerre la Reine Blanche **1998** £8.95 (WS)

Sancerre Laporte **1997** £8.60 (PIP)

Sancerre le Croix au Garde, Pellé **1997** £8.99 (YOU) £9.40 (MV)

Sancerre les Baronnes, Henri Bourgeois **1997** £8.95 (CON) £10.35 (UB)

Sancerre la Gravelière, Mellot **1997** £8.12 (PEN)

Sancerre Paul Prieur **1996** £8.50 (HA) £9.11 (DOM) £9.29 (BAL)

Sancerre Roger **1997** £9.95 (BEN)

Sancerre Vacheron **1998** £9.99 (MAJ) Saumur Blanc Château du Hureau **1996** £8.99 (NI) £9.60 (MV) £11.40 (TW)

Savennières Château d'Epiré **1997** £8.90 (GAU)

Savennières Clos de la Coulaine, Château de Pierre Bise **1991** £9.99 (RAE)

Savennières Clos du Papillon, Baumard **1995** £9.95 (CON) £11.60 (UB) £12.50 (ROB) £13.40 (TAN)

Savennières Clos du Papillon, Domaine du Closel **1997** £9.95 (AD)

Savennières Domaine du Closel, Mme de Jessey **1997** £8.95 (YAP)

Savennières Roche-aux-Moines, Domaine Aux Moines **1995** £9.85 (RSJ)

Vouvray Brédif **1997** £8.50 (CRO) £8.99 (VA) £9.50 (STA) £9.95 (BER)

Vouvray Château Gaudrelle **1997** £8.95 (LEA)

Vouvray Clos du Bourg, Huet **1993** £9.70 (GAU) £17.95 (FORT)

Vouvray le Haut Lieu, Huet **1995** £8.29 (WAT) £9.75 (RAE) £9.95 (ROB) £10.28 (REI)

£10.00 → £14.99

Menetou-Salon Morogues les Blanchais, Pellé **1996** £14.00 (NO)

Pouilly-Fumé en Chailloux, Didier Dagueneau **1997** £14.10 (FA) £15.10 (TAN) £18.25 (ROB) £21.09 (TW)

Pouilly-Fumé Château de Tracy **1997** £11.90 (AV) £11.95 (LEA) £11.99 (POR)

Pouilly-Fumé Château de Tracy **1996** £10.25 (BALL) £10.28 (JER) £10.95 (AD) £11.39 (ROS) £11.93 (CB)

Pouilly-Fumé Château du Nozet, de Ladoucette **1997** £14.99 (MAJ) £15.00 (WS) £16.95 (NA) £17.50 (ROB)

Pouilly-Fumé Château du Nozet, de Ladoucette **1995** £14.15 (COC)

Pouilly-Fumé Clos des Chadoux, Serge Dagueneau **1994** £12.90 (JU)

Pouilly-Fumé Clos Joanne d'Orion, Gitton **1995** £10.75 (HIG)

Pouilly-Fumé Cuvée Prestige, Châtelain **1995** £14.95 (BAL)

Pouilly-Fumé Cuvée Prestige, Pabiot **1996** £12.44 (LAY)

Pouilly-Fumé Silex, Didier Dagueneau **1997** £14.95 (GAU) £23.89 (FA) £25.50 (TAN) £28.99 (YOU) £38.01 (TW)

Pouilly-Fumé Villa Paulus, Masson-Blondelet **1997** £14.60 (NO)

Sancerre André Dézat **1996** £10.95 (ROB)

Sancerre Chavignol la Grande Côte, Cotat **1997** £14.95 (RAE)

Sancerre Chavignol le Manoir, André Neveu **1997** £10.19 (BIB)

Sancerre Clos des Roches, Vacheron **1997** £11.25 (ELL) £12.50 (ROB)

Sancerre Comte Lafond, Château du Nozet **1997** £14.99 (MAJ) £15.91 (PLAY)

Sancerre Culs de Beaujeu, Cotat **1997** £13.95 (RAE) £14.95 (BAL)

Sancerre Cuvée François de la Grange,
Natter **1995** £11.99 (RAE)
Sancerre les Perriers, Vatan **1998** £10.25
(YAP)
Sancerre les Romains, Gitton **1995**
£10.99 (HIG)
Sancerre Roger **1996** £11.69 (TW)
Savennières Château de Chamboureau,
Soulez **1995** £11.25 (YAP)
Savennières Coulée-de-Serrant Château
de la Roche-aux-Moines, Nicolas Joly
1992 £12.99 (DI)
Savennières Domaine du Closel, Mme de
Jessey **1995** £12.00 (FORT)
Vouvray Aigle Blanc, Poniatowski **1986**
£10.95 (VA) £12.75 (UB)
Vouvray Brédif **1997** £10.41 (PLAY)
Vouvray Clos du Bourg, Huet **1995**
£10.39 (JON)
Vouvray Clos Naudin, Foreau **1993**
£10.50 (DI)
Vouvray le Mont, Huet **1995** £10.95 (JU)

£15.00 → £19.99

Pouilly-Fumé Pur Sang, Didier Dagueneau
1997 £17.04 (FA) £18.70 (TAN)
Sancerre Cuvée Harmonie, Pinard **1995**
£18.00 (JU)
Sancerre Cuvée LC, Crochet **1995**
£18.90 (JU)
Sancerre les Baronnes, Henri Bourgeois
1996 £15.63 (NO)
Savennières Clos des Maurières, Domaine
des Forges **1994** £15.46 (NO)
Savennières Roche-aux-Moines, Château
de Chamboureau **1996** £16.45 (NO)
Savennières Roche-aux-Moines, Soulez
1995 £15.25 (YAP)

£20.00 → £29.99

Pouilly-Fumé Silex, Didier Dagueneau
1994 £22.91 (FA) £27.95 (ROB)
Savennières Coulée-de-Serrant, Nicolas
Joly **1996** £24.99 (RAE) £28.50 (BAL)
£34.58 (MI)

- *Wines are listed in A–Z order within each price band.*
- *For each wine, vintages are listed in descending order.*
- *Each vintage of any wine appears only once.*

Savennières Coulée-de-Serrant, Nicolas
Joly **1991** £21.95 (UB) £30.00 (YAP)
Vouvray Clos du Bourg, Huet **1971**
£24.95 (RAE) £38.48 (REI)

£30.00 → £39.99

Pouilly-Fumé Baron de L, Château du
Nozet **1996** £33.11 (PLAY) £35.90 (NA)
Pouilly-Fumé Baron de L, Château du
Nozet **1994** £32.50 (FORT) £33.00 (WRI)
£33.50 (STA)
Savennières Coulée-de-Serrant, Nicolas
Joly **1990** £33.49 (REI) £57.50 (MI)
Savennières Liquoreux Coulée-de-
Serrant, Nicolas Joly **1995** £33.00 (JU)
Vouvray le Haut Lieu, Huet **1978** £31.00
(CRO)

Over £60.00

Savennières Coulée-de-Serrant, Nicolas
Joly **1969** £62.00 (CRO)
Vouvray le Haut Lieu, Huet **1949** £60.12
(FA)

SPARKLING

Under £8.00

Montlouis Brut Domaine des Liards,
Berger Frères **Non-vintage** £7.95 (JU)
£8.75 (YAP)
Saumur Brut Bouvet-Ladubay **Non-
vintage** £7.95 (JU) £8.49 (MAJ) £9.95 (ROB)
Saumur Brut La Grande Marque **1996**
£5.99 (POR)
Saumur Brut La Grande Marque **1993**
£7.09 (JON)
Saumur Rosé Excellence, Bouvet-Ladubay
Non-vintage £7.95 (ROB)

£8.00 → £9.99

Montlouis Demi-sec Domaine des Liards,
Berger Frères **Non-vintage** £8.75 (YAP)
Saphir Bouvet-Ladubay **1995** £8.49 (NI)
Saumur Cuvée Flamme, Gratien & Meyer
Non-vintage £9.50 (CRO)
Vouvray Brut Brédif **Non-vintage** £9.99
(JON)
Vouvray Brut Jarry **Non-vintage** £8.95
(YAP)
Vouvray Pétillant Brut, Huet **Non-
vintage** £9.95 (JU) £9.99 (RAE) £10.50
(GAU)
Vouvray Pétillant Brut, Huet **1997** £8.95
(WS)

Over £10.00

Crémant de Loire Château Langlois **Non-vintage** £11.25 (BEN)
Vouvray Foreau **Non-vintage** £10.90 (GAU)
Vouvray Mousseux Méthode Traditionelle, Huet **1959** £75.00 (RAE)

MEDIUM & SWEET WHITE

Under £7.00

Coteaux du Layon Domaine des Forges, Branchereau **1997** £6.95 (AD)
Coteaux du Layon Domaine des Forges, Branchereau **1996** £6.95 (BU) £10.99 (YOU) £11.94 (NO) £12.50 (MV)
Coteaux du Layon Domaine du Petit Val **1990** £6.95 (JU)
Vouvray Demi-Sec Château Moncontour **1998** £5.72 (STE) £6.35 (NA)
Vouvray Demi-Sec Château Moncontour **1995** £5.50 (BALL) £8.25 (ROB)

£7.00 → £8.99

Coteaux de l'Aubance Domaine Richou **1997** £7.50 (WAT)
Coteaux du Layon Beaulieu, Chéné **1989** £8.90 (JU)
Coteaux du Layon Château de Bellevue, Tijou et Fils **1994** £7.44 (HIG)
Coteaux du Layon Chaume Château de Bellevue, Tijou **1993** £8.62 (HIG)
Coteaux du Layon Chaume Château Soucherie, Tijou **1993** £8.85 (WAT)
Coteaux du Layon Domaine du Petit Val **1996** £7.80 (TAN)
Coteaux du Layon Rablay, Château la Tomaze **1995** £8.75 (YAP)
★ Coteaux du Layon St Aubin de Luigné, Domaine des Forges **1997** £8.25 (WRI) £10.80 (TAN)
Montlouis Domaine des Liards Vieilles Vignes, Berger Frères **1998** £7.50 (YAP)
Montlouis Domaine des Liards Vieilles Vignes, Berger Frères **1997** £8.50 (LAY)
Montlouis Moelleux Deletang **1986** £8.99 (RAE)
Touraine Azay-le-Rideau Moelleux, Pibaleau **1995** £7.99 (WAT)
Vouvray Château Gaudrelle **1997** £7.40 (TAN)
Vouvray Demi-Sec Gilles Champion **1993** £8.96 (LAY)

£9.00 → £12.99

Bonnezeaux 1ère Trie, Domaine du Petit Val **1996** £11.50 (TAN)
Bonnezeaux 1ère Trie, Domaine du Petit Val **1990** £10.90 (JU)
★ Coteaux du Layon Beaulieu l'Anclaie, Bise 50cl **1996** £10.95 (LEA)
Coteaux du Layon Chaume, Branchereau **1996** £10.00 (MV)
Coteaux du Layon Chaume le Cerisier, Château de la Roulérie **1994** £11.03 (NO)
Coteaux du Layon Chaume les Onnis, Domaine des Forges **1997** £11.95 (TAN)
Coteaux du Layon Chaume St Lambert, Domaine des Maurières **1995** £10.76 (NO)
Coteaux du Layon Clos de Ste-Catherine, Baumard **1994** £10.20 (SOM)
Coteaux du Layon Rablay, Château la Tomaze **1990** £11.25 (YAP)
Coteaux du Layon St Lambert Cuvée d'Adrien, Domaine du Sauveroy **1988** £12.30 (NO)
Montlouis Domaine des Liards Vendange Tardive, Berger Frères **1990** £12.90 (JU)
Montlouis Moelleux, Dominique Moyer **1995** £12.80 (LAY)
Quarts-de-Chaume Château de Bellerive **1992** £9.95 (WS)
Vouvray Clos de Bourg Demi-Sec, Huet **1996** £11.66 (BIB) £14.04 (TW)
Vouvray Clos Naudin Demi-Sec, Foreau **1995** £11.40 (GAU)
Vouvray le Haut Lieu Demi-Sec, Huet **1989** £11.90 (JU) £12.30 (RAE)
Vouvray le Mont Demi-Sec, Huet **1993** £9.50 (WS) £9.58 (REI)
Vouvray Moelleux Jean-Pierre Laisement **1995** £11.29 (LAY)

£13.00 → £15.99

Bonnezeaux la Montagne Domaine du Petit Val, Goizil **1997** £14.50 (MV) £15.00 (FORT)
Coteaux du Layon Beaulieu Vieilles Vignes, Château du Breuil **1995** £15.89 (LAY)
Coteaux du Layon Chaume les Onnis, Domaine des Forges **1995** £13.50 (JU) £19.90 (CRO)
Coteaux du Layon Ravouin-Gesbron **1970** £14.75 (WS)
Jasnières les Truffières, Pinon **1989** £14.50 (YAP)

Montlouis Domaine des Liards Vendange
Tardive, Berger Frères **1995** £13.50 (YAP)
Vouvray Clos Naudin Moelleux, Foreau
1988 £14.45 (DI)
Vouvray le Mont Moelleux, Huet **1995**
£13.45 (WAT) £13.99 (RAE) £15.95 (ROB)
Vouvray Moelleux Domaine Peu de la
Moriette **1996** £14.50 (PIP)

£16.00 → £19.99

Coteaux de Saumur Moelleux, Château
du Hureau **1996** £18.56 (TW)
Coteaux du Layon Chaume Cuvée
Corentine, Château de la Roulérie
1989 £19.75 (YAP) £24.53 (NO)
Coteaux du Layon Cuvée Privilège,
Branchereau **1995** £19.95 (GAU)
Coteaux du Layon Domaine de la Motte,
Sorin **1990** £18.60 (NO)
Coteaux du Layon Rablay Cuvée des Lys,
Château la Tomaze **1990** £17.50 (YAP)
£19.43 (NO)
Montlouis Domaine des Liards Grains
Nobles de Pineau, Berger Frères **1990**
£18.00 (JU) £22.75 (YAP)
Quarts-de-Chaume Baumard **1996**
£18.55 (SOM) £21.31 (RAE)
Quarts-de-Chaume Château de Bellerive
1990 £19.00 (JU) £31.51 (NO)
Quarts-de-Chaume Lalanne **1986** £16.50
(WS)
Sancerre Vendange du 27 Octobre,
Crochet **1995** £19.50 (JU)
Vouvray Aigle Blanc Réserve, Poniatowski
1976 £17.00 (CRO)
Vouvray Clos Naudin Moelleux, Foreau
1996 £18.95 (AD)

£20.00 → £29.99

Anjou Moulin, Touchais **1979** £22.50 (WRI)
Bonnezeaux Château de Fesles 50cl
bottle **1997** £23.99 (OD)
Bonnezeaux Château de Fesles 50cl
bottle **1996** £25.00 (MI)
Bonnezeaux la Montagne Domaine du
Petit Val, Goizil **1990** £27.60 (NO)

• *All prices for each wine are
listed together in ascending
order.*
• *Price bands refer to the
lowest price for which the
wine is available.*

Coteaux du l'Aubance les Trois
Demoiselles, Richou **1990** £24.32 (NO)
Coteaux du Layon Chaume Cuvée
Privilège, Branchereau **1994** £22.33 (NO)
Coteaux du Layon Chaume, Domaine
Grosset **1990** £23.37 (NO)
Coteaux du Layon Chaume les Aunis
Cuvée Margaux, Château de la Roulérie
1989 £21.66 (NO)
Coteaux du Layon Clos de Ste-Catherine,
Baumard **1995** £22.50 (UB)
Coteaux du Layon Domaine des
Maurières **1990** £27.96 (NO)
Coteaux du Layon Faye d'Anjou, Château
Montbenault **1976** £21.66 (NO)
Montlouis les Batisses, Deletang **1990**
£21.00 (WS)
Quarts-de-Chaume Bise **1996** £22.40 (RSJ)
Quarts-de-Chaume Château de
l'Echarderie **1989** £25.00 (YAP) £27.54
(NO)
Quarts-de-Chaume Lalanne **1989** £29.40
(NO)
Vouvray Clos du Bourg Moelleux, Huet
1996 £23.60 (AD)
Vouvray Clos du Bourg Moelleux, Huet
1990 £23.70 (GAU) £29.00 (JU)
Vouvray Clos Naudin Demi-Sec, Foreau
1973 £21.00 (CRO)
Vouvray Cuvée Constance, Huet **1993**
£29.60 (RAE) £29.90 (GAU)
Vouvray le Haut Lieu Moelleux, Huet
1989 £25.00 (BU) £35.00 (JU)
Vouvray le Mont Moelleux, Huet **1990**
£22.21 (NO) £31.40 (GAU)
Vouvray Moelleux Domaine Peu de la
Moriette **1989** £28.00 (CRO)
Vouvray Réserve Personelle, Château
Gaudrelle **1990** £29.00 (JU)
Vouvray Réserve Spéciale, Château
Gaudrelle **1989** £22.00 (JU)

£30.00 → £39.99

Vouvray Brédif **1961** £38.19 (REI)
Vouvray Clos de Bourg Demi-Sec, Huet
1989 £39.00 (CRO)

£40.00 → £49.99

Anjou Moulin, Touchais **1962** £41.13 (REI)
Anjou Rablay, Maison Prunier ½ bottle
1928 £45.00 (CRO)
Bonnezeaux Château de Fesles **1990**
£41.13 (TW)
Bonnezeaux la Chapelle, Château de
Fesles **1989** £43.04 (NO)

Quarts-de-Chaume Domaine des
  Maurières **1990** £41.44 (NO)
Vouvray Clos du Bourg Moelleux , Huet
  1962 £46.82 (REI) £48.50 (RAE)
Vouvray Cuvée Constance, Huet **1995**
  £41.13 (TW) £60.72 (NO)
Vouvray Doux Brédif **1964** £44.00 (CRO)

£50.00 → £99.99

Anjou Moulin, Touchais **1947** £62.00 (UB)
Bonnezeaux Château des Gauliers, Mme
  Fourlinnie **1959** £68.00 (CRO) £82.91
  (NO)
Quarts-de-Chaume Baumard **1978**
  £84.00 (NO)
Vouvray Brédif **1947** £84.00 (CRO)
Vouvray le Haut Lieu Moelleux, Huet
  1959 £50.00 (CRO)

Over £100.00

Bonnezeaux Château des Gauliers, Mme
  Fourlinnie **1953** £105.00 (CRO)
Vouvray le Haut Lieu Moelleux, Huet
  1947 £125.00 (RAE)
Vouvray le Haut Lieu Moelleux, Huet
  1924 £146.88 (REI) £176.25 (TW)

ROSÉ

Under £6.00

Anjou Rosé Cellier de la Loire **1993**
  £3.99 (NI)
Cabernet d'Anjou Château de la
  Genaiserie **1997** £4.95 (WS)
Sancerre Rosé Chavignol Domaine
  Delaporte ½ bottle **1998** £5.40 (LEA)

£6.00 → £8.99

Reuilly Pinot Gris, Beurdin **1997** £6.75
  (AD) £7.80 (BAN)
Reuilly Pinot Gris, Cordier **1996** £7.75
  (YAP)
Sancerre Pinot-Rosé, Crochet **1995**
  £8.75 (JU)
Sancerre Rosé Domaine Pastou **1996**
  £8.13 (JER)
Sancerre Rosé le Rabault, Mellot **1997**
  £8.12 (PEN)
Sancerre Rosé les Baronnes, Henri
  Bourgeois **1996** £8.95 (CON)
Sancerre Rosé les Cailleries, Vacheron
  1998 £8.95 (WS)
Sancerre Rosé les Romains, Vacheron
  1998 £8.69 (STE) £9.65 (NA)

Over £9.00

Sancerre Rosé André Dezat **1997** £9.49
  (JON) £9.50 (CRO) £10.25 (FORT)
Sancerre Rosé Cotat **1996** £9.99 (RAE)
Sancerre Rosé Domaine de la Mercy
  Dieu, Bailly-Reverdy **1998** £9.35 (LAY)
Sancerre Rosé Domaine de Montigny,
  Natter **1998** £9.89 (LAY)
Sancerre Rosé les Romains, Vacheron
  1995 £11.99 (BEN)

RED

Under £5.00

Bourgueil la Hurolaie, Caslot-Galbrun
  1995 £4.99 (TES)
Bourgueil les Garennes, Caves des Grands
  Vin de Bourgueil **1996** £4.95 (JU)
Chinon les Aubuis, Caves des Vins de
  Rabelais **1997** £4.99 (VIC) £4.99 (THR)
  £4.99 (WR) £4.99 (BOT) £5.60 (AD)
Gamay du Haut Poitou Cave Co-op.
  Non-vintage £3.99 (MORR)
Saumur Cave des Vignerons de Saumur
  1997 £4.95 (AD)
VdP du Jardin de la France Gamay, Cave
  du Haut-Poitou **1997** £3.85 (CON)

£5.00 → £6.99

Anjou Rouge Tijou **1996** £5.48 (HIG)
Anjou Rouge Vieilles Vignes, Domaine
  Richou **1996** £6.25 (WAT)

Bourgueil Domaine de la Grive **1997**
  £5.95 (BER) £6.35 (TAN)
Bourgueil Vieilles Vignes, Lamé-Delille-
  Boucard **1993** £6.75 (WAT)
Chinon Couly-Dutheil **1997** £5.49 (MAJ)
Chinon Domaine de la Perrière, Baudry
  1997 £6.50 (RSJ)
Gamay de Touraine Domaine de la
  Charmoise, Marionnet **1997** £6.75 (BAL)
Saumur Cave des Vignerons de Saumur
  1998 £5.50 (YAP)

Saumur-Champigny Château des Chaintres 1996 £6.75 (WS)

Saumur-Champigny Château Villeneuve 1997 £6.95 (RSJ) £7.60 (PIP) £7.79 (JON)

Saumur-Champigny Domaine de Nerleux 1997 £6.75 (RSJ) £7.35 (HAH)

Saumur Domaine du Langlois-Château 1994 £5.95 (DI)

£7.00 → £8.99

Anjou-Villages Domaine Ogereau 1994 £7.99 (BAL)

★ Anjou-Villages Domaine des Rochelles, Lebreton 1997 £7.35 (RSJ) £7.80 (TAN)

Bourgueil les Cent Boisselées, Druet 1996 £8.40 (AD) £9.95 (YAP)

Bourgueil Domaine les Galichets 1996 £7.70 (RSJ)

Cabernet d'Anjou Clos de Coulaine 1990 £7.20 (GAU)

Menetou-Salon Domaine de Chatenoy, Clement 1998 £8.50 (DI)

Reuilly Pinot Noir, Beurdin 1997 £7.80 (BAN) £9.25 (FORT)

★ St-Nicolas-de-Bourgueil Cuvée Estelle Cognard-Taluau 1997 £7.80 (HAH)

St-Nicolas-de-Bourgueil Taluau 1996 £7.52 (GW)

Sancerre les Cailleries, Vacheron 1996 £8.50 (WS) £9.95 (BER)

Saumur-Champigny Domaine Dubois 1995 £7.35 (GAU)

Saumur-Champigny Domaine des Roches Neuves 1997 £7.05 (RSJ)

Saumur-Champigny Grande Cuvée Château du Hureau, Vatan 1996 £7.99 (NI) £8.03 (GW) £10.52 (TW)

Saumur Château Fouquet, Domaine Filliatreau 1996 £7.35 (YAP)

Touraine Château de Chenonceau 1995 £8.17 (PEN)

£9.00 → £10.99

Bourgueil Beauvais, Druet 1995 £10.50 (MV)

Bourgueil Domaine des Ouches 1993 £9.60 (PIP)

Chinon Clos de Danzay, Druet 1994 £9.90 (UB)

Chinon Couly-Dutheil 1995 £9.99 (VA)

Chinon Vieilles Vignes, Domaine Philippe Alliet 1996 £9.95 (LEA)

St-Nicolas-de-Bourgueil les Malgagnes, Domaine Amirault 1995 £9.95 (LEA)

Sancerre André Dezat 1997 £9.40 (TAN)

Sancerre Domaine de Montigny, Natter 1995 £10.95 (RAE)

Sancerre la Croix du Roi, Crochet 1995 £10.95 (JU)

Sancerre les Baronnes, Henri Bourgeois 1996 £9.99 (CON)

Sancerre les Cailleries, Vacheron 1997 £9.41 (STE) £10.45 (NA)

Saumur-Champigny Château du Hureau, Vatan 1996 £9.20 (MV)

Saumur-Champigny Domaine des Roches Neuves 1996 £10.67 (NO)

Saumur-Champigny Terres Chauds, Domaine des Roches Neuves 1995 £9.99 (MAJ)

£11.00 → £12.99

Anjou Rouge Château de la Roche, Nicolas Joly 1990 £11.99 (RAE) £12.50 (GAU)

Bourgueil Beauvais, Druet 1993 £11.50 (JU) £11.75 (YAP)

Chinon Clos de l'Echo, Couly-Dutheil 1989 £11.15 (WAT)

Chinon Clos de le Cure, Joguet 1996 £11.52 (TW)

Chinon Clos du Chêne Vert, Joguet 1992 £11.50 (JU)

Chinon Cuvée des Varennes du Grand Clos, Joguet 1996 £11.10 (HAH)

Chinon Cuvée des Varennes du Grand Clos, Joguet 1995 £11.60 (GAU) £11.95 (JU) £13.49 (YOU)

Sancerre Cotat 1992 £11.99 (RAE)

Sancerre les Cailleries, Vacheron 1995 £12.16 (REI)

Saumur-Champigny Cuvée les Poyeux, Foucault et Fils 1992 £12.50 (BAL)

£13.00 → £14.99

Bourgueil Grand Mont, Druet 1993 £13.25 (YAP)

Bourgueil Grand Mont, Druet 1990 £14.00 (JU)

Chinon Clos de la Dioterie, Joguet 1997 £14.70 (GAU)

Chinon Clos de la Dioterie, Joguet 1996 £14.95 (HAH) £16.00 (MV) £19.09 (TW)

Chinon Domaine de la Chapellerie, Olek 1985 £14.50 (CRO)

Over £15.00

Chinon Clos de l'Echo, Couly-Dutheil 1990 £21.00 (CRO)

Saumur-Champigny Domaine des Roches Neuves 1994 £15.57 (PLA)

RHÔNE

Is the Rhône succumbing to New World lushness? If it trickles down to the lesser wines, I'm all in favour

The Australians have won the battle in Bordeaux. Will the Rhône be next? What battle? The battle to define the major wine styles. Look at the way flavours of claret have changed over the last few years: many leading châteaux – not all of them, but enough – have very quietly changed their winemaking techniques to produce the sort of rich, fleshy wines in which Australia specializes. (California makes similarly lush Cabernets, but we don't see so many of them here because they've always been more expensive.) Bordeaux may rule in the investment market, but when it comes to defining the style of Cabernet Sauvignon, Australia has won hands down.

Is the same thing happening in the Rhône? Northern Rhône Syrah has always been known for its relative slowness to evolve, its tannin, its lean pepperiness that blossoms after a few years into smoke and herbs and spice. Innovations take time to be accepted in the Rhône, but we're beginning to see a new momentum towards more luscious fruit, more approachable tannins, wines that can be drunk with greater pleasure, earlier. They're not cheap, these new wines, because they're being made by producers who know that you don't get taken seriously by undercharging. And they're not direct imitations of Australian Shiraz; they're firmly French, but they give more than a nod in the direction of New World ripeness and softness.

If this style takes over at the top (and it probably will, in time) it will eventually penetrate to the simpler wines. And, given their tendency to thin, dilute fruit, that can't happen too soon for me.

GRAPE VARIETIES

CARIGNAN (red) This grape is much maligned because in the far South it used to, and often still does, produce raw, fruitless wines that are the mainstay of the cheapest bulk wines. But old Carignan vines can produce strong, tasty, flavoursome wines that age well.

CINSAUT (red) This widely planted grape is now out of favour because of its inability to age. But it can add pepperiness and acidity to the blend, as at Château Rayas. Cinsaut often makes a successful contribution to rosé blends.

CLAIRETTE (white) Makes sparkling Crémant de Die, but is a bit dull unless livened up with the aromatic Muscat. In the South it makes big, strong whites that can be creamy, but more often dull and nutty. Needs careful handling and early drinking.

COUNOISE (red) Rich, spicy, floral flavours, and highly regarded at *Beaucastel* and *Durieu* in Châteauneuf-du-Pape. Could be promising.

GRENACHE (red) You won't see this grape in lights on Rhône labels much: it's mostly used for blending, giving loads of alcohol and a gentle, juicy, spicy fruit perked up by a whiff of pepper. It achieves its greatest power at Châteauneuf-du-Pape.

GRENACHE BLANC (white) Widely planted in the southern Rhône, producing rich, appley wines with a strong scent of aniseed. Good, but soft, so drink young.

MARSANNE (white) The dominant of the two grapes that go to make white Hermitage and Crozes-Hermitage, as well as white St-Joseph and St-Péray. Marsanne is

> **ON THE CASE**
> Rhône wines currently look rather
> good value compared to Bordeaux,
> but prices are starting to go up.
> Now could be the time to buy
> for the future

weighty and can be flabby, but at its best it is rich and scented. Further south it makes burly, lanoliny wine, but is capable of rich, exotic peach and toffee flavours, too.

MOURVÈDRE (red) This vine relishes ample warmth and sunshine. It contributes backbone and tannin to the blends of the South, and develops wonderful smoky, leathery, meaty flavours as it ages.

MUSCAT (white) Used to great effect blended with Clairette to make the sparkling Clairette de Die, but more famous for sweet Muscat de Beaumes-de-Venise.

ROUSSANNE (white) Altogether more delicate and fragrant than the Marsanne. Found chiefly in Hermitage and St-Péray in

the North, though it also makes light, fragrant wines further south in Châteauneuf. Look out for *Beaucastel*'s Roussanne *Vieilles Vignes* – pricy but superb.

SYRAH (red) The whole of the northern Rhône is dominated by Syrah – and it makes some of the blackest, most startling, pungent red wine in France. From Hermitage and Cornas, it rasps with tannin and tar and woodsmoke, backed by the deep, ungainly sweetness of black treacle. But give it five or ten years, and those raw fumes will have become sweet and pungent, full of raspberries, brambles and cassis.

VIOGNIER (white) The grape of Condrieu and Château-Grillet. It has one of the most memorable flavours of any white grape, blending the rich, musky scent of overripe apricots with that of spring flowers. The wine is made dry, but it is so rich you would hardly believe it. Sweet versions are making a comeback now. Viognier is a bit of a cult, with plantings increasing in the southern Rhône, California and Australia, and many are pretty good.

WINE REGIONS

CHÂTEAU-GRILLET, AC (white; north) This single property is one of the smallest ACs in France. Wildly expensive, it's 100 per cent Viognier and is often surpassed in freshness and quality by top Condrieus. But unlike Condrieu, it can age interestingly.

CHÂTEAUNEUF-DU-PAPE, AC (red, white; south) This can be delicious, deep, dusty red, almost sweet and fat, low in acidity, but kept appetizing by back-room tannin. *Can* be. It can also be fruit-pastilly and pointless, or dark, tough and stringy. Thirteen different red and white grapes are permitted, and the resulting flavour is usually slightly indistinct, varying from one property to another. Around one-third of

the growers make good wine – and as much as two-thirds of the wine sold probably exceeds the permitted yields. So it makes sense always to go for a domaine wine and certainly not one bottled away from the region. Best: *Pierre André, Lucien Gabriel Barrot, Henri Bonneau, Bosquet des Papes, les Cailloux, Chante-Cigale, Chante-Perdrix, Chapoutier*'s *la Bernadine, Château de Beaucastel, Château Fortia, Château de la Gardine, Château Rayas, Château St-André, les Clefs d'Or, Clos du Mont Olivet, Clos des Papes, Paul Coulon, Domaine Durieu, Domaine du Grand Tinel, Domaine de Mont Redon, Domaine St-Benoît, Domaine du Vieux Télégraphe, Font du Loup, Font Michelle, la Gardine, la Janasse, Gabriel Meffre, Monpertuis, la Nerthe, Quiot, le Vieux Donjon.*

Few whites are made, but they can be outstandingly perfumed with a delicious nip of acidity, leaving you wondering how on earth such aromatic wines could come from such a hot, arid region. In its youth, the wine has a perfumed rush of springtime madness. Then it closes up for a few years, emerging at seven years as a rich, succulent, nutty mouthful. Best: *Château de Beaucastel* (its pure Roussanne *Vieilles Vignes* – and the Viognier white), *Clefs d'Or, Clos des Papes, Font de Michelle, Grand Tinel, Mont Redon, Nalys, Rayas, Vieux Télégraphe*.

CLAIRETTE DE DIE, AC (sparkling; south) Made half from Clairette, half from Muscat, this is delicious, light and off-dry. It used to be called Clairette de Die Tradition, and the much duller Champagne-method sparkler is now called Crémant de Die. The still wine is Coteaux Diois.

CONDRIEU, AC (white; north) An appellation on a roll, with new plantings, better quality and lots of chic. The apricot scent leaps out of the glass, and there's an exciting balance of succulent fruit and gentle acidity. Viognier is the only grape. Always best young. Top names: *Chapoutier, Château du Rozay, Cuilleron, Delas, Dumazet, Pierre Gaillard, Guigal's La Doriane, Multier* (who, like some others, is using new oak), *Niero-Pinchon, Alain Paret, André Perret, Jean Pinchon, Rostaing* and *Georges Vernay*.

CORNAS, AC (red; north) Black and tarry tooth-staining wine. It's usually rather hefty, jammy even, and lacks some of the fresh fruit of Hermitage, yet at ten years old it's impressive. Excellent blockbusters are made by *Auguste Clape, Robert Michel* and *Noël Verset*. It's also worth looking for *René Balthazar, Colombo* (*Domaine des Ruchets*), *Courbis, Delas, Jaboulet, Juge, Lemenicier, Allemand, Jean Lionnet* (especially *Cuvée Rochepertuis*), *Alain Voge*.

COSTIÈRES DE NÎMES, AC (red, rosé; south) There are good rosés and meaty,

smoky reds here, at prices that are still reasonable. Try *Ch. de Campuget, Ch. Mourgues du Grés, Ch. de la Tuilerie, Dom. de l'Amarine, Mas de Bressades, Mas Carlot* (especially its top wines under the *Ch. Paul Blanc* label).

COTEAUX DU TRICASTIN, AC (red, white; south) Fast-improving, good-value, spicy, fruity reds, and fresh, fruity and quite full-flavoured whites, not as exciting as the reds. Best producers (reds): *Dom. de Grangeneuve, Dom. Saint-Luc, Dom. du Vieux Micocoulier, Prods. Réunis Ardéchois* (co-op; also good white), *Tour d'Elyssas* (100 per cent Syrah).

CÔTE-RÔTIE, AC (red; north) Together with Hermitage, the greatest wine of the northern Rhône. It can have exceptional finesse, thanks to the occasional addition of a dash of Viognier. The top wines, like Guigal's La Landonne, are now international blue chips. The top growers are *Barge, Burgaud, Champet, Chapoutier, Clusel-Roch, Delas, Gaillard, Gerin, Guigal, Jaboulet, Jamet, Jasmin* and *Rostaing*.

CÔTES DU LUBÉRON, AC (red, white; south) Lubéron makes decent reds, usually rather light, but capable of stronger personality. The *Val Joanis* rosé is one of the best in the South. Try also *Château de Canorgue, Château de l'Isolette, Mas du Peyroulet, Val Joanis* (also to be seen under the names of *Domaines Chancel* or *Domaine de la Panisse*), *la Vieille Ferme*. The whites are usually pleasant and light but little more, though much more fragrant, interesting styles come from *Château de l'Isolette, Mas du Peyroulet, Val Joanis* and *la Vieille Ferme*.

CÔTES DU RHÔNE, AC (red, white) Well-made basic Côtes du Rhône reds are delicious when young, wonderfully fresh and fruity, like a soft Beaujolais. Or they can be fierce, black, grapeskins-and-alcohol monsters. Many of the weightiest are made by Châteauneuf growers (*Cru de Coudoulet* from *Beaucastel*, *Château de Fonsalette* from *Rayas*) or northern Rhône producers like *Guigal* and *Clape*. *Château du Grand Moulas* is spicy and attractive, with plenty of body. Also good: *Château de Goudray*, *Château de Ruth*, *Clos du Père Clément*, *Domaine des Aussellons*, *Domaine de Bel Air*, *Domaine de la Cantharide*, *Domaine de St-Estève*, *Jean Lionnet* and *Chapoutier*'s rosé. Whites are generally fresh and fruity.

CÔTES DU RHÔNE-VILLAGES, AC

(red, white; south) Good, full reds that can also age, combining earthy, dusty southern heat with spicy, raspberry fruit. They come from villages, 17 of which can add their names on the label, including Cairanne, Chusclan, Valréas, Beaumes-de-Venise and Rasteau. These wines often offer excellent value. Best: *Dom. Pélaquié* (Laudun); *Dom. de Grangeneuve*, *Dom. la Soumade* (Rasteau); *Jean-March Antran*, *Jean-Pierre Cartier*, *Château de Trignon*, *Dom. de Boisson*, *Dom. St-Antoine*, *Dom. de Verquière* (Sablet); *Dom. de l'Ameillaud*, *Dom. Brusset*, *Dom. l'Oratoire St-Martin*, *Dom. de la Présidente*, *Dom. Rabasse-Charavin*, *Marcel Richaud* (Cairanne); *Dom. Ste-Anne* (St-Gervais); *Dom. de Cabasse*, *Dom. Courançonne* (Séguret); *Roger Combe*, *Dom. des Grands Devers*, *le Val des Rois* (Valréas). The whites are increasingly fresh, fruity and gulpable, especially from the villages of Laudun and Chusclan. *Dom. Pélaquié* is tops, and *Dom. Ste-Anne* is good.

CÔTES DU VENTOUX, AC

(red, white, rosé; south) Good area producing lots of fresh, juicy wine; the red is the best. Can even be quite special. Best: *Domaine des Anges*, *Jaboulet*, *Pascal*, *la Vieille Ferme*, *Vieux Lazaret*.

CROZES-HERMITAGE, AC

(red, white; north) Red that varies from the light and juicy to well-structured smoky wine recognizable as a lesser cousin of the great Hermitage. *Etienne Pochon* (*Château Curson*), *Chapoutier*'s *les Meysonniers* and

Varonniers, *Graillot*'s *Guiraude*, *Jaboulet*'s *Thalabert* are tops. Also good are *Albert Belle*, *Cave des Clairmonts*, *Cave de Tain*, *Bernard Chave*, *Laurent Combier*, *Stéphane Cornu*, *Domaine des Entrefaux*, *Fayolle*, *Pradelle* and *Vidal-Fleury*. The white is generally rather dull and strong, but there are good ones from *Château Curson*, *Combier*, *Entrefaux*, *Fayolle*, *Graillot*, *Jaboulet*, *Pradelle* and the *Tain co-op*.

GIGONDAS, AC

(red; south) Big, chunky, plummy wines that can be short on finesse. This is Grenache country, and proud of it. Best: *Clos des Cazaux*, *Dom. de Cayron*, *Dom. les Gouberts*, *Dom. de Longue-Toque*, *Dom. l'Oustau Fauquet*, *Dom. les Pallières*, *Dom. Raspail-Ay*, *Dom. de Santa Duc*, *Dom. de St-Gayan*.

HERMITAGE, AC

(red, white; north) Grand, burly red; strong and fierily tough when young, it matures to a rich, brooding magnificence. There is always a medicinal or smoky edge, and an unmatchable depth of raspberry and blackcurrant fruit. Although many people produce Hermitage of sorts, the stars are *Chave, Paul Jaboulet Aîné* and *Chapoutier's le Pavillon*. Also good: *Belle, Delas Cuvée Marquise de la Tourette, Desmeure, Faurie, Jean-Louis Grippat, Guigal* and *Sorrel*. The white is often heavy and dull, but it ages to a soft, rich nuttiness. *Chave* makes magnificent white Hermitage even in modest vintages, and other good producers include *Chapoutier, Desmeure, Ferraton, Grippat, Guigal* and *Marc Sorrel*.

LIRAC, AC (red, white, rosé; south) A good, often underrated area making light, attractive wines. Reds are packed with fruit, often tinged with a mineral edge. The rosés are fresh. Whites are best young. Best: *Ch. d'Aquéria, Dom. des Causses et St-Eymes, Dom. de Ch. St-Roch, Dom. la Fermade, Dom. les Garrigues, Dom. de la Tour, Maby.*

MUSCAT DE BEAUMES-DE-VENISE, AC (fortified white; south) The only Rhône village growing Muscat. This golden sweet wine – a *vin doux naturel* – is supremely delicious. Grapy, fresh, rich but not cloying. Best: *Dom. de Coyeux, Dom. Durban, Jaboulet, Beaumes-de-Venise co-op.*

RASTEAU, AC (fortified red, fortified white; south) Rasteau makes a few big, port-like fortified wines – *vins doux naturels* – but if you want that sort of thing you're probably better off with port itself. Young reds can have a delightful raspberry scent from the Grenache Noir. The whites are made from Grenache Blanc and can be frankly unpleasant. Production is small. Try *Dom. de la Soumade, Rasteau co-op.*

ST-JOSEPH, AC (red; north) Almost smooth and sweet compared to their tougher neighbours, these reds can be fairly big, fine wines, stacked with blackcurrant in good years. *Chave, Courbis, Coursodon, Cuilleron, Philippe Faury, Gripa, Grippat, Jaboulet, Didier Morion* and *Trollat* are leading names. The co-op at *St-Désirat Champagne* makes lovely Beaujolais-type St-Joseph. The white is decent and nutty. *Grippat* is good, but *Florentin*, an old-style oxidative, headbanging white, is more controversial. White Crozes is usually better value.

ST-PÉRAY, AC (white; north) Usually rather stolid and short on freshness. Quality is improving from the likes of *Chaboud, Domaine de Fauterie, Grippat* and Comas estates such as *Clape, Lionnet* and *Voge*.

TAVEL, AC (rosé; south) Quite expensive, certainly tasty, rosés, but mostly they're too big and alcoholic to be very refreshing. Any of the Rhône grapes will do, but generally it's Grenache-dominated, with the addition of a little Cinsaut. Best producers: *Château d'Aquéria, Château de Trinquevedel, Domaine de la Forcadière, Domaine de la Genestière.*

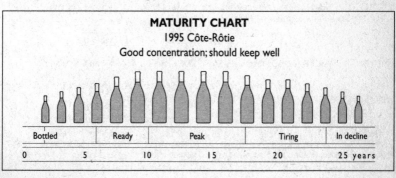

MATURITY CHART
1995 Côte-Rôtie
Good concentration; should keep well

Bottled	Ready	Peak	Tiring	In decline

| 0 | 5 | 10 | 15 | 20 | 25 years |

VACQUEYRAS, AC (red, white, rosé; south) Reds and rosés of character and structure. Some white wine is also produced, but it tends to be heavy. Cinsaut fanatic *Ch. de Montmirail* is good, as are *Clos des Cazaux, Dom. de la Fourmone, Dom. la Garrigue, le Sang des Cailloux.*

VIN DE PAYS DES COLLINES RHODANIENNES (red; north) A usually impressive and expanding northern Rhône area, particularly for inexpensive, tasty Syrah-based reds, though the lighter, softer Gamays can also be good.

VIN DE PAYS DES COTEAUX DE L'ARDÈCHE (red, white; south) A source of delicious Nouveau-style Gamay, first-class Syrah, good Cabernet, plus Sauvignon, Pinot Noir – and Chardonnay, both for *Louis Latour's* decent *Chardonnay de l'Ardèche* and the local co-ops (which give higher quality for far lower prices). This was one of the first vin de pays regions to smarten up its act; as happens to pioneers, it's been rather overtaken in the fashion stakes by others, notably those in the Languedoc. But it's still making good stuff, and it's worth looking out for.

RHÔNE VINTAGES

1998   Good in the North, and even better in the South. Reds are good and ripe.

1997   A year that looks like turning out as well as or better than 1996, at least in the South. Reds look set to age well.

1996   This looks superb for the northern reds, which have bags of tannin, fruit and acidity and will last, and for the whites from the whole region, some of which are stunning. Quality is less even in the South and the reds lack the intensity of those in the North.

1995   Top growers made very good wines, and there will be great wines in the North from those who, like Chapoutier and Chave, picked late.

1994   There were succulent reds and lively, flowery whites this year. A very good year but not a great one.

1993   Châteauneuf-du-Pape and Côtes du Rhône did best. In the North attractive whites but raw and rather dilute reds from Hermitage, Crozes and Cornas.

1992   A poor year; buy only from top growers and drink up quickly.

1991   Côte-Rôtie is generally better than in 1990. The South was only moderately good.

1990   The North was more successful than the South. Choose 1990 for the North (though Côte-Rôtie is dodgy); 1989 for the South.

1989   Some poor Hermitage and Cornas. Concentrated Châteauneuf-du-Pape.

1988   Best in Côte-Rôtie, Hermitage and Châteauneuf-du-Pape. Some is too tannic.

1987   The few good wines should have been drunk by now, though Côte-Rôtie and Hermitage provided some very good bottles, now drinking well.

1985   Brilliant Côte-Rôtie, St-Joseph and Cornas. Châteauneuf is delicious and juicy.

1983   Outstanding dark, rich, complex Hermitage and very good Côte-Rôtie for keeping. Southern reds are good, though some are a bit tough.

RHÔNE PRICES

RED

Under £4.00

Côtes du Ventoux la Falaise 1997 £3.92 (ROS)

Côtes du Ventoux les Cailloux 1995 £3.49 (OD)

£4.00 → £4.99

Côtes du Rhône Château du Grand Moulas 1997 £4.95 (BALL) £4.99 (POR) £5.50 (HAH)

Côtes du Rhône Cuvée des Capucines, Domaine de Vieux Chêne 1993 £4.95 (JU)

Côtes du Rhône Domaine des Moulins 1997 £4.99 (VIC) £4.99 (THR) £4.99 (WR) £4.99 (BOT) £5.30 (NEZ) £5.69 (YOU)

Côtes du Rhône Jaume 1996 £4.75 (WS)

Côtes du Rhône Meffre **Non-vintage** £4.49 (VIC) £4.49 (THR) £4.49 (WR)

Côtes du Rhône-Villages Cairanne, Domaine de l'Ameillaud 1997 £4.55 (HAH)

Côtes du Rhône-Villages Château la Courançonne 1996 £4.99 (SAI)

Côtes du Rhône-Villages Domaine de Hauterive 1996 £4.99 (CO)

Côtes du Ventoux Jaboulet 1997 £4.85 (WS) £4.99 (OD) £5.63 (PLA)

Côtes du Ventoux Jaboulet 1995 £4.65 (NI)

Côtes du Vivarais Domaine de Belvezet 1995 £4.99 (JON)

VdP des Collines Rhodaniennes Syrah, Cave de Tain l'Hermitage **Non-vintage** £4.59 (CON)

VdP de la Principauté d'Orange Cuvée des Templiers, Rieu Herail 1996 £4.70 (JER)

★ Vacqueyras Vignerons de Beaumes-de-Venise 1997 £4.99 (MAJ)

£5.00 → £5.99

Coteaux du Tricastin Domaine de Vieux Micocoulier 1993 £5.91 (CHA)

Côtes du Rhône Belleruche, Chapoutier 1996 £5.62 (PEN) £5.99 (CON)

Côtes du Rhône Caves des Vignerons de Vacqueyras 1997 £5.15 (TAN)

Côtes du Rhône Château du Grand Moulas 1998 £5.75 (TAN) £5.80 (AD)

Côtes du Rhône Château St-Estève 1997 £5.75 (WS)

Côtes du Rhône Coudoulet de Beaucastel 1995 £5.29 (CAV) £8.95 (FORT) £8.99 (RAE) £9.50 (GAU) £9.95 (ROB) £11.99 (VA)

Côtes du Rhône Cuvée des Capucines, Domaine de Vieux Chêne 1994 £5.35 (JU)

Côtes du Rhône Domaine de l'Ameillaud 1996 £5.68 (JER)

Côtes du Rhône Domaine de la Mordorée 1997 £5.75 (BAL) £5.95 (LEA) £6.29 (YOU)

Côtes du Rhône Domaine de l'Amandier 1995 £5.35 (CON)

Côtes du Rhône Domaine St-Gayan, Roger Meffre 1997 £5.95 (YAP)

Côtes du Rhône la Haie aux Grives, Domaine Vieux Chêne 1995 £5.75 (JU)

Côtes du Rhône Parallèle 45, Jaboulet 1997 £5.99 (OD) £6.69 (PLA) £6.90 (GAU)

Côtes du Rhône Rasteau, Chapoutier 1994 £5.79 (ROS)

Côtes du Rhône-Villages Sablet, Château du Trignon 1997 £5.49 (MAJ) £7.03 (GW)

Côtes du Ventoux la Vieille Ferme 1996 £5.29 (FLE) £5.70 (CB)

Crozes-Hermitage Louis Mousset 1996 £5.29 (CO)

Lirac la Fermade, Domaine Maby 1996 £5.35 (WS) £7.50 (YAP)

MERCHANTS SPECIALIZING IN THE RHÔNE

see Merchant Directory (page 413) for details

Adnams (AD), Bennetts (BEN), Berry Bros & Rudd (BER), Bibendum (BIB), Anthony Byrne (BY), Direct Wine Shipments (DI), Ben Ellis (ELL), Farr Vintners (FA), Gelston Castle, Justerini & Brooks (JU), Lay & Wheeler (LAY), Oddbins (OD), James Nicholson (NI), Nobody Inn (NO), Raeburn Fine Wines (RAE), Reid Wines (REI), Savage Selection (SAV), T&W Wines (TW), Tanners (TAN), The Ubiquitous Chip (UB), Wine Society (WS), Yapp Brothers (YAP), Noel Young (YOU).

Vacqueyras Cuvée du Marquis de Fonseguille **1996** £5.99 (CO)

VdP des Coteaux de la Cèze, Domaine Maby **1996** £5.75 (YAP)

£6.00 → £6.99

Coteaux du Tricastin Domaine de Grangeneuve **1997** £6.10 (YAP)

Côtes du Rhône Domaine Cros de la Mure **1997** £6.25 (WS)

★ Côtes du Rhône Domaine de St Georges **1994** £6.10 (PIP)

Côtes du Rhône Guigal **1996** £6.99 (BO) £7.99 (UN)

Côtes du Rhône Rascasses, Berard **1990** £6.49 (WAT)

Côtes du Rhône Vidal-Fleury **1995** £6.95 (ROB)

Côtes du Rhône-Villages Cairanne Réserve de Seigneurs de St Martin, Alary **1996** £6.70 (GAU)

Côtes du Rhône-Villages Château du Grand Moulas **1997** £6.95 (TAN) £7.15 (AD)

Côtes du Rhône-Villages Château du Grand Moulas **1996** £6.99 (POR)

Côtes du Rhône-Villages Jaboulet **1995** £6.50 (WS) £6.50 (FORT) £6.99 (NI)

Côtes du Rhône-Villages Valréas, Bouchard **1996** £6.50 (WS)

Côtes du Ventoux le Mont, la Vieille Ferme **1995** £6.75 (ROB)

Crozes-Hermitage Cave de Vins Fins à Tain-Hermitage **1997** £6.95 (BU) £6.99 (AME)

Crozes-Hermitage Cave de Vins Fins à Tain-Hermitage **1996** £6.49 (SAI) £7.95 (ROB)

★ Crozes-Hermitage Cave des Clairmonts, Borja **1997** £6.99 (WAI)

Crozes-Hermitage Cave des Clairmonts, Borja **1996** £6.99 (JON) £7.80 (MV)

Crozes-Hermitage Domaine du Colombier **1996** £6.99 (WAT) £10.52 (TW)

Crozes-Hermitage Pochon **1996** £6.95 (WS) £7.90 (JU)

Lirac les Queyrades, Mejan **1996** £6.90 (TAN) £6.95 (AD)

Stars (★) indicate wines selected by Oz Clarke in the Best Buys section which begins on page 9.

Vacqueyras Domaine le Clos des Cazaux **1997** £6.95 (AD)

Vacqueyras Pascal **1990** £6.39 (NLW)

VdP des Coteaux de l'Ardèche Syrah, Cave de St-Désirat **1998** £6.15 (YAP)

VdP de la Principauté d'Orange, Domaine de la Janasse **1997** £6.49 (MAJ)

VdP de la Principauté d'Orange, Domaine de la Janasse **1996** £6.95 (BU)

£7.00 → £7.99

Côtes du Rhône Château des Tours **1995** £7.50 (WS)

Côtes du Rhône Coudoulet de Beaucastel **1996** £7.25 (FA) £8.49 (OD) £8.89 (RAE) £8.95 (WS) £10.49 (BOT) £11.00 (MV)

Côtes du Rhône Domaine Cros de la Mure **1996** £7.40 (MV)

Côtes du Rhône Guigal **1995** £7.23 (BY) £7.34 (REI) £7.90 (BEN) £7.99 (CB) £8.50 (CRO) £9.99 (AV)

Côtes du Rhône Guigal **1994** £7.07 (FLE) £7.40 (UB) £7.75 (BU) £7.99 (CB)

Côtes du Rhône Jaboulet **1995** £7.30 (HAH)

Côtes du Rhône Mataro, Domaine le Clos des Cazaux **1995** £7.50 (JU)

Côtes du Rhône Rasteau, Chapoutier **1996** £7.95 (AD) £8.78 (STE)

Côtes du Rhône-Villages Cairanne, Rabasse-Charavin **1996** £7.49 (YOU)

Côtes du Rhône-Villages Rasteau, Chapoutier **1996** £7.20 (TAN) £7.49 (DI)

Côtes du Rhône-Villages Rasteau, Château du Trignon **1995** £7.50 (JU)

Côtes du Rhône-Villages Rasteau, Domaine la Soumade **1997** £7.99 (AME)

Crozes-Hermitage Domaine des Entrefaux **1997** £7.61 (BY) £7.90 (TAN) £8.00 (PIP)

Crozes-Hermitage Domaine des Remizières, Desmeure **1996** £7.50 (BALL)

Crozes-Hermitage Jaboulet **1996** £7.70 (HAH)

Crozes-Hermitage les Jalets, Jaboulet **1996** £7.85 (COC) £7.93 (REI) £10.00 (FORT)

Crozes-Hermitage les Pierrelles, Albert Belle **1996** £7.99 (OD)

Crozes-Hermitage les Pierrelles, Albert Belle **1995** £7.50 (WS)

Gigondas Domaine Raspail **1993** £7.55 (HA)

★ Vacqueyras Château de Roques **1996** £7.10 (HAH)

Vacqueyras Cuvée des Templiers, Domaine le Clos des Cazaux **1995** £7.95 (JU)

Vacqueyras Domaine le Couroulu **1994**
£7.79 (COC) £7.99 (AME) £8.60 (BER)
Vacqueyras Domaine des Genets, Delas
1996 £7.34 (JER)
Vacqueyras Jaboulet **1996** £7.65 (CON)

£8.00 → £8.99

Châteauneuf-du-Pape Château de
Beaucastel **1993** £14.00 (JU) £15.99 (YOU)
Châteauneuf-du-Pape Clos du Caillou
1996 £8.95 (SOM) £12.89 (YOU)
Côtes du Rhône-Villages Cuvée de l'Ecu,
Château du Grand Moulas **1997** £8.50
(TAN)
Côtes du Rhône-Villages Domaine Ste-
Anne **1997** £8.50 (TAN)
Côtes du Rhône-Villages Rasteau,
Domaine la Soumade **1995** £8.75 (PIP)
Crozes-Hermitage Delas **1997** £8.30 (NEZ)
Crozes-Hermitage Domaine du Colombier
1998 £8.72 (BIB)
Crozes-Hermitage Domaine du Colombier
1995 £8.69 (YOU) £10.52 (TW)
Crozes-Hermitage Graillot **1997** £8.97 (BY)
Crozes-Hermitage Jaboulet **1994** £8.55
(WHI)
Crôzes-Hermitage la Petite Ruche,
Chapoutier **1997** £8.50 (TAN) £9.86
(STE) £9.95 (BEN) £10.95 (NA) £10.99 (VA)
Crozes-Hermitage les Meysonniers,
Chapoutier **1996** £8.99 (OD) £9.49 (CON)
Crozes-Hermitage les Meysonniers,
Chapoutier **1995** £8.71 (FA) £8.99 (DI)
£9.90 (GAU) £10.53 (STE) £11.70 (NA)
Gigondas Cuvée de la Tour Sarrazine,
Domaine le Clos des Cazaux **1996**
£8.03 (JER) £8.90 (TAN)
St-Joseph Cave de St-Désirat **1996** £8.95
(WAI)

St-Joseph Deschants, Chapoutier **1995**
£8.22 (CAV) £10.49 (CON) £11.26 (JER)
£11.59 (JON) £11.97 (STE) £12.25 (STA)
St-Joseph le Grand Pompée, Jaboulet **1996**
£8.99 (OD) £10.05 (HAH) £11.40 (PLA)

St-Joseph le Grand Pompée, Jaboulet
1995 £8.99 (NI)
Vacqueyras Cuvée des Templiers,
Domaine le Clos des Cazaux **1993**
£8.75 (ROB)
Vacqueyras Domaine du Clos du Caveau
1995 £8.99 (PHI)
Vacqueyras Domaine le Couroulu **1995**
£8.00 (BER) £8.95 (STA)
Vacqueyras Domaine le Clos des Cazaux
1996 £8.10 (TAN)
Vacqueyras Domaine le Sang des Cailloux
1997 £8.70 (PIP)

£9.00 → £9.99

Châteauneuf-du-Pape Clos du Caillou
1997 £9.75 (BAN)
Châteauneuf-du-Pape Domaine de
Farguerol **1996** £9.35 (CON)
Châteauneuf-du-Pape Domaine du Père
Caboche **1997** £9.99 (OD)
Châteauneuf-du-Pape Domaine de la
Solitude **1997** £9.49 (SO)
Châteauneuf-du-Pape les Celliers des
Princes **1995** £9.99 (CO)
Côtes du Rhône Coudoulet de Beaucastel
1994 £9.90 (CRO)
Côtes du Rhône-Villages Cuvée St-Gervais,
Domaine Ste-Anne **1997** £9.50 (LEA)
Crozes-Hermitage Chapoutier **1996**
£9.85 (PHI) £13.50 (AV)
Crozes-Hermitage Château Curson,
Pochon **1996** £9.95 (YOU)
★ Crozes-Hermitage Cuvée Alberic Bouvet,
Gilles Robin **1997** £9.69 (GW)
Crozes-Hermitage Domaine de Thalabert,
Jaboulet **1996** £9.40 (CAV) £10.99 (OD)
£11.30 (GAU) £11.49 (CON) £11.90 (TAN)
Crozes-Hermitage Tour d'Albon, Delas
1995 £9.75 (PEN)
Crôzes-Hermitage la Petite Ruche,
Chapoutier **1996** £9.99 (POR)
Gigondas Château du Trignon **1995**
£9.50 (WS)
Gigondas Cuvée Pierre Aiguille, Jaboulet
1996 £9.95 (CON) £10.25 (HAH)
Gigondas Domaine du Cayron **1997**
£9.90 (GAU) £11.95 (AD)
Gigondas Domaine de Gour de Chaulé
1995 £9.50 (JU)
Gigondas Domaine Santa Duc **1996** £9.50
(FORT) £10.89 (YOU) £10.99 (DI) £11.20
(AV) £11.85 (BAN)
Gigondas Domaine les Tourelles,
Cuillerat **1996** £9.99 (HIG)

Gigondas Guigal **1996** £9.99 (MAJ)

Gigondas Jaboulet **1993** £9.25 (NI)

Lirac Cuvée de la Reine des Bois, Domaine de la Mordorée **1996** £9.00 (ELL) £9.50 (BAL) £9.95 (LEA)

Lirac Sabon **1995** £9.50 (PIP) £9.95 (STA)

St-Joseph Cave de St-Désirat **1997** £9.75 (YAP)

St-Joseph Chapoutier **1997** £9.99 (OD)

St-Joseph Clos de la Cuminaille, Gaillard **1995** £9.95 (LEA) £12.60 (CRO)

St-Joseph Coursodon **1996** £9.99 (WR)

St-Joseph François de Tournon, Delas **1994** £9.95 (WS)

St-Joseph Larmes du Père, Paret **1995** £9.95 (PHI)

St-Joseph Larmes du Père, Paret **1994** £9.49 (AME)

Vacqueyras Château des Tours **1996** £9.95 (NI) £10.60 (YAP)

Vacqueyras Cuvée Spéciale, Pascal **1993** £9.45 (VIN)

£10.00 → £11.99

Châteauneuf-du-Pape Chante-Cigale **1996** £11.99 (AME) £12.95 (YAP)

Châteauneuf-du-Pape Château des Fines Roches **1996** £10.99 (BO) £13.99 (UN)

Châteauneuf-du-Pape Château Fortia **1994** £11.00 (WS) £12.95 (AV)

Châteauneuf-du-Pape Domaine de Beaurenard **1997** £11.55 (NEZ)

Châteauneuf-du-Pape Domaine Font de Michelle **1996** £11.75 (BALL) £12.80 (TAN)

Châteauneuf-du-Pape Domaine Grand Tinel **1995** £10.50 (JU) £10.55 (AV) £16.90 (CRO)

Châteauneuf-du-Pape Domaine de Nalys **1997** £10.96 (BY)

Châteauneuf-du-Pape Domaine de Nalys **1995** £11.26 (COC)

Châteauneuf-du-Pape Domaine de la Roquette, Brunier **1996** £11.50 (TAN) £13.40 (PIP)

Châteauneuf-du-Pape Domaine de la Solitude **1994** £11.80 (AV)

Châteauneuf-du-Pape Domaine Versino **1995** £11.65 (JER)

Châteauneuf-du-Pape Domaine du Vieux Télégraphe **1996** £10.99 (LAY) £13.50 (TAN) £14.95 (BER) £15.99 (PHI)

Châteauneuf-du-Pape les Galéans, Brunier **1994** £11.00 (WS) £12.95 (BER)

Châteauneuf-du-Pape Lucien Barrot **1996** £11.99 (POR)

Châteauneuf-du-Pape Lucien Barrot **1995** £11.99 (BAL) £12.00 (MV)

Châteauneuf-du-Pape Vieux Donjon, Michel **1995** £10.18 (FA) £14.50 (CRO) £16.50 (GAU)

Châteauneuf-du-Pape Vieux Mas des Papes, Brunier **1996** £10.99 (POR)

Cornas Chapoutier **1995** £11.16 (FA)

Côte-Rôtie Clusel-Roch ½ bottle **1995** £10.95 (LEA)

Crozes-Hermitage Domaine de Thalabert, Jaboulet **1995** £10.67 (FA) £10.95 (NI) £11.49 (CON) £17.25 (FORT)

Crozes-Hermitage Domaine de Thalabert, Jaboulet **1994** £10.75 (WS)

Gigondas Chapoutier **1996** £10.99 (UB)

Gigondas Château du Trignon **1997** £11.50 (ELL)

Gigondas Domaine du Cayron **1995** £10.50 (JU)

Gigondas Domaine les Gouberts **1996** £10.95 (LEA)

Gigondas Domaine du Grand Montmirail **1993** £10.25 (YAP) £12.90 (VIN)

Gigondas Domaine les Pallières **1993** £11.26 (COC) £12.60 (PIP)

Gigondas Domaine St-Gayan, Roger Meffre **1995** £10.50 (YAP) £10.99 (JON)

Gigondas Domaine Santa Duc **1997** £10.90 (GAU)

Gigondas Guigal **1995** £10.83 (BY) £13.60 (UB)

Lirac Cuvée de la Reine des Bois, Domaine de la Mordorée **1997** £10.75 (BEN)

St-Joseph Clos de la Cuminaille, Gaillard **1997** £10.95 (LEA)

St-Joseph Clos de l'Arbalestrier, Florentin **1994** £11.00 (WS) £11.06 (RAE)

St-Joseph Graillot **1997** £10.40 (BY)

St-Joseph Graillot **1996** £10.19 (LAY) £19.50 (CRO)

St-Joseph Gripa **1994** £11.75 (CON) £14.70 (BEN)

St-Joseph le Grand Pompée, Jaboulet **1994** £11.25 (UB)

St-Joseph Faurie **1995** £10.90 (JU)

St-Joseph Vidal-Fleury **1991** £10.95 (ROB)

Vacqueyras Château des Tours **1997** £10.49 (DI)

Vacqueyras Château des Tours **1995** £10.18 (RAE) £11.00 (ELL)

Vacqueyras Grenat Noble, Domaine le Clos des Cazaux **1995** £11.90 (JU) £12.95 (GAU)

£12.00 → £13.99

Châteauneuf-du-Pape Château Fortia
1995 £12.99 (YOU) £13.95 (DI)

Châteauneuf-du-Pape Château la Nerthe
1996 £13.99 (NI)

Châteauneuf-du-Pape Clos des Papes,
Avril 1996 £13.61 (GAU) £14.50 (RAE)

Châteauneuf-du-Pape Clos du Mont
Olivet 1996 £12.39 (YOU)

Châteauneuf-du-Pape Clos du Mont
Olivet 1995 £12.20 (AV) £13.99 (JON)
£13.99 (POR) £14.95 (RES)

Châteauneuf-du-Pape Domaine du Père
Caboche 1996 £12.75 (YAP)

Châteauneuf-du-Pape Domaine de la
Roquette, Brunier 1995 £13.86 (LAY)

Châteauneuf-du-Pape Domaine de la
Roquette, Brunier 1994 £12.50 (FORT)

Châteauneuf-du-Pape Domaine Terre
Ferme, Bérard 1992 £13.75 (WAT)

Châteauneuf-du-Pape Domaine Versino
1994 £13.22 (JER)

Châteauneuf-du-Pape Domaine du Vieux
Télégraphe 1997 £13.45 (HAH)

Châteauneuf-du-Pape Domaine du Vieux
Télégraphe 1995 £12.75 (BALL) £15.67
(ELL) £18.50 (JU) £22.50 (ROB)

Châteauneuf-du-Pape la Bernardine,
Chapoutier 1996 £13.99 (OD) £14.95
(DI) £15.59 (YOU) £19.70 (BEN)

Châteauneuf-du-Pape la Bernardine,
Chapoutier 1995 £13.12 (FA) £13.50
(CON)

Châteauneuf-du-Pape les Cailloux, Brunel
1996 £12.49 (YOU) £12.99 (POR)

Châteauneuf-du-Pape les Cailloux, Brunel
1995 £12.55 (AV)

Châteauneuf-du-Pape les Cèdres, Jaboulet
1995 £12.50 (NI) £15.60 (COC)

Châteauneuf-du-Pape Lucien Barrot 1994
£12.00 (MV)

Châteauneuf-du-Pape Mont-Redon 1995
£12.63 (FA) £13.99 (POR)

Châteauneuf-du-Pape Mont-Redon 1994
£12.65 (UB)

Châteauneuf-du-Pape Réserve, Sabon
1996 £13.49 (YOU)

Châteauneuf-du-Pape Vieux Donjon,
Michel 1997 £13.50 (YAP)

Cornas Delas 1994 £13.00 (WS)

Cornas La Geynale, Robert Michel 1994
£13.51 (REI)

Cornas les Ruchets, Colombo 1995
£13.30 (SOM) £23.59 (YOU) £28.50 (FORT)

Cornas Robert Michel 1984 £13.50 (GAU)

Côte-Rôtie Chapoutier 1994 £13.61 (FA)
£20.90 (GAU) £26.51 (STE) £29.45 (NA)

Côtes du Rhône Coudoulet de Beaucastel
1990 £12.75 (ROB)

Crozes-Hermitage Desmeure 1996
£12.10 (HAH)

Crozes-Hermitage Graillot 1995 £13.50
(FORT)

Crôzes-Hermitage la Petite Ruche,
Chapoutier 1992 £12.50 (CRO)

Gigondas Domaine les Pallières 1988
£12.50 (FLE)

St-Joseph Clos de la Cuminaille, Gaillard
1994 £12.95 (ROB)

St-Joseph Clos de l'Arbalestrier, Florentin
1991 £13.95 (RAE)

St-Joseph Grippat 1996 £13.75 (YAP)

St-Joseph les Pierres, Pierre Gaillard
1995 £12.50 (JU)

St-Joseph Pascal 1995 £13.45 (VIN)

£14.00 → £15.99

Châteauneuf-du-Pape Château de
Beaucastel 1996 £14.59 (FA) £15.86
(REI) £17.95 (TAN) £18.48 (FLE) £20.07
(CAV) £22.50 (AD) £23.00 (MV)

Châteauneuf-du-Pape Château de
Beaucastel 1994 £14.95 (NI) £19.00 (RAE)
£19.00 (FA) £20.00 (BU) £24.95 (WR)
£24.95 (BOT) £25.00 (MV) £26.95 (BEN)

Châteauneuf-du-Pape Château Fortia
1984 £15.86 (REI)

Châteauneuf-du-Pape Clos des Papes,
Avril 1995 £15.67 (ELL)

Châteauneuf-du-Pape Cuvée Etienne
Gonnet, Domaine Font de Michelle
1993 £15.00 (JU) £15.98 (LAY)

Châteauneuf-du-Pape Domaine de la
Mordorée 1995 £14.95 (BAL)

Châteauneuf-du-Pape Domaine Font de
Michelle 1997 £15.49 (THR) £15.49 (WR)

Châteauneuf-du-Pape Domaine du Vieux
Télégraphe 1994 £15.00 (JU) £15.18
(JER) £18.50 (BEN) £19.00 (CRO)

> • Wines are listed in A–Z
> order within each price
> band.
> • For each wine, vintages are
> listed in descending order.
> • Each vintage of any wine
> appears only once.

Cornas Jaboulet 1995 £14.55 (HAH)
£20.39 (PLA)

Cornas la Chaillot, Allemand 1992 £14.00
(JU)

Cornas le Reynard, Allemand 1993
£15.60 (TAN) £15.95 (RAE)

Cornas Noël Verset 1996 £14.51 (REI)

Cornas Noël Verset 1993 £15.95 (RAE)
£16.29 (JON)

Cornas Rochepertuis, Jean Lionnet 1991
£14.90 (JU)

Côte-Rôtie les Jumelles, Jaboulet 1983
£14.59 (FA) £41.13 (WY)

Gigondas Chapoutier 1997 £14.85 (STE)
Gigondas Domaine Santa Duc 1995
£15.00 (CRO)

Gigondas Jaboulet 1996 £14.50 (STA)

Hermitage Domaine des Remizières 1995
£14.88 (RAE) £17.50 (ELL)

St-Joseph Chave 1998 £15.00 (YAP)

St-Joseph Grippat 1986 £15.00 (CRO)

£16.00 → £19.99

Châteauneuf-du-Pape Château de
Beaucastel 1995 £18.95 (NI) £22.95
(ROB) £26.50 (POR) £30.00 (FORT)

Châteauneuf-du-Pape Château de
Beaucastel 1991 £17.50 (BU)

Châteauneuf-du-Pape Clos du Caillou
1995 £16.95 (PHI)

Châteauneuf-du-Pape Clos du Caillou
1994 £16.50 (ROB)

Châteauneuf-du-Pape Cuvée de la Reine
des Bois, Domaine de la Mordorée
1996 £18.95 (LEA)

Châteauneuf-du-Pape Domaine Font de
Michelle 1995 £19.25 (NO)

Châteauneuf-du-Pape la Bernardine,
Chapoutier 1997 £17.95 (WAI)

Châteauneuf-du-Pape les Cèdres, Jaboulet
1996 £17.38 (PLA)

Châteauneuf-du-Pape Mont-Redon 1989
£17.00 (WS)

Châteauneuf-du-Pape Réserve, Sabon
1995 £16.95 (STA)

Cornas Chapoutier 1996 £17.64 (STE)

Cornas Clape 1992 £18.73 (PLAY) £33.40
(UB)

Cornas Colombo 1991 £16.00 (JU)

Cornas Jaboulet 1996 £16.90 (TAN)

Cornas Jaboulet 1984 £17.04 (REI)

Cornas la Geynale, Robert Michel 1995
£18.80 (CRO)

Cornas Rochepertuis, Jean Lionnet 1993
£18.69 (YOU)

Côte-Rôtie Brune et Blonde, Gaillard
1995 £17.00 (JU) £19.34 (FLE)

Côte-Rôtie Burgaud 1995 £18.00 (JU)
£19.99 (YOU) £22.00 (YAP)

Côte-Rôtie Burgaud 1992 £19.00 (JU)

Côte-Rôtie Chapoutier 1996 £18.95 (DI)
£24.95 (UB)

Côte-Rôtie Chapoutier 1990 £18.45 (BER)

Côte-Rôtie Clusel-Roch 1996 £17.00 (WS)

Côte-Rôtie Clusel-Roch 1994 £17.95 (LEA)
£20.00 (JU)

Côte-Rôtie Cuvée du Plessy, Gilles Barge
1996 £16.99 (RAE) £19.10 (TAN)

Côte-Rôtie Cuvée du Plessy, Gilles Barge
1994 £17.45 (REI) £20.00 (BU)

Côte-Rôtie Gaillard 1991 £17.90 (BER)

Côte-Rôtie Jamet 1993 £17.99 (MAJ)

Côte-Rôtie la Viaillère, Dervieux-Thaize
1987 £19.39 (REI)

Côte-Rôtie la Viaillère, Champet 1996
£19.25 (YAP)

Côte-Rôtie la Viaillère, Champet 1995
£16.50 (JU)

Côte-Rôtie René Rostaing 1996 £16.06
(FA) £19.95 (AD)

Côte-Rôtie Seigneur de Maugiron, Delas
1989 £19.39 (PEN)

Côte-Rôtie de Vallouit 1980 £19.00 (CRO)

Côtes du Rhône Château de Fonsalette
1994 £19.65 (UB) £21.15 (CAV)

Côtes du Rhône Château de Fonsalette
1993 £19.39 (TW)

Crozes-Hermitage Domaine de
Thalabert, Jaboulet 1990 £16.00 (COC)
£35.00 (CRO)

Gigondas Domaine les Gouberts 1985
£18.50 (CRO)

Hermitage Desmeure 1995 £17.50 (GAU)

Hermitage Domaine du Colombier 1996
£19.97 (JER)

Hermitage Domaine des Remizières 1994
£17.95 (RAE)

Hermitage Guigal 1994 £18.60 (BY)

Hermitage la Sizeranne, Chapoutier 1994
£19.80 (REI) £22.99 (UN) £23.70 (TAN)
£24.99 (POR) £32.10 (AV) £33.90 (NA)

Hermitage Marquise de la Tourette, Delas
1994 £19.39 (PEN)

Hermitage de Vallouit 1982 £17.50 (CRO)

St-Joseph Clos de la Cuminaille, Gaillard
1989 £16.06 (FA)

St-Joseph le Grand Pompée, Jaboulet
1985 £19.39 (REI)

St-Joseph Réserve Personnelle, Jaboulet
1985 £18.00 (CRO)

£20.00 → £24.99

Châteauneuf-du-Pape Château Pignan 1994 £23.50 (CAV)
Châteauneuf-du-Pape Clos des Papes, Avril 1994 £24.50 (ROB)
Châteauneuf-du-Pape Vidal-Fleury 1985 £22.00 (CRO)
Cornas Clape 1997 £22.75 (YAP)
Cornas Delas 1985 £22.50 (BU)
Cornas Jaboulet 1976 £22.50 (BU) £29.00 (CRO)
Cornas les Ruchets, Colombo 1996 £22.91 (FA) £24.25 (BAN) £30.79 (TW)
Cornas Robert Michel 1983 £20.56 (REI)
Côte-Rôtie Barge 1983 £22.00 (CRO)
Côte-Rôtie Brune et Blonde, Guigal 1995 £20.32 (BY) £21.25 (MI) £23.95 (POR)
Côte-Rôtie Brune et Blonde, Guigal 1992 £20.75 (CON) £23.00 (JU) £32.31 (TW)

Côte-Rôtie Brune et Blonde, Vidal-Fleury 1994 £23.41 (HA)
Côte-Rôtie Champet 1993 £20.15 (PIP)
Côte-Rôtie Chapoutier 1995 £21.95 (DI) £23.32 (REI) £25.85 (CAV) £28.95 (BEN)
Côte-Rôtie Chapoutier 1991 £24.75 (FORT) £26.00 (CRO)
Côte-Rôtie Côte Blonde, René Rostaing 1994 £22.91 (REI) £37.00 (CRO)
Côte-Rôtie Côte Blonde, René Rostaing 1993 £24.95 (NI) £26.00 (JU)
Côte-Rôtie Côte Brune, Gentaz-Dervieux 1993 £23.95 (RAE) £25.99 (JON)
Côte-Rôtie Gentaz-Dervieux 1993 £23.00 (WS)
Côte-Rôtie Guigal 1995 £23.50 (AME)
Côte-Rôtie Guigal 1994 £21.79 (UN)
Côte-Rôtie Jasmin 1996 £23.50 (YAP)
Côte-Rôtie la Landonne, Rostaing 1994 £23.90 (NI) £28.00 (JU)
Côte-Rôtie la Viaillère, Rostaing 1996 £22.91 (FA) £29.95 (RES)
Côte-Rôtie les Jumelles, Jaboulet 1995 £24.50 (AD) £25.00 (FLE) £32.31 (PLA)

Côte-Rôtie René Rostaing 1995 £20.56 (REI) £22.00 (JU) £32.00 (CRO)
Côte-Rôtie de Vallouit 1991 £24.87 (FA)
Côte-Rôtie de Vallouit 1983 £20.00 (CRO)
Côtes du Rhône Château de Fonsalette 1986 £23.00 (CRO)
Crozes-Hermitage Domaine de Thalabert, Jaboulet 1989 £20.49 (YOU) £20.56 (REI) £32.00 (CRO)
Gigondas Domaine les Pallières 1983 £23.00 (CRO)
Gigondas Jaboulet 1979 £21.00 (CRO)
Hermitage Albert Belle 1996 £24.95 (BEN)
Hermitage Bernard Faurie 1996 £20.40 (HAH)
Hermitage Bernard Faurie 1991 £23.00 (JU)
Hermitage Chapoutier 1976 £22.50 (BU)
Hermitage Chave 1995 £20.99 (AME) £75.00 (BEN) £88.13 (CAV)
Hermitage Chave 1993 £23.00 (WS) £30.12 (PLAY) £35.00 (YAP) £40.00 (FORT)
Hermitage Domaine du Colombier 1994 £20.39 (YOU) £22.00 (JU) £25.26 (TW)
Hermitage Domaine Ferraton 1985 £21.00 (CRO)
Hermitage Domaine des Remizières 1991 £22.21 (TW)
Hermitage Guigal 1995 £21.25 (MI)
Hermitage Guigal 1993 £24.83 (PLAY)
Hermitage Guigal 1991 £24.50 (ROB) £35.25 (TW)
Hermitage la Chapelle, Jaboulet 1992 £23.85 (COC) £23.99 (WR) £27.50 (STA) £32.31 (PLA)
Hermitage la Sizeranne, Chapoutier 1996 £21.95 (DI) £24.87 (FA) £24.90 (GAU) £27.02 (CAV)
Hermitage la Sizeranne, Chapoutier 1991 £24.95 (ROB) £25.00 (CRO) £27.00 (JU)
Hermitage Vidal-Fleury 1991 £20.50 (ROB)
St-Joseph le Berceaux, Bernard Gripa 1994 £20.56 (TW)

£25.00 → £29.99

Châteauneuf-du-Pape Barbe Rac, Chapoutier 1992 £29.00 (CRO) £45.24 (REI)
Châteauneuf-du-Pape Domaine du Vieux Télégraphe 1985 £29.96 (REI)
Châteauneuf-du-Pape Domaine du Vieux Télégraphe 1976 £26.50 (CRO)
Châteauneuf-du-Pape la Grappe des Papes, Jaboulet 1969 £29.00 (CRO)
Châteauneuf-du-Pape les Cailloux, Brunel 1990 £29.00 (CRO)

Cornas Clape **1996** £25.00 (FORT) £28.90 (CRO)

Côte-Rôtie Brune et Blonde, Guigal **1983** £26.83 (FA) £30.55 (WY) £35.00 (CRO)

Côte-Rôtie Chapoutier **1989** £29.95 (DI)

Côte-Rôtie Côte Blonde, René Rostaing **1996** £28.79 (FA)

Côte-Rôtie Côte Brune, Gentaz-Dervieux **1992** £26.50 (ROB)

Côte-Rôtie Gentaz-Dervieux **1980** £29.00 (CRO)

Côte-Rôtie Jamet **1988** £26.00 (CRO)

Côte-Rôtie Jasmin **1994** £25.00 (YAP)

Côte-Rôtie la Landonne, Guigal **1983** £25.00 (CRO) £205.63 (FA) £293.75 (CAV)

Côte-Rôtie la Landonne, Rostaing **1996** £26.65 (AD) £27.32 (FA) £27.95 (WAI) £36.95 (RES)

Côte-Rôtie la Viaillère, Rostaing **1995** £26.00 (JU)

Côte-Rôtie les Grandes Places, Clusel-Roch **1993** £29.00 (JU) £29.95 (LEA)

Côte-Rôtie les Jumelles, Jaboulet **1996** £25.05 (HAH) £25.80 (TAN)

Côte-Rôtie les Jumelles, Jaboulet **1986** £28.00 (JU)

Côte-Rôtie Rose Pourpe, Gaillard **1995** £27.00 (JU)

Hermitage Chave **1992** £28.89 (CAV)

Hermitage Desmeure **1983** £27.00 (CRO)

Hermitage Grippat **1997** £28.50 (YAP)

Hermitage Guigal **1990** £25.00 (BU) £41.12 (CAV)

Hermitage la Chapelle, Jaboulet **1996** £28.99 (OD) £33.70 (TAN) £37.50 (CON)

Hermitage la Chapelle, Jaboulet **1995** £28.75 (NI) £35.00 (FORT) £38.68 (CAV) £48.37 (FA)

Hermitage la Chapelle, Jaboulet **1994** £26.97 (REI) £29.00 (YOU) £31.00 (WS)

Hermitage la Sizeranne, Chapoutier **1990** £27.00 (JU) £27.50 (RES)

Hermitage le Gréal, Sorrel **1996** £25.90 (GAU)

Hermitage Sorrel **1990** £27.75 (ROB)

St-Joseph Jaboulet **1978** £27.00 (CRO)

- *All prices for each wine are listed together in ascending order.*
- *Price bands refer to the lowest price for which the wine is available.*

£30.00 → £49.99

Châteauneuf-du-Pape Barbe Rac, Chapoutier **1996** £49.50 (BEN)

Châteauneuf-du-Pape Barbe Rac, Chapoutier **1995** £41.99 (YOU) £44.24 (REI)

Châteauneuf-du-Pape Barbe Rac, Chapoutier **1993** £37.50 (RES)

Châteauneuf-du-Pape Barbe Rac, Chapoutier **1991** £38.68 (CAV) £47.00 (BEN)

Châteauneuf-du-Pape Château de Beaucastel **1990** £42.50 (FA) £49.50 (CRO) £59.95 (RES) £60.00 (FORT)

Châteauneuf-du-Pape Château de Beaucastel **1988** £30.75 (FA) £37.00 (CRO) £40.00 (FORT) £94.00 (UB)

Châteauneuf-du-Pape Château Fortia **1975** £33.49 (REI)

Châteauneuf-du-Pape Château Pignan **1995** £48.47 (CAV)

Châteauneuf-du-Pape Château Pignan **1986** £32.00 (CRO)

Châteauneuf-du-Pape Château Rayas **1994** £36.50 (DI) £50.33 (FA)

Châteauneuf-du-Pape Château Rayas **1993** £39.72 (TW) £76.38 (CAV)

Châteauneuf-du-Pape Clos des Papes, Avril **1985** £37.50 (RES)

Châteauneuf-du-Pape Clos du Mont Olivet **1978** £40.00 (CRO)

Châteauneuf-du-Pape Clos Pignan, Reynaud **1988** £46.82 (REI)

Châteauneuf-du-Pape Domaine Bosquet des Papes **1985** £34.00 (CRO)

Châteauneuf-du-Pape Domaine du Vieux Télégraphe **1989** £39.95 (WY)

Cornas Clape **1990** £48.00 (CRO)

Cornas Jaboulet **1978** £48.76 (REI)

Cornas les Ruchets, Colombo **1994** £32.31 (TW)

Côte-Rôtie Brune et Blonde, Guigal **1985** £33.49 (REI) £35.00 (BEN) £40.00 (CRO)

Côte-Rôtie Brune et Blonde, Vidal-Fleury **1990** £33.76 (NO)

Côte-Rôtie Chapoutier **1978** £35.00 (CRO)

Côte-Rôtie Côte Blonde, René Rostaing **1995** £31.14 (REI)

Côte-Rôtie Côte Blonde, René Rostaing **1988** £49.00 (JU)

Côte-Rôtie Gentaz-Dervieux **1991** £38.00 (CRO)

Côte-Rôtie la Landonne, Guigal **1993** £41.54 (BY) £60.12 (FA) £117.50 (TW)

Côte-Rôtie la Landonne, René Rostaing
1995 £30.99 (NI) £75.00 (RES)
Côte-Rôtie la Landonne, René Rostaing
1988 £49.00 (JU) £61.00 (CRO)
Côte-Rôtie la Mordorée, Chapoutier
1994 £42.50 (FA) £57.99 (YOU)
Côte-Rôtie la Mouline, Guigal **1993**
£41.54 (BY) £90.00 (ROB)
Côte-Rôtie les Jumelles, Jaboulet **1991**
£39.00 (WS)
Côte-Rôtie les Jumelles, Jaboulet **1985**
£35.25 (WY)
Côte-Rôtie René Rostaing **1991** £34.00
(CRO) £49.95 (RES)
Côte-Rôtie de Vallouit **1978** £31.00 (YOU)
Côtes du Rhône Château de Fonsalette
1995 £38.68 (CAV) £41.13 (REI)
Crozes-Hermitage Domaine de
Thalabert, Jaboulet **1978** £42.89 (REI)
Gigondas Domaine les Gouberts **1981**
£34.00 (CRO)
Gigondas Jaboulet **1970** £32.00 (CRO)
Hermitage Bernard Faurie **1985** £42.00 (PIP)
Hermitage Chave **1974** £41.13 (REI)
Hermitage Guigal **1983** £32.90 (WY)
Hermitage Guigal **1982** £35.00 (CRO)
Hermitage Jaboulet **1983** £38.19 (REI)
Hermitage Jaboulet **1976** £30.00 (CRO)
Hermitage la Chapelle, Jaboulet **1991**
£31.99 (YOU) £34.08 (CAV) £35.00 (JU)
Hermitage la Chapelle, Jaboulet **1988**
£30.58 (FA) £48.47 (CAV) £60.00 (NO)
Hermitage la Chapelle, Jaboulet **1983**
£45.43 (FA) £65.00 (WS) £68.05 (CAV)
£70.00 (JU) £70.50 (REI) £78.15 (NO)
£94.00 (WY) £125.00 (RES) £135.00 (UB)
Hermitage le Gréal, Sorrel **1986** £31.95
(RES)
Hermitage les Bessards, Delas **1991**
£35.00 (RES)
Hermitage les Bessards, Delas **1990**
£35.25 (PEN)
Hermitage Marquise de la Tourette, Delas
1983 £45.00 (CRO)

£50.00 → £99.99

Châteauneuf-du-Pape Barbe Rac,
Chapoutier **1994** £68.15 (CAV)
Châteauneuf-du-Pape Barbe Rac,
Chapoutier **1990** £91.00 (CRO)
Châteauneuf-du-Pape Château de
Beaucastel **1989** £52.29 (FA) £58.50
(BEN) £59.95 (TAN) £62.00 (CRO)
Châteauneuf-du-Pape Château de
Beaucastel **1981** £54.25 (FA) £62.86 (REI)

Châteauneuf-du-Pape Château de
Beaucastel **1978** £76.38 (REI) £92.00
(CRO) £100.00 (FORT)
Châteauneuf-du-Pape Château Fortia
1978 £67.00 (CRO) £89.95 (RES)
Châteauneuf-du-Pape Château Pignan
1985 £60.00 (CRO)
Châteauneuf-du-Pape Château Rayas
1992 £52.88 (CAV)
Châteauneuf-du-Pape Château Rayas
1986 £79.70 (FA)
Châteauneuf-du-Pape Château Rayas
1974 £56.00 (CRO)
Châteauneuf-du-Pape Hommage à Jacques
Perrin, Château de Beaucastel **1995**
£90.00 (MV) £105.00 (YOU) £150.00 (FORT)
Châteauneuf-du-Pape Hommage à Jacques
Perrin, Château de Beaucastel **1994**
£82.00 (JU) £90.00 (MV) £120.00 (FORT)
£141.00 (FA)
Châteauneuf-du-Pape Mont-Redon **1961**
£76.96 (REI)
Côte-Rôtie Gentaz-Dervieux **1985**
£55.00 (CRO)
Côte-Rôtie Jasmin **1985** £55.95 (RES)
Côte-Rôtie la Landonne, Guigal **1986**
£80.00 (JU) £105.00 (CRO) £117.50 (REI)
£117.50 (CAV) £120.00 (ROB) £146.88
(TW)
Côte-Rôtie la Landonne, Guigal **1981**
£74.81 (FA) £115.00 (BU) £170.38 (NO)
Côte-Rôtie la Mordorée, Chapoutier
1996 £68.99 (YOU) £75.00 (BEN)
Côte-Rôtie la Mordorée, Chapoutier
1990 £75.00 (CRO)
Côte-Rôtie la Mouline, Guigal **1994**
£89.50 (FA)
Côte-Rôtie la Mouline, Guigal **1987**
£68.00 (JU) £95.00 (NO) £125.00 (CRO)
Côte-Rôtie la Turque, Guigal **1987**
£98.00 (JU) £117.50 (CAV) £176.25 (REI)
Côte-Rôtie les Jumelles, Jaboulet **1971**
£59.00 (YOU)
Côtes du Rhône Château de Fonsalette
1978 £76.38 (CAV)
Ermitage le Pavillon, Chapoutier **1996**
£79.50 (YOU)
Ermitage le Pavillon, Chapoutier **1992**
£58.00 (JU) £79.50 (BEN)
Hermitage Chave **1989** £87.54 (FA)
£111.62 (CAV)
Hermitage Chave **1983** £71.00 (CRO)
£77.75 (FA) £99.88 (CAV) £125.00 (RES)
Hermitage la Chapelle, Jaboulet **1979**
£51.00 (CRO) £65.00 (RES)

£100.00 → £149.99

Châteauneuf-du-Pape Château Rayas
1988 £109.08 (FA) £146.88 (CAV)
Côte-Rôtie la Landonne, Guigal **1982**
£138.45 (FA) £176.25 (CAV) £189.76
(NO) £190.00 (JU)
Côte-Rôtie la Turque, Guigal **1994**
£110.00 (YOU)
Ermitage le Pavillon, Chapoutier **1995**
£125.00 (CRO)
Hermitage Chave **1990** £141.00 (CAV)
£145.00 (BEN)
Hermitage Chave **1966** £135.00 (CRO)
Hermitage Jaboulet **1955** £117.50 (CAV)
Hermitage la Chapelle, Jaboulet **1990**
£138.45 (FA) £160.00 (BEN) £161.56 (CAV)

£150.00 → £249.99

Châteauneuf-du-Pape Château Rayas
1989 £210.00 (BEN) £376.95 (UB)
Châteauneuf-du-Pape Hommage à Jacques
Perrin, Château de Beaucastel **1990**
£193.88 (FA) £220.00 (CRO)
Côte-Rôtie la Landonne, Guigal **1991**
£175.00 (RES) £177.62 (FA) £195.00 (ROB)
Côte-Rôtie la Landonne, Guigal **1985**
£211.50 (FA) £220.00 (JU) £260.00 (CRO)
Côte-Rôtie la Mouline, Guigal **1983**
£205.63 (FA) £230.00 (JU) £232.77 (NO)
£250.00 (CRO) £293.75 (CAV)
Côte-Rôtie les Jumelles, Jaboulet **1955**
£199.75 (TW)
Ermitage le Pavillon, Chapoutier **1989**
£229.13 (CAV)
Hermitage Chave **1978** £150.00 (NO)
Hermitage Chave **1971** £160.39 (REI)
Hermitage la Chapelle, Jaboulet **1978**
£225.00 (RES) £230.00 (CRO) £235.00
(YOU) £264.38 (CAV)

Over £250.00

Châteauneuf-du-Pape Château Rayas
1978 £270.25 (CAV)
Côte-Rôtie la Turque, Guigal **1985**
£311.38 (FA)

> *Please remember that*
> **Oz Clarke's Wine Guide**
> *is a price* **guide** *and not a*
> *price list. It is not meant to*
> *replace up-to-date*
> *merchants' lists.*

WHITE

Under £6.00

Côtes du Rhône Belleruche, Chapoutier
1997 £5.62 (PEN) £7.43 (STE) £8.25 (NA)
Côtes du Rhône Jaume **1998** £4.95 (WS)
VdP des Coteaux de l'Ardèche
Chardonnay, Latour **1997** £5.41 (COC)
VdP des Coteaux de l'Ardèche
Chardonnay, Latour **1996** £4.95 (POR)
£5.49 (PEN) £6.25 (FORT) £7.40 (TAN)

£6.00 → £7.99

Côtes du Rhône Belleruche, Chapoutier
1996 £6.49 (CON)
Côtes du Rhône Domaine St-Gayan,
Roger Meffre **1998** £6.75 (YAP)
Côtes du Rhône Guigal **1997** £7.99 (UN)
£9.55 (AV)
Côtes du Rhône Guigal **1996** £7.49 (JON)
Côtes du Rhône Parallèle 45, Jaboulet
1997 £6.45 (PLA)
Côtes du Rhône-Villages Blanc de Blancs,
Château du Grand Moulas **1998** £6.95
(AD)
Côtes du Rhône-Villages, Domaine du
Vieux Chêne **1996** £6.95 (JU)
Crozes-Hermitage Domaine des
Entrefaux **1997** £7.61 (BY) £7.90 (TAN)
£8.00 (PIP)
Crozes-Hermitage Pradelle **1996** £6.75
(BALL)
VdP des Coteaux de l'Ardèche Viognier,
Duboeuf **1998** £6.25 (NEZ)

£8.00 → £9.99

Châteauneuf-du-Pape Mont-Redon **1997**
£9.95 (WS)
Côtes du Rhône Coudoulet de Beaucastel
1997 £8.71 (FA) £10.60 (TAN) £11.55
(AD) £12.50 (MV)
Crozes-Hermitage Domaine du
Colombier **1998** £9.29 (BAL)
Crozes-Hermitage la Mule Blanche,
Jaboulet **1997** £9.70 (GAU) £9.95 (TAN)
£10.60 (STA)
Crozes-Hermitage la Mule Blanche,
Jaboulet **1996** £8.25 (WS) £9.25 (HAH)
Lirac Cuvée de la Reine, Domaine de la
Mordorée **1997** £9.95 (LEA)
St-Joseph Deschants, Chapoutier **1996**
£9.50 (DI)
St-Péray Thières **1994** £9.50 (YAP)
St-Joseph Perret **1994** £9.95 (BAL)

£10.00 → £14.99

Châteauneuf-du-Pape Château Fortia
1996 £12.50 (AV)
Châteauneuf-du-Pape Domaine de la
Roquette, Brunier 1997 £12.90 (TAN)
Châteauneuf-du-Pape la Bernadine,
Chapoutier 1997 £13.45 (UB) £13.99
(YOU)
Châteauneuf-du-Pape la Bernadine,
Chapoutier 1995 £13.95 (DI) £14.95
(CON)
Châteauneuf-du-Pape la Bernadine,
Chapoutier 1994 £12.63 (PEN)
Châteauneuf-du-Pape les Cèdres, Jaboulet
1997 £14.75 (STA)
Châteauneuf-du-Pape les Cèdres, Jaboulet
1996 £11.79 (YOU) £12.34 (REI)
Côtes du Rhône Coudoulet de Beaucastel
1996 £10.50 (CRO) £10.75 (FORT)
£11.50 (GAU) £11.57 (REI)
Côtes du Rhône Viognier Clos de la
Cuminaille, Pierre Gaillard 1997 £14.95
(LEA)
Crozes-Hermitage Château Curson,
Pochon 1995 £10.50 (JU)
Crozes-Hermitage Graillot 1997 £11.25
(YAP)
Hermitage Domaine des Remizières 1986
£14.95 (RAE) £17.45 (UB)
Hermitage les Nobles Rives 1996 £14.99
(YOU)
Lirac Cuvée de la Reine, Domaine de la
Mordorée 1998 £10.75 (BEN)
St-Joseph Clos de l'Arbalestrier, Florentin
1995 £11.95 (RAE)
St-Joseph Grippat 1996 £13.50 (YAP)
St-Joseph le Grand Pompée, Jaboulet
1995 £10.52 (REI)
St-Joseph Bernard Gripa 1993 £11.75
(CON) £16.39 (TW)
St-Joseph Perret 1997 £11.50 (MV)
St-Joseph Perret 1996 £11.00 (JU) £11.03
(WT)

£15.00 → £19.99

Châteauneuf-du-Pape Château de
Beaucastel 1997 £19.20 (TAN) £19.30
(GAU)
Châteauneuf-du-Pape Château de
Beaucastel 1996 £16.06 (FA) £17.85
(PLAY) £19.00 (RAE) £20.95 (BAL) £21.00
(MV) £22.50 (FORT) £22.99 (YOU)
Châteauneuf-du-Pape Domaine Font de
Michelle 1996 £15.35 (JU)

Châteauneuf-du-Pape Domaine du Vieux
Télégraphe 1997 £15.60 (TAN)
Châteauneuf-du-Pape Domaine du Vieux
Télégraphe 1996 £15.39 (JON) £16.95 (JU)
Châteauneuf-du-Pape Domaine du Vieux
Télégraphe 1994 £16.15 (HAH)
Châteauneuf-du-Pape Mont-Redon 1996
£15.15 (UB)
Condrieu Coteau de Chéry, Perret 1998
£18.90 (GAU)
Condrieu Delas 1994 £18.57 (PEN)
Condrieu les Ceps du Nebaudon, Paret
1997 £19.95 (AD)
Condrieu Perret 1996 £19.79 (WT)
Condrieu Pinchon 1993 £18.95 (RAE)
Côtes du Rhône Viognier, Gaillard 1996
£16.00 (JU)
Hermitage Chante-Alouette, Chapoutier
1996 £19.39 (REI) £19.95 (DI) £22.35 (UB)
Hermitage Chevalier de Stérimberg,
Jaboulet 1996 £17.90 (TAN) £32.20 (PLA)

£20.00 → £29.99

Château Grillet 1995 £28.79 (FA)
Châteauneuf-du-Pape Château de
Beaucastel 1995 £21.00 (MV)
Châteauneuf-du-Pape Château de
Beaucastel 1987 £28.79 (REI)
Châteauneuf-du-Pape Château Rayas
1994 £24.95 (DI) £41.13 (TW)
Châteauneuf-du-Pape Vieilles Vignes,
Château de Beaucastel 1992 £27.95 (NI)
Condrieu Barge 1997 £21.40 (TAN)
Condrieu Chapoutier 1996 £23.04 (STE)
Condrieu Chapoutier 1995 £20.75 (DI)
£20.99 (CON) £30.95 (RES)
Condrieu Chapoutier 1994 £21.75 (BEN)
Condrieu Château du Rozay 1996 £25.00
(YAP)
Condrieu Clos Chanson, Perret 1997
£20.99 (YOU)
Condrieu Coteau de Chéry, Perret 1996
£24.00 (JU) £26.25 (FORT)
Condrieu Coteau du Chéry, Clusel-Roch
1997 £20.95 (LEA)
Condrieu Dumazet 1989 £21.74 (REI)
Condrieu Gaillard 1997 £20.60 (BAN)
Condrieu Guigal 1995 £21.67 (MI) £21.69
(UN) £23.35 (HAH)
Condrieu la Bonnette, Rostaing 1997
£23.95 (LAY) £23.99 (YOU)
Condrieu la Bonnette, Rostaing 1996
£23.40 (HAH) £24.00 (JU)
Condrieu les Ceps du Nebaudon, Paret
1996 £26.53 (NO)

Condrieu Perret **1992** £21.09 (PLAY)
Condrieu Vernay **1996** £22.75 (YAP)
  Côtes du Rhône Château de Fonsalette **1995** £21.54 (CAV)
Hermitage Domaine des Remizières **1993** £22.21 (TW)
Hermitage Faurie **1996** £20.60 (HAH)
Hermitage Faurie **1995** £22.00 (IU)
Hermitage Grippat **1996** £22.50 (YAP)
Hermitage Grippat **1986** £24.95 (BEN)
Hermitage les Rocoules, Sorrel **1996** £23.75 (GAU)

£30.00 → £39.99

Château Grillet **1997** £34.00 (YAP)
Châteauneuf-du-Pape Vieilles Vignes, Château de Beaucastel **1997** £42.00 (MV)
Châteauneuf-du-Pape Vieilles Vignes, Château de Beaucastel **1996** £30.75 (FA) £33.49 (REI) £38.00 (BAL) £50.88 (PLAY)
Châteauneuf-du-Pape Vieilles Vignes, Château de Beaucastel **1995** £39.00 (IU) £47.59 (NO)
Condrieu les Chaillets Vieilles Vignes, Cuilleron **1996** £38.95 (RES)
Hermitage Chave **1996** £37.50 (FORT)
Hermitage Chave **1994** £33.00 (YAP) £38.68 (CAV)

Over £40.00

Château Grillet **1990** £45.00 (BU)
Château Grillet **1989** £79.00 (UB)
Châteauneuf-du-Pape Château Rayas **1990** £40.00 (WS) £70.50 (CAV)
Hermitage Chave **1979** £88.12 (WY)
Hermitage de l'Orée, Chapoutier **1995** £67.50 (BEN) £99.88 (CAV)

ROSÉ

Under £10.00

Côtes du Rhône Domaine du Vieux Chêne **1996** £5.50 (IU)
Lirac Rosé la Fermade, Domaine Maby **1998** £7.00 (YAP)
Tavel Canto Perdrix, Domaine Mejan-Taulier **1997** £6.95 (BALL)
Tavel Domaine de la Mordorée **1997** £9.50 (LEA)
Tavel Domaine de Valéry, André Méjan **1996** £7.50 (IU)
Tavel l'Espiègle, Jaboulet **1995** £9.95 (UB)
Tavel la Forcadière, Domaine Maby **1997** £5.95 (WS) £7.75 (YAP)

SPARKLING

Under £10.00

Clairette de Die Brut Archard-Vincent **Non-vintage** £9.50 (YAP)
Clairette de Die Tradition Demi-sec Archard-Vincent **Non-vintage** £9.25 (YAP)

c. £21.00

St-Péray Mousseux Brut, Clape **1996** £21.00 (IU)

FORTIFIED

£6.00 → £9.99

Muscat de Beaumes-de-Venise Cave Co-op. de Beaumes-de-Venise **1993** £7.99 (OD)
Muscat de Beaumes-de-Venise Cave des Vignerons à Vacqueyras **Non-vintage** £8.73 (STE) £8.95 (BALL) £8.95 (POR) £9.33 (PLAY) £9.39 (JON) £9.70 (NA)
Muscat de Beaumes-de-Venise Chapoutier ½ bottle **1997** £7.99 (DI)
Muscat de Beaumes-de-Venise Chapoutier ½ bottle **1995** £7.95 (CON)
Muscat de Beaumes-de-Venise Domaine de Coyeux ½ bottle **1997** £6.25 (AD)
Muscat de Beaumes-de-Venise Domaine de Durban ½ bottle **1997** £7.50 (YAP)
Muscat de Beaumes-de-Venise Jaboulet ½ bottle **1997** £6.50 (WS)
Rasteau Domaine la Soumade **1995** £9.50 (ROB) £16.74 (TW)

£10.00 → £13.99

Muscat de Beaumes-de-Venise Domaine de Coyeux **1996** £10.35 (AV) £10.95 (IU) £12.93 (CB)
Muscat de Beaumes-de-Venise Domaine de Durban **1997** £11.50 (SOM) £11.95 (YAP) £12.20 (PIP)
Muscat de Beaumes-de-Venise Domaine des Bernardins **1997** £13.85 (PIP)
Muscat de Beaumes-de-Venise Jaboulet **1997** £11.25 (WS) £14.98 (PLA)
Muscat de Beaumes-de-Venise Jaboulet **1996** £12.25 (FORT)
Muscat de Beaumes-de-Venise Vidal-Fleury **1996** £13.95 (SOM)
Rasteau Domaine la Soumade **Non-vintage** £12.70 (PIP)

SOUTHERN FRANCE

Pick your way through the South and you'll find some gems. But there's fool's gold there as well, for the unwary

There's a mistake it's all too easy to make with southern French wines, and that's to assume that because the weather's pretty reliable, and because there's so much high-tech, Aussie-style winemaking, that all the wines are automatically good. It's not true. They're not.

A lot are, of course. Compared to a few years ago, a staggering number are reliably good. But good quality, vintage after vintage isn't simply a question of bunging new wine into new oak and hoping it will taste fashionable enough to pass muster. There are small matters like balance to be attended to. For all that the South of France is constantly compared to Australia, it is not Australia. It is perfectly possible to find over-extracted, over-oaked wines here because the winemakers are trying too hard to keep up with trends and not trying hard enough to understand their vineyards and what the latter are really capable of.

That being said, the good wines are stunning. This is one of the best places in the world to find smoky Syrah at an affordable price, or dusty, raspberryish blends, or all sorts of herb-flavoured reds from both vin de pays and appellation regions. Whites divide more sharply into international tastes like Chardonnay and Sauvignon, and traditional, often excellent, often pricy, local blends. Take your pick.

WINE REGIONS

BANDOL, AC (Provence; red, white) Herby, tobaccoey, long-lived wines of world class, based on Mourvèdre. Some, like *Tempier*, are being made in a more supple style. The serious spicy rosés (made from younger vines) can also be excellent. Best estates: *Ch. de Pibarnon, Ch. Pradeaux, Dom. Bastide Blanche, Dom. de Belouve, Dom. du Cagueloup, Dom. le Galantin, Dom. Ray-Jane, Dom. Tempier, Dom. Terrebrune, Dom. de la Tour du Bon, Ste-Anne*. The whites can be delicious, with a lovely aniseed-and-apple bite to them. *Ch. de Pibarnon* and *Dom. Lafran Veyrolles* are among the most interesting.

BANYULS, AC (Languedoc-Roussillon; vin doux naturel, red) Grenache-based wine that can assume many guises: red or tawny, sweet or dryish, and can come, too, in an oxidized *rancio* style with burnt caramel flavours – something of an acquired taste. *Dom. de la Rectorie, Mas Blanc* and *Mas Casa Blanca* are good. Wines aged for two-and-a-half years in wood may be labelled *grand cru*.

LES BAUX-DE-PROVENCE , AC (Provence; red, rosé) More characterful than their neighbours in Coteaux d'Aix-en-Provence, though limits on the use of Cabernet mean that *Domaine de Trévallon* has been demoted to vin de pays. *Mas de la Dame, Mas de Gourgonnier* and *Mas Ste-Berthe* are also good.

BÉARN, AC (South-West; red, rosé, white) The reds are mainly from the Tannat grape, with other local varieties and both Cabernets thrown in. In spite of this they are basically undistinguished but you could try the wines of the *Vignerons de Bellocq* co-op, or the co-op at *Crouseilles*. *Domaine Guilhemas* is also worth a punt.

BELLET, AC (Provence; red, white) An unusual nutty Rolle and Chardonnay white with a good local reputation. *Château de*

Crémat and *Château de Bellet* are worth seeking out, though like everything else near Nice, they're expensive. There are also a few good, dark reds made at *Château de Bellet* and *Château de Crémat*.

BERGERAC, AC (South-West; red, rosé) Bergerac is a kind of Bordeaux understudy: the rosés are often extremely good, deep in colour, dry and full of fruit; a good red can be a better bet than basic Bordeaux, and often cheaper. Bergerac Rouge is usually at its best at between one and four years old, depending on vintage and style. *Château la Jaubertie* goes from strength to strength. *Château le Barradis* and *Château Belingard* are also good, and *Château Court-les-Mûts* makes a delicious rosé and a good red.

BERGERAC SEC, AC (South-West; white) Bordeaux lookalikes. *Château Belingard, Château Court-les-Mûts* and *Château de Panisseau* are good but the star is *Château la Jaubertie* where tremendous flavour and panache are extracted from a Sauvignon, Sémillon and Muscadelle blend, and from a straight Sauvignon as well.

BUZET, AC (South-West; red, white) Claret lookalikes that can combine a rich blackcurrant sweetness with an arresting grassy greenness. They are for drinking at between one and five years old, depending on the vintage and the style. Look out for the wines of the co-op, which dominates the area: its *Baron d'Ardeuil, Château de Gueyze* and *Château Padère* are all pretty special.

CABARDÈS, VDQS (Languedoc-Roussillon; red) The aromatic originality and liveliness of these wines derives from the marriage of southern and south-western grape varieties, such as Merlot, Cabernet, Fer Servadou and Cot (Malbec). Best producers include *de Brau, Château de la Bastide, Château de Rayssac, Domaine Jouclary* and *Ventenac.*

CAHORS, AC (South-West; red) Increasingly supple these days: the 'black wine' of yore has pretty well vanished, and actually that's no bad thing. Modern Cahors is likely to combine raisiny, plummy fruit with flavours of spices, tobacco and prunes, soft tannins and the potential for longevity. The grapes are largely Auxerrois (Bordeaux's Malbec), plus Merlot and Tannat. Good names: *Château des Bouysses* from the *Côtes d'Olt* co-op, *Château de Cayrou, Château de Chambert, Château de Haute-Serre, Château de Poujol, Château St-Didier, Château de Treilles, Clos la Coutale, Clos de Gamot, Clos Triguedina, Domaine du Cèdre, Domaine Eugénie, Domaine de Gaudou, Domaine de Paillas* and *Domaine de Quattre.*

CASSIS, AC (Provence; red, white, rosé) The white dominates the AC – they say locally you should be able to taste the sea salt. Rosés are good, but red is increasingly rare. Look out for *Dom. du Bagnol, Dom. de la Ferme Blanche, Domaine du Paternel* and *Clos Ste-Magdelaine.*

CLAIRETTE DU LANGUEDOC, AC (Languedoc-Roussillon; white) The Clairette can be a difficult grape to vinify, but the quality of wines like *Dom. de la Condamine Bertrand,* the co-op at *Cabrières* and *Domaine St-André* show what can be done.

COLLIOURE, AC (Languedoc-Roussillon; red) Startling, intense reds dominated by Grenache, with increasing contributions from Mourvèdre. Best: *Clos des Paulilles, Dom. du Mas Blanc, Dom. de la Rectorie, Mas Casa Blanca.*

CORBIÈRES, AC (Languedoc-Roussillon; red, white, rosé) Reds range from juicy upfront wines produced using carbonic maceration to powerful, serious, traditionally made bottles like *la Voulte-Gasparets.* Others: *Caraguilhes, Château les Aiguilloux, Château Bories-Azea, Château Cabriac, Château Hélène, Château les Ollieux,*

Domaine Dohin le Roy, Dom. du Révérend, Étang des Colombes, Fontsainte, les Palais, St-Auriol, Villemajou. There is less white, but it's increasingly good.

COTEAUX D'AIX-EN-PROVENCE, AC (Provence; red, white, rosé) An increasing use of Cabernet and Syrah and subtle use of new oak are combining to make interesting reds and rosés in a semi-Bordelais style – such as *Château Vignelaure.* Also good: *Château Crémade, Château de Calissanne, Château du Seuil, Domaine de la Courtade, Domaine des Glauges.* There is little white, and frankly it's not that thrilling.

COTEAUX DU LANGUEDOC, AC

(Languedoc-Roussillon; red, white) This sprawling appellation incorporates 12 demarcated *terroirs* that may state their names on the labels. Among the better ones for reds are St-Saturnin, Pic St-Loup and La Clape. The classic southern grapes are used, and the growing presence of Syrah and Mourvèdre can be discerned in the complexity and breed of many wines. Best: *d'Aupilhac, Calage, Capion, Château Moujan, Domaine de Brunet, Domaine de la Coste, Domaine l'Aiguelière, Domaine de Cazeneuve, Domaine de l'Hortus,* especially the rosé, *Domaine de Payre-Rose, Domaine de la Roque, Flaugergues, Olivier Jullien, Lascaux, Pech-Céleyran, Pech-Redon, de Terre-Mégère* and the co-ops at *Cabrières, Gabian (la Carignano), Montpeyrous, Neffiès* and *St-Saturnin.* White wine-making is also being taken more and more seriously. Best: *Boscary, Chamayrac, Château de Granoupiac, Claude Gaujal, Mas Jullien, Terre Mégère* and the co-ops at *Pine, Pomérols* and *St-Saturnin* (for its *le Lucian*).

COTEAUX VAROIS, AC (Provence; red, rosé, white) Quality is improving here. Try *Château de Miraval* for white, or *Château la Calisse, Château Routas, Château St-Estève, Château St-Jean de Villecroze, Domaine des Alysses, Domaine du Loou* and *Domaine de Triennes.*

INSTANT CELLAR: REGIONAL CHARACTER

- **1995 Faugères La Bastide, Gilbert Alquier, £9.95, Ballantynes** The top wine from the top producer in this appellation. Spicy, leathery and intense.
- **1995 Irouléguy, Harri Gorri, Domaine Brana, £8.99, Ballantynes** Crisp white from the Pyrenees.
- **1995 Vin de Pays de l'Hérault, Mas de Daumas Gassac Rouge, £16.95, Berry Bros & Rudd** I couldn't leave this out. Terrifically complex stuff.
- **1996 Minervois, Château Maris Prestige, £6.95, Balls Brothers** Classy, spicy red from a newish estate.
- **1997 Pacherenc de Vic-Bilh sec, Ch. de Viella £6.95, Bennetts** Dry, rich, spicy white.
- **1991 Bandol, Domaine Tempier, £11.75, Direct Wine Shipments** Herby and glorious.
- **1996 Vin de Pays d'Oc Aramon, Terrasses de Landoc, £4.59, Philglas & Swiggot** Juicy, rich red from a grape variety that used to be thought fit only for vinegar.

CÔTES DE BERGERAC, AC (South-West; red, rosé) This is to Bergerac what Bordeaux Supérieur is to Bordeaux: from the same region, but with slightly higher minimum alcohol. Many are still sold as basic Bergerac, although the excellent *Château Court-les-Mûts* now uses this AC.

CÔTES DE DURAS, AC (South-West; red, white) Light, grassy claret lookalikes. *Château de Pilar* and *le Seigneuret* from the co-op are quite good and cheap. Also fairly good Sauvignon-based white that can be as fresh as good Bordeaux Blanc, but just a little chubbier. *Château de Conti* is good, as is *le Seigneuret* from the co-op.

CÔTES DU FRONTONNAIS, AC

(South-West; red, rosé) At their best these are silky and plummy, sometimes with a touch of raspberry and liquorice, but always with a twist of fresh black pepper. The Négrette grape dominates, and is wonderfully tasty. Best producers are *Château Bellevue-la-Forêt, Château Flotis, Château Montauriol, Château la Palme* and *Domaine de Baudare.*

CÔTES DE LA MALEPÈRE, VDQS

(Languedoc-Roussillon; red) The grape varieties are similar to those of Cabardès, with the addition of Cabernet Franc. Best: *Cave du Razès, Ch. de Festes, Dom. de Matibat.*

CÔTES DU MARMANDAIS, AC

(South-West; red) Simple, soft, fruity wines for drinking young, made from Cabernet Sauvignon, Cabernet Franc, Merlot, Fer and Abouriou. A few are designed for more serious aging, but it doesn't suit them.

CÔTES DE PROVENCE, AC

(Provence; red, white, rosé) Getting left behind in the race for quality, although among the overpriced rosés made for the tourists there are many top-grade red and pink wines made by growers who take their calling seriously. They include *Aumerade, Commanderie de Peyrassol, Château de Selle, Domaines de la Bernarde, Domaine de Courtade, Jas d'Esclans, Mas de Cadenet, Presqu'île de St-Tropez, Richeaume, Rimauresq* and *St-Baillon.* For whites, *Castel Roubine, Château Ferry-Lacombe, Clos Bernarde, Domaine Arnaude, Domaine Richeaume, de Rasque, Réal Martin* and *St-André de la Figuière* are the leading lights.

CÔTES DU ROUSSILLON AND CÔTES DU ROUSSILLON VILLAGES, AC

(South-West; red, white) Distinctly up-and-coming for reds, although whites lag behind. Carignan still dominates the vineyards, though the tastier Syrah is increasing. The Villages AC covers 32 villages in the North. Try *Château de Casenove, Domaine Cazes, Domaine Gauby, Domaine Laporte, Domaine Piquemal, Domaine Sarda-Malet, Domaine des Schistes, Les Hauts de Força Réal, Mas Crémat, Mas de la Garrigue.*

CÔTES DE ST-MONT, VDQS

(South-West; red, white) These reds are increasingly made in a fresh, blackcurranty, modern style. By far the best examples come from the *Plaimont* co-op.

FAUGÈRES, AC (Languedoc-Roussillon;

red) The grapes here are Grenache, Syrah, Mourvèdre and Carignan. The wines have real depth, class and character in which cassis, black cherries and liquorice predominate. In mature Faugères wines, complex game and leather aromas can often emerge. Best producers: *Alquier, Château de Chenaie, Louison, Lubac, Ollier-Taillefer, Vidal* and the co-op at *Laurens* must be in anyone's top ten.

FITOU, AC (Languedoc-Roussillon; red)

A highly variable, old-style red in which Carignan has traditionally been dominant, but Grenache and, increasingly, Syrah and Mourvèdre are being used to add interest. *Paul Colomer* and *Robert Daurat-Fort* are the leading lights, along with co-ops at *Villeneuve* and at *Tuchan,* where the *Caves de Mont Tauch* is producing some of the most serious Fitou of all.

GAILLAC, AC (South-West; red, white).

The white, based on the bracing Mauzac grape, can be *moelleux* (medium-sweet), *perlé* (very faintly bubbly) or dry; the dry is usually a little neutral, though a few have a quite big apple-and-liquorice fruit. The sparkling wines can be superb: peppery, honeyed, apricotty and appley all at the same time. From *Boissel-Rhodes, Canto Perlic* (a newcomer), *Cros* or *Robert Plageoles,* they are very good value. Other still wine producers to look out for are *Château Larroze, Domaine du Bosc-Long* and *Domaine de Labarthe.* The co-op at *Labastide-de-Lévis* is improving. There are two styles of red, Duras plus Fer Servadou and Syrah, or Duras plus Merlot and Cabernet. *Domaine Jean Cros* is delicious. Other producers worth a look are: *Labarthe, Lastours, Larroze, Mas Pignou.*

IROULÉGUY, AC (South-West; red)
This comes from the foothills of the
Pyrénées, and it's mostly quite rough and
rustic, Tannat-based red, supplemented by
both Cabernets. Try *Domaine Brana* and
Domaine Ilarria.

JURANÇON, AC (South-West; white)
This can be sweet, medium or dry. The dry
wines are light and can be ravishingly
perfumed, while the sweet wines are
honeyed, raisiny and peachy, yet with a lick
of acidity. The pace-setter is *Henri
Ramonteu*; others are *Clos Lapeyre, Clos
Thou* (dry), *Clos Uroulat* (sweet), *Clos de la
Vierge* (dry), *Cancaillaü* (sweet), *Cru
Lamouroux* (sweet), *Dom. Bru-Baché* (dry),
*Dom. Castera, Dom. de Cauhapé, Dom.
Larrédya, Dom. de Souch*.

LIMOUX, AC (South-West; white)
Sparkling Blanquette de Limoux is mostly
from the Mauzac grape; Crémant de
Limoux has more Chardonnay, and is less
rustic. The still wines are based on barrel-
fermented Chardonnay, and tend to be
expensive. Best producers include: *Antech,
Caves du Sieur d'Arques, Philippe Collin,
Delmas, Sev Dervin* and *Robert*.

MADIRAN, AC (South-West; red)
Attractive, generally rather rustic reds based
on the Tannat grape, along with the
Cabernets and occasionally Fer. Good ones
include *Château d'Arricau-Bordes, Château
d'Aydie* (alias *Domaine Laplace*), *Château
Bouscassé, Château de Crouseilles, Château
Montus, Château Peyros, Domaine
Berthoumieu, Domaine du Crampilh, Domaine
Damiens, Domaine Meinjarre, Domaine
Mouréou* and *Laffitte-Teston*.

MAURY, AC (Languedoc-Roussillon; *vin
doux naturel*, red) Grenache without the
finesse of Banyuls, but more explosive in its
nutty, toffee, prunes-in-brandy intensity. It
can also be made in the oxidized *rancio*
style. The ones to try are *Mas Amiel* and the
co-op at *Maury*.

MINERVOIS, AC (Languedoc-
Roussillon; red, white, rosé) Interesting reds
with good peppery berry fruit. A handful of
crus – wines from areas a cut above the
rest – is planned; first will be La Livinière,
with wines based on Syrah. Best include the
co-op at *la Livinière*, plus *Château du Donjon,
Château Fabas, Château de Gourgazaud,
Château d'Oupia, la Combe Blanche,
Domaine Maris, Ste-Eulalie, la Tour Boisée,
Villerambert-Julien* and the co-ops at *Peyriac*
and *Azillanet*. White Minervois is improving,
and is increasingly good and aromatic.
Minervois Noble is sweet, late-picked white,
usually fresh and with good acidity.

MONBAZILLAC, AC (South-West;
white) These sweet wines are never as rich
or weighty as a top Sauternes, but the
massive improvements in quality in
Sauternes have spurred the producers here
to sharpen up their act, too. The best are
very good indeed, and include *Château La
Fonrousse, Château Haut-Bernasse, Château
les Hébras, Château du Treuil-de-Nailhac* and
Clos Fontindoule. Grab any 1990s you can
still find: coming from one of the hottest,
most botrytized vintages for years, the best
are terrific.

MONTRAVEL, AC (South-West; white)
Dry white from the Dordogne. Côtes de
Montravel is medium-sweet *moelleux* from
the same area; Haut-Montravel is a separate
area and sweeter. All are mostly sold as
Bergerac or Côtes de Bergerac.

MUSCAT (*vin doux naturel*; white) Not a
region but a grape. Wines range from the
syrupy *Tradition* made by the *Frontignan* co-
op to the elegant *Château de la Peyrade*
(Frontignan), *Domaine de la Capelle*
(Mireval), *Grés St-Paul* (Lunel), *Domaine de
Barroubie* and the co-op in *St-Jean-de-
Minervois*. All of these are made from the
Muscat à Petits Grains which gives more
finesse than the Muscat d'Alexandrie, used
in Muscat de Rivesaltes (*Cazes* and *Brial* are
the names to go for here).

PACHERENC DU VIC-BILH, AC
(South-West; white) One of France's most esoteric whites, a blend of Gros and Petit Manseng and Arrufiac – a grape peculiar to the AC. At its best when dry and pear-skin-perfumed – and sometimes when rich and sweet. Best: *Château d'Aydie, Château Bouscassé, Domaine du Crampilh* and *Domaine Damiens.*

PALETTE, AC (Provence; red, white, rosé) A tiny AC dominated by *Château Simone.* The rosé beats the others.

PÉCHARMANT, AC (South-West; red)
The best red wine of Bergerac, this must be aged for a minimum of a year before sale to distinguish it from Bergerac, which can be sold after only six months. It is deliciously blackcurranty when young, and at its best is good claret lookalike stuff. *Château de Tiregand* is very good indeed, but *Domaine du Haut-Pécharmant* is even better, resembling a decent Médoc.

ST-CHINIAN, AC (Languedoc-Roussillon; red, rosé) Improving and often very attractive wines. Among the top must be *Ch. Cazal-Viel, Ch. Coujan, Ch. Milhau-Lacugue, Dom. des Jougla, Dom. Madalle* and *la Dournie* (especially for its brilliant rosé). The co-ops at *Berlou, Roquebrun* and *Roueire* are outstanding.

VIN DE CORSE, AC (Corsica; red, white, rosé) Still lagging far behind the mainland in quality. *Dom. de Torraccia* makes a tasty red redolent of spices and rosemary. Also good: *d'Alzeto, Capitoro, Clos Landry, Dom. Filippi* and *Dom. Peraldi.* Most wines of better than vin de table status take the all-island designation Vin de Pays de l'Île de Beauté.

VINS DE PAYS (red, white, rosé) This is where it's all happening. The most innovative winemakers love the vin de pays classification for the freedom it gives them. There's plenty of Cabernet Sauvignon being used here, but some of the most exciting flavours come from Syrah and the other good grapes of the South, like Grenache or Mourvèdre. There are some excellent varietals, particularly Syrah, Cabernet Sauvignon and Chardonnay. Australian influence in the winemaking is producing clear flavours and some creamy new oak. In the Pays d'Oc look for *de l'Aigle, du Bosc, Chais Baumière, Cousserges, Domaine de l'Arjolle, Domaine de la Colombette, Domaine la Condamine-l'Evêque, Domaine de la Jonction, Domaine de Limbardie, Domaine Virginie, L'Enclos Domeque, Fortant de France, la Grange des Quatre Sous, Peyrat, Raissac, Richemont, Rives de l'Argent Double* and *Top Forty Barrel-Fermented Chardonnay* (from Waitrose).

In the Gard, seek out *Domaine de Gournier, Domaine de Monpertuis, Listel* and *Mas Montel;* and, in the Roussillon, *Chichet, Laporte* and *Vaquer.* In the Vaucluse, look for *Domaine de l'Ameillaud.*

In the Hérault, *Domaine de Limbardie, Domaine de Poujol* and *Mas de Daumas Gassac;* the latter's reds are explosively concentrated. There's also a Viognier-based white. From the Comté Tolosan, *Ribeton* makes good white; from the Comtés Rhodaniens, *les Vignerons Ardéchois* have a tasty Viognier. Look also for *Teisserenc* in the Côtes de Thongue, *Domaine d'Aupilhac* from Mont Baudille, and *Domaine de la Jasse Grande Olivette* from the Cevennes.

On the western side of France the Charente produces some good, grassy-fresh whites with fairly sharp acidity – which sometimes gets the better of the fruit. The region here is Vin de Pays Charentais. The equivalent from Armagnac country is Vin de Pays des Côtes de Gascogne. The Ugni Blanc is the major grape, and the Colombard adds a touch of class. Look for the co-op at *Plaimont,* though quality is variable. The *Grassa* family estates – notably *Domaines de Plantérieu* and *de Tariquet* – are worth seeking out. Also good are *Domaine le Puts, Domaine St-Lannes* and *San Guilhem.*

SOUTHERN FRANCE PRICES

RED

Under £4.00

Corbières Château de Lastours 1994
£3.49 (VIC) £3.49 (THR) £3.49 (WR)

Côtes du Roussillon-Villages Château de
Pena 1997 £3.60 (WS) £4.99 (DI)

Faugères Domaine Roque Gabarron
1997 £3.95 (WS)

Fitou Caves du Mont Tauch 1995 £3.99
(MAR)

Minervois Château d'Oupia 1997 £3.95
(SOM) £5.50 (PIP)

Minervois Domaine du Moulin Rigaud
1997 £3.95 (WS)

Minervois Domaine les Combelles 1994
£3.99 (CO)

VdP du Comté Tolosan, Domaine de
Baudare 1996 £3.69 (GW)

VdP des Coteaux de Murviel, Domaine de
Limbardie 1997 £3.50 (SOM) £3.95 (WS)
£4.95 (HAH) £4.95 (TAN)

VdP des Côtes de Thongue Syrah, la
Condamine l'Évêque 1998 £3.95 (WS)

★ VdP du Gers Jean des Vignes 1997 £3.75
(SAV)

VdP de l'Hérault Cabernet/Syrah,
Domaine Montrose 1995 £3.95 (JU)

VdP de l'Hérault Figaro 1997 £3.35 (SOM)
£3.49 (THR) £3.49 (WR) £3.49 (BOT)

VdP de l'Hérault Terrasses de Guilhem
1997 £3.95 (SOM)

VdP d'Oc Cépage Merlot, Domaine des
Fontaines 1997 £3.89 (WAI)

VdP d'Oc Merlot, Domaine Virginie 1995
£3.95 (JU)

★ VdP d'Oc Syrah/Mourvèdre, Goûts et
Couleurs 1997 £3.99 (SOM)

£4.00 → £4.99

Bergerac Château le Raz 1996 £4.99 (YOU)

Bergerac Château Tour de Gendres 1995
£4.95 (JU)

Cabardès Château Rivals 1996 £4.99 (CON)

Cahors Clos la Coutale 1996 £4.75 (WS)
£7.65 (WT)

Corbières Château de Lastours 1996
£4.99 (POR)

Corbières Château de Montrabech 1996
£4.19 (JON) £4.25 (BALL) £4.65 (TAN)

Corbières Domaine du Trillol, Sichel
1995 £4.25 (BO) £5.30 (TAN)

Costières de Nîmes Château de Campuget
1998 £4.99 (POR) £4.99 (YOU)

Coteaux d'Aix-en-Provence Château de
Fonscolombe 1997 £4.95 (POR)

Coteaux d'Aix-en-Provence Château de
Fonscolombe 1997 £4.89 (JON)

Coteaux du Languedoc Château de
Lascaux 1997 £4.99 (OD) £5.95 (LEA)

Coteaux du Languedoc La Clape, Château
Pech-Céleyran 1996 £4.30 (WS) £4.50
(BALL) £5.09 (JON) £5.30 (TAN)

Coteaux du Languedoc La Méjanelle,
Château de Calage 1997 £4.95 (WS)

Coteaux du Languedoc les Vignerons de
la Carignano 1996 £4.11 (FRI)

Côtes de la Malepère Château Malvies
1997 £4.37 (STE) £4.95 (NA)

Côtes de Provence Domaine Hilaire
Houchart 1998 £4.50 (WS)

Côtes de St-Mont, les Hauts de Bergelle
1997 £4.95 (TAN)

Côtes de St-Mont, Producteurs Plaimont
1996 £4.10 (HAH)

Côtes de St-Mont, Producteurs Plaimont
1996 £4.09 (JON) £4.25 (WS) £4.35 (AD)

MERCHANTS SPECIALIZING IN SOUTHERN FRANCE
see Merchant Directory (page 413) for details

Most good merchants have some. For
particularly good lists try the following
merchants: Adnams (AD), Averys of Bristol
(AV), Ballantynes (BAL), Bibendum (BIB),
Anthony Byrne (BY) – always enterprising,
Cockburns of Leith (COC), Direct Wine (DI),
Ben Ellis (ELL), First Quench Group (BOT,
THR, VIC, WR), Fuller's (FUL), Gauntleys (GAU),
Gelston Castle, Lay & Wheeler (LAY),
Majestic (MAJ), Oddbins (OD), The Nobody
Inn (NO), James Nicholson (NI), Thos.
Peatling, Terry Platt (PLA), Raeburn Fine
Wines (RAE), Reid Wines (REI), Sainsbury's
(SAI), Savage Selection (SAV), Somerfield (SO),
Tanners (TAN), Ubiquitous Chip (UB), Wine
Society (WS), Yapp Brothers (YAP).

Côtes du Frontonnais Château Baudare **1996** £4.52 (GW)

Côtes du Frontonnais Château Bellevue-la-Forêt **1996** £4.69 (UN)

Côtes du Roussillon-Villages Vignerons Catalans **Non-vintage** £4.49 (MAR)

Gaillac Domaine de Labarthe **1996** £4.25 (SOM)

Marcillac Domaine du Cros, Teulier **1995** £4.75 (WS)

Minervois Château de Fabas **1996** £4.70 (DOM)

Minervois Château de Gourgazaud **1995** £4.99 (REI)

Minervois Domaine de Ste-Eulalie **1997** £4.30 (WS) £4.49 (THR) £4.49 (WR)

Minervois Domaine de Ste-Eulalie **1995** £4.85 (HAH) £4.95 (POR) £4.99 (JON)

Minervois Domaine la Tour Boisée **1997** £4.19 (WAT)

Pic St Loup Mas Bruguière **1997** £4.75 (SOM)

St-Chinian Château Maurel Fonsalade **1997** £4.75 (WS)

VdP de l'Aude Cabernet Sauvignon, Domaine du Puget **1997** £4.52 (CB)

VdP des Coteaux de Bessilles Cuvée Traditionelle, Domaine St-Martin de la Garrigue **1995** £4.45 (JU)

VdP des Côtes de Gascogne Cabernet Sauvignon, Brumont **1998** £4.00 (BY)

VdP des Côtes de Thongue Cabernet Sauvignon, la Condamine l'Évêque **1997** £4.39 (JON) £4.50 (LEA)

VdP des Côtes de Thongue Syrah, la Condamine l'Évêque **1997** £4.39 (JON) £4.50 (LEA) £4.75 (TAN)

VdP des Côtes de Thongue Champs de Coq, Domaine Boyer **1995** £4.95 (JU)

VdP des Côtes de Thongue, Domaine Boyer **1996** £4.50 (JU)

VdP de l'Hérault Cabernet Sauvignon, Domaine de Capion **1997** £4.35 (SOM)

VdP de l'Hérault, Domaine de Chapître **1997** £4.30 (MV)

> • Wines are listed in A–Z order within each price band.
> • For each wine, vintages are listed in descending order.
> • Each vintage of any wine appears only once.

VdP de l'Hérault Merlot, Domaine de Moulines **1995** £4.95 (ROB)

VdP de l'Hérault Terrasses de Guilhem **1996** £4.22 (FLE) £4.89 (PHI) £5.69 (PLAY)

VdP d'Oc Cabernet Sauvignon, Chais Baumière **1997** £4.99 (SAI)

VdP d'Oc Merlot, Domaine de Terre Megère **1997** £4.95 (LEA)

VdP d'Oc Merlot, Domaine Virginie **1997** £4.79 (JON)

VdP d'Oc Merlot, Domaine Virginie **1996** £4.52 (REI) £5.00 (MV) £5.45 (BEN)

VdP d'Oc Syrah, Domaine de la Jonction **1997** £4.47 (CB)

VdP d'Oc Syrah Domaine St Marc, Foncalieu **1997** £4.29 (SAI)

★ VdP d'Oc Viognier Domaine de la Ferrandière **1997** £4.95 (WAT)

VdP du Var les Trois Chênes, Domaine de l'Hermitage **1995** £4.39 (CON)

VdP du Vaucluse Domaine Michel **1998** £4.85 (AD)

VdP du Vaucluse Domaine du Vieux Chêne **1996** £4.50 (JU)

£5.00 → £5.99

Bergerac Château Tour de Gendres **1998** £5.32 (GW)

Bergerac Domaine du Gouyat **1997** £5.09 (JON)

Cahors Château du Cèdre **1994** £5.99 (GW)

Cahors Château St-Didier-Parnac, Rigal **1996** £5.49 (OD)

Cahors Chevaliers de Lagrezette **1996** £5.39 (CAV)

Corbières Château la Baronne **1996** £5.49 (JON) £6.99 (TW)

Corbières Château Cascadais **1995** £5.75 (BAL)

Corbières Domaine Baillat **1995** £5.50 (JU)

Corbières Domaine du Grand Crès **1995** £5.95 (WS)

Costières de Nîmes Château Mourgues du Grès **1997** £5.39 (NI)

Coteaux du Languedoc La Clape, Château Pech-Céleyran **1997** £5.45 (AD)

Coteaux du Languedoc Domaine de Terre Megère **1997** £5.50 (LEA)

Côtes de Bergerac Château le Tour des Gendres **1997** £5.75 (BAL)

Côtes de Duras Domaine de Laulan **1998** £5.03 (GW)

Côtes du Frontonnais Château le Roc **1996** £5.25 (LEA)

Côtes du Lubéron Château Val Joanis
1996 £5.42 (BY)

Côtes du Roussillon Cuvée des Rocailles,
Domaine Gauby **1995** £5.90 (GAU)

Côtes du Roussillon Domaine Gauby
1997 £5.95 (WS)

Côtes du Roussillon Domaine Piquemal
1996 £5.49 (NI) £5.95 (LEA) £5.99 (BAL)

Fitou Château de Ségure **1996** £5.29 (SAI)

Fitou Domaine d'Estradelle **1995** £5.25
(CON)

Minervois Château d'Oupia **1996** £5.69
(YOU)

Minervois Cuvée Opera, Château
Villerambert Julien **1995** £5.70 (TAN)

Minervois Domaine Piccinini **1995** £5.45
(JU)

Pic St Loup Mas Bruguière **1996** £5.90
(GAU) £5.99 (PHI) £6.99 (YOU) £10.95
(ROB)

Pic St Loup Terres Rouge, Château de
Cazeneuve **1997** £5.95 (BAL)

St-Chinian Château Viranel **1995** £5.99
(BAL)

VdP des Bouches-du-Rhône Domaine de
Lunard **1995** £5.50 (WS)

VdP des Coteaux de Bessilles Cuvée
Bronzinelle, Domaine St-Martin de la
Garrigue **1995** £5.95 (JU) £6.29 (YOU)

VdP des Coteaux de Murviel, Domaine de
Limbardie **1996** £5.00 (MV)

VdP des Côtes Catalanes Cuvée Pierre
Audonnet, Domaine Piquemal **1997**
£5.50 (LEA)

VdP des Côtes Catalanes Cuvée Pierre
Audonnet, Domaine Piquemal **1996**
£5.29 (YOU)

VdP des Côtes de Thongue Cuvée de
l'Arjolle, Teisserenc **1995** £5.45 (JU)

VdP de l'Hérault Cabernet/Syrah Barrel-
Fermented, Domaine Montrose **1996**
£5.45 (JU)

VdP de l'Hérault, Domaine du Poujol
1998 £5.58 (BIB)

VdP d'Oc Cuvée Pierre Elie, Les Chemins
de Bassac **1994** £5.99 (BAL)

VdP d'Oc Domaine de Granoupiac **1995**
£5.39 (NI)

VdP d'Oc Laperouse **1995** £5.75 (ROB)

VdP d'Oc les Chemins de Bassac **1995**
£5.49 (BAL) £5.50 (LEA) £6.75 (PHI)

VdP de Vaucluse Domaine des Tours,
Reynaud **1997** £5.95 (LEA)

VdP de Vaucluse Merlot, Domaine du
Vieux Chêne **1996** £5.45 (JU)

£6.00 → £7.99

Bergerac Château de la Colline, Martin
1996 £6.46 (HIG)

Cahors Château du Cèdre **1997** £7.50 (LEA)

Cahors Château de Chambert **1996**
£7.99 (DI)

Cahors Clos de Gamot **1992** £7.55 (WAT)

Cahors Domaine de Paillas **1994** £7.99
(RAE)

Cahors Domaine de la Pineraie **1994**
£6.30 (SOM) £6.40 (COC)

★ Corbières Cuvée Hélène de Troie,
Château Hélène **1995** £7.79 (WAT)

Costières de Nîmes Château Mourgues
du Grès **1995** £6.99 (VA)

Costières de Nîmes Château de Rozier
1995 £6.99 (GW)

Coteaux d'Aix-en-Provence Château
Vignelaure **1995** £7.50 (NI)

Coteaux d'Aix-en-Provence Mas de la
Dame **1996** £6.99 (YOU)

Coteaux du Languedoc Château de
Lascaux **1996** £6.76 (DOM)

Coteaux du Languedoc Montpeyroux,
Domaine d'Aupilhac **1996** £6.95 (WS)

Côtes de Bergerac Château la Borderie
1995 £7.34 (TW)

Côtes de Provence Château St Baillon
1996 £6.80 (BIB)

Côtes du Frontonnais Cuvée Réservée,
Château le Roc **1992** £7.99 (BAL)

Côtes du Lubéron Château de Canorgue
1997 £7.75 (YAP)

Côtes du Marmandais Château de
Beaulieu **1996** £6.44 (STE) £7.15 (NA)

Côtes du Roussillon Château de Jau **1997**
£6.03 (GW)

Côtes du Roussillon Élevé en Fûts,
Domaine Gauby **1995** £7.50 (RAE)

Faugères Château de Grézan **1995** £6.49
(POR)

Faugères Gilbert Alquier **1997** £7.30 (TAN)
£7.99 (BO)

Faugères Gilbert Alquier **1995** £7.49 (JON)

Faugères Réserve la Maison Jaune, Alquier
1995 £7.99 (RAE) £8.95 (BAL) £11.95 (ROB)

Madiran Château d'Aydie **1995** £7.05 (NO)

Madiran Château Bouscassé, Brumont
1994 £7.94 (BY)

Madiran Château Pichard **1995** £6.50 (WS)

Madiran Cuvée du Couvent, Domaine
Capmartin **1994** £7.83 (GW)

Madiran Domaine de Mouréou **1995**
£6.30 (TAN) £6.50 (PIP)

Minervois Château d'Oupia **1995** £6.45
(PHI)

Pécharmant Château de Tiregand **1995**
£6.90 (TAN)

Pic St Loup Château de Cazeneuve **1996**
£6.75 (BAL)

VdP des Côtes de Thongue Cabernet de
l'Arjolle, Domaine Teisserenc **1995**
£7.95 (JU)

VdP d'Oc les Chemins de Bassac **1994**
£7.53 (WT)

VdP d'Oc Merlot Fûts de Chêne,
Domaine la Fadèze **1996** £6.49 (LAY)

VdP des Sables du Golfe du Lion,
Domaine du Bosquet **1996** £6.75 (NEZ)

£8.00 → £9.99

Bandol Domaine de l'Hermitage **1996**
£8.85 (CON)

Bandol Domaine de la Tour du Bon **1997**
£9.55 (BIB)

Bandol Mas de la Rouvière, Bunan **1996**
£9.50 (YAP)

les Baux-de-Provence la Chapelle de
Romanin **1995** £9.99 (PHI)

Bergerac Cuvée la Gloire de Mon Père,
Château Tour de Gendres **1995** £8.95
(LEA)

Cahors Château du Cayrou, Jouffreau
1988 £8.15 (WAT)

Cahors Château de Chambert **1993**
£8.75 (DI)

Coteaux d'Aix-en-Provence Mas de
Gourgonnier **1996** £8.95 (UB)

Côtes du Lubéron Château Val Joanis
1990 £8.50 (CRO)

Côtes du Roussillon Domaine Piquemal
1994 £8.95 (ROB)

Faugères le Moulin Couderc, V Fonteneau
1995 £8.99 (BEN) £9.29 (BAL)

Faugères Reserve la Maison Jaune, Alquier
1993 £9.99 (RAE)

Madiran Chapelle l'Enclos, Domaine
Ducournau **1993** £8.50 (WS)

Minervois Château Villerambert, Julien
1995 £8.30 (TAN)

> • *All prices for each wine are
> listed together in ascending
> order.*
> • *Price bands refer to the
> lowest price for which the
> wine is available.*

Pic St Loup les Nobles Pierres, Château
de Lascaux **1996** £8.95 (LEA)

VdP des Côtes Catalanes le Credo
Cabernet/Merlot, Domaine Cazes
1994 £9.99 (CON)

VdP du Mont Baudile Carignan, Domaine
d'Aupilhac **1997** £8.95 (LEA)

VdP d'Oc Pinot Noir les Pomaredes,
Clovallon **1996** £9.25 (BEN)

VdP d'Oc Syrah, Clovallon **1995** £8.99
(BEN) £9.29 (BAL)

£10.00 → £14.99

Bandol Château de la Rouvière, Bunan
1996 £11.95 (YAP)

Bandol Château Vannières **1988** £14.90
(GAU)

Bandol Cuvée Migoua **1995** £14.90 (GAU)
£15.49 (YOU)

Bandol Cuvée Tourtine, Tempier **1995**
£13.51 (REI) £14.90 (GAU)

★ Bandol Château de Pibarnon **1996** £13.06
(BY) £13.95 (FORT)

Bandol Château de Pibarnon **1993** £13.70
(FLE)

Bandol Domaine Tempier **1995** £10.58
(REI) £10.80 (GAU) £12.99 (DI)

Bandol Mas de la Rouvière, Bunan **1991**
£12.50 (ROB)

Cahors Château du Cayrou, Jouffreau
1983 £14.00 (CRO)

Cahors Prince Probus, Clos Triguedina
1995 £14.95 (NO)

Collioure Domaine de la Rectorie **1994**
£11.90 (GAU)

Coteaux du Languedoc Prieuré de St-Jean
de Bébian **1996** £10.38 (GAU) £13.42 (BIB)

Coteaux du Languedoc Prieuré de St-Jean
de Bébian **1995** £12.00 (WS) £13.79
(YOU) £14.90 (GAU)

Coteaux du Languedoc Prieuré de St-Jean
de Bébian **1994** £12.95 (BAL)

Madiran Château Montus, Brumont **1995**
£11.16 (REI) £11.43 (BY)

Madiran Château de Peyros **1982** £12.50
(CRO)

Pécharmant Château de Tiregand **1985**
£11.50 (CRO)

VdP des Bouches-du-Rhône Domaine de
Trévallon **1994** £14.95 (NI)

VdP de l'Hérault, Mas de Daumas Gassac
1996 £12.14 (FA) £14.99 (NI) £16.95 (AD)

VdP de l'Hérault, Mas de Daumas Gassac
1995 £13.12 (FA) £15.20 (FLE) £16.95 (PHI)
£16.95 (FORT) £18.00 (JU) £28.85 (UB)

£15.00 → £19.99

Bandol Château Vannières **1985** £17.90 (GAU)

Bandol Cuvée Tourtine, Tempier **1996** £15.00 (WS)

Cahors Château du Cayrou, Jouffreau **1982** £15.10 (REI)

Madiran Cuvée Prestige Château Montus, Brumont **1996** £16.06 (FA) £20.23 (BY)

Madiran Vieilles Vignes Château Bouscassé, Brumont **1996** £15.73 (BY)

Minervois Château d'Oupia **1992** £18.35 (NO)

Palette Château Simone **1995** £17.75 (YAP)

VdP des Bouches-du-Rhône Domaine de Trévallon **1995** £19.00 (FA)

VdP de l'Hérault, Mas de Daumas Gassac **1993** £16.99 (WR) £17.50 (ROB)

VdP de l'Hérault, Mas de Daumas Gassac **1986** £19.92 (REI) £29.95 (ROB)

£20.00 → £29.99

Bandol Château Vannières **1975** £25.90 (GAU)

Coteaux d'Aix-en-Provence Château Vignelaure **1982** £29.96 (REI)

Madiran Cuvée Prestige Château Montus, Brumont **1995** £25.85 (FA) £66.31 (NO)

Palette Château Simone **1994** £22.95 (FORT)

VdP des Bouches-du-Rhône Domaine de Trévallon **1995** £25.00 (FORT) £26.00 (CRO)

VdP de l'Hérault, Domaine de la Grange des Pères **1996** £23.50 (AD)

Over £30.00

les Baux-de-Provence Domaine de Trévallon **1990** £44.00 (CRO)

Madiran Vieilles Vignes Château Bouscassé, Brumont **1995** £48.65 (NO)

VdP de l'Hérault, Mas de Daumas Gassac **1985** £31.00 (CRO)

DRY WHITE

Under £4.00

Bergerac Château le Fagé **1997** £3.99 (MORR)

Côtes de St-Mont, les Hauts de Bergelle **1997** £3.70 (SOM) £4.95 (TAN)

Côtes de St-Mont, Producteurs Plaimont **1997** £3.95 (WS) £3.99 (JON) £4.10 (HAH)

Côtes de St-Mont, Producteurs Plaimont **1996** £3.75 (BALL)

VdP des Côtes de Thau Terret, Lurton **1996** £3.99 (NI)

VdP des Côtes de Gascogne Domaine de Planterieu **1998** £3.99 (WAI)

VdP des Côtes de Gascogne Domaine de Rieux **1998** £3.99 (POR) £4.15 (HAH) £4.40 (AD) £4.50 (TAN)

VdP des Côtes de Gascogne Domaine de Tariquet **1997** £3.99 (THR) £3.99 (WR)

VdP des Côtes de Gascogne le Prada **1998** £3.60 (WS)

VdP des Côtes de Gascogne Producteurs Plaimont **1997** £3.89 (JON) £4.30 (PIP)

VdP du Gers, Producteurs Plaimont **1998** £2.99 (MAR)

VdP de l'Hérault Grenache, Bésinet **1998** £3.60 (WS)

VdP des Landis Domaine d'Espérance **1997** £3.99 (BAL)

VdP d'Oc Laperouse **1995** £3.99 (VIC) £3.99 (THR) £3.99 (WR) £3.99 (BOT)

VdP d'Oc Sauvignon, Domaine des Fontanelles **1998** £3.99 (MAJ)

VdP des Terroirs Landais Domaine de Laballe **1997** £3.99 (BAL)

£4.00 → £4.99

Coteaux d'Aix-en-Provence Château de Fonscolombe **1997** £4.89 (JON) £4.95 (POR)

Côtes de St-Mont, Producteurs Plaimont **1998** £4.35 (AD)

VdP des Coteaux des Baronnies Chardonnay, Bellefontaine **1998** £4.49 (YOU)

VdP des Côtes de Gascogne Domaine de Maubet **1997** £4.29 (CON)

VdP des Côtes de Gascogne Gros Manseng, Brumont **1998** £4.00 (BY)

VdP des Côtes de Pérignan Chardonnay, Château Pech-Céleyran **1997** £4.50 (WS)

VdP des Côtes de Gascogne Domaine de Rieux **1997** £4.32 (GW) £5.29 (REI)

VdP des Côtes de Gascogne Domaine San de Guilhem **1997** £4.80 (MV)

VdP des Côtes de Thongue Chasan Blanc, Domaine de la Croix Belle **1997** £4.95 (LEA)

VdP des Côtes de Thongue Grenache, Domaine Boyer **1996** £4.75 (JU)

VdP de l'Hérault Chardonnay, Domaine Montrose **1997** £4.99 (YOU)

VdP de l'Hérault Chardonnay, Domaine Pourthié **1997** £4.99 (BAL)

VdP de l'Hérault Marsanne, du Bosc **1997** £4.50 (WS) £4.99 (BAL)

VdP de l'Hérault Muscat Sec, Bésinet **1997** £4.25 (WS)

VdP de l'Hérault Terret, Domaine Gourg du Laval **1996** £4.50 (JU)

VdP d'Oc Blanc sur lie, les Domaines Virginie **1997** £4.70 (MV)

VdP d'Oc Chardonnay, Domaine de Gourgazaud **1998** £4.95 (WS)

VdP d'Oc Chardonnay Domaine Montgaillard, Duboeuf **1995** £4.99 (NI)

VdP d'Oc Chardonnay, James Herrick **1997** £4.99 (MORR) £4.99 (SAI) £4.99 (BO) £4.99 (CO) £4.99 (SAF) £4.99 (THR) £4.99 (WR)

VdP d'Oc Chardonnay, Philippe de Baudin (alias Chais Baumière) **1997** £4.99 (SAI) £5.29 (SAF)

VdP d'Oc Laperouse **1996** £4.49 (CO)

VdP d'Oc Marsanne, Domaines Virginie **1997** £4.99 (YOU) £5.00 (MV) £6.25 (BALL) £8.22 (NO)

VdP d'Oc Roussanne, Domaines Virginie **1997** £4.99 (YOU) £5.00 (MV) £5.45 (BEN) £5.49 (LAY)

VdP d'Oc Sauvignon Blanc Domaine des Salices, Lurton **1996** £4.49 (NI)

VdP d'Oc Sauvignon Blanc, Philippe de Baudin **1997** £4.99 (SAI)

VdP d'Oc Sauvignon Blanc, Domaine de la Belonette **1997** £4.79 (JON)

VdP du Vaucluse Domaine du Vieux Chêne **1996** £4.50 (JU)

£5.00 → £6.99

Bergerac Château de la Colline, Martin **1996** £5.88 (HIG)

Bergerac Château Tours des Gendres **1995** £5.45 (JU)

Bergerac Cuvée des Conti, Château Tours des Gendres **1997** £6.25 (LEA) £6.29 (YOU)

Bergerac Sec Château de Tiregand **1998** £5.10 (TAN)

Costières de Nîmes Cuvée St Marc, Château de Bellecoste **1997** £6.95 (LEA)

Coteaux du Languedoc Picpoul de Pinet, Domaine St Peyre **1997** £5.25 (PIP)

Coteaux du Languedoc Cuvée Classique, Château de Lascaux **1998** £6.50 (LEA) £6.99 (BEN)

Côtes du Lubéron Château Val Joanis **1998** £5.42 (BY)

Côtes du Lubéron la Vieille Ferme **1997** £5.70 (CB)

Côtes du Lubéron la Vieille Ferme **1996** £6.45 (ROB)

Côtes du Roussillon Domaine Gauby **1995** £5.90 (GAU)

Jurançon Sec Domaine de Bru-Braché **1996** £6.49 (GW)

Jurançon Sec Domaine Castera **1996** £6.99 (GW) £9.50 (ROB)

VdP des Côtes de Thongue Chardonnay, Domaine de la Croix Belle **1997** £5.95 (LEA)

VdP des Côtes de Thongue Muscat Sec de Petits Grains, Teisserenc **1996** £5.50 (JU)

VdP des Côtes de Thongue Viognier, la Condamine l'Évêque **1998** £6.40 (TAN) £6.95 (LEA)

VdP de la Haute Vallée de l'Orb Oaked Chardonnay, Domaine de la Croix Ronde **1995** £6.75 (HIG)

VdP de l'Hérault Chardonnay Barrel-Fermented, Domaine Montrose **1996** £5.95 (JU)

VdP de l'Hérault, Château St Martin de la Garrigue **1996** £5.95 (JU)

VdP de l'Hérault Sauvignon Blanc, Domaine Gourg du Laval **1995** £5.45 (JU)

VdP de l'Hérault Terret Blanc, Domaine la Fadèze **1998** £5.70 (LAY)

VdP de l'Hérault Viognier, Domaine du Bosc **1997** £5.95 (WS) £5.99 (BAL)

VdP d'Oc Chardonnay, Domaine Virginie **1997** £5.40 (HAH) £5.59 (JON) £5.90 (MV)

VdP d'Oc Chardonnay, Domaine Virginie **1996** £5.29 (REI) £5.45 (JU)

VdP d'Oc Chardonnay/Viognier, Domaine de la Baume **1996** £6.99 (SAF)

VdP d'Oc Marsanne, Domaine Virginie **1998** £5.10 (TAN) £5.45 (BEN)

VdP d'Oc Viognier, Domaine St Hilaire **1997** £6.49 (GW) £7.40 (PIP)

VdP d'Oc Viognier, Domaine Virginie **1997** £6.20 (MV)

VdP du Vaucluse Roussanne, Domaine du Vieux Chêne **1996** £5.90 (JU)

£7.00 → £9.99

Bandol Domaine de l'Hermitage **1995** £8.85 (CON)

Bandol Mas de la Rouvière, Bunan **1997** £8.95 (YAP)

Coteaux du Languedoc Domaine d'Aupilhac **1997** £8.95 (LEA)

Jurançon Sec Domaine Cauhapé **1997** £7.95 (WS) £8.49 (POR) £8.60 (MV)

Limoux Chardonnay, Domaine de l'Aigle Cuvée Classique **1997** £8.50 (LEA)

Limoux Chardonnay, Domaine de l'Aigle Cuvée Classique **1996** £7.30 (TAN) £7.95 (PIP)

Pacherenc du Vic-Bilh Domaine Boucassé **1995** £7.93 (REI)

VdP des Côtes de Thongue Viognier/Sauvignon Blanc, Equinoxe de l'Arjolle **1996** £7.85 (JU)

VdP d'Oc Chardonnay, Clovallon **1995** £9.95 (BAL)

VdP d'Oc Chardonnay, des Rives de l'Argent Double **1995** £7.63 (CB)

£10.00 → £19.99

Bandol Château de Pibarnon **1995** £11.30 (GAU)

Bandol Château de la Rouvière, Bunan **1996** £10.75 (YAP)

Cassis Clos Ste-Magdeleine, Sack **1997** £10.50 (YAP)

Palette Château Simone **1996** £17.75 (YAP)

VdP des Bouches-du-Rhône Domaine de Trévallon **1996** £16.06 (FA) £40.00 (FORT)

VdP de l'Hérault, Mas de Daumas Gassac **1995** £11.21 (NO) £17.95 (ROB)

VdP d'Oc Viognier, Clovallon **1997** £11.95 (BEN)

Over £20.00

Coteaux d'Aix-en-Provence Domaine de Trévallon **1995** £22.50 (NI)

Côtes de Provence Clos Mireille Blanc de Blancs, Domaines Ott **1994** £20.00 (FORT)

VdP de l'Hérault, Mas de Daumas Gassac **1996** £28.85 (UB)

SWEET WHITE

Under £5.00

Gaillac Domaine de Labarthe **1996** £4.60 (SOM)

£6.50 → £11.99

Jurançon Vendange Tardive du 2 Novembre, Domaine Cauhape ½ bottle **1995** £8.87 (NO) £9.50 (BEN)

Jurançon Domaine Bellegarde, Labasse **1997** £9.75 (YAP)

Jurançon Domaine Bellegarde, Labasse **1996** £11.50 (ROB)

Monbazillac Château Septy **1995** £7.49 (JON) £7.58 (CB)

Monbazillac Château Theulet 50cl bottle **1995** £8.95 (WS) £9.45 (ELL) £10.95 (ROB)

Monbazillac Château Theulet **1996** £9.25 (NA)

★ Saussignac Cuvée Flavie, Château des Eyssards **1995** £6.95 (AD)

£12.00 → £24.99

Monbazillac Château Tirecul la Gravière **1994** £19.00 (FA)

Monbazillac Château Tirecul la Gravière 50cl bottle **1994** £13.12 (FA) £14.50 (JU) £15.95 (LEA) £18.50 (CRO)

Pacherenc du Vic-Bilh Vendange Décembre Château Bouscassé, Brumont ½ bottle **1989** £23.90 (NO)

★ Saussignac Clos d'Yvigne **1995** £13.95 (JU)

Over £25.00

Monbazillac Cuvée Madame, Château Tirecul la Gravière 50cl bottle **1995** £74.81 (FA)

Monbazillac Château Cuvée Madame, Tirecul la Gravière 50cl bottle **1992** £35.00 (JU)

Pacherenc du Vic-Bilh Vendange Décembre Château Bouscassé, Brumont **1990** £42.30 (REI)

ROSÉ

Under £5.00

Cabardès Château Rivals **1997** £4.99 (CON)

Coteaux d'Aix-en-Provence Château de Fonscolombe **1997** £4.89 (JON)

Côtes de Provence Domaine Hilaire Houchart **1998** £4.25 (WS)

Stars (★) indicate wines selected by Oz Clarke in the Best Buys section which begins on page 9.

Côtes du Frontonnais Château le Roc
1998 £4.95 (LEA)
VdP des Coteaux de Murviel, Domaine de
Limbardie **1998** £3.50 (SOM)
VdP des Côtes de Thongue Cuvée de
l'Arjolle, Domaine Teisserenc **1996**
£4.95 (JU) £5.50 (CRO)
VdP de l'Hérault, Domaine Montrose
1996 £4.45 (JU)
VdP d'Oc Syrah, Domaines Virginie **1996**
£3.95 (BALL)
VdP des Sables du Golfe du Lion Gris de
Gris, Listel **Non-vintage** £4.43 (GW)
VdP du Var les Trois Chenes, Domaine de
l'Hermitage **1996** £4.39 (CON)
VdP du Vaucluse Domaine du Vieux
Chêne **1996** £4.60 (JU)

£5.00 → £9.99

Bandol Domaine de l'Hermitage **1997**
£7.99 (CON)
Bandol Mas de la Rouvière **1997** £8.95 (YAP)
Bandol Mas de la Rouvière **1995** £9.25 (UB)
Bergerac Château de la Colline, Martin
1996 £5.88 (HIG)
Bergerac Château Tour de Gendres **1998**
£5.32 (GW)
Côteaux du Languedoc Château de
Lascaux **1998** £5.95 (LEA) £5.99 (BEN)
Côtes du Lubéron Château Val Joanis
1998 £5.42 (BY)
Côtes de Provence Carte Noire, Vignerons
de St-Tropez **1998** £5.75 (NEZ)
Côtes de Provence Château la Moutete
1997 £5.59 (CON)
VdP des Côtes de Thongue Meridiene,
Domaine de l'Arjolle **1996** £8.50 (JU)
VdP d'Oc les Chemins de Bassac **1995**
£7.11 (WT)

Over £15.00

Côtes de Provence Château de Selle,
Domaines Ott **1997** £19.19 (PLAY)
Côtes de Provence Château de Selle,
Domaines Ott **1996** £18.75 (FORT)
Palette Château Simone **1994** £16.75 (YAP)

Please remember that
Oz Clarke's Wine Guide
is a price **guide** *and not a*
price **list***. It is not meant to*
replace up-to-date
merchants' lists.

SPARKLING

Under £9.00

Blanquette de Limoux Domaine des
Martinolles **1994** £7.47 (STE)
Crémant de Limoux Cuvée St Laurent,
Antech **1994** £7.25 (WS)
★ Domaine de l'Aigle Brut Tradition **NV**
£8.95 (PIP)

VINS DOUX NATURELS

Under £7.00

Muscat de Mireval Domaine du Moulinas
½ bottle **Non-vintage** £6.36 (NO)
Muscat de Rivesaltes Domaine Cazes ½
bottle **1996** £4.99 (CON) £6.75 (FORT)
Muscat de Rivesaltes Domaine Cazes ½
bottle **1993** £5.69 (YOU)
Muscat de Rivesaltes Domaine Piquemal
1997 £6.99 (BAL) £9.95 (LEA)

£7.50 → £9.99

Maury Vintage Mas Amiel ½ bottle **1996**
£7.95 (LEA)
Muscat de Frontignan, Château de la
Peyrade **Non-vintage** £7.90 (CRO)
£9.10 (ELL)
Muscat de Frontignan, Château de la
Peyrade **1994** £8.95 (PHI)
Muscat de Rivesaltes Domaine Cazes
1996 £9.99 (CON) £11.45 (ROB)

£10.00 → £19.99

Maury 15 Ans d'Age, Mas Amiel **Non-
vintage** £15.95 (LEA)
Maury Vintage Mas Amiel **1996** £11.95
(LEA)
Muscat de Rivesaltes Chapoutier **1996**
£13.89 (NO)
Muscat de Rivesaltes Domaine Cazes
1995 £11.45 (ROB)
Muscat de Rivesaltes Gauby **1995** £10.99
(RAE)
Rivesaltes Tuile Domaine Cazes **1984**
£11.95 (CON)

Over £20.00

Banyuls Grand Cru, Castell des Hospices
1982 £20.86 (NO)
Banyuls Vieilles Vignes, Domaine du Mas
Blanc **1981** £21.00 (WS)
Banyuls Vieilles Vignes, Domaine du Mas
Blanc **1978** £28.00 (CRO)

VINS DE PAYS

**From being a name for simple country wines, vin de pays has developed
into a catch-all category that includes some real stars**

In the last few years I've had to rethink my ideas about what vin de pays should mean; and I don't think I'm alone. Vins de pays as a category were set up some decades ago as a way of giving respectability and a sense of ambition to wines which were obviously better than basic blended table wine, but which could not yet aspire to the dizzy heights of VDQS (Vin Delimité de Qualité Supérieure) or AC. It was an extremely worthy, sensible move, and recognized the value of wines that reflected the character of their region, while remaining simple and rustic.

Does it still mean that? Well, in law it does. In practice it has frequently come to mean something different: particularly in the South, a vin de pays can be just about anything. It can be a modern, fruit-driven wine, a varietal or a blend, which is made using techniques or grape varieties which are not permitted for AC wines in that region. So Cabernet Sauvignon, which is severely restricted for AC wines in the Midi, can be grown by the acre for vins de pays. Likewise Syrah; likewise Chardonnay and Sauvignon Blanc and Viognier.

But vins de pays can be something else, as well. Say you've found a sensational piece of land in a vin de pays area, and you want to plant it with your own idiosyncratic grape mix (again, not one that the AC authorities would necessarily approve of) and make something world class. It'll still be vin de pays. And none the worse for that.

Vins de pays come in three categories:

VINS DE PAYS RÉGIONAUX

There are four of these. Vin de Pays du Jardin de la France covers the whole Loire basin across almost to Chablis and down to the Charente. Vin de Pays du Comté Tolosan is for the South-West, starting just below Bordeaux, and covering Bergerac, Cahors, the Tarn and down to the Pyrénées, but not including the Aude and Pyrénées Orientales. Vin de Pays des Comtés Rhodaniens includes the northern Rhône and Savoie; Vin de Pays d'Oc covers Provence and the Midi all the way down to the Spanish border.

VINS DE PAYS DÉPARTEMENTAUX

These are also large groupings, and each one is defined by the boundaries of the *département*. So, for instance, any wine of vin de pays quality grown in the *département* of Vaucluse will qualify for the title 'Vin de Pays du Vaucluse'.

VINS DE PAYS DE ZONE

These are the most tightly controlled of the categories, and can apply to actual communes or carefully defined localities. The allowed yield is lower and there may be more control on grape varieties. So, for example, we could have a Vin de Pays de la Vallée du Paradis which is in the Aude, and could also be sold as Vin de Pays de l'Aude, or as Vin de Pays d'Oc.

MERCHANTS SPECIALIZING IN VINS DE PAYS
see Merchant Directory (page 413) for details

Most merchants have some vins de pays on their lists, but for particularly good ranges try the following: Adnams (AD), Avery's of Bristol (AV), Bibendum (BIB), Anthony Byrne (BY), First Quench Group (BOT, THR, VIC, WR), Lay & Wheeler (LAY), Majestic (MAJ), James Nicholson (NI), Oddbins (OD), Thos. Peatling, The Ubiquitous Chip (UB), Wine Society (WS).

GERMANY

**Think you might like to risk German wines again? Here's how to
go about it with minimum risk and
maximum enjoyment**

Okay, let's suppose you've decided to take note of what I've been saying for years, that fine German wines are some of the most fascinating whites in the world. What next? How do you find your way through the maze of unpronounceable names at hugely varying prices, to find something that might be a benchmark wine? Well, there are ways. First, look for the word Riesling on the label. There are other good grapes in Germany, but Riesling is where you should start. Next, go to

Waitrose or Oddbins or Wine Rack or a serious local independent, and look for something at around the £7 level. Buy a Kabinett or Spätlese (the latter will probably be sweeter) from the Mosel, Rheingau or Pfalz, and try and get something at least five years old. Take it home and open it. Don't blame it for not being dry. Concentrate instead on the flavour – honey? peaches? – and on the structure. Look for a taut, tense balance of sweetness and acidity. Then have another glass. And then another…

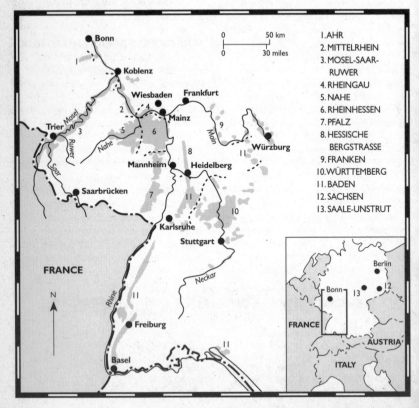

1. AHR
2. MITTELRHEIN
3. MOSEL-SAAR-RUWER
4. RHEINGAU
5. NAHE
6. RHEINHESSEN
7. PFALZ
8. HESSISCHE BERGSTRASSE
9. FRANKEN
10. WÜRTTEMBERG
11. BADEN
12. SACHSEN
13. SAALE-UNSTRUT

QUALITY CONTROL

You'll see one of these terms on every German wine label: they are simply a way of classifying wine according to the ripeness of the grapes when they are picked.

DEUTSCHER TAFELWEIN Basic German table wine of supposedly tolerable quality; low natural alcohol, sugared at fermentation to increase it, no specific vineyard origin stated. Usually little more than sugar-water. However, at the other end of the price spectrum are expensive 'designer table wines' from adventurous producers who may age them in oak.

LANDWEIN Rarely seen German version of vin de pays; table wine from one of 20 designated areas. It can be Trocken (dry) or Halbtrocken (half-dry).

QbA (Qualitätswein bestimmter Anbaugebiete) Literally 'quality wine from designated regions' – Ahr, Hessische Bergstrasse, Mittelrhein, Nahe, Rheingau, Rheinhessen, Pfalz, Franken, Württemberg, Baden, Mosel-Saar-Ruwer, Saale-Unstrut and Sachsen. Quality varies from poor to very good, depending on the producer. Anything labelled Liebfraumilch, Niersteiner Gutes Domtal or Piesporter Michelsberg is unlikely to be worth a second glance. Go for top estates only, but 1997 yielded some splendidly concentrated QbAs.

QmP (Qualitätswein mit Prädikat) Literally, quality wine with special attributes. There are six categories, in order of increasing ripeness of the grapes: Kabinett, Spätlese, Auslese, Beerenauslese, Trockenbeeren-auslese and Eiswein. Drier wines (usually Kabinett or Spätlese) may be either Trocken (dry) or Halbtrocken (half-dry). Not all styles are made every year.

KABINETT Made from ripe grapes. Usually lighter in alcohol than ordinary QbA, and often delicious.

SPÄTLESE From late-picked (therefore riper) grapes. Often moderately sweet, though there are now dry versions.

AUSLESE From selected bunches of very ripe grapes. Usually sweet and sometimes touched by 'noble rot', a fungus that concentrates the sugar and acidity in the grapes. In many southern regions, such as Baden, they are fermented dry, making rich and powerful wines.

BEERENAUSLESE (BA) Wines made from selected single grapes almost always affected by the noble rot fungus. Beerenauslese from new, non-Riesling grapes can be dull. But Riesling Beerenauslese, and many a Scheurebe or Silvaner, will be astonishing.

EISWEIN Just that – 'ice wine' – often picked before a winter dawn when the grapes are frozen. They are dashed to the winery by the frost-bitten pickers; once there, quick and careful pressing removes just the slimy-sweet concentrate; the water, in its icy state, stays separate. Eiswein always has a high acidity that needs to be tamed by bottle age, though you do lose the lovely frosty, green apple flavours of youth.

TROCKENBEERENAUSLESE (TBA) 'Shrivelled selected berries' – that's a pedestrian translation of one of the world's great tastes. Individually picked grapes, shrivelled by noble rot, produce small amounts of intensely sweet juice, making TBAs among the sweetest wines in the world. The risks and the costs are both enormous. The vines are making a glass of wine each instead of a bottle, and the weather can easily ruin it all anyway. That's why TBAs are expensive – usually starting at £20 a half bottle ex-cellars. But, even then, a grower won't make money; it's his pride that makes him do it. And the wines can age for as long as you or I.

GRAPE VARIETIES

DORNFELDER (red) At its best this produces deep-coloured reds with great fruit concentration and firm structure. Made in two styles: reminiscent of Beaujolais and for early drinking or aged in barriques for longer keeping. Best: *Knipser, Lergenmüller, Lingenfelder Onyx, Messmer, Siegrist, Heinrich Vollmer* (Pfalz).

MÜLLER-THURGAU (white) The most widely planted German grape, propagated in 1883 to get Riesling style plus big yields. Well, you can't do it. It produces soft, potpourri-scented wines of no distinction, but it produces plenty of them. Occasionally it's made dry and aged in oak; this style is particularly successful in Baden when yields are severely reduced. For the oaked style try *Gunderloch, Karl H Johner, Dr Loosen. Juliusspital* in Franken makes a deceptively fragile unoaked version.

RIESLANER (white) A sensational crossing of Riesling and Silvaner, but not widely planted. Ripe it tastes of apricots; unripe it tastes, less appealingly, of grass and gooseberries. Best as dessert wine from the Pfalz (especially *Müller-Catoir*) and Franken. Best producers: *Juliusspital, Rudolf Fürst, Robert Schmitt, Schmitt's Kinder* (Franken).

RIESLING (white) Most of Germany's best wines (except in Baden-Württemberg, where the soils are usually unsuitable) are made from this grape. When yields are controlled it produces wonderful flavours: from steely, slaty and dry as sun-bleached bones, through apples, peaches, apricots – more or less sweet according to the ripeness of the grapes and the intentions of the winemaker – and finally arriving at the great sweet wines. These can be blinding in their rich, honeyed concentration of peaches, pineapples, mangoes and even raisins, with acidity like a streak of fresh lime that makes them the most appetizing of sweet wines.

RULÄNDER (white) The French Pinot Gris. It can be strong, sweetish, broadshouldered, with a whiff of spice and a splash of honey. When made dry it is often aged in small oak barriques and can make exciting drinking. Best: *Schlossgut Diel* (Nahe); *Koehler-Ruprecht, Müller-Catoir, Münzberg* (Pfalz); *Bercher, Dr Heger, Karl H Johner, Salwey, Stigler* (Baden); *Johann Ruck* (Franken).

SCHEUREBE (white) A tricky grape. When it's unripe, it can pucker your mouth with its rawness. But properly ripe, there's honey, and a crackling, peppery fire which, in the Pfalz, Baden and Franken, produces dry wines as well as sweeter, sometimes outstanding Auslese and Beerenauslese.

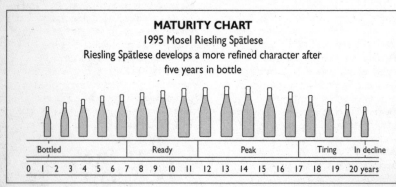

MATURITY CHART

1995 Mosel Riesling Spätlese

Riesling Spätlese develops a more refined character after five years in bottle

Bottled	Ready	Peak	Tiring	In decline

0 1 2 3 4 5 6 7 8 9 10 11 12 13 14 15 16 17 18 19 20 years

Best producers: *Darting, Lingenfelder, Messmer, Müller-Catoir* (Pfalz); *Andreas Laible, Wolff-Metternich* (Baden); *Rudolf Fürst, Wirsching* (Franken).

SILVANER (white) A workhorse grape, often dull, fat and vegetal, but can be impressive in Franken, where it develops honeyed weight with age. It suits the local porky cookery; good with asparagus, too. *Juliusspital* and *Lingenfelder Ypsilon* are good.

SPÄTBURGUNDER (red) There is a new, deeply coloured, rich and powerful style of this, the Pinot Noir of Burgundy.

Top producers: *Meyer-Näkel* (Ahr); *August Kesseler* (Rheingau); *Knipser, Koehler-Ruprecht, Lingenfelder* (Pfalz); *Bercher, Dr Heger, Bernhard Huber, Karl H Johner* (Baden); *Rudolf Fürst* (Franken); *Dautel* (Württemberg).

WEISSBURGUNDER or **WEISSER BURGUNDER** (white) Can produce soft, creamy wines with a peach, melted butter, caramel and nuts flavour. Best: *Dönnhoff* (Nahe); *Heyl zu Herrnsheim, Schales* (Rheinhessen); *Bergdolt, Müller-Catoir, Rebholz, Wehrheim* (Pfalz); *Bercher, Dr Heger, Karl H Johner, Franz Keller, Salwey* (Baden).

WINE REGIONS AND STYLES

AHR This small area contrives to be famous for red wines, though their flavour and colour are pretty light, and the Rieslings are in fact more interesting. Top producers: *Deutzerhof, Meyer-Näkel*.

BADEN Dry Ruländer and Weisser Burgunder can be really special here in the balmy South. The Pinot family generally – even Spätburgunder – is on top, although the Ortenau area has fine dry Riesling. The area is dominated by the vast *Badische Winzerkeller* co-operative. Top names: *Bercher, Dr Heger, Bernhard Huber, Karl H Johner, Franz Keller, Andreas Laible, Schloss Neuweier, Salwey, Seeger, Wolff-Metternich*.

BEREICH A collection of villages, usually trading on the name of the most famous of them. Bereich wine is usually dull, dull, dull.

DEUTSCHER SEKT Often a sure route to intestinal distress and sulphur-led hangover, although *Deinhard* makes a decent Riesling version called *Lila; Dr Richter*'s and *Georg Breuer*'s are outstanding, but expensive. Interesting but rare smaller brands are *Graeger, Menger-Krug, Schloss Vaux*. Avoid at all costs the stuff made from imported wines, labelled Sekt (not Deutscher Sekt), or worse, Schaumwein.

FRANKEN (Franconia) Dry wine country. The slightly earthy, slightly vegetal, big and beefy Franken wines in their flagon-shaped 'Bocksbeutel' bottles are usually based on Silvaner or Müller-Thurgau. Quality is mixed, with only a few wines worth the high prices. Top names: *Rudolf Fürst, Juliusspital, Johann Ruck, Egon Schäffer, Schmitt*'s *Kinder, Robert Schmitt, Wirsching*.

GROSSLAGE An area smaller than a Bereich, but bigger than a single vineyard. The names sound like those of single vineyards (Piesporter Michelsberg is a Grosslage). Gross deceit is more like it.

HALBTROCKEN Half-dry. The wines need to have more body to balance the acidity, so the best Halbtrockens are from the Rheingau or Pfalz – not the Mosel.

HESSISCHE BERGSTRASSE A tiny side valley of the Rhine from which hardly anything is exported. Generally good Rieslings. Best: *Staatsweingut Bergstrasse*.

LIEBFRAUMILCH Liebfraumilch was a brilliant invention, innocuous and grapy and the perfect beginner's wine. Now mostly cheap sugar-water. *Blue Nun,* always one of the better ones, is no longer labelled Lieb.

INSTANT CELLAR: THRILLING RIESLING

- **1997 Riesling Kabinett 'Dr L', Loosen, £5.99, Waitrose** Entry-level Riesling from the Mosel – a taste of what it's all about.
- **1990 Ayler Kupp Riesling Auslese, W V Ayl, £7.85, Averys** Nine years old already, but I'd still give it a bit longer.
- **1994 Graacher Himmelreich Riesling Spätlese, Friedrich Wilhelm Gymnasium, £10.30, Averys** Top grower, top vineyard.
- **1995 Erdener Treppchen Riesling Kabinett, Dr Loosen, £12.30, Nobody Inn** All the delicacy of a Mosel, plus taut structure and great depth.
- **1983 Wallufer Walkenberg Riesling Spätlese, Becker, £15, Gelston Castle** Gloriously mature Rheingau Riesling with some weight.
- **1989 Forster Kirchenstück Riesling Kabinett, Dr von Bassermann-Jordan, £8.50, Justerini & Brooks** Mature Riesling from the Pfalz.
- **1997 Trittenheimer Apotheke Riesling Auslese, Grans-Fassian, £8.99, Majestic** Glorious Mosel Auslese with ripe fruit and taut acidity.

MITTELRHEIN The Rhine at its most beautiful; tourists flock there and drink most of its wine, but *Toni Jost*'s racy Rieslings still get away. Also good: *Fritz Bastian, Dr Randolph Kauer, Helmut Madess.*

MOSEL-SAAR-RUWER When they are made from Riesling and come from one of the many steep, slaty, south-facing sites in the folds of the river, these northerly wines are unlike any others. Think of a thrilling spring flowers flavour, allied to an alcohol level so low that it leaves your head clear. The lightest yet most intense Rieslings in the world, with a minerally character from the slate soil. The Saar and the Ruwer both need the warmest years to show at their best, and both can be longer-maturing, with even more steel. Best: *Joh. Jos. Christoffel, Fritz Haag, Reinhold Haart, von Hövel, Karthäuserhof, von Kesselstatt, Dr Loosen, Joh.*

Jos. Prüm, Max Ferd. Richter, Schloss Saarstein, Willi Schaefer, von Schubert, Selbach-Oster, Dr Wagner, Dr Weins-Prüm, Zilliken.

NAHE At their best the Rieslings have quite high acidity and a mineral edge, but quality is not uniformly good. *Paul Anheuser, Dönnhoff, Crusius, Schlossgut Diel, Emrich-Schönleber, Kruger-Rumpf* and *Mathern* are all tops. The *Staatliche Weinbaudomäne* is still struggling to regain top form.

PFALZ (Formerly the Rheinpfalz.) The northern half includes extremely good villages like Forst, Wachenheim, Deidesheim and Ruppertsberg. There's lots of fiery Riesling, and Scheurebe is excellent. The South is Germany's most dynamic region, with fewer big names to fly its flag but an astonishing overall improvement in quality. Look for *Bergdolt, Josef Biffar, Dr Bürklin-Wolf, Knipser, Koehler-Ruprecht, Lingenfelder, Messmer, Georg Mosbacher, Müller-Catoir, Pfaffingen-Fuhrmann-Eymael, Rebholz, Karl Schaefer, Wehrheim, Werlé Erben.*

RHEINGAU Some of Germany's most famous vineyards and renowned aristocratic wine estates are here, and its supremely elegant Rieslings once defined top-quality German wines. However, many of the big estates here have been resting on their laurels for years. The best sign recently has been the (still unofficial) classification of top vineyards. Look for these producers: *Georg Breuer, Domdechant Werner, August Eser, Johannishof, August Kesseler, Franz Künstler, Josef Leitz, Schloss Reinhartshausen, Balthasar Ress, J Wegeler-Erben (Deinhard), Robert Weil.* All are worth their high prices.

RHEINHESSEN The contrast between Rheinhessen's regular products and its top wines could not be more extreme. It is one of the main sources of Liebfraumilch, yet Nierstein's top Rieslings can match anything from the Rheingau. Top producers: *Gunderloch, Heyl zu Herrnsheim, Keller, St Antony, Schales, Georg Albrecht Schneider.*

SAALE-UNSTRUT The largest wine region in what used to be East Germany. The climate is similar to Franken, the grapes mainly Müller-Thurgau and Silvaner. *Lutzkendorf* has good Riesling and Traminer.

SACHSEN Germany's smallest wine-growing region, formerly part of the GDR. Müller-Thurgau dominates, but the best dry wines come from Weissburgunder, Kerner, Grauburgunder, Traminer and Riesling. *Klaus Zimmerling* is the best bet, but *Schloss Proschwitz* and *Jan Ulrich* are also good.

SEKT bA (Sekt bestimmter Anbaugebiete). Germany's best sparkling wine comes from private estates. If the wine comes from one specific region it can be labelled accordingly – for instance, Rheinhessen Sekt – and is generally a step above Deutscher Sekt. Riesling Sekt bA is especially worth looking out for. Try *Schloss Wachenheim* or *Winzersekt,* or *Dr Richter's.*

TROCKEN Dry: the driest German wines, austere and acidic in unripe vintages. The richer, more alcoholic wines of the Pfalz, Baden and Franken suit dryness best, as do fat, ripe years like 1997.

WÜRTTEMBERG Most is drunk on the spot. Its claim to fame – if fame is the right word – is red. The best grape is Lemberger, dark, spicy and suited to oak aging. Best: *Graf Adelmann, Dautel, Haidle, Hohenlohe-Öhringen, Graf von Neipperg.*

PRODUCERS WHO'S WHO

GEORG BREUER ★★★★ (Rheingau) Convincing promoter of dry Rheingau Riesling. Rüdesheimer Berg Schlossberg and Rauenthaler Nonnenberg are best.

H DÖNNHOFF ★★★★★ (Nahe) Classic Rieslings of great aromatic subtlety and racy intensity. Sensational Auslese and Eiswein.

GUNDERLOCH ★★★★★ (Rheinhessen) Explosively fruity, rich, seductive Rieslings from the great Nackenheimer Rothenberg. Jean Baptiste Kabinett is good value; also Beerenauslese and Trockenbeerenauslese of other-worldly concentration and density.

FRITZ HAAG ★★★★ (Mosel-Saar-Ruwer) Wines of crystalline clarity and racy refinement from Brauneberger Juffer-Sonnenuhr.

VON HÖVEL ★★★★ (Mosel-Saar-Ruwer) These have taken a dramatic jump up in quality in recent years. Best are the succulent, beautifully balanced wines from Oberemmeler Hütte.

KARTHÄUSERHOF ★★★★★ (Mosel-Saar-Ruwer) Large Ruwer property making wines of concentration and character.

VON KESSELSTATT ★★★ (Mosel-Saar-Ruwer) Huge estate showing big improvements. Look for Rieslings from Graach, Piesport and Wiltingen.

KOEHLER-RUPRECHT ★★★★★ (Pfalz) Powerful dry Rieslings plus excellent oak-aged whites and Germany's best Pinot Noir reds, sold under the Philippi label.

FRANZ KÜNSTLER ★★★★★ (Rheingau) Powerful and long-lived Rieslings. Best are the majestic dry and dessert wines from the Hochheimer Hölle.

DR LOOSEN ★★★★★ (Mosel-Saar-Ruwer) Rieslings, Spätlesen and Auslesen from Urziger Würzgarten, Erdener Prälat and Treppchen are tops. For value, try wines without vineyard names.

EGON MÜLLER ★★★★★ (Mosel-Saar-Ruwer) The ultimate in Riesling Auslese, Beerenauslese,

Trockenbeerenauslese and Eiswein. No honey tastes this good. World-class prices.

MÜLLER-CATOIR ★★★★★ (Pfalz) Highly expressive, rich, dry and naturally sweet wines. Superb Scheurebe and Rieslaner as well as Rieslings.

JOH. JOS. PRÜM ★★★★★ (Mosel-Saar-Ruwer) Wines that need time to show their best; after a few years of aging they are supremely elegant. Wehlene Sonnenuhrs can age for decades without losing vigour.

WILLI SCHAEFER ★★★★ (Mosel-Saar-Ruwer) Small production; wines of great depth and elegance from Graach.

VON SCHUBERT ★★★★★ (Mosel-Saar-Ruwer) The Maximin Grünhaus estate makes exquisitely delicate, fragrant Rieslings that gain enormously with long aging.

SELBACH-OSTER ★★★★ (Mosel-Saar-Ruwer) Superbly poised, concentrated Rieslings from Zeltingen.

WEINGUT ROBERT WEIL ★★★★ (Rheingau) Classic Rieslings which combine opulent fruit with clarity and crisp acidity. Best are the Kiedricher Gräfenbergs.

ZILLIKEN ★★★★ (Mosel-Saar-Ruwer) Racy Saar Rieslings with minerally intensity. Fashionable Eiswein.

GERMAN VINTAGES

1998 'Surprisingly good', according to the growers – it rained, in other words. But quality does look impressive, especially in the Mosel.

1997 Rich, concentrated wines: lots of Spätlesen and Auslesen. Some top estates had to declassify Spätlesen to QbA in order to have enough. Not an Eiswein year: too warm.

1996 Higher acidity than the 1997s, and will take longer to mature. At the moment a lot are rather closed.

1995 The best vintage since 1990. Lots of excellent Spätlesen and Auslesen.

1994 Strongest in the Mosel-Saar-Ruwer, but quite good generally. Outstanding at BA and TBA level.

1993 Rich, even opulent wines that have developed quite quickly. Best in the Rheingau, Pfalz and Mosel. Very good for dry Riesling. Drink now and for the next few years.

1992 Good, but a bit low on acidity. Don't keep them too long.

1991 The best are showing well now.

1990 Fantastic wines that will age and age.

1989 A mixed vintage: Kabinett and Spätlesen mostly want drinking. Best in the Mosel-Saar-Ruwer, Nahe and Pfalz.

1988 Very good to very, very good, and drinking beautifully now.

GERMANY PRICES

Kab.	=	Kabinett
Spät.	=	Spätlese
Aus.	=	Auslese
BA	=	Beerenauslese
TBA	=	Trockenbeerenauslese

RHINE WHITE

Under £4.00

Devil's Rock Riesling, St Ursula **1997** £3.89 (MORR)

Devil's Rock Riesling, St Ursula **1996** £3.99 (CO) £3.99 (SAF)

Liebfraumilch Black Tower **1997** £3.99 (VIC) £3.99 (THR) £3.99 (WR) £3.99 (BOT) £3.99 (SO) £3.99 (ASD)

Liebfraumilch Blue Nun **1997** £2.99 (MORR) £3.99 (THR) £3.99 (WR) £3.99 (BOT)

Liebfraumilch Blue Nun **1996** £3.99 (CO) £3.99 (SAF)

Morio Muskat St Georg, Pfalz **1997** £3.59 (SAF)

Niersteiner Gutes Domtal, R Müller **1997** £3.71 (PEN)

Rüdesheimer Rosengarten, R Müller **1998** £3.72 (GW)

£4.00 → £4.99

Niersteiner Auflangen Riesling Spät., R Müller **1997** £4.70 (HAH) £4.95 (AD) £4.95 (POR)

Niersteiner Gutes Domtal, Langenbach **1997** £4.44 (PLAY)

Oppenheimer Krötenbrunnen, R Müller **1996** £4.47 (CB)

Ruppertsberger Hoheburg Riesling Kab., Winzerverein **1997** £4.75 (WS)

£5.00 → £5.99

Deidesheimer Hofstück Kab., R Müller **1993** £5.60 (UB)

Johannisberger Erntebringer Riesling Kab., R Müller **1996** £5.39 (JON) £5.58 (GW)

Kreuznacher Kronenberg Kab., Zentralkellerei **1997** £5.20 (AD)

Niersteiner Spiegelberg Riesling Spät., R Müller **1997** £5.49 (UN)

Niersteiner Spiegelberg Riesling Aus., R Müller **1994** £5.49 (PEN)

Riesling QbA, Wolf **1998** £5.81 (STE)

£6.00 → £6.99

Deidesheim Riesling, von Buhl **1996** £6.50 (JU)

Forster Riesling, Bürklin-Wolf **1996** £6.95 (WRI) £7.99 (CON)

Niersteiner Bergkirche Riesling Kab., Guntrum **1995** £6.85 (CON)

Niersteiner Hölle Riesling Kab., Senfter **1994** £6.86 (COC)

Niersteiner Oelberg Riesling Spät., Senfter **1997** £6.95 (WS)

Riesling Qba, Dönnhoff **1997** £6.80 (TAN)

Riesling Kab., Gunderloch **1995** £6.50 (JU)

Scheurebe Kab. Louis Philipp, Guntrum **1997** £6.45 (STA)

£7.00 → £7.99

Deidesheimer Leinhöhle Riesling Kab., Bassermann-Jordan **1989** £7.95 (JU)

Forster Pechstein Riesling Kab., von Buhl **1995** £7.99 (NI)

Forster Riesling, Bürklin-Wolf **1994** £7.85 (DI)

Hattenheimer Schützenhaus Riesling Kab., Ress **1996** £7.83 (MON)

Johannisberger Vogelsang Riesling Kab., Eser **1994** £7.99 (NI)

MERCHANTS SPECIALIZING IN GERMANY

see Merchant Directory (page 413) for details

Adnams (AD), Averys (AV), Bennetts (BEN), Berry Bros (BER), Bibendum (BIB), Butlers (BU) – particularly old vintages, Cockburns of Leith (COC), Direct Wine (DI), Gelston Castle, Douglas Henn-Macrae, S H Jones (JON), Justerini & Brooks (JU), Lay & Wheeler (LAY), Montrachet (MON), Oddbins (OD), Majestic (MAJ), James Nicholson (NI), Nobody Inn (NO), Thos. Peatling, Reid (REI), Tanners (TAN), Ubiquitous Chip (UB), Waitrose (WAI), Waterloo Wine Company (WAT), Wine Society (WS).

Rheingau Riesling Kab., von Simmern
  1992 £7.39 (JON)
Riesling Kab., Robert Weil 1997 £7.99 (DI)
Riesling QbA, J L Wolf 1997 £7.45 (NO)
Schloss Schönborn Riesling Kab.,
  Schönborn 1990 £7.90 (JU)

£8.00 → £8.99

Armand Kab., von Buhl 1995 £8.99 (NI)
  £11.57 (TW)
Eltviller Sonnenberg Riesling Kab., von
  Simmern 1996 £8.30 (PIP)
Eltviller Sonnenberg Riesling Kab., von
  Simmern 1985 £8.49 (WAT)
Forster Stift Kab., Bassermann-Jordan
  1988 £8.99 (RAE)
Freinsheimer Halbtrocken Riesling Spät.,
  Lingenfelder 1994 £8.39 (NI)
Geisenheimer Schlossgarten Riesling Spät.,
  Schönborn 1989 £8.95 (JU) £8.99 (RAE)
Hattenheimer Nussbrunnen Riesling Kab.,
  von Simmern 1993 £8.85 (JU)
Hochheimer Hölle Riesling Kab.,
  Domdechant Werner'sches 1994
  £8.95 (JU)
Kreuznacher Kahlenberg Riesling Spät.,
  Paul Anheuser 1995 £8.13 (MON)
Niersteiner Pettenthal Riesling Kab.,
  Balbach 1996 £8.80 (TAN) £8.90 (JU)
Rauenthaler Baiken Riesling Kab.,
  Staatsweingüter Eltville 1986 £8.99 (WAT)
Riesling Spät. Trocken, Lingenfelder 1997
  £8.71 (MON)
Schlossböckelheimer Kupfergrube
  Riesling Kab., Staatliche
  Weinbaudomäne 1994 £8.00 (LAY)
Schlossböckelheimer Kupfergrube
  Riesling Spät., Staatliche
  Weinbaudomäne 1995 £8.19 (JON)

£9.00 → £9.99

Deidesheimer Hohenmorgen Riesling
  Spät., Bassermann-Jordan 1988 £9.95
  (RAE) £10.99 (JON)
Deidesheimer Leinhöhle Riesling Spät.,
  Bassermann-Jordan 1989 £9.90 (JU)
Erbacher Marcobrunnen Riesling Kab.,
  von Simmern 1993 £9.45 (JU)
Freinsheimer Goldberg Riesling Aus.,
  Lingenfelder 1994 £9.95 (FORT)
Hochheimer Reichestal Riesling Kab.,
  Franz Kunstler 1996 £9.00 (JU)
Nackenheimer Rothenberg Rieslng Kab.
  Jean Baptiste, Gunderloch 1994 £9.82
  (NO) £9.90 (JU)

Oberhäuser Leistenberg Riesling Kab.,
  Dönnhoff 1997 £9.20 (TAN)
Rauenthaler Rothenberg Riesling Kab.,
  Eser 1994 £9.90 (JU)
Riesling Kab., Robert Weil 1996 £9.95
  (WAI)
Schloss Johannisberger Riesling Kab.
  Halbtrocken, Schloss Johannisberg
  1990 £9.52 (NO)
Schloss Vollrads Blau-Gold, Schloss
  Vollrads 1989 £9.50 (UB)
Wachenheimer Rechbächel Riesling Kab.,
  Bürklin-Wolf 1994 £9.95 (BER)

£10.00 → £11.99

Forster Jesuitengarten Riesling Spät., von
  Buhl 1995 £11.50 (JU)
Forster Pechstein Riesling Kab., J L Wolf
  1996 £10.45 (AV)
Grosskarlbacher Burgweg Scheurebe
  Kab., Lingenfelder 1993 £10.50 (FORT)
Hattenheimer Pfaffenberg Riesling Spät.,
  Schönborn 1989 £11.90 (JU)
Hochheimer Domdechaney Riesling Spät.,
  Staatsweingüter Eltville 1985 £11.16 (REI)
Hochheimer Kirchenstück Riesling Spät.,
  Geheimrat Aschrott'sche 1994 £10.50
  (JU)
Hochheimer Reichestal Riesling Kab.,
  Franz Kunstler 1997 £11.95 (BER)
Johannisberger Goldatzel Riesling Kab.,
  Johannishof 1993 £11.95 (ROB)
Johannisberger Klaus Riesling Spät.,
  Schönborn 1990 £11.90 (JU)
Nackenheimer Rothenberg Rieslng Kab.
  Jean Baptiste, Gunderloch 1995 £10.90
  (JU)
Niederhauser Hermannshöhle Riesling
  Spät., Dönnhoff 1993 £11.95 (JU)
Oberhäuser Leistenberg Riesling Kab.,
  Dönnhoff 1996 £10.20 (JU)
Oppenheimer Herrenberg Scheurebe
  Spät., Guntrum 1993 £11.16 (TW)
Rüdesheimer Bischofberg Halbtrocken
  Riesling Kab., Leitz 1994 £10.95 (ROB)
Schloss Vollrads Riesling Kab., Schloss
  Vollrads 1989 £10.14 (NO)

£12.00 → £14.99

Erbacher Marcobrunnen Riesling Spät.,
  von Simmern 1992 £14.95 (AD)
Forster Jesuitengarten Riesling Spät., von
  Buhl 1997 £13.81 (TW)
Forster Kirchenstück Riesling Spät.,
  Bassermann-Jordan 1996 £14.84 (BIB)

Forster Kirchenstück Riesling Spät.,
Bassermann-Jordan 1994 £13.49 (CON)
£15.16 (TW)
Forster Ungeheuer Riesling Spät.,
Bassermann-Jordan 1986 £13.25 (UB)
Hochheimer Kirchenstück Riesling Spät.,
Domdechant Werner'sches 1994
£12.95 (BER) £13.95 (JU)
Kreuznacher Brückes Riesling Spät., von
Plettenberg 1985 £12.65 (UB)
Niederhäuser Hermannsberg Riesling
Spät., Staatliche Weinbaudomäne 1985
£13.75 (WAT)
Niederhauser Hermannshöhle Riesling
Spät., Dönnhoff 1994 £13.85 (AD)
Niersteiner Oelberg Riesling Aus., Senfter
1990 £14.50 (ROB)
Rauenthaler Baiken Riesling Spät., von
Simmern 1992 £14.95 (AD)
Riesling Kab., Robert Weil 1991 £12.50
(ROB)
Wachenheimer Belz Riesling Aus., J L
Wolf 1996 £12.99 (NI)
Wachenheimer Böhlig Riesling Aus.,
Bürklin-Wolf 1990 £13.95 (DI)
Wachenheimer Gerümpel Riesling Spät.,
Bürklin-Wolf 1989 £13.40 (PIP)
Wachenheimer Gerümpel Riesling Spät., J
L Wolf 1996 £12.20 (NO)
Wallufer Walkenberg Riesling Spät.,
Schönborn 1990 £13.90 (JU)

£15.00 → £19.99

Deidesheimer Hohenmorgen Riesling
Aus., Bassermann-Jordan 1989 £15.50
(CON) £18.90 (JU)
Erbacher Marcobrunn Riesling Spät., von
Simmern 1994 £15.00 (BU)
Erbacher Siegelsberg Riesling Spät.,
Auguste Eser 1994 £15.50 (JU)
Forster Ungeheuer Riesling Aus., von
Buhl 1997 £17.92 (TW)
Geisenheimer Rothenberg Riesling Aus.,
Deinhard 1989 £17.90 (JU)
Hallgartener Schonhell Riesling Spät.,
Lowenstein 1983 £15.40 (UB)

• All prices for each wine are
listed together in ascending
order.
• Price bands refer to the
lowest price for which the
wine is available.

Hochheimer Herrenberg Riesling Aus.,
Nagler 1983 £17.35 (UB)
Niersteiner Hipping Riesling Aus., Balbach
1996 £15.00 (JU)
Oberhäuser Brücke Riesling Aus.,
Dönnhoff 1993 £17.50 (JU)
Schlossbockelheimer Kupfergrube Riesling
Spät., Dönnhoff 1996 £16.00 (JU)
Wachenheimer Mandelgarten Scheurebe
Aus., Bürklin-Wolf 1983 £17.95 (UB)

£20.00 → £24.99

Eltviller Sonnenberg Riesling Aus., J B
Becker 1995 £23.50 (JU)
Nackenheimer Rothenberg Riesling Aus.,
Gunderloch 1995 £22.00 (JU)
Niersteiner Oelberg Eiswein, Balbach ½
bottle 1996 £24.00 (JU)
Schloss Johannisberger Riesling Kab.,
Schloss Johannisberg 1985 £20.50 (NO)
Schloss Vollrads Riesling Kab., Schloss
Vollrads 1971 £22.50 (BU)

Over £25.00

Deidesheimer Hohenmorgen Riesling BA,
Bassermann-Jordan 1994 £110.00 (JU)
Erbacher Marcobrunn Riesling Aus.,
Schönborn 1990 £49.00 (JU)
Forster Jesuitengarten Riesling BA, von
Buhl 1994 £82.25 (TW) £90.00 (JU)
Forster Jesuitengarten Riesling TBA,
Basserman-Jordan 1989 £175.00 (JU)
Forster Kirchenstuck Riesling BA, von
Buhl 1996 £68.00 (JU)
Forster Ungeheuer Riesling Eiswein, von
Buhl 1996 £72.00 (JU)
Geiseneimer Kläuserweg Riesling TBA,
Deinhard 1971 £146.88 (REI)
Grosskarlbacher Burgweg Scheurebe
TBA ½ bottle, Lingenfelder 1985
£50.00 (FORT)
Hochheimer Hölle Riesling BA, Franz
Kunstler ½ bottle 1996 £41.00 (JU)
Hochheimer Reichestal Riesling Eiswein,
Franz Kunstler ½ bottle 1996 £53.00 (JU)
Hochheimer Riesling Aus., Domdechant
Werner's 1994 £25.00 (JU)
Nackenheimer Rothenberg Riesling BA,
Gunderloch ½ bottle 1996 £34.00 (JU)
Niersteiner Pettenthal Riesling BA,
Balbach 1989 £36.00 (JU)
Oberhäuser Brücke Riesling Eiswein,
Dönnhoff ½ bottle 1995 £78.00 (JU)
Wallufer Walkenberg Riesling TBA, J B
Becker 1994 £136.00 (JU)

RHINE RED

Under £7.00

Grosskarlbacher Osterberg Dornfelder
Trocken, Lingenfelder 1993 £6.99 (NI)

Over £10.00

Spätburgunder QbA, Lingenfelder 1996
£10.28 (MON)
Spätburgunder QbA, Lingenfelder 1993
£12.50 (FORT)
Wallufer Walkenberg Spätburgunder Spät.
Trocken, J B Becker 1994 £17.90 (JU)

MOSEL WHITE

£3.00 → £5.99

Deinhard Green Label 1996 £4.39 (WHI)
Ockfener Bockstein Riesling, Dr Wagner
1997 £5.45 (WAI)
Piesporter Michelsberg R Müller 1997
£4.91 (CB)
Piesporter Michelsberg Reh 1998 £3.99
(MAR)
Piesporter Michelsberg Schneider 1996
£3.59 (WHI)

Piesporter Treppchen Riesling Kab., R
Müller 1996 £5.29 (PEN)
Piesporter Treppchen Riesling Kab., R
Müller 1995 £4.64 (GW)
Reiler vom Heissen Stein Kab., R Müller
1997 £4.69 (JON)
Reiler vom Heissen Stein Kab., R Müller
1996 £4.95 (POR)
Riesling Dr 'L', Dr Loosen 1997 £5.99
(YOU)

£6.00 → £7.99

Bernkasteler Badstube Riesling Kab., F-
W-Gymnasium 1996 £7.09 (JON)
Erdener Treppchen Riesling Kab.,
Mönchhof 1989 £7.50 (JU)
Falkensteiner Hofberg Riesling, F-W-
Gymnasium 1991 £6.85 (UB)
Graacher Himmelreich Riesling Kab., F-
W-Gymnasium 1995 £7.49 (JON)
Kaseler Kehrnägel Riesling Trocken,
Bischöfliches Konvikt 1992 £7.85 (UB)
Oberemmeler Hutte Riesling Kab., von
Hövel 1997 £7.35 (WS)
Ockfener Bockstein Riesling Kab., Zilliken
1996 £7.95 (AD)
Ockfener Bockstein Riesling Spät.,
Rheinart 1996 £7.63 (PLA)
Reiler Mullay Hofberg Riesling Spät., R
Müller 1997 £7.99 (CB)
Riesling Dr 'L', Dr Loosen 1998 £6.26 (STE)
Riesling Dr 'L', Dr Loosen 1996 £6.49 (NI)
Riesling, Fritz Haag 1996 £7.95 (JU)
Riesling Kab. Dr 'L', Dr Loosen 1997
£7.95 (ELL)
Riesling Kab. Dr 'L', Dr Loosen 1996
£7.09 (CON) £7.49 (WR) £7.49 (BOT)
Riesling QbA, Dr Loosen 1997 £6.25
(JON) £7.01 (PLAY) £7.12 (NO)
Riesling QbA, Dr Loosen 1996 £7.50 (ROB)
Riesling QbA, Dr Loosen 1995 £6.59 (PHI)
Riesling, Zilliken 1996 £6.95 (JU) £6.99
(YOU)
Saarburger Rausch Riesling Kab., Zilliken
1997 £7.49 (POR) £7.95 (WS)
Scharzhofberger Riesling Kab., Kesselstatt
1995 £7.50 (STA)
Scharzhofberger Riesling Spät., Kesselstatt
1996 £7.95 (SAF)
Serriger Schloss Saarsteiner Riesling Kab.,
Schloss Saarstein 1997 £6.95 (WS)
Urziger Würzgarten Riesling Kab., R
Müller 1992 £6.35 (PEN)
Zeltinger Schlossberg Riesling Kab.,
Selbach-Oster 1991 £7.50 (RAE)

£8.00 → £9.99

Brauneberger Juffer Riesling Kab., Richter
1994 £8.23 (MON)
Erdener Treppchen Riesling Kab., Dr
Loosen 1997 £9.99 (YOU) £10.35 (PIP)
£10.99 (JON)
Erdener Treppchen Riesling Kab.,
Mönchhof 1994 £8.81 (BIB)
Graacher Himmelreich Riesling Kab., J J
Prüm 1992 £9.95 (JU) £12.87 (TW)
Graacher Himmelreich Riesling Spät., F-
W-Gymnasium 1995 £9.99 (JON)
Graacher Himmelreich Riesling Spät., Max
Ferd Richter 1996 £9.95 (FORT)
Josephshofer Riesling Spät., Kesselstatt
1989 £9.50 (JU)
Maximin-Grünhäuser Abtsberg Riesling,
Schubert 1992 £9.95 (JU)
Ockfener Bockstein Riesling Kab., Zilliken
1997 £9.35 (LAY)
Ockfener Bockstein Riesling Spät., Dr
Fischer 1989 £9.00 (JU)
Riesling Kab., J J Prüm 1996 £9.99 (YOU)
Riesling Spät. Dr 'L', Dr Loosen 1997
£9.27 (STE) £10.30 (NA)
Riesling Spät. Dr 'L', Dr Loosen 1996
£8.95 (CON)
Saarburger Rausch Riesling Kab., Zilliken
1994 £8.90 (JU)
Scharzhofberger Riesling Spät., Kesselstatt
1994 £9.99 (NI)
Trittenheimer Apotheke Riesling Spät., F-
W-Gymnasium 1995 £9.95 (POR)
Urziger Wurzgarten Riesling Spät.,
Mönchhof 1990 £9.95 (JU)
Wehlener Sonnenuhr Riesling Aus., Dr
Loosen 1997 £9.33 (NO)
Wehlener Sonnenuhr Riesling Kab., Dr
Loosen 1996 £9.79 (CON) £9.95 (WRI)
£9.99 (REI) £12.99 (PHI)
Wehlener Sonnenuhr Riesling Kab., J J
Prüm 1996 £8.95 (WRI) £13.92 (REI)
£15.04 (TW)
Wehlener Sonnenuhr Riesling Kab.,
Richter 1991 £8.32 (MON)

Please remember that
Oz Clarke's Wine Guide
*is a price **guide** and not a*
*price **list**. It is not meant to*
replace up-to-date
merchants' lists.

Wehlener Sonnenuhr Riesling Kab.,
Weins Prüm 1995 £8.95 (COC)
Wehlener Sonnenuhr Riesling Spät., Licht-
Bergweiler 1989 £9.00 (JU)
Wiltinger Braune Kupp Riesling Kab.,
Egon Müller 1990 £9.95 (JU)

£10.00 → £11.99

Brauneberger Juffer Sonnenuhr Riesling
Spät., Fritz Haag 1996 £11.99 (RAE)
£13.50 (JU)
Brauneberger Juffer Sonnenuhr Riesling
Spät., H Thanisch 1994 £10.79 (UN)
Eitelsbacher Karthäuserhofberg Riesling
Kab., Karthäuserhof 1997 £10.20 (TAN)
£10.58 (MON)
Erdener Treppchen Riesling Kab., Dr
Loosen 1996 £10.95 (BER)
Graacher Himmelreich Riesling Kab., J J
Prüm 1994 £10.95 (JU)
Graacher Himmelreich Riesling Spät., F-
W-Gymnasium 1990 £10.10 (AV)
£10.49 (YOU) £13.75 (ROB)
Josephshofer Riesling Spät., Kesselstatt
1995 £10.95 (STA)
Maximin-Grünhäuser Abtsberg Riesling
Kab., Schubert 1996 £11.90 (JU) £15.86
(REI)
Piesporter Goldtröpfchen Riesling Spät.,
Haart 1996 £11.50 (JU)
Piesporter Goldtröpfchen Riesling Spät.,
Kesselstatt 1996 £10.95 (STA)
Scharzhofberger Riesling Spät., von Hövel
1995 £10.55 (AV)
Serriger Schloss Saarsteiner Riesling Spät.,
Schloss Saarstein 1997 £10.97 (MON)
Urziger Wurzgarten Riesling Spät.,
Mönchhof 1995 £11.50 (JU)
Wehlener Sonnenuhr Riesling Kab., Dr
Loosen 1997 £11.16 (PLAY)
Wehlener Sonnenuhr Riesling Kab., J J
Prüm 1993 £11.50 (JU) £16.45 (ROB)
Wehlener Sonnenuhr Riesling Spät., Dr
Loosen 1996 £10.29 (JON)

£12.00 → £14.99

Brauneberger Juffer Riesling Aus., Richter
1985 £14.00 (FORT)
Brauneberger Juffer Sonnenuhr Riesling
Aus., Fritz Haag 1992 £13.99 (RAE)
Brauneberger Juffer Sonnenuhr Riesling
Spät., Fritz Haag 1995 £14.20 (LAY)
£15.00 (JU)
Eitelsbacher Karthäuserhofberg Riesling
Aus., Karthäuserhof 1997 £13.22 (MON)

Enkircher Batterieberg Riesling Spät.
Halbtrocken, Immich-Batterieberg
1994 £13.95 (AD)

Erdener Treppchen Riesling Spät., Dr
Loosen **1994** £14.82 (NO)

Graacher Domprobst Riesling Aus.,
Richter **1997** £13.71 (MON)

Graacher Himmelreich Riesling Spät., J J
Prüm **1994** £13.45 (WAI)

Kaseler Kehrnagel Riesling Aus., Simon
1983 £13.75 (WAT)

Kaseler Nies'chen Riesling Aus.,
Kesselstatt **1989** £13.10 (UB)

Maximin-Grünhäuser Abtsberg Riesling
Kab., Schubert **1997** £12.95 (AD)

Maximin-Grünhäuser Abtsberg Riesling
Spät., Schubert **1996** £13.69 (LAY)

Maximin-Grünhäuser Abtsberg Riesling
Spät., Schubert **1988** £14.96 (CB)
£19.95 (ROB)

Maximin-Grünhäuser Herrenberg Riesling
Kab., Schubert **1994** £12.75 (CB)

Piesporter Goldtröpfchen Riesling Spät.,
Haart **1995** £13.90 (JU)

Scharzhofberger Riesling Aus., Kesselstatt
1995 £13.02 (GW)

Scharzhofberger Riesling Kab. Fuder 21,
Egon Müller **1994** £13.90 (JU)

Scharzhofberger Riesling Kab., Egon
Müller **1996** £13.15 (HAH)

Scharzhofberger Riesling Spät., Egon
Müller **1996** £14.50 (FORT) £15.60
(HAH) £15.95 (JU)

Serriger Herrenberg Riesling Aus., Simon
1983 £13.99 (WAT)

Wehlener Sonnenuhr Riesling Kab.,
Weins Prüm **1993** £13.95 (UB)

Wehlener Sonnenuhr Riesling Spät., Dr
Loosen **1995** £12.99 (YOU)

Wiltinger Braune Kupp Riesling Spät.,
Mönchhof **1990** £14.50 (JU)

Zeltinger Sonnenuhr Riesling Aus.,
Selbach-Oster **1996** £14.50 (RAE)
£17.00 (MV)

Zeltinger Sonnenuhr Riesling Spät.,
Selbach-Oster **1995** £12.00 (MV) £12.50
(FORT)

£15.00 → £19.99

Bernkasteler Badstube Riesling Spät., J J
Prüm **1990** £17.51 (TW)

Bernkasteler Doctor Riesling Kab., H
Thanisch **1996** £19.29 (UN)

Bernkasteler Doctor Riesling Spät., H
Thanisch **1997** £16.99 (WAI)

Brauneberger Juffer Sonnenuhr Riesling
Aus., Fritz Haag **1995** £15.99 (RAE)
£18.20 (LAY) £19.50 (JU)

Eitelsbacher Karthäuserhofberg Riesling
Aus., Karthäuserhof **1995** £19.50 (JU)

Erdener Treppchen Riesling Aus.,
Mönchhof **1990** £15.66 (BIB)

Graacher Himmelreich Riesling Spät., J J
Prüm **1995** £18.33 (TW)

Graacher Himmelreich Riesling Spät., J J
Prüm **1985** £17.50 (FORT)

Kaseler Nies'chen Riesling Aus.
Goldkapsul, Bischöfliches
Priesterseminar **1989** £18.50 (JU)

Maximin-Grünhäuser Abtsberg Riesling
Spät., Schubert **1993** £16.00 (WS)

Maximin-Grünhäuser Abtsberg Riesling
Aus., Schubert **1996** £18.40 (LAY)
£21.00 (JU)

Maximin-Grünhäuser Abtsberg Riesling
Aus., Schubert **1992** £19.95 (AD)

Maximin-Grünhäuser Herrenberg Riesling
Aus., Schubert **1995** £18.00 (RAE)

Scharzhofberger Riesling Kab., Egon
Müller **1989** £16.95 (ROB)

Scharzhofberger Riesling Spät. Fuder 17,
Egon Müller **1993** £17.50 (JU)

Urziger Würzgarten Riesling Aus., Dr
Loosen **1997** £17.99 (YOU)

Urziger Würzgarten Riesling Aus., Dr
Loosen **1996** £18.25 (CON)

Urziger Würzgarten Riesling Kab., Dr
Loosen **1996** £15.95 (AD)

Urziger Würzgarten Riesling Spät., Dr
Loosen **1996** £15.99 (NI) £17.99 (JON)

Wehlener Sonnenuhr Riesling Aus., Dr
Loosen **1995** £18.68 (NO)

Wehlener Sonnenuhr Riesling Aus., S A
Prüm-Erben **1989** £19.50 (DI)

Wehlener Sonnenuhr Riesling Aus., J J
Prüm **1993** £15.00 (WS) £18.00 (JU)

Wehlener Sonnenuhr Riesling Spät., J J
Prüm **1995** £16.50 (JU) £20.27 (TW)

£20.00 → £29.99

Bernkasteler Doctor Riesling Aus.,
Deinhard **1990** £21.76 (PLAY)

Bernkasteler Doctor Riesling Spät., H
Thanisch **1989** £26.00 (JU) £28.79 (REI)

Brauneberger Juffer Sonnenuhr Riesling
Aus. Fuder 11, Fritz Haag **1994** £23.00
(JU)

Brauneberger Juffer Sonnenuhr Riesling
Aus. Goldkapsul Fuder 4, Fritz Haag
1989 £28.00 (JU)

Brauneberger Juffer Sonnenuhr Riesling
Aus. Goldkapsul, Fritz Haag 1996
£24.99 (RAE)

Eitelsbacher Karthäuserhofberg Riesling
Aus. Fuder 30, Karthäuserhof 1995
£23.00 (JU)

Erdener Prälat Riesling Aus., Dr Loosen
1997 £24.99 (YOU)

Erdener Treppchen Riesling Aus., Dr
Loosen 1995 £25.55 (AV) £27.49 (NO)

Graacher Himmelreich Riesling Aus., J J
Prüm 1995 £21.03 (TW)

Maximin-Grünhäuser Abtsberg Riesling
Aus., Schubert 1990 £28.79 (REI)
£29.50 (ROB)

Maximin-Grünhäuser Abtsberg Riesling
Aus. Fuder 117, Schubert ½ bottle
1995 £24.00 (JU)

Maximin-Grünhäuser Herrenberg Riesling
Aus., Schubert 1994 £28.50 (FORT)

Mulheimer Helenenkloster Riesling
Eiswein, Richter ½ bottle 1995 £25.26
(MON) £30.00 (FORT)

Piesporter Goldtröpfchen Riesling Aus.,
Haart 1994 £24.50 (JU)

Saarburger Rausch Riesling Aus., Zilliken
1995 £21.00 (JU)

Scharzhofberger Riesling Spät., Egon
Müller 1991 £26.15 (UB)

Urziger Würzgarten Riesling Aus., Dr
Loosen 1995 £22.91 (NO)

Wehlener Sonnenuhr Riesling Aus., J J
Prüm 1996 £25.26 (REI)

Zeltinger Sonnenuhr Riesling Aus.,
Selbach-Oster 1997 £21.00 (MV)

£30.00 → £59.99

Bernkasteler Doctor Riesling Aus.,
Bergweiler 1985 £57.00 (UB)

Eitelsbacher Karthäuserhofberg Riesling
Eiswein, Karthäuserhof ½ bottle 1995
£49.00 (JU)

Erdener Prälat Riesling Aus. Goldkapsul,
Dr Loosen 1995 £34.83 (NO)

Erdener Treppchen Riesling Aus.
Goldkapsul, Dr Loosen 1994 £50.71
(NO)

Maximin-Grünhäuser Abtsberg Riesling
Aus. Fuder 96, Schubert 1989 £47.00 (JU)

Maximin-Grünhäuser Herrenberg Riesling
Aus., Schubert 1976 £40.00 (CRO)

Mulheimer Helenenkloster Riesling Eiswein,
Richter ½ bottle 1993 £49.50 (UB)

Piesporter Goldtröpfchen Riesling Aus.
Goldkapsul, Haart 1995 £37.00 (JU)

Scharzhofberger Aus. Fuder 29, Egon
Müller 1990 £59.00 (JU)

Scharzhofberger Riesling Aus. Fuder 20,
Egon Müller 1993 £59.00 (JU)

Wehlener Sonnenuhr Riesling Aus.
Goldkapsul, J J Prüm 1995 £43.00 (JU)
£55.87 (TW)

Over £60.00

Bernkasteler Doctor Riesling Aus., H
Thanisch 1989 £98.00 (JU)

Bernkasteler Graben Riesling Eiswein,
Deinhard ½ bottle 1959 £70.50 (REI)

Brauneberger Juffer Sonnenuhr Riesling
BA, Fritz Haag 1995 £120.00 (JU)

Eitelsbacher Marienholz Riesling Eiswein,
Bischöfliches Konvikt 1989 £85.00 (JU)

Maximin-Grünhäuser Abtsberg Riesling
BA, Schubert 1995 £80.00 (RAE)

Maximin-Grünhäuser Abtsberg Riesling
Eiswein, Schubert 1993 £180.00 (JU)

Maximin-Grünhäuser Abtsberg Riesling
BA, Schubert 1989 £220.00 (JU)

Maximin-Grünhäuser Abtsberg TBA,
Schubert 1995 £200.00 (RAE)

Maximin-Grünhäuser Herrenberg Riesling
Aus., Schubert 1989 £65.00 (UB)

Maximin-Grünhäuser Herrenberg Riesling
BA, Schubert 1995 £71.00 (RAE)

Maximin-Grünhäuser Herrenberg Riesling
TBA, Schubert 1989 £330.00 (JU)

Ockfener Bockstein Riesling BA, Fischer
1989 £70.00 (JU)

Ockfener Bockstein Riesling Eiswein,
Fischer 1989 £85.00 (JU)

Scharzhofberger Riesling Aus. Goldkapsul
Fuder 23, Egon Müller 1993 £140.00 (JU)

Urziger Würzgarten Riesling TBA,
Mönchhof ½ bottle 1994 £165.00 (JU)

Wehlener Sonnenuhr BA, J J Prüm 1971
£88.13 (REI)

OTHER GERMAN WHITE

c. £8.00

Schloss Castell Silvaner Trocken, Fürstlich
Castell'sches Domänenamt 1995 £7.95
(TAN)

GERMAN SPARKLING

c. £8.00

Henkell Trocken **Non-vintage** £7.69 (UN)

ITALY

Don't despise Soave and its brethren: they may not taste of upfront fruit and spice, but there's a lot to be said for subtlety

I want to think for a moment about Italy's most neutral whites. Why? Why should anyone want to spend more than a nanosecond on Soave? Isn't it the most boring joke wine ever created, fit only for those who daren't tackle anything invented in the last 20 years? Not in my book, it isn't. Well, some is. Not all.

There are times when a break from new oak and tropical fruit can be just what you want – times when you want something light, refreshing, not too assertive. The sort of wine that murmurs 'Oh, you're so right' as it goes down, rather than the sort that argues the whole way. But of course this sort of wine must be from a very good

grower: if a wine is going to agree with you, you have to make sure you respect its credentials. And, you know, some Soave is just wonderful. Subtle, with considerable depth, and if you pick a top single-vineyard wine, remarkable aging ability. I had a ten-year old single-vineyard Soave recently, and it was just sensational.

Verdicchio's another. Clean, leafy, nutty – Waitrose has a nice one. Frascati fits the bill when it's fresh – it has a terrific sour-milk tang – but it seems to suffer from staleness problems all too often. Orvieto I find it harder to get excited about, and Lugana's a bit four-square. But one can't have everything. Wouldn't you agree?

GRAPE VARIETIES

AGLIANICO (red) A southern grape at its most impressive in Aglianico del Vulture (Basilicata) and Taurasi (Campania).

BARBERA (red) The most prolific grape of the North-West, with high acidity and a sweet-sour, raisiny taste or even a brown-sugar sweetness. Some are lighter but intensely fruity. The grape does best in the Langhe hills around Alba in the hands of *Altare, Conterno-Fantino, Aldo Conterno, Gaja.*

BONARDA (red) Low acid, rich, plummy reds, often with a liquoricy, chocolaty streak. It's found most often in Emilia-Romagna where it is blended with Barbera as Gutturnio; also found in the Oltrepò Pavese.

CABERNET FRANC (red) Fairly widely grown in the North-East of Italy, especially in Alto Adige, Trentino, Veneto and Friuli. It can make gorgeous grassy, yet juicy-fruited reds – wines that are easy to drink young but also capable of aging.

CABERNET SAUVIGNON (red) Still important in the North-East and Tuscany, but no longer seen as a universal panacea. Check out new Bordeaux-inspired *Tassinaia* and *Lupicaia* from *Tenuta del Terriccio.*

CANNONAU (red) Sardinian name for Grenache. Makes warm, full-blooded wine, sometimes DOC, usually inexpensive. Look for *Argiolas, Giuseppe Gabbas, Giggi Picciau, Meloni, Sella & Mosca, Tonino Arcadu.*

CHARDONNAY (white) The typical Italian style is unoaked: lean, floral and sharply balanced from the Alto Adige, more neutral from elsewhere. Try *Zeni* (Trentino) and *Gradnik* (Friuli). Oak-aged styles can be spicy and exciting, or just overoaked. Try *Gaja, Marchesi di Gresy* and *Pio Cesare* in Piedmont, *Zanella* in Lombardy, *Maculan* in the Veneto and *Caparzo (Le Grance)* and *Avignonesi (Il Marzocco)* in Tuscany. Many vary from year to year, and producers don't all have their winemaking sorted out.

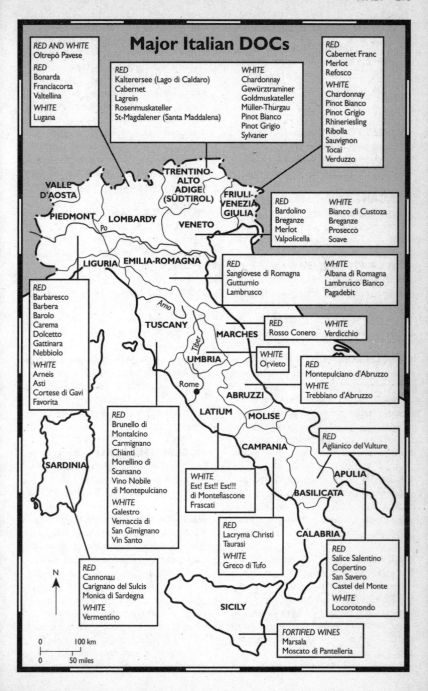

Major Italian DOCs

RED AND WHITE
Oltrepò Pavese

RED
Bonarda
Franciacorta
Valtellina

WHITE
Lugana

RED
Kalterersee (Lago di Caldaro)
Cabernet
Lagrein
Rosenmuskateller
St-Magdalener (Santa Maddalena)

WHITE
Chardonnay
Gewürztraminer
Goldmuskateller
Müller-Thurgau
Pinot Bianco
Pinot Grigio
Sylvaner

RED
Cabernet Franc
Merlot
Refosco

WHITE
Chardonnay
Pinot Bianco
Pinot Grigio
Rhineriesling
Ribolla
Sauvignon
Tocai
Verduzzo

VALLE
D'AOSTA

TRENTINO-
ALTO
ADIGE
(SÜDTIROL)

FRIULI-
VENEZIA
GIULIA

PIEDMONT   LOMBARDY

Po

VENETO

LIGURIA   EMILIA-ROMAGNA

RED
Bardolino
Breganze
Merlot
Valpolicella

WHITE
Bianco di Custoza
Breganze
Prosecco
Soave

RED
Sangiovese di Romagna
Gutturnio
Lambrusco

WHITE
Albana di Romagna
Lambrusco Bianco
Pagadebit

Arno

TUSCANY   MARCHES

RED
Rosso Conero

WHITE
Verdicchio

RED
Barbaresco
Barbera
Barolo
Carema
Dolcetto
Gattinara
Nebbiolo

WHITE
Arneis
Asti
Cortese di Gavi
Favorita

Tiber

UMBRIA

WHITE
Orvieto

RED
Montepulciano d'Abruzzo

WHITE
Trebbiano d'Abruzzo

Rome

ABRUZZI

LATIUM   MOLISE

RED
Brunello di
Montalcino
Carmignano
Chianti
Morellino di
Scansano
Vino Nobile
di Montepulciano

WHITE
Galestro
Vernaccia di
San Gimignano
Vin Santo

CAMPANIA

RED
Aglianico del Vulture

SARDINIA

WHITE
Est! Est!! Est!!!
di Montefiascone
Frascati

APULIA

BASILICATA

RED
Lacryma Christi
Taurasi

WHITE
Greco di Tufo

CALABRIA

RED
Salice Salentino
Copertino
San Savero
Castel del Monte

WHITE
Locorotondo

N

RED
Cannonau
Carignano del Sulcis
Monica di Sardegna

WHITE
Vermentino

SICILY

FORTIFIED WINES
Marsala
Moscato di Pantelleria

0   100 km

0   50 miles

ON THE CASE
Don't confuse Vino Nobile di Montepulciano with Montepulciano d'Abruzzo: the first is one of the priciest reds in Italy, the second one of the cheapest

DOLCETTO (red) Usually light and refreshing with a bitter-cherry twist, though some producers in Alba, notably *Mascarello*, make it with attitude. Only age the best.

GARGANEGA (white) The principal grape of Soave, soft yet green-apple fresh when well made. Too much characterless Trebbiano Toscano spoils cheaper blends.

GEWÜRZTRAMINER (white) Most plantings are of the less flavoursome Traminer, rather than the spicier, more memorable Gewürztraminer of Alsace. Lovely at its best, needing some time in bottle to develop perfume.

GRECO/GRECHETTO (white) Greco makes crisp, pale and refreshing wines with lightly spicy overtones in the South. Grechetto is part of the same family and its delicious, nutty, aniseed character adds dramatically to Trebbiano-dominated blends in central Italy. It sometimes surfaces under its own colours in Umbria: try *Adanti*.

LAGREIN (red) Local grape of the Alto Adige and Trentino, making delicious, dark reds, strongly plum-sweet when young, aging slowly to a smoky, creamy softness. It also makes a good rosé, Lagrein Kretzer.

MALVASIA (white) This name and Malvoisie apply to a range of grape varieties, some not related. Malvasia is found mostly in Tuscany, Umbria and Latium, giving a full, creamy nuttiness to dry whites like Frascati. It also produces brilliant, rich dessert wines with the density of thick brown-sugar syrup and the sweetness of raisins in Sardinia and the islands of Lipari north of Sicily.

MERLOT (red) Widely planted in the North-East. Often good in Friuli; provides lots of jug wine in the Veneto but when blended with Cabernet Sauvignon by *Loredan Gasparini* (Venegazzù) or *Fausto Maculan* (Trentino) achieves greater stature. Other Cabernet/Merlot blends are produced by *Mecvini* in the Marches and Trentino's *Bossi Fedrigotti* (Foianeghe). *Avignonesi* and *Castello di Ama* in Tuscany are promising, while *Ornellaia*'s *Masseto* (also Tuscany) is outstanding. It is becoming extremely fashionable.

MONTEPULCIANO (red) A much underrated grape. Yes, it is tough, and yes it is tannic, but it also has lots of plummy, herby fruit behind that toughness. *Banfi* in Montalcino has high hopes for it.

MOSCATO (white) The Alto Adige has various Muscats, including Rosenmuskateller and Goldmuskateller, making dry wines to equal the Muscats of Alsace and sweet ones of unrivalled fragrance. But it is at its best in Piedmont with the delicious, grapy, sweetish fizz, Asti, and Moscato Naturale, a heartily perfumed sweet wine. Moscato is best young, but *Ivaldi*'s Passito from Strevi can age beautifully. It also makes fine dessert wines on the island of Pantelleria, near Sicily.

MÜLLER-THURGAU (white) On the high, steep Alpine vineyards of the Alto Adige this can produce glacier-fresh flavours; not bad in Trentino and Friuli too.

NEBBIOLO (red) The big, tough grape of the North-West, making – unblended – the famous Barolos and Barbarescos as well as Gattinara, Ghemme, Carema, Spanna and plain Nebbiolo. This is a surly, fierce grape, producing wines that can be dark, chewy, unyielding and harsh behind a shield of tannin and acidity for the first few years; but which then blossom out into a remarkable richness full of chocolate, raisins, prunes, and an austere perfume of tobacco, pine and herbs. The newer style still has a fairly hefty whack of tannin, but clever wine-making sheaths this in sleek and velvety fruit. These are ready much sooner. A few growers (*Altare*, *Clerico*, *Conterno-Fantino* and *Voerzio*) are producing some superb vini da tavola by aging their wine in barriques, or blending it with Barbera, or both, as in *Sebaste*'s *Briccoviole*.

PINOT BIANCO (white) Produces some of its purest, honeyed flavours in the Alto Adige, and can do very well in Friuli where the best are buttery and full.

RHEINRIESLING/RIESLING RENANO (white) The true German Riesling is grown in the Alto Adige for sharp, green, refreshing, steely dry wines. It can be OK, and slightly fatter, in Friuli and Lombardy. Riesling Italico, nothing to do with real Riesling, is the lesser Olasz/Laski/Welsch Rizling, still good if it's fresh.

SANGIOVESE (red) The mainstay of Chianti and all the other major Tuscan DOCGs. The wines have in common an austere, tea-like edge balanced by rich fruit. But the grape changes character when planted in the cool hills of Chianti, the warm clay soil of the coastal strip or the arid slopes of Montalcino. This sensitivity also explains why many vineyards in Chianti Classico don't produce the quality they should: the soil is too rich, the slopes too gentle and the density of planting too high. This is the lesson people are now learning.

SAUVIGNON BLANC (white) Spicy, grassy and refreshing from the Alto Adige and Friuli, though the style is usually more subtle than New World Sauvignon. Try *Avignonesi*, *Banfi*, *Castellare* and *Volpaia*.

SCHIAVA (red) Light reds with a unique taste that veers between smoked ham and strawberries. It's found in the Alto Adige, where the locals call it Vernatsch.

SYLVANER (white) Grown very high in the northern valleys of the Alto Adige, at its best this is dry, lemon-crisp and delicious.

TREBBIANO (white) Trebbiano Toscano is a wretched thing: easy to grow, yielding mountains of grapes which go into an awful lot of fruitless, oxidized, sulphured wine. Trebbiano di Soave, the Veneto clone, is much better. Lugana can be a Trebbiano DOC of character (*Zenato*'s is good). Abruzzi's strain *can* be tasty from *Pepe*, *Tenuta del Priore* and *Valentini*.

VERNACCIA (white) We mostly just see two types of Vernaccia. In Sardinia Vernaccia di Oristano is a sort of Italian sherry, best dry – when it has a marvellous mix of floral scents, nutty weight and taunting sourness – but also medium and sweet. Vernaccia di San Gimignano *can* be Tuscany's best traditional white – full, golden, peppery but with a softness of hazelnuts and angelica. *Fagiuoli* and *Teruzzi & Puthod* show what can be done.

WINE REGIONS

AGLIANICO DEL VULTURE, DOC (Basilicata; red) Superb, thick-flavoured red from gaunt Monte Vulture, in the wilds of Italy's 'instep'. The colour isn't particularly deep, but the tremendous almond paste and chocolate fruit is matched by a tough, dusty feel and quite high acidity. What's more, it's *not* very expensive. *Fratelli d'Angelo* (especially barriqued *Canneto d'Angelo*) and *Paternoster* are both good.

ALBANA DI ROMAGNA, DOCG (Emilia-Romagna; white) Can be dry or sweet, still or slightly fizzy, or very fizzy, and usually uninspiring. At its best, the dry version can be delicately scented with an almondy finish. The only good producers are *Fattoria Paradiso* and *Zerbina*.

ALTO ADIGE various **DOCs** (red, white, rosé) Wines from these dizzily steep slopes are much more Germanic than Italian. The reds are attractive light wines made from the Vernatsch/Schiava grape, especially Kalterersee and St Magdalener. Cabernet, Pinot Nero, Lagrein and the tea-rose-scented Rosenmuskateller all make reds – and rosés – with stuffing and personality. Whites are light, dry and intensely fresh wines with spice and plenty of fruit, providing the producers haven't been too greedy about yields, which some of them are. Best: *Castello Schwanburg, Haas, Hofstätter, Lageder, Tiefenbrunner, Walch,* and *St Michael-Eppan, Schreckbichl* and *Terlan* co-ops.

ARNEIS (Piedmont; white) Potentially stunning, apples-pears-and-liquorice-flavoured wines from an ancient white grape of the same name, with high prices to match. They have something of the structure of dry Mosel Riesling. Best producers: *Arneis di Montebertotto* by *Castello di Neive, Deltetto, Bruno Giacosa, Malvirà, Negro, Vietti, Voerzio.*

ASTI, DOCG (Piedmont; white) At its best it's wonderfully frothy, fruit-bursting young wine. Go for *Canelli, Cantina Duca d'Asti, Martini, Elio Perrone, Santo Stefano,* and don't even think of aging it.

BARBARESCO, DOCG (Piedmont; red) Toughness and tannin are the hallmarks of the Nebbiolo, Barbaresco's only grape, but there's also a delicious soft, strawberryish maturity, edged with smoke, herbs and pine. Expect more softness and finesse than in Barolo. Best: *Luigi Bianco, Castello di Neive, Cigliuti, Giuseppe Cortese, Gaja, Bruno Giacosa, Glicine, Marchesi di Gresy, Moresco, Pasquero, Pelissero, Pertinace, Pio Cesare, Produttori del Barbaresco, Roagna, Scarpa, La Spinona* and *Vietti.*

BARBERA, DOC (Piedmont and others; red) Italy's second most widely planted red vine after Sangiovese makes a good, gutsy wine, usually with a resiny, herby bite, insistent acidity and forthright, dry raisin sort of fruit. It is best in Piedmont as Barbera d'Alba or d'Asti, and also in Lombardy under the Oltrepò Pavese DOC.

BARDOLINO, DOC (Veneto; red, rosé) Pale-pinky reds with a frail, wispy cherry

ITALIAN CLASSIFICATIONS

Little more than 13 per cent of the massive Italian wine harvest comes under the heading of DOC or DOCG, and the regulations are treated in a fairly cavalier manner by many growers. Some producers choose to operate outside the regulations and classify their – frequently exceptional – wine simply as vino da tavola, the lowest grade. A new law means that more of these will come under the DOC umbrella.

Vino da Tavola   This currently applies to absolutely basic stuff but also to maverick wines of the highest class such as Gaja's Piedmontese Chardonnay.

Indicazione Geografiche Tipici (or IGT for short)   This applies to wines which are typical of their regions, but which do not qualify for DOC. It is equivalent to vin de pays.

Denominazione di Origine Controllata (DOC)   This applies to wines from specified grape varieties, grown in delimited zones and aged by prescribed methods. Most of Italy's traditionally well-known wines are DOC, but more are added every year.

Denominazione di Origine Controllata e Garantita (DOCG)   The top tier – a tighter form of DOC with more stringent restrictions on grape types, yields and a tasting panel. The new law is supposed to give recognition to particularly good vineyard sites.

fruit and a slight bitter snap to the finish. There are also a few fuller, rounder wines like *Boscaini's Le Canne* which can take some aging. Also *Arvedi d'Emilei, Cavalchina, Gardoni, Guerrieri-Rizzardi, Lenotti, Masi* (*Fresco* and *La Vegrona*), *Portalupi, Le Vigne di San Pietro, Zeni*.

BAROLO, DOCG (Piedmont; red) The remarkable flavours of the Nebbiolo – plums and cherries, tobacco and chocolate, liquorice and violets – whirl like a maelstrom in the best wines. The modernization of wine-making has accentuated these flavours, and made wines that are drinkable in five years rather than 20.

Producers are fighting for official classification of the top sites: single vineyard wines can be the absolute best (and absolute most expensive) but because anyone's free to put any old vineyard on, standards are not consistent. Best producers: *Altare, Azelia, Borgogno, Bovio, Brovia, Cavallotto, Ceretto, Clerico, Aldo* and *Giacomo Conterno, Conterno-Fantino, Cordero di Montezemolo, Fontanafredda* (only its *cru* wines), *Bruno Giacosa, Marcarini, Bartolo* and *Giuseppe Mascarello, Pio Cesare, Pira, Prunotto, Ratti, Rocche dei Manzoni, Sandrone, Scarpa, Scavino, Sebaste, Vajra, Vietti* and *Voerzio* (*Roberto* and *Gianni*).

BIANCO DI CUSTOZA, DOC (Veneto; white) A Soave lookalike, though generally better. *Gorgo, Portalupi, Santa Sofia, Tedeschi, Le Tende, Le Vigne di San Pietro, Zenato* are good.

BOLGHERI, DOC (Tuscany; red, white, rosé) A DOC for all colours, including reds based on Cabernet, Merlot or Sangiovese in various combinations, and even a special category for *Sassicaia*, previously a vino da tavola. It has intense Cabernet character but higher acidity and slightly leaner profile than most New World Cabernets. It needs eight to ten years to approach its best. 1990, '92, '94 and '96 are excellent. Pre-1994 vintages are labelled as vino da tavola.

BREGANZE, DOC (Veneto; red, white) Little-known but quite good wines from near Vicenza. *Maculan* is best, and makes a stunning dessert wine, *Torcolato*.

BRUNELLO DI MONTALCINO, DOCG (Tuscany; red) A big, strong neighbour of Chianti. In the right hands it can achieve an amazing combination of flavours: blackberries, raisins, pepper, acidity, tannin and a haunting sandalwood perfume, all bound together by the austere richness of liquorice and fierce black chocolate. Tops: *Altesino, Argiano, Biondi Santi, Campogiovanni, Caparzo, Casanova, Case Basse, Il Casello, Castelgiocondo, Col d'Orcia, Colombini, Costanti, Il Greppone Mazzi, Pertimali, Poggio Antico, Il Poggione, Sassetti, Talenti, Val di Suga, Villa Banfi*. Barbaresco star *Angelo Gaja* has been here since 1994.

CAREMA, DOC (Piedmont; red) The most refined of the Nebbiolo wines. *Luigi Ferrando* is the best producer; the wines need five to six years to be at their best.

CARMIGNANO, DOCG (Tuscany; red) A small enclave inside the Chianti zone where the soft, clear blackcurranty fruit of Cabernet Sauvignon makes a delicious blend with the somewhat stark flavours of the Sangiovese. There is also some good toasty, creamy rosé and some sweet *vin santo*. *Capezzana* is the original estate and the only one which is regularly seen here.

CHIANTI, DOCG and CHIANTI CLASSICO, DOCG (Tuscany; red) There are two basic styles of Chianti. The first is the sharp young red with a rather attractive taste: almost a tiny bit sour, but backed up by good, raisiny-sweet fruit, a rather stark, peppery bite and tobacco-like spice. The second type has usually been matured for several years. Expect a range of slightly raw strawberry, raspberry and blackcurrant flavours backed up by a herby, tobaccoey spice and a grapeskins roughness that is demanding but exciting. Chianti

Classico's separate DOCG allows for pure Sangiovese wines, should the producer wish, thus potentially bringing many SuperTuscans back into the fold. Not many seem to want to come. Best: *Badia a Coltibuono, Castellare, Castell'in Villa, Castello di Ama, Castello dei Rampolla, Castello di San Polo in Rosso, Castello di Volpaia, Felsina Berardenga, Fontodi, Monsanto, Montesodi* and *Nipozzano (Frescobaldi), Isole e Olena, Pagliarese, Riserva Tenute del Marchese* and *Peppoli* (both *Antinori*), *Riecine, San Felice, Selvapiana, Vecchie Terre di Montefili, Vicchiomaggio, Villa di Vetrice.*

The Chianti territory is divided into seven sub-zones: Classico, Colli Aretini, Colli Fiorentini, Colli Senesi, Colline Pisane, Montalbano and Rufina. Most wines, however, are simply labelled 'Chianti'.

COLLI EUGANEI, DOC (Veneto; red, white) *Vignalta* produces a Cabernet Riserva and Merlot-based *Gemola* of good concentration.

COPERTINO, DOC (Apulia; red) The blend of Negroamaro and Malvasia Nera produces robust reds that can be elegant, and great bargains. Try the *Copertino* co-op.

DOLCETTO, some **DOC** (Piedmont; red) At its best, delicious. It's a full but soft, fresh, and dramatically fruity red, usually for gulping down fast and young, though some will age. The sub-regions of Asti and Acqui tend to produce the lightest. *Altare, Castello di Neive, Clerico, Aldo Conterno, Giacomo Conterno, Marcarini, Mascarello, Oddero, Pasquero, Prunotto, Ratti, Sandrone, Scavino, Vajra, Vietti* and *Voerzio* are wonderful.

ERBALUCE DI CALUSO, DOC (Piedmont; white) Half the price of Gavi, with a soft, creamy flavour. *Boratto, Ferrando* and *Marbelli* are good; *Boratto* also makes a rich but refreshing Caluso Passito.

FIANO DI AVELLINO, DOC (Campania; white) Inexplicably famous,

though *Mastroberardino*'s single-vineyard *Vignadora* has a brilliant spring flowers scent and honey, peaches and pearskins taste.

FRANCIACORTA, DOCG (Lombardy; red, white) Champagne method fizz made from Pinots Bianco and Nero and Chardonnay grapes. Best are *Bellavista* and *Ca' del Bosco*, though *Cavalleri, Monte Rosa, Ricci Curbastro* and *Uberti* are also recommended. The DOC of Terre di Franciacorta makes fine still white from Pinot and Chardonnay, and tasty red.

FRASCATI, DOC (Latium; white) Most is bland and stale, though the best has a lovely, fresh, nutty feel with an attractive tang of slightly sour cream. *Colli di Catone, Villa Catone* and *Villa Romana* are reliable. Or try *Fontana Candida*'s limited releases, *San Marco's Racemo* and *Villa Simone.*

FRIULI, some **DOC** (red, white) Six different zones, of which Friuli Grave DOC produces the most. The reds are marked by vibrant fruit. Refosco has a memorable taste in the tar-and-plums mould – sharpened up with a fresh grassy acidity. Best: *Borgo Conventi, Ca' Ronesca, Collavini, La Fattoria, Pintar, Russiz Superiore.* Very good fruity and fresh varietal whites come from *Abbazia di Rosazzo, Attems, Borgo Conventi, Collavini, Dri, Eno Friulia, Gravner, Jermann, Livio Felluga* (especially *Molamatta*), *Puiatti, Ronchi di Cialla, Schiopetto, Villa Russiz, Volpe Pasini.* The almost mythical Picolit sweet wine is beautifully made by *Al Rusignul.*

GALESTRO (Tuscany; white) A name created to mop up the Trebbiano and Malvasia no longer used in red Chianti. Low alcohol, simple, lemony, greengage taste, high-tech style, best on its home territory.

GATTINARA, DOCG (Piedmont; red) Nebbiolo-based red that can be good but often has an unappealingly volatile character. *Antoniolo, Brugo, Dessilani* and *Travaglini* are reliable.

GAVI, DOC (Piedmont; white) Cortese is the grape, its wine dry and sharp, like Sauvignon minus the tang, and fairly full, like Chardonnay without the class. Best: *Arione, Ca' Bianca, Chiarlo (Fior di Rovere), Deltetto*.

KALTERERSEE/LAGO DI CALDARO, DOC (Alto Adige; red) Good, light, soft red with an unbelievable flavour of home-made strawberry jam and woodsmoke, made from the Schiava (alias Vernatsch) grape. It is best as a young gulper. Best producers: *Gries* co-op, *Lageder, Muri-Gries, Hans Rottensteiner, St Michael-Eppan* co-op, *Tiefenbrunner* and *Walch*.

LACRYMA CHRISTI DEL VESUVIO, DOC (Campania; red, white) The most famous wine of Campania and Naples. It can be red, white, dry or sweet: *Mastroberardino*'s is the best.

LAGREIN DUNKEL, some **DOC** (Alto Adige; red) Dark, chewy red with a tarry roughness jostling with chocolate-smooth ripe fruit. Look for the *Gries* co-op, *Lageder, Muri-Gries, Niedermayr* and *Tiefenbrunner* (also very good pink Lagrein Kretzer).

LAMBRUSCO, some **DOC** (Emilia-Romagna; red, white) Good Lambrusco – lightly fizzy, low in alcohol, dry to vaguely sweet – should *always* have a sharp, almost rasping acid bite to it. Look for a DOC, from Sorbara, Santa Croce or Castelvetro. Most here is not DOC and softened for the UK market, but *Cavicchioli* is proper stuff.

LANGHE, DOC (Piedmont, red, white) This recent DOC covers wines previously sold as vino da tavola. Look for tasty young Langhe Nebbiolo from good Barolo and Barbaresco producers at attractive prices.

LUGANA, DOC (Lombardy; white) The Trebbiano di Lugana grape makes whites of solid structure and some fruity flavours from *Ca' dei Frati, Premiovini, Provenza, Visconti* and *Zenato*.

MARSALA (Sicily; fortified) This has, at its best, a delicious, deep brown-sugar sweetness allied to a cutting, lip-tingling acidity that makes it surprisingly refreshing for a fortified dessert wine. The rare dry Marsala Vergine is also good. But a once-great name is now in decline. A few good producers keep the flag flying: *De Bartoli* outclasses all the rest, and even makes an intense, beautifully aged, but *unfortified* non-DOC range called *Vecchio Samperi*. His *Josephine Dore* is in the style of *fino* sherry.

MONTEFALCO, DOC and **SAGRANTINO DI MONTEFALCO, DOCG** (Umbria; red) Montefalco Rosso is tasty and often stylish. Sagrantino is a red of great size and strength, that comes in a dry version or as sweet Passito, using semi-dried grapes. Both can age impressively from *Adanti, Antonelli* and *Caprai*.

MONTEPULCIANO D'ABRUZZO, DOC (Abruzzi; red) Good ones are citrus-fresh and plummily rich, juicy yet tannic, ripe yet with a tantalizing sour bite. Best: *Casal Thaulero* co-op, *Colle Secco, Illuminati, Mezzanotte, Pepe* and *Valentini*.

MORELLINO DI SCANSANO, DOC (Tuscany, red) A similar grape-mix to that of Chianti gives austere wines with earthy tannins, deep, ripe fruit, and tarry spice. *Le Sentinelle Riserva* from *Mantellassi* is good.

MOSCATO D'ASTI, DOCG (Piedmont; white) Sweet, slightly fizzy wine that captures all the crunchy green freshness of a fistful of ripe table grapes. Heavenly ones come from the following: *Ascheri, Michele Chiarlo, Dogliotti, Gallo d'Oro, Gatti, Bruno Giacosa, Rivetti, Vietti, I Vignaioli di Santo Stefano*.

MOSCATO PASSITO DI PANTELLERIA (Pantelleria; white) Big, heavy wine with a great wedge of rich Muscat fruit and a good slap of alcoholic strength.

OLTREPÒ PAVESE, some **DOC** (Lombardy; red, white, rosé) This covers just about anything, including dry whites, sweet whites and fizz. Almost the only wine we see is non-DOC Champagne-method fizz based on Pinot Grigio/Nero/Bianco, and some red, which is good, substantial stuff.

ORVIETO, DOC (Umbria; white) Generally modern, pale and dry, sometimes peach-perfumed and honeyed. Best: *Antinori* (*Cervaro della Sala* vino da tavola), *Barberani*, *Bigi* (*Cru Torricella Secco* and medium-sweet *Cru Orzalume Amabile*), *Decugnano dei Barbi*, *Palazzone*, *Scambia*. Sweet, unctuous, noble rot-affected wines (*Antinori*'s *Muffato della Sala* and *Barberani*'s *Calcaia*) are rarely seen but delicious.

PIEMONTE, DOC (Piedmont, red, white) Applies to quality wines not covered by the other DOCs of Piedmont. The reds include Barbera, Bonarda, Brachetto and Grignolino. Whites, which may be sparkling, come from Chardonnay, Cortese, Moscato, Pinot Bianco, Pinto Grigio and Pinot Nero.

POMINO, DOC (Tuscany; red, white) The DOC also includes some sweet *vin santo*. The red, based on Sangiovese with Canaiolo, Cabernet and Merlot, becomes rich, soft, velvety and spicy with age. The only producers are *Frescobaldi* and *Giuntini*.

PROSECCO, some **DOC** (Veneto; white) Still or sparkling, it's a lovely fresh, bouncy, light white, often off-dry. The best is labelled Cartizze. Try *Canevel, Carpenè Malvolti, Le Case Bianche, Collavini, Zonin*.

ROSSO CONERO, DOC (Marches; red) Very good, sturdy red full of herb and fruit flavours, sometimes with some oak for richness. Best: *Bianchi, Garofoli, Marchetti, Mecvini* and *San Lorenzo* (*Umani Ronchi*).

ROSSO DI MONTALCINO, DOC (Tuscany; red) DOC for producers of Brunello who want a second wine, perhaps for declassifying part of their crop. Softer, more approachable and cheaper than Brunello di Montalcino.

ROSSO DI MONTEPULCIANO, DOC (Tuscany; red) This is the DOC for 'lesser' Montepulciano, aged for less time in the cellar. Much the same style as big brother, but lighter, more approachable and drinkable younger.

SALICE SALENTINO, DOC (Apulia; red) Impressive wines, deep in colour, ripe and chocolaty, acquiring hints of roast chestnuts and prunes with age. Look for *Candido, Leone De Castris, Taurino, Vallone*.

SOAVE, DOC (Veneto; white) Usually attractive, soft, fair-priced white; slightly nutty, even creamy. Drink it as young as possible. *Bertani, Pasqua* and *Zenato* make a lot of decent basic stuff. On a higher level are *Anselmi* (try *Capitel Foscarino*) and *Pieropan*, especially single-vineyard wines *Calvarino* and *La Rocca*. Other good ones are *Bolla*'s *Castellaro, Boscaini, Costalunga, Inama, Lenotti, Santi*'s *Monte Carbonare, Tedeschi*'s *Monte Tenda, Zenato* and the local co-operative's *Costalta. Anselmi* also makes a *Recioto di Soave I Capitelli* which is shockingly good in its pungent sweet-sour way, and *Pieropan*'s unoaked *Recioto di Soave* is gorgeously redolent of apricots. Quality is better than it used to be, though it still pays to look for a top producer.

SPANNA (Piedmont; red) A Nebbiolo-based wine with a lovely raisin and chocolate flavour in the old style. Even cheap Spannas are a pretty good bet.

TAURASI, DOCG (Campania; red) Remarkable, plummy yet bitingly austere red, sometimes short on fruit or long on tannin, but generally worth trying. *Mastroberardino* is the top name.

TOCAI, DOC (Friuli, Veneto; white) Full, aromatic, softly nutty, honeyed wines. Best producers include: *Abbazia di Rosazzo, Borgo Conventi, Cà Bolani, Caccese, Collavini, Livio Felluga, Lazzarini, Maculan, Schiopetto, Villa Russiz, Volpe Pasini*.

TORGIANO, DOC and DOCG

(Umbria; red) The region's fame rests on *Lungarotti*. The reds are strong, plummy, sometimes overbearing, usually carrying the trade name *Rubesco*. Quality is perhaps not as tip-top as it once was. Single-vineyard *Monticchio* and *San Giorgio* Cabernet Sauvignon are exciting. Torgiano Rosso Riserva is DOCG. White wines are clean and good. Lungarotti also makes good *flor*-affected sherry-type wine called *Solleone*.

TRENTINO, DOC (red, white) Some of

Italy's best Pinot Bianco and Chardonnay comes from here, as well as some interesting whites from Riesling, Müller-Thurgau and excellent dry Muscat. But until they stop grossly overproducing we're never going to see the full potential. Trento Classico DOC applies to Champagne-method sparkling wines. Look especially for *Conti Martini, Gaierhof, Istituto di San Michele, Mandelli, Pojer e Sandri, Spagnolli* and *Zeni*. Fair *vin santo* comes from *Pisoni* and *Simoncelli*. Reds are made either from local grape varieties such as Lagrein, Teroldego and Marzemino, or the likes of Cabernet, Merlot and Pinot Noir. Go for *Conti Martini, Foradori, Guerrieri-Gonzaga, Istituto di San Michele, Pojer e Sandri, de Tarczal* and *Zeni*.

VALPOLICELLA, DOC (Veneto; red)

This *should* have delicious, light, cherry fruit and a bitter almond twist to the finish – a bit fuller and deeper than Bardolino with a hint more sourness. Superiore has been aged for a year before release. Most of the commercial stuff is compared locally to twice-skimmed milk – i.e. insipid. Producers with good flavours: *Allegrini, Boscaini, Corte Sant'Alda, Guerrieri-Rizzardi, Masi, Quintarelli, Le Ragose, Santi, Tedeschi, Zenato*.

There are a few single-vineyard wines, like *Masi*'s *Serègo Alighieri*, which are way ahead. They cost more, but *Allegrini*'s *La Grola* or *Tedeschi*'s *Ca' Nicalo* show what Valpolicella should be about. You might also look for wine made by the traditional *ripasso* method, in which new wine is pumped over the skins and lees of Recioto or Amarone, starting a re-fermentation and adding an exciting sweet-sour dimension. Try *Masi, Quintarelli* and *Tedeschi*.

Best of all is the weird and wonderful Recioto Amarone della Valpolicella. It's made from half-shrivelled grapes and has a brilliant array of flavours – sweet grapeskins, chocolate, plums and woodsmoke – and a shocking, penetrating bruised sourness. The good stuff is about three times the price of simple Valpolicella, but it's still good value. Wine labelled simply as 'Recioto della Valpolicella' will be sweet and may still be excellent – but a little less strangely special. Best: *Allegrini, Bertani, Masi, Quintarelli, Le Ragose* and *Tedeschi*.

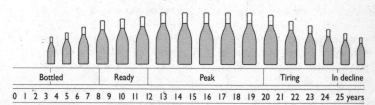

MATURITY CHART
1990 Barolo
A superb year in Piedmont, but patience is needed for the tannins to soften

Bottled	Ready	Peak	Tiring	In decline

0 1 2 3 4 5 6 7 8 9 10 11 12 13 14 15 16 17 18 19 20 21 22 23 24 25 years

VALTELLINA, DOC (Lombardy; red)
Slightly stringy Nebbiolo, not much seen
over here.

VERDICCHIO, DOC (Marches; white)
Reliable rather than exciting – usually
extremely dry, lean, clean, nutty with a
streak of dry honey, sharpened by slightly
green acidity. *Fazi-Battaglia's* single-vineyard
vino da tavola *Le Moie* shows the potential.
There is also some fizz. The two leading
areas are Verdicchio dei Castelli di Jesi and
Verdicchio di Matelica. The rarer Matelica
wines often have more flavour. *Bucci,
Garafoli* and *Umani Ronchi* use new oak for
their best wines. Also: *Brunori, Fabrini, Fazi-
Battaglia, Mecvini, Monte Schiavo, Zaccagnini.*

VERDUZZO, DOC (Friuli and Veneto)
This is usually a soft, nutty, low-acid yet
refreshing light white. The DOC also
includes a lovely, gentle fizz, and some of
Italy's best sweet wines, in particular
Abbazia di Rosazzo's Amabile and *Dri's
Verduzzo di Ramandolo.*

**VERNACCIA DI SAN GIMIGNANO
DOCG** (Tuscany) Can be attractively
nutty, but is too often a model of bland
neutrality. Good: *Fagiuoli, Falchini, Frigeni,
San Quirico, Teruzzi & Puthod* and *La Torre.*

**VINO NOBILE DI
MONTEPULCIANO, DOCG**
(Tuscany) Like Chianti only more so: more
pepper, acid and tannin, and a higher price,
but the best has a marvellous dry fragrance
reminiscent almost of sandalwood, backed
up by good Sangiovese spice, and a strong
plumskins-and-cherries fruit. Best
producers: *Avignonesi, Bindella, Boscarelli, La
Casalte, Fassati, Fattoria di Casale, Fattoria
del Cerro, Fognano, Poliziano* and *Trerose.*

VIN SANTO Can be one of the great
sweet wines, but too often vaguely raisiny
and very dull. It *should* have all kinds of
splendid, rich fruit flavours – apricots,
apples, the chewiness of toffee, smoke and
liquorice. Try *Avignonesi, La Calonica* or *Isole
e Olena* in Tuscany or *Adanti* in Umbria.

PRODUCERS WHO'S WHO

ABBAZIA DELL'ANNUNZIATA
★★★★ (Piedmont) One of the great
producers of Barolo. All the wines are full of
excitement and strongly perfumed, and
they develop wonderfully in the bottle.

ALLEGRINI ★★★★★ (Veneto)
Splendid single-vineyard Valpolicellas,
especially La Grola, Fieramonte and Palazzo
della Torre. Top Amarone and Recioto.
Also excellent vino da tavola, La Poja.

ELIO ALTARE ★★★★ (Piedmont)
New wave producer – wines of firm
structure and tannin behind perfumed fruit.
Highly successful Barolo Vigna Arborina,
very good Dolcetto and barrique-aged
Barbera Vigna Larigi.

ALTESINO ★★★★ (Tuscany) Excellent
Brunello and some good vini da tavola,

notably under the names of Alte d'Altesi
and Palazzo Altesi.

CASTELLO DI AMA ★★★★
(Tuscany) Excellent single-vineyard Chianti
Classico: San Lorenzo, La Casuccia,
Bellavista; also a Merlot, Vigna L'Apparita.

ANSELMI ★★★★★ (Veneto) Soave
with character. Cru Capitel Foscarino is as
good as it gets – as is his Recioto I Capitelli.

ANTINORI ★★★★ (Tuscany) One of
the great names of Chianti. Excellent
Chianti Classico from estates Pèppoli and
Badia a Passignano; also Tignanello, the
archetypal barrique-aged Sangiovese/
Cabernet blend. Solaia has more Cabernet.
Orvieto estate, Castello della Sala, makes
wonderful vino da tavola white, Cervaro
della Sala. Brother Ludovico Antinori makes

Ornellaia, a Cabernet-based vino da tavola. High price, high quality.

AVIGNONESI ★★★★ (Tuscany) Serious Vino Nobile, and two excellent Chardonnays: Terre di Cortona, without oak, and Il Marzocco, oak-fermented and aged wine of considerable depth. I Grifi is barrel-aged Prugnolo and Cabernet Franc.

BADIA A COLTIBUONO ★★★ (Tuscany) Produces good Chianti and even better 'Sangioveto', a vino da tavola made from old vines.

BANFI ★★★ (Tuscany) US-owned Montalcino winery making international styles. Brunello Poggio all'Oro is best, Tavernelle Cabernet good, others sound.

FATTORIA DEI BARBI ★★★★ (Tuscany) Traditional methods produce serious Brunello and Rosso di Montalcino, as well as Brusco dei Barbi, and a single-vineyard wine, Vigna Fiore.

BIONDI SANTI ★★★ (Tuscany) A legendary family making a fabulously priced, but not necessarily legendary wine; old vintages are wonderful, and new ones seem to be on the up.

BOLLA ★★★ (Veneto) Large scale producer of Soave and Valpolicella. Skip the basic wines and go for Valpolicella Jago.

BRAIDA-GIACOMO BOLOGNA ★★★ (Piedmont) Saw early the potential of Barbera in barrique: deep, balanced and rich cru Bricco dell' Uccellone impresses. Equally good Bricco della Bigotta. Unoaked, youthful Barbera, La Monella. Good Moscato d'Asti and Brachetto d'Acqui.

CA'DEL BOSCO ★★★ (Lombardy) Good fizz from Franciacorta. Also vino da tavola called Maurizio Zanella, blended from both Cabernets and Merlot, which is expensive but terrific.

INSTANT CELLAR:
SOUTHERN ITALIAN VALUE

- **1995 Rosso del Salento, Notarpanaro Taurino, Puglia, £6.40, Averys** A single-vineyard red from the Salento peninsula, rich with a bitter twist to the finish.
- **1998 Greco, Basilicata, £5.35, Averys** The nutty, elegant white Greco grape from Puglia. Lightly aromatic.
- **1997 Falerno del Massico Bianco, Villa Matilde, £7.99, Liberty Wines** Rich fruit with good acidity from Campania.
- **1998 Primitivo di Puglia, Allora, £5.20, Bibendum** Rich, figgy fruit.
- **1997 Rosso del Salento, La Forza, £4.29, Bordeaux Direct** Easy-going juicy red from the South of Italy.
- **1994 Copertino Riserva, Cantina Sociale, £6.99, Valvona & Crolla** Earthy, inky red.
- **1995 Regaleali Rosso, Conte Tasca d'Almerita, £6.99, Direct Wine Shipments** Herbs and blackberries from Sicily.
- **1994 Rosso del Salento, Capello di Prete, Francesco Candido, £6.99, Noel Young** Rich, oak-aged red from the Salento Peninsula in the South of Italy.

CAPARZO ★★★★ (Tuscany) High quality producer of Brunello di Montalcino and Rosso di Montalcino; also an oak-fermented Chardonnay called Le Grance, and Ca' del Pazzo, a barrique-aged blend of Cabernet Sauvignon and Sangiovese.

TENUTA DI CAPEZZANA ★★★★ (Tuscany) The leader in Carmignano, also a very good Bordeaux blend, Ghiaie della Furba. Good but expensive pink, Vin Ruspo.

CASTELLARE ★★★★ (Tuscany) Nice Chianti, splendid vino da tavola I Sodi di San Niccolò, with a little Malvasia Nera adding perfume to the Sangiovese.

CERETTO ★★★★ (Piedmont) Barolo Bricco Rocche Bricco Rocche (yes) and Barbaresco Bricco Asili are legendary with prices to match. Light Barbera and Dolcetto. Arneis is disappointing.

FATTORIA DEL CERRO ★★★

(Tuscany) Traditional producer of Vino Nobile, now working with barriques. Its best wine remains the DOCG Vino Nobile.

CLERICO ★★★★★ (Piedmont) Top

modern producer; fine Nebbiolo-Barbera blend Arte, Barolo from two *crus* (Bricotto Bussia, Ciabot Mentin Ginestra).

ALDO CONTERNO ★★★★★

(Piedmont) Great Barolo, traditionally made, slow to mature but worth the wait. Powerful Barbera, Dolcetto also good.

GIACOMO CONTERNO ★★★★★

(Piedmont) Aldo's brother, making excellent traditional Monfortino Barolo.

CONTERNO FANTINO ★★★★

(Barolo, Monforte) Guido Fantino and Diego Conterno have earned a reputation for fine Barolo from the Ginestra hillside. Rich but forward, perfumed wines.

PAOLO CORDERO DI MONTEZEMOLO ★★★ (Piedmont)

The accent is on fruit. Standard-bearer is *cru* Monfalletto from La Morra. *Cru* Enrico VI is from Castiglione Falletto, refined, elegant, scented. Also Barbera and Dolcetto.

CARLO DELTETTO ★★★ (Roero,

Canale) Good understated, intriguing whites from Arneis and Favorita. Reliable Roero and Gavi.

FELSINA BERARDENGA ★★★

(Tuscany) Winery very much on the up. Vigneto Rancia single-vineyard Chianti, I Sistri barrique-aged Chardonnay. Fontalloro Sangiovese aged in barrique for a year.

FONTODI ★★★ (Tuscany) Sleek

Sangiovese, in the form of single-estate Chianto Classico or vino da tavola red Flaccianello (plus white Meriggio, Pinot Bianco, Sauvignon and Traminer).

FRESCOBALDI ★★★ (Tuscany) The

best Frescobaldi estate is Castello di Nipozzano. Also excellent Pomino, including an oak-aged white, Il Benefizio. Excellent Brunello from the Castelgiocondo estate, plus good white under the Capitolato label and fine Cabernet Mormoreto red. Latest is a joint venture with Mondavi of California to produce a high-priced red, Luce delle Vite.

ANGELO GAJA ★★★★★ (Piedmont)

Uses barriques for most wines, including all Barbarescos: Costa Russi, Sorì San Lorenzo, Sorì Tildìn. In the vanguard of Piedmontese Cabernet (Darmagi) and Chardonnay (Gaia and Rey) production. Also makes two Barberas, two Dolcettos, Freisa and a top Barolo from the Marenca Rivette vineyard.

BRUNO GIACOSA ★★★★★

(Piedmont) Traditional wines of, at their best, mind-blowing quality, especially Barbaresco *cru* Santo Stefano and, best of

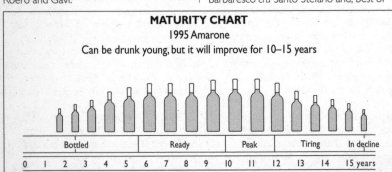

MATURITY CHART
1995 Amarone
Can be drunk young, but it will improve for 10–15 years

Bottled	Ready	Peak	Tiring	In decline

| 0 | 1 | 2 | 3 | 4 | 5 | 6 | 7 | 8 | 9 | 10 | 11 | 12 | 13 | 14 | 15 years |

all, Vigna Rionda Barolo. Rich, concentrated but not overbearing, elegant. Also white Arneis and good fizz.

MARCHESI DI GRESY ★★★★★
(Piedmont) The leading site, Martinenga, produces Barbaresco, two *crus* – Camp Gros and Gaiun – and a non-wood-aged Nebbiolo called Martinenga; all are elegant. Notable Sauvignon and Chardonnay, too.

ISOLE E OLENA ★★★★ (Tuscany)
Fine Chianti Classico. Also Cepparello, a rich pure Sangiovese wine, made from the oldest vines of the estate; outstanding sweet *vin santo* and a superb Syrah.

JERMANN (Friuli-Venezia Giulia) ★★★★
Characterful, subtle vini da tavola: oak-aged Vintage Tunina and Chardonnay 'Where the Dreams have no End'. Plain Pinot Grigio and Riesling are also very good.

LAGEDER ★★★ (Alto Adige)
Straightforward varietals are – well, straightforward. Single vineyard wines are far better: Sauvignon Lehenhof and Pinot Grigio Benefizium Porer.

LUNGAROTTI ★★★ (Umbria) The
main name in Torgiano. Also Chardonnays, Miralduolo and Vigna I Palazzi. San Giorgio is Cabernet plus Sangiovese.

GIUSEPPE MASCARELLO ★★★★★
(Piedmont) Superb *cru* Barolo Monprivato. Also Villero and other *crus*. Barbera d'Alba Ginestra is notable. Excellent inky Dolcetto.

MASI ★★★★ (Veneto) Very good Soave
and Valpolicella, especially Valpolicella Campo Fiorin. Brilliant Amarone and Recioto. Toar is oaky, cherryish new red vino da tavola.

MASTROBERARDINO ★★★★
(Campania) Leading southern producer. Noteworthy Taurasi, and whites including Fiano di Avellino and Greco di Tufo.

> ### ON THE CASE
> Famous DOCs and DOCGs can be outrageously expensive, famous growers even more so. Check out wines from Apulia, Basilicata and Abruzzo instead

MONTEVERTINE ★★★★ (Tuscany)
Outstanding Le Pergole Torte, a barrique-aged Sangiovese vino da tavola, needs at least five years to open up. Il Sodaccio Sangiovese/Canaiolo can be drunk young.

CASTELLO DI NEIVE ★★★★
(Piedmont) Impeccable, finely crafted, austerely elegant Barbaresco from Santo Stefano. Barrique-aged Barbera from single *cru* Mattarello and firm, classic Dolcetto from three sites, the best of which is Basarin. Revelatory Arneis.

FRATELLI ODDERO ★★★
(Piedmont) Barolo, Barbera and Dolcetto from vineyards in prime sites in the area, plus Barbaresco from bought-in grapes. Good roundness, balance, style and value.

PIEROPAN ★★★★★ (Veneto)
Stunning Soave, in particular La Rocca and Calvarino, both single vineyards. Recioto Le Colombare is divine.

PIO CESARE ★★★ (Piedmont) Full
spread of Barolo, Barbaresco, Nebbiolo d'Alba, Dolcetto, Barbera, Grignolino and Gavi. Wines are gaining elegance, losing a bit of punch but gaining harmony and balance. Experiments with barriques; also makes Nebbio (young-drinking Nebbiolo) and Piodilei (barriqued Chardonnay).

POJER & SANDRI ★★★ (Trentino)
Good quality in reds and whites, and particularly good spumante.

QUINTARELLI ★★★★★ (Veneto)
Revelatory Valpolicella, especially Amarone and Recioto, though all are splendid.

ITALIAN VINTAGES

1998 Patchy: go for Piedmontese reds and Tuscan reds, above all. Top Veneto growers will have made decent stuff.

1997 A very good year, but variable: some reds have low acidity and a slightly raisiny character. Central Italy produced excellent whites. Quantity is down, prices up.

1996 Very good for Piedmontese reds, pretty good for Tuscan reds. Variable elsewhere.

1995 Excellent Barolo and Barbaresco, though Dolcetto was below par. Valpolicella was very good, and there'll be wonderful Amarone and Recioto. Also very good for Central Italian reds, though whites had a less good year all over the country.

1994 Central Italy came off best, with good quality across the board. North-eastern whites are also pretty good. In the North-West, Dolcetto, Moscato and Arneis are very good, but Barbera and Nebbiolo are less so.

1993 Best in the North-East, where the whites have more richness, perfume, length – well, more of everything – than the 1992s, while the reds are excellent. Central Italy looks fair, and the North-West patchy, though Dolcetto was generally successful.

1992 Light, early-drinking wines were made across most of the country, though Carmignano is nearly as good as in 1990, and the Marches were also fortunate.

1991 A very fragmented year. Fair to good overall in the North-West. Tuscany was outstanding, and the Marches, Torgiano, Veneto, Friuli are very good, Trentino-Alto-Adige less so.

1990 A fabulous vintage pretty well everywhere: wines of tremendous colour, richness and perfume, Barolo and Barbaresco for long aging and delicious Barbera. Wonderful Dolcetto again. Tuscan wines are built to last.

1989 Barbera d'Asti is very good, and at its peak. Reds from elsewhere are less concentrated.

1988 Dolcetto and Barbera have concentration and fruit. Nebbiolo is patchier. Tremendous quality in Central Italy and the North-East.

1987 Patchy Barolo and Barbaresco. Central Italian reds are reasonable, in particular Carmignano; young Chiantis were good but aren't young any more.

1986 Barbaresco and Barolo are overshadowed by the great 1985s, but the quality is good. Chianti Riserva is very good, and Amarone Valpolicella is lovely and drinking beautifully now.

1985 Big rich wines in Central Italy. An exciting vintage in the North-West, when more growers decided to emphasize fruit and perfume.

1983 Almost all fading now. Top Amarone is still good

1982 Excellent, big ripe reds from Barolo which are still drinking. Everything else should have been drunk by now.

REGALEALI ★★★★ (Sicily) Wonderful vini da tavola from local varieties: red Rosso del Conte and white Nozze d'Oro. Top Chardonnay. Good standard range, too.

RICASOLI ★★★ (Tuscany) Chianti is currently looking good. Also makes a host of other Tuscan wines at Brolio.

GIUSEPPE RIVETTI ★★★ (Piedmont) Smallish quantities of magical Moscato d'Asti which sell out in a flash.

RUFFINO ★★★ (Tuscany) Large Chianti house. Riserva Ducale is its best-known wine. Good vini da tavola include lively Cabreo il Borgo (Cabernet) and succulent, oaky Chardonnay, Cabreo la Pietra. Romitorio di Santedame is Prugnolo (alias Sangiovese) and Colorino.

LUCIANO SANDRONE ★★★★ (Piedmont) A small producer making tiny quantities of perfumed new-style Barolo with lovely raspberry and black cherry flavours. Also excellent Dolcetto.

TENUTA SAN GUIDO ★★★★★ (Tuscany) Never heard the name? You may have heard of Sassicaia, Italy's leading Cabernet. It used to be vino da tavola; now it has the DOC of Bolgheri.

PAOLO SCAVINO ★★★★ (Piedmont) Hailed as one of the emerging masters of Barolo: superb wines which combine purity of fruit with depth and structure. Barolo Bric' del Fiasc' is his top wine; Cannubi and straight Barolo are not far behind. Delicious Dolcetto and Barbera.

MARIO SCHIOPETTO ★★★★ (Collio) Lovely whites from Pinot Grigio, Tocai etc., and white Rosis vino da tavola.

TERUZZI & PUTHOD ★★★★ (Tuscany) Commonly acknowledged to be the best producer of Vernaccia di San Gimignano. Its most expensive wine is the oak-aged Terre di Tufo. Whites include Terre di Tufi and Carmen.

VIETTI ★★★★★ (Barolo, Castiglione Falletto) Classically perfect wines of their type, with a punch of acidity and tannin, plus elegance and class. Barolo (straight plus *crus* Rocche, Villero and Brunate) and Barbaresco (*normale* plus *crus* Masseria, Rabajà) are all intensely complex. Also, very good Dolcetto and Barbera, one of the top Moscatos d'Asti and very good Arneis.

ROBERTO VOERZIO ★★★★ (Piedmont) Ultra-modern fine wines full of fruit and perfume, made with great skill, giving Roberto (brother Gianni is also on the up) a reputation as a rising star. Barolo, Dolcetto d'Alba, Barbera d'Alba, Freisa, and delicious barrique-aged Barbera/ Nebbiolo blend Vignaserra. Fine Arneis.

CASTELLO DI VOLPAIA ★★★ (Tuscany) Leading Chianti estate with elegant wines. Balifico Sangiovese/Cabernet is exotic and oaky-rich; Coltassala is lovely, austere Sangiovese that needs time.

WINE-FINDER: ITALY

In the Price Guides on the next 15 pages, we have divided Italy into the following geographical regions: North-West, North-East, Central and Southern. If you are unsure which part of the country the wine you're looking for comes from, this guide should help. See also the map on page 293.

Asti – *North-West Sparkling*
Barbaresco – *North-West Red*
Barbera – *North-West Red*
Barolo – *North-West Red*
Brunello di Montalcino – *Central Red*
Chianti – *Central Red*
Dolcetto – *North-West Red*
Frascati – *Central White*
Vino Nobile di Montepulciano – *Central Red*
Montepulciano d'Abruzzo – *Southern Red*
Orvieto – *Central White*
Soave – *North-East White*
Valpolicella – *North-East Red*
Verdicchio – *Central White*

ITALY PRICES

NORTH-WEST RED

Under £5.00

Barbera d'Asti Ceppi Storici 1996 £4.99
(CO) £7.20 (TAN) £7.30 (PIP)
Barbera d'Asti Superiore, Araldica 1996
£4.99 (VA)

£5.00 → £5.99

Barbera d'Alba Punset 1994 £5.99 (WAT)
Barbera d'Asti Gemma 1995 £5.25 (BALL)
Barbera del Piemonte, Giordano 1997
£5.25 (PEN)
Dolcetto d'Alba Gemma 1996 £5.95
(BALL) £6.50 (CON)
Valtellina Sfursat Negri 1995 £18.49
(YOU)

£6.00 → £6.99

Barbera d'Asti Ceppi Storici 1993 £6.02
(ROS)
Dolcetto d'Asti Alasia 1995 £6.15 (BEN)
Dolcetto di Dogliani, Francesco Boschis
1996 £6.90 (JU)
Nebbiolo delle Langhe Settimo 1995
£6.49 (WAT) £8.99 (DI)

£7.00 → £7.99

Barbera d'Alba Fontanafredda 1996 £7.25
(FORT)
Barbera d'Alba Nicolello 1994 £7.88 (COC)
Barolo Fratelli Giacosa 1992 £7.99 (TES)
Dolcetto d'Alba Cascina Morassino,
Bianco Mauro 1996 £7.64 (PEN)
Dolcetto d'Alba Elio Altare 1996 £7.90 (JU)
Dolcetto d'Alba Gemma 1997 £7.19 (JON)
Dolcetto d'Alba Prunotto 1998 £7.00 (NEZ)
Nebbiolo delle Langhe Cascina Morassino
1995 £7.64 (PEN) £9.25 (ROB)
Nebbiolo delle Langhe Produttori del
Barbaresco 1996 £7.99 (VA)
Spanna Dessilani 1995 £7.95 (RAE)

£8.00 → £9.99

Barbera d'Alba Rocca Albino 1995 £8.90
(JU)
Barbera d'Alba Altare 1996 £8.50 (JU)
Barbera d'Alba Vigna Vigia, Bricco
Maiolica 1996 £9.95 (LEA)
Barbera d'Asti Litina Superiore, Cascina
Castle't 1996 £8.79 (YOU)
Barbera del Monferrato la Monella,
Bologna 1997 £8.95 (TAN)
Oltrepò Pavese Barbera, Castello di
Luzzano 1991 £8.95 (RAE)
Barolo Terre del Barolo 1994 £9.17 (FLE)
Barolo Terre del Barolo 1993 £8.99 (CO)
Dolcetto d'Alba Aldo Conterno 1996
£8.50 (CRO) £10.99 (VA) £11.40 (HAH)
Dolcetto d'Alba Ascheri 1996 £8.50 (ROB)
Dolcetto d'Alba Azelia 1996 £8.50 (JU)
Dolcetto d'Alba Diano Bricco Maiolica
1994 £8.95 (LEA)
Dolcetto d'Alba Sandrone 1997 £8.95
(TAN)
Dolcetto d'Alba Vajra 1991 £9.75 (BU)
Dolcetto d'Alba Vietti 1996 £8.95 (FORT)
Dolcetto di Dogliani Sori S. Martino,
Boschis 1996 £8.00 (JU) £8.49 (YOU)
Gutturnio dei Colli Piacentini, Castello di
Luzzano 1991 £9.95 (RAE)
Inferno Nino Negri 1995 £8.89 (VA)
Nebbiolo delle Langhe Vajra 1997 £9.50
(WS) £11.95 (PHI) £12.49 (LIB)
Oltrepò Pavese Vino Cuore, Cabanon
1995 £9.30 (JER)

£10.00 → £12.49

Barbaresco Campo Quadro, Punset 1992
£12.25 (WAT)
Barbaresco Punset 1989 £11.55 (WAT)
Barbera d'Alba Aldo Conterno 1994
£12.10 (SOM) £15.75 (ROB)
Barbera d'Alba Conca Tre Pile, Aldo
Conterno 1995 £10.18 (FA) £14.99 (VA)

MERCHANTS SPECIALIZING IN ITALY

see Merchant Directory (page 413) for details

Adnams (AD), Bennetts (BEN), Bibendum
(BIB), Butlers Wine Cellar (BU), Anthony
Byrne (BY), Cockburns of Leith (COC),
Direct Wine (DI), Lay & Wheeler (LAY), Lea
& Sandeman (LEA), Liberty (LIB), James
Nicholson (NI), Reid Wines (REI), Roberson
(ROB), T&W (TW), Ubiquitous Chip (UB),
Valvona & Crolla (VA), Wine Treasury (WT).

Barolo Ascheri **1993** £10.72 (FLE)

Barolo Cordana, Castiglione Falletto **1994**
£10.40 (SOM) £12.49 (YOU) £14.50 (PIP)

Barolo Fontanafredda **1994** £10.99 (THR)
£10.99 (WR) £10.99 (BOT) £14.95 (STA)

Dolcetto d'Alba Aldo Conterno **1997**
£10.95 (LIB) £10.99 (BEN)

Dolcetto d'Alba Priavino, Voerzio **1997**
£10.99 (VA)

Dolcetto d'Alba Vajra **1998** £10.49 (LIB)

Dolcetto d'Alba Vigneto del Fiasc, Paolo
Scavino **1996** £10.99 (VA)

Dolcetto Sandrone **1997** £11.84 (WT)

Nebbiolo d'Alba Il Cumot, Bricco
Maiolica **1996** £10.95 (LEA)

Nebbiolo d'Alba San Michele, Vietti **1995**
£10.00 (FORT)

Nebbiolo Marengo **1996** £10.99 (YOU)
£11.50 (JU)

Ronco di Mompiano, Pasolini **1985**
£11.50 (CRO)

Ruche di Castagnole Monferrato, Casa
Brina **1995** £11.99 (BO)

Ruche di Castagnole Monferrato, Casa
Brina **1993** £10.80 (NO)

£12.50 → £14.99

Barbaresco Cascina Morassino **1993**
£14.22 (PEN) £15.99 (VA)

Barbaresco Nicolello **1989** £12.90 (PIP)
£13.70 (COC) £14.28 (PLAY)

Barbera d'Alba Vin del Ross, Bussia
Soprana **1993** £14.50 (BAL) £18.14 (NO)

Barbera d'Alba Aldo Conterno **1995**
£14.99 (VA)

Barbera d'Asti Superiore Arbest, Bava
1993 £13.16 (TW)

Barbera Passum Passito, Cascina Castle't
1996 £13.99 (YOU)

Barolo Ascheri **1994** £12.75 (REI) £13.49
(VA) £13.50 (HED) £13.75 (AD) £13.95
(RES) £13.95 (STA)

Barolo Azelia **1993** £14.50 (JU)

Barolo Batasiolo **1994** £14.95 (UB)

Barolo Gemma **1994** £12.95 (BALL)

Barolo Gemma **1993** £13.95 (CON)

Barolo Nicolello **1993** £13.70 (COC)
£14.99 (DI)

Barolo Oddero **1992** £13.95 (ROB)

Barolo Settimo **1993** £13.35 (WAT)
£17.99 (DI)

Monpra Conterno Fantino **1993** £14.45
(SOM)

Nebbiolo d'Alba Pio Cesare **1995** £14.75
(FORT)

£15.00 → £19.99

Barbaresco Martinenga, Marchesi di
Gresy **1989** £18.50 (BAL)

Barbaresco Santo Stefano, Castello di
Neive **1993** £16.95 (VA)

Barbaresco Sori Paitin, Paitin **1993** £16.16
(JER)

Barbera d'Alba Sandrone **1996** £15.60
(WT)

Barbera d'Alba Aldo Conterno **1996**
£16.39 (LIB)

Barbera d'Alba Conca Tre Pile, Aldo
Conterno **1996** £16.95 (BEN)

Barbera d'Alba Giada, Oberto **1996**
£16.49 (VA)

Barbera d'Alba Vietti **1995** £16.45 (PEN)

Barolo Arborina, Elio Altare **1993** £19.90
(JU)

Barolo Bava **1991** £19.33 (TW)

Barolo Bava **1990** £15.86 (PEN)

Barolo Bricco Boschis Riserva San
Giuseppe, Cavallotto **1993** £18.95 (AD)

Barolo Bricco Fiasco, Azelia **1993** £17.00
(JU)

Barolo Brunate, Marengo **1993** £16.00 (JU)

Barolo Chiarlo **1993** £16.55 (AV)

Barolo Ciabot Mentin Ginestra, Clerico
1993 £19.00 (JU)

Barolo Oberto **1994** £19.99 (VA)

Barolo Riserva Borgogno **1993** £18.50 (VA)

Barolo Paulo Scavino **1993** £17.50 (JU)
£26.95 (ROB)

Barolo Vigna Rocche, Corino **1993**
£16.00 (JU)

Barolo Zonchera Ceretto **1994** £19.00
(TAN)

Barolo Zonchera Ceretto **1993** £17.95
(DI) £18.95 (ROB)

Cabernet del Piemonte I Fossaretti,
Bertelli **1993** £18.00 (JU)

Freisa delle Langhe Vajra **1997** £19.95 (LIB)

Monpra Conterno Fantino **1995** £19.99
(VA)

Nebbiolo d'Alba San Michele, Vietti **1993**
£15.13 (PEN)

Sito Moresco, Gaja **1995** £17.76 (LAY)
£18.95 (DI) £19.95 (BEN)

> Stars (★) indicate wines
> selected by Oz Clarke in the
> Best Buys section which begins
> on page 9.

Sito Moresco, Gaja **1992** £16.49 (VA)
Sitorey, Gaja **1994** £16.99 (DI) £18.04
(REI) £22.34 (NO) £22.95 (RES)
St Marsan, Bertelli **1995** £16.50 (JU)
Vignaserra Voerzio **1994** £16.50 (SOM)

£20.00 → £29.99

Barbaresco Bricco Asili, Ceretto **1995**
£25.85 (FA)
Barbaresco Montestefano, Prunotto **1993**
£25.95 (ROB)
Barbaresco Pio Cesare **1995** £23.00 (FORT)
Barolo Bussia, Prunotto **1993** £27.00
(CRO) £35.00 (ROB)
Barolo Bussia Soprana, Aldo Conterno
1994 £29.60 (SOM) £34.25 (LIB) £34.56
(NO) £36.95 (BEN) £40.50 (RES)
Barolo Conteisa Cerequio, Gromis **1993**
£27.24 (LAY) £32.08 (MI)
Barolo Pio Cesare **1995** £22.00 (FORT)
Bricco dell'Uccellone, Giacomo Bologna
1995 £23.80 (TAN) £26.00 (CRO)
Nebbiolo delle Langhe Il Favot, Aldo
Conterno **1994** £21.00 (PHI)
Sitorey, Gaja **1993** £23.00 (FORT)

£30.00 → £39.99

Barbaresco Gaja **1994** £38.00 (LAY)
£39.00 (VA) £43.95 (BEN)
Barolo Bussia Soprana, Aldo Conterno
1995 £34.25 (LIB) £35.00 (WS)
Barolo Bussia Soprana, Aldo Conterno
1993 £31.99 (YOU) £36.75 (BEN) £37.49
(VA) £38.19 (REI) £44.50 (ROB)

Barolo Aldo Conterno **1993** £38.25 (NI)
Barolo Lazzarito, Fontanafredda **1990**
£33.95 (RES)
Barolo Riserva Marchesi di Barolo **1990**
£33.29 (FRI)
Barolo Zonchetta, Ceretto **1969** £35.00
(BU)
Darmagi Gaja **1986** £61.10 (TW) £65.00
(CRO)
Maurizio Zanella, Ca' del Bosco **1995**
£35.00 (VA) £37.01 (REI)

£40.00 → £49.99

Barbaresco Gaja **1993** £43.90 (LAY)
£48.00 (VA) £52.00 (RES) £60.00 (FORT)
Barolo Bricco Bussia Colonello, Aldo
Conterno **1993** £45.24 (REI) £48.50 (VA)
Barolo la Serra di la Morra, Voerzio **1995**
£49.40 (WT)
Barolo Pio Cesare **1964** £42.89 (REI)
Barolo Sperss, Gaja **1994** £46.84 (LAY)
£53.50 (BEN) £76.86 (CAV)
Barolo Vigna del Gris, Conterno-Fantino
1990 £48.00 (BEN)

£50.00 → £99.99

Barbaresco Costa Russi, Gaja **1993**
£79.95 (LAY) £115.00 (VA)
Barbaresco Gaja **1995** £62.08 (MI) £84.70
(CAV)
Barbaresco Gaja **1990** £77.00 (CRO)
£84.64 (NO) £110.00 (VA)
Barbaresco Gallina di Neive, Bruno
Giacosa **1995** £95.00 (VA)
Barbaresco Santo Stefano, Castello di
Neive **1990** £50.16 (FA)
Barbaresco Sori San Lorenzo, Gaja **1986**
£75.00 (NO)
Barolo Borgogno **1985** £55.00 (VA)
Barolo Bricco Rocche Brunate, Ceretto
1990 £60.00 (VA)
Barolo Aldo Conterno **1969** £50.00 (BU)
Barolo Conterno Riserva Speciale
Monfortino **1967** £65.00 (VA)
Barolo la Serra di la Morra, Voerzio **1996**
£57.20 (WT)
Barolo Marchesi di Barolo **1968** £50.00 (BU)
Barolo Monprivato, Mascarello **1982**
£61.69 (REI)
Barolo Riserva Borgogno **1971** £65.00 (VA)
Barolo Sperss, Gaja **1991** £62.50 (FORT)
£68.00 (VA) £69.50 (RES)
Barolo Vigna Giachini, Corino **1990**
£55.00 (VA)
Darmagi Gaja **1993** £53.60 (LAY) £79.95
(RES)
Darmagi Gaja **1989** £80.00 (VA)

£100.00 → £149.99

Barbaresco Sori San Lorenzo, Gaja **1971**
£111.63 (REI)
Barolo Bricco Bussia Colonello, Aldo
Conterno **1990** £135.00 (VA)
Barolo Aldo Conterno **1971** £100.00 (VA)
Barolo Sperss, Gaja **1990** £102.28 (NO)
£125.00 (VA) £130.42 (MI)

Over £200.00

Barbaresco Sorì Tildìn, Gaja 1989
£200.00 (VA)
Barolo Granbussia, Aldo Conterno 1990
£219.00 (VA)
Barolo Monfortino, Giacomo Conterno
1990 £209.00 (VA)

NORTH-WEST WHITE

Under £6.00

Chardonnay del Piemonte, Alasia 1997
£4.99 (UN) £5.79 (YOU) £5.99 (BEN)
Chardonnay del Piemonte, Giordano
1997 £5.62 (PEN)
Cortese del Piemonte, Araldica 1998
£4.59 (VA)
Gavi Arione Vini 1996 £5.80 (AV)
Moscato d'Asti, Araldica Non-vintage
£3.50 (WS) £4.34 (ROS)

£6.00 → £7.99

Arneis del Roero, Malvirà 1997 £7.49 (YOU)
Gavi Castello di Tassarolo 1997 £7.99 (MAJ)
Gavi Giordano 1997 £7.04 (PEN)
Gavi La Chiara 1996 £7.50 (BALL) £7.85
(CON)
Gavi La Raia 1998 £6.58 (BIB)
Moscato d'Asti Bricco Quaglia, la
Spinetta-Rivetti 1997 £7.95 (SOM)
Verbesco Chiarlo 1995 £6.50 (CRO)

£8.00 → £9.99

Erbaluce di Caluso La Rustia, Orsolani
1996 £9.95 (ROB)
Gavi Fontanafredda 1995 £8.95 (ROB)
★ Langhe Il Fiore, Serre dei Fiori 1998
£9.90 (TAN)
Moscato d'Asti Sourgal, Elio Perrone
1996 £8.05 (REI)
Moscato d'Asti Bricco Quaglia, la
Spinetta-Rivetti 1998 £8.95 (BAL)

£10.00 → £19.99

Arneis Blange Ceretto 1996 £11.99 (DI)
£12.49 (PLAY)
Chardonnay del Piemonte Giarone,
Bertelli 1993 £15.90 (JU)
Erbaluce di Caluso Passito, Boratto 1990
£16.95 (VA)
Gavi Pio Cesare 1997 £11.95 (FORT)
Rossj-Bass Gaja 1997 £18.95 (LAY)
St Marsan, Bertelli 1995 £14.90 (JU)

Over £20.00

Alteni di Brassica, Gaja 1993 £33.49 (TW)
Chardonnay Gaia & Rey, Gaja 1994
£54.64 (REI)
Chardonnay Rossj Bass, Gaja 1997
£22.50 (BEN) £23.99 (VA)
Gavi dei Gavi, la Scolca 1995 £22.95 (ROB)

NORTH-WEST SPARKLING

Under £6.00

Asti Baldovino Non-vintage £5.28 (PLA)
Asti Calissano Non-vintage £5.99 (JON)
£5.99 (POR)
★ Asti Gianni Non-vintage £4.49 (MORR)
Asti Martini Non-vintage £5.49 (TES)
£5.49 (WAI) £5.49 (SO) £5.49 (UN) £5.49
(CO) £5.49 (SAF) £5.49 (THR) £5.49 (WR)
£5.49 (BOT) £5.49 (ASD) £5.99 (OD)
£6.75 (WRI) £6.90 (STA) £6.92 (PLA)
£7.71 (VIN)

£6.00 → £9.99

Asti Arione Non-vintage £6.55 (AV)
Asti Cascina Castle't 1997 £6.79 (YOU)
Asti Cinzano Non-vintage £6.25 (COC)
Asti Fontanafredda Non-vintage £8.25
(UB) £8.79 (VA) £9.00 (FORT)
Malvasia Cantine Gemma Non-vintage
£8.25 (CON)

Over £15.00

Franciacorta Brut, Ca' del Bosco Non-
vintage £15.00 (CRO) £15.99 (VA)

NORTH-EAST RED

Under £5.00

Breganza Rosso, Bartolomeo da Breganze
1997 £4.99 (YOU)
Colli Berici Merlot La Casona 1995 £4.35
(CON)
Valpolicella Campagnola 1997 £4.32 (STE)
Valpolicella Campagnola 1996 £4.50 (ROB)
Valpolicella Classico Superiore Zenato
1996 £4.99 (THR) £4.99 (WR) £4.99
(BOT) £5.36 (STE) £5.65 (HED) £5.95 (NA)
Valpolicella Lenotti 1996 £4.99 (DI)
Valpolicella Rocca Merlata 1997 £3.95
(BALL)
Valpolicella Rocca Merlata 1996 £3.95
(HAH)

£5.00 → £5.99

Trentino Marzemino Letrari **1997** £5.75 (WS)

Trentino Merlot Mezzacorona **1997** £5.90 (COC)

Valpolicella Classico Allegrini **1997** £5.25 (WS) £5.60 (SOM) £6.59 (YOU) £6.99 (VA) £7.90 (CRO)

Valpolicella Classico Allegrini **1996** £5.95 (BU) £6.99 (PHI)

Valpolicella Classico Masi **1996** £5.49 (OD)

Valpolicella Classico Superiore Masi **1996** £5.99 (YOU) £6.50 (PIP)

Valpolicella Classico Superiore Tedeschi **1995** £5.75 (NLW)

Valpolicella Classico Superiore Valverde, Tedeschi **1995** £5.86 (COC)

Venegazzù Cabernet Sauvignon Venegazzù **1997** £5.50 (AV)

£6.00 → £7.99

Bardolino Classico Ca' Bordenis **1996** £6.50 (STA)

Bardolino le Vigne di San Pietro **1997** £7.75 (LIB)

Campo Fiorin Masi **1995** £7.49 (OD) £8.70 (PIP) £9.99 (DI)

Colli Orientali del Friuli Merlot Petrussa **1996** £7.95 (CON)

Teroldego Rotaliano Dorigati **1994** £6.85 (CON)

Valdadige Cabernet Cantina Sociale Della Valdadige Veronese **1995** £6.95 (LEA)

Valpolicella Classico Allegrini **1998** £6.99 (VA)

russizValpolicella Classico Allegrini **1995** £7.95 (JU)

Valpolicella Classico Antanel, Spinosa **1997** £7.25 (BEN)

★ Valpolicella Superiore Ripassa, Zenato **1995** £7.99 (WR) £7.99 (BOT)

£8.00 → £9.99

Breganze Rosso, Maculan **1994** £9.99 (DI)

Cabernet Sauvignon Morago **1994** £8.93 (CB)

Teroldego Rotaliano Foradori **1997** £9.95 (BAL)

Teroldego Rotaliano Foradori **1996** £8.69 (YOU)

Valpolicella Classico la Grola, Allegrini **1993** £9.70 (SOM) £12.25 (PHI)

Valpolicella Classico Superiore Acinatico, Stafano Accordini **1996** £8.90 (TAN)

£10.00 → £12.99

Amarone della Valpolicella Classico, Campagnola **1995** £12.99 (VIC) £12.99 (THR) £12.99 (BOT)

Amarone della Valpolicella Classico, Tedeschi **1995** £11.99 (MAJ) £12.99 (SAF)

Collio Cabernet Franc, Russiz Superiore **1996** £11.45 (NEZ)

Valpolicella Classico la Grola, Allegrini **1996** £12.25 (FORT)

Valpolicella Classico Palazzo della Torre, Allegrini **1995** £10.28 (REI) £10.99 (PHI)

Valpolicella Classico Superiore La Grola, Allegrini **1995** £11.00 (NO) £11.50 (PIP)

£13.00 → £14.99

Amarone della Valpolicella Classico, Tedeschi **1996** £13.99 (POR)

Amarone della Valpolicella Corte Rubini, Lamberti **1994** £14.90 (UB)

Amarone della Valpolicella Masi **1995** £14.99 (OD) £17.75 (PIP) £18.99 (DI)

Teroldego Rotaliano Diedri, Dorigati **1993** £13.50 (CON)

£15.00 → £19.99

Amarone della Valpolicella Capitel Monte Olmi, Tedeschi **1995** £19.35 (AV)

Amarone della Valpolicella Classico, Zenato **1993** £17.99 (WR)

Amarone della Valpolicella Classico, Allegrini **1993** £16.95 (SOM) £19.90 (VA)

Amarone della Valpolicella Tommasi **1993** £15.95 (AD)

Conte Federico, Bossi Fedrigotti **1990** £18.58 (NO)

Recioto della Valpolicella Classico Capitel Monte Fontana, Tedeschi **1993** £15.00 (AV)

Teroldego Rotaliano Vigneto Sgarzon Foradori **1996** £15.95 (BAL)

Valpolicella Classico Superiore Quintarelli **1992** £15.82 (BIB)

Over £20.00

Amarone della Valpolicella Capitel Monte Olmi, Tedeschi **1993** £21.50 (VA)

Amarone della Valpolicella Le Ragose **1986** £23.50 (ROB)

La Poja, Allegrini **1993** £22.99 (YOU) £23.90 (VA) £24.50 (STA) £26.80 (NO)

La Poja, Allegrini **1992** £26.50 (ROB)

Recioto della Valpolicella Quintarelli **1986** £42.50 (VA)

NORTH-EAST WHITE

Under £4.00

Chardonnay del Veneto, Canaletto 1997
£3.99 (BAL)
Friuli Grave Tocai Friulano San Simone
1996 £3.95 (JU)
Lugana San Benedetto, Zenato 1996
£2.99 (WR) £2.99 (BOT)
Soave Rocca Merlata 1997 £3.95 (HAH)
Soave Via Nova 1997 £3.50 (WS)

£4.00 → £4.99

Friuli Grave Sauvignon San Simone 1997
£4.75 (WAI)
★ Pinot Grigio La Vis 1998 £4.99 (VA)
Sauvignon La Casona 1996 £4.65 (CON)
Soave Campagnola 1998 £4.70 (NA)
Soave Campagnola 1996 £4.50 (ROB)
Soave Classico Superiore Zenato 1998
£4.99 (THR) £4.99 (WR) £4.99 (BOT)
Soave Classico Vigneto Colombara,
Zenato 1997 £4.95 (WAI) £5.65 (HED)
Trentino Pinot Grigio Ca'vit 1996 £4.99
(NLW)

£5.00 → £5.99

Colli Bolognesi Pinot Grigio Valdadige San
Vito 1997 £5.58 (JER)
Friuli Grave Pinot Grigio San Simone
1996 £5.45 (JU)
Lugana Ca' dei Frati 1997 £5.95 (WS)
£6.85 (SOM)
Lugana San Benedetto, Zenato 1997
£5.76 (STE) £6.40 (NA)
Lugana Villa Flora Riserva, Zenato 1998
£5.25 (WAI)
Pinot Grigio Bidoli 1998 £5.03 (GW)
Pinot Grigio Le Due Terre 1998 £5.70
(TAN)

Pinot Grigio Le Due Terre 1997 £5.89
(JON)
Soave Classico Anselmi 1997 £5.99 (SAI)
£9.25 (FORT)
Soave Classico Monte Tenda, Tedeschi
1996 £5.35 (AV)
Soave Classico Superiore Castelcerino
1997 £5.50 (TAN) £5.79 (JON)
Soave Classico Superiore Masi 1997
£5.39 (YOU) £6.75 (DI)
Soave Classico Vigneto Colombara,
Zenato 1998 £5.36 (STE) £5.95 (NA)

£6.00 → £7.99

Bianco di Custoza Gardoni 1995 £7.50
(ROB)
Bianco di Custoza le Vigne di San Pietro
1997 £7.89 (LIB)
Capitel San Rocco Bianco, Tedeschi 1995
£6.75 (AV)
Colli Orientali del Friuli Bianco Solivo,
Cantarutti 1995 £6.66 (JER)
Friuli Grave Pinot Grigio Le Fredis 1996
£6.75 (CON)
Soave Classico Col Baraca, Masi 1997
£7.60 (PIP)
Soave Classico San Vincenzo, Anselmi
1997 £7.99 (NI) £7.99 (PHI)
Soave Classico Suavia 1998 £6.56 (BIB)
Soave Classico Superiore Masi 1998
£6.11 (PIP)
Soave Classico Superiore Pieropan 1996
£6.60 (SOM)

£8.00 → £9.99

Collio Pinot Grigio Puiatti 1997 £9.50
(SOM)
Collio Sauvignon Vigna del Lauro 1996
£8.32 (JER)
Dindarello Maculan ½ bottle 1996 £9.58
(REI)

Lugana I Frati, Ca' dei Frati 1996 £8.50
(TAN)

Lugana Il Brolettino, Ca' dei Frati 1997
£9.90 (PIP) £10.99 (PHI)

Recioto di Soave le Colombare, Pieropan
1995 £9.95 (WS)

Soave Classico Capitel Foscarino, Anselmi
1997 £9.49 (NI)

Soave Classico San Vincenzo, Anselmi
1996 £8.75 (ROB)

Soave Classico Superiore Pieropan 1997
£8.25 (STA) £8.70 (TAN)

Soave Classico Vigneto la Rocca, Pieropan
1997 £9.95 (AD)

Soave Classico Vigneto la Rocca, Pieropan
1996 £8.95 (WS) £8.99 (VA) £10.99 (PHI)

£10.00 → £11.99

Collio Pinot Grigio Russiz Superiore
1997 £10.55 (NEZ)

Collio Pinot Grigio Puiatti 1995 £11.50 (JU)

Pinot Bianco Jermann 1996 £11.55 (SOM)
£13.69 (REI) £14.17 (NO) £14.95 (ROB)

Recioto di Soave I Capitelli, Anselmi ½
bottle 1995 £11.16 (REI) £11.95 (ROB)

Soave Classico Capitel Croce, Anselmi
1996 £10.49 (VA) £10.99 (NI) £10.99
(YOU) £11.75 (BU)

Soave Classico Vigneto Calvarino,
Pieropan 1996 £10.59 (JON)

£12.00 → £14.99

Chardonnay Jermann 1997 £12.99 (YOU)
£14.49 (VA)

Collio Pinot Bianco Schiopetto 1997
£14.50 (FORT) £15.49 (VA)

Collio Riesling Renano, Schiopetto 1997
£12.99 (YOU)

Collio Tocai Schiopetto 1997 £12.50
(BAN) £15.49 (VA)

Pinot Bianco Jermann 1995 £12.99 (NI)

Pinot Grigio Jermann 1997 £13.95 (BEN)
£13.99 (VA) £15.15 (UB)

Pinot Grigio Jermann 1996 £13.81 (REI)
£14.25 (STA)

Recioto di Soave le Colombare, Pieropan
1993 £13.99 (PHI)

Over £17.00

Recioto di Soave I Capitelli, Anselmi 1996
£17.99 (VA) £20.00 (BU)

Torcolato Maculan 1995 £26.44 (REI)

Vintage Tunina Jermann 1995 £23.50 (STA)

Vintage Tunina Jermann 1996 £22.91 (REI)
£24.95 (ROB)

NORTH-EAST SPARKLING

Under £9.00

Prosecco di Conegliano Carpenè Malvolti
Non-vintage £7.95 (LEA) £8.69 (VA)

CENTRAL RED

Under £4.00

★ Montepulciano d'Abruzzo, Miglanico
1997 £3.99 (UN)

Rosso Conero San Lorenzo, Umani Ronchi
1995 £3.99 (VIC) £3.99 (THR) £3.99 (WR)
£3.99 (BOT) £5.80 (SOM) £7.95 (RES)

Sangiovese di Toscana Cecchi 1997 £3.99
(WAI) £3.99 (SAI) £3.99 (VIC) £3.99 (THR)
£3.99 (WR) £3.99 (BOT)

£4.00 → £4.99

Bolgheri Poggio Fiorito, le Macchiole
1997 £4.95 (LEA)

Chianti Querceto 1996 £4.95 (JU)

Chianti Rufina Grati 1997 £4.49 (MAJ)
£4.95 (WS)

Chianti Rufina Villa di Vetrice 1996 £4.99
(POR) £5.50 (TAN) £5.80 (HAH) £5.99
(YOU) £6.45 (ROS)

Montepulciano d'Abruzzo, Roxan 1997
£4.99 (AME) £5.75 (LAY)

Montepulciano d'Abruzzo Cornacchia
1997 £4.99 (VA) £4.99 (MAJ) £4.99 (BO)
£5.39 (PEN) £5.99 (BU)

Montepulciano d'Abruzzo Umani Ronchi
1997 £4.54 (FLE) £4.79 (YOU) £4.95 (RES)

Parrina Rosso La Parrina 1995 £4.99 (NI)

£5.00 → £5.99

Chianti Classico Rocca delle Macie 1997
£5.69 (NI) £6.99 (MAJ)

Chianti Classico Otto Santi 1996 £5.99
(CO)

Chianti Rufina Riserva Villa di Vetrice 1995
£5.99 (VIC) £5.99 (THR) £5.99 (BOT)

Chianti Rufina Riserva Villa di Vetrice 1993
£5.95 (WS) £6.99 (YOU) £7.50 (PIP)

Chianti Rufina Villa di Vetrice 1995 £5.20
(SOM) £5.59 (JON)

Parrina Rosso La Parrina 1997 £5.99 (VA)
£6.99 (BEN) £6.99 (LIB)

Parrina Rosso La Parrina 1996 £5.25 (SOM)
£5.99 (YOU) £6.49 (LIB) £6.95 (ROB)

Santa Cristina, Antinori 1997 £5.69 (NEZ)
£6.99 (DI)

£6.00 → £6.99

Carmignano Barco Reale, Capezzana
1997 £6.99 (VA) £7.99 (LIB) £8.00 (FLE)
£8.35 (HED) £8.40 (HAH)
Chianti Classico le Capanne, Querceto
1995 £6.50 (JU)
Chianti Classico Villa Cafaggio **1997**
£6.99 (UN) £8.50 (AS)
Chianti Colli Senesi Cecchi **1997** £6.99
(WAI)
Chianti Rufina Selvapiana **1996** £6.95 (WS)
£8.49 (LIB) £9.95 (FORT)
Chianti Rufina Villa di Vetrice **1997** £6.30
(PIP)
Montepulciano d'Abruzzo Cornacchia
1996 £6.07 (JER)
Montescudaio Rosso delle Miniere,
Fattoria di Sorbaiano **1997** £6.45 (CON)
Morellino di Scansano le Pupille **1997**
£6.95 (WS) £8.99 (YOU) £9.65 (HED)
Rosso Conero San Lorenzo, Umani
Ronchi **1996** £6.59 (VA) £7.50 (TAN)
Val di Cornia Gualdo del Re **1997** £6.95
(LEA)

£7.00 → £7.99

Chianti Classico Aziano, Ruffino **1996**
£7.59 (COC)
Chianti Classico Brolio **1996** £7.50 (WS)
£7.99 (VA)
Chianti Classico la Lellera, Matta **1995**
£7.75 (WHI)
Chianti Classico Montiverdi **1994** £7.79
(CON)
Chianti Classico Nozzole **1995** £7.64 (JER)
Chianti Rufina Riserva Villa di Vetrice
1988 £7.07 (ROS)
Chianti Classico San Jacopo, Vicchiomaggio
1996 £7.94 (PEN) £9.14 (COC)
Chianti Rufina Selvapiana **1995** £7.26 (FLE)
Rosso di Montalcino Altesino **1995** £7.99
(POR)
Rosso di Montalcino Campo ai Sassi,
Frescobaldi **1996** £7.99 (OD)
Rosso di Montepulciano Dei **1997** £7.95
(LEA)
Rosso Piceno Vigna Piediprato, Pilastri
1995 £7.49 (BAL) £7.90 (BEN)
Rubesco Rosso di Torgiano Lungarotti
1993 £7.95 (ROB)
Vino Nobile di Montepulciano Cerro
1997 £7.49 (OD)
Vino Nobile di Montepulciano Fassati
1995 £7.99 (MAJ)

£8.00 → £8.99

Bolgheri Vigneto le Contessine, le
Macchiole **1997** £8.50 (LEA)
Castelrapiti Montellori **1992** £8.95 (BAN)
£10.15 (SOM)
Chianti Classico Castello dei Rampolla
1996 £8.32 (CAV) £10.95 (BAL)
Chianti Classico Castello di Fonterutoli
1996 £8.99 (BAL) £9.49 (VA) £10.99 (PHI)
Chianti Classico Castello di Volpaia **1996**
£8.95 (AD)
Chianti Classico Fontodi **1996** £8.50 (WS)
£10.95 (LIB) £11.50 (CRO) £11.99 (PHI)
Chianti Classico Riserva Antinori **1996**
£8.99 (NEZ)
Chianti Classico Riserva Antinori **1995**
£8.49 (NLW) £8.65 (HAH)
Chianti Classico Riserva Villa Antinori
1995 £8.20 (TAN) £8.99 (VA) £8.99 (WR)
Chianti Classico Villa Cafaggio **1996**
£8.35 (WRI)
Chianti Colli Senesi Villa Sant' Anna **1995**
£8.95 (LEA)
Chianti Rufina Castello di Nipozzano
1996 £8.99 (MAJ)
Chianti Rufina Riserva Selvapiana **1995**
£8.95 (WS) £11.90 (BEN) £11.95 (LIB)
Le Volte, Tenuta dell'Ornellaia **1996**
£8.50 (DI) £9.22 (REI) £9.79 (YOU)
Le Volte, Tenuta dell'Ornellaia **1994**
£8.18 (NO)
Montefalco Rosso Caprai **1995** £8.49
(BAL) £9.49 (LIB) £9.75 (HED) £9.99 (VA)
Morellino di Scansano le Pupille **1998**
£8.99 (VA) £9.39 (LIB)
Parrina Reserva, La Parrina **1995** £8.39
(YOU) £10.95 (STA)
Rosso di Montalcino Argiano **1997** £8.40
(SOM) £8.50 (WS) £9.79 (VA) £9.99 (PHI)
£10.49 (LIB) £10.50 (BEN) £10.75 (HED)
Rosso Piceno Vigna Piediprato, Pilastri
1997 £8.80 (BEN)
Tignanello Antinori **1990** £8.71 (CAV)
£52.88 (REI) £125.00 (VA)

£9.00 → £9.99

Carmignano Villa di Capezzana **1995**
£9.75 (WS) £21.80 (TAN)
Chianti Classico Fontodi **1997** £9.99 (VA)
£12.95 (BEN) £12.95 (LIB)
Chianti Classico Riserva Monsanto **1986**
£9.95 (RAE)
Chianti Classico Villa Antinori **1995** £9.99
(DI)

Montescudaio Rosso delle Miniere,
Fattoria di Sorbaiano **1995** £9.95 (BALL)
£10.80 (TAN) £11.99 (VA) £12.49 (JON)
Pomino Rosso Frescobaldi **1994** £9.99 (OD)
Rosso Conero Fattoria le Terrazze **1993**
£9.28 (TW)
Rosso di Montalcino Argiano **1996** £9.95
(ROB)
Rosso di Montalcino, Lisini **1996** £9.99 (RAE)
Rosso di Montalcino Vigna della Fonte,
Ciacci Piccolomini d'Aragona **1995**
£9.25 (NO)
Rosso di Montalcino Villa Banfi **1997**
£9.99 (VA)
Sangioveto Badia a Coltibuono **1983**
£9.77 (FLE)
Vino Nobile di Montepulciano Avignonesi
1995 £9.45 (WAI) £10.35 (STE) £11.50
(NA)
Vino Nobile di Montepulciano Bindella
1996 £9.99 (BIB)
Vino Nobile di Montepulciano le Casalte
1993 £9.80 (SOM)

£10.00 → £11.99

Arquata Rosso dell'Umbria, Adanti **1991**
£11.99 (CON)
Campovecchio Rosso, Castel de Paolis
1996 £10.95 (BAL)
Carmignano Villa di Capezzana **1996**
£10.99 (VA) £12.99 (LIB)
Chianti Classico Castello di Ama **1995**
£11.73 (WT)
Chianti Classico Felsina Berardenga **1996**
£10.99 (PHI) £11.75 (LIB) £11.80 (PIP)
£11.99 (BEN) £12.95 (VA) £13.95 (RES)
Chianti Classico Isole e Olena **1997** £10.50
(WS) £10.99 (SOM) £11.99 (VA) £13.37
(FLE) £13.75 (STA) £13.75 (BEN) £13.95 (LIB)
Chianti Classico Isole e Olena **1996** £10.99
(YOU) £13.75 (FORT) £14.50 (TAN)
Chianti Classico Pèppoli, Antinori **1996**
£10.99 (VA)
Chianti Classico Riserva Ducale, Ruffino
1995 £11.49 (VA)

- *Wines are listed in A–Z
  order within each price
  band.*
- *For each wine, vintages are
  listed in descending order.*
- *Each vintage of any wine
  appears only once.*

Chianti Classico Vecchie Terre di
Montefili **1995** £11.50 (RAE)
Le Volte, Tenuta dell'Ornellaia **1997**
£11.13 (PIP)
Parrina Reserva, La Parrina **1997** £10.95
(BEN) £10.95 (LIB)
Rosso Conero Cumaro, Umani Ronchi
1994 £10.35 (SOM) £12.34 (REI) £14.95
(RES)
Rosso di Montalcino Col d'Orcia **1997**
£10.35 (VA)
Rosso di Montalcino Costanti **1995**
£10.80 (SOM) £14.95 (PHI)
Vino Nobile di Montepulciano Avignonesi
1994 £10.95 (HED)
Vino Nobile di Montepulciano Dei **1995**
£10.95 (LEA)
Vino Nobile di Montepulciano Poliziano
1996 £10.99 (PHI)
Vino Nobile di Montepulciano Poliziano
1995 £11.59 (JON) £11.80 (NO) £12.60
(PIP)
Vino Nobile di Montepulciano Riserva,
Avignonesi **1993** £11.99 (WR) £11.99
(BOT) £12.04 (REI)
Vino Nobile di Montepulciano Trerose
1995 £11.99 (DI)

£12.00 → £14.99

Bongoverno Farneta **1986** £14.21 (NO)
Brunello di Montalcino Promis, Pieve
Santa Restituta **1996** £13.90 (LAY)
Carmignano Riserva, Villa di Capezzana
1995 £12.99 (LIB)
Chianti Classico Riserva Castello di
Volpaia **1996** £12.50 (AD)
Chianti Classico Riserva Ducale, Ruffino
1993 £13.20 (COC) £16.95 (VA)
Chianti Classico Riserva Felsina
Berardenga **1994** £13.99 (VA) £15.75
(LIB) £15.95 (STA) £15.95 (BEN)
Chianti Classico Riserva Marchese
Antinori **1995** £13.95 (VA) £15.99 (DI)
Chianti Classico Riserva Nozzole **1994**
£13.32 (JER)
Chianti Classico Riserva Querciabella
1994 £14.50 (LEA) £15.45 (GW)
Chianti Classico Riserva Santa Cristina,
Antinori **1990** £12.00 (CRO)
Chianti Classico Riserva Ser Lapo,
Castello di Fonterutoli **1994** £12.99 (NI)
£15.69 (VA) £15.99 (PHI) £20.50 (RES)
Chianti Rufina Riserva Bucerchiale,
Selvapiana **1995** £13.95 (WS) £16.75
(LIB) £17.95 (FORT)

Federico Primo Gualdo del Re **1994** £13.71 (JER)

Il Latini, Il Vivaio **1994** £13.50 (WS) £17.96 (LAY)

Montepulciano d'Abruzzo Emidio Pepe **1995** £13.49 (VA)

Morellino di Scansano Riserva, le Pupille **1996** £14.39 (LIB) £14.99 (VA)

Rosso Conero Cumaro, Umani Ronchi **1995** £12.59 (YOU) £12.99 (VA) £14.30 (TAN)

Rosso Conero Cumaro, Umani Ronchi **1991** £12.99 (PHI)

Tavernelle Villa Banfi **1994** £13.84 (PEN)

Vigna il Vallone Villa Sant' Anna **1993** £14.50 (LEA)

Vino Nobile di Montepulciano le Casalte **1997** £12.50 (BU)

Vino Nobile di Montepulciano le Casalte **1996** £12.49 (AME)

Vino Nobile di Montepulciano Vigneto Caggiole, Poliziano **1994** £14.12 (NO)

£15.00 → £19.99

Brancaia, La Brancaia **1995** £16.95 (BAL) £19.95 (LEA)

Brunello di Montalcino Argiano **1994** £15.75 (WS) £16.90 (SOM) £19.95 (LIB) £19.95 (VA) £21.00 (STA) £22.50 (BEN)

Brunello di Montalcino Castelgiocondo **1993** £19.00 (TAN) £20.80 (PIP)

Brunello di Montalcino Friggiali **1993** £17.09 (WT)

Brunello di Montalcino Poggio Antico **1991** £19.95 (WAI) £23.00 (ROB)

Brunello di Montalcino Quercecchio **1993** £16.75 (BALL)

Brunello di Montalcino Quercecchio **1991** £18.25 (CON)

Brunello di Montalcino Val di Suga **1993** £17.82 (COC) £18.98 (PLAY) £19.95 (DI)

Brunello di Montalcino Villa Banfi **1993** £16.84 (PEN) £17.95 (VA) £18.69 (BO)

Brunesco di San Lorenzo Cappelli **1988** £18.75 (WS)

Cepparello, Isole e Olena **1993** £19.00 (CRO) £21.25 (BEN) £21.50 (VA)

Chianti Classico Cipressone, Montiverdi **1988** £19.25 (CON)

Chianti Classico Riserva Carpineto **1990** £16.50 (AV)

Chianti Classico Riserva Castell'in Villa **1993** £15.79 (CB)

Chianti Classico Riserva Castell'in Villa **1988** £15.30 (UB)

Chianti Classico Riserva Castello dei Rampolla **1995** £15.67 (CAV) £17.50 (BAL)

Chianti Classico Riserva Castello di Fonterutoli **1995** £19.49 (YOU) £19.50 (BAL) £20.99 (VA) £22.50 (BU) £23.50 (RES)

Chianti Classico Riserva Fontodi **1995** £16.49 (LIB) £16.95 (BEN) £16.95 (VA)

Chianti Classico Riserva Il Picchio, Querceto **1991** £17.00 (JU)

Chianti Classico Riserva, Fattoria Ormanni **1995** £16.95 (BEN)

Chianti Classico Riserva Ser Lapo, Castello di Fonterutoli **1995** £18.99 (PHI)

Chianti Classico Riserva Vigna del Sorbo, Fontodi **1995** £16.50 (WS) £21.95 (VA)

Chianti Classico Riserva Vigna del Sorbo, Fontodi **1994** £16.75 (SOM) £20.75 (LIB)

Chianti Classico Riserva Vigneto Rancia, Felsina Berardenga **1994** £17.75 (WS) £17.99 (YOU) £19.25 (LIB) £19.80 (BEN)

Chianti Classico Villa Antinori **1961** £15.00 (BU)

Chianti Colli Senesi la Torre **1979** £16.50 (BU)

Coltassala Castello di Volpaia **1994** £16.95 (AD)

Concerto Fonterutoli **1994** £19.95 (BAL) £19.95 (VA) £23.50 (RES)

Elegia Poliziano **1995** £19.99 (VA) £20.27 (REI)

Flaccianello della Pieve, Fontodi **1995** £19.99 (VA) £24.25 (LIB)

Fontalloro, Felsina Berardenga **1993** £16.95 (SOM) £21.84 (NO) £22.50 (PHI)

Ghiaie della Furba, Capezzana **1995** £15.85 (SOM) £21.00 (TAN)

Grifi Avignonesi **1995** £15.08 (STE) £16.75 (NA) £16.99 (WR) £16.99 (BOT)

Il Querciolaia, Querceto **1991** £18.00 (JU)

Lamaione Merlot Frescobaldi **1995** £17.99 (OD)

Palazzo Altesi, Altesino **1995** £16.95 (POR) £17.95 (LEA)

Quercia Grande, Capaccia **1993** £19.95 (CON) £19.95 (VA)

Rosso della Rocca Meleta **1992** £18.75
(LAY)
Rosso di Montalcino Costanti **1994**
£16.50 (BU)
Rosso Miani, Miani **1994** £16.95 (BAL)
San Giorgio Lungarotti **1987** £17.89 (VA)
Sangioveto Badia a Coltibuono **1980**
£15.00 (CRO)
Vino Nobile di Montepulciano Riserva, Il
Macchione **1991** £15.95 (BER)
Vino Nobile di Montepulciano Vigna
Asinone, Poliziano **1993** £17.49 (VA)
£19.95 (RES)

£20.00 → £24.99

Brunello di Montalcino Argiano **1993**
£24.99 (PHI)
Brunello di Montalcino Casanova di Neri
1993 £23.95 (LEA)
Brunello di Montalcino Costanti **1994**
£24.00 (WS) £26.95 (BEN) £26.95 (LIB)
Brunello di Montalcino Fattoria dei Barbi
1993 £22.50 (PIP) £23.99 (VA) £24.95 (RES)
Brunello di Montalcino Friggiali **1990**
£21.89 (NO)
Brunello di Montalcino Poggio Antico
1993 £22.95 (VA)
Brunello di Montalcino Riserva,
Castelgiocondo **1980** £22.00 (CRO)
Camartina Querciabella **1994** £24.95 (LEA)
Cepparello, Isole e Olena **1995** £24.95 (VA)
£25.49 (LIB) £26.50 (BEN) £31.33 (CAV)
Chianti Classico Riserva Santa Cristina,
Antinori **1983** £21.00 (CRO)
Chianti Classico Riserva Vecchie Terre di
Montefili **1990** £23.99 (RAE)
Chianti Classico Vignamaggio **1971**
£20.00 (BU)
Chianti Rufina Selvapiana **1990** £24.00
(CRO)
Cignale Querceto **1991** £21.00 (JU)
Flaccianello della Pieve, Fontodi **1996**
£24.95 (VA) £25.75 (LIB)
Fontalloro, Felsina Berardenga **1994**
£23.95 (LIB) £23.95 (VA) £24.50 (BEN)
Ghiaie della Furba, Capezzana **1994**
£24.35 (PLAY)
Monte Vertine Riserva, Monte Vertine
1993 £20.56 (REI)
Ornellaia Tenuta dell'Ornellaia **1994**
£24.95 (DI) £29.95 (RES) £32.00 (VA)
Rosso Miani, Miani **1995** £20.68 (NO)
Sammarco Castello dei Rampolla **1994**
£23.50 (CAV)
San Giorgio Lungarotti **1981** £24.00 (CRO)

Sangioveto Badia a Coltibuono **1982**
£22.91 (REI)
Le Stanze Cabernet Sauvignon, Poliziano
1995 £20.27 (REI)
Syrah Isole e Olena **1995** £22.49 (LIB)
Tignanello Antinori **1991** £23.95 (DI)
£45.00 (VA)
Vino Nobile di Montepulciano Bindella
1986 £20.00 (CRO)

£25.00 → £29.99

Brunello di Montalcino Altesino **1993**
£27.99 (POR)
Brunello di Montalcino Costanti **1993**
£26.95 (BEN) £27.60 (HAH) £29.95 (RES)
Brunello di Montalcino Costanti **1991**
£26.00 (PHI) £27.95 (ROB)
Brunello di Montalcino Rennina, Pieve
Santa Restituta **1994** £27.35 (LAY)
Brunello di Montalcino Villa Banfi **1983**
£26.44 (REI)
Cabernet Sauvignon Isole e Olena **1995**
£26.95 (LIB)
Cepparello, Isole e Olena **1988** £27.00
(CRO)
Coltassala Castello di Volpaia **1987**
£26.44 (REI)
Guado al Tasso, Antinori **1995** £28.00
(CRO) £32.00 (VA) £35.64 (FA)
Guado al Tasso, Antinori **1993** £26.50
(VA) £29.50 (ROB)
Ornellaia Tenuta dell'Ornellaia **1993**
£27.99 (YOU) £31.95 (LEA) £34.50 (ROB)
Ornellaia Tenuta dell'Ornellaia **1992**
£25.60 (PIP) £28.95 (PHI) £45.00 (VA)
Saffredi le Pupille **1995** £25.95 (LIB)
£28.50 (HED)
Sammarco Castello dei Rampolla **1993**
£25.50 (BAL)
Sangioveto Badia a Coltibuono **1995**
£28.50 (AV)
Tignanello Antinori **1995** £25.00 (CRO)
£26.40 (TAN) £28.25 (HAH) £28.99 (WR)
£29.99 (YOU) £32.50 (BAL) £34.66 (FA)
Tignanello Antinori **1994** £26.75 (DI)
£27.50 (FORT) £28.99 (JON) £29.95 (ROB)

> • All prices for each wine are
> listed together in ascending
> order.
> • Price bands refer to the
> lowest price for which the
> wine is available.

£30.00 → £39.99

Alte d'Altesi, Altesino **1988** £33.00 (CRO)
Cepparello, Isole e Olena **1990** £33.00 (CRO)
Chianti Classico Badia a Coltibuono **1959** £41.13 (REI)
Chianti Classico Riserva Felsina Berardenga **1990** £33.00 (CRO)
Montepulciano d'Abruzzo Emidio Pepe **1979** £39.00 (VA)
Ornellaia Tenuta dell'Ornellaia **1995** £30.00 (VA) £33.19 (FA) £41.20 (TAN) £41.61 (CAV) £44.00 (LEA) £45.00 (FORT)
Le Pergole Torte, Monte Vertine **1995** £31.95 (LEA)
San Giorgio Lungarotti **1978** £30.00 (CRO)
Tignanello Antinori **1980** £35.00 (YOU)
Vino Nobile di Montepulciano Fassati **1970** £39.00 (CRO)

£40.00 → £49.99

Brunello di Montalcino Fattoria dei Barbi **1968** £47.50 (BU)
Brunello di Montalcino Rennina, Pieve Santa Restituta **1990** £45.00 (MI)
Brunello di Montalcino Sugarille, Pieve Santa Restituta **1990** £43.39 (NO) £78.33 (MI)
Chianti Classico Brolio **1966** £41.13 (REI)
Chianti Classico Riserva Santa Cristina, Antinori **1964** £41.13 (REI)
Chianti Classico Riserva Villa Antinori **1964** £41.13 (REI)
Fontalloro, Felsina Berardenga **1990** £49.00 (VA)
Il Carbonaione, Podere Poggio Scalette **1994** £41.61 (CAV)
Masseto Tenuta dell'Ornellaia **1993** £43.48 (CB) £55.00 (RES) £55.00 (FORT)
Masseto Tenuta dell'Ornellaia **1992** £44.50 (VA) £65.00 (ROB) £85.00 (BU)
Montepulciano d'Abruzzo Emidio Pepe **1990** £49.00 (VA)
Sassicaia Tenuta San Guido **1995** £47.70 (TAN) £55.22 (FA) £69.00 (BAL) £72.50 (BEN) £85.00 (VA)
Sassicaia Tenuta San Guido **1994** £42.99 (WR) £42.99 (BOT) £43.12 (NO) £44.00 (DI) £50.00 (ROB)
Sassicaia Tenuta San Guido **1993** £49.50 (BEN) £51.76 (PLAY) £58.95 (ROB) £65.00 (VA)
Solaia Antinori **1995** £44.00 (CRO) £50.00 (YOU)
Tignanello Antinori **1982** £48.00 (VA)

£50.00 → £69.99

Chianti Classico Riserva Badia a Coltibuono **1968** £50.00 (CRO)
Sassicaia Tenuta San Guido **1989** £52.88 (REI) £99.00 (VA) £117.50 (CAV)
Solaia Antinori **1994** £50.00 (VA) £59.95 (ROB)
Solaia Antinori **1988** £61.12 (NO) £71.87 (FA)
Solaia Antinori **1986** £68.00 (VA)
Tignanello Antinori **1985** £67.95 (FA) £145.00 (VA)

£70.00 → £99.99

Brunello di Montalcino Riserva, Biondi-Santi **1970** £70.00 (CRO)
Guado al Tasso, Antinori **1990** £97.33 (FA)
Masseto Tenuta dell'Ornellaia **1987** £99.88 (REI)
Ornellaia Tenuta dell'Ornellaia **1990** £90.00 (BEN) £111.63 (REI) £139.00 (VA)
Ornellaia Tenuta dell'Ornellaia **1988** £95.00 (FORT)
Sassicaia Tenuta San Guido **1981** £88.13 (REI) £159.00 (VA)
Tignanello Antinori **1988** £85.00 (VA)

£100.00 → £149.99

Brunello di Montalcino Biondi-Santi **1988** £100.00 (VA)
Sassicaia Tenuta San Guido **1988** £110.00 (CRO) £185.00 (VA)

Over £150.00

Brunello di Montalcino Riserva, Biondi-Santi **1990** £165.00 (VA)
Sassicaia Tenuta San Guido **1990** £229.00 (VA)
Solaia Antinori **1990** £195.00 (VA)

CENTRAL WHITE

Under £4.50

Est! Est!! Est!!! di Montefiascone, Bigi
1998 £3.15 (MORR)
Frascati Superiore San Matteo 1997
£4.49 (YOU)
Frascati Superiore Satinata, Colle di
Catone 1998 £3.99 (ASD)
Grechetto dell'Umbria, Il Vignolo 1997
£4.40 (SOM)
Orvieto Classico Secco Cardeto 1997
£4.46 (STE) £4.95 (NA)
Trebbiano d'Abruzzo Villa Leoni 1995
£4.41 (JER)
Verdicchio dei Castelli di Jesi Classico,
Umani Ronchi 1997 £4.20 (NI) £4.94
(FLE) £6.63 (NO)

£4.50 → £5.49

Est! Est!! Est!!! di Montefiascone, Bigi
1997 £4.99 (UN)
Frascati Superiore Fontana Candida 1997
£4.99 (NI) £6.25 (STA)
Frascati Superiore Satinata, Colle di
Catone 1996 £5.45 (JU) £5.99 (VIC)
£5.99 (THR) £5.99 (WR) £5.99 (BOT)
Orvieto Classico Abboccato Antinori
1998 £4.99 (VIC) £4.99 (THR) £4.99 (BOT)
Orvieto Classico Abboccato Antinori 1997
£5.49 (JON) £5.49 (YOU) £5.70 (TAN)
Orvieto Classico Campogrande Castello
della Sala, Antinori 1997 £5.49 (YOU)
Orvieto Classico Secco Antinori 1997
£4.99 (VIC) £4.99 (THR) £4.99 (WR) £4.99
(BOT) £5.49 (JON) £5.50 (TAN)
Orvieto Classico Secco Bigi 1996 £5.17
(ROS)
Orvieto Secco Barberani 1997 £5.25 (WS)
Verdicchio dei Castelli di Jesi Classico,
Brunori 1997 £5.49 (BIB)
Vernaccia di San Gimignano Signano 1998
£4.95 (WS)
Vernaccia di San Gimignano Strozzi 1997
£5.49 (BAL)

£5.50 → £6.99

Bianco di Avignonesi, Avignonesi 1996
£6.87 (REI)
Bianco Villa Antinori 1998 £5.99 (NEZ)
£6.59 (VA)
Bianco Villa Antinori 1996 £5.70 (HAH)
Chardonnay Villa di Capezzana 1998
£6.99 (LIB)

Frascati Superiore Monteporzio 1997
£5.99 (VA)
Grechetto dell'Umbria Adanti 1996 £6.25
(BALL)
Montefalco Bianco, Adanti 1996 £6.49
(CON) £6.69 (JON)
Montescudaio Bianco, Fattoria di
Sorbaiano 1994 £5.59 (CON)
Orvieto Classico Abboccato Antinori
1994 £5.85 (ROB)
Orvieto Classico Amabile Bigi 1998 £5.99
(VA)
Orvieto Classico Antinori 1997 £5.99
(DI) £6.35 (CB) £7.80 (CRO)
Orvieto Classico Campogrande Castello
della Sala, Antinori 1998 £5.50 (NEZ)
Orvieto Classico Secco Antinori 1994
£5.95 (ROB)
Orvieto Classico Secco Campogrande,
Antinori 1997 £5.99 (DI)
Orvieto Classico Vigneto Torricella, Bigi
1997 £5.50 (SOM) £6.95 (STA) £7.49
(VA) £7.50 (AD) £7.95 (FORT)
Orvieto Secco Antinori 1998 £5.99 (VA)
Orvieto Secco Antinori 1996 £5.59 (NLW)
Orvieto Secco Bigi 1997 £5.99 (VA)
Toscano Villa Antinori, Antinori 1996
£6.95 (HAH)
Verdicchio dei Castelli di Jesi Classico
Casal di Serra, Umani Ronchi 1997
£5.80 (SOM) £6.79 (VA) £6.95 (BU) £6.99
(NI) £7.25 (STA) £7.25 (FORT)
Verdicchio dei Castelli di Jesi Classico
Villa Bianchi, Ronchi 1997 £5.70 (TAN)
Verdicchio di Matelica, Fattoria
Monacesca 1996 £6.36 (JER) £8.49 (BAL)
Verdicchio di Matelica, Filli Bisci 1995
£5.95 (JU)
Vernaccia di San Gimignano Falchini 1997
£5.99 (RAE)
Vernaccia di San Gimignano Teruzzi e
Puthod 1997 £6.35 (SOM) £7.29 (YOU)
£7.60 (PIP) £8.25 (ROB) £12.99 (VA)

£7.00 → £9.99

Borro Lastricato Selvapiana 1998 £7.99 (LIB)
Frascati Superiore Campovecchio, Castel
de Paolis 1997 £9.95 (BAL)
Orvieto Classico Campo del Guardiano, Il
Palazzone 1995 £7.35 (JU)
Pinot Bianco Gualdo del Re 1996 £7.64 (JER)
Verdicchio dei Castelli di Jesi Classico,
Coroncino 1997 £9.96 (LAY)
Vernaccia di San Gimignano Fiore,
Montenidoli 1997 £9.96 (BIB)

£10.00 → £12.99

Chardonnay I Sistri, Felsina Berardenga **1996** £10.25 (SOM) £12.79 (YOU) £13.49 (LIB) £13.50 (STA) £13.95 (BEN) £13.99 (VA)

Frascati Colle Gaio, Colli di Catone **1994** £12.99 (VA)

Frascati Superiore Castel de Paolis **1996** £12.50 (BAL)

Pomino il Benefizio, Frescobaldi **1995** £12.99 (VA)

Vin Santo Brolio ½ bottle **1988** £10.02 (NO)

Vin Santo Villa di Vetrice **1979** £12.20 (TAN) £17.11 (ROS)

£13.00 → £19.99

Cervaro della Sala, Antinori **1997** £18.00 (NEZ)

Chardonnay Isole e Olena **1997** £15.95 (LIB) £16.99 (VA)

Il Marzocco, Avignonesi **1995** £13.51 (REI)

Vernaccia di San Gimignano Terre di Tufi, Teruzzi e Puthod **1996** £14.95 (LEA) £14.95 (ROB)

Vin Santo Antinori **1993** £19.95 (LEA)

Vin Santo Selvapiana 50cl bottle **1991** £19.49 (LIB) £20.99 (VA)

Over £20.00

Batàr Querciabella **1997** £24.95 (LEA)

Cervaro della Sala, Antinori **1996** £22.50 (BAL) £22.95 (VA) £23.50 (ROB)

Cervaro della Sala, Antinori **1991** £20.95 (DI)

Trebbiano d'Abruzzo Valentini **1993** £24.95 (BAL)

Vin Santo Avignonese ½ bottle **1987** £55.23 (REI)

Vin Santo Isole e Olena **1993** £21.95 (LIB)

CENTRAL ROSÉ

c. £8.00

Carmignano Vinruspo Rosato, Capezzana **1998** £7.95 (LIB)

CENTRAL SPARKLING

Under £6.00

Lambrusco di Modena, Cavicchioli **Non-vintage** £5.49 (YOU)

Lambrusco Grasparossa di Castelvetro **1994** £5.50 (PHI)

SOUTHERN RED

Under £5.00

Carignano del Sulcis, Santadi **1995** £2.99 (WR) £2.99 (BOT) £5.85 (HED) £6.20 (PIP)

Copertino Eloquenzia, Masseria Monaci **1995** £4.35 (SOM) £5.95 (POR)

Salice Salentino Riserva Candido **1994** £4.95 (WS) £5.97 (NO) £5.99 (YOU) £6.40 (REI) £6.70 (TAN)

Salice Salentino Vallone **1995** £4.99 (BO) £4.99 (POR) £5.49 (AME) £5.50 (BU) £6.00 (LAY) £6.09 (JON)

Salice Salentino Vallone **1994** £4.50 (SOM) £4.99 (BAL) £5.29 (YOU) £20.95 (NO)

Settesoli Rosso **1997** £4.89 (COC)

£5.00 → £5.99

Aglianico del Taburno, Cantina del Taburno **1993** £5.75 (WS)

Barbaglio Santa Barbara **1994** £5.75 (BALL)

Barbaglio Santa Barbara **1993** £5.99 (CON)

Cappello di Prete, Candido **1994** £5.50 (WS) £7.45 (ROB) £7.58 (REI) £7.99 (VA)

Cirò Classico Librandi **1997** £5.99 (VA)

Copertino Riserva, Cantina Copertino **1994** £5.60 (SOM) £6.43 (NO) £6.99 (VA)

Rosso Brindisi Santa Barbara **1993** £5.15 (TAN)

Rosso del Salento Cappello di Prete **1990** £5.65 (CON)

Rosso del Salento Notarpanaro Taurino **1993** £5.99 (MAJ)

Salice Salentino Riserva Candido **1993** £5.45 (SOM)

Salice Salentino Vallone **1996** £5.02 (ROS)

£6.00 → £7.99

Aglianico del Vulture, Fratelli d'Angelo **1995** £7.59 (YOU) £8.49 (VA) £8.50 (ROB)

Cannonau di Sardegna Costera, Argiolas **1995** £7.45 (ROB)

Carignano del Sulcis, Santadi **1991** £6.50 (STA)

Corvo Rosso Duca di Salaparuta **1966** £6.99 (VA)

Corvo Rosso Duca di Salaparuta **1994** £6.25 (COC)

Pier delle Vigne Rosso delle Murge, Botromagno **1992** £6.99 (BAL)

Regaleali Rosso, Tasca d'Almerita-Regaleali **1997** £7.56 (COC)

Regaleali Rosso, Tasca d'Almerita-Regaleali **1996** £7.25 (LEA) £7.66 (PIP)

Regaleali Rosso, Tasca d'Almerita **1993**
£7.65 (ROB)
Rosso del Salento Cappello di Prete **1994**
£7.09 (JON) £7.30 (PIP)
Salice Salentino Candido **1994** £6.49 (VA)
Simposia Masseria Monaci **1994** £7.99 (BAL)
Vigna Virzi Rosso, Spadafora **1997** £6.40
(SOM) £7.95 (LIB)

£8.00 → £9.99

Aglianico del Vulture, Fratelli d'Angelo
1996 £8.40 (TAN) £8.49 (VA)
Aglianico del Vulture, Paternoster **1995**
£8.95 (BU)
Alezio Rosso Mjere, Michele Calò **1994**
£9.95 (ROB)
Carignano del Sulcis Rocca Rubia Riserva,
Santadi **1994** £8.95 (HED) £9.99 (YOU)
£10.49 (NO) £10.95 (ROB) £10.99 (VA)
Don Pietro Rosso, Spadafora **1996** £8.45
(SOM) £10.49 (LIB)
Pier delle Vigne Rosso delle Murge,
Botromagno **1994** £8.25 (BU)

£10.00 → £14.99

Alezio Rosso Mjere, Michele Calò **1995**
£10.50 (ROB)
Carignano del Sulcis Rocca Rubia Riserva,
Santadi **1995** £10.99 (PHI)
Graticciaia Vallone **1992** £12.75 (SOM)
Planeta Merlot **1995** £14.69 (REI) £14.99
(YOU) £15.69 (VA)

£15.00 → £19.99

Graticciaia Vallone **1993** £15.99 (AME)
£16.95 (POR)
Terre Brune, Santadi **1995** £16.49 (YOU)
£18.90 (VA) £18.95 (PHI)
Turriga Argiolas **1993** £18.45 (STE) £19.25
(LEA) £20.50 (NA)

Over £20.00

Corvo Rosso Duca di Salaparuta **1964**
£33.49 (REI)
Taurasi Riserva Mastroberardino **1981**
£21.00 (CRO)

> *Please remember that*
> ***Oz Clarke's Wine Guide***
> *is a price **guide** and not a*
> *price list. It is not meant to*
> *replace up-to-date*
> *merchants' lists.*

SOUTHERN WHITE

Under £5.00

Cent'Are Alcamo Bianco Duca di
Castelmonte **1996** £4.40 (CRO) £5.10
(AV)
Chardonnay del Salento Barrique
Cantele/Kym Milne **1997** £4.75 (WS)
Chardonnay del Salento le Trulle **1996**
£4.49 (OD)
Gravina Bianco, Botromagno **1997** £4.75
(WS) £4.90 (NO) £4.99 (BAL)
Settesoli Bianco **1997** £4.89 (COC)

£5.00 → £7.99

Alcamo Spadafora **1997** £5.95 (LIB)
Corvo Bianco Duca di Salaparuta **1997**
£6.25 (COC) £6.99 (VA)
Greco di Tufo Feudi di San Gregorio **1997**
£7.99 (POR) £8.59 (YOU) £8.99 (VA)
Regaleali Bianco **1997** £6.96 (COC) £7.05
(PIP) £7.75 (DI)
Regaleali Bianco **1995** £7.65 (ROB)
Regaleali Tasca d'Almerita **1998** £7.49
(VA)

Over £8.00

Don Pietro Bianco, Spadafora **1997** £8.75
(LIB)
Greco di Tufo Feudi di San Gregorio
1995 £9.50 (ROB)
Lacryma Christi del Vesuvio,
Mastroberardino **1997** £8.99 (VA)

SOUTHERN ROSÉ

Under £6.00

Vigna Flaminio Brindisi Rosato, Vallone
1995 £4.75 (SOM) £5.75 (BAL)

SOUTHERN FORTIFIED

Under £7.00

Marsala Superiore Garibaldi Dolce,
Pellegrino **Non-vintage** £6.10 (AV)
£6.95 (DI)

Over £11.00

Moscato Passito di Pantelleria Bukkuram,
de Bartoli **Non-vintage** £24.69 (VA)
Vecchio Samperi 10-year-old, de Bartoli
Non-vintage £11.75 (REI)

NEW ZEALAND

**The Sauvignon Blancs are classics, but other styles are still finding their feet.
If you haven't tried them for a while, take another look**

It's hard to believe it of New Zealand, because the wines have been around a fair while now; the Sauvignon Blancs have even become established as classics. But actually, a lot are wines still in evolution.

Yes, of course; all wines everywhere are always in evolution: either they're getting slowly better as techniques and knowledge improve, or they're getting slowly worse if stagnation and lack of investment are the orders of the day. But a lot of New Zealand's wines have yet to find their feet. I mean particularly the reds. Every year they get more deft as producers select their sites better and get riper fruit. So if you tried them a few years ago and weren't that thrilled, it could be time to try them again. Many will be totally different to how you remember them.

Not that prices are ever going to be low, but names like Montana are delivering good-value flavour. So look beyond Sauvignon.

GRAPES & FLAVOURS

CABERNET SAUVIGNON (red) Only really succeeds in the hotter North Island, where Waiheke, Matakana and Hawke's Bay can make it well in warm years. Elsewhere a lot is being pulled out, and producers are focusing on blends instead, or on Merlot and Pinot Noir. Try *Babich Patriarch, Delegat's, Esk Valley, Heron's Flight, Matua Ararimu, Sacred Hill Basket Press Reserve, Stonyridge Larose, Te Mata Coleraine, Twin Bays Fenton, Vavasour Reserve, Vidal, Villa Maria Reserve, Waiheke Vineyards Te Motu.*

CHARDONNAY (white) Styles range from the soft peaches-and-cream of Gisborne to the grapefruit of Hawke's Bay and the light, zesty wines of Marlborough. Auckland, Nelson, Wairarapa and Canterbury all have less defined styles. The best producers are: *Babich Irongate, Chard Farm, Church Road, Cloudy Bay, Collards Rothesay* and *Hawke's Bay, Corbans Marlborough Private Bin* and *Gisborne Cottage Block, Delegats, Hunter's, Kumeu River, Matua Valley Ararimu, Montana Ormond Estates, Morton Estate Black Label, Neudorf, Nobilo Dixon* and *Marlborough, Te Mata, Vidal* and *Villa Maria.*

CHENIN BLANC (white) Not widely imported here, and generally sound but not thrilling. Best: *Millton Vineyard*'s Chenin is a serious heavyweight, whereas *Collards* and *Esk Valley* are lighter, more supple wines.

GEWÜRZTRAMINER (white) Usually well-structured with some elegance. Try: *Rippon, Villa Maria, Montana 'P'* from Patutahi Estate, *Vidal, Stonecroft.*

MERLOT (red) Increasingly popular in NZ. A lot is blended with Cabernet although there is an emerging band of top varietals: try *Delegat's, Corbans* and the concentrated *Vidal.*

MÜLLER-THURGAU (white) The mainstay of bag-in-the-box production. Good ones in bottle include the White Cloud blend from *Nobilo,* and delicately fruity wines from *Babich* and *Montana.* Also good are *Collards* and *Matua Valley.*

PINOT NOIR (red) With California, NZ is the best New World source of this. None is as good as great Burgundy, but then nor is most Burgundy. *Martinborough Vineyard* is closest to the Burgundy benchmark. Try also *Ata Rangi, Chard Farm, Dry River*, Also: *Corbans, Giesen Estate, Neudorf, Palliser, Mark Rattray, Rippon, St Helena* and *Waipara Springs*.

RIESLING (white) There's potential here for very good quality, but the grape's image problem is holding growers back. Try *Corbans Amberley, Dry River, Giesen, Hunter's, Neudorf, Palliser, Redwood Valley* and *Seifried*. For off-dry wines try *Collards, Millton, Montana* and *Stoneleigh*. The best sweet botrytized ones are made by *Corbans, Palliser* and *Villa Maria*.

SAUVIGNON BLANC (white) This is what made NZ famous, and it's still the country's best wine. It can be divided into the pungently aromatic, herbaceous and zesty South Island (mainly Marlborough)

styles, and the fleshier, riper and softer wines with stone-fruit flavours made on the North Island. There's increasingly a move towards single vineyard wines, and an emphasis on terroir. Marlborough is becoming divided into Wairau Valley (tightly structured wines) and Awatere (richer, riper, more powerful). Best of the South include: *Cloudy Bay, Corbans, Hunter's, Jackson Estate, Merlen, Montana Brancott Estate, Selaks, Stoneleigh, Vavasour Awatere, Villa Maria Wairau Valley* and *Wairau River*. Best North Island: *Matua Valley, Morton Estate, Palliser* and *Vidal*.

SEMILLON (white) This is riper, and less aggressively grassy than it used to be. *Villa Maria* and *Collards* are the best. *Selaks'* Sauvignon-Semillon is clearly the best of the blends.

WINE REGIONS

AUCKLAND (North Island) A catch-all area that includes such sub-regions as Kumeu/Huapai, Waiheke Island (robust Bordeaux blends from *Stonyridge, Te Motu* and *Goldwater*), Henderson and Northland/Matakana. *Kumeu River, Matua Valley, Nobilo, Selaks, Babich, Corbans, Delegat's, Villa Maria* – a whole range of stars are here.

CANTERBURY (South Island) This is dominated by *Giesen*, with a particular reputation for sweet botrytized Riesling. The sub-region of Waipara can boast Pinot Noir specialist *Mark Rattray Vineyards*, plus *Waipara Springs* and *Pegasus Bay*.

CENTRAL OTAGO (South Island) A fast-growing region in which Pinot Noir is rapidly becoming the most planted vine. *Rippon, Gibbston* and *Chard Farm* are the leading producers.

GISBORNE (North Island) Local growers and winemakers have dubbed this region the Chardonnay capital of NZ. Gisborne is also a spiritual home of Gewürztraminer,

and (less promisingly) a centre of bulk production of Müller-Thurgau. There are approximately as many wine styles here as there are wineries. Reds are less exciting than whites, although expanding vineyards of Pinot Noir are now being grown for good Champagne-method sparklers.

HAWKE'S BAY (North Island) Potentially NZ's greatest wine region. Chardonnay, Cabernets Sauvignon and Franc and Merlot are the leading grapes, though there's also good Sauvignon Blanc, generally softer and riper than that of Marlborough. Star names: *Te Mata, Church Road, Brookfields, Esk Valley, Ngatarawa, Vidal, C J Pask* and *Waimarama*. *Babich, Cooks, Matua Valley, Mills Reef, Morton Estate* and *Villa Maria* also use grapes from here. Sub-region Gimblett Road is terrifically trendy.

MARLBOROUGH (South Island) NZ's biggest region by far specializes in Sauvignon Blanc and makes the archetypal NZ style, all gooseberries and cut grass. Riesling does well here, making wines from dry to sweet;

Chardonnay is more difficult, but complex and distinctive when successful. Reds have fared less well although Pinot Noir is in great demand when it can be spared from the buoyant Champagne-method fizz industry. There's good botrytized wine here as well. Best: *Cellier Le Brun* (for fizz), *Cloudy Bay, Corbans, Grove Mill, Hunter's, Jackson Estate, Nautilus, Selaks* and *Vavasour.*

NELSON (South Island) *Neudorf,* making subtle, nutty Chardonnay, and *Seifried,* with complex Riesling, are the leading lights in this South Island region.

WAIRARAPA (North Island) This includes the sub-region of Martinborough, which is the source of some of NZ's most exciting Pinot Noirs. *Martinborough Vineyard, Ata Rangi* and *Dry River* are the Pinot stars, all making small quantities from low-yielding vines; *Palliser Estate* makes concentrated Chardonnay and Sauvignon Blanc, and there's promising Riesling and Pinot Gris, too.

PRODUCERS WHO'S WHO

ALLAN SCOTT ★★★(★) Lively Marlborough Sauvignon Blanc, pungent Riesling and elegant Chardonnay.

ATA RANGI★★★★ Good subtle Pinot Noir, an intense Cabernet/Merlot/Shiraz blend called Célèbre, and nice Chardonnay.

BABICH ★★★(★) Fresh Fumé Vert (Chardonnay, Semillon, Sauvignon), zesty Marlborough Sauvignon, elegant Irongate Chardonnay and Cabernet/Merlot. The Syrah so far is less noteworthy.

CELLIER LE BRUN ★★★★(★) Excellent, Champenois-run specialist sparkling wine producer.

CLOUDY BAY ★★★★★ Excellent, complex Sauvignon, fattened with a little Semillon. Top Champagne-method fizz under the Pelorus brand, with the ability to age well, and Chardonnay is also good.

COLLARDS ★★★★ A top Chardonnay maker. There's buttery Chenin Blanc and luscious botrytized Riesling when the vintage allows.

CORBANS ★★★(★) Very good Private Bin Chardonnay, and reliable to good quality across the whole range. New are single-vineyard Cottage Block Chardonnay and Pinot Noir.

DELEGAT'S ★★★★ Look out for the Marlborough range: it's called Oyster Bay. Fine Chardonnay and Cabernet with a good botrytized Riesling. Proprietor's Reserve wines are limited-release.

DE REDCLIFFE ★★★ State-of-the-art winery producing good, consistent Chardonnay and Riesling with occasionally very good oak-aged Sauvignon Blanc. Look out for the Bordeaux-blend reds.

DRY RIVER ★★★★★ Micro-winery making mega quality. The Pinot Noir, Gewürztraminer and Pinot Gris are among the best in the country; Chardonnay and botrytized styles are also up with the leaders.

ESK VALLEY ESTATE ★★★ Reds are based on blends of Bordeaux varieties, but the blend changes according to the year. Decent Chardonnay. Look out for single vineyard The Terraces.

FROMM ★★★ New set-up based in Blenheim and showing great promise. Chardonnay is elegant, Cabernet Sauvignon ripe and Pinot Noir worth watching. The wine-making here seems to have a nice sure touch.

GIBBSTON VALLEY ★★★ Small Otago winery making good Pinot Noir and

Chardonnay. Sauvignon Blanc is somewhat more variable.

GIESEN ★★★(★) Elegant lime-fruited dry and luscious sweet Riesling are the wines to look for here. There's also big, buttery Chardonnay.

GOLDWATER ★★★★ Big Waiheke reds, plus good Chardonnay. Sauvignon Blanc is called Dog Point.

GROVE MILL ★★★(★) Weighty Riesling and rich Chardonnay from Marlborough. Top reds in good years.

HUNTER'S ★★★★(★) Jane Hunter makes top-of-the-line Sauvignon Blanc and elegant Chardonnay. Fizz is slightly dull.

JACKSON ESTATE ★★★★ Classic Marlborough Sauvignon Blanc, complex Chardonnay and rather good vintage sparkling wine.

KUMEU RIVER ★★★★(★) Excellent single-vineyard Chardonnay from Mate's Vineyard. Good North Island Sauvignon Blanc and a Merlot-Cabernet blend.

MARTINBOROUGH VINEYARDS ★★★★ NZ's best-known Pinot Noir, big and complex Chardonnay, lovely Riesling.

MATUA VALLEY ★★★★ Look for top Ararimu Chardonnay and Cabernet. There's also luscious Sauvignon and Gewürztraminer, and good Shingle Peak range from Marlborough.

MILLS REEF★★★ Big, ripe Hawke's Bay Chardonnay, stylish limy Riesling and rich, ripe, mouthfilling fizz.

THE MILLTON VINEYARD ★★★★ New Zealand's first organic winemaker. There's lush, smoky, medium-dry Riesling (look out for Opou Vineyard), big, rich Chenin Blanc and balanced Chardonnay.

INSTANT CELLAR: NZ RED UPDATE

- 1997 Pinot Noir, Martinborough, £13.49, Bottoms Up, Thresher, Wine Rack, Victoria Wine The NZ Pinot that has to be top of the list.
- 1996 Coleraine, Te Mata, £18.99, Amey's Yes, it's pricy, but how could I leave this out?
- 1992 Awatea Hawkes Bay Cabernet/ Merlot, Te Mata, £13.49, Amey's Stunning, and only bettered by Coleraine.
- 1995 Célèbre, Ata Rangi, £17.49, S H Jones Refined blend of Cabernet, Merlot and Syrah from Martinborough. Syrah in NZ? Sounds unlikely, but it depends where you plant it.
- 1996 Cabernet/Merlot, C J Pask, Hawkes Bay, £8.20, Lay & Wheeler Plummy and vibrant. Blends of Cabernet are nearly always better than pure Cabernet in New Zealand.
- 1997 Pinot Noir, Isabel Estate, £12.50, Morris & Verdin Low yields and good ripeness give a smoky plum and cherry-flavoured wine.
- 1996 Cabernet Sauvignon, Montana Fairhall Estate, Marlborough, £11.99, Oddbins Minty, spicy Cabernet that's exclusive to Oddbins and that will age well.
- 1997 Cabernet Sauvignon, Redwood Valley, £8.70, New Zealand Wines Direct Mulberry and blackcurrant flavours from the northern corner of the South Island.

MISSION ★★★(★) A quality drive here has produced a range of impressive Chardonnays, delicate Riesling and an occasional sweet botrytis style when the year allows.

MONTANA ★★★(★) Top Champagne-method fizz, Lindauer; good Chardonnay and botrytized Riesling. Look out for new Pinot Noir, and single vineyard wines called 'O', 'R' and 'P', after the initial letter of their vineyards' names.

MORTON ESTATE ★★★★ Chardonnay at this estate, especially Black Label, is reliable and attractive. There's also fresh Sauvignon Blanc and Gewürztraminer, and impressive Champagne-method fizz. Reds are pretty good.

NAUTILUS ★★★★ Tight, quality-focused range includes top Marlborough Chardonnay, Sauvignon Blanc and firm, bottle-fermented fizz.

NEUDORF ★★★★ Remarkably subtle Burgundian-style Chardonnay; nice Sauvignon Blanc, too, and Pinot Noir.

NGATARAWA ★★★ Attractive Chardonnay, Cabernet/Merlot and botrytized Riesling. The Glazebrook label is top of the range.

NOBILO ★★★(★) Good Dixon Vineyard Chardonnay. Stylish Sauvignon. Popular White Cloud is a reliable Müller-Thurgau and Sauvignon blend.

PALLISER ★★★★ Some nice Sauvignon, Pinot Noir and concentrated Chardonnay.

C J PASK ★★★(★) Flavoursome reds from Cabernet, Merlot and Pinot Noir; also makes good Chardonnay from excellent vineyard sites.

PEGASUS BAY ★★★(★) Great Riesling, unconventional Sauvignon Blanc-Semillon and big, chewy Pinot Noir.

MARK RATTRAY VINEYARDS ★★★★ Very good Waipara-based Pinot Noir producer. Excellent Chardonnay.

RIPPON VINEYARD ★★★ Organic vineyard with a promising Pinot Noir. There's also some Syrah. Whites include decent Chardonnay and Sauvignon Blanc.

ST CLAIR ★★★(★) Classic Marlborough Sauvignon Blanc, elegant Chardonnay and pungent medium dry Riesling.

ST HELENA ★★★(★) Good Chardonnay, Pinot Gris and Pinot Blanc.

ST NESBIT ★★★ A red specialist with a consistently good Cabernet/Merlot blend.

> ### ON THE CASE
> If you want to splash out, look for single-vineyard wines. They're pricy, but they can compete with almost anything the world can offer

SEIFRIED ESTATE ★★★ A winery making very good Riesling, more complex than most. Sauvignon Blanc, too, is distinguished and well-made.

SELAKS ★★★★ Great Sauvignon and Sauvignon/Semillon. Founder's Selection is the top label.

STONYRIDGE ★★★★★ NZ's top red producer. Intense, ripe Cabernet blend (Larose) with less intense version as the second label.

TE MATA ★★★★★ Coleraine and Awatea are sought-after Cabernet/Merlot blends. There's also Burgundian-style Chardonnay under the Elston label, and one of NZ's first Syrahs.

VAVASOUR ★★★★ Top Chardonnay and reds and very good Sauvignons. The Vavasour label is used for the top wines; those under the Dashwood label have less aging ability.

VIDAL ESTATE ★★★ The Gewürztraminer here is very good, long and structured. Chardonnay is also worth seeking.

VILLA MARIA ★★★★ Villa Maria owns Vidal and Esk Valley, though they are independently run. From this label there's top Sauvignon Blanc (look especially for single vineyard wines) and botrytized Riesling.

WAIPARA SPRINGS WINES ★★★ Good Chardonnay from a youngish label. Sauvignon Blanc looks promising.

NEW ZEALAND PRICES

RED

Under £7.00

Cabernet Sauvignon Montana Marlborough **1995** £5.63 (FLE)

Cabernet Sauvignon Stoneleigh Marlborough **1996** £6.99 (TES)

Cabernet Sauvignon/Merlot Montana Timara **1997** £4.99 (THR) £4.99.(WR)

Dry Red Waimanu North Island **1998** £4.49 (UN)

£7.00 → £8.99

Cabernet Franc Kim Crawford Wicken Hawkes Bay **1998** £7.45 (SOM) £8.99 (LIB) £9.69 (VA) £9.70 (NO)

Cabernet Sauvignon Nobilo **1994** £8.70 (AV) £9.41 (ROS)

Cabernet Sauvignon C J Pask **1996** £7.80 (HAH) £8.50 (TAN) £8.95 (POR) £9.99 (JON)

Cabernet Sauvignon Redwood Valley **1995** £8.81 (DOM)

Cabernet Sauvignon Selaks Hawkes Bay **1996** £7.34 (STE) £8.15 (NA)

Cabernet Sauvignon/Merlot Aotea **1995** £8.52 (PLAY) £8.95 (ROB)

Cabernet Sauvignon/Merlot Matua Valley Hawkes Bay **1996** £7.83 (STE) £8.70 (NA) £11.69 (TW)

Cabernet Sauvignon/Merlot Montana Church Road **1996** £8.99 (SAF) £8.99 (VIC) £8.99 (THR) £8.99 (WR) £8.99 (BOT)

Cabernet Sauvignon/Merlot Montana McDonald Church Road **1996** £8.95 (COC) £10.20 (PIP)

Cabernet Sauvignon/Merlot C J Pask Hawke's Bay **1996** £7.95 (AD) £8.95 (BALL) £8.95 (POR) £9.99 (JON)

Cabernet Sauvignon/Merlot Te Mata **1997** £7.99 (AME) £9.02 (GW) £11.69 (TW)

Cabernet Sauvignon/Merlot Te Mata **1996** £8.99 (GW) £9.20 (HAH) £9.95 (BALL)

Merlot Matua Valley Dartmoor Smith Hawkes Bay **1995** £8.46 (STE) £13.34 (REI)

Merlot Sacred Hill Whitecliff **1998** £7.99 (FUL)

Pinot Noir Jackson Estate **1996** £8.95 (HED) £9.95 (POR) £10.88 (PLAY)

★ Ram Paddock Red, Waipara West **1996** £8.59 (WAT) £8.99 (DI)

Syrah Babich Mara Estate **1996** £7.69 (CON)

Two Terrace Red Waipara West **1997** £7.25 (NZW)

£9.00 → £10.99

Cabernet Sauvignon Redwood Valley **1997** £9.00 (NZW) £9.50 (STA) £10.30 (UB)

Cabernet Sauvignon/Merlot Dashwood **1994** £9.95 (NI) £11.57 (TW)

Cabernet Sauvignon/Merlot Lincoln Vineyards **1995** £9.95 (ROB)

Cabernet Sauvignon/Merlot C J Pask Hawke's Bay **1995** £10.20 (AV)

Cabernet Sauvignon/Merlot de Redcliffe **1995** £9.25 (CON)

Cabernet Sauvignon/Merlot Villa Maria Private Bin **1994** £9.75 (ROB)

Merlot Kim Crawford Hawkes Bay **1998** £9.95 (LIB)

Merlot Matua Valley Smith Dartmour **1995** £9.40 (NA)

Merlot/Cabernet Sauvignon Gunn Estate **1997** £9.00 (MV)

Pinot Noir Hunter's **1996** £9.99 (DI) £12.40 (CRO)

Pinot Noir Isabel Estate **1997** £10.99 (PHI) £12.49 (POR) £12.50 (BEN) £12.50 (MV)

Pinot Noir Martinborough **1996** £10.25 (SOM) £10.50 (CRO) £12.95 (CON) £12.95 (FORT) £12.99 (JON) £13.11 (NO)

MERCHANTS SPECIALIZING IN NEW ZEALAND
see Merchant Directory (page 413) for details

Nobody has very many (except New Zealand Wines Direct), but for a wider-than-average choice, try: Adnams (AD), Averys of Bristol (AV), Ballantynes (BAL), Anthony Byrne (BY), Cockburns of Leith (COC), First Quench Group (BOT, THR, VIC, WR), New Zealand Wines Direct (NZW), Lay & Wheeler (LAY), Tanners (TAN), The Ubiquitous Chip (UB), Wine Society (WS), Noel Young (YOU).

Pinot Noir Montana Reserve Marlborough **1997** £9.99 (UN) £9.99 (OD)
Pinot Noir Palliser Estate **1996** £10.95 (JU) £10.99 (PHI) £11.99 (YOU)
Pinot Noir de Redcliffe **1996** £9.25 (CON)
Pinot Noir St Helena **1995** £10.99 (YOU) £11.50 (BAL)
Pinot Noir Te Kairanga **1997** £10.28 (BIB)

£11.00 → £14.99

Cabernet Sauvignon/Merlot Mills Reef Elspeth **1995** £12.46 (PEN)
Cabernet Sauvignon/Merlot Montana Church Road Reserve **1996** £11.50 (CON)
Cabernet Sauvignon/Merlot Morton Estate Black Label **1995** £13.35 (NEZ)
Cabernet Sauvignon/Merlot Ngatarawa Glazebrook **1996** £13.75 (FORT)
Cabernet Sauvignon/Merlot Te Mata Estate Awatea **1995** £13.60 (TAN) £14.00 (WS) £14.95 (ROB)
Merlot/Cabernet Franc Redmetal Vineyards **1997** £14.00 (NZW)
Merlot/Cabernet Sauvignon Kumeu River **1996** £12.50 (BEN)
Pinot Noir Fromm La Strada **1997** £14.94 (LAY)
Pinot Noir Isabel Estate **1996** £12.49 (YOU) £12.95 (BALL)
Pinot Noir Martinborough **1997** £12.95 (PHI) £12.99 (YOU) £13.49 (THR) £13.49 (WR) £13.49 (BOT) £14.50 (AD)
Pinot Noir Martinborough **1995** £11.99 (NI) £12.81 (NO)
★ Pinot Noir Palliser Estate **1997** £11.05 (BY) £11.49 (VIC) £11.49 (THR) £11.49 (WR) £11.49 (BOT)
Pinot Noir St Helena **1997** £12.85 (PIP)
Syrah Te Mata Bullnose **1996** £12.93 (PEN) £12.95 (POR)

£15.00 → £19.99

Cabernet Sauvignon C J Pask Reserve **1995** £15.50 (CRO)
Cabernet Sauvignon/Merlot Te Mata Coleraine **1996** £18.99 (AME) £19.30 (TAN) £19.49 (POR)
Cabernet Sauvignon/Merlot Te Mata Coleraine **1995** £19.35 (GW)
Celebre Ata Rangi **1996** £15.08 (FA) £15.90 (TAN) £17.50 (FORT)
Celebre Ata Rangi **1995** £16.50 (BEN) £17.49 (JON)
Pinot Noir Ata Rangi **1997** £19.95 (STA) £20.70 (HAH)

Pinot Noir Ata Rangi **1996** £19.50 (FORT) £19.95 (LEA) £19.99 (JON) £20.50 (ROB)
Pinot Noir Dry River **1996** £18.75 (RAE) £20.99 (YOU) £21.00 (JU) £21.50 (ELL)
Pinot Noir Neudorf Moutere **1995** £16.00 (WS)
Pinot Noir Rippon Vineyard **1996** £15.00 (NZW)

£20.00 → £29.99

Cabernet Sauvignon/Merlot Waiheke Vineyards Te Motu **1996** £23.00 (NZW)
Cabernet Sauvignon/Merlot Waiheke Vineyards Te Motu **1994** £22.91 (FA)
Cabernet Sauvignon/Merlot Goldwater Estate Waiheke Island **1996** £23.95 (AV)
Larose Stonyridge **1997** £29.00 (NZW) £31.60 (TAN) £34.50 (STA)
Pinot Noir Martinborough Reserve **1994** £25.70 (NO) £39.00 (CRO)

Over £30.00

Larose Stonyridge **1996** £35.00 (ROB) £40.06 (PLAY)

WHITE

Under £4.00

Dry White Montana Timara **1998** £3.99 (SAF)
Dry White Montana Timara **1997** £3.99 (VIC) £3.99 (THR) £3.99 (WR) £3.99 (BOT)
Dry White Waimanu Gisborne **1998** £3.99 (UN)

£4.00 → £4.99

Chardonnay Cooks Hawke's Bay **1998** £4.99 (WAI)
★ Riesling Stoneleigh **1997** £4.99 (THR)
Sauvignon Blanc Cooks Marlborough **1997** £4.99 (THR) £4.99 (JON) £5.49 (NLW)
Sauvignon Blanc/Semillon Montana Azure Bay **1997** £4.99 (VIC) £4.99 (THR)
White Cloud Nobilo **1997** £4.49 (CO)
White Cloud Nobilo **1996** £4.95 (AV) £4.96 (ROS) £5.03 (GW) £5.50 (CRO)

£5.00 → £5.99

Chardonnay Cooks Gisborne **1997** £5.49 (VIC) £5.49 (THR) £5.49 (WR) £5.49 (BOT)
Chardonnay Cooks Gisborne **1996** £5.79 (JON)
Chardonnay Cooks Hawke's Bay **1997** £5.49 (TES)

Chardonnay Corbans Gisborne 1998
£5.95 (AD)
Chardonnay Corbans Gisborne 1997
£5.49 (UN) £5.99 (NLW) £6.90 (AS)
Chardonnay Delegat's Hawkes Bay 1997
£5.90 (FLE)
Chardonnay Montana Marlborough 1998
£5.49 (BO) £5.95 (COC) £5.99 (CO) £5.99
(OD) £5.99 (SAF) £5.99 (VIC) £5.99 (THR)
Gewürztraminer Matua Valley 1997
£5.39 (NI)
Riesling Stoneleigh 1996 £5.60 (UB)
Riesling Villa Maria Private Bin 1998 £5.49
(VIC) £5.49 (THR) £5.49 (WR) £5.49 (BOT)
Sauvignon Blanc Delegat's Marlborough
Gold 1998 £5.49 (MAJ)
Sauvignon Blanc Montana Marlborough
1998 £5.49 (BO) £5.95 (COC) £5.99 (TES)
£5.99 (PHI) £5.99 (SO) £5.99 (SAI) £5.99
(CO) £5.99 (OD) £5.99 (THR) £5.99 (WR)
Sauvignon Blanc C J Pask Hawkes Bay
1997 £5.99 (POR) £6.15 (HAH) £6.50
(BALL) £6.95 (AD) £6.99 (JON)
Sauvignon Blanc Stoneleigh Marlborough
1998 £5.99 (NLW)
Sauvignon Blanc Stoneleigh Marlborough
1997 £5.99 (SAI) £5.99 (THR) £5.99
(WR)
Semillon/Chardonnay Babich Gisborne
1998 £5.43 (COC)

£6.00 → £6.99

Chardonnay Aotea 1996 £6.95 (NZW)
£7.25 (STA) £8.64 (CB)
Chardonnay Babich Hawke's Bay 1994
£6.99 (COC) £7.95 (CON)
Chardonnay Delegat's Oyster Bay 1998
£6.99 (MAJ)
Chardonnay Kumeu River Brajkovich
1997 £6.76 (FA) £8.99 (BEN)
Chardonnay Nobilo Fall Harvest
Gisborne 1996 £6.99 (DI)
Chardonnay Nobilo Gisborne 1996 £6.91
(ROS)
Chardonnay C J Pask 1997 £6.99 (POR)
£7.65 (HAH) £7.95 (AD) £8.75 (BALL)
Chardonnay Stoneleigh 1996 £6.99 (TES)
£6.99 (VIC) £6.99 (THR) £6.99 (WR)

Stars (★) indicate wines
selected by Oz Clarke in the
Best Buys section which begins
on page 12.

Chardonnay Villa Maria Private Bin 1998
£6.99 (BO) £6.99 (OD) £6.99 (SAF)
Gewürztraminer Villa Maria Private Bin
1998 £6.49 (POR)
Riesling Allan Scott 1997 £6.99 (YOU)
£7.50 (FORT)
Riesling Jackson Estate Dry Marlborough
1998 £6.95 (HED) £7.50 (TAN)
Sauvignon Blanc Allan Scott Moa Ridge
1997 £6.99 (YOU)
Sauvignon Blanc Aotea 1998 £6.50 (NZW)
£6.50 (STA)
Sauvignon Blanc Aotea 1997 £6.95 (ROB)
£6.95 (FORT) £7.00 (MV) £7.87 (CB)
Sauvignon Blanc Babich Marlborough
1998 £6.49 (AME)
Sauvignon Blanc Chancellor 1997 £6.15
(GW)
Sauvignon Blanc Corbans Marlborough
1997 £6.30 (AS)
Sauvignon Blanc Kim Crawford
Marlborough 1998 £6.75 (SOM) £7.49
(TES) £7.99 (LIB) £8.49 (VA) £8.56 (FLE)
Sauvignon Blanc Dashwood 1997 £6.99
(THR) £6.99 (WR) £6.99 (BOT) £7.40 (CRO)
£8.20 (HAH) £8.99 (CB) £8.99 (YOU)
Sauvignon Blanc Delegat's Oyster Bay
1998 £6.49 (MAJ) £7.25 (BER)
Sauvignon Blanc Grove Mill Marlborough
1998 £6.99 (OD) £7.95 (CON) £8.25 (PHI)
Sauvignon Blanc Matua Valley Hawkes Bay
1998 £6.62 (STE) £7.35 (NA)
Sauvignon Blanc Matua Valley Hawkes Bay
1996 £6.39 (NI) £6.66 (ROS) £6.99 (GW)
£7.23 (PEN)
Sauvignon Blanc Ngatarawa Stables 1997
£6.99 (YOU)
Sauvignon Blanc Seifried 1998 £6.95 (WS)
£9.25 (STA)
Sauvignon Blanc Villa Maria Private Bin
1998 £6.99 (TES) £6.99 (WAI) £6.99 (SAI)
£6.99 (BO) £6.99 (SAF) £6.99 (VIC) £6.99
(THR) £6.99 (WR) £6.99 (BOT) £7.25 (ELL)
Sauvignon Blanc Wairau River 1997 £6.85
(SOM) £7.93 (REI) £7.99 (VIC) £7.99 (THR)
£7.99 (WR) £8.50 (LEA) £10.95 (FORT)

£7.00 → £7.99

Chardonnay Babich Hawke's Bay 1995
£7.90 (JU) £8.50 (TAN)
Chardonnay Coopers Creek 1998 £7.49
(SO)
Chardonnay Kim Crawford Unoaked
Marlborough 1998 £7.49 (SAF) £7.99
(LIB) £7.99 (YOU) £8.40 (NO) £8.49 (VA)

Chardonnay Kim Crawford Unoaked
Marlborough 1997 £7.75 (CON)
Chardonnay Hunter's 1995 £7.99 (DI)
£12.05 (PIP) £12.49 (WR) £12.49 (BOT)
£12.53 (GW) £12.90 (JU)
Chardonnay Matua Valley Eastern Bays
Gisborne/Hawkes Bay 1997 £7.25 (WS)
Chardonnay Mills Reef 1994 £7.73 (PEN)
Chardonnay Montana Church Road
Reserve 1997 £7.99 (TES)
Chardonnay Montana Marlborough 1997
£7.10 (PIP)
Chardonnay Nobilo Poverty Bay 1997
£7.80 (MV)
Chenin Blanc Esk Valley Wood-aged
1997 £7.64 (PLAY)
Gewürztraminer Lawson's Dry Hills
1998 £7.49 (TES) £7.64 (BIB)
Gewürztraminer Montana Reserve
Gisborne 1997 £7.99 (THR) £7.99 (BOT)
Riesling Coopers Creek Hawkes Bay
1997 £7.99 (CON)
Riesling Kim Crawford Dry Marlborough
1998 £7.99 (LIB) £7.99 (YOU)
Riesling Grove Mill Marlborough 1998
£7.99 (PHI)
Riesling Jackson Estate Dry Marlborough
1997 £7.29 (YOU) £9.34 (TW)
Riesling Montana Awatere Reserve 1997
£7.99 (OD)
Riesling Palliser Estate 1998 £7.16 (BY)
Sauvignon Blanc Allan Scott 1998 £7.99
(LAY)
Sauvignon Blanc Clifford Bay Estate 1998
£7.05 (FRI)
Sauvignon Blanc Coopers Creek
Marlborough 1998 £7.49 (SO)
Sauvignon Blanc Dashwood 1998 £7.99
(BO)
Sauvignon Blanc Forrest Estate 1998
£7.95 (AD) £7.99 (BEN) £7.99 (YOU)
Sauvignon Blanc Goldwater Estate
Marlborough 1998 £7.99 (AV) £7.99
(MAJ) £7.99 (SAF) £7.99 (YOU)
Sauvignon Blanc Grove Mill Marlborough
1997 £7.05 (DOM) £7.11 (ROS)
Sauvignon Blanc de Gyffarde Marlborough
1996 £7.99 (CON)
Sauvignon Blanc Jackson Estate 1998 £7.99
(POR) £8.35 (NO) £8.49 (BO) £8.80 (CRO)
£8.92 (PLA) £8.95 (HED) £8.99 (TES) £8.99
(WAI) £8.99 (PHI) £8.99 (AME) £8.99 (OD)
£9.25 (WRI) £9.70 (AD) £9.96 (PLAY)
Sauvignon Blanc Lawson's Dry Hills 1998
£7.64 (BIB)

Sauvignon Blanc Ngatarawa Stables 1996
£7.49 (AME)
Sauvignon Blanc Te Mata Castle Hill 1997
£7.99 (AME) £7.99 (POR) £9.02 (GW)
Sauvignon Blanc Tui Vale 1997 £7.64 (JER)
Sauvignon Blanc Villa Maria Cellar
Selection 1998 £7.99 (OD)
Sauvignon Blanc Wairau River 1998 £7.90
(CRO) £7.99 (YOU) £8.50 (LEA)

£8.00 → £8.99

Chardonnay Dashwood 1997 £8.45 (HAH)
Chardonnay Jackson Estate Marlborough
1997 £8.95 (HED) £8.99 (POR) £9.69 (PLA)
£9.70 (TAN) £9.85 (WRI) £10.15 (PIP)
Chardonnay Morton Estate Hawkes Bay
1996 £8.99 (YOU) £9.95 (ROB)
Chardonnay Redwood Valley 1996 £8.50
(WS) £9.00 (NZW) £10.52 (REI)
Chardonnay Wairau River 1994 £8.20
(SOM) £9.34 (REI)
Chenin Blanc Esk Valley 1996 £8.50 (UB)
Pinot Blanc St Helena 1996 £8.13 (PEN)
£9.35 (PIP)
Riesling Kim Crawford Dry Marlborough
1997 £8.99 (REI)
Riesling Millton Opou Vineyard 1996
£8.95 (ROB)
Riesling Sandihurst Wines 1997 £8.10 (NO)
Riesling Waipara West 1997 £8.99 (DI)
Sauvignon Blanc Allan Scott 1997 £8.99
(YOU) £9.25 (HAH) £9.25 (FORT) £9.95
(BALL) £9.99 (JON)
Sauvignon Blanc Coopers Creek
Marlborough 1997 £8.35 (CON) £9.25
(BALL)
Sauvignon Blanc Dashwood 1996 £8.30 (NI)
Sauvignon Blanc Esk Valley 1997 £8.20
(PLAY)
Sauvignon Blanc de Gyffarde 1998 £8.13
(PEN)
Sauvignon Blanc Hunter's 1998 £8.90 (CRO)
£9.49 (YOU) £9.90 (WRI) £9.95 (AME) £9.95
(WS) £9.99 (OD) £10.99 (PHI) £12.02 (STE)
Sauvignon Blanc Isabel Estate 1998 £8.99
(POR) £8.99 (YOU) £9.35 (BU) £9.95 (ROB)
Sauvignon Blanc Jackson Estate 1997
£8.75 (ROS) £9.39 (JON) £11.40 (TW)
Sauvignon Blanc Mills Reef 1996 £8.01 (PEN)
Sauvignon Blanc Neudorf Nelson 1997
£8.13 (FA) £9.95 (ELL)
★ Sauvignon Blanc Palliser Estate 1998
£8.05 (BY) £8.95 (YOU) £9.00 (FLE) £9.99
(PHI) £9.99 (VIC) £9.99 (THR) £9.99 (WR)
£9.99 (BOT)

Sauvignon Blanc de Redcliffe Marlborough
1996 £8.25 (CON)
Sauvignon Blanc Redwood Valley **1998**
£8.17 (DOM) £8.70 (NZW) £12.65 (NO)
Sauvignon Blanc Selaks Drylands Vineyard
1998 £8.78 (STE) £9.95 (NA)
Sauvignon Blanc Te Mata Castle Hill **1996**
£8.46 (PEN) £8.99 (GW)
Sauvignon Blanc Villa Maria Reserve
Wairau Valley **1998** £8.80 (CRO) £9.99
(POR) £9.99 (SAF)
Sauvignon Blanc/Semillon Selaks **1997**
£8.87 (STE) £9.85 (NA)

£9.00 → £10.99

Chardonnay Dashwood **1996** £9.79
(YOU)
Chardonnay Forrest Estate **1997** £9.99
(YOU)
Chardonnay Grove Mill Marlborough
1995 £9.65 (CON)
Chardonnay Isabel Estate **1997** £10.95
(BALL)
Chardonnay Isabel Estate **1996** £10.50
(MV) £12.95 (PHI)
Chardonnay Jackson Estate Marlborough
1998 £10.86 (PLAY)
Chardonnay Jackson Estate Marlborough
1996 £9.40 (CRO) £9.79 (AME) £9.95 (JU)
Chardonnay Kumeu River Brajkovich
1996 £10.90 (CRO)
Chardonnay Martinborough Vineyards
1996 £10.99 (AME) £11.99 (JON) £11.99
(YOU) £12.50 (AD)
Chardonnay Martinborough Vineyards
1995 £10.80 (CRO) £13.09 (NO)
Chardonnay Matua Valley Eastern Bays
Gisborne/Hawkes Bay **1996** £10.52 (TW)
Chardonnay Montana McDonald Church
Road **1997** £10.20 (PIP)
Chardonnay Montana Ormond Estate
Gisborne **1996** £10.25 (COC) £10.99
(CON) £10.99 (VIC) £10.99 (THR)
Chardonnay Palliser Estate **1995** £10.49
(THR) £10.49 (WR) £10.49 (BOT)
Chardonnay Palliser Estate Martinborough
Vineyard **1995** £10.90 (JU)
Chardonnay C J Pask **1996** £9.49 (JON)
Chardonnay de Redcliffe Mangatawiri
1995 £9.25 (CON)
Chardonnay Seifried Barrel-Fermented
1997 £9.11 (DOM)
Chardonnay Selaks Founders **1997** £9.41
(STE) £10.45 (NA)
Chardonnay Te Kairanga **1997** £9.01 (BIB)

Chardonnay Vavasour **1997** £10.99 (NI)
£11.49 (YOU)
★ Chardonnay Waipara West **1996** £9.99
(WAT) £10.75 (DI)
Chardonnay Wairau River **1996** £9.34
(REI) £10.95 (LEA)
Gewürztraminer Hunter's **1997** £9.65 (PIP)
Pinot Gris St Helena **1995** £9.29 (BAL)
Riesling Hunter's Rhine **1996** £10.39
(GW)
Riesling Neudorf Moutere **1997** £9.95
(STA) £9.95 (ELL)
Sauvignon Blanc Cloudy Bay **1998** £9.95
(NI) £10.95 (HAH) £12.00 (MORR) £12.49
(CON) £12.87 (PLAY) £13.99 (VA)
Sauvignon Blanc Collards Marlborough
1997 £9.99 (PHI)
Sauvignon Blanc Dry River **1997** £10.95
(JU) £10.99 (YOU)
Sauvignon Blanc Highfield Marlborough
1996 £9.95 (ROB)

Sauvignon Blanc Hunter's **1997** £10.25
(PIP) £11.02 (GW) £13.80 (UB)
Sauvignon Blanc Hunter's Wood-Aged
1996 £10.49 (YOU) £11.90 (TAN)
Sauvignon Blanc Montana Brancott Estate
1996 £10.25 (COC)
Sauvignon Blanc Nautilus Marlborough
1998 £9.68 (STE) £10.10 (PIP) £10.75 (NA)
Sauvignon Blanc Neudorf Nelson **1996**
£9.95 (BAL) £9.95 (RAE)
Sauvignon Blanc Redwood Valley **1997**
£9.75 (FORT)
Sauvignon Blanc Seifried **1997** £9.40 (JER)
Sauvignon Blanc Torlesse Wines
Marlborough **1998** £9.00 (NZW) £9.45
(STA)
Sauvignon Blanc Vavasour **1998** £9.49 (BO)
Sauvignon Blanc Vavasour **1997** £9.99
(LLO) £10.59 (YOU) £10.99 (NI)
Sauvignon Blanc Villa Maria Reserve
Wairau Valley **1997** £9.99 (VIC) £9.99
(THR) £9.99 (WR) £9.99 (BOT)
Semillon Kim Crawford Hawkes Bay
1996 £10.65 (NO) £10.99 (LIB)

£11.00 → £12.99

Chardonnay Babich Irongate **1996** £12.50
(CON) £12.60 (TAN)
Chardonnay Cloudy Bay **1997** £11.95 (NI)
£13.75 (WRI) £14.99 (CON) £16.95 (AD)
Chardonnay Hunter's **1996** £11.99 (YOU)
Chardonnay Jackson Estate Reserve **1996**
£11.79 (AME)
Chardonnay Kumeu River **1996** £11.16 (FA)
£14.50 (WS) £14.95 (BEN) £18.90 (CRO)
Chardonnay Montana Church Road
Reserve **1996** £11.99 (WR) £11.99 (BOT)
Chardonnay Redwood Valley **1997**
£11.25 (FORT)
★ Chardonnay Te Mata Elston **1997** £12.95
(POR) £13.69 (VIC) £13.69 (THR) £13.69
(BOT) £16.22 (TW) £14.50 (BALL)
Sauvignon Blanc Vavasour **1996** £12.99 (VA)
Sauvignon Blanc/Semillon Kumeu River
1997 £11.25 (BEN)
Semillon Kim Crawford Hawkes Bay
1997 £12.99 (YOU) £17.25 (FORT)

£13.00 → £15.99

Chardonnay Kim Crawford Tietjen
Gisborne **1997** £14.39 (YOU) £14.95 (LIB)
Chardonnay Dry River **1996** £15.99 (RAE)
£16.95 (JU) £16.99 (YOU)
Chardonnay Hunter's **1997** £13.23 (STE)
£14.70 (NA)
Chardonnay Kumeu River Mate's Vineyard
1996 £13.61 (FA) £27.80 (CRO)
Chardonnay Ngatarawa Glazebrook
1995 £13.75 (FORT)
Chardonnay Te Mata Elston **1996** £13.49
(AME) £14.00 (WS)
Sauvignon Blanc Cloudy Bay **1997** £14.10
(FA) £29.95 (UB)

Over £16.00

Chardonnay Kumeu River Mate's Vineyard
1997 £16.50 (ELL) £17.95 (BEN)
Chardonnay Morton Estate Reserve **1996**
£17.99 (YOU)
Semillon Kim Crawford Oak-Aged **1996**
£16.75 (ROB)

> *Please remember that*
> **Oz Clarke's Wine Guide**
> *is a price **guide** and not a
> price **list**. It is not meant to
> replace up-to-date
> merchants' lists.*

SPARKLING

Under £7.50

Lindauer Brut **Non-vintage** £7.49 (MORR)
£7.49 (TES) £7.49 (WAI) £7.49 (BO) £7.49
(POR) £7.49 (CO) £7.49 (OD) £7.49 (SAF)
£7.49 (THR) £7.49 (WR) £7.49 (ASD)
£7.50 (CRO) £7.99 (JON) £8.50 (ROB)
Lindauer Rosé **Non-vintage** £7.49 (TES)
£7.49 (THR) £7.49 (BOT) £7.50 (CRO)

£7.50 → £9.99

★ Deutz Marlborough Cuvee Brut Non-
Vintage **Non-vintage** £9.99 (TES) £9.99
(BO) £10.90 (CRO) £10.99 (OD) £10.99
(VIC) £10.99 (THR) £10.99 (WR) £10.99
(BOT)
Lindauer Special Reserve **Non-vintage**
£8.99 (TES) £8.99 (OD) £8.99 (VIC) £8.99
(THR) £8.99 (WR) £8.99 (BOT)
Terrace Road, Cellier Le Brun **Non-
vintage** £9.95 (HED)

£10.00 → £12.99

Daniel Le Brun Brut **Non-vintage**
£12.95 (HED) £12.99 (POR) £13.50
(FORT) £14.99 (YOU) £16.50 (ROB)
Daniel Le Brun Brut Tache **Non-vintage**
£12.95 (PHI) £12.95 (ROB)
Deutz Marlborough Cuvee Blanc de
Blancs Vintage **1991** £11.99 (OD)
Miru Miru, Hunter's **1996** £10.99 (DI)
£12.49 (YOU) £12.99 (MAJ)
Miru Miru, Hunter's **1995** £10.90 (CRO)
Morton Estate Brut **Non-vintage** £10.99
(YOU)
Nautilus Cuvee **Non-vintage** £11.12
(STE) £12.35 (NA)
Pelorus **1994** £12.14 (FA) £13.56 (PLAY)
£13.82 (NO) £14.90 (CRO) £14.99 (VA)
Pelorus **1993** £11.16 (NO) £12.99 (RAE)
£13.50 (BALL) £13.55 (HAH) £13.90 (JU)
£13.95 (FORT) £14.99 (PHI) £15.45 (LEA)
£16.45 (CB) £17.04 (TW)
Pelorus Blanc de Blancs **Non-vintage**
£10.74 (NO) £11.90 (CRO) £12.99 (PHI)

£13.00 → £15.99

Miru Miru, Hunter's **Non-vintage**
£13.95 (JU)
Pelorus **Non-vintage** £15.50 (MV)

c. £25.00

Pelorus **1992** £24.85 (UB)

PORTUGAL

Anyone who wants stylish wines but has a rather unstylish budget should head straight for the Portuguese shelves. Nobody will believe you paid so little for so much

You want to know about the next big thing in wine? This is it. This is where you go for great flavours, bags of character, serious reds that will take some aging but are delicious when you buy them, and even (heaven be praised) good whites. And what's more, the prices are terrific.

Do I sound enthusiastic? That's because I am. Some of the prices are low – around the £4–5 mark. Some are higher – £7–8. Some are over £10. But don't worry, because whatever price bracket you happen to favour, you'll find value.

There are some short cuts to finding the most modern styles. José Maria da Fonseca is a pretty big producer with lots of brands, and you won't go far wrong with any of them; Sogrape is pretty reliable, too. From the South, José Neiva is a very good winemaker with a hand in a number of co-ops. Peter Bright (or Bright Brothers) is another leading name; and J P Vinhos, too.

If you feel like branching out, look for single-estate wines from the South – Alentejo, Ribatejo and Estremadura. And from the Douro Valley: the great home of port planted so many good new vineyards in the 1980s that there are more top grapes around than the port market can mop up. And that's good news for anyone who likes the rich, spicy flavours of Douro table wine.

Most high street chains and the better supermarkets should have some good examples. And there are great producers queuing up to get their wines into Britain, so don't turn a wine down just because you haven't heard of the name. It could be the wine you've been waiting for all your life.

WINE REGIONS

ALENTEJO (red, white) This broad region includes the DOCs of Borba, Redondo, Reguengos and Vidigueira: those regions in the South, near Spain. There's not a great deal of regional difference but there are quality differences. Cheap and cheerful co-op wines are good value: look for soft chocolate-and-cherries reds and increasingly fresh whites. Single estate wines are often very serious, with complex flavours and good concentration. The names to go for include *José Maria da Fonseca, J P Vinhos, Herdade de Esporão, Fonseca, J S Rosado Fernandes, Paço dos Infantes, Cartuxa, Reguengos de Monsaraz, Pêra Manca, Cortes de Cima, Dom Martinho,* and *Quinta do Carmo.*

ALGARVE (red, white) Mostly undistinguished, alcoholic reds. There are four DOCs here, Lagos, Portimão, Lagoa and Tavira, and none of them deserves its status. Among producers, the *Lagoa* co-op is probably the best bet.

BAIRRADA, DOC (red, white) The reds produced here frequently overshadow the more famous Dão wines. They're apt to be tannic, but the Baga grape gives sturdy, peppery, plum-and-blackcurrant fruit. The best Bairrada wines age remarkably well. The top red producers are: *Caves São João, Caves Aliança, Sogrape* (look for its *Nobilis*), *Luís Pato, Casa de Saima, Gonçalves Faria, Sidonia de Souza,* co-ops at *Vilharino do Bairro, Cantanhede* and *Mealhada.*

There are also some increasingly good dry whites available. *Sogrape* and *Caves Aliança* are the best producers to try for these.

BUCELAS, DOC (white) Popular in Wellington's day, this dry white was almost extinct, with *Caves Velhas* left as the sole producer. *Prova Régia* is a new arrival, but lacks concentration.

CARCAVELOS, DOC (fortified) Just when Carcavelos looked as if it was about to disappear for ever, along comes a new vineyard. *Quinta dos Pesos* is making a good, nutty, fortified version rather like an aged Tawny port.

COLARES, DOC (red) Based on the scented Ramisco grape, the young wine has fabulous cherry perfume but is *numbingly* tannic. As it ages it gets an exciting rich pepper-and-bruised-plums flavour; current vintages of *Chitas* (aka *Paulo da Silva*), and the vinhos de mesa of *Beira Mar Garrafeira* and *Casal da Azenha* are 1984, 1987 and 1988 respectively.

DÃO, DOC (red, white) Getting a bit left behind these days, as the regions of the South and the far North come to the fore. A bit more modernity wouldn't hurt, guys. Best buys are from *Sogrape, Caves São João, Caves Aliança, José Maria da Fonseca, Quinta das Maias, Quinta da Alameda* and *Quinta dos Roques*.

White Dão was traditionally (and mostly still is) yellow, tired and heavy. But a few companies are now making a lighter, fresher, fruitier style. White *Grão Vasco* from *Sogrape* is good and lemony.

DOURO, DOC (red, white) Famous these days for table wine as well as Port. The flavour of the table wines can be delicious – soft and glyceriny, with a rich raspberry-and-peach fruit, and a perfume somewhere between liquorice, smoky bacon and cigar tobacco. *Ferreira* (under the ownership of *Sogrape*) produces a number, from the rare and expensive *Barca Velha*, through *Reserva Especial*, to the young and fruity *Esteva*. Other port shippers are beginning to follow suit; good wines are

Redoma from *Niepoort*, and *Quinta de la Rosa*. Look out also for *Quinta da Cismeira, Calços do Tanha, Seara d'Ordem* among the producers of easy-drinking Douro wines, and *Quinta do Côtto Grande Escolha, Quinta do Crasto, Quinta do Vale da Raposa, Duas Quintas, Quinta do Fojo* and *Vinha de Gaivosa* for the more heavyweight styles.

Nearly all the best table wines are red, though among the whites *Sogrape's Planalto* and *Douro Reserva, Esteva* from *Ferreira* and *Quinta do Valprado Chardonnay* are well worth trying.

ON THE CASE

How do you spot a single-estate table wine? Look for the word 'Quinta', which means farm or estate. This doesn't mean that anything not so labelled should be despised, though

ESTREMADURA (red, white) Alias Oeste. It covers the following IPRs: Arruda, Alenquer, Óbidos, Torres Vedras, Alcobaça and Encostas d'Aire – and the region of Estremadura. Private estates here are making terrific quality. There's that same cherries-and-chocolate fruit in the reds that you get all over the South (the chocolate comes from aging in Portuguese oak, rather than the more international-style American or French oak). Look out for *João Pato*, *Bright Brothers*, *Quinta da Boa Vista*'s brands *Espiga*, *Quinta das Setencostas* and *Palha Canas*. *Quinta de Abrigada*, *Quinta de Pancas*, *Beira Mar* and *Casal de Azenha* are also good, as are *Alta Mesa* and *Portada* among the cheaper brands. Whites can be nicely aromatic, but need drinking young.

MADEIRA, DOC (fortified) Each Madeira style is supposedly based on the grape from which it takes its name: there are four of them, and they are Malmsey (Malvasia), Bual, Verdelho and Sercial. In practice cheaper Madeiras, those of up to five years old, are almost all made from the inferior Tinta Negra Mole. At least these are now calling themselves, more honestly, 'Pale Dry', 'Dark Rich', and so on. So anything calling itself Sercial, Verdelho or whatever should be made 85 per cent from that grape.

The Malmsey grape makes the sweetest Madeira, reeking sometimes of Muscovado sugar, dark, rich and brown, but with a smoky bite and surprisingly high acidity that makes it positively refreshing after a long meal. The Bual grape is also rich and strong, less concentrated, sometimes with a faintly rubbery whiff and higher acidity. Verdelho makes pungent, smoky, medium-sweet wine with more obvious, gentle fruit, and the Sercial makes dramatic dry wine, savoury, spiry, tangy, with a steely, piercing acidity. To taste what Madeira is all about you need a 10-year-old; really good Madeira should be two or three times that age.

Blandy, Cossart Gordon, Rutherford & Miles and *Leacock* are all good producers, and all under the same ownership anyway. *Henriques & Henriques* is the most widely available of the Portuguese-owned houses.

PORT (DOURO, DOC) (fortified) Port falls into two broad categories: that aged in bottle (vintage and single-quinta vintage) and that aged in wood, which is bottled when ready to drink: ruby, tawny, late-bottled vintage, crusted, vintage character and branded ports.

That's the basic outline. The simplest and cheapest port available in Britain is labelled 'Ruby' and 'Tawny'. Ruby is a tangy, tough, but warmingly sweet wine to knock back uncritically. Cheap Tawny at around the same price as Ruby is simply a mixture of light Ruby and White ports, and is almost never as good as the Ruby would have been, left to itself.

Calling these inferior concoctions 'Tawnies' is very misleading because there's a genuine 'Tawny', too. Proper Tawnies are kept in wooden barrels for at least five, but preferably ten or more years, to let a delicate flavour of nuts, brown sugar and

PORTUGUESE CLASSIFICATIONS

Portugal's wines are divided into four tiers of quality. At the top are **Denominaçoes de Origem Controlada** or DOCs. **Indicaçãos de Proveniência Regulamentada** or IPRs, are similar to the French VDQS. **Vinhos Regionais** are regional wines, and **Vinhos de Mesa** are table wines.

raisins develop. Most of these more expensive Tawnies carry an age on the label: 10, 20, 30 or even 40 years old. Those without an age are usually best avoided, though there are some good brands like *Harvey's Director's Bin Very Superior Old Tawny* or *Delaforce's His Eminence's Choice*. For aged Tawnies try *Noval, Cockburn, Ferreira, Fonseca, Dow, Taylor's, Graham, Quinta da Ervamoira* from *Ramos Pinto, Churchill, Poças, Quinta de la Rosa, Croft*. Colheitas – single-vintage Tawnies – are increasingly available, usually from Portuguese houses, and can be really delicious. Look for *Kopke, Messias, Noval, Niepoort, Barros, Poças, Warre*.

Vintage ports are the opposite of Tawnies, since the object here is to make a big, concentrated rather than a delicate mouthful. Vintage years are 'declared' by port shippers when the quality seems particularly good – usually about three times a decade. The wines will age for a decade or two in bottle to develop an exciting, complex tangle of flavours; blackcurrant, plums, minty liquorice, pepper and herbs, cough mixture and a lot more.

If you want a peek at what a declared Vintage port can be like, buy single-quinta vintage wine. These are usually from the best vineyards in the less brilliant years; they mature faster and can be extremely good. Look particularly for Taylor's *Quinta da Vargellas*, Dow's *Quinta do Bomfim*, Warre's *Quinta da Cavadinha*, Fonseca's *Quinta do Panascal*, Niepoort's *Quinta do Passadouro*, Croft's *Quinta da Roêda*, Delaforce's *Quinta da Corte*, Cockburn's *Quinta da Eira Velha* and *Quinta dos Canais*, Churchill's *Quinta da Agua Alta* and *Quinta do Vesúvio, Quinta de la Rosa, Quinta do Crasto*.

Vintage Character and Late Bottled Vintage are usually short on personality. The best are from *Fonseca, Niepoort, Smith Woodhouse, Ramos Pinto, Warre*. Crusted port is more interesting: *Churchill's* and *Dow's* are good.

White port, sweet or dry, is seldom exciting. Barros *Very Old Dry White* is special.

RIBATEJO (red, white) An exciting area, the source of both inexpensive brands and some of Portugal's best *garrafeira* (reserve-style) wines – in particular *Romeira* of *Caves Velhas*. The region includes the IPRs Tomar, Santarém, Cartaxo, Almeirim, Chamusca and Coruche, but Ribatejo is the name we see most on labels. There are lovely chocolaty reds, and fresh whites. Decent brands include red and white *Lezíria, Segada, Falcoaria* and *Torre Velha*. Classier wines: *Quinta das Varandas, Quinta da Lagoalva, Bright Bros* at *Quinta da Granja*, the Margaride estate (*Casal do Monteiro, Dom Hermano, Margarides* and *Convento da Serra*), *Quinta do Casal Branco*.

SETÚBAL, DOC (fortified) This is good, but it's always a little spirity and never quite as perfume-sweet as one would like, perhaps because they don't use the best sort of Muscat. It comes in a 6-year-old and a 25-year-old version, and the wines do

---

INSTANT CELLAR: DOURO VALLEY

• **Quinta da Ervamoira 10-Year-Old Tawny, Adriano Ramos Pinto, £19.85, Bennetts** A single-quinta tawny port from a Portuguese port house under French ownership. And very well made it is too.
• **1995 Quinta do Crasto Reserva, £7.99, Fuller's** This is the table wine, though the same estate makes excellent port as well. This is very stylish and spicy.
• **1996 Quinta do Fojo, £10.95, Hedley Wright** Rich, supple red that will go on improving.
• **1996 Quinta Vale Dona Maria, £15, Millésima** Well made red, all spices and figs and plums.
• **1996 Esteva Tinto, Ferreira, £5.50, Nadder Wines** Light, juicy stuff, for when you don't want the heavyweights.
• **1996 Quinta do Vale da Raposa, £7.74, Savage Selection** Very concentrated and rich table wine, from very old vines.
• **1996 Vila Freire Tinto, £5.75, Wine Society** Terrific depth and structure.

gain in concentration with age – the 25-year-old has a lot more character and less overbearing spiritiness. You can still occasionally find older wines like *José Maria da Fonseca*, or its intense, pre-phylloxera *Torna Viagem*, with a powerful treacle toffee character balanced by a sharp acidic tang.

TERRAS DO SADO (red, white) This region, that includes the Setúbal DOC, is where international grapes have made most inroads. The oak-aged *Cova da Ursa* Chardonnay is the sort of thing. Others use local varieties. From *J P Vinhos* look for *J P Barrel Selection, Meia Pipa, Má Partilho*; also *Pasmados, Primum* and *Quinta do Camarate* from *José Maria da Fonseca Sccrs*.

VINHO VERDE, DOC (red, white) Roughly half of all Vinho Verde produced is

red, wonderfully sharp, harsh even, but hardly ever seen outside Portugal. Try *Ponte da Lima*, if you feel brave.

But the wine we see is white, and *Verde* means green-youthful, un-aged, not the colour of a croquet lawn. Ideally, the whites are bone dry, positively tart, often aromatic, and brilliantly suited to heavy, oily northern Portuguese food. But we almost always get the wines slightly sweetened and softened, which is a pity, because they're then not nearly so distinctive.

Authentic versions come from *Palácio da Brejoeira, Solar das Bouças, Quinta de Tamariz, Quinta da Franqueira, Quinta da Azevedo, Casa de Sezim, Grinalda* and *Terras da Corga. Gazela* is off-dry, as is *Aveleda*. All Vinho Verde should be drunk young. Look for wines from the Alvarinho or Loureiro grapes, which are the best.

PRODUCERS WHO'S WHO

CAVES ALIANÇA ★★★★ (Bairrada) Up-to-date and quality oriented. Making good stuff in the Alentejo (red Monte da Terrugem) as well as in Bairrada.

QUINTA DA AVELEDA ★★★ (Vinho Verde) Largest producer of Vinho Verde, with commercially sweetened Casal Garcia and Aveleda, as well as excellent dry Grinalda and varietal Loureiro. Now Charamba red Douro, too.

BRIGHT BROTHERS ★★★★ (Several) Aussie Peter Bright gets his fingers into everything. Great Palmela and Cartaxo.

CHURCHILL GRAHAM ★★★★ (Port) Intense and concentrated Churchill's Vintage, LBV, 10-Year-Old Tawny and single-quinta Agua Alta.

COCKBURN ★★★★ (Port) Special Reserve is good Vintage Character, and the 10-Year-Old Tawny is complex. Look for Quinta dos Canais 1992, and Cockburn 1994.

QUINTA DO CRASTO ★★★★ (Port/Douro) Estate focusing on vintage port and table wines. Quality is very high, since there's both dedication and plenty of cash for investment. All the wines age well.

CROFT ★★(★) (Port) Quinta da Roêda is lovely single-quinta vintage, but many wines are over-delicate. 1994 is Croft's best Vintage for ages.

DELAFORCE ★★(★) (Port) Tawny His Eminence's Choice is its best-known wine. Good 1994 Vintage and 1984 Quinta da Corte.

DOW ★★★★★ (Port) Deft, complex wines made in a relatively dry style. Its 1994 Vintage is a triumph. Look also for the 10-Year-Old Tawny.

HERDADE DE ESPORÃO ★★★★ (Alentejo) Australian wine-making plus a combination of local and international grapes. Esporão Reserva and Aragonês are very good reds.

MATURITY CHART
Vintage Ports

1983   A vintage for mid-term drinking

Bottled			Ready	Peak		Tiring	In decline

0	5	10	15	20	25	30 years

1985   An excellent vintage for laying down

Bottled			Ready	Peak		Tiring	In decline

0	5	10	15	20	25	30	35 years

1991   1991 ports are likely to be ready before the 1985s

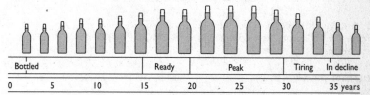

Bottled			Ready	Peak		Tiring	In decline

0	5	10	15	20	25	30 years

1994   Possibly even better than 1991

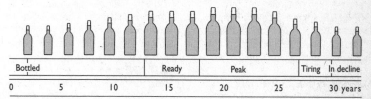

Bottled			Ready	Peak		Tiring	In decline

0	5	10	15	20	25	30 years

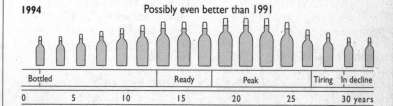

FERREIRA ★★★★ (Port/Douro) Elegant, early-maturing Vintages and two superb Tawnies: 10-year-old Quinta do Porto and 20-year-old Duque de Bragança. Makes some of the top Douro table wines, too.

FONSECA GUIMARAENS ★★★★★ (Port) Fonseca's wines are sweeter and less austere than sister company Taylor's. The Vintage ports are often outstanding, as is the 1994, and the quality of its commercial releases is reassuring.

JOSÉ MARIA DA FONSECA SCCRS ★★★★ (Countrywide) Delicious range of table wines, particularly Quinta de Camarate red and white and expensive red, Primum, all from Setúbal. Not connected to Fonseca port.

GRAHAM ★★★★★ (Port) Usually rich and sweet. Apart from Vintage there is Malvedos, produced in off-vintage years, and fine Tawnies. Very good 1994 Vintage. Six Grapes is attractive Vintage Character.

HENRIQUES & HENRIQUES ★★★★ (Madeira) Good quality across the board.

J P VINHOS ★★★★ (Setúbal) Brilliant winemaking. Look for João Pires Branco, red Tinto da Ânfora, red Quinta da Bacalhôa and Cova da Ursa Chardonnay.

MADEIRA WINE COMPANY ★★★★ (Madeira) Blandys, Cossart Gordon, Rutherford & Miles and Leacock are grouped together under this ownership. Rutherford & Miles and Cossart Gordon wines are slightly drier; otherwise there's not much between them.

NIEPOORT ★★★★★ (Port) Subtle aged Tawnies, traditional LBVs, Colheitas and long-lasting Vintage (especially 1994), plus single-quinta Quinta do Passadouro.

QUINTA DO NOVAL ★★★ (Port) Noval's Nacional wines, made from ungrafted vines, are legendary and fetch a stratospheric price at auction. Other Noval wines don't attempt such heights, but are good, especially the 1982 Colheita and Over 40-Year-Old Tawny.

OFFLEY FORRESTER ★★★(★) (Port) Famous for 'Boa Vista' Vintage and LBV ports. Vintage can be insubstantial. Excellent Baron de Forrester Tawnies.

QUINTA DE PANCAS ★★★(★) (Oeste) Good wine-making in a relatively international style. There's a quite oaky Casa de Pancas Chardonnay and ripe Cabernet.

RAMOS PINTO ★★★ (Port/Douro) There are delicious Tawnies from two single-quintas – Ervamoira and Bom Retiro – both of which are elegant, nutty and delicate. Duas Quintas is good Douro red.

SANDEMAN ★★★ (Port) Not top flight, although the 20-Year-Old Tawny is attractive.

SMITH WOODHOUSE ★★★★ (Port) Some delicious Vintage and LBVs. Concentrated Vintage wines which tend to mature early, though 1994 is gutsy. Full-flavoured Crusted.

SOGRAPE ★★★★ (North) Producer of Mateus Rosé, plus excellent Grão Vasco white Dão and many others with emphasis on fruit. Very go-ahead.

TAYLOR, FLADGATE AND YEATMAN ★★★★(★) (Port) Quinta de Vargellas is still one of the best single-quinta wines on the market, and the 10-Year-Old Tawny is superb.

WARRE ★★★★★ (Port) Serious wines: good LBVs and Vintage (especially in 1994) and fine 'Nimrod' Tawny. Quinta da Cavadinha is a single-quinta wine, and the 1986 Colheita is subtle.

PORT VINTAGES

Not every year produces a crop of fine enough quality for vintage-dated wine to be made, and a few houses may not make Vintage port even in a generally good year. Announcing the intention to bottle Vintage port is known as 'declaring'. It all depends on the quality the individual house has produced, although it is extremely rare for a house to declare two consecutive years.

1998 A small vintage which will probably all be needed for tawnies and the like.

1997 Varied in quality. Declarations include *Dow, Warre, Fonseca* and *Taylor*.

1996 Seems an elegant, useful year rather than gutsy.

1995 A vintage with a lot of colour and tannin, but slightly unbalanced. Above average, but missed being top grade.

1994 Excellent year, declared by almost all houses. They're ripe, fleshy and intense, with lovely fruit. They're also much more expensive than the last generally declared year, 1991.

1992 Declared by four shippers: *Fonseca, Taylor, Niepoort* and *Burmester*. Rich, fruity wines, lusher than the 1991s. Cynics note that 1992 was Taylor's tercentenary.

1991 Generally declared, but quantities were small. The wines need at least ten years.

1987 *Ferreira, Martinez, Niepoort* and *Offley* declared this small but good vintage. Most shippers opted instead for single-quinta wines for medium-term drinking.

1985 Declared by every important shipper. The quality is exceptionally good, with a juicy ripeness of fruit. *Croft, Offley* and *Cockburn* are very good, and *Fonseca* is rich and lush. My favourites are *Graham, Warre, Dow, Gould Campbell* and *Churchill*.

1983 Marvellous wine, strong and aggressive, but with a deep, brooding sweetness which is all ripe, clean fruit. Not one of the most fragrant vintages, but it will be a sturdy classic.

1982 Not as good as it was at first thought. Most need to be drunk.

1980 A good vintage, developing a delicious, drier-than-usual style. They're ready to drink now, but there's no hurry.

1977 Brilliant wine, now mature. The flavour is a marvellous mixture of great fruit sweetness and intense spice and herb fragrance.

1975 These in general don't have the stuffing that a true vintage style demands, but many are excellent for drinking now. *Noval, Taylor, Dow, Warre* and *Graham* need no apologies. Most of the others do.

1970 Exceptional, balanced port, now good to drink, sweet and ripe with a fascinating citrus freshness — and it'll last. All the top houses are special, led by *Fonseca, Taylor, Warre, Graham* and *Dow*, but lesser houses like *Cálem* and *Santos Junior* are also excellent.

1966 This has gained body and oomph and can be drunk with pleasure; a very good year. *Fonseca* is the star at the moment.

1963 The classic year. It's big, deep, and spicy, with remarkable concentration of flavours.

PORTUGAL PRICES

RED

Under £4.00

Alentejo Montado, Fonseca 1997 £3.95 (WS)

Douro Vila Regia 1996 £3.99 (SAF) £4.75 (ELL)

Ramada Tinto 1995 £3.49 (THR) £3.49 (BOT)

Tinto da Ânfora J P Vinhos **Non-vintage** £2.99 (VIC) £2.99 (THR) £2.99 (WR)

£4.00 → £4.99

Alentejo Alandra, Esporão 1997 £4.29 (VIC) £4.29 (THR) £4.29 (WR) £4.29 (BOT)

Bairrada Reserva Caves Aliança 1995 £4.69 (PEN)

Bairrada Reserva Dom Ferraz 1996 £4.29 (VIC) £4.29 (THR) £4.29 (WR) £4.29 (BOT)

Beiras Piornos 1996 £4.25 (AD)

★ Beiras Baga, Bela Fonte 1998 £4.99 (UN)

Dão Dom Ferraz 1997 £4.99 (TES)

Dão Grão Vasco 1997 £4.28 (STE)

Dão Reserva, Caves Aliança 1994 £4.69 (PEN)

Dão Reserva Dom Ferraz 1997 £4.99 (UN)

Dão Reserva Dom Ferraz 1995 £4.29 (THR) £4.29 (WR) £4.29 (BOT) £5.40 (TAN)

Dão Terras Altas J M da Fonseca 1994 £4.49 (MAJ)

Douro Quinta de la Rosa 1996 £4.85 (SOM) £6.40 (TAN) £6.45 (PLA) £6.50 (BU) £6.50 (MV) £6.60 (BEN) £6.95 (BALL) £7.03 (GW)

Douro Vila Regia 1997 £4.01 (STE) £4.45 (NA)

Periquita J.M. da Fonseca 1996 £4.49 (MAJ) £5.29 (YOU)

Quinta das Setencostas 1998 £4.25 (BO)

Quinta das Setencostas 1997 £4.99 (OD)

£5.00 → £5.99

Beira Mar Reserva, da Silva 1988 £5.95 (ROB) £7.95 (VIN)

Dão Duque de Viseu 1994 £5.99 (CO)

Dão Duque de Viseu 1992 £5.95 (WS)

Dão Garrafeira Grão Vasco 1994 £5.00 (STE) £5.55 (NA)

Douro Duas Quintas 1995 £5.99 (MAJ) £6.15 (STA) £6.35 (HAH)

Douro Duas Quintas 1994 £5.95 (POR)

Douro Esteva, Ferreira 1996 £5.22 (STE) £5.80 (NA)

Douro Quinta de la Rosa 1995 £5.99 (RAE) £6.17 (REI) £6.35 (CON) £6.49 (YOU) £6.90 (UB) £6.95 (ROB) £6.99 (GW)

★ Douro Quinta do Crasto 1997 £5.85 (SOM) £5.95 (AD) £6.49 (YOU) £6.76 (SAV) £6.99 (VA) £8.81 (TW)

Quinta da Camarate, J.M. da Fonseca 1992 £5.50 (WS)

Quinta da Lagoalva Tinto 1994 £5.99 (OD)

Tinto da Ânfora J P Vinhos 1992 £5.49 (MAJ)

£6.00 → £6.99

Alentejo Vinha do Monte Sogrape 1997 £6.26 (STE) £6.95 (NA)

Beira Mar Garrafeira, da Silva 1989 £6.90 (TAN)

Dão Duque de Viseu 1997 £6.48 (STE) £7.20 (NA)

Dão Quinta das Maias 1995 £6.95 (POR)

Dão Terras Altas J M da Fonseca 1993 £6.00 (PIP)

★ Douro Quinta de la Rosa 1997 £6.50 (MV)

Garrafeira da Silva 1989 £6.29 (UN)

Quinta da Lagoalva Tinto 1993 £6.50 (ROB)

Reguengos Esporão Reserva 1994 £6.99 (OD) £8.95 (ROB)

MERCHANTS SPECIALIZING IN PORTUGAL

see Merchant Directory (page 413) for details

Nearly all merchants sell some port, but only a few have interesting Portuguese table wines. Adnams (AD), Bibendum (BIB) – especially port, on fine wine list, Cockburns of Leith (COC) – especially port, Direct Wine (DI) – for port and Madeira, Farr Vintners (FA) – for Vintage port, First Quench Group (BOT, THR, VIC, WR), Justerini & Brooks, Lay & Wheeler (LAY), Laymont & Shaw, Oddbins (OD), Peatling, Raeburn Fine Wines (RAE) – old colheitas from *Niepoort*, Reid Wines (REI) – particularly for port, T&W Wines (TW) – including ports back to 1937, Tanners (TAN) – particularly port, Wine Society (WS), Peter Wylie Fine Wines (WY) – old ports and Madeiras.

£7.00 → £9.99

Bairrada Luis Pato 1996 £8.25 (LAY)
Bairrada Reserva Casa de Saima 1991
  £8.99 (RAE)
Beira Mar Garrafeira, da Silva 1987 £8.50
  (VIN)
Dão Fonte do Ouro, Sociedade Agricola
  Boas Quintas 1995 £7.99 (BEN) £8.50 (BU)
Dão Quinta das Maias 1996 £8.25 (WRI)
  £8.75 (BU)
Dão Quinta dos Roques Reserva 1995
  £7.95 (LEA)
Douro Quinta do Crasto Reserve 1996
  £8.95 (AD) £9.75 (PIP) £11.69 (TW)
  £15.00 (MI)
Douro Vale da Raposa 1996 £9.58 (MI)
Pasmados J M da Fonseca 1993 £7.90 (PIP)
Quinta da Bacalhôa 1996 £8.32 (PLAY)
Quinta da Camarate, J M da Fonseca
  1993 £7.60 (PIP)
Quinta da Pacheca 1996 £7.92 (MI)
Romeira Garrafeira 1991 £7.75 (BU)
Trás-os-Montes Quinta do Bons Ares,
  Ramos Pinto 1992 £9.95 (JU)

£10.00 → £19.99

Alentejo Quinta do Carmo 1994 £11.95
  (TAN)
Alentejo Quinta do Carmo 1993 £10.90
  (CRO) £16.22 (NO)
Cartuxa Tinto 1995 £10.95 (BEN) £10.95
  (WRI)
Cartuxa Tinto 1989 £13.00 (CRO)
Dão Porta dos Cavaleiros 1975 £19.39
  (REI)
Douro Duas Quintas Reserva, Ramos
  Pinto 1992 £14.95 (JU)
Douro Quinta do Crasto 1987 £17.99
  (YOU)
Periquita J M da Fonseca 1987 £10.50
  (CRO)
Periquita J M da Fonseca 1976 £18.00
  (CRO)
Reserva Especial, Ferreira 1990 £17.50
  (NA) £18.51 (REI)
Reserva Especial, Ferreira 1986 £17.04 (REI)

Over £20.00

Barca Velha, Ferreira 1991 £33.48 (STE)
  £39.50 (NA)
Barca Velha, Ferreira 1985 £32.31 (REI)
Barca Velha, Ferreira 1982 £62.00 (CRO)
Dão Reserva Caves São João 1978
  £25.00 (CRO)

WHITE

Under £4.00

Ramada Branco 1996 £3.49 (VIC) £3.49
  (THR) £3.49 (WR) £3.49 (BOT)
Vinho Verde Casal Mendes Caves Aliança
  Non-vintage £3.39 (BO) £4.25 (CON)
  £4.31 (ROS)
Vinho Verde Gazela, Sogrape **Non-
  vintage** £3.99 (OD) £4.05 (STE) £4.23
  (FLE) £4.30 (TAN) £4.50 (NA)

£4.00 → £4.99

Albis Fonseca 1997 £4.65 (WS)
Dão Grão Vasco 1998 £4.28 (STE) £4.75
  (NA)
João Pires Branco 1997 £4.49 (MAJ) £4.79
  (JON)
João Pires Branco 1996 £4.52 (GW) £4.75
  (CON) £4.85 (PIP) £4.95 (JU)

Over £5.00

Albis Fonseca 1996 £6.06 (PIP)
Bairrada Quinta de Pedravites 1998
  £6.50 (NA)
Bairrada Reserva Sogrape 1997 £7.50 (NA)
Cova da Ursa Chardonnay, J.P. Vinhos
  1997 £7.99 (YOU)
Dão Terras Altas J M da Fonseca 1996
  £6.01 (PIP)
Douro Duas Quintas Branco, Ramos
  Pinto 1995 £6.95 (JU)
Douro Reserva Sogrape 1998 £6.71 (STE)
Dry Palmela Moscato, João Pires 1995
  £5.45 (UB)
João Pires Catarina 1997 £6.04 (PIP)

ROSÉ

Under £4.50

Mateus Rosé **Non-vintage** £3.49 (ASD)
  £3.99 (MORR) £3.99 (TES) £3.99 (SO)
  £3.99 (UN) £3.99 (CO) £3.99 (SAF) £3.99
  (VIC) £3.99 (THR) £3.99 (WR) £3.99 (BOT)
Nobilis Bairrada, Sogrape 1998 £4.19 (STE)

FORTIFIED

Under £17.00

Moscatel de Setúbal 20-year-old J.M. da
  Fonseca **Non-vintage** £16.96 (PIP)
  £20.00 (FORT) £21.08 (NO) £22.50 (TAN)

PORT PRICES

Under £6.00

Churchill's Finest Vintage Character ½ bottle **Non-vintage** £5.50 (LEA) £6.76 (VIN)

Cockburn's Special Reserve ½ bottle **Non-vintage** £4.85 (SAF)

£6.00 → £6.99

Cockburn's Fine Ruby **Non-vintage** £6.16 (HA) £7.10 (COC) £7.39 (WHI) £7.49 (SAF) £7.55 (UN) £7.59 (VIC) £7.59 (THR) £7.59 (WR) £7.59 (BOT)

Graham Ruby **Non-vintage** £6.50 (NI)

Niepoort Ruby **Non-vintage** £6.99 (RAE) £7.14 (BIB) £7.75 (BO) £9.95 (GAU)

Quinta de la Rosa **1996** £6.60 (ELL)

Quinta do Noval Extra Dry White **Non-vintage** £6.80 (PLA)

Quinta do Noval Old Coronation Ruby **Non-vintage** £6.25 (COC)

Royal Oporto **Non-vintage** £6.29 (YOU) £7.95 (VIN)

Sandeman Fine Old White **Non-vintage** £6.99 (VIC) £6.99 (THR) £6.99 (WR) £6.99 (BOT) £7.75 (BO)

Sandeman Tawny **Non-vintage** £6.99 (OD)

★ Smith Woodhouse Vintage Character **Non-vintage** £6.99 (OD) £13.55 (NO)

Van Zellers Ruby **Non-vintage** £6.59 (WHI)

£7.00 → £8.99

Churchill's Late Bottled **1992** £8.79 (HED) £9.95 (AS)

Churchill's Late Bottled **1990** £8.99 (YOU) £10.49 (BO) £10.50 (STA) £11.88 (VIN)

Churchill's Dry White **Non-vintage** £8.99 (HED) £9.25 (BO) £9.49 (WAI) £9.49 (SOM) £9.95 (AME) £9.95 (LEA) £10.05 (PIP) £10.20 (TAN) £10.50 (STA) £10.99 (PHI) £11.63 (TW) £11.95 (VIN)

Churchill's Finest Vintage Character **Non-vintage** £8.68 (PLAY) £9.93 (PIP) £9.95 (LEA) £11.63 (TW) £12.95 (VIN)

Cockburn's Special Reserve **Non-vintage** £7.20 (HA) £8.40 (COC) £8.55 (UN) £8.55 (SAF) £8.59 (VIC) £8.59 (THR) £8.59 (WR) £8.59 (BOT) £8.69 (WAI) £8.89 (WHI)

Dow's Fine Ruby **Non-vintage** £7.99 (GW) £8.50 (ROB) £9.60 (JER)

Dow's Late Bottled **1991** £8.49 (OD) £8.50 (GW) £9.49 (WAI) £11.26 (JER)

Fonseca Bin 27 **Non-vintage** £7.99 (BAL) £8.35 (COC) £8.89 (ROS) £8.99 (DI) £8.99 (YOU) £9.35 (WRI) £9.69 (NLW) £9.95 (PHI) £10.95 (FORT) £10.95 (VIN)

Graham Late Bottled **1991** £8.65 (NI) £10.49 (WAI) £10.49 (GW) £10.49 (SAF) £10.53 (WAT) £11.20 (HAH) £12.34 (REI) £16.10 (NO)

Graham Tawny **Non-vintage** £8.79 (BO) £8.94 (PLAY)

Martinez Dry White **Non-vintage** £8.95 (CON) £12.45 (VIN)

Martínez Fine Tawny **Non-vintage** £7.49 (CON) £11.48 (VIN)

Niepoort Vintage Character **Non-vintage** £8.61 (BIB) £8.99 (RAE) £10.69 (PEN)

Quinta do Noval Late Bottled **Non-vintage** £7.95 (COC) £9.68 (FLE) £10.09 (UN)

Ramos-Pinto Ruby **Non-vintage** £8.40 (BEN)

Taylor First Estate **Non-vintage** £7.99 (BO) £8.99 (NLW)

Warre's Warrior **Non-vintage** £8.29 (TES) £8.29 (SAF) £8.39 (UN) £8.48 (ROS) £8.49 (VIC) £8.49 (THR) £8.49 (WR) £8.49 (BOT) £9.28 (GW) £9.60 (JER)

£9.00 → £10.99

Cálem Late Bottled **1992** £9.75 (CON)

Churchill's Traditional Late Bottled **1992** £9.95 (HED) £11.85 (PHI) £11.95 (LEA) £12.15 (PIP)

Cockburn's Anno Late Bottled **1993** £9.99 (UN)

Cockburn's Late Bottled **Non-vintage** £9.08 (HA)

Dow's Late Bottled **1994** £9.49 (AME)

Dow's Late Bottled **1992** £9.75 (VIC) £9.75 (THR) £9.75 (BOT)

Fonseca Late Bottled **1994** £10.95 (DI)

Fonseca Late Bottled **1992** £10.95 (BALL) £10.99 (BEN) £11.25 (ELL)

Fonseca Late Bottled **1990** £9.35 (COC) £9.90 (CRO)

Graham 10-year-old Tawny **Non-vintage** £10.95 (NI) £15.49 (OD) £20.56 (TW)

Graham Late Bottled **1992** £10.49 (THR)
£10.49 (WR) £10.59 (UN) £10.75 (BO)
£11.40 (TAN) £11.49 (CB) £12.75 (FORT)
Graham Late Bottled **1990** £10.49 (TES)
£10.60 (COC)
Niepoort ½ bottle **1992** £10.95 (RAE)
£13.50 (ROB)
Niepoort Late Bottled **1994** £9.95 (RAE)
£10.49 (AME)
Niepoort Late Bottled **1992** £10.75 (BO)
Niepoort Senior Fine Old Tawny **Non-
vintage** £9.89 (BIB) £10.65 (RAE) £12.34
(PEN) £12.53 (PIP)
Quinta de la Rosa **Non-vintage** £9.95
(ROS)
Quinta de la Rosa **1991** £10.98 (SOM)
Quinta do Noval Late Bottled **1991** £9.95
(HAH) £9.99 (YOU)
Ramos-Pinto Late Bottled **Non-vintage**
£10.99 (JON)
Ramos-Pinto Late Bottled **1989** £9.80
(HAH) £9.99 (BO)
Ramos Pinto Quinta da Urtiga **Non-
vintage** £9.09 (JON)
Taylor Chip Dry White Port **Non-
vintage** £9.95 (COC) £11.15 (STA)
£11.25 (BALL) £11.80 (BEN) £12.25 (NA)
Taylor Late Bottled **Non-vintage** £10.49
(VIC) £10.49 (THR) £10.49 (WR)
Taylor Late Bottled **1994** £9.98 (WAT)
£10.49 (MAJ) £11.50 (STA) £12.65 (NA)
Taylor Late Bottled **1992** £9.99 (BO)
£10.49 (UN) £10.59 (WAI) £10.59 (SAF)
£11.30 (TAN) £11.90 (GAU) £13.95 (VIN)
Taylor Late Bottled **1991** £10.95 (BALL)
£13.75 (JU)

£11.00 → £12.99

Cálem Colheita **Non-vintage** £12.65
(CON)
Cálem Colheita **1987** £12.75 (COC)
£16.99 (UN)
Cálem Late Bottled **1983** £11.75 (REI)
Churchill's 10-year-old Tawny **Non-
vintage** £12.95 (HED) £14.49 (PLAY)
£14.50 (LEA) £14.95 (STA) £16.70 (VIN)

> *Please remember that*
> **Oz Clarke's Wine Guide**
> *is a price guide and not a
> price list. It is not meant to
> replace up-to-date
> merchants' lists.*

Churchill's Crusted Port **Non-vintage**
£11.75 (HED) £13.99 (JON) £14.50 (WRI)
Churchill's Crusted Port **1988** £11.37
(PLAY) £13.50 (FORT) £13.95 (LEA)
£15.30 (PIP) £15.76 (VIN) £16.50 (PHI)
Croft Late Bottled **1990** £11.95 (JU)
Delaforce His Eminence's Choice **Non-
vintage** £12.00 (JU)
Dow's Trademark **Non-vintage** £11.25
(FORT)
Dow's Vintage Character **Non-vintage**
£12.24 (JER)
Feuerheerd **1982** £12.34 (REI) £13.99
(YOU) £14.50 (BU)
Fonseca 10-year-old Tawny **Non-
vintage** £12.90 (CRO) £13.45 (DI)
£15.95 (BEN)
Graham Late Bottled **1989** £12.25 (JU)
Graham Malvedos **1984** £12.99 (NI)
£20.49 (WHI) £21.00 (JON) £21.00 (THR)
£21.00 (WR) £21.00 (BOT) £21.21 (PLAY)
£21.49 (AME) £21.74 (PEN) £21.75 (FORT)
£22.21 (ROS) £22.80 (HAH) £28.14 (TW)
Graham Six Grapes Vintage Character
Non-vintage £11.99 (WAI) £11.99
(JON) £11.99 (WR) £11.99 (BOT) £12.50
(JU) £16.96 (NO)
Martinez ½ bottle **1994** £12.50 (CON)
Niepoort ½ bottle **1987** £11.95 (RAE)
Quarles Harris **1983** £12.73 (FA) £19.00
(JU) £19.54 (PLAY) £56.42 (VIN)
Quinta da Eira Velha ½ bottle **1994**
£12.50 (CON)
Quinta de la Rosa **1990** £12.99 (RAE)
Quinta de la Rosa **1988** £37.29 (VIN)
Quinta do Noval **1978** £11.75 (FA)
Quinta do Noval 10-year-old Tawny
Non-vintage £12.56 (PLA) £13.95
(WAI) £14.50 (FORT) £14.99 (UN)
Sandeman Late Bottled **1994** £11.99 (NLW)
Taylor Late Bottled **1989** £11.00 (PLAY)
Wellington Wood Port **Non-vintage**
£11.75 (BER)

£13.00 → £14.99

★ Cálem 10-year-old Tawny **Non-vintage**
£13.99 (UN)
Churchill's Traditional Late Bottled **1990**
£13.45 (TW)
Croft Quinta da Roeda **1980** £14.04 (PLA)
Delaforce Quinta da Corte **1984** £13.99
(OD)
Dow's 10-year-old Tawny **Non-vintage**
£14.99 (GW) £14.99 (VIC) £14.99 (THR)
£14.99 (WR) £14.99 (BOT) £16.50 (ROB)

Dow's 20-year-old Tawny **Non-vintage**
£14.85 (HAH) £21.75 (GW) £23.49 (SAF)
£23.50 (WAI)

Ferreira Quinta do Porto 10-year-old
Tawny **Non-vintage** £13.95 (YOU)

Fonseca Late Bottled **1983** £14.55 (WAI)

Martinez 10-year-old Tawny **Non-vintage** £14.95 (RAE) £14.99 (CON)
£14.99 (AME) £15.50 (PIP)

Niepoort 10-year-old Tawny **Non-vintage** £14.19 (BIB) £14.95 (RAE)
£17.90 (GAU)

Quinta de la Rosa **1994** £14.59 (NI)
£21.00 (JU)

Royal Oporto **1982** £13.49 (TES)

Tanners Crusted **Non-vintage** £13.95
(TAN)

Taylor 10-year-old Tawny **Non-vintage**
£14.75 (ROS) £14.95 (TAN) £15.00 (PLA)
£15.59 (BO) £15.75 (WHI) £16.25 (BALL)
£16.45 (PEN) £16.45 (WRI) £16.49 (MAJ)
£16.49 (VIC) £16.49 (THR) £16.49 (WR)
£16.49 (BOT) £16.75 (STA) £17.20 (BEN)
£17.50 (FORT) £17.50 (GAU) £17.99 (VIN)

Warre's ½ bottle **1980** £13.50 (ROB)
£15.27 (WY) £21.54 (FA)

Warre's Late Bottled **Non-vintage**
£14.99 (JON)

Warre's Late Bottled **1984** £14.39 (WHI)
£14.80 (HAH)

Warre's Traditional Late Bottled **1984**
£13.99 (SAF) £14.45 (WAI) £15.95 (CON)
£15.99 (AME)

£15.00 → £16.99

Cálem Quinta da Foz **1987** £15.99 (UN)

Churchill's Crusted Port **1987** £16.00
(WR) £16.00 (BOT)

Churchill's Quinta do Agua Alta **1983**
£16.44 (PLA) £26.50 (HED)

Cockburn's 20-year-old Tawny **Non-vintage** £16.20 (HA)

Croft Quinta da Roeda **1983** £15.95 (POR)

Delaforce **1982** £15.86 (REI)

Fonseca Guimaraens **1984** £16.95 (DI)
£17.05 (ROS) £17.90 (COC) £19.29 (JER)
£19.42 (PEN) £19.70 (HAH) £20.50 (PHI)
£20.56 (REI) £20.75 (WRI) £21.75 (FORT)
£21.90 (GAU) £23.50 (ELL)

Fonseca Guimaraens Quinta do Panascal
1986 £16.43 (STE) £17.50 (FORT) £17.50
(GAU) £18.00 (VIC) £18.00 (THR) £18.00
(WR) £18.00 (BOT) £18.25 (NA)

Graham **1991** £15.85 (NI) £27.95 (ROB)
£30.00 (JU) £30.90 (LAY) £38.78 (TW)

Graham **1989** £16.10 (NO)

Offley Boa Vista **1982** £16.95 (ROB)

Quinta da Ervamoira 10-year-old Tawny
Non-vintage £15.75 (PHI) £16.99 (JON)

Quinta do Noval **1982** £15.18 (FA) £17.00
(COC) £20.00 (CRO) £20.50 (BALL)
£22.00 (PEN) £23.50 (FORT)

Rebello Valente **1985** £16.65 (FA) £25.00
(JU)

Royal Oporto **1980** £15.86 (REI)

Warre's Late Bottled **1981** £16.33 (PEN)

Warre's Traditional Late Bottled **1996**
£15.95 (AD)

Warre's Traditional Late Bottled **1986**
£16.25 (FORT)

£17.00 → £18.99

Churchill's **1982** £18.21 (REI) £29.37 (NO)
£33.50 (PHI)

Churchill's Quinta do Agua Alta **1992**
£18.50 (AS)

Croft Quinta da Roeda **1978** £17.92 (REI)
£28.33 (MI)

Dow Quinta do Bomfim **1986**£18.99 (GW)
£19.66 (LAY) £20.00 (AD) 20.97 (PEN)

Gould Campbell **1980** £18.75 (BER)

Niepoort **1991** £18.95 (RAE)

Niepoort Colheita **1985** £17.99 (RAE)
£21.90 (GAU)

Sandeman **1982** £18.20 (COC) £21.99
(NLW)

Taylor Quinta de Vargellas **1986** £18.15
(COC) £18.79 (PLA) £19.99 (UN) £19.99
(BO) £20.00 (VIC) £20.00 (THR) £20.00
(WR) £20.00 (BOT) £20.20 (TAN) £20.25
(STE) £20.27 (PLAY) £20.75 (HAH) £21.90
(GAU) £21.95 (AD) £22.50 (NA)

Warre's Late Bottled **1986** £17.95 (PIP)

Warre's Quinta da Cavadinha **1987**
£18.79 (CON) £19.99 (BO) £20.95 (LAY)
£21.49 (VIC) £21.49 (THR) £21.49 (WR)
£21.49 (BOT) £26.20 (PIP)

£19.00 → £20.99

Cockburn **1994** £19.32 (HA) £21.54 (FA)
£26.93 (CAV) £41.95 (VIN)

Cockburn **1991** £19.12 (HA) £21.15 (CB)
£22.00 (COC) £22.52 (CAV) £23.00 (JON)

Croft **1982** £19.95 (BAL)

Delaforce **1975** £20.00.(WR) £20.00 (BOT)

Dow Quinta do Bomfim **1984** £19.95 (WAI)
£19.99 (OD) £19.99 (VIC) £19.99 (THR)
£19.99 (WR) £19.99 (BOT) £20.99 (GW)

Fonseca **1980** £19.58 (FA) £24.50 (COC)
£29.38 (WY) £29.50 (CON)

Fonseca Guimaraens **1982** £19.00 (VIC) £19.00 (THR) £19.00 (WR) £19.99 (SAF)
Gould Campbell **1994** £20.52 (NI) £24.00 (JU)
Gould Campbell **1991** £21.35 (PIP)
Gould Campbell **1983** £19.00 (JU) £22.88 (NO)
Graham 20-year-old Tawny **Non-vintage** £20.50 (NI) £35.13 (TW)
Graham Malvedos **1986** £19.99 (OD) £22.49 (THR) £22.49 (WR) £22.49 (BOT)
Harvey **1985** £19.95 (CON)
Martinez **1994** £19.95 (LAY) £20.00 (JU) £21.00 (PIP) £27.07 (NO)
Niepoort **1992** £19.95 (RAE) £20.83 (ROS)
Quinta de la Rosa **1995** £19.00 (MV) £20.99 (YOU)
Sandeman **1980** £19.99 (ROB) £21.54 (CAV)
Smith Woodhouse **1983** £19.00 (JU) £24.00 (VIC) £24.00 (THR) £24.00 (WR)
Taylor Quinta de Vargellas **1987** £20.50 (FORT)
Taylor Quinta de Vargellas **1984** £19.39 (REI) £19.50 (JU) £19.99 (MAJ) £20.75 (WRI) £21.00 (BALL)
Warre **1980** £19.58 (FA) £23.50 (BAL) £26.44 (REI) £35.39 (AV) £40.93 (VIN)

Warre's Late Bottled **1982** £20.77 (NO)
Warre's Quinta da Cavadinha **1986** £19.95 (WAI) £19.99 (WHI) £19.99 (OD) £19.99 (SAF) £20.36 (ROS) £20.99 (AME)
Warre's Quinta da Cavadinha **1984** £20.79 (PEN) £21.95 (ROB) £22.20 (GW)

£21.00 → £22.99

Churchill's **1991** £21.00 (JU) £34.66 (TW)
Churchill's Quinta do Agua Alta **1995** £21.50 (TAN) £27.60 (STA)
Churchill's Quinta do Agua Alta **1990** £22.99 (PHI)
Cockburn **1985** £21.51 (HA) £25.46 (CAV) £27.00 (JU) £29.00 (JON) £30.00 (UN)
Croft **1985** £21.54 (FA) £22.50 (BAL) £23.95 (ROB) £29.15 (AV) £67.45 (VIN)

Croft **1977** £22.33 (CB) £33.00 (BER) £38.68 (CAV) £39.00 (BAL) £45.00 (VIC) £45.00 (THR) £45.00 (WR) £45.00 (BOT)
Delaforce **1985** £21.50 (POR) £25.00 (JU) £27.00 (VIC) £27.00 (THR) £27.00 (BOT)
Gould Campbell **1985** £22.21 (ROS) £24.20 (TAN) £26.50 (JON) £27.20 (PLAY)
Niepoort **1987** £22.00 (RAE) £23.50 (BIB)
Niepoort Colheita **1982** £22.95 (PHI)
Niepoort Colheita **1978** £21.95 (RAE) £37.90 (GAU)
Quinta da Eira Velha **1994** £22.50 (CON) £25.32 (NO)
Quinta do Noval **1985** £22.05 (PLAY) £22.52 (CAV) £25.49 (BO) £28.00 (CRO) £28.50 (WRI) £31.26 (VIN) £32.50 (PHI)
Quinta do Noval **1975** £22.25 (WAT)
Ramos-Pinto **1983** £21.98 (GW) £24.95 (RES) £28.50 (POR)
Sandeman **1985** £21.95 (ROB) £23.01 (CAV) £27.50 (FORT)
Smith Woodhouse **1994** £21.74 (CB) £24.00 (JU) £24.50 (PIP) £26.73 (REI)
Taylor Quinta de Vargellas **1982** £21.99 (TES) £29.96 (TW)
Warre **1994** £22.90 (NI) £31.33 (JER) £33.78 (FA) £34.12 (PLAY) £35.00 (CON) £35.00 (JU) £40.00 (BALL)
Warre **1991** £22.50 (ROB) £24.50 (CON) £24.50 (STA) £28.00 (JU) £57.99 (VIN)
Warre **1983** £22.25 (WAT) £23.50 (ROB) £25.00 (JU) £25.46 (CAV) £25.95 (COC) £27.50 (BALL) £27.91 (REI) £35.00 (FORT) £36.00 (VIC) £36.00 (THR) £36.00 (BOT) £37.50 (JON) £38.35 (HAH) £44.65 (VIN)
Warre's Quinta da Cavadinha **1982** £22.20 (GW)

£23.00 → £24.99

Cálem 20-year-old Tawny **Non-vintage** £24.99 (UN)
Dow **1991** £24.55 (LAY) £28.00 (JU)
Fonseca Guimaraens **1995** £24.95 (RES) £24.95 (DI) £27.81 (GAU) £29.38 (REI) £29.96 (CB) £30.90 (TAN) £33.20 (AV)

> • Wines are listed in A–Z order within each price band.
> • For each wine, vintages are listed in descending order.
> • Each vintage of any wine appears only once.

Fonseca Guimaraens **1991** £23.50 (ROB)
Graham **1994** £23.42 (NI) £37.70 (FA)
£42.50 (CON) £47.00 (JU) £55.00 (BALL)
Graham **1983** £23.50 (ROB) £31.33 (CAV)
£32.50 (FORT) £36.45 (PLAY) £36.50
(BAL)
Graham **1980** £24.50 (ROB) £31.82 (CAV)
£34.45 (PLAY) £40.00 (VIC) £40.00 (THR)
£40.00 (WR) £40.00 (BOT) £42.12 (TW)
Graham Malvedos **1987** £24.99 (BO)
Quinta do Noval Nacional **1975** £23.50
(NO)
Sandeman **1994** £24.99 (NLW)
Sandeman Imperial 20-year-old Tawny
Non-vintage £23.50 (LEA) £23.50 (OD)
Smith Woodhouse **1980** £23.00 (VIC)
£23.00 (THR) £23.00 (WR) £23.00 (BOT)
Taylor **1980** £24.50 (COC) £29.95 (ROB)
£31.73 (REI) £37.94 (PLAY) £42.12 (TW)
Warre **1985** £23.50 (FA) £25.95 (RES)
£28.00 (JU) £29.50 (UN) £29.95 (CON)
£30.35 (CAV) £31.00 (BER) £31.50 (LAY)
£32.00 (VIC) £32.00 (THR) £32.00 (WR)
£34.17 (PLAY) £34.95 (STA) £35.00 (BALL)
£36.90 (HAH) £37.95 (DI) £39.50 (BAL)

£25.00 → £29.99

Barros **1985** £27.20 (AV)
Churchill's **1994** £25.00 (JU) £29.95 (PHI)
£38.95 (VIN)
Churchill's **1985** £25.00 (JU) £33.25 (HED)
£34.95 (STA) £35.50 (AD) £37.85 (WRI)
Delaforce **1994** £25.00 (JU)
Dow **1985** £25.46 (FA) £28.00 (JU) £29.95
(CON) £32.00 (VIC) £32.00 (THR) £32.00
(WR) £32.00 (BOT) £32.50 (MI) £34.00
(RES) £38.80 (PLAY) £40.80 (AV)
Dow **1983** £25.00 (BALL) £25.00 (JU)
£25.46 (FA) £27.50 (CON) £34.00 (NO)
£37.50 (ROB) £39.10 (HAH)
Fonseca **1983** £25.00 (JU) £26.95 (COC)
£27.91 (FA) £31.00 (CRO) £39.95 (DI)
£45.00 (JON) £48.00 (VIC) £48.00 (THR)
Fonseca **1975** £29.95 (ROB) £32.70 (PLAY)
Fonseca Guimaraens **1978** £28.95 (BALL)
Gould Campbell **1970** £25.46 (FA)
Graham Malvedos **1995** £27.00 (JU)
£29.38 (REI) £31.70 (TAN) £33.00 (RES)
Graham Malvedos **1979** £29.38 (TW)
Hoopers **1985** £27.91 (VIN)
Martinez **1985** £26.31 (NO)
Martinez 20-year-old Tawny **Non-
vintage** £25.00 (CON)
Niepoort **1982** £27.60 (RAE)
Niepoort **1980** £29.60 (RAE)

Niepoort 20-year-old Tawny **Non-
vintage** £29.90 (GAU)
Niepoort Colheita **1987** £29.95 (PHI)
Offley Boa Vista **1977** £26.05 (JER)
Offley Boa Vista **1966** £29.96 (REI)
Quarles Harris **1994** £28.89 (JER)
Quarles Harris **1985** £25.00 (VIC) £25.00
(THR) £25.00 (WR) £25.00 (BOT)
Quarles Harris **1980** £28.00 (VIC) £28.00
(THR) £28.00 (WR) £28.00 (BOT)
Quinta do Noval **1991** £25.00 (JU)
Quinta do Noval 20-year-old Tawny
Non-vintage £26.91 (PLA) £28.06 (NO)
£33.00 (FORT)
Quinta do Vesuvio **1995** £29.86 (FA)
£29.96 (CB) £30.00 (FORT) £31.14 (REI)
£31.82 (PLAY) £33.00 (RES) £34.45 (HAH)
Quinta do Vesuvio **1990** £27.50 (CON)
Rebello Valente **1970** £27.67 (REI)
Rebello Valente **1960** £29.50 (BU)
Royal Oporto **1985** £29.76 (VIN)
Sandeman **1977** £29.50 (ROB) £35.00 (JU)
£39.95 (NI)
Smith Woodhouse **1985** £25.00 (JU)
£27.00 (VIC) £27.00 (THR) £28.00 (UN)
Taylor **1983** £25.95 (ROB) £26.95 (COC)
£27.42 (FA) £35.00 (CRO) £35.25 (CAV)
£45.00 (JON) £45.00 (FORT) £48.00 (VIC)
£48.00 (THR) £48.00 (WR) £48.00 (BOT)
Taylor Quinta de Vargellas **1995** £27.81
(GAU) £28.00 (JU) £29.38 (REI) £30.90
(TAN) £32.20 (HAH)
Taylor Quinta de Vargellas **1991** £26.92
(ELL)

£30.00 → £39.99

Cálem **1970** £32.50 (CON) £52.75 (COC)
Cockburn **1970** £34.51 (HA) £38.68 (CAV)
£42.50 (ROB) £43.48 (WY) £45.12 (PLAY)
Croft **1994** £33.29 (FA)
Croft **1970** £38.68 (CAV) £41.13 (WY)
£50.00 (JU)
Delaforce **1977** £35.00 (VIC) £35.00 (THR)
£35.00 (WR) £35.00 (BOT)
Dow **1994** £35.00 (JU) £36.72 (CAV)
£37.21 (FA) £38.90 (LAY) £40.00 (CON)
£45.00 (BALL)
Dow **1980** £30.79 (LAY) £34.00 (THR)
£34.00 (WR) £34.00 (BOT) £34.26 (PLAY)
Dow **1960** £35.25 (REI)
Fonseca **1993** £37.99 (BO)
Fonseca **1985** £33.95 (COC) £35.00 (ROB)
£39.17 (FA) £43.08 (CAV) £51.50 (STA)
£53.00 (JON) £55.00 (BER) £55.00 (FORT)
£56.00 (THR) £56.00 (WR) £56.00 (BOT)

Fonseca 20-year-old **Non-vintage**
£31.45 (BEN) £31.50 (FORT) £32.75 (PIP)
Gould Campbell **1977** £32.31 (CAV)
£35.25 (REI) £38.00 (BER) £40.00 (FORT)
Graham **1985** £36.00 (WR) £36.00 (BOT)
£37.21 (FA) £39.17 (CAV) £39.17 (MI)
£45.00 (BAL) £46.41 (REI) £55.00 (FORT)
Graham **1960** £38.78 (REI) £45.00 (BU)
Martinez **1991** £35.00 (VIN)
Offley Boa Vista **1985** £37.25 (VIN)
Quarles Harris **1977** £31.50 (JON) £39.00
(PHI) £39.00 (VIC) £39.00 (THR) £39.00
(WR) £39.00 (BOT) £78.14 (VIN)
Quinta do Noval **1970** £37.70 (CAV)
£48.00 (BER)
Quinta do Vesuvio **1996** £32.99 (PHI)
£34.50 (HAH)
Quinta do Vesuvio **1994** £35.25 (FA)
£42.50 (CON) £45.00 (JU)
Quinta do Vesuvio **1992** £32.94 (LAY)
£35.00 (JU)
Sandeman **1970** £33.50 (ROB) £35.25
(CAV) £36.00 (BAL)
Sandeman **1960** £35.00 (BU)
Taylor **1985** £32.31 (PLA) £38.68 (FA)
£39.95 (CON) £43.08 (CAV) £45.90 (LAY)
£53.00 (JON) £55.00 (RES) £56.00 (THR)
£56.00 (WR) £60.00 (FORT) £88.95 (VIN)
Taylor **1975** £39.95 (RES)
Taylor 20-year-old Tawny **Non-vintage**
£33.01 (PLAY) £33.50 (UN) £33.60 (TAN)
£34.00 (VIC) £34.00 (THR) £34.90 (GAU)
£34.95 (ROB) £35.00 (BEN) £36.72 (VIN)
Taylor Quinta de Vargellas **1972** £38.99
(VIN)
Warre **1977** £35.00 (CON) £35.20 (AV)
£37.21 (FA) £42.50 (ROB) £43.08 (CAV)
£44.90 (NI) £44.99 (OD) £45.00 (THR)
£45.00 (BOT) £55.00 (JON) £72.56 (VIN)
Warre **1960** £35.25 (REI) £41.13 (WY)
£61.69 (TW)

£40.00 → £49.99

Cálem **1994** £42.50 (WRI)
Dow **1977** £42.10 (FA) £44.58 (MI) £46.51
(CAV) £48.00 (THR) £48.00 (WR) £48.00
(BOT) £49.50 (BEN) £55.00 (BER)
Dow **1970** £49.50 (BAL) £52.87 (CAV)
£68.15 (REI) £75.00 (BER)
Fonseca **1992** £46.02 (FA) £49.95 (CON)
£57.77 (CAV) £58.75 (WRI) £66.39 (REI)
£88.10 (TAN)
Offley Boa Vista **1963** £45.00 (BU)
Warre **1970** £48.00 (JU) £48.50 (ROB)
£48.96 (CAV) £50.00 (FLE) £57.60 (LAY)

£50.00 → £74.99

Cálem 40-year-old Tawny **Non-vintage**
£52.50 (CON)
Cockburn **1963** £60.00 (JU) £65.00 (HED)
£65.00 (BU) £70.50 (CAV) £86.19 (PLAY)
Cockburn **1955** £70.50 (FA) £80.00 (BU)
£118.00 (RES) £129.25 (WY) £173.90 (REI)
Croft **1966** £55.00 (BAL) £61.69 (REI)
Croft **1950** £52.88 (REI)
Dow **1966** £64.63 (REI)
Dow **1950** £50.00 (CRO)
Fonseca **1994** £65.00 (WRI) £85.00 (CON)
£85.19 (FA) £89.90 (LAY) £93.02 (CAV)
Fonseca 40-year-old **Non-vintage**
£59.95 (DI)
Graham **1977** £52.87 (FA) £58.75 (CAV)
£65.00 (ROB) £69.95 (AD) £75.00 (FORT)
£82.00 (STA)
Graham **1970** £60.00 (JU) £69.50 (BU)
£70.00 (RES) £70.50 (CAV) £75.70 (AV)
£85.00 (FORT) £101.05 (TW)
Graham **1966** £66.50 (ROB) £70.50 (REI)
£75.95 (BEN) £80.78 (CAV) £100.00
(FORT)
Graham 40-year-old Tawny **Non-vintage** £65.00 (JU) £78.96 (TW)
Martinez **1963** £57.50 (BU)
Niepoort Colheita **1963** £54.00 (RAE)
Quinta do Noval **1966** £57.28 (CAV)
£65.00 (ROB)
Quinta do Noval **1963** £69.50 (RES)
£70.00 (ROB)
Quinta do Noval 40-year-old Tawny **Non-vintage** £65.00 (FORT)
Quinta do Vesuvio **1989** £55.10 (AV)
Ramos-Pinto Tawny **1937** £55.00 (CRO)
Sandeman **1966** £53.85 (CAV)
Sandeman **1963** £66.09 (CAV) £99.95 (VIN)
Taylor **1977** £65.60 (FA) £67.56 (CAV)
£70.50 (WY) £75.00 (CON) £75.00 (ROB)

Taylor **1970** £62.25 (ROB) £68.75 (BEN)
£76.38 (REI) £76.86 (CAV) £79.90 (WY)
£100.00 (FORT) £109.96 (VIN) £112.80
(TW)

Taylor **1966** £69.50 (ROB) £75.00 (SOM)
£77.84 (CAV) £127.49 (TW)
Taylor 30-year-old Tawny **Non-vintage**
£54.34 (VIN)
Taylor 40-year-old Tawny **Non-vintage**
£70.50 (PEN) £75.99 (UN) £76.00 (STA)
£78.50 (GAU) £80.00 (FORT) £82.54 (VIN)
Warre **1966** £58.75 (PLA)
Warre **1963** £73.50 (ROB) £75.00 (BU)
£75.00 (SOM) £78.00 (BEN) £97.50 (RES)
£115.00 (FORT) £131.37 (TW)

£75.00 → £99.99

Cockburn **1912** £76.37 (WY)
Croft **1963** £95.00 (RES) £126.90 (VIN)
Croft **1955** £80.00 (BU) £102.81 (CAV)
£135.12 (WY) £164.50 (SOM)
Dow **1963** £75.00 (RES) £90.08 (FA)
Fonseca **1977** £80.00 (SOM) £88.12 (FA)
£97.92 (CAV) £99.88 (REI) £145.00
(FORT)
Fonseca **1970** £75.00 (ROB) £75.00 (JU)
£77.84 (CAV) £85.00 (RES) £89.00 (AD)
£98.00 (NO) £100.00 (FORT)
Fonseca **1966** £78.75 (BEN) £125.00 (RES)
Niepoort Colheita **1934** £99.50 (RAE)
Quinta do Noval **1955** £75.00 (BU)
£111.63 (REI)
Quinta do Noval **1947** £95.00 (CRO)
£182.13 (REI)
Taylor **1994** £85.00 (CON) £85.19 (FA)
£90.57 (CAV)
Taylor **1992** £80.29 (FA) £87.15 (CAV)
£95.00 (JU) £100.00 (CON)
Taylor **1963** £92.00 (CRO) £110.00 (SOM)
£115.00 (RES) £127.00 (ROB) £130.00
(JU) £139.04 (FA) £151.77 (CAV) £173.90
(REI) £192.90 (AV) £200.00 (FORT)
Taylor ½ bottle **1994** £90.08 (FA)
Warre **1958** £99.50 (RES)

£100.00 → £149.99

Cockburn **1927** £129.25 (WY)
Ferreira **1945** £146.88 (REI) £176.25 (CAV)
Fonseca **1963** £139.00 (VIN) £155.00 (ROB)
£161.56 (CAV) £170.38 (WY) £175.00 (RES)
£179.95 (AV) £205.63 (REI) £225.00 (FORT)
Graham **1963** £145.00 (BEN)
Quinta do Noval Nacional **1978** £139.83
(TW)
Quinta do Noval Nacional **1960** £148.83
(FA) £411.25 (TW)
Rebello Valente **1924** £135.12 (WY)
Sandeman **1927** £143.94 (REI)
Taylor **1924** £146.88 (REI) £182.12 (WY)

£150.00 → £199.99

Cockburn **1947** £170.37 (WY)
Cockburn **1935** £199.50 (POR) £217.37
(WY) £217.38 (REI) £258.50 (CAV)
Dow **1945** £176.25 (REI) £395.00 (VIN)
Graham **1955** £150.00 (ROB) £150.00 (SOM)
Graham **1942** £190.00 (BEN)
Quinta do Noval Nacional **1987** £159.80
(NO)
Quinta do Noval Nacional **1980** £164.50
(TW)
Ramos-Pinto **1945** £164.50 (REI)
Rebello Valente **1927** £182.13 (REI)
Sandeman **1947** £193.87 (WY) £385.00
(FORT)
Taylor **1955** £166.46 (CAV) £176.25 (WY)
£195.00 (JU) £235.00 (RES) £245.00 (FORT)
Taylor **1930** £176.25 (REI)

£200.00 → £299.99

Croft **1945** £252.62 (WY) £252.63 (REI)
Croft **1935** £264.38 (REI)
Croft **1920** £264.37 (WY)
Dow **1938** £264.38 (REI)
Dow **1927** £250.00 (BEN) £264.38 (REI)
Fonseca **1955** £223.25 (CAV)
Graham **1927** £205.63 (REI)
Quinta do Noval Nacional **1994** £293.75
(FA)
Quinta do Noval Nacional **1970** £225.00
(ROB) £246.75 (REI) £300.80 (NO)
£352.50 (TW)
Quinta do Noval Nacional **1967** £200.00
(FORT) £235.00 (NO)
Sandeman **1945** £264.38 (REI)
Sandeman **1935** £205.63 (REI) £282.00 (WY)
Taylor **1920** £299.62 (WY)
Warre **1945** £225.60 (REI)
Warre **1920** £205.62 (WY)

Over £300.00

Dow **1924** £346.62 (WY)
Graham **1945** £411.25 (REI)
Martinez **1931** £446.50 (CAV)
Quinta do Noval Nacional **1966** £347.80
(NO)
Quinta do Noval Nacional **1963** £490.00
(JU) £658.00 (NO) £705.00 (TW) £705.00
(CAV)
Quinta do Noval Nacional **1955** £393.63
(WY)
Taylor **1948** £411.25 (CAV) £417.13 (REI)
Taylor **1945** £354.46 (FA) £550.00 (FORT)
Warre **1947** £375.00 (RES)

MADEIRA PRICES

Under £9.00

3-year-old Medium Dry Henriques &
Henriques **Non-vintage** £8.95 (STA)
£9.35 (ROS) £9.75 (FORT) £9.95 (LEA)
Duke of Clarence Blandy **Non-vintage**
£8.50 (NI) £8.95 (CON) £8.99 (GW)
£8.99 (SAF) £9.10 (HAH) £9.49 (THR)
£9.50 (ROB) £9.95 (JU) £11.16 (TW)
£11.54 (VIN)
Duke of Cumberland Blandy **Non-vintage**
£8.50 (NI) £9.10 (WAT) £9.49 (THR) £9.49
(WR) £9.50 (ROB) £11.54 (VIN)
Duke of Sussex Blandy **Non-vintage**
£8.50 (NI) £8.99 (GW) £9.10 (HAH) £9.49
(THR) £9.49 (WR) £9.95 (JU) £11.54 (VIN)
Sercial Blandy **Non-vintage** £8.99 (GW)

£9.00 → £9.99

3-year-old Medium Rich Henriques &
Henriques **Non-vintage** £9.00 (ELL)
£9.35 (ROS) £9.95 (LEA) £12.38 (VIN)
Duke of Cambridge Blandy **Non-vintage**
£9.95 (JU) £11.54 (VIN)
Sercial Old Custom House Rutherford &
Miles **Non-vintage** £9.95 (ROB)

£10.00 → £14.99

10-year-old Malmsey Blandy **Non-vintage** £14.50 (NI) £15.76 (WAT)
£15.95 (WAI) £16.20 (HAH) £16.99 (JON)
£20.33 (CB)
10-year-old Verdelho Henriques &
Henriques **Non-vintage** £14.80 (COC)
£17.75 (FORT) £17.95 (LEA)
5-year-old Bual Blandy **Non-vintage**
£11.90 (HAH)
5-year-old Bual Cossart Gordon **Non-vintage** £12.95 (CON) £12.95 (JU)
5-year-old Finest Full Rich Henriques &
Henriques **Non-vintage** £10.45 (COC)
5-year-old Finest Medium Dry Henriques
& Henriques **Non-vintage** £10.45
(COC) £10.99 (AME) £11.95 (LEA)
5-year-old Malmsey Cossart Gordon
Non-vintage £12.95 (CON) £13.50 (DI)
£14.75 (FORT) £14.92 (CB) £14.95 (AD)
5-year-old Sercial Blandy **Non-vintage**
£11.17 (WAT)
5-year-old Sercial Cossart Gordon **Non-vintage** £12.95 (JU) £13.50 (DI) £14.20
(HAH) £14.75 (FORT) £14.92 (CB)

£15.00 → £24.99

10-year-old Bual Cossart Gordon **Non-vintage** £17.95 (DI)
10-year-old Malmsey Henriques &
Henriques **Non-vintage** £15.33 (NO)
£15.50 (CRO) £15.95 (HED) £16.49 (AME)
£16.95 (AS) £17.00 (ELL) £17.95 (LEA)
10-year-old Verdelho Cossart Gordon
Non-vintage £19.50 (AD)
Bual Henriques & Henriques **Non-vintage** £16.13 (NO)
Verdelho Henriques & Henriques **Non-vintage** £15.33 (NO)

£25.00 → £49.99

15-year-old Malmsey Cossart Gordon
Non-vintage £25.00 (JU)
Sercial Henriques & Henriques **1940**
£43.08 (FA)

£50.00 → £99.99

Bual Blandy **1954** £55.00 (BOT) £120.00 (JU)
Bual Blandy **1920** £99.88 (FA)
Bual Henriques & Henriques **1954** £58.75
(REI) £93.00 (JU)
Malmsey Cossart Gordon **1954** £93.00 (JU)
Malmsey Henriques & Henriques **1954**
£93.00 (JU) £110.00 (CRO)
Malmsey Justino Henriques **1933** £73.44
(REI)
Sercial Solera 1860 Cossart Gordon
Non-vintage £99.88 (REI)
Sercial Vintage Cossart Gordon **1940**
£99.88 (REI)
Verdelho Henriques & Henriques **1934**
£60.71 (FA) £88.13 (REI) £170.00 (JU)

Over £100.00

Bual Blandy **1911** £205.63 (REI)
Bual Vintage Cossart Gordon **1920**
£193.88 (REI)
Bual Vintage Cossart Gordon **1914**
£188.00 (TW)
Bual Vintage Leacocks **1914** £305.50 (WY)
Malmsey Cossart Gordon **1933** £211.50
(WY)
Malmsey Powers **1954** £175.00 (JU)
Sercial Henriques & Henriques **1944**
£130.00 (CRO) £130.00 (JU)
Verdelho Vintage Rutherford & Miles
1934 £240.88 (REI)

SOUTH AFRICA

This isn't a bargain basement area at the moment. You've got to spend more to get the best flavours

South Africa produces an awful lot of wine. You can hardly expect it all to be the same quality.

South Africa is, in fact, the world's seventh largest wine producer. It's also had a series of difficult vintages – 1996, 1997 and 1998 all had their problems – and the net result is that the wines to look for are the more up-market ones. Sorry, but there it is. The least expensive wines are not the ones to pick at the moment. Single-estate wines are much better, and show just what the country is capable of. They're easy to spot – you'll either see the words 'estate wine' on the label or the word 'estate' will form part of the producer's name.

Pinot Noir is looking increasingly good; Pinotage, too, as it gets less odd-tasting and more balanced. Reds generally are becoming more approachable, though some wines display more winemaking than actual wine. But South Africa is by no means the only country to fall into that particular trap.

GRAPE VARIETIES

CABERNET SAUVIGNON, CABERNET FRANC AND BORDEAUX BLENDS (red) Good ones have clean, minty aromas and fresh fruit, though seldom as soft and seductive as, say, Chilean versions. Old-style ones persist with a tough greenness or a dusty dryness. Bordeaux blends tend to be best Best Cabernets include: *L'Avenir, Avontuur Reserve, Backsberg, Bellingham, Beyerskloof, Blaauwklippen Reserve, Neil Ellis, Glen Carlou, Hartenberg, Haute Provence, Jacques Kruger, Landskroon Cabernet Franc, Le Bonheur, Lievland, Mouton-Excelsior, Nederburg, Plaisir de Merle, Springfield, Swartland Co-op, Thelema, De Trafford, Vergelegen.* Blends: *Avontuur Baccarat, Buitenverwachting Grand Vin, Clos Malverne Devonet, Fairview Charles Gerard Red Reserve, Glen Carlou Les Trois, Grangehurst, Groot Constantia Gouverneur's Reserve, Klein Constantia Marlbrook, Lievland DVB, Meerlust, Nederburg Auction, Rustenberg Gold, Villiera Cru Monro, Welgemeend, Zonnebloem Lauréat.*

CHARDONNAY (white) The best wines have lingering lemon-lime freshness with subtle oak. Inevitably, there's some over-oaking disguising some underpowered wine-making, too. Try: *Alphen, Backsberg, Graham Beck Lone Hill, Bellingham Reserve, Blaauwklippen, Bouchard Finlayson, Buitenverwachting, De Leuwen Jagt, De Wetshof Bateleur, Dieu Donné, Neil Ellis, Hamilton Russell, Haute Provence, Jordan, Klein Constantia, Glen Carlou Reserve, Groot Constantia, Louisvale, Van Loveren, Meerlust, Morgenhof, Mulderbosch, Nederburg Auction, Rustenberg, Schoon Gevel, Slaley Sentinel, Simonsig, Springfield, Stellenryck, Thelema, Vergelegen Les Enfants, Weltevrede, Zandvliet, Zevenwacht Zevenrivieren, Zonnebloem.*

CHENIN BLANC (white) Usually simple entry-level stuff, though a few take it more seriously. Best: *Hamilton Russell, Boland, Glen Carlou, Boschendal, Leopard's Rock, Môreson-Matin Soleil, Villiera, Wildekrans, Van Zylshof.*

WINE OF ORIGIN

Every bottle of wine sold in South Africa must bear the Wine of Origin seal. This certifies the wine's area of origin, grape variety (or varieties) and vintage.

CINSAUT (red) Crossed with Pinot Noir, it produced the Pinotage. By itself it mostly gives light, undistinguished reds, although *Rosenview* is attractive.

MERLOT (red) By itself Merlot makes rich, ripe, easy reds – even better aged in new oak. Increasingly popular. Good ones include *Avontuur Reserve, Bellingham, Boschendal, De Trafford, Drostdy-Hof, Fairview Reserve, Glen Carlou, Hoopenburg, Jacana, Meerlust, Morgenhof, Steenberg, Thelema, Uiterwyk, Saxenburg, Thelema, Vergelegen, Villiera, Warwick, Wildekrans* and *Zonnebloem*.

MUSCAT (white) Sweet Muscadels are usually the best bet, and include: *De Leuwen Jagt, Klein Constantia Vin de Constance, KWV, Van Loveren Blanc de Noir, Nederburg Eminence, Vredendal*.

PINOTAGE (red) The abrasive, estery styles of old are being taken over by cleaner, more intense fruit. Pinotage is suddenly very fashionable: huge amounts are being planted. Good ones are *Avontuur, Beyerskloof, Beyers Truter, Clos Malverne, Grangehurst, Jacana, Kanonkop, KWV Cathedral Cellars, Simonsig, Swartland co-op, Warwick* and *Wildekrans*.

PINOT NOIR (red) The coolest parts of the country are producing supple and understated Pinot Noirs of world class. Best are: *Bouchard Finlayson, Glen Carlou, Hamilton Russell, Haute Cabrière*.

> **ON THE CASE**
> *Wine styles are still evolving rapidly in South Africa, so it's always worth trying new wines*

RIESLING (white) Sweet ones are excellent; the dry and off-dry ones can be too. Best dry: *Buitenverwachting, Neethlingshof*. Best off-dry: *De Leuwen Jagt, Hartenburg, Klein Constantia, Lievland, Sinnya*. Best sweet botrytized Rieslings: *Danie De Wet Edeloes, KWV Noble Late Harvest, Nederburg Noble Late Harvest* and *Neetlingshof Noble Late Harvest*.

SAUVIGNON BLANC (white) Showing vast improvements, and challenging Chile on quality. Lovely pungent, ripe wines come from *Bellingham, Neil Ellis, Klein Constantia, Morgenhof, Mulderbosch, Saxenburg, Springfield, Thelema, Villiera*.

SHIRAZ (red) Shiraz can make savoury, raspberry-fruited wines, although perhaps lacking the fleshy sweetness of the best of the Rhône and Australia. Best: *Fairview, Klein Constantia, Hartenberg, La Motte, Lievland, Saxenburg, Sentinel, Thelema, Zonnebloem*.

SPARKLING WINES 'Methode Cap Classique' is the name for Champagne-method fizz. Best: *Graham Beck, Blaauwklippen Barouche, Boschendal, Pierre Jourdan* (from *Cabrière*), *Charles de Fere Tradition, Pongrácz* and *J C Le Roux Chardonnay*.

WINES & WINE REGIONS

CONSTANTIA South Africa's oldest existing wine region is one of its most dynamic. *Steenberg's* Sauvignon Blanc, *Buitenverwachting* and *Klein Constantia* are the names to watch.

DURBANVILLE Cape Town is threatening the vineyards of Durbanville. Sauvignon Blanc is particularly good.

FRANSCHHOEK White grapes rule, yet the new reds are promising. Look for *Cabrière* fizz and Pinot Noir, *Bellingham's* fantastic new Cabernet Franc, *Dieu Donné* and *Haute Provence* Cabernet Sauvignon.

OLIFANTS RIVER Irrigated bulk wine area, making some good everyday stuff as well.

PAARL The *KWV* is based in the town of Paarl, as is *Nederburg*. There is also *Backsberg, Villiera, Glen Carlou, Fairview, De Leuwen Jagt* and *Landskroon*, with good wines from almost every variety. *Villiera* even has a good Sauvignon, and *Glen Carlou* one of South Africa's best Pinot Noirs.

ROBERTSON A region rapidly gaining a reputation for Chardonnay. *Astonvale, Leopard's Rock, Van Loveren, Sinnya, Springfield Estate, Weltevrede, Danie de Wet, Zandvliet, Van Zylshof* are names to look for.

STELLENBOSCH The heart of the wine industry. Both reds and whites are successful. Look for: *Avontuur, Bertrams,* *Beyerskloof, Blaauwklippen, Clos Malverne, Neil Ellis, Grangehurst Winery, Hartenberg, Kanonkop, Lievland, Meerlust, Morgenhof, Mulderbosch, Neetlingshof, Rust-en-Vrede, Saxenburg, Simonsig, Stellenzicht, Thelema, Vergelegen, Vriesenhof, Zevenwacht.*

SWARTLAND Hot and dry; Chenin Blanc, Sauvignon Blanc, Colombard and Pinotage do best. The *Swartland* and *Riebeek co-ops* and *Allesverloren* estate lead.

WALKER BAY Some of the best Pinot Noir comes from here and there's good Chardonnay, too. Top names: *Hamilton-Russell, Bouchard Finlayson, Wildekrans, Southern Right.*

PRODUCERS WHO'S WHO

BACKSBERG ★★★★ Luscious Chardonnay and superb reds, including top Malbec and Pinotage.

BELLINGHAM ★★★★★ Super flinty Sauvignon and an elegant, peachy Chardonnay. Cabernet Franc is stunning.

BOSCHENDAL ★★★★(★) Stronger on reds than whites. Look for intense, peppery Shiraz, juicy, chocolaty Merlot, and superb Lanoy red blend.

BOUCHARD FINLAYSON ★★★★★ Burgundian-style Chardonnays and some of South Africa's best Pinot Noir.

CABRIÈRE ESTATE ★★★★ Assertively dry and steely Pierre Jourdan Brut, elegant Blanc de Blancs, and perfumed, raspberry-packed Pinot Noir.

CATHEDRAL CELLAR ★★★ KWV's top range. Good New World-style Cabernet Sauvignon, vibrant Pinotage and grassy Sauvignon Blanc.

CLOS MALVERNE ★★★(★) Makes a lovely Pinotage and a very good value blend by the name of Devonet from Cabernet and Merlot.

DE WETSHOF ★★★(★) Danie de Wet makes Chardonnays with great elegance and poise, and spicy Rhine Riesling.

NEIL ELLIS WINES ★★★(★) Top negociant producing excellent Sauvignon from Elgin and Darling. Tropical-tasting Chardonnay, intense Cabernet.

FAIRVIEW ★★★★(★) Great Cabernet, Shiraz, Merlot, and new Zinfandel/Cinsaut blend. The Sauvignon/Semillon blend is the top white.

GLEN CARLOU ★★★★ Tropically rich, leesy Chardonnay and impressive red Bordeaux blends.

HAMILTON RUSSELL ★★★★★ Elegant Chardonnay and supple, ripe, even silky Pinot Noir that brilliantly straddle Old and New Worlds.

HAUTE PROVENCE ★★★(★) Newish Franschhoek winery with excellent reds and whites, including a Burgundian-style Chardonnay and a cedary Cabernet that will improve with age.

JORDAN VINEYARD ★★★
International styles made with great aplomb. Look for the Chardonnays.

KANONKOP ★★★★★ Pinotage king of
the Cape. There's also rich, mouthfilling Cabernet and complex Paul Sauer Bordeaux blend.

KLEIN CONSTANTIA ★★★★
Stunning Sauvignon Blanc, toasty Chardonnay and claret-style Marlbrook red.

LA MOTTE ★★★★ Excellent reds, in
particular big spicy Shiraz and ripe oak-splashed Cabernet.

LOUISVALE ★★★ Buttery, biscuity
Chardonnay and a good Cabernet/Merlot.

MEERLUST ★★★★ Look for stunning
Chardonnay, complex Rubicon Cabernet blend and a range of grappa.

PLAISIR DE MERLE ★★★(★) Rapidly
improving Chardonnay and Cabernet.

RUSTENBERG ★★★ Cabernet blends
that cellar well. Whites haven't been up to the same standard, but could be improving.

SIMONSIG ★★★★ Concentrated,
unwooded Pinotage and brilliant Shiraz.

SPRINGFIELD ESTATE ★★★
Cabernets are very good and age well; Sauvignon is good and lean, Chardonnay complex.

STEENBERG ★★★(★) Constantia's
rising star. Crisp, nettly Sauvignon Blanc and powerful, inky Merlot.

THELEMA ★★★★ First-rate Sauvignon
Blanc and Chardonnay, gutsy Cabernet Reserve and fruit-driven Cabernet/Merlot.

INSTANT CELLAR:
SINGLE-ESTATE WINES

- **1998 Semillon, Stellenzicht Reserve, £12, Averys** Trademark toastiness and lemon.
- **1998 Pinot Noir, Hamilton Russell, £14.55, Averys** Finely tuned supple fruit.
- **1996 Cabernet Franc, Warwick, £9.95, Ballantynes** Succulent and beautifully made.
- **1996 Shiraz, Saxenburg Private Collection, £11.95, Berry Bros. & Rudd** Dense and spicy with very good structure.
- **Marlbrook, Klein Constantia, £8.83, Cape Province** A Merlot-based Bordeaux blend, nicely plummy.
- **Cabernet Sauvignon, Plaisir de Merle, £11.28, Cape Province** Supple, ripe, round.
- **1994 Cabernet/Merlot, Klein Gustrouw, £8.97, Corney & Barrow** Sweetly berried fruit with a touch of tarriness.
- **1995 Les Trois, Glen Carlou, £9.50, Direct Wine Shipments** Top Bordeaux blend.
- **1996 Chardonnay, Meerlust, £21, Justerini & Brooks** Expensive but good: elegant and intense.
- **1996 Sauvignon Blanc, Buitenverwachting, £7.85, Lay & Wheeler** Ripe and pungent.

VERGELEGEN ★★★(★) Massive
investment is producing good results: supple Cabernet and rich Chardonnay. Look out for the Merlot.

VILLIERA ★★★★ Consistently excellent
Merlot and a new Chenin that nudges ahead of the tangy Sauvignon.

VRIESENHOF ★★★(★) Very intense
Chardonnay; super Kallista Bordeaux blend.

WARWICK ★★★★(★) Red specialist
making fabulous bush-trained Pinotage, dense, mouthfilling Cabernet Franc and a complex Bordeaux blend called Trilogy.

WELGEMEEND ESTATE ★★★★
Tremendous reds from Bordeaux grape varieties, including otherwise rarely seen Malbec and Petit Verdot.

SOUTH AFRICA PRICES

RED

Under £4.50

Adelberg Simonsig Estate 1997 £3.95 (WS)
Cabernet/Shiraz Van Loveren 1998 £3.99 (SOM)
Cape Red Drostdy-Hof 1996 £3.99 (NI)
Roodeberg KWV 1995 £4.49 (WAI)

£4.50 → £4.99

Adelberg Simonsig Estate 1996 £4.83 (PEN)
Adelberg Simonsig Estate 1995 £4.81 (ROS)
Cabernet Sauvignon KWV 1997 £4.99 (UN)
Cabernet Sauvignon KWV 1996 £4.93 (COC) £4.99 (VIC) £4.99 (THR) £4.99 (WR) £4.99 (BOT) £5.25 (CAP)
Cinsaut/Pinotage Kumala 1997 £4.59 (SAF)
Dry Red Stormy Cape, Thelema 1996 £4.50 (WS) £5.59 (NI)
Le Pavillon Boschendal Non-vintage £4.75 (UB) £4.76 (PLA) £9.75 (BALL)
Le Pavillon Boschendal 1998 £5.50 (NA)
Pinotage Kleinbosch Young Vatted 1998 £4.99 (SAF)
Pinotage Klippenkop 1997 £4.99 (CON)
Pinotage KWV 1997 £4.99 (COC) £4.99 (THR) £4.99 (WR) £4.99 (BOT) £5.49 (UN)
Zinfandel/Cinsaut Kopland 1997 £4.95 (JU)

£5.00 → £5.99

Cabernet Sauvignon Nederburg 1995 £5.49 (NLW) £5.93 (COC)
Chateau Libertas 1995 £5.49 (NLW)
Edelrood Nederburg 1995 £5.93 (COC)
Merlot Bellingham 1997 £5.99 (SAI)
Merlot De Leuwen Jagt 1990 £5.86 (PEN)
Pinotage Backsberg 1995 £5.99 (COC) £6.55 (WHI)
Pinotage Bellingham 1997 £5.29 (THR) £5.29 (WR) £5.29 (BOT) £6.59 (YOU)
Pinotage Beyerskloof 1997 £5.20 (SOM) £5.49 (OD) £5.99 (WR) £5.99 (BOT)

Pinotage Clos Malverne 1998 £5.99 (SOM) £6.95 (POR) £6.99 (YOU)
Pinotage Drostdy-Hof 1996 £5.36 (STE)
Pinotage Fairview 1998 £5.99 (SAI) £6.29 (GW) £6.95 (AD)
Pinotage Fairview 1997 £5.99 (SAF)
Pinotage Kopland 1996 £5.95 (JU)
Pinotage Nederburg 1996 £5.20 (COC) £5.79 (NLW) £6.02 (CAP)
Pinotage Nederburg 1995 £5.65 (UB)
Roodeberg KWV 1996 £5.10 (COC) £5.72 (CAP) £5.99 (UN)
Shiraz Fairview 1996 £5.99 (TES) £5.99 (SAF) £6.45 (BER) £6.59 (GW)
Shiraz KWV 1996 £5.34 (CAP)
Shiraz Sentinel 1997 £5.99 (OD)

£6.00 → £6.99

Cabernet Franc/Merlot Fairview 1996 £6.99 (GW)
Cabernet Sauvignon Backsberg 1995 £6.85 (COC) £7.29 (CAP)
Cabernet Sauvignon Fairview 1995 £6.99 (GW) £7.45 (JU)
Cabernet Sauvignon L'Avenir 1996 £6.75 (SOM) £7.99 (YOU)
Cabernet Sauvignon Zonnebloem 1994 £6.95 (NA) £7.14 (PLAY) £7.19 (CAP) £9.34 (TW)
Merlot Fairview 1996 £6.95 (AD) £7.03 (GW)
Merlot Fairview 1995 £6.95 (JU)
Pinotage Clos Malverne Reserve 1998 £6.99 (WAI)
Pinotage Drostdy-Hof 1995 £6.75 (ROB)
Pinotage Groot Constantia 1995 £6.22 (CAP)
Pinotage Meerendal 1994 £6.49 (MAJ)
Pinotage Simonsig 1996 £6.45 (ROS)
Pinotage Wildekrans 1996 £6.10 (SOM)
Pinotage Zonnebloem 1995 £6.25 (BALL) £6.60 (WRI) £7.12 (CAP)
Shiraz KWV 1991 £6.23 (BY)

MERCHANTS SPECIALIZING IN SOUTH AFRICA
see Merchant Directory (page 413) for details

Averys (AV), Bibendum (BIB), Cape Province Wines (CAP), Cockburns of Leith (COC), Direct Wine (DI), First Quench Group (BOT, THR, VIC, WR), Lay & Wheeler (LAY),

Oddbins (OD), Thos. Peatling, Terry Platt (PLA), Roberson (ROB), Sainsbury's (SAI), Tanners (TAN), The Ubiquitous Chip (UB), Waitrose (WAI).

Shiraz/Merlot Groot Constantia 1993 £6.69 (JON)
Tinta Barocca Rust-en-Vrede 1996 £6.95 (ROB)
Zinfandel/Cinsaut Fairview 1997 £6.45 (AD)

£7.00 → £7.99

Cabernet Sauvignon Backsberg 1994 £7.15 (WHI)
Cabernet Sauvignon Delheim 1994 £7.29 (WR)
Cabernet Sauvignon Groot Constantia 1995 £7.69 (CAP)
Cabernet Sauvignon La Cotte Reserve 1996 £7.50 (BU)
Cabernet Sauvignon/Merlot Jordan Chameleon 1996 £7.75 (WRI) £7.95 (STA)
Cabernet Sauvignon Springfield Estate 1997 £7.34 (BIB)
Cabernet Sauvignon Villiera 1995 £7.79 (VIC) £7.79 (THR) £7.79 (WR) £7.79 (BOT)
Cabernet Sauvignon Vriesenhof 1995 £7.60 (TAN)
Cabernet Sauvignon/Merlot Louisvale 1996 £7.49 (POR) £9.45 (AD)
Klein Babylonstoren Backsberg 1996 £7.99 (MORR)

Laureat Zonnebloem 1994 £7.50 (WRI) £8.50 (CAP)
Marlbrook Klein Constantia 1991 £7.99 (DI)
Merlot Cathedral Cellar 1995 £7.99 (MORR)
Merlot Fairview Reserve 1993 £7.99 (GW)
Merlot Warwick 1991 £7.99 (RAE)
Pinotage Neil Ellis 1996 £7.04 (PEN)
Pinotage Simonsig 1997 £7.76 (CB)
Pinotage Vriesenhof Paradyskloof 1997 £7.20 (TAN)
Pinotage/Cabernet Franc Overgaauw 1995 £7.25 (BALL)
Ruby Cabernet Robertson Winery 1998 £7.63 (BY)
Shiraz Backsberg 1995 £7.77 (BY)
Shiraz Fairview 1995 £7.45 (JU)
Shiraz Simonsig 1997 £7.18 (ROS) £7.37 (CAP)
Tinta Barocca Allesverloren 1991 £7.37 (COC)

£8.00 → £8.99

Auret Clos Malverne 1996 £8.52 (NO)
Cabernet Franc Warwick 1993 £8.68 (NO)
Cabernet Sauvignon Neil Ellis 1996 £8.99 (MAJ)

Cabernet Sauvignon Haute Provence
1996 £8.99 (OD)

Cabernet Sauvignon Klein Constantia
1995 £8.46 (CAP) £8.95 (AD) £9.30 (TAN)

Cabernet Sauvignon Klein Constantia
1994 £8.99 (JON) £10.50 (AV)

Cabernet Sauvignon Laborie **1997** £8.64
(CAP)

Cabernet Sauvignon Robertson Winery
1998 £8.52 (BY)

Cabernet Sauvignon Springfield Estate
1995 £8.60 (NO)

Cabernet Sauvignon/Merlot Louisvale
1995 £8.84 (PLAY) £9.50 (ROB)

Kallista Vriesenhof **1995** £8.30 (TAN)
£8.95 (LEA) £8.95 (ROB)

Klein Babylonstoren Backsberg **1994**
£8.45 (PLA)

Marlbrook Klein Constantia **1994** £8.46
(CAP) £9.25 (WRI)

Merlot Boschendal **1996** £8.50 (CRO)

Merlot Jordan **1996** £8.95 (CON) £9.10 (PIP)

Merlot Jordan **1995** £8.26 (FLE) £8.99 (YOU)
£9.69 (JER)

Merlot Warwick **1995** £8.52 (REI)

Millennium La Motte **1993** £8.99 (NI)

Pinot Noir Muratie Estate **1997** £8.95
(STA) £9.47 (PLAY)

Pinotage Clos Malverne Reserve **1997**
£8.49 (YOU) £8.75 (CON)

Pinotage Meerendal **1995** £8.73 (CAP)

Pinotage Warwick Traditional Bush Vine
1995 £8.90 (GAU)

Pinotage Wildekrans **1995** £8.95 (BER)

Red Wellington Claridge **1995** £8.96
(LAY) £9.99 (YOU)

Shiraz Allesverloren **1994** £8.95 (STA)
£8.96 (CAP)

Shiraz Delheim **1993** £8.45 (ROB)

Shiraz Fairview Reserve **1997** £8.03 (GW)

Shiraz Rust-en-Vrede **1995** £8.11 (FLE)

Shiraz Stellenzicht **1996** £8.65 (AV)

Shiraz Stellenzicht **1995** £8.07 (CAP)

Tinta Barocca Allesverloren **1995** £8.52
(CAP) £8.90 (WRI)

Tinta Barocca Allesverloren **1994** £8.80
(PLA)

£9.00 → £9.99

Cabernet Franc Warwick **1996** £9.95
(BAL) £9.95 (RAE)

Cabernet Sauvignon Alto **1991** £9.41
(STE) £10.45 (NA)

Cabernet Sauvignon Bellingham **1996**
£9.02 (CAP)

Cabernet Sauvignon De Trafford **1996**
£9.72 (BIB)

Cabernet Sauvignon Neil Ellis **1995** £9.95
(ROB)

Cabernet Sauvignon Jordan **1996** £9.50
(CON) £9.75 (PIP) £9.95 (STA)

Cabernet Sauvignon Kanonkop **1995**
£9.90 (SOM)

Cabernet Sauvignon/Merlot Jordan
Chameleon **1995** £9.30 (JER)

Cabernet Sauvignon Overgaauw **1994**
£9.90 (UB)

Cabernet Sauvignon Plaisir de Merle **1996**
£9.99 (MAJ)

Cabernet Sauvignon Plaisir de Merle **1995**
£9.99 (TES) £10.99 (SAF) £12.75 (UB)

Cabernet Sauvignon Stellenryck **1991**
£9.99 (NI)

Cabernet Sauvignon Warwick **1996**
£9.49 (WAI)

Faithful Hound Mulderbosch **1994** £9.75
(NO) £10.50 (CRO)

Gouverneurs Reserve Groot Constantia
1994 £9.00 (COC)

Merlot Boschendal **1995** £9.40 (HAH)

Merlot Glen Carlou **1997** £9.90 (STA)

Merlot Glen Carlou **1995** £9.40 (NO)
£9.99 (YOU)

Merlot Steenberg **1997** £9.70 (NO) £9.99
(WAI) £10.95 (DI)

Merlot Thelema **1995** £9.99 (SOM) £10.50
(FLE) £11.42 (NO) £11.66 (CAP) £11.99
(YOU) £12.50 (BEN) £13.95 (ROB) £14.99
(PHI)

Pinotage Kanonkop **1997** £9.40 (SOM)
£12.75 (FORT)

Pinotage Longridge **1995** £9.96 (HED)

Pinotage Uiterwyk **1995** £9.69 (YOU)
£10.19 (LAY)

Pinotage Warwick Traditional Bush Vine
1996 £9.39 (YOU) £9.95 (WS)

Shiraz La Motte **1994** £9.50 (LEA)

Trilogy Warwick **1995** £9.89 (YOU) £9.95
(RAE) £9.99 (WR) £9.99 (BOT) £10.16 (REI)

Trilogy Warwick **1993** £9.15 (GAU)

£10.00 → £12.99

Cabernet Sauvignon Beyerskloof **1995**
£11.99 (OD)

Cabernet Sauvignon Haute Provence
1995 £10.56 (NO)

Cabernet Sauvignon Jordan **1995** £10.77
(JER)

Cabernet Sauvignon Kanonkop **1994**
£12.99 (SAF)

Cabernet Sauvignon Rust-en-Vrede 1992
£10.93 (CAP)
Cabernet Sauvignon Stellenryck
Collection 1993 £10.50 (WRI)
Cabernet Sauvignon Thelema 1995
£12.75 (SOM) £14.57 (NO) £14.88 (CAP)
£14.99 (YOU) £15.95 (BEN) £15.99 (SAI)
Cabernet Sauvignon/Merlot Simonsig
Tiara 1994 £12.95 (WRI)
Cabernet/Merlot Grangehurst Reserve
1995 £11.75 (BIB)
Merlot Meerlust 1995 £11.99 (PHI) £13.90
(TAN) £13.99 (POR) £14.80 (BEN)
Merlot Thelema 1994 £11.95 (BU) £12.99
(NI)
Millennium La Motte 1994 £10.25 (BALL)
Paul Sauer Kanonkop 1995 £11.25 (SOM)
£15.25 (FORT)
Pinot Noir Bouchard Finlayson Galpin's
Peak 1997 £11.95 (WAI) £12.27 (BIB)
£12.95 (PHI) £14.00 (FORT)
Pinot Noir Hamilton Russell 1997 £12.75
(COC) £14.00 (AV) £16.41 (PLAY) £18.40
(TAN)
Pinot Noir Meerlust 1993 £10.95 (BU)
£12.50 (WRI)
Pinotage Beyerskloof 1995 £10.83 (NO)
Pinotage Kanonkop 1994 £11.50 (JU)
Pinotage L'Avenir 1997 £11.30 (NO)
£11.49 (YOU)
Rubicon Meerlust 1996 £11.99 (PHI)
Shiraz Zandvliet 1991 £10.00 (CAP)
Trilogy Warwick 1994 £10.95 (BAL)
Veenwouden 1995 £12.99 (OD)

£13.00 → £15.99

Cabernet Sauvignon Beyerskloof 1993
£13.85 (NO)
Cabernet Sauvignon Meerlust 1991
£14.50 (BU)
Cabernet Sauvignon Thelema 1993 £14.50
(BU) £15.57 (REI) £15.99 (NI) £17.00 (CRO)
Estate Wine Rust-en-Vrede 1995 £14.15
(LAY)
Merlot Meerlust 1994 £14.75 (FORT)
Paul Sauer Kanonkop 1992 £15.37 (NO)
Pinot Noir Hamilton Russell 1996 £14.03
(ROS) £15.25 (WRI) £15.75 (DI) £26.75 (UB)
Pinot Noir Hamilton Russell 1995 £13.95
(POR) £14.39 (JON) £14.80 (CRO)
Rubicon Meerlust 1994 £14.50 (FORT)
£15.25 (WRI)
Rubicon Meerlust 1992 £13.50 (ROB)
£16.00 (CRO)
Shiraz Hartenberg 1995 £15.95 (BER)

Over £16.00

Cabernet Sauvignon Agusta 1997 £16.75
(LIB)
Cabernet Sauvignon Warwick 1992
£20.00 (CRO)
Merlot Uiterwyk 1993 £18.52 (NO)
Pinot Noir Hamilton Russell Ashbourne
1997 £17.50 (FORT)
Pinotage Clos Malverne Reserve 1994
£18.14 (NO)
Pinotage Kanonkop 1995 £19.00 (CRO)

WHITE

Under £4.00

★ Chardonnay Danie de Wet Sur Lie 1998
£3.99 (OD)
Chenin Blanc Klippenkop 1997 £3.99
(CON) £4.99 (JER)
Chenin Blanc KWV 1998 £3.60 (COC)
£3.99 (UN) £3.99 (VIC) £3.99 (THR) £3.99
(WR) £3.99 (BOT)
Chenin Blanc Riebeek 1998 £3.99 (MORR)
★ Chenin Blanc Ryland's Grove 1998 £3.99
(TES)

Chenin Blanc SwartlandWine Cellar Reserve **1998** £3.99 (SAF)
Colombard Namaqua **1998** £3.25 (SOM)
Pinot Gris Van Loveren **1998** £3.99 (MORR)
Steen Drostdy-Hof **1996** £3.99 (NI)

£4.00 → £5.99

Chardonnay Avontuur **1998** £5.95 (WS)
Chardonnay De Leuwen Jagt **1993** £5.61 (PEN)
Chardonnay De Wetshof Lesca **1998** £5.99 (SAI)
Chardonnay Drostdy-Hof **1998** £5.36 (STE)
Chardonnay Fairview **1998** £5.99 (UN)
Chardonnay Fairview **1997** £5.99 (OD)
Chardonnay Nederburg **1996** £5.79 (NLW)
Chardonnay Rietvallei **1996** £5.36 (STE)
Chardonnay Sentinel **1997** £5.99 (OD)
Chardonnay Zonnebloem **1997** £5.58 (STE) £7.45 (NA) £7.72 (PLAY) £7.84 (CAP)
Chenin Blanc Klippenkop **1998** £4.22 (FLE) £4.75 (PIP)
Chenin Blanc KWV **1996** £4.32 (CAP)
Chenin Blanc Long Mountain **1996** £4.35 (UB)
Chenin Blanc Riebeek **1997** £4.75 (CON)

Chenin Blanc Simonsig **1997** £4.58 (PEN)
Chenin Blanc Thelema Stormy Cape **1998** £4.50 (WS) £4.55 (SOM)
Chenin Blanc Van Zylshof **1997** £4.37 (ROS) £5.00 (FORT)
Chenin Blanc Villiera **1997** £5.49 (THR)
Chenin/Chardonnay Arniston Bay **1998** £4.49 (MORR) £4.49 (THR) £4.49 (WR)
Riesling Hartenberg Weisser **1997** £5.99 (VIC) £5.99 (THR) £5.99 (WR)
Sauvignon Blanc Bellingham **1998** £5.39 (YOU)
Sauvignon Blanc KWV **1998** £4.48 (COC) £4.79 (THR) £4.79 (WR) £4.79 (BOT)
Sauvignon Blanc Nederburg **1996** £5.65 (UB)
Sauvignon Blanc Simonsig **1998** £5.32 (ROS) £5.82 (DOM) £6.19 (JON)
Sauvignon Blanc Two Oceans **1997** £4.79 (BAL)
Sauvignon Blanc Wildekrans **1997** £5.49 (POR)
Sauvignon/Chenin Blanc Kopland **1996** £4.55 (JU)
Semillon Fairview **1997** £5.99 (SAF) £6.03 (GW) £6.50 (AD)

£6.00 → £7.99

Buiten Blanc Buitenverwachting 1999
£6.05 (NEZ)
Chardonnay Agusta Unwooded 1998
£7.49 (VA) £7.50 (SOM)
Chardonnay Backsberg 1997 £7.10 (COC)
£7.55 (CAP)
Chardonnay Boschendal 1998 £6.42 (CAP)
Chardonnay Brampton 1996 £7.95 (LEA)
Chardonnay Cathedral Cellar 1996 £7.99
(MORR)
Chardonnay Claridge 1996 £7.99 (LAY)
Chardonnay Claridge 1995 £7.20 (FLE)
Chardonnay Delheim 1998 £6.99 (WR)
Chardonnay Dieu Donné Vineyards 1996
£7.25 (JU)
Chardonnay Fairview 1996 £7.95 (JU)
Chardonnay Groot Constantia 1996
£7.02 (CAP)
Chardonnay Jordan 1997 £7.99 (WAI) £8.49
(YOU) £8.50 (WRI) £8.70 (PIP) £8.95 (STA)
Chardonnay Laborie 1998 £6.25 (CAP)
Chardonnay Laborie 1995 £6.69 (JON)
Chardonnay L'Avenir 1997 £7.99 (YOU)
Chardonnay Le Bonheur 1996 £7.99 (BAL)
Chardonnay Louisvale Chavant Oaked
1997 £6.75 (WS) £8.49 (POR)
Chardonnay Louisvale Chavant Oaked
1995 £6.80 (HAH)
Chardonnay Louisvale Chavant Unoaked
1995 £7.95 (ROB)
Chardonnay Nederburg 1997 £6.02 (CAP)
Chardonnay Neil Ellis 1997 £7.99 (MAJ)
Chardonnay/Sauvignon Blanc Jordan
Chameleon 1998 £6.60 (WRI) £6.95
(STA) £7.00 (PIP)
Chardonnay Simonsig 1997 £7.64 (DOM)
Chardonnay Simonsig 1996 £7.95 (POR)
£10.35 (UB)
Chardonnay Uiterwyk 1996 £6.95 (BER)
Chardonnay Vergelegen 1997 £6.99 (SAF)
Chardonnay Vriesenhof 1997 £7.30 (TAN)
Chardonnay Warwick 1998 £6.99 (WAI)
Chardonnay Zevenwacht 1996 £6.99 (YOU)
Riesling Klein Constantia Rhine 1997
£6.40 (BEN)
Riesling Klein Constantia Rhine 1996
£6.25 (BAL) £9.95 (BER)
Sauvignon Blanc Brampton 1997 £6.95
(WS) £6.99 (SAF) £6.99 (YOU)
Sauvignon Blanc Buitenverwachting 1998
£7.33 (NEZ)
Sauvignon Blanc Jordan 1998 £7.95 (STA)
Sauvignon Blanc Jordan 1997 £7.50 (CON)

FAIRVIEW

TOWER OF QUALITY

GROWN, MADE & BOTTLED
AT FAIRVIEW BY CHARLES BACK.

FIND STOCKISTS IN THIS GUIDE

FOR MORE INFORMATION
CONTACT
CHARLES HAWKINS

TEL: 01572 823030 · FAX: 01572 823040

Sauvignon Blanc Jordan 1996 £7.34 (JER)
Sauvignon Blanc Klein Constantia 1997
£7.99 (CAP) £8.39 (BO) £8.40 (WRI)
£8.50 (TAN) £8.50 (FORT) £9.15 (PLAY)
Sauvignon Blanc L'Ormarins 1998 £6.78
(CAP) £7.10 (WRI)
Sauvignon Blanc Uiterwyk 1998 £6.59 (LAY)
Sauvignon Blanc Uitkyk 1997 £6.29 (COC)
Sauvignon Blanc Villiera 1997 £6.49 (VIC)
£6.49 (THR) £6.49 (WR) £6.49 (BOT)
Sauvignon/Chardonnay Uiterwyk
Rosenburg 1997 £7.25 (WRI)

£8.00 → £9.99

Chardonnay Boschendal Reserve 1997
£8.99 (YOU)
Chardonnay Bouchard Finlayson Oak
Valley 1997 £9.95 (WS)
Chardonnay Bouchard Finlayson Oak
Valley 1996 £9.99 (SAF)
Chardonnay Brampton 1997 £8.50 (BEN)
Chardonnay Buitenverwachting 1997
£8.99 (YOU)
Chardonnay Delaire 1997 £8.99 (SAF)
£9.99 (WR) £9.99 (BOT)
Chardonnay Hamilton Russell 1997 £9.72
(ROS) £9.95 (DI) £10.40 (AV) £12.00 (FLE)
£12.00 (WRI) £12.17 (PLAY) £12.25 (BALL)

Chardonnay Hamilton Russell **1996** £9.99
(RAE) £10.95 (POR)
Chardonnay Jordan **1996** £8.50 (CON)
£9.60 (JER)
Chardonnay Klein Constantia **1997** £8.15
(UN) £8.95 (FORT)
Chardonnay Klein Constantia **1996** £8.99
(JON)
★ Chardonnay Longridge **1998** £8.99 (OD)
Chardonnay Plaisir de Merle **1996** £8.99
(TES) £8.99 (MAJ)
Chardonnay Vergelegen Reserve **1996**
£9.99 (OD)
Chardonnay Warwick **1997** £8.49 (BAL)
Sauvignon Blanc Bouchard Finlayson **1996**
£9.95 (NO)
Sauvignon Blanc Buitenverwachting **1997**
£8.79 (YOU)
Sauvignon Blanc Klein Constantia **1996**
£8.99 (JON)
Sauvignon Blanc Mulderbosch **1998** £9.40
(CRO) £11.98 (ROB)
Sauvignon Blanc Neil Ellis **1998** £8.25 (ROB)
Sauvignon Blanc Neil Ellis **1996** £8.75 (UB)
Sauvignon Blanc Steenberg **1997** £9.69
(NO) £9.81 (REI)
Sauvignon Blanc Thelema **1998** £8.85 (SOM)
£9.99 (PHI) £10.50 (FLE) £10.79 (YOU)
£10.95 (BEN) £10.99 (SAI) £11.95 (LEA)
Sauvignon Blanc Zonnebloem **1997** £9.34
(TW)

£10.00 → £11.99

Chardonnay Bouchard Finlayson
Kaaimansgat **1998** £10.14 (BIB)
Chardonnay Bouchard Finlayson Walker
Bay **1997** £11.75 (FORT)
Chardonnay Glen Carlou Reserve **1997**
£10.95 (STA)
Chardonnay Glen Carlou Reserve **1996**
£10.66 (NO)
Chardonnay Hamilton Russell **1995**
£11.99 (JON)
Chardonnay Longridge **1996** £10.50 (BALL)
Chardonnay Overgaauw **1996** £10.80 (UB)
Chardonnay Thelema **1997** £10.05 (SOM)
£10.88 (FLE) £12.49 (SAI) £12.50 (BEN)
Chardonnay Thelema **1996** £11.95 (BU)
£12.99 (NI) £13.99 (PHI)
Sauvignon Blanc Mulderbosch Barrel-
Fermented **1995** £10.47 (NO)
Sauvignon Blanc Thelema **1997** £10.50
(NO) £10.95 (BU) £12.50 (ROB)
Vin de Constance Klein Constancia ½ litre
1988 £11.95 (GAU)

£12.00 → £15.99

Chardonnay Agusta Count **1998** £12.99
(LIB)
Chardonnay Springfield Estate Methode
Ancienne **1997** £12.34 (BIB) £12.99 (SAI)

Over £19.00

Chardonnay Meerlust **1996** £19.85 (WRI)
£20.00 (FORT)

ROSÉ

Under £6.00

Cabernet Sauvignon Blanc de Noir KWV
1996 £4.77 (CAP)
Rosé Nederburg **1996** £5.52 (CAP)

SPARKLING

Under £7.00

Graham Beck Brut **Non-vintage** £6.99
(SAF) £9.25 (FORT)
KWV Mousseux Blanc Cuvée Brut **Non-
vintage** £6.04 (CAP)
Laborie Blanc de Noir **1997** £6.97 (CAP)
Nederburg Premiere Cuvée Brut **Non-
vintage** £6.72 (CAP)

Over £8.50

Boschendal Brut Vintage **1993** £11.07 (STE)
Boschendal Brut Vintage **1992** £10.90 (CAP)
Boschendal Le Grand Pavillon Blanc de
Blancs **Non-vintage** £9.00 (CRO)
Pongrácz Cap Classique **Non-vintage**
£9.90 (CAP) £10.29 (JON)
Simonsig Kaapse Vonkel **1996** £10.13 (CAP)
Simonsig Kaapse Vonkel **1993** £9.05 (NO)

FORTIFIED

Under £5.00

Cavendish Cape Medium Dry **Non-
vintage** £4.54 (COC) £5.07 (CAP)
Cavendish Fine Old Ruby **Non-vintage**
£4.95 (COC) £6.03 (CAP)

Over £5.00

Cavendish Cape Cream **Non-vintage**
£5.27 (CAP)
Cavendish Vintage **1979** £9.55 (CAP)
Cavendish Vintage **1963** £8.84 (PEN)

SPAIN

Prices in Rioja have shot up, and all the top regions seem to be grooming themselves for superstardom. But does that really help us? I dunno

Frankly, I'm a bit puzzled by Spain at the moment. On the one hand even wines at the cheapest level have pretty much got the winemaking sorted out, and are fresh and clean. The wines at the top level are better than ever before, with regions like Ribera del Duero revelling in their star status. In fact stardom is very much the fashion in Spain at the moment: new cult wineries are springing up with a rapidity we're more used to seeing in California. But gosh, they're expensive. Top Spanish wines have got the bit between their teeth on price. And I can't honestly blame them: they match themselves against the glitziest wines of Italy, or France, or Australia, or the US,

and they think, 'Why not us? If there's a worldwide appetite for expensive wine, why not cash in?'

On the other hand at the less pricy end, where there are plenty of good juicy young reds, not overaged (and that, believe me, is a revolution), there's not that much that's of real interest. Nice soft gluggable everyday wines, yes. But I wonder if there's a danger of Spain squeezing out the middle ground. It can happen: everybody making good and good-value wine starts to think they should be charging a fortune. The cheaper end becomes mass-produced and simple. Overall prices rise faster than overall quality. I hope it won't happen in Spain.

GRAPE VARIETIES

AIRÉN (white) These days Airén is the mainstay of the cheap, fresh whites of La Mancha – even though the reds seem to have taken a bigger hold of the British imagination. Never mind. It's a perfect example of how modern winemaking can turn what was always the world's dullest grape (apart from Ugni Blanc) into something perfectly drinkable.

ALBARIÑO (white) Lovely, peachy, fresh wines with elegant acid balance from Rías Baixas. From being a rarity it's suddenly everywhere. Why? The growers have realized they can get good money for it. It's also grown over the border in Portugal for Vinho Verde, but it's called Alvarinho there.

BOBAL (red) Quite good deep-coloured, fruity red and stylish rosados in Utiel-Requena and Valencia. It has reasonable acidity and relatively low alcohol, which keep the wines comparatively fresh and appetizing.

CABERNET SAUVIGNON (red) Not a native Spanish variety, but making inroads in Penedés and Navarra, where it is generally rich and heavy with oak. Still officially experimental in Rioja, but probably not forever.

CARIÑENA (red) A source of dark and prodigiously tannic wine. It plays only a small part in the DO wine which carries its name, and most Cariñena (it's the same as the Carignan of southern France) is grown in Catalonia, usually as a beefy blender. It is also a minority grape in Rioja under the name Mazuelo. With its high tannin and acidity, and its aroma of ripe plums and cherries, it complements Tempranillo and adds to its aging potential.

CHARDONNAY (white) Usually made in a rich, oaky style, but often blended as well. Found a lot in Navarra and Penedés.

GARNACHA (red) This, known as Grenache in France, grows everywhere in Spain except Andalusia, and makes big, broad, alcoholic, sometimes peppery or spicy wines. The wines are dark, and don't last well, but they can be delicious young. The greatest examples are to be found in Priorato.

GARNACHA BLANCA (white) This makes wines that are high in alcohol, low in acidity and with a tendency to oxidize, so they are usually blended in with wines of higher acidity, like Viura.

GRACIANO (red) On the verge of extinction, the excellent Graciano grape has been rescued by the DOC upgrade in Rioja, where conscientious winemakers are seeking it out once again for the extra quality it gives to the wine.

MALVASÍA (white) This interesting, aromatic, flavourful grape tends, in Spain, to produce wines of low acidity that turn yellow and oxidize rapidly. When well made, it's full-bodied, fairly strongly scented, spicy or musky, often with a hint of apricots, and sometimes slightly nutty as well. Malvasia helps *Marqués de Murrieta* and *CVNE* white Riojas taste the way all white Rioja used to. But Malvasia is also still widely grown in the Canary Islands where it makes light, fresh whites, sometimes mixed with Viura/Macabeo.

MENCÍA (red) Mainly used in light, fruity young wines in Ribeiro and Bierzo.

MERSEGUERA (white) Valencia's mainstay white grape, also grown in Alicante and Tarragona, produces light, delicately aromatic and characterful wines.

MONASTRELL (red) Used to add body and guts to many Catalonian Tempranillo blends. It's grown right down the eastern seaboard in Alicante, Jumilla, Almansa, Yecla and Valencia – usually dry and stolid but sometimes made sweet. Jumilla's *Altos de Pío* is traditional, Yecla's *Pozuelo* more elegant.

MOSCATEL (white) Almost all Spanish Moscatel is the second-line Muscat of Alexandria rather than the top-quality Muscat à Petits Grains. But it makes a lot of good wine – rich and brown in Málaga, or fresh and grapy in Valencia. *Torres* makes a good, off-dry, aromatic version mixed with Gewürztraminer in Penedés, as does *de Muller* in Tarragona. Muscat de Chipiona from *Burdon* is rich and peachy. Also used to sweeten cream sherries.

PALOMINO (white) This is the dominant grape of the sherry region, making up all of the dry sherries, and an increasing proportion of the others. Although it produces great fortified wine it is not in itself a great grape. It plays a minor role in Montilla-Moriles. As a table wine grape, it produces dull, fat stuff, even with modern winemaking techniques, but in the sherry bodegas it reacts brilliantly to the *flor* yeast which imparts to *fino* that characteristic bone-dry, stark-sour nose.

PARELLADA (white) Touted as the provider of all the perfume and finesse in Catalonia's whites and in Cava fizz, but Parellada doesn't honestly have much to say for itself, except from the best producers: *Torres Viña Sol* is refreshing and lemony; also good are *Ferret i Mateu* and *Miret*.

PEDRO XIMÉNEZ (white) This used to be the chief component of sweet sherries, and is sometimes made into dessert wine, deeply coloured and thick. It covers most of the nearby Montilla-Moriles vineyards, as well as providing richness in Málaga; otherwise used for rather dull dry whites.

TEMPRANILLO (red) The fine red grape of Rioja and Navarra crops up all over Spain as far south as the province of

ON THE CASE

For really stylish Spanish red, go to Ribera del Duero. But tuck the bottles away in a corner for a few years more: these are wines that need lots of aging to show their best

Cádiz, but with a different name in almost every region. It's known as Cencibel on the plains of La Mancha and Valdepeñas, and as Tinto Fino in Ribera del Duero; elsewhere it may be Tinto de Madrid, Tinto de Toro, Tinto del País, and so on.

The wines have a spicy, herby, tobacco-like character, with plenty of sweet strawberry or sour cherry fruit, firm acidity and some tannin. Tempranillo makes vibrantly fruity wines ideally for gulping down young, as well as more robust wines suitable for aging – and it mixes brilliantly with oak. It's often blended, especially with Garnacha.

VERDEJO (white) One of Spain's more interesting white grapes. In Rueda it makes soft, creamy and slightly nutty white, sometimes a touch honeyed, with good, green acidity.

VIURA (white) The main white grape of Rioja, made nowadays apple-fresh and clean and, at best, rather neutral; at worst it is sharp and grapefruity. It achieves similarly mixed results, under the name Macabeo, in Catalonia. Made in this light, modern style, it's a wine for gulping down young, in its first year. But if you take the trouble to blend it with Malvasía, top it up with a slug of acidity and leave it to age for a while in oak barrels, Viura can make wonderful, rich, almost Burgundy-like white Rioja.

XAREL-LO (white) One of the three main white grapes of Catalonia, this is heavier, more alcoholic and even less aromatic than the barely aromatic Parellada and Macabeo, with which it is blended.

WINE REGIONS

ALELLA, DO (white) Catalan region whose best-known wine is the off-dry, very fruity *Marqués de Alella*. Also look for the light, pineapple-fresh Chardonnay and appley *Marqués de Alella Seco*, as well as the sparkling, greengagy *Parxet*, which beats most famous Cavas hands down.

ALICANTE, DO (red) Heavy, earthy reds made in south-east Spain from Monastrell and mostly useful for blending.

ALMANSA, DO (red) Strong spicy reds from Monastrell and Garnacha, and even better reds from Tempranillo. *Bodegas Piqueras* makes very good wines under the *Castillo de Almansa* and *Marius* labels.

AMPURDÁN-COSTA BRAVA, DO (red, white, rosado) Suddenly there are some good juicy reds being exported from here. The best are very good indeed. Look for *Cellars Santamaría*.

BIERZO, DO (red) Emergent zone for the promising Mencía grape. Older wines are blends from before it became a DO. The *Vinos del Bierzo* co-op is good.

BINISSALEM, DO (red, white, rosado) Young and *crianza* reds and light young whites and rosados from Mallorca. The main producer is *Bodegas Franja Roja*.

BULLAS, DO (red) In the province of Murcia, making great big heady Monastrell reds, mostly from co-operatives.

CALATAYUD, DO (red) Mainly Garnacha reds, plus some Tempranillo, usually for drinking young.

CAMPO DE BORJA, DO (red) Hefty alcoholic reds made from Cariñena and Garnacha, now making way for lighter reds and good rosados. *Bodegas Bordejé* and the *Borja* and *Santo Cristo* co-ops look promising.

CANARY ISLANDS There are eight DOs in the islands: Abona, El Hierro, Lanzarote, La Palma, Tacoronte-Acentejo, Valle de Güímar, Valle de la Orotava and Ycoden-Daute-Isora. Most of the wines are white (Tacoronte-Acentejo is the only serious producer of red) and mainly pleasant enough for the beach. There is still

SPANISH CLASSIFICATIONS

Denominación de Origen Calificada (DOC) is a new super-category (equivalent to the Italian DOCG) for wines which have a long tradition of high quality and are prepared to submit themselves to more rigorous quality scrutiny. So far there's only one DOC, and that's Rioja.

Denominación de Origen (DO) is roughly equivalent to the French AC: the basic quality wine designation. There are 51 of them.

Country wines fall into two groups: there are **Vinos Comarcales**: perhaps 'county wines' is the nearest translation into English. These have some local significance but few pretensions to promotion. The second and more important group comprises 22 **Vinos de la Tierra**, which translates as 'country wines', like French vins de pays. These are smaller areas, more tightly controlled and, in many cases, with ambitions to apply for DO status at some time in the future.

Vino de Mesa, basic table wine, doesn't usually carry any kind of regional name, nor a vintage date. A few maverick winemakers such as the Marqués de Griñón in Toledo and the Yllera family in Rueda use a legal nicety to put a general regional name on the label.

some sweet, fortified Malvasia, but it's not seen outside the islands.

CARIÑENA, DO (red) The best here are the pleasant, full, soft reds, mostly made from the fat, jammy Garnacha. Whites and rosados can be pleasant, but are mostly dull. The reds of the *Bodegas San Valero* co-op are sold here as *Don Mendo* and *Monte Ducay*.

CAVA, DO (white, rosado) The Spanish name for Champagne-method fizz, nearly all of which is from Catalonia. When Cava was promoted to DO status, several regions lost the right to use the name, and their wines (some, admittedly excellent) must now be called *Método Tradicional*. However, the two biggest outsiders, *Bodegas Inviosa* in Extremadura and *Torre Oria* in Valencia have permission to continue using the name.

Most Cava is much less earthy and old-fashioned than it used to be, though it doesn't improve with bottle age. Most appetizing are *Cavas Hill Reserva Oro Brut Natur*, *Codorníu Première Cuvée Brut*, *Juvé y Camps*, *Mont Marçal Cava Nature* (and *Chardonnay*), *Parxet*, *Raïmat*, *Segura Viudas* and *Rovellats*, *Freixenet* and its subsidiary company *Condé de Caralt*.

CIGALES, DO (red, rosado) Near Ribera del Duero, famed for rosados but with some serious reds as well, made from Tempranillo/Garnacha mixes.

CHACOLÍ, DO (red, white) There are two of these, in neighbouring Basque provinces: Chacolí de Getaria (the local spelling is Getariako Txakolina) and Chacolí de Bizcaia/Vizcaya (Bizkaiko Txakolina). The wines are sharp, fresh and uncomplicated, suited to the local seafood.

CONCA DE BARBERÁ, DO (red, white) The fresh, fruity *Santara* brand comes from here, via flying winemaker Hugh Ryman. *Concavins* also makes a decent Merlot.

CONDADO DE HUELVA, DO (white, fortified) Wines not unlike Montilla are made and mostly drunk locally.

COSTERS DEL SEGRE, DO (red, white) Formerly a virtual one-producer DO, in the form of *Raïmat*, whose ripe, oaky, plummy reds have been a hit here for years. Whites include the light, lemony, gently oaked Chardonnay, as well as a good sparkler, Chardonnay Brut. *Castell del Remei*, producing Cabernet, Merlot, Chardonnay, Macabeo and Tempranillo, is now also in Britain.

JUMILLA, DO (red) Super-ripe reds, usually sold in bulk for beefing up blends elsewhere. However, French investment is now creating a new fresh-flavoured red style. The *Condestable* brands, *Castillo Jumilla* and *Con Sello* are quite good and gentle as is

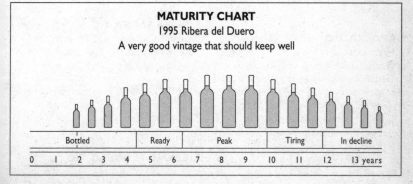

MATURITY CHART
1995 Ribera del Duero
A very good vintage that should keep well

| Bottled | Ready | Peak | Tiring | In decline |

| 0 | 1 | 2 | 3 | 4 | 5 | 6 | 7 | 8 | 9 | 10 | 11 | 12 | 13 years |

the ripe, plummy *Taja* from French merchants *Mahler-Besse*.

MÁLAGA, DO (fortified) A bigger rarity than ever, now that *Scholtz Hermanos* has closed, leaving only one producer, *Bodega López Hermanos*, of any size. Málaga is (was?) usually full, brown and sweet in a raisiny, but not a gooey way, and is slightly smoky too.

LA MANCHA, DO (red, white) Spain's enormous central plateau has learnt how to make good fresh flavours in spite of searing summer heat. All new vineyards have to be of red grapes, usually Cencibel or Cabernet; whites are mostly Airén. Reds have soft tannins and whites are fresh, but need drinking young. *Vinícola de Castilla, Bodegas Cueva del Granero, Rodríguez & Berger, Arboles de Castillejo* from *Bodegas Torres Filoso, Casa la Teja, Castillo de Alhambra, Lazarillo, Señorío de Guadianeja, Viña Santa Elena, Yuntero, Zagarrón, Castillo de Manzanares, Tierra Seca* and *Casa Gualda* are all producing the goods.

MÉNTRIDA, DO (red) Strong, sturdy reds produced bang in the middle of Spain and seldom travelling much further.

MONTILLA-MORILES, DO (fortified) Montilla wines are usually thought of as lower-priced – and lower-strength – sherry lookalikes but there is a great deal of reasonably good wine here, even if it lacks the bite of really good sherry.

NAVARRA, DO (red, white, rosado) The neighbouring region to Rioja grows the same grapes, but with more Garnacha.

There are many more individual estates making wine than there used to be. Look for *Magaña, Chivite, Bodegas Príncipe de Viana*, which also uses the label *Agramont*. *Monte Ory* by *Luís Muga, Bodegas Ochoa, Vinícola Navarra* (especially *Castillo de Tiebas), Senorío de Sarria, Bodegas Irache, Palacio de la Vega, Castillo de Monjardin,* *Guelbenzu* and *Nekeas*. Styles range from young and juicy through hefty, unoaked Garnacha to oak-aged blends. Young and fresh white Navarra, made with Viura plus Chardonnay, is pleasant and slurpable.

PENEDÉS, DO (red, white, rosado) Catalonia's leading region, though no longer as exciting as it used to be. *Torres* wines run from the rich, rather sweetly oaky basic reds, right up to the exciting Cabernet Sauvignon-based *Mas La Plana* and the 100 per cent Pinot Noir *Mas Borras*. Torres also extracts a lean, lemony, sharply refreshing flavour from Parellada. *Jean León* makes a rich, oaky, pineappley Chardonnay and a rich Cabernet. Also look out for are *Cavas Hill, Ferret i Mateu, Masía Bach, Mont Marçal, Vallformosa, René Barbier, Jaume Serra*.

PRIORATO, DO (red) You need 13.5 degrees of alcohol here to get your DO. The reds from Garnacha and Cariñena are renowned – rich and full-bodied in style, and *Masía Barril, Scala Dei* and *de Muller* are worth trying. Also look for *Masia Duch, Clos Dofí, Clos Martinet, Clos de l'Obac, Clos Mogador* and, for pools winners, *Clos l'Ermita*.

RÍAS BAIXAS, DO (red, white) Fresh and fragrant Albariño is the star grape here: *Martín Codax, Condado de Tea, O Rosal, Bodegas Morgadío, Santiago Ruiz, Granja Fillaboa* and *Lagar de Cervera* are all good. Some wines are oaked, which is generally a mistake.

RIBEIRA SACRA, DO (white) Newish Galician DO making excellent and good value whites from Godello, Albariño, Treixadura and others.

RIBEIRO, DO (red, white) There is fresh white wine made from Treixadura and Torrontés here: try *Casal da Barca* from *Bodega Alanis*.

RIBERA DEL DUERO, DO (red) The big name in this big-name region is *Vega*

Varietals are the spice of life

**Paul Masson Merlot Zinfandel and Semillon Chardonnay
are now available in outlets across the country**

SupremeCorq®. The closure that keeps wine as the winemaker *intended*.

The difference between a wine being "magnificent" and "musty" is often the length of the cork. Which is why hundreds of wineries have chosen to bottle their wines with SupremeCorq. SupremeCorq is a revolutionary cork that virtually eliminates the leakage and off-flavours associated with traditional closures. It opens with a regular corkscrew, won't break, and is recyclable. In short, it is perhaps the wine world's most perfect seal. Look for them topping off bottles in pubs, fine restaurants and wine shops worldwide. Visit us at: www.supremecorq.com.

SUPREME**CORQ**®

T H E   N E W   T R A D I T I O N ™

A NEW WORLD WINE, 200 YEARS IN THE MAKING

NEDERBURG WAS ESTABLISHED AT THE FOOT OF THE KLEIN DRAKENSTEIN MOUNTAINS IN 1791, MAKING IT ONE OF THE OLDEST OF THE 'NEW WORLD' WINES. THROUGH THE YEARS NEDERBURG'S GUIDING PHILOSOPHY HAS BEEN THAT GOOD WINES START IN THE VINEYARD. A PHILOSOPHY ECHOED BY A LONG-TERM COMMITMENT TO RESEARCH INTO CLONAL DEVELOPMENT AT ITS ERNITA NURSERY. THE RESULT HAS BEEN THE CREATION OF A RANGE OF WINES THAT HAVE WON MORE LOCAL AND INTERNATIONAL AWARDS THAN ANY OTHER WINE LABEL IN SOUTH AFRICA.

Nederburg
THE WINEMASTERS
ESTABLISHED 1791

SANTA CAROLINA

A CHILEAN FULL HOUSE
@ THE 1999 INTERNATIONAL
WINE CHALLENGE

GRAN RESERVA CABERNET SAUVIGNON 1996

1997

GOLD

SILVER

GRAN RESERVA MERLOT 1996

BRONZE

GRAN RESERVA CHARDONNAY

friendship, warmth and laughter

from only £2.99

Sainsbury's

making life taste better

A fresh breeze from the Cape
TWO OCEANS

SAUVIGNON BLANC

Light, crisp
and remarkably fresh.

CABERNET SAUVIGNON
MERLOT
Medium-bodied, fruity
and full of berry aromas.

Available nationally from
Londis, Spar and all good convenience stores.

PERCY FOX & CO
Established 1886
WINE   SHIPPERS

For further information call 01279 633542

Europe's most exclusive reds and whites

Quality you didn't know existed

Sicilia. Its wines are arguably the best in Spain, and unquestionably the most expensive. *Pesquera* from Alejandro Fernández is also something of a cult and fetches high prices (usually too high). Others making classy, oak-aged reds include *Félix Callejo, Señorío de Nava, Viña Pedrosa, Balbás, Vega Izan, Ribeño, La Cepa Alta* and *Pago de Carraovejas.* The *Protos* co-op is reliable.

RIOJA, DOC (red, white) Classic reds that taste of oak and vanilla toffee, plus rather light, sometimes peppery fruit with a strawberry jam sweetness.

Single estate wines (from *Remelluri, Contino, Barón de Ley, Martínez Bujanda's Finca Valpiedra*) are on the increase, which is a welcome development, and it's not unusual for producers to add some Cabernet to the blend. Otherwise the red blend is Tempranillo (for elegance), Garnacha (for fatness), and perhaps some of the two minority grapes, Graciano and Mazuelo. The Rioja Alavesa region makes more delicate, scented wines; Rioja Alta is firmer, leaner, slower to show its character but slower to lose it too, and the lower, hotter Rioja Baja grows mostly Garnacha, which gets super-ripe and rather lumpish. Best are *Remelluri, Bodegas Riojanas, Barón de Ley, Campo Viejo, El Coto, CVNE, Faustino, López de Heredia, Marqués de Cáceres, Marqués de Murrieta, Martínez Bujanda, Montecillo, Muga, Olarra, La Rioja Alta, Palacio, Campillo, Amézola de la Mora, Viña Ijalba, Bodegas Bretón* and *Marqués de Riscal. Viña Paterna* makes the epitome of the unoaked style.

White Rioja *can* be buttery and rich, slightly Burgundian. *Marqués de Murrieta* still makes a very good example of this style, and so, with rather less oak, does *CVNE* with its *Monopole* and *Reserva,* and *Bodegas Riojanas* with its *Monte Reál. López de Heredia* makes an old-fashioned style, while *Navajas, Viña Soledad* from *Franco Españolas* and *Siglo Gold* from *AGE* are all oak aged. The best new white Riojas are full of fresh, breath-catching raw fruit.

RUEDA, DO (white) A brilliant source of light table wines, picked early and fresh and fermented cool. The local grape, the

---

RIOJA CLASSIFICATIONS

Rioja is divided into three geographical sub-regions: Rioja Alta, Rioja Alavesa and Rioja Baja: most wines will be a blend from all three. The wine's age, indicated on the label, falls into one of four categories.

Sin crianza Without aging, or with less than a year in wood; wine sold in its first or second year. (The words *sin crianza* are not seen on the label.)

Crianza With a minimum of 12 months in wood and some further months in bottle; cannot be sold before its third year. Whites will have had a minimum of six months in cask before bottling.

Reserva Selected wine from a good harvest with a minimum of 36 months' aging, in cask and bottle, of which 12 months minimum in cask. It cannot leave the bodega until the fifth year after the vintage. Whites have at least six months in cask, and 24 months' aging in total.

Gran Reserva Wine from an excellent vintage (supposedly) that will stand up to aging: 24 months minimum in cask and 36 months in bottle, or vice-versa. It cannot leave the bodega until the sixth year after the vintage. White wines have six months in cask and 48 months' aging in total.

Verdejo, makes soft, full, nutty wines, sometimes padded out with the dull Palomino, or sharpened up with the more acid Viura. Most are best young, but there are oaked ones. Look for *Marqués de Griñon*, made at *Bodegas Castilla La Vieja, Bodegas con Class, Marqués de Riscal, Alvarez y Díez, Belondrade y Lurton*.

SHERRY (JEREZ-XÉRÈS-SHERRY, DO) (fortified) There are two basic sherry

styles, *fino* and *oloroso*, each with sub-divisions. *Fino*, from Jerez or Puerto de Santa Maria, should be pale and dry, with an unnerving dry austerity. The tang comes from a layer of natural yeast, called *flor*, that forms on the surface of the wine in the barrels. The lightest wines are selected for *fino*, which is drunk cool and fresh, often as an apéritif.

Manzanilla is a form of *fino* matured by the sea at Sanlúcar de Barrameda. It can be almost savoury-dry, and you might imagine a whiff of sea salt – if you catch it fresh enough. Best: *Barbadillo, Caballero, Diez-Merito, Don Zoilo, Garvey, La Gitana, Hidalgo, La Ina, Inocente, Lustau, La Riva, Sanchez Romate, Tío Pepe*. Good Puerto *fino* comes from *Burdon* and *Osborne*.

In Britain there can be a problem with freshness: *fino* and *manzanilla* won't usually keep longer than six months in bottle.

Real *amontillado* begins life as *fino*, aged in cask until the flor dies and the wine deepens and darkens to a tantalizing, nutty dryness. In the natural state, as drunk in Spain, it is *completely* dry, and a proper *amontillado* will usually say *seco* ('dry'), on the label. But we've adulterated the word in English to mean a bland, downmarket drink of no interest. Look out for *almacenista* sherries, wines from small stockholders, which can be wonderful.

Look out also for *Solear* from *Barbadillo, La Goya Manzanilla Pasada* and *Amontillado Fino Zuleta (Delgado Zuleta), Amontillado del Duque (González Byass), Hidalgo Manzanilla Pasada, Valdespino's Amontillado Coliseo* and *Don Tomás. (Manzanilla pasada has extra*

INSTANT CELLAR: POWERFUL REDS

- 1995 Marqués de Vannos, Ribera del Duero, £9.95, Adnams Rich, plummy, spicy.
- 1995 Pesquera Crianza, Ribera del Duero £10.95, Ballantynes The wine that started the current ball rolling in Ribera del Duero.
- 1996 Cellers Scala Dei Negre, Priorato, £5.99, Ballantynes Immensely rich Garnacha from Priorato.
- 1996 Farina Gran Colegiata, Toro, £7.99, Cockburns of Leith This is less hefty than it used to be, and more supple, but it's still good.
- 1995 Hacienda Monasterio, Ribera del Duero, £15.65, Corney & Barrow Still young, and with plenty of concentration.
- 1993 Marqués de Griñon, Rioja, £9.50, Croque-en-Bouche Subtlety and finesse as well as power.
- 1995 Vega Sicilia Alion, Ribera del Duero, £17.95, Direct Wine Shipments Rich and refined red from a new estate owned by Vega Sicilia.
- 1994 Valdepusa Petit Verdot, Marqués de Griñon, £12.25, Ben Ellis A rare chance to taste this grape alone.
- 1996 Teofilo Reyes, Ribera del Duero, £14.20, Gauntleys Luscious violets and blackcurrants backed up by big tannins.
- 1994 Muga Reserva, Rioja, £8.60, Moreno Very traditional red Rioja.

---

barrel age, and should be wonderful.)

Real *olorosos*, made from richer, fatter wines without any flor, are deep and dark, packed with violent burnt flavours – and usually dry, though you may find *oloroso dulce* (sweet). In Britain most are sweetened with Pedro Ximénez or Moscatel. They usually come as 'Milk', 'Cream' or 'Brown'. Pale Creams are sweetened (inferior) *fino*, and are some of the dullest drinks around. For the real, dry thing, once again, look for *almacenista olorosos* from *Lustau*. There are a few good, concentrated sweetened *olorosos* around, like *Apostoles* and *Matusalem*, both from *González Byass, Solera 1842 (Valdespino)*.

Dry: *Barbadillo, Don Zoilo, Sandeman, Valdespino Don Gonzalo, Williams & Humbert Dos Cortados*. These intense old wines are one of today's great bargains.

SOMONTANO, DO (red, white, rosado) The most exciting of Spain's newer regions, with a long tradition of both Spanish and international grape varieties. *Enate* and *Vinos del Vero* are the star producers, making substantial, ageworthy reds and good whites from Chardonnay and Gewürztraminer. Look also for the *Co-operativa de Sobrarbe* under the *Camporocal* label, *Covisa, Bodegas Pirineos*.

TARRAGONA, DO (red, white, rosado) There is some progress discernible here, in the form of *crianzas* made from Cabernet Sauvignon, Garnacha and Tempranillo.

TERRA ALTA, DO (red) Decent Tempranillo. Good producers include the *Gandesa* co-op, *Ferrer Escod*.

TIERRA DE BARROS, Vino de la Tierra (red) One major bodega (*Inviosa*) has blazed a trail with its excellent *Lar de Barros* from Cencibel and Cabernet Sauvignon. *Viniberia* heads the followers.

TORO, DO (red) This makes good beefy fruity reds from the Tinto de Toro – yet another alias for the Tempranillo. The best wines still probably come from *Bodegas Fariña*, whose *Gran Colegiata* is aged French-style in small oak barrels. *Bodegas Frutos Villar* and the co-op at *Morales* offer good value at lower prices. But lately the wines have become softer, sadly.

UTIEL-REQUENA, DO (red, rosado) The reds, from the Bobal grape, are robust, rather hot and southern. The rosados *can* be better – delicate and fragrant.

VALDEORRAS, DO (red, white) The reds are best young. The ordinary whites, fresh and fruity at their best, are made from Palomino and Doña Blanca, but there is work being done with Godello.

VALDEPEÑAS, DO (red, white) The best reds here are from Cencibel (Tempranillo) and turn out deep and herby with good strawberry fruit – and excellent value at very low prices, even for *gran reservas* with a decade's aging, which is what the region is famous for. Look for the soft wines, aged in new oak, of *Señorío de Los Llanos, Viña Albali* from *Bodegas Felix Solís, Bodegas Luis Megia* (including *Marqués de Gastañaga*) and *Casa de la Viña*.

VALENCIA, DO (red, white, rosado) Large quantities of wines fine for the beach. Some low-priced reds from *Schenk* and *Gandía Pla* can be good, and sweet Moscatels can be tasty and good value. Gandía's *Castillo de Liria,* is an attractive red.

VALLE DE MONTERREI, DO (white) Another of Galicia's new 'superwhite' DOs. Good value whites from Godello, Doña Blanca and even Palomino.

YECLA, DO (red, white) Fairly full-bodied reds and more dubious whites. Some decent wines from *Bodegas Castaño*, from the cheap and cheerful *Dominio de Espinal* to the better *Pozuelo Reserva*.

PRODUCERS WHO'S WHO

ANTONIO BARBADILLO ★★★★(★) (Sanlúcar de Barrameda) Top *manzanilla* bodega producing consistently fresh wines. Older Amontillados are superb, too, and a touch lighter than Jerez versions. Buy the *manzanilla* in half bottles.

CAMPO VIEJO ★★★ (Rioja) Decent Riojas, soft, traditional *reservas*, and varietals. Albor is unoaked.

VINÍCOLA DE CASTILLA ★★★ (La Mancha) Up-to-date producer of white and oaky red Señorío de Guadianeja. Soft red Castillo de Alhambra is good value.

JULIÁN CHIVITE ★★★ (Navarra) Clean white from Viura, attractive *rosado* from Garnacha, and a good Tempranillo-based red, all under the Gran Feudo label.

CODORNÍU ★★★ (Penedés) Giant Cava company making likeably reliable fizz. Good soft and honeyed Anna de Codomíu, and a very good, creamy Chardonnay Cava.

CONTINO (SOCIEDAD VINÍCOLA LASERNA) ★★★★(★) (Rioja) Excellent, single-vineyard wines. Big, plummy and spicily complex.

CVNE ★★★(★) (Rioja) Excellent *crianza* and *reserva* whites (Monopole and CVNE Reserva). Best reds are Imperial and Viña Real, *reservas* upwards. Younger reds are currently looking a bit uninspired.

DOMECQ ★★★★(★) (Jerez) Leading sherry house, with top *fino* La Ina, Botaina *amontillado* and Rio Viejo *oloroso*. Also makes respectable Rioja.

FAUSTINO MARTÍNEZ ★★★ (Rioja) Good reds. Look out also for the new Campillo bodega.

FREIXENET ★★ (Penedés) High-tech Cava firm best known for Cordon Negro, but also good value Carta Nevada, Vintage Brut Nature, and upmarket Brut Barroco.

GONZÁLEZ BYASS ★★★★★ (Jerez) Producer of the best-selling (and very good) fino Tío Pepe. Gonzalez Byass makes an impressive top range of wines, and a Rioja, Bodegas Beronia.

CAVAS HILL ★★(★) (Penedés) Table wines as well as fresh, clean Cava Reserva Oro Brut Natur. Look out for Blanc Cru and Oro Penedés Blanco Suave whites, and Rioja-style reds, Gran Civet and Gran Toc.

JEAN LEÓN ★★★★ (Penedés) Some of Spain's most 'Californian' wines: super-oaky, pineapple-and-honey Chardonnay, and soft, blackcurranty Cabernet Sauvignon.

LOS LLANOS ★★★ (Valdepeñas) Reliable bodega producing wonderfully soft, oaky reds and uncomplicated whites.

LÓPEZ DE HEREDIA ★★★★ (Rioja) Rich, complex whites, Viña Tondonia and Viña Gravonia, and delicate, ethereal reds, Viña Cubillo and Viña Tondonia. The most traditional of all Riojan bodegas.

LUSTAU ★★★★ (Jerez) 'Reviving Traditional Sherry Values', to use its own phrase, with its range of *almacenista* wines.

MARQUÉS DE CÁCERES ★★★(★) (Rioja) Whites are cool-fermented and fresh, and reds have less wood-aging than usual, but still keep an attractive style.

MARQUÉS DE GRIÑÓN ★★★★ (Toledo) Very good Cabernet, aided by advice from Professor Émile Peynaud from Bordeaux. Also a joint venture with Berberana in Rioja which is looking good.

MARQUÉS DE MURRIETA ★★★★ (Rioja) A remarkable, ultra-traditional winery with wines oak-aged far longer than in any other Rioja bodega; Etiqueta Blanca wines, the youngest, spend at least two years in barrel, and are richly oaky, pungent and lemony. The red is soft and fruity-oaky, while the *reservas* are deep and complex. Castillo Ygay wines (the best from the very top years) may sit in barrel for 40 years.

MARTÍNEZ BUJANDA ★★★ (Rioja) Super-fresh and lively Valdemar white and strongly oaky *reserva* and *gran reserva* Condé de Valdemar. New-style Rioja at its best.

MONTECILLO ★★★(★) (Rioja) Aromatic white Viña Cumbrero, a raspberry and oak red, Viña Cumbrero *crianza*, and a *reserva*, Viña Monty.

MUGA ★★★(★) (Rioja) This bodega has a sternly traditional image. For reds, this traditionalism does nothing but good, and the *crianza* is fragrant and delicate, while the Prado Enea *reserva* or *gran reserva* is more complex, but still subtle and elegant. It's not cheap, though.

VIÑA PESQUERA ★★★(★) (Ribera del Duero) US wine writer Robert Parker likened this to Château Pétrus. Made from Tinto Fino and Garnacha, it's good but not *that* good, oaky and aromatic, with rich savoury fruit.

PRÍNCIPE DE VIANA ★★★(★) (Navarra) Innovative bodega which used to be a co-op, and became known as Bodegas Cenalsa. Agramont is its best-known UK brand, and look out for new Bodegas Guelbenzu, a Cabernet/Tempranillo estate in Cascante.

RAÏMAT ★★★ (Costers del Segre) The Raïmat Chardonnay Cava is honeyed, with grassy acidity. Abadía is an oak-enhanced blend of Cabernet, Tempranillo and Garnacha. Also Cabernet Sauvignon, Pinot Noir and Merlot.

REMELLURI ★★★★(★) (Rioja) Single-estate wine, not that common in Rioja; the bodega makes a fine, meaty *reserva*, barrel-aged for two to three years. Into bio-dynamic viticulture, which involves incredible degrees of care of the vines.

LA RIOJA ALTA ★★★★ (Rioja) A traditional bodega, firm believer in long barrel-aging: over half the wines qualify as *reserva* or *gran reserva*. Even the Viña Alberdi *crianza* has a delightfully oaky flavour. It makes two styles of *reserva*, the elegant Viña Arana and the rich Viña Ardanza. In the best years, it makes exceptional *gran reservas*.

RIOJANAS ★★★(★) (Rioja) The best reds here are the *reservas*: the light, elegant, plummy Viña Albina and the richer, more concentrated Monte Reál. White Monte Reál *crianza* is soft and peachy, with just enough oak to fatten it.

MIGUEL TORRES ★★★★ (Penedés) Viña Sol is a super-fresh modern white. Gran Viña Sol is Parellada and Chardonnay, fresh and pineappley, enriched with hints of vanilla oak. Gran Viña Sol Green Label pairs Parellada with Sauvignon Blanc, like oakier Sancerre. The superstar white is Milmanda Chardonnay. Viña Esmeralda is Gewürztraminer and Muscat d'Alsace.

Mas la Plana Cabernet Sauvignon is the top red. Viña Magdala is Pinot Noir and Tempranillo, Gran Sangredetoro is mainly Garnacha, Mas Borras is Pinot Noir, Las Torres is Merlot and Coronas Tempranillo is least exciting. Look out for the newest addition, Grandes Murallas, a blend of four red varieties made very much in the current mode: highly extracted, highly concentrated.

VALDESPINO ★★★★★ (Jerez) Family-owned bodega making a range of top-class, dry sherries. Inocente is superb, characterful *fino*. The Pedro Ximénez Solera Superior is one of the few examples of sherry's great sweetening wine bottled by itself. *Amontillados* and *olorosos* from here are about as good as you can get.

BODEGAS VEGA SICILIA ★★★★(★) (Ribera del Duero) Makers of Spain's most famous and expensive red wine – Vega Sicilia Unico, sometimes kept in barrel for ten years. The younger Valbuena offers a cheaper glimpse of Vega Sicilia's glories. Cheaper, you understand. Not cheap. Newest is more modern Alion, from a separate winery.

VICENTE GANDÍA ★★(★) (Valencia) Perhaps this DO's most go-ahead producer. Fresh white Castillo de Liria and juicy red and rosado from Bobal.

SPAIN PRICES

RIOJA RED

Under £5.00

Alaveses Orobio Tempranillo 1998 £4.79 (BO) £6.75 (LIB)
Alaveses Orobio Tempranillo 1997 £4.99 (TES) £5.59 (LIB)
Berberana Carta de Oro 1996 £4.99 (UN)
Berberana Carta de Plata 1996 £4.95 (NA)
Berberana Tempranillo 1997 £4.99 (SAF)
Berberana Tempranillo 1996 £4.99 (CO)
Bodegas Muerza Vega 1997 £4.99 (BAL) £5.35 (COC)
Campo Viejo Albor 1997 £3.99 (YOU)
Faustino Rivero Orla Dorado Tinto Sin Crianza 1997 £4.95 (TAN)
★ Martinez Bujanda Valdemar 1998 £4.99 (VIC) £4.99 (THR) £4.99 (WR) £4.99 (BOT)

£5.00 → £5.99

Bodegas Muerza Vega 1994 £5.19 (JER)
CVNE 1996 £5.58 (GW) £6.95 (PIP) £7.16 (STE) £7.95 (NA) £8.42 (BIB)
CVNE 1995 £5.29 (GW) £5.75 (UB) £5.79 (BO) £5.99 (MOR) £6.09 (JON) £8.75 (VIN)
El Coto Crianza 1995 £5.95 (ROB)
El Coto Crianza 1994 £5.50 (PHI)
Marqués de Cáceres Crianza 1995 £5.99 (POR) £6.50 (HAH) £6.64 (LAY) £6.67 (COC) £7.04 (PLA) £7.79 (STE) £7.95 (NA)
Marqués de Griñon 1997 £5.49 (TES) £5.49 (MAJ)
Martinez Bujanda Conde de Valdemar Crianza 1996 £5.99 (VIC) £5.99 (THR) £5.99 (WR) £5.99 (BOT) £7.95 (CON)
Palacio y Hermanos Cosme 1996 £5.75 (WAI) £6.49 (SAF) £6.79 (UN) £7.50 (WS) £9.22 (TW)
Paternina Banda Azul 1995 £5.99 (SAF) £6.78 (COC)
Viña Salceda Crianza 1995 £5.75 (BALL) £6.09 (JON) £6.60 (TAN) £6.75 (WS)

£6.00 → £6.99

Alaveses Artadi Viñas de Gain 1995 £6.49 (BO) £7.50 (WS) £9.79 (YOU) £9.95 (LIB)
Amezola de la Mora Amezola Crianza 1995 £6.75 (WS) £7.25 (BER) £7.39 (JON) £7.49 (BO) £8.67 (BIB)
Amezola de la Mora Amezola Crianza 1994 £6.99 (RAE) £6.99 (THR) £6.99 (WR)
Berberana Reserva 1995 £6.99 (MAJ)
Campo Viejo 1996 £6.26 (STE) £6.95 (NA)
CVNE Viña Real 1996 £6.03 (GW) £7.74 (STE) £8.60 (NA) £9.40 (BIB)
CVNE Viña Real 1995 £6.49 (MOR) £6.95 (BALL)
El Coto Crianza 1996 £6.17 (STE)
Gran Condal Reserva 1991 £6.99 (CO)
La Rioja Alta Viña Alberdi 1994 £6.85 (JER) £7.99 (PHI) £8.95 (ROB)
Lan Crianza 1996 £6.66 (BY)
Marqués de Cáceres Crianza 1996 £6.59 (WHI)
Marqués de Cáceres Crianza 1994 £6.20 (TAN) £6.23 (ROS) £6.25 (BALL) £6.80 (CRO) £6.85 (MOR) £7.50 (STA)
Martinez Bujanda Conde de Valdemar Crianza 1995 £6.70 (TAN)
Martinez Bujanda Conde de Valdemar Reserva 1992 £10.22 (PLA) £10.99 (VIN)
Palacio Glorioso Crianza 1996 £6.49 (OD)
Palacio y Hermanos Cosme 1997 £6.99 (OD)
Viña Berceo 1994 £6.19 (NLW)

£7.00 → £7.99

Alaveses Artadi Viñas de Gain 1996 £7.99 (MAJ) £7.99 (GAU)
Alaveses Artadi Viñas de Gain 1994 £7.99 (CON) £10.52 (TW)
Amezola de la Mora Amezola Crianza 1992 £7.75 (JU)
Baron de Oña Torre de Oña Reserva 1991 £7.93 (JER)

MERCHANTS SPECIALIZING IN SPAIN
see Merchant Directory (page 413) for details

Adnams (AD), Ballantynes, Bibendum (BIB), Direct Wine (DI),Cockburns of Leith (COC) – particularly sherry, Lay & Wheeler (LAY), Laymont & Shaw, Lea & Sandeman (LEA),

Moreno Wines (MOR) – a mostly Spanish list, Thos. Peatling, Reid Wines (REI) – good sherries, Roberson (ROB), Tanners (TAN), Wine Society (WS).

Campo Viejo Reserva **1993** £7.49 (POR)
Faustino V Reserva **1994** £7.49 (VIC) £7.49
(THR) £8.49 (MOR) £8.80 (UB) £9.99 (WHI)
Faustino V Reserva **1993** £7.55 (SAF)
Faustino V Reserva **1992** £7.55 (TES)
£7.69 (CON)
La Rioja Alta Viña Alberdi **1995** £7.00
(SOM) £8.49 (POR)
Marqués de Murrieta Reserva **1991** £7.95
(CON) £10.68 (PLA)
Marqués de Riscal Reserva **1994** £8.75
(MOR) £8.95 (WS) £9.99 (VA) £11.69 (REI)
Martinez Bujanda Conde de Valdemar
Reserva **1993** £7.99 (THR) £7.99 (WR)
£7.99 (BOT) £8.40 (TAN) £8.93 (PEN)
Muga Reserva **1994** £7.81 (PEN) £7.99
(BAL) £8.60 (MOR)
Viña Salceda Reserva **1994** £7.95 (WS)
£8.99 (DI) £10.68 (NO) £10.95 (LEA)

£8.00 → £8.99

CVNE Reserva **1991** £8.99 (BOT) £9.15
(WAT)
Marqués de Murrieta **1993** £8.39 (MORR)
Marqués de Murrieta Reserva **1993** £8.99
(NI) £9.40 (JON) £9.49 (MOR) £9.75 (RAE)
£9.99 (SAF) £10.25 (ROB) £10.80 (UB)
£10.95 (AD) £11.20 (AV) £11.46 (TW)
Marqués de Riscal **1995** £8.99 (UN)
Marqués de Riscal Reserva **1995** £8.62
(GW) £8.99 (MAJ)
Marqués de Vargas Reserva **1994** £8.99
(DI) £11.95 (TAN) £12.95 (LEA)
Martinez Bujanda Conde de Valdemar
Reserva **1994** £8.99 (UN)
Muga Reserva **1995** £8.49 (MAJ) £8.75
(WHI) £9.15 (PIP)
Muga Reserva **1992** £8.99 (JON)
Remelluri **1994** £8.95 (FLE)

£9.00 → £9.99

La Rioja Alta Viña Arana Reserva **1991**
£9.50 (WS) £10.28 (JER) £12.99 (PHI)
Lagunilla Gran Reserva **1989** £9.74 (PLA)
López de Heredia Viña Bosconia **1990**
£9.95 (BAL) £10.75 (MOR)
Marqués de Cáceres Reserva **1993** £9.25
(HAH)
Marqués de Cáceres Reserva **1990** £9.99
(POR)
Marqués de Cáceres Reserva **1989** £9.61
(ROS)
Marqués de Murrieta Reserva **1995** £9.99
(MAJ) £9.99 (POR) £10.49 (STE) £10.60
(WRI) £11.65 (NA) £11.71 (PLAY)

Marqués de Murrieta Reserva **1994** £9.75
(RAE) £10.95 (BEN)
Marqués de Murrieta Reserva **1992** £9.49
(SAI) £9.49 (BOT) £9.50 (JU)
Marqués de Riscal Reserva **1991** £9.18 (FLE)
Martinez Bujanda Garnacha **1990** £9.99
(NI) £12.00 (WR) £12.00 (BOT)
Montecillo Gran Reserva **1989** £9.99 (OD)
Remelluri **1995** £9.70 (SOM) £9.95 (WS)
£11.99 (YOU) £12.50 (ELL) £19.00 (CRO)
Urbina Gran Reserva **1990** £9.95 (POR)
£10.09 (JON) £10.65 (AD)
Viña Ijalba, Múrice Crianza **1995** £9.02
(PLAY)

£10.00 → £11.99

Baron de Oña Torre de Oña Reserva **1994**
£10.50 (STA) £10.79 (AME) £10.95 (LAY)
Campo Viejo Gran Reserva **1991** £11.39
(STE) £12.65 (NA)
Campo Viejo Gran Reserva **1989** £10.95
(POR)
Conde de la Salceda Gran Reserva **1987**
£10.95 (DI)
CVNE Viña Real Reserva **1991** £11.49
(MOR) £11.70 (PIP) £12.50 (TAN) £12.54
(GW) £13.50 (STA)
CVNE Viña Real Reserva **1989** £11.69
(GW) £12.09 (JON) £12.16 (REI) £12.49
(BOT) £12.69 (ROS)
Faustino I Gran Reserva **1991** £11.20
(COC) £11.85 (MOR)
Faustino I Gran Reserva **1988** £11.69 (CON)
Faustino I Gran Reserva **1987** £10.99 (BOT)
La Rioja Alta Viña Arana Reserva **1993**
£11.25 (BER)
La Rioja Alta Viña Ardanza Reserva **1990**
£10.00 (NO) £11.25 (SOM) £11.80 (COC)
£11.95 (POR) £11.99 (JON) £12.25 (MOR)
£12.99 (AME) £13.50 (AD) £13.50 (STA)
£14.50 (BEN)
La Rioja Alta Viña Ardanza Reserva **1989**
£10.77 (JER) £10.95 (JU) £11.90 (CRO)
£11.99 (SAI) £13.50 (PHI) £13.55 (AV)
£13.95 (FORT)

> • Wines are listed in A–Z
>   order within each price
>   band.
> • For each wine, vintages are
>   listed in descending order.
> • Each vintage of any wine
>   appears only once.

López de Heredia Viña Tondonia Reserva
1991 £11.95 (BAL) £13.95 (MOR)

Marqués de Cáceres Gran Reserva **1987**
£11.99 (MOR)

Marqués de Cáceres Reserva **1991**
£10.15 (MOR) £10.85 (UB) £11.50 (STA)

Marqués de Griñon **1990** £11.90 (CRO)

Marqués de Murrieta Castillo Ygay Gran
Reserva Especial **1993** £10.95 (WAI)

Marqués de Murrieta Reserva Especial
1994 £10.99 (MAJ) £13.50 (BEN) £13.90
(AD)

Marqués de Murrieta Reserva Especial
1991 £10.49 (NI) £11.49 (MOR) £12.50
(FORT) £12.75 (JU) £13.50 (BOT) £14.34
(TW)

Muga Prado Enea Gran Reserva **1991**
£11.99 (MAJ)

Palacio Glorioso Reserva **1989** £11.63 (TW)

Paternina Gran Reserva **1991** £10.50 (COC)

Remelluri Reserva **1995** £11.60 (NO)
£11.99 (MOR) £12.75 (HED)

£12.00 → £13.99

Alaveses Artadi Pagos Viejos Reserva
1993 £12.95 (CON)

Amezola Gran Reserva **1990** £12.99 (RAE)

Amezola Gran Reserva **1988** £13.95 (JU)

Contino Reserva **1994** £13.70 (MOR)
£13.85 (WAT) £13.95 (STE) £15.50 (NA)

Contino Reserva **1991** £12.59 (PIP)
£13.95 (ROB) £14.99 (BOT)

CVNE Imperial Reserva **1991** £12.73 (PIP)
£12.83 (STE) £14.25 (STA) £14.25 (NA)

CVNE Imperial Gran Reserva **1989** £12.40 (GW)
£12.49 (MOR) £12.65 (WAT) £13.95 (ROB)

Faustino I Gran Reserva **1992** £12.25 (UB)
£12.69 (OD) £13.99 (WHI)

Marqués de Murrieta Castillo Ygay Gran
Reserva Especial **1991** £12.95 (ROB)
£12.95 (BALL)

Marqués de Murrieta Reserva **1984**
£13.00 (CRO)

Marques de Vargas Reserva **1995** £13.95
(LEA)

Martinez Bujanda Conde de Valdemar
Gran Reserva **1993** £12.49 (VIC) £12.49
(THR) £12.49 (WR) £12.49 (BOT)

Martinez Bujanda Conde de Valdemar
Gran Reserva **1991** £13.85 (PLA)

Martinez Bujanda Garnacha **1987** £13.51
(PEN)

Muga Reserva **1991** £12.25 (WHI)

Remelluri **1996** £12.95 (AD)

Viña Salceda Reserva **1995** £13.95 (LEA)

£14.00 → £15.99

Alaveses Artadi Viñas El Pison Reserva
1994 £15.98 (TW) £18.99 (BO)

CVNE Imperial Gran Reserva **1989**
£15.50 (PIP) £15.75 (MOR) £17.95 (FORT)

CVNE Imperial Gran Reserva **1988**
£15.86 (PEN) £19.99 (BOT)

CVNE Viña Real Gran Reserva **1989**
£14.35 (MOR) £20.22 (PIP)

CVNE Viña Real Gran Reserva **1988**
£14.50 (GW) £15.50 (STA) £18.49 (BOT)

La Rioja Alta Reserva 904 **1987** £15.90
(CRO)

Marqués de Cáceres Gran Reserva **1989**
£14.65 (UB)

Marqués de Riscal Gran Reserva **1989**
£15.99 (SAF)

Martinez Bujanda Conde de Valdemar
Gran Reserva **1992** £14.99 (UN)

Martinez Lacuesta Gran Reserva **1980**
£14.00 (WRI)

Muga Prado Enea Gran Reserva **1989**
£15.10 (SOM) £16.35 (MOR) £19.15 (PIP)

Palacio Glorioso Reserva **1982** £14.69 (TW)

£16.00 → £19.99

Alaveses Artadi Viñas El Pison Reserva
1992 £19.95 (CON)

CVNE Imperial Gran Reserva **1991**
£17.96 (STE) £19.95 (NA)

CVNE Imperial Gran Reserva **1990**
£16.60 (TAN) £18.95 (STA)

CVNE Imperial Reserva **1994** £16.60 (PIP)

La Rioja Alta Reserva 904 Gran Reserva
1989 £17.95 (SOM) £19.10 (MOR) £19.95
(POR) £20.70 (BEN) £21.50 (FORT) £22.70
(LAY) £25.90 (UB)

La Rioja Alta Reserva 904 Gran Reserva
1987 £16.95 (JU) £17.14 (JER) £19.99 (JON)

Marqués de Murrieta Castillo Ygay Gran
Reserva **1989** £16.99 (NI) £18.50 (MOR)
£18.95 (POR)

Marqués de Murrieta Castillo Ygay Gran
Reserva Especial **1989** £19.15 (HAH)
£19.50 (BOT)

Marqués de Murrieta Castillo Ygay Gran
Reserva **1989** £19.92 (PLA) £19.95 (AD)
£27.28 (PLAY)

Marqués de Murrieta Castillo Ygay Gran
Reserva **1987** £19.50 (JU)

Marqués de Murrieta Ygay Reserva **1989**
£19.50 (FORT)

Marqués de Riscal Gran Reserva **1991**
£16.25 (MOR)

Martinez Bujanda Conde de Valdemar
Reserva **1986** £16.00 (CRO)
Muga Prado Enea Gran Reserva **1987**
£18.99 (JON)
Viña Lanciano Reserva **1995** £17.25 (BY)

£20.00 → £29.99

Contino Reserva **1985** £28.79 (REI)
CVNE Imperial Gran Reserva **1987**
£20.95 (BALL)
La Rioja Alta Reserva 904 **1985** £24.00
(CRO)
López de Heredia Viña Bosconia Gran
Reserva **1976** £29.50 (MOR)
López de Heredia Viña Tondonia Gran
Reserva **1978** £25.50 (BAL) £31.49
(MOR)
Marqués de Murrieta Castillo Ygay **1989**
£21.00 (CRO)
Marqués de Murrieta Gran Reserva **1983**
£26.00 (CRO)
Marqués de Murrieta Ygay Reserva **1986**
£21.50 (FORT)
Marqués de Riscal **1969** £20.46 (FA)
Martinez Bujanda Conde de Valdemar
Gran Reserva **1981** £23.00 (CRO)
Muga Prado Enea Gran Reserva **1985**
£21.74 (PEN)

£30.00 → £49.99

Alaveses Artadi Viñas El Pison Reserva
1995 £33.95 (LIB)
Berberana Gran Reserva **1970** £39.00
(CRO)
Bilbainas Viña Pomal **1960** £34.66 (FA)
La Rioja Alta Reserva 890 Gran Reserva
1982 £37.70 (JER) £41.42 (REI) £41.99
(MOR) £45.95 (POR)
López de Heredia Viña Bosconia Gran
Reserva **1973** £32.50 (BAL) £43.75 (MOR)
López de Heredia Viña Tondonia Gran
Reserva **1968** £46.00 (BAL) £58.55 (MOR)
Marqués de Murrieta Castillo Ygay **1978**
£34.95 (BOT)
Marqués de Murrieta Castillo Ygay Gran
Reserva **1985** £31.50 (ROB)

> • All prices for each wine are
> listed together in ascending
> order.
> • Price bands refer to the
> lowest price for which the
> wine is available.

£50.00 → £69.99

CVNE Imperial Gran Reserva **1970**
£52.70 (REI) £59.99 (BOT)
CVNE Viña Real Gran Reserva **1973**
£59.99 (BOT)
López de Heredia Viña Tondonia Gran
Reserva **1964** £53.00 (BAL) £60.59 (MOR)
Marqués de Murrieta Castillo Ygay Gran
Reserva **1968** £65.00 (CRO) £66.00 (ROB)

Over £70.00

López de Heredia Viña Tondonia Gran
Reserva **1954** £75.00 (MOR)
Marqués de Murrieta Castillo Ygay Gran
Reserva **1964** £78.00 (RAE) £82.00
(MOR) £95.00 (JU) £98.50 (ROB)
Marqués de Murrieta Castillo Ygay Gran
Reserva **1942** £110.00 (CRO)

RIOJA WHITE

Under £4.00

Campo Viejo Albor **1997** £3.99 (YOU)
Marqués de Cáceres **1997** £3.99 (POR)
£4.31 (ROS) £4.39 (BO) £4.50 (TAN)
£4.55 (HAH) £4.65 (DI) £4.99 (MOR)

£4.00 → £4.99

Berberana Carta de Oro **1995** £4.29 (CO)
Marqués de Cáceres **1998** £4.25 (COC)
£4.95 (STE) £4.95 (NA) £5.19 (NLW)
Marqués de Cáceres **1996** £4.50 (BALL)
£4.65 (DI) £4.75 (STA) £4.90 (CRO)
Marqués de Cáceres Satinela Semi-Dulce
1997 £4.60 (UB)
Marqués de Cáceres Satinela Semi-Dulce
1994 £4.79 (DI)
Marqués de Cáceres sin Crianza **1994**
£4.99 (DI)
Marqués de Murrieta Misela de Murrieta
1994 £4.95 (WS) £5.95 (JU) £9.26 (NO)

£5.00 → £5.99

Alaveses Artadi Blanco **1996** £5.49 (CON)
El Coto **1998** £5.99 (UN)
El Coto **1997** £5.75 (ROB)
Faustino V **1993** £5.55 (SAF)
Marqués de Cáceres Antea **1994** £5.99
(DI)
Marqués de Cáceres sin Crianza **1997**
£5.95 (VIN)
Muga **1997** £6.15 (MOR) £6.17 (PEN)
Olarra Añares Seco **1996** £5.35 (CON)

£6.00 → £7.99

CVNE Monopole 1996 £7.50 (BALL)
CVNE Monopole 1995 £7.70 (TAN) £9.75 (UB)
CVNE Monopole 1993 £7.05 (REI)
CVNE Monopole Barrel Fermented 1996 £6.55 (SAF) £7.10 (PIP) £7.83 (STE) £8.70 (NA)
CVNE Monopole Barrel Fermented 1995 £6.99 (MOR) £7.53 (GW)
Faustino V 1992 £6.90 (UB)
La Rioja Alta Viña Ardanza Reserva 1989 £7.95 (JU) £9.85 (ROB)
Marqués de Murrieta Reserva 1994 £7.95 (WS) £7.99 (MAJ) £7.99 (POR) £9.90 (CRO)
Marqués de Murrieta Reserva 1992 £7.99 (RAE) £8.95 (JU) £8.99 (VIC) £8.99 (THR) £8.99 (BOT) £9.49 (AV) £9.50 (UB) £9.69 (TW)
Martinez Bujanda Conde de Valdemar 1995 £6.50 (NI) £7.95 (CON)
Muga 1998 £6.69 (JON)
Navajas 1994 £6.50 (MOR)
Navajas 1993 £6.39 (YOU) £6.50 (MOR) £7.99 (POR)
Navajas 1989 £6.30 (UB)
Paternina Banda Dorada 1997 £6.50 (COC)

£8.00 → £11.99

CVNE Reserva 1994 £8.99 (MOR)
La Rioja Alta Viña Ardanza Reserva 1993 £8.99 (MOR)
López de Heredia Tondonia Reserva 1987 £11.95 (BAL)
Marqués de Murrieta 1994 £8.95 (BEN)
Marqués de Murrieta 1992 £8.49 (NI)
Marqués de Murrieta Reserva 1995 £8.50 (WRI) £9.95 (WAI)
Marqués de Murrieta Reserva 1991 £8.64 (PLA)
Marqués de Murrieta Reserva Especial 1993 £8.50 (FORT)
Martinez Bujanda Conde de Valdemar 1996 £9.95 (VIC) £9.95 (WR) £9.95 (BOT)
Martinez Bujanda Conde de Valdemar 1994 £9.15 (PLA) £11.59 (VIN)

£12.00 → £19.99

López de Heredia Tondonia Reserva 1991 £13.95 (MOR)
Marqués de Murrieta 1990 £14.00 (CRO)
Marqués de Murrieta Ygay Gran Reserva 1991 £12.61 (NO)

£20.00 → £29.99

Marqués de Murrieta Castillo Ygay 1986 £21.95 (BOT)
Marqués de Murrieta Gran Reserva 1986 £20.00 (MOR)
Marqués de Murrieta Ygay Gran Reserva 1978 £24.00 (JU) £24.95 (ROB)

Over £30.00

López de Heredia Tondonia Gran Reserva 1976 £31.49 (MOR)
López de Heredia Tondonia Gran Reserva 1964 £53.00 (BAL) £65.00 (MOR)
López de Heredia Tondonia Gran Reserva 1957 £68.95 (MOR)
Marqués de Murrieta Castillo Ygay 1962 £35.00 (BEN)
Marqués de Murrieta Ygay Gran Reserva 1970 £37.99 (NO)
Marqués de Murrieta Ygay Gran Reserva 1962 £50.00 (CRO)

RIOJA ROSÉ

Under £5.50

Alaveses Artadi Rosado 1996 £5.49 (CON)
Marqués de Cáceres Rosado 1998 £4.95 (NA) £5.09 (STE) £5.75 (NLW)
Marqués de Cáceres Rosado 1997 £3.99 (POR) £4.80 (COC)
Marqués de Cáceres Rosado 1996 £3.95 (DI)

NAVARRA RED

Under £4.00

Baso 1996 £3.50 (SOM) £4.00 (CRO)
Orvalaiz Tempranillo 1996 £3.99 (JON)

£4.00 → £4.99

Baso 1998 £4.33 (FLE)
Baso 1997 £4.35 (BEN) £4.49 (YOU)
Baso 1993 £4.89 (PHI)
Bodegas Principe de Viana Agramont 1996 £4.99 (OD) £4.99 (WAI)
Guelbenzu Jardin 1997 £4.99 (MAJ)
Guelbenzu Jardin 1996 £4.74 (GW) £4.95 (WS) £4.99 (POR) £4.99 (MOR) £5.19 (BO) £5.35 (BAL) £6.49 (VA) £6.75 (ROB)
Guelbenzu Jardin 1995 £4.99 (NI)

Julián Chivite Gran Feudo **1996** £4.97 (ROS)
Julián Chivite Gran Feudo **1995** £4.99 (DI)
  £5.56 (COC) £5.99 (OD) £7.00 (PLAY)
Las Campanas Cabernet Sauvignon **1995**
  £4.49 (YOU)

£5.00 → £6.99

Bodegas Piedemonte Cabernet Sauvignon
  Crianza **1993** £5.95 (CON)
Castillo de Monjardin Merlot **1996** £6.95
  (POR)
Castillo de Monjardin Merlot **1995** £5.50
  (SOM) £6.75 (WRI) £7.55 (PHI)
Castillo de Monjardin Merlot **1994** £5.88
  (JER) £6.29 (REI) £6.59 (YOU) £6.95 (JU)
Guelbenzu Crianza **1996** £5.99 (MAJ)
Guelbenzu Crianza **1995** £5.99 (MOR)
  £6.03 (GW) £7.20 (TAN)
Guelbenzu Crianza **1994** £5.99 (NI)
Julián Chivite Gran Fuedo Reserva **1994**
  £5.99 (DI) £6.29 (VIC) £6.29 (THR) £6.29
  (BOT)
Ochoa **1997** £5.10 (UB) £5.43 (GW)
Ochoa Tempranillo **1996** £6.89 (BO) £6.99
  (UN) £6.99 (MAJ) £7.80 (PIP) £7.95 (FORT)
Ochoa Tempranillo **1995** £6.33 (ROS)
  £6.99 (MOR) £7.03 (GW) £7.09 (JON)
  £7.15 (WAT) £7.64 (REI) £7.74 (PLA) £7.75
  (BALL) £7.90 (TAN) £7.97 (STE) £8.20 (LAY)
  £8.85 (NA)
Palacio de la Vega Cabernet/Tempranillo
  Crianza **1995** £5.99 (UB)

£7.00 → £10.99

Julián Chivite Gran Fuedo Reserva **1995**
  £7.00 (WRI)
Ochoa Merlot **1995** £9.10 (PIP)
Ochoa Merlot **1994** £8.50 (BALL)
Ochoa Merlot **1993** £8.99 (BOT)
Ochoa Reserva **1994** £10.36 (PIP)
Ochoa Reserva **1992** £8.99 (WAT) £9.90
  (TAN)
Ochoa Tempranillo **1993** £7.99 (BOT)

NAVARRA WHITE

Under £6.00

Bodegas Principe de Viana Agramont
  1998 £4.99 (OD)
Julián Chivite Gran Feudo Blanco **1996**
  £5.99 (DI)
Nekeas Vega Sindoa Chardonnay **1997**
  £5.99 (FLE)
Ochoa **1996** £5.15 (UB)

Over £8.00

Ochoa Vino Dulce de Moscatel 50cl **1997**
  £8.75 (MOR)
Ochoa Vino Dulce de Moscatel 50cl **1996**
  £8.08 (ROS) £9.91 (STA)

OTHER SPANISH RED

Under £4.00

Bodegas Inviosa Lar de Barros Tempranillo,
  Ribera del Guadiana **1997** £3.85 (SOM)
  £4.40 (TAN)
Bodegas Piqueras Marius Tinto Reserva,
  Almansa **1991** £3.99 (POR) £4.95 (LEA)
  £4.99 (JON) £5.15 (UB) £5.25 (TAN)
Castillo de Liria Vicente Gandia, Valencia
  Non-vintage £3.49 (BOT)
Elegido, Vino de Mesa **1997** £3.20 (SOM)
Los Llanos Señorio de los Llanos Reserva,
  Valdepeñas **1993** £3.95 (WS) £4.10 (SOM)
  £4.29 (TES) £4.99 (POR) £5.50 (BEN)
Muruve Frutos Villar, Toro **1997** £3.79
  (SAF)
Vitorianas Don Darias, Vino de Mesa
  Non-vintage £3.49 (ASD) £3.79 (TES)
  £3.79 (SAF)
Vitorianas Don Hugo, Alto Ebro, Vino de
  Mesa **Non-vintage** £3.49 (WAI)

£4.00 → £4.99

Bodegas Inviosa Lar de Barros Tempranillo,
  Ribera del Guadiana **1995** £4.99 (PHI)
Bodegas Piqueras Castillo de Almansa,
  Almansa **1991** £4.99 (DI)
Bodegas Piqueras Marius Tinto Reserva,
  Almansa **1993** £4.95 (LEA)
Bodegas Piqueras, Piqueras **1995** £4.01
  (ROS) £4.75 (LEA)
Fariña Dama, Toro **1995** £4.99 (SAI)
Felix Solis Viña Albali Reserva, Valdepeñas
  1993 £4.49 (UN)
Fuente del Ritmo, La Mancha **1996** £4.99
  (VIC) £4.99 (THR) £4.99 (BOT)
Los Llanos Señorio de los Llanos Reserva,
  Valdepeñas **1994** £4.40 (COC)
Los Llanos Señorio de los Llanos,
  Valdepeñas **1994** £4.49 (JON) £4.85 (UB)
Muruve Frutos Villar, Toro **1996** £4.31
  (JER) £4.99 (YOU)
Ryman Santara Cabernet/Merlot, Conca
  de Barberà **1998** £4.99 (CO)
Torres Sangredetoro, Penedés **1997**
  £4.99 (MORR) £4.99 (DI) £5.99 (MOR)

£5.00 → £5.99

Abadia Retuerta Primicia, Vina de Mesa 1996 £5.99 (DI) £6.49 (YOU)

Cellers Scala Dei Negre, Priorato 1996 £5.99 (BAL) £5.99 (MOR) £6.99 (YOU)

Condé de Caralt Reserva, Penedés 1994 £5.49 (MOR)

Covisa Viñas del Vero Pinot Noir, Somontano 1997 £5.49 (OD)

Fariña Gran Colegiata, Toro 1995 £5.79 (COC)

Felix Solis Viña Albali Gran Reserva, Valdepeñas 1996 £5.00 (MORR)

Felix Solis Viña Albali Gran Reserva, Valdepeñas 1991 £5.99 (ASD)

Los Llanos Señorio de los Llanos Gran Reserva, Valdepeñas 1995 £5.95 (JU)

Los Llanos Señorio de los Llanos Gran Reserva, Valdepeñas 1990 £5.20 (SOM) £5.49 (MAJ) £5.86 (PEN) £5.99 (JON) £5.99 (POR) £6.75 (BEN)

Los Llanos Señorio de los Llanos Reserva, Valdepeñas 1992 £5.95 (ROB)

Manuel Sancho Mont Marçal Cabernet Sauvignon, Penedés 1991 £5.99 (CON)

Marques de Velilla, Ribera del Duero 1996 £5.49 (NI) £5.49 (WR) £5.49 (BOT) £5.49 (YOU) £5.99 (MOR)

Masía Bach, Penedés 1996 £5.49 (SAF)

Torres Coronas, Penedés 1996 £5.29 (DI) £5.49 (SAF) £5.59 (JON) £5.99 (UN) £5.99 (MOR)

Torres Coronas, Penedés 1995 £5.08 (COC) £5.49 (TES) £5.78 (PEN) £6.95 (BALL)

Torres Gran Sangredetoro, Penedés 1995 £5.75 (DI) £7.50 (WRI) £7.50 (STA)

Torres Gran Sangredetoro, Penedés 1994 £5.99 (VIC) £5.99 (THR) £5.99 (WR) £5.99 (BOT) £6.55 (UB) £6.81 (COC) £6.99 (MOR)

Torres Sangredetoro, Penedés 1996 £5.29 (TES) £5.43 (ROS) £5.46 (PEN)

£6.00 → £7.99

Abadia Retuerta Rivola, Vina de Mesa 1996 £6.65 (SOM) £7.50 (DI) £7.75 (ROB)

Bodegas Inviosa, Lar de Lares Gran Reserva, Ribera del Guadiana 1993 £6.90 (TAN)

Bodegas Valduero Crianza, Ribera del Duero 1994 £6.99 (VIC) £6.99 (THR) £6.99 (WR) £6.99 (BOT) £7.05 (JER) £9.90 (JU)

Cellers Santamaria Gran Recosind, Ampurdan Costa Brava 1990 £6.99 (BAL)

Condado de Haza, Ribera del Duero 1995 £7.99 (NI) £10.75 (MOR)

Cosecheros Abastecedores Pata Negra Gran Reserva, Valdepeñas 1991 £6.49 (POR) £6.50 (CRO) £6.95 (PHI) £7.45 (WRI) £7.45 (BEN) £7.99 (CB)

Cosecheros Abastecedores Pata Negra Gran Reserva, Valdepeñas 1987 £6.45 (JU) £6.80 (UB) £9.50 (CRO)

Enate Crianza, Somontano 1996 £7.20 (CRO)

Enate Crianza, Somontano 1995 £6.49 (OD)

Enate Crianza, Somontano 1994 £7.15 (AV)

Enrique Mendoza Viña Alfaz Seleccion, Alicante 1996 £7.50 (LEA)

Masía Barril Típico, Priorato 1991 £7.99 (BO) £9.50 (MOR)

Raïmat Cabernet Sauvignon, Costers del Segre 1994 £6.99 (THR) £6.99 (WR)

Raïmat Cabernet Sauvignon, Costers del Segre 1993 £6.75 (WS)

René Barbier Reserva, Penedés 1993 £7.50 (ROB)

Protos, Ribera del Duero 1996 £7.69 (COC)

Señorio de Nava Crianza, Ribera del Duero 1997 £6.99 (UN)

Torres Coronas, Penedés 1997 £6.17 (STE) £6.85 (NA)

Torres Coronas, Penedés 1994 £6.99 (TW)

Torres Gran Sangredetoro, Penedés 1996 £6.49 (CO)

Torres Gran Sangredetoro, Penedés 1993 £6.46 (PEN)

Torres Las Torres Merlot, Penedés 1997 £6.99 (MOR)

£8.00 → £9.99

Bodegas Inviosa, Lar de Lares Gran Reserva, Ribera del Guadiana 1992 £8.99 (PHI)

Bodegas Valduero Crianza, Ribera del Duero 1995 £9.50 (ROB)

Bodegas Valduero Crianza, Ribera del Duero 1990 £8.23 (PEN)

Cellers Scala Dei Crianza, Priorato 1993 £8.99 (MOR)

Fariña Gran Colegiata Reserva, Toro 1991 £8.90 (TAN)

Stars (★) indicate wines selected by Oz Clarke in the Best Buys section which begins on page 9.

Fernandez Condado de Haza, Ribera del
Duero **1996** £9.99 (YOU) £10.90 (CRO)
£10.99 (PHI) £10.99 (VA)

Masía Barril Típico, Priorato **1993** £8.40
(TAN) £8.99 (MOR)

Mauro, Vino de Mesa **1995** £8.99 (NI)
£12.49 (MOR)

Pesquera Crianza, Ribera del Duero **1995**
£9.69 (REI) £9.99 (NI) £10.39 (BAL)
£10.99 (DI) £12.85 (MOR) £12.99 (VA)

Ribeño, Ribera del Duero **1994** £8.21 (PEN)

Torres Gran Coronas, Penedés **1996**
£8.87 (ROS)

Torres Gran Coronas, Penedés **1995**
£9.50 (STE) £10.55 (NA)

Torres Gran Coronas, Penedés **1994**
£8.49 (CO) £8.99 (JON) £8.99 (POR)
£9.25 (MOR) £9.75 (STA)

Torres Gran Coronas, Penedés **1993**
£8.95 (CON) £9.50 (PIP)

Torres Gran Coronas, Penedés **1991**
£8.60 (PEN)

Yllera Tinto Vino de Mesa de Castilla y
Léon, Los Curros **1992** £8.95 (ROB)

£10.00 → £19.99

Bodegas Valduero Reserva, Ribera del
Duero **1994** £10.48 (JER) £12.95 (STA)

Bodegas Valduero Reserva, Ribera del
Duero **1991** £13.95 (JU)

Cellers Santamaria Gran Recosind Gran
Reserva, Ampurdan Costa Brava **1988**
£10.99 (RAE)

Cellers Scala Dei Negre, Priorato **1992**
£11.95 (ROB)

Costers del Siurana Miserere, Priorato
1994 £12.95 (JU) £24.06 (NO) £24.50
(FORT)

Jean León Cabernet Sauvignon, Penedés
1991 £11.95 (DI)

Jean León Cabernet Sauvignon, Penedés
1979 £18.21 (PEN)

Masía Barril Priorato Extra, Priorato
1995 £10.65 (MOR)

Mauro Crianza, Ribera del Duero **1995**
£13.50 (LEA)

Mauro Crianza, Ribera del Duero **1994**
£12.90 (JU)

Mauro, Vino de Mesa **1996** £13.90 (GAU)

Pesquera Crianza, Ribera del Duero **1996**
£11.90 (TAN) £14.99 (OD) £16.00 (GAU)

Pesquera Crianza, Ribera del Duero **1993**
£14.95 (UB)

Pesquera Crianza, Ribera del Duero **1992**
£13.79 (CON)

Pesquera Crianza, Ribera del Duero **1988**
£19.00 (FA)

Pesquera Reserva, Ribera del Duero
1993 £13.99 (NI)

Ribeño, Ribera del Duero **1995** £11.16 (REI)

Torres Coronas, Penedés **1985** £17.04
(REI) £19.00 (VA)

Torres Gran Coronas Black Label (Mas La
Plana), Penedés **1994** £19.99 (POR)

Torres Gran Coronas Black Label (Mas La
Plana), Penedés **1993** £16.95 (DI)
£19.99 (MOR) £20.20 (TAN) £21.50 (STA)
£22.00 (UB) £25.26 (TW) £26.78 (PLAY)

Torres Gran Coronas Black Label (Mas La
Plana), Penedés **1990** £16.95 (DI)
£19.99 (CON) £20.97 (REI) £21.50 (WRI)

Torres Gran Coronas Black Label (Mas La
Plana), Penedés **1989** £22.75 (ROB)

Torres Gran Coronas Black Label (Mas La
Plana), Penedés **1988** £19.99 (RAE)
£21.25 (JON)

Torres Mas Borras Pinot Noir, Penedés
1994 £13.75 (PIP)

Viña Pedrosa Reserva, Ribera del Duero
1994 £14.69 (MOR)

Viña Pedrosa Reserva, Ribera del Duero
1992 £15.99 (RAE)

Viña Sastre Reserva, Ribera del Duero
1992 £19.75 (ROB)

£20.00 → £29.99

Alvaro Palacios Dofi, Priorato **1996**
£25.85 (FA) £39.99 (DI)

Clos Mogador, Priorato **1995** £21.50 (BAL)
£32.00 (MOR)

Clos Mogador, Priorato **1992** £21.00 (CRO)

Costers del Siurana Clos de l'Obac,
Priorato **1995** £25.85 (JER) £34.00 (JU)

Costers del Siurana Clos de l'Obac,
Priorato **1992** £28.79 (REI) £29.75 (WRI)

Costers del Siurana Dolc de l'Obac,
Priorato **1994** £29.00 (JU) £53.89 (NO)
£54.63 (REI)

Costers del Siurana Miserere, Priorato
1995 £28.50 (CRO)

£30.00 → £49.99

Alvaro Palacios Dofi, Priorato **1995**
£39.60 (MOR)

Alvaro Palacios Dofi, Priorato **1994**
£41.74 (NO) £59.95 (BOT)

Costers del Siurana Clos de l'Obac,
Priorato **1994** £30.66 (NO) £32.50 (FORT)

Pesquera Crianza, Ribera del Duero **1985**
£32.31 (REI)

Pesquera Reserva, Ribera del Duero
1994 £36.62 (FA)
Pesquera Reserva, Ribera del Duero
1986 £49.00 (CRO)
Torres Gran Coronas Black Label (Mas La
Plana), Penedés **1983** £32.00 (CRO)
Torres Gran Coronas Black Label (Mas La
Plana), Penedés **1981** £49.94 (REI)
Vega Sicilia Valbuena 3rd year, Ribera del
Duero **1983** £47.00 (CRO)
Vega Sicilia Valbuena 5th year, Ribera del
Duero **1993** £35.00 (DI) £35.50 (TAN)
Vega Sicilia Valbuena 5th year, Ribera del
Duero **1992** £42.50 (MOR) £52.50 (BER)
Vega Sicilia Valbuena, Ribera del Duero
1993 £36.00 (MV) £39.50 (RAE) £44.00
(FORT)
Vega Sicilia Valbuena, Ribera del Duero
1992 £43.50 (LEA)
Vega Sicilia Valbuena, Ribera del Duero
1990 £39.36 (PLA)

£50.00 → £99.99

Alvaro Palacios l'Ermita, Priorato **1996**
£96.35 (FA)
Torres Gran Coronas Black Label (Mas La
Plana), Penedés **1976** £52.00 (CRO)
Vega Sicilia, Ribera del Duero **1985**
£87.54 (FA) £97.00 (UB)
Vega Sicilia, Ribera del Duero **1979**
£99.29 (FA)
Vega Sicilia Unico, Ribera del Duero **1986**
£60.30 (TAN) £62.00 (MV) £65.00 (BU)
£69.00 (CRO) £70.00 (FORT) £72.00 (MOR)
Vega Sicilia Unico, Ribera del Duero **1985**
£75.00 (ROB)
Vega Sicilia Unico, Ribera del Duero **1981**
£89.00 (CRO) £90.00 (BU) £91.65 (RAE)
£95.00 (MV) £103.00 (MOR) £115.00 (BER)

£100.00 → £124.99

Vega Sicilia, Ribera del Duero **1968**
£117.62 (FA)
Vega Sicilia Unico, Ribera del Duero **1970**
£110.00 (FORT) £115.74 (REI) £130.00 *
(BEN) £130.00 (ROB)

Please remember that
Oz Clarke's Wine Guide
*is a price guide and not a
price list. It is not meant to
replace up-to-date
merchants' lists.*

Over £125.00

Alvaro Palacios l'Ermita, Priorato **1995**
£147.99 (MOR)
Alvaro Palacios l'Ermita, Priorato **1994**
£154.47 (NO)
Vega Sicilia, Ribera del Duero **1982**
£145.00 (UB)
Vega Sicilia Unico, Ribera del Duero **1962**
£205.63 (REI)

OTHER SPANISH WHITE

Under £4.00

Alanis Solana (Torrontés & Treixadura),
Ribeiro **1995** £3.19 (MORR)
★ Basa, Rueda **1998** £3.95 (CRO) £4.33 (FLE)
£4.50 (BEN) £4.95 (AD)
Basa, Rueda **1996** £3.60 (SOM) £4.69 (PHI)
Pazo Ribeiro Blanco, Ribeiro **1998** £3.70
(SOM)
Lurton Rueda, Rueda **1996** £2.99 (THR)
£2.99 (WR) £2.99 (BOT) £5.39 (JER)
Ryman Santara Chardonnay, Conca de
Barberà **1996** £3.99 (CO) £3.99 (VIC)
£3.99 (THR) £3.99 (WR)

£4.00 → £4.99

Basa, Rueda **1997** £4.49 (YOU) £5.10 (PIP)
£5.95 (ROB)
Bodegas Alvear Medium Dry, Montilla
Non-vintage £4.45 (TAN)
Castillo de Liria Moscatel de Valencia
Gandia, Valencia **Non-vintage** £4.25
(TAN)
Covisa Viñas del Vero Chardonnay,
Somontano **1997** £4.99 (UN)
Covisa Viñas del Vero Chenin Blanc,
Somontano **1992** £4.65 (UB)
Los Llanos Armonioso, Valdepeñas **1995**
£4.30 (UB)
Palacio de Bornos, Rueda **1998** £4.00
(SOM) £5.49 (JON)
Torres San Valentin, Penedés **1997** £4.49
(DI)
Torres Viña Esmeralda, Penedés **1997**
£4.99 (DI) £5.25 (WHI) £5.95 (WRI) £5.95
(TAN) £5.99 (AME) £5.99 (MOR)
Torres Viña Sol, Penedés **1998** £4.29
(VIC) £4.29 (THR) £4.29 (WR) £4.29 (BOT)
£4.39 (MORR) £4.50 (POR) £4.58 (COC)
£4.95 (STE) £5.49 (BO) £5.50 (NA)
Torres Viña Sol, Penedés **1997** £4.49
(TES) £4.49 (CO) £4.49 (DI) £5.29 (MOR)

£5.00 → £5.99

Alvarez y Diez Mantel Verdejo/Sauvignon Blanc, Rueda 1998 £5.49 (BO)
Bodegas Valduero Azumbre Blanco, Ribera del Duero 1996 £5.45 (JU)
Covisa Viñas del Vero Chardonnay, Somontano 1991 £5.60 (UB)
Marqués de Alella, Alella Clasico 1997 £5.25 (WS) £5.99 (MOR) £5.99 (YOU)
Marqués de Riscal, Rueda 1998 £5.49 (MAJ)
Torres Gran Viña Sol, Penedés 1997 £5.75 (DI) £5.85 (WHI) £6.49 (POR) £6.49 (SAF) £6.65 (MOR) £6.70 (WRI)
Torres Gran Viña Sol, Penedés 1993 £5.60 (CRO)
Torres Viña Esmeralda, Penedés 1998 £5.29 (VIC) £5.29 (THR) £5.29 (WR) £5.29 (BOT) £5.49 (POR) £5.85 (STE) £5.95 (STA) £5.99 (BO) £6.25 (PIP) £6.50 (NA)
Torres Viña Esmeralda, Penedés 1996 £5.43 (NO) £5.50 (UB) £5.52 (PEN) £5.65 (CON) £5.73 (ROS) £5.95 (JU) £6.75 (ROB) £7.64 (TW)
Torres Viña Esmeralda, Penedés 1994 £5.69 (JON)

£6.00 → £9.99

Belondrade y Lurton, Rueda 1995 £9.95 (RAE) £10.50 (BALL)
Covisa Viñas del Vero Barrel-Fermented Chardonnay, Somontano 1996 £6.49 (OD)
Covisa Viñas del Vero Barrel-Fermented Chardonnay, Somontano 1995 £6.59 (GW) £7.50 (BALL)
Covisa Viñas del Vero Gewürztraminer, Somontano 1997 £7.03 (GW)
Enate, Somontano 1996 £7.90 (CRO)
Lagar de Fornelos Lagar de Cervera, Rías Baixas 1998 £7.65 (SOM) £9.30 (WRI) £9.30 (STA) £9.45 (HED) £9.59 (JON) £9.70 (PIP) £9.85 (PHI)
Lagar de Fornelos Lagar de Cervera, Rías Baixas 1997 £6.64 (JER) £7.69 (YOU) £8.05 (REI) £8.95 (TAN)
Lagar de Fornelos Lagar de Cervera, Rías Baixas 1996 £8.50 (JU)
Manuel Sancho Mont Marçal Chardonnay, Penedés 1995 £6.25 (CON)
Marqués de Alella, Alella Clasico 1998 £6.49 (POR)
Marqués de Alella, Allier 1995 £7.95 (ROB) £14.99 (MOR)

Marqués de Riscal, Rueda 1997 £6.33 (PLA)
Pazo de Barrantes Albariño, Rias Baixas 1997 £9.99 (RAE) £10.35 (HAH) £10.75 (FORT)
Pazo de Barrantes Albariño, Rias Baixas 1996 £9.51 (PLA)
Torres Fransola, Penedés 1997 £9.50 (DI) £10.35 (MOR) £10.50 (STA)
Torres Gran Viña Sol, Penedés 1998 £6.29 (VIC) £6.29 (THR) £6.29 (WR) £6.29 (BOT) £6.50 (PIP) £6.62 (STE) £7.35 (NA)
Torres Gran Viña Sol, Penedés 1996 £6.11 (ROS) £6.55 (HAH) £7.99 (TW)
Torres Moscatel Malvasia de Oro, Penedés Non-vintage £7.21 (NO)
Txakolina Txomin Etxaniz, Getariako Txakolina 1998 £8.50 (WS)

£10.00 → £14.99

Belondrade y Lurton, Rueda 1996 £11.46 (BIB)
Cellers Puig & Roca, Augustus Chardonnay, Penedés 1998 £10.99 (DI)
Cellers Puig & Roca, Augustus Chardonnay, Penedés 1997 £10.95 (DI)
Cellers Puig & Roca, Augustus Chardonnay, Penedés 1996 £13.25 (MOR) £11.00 (WS)
Enate Barrel-Fermented Chardonnay, Somontano 1996 £10.60 (AV) £12.09 (PLAY)
Jean León Chardonnay, Penedés 1995 £14.69 (REI)
Jean León Chardonnay, Penedés 1992 £13.60 (DI) £14.10 (PEN)
Torres Fransola, Penedés 1996 £10.28 (REI)
Torres Milmanda Chardonnay, Penedés 1996 £14.99 (MOR)
Txakolina Etxaniz Txomin, Getariako Txakolina 1994 £12.95 (ROB)

Over £15.00

★ Olivares Dulce Monastrell 1996 £16.99 (MOR)
Scholtz Solera 1885, Málaga Non-vintage £24.00 (CRO)
Torres Milmanda Chardonnay, Penedés 1997 £16.95 (DI)
Torres Milmanda Chardonnay, Penedés 1995 £15.10 (NO) £16.27 (REI)
Torres Milmanda Chardonnay, Penedés 1994 £20.75 (UB)
Torres Milmanda Chardonnay, Penedés 1988 £19.99 (RAE)

OTHER SPANISH ROSÉ

Under £4.00

Chivite Gran Feudo, Navarra **1997** £2.99 (VIC) £2.99 (THR) £2.99 (WR) £2.99 (BOT)
Torres de Casta, Penedés **1996** £3.49 (DI)

£5.00 → £5.99

Ochoa Rosé, Navarra **1998** £5.49 (UN) £5.52 (GW)
Ochoa Rosé, Navarra **1997** £5.95 (FORT)
Ochoa Rosé, Navarra **1996** £5.20 (UB)
Torres de Casta, Penedés **1997** £5.49 (POR)
Torres de Casta, Penedés **1994** £5.15 (UB)

c. £6.50

Chivite Gran Feudo, Navarra **1998** £6.09 (PLAY)

SPANISH SPARKLING

Under £6.00

★ Bodegas Inviosa Bonaval Brut, Cava **Non-vintage** £5.99 (YOU) £6.50 (FLE) £6.50 (PHI) £6.95 (AD)
Castellblanch Extra Seco, Cava **Non-vintage** £5.99 (VIC) £5.99 (THR) £5.99 (WR) £5.99 (BOT)
Codorníu Brut, Cava **Non-vintage** £5.99 (ASD)
Freixenet Extra Brut, Cava **Non-vintage** £5.99 (UB)
Palau Brut, Cava **Non-vintage** £4.99 (BO)
Palau Rosé **Non-vintage** £5.49 (CON)
Segura Viudas Brut, Cava **Non-vintage** £5.49 (UN)
Segura Viudas Brut Reserva, Cava **Non-vintage** £5.99 (OD) £6.49 (YOU) £6.50 (DI)
★ Somerfield Cava Brut Rosé **Non-vintage** £4.99 (SO)
Sumarroca Extra Brut, Cava **1994** £5.95 (WS)

£6.00 → £6.99

★ ASDA Vintage Cava **1996** £6.49 (ASD)
Castellblanch Brut Zero, Cava **Non-vintage** £6.09 (JON)
Castellblanch Rosado **Non-vintage** £6.09 (JON)
Condé de Caralt Brut, Cava **Non-vintage** £6.50 (CRO) £6.54 (GW)
Condé de Caralt Semi-seco, Cava **Non-vintage** £6.99 (MOR)
Freixenet Carta Nevada, Cava **Non-vintage** £6.49 (BO) £7.20 (PIP) £7.45 (WHI) £7.49 (MOR)
Freixenet Cordon Negro Brut, Cava **Non-vintage** £6.95 (BALL) £7.16 (STE) £7.39 (BO) £7.45 (WHI) £7.49 (WAI) £7.49 (MOR) £7.49 (CO) £7.49 (SAF) £7.49 (VIC) £7.49 (THR) £7.49 (WR) £7.49 (BOT) £7.49 (ASD) £7.95 (NA) £7.99 (MAJ)
Freixenet Cordon Negro Brut, Cava **1993** £6.95 (POR) £7.20 (PIP) £7.23 (PLA) £7.65 (UB)
Marqués de Monistrol Brut, Cava **Non-vintage** £6.50 (ELL)
Raventos I Blanc Cava l'Hereau **Non-vintage** £6.65 (WAT)
Torre del Gall Brut, Cava **1994** £6.25 (SOM)

£7.00 → £7.99

Condé de Caralt Blanc de Blancs, Cava **Non-vintage** £7.99 (MOR)
Codorníu Cuvée Raventos Chardonnay Brut **Non-vintage** £7.99 (ASD)
Freixenet Brut Rosé, Cava **Non-vintage** £7.45 (WHI) £7.49 (MOR) £7.61 (STE)
Freixenet Cordon Negro Brut, Cava **1992** £7.95 (ROB)
Juvé y Camps Brut, Cava **1994** £7.45 (STA)
Segura Viudas Brut, Cava **1994** £7.99 (SAF)
Torre del Gall Gran Reserva **1992** £7.99 (RAE)

£8.00 → £9.99

Freixenet Brut Nature, Cava **1996** £8.99 (MAJ)
Juvé y Camps Brut, Cava **1993** £8.30 (UB)
Juvé y Camps Reserva de la Familia, Cava **1993** £9.01 (JER)
Raventos I Blanc Cava Brut Reserva **Non-vintage** £8.25 (WAT)

Over £10.00

Freixenet Cordon Negro Brut, Cava **1991** £15.95 (UB)
Juvé y Camps Reserva de la Familia, Cava **Non-vintage** £10.99 (MOR)
Juvé y Camps Reserva de la Familia, Cava **1994** £10.50 (PHI) £10.95 (ROB) £11.75 (FORT)
Juvé y Camps Reserva de la Familia Brut Natural, Cava **1995** £11.95 (LA)
Raventos I Blanc Cava Gran Reserva Personal MRN **1992** £14.55 (WAT)

SHERRY PRICES

DRY

Under £4.00

la Gitana Manzanilla, Hidalgo ½ bottle
£3.15 (SOM) £3.16 (PLA) £3.25 (TAN)
£3.25 (BALL) £3.38 (JER) £3.49 (OD) £3.94
(REI) £3.99 (YOU) £4.25 (PHI) £5.99 (JON)

£4.00 → £4.99

Amontillado de Sanlúcar, Barbadillo £4.99
(WHI) £5.29 (GW) £6.96 (CB) £8.29 (NO)
Amontillado Hidalgo £4.99 (MAJ) £8.49
(YOU)
Amontillado Napoleon, Hidalgo £4.01 (JER)
£6.30 (NI) £7.59 (JON) £7.95 (AD)
Fino Barbadillo £4.99 (CON) £5.25 (PLAY)
Fino de Sanlúcar, Barbadillo £4.99 (WHI)
£5.49 (AME)
Fino Hidalgo £4.69 (PLA) £4.99 (NI) £4.99
(MAJ) £5.25 (HAH) £5.45 (PIP)
Lustau Puerto Fino ½ bottle £4.50 (SOM)
£5.25 (BALL) £5.50 (BEN) £5.60 (MOR)
Manzanilla de Sanlúcar, Barbadillo £4.99
(CON) £5.29 (GW) £5.29 (OD) £5.45 (ROS)
£5.49 (AME) £5.49 (VIC) £5.49 (THR) £5.49
(BOT) £6.15 (MOR) £6.70 (CB) £6.95 (ROB)
Oloroso Seco Barbadillo £4.99 (CON)
£5.20 (COC) £13.50 (JU)
Valdespino Fino £4.68 (WAT) £4.95 (LEA)

£5.00 → £6.99

Elegante, González Byass £5.10 (COC) £5.75
(WHI) £5.89 (TES) £5.89 (UN) £5.89 (SAF)
£5.89 (VIC) £5.89 (THR) £5.99 (YOU)
Fino de Balbaina, Barbadillo £5.29 (GW)
Fino Superior, Hidalgo £6.25 (NI) £8.50
(TAN) £9.11 (JER) £9.99 (LAY)
la Gitana Manzanilla, Hidalgo £5.99 (NI)
£5.99 (WAI) £5.99 (MAJ) £6.35 (PIP) £6.50
(AD) £6.75 (HAH) £6.95 (ROB) £7.64 (TW)
Harvey's Dune £5.99 (CON) £5.99 (WHI)
£5.99 (THR) £5.99 (WR) £5.99 (BOT)
Harvey's Manzanilla £6.03 (HA)
la Ina, Domecq £6.24 (HA) £6.50 (COC)
£6.97 (WAT) £7.05 (HAH) £7.25 (WRI)
£7.35 (UN) £7.75 (ROB) £7.75 (FORT)
Inocente Fino, Valdespino £6.91 (WAT)
£7.49 (OD) £7.95 (AD) £7.95 (LEA)
Lustau Puerto Fino £5.00 (NO) £7.65 (CON)
£8.49 (BAL) £8.95 (DI) £8.99 (PHI) £8.99
(AME) £8.99 (BEN) £8.99 (YOU) £9.00 (MV)

Manzanilla Pasada Solear, Barbadillo £6.99
(CON) £6.99 (SAF) £7.04 (PEN) £7.75 (STA)
Mariscal Manzanilla, Hidalgo £5.95 (TAN)
Ostra Manzanilla £6.95 (LAY)
San Patricio Fino, Garvey £6.76 (ROS)
£6.95 (WRI) £7.45 (COC)
Tio Pepe, González Byass £6.90 (COC)
£7.49 (WHI) £7.56 (PLAY) £7.59 (YOU)
£7.65 (WRI) £7.75 (STA) £7.79 (TES)
£7.79 (WAI) £7.79 (UN) £7.79 (OD) £7.79
(SAF) £7.95 (ROB) £7.95 (FORT) £8.37
(VIN) £8.95 (HAH)
Valdespino Manzanilla Deliciosa £6.49
(OD) £6.95 (LEA)

£7.00 → £8.99

Don Zoilo Manzanilla £7.35 (COC) £8.25
(WRI)
Dos Cortados Old Dry Oloroso,
Williams & Humbert £8.99 (UN) £9.50
(COC) £9.99 (WAI) £9.99 (YOU)
Fino Superiore El Cuadrado, Hidalgo
£7.95 (AD)
la Guita Manzanilla, Hidalgo £7.99 (DI)
Harvey's Palo Cortado £8.12 (HA)
Lustau Fino £8.40 (PLA)
Manzanilla Pasada de Sanlúcar, Hidalgo
£8.50 (TAN) £9.19 (JON) £9.99 (LAY)
£9.99 (YOU) £10.93 (TW) £10.99 (BEN)
Oloroso Anada 1918 Solera, Emilio
Lustau ½ bottle £7.99 (BO) £7.99 (DI)
£8.49 (BAL) £8.81 (REI) £8.99 (BEN)
Oloroso Especial, Hidalgo £7.95 (NI)
£8.50 (BU) £10.34 (TW)
Oloroso Seco, Hidalgo £8.09 (JON) £8.50
(TAN) £8.95 (AD)
Oloroso Seco Napoleon, Hidalgo £8.05
(PIP) £9.50 (BEN) £9.65 (LAY)
Palo Cortado del Carrascal, Valdespino
£8.49 (OD) £9.95 (LEA)
Puerto Fino Reserva, Lustau £8.95 (ROB)
£8.99 (GW) £9.34 (REI)
Tio Pepe Lustau £7.25 (CON)

£9.00 → £9.99

Don Gonzalo Old Dry Oloroso,
Valdespino £9.28 (WAT) £9.95 (LEA)
Fino Quinta Osborne £9.50 (FORT)
Jerez Cortado, Hidalgo £9.69 (JON) £9.80
(TAN) £9.80 (PIP) £9.95 (AD) £11.49 (LAY)
Lustau Dry Oloroso £9.25 (STA)
Palo Cortado Vides £9.00 (MV) £11.95 (JU)

£10.00 → £19.99

Amontillado del Duque, González Byass
£18.95 (COC) £22.00 (MOR) £22.50 (FORT)

Amontillado Very Old Dry Coliseo,
Valdespino £19.95 (LEA)
Fino Amontillado de Jerez, Alberto
Lorente Piaget £11.70 (JU)
Palo Cortado Cardenal, Valdespino
£14.50 (LEA)

Over £20.00

Amontillado Viejo, Hidalgo £21.50 (NI)
£23.95 (BALL) £28.20 (TAN) £28.75 (HAH)

MEDIUM

Under £5.00

Amontillado Valdespino £4.68 (WAT)
£4.79 (OD) £4.95 (LEA)
Tanners Medium Sherry £4.95 (TAN)

£5.00 → £6.99

Amontillado Martial, Valdespino £5.35 (AS)
Caballero Amontillado, González Byass
£5.89 (TES) £5.89 (SAF)
Croft Particular £6.49 (SAF) £6.49 (THR)
Dry Sack, Williams & Humbert £5.49 (TES)
£6.40 (COC) £6.95 (FORT) £6.99 (YOU)
Harvey's Club Amontillado £5.49 (WAI)
£5.59 (THR) £5.59 (BOT) £5.65 (SAF)
£5.99 (CON) £6.49 (YOU) £6.50 (ROB)
La Concha Amontillado, González Byass
£5.10 (COC) £5.29 (WAI) £5.75 (WHI)
£5.89 (SAF) £5.89 (VIC) £5.89 (THR)

£7.00 → £10.99

Amontillado del Puerto, José Luis
Gonzalez Obregon ½ bottle £9.00 (MV)
Harvey's Fine Old Amontillado £8.11 (HA)
Oloroso de Jerez Almacenista Viuda de
Antonio Borrego, Lustau £8.95 (FORT)
Oloroso Solera 1842, Valdespino £8.49
(OD) £9.28 (WAT) £9.40 (TAN) £9.95 (LEA)

£11.00 → £19.99

Amontillado del Puerto, Loreto Colosio
Molleda £11.95 (JU)
Apostoles Oloroso, González Byass
£18.95 (COC) £21.50 (ROB) £23.59 (VIN)
Sandeman Royal Corregidor Oloroso
£12.95 (ROB) £13.25 (FORT) £17.00 (CRO)

Over £20.00

Amontillado Almacenista, Lustau £48.37
(FA)
Old Amoroso, Sandeman £28.79 (REI)

SWEET

Under £5.50

Cabrera Rich Cream, Palomino & Vergara
£4.59 (YOU)
Hidalgo Cream £5.45 (PIP)

£5.50 → £6.99

Croft Original Pale Cream £6.20 (COC)
£6.49 (CON) £6.49 (TES) £6.49 (WAI) £6.49
(WHI) £6.49 (UN) £6.49 (OD) £6.49 (SAF)
£6.49 (THR) £6.49 (WR) £6.49 (BOT) £6.90
(HAH) £6.95 (WRI) £6.95 (ROB) £6.95
(BALL) £6.95 (JU) £6.99 (VIN) £6.99 (YOU)
Harvey's Bristol Cream £6.26 (HA) £6.39
(CON) £6.49 (UN) £6.49 (OD) £6.49 (SAF)
£6.49 (THR) £6.49 (BOT) £6.59 (TES) £6.59
(WAI) £6.59 (BO) £6.60 (COC) £6.63 (PLAY)
£6.85 (VIN) £6.89 (WHI) £6.95 (BALL) £6.99
(YOU) £7.50 (WRI) £7.95 (HAH) £7.95 (ROB)

£7.00 → £9.99

Lustau's Old East India £9.95 (PHI) £9.95
(COC) £9.99 (BO) £10.95 (DI) £10.99
(BEN) £10.99 (BU) £10.99 (GW) £10.99
(YOU) £11.00 (MV) £11.50 (FORT) £11.55
(MOR) £11.75 (HIG)
Old Oloroso Jerez Cream, Valdespino
£7.60 (LEA)
Pedro Ximenez, Barbadillo £8.99 (CON)
Pedro Ximenez Solera Superior,
Valdespino £7.49 (OD) £7.87 (WAT)
Pedro Ximénez Viejo, Hidalgo £8.50
(TAN) £8.70 (PIP) £8.99 (MAJ) £9.99 (YOU)

Over £18.00

Matusalem Oloroso, González Byass
£18.95 (COC) £20.95 (AD) £22.00 (MOR)
£22.50 (ROB) £22.50 (FORT) £23.59 (VIN)
Rich Old Oloroso, Sandeman £28.79 (REI)

UNITED KINGDOM

**English winemakers continue to battle with the weather,
but they're making progress on the quality front**

If you want a difficult life, become an English winemaker. Wet springs, cold summers, rainy autumns – small wonder there's still little consensus on what England does best, winewise.

And yet in spite of the weather, in spite of the unwillingness of too many of us to take our home-grown wines seriously, in spite of the fact that much of the world can undercut English wines on price without even trying, the best wines from England are very good indeed.

For some years now Breaky Bottom has been, to my mind, at the top of the tree. Its Seyval Blanc ages for years (seven or eight, easily) to become toasty and smoky and honeyed – put a bottle in front of your most knowledgeable friends and see how many get it right. Not many, I suspect.

England's even making some good reds these days – Denbies, for example. And some good sparklers. But because competing on price is difficult, the best buys are not the cheapest.

GRAPE VARIETIES

BACCHUS (white) Sharp, strong flavours of gooseberry, elderflower and orange rind. Best: *Lamberhurst, Partridge Vineyard, Sandhurst, Staverton, Three Choirs, Wyken.* Good sweet ones: *Chiltern Valley, Cane End.*

FABER (white) Fragrant with good acidity.

HUXELREBE (white) Has a grapefruit-pith taste and a greenish bite. For this reason it is often softened up by blending. Best: *Biddenden, Bothy* (blended with Perle), *Monnow Valley* (blended with Seyval Blanc), *Staple St James, Three Choirs. Davenport* rosé blends it with Triomphe d'Alsace.

KERNER (white) *Carr-Taylor* blends this with Reichensteiner for fizz; *Elham Valley* blends it with Seyval Blanc, likewise for fizz.

MADELEINE ANGEVINE (white) A fruit-juicy character is matched by good acidity, elderflower-perfumed or more honeyed but appley. *Halfpenny Green* and *Sharpham* are good.

MÜLLER-THURGAU (white) This used to be the English workhorse, but is now much less planted. *Breaky Bottom, Bruisyard, Elham Valley, Penshurst, St George's, St Nicholas, Staple St James, Tenterden* and *Wootton* are good. And it can make very attractive, slightly sweet wine, as at *Rowney.*

ORTEGA (white) *Hidden Spring* is concentrated, and *Biddenden,* in particular, makes a delicious, slightly sweet but tremendously fruity elderflower-and-apricot-tasting example. It is usually blended (as at *Rock Lodge*).

PINOT NOIR (red) Used mostly for rosé and sparkling wine; or indeed sparkling rosé. *Denbies* Pinot Noir is rich and savoury; *Thames Valley's* is a good contender and *Carr Taylor* makes good rosé fizz; *Chiddingstone* blends it with Pinot Meunier to make a delicious Blanc de Noirs; *Bodiam Castle* makes a tasty rosé, as well as a dry, honeyed Blanc de Pinot Noir white; *Biddenden* and *Tenterden* use it for rosé blends. *Three Choirs* rosé from Pinot Noir has earthy raspberry-and-morello-cherry fruit; *Conghurst's* grapy, herbaceous rosé is also good, and *Denbies, Nyetimber* and *South Ridge* sparklers are notable.

REICHENSTEINER (white) Usually dull when dry, but slightly sweet, it can develop a pleasant, smoky, quince-and-peaches taste and age well. *Carr Taylor* and *Rock Lodge* use it for Champagne-method fizz, *Northbrook Springs* is barrel fermented. *Nutbourne Manor* and *Three Choirs* are also good.

SCHEUREBE (white) Good grapefruity, curranty wines in good years. It goes into *Thames Valley's Clocktower Selection Botrytis,* when it's made, along with Reichensteiner.

SCHÖNBURGER (pink) Fat wine by English standards, with a pear-lychee flavour and good acidity. Best: *Carr Taylor, Coxley, Nutborne Manor, Saxon Valley, Three Choirs, Woolding, Wootton.*

SEYVAL BLANC (white) *Breaky Bottom* is the most successful – dry and Sauvignon-like when young, honeyed like Burgundy after four to five years – but Seyval Blanc is generally best blended or made sweetish.

Three Choirs and *Hidden Spring* blend it, while *Tenterden* makes a good oaked Reserve. *Thames Valley* is oaked. *Elham Valley* uses it in good fizz. Other good ones: *Headcorn, Penshurst, Shawsgate, Wootton.*

OTHER REDS *Beenleigh Manor* has a good reputation for Cabernet and Merlot grown under plastic; there is also some potential in Dunkelfelder and Dornfelder, plus plantings of Léon Millet and Maréchal Foch, both more commonly seen in Canada. Gamay is being used by *Thames Valley* for a sparkler. *Dunkery's Prometheus* (from Somerset) is delicious, as is *Chapel Down's* Epoch 1. *Wyken's* red is pretty good.

OTHER WHITES There's Gewürz-traminer at *Barton Manor,* and Ehrenfelser at *Penshurst; Wootton's* Auxerrois is a pungent, salty-sappy. *Carr Taylor* has Pinot Blanc for concentrated *Kemsley Dry.* The best Chardie is *Denbies'. Nyetimber* and *Thames Valley* are also good. Try *Denbies* Riesling.

UNITED KINGDOM PRICES

WHITE

Under £5.00

Chapel Down, Epoch V **1996** £4.99 (SAF)
£5.49 (BO)
Denbies Surrey Gold **Non-vintage** £4.69
(WAI)
Three Choirs **1997** £4.99 (NO)
Three Choirs **1996** £3.99 (CON)
Three Choirs Premium Dry **1994** £4.99
(CON)

DANEBURY

Danebury Vineyards Limited,
Nether Wallop,
Stockbridge,
Hampshire SO20 6JX,
England.

Tel: +44 (0)1264 781851
Fax: +44 (0)1264 782212

£5.00 → £5.99

Astley Severn Vale **1997** £5.80 (TAN)
Three Choirs Medium Dry **1997** £5.20
(TAN)
Three Choirs Medium Dry **1996** £5.09
(JON)

Over £6.00

Breaky Bottom Fumé Seyval Blanc **1993**
£7.95 (ROB)
Chapel Down Ortega Oaked **1995** £7.86
(NO)
Chiddingstone Seyval/Kerner **1996** £6.95
(FORT)

Sharpham Barrel-Fermented Dry **1995**
£9.80 (NO)
Sharpham Estate Selection **1996** £8.35
(PIP)
Wroxeter Roman Vineyard Madeleine
Angevine, Medium Dry **1996** £6.70
(TAN)

RED

Over £5.00

Beenleigh Red **1994** £17.50 (NO)
Chapel Down Epoch I **1997** £5.69
(WAI)
Chapel Down Epoch I **1996** £5.99 (BO)
Chapel Down Epoch Reserve **1996** £8.75
(FORT)

SPARKLING

Under £12.00

Carr Taylor **Non-vintage** £10.50 (CRO)

Three Choirs Vintage Reserve **Non-
vintage** £9.99 (CON)
★ Warden Vineyard Extra Brut **1996**
£11.95 (HED)

c. £18.00

★ Nyetimber Classic Blend Brut **1992**
£17.75 (FORT)

MERCHANTS SPECIALIZING IN UNITED KINGDOM
see Merchant Directory (page 413) for details

Nobody has very long lists of English wines,
but the following have a fair selection:
Averys of Bristol (AV), Benedict's, The
Nobody Inn (NO), Thos. Peatling, Terry Platt

(PLA) – well, wines from Wales actually,
Safeway (SAF), Tanners (TAN), Tesco (TES),
Unwins (UN), The Wine Society (WS).
Otherwise buy direct from the vineyard.

UNITED STATES

There's no bargain-basement wine in California. Good stuff is very expensive, and very good stuff is very, very, very expensive

Yes, I know. I know that last year I predicted that prices of California wine might fall – well, predicted is perhaps too strong a word. 'Hoped', maybe. Or even, um, 'fantasized'.

Either way, there doesn't seem to be much sign of it happening. Not yet. And the California wines we get here are frankly not terrifically good value compared to countries like Chile, Argentina or Italy.

At least, that's true at the cheaper end. If you want to pay a bit more, there are some great flavours to be had: silky, strawberryish Pinot Noir from Carneros, for example, and rich, berryish Zinfandels.

But it's not that easy to find a big selection at a UK merchant. Why? Price, I suppose. Isn't that what it always comes

down to? Australia, even now that prices there are higher than they were, is still delivering more flavour to the pound. Maybe it's just that Australia is keener to sell to us: California has that huge market on its doorstep and is choc-a-bloc with winemakers all keen to make wine that sells for $10 more than the wine from next door. The cheaper end of the market has been pretty much sewn up by the big companies (and when I say big I mean mega), and while quality is perfectly good you're not going to die of excitement.

So, if you're going to drink California wine, expect to pay if you want something interesting. For something sensational you'll have to pay much, much more. But that's another story.

GRAPE VARIETIES

BARBERA (red) The Italian variety most grown in California. Look for *Louis M Martini, Sebastiani, Il Podere dell' Olivos* and *Bonny Doon, Monteviña* and *Preston Vineyards*.

CABERNET SAUVIGNON (red) Still the top grape for premium California reds. Napa Cabernet is the classic, rich, tannic yet seductive at a young age. For the top wines, complexity and finesse are the new watchwords, especially for wines from hillside vineyards (as opposed to the flat floor of the Napa). Washington State Cab continues to improve as the vines age, yielding more concentration. For cellaring (never as long as for the equivalent quality Bordeaux), try: *Beaulieu Vineyards Georges de Latour Private Reserve, Beringer Reserve, Bernardus, Buena Vista, Burgess, Cain, Carmenet Vin de Garde Reserve, Caymus*

Special Selection, Chimney Rock, Clos du Val, Conn Creek, Cuvaison, Dalla Valle, Diamond Creek, Dominus, Dunn, Franciscan, Grgich Hills, Groth, Heitz Bella Oaks, Kenwood Artist Series, La Jota, Laurel Glen, Louis M Martini, Robert Mondavi Reserve and *Opus One, Chateau Montelena, Newton, Niebaum-Coppola, Raymond Private Reserve, Ridge Monte Bello, Sequoia Grove, Shafer Hillside Select, Spottswoode, Stag's Leap Cask 23, Sterling Vineyards Diamond Mountain Ranch, Stonestreet* (California); *Ste Chapelle* (Idaho); *Fall Creek Vineyards, Llano Estacado, Messina Hof, Oberhellmann, Pheasant Ridge* (Texas); *Arbor Crest, Hogue Cellars, Chateau Ste Michelle, Columbia, Staton Hills* (Washington). For light Cabernet, try: *Beringer, Caymus Liberty School, Chateau Souverain, Clos du Bois, Cosentino, Fetzer, Estancia, Foppiano, Kendall-Jackson* (California); *Columbia Crest* (Washington).

CHARDONNAY (white) This is less relentlessly oaky than it was, and more interesting as a result. Many of the more popular brands – such as *Kendall-Jackson* and *Sebastiani* – have a slightly sweet finish to make them more commercial. The best can age, but seldom need to, they are so attractive young. For balance and poise look for: *Acacia, Arrowood, Beringer, Buena Vista, Chalone, Chateau St Jean, Cuvaison, Dehlinger, Far Niente, Flora Springs, Franciscan, Kistler, Kunde, Mondavi Reserve, Newton, Raymond Reserve, Renaissance, Signorello, Simi* and *Sonoma-Cutrer* (California); *Bridgehampton* (NY); *Prince Michel* (Virginia). For simpler wines, try *Callaway, Clos du Bois, Estancia, Matanzas Creek, Kendall-Jackson, Morgan, Mirassou, Phelps, Monterey Vineyards, Wente* (California); *Fall Creek* (Texas); *Chateau Ste Michelle, Columbia Crest, Hogue Cellars* (Washington).

GEWÜRZTRAMINER (white) It's really too hot in California for this grape, although a few people keep trying. Look for *Adler Fels* (sometimes), *Handley Cellars, Lazy Creek, Obester, Rutherford Hill* (California); *Llano Estacado* (Texas); *Columbia, Chateau Ste Michelle* (Washington).

MERLOT (red) When it's good it's very, very good, full of lovely black cherry fruit with a pleasing brambly edge. But it's frighteningly fashionable, and too many are overcropped and insipid. Best are *Arrowood, Bellerose, Clos du Val, Crichton Hall, Cuvaison, Duckhorn, Geyser Peak, Gundlach-Bundschu, Monticello Cellars, Murphy-Goode, Newton, St Francis, Pine Ridge, Ridge Santa Cruz, Silverado, Sinskey, St Clement, Sterling, Swanson, Vichon,* (California); *Bedell Cellars, Bridgehampton, Peconic Bay* (New York); *Chateau Ste Michelle, Columbia, Columbia Crest, Hogue Cellars, Leonetti, Staton Hills, Paul Thomas* (Washington).

PETITE SIRAH (red) This is emphatically not the same as the great red Syrah grape of the Rhône Valley or the Shiraz of

Australia. It produces big, stark, dry, almost tarry wines – impressive, but needing a good winemaker. *Ridge* is superb. Also look for *Concannon, Christopher Creek, Foppiano* and *Stag's Leap.*

PINOT GRIS (white) Oregon's other speciality, after Pinot Noir. Most are light and spicy, but less vinous than Alsace versions. Try *Elk Cove, Erath, Eyrie, Ponzi.*

PINOT NOIR (red) At its best (which means from a handful of producers in California and Oregon) US Pinot is almost as good as very good Burgundy. Most, though, settles for charm rather than excitement, and lesser wines can be dilute and over-oaked. Try *Acacia, Au Bon Climat Cuvée Isabelle, Bouchaine, Byron, Calera, Carneros Creek, Chalone, Dehlinger, Fetzer, De Loach, The Famous Gate, Gary Farrel, Iron Horse, Kendall-Jackson, Kistler, Lazy Creek, Robert Mondavi, Patz & Hall, Rochioli, Lane Tanner, Saintsbury, Sanford, Sinskey, Rod Strong, Whitcraft, Wild Horse, Zaca Mesa, ZD* (California); *Bridgehampton* (NY); *Adelsheim, Amity, Archery Summit, Bethel Heights, Broadley, Drouhin, Erath, Eyrie, Scott Henry, King Estate, Panther Creek, Rex Hill, Sokol Blosser, Ken Wright* (Oregon).

RIESLING (white) This grape likes cool spots, which means that it all too often makes dull wines in California. *Renaissance* is streets ahead; other good ones are *Alexander Valley Vineyards, Konocti, Navarro* (California); *Lamoureux Landing, Wagner Vineyards* (New York); *Amity* (Oregon); *Chateau Morrisette, Prince Michel* (Virginia); *Hogue Cellars, Columbia Cellars, Chateau Ste Michelle, Kiona* (Washington).

SAUVIGNON BLANC/FUMÉ BLANC (white) Generally riper and broader than the New Zealand or Loire prototypes, and often oaked, usually to excess. Try *Beringer, Cakebread Cellars, Chalk Hill, Chateau Potelle, Chateau St Jean, Dry Creek Vineyards Reserve, Ferrari-Carano,*

Geyser Peak, Hanna, Kunde, Markham, Robert Mondavi, Murphy-Goode, Renaissance, Sanford, Simi, Stag's Leap, Sterling, Voss, William Wheeler (California); *Hargrave* (NY); *Arbor Crest, Columbia* (Washington).

SEMILLON (white) Usually added to Sauvignon Blanc for complexity (try *Carmenet, Clos du Val, St Supéry* and *Vichon* in California). For stand-alone Semillon try *Alderbrook, Ahlgren* (California); *Chateau Ste Michelle* (Washington).

SYRAH/RHÔNE VARIETIES (red) There has been an explosion of interest in these. Most eyes are on Syrah, but there is also Mourvèdre, Cinsaut, Grenache and Carignan. Whites include Viognier and Marsanne. The best are from California: *Bonny Doon, Cline, Duxoup, Fetzer, Kendall-*

Jackson, Jade Mountain, Jensen, La Jota, McDowell Valley, Joseph Phelps Mistral series, *RH Phillips, Il Podere dell' Olivos, Preston Vineyards, Qupé, Santino, Zaca Mesa.* In Washington: *Columbia, Columbia Crest.*

ZINFANDEL (red) This comes in 'white' (i.e. pink and sweetish), but the best are all red and share ripe, red-berries fruit. Big Zins include: *Chateau Potelle, Cline Cellars, Deer Park, Peter Franus, Kendall-Jackson Ciapusci Vineyard, Kunde, La Jota, Martinelli, Murrieta's Well, Preston Vineyards, A Rafanelli, Ravenswood, Ridge Lytton Springs, Rosenblum, Shenandoah, Storybook Mountain, Joseph Swan.* Lighter ones: *Buehler, Buena Vista, Burgess, Clos du Val, Fetzer, Haywood, Howell Mountain, Kendall-Jackson Kenwood, Mariah Vineyard, Louis M Martini, Nalle, Quivira, Renaissance.*

WINE REGIONS

CARNEROS (California; red, white) One of California's top spots for Pinot Noir and Chardonnay. It crosses the southern end of Napa and Sonoma. Look for *Acacia, Buena Vista, Carneros Creek, Domaine Carneros, Saintsbury.*

CENTRAL VALLEY (California; red, white) Huge and hot. This is where much of California's everyday jug wine comes from, and it's usually drinkable. Chardonnay, especially, is much improved.

LAKE COUNTY (California; red, white) Good Cabernet Sauvignon and Sauvignon Blanc territory. *Guenoc, Konocti* and *Louis M Martini* have vines here.

LIVERMORE VALLEY (California; red, white) Currently reviving. Stars include *Bonny Doon, Concannon, Wente.*

MENDOCINO COUNTY (California; red, white) The cool Anderson Valley is becoming a sparkling wine star, led by *Roederer Estate,* the US offshoot of

Champagne Roederer, and *Handley Cellars.* Elegant Riesling, Gewürztraminer, Pinot Noir and Chardonnay comes from here, too. Some Cabernet Sauvignon is good.

MISSOURI (red, white) Grows both standard vinifera grapes and a range of French hybrids like Vidal, as well as native American grapes like Cynthiana/Norton. *Stone Hill Winery's* Norton red is pretty good; there are also some suitably pleasing Rieslings from *Mount Pleasant Vineyard.*

MONTEREY COUNTY (California; red, white) The North is top Pinot Noir country (*Calera, Chalone*) and Carmel Valley is giving nice Cabernets. *Jekel* makes excellent Chardonnay and Riesling in Arroyo Seco.

NAPA COUNTY (California; red, white) This is California's classic wine country. Napa's strong suit is red – Cabernet Sauvignon and Merlot – with Pinot Noir in Carneros. Star producers are too many to list, but include *Beaulieu, Beringer, Clos du Val, Diamond Creek, Dominus, Heitz,*

Mondavi, Newton, Opus One, Phelps, Spottswoode, Stag's Leap.

NEW MEXICO (red, white) Good producers here are *Anderson Valley*, especially for Chardonnay, and a fizz from *Devalmont Vineyards* under the Gruet label.

NEW YORK STATE (red, white) Long Island Chardonnays are very different from those of California, with more austere flavours, a bit like ripe Chablis. There's also decent Chardonnay and good Riesling coming from the Finger Lakes and the Hudson River Valley areas. Try *Bedell Cellars, Bridgehampton, Brotherhood, Hargrave, Lenz, Pindar* and *Wagner.*

OREGON (red, white) Most famous for Pinot Noir, which is patchy but excellent at its best. Next comes Pinot Gris, which can often be charming. Riesling can also be quite good, although it is a little short on that floral intensity one looks for in a great Riesling. For Pinot Gris, try *Elk Cove, Erath, Eyrie* or *Ponzi.* Oak Knoll has the best Riesling. For Pinot Noir, go for *Adelsheim, Amity, Archery Summit, Broadley, Drouhin, Erath, Eyrie, Scott Henry, King Estate, Panther Creek, Rex Hill, Sokol Blosser, Ken Wright.*

SAN LUIS OBISPO COUNTY (California; red, white) Has some good sites for Pinot Noir and Chardonnay, and there are a few surprising old Zinfandel vineyards. Edna Valley is the chief sub-region with a

deserved reputation for Chardonnay. *Maison Deutz* makes good fizz.

SANTA BARBARA COUNTY (California; red, white) Some outstanding Pinot Noirs from the Santa Maria and Santa Ynez valleys, plus some good Sauvignon and Merlot. Best names: *Au Bon Climat, Firestone, Qupé, Sanford, Zaca Mesa.*

SANTA CRUZ MOUNTAINS (California; red, white) Pinot Noir here is promising, but still patchy. *David Bruce* and *Santa Cruz Mountain Winery* have had various degrees of success. *Mount Eden* and *Ridge Vineyards* are good for Cabernet.

SIERRA FOOTHILLS (California; red, white) California's gold country was one its busiest wine zones until Prohibition, but only a few Zinfandel vineyards survived. These are the basis of the area's reputation, plus good Sauvignon Blanc and Barbera. Best are *Amador Foothill Winery, Boeger Winery, Monteviña, Renaissance* (stunning Riesling), *Santino* and *Shenandoah Vineyards.*

SONOMA COUNTY (California; red, white) Sonoma Valley is the main sub-region, but there are many others, in particular Alexander Valley, Chalk Hill, Dry Creek, Knight's Valley, and the Russian River Valley (including its sub-region Green Valley). Cabernet Sauvignon is the star grape, and it and Chardonnay are usually a little fruitier and softer than they are in

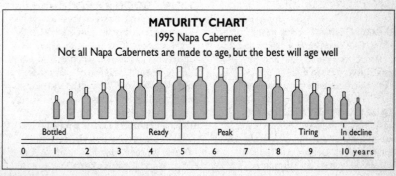

MATURITY CHART
1995 Napa Cabernet
Not all Napa Cabernets are made to age, but the best will age well

Bottled		Ready		Peak			Tiring	In decline

0	1	2	3	4	5	6	7	8	9	10 years

Napa. There's also some first rate Pinot Noir emerging from the lower Russian River Valley. Look for *Carmenet, Chateau St Jean, Dehlinger, De Loach, Iron Horse, Jordan, Kistler, Simi, Sonoma-Cutrer, Williams-Selyem*.

TEXAS (red, white) Texas wines continue to surprise. Cabernet Sauvignons from Texas have a drink-me-now rich fruitiness and the Chardonnays and Sauvignon Blancs are looking better every year. In short, it's goodbye Chateau Redneck. The best

producers currently are: *Fall Creek, Llano Estacado, Messina Hof, Oberhellmann* and *Pheasant Ridge*.

VIRGINIA (red, white) Growing good wine grapes in Virginia's hot, humid climate is a man-over-nature drama. Besides the heat and the humidity, there is the occasional hurricane. Nevertheless, there are some good Rieslings and Chardonnays. Top producers are *Chateau Morrisette, Ingleside Plantation* and *Prince Michel*.

WASHINGTON STATE (red, white) Intense, clear fruit is the hallmark here for Cabernet, Merlot, Sauvignon Blanc, Semillon, Riesling and Chardonnay, and quality is improving year by year. Good names include *Arbor Crest, Chaleur, Chateau Ste Michelle, Columbia, Columbia Crest, Hogue Cellars, Staton Hills, Leonetti, Paul Thomas, Woodward Canyon*.

PRODUCERS WHO'S WHO

ACACIA ★★★(★) (Carneros/Napa) Attractive Pinot Noir and Chardonnay. Reserve wines go heavy on the oak.

ADLER FELS ★★(★) (Sonoma) A quirky winery, taking chances that sometimes miss. Top Gewürztraminer and an unusual Riesling sparkler.

ARROWOOD ★★★★ (Sonoma) Superb Cabernet Sauvignon and Merlot, providing you like oak.

AU BON CLIMAT ★★★★(★) (Santa Barbara) Fine Pinot Noir with intense black cherry fruit. Chardonnay can also be impressive. The Podere dell' Olivos label is for quirky, characterful Italian varietals.

BEAULIEU VINEYARDS ★★★ (Napa) Top-of-the-line George de Latour Private Reserve Cabernet Sauvignon is still marvellous. Also lean, supple Carneros Chardonnay, and cheaper Beautour Cab.

BERINGER ★★★★(★) (Napa) Reserve Cabernets are top of the line. Sbragia Chardonnay (named after the winemaker) is rich and loaded with buttery oak. The second label, Napa Ridge, is good value.

BETHEL HEIGHTS ★★★(★) (Oregon) Impressive, intense Pinot Noirs. The Reserves can be among Oregon's finest and most concentrated.

BONNY DOON ★★★(★) (Santa Cruz) One of California's most innovative winemakers, Grenache (Le Cigare Volant) and Mourvèdre (Old Telegram, a pun on Châteauneuf's Vieux Télégraphe, if you hadn't guessed) and a line of Italian styles called Ca' Del Solo. New ideas and new wines appear every year.

BRIDGEHAMPTON ★★★(★) (New York) First-class Chardonnay from Long Island as well as a fresh, light quaffable Pinot Noir and a fruity, forward Merlot.

BUENA VISTA ★★★(★) (Sonoma/Carneros) Balanced, understated Merlot, Pinot Noir and Cabernet Sauvignon. Reserve wines have great intensity and depth. Very good Lake County Sauvignon Blanc.

CAIN CELLARS ★★★★(★) (Napa) Superb Cain Five Bordeaux blend red, and excellent across the board.

CALERA ★★★★(★) (San Benito) Possibly the best Pinot Noir in California. Rich and intense; Jensen Vineyard is tops. Also fine Viognier and Chardonnay.

CAYMUS ★★★★ (Napa) Benchmark California Cabernet which shows no sign of faltering. Special Selection is the top wine. Liberty School is the second label.

CHALONE ★★★★(★) (Monterey) Individualistic, ageworthy Pinot Noir and harmonious Chardonnay. Also some nice Pinot Blanc and Chenin Blanc.

CHATEAU MONTELENA ★★★★(★) (Napa) Chardonnay and Cabernet that both need time and repay the wait.

CHATEAU POTELLE ★★★(★) (Napa) Very good Sauvignon Blanc and Cabernet, outstanding Zinfandel.

CHATEAU ST JEAN ★★★(★) (Sonoma) Rich Chardonnay, outstanding Cabernet and Merlot, and justly famous botrytized Rieslings.

CHATEAU STE MICHELLE ★★★(★) (Washington) Consistently good with Cabernet Sauvignon and Merlot being the real strengths; pretty good bubbly.

CHIMNEY ROCK ★★★(★) (Napa) Powerful yet elegant Cabernet Sauvignon and Bordeaux blend called Elevage with deep, rich and complex fruit.

CLOS DU BOIS ★★★(★) (Sonoma) Consistently good Merlots, Chardonnays and a Bordeaux-style blend called Marlstone.

CLOS DU VAL ★★★(★) (Napa) Elegant, ageworthy, well-balanced reds. Best are Cabernet and Zinfandel.

COLUMBIA ★★★★ (Washington) Reds are excellent: Syrah, soft, peppery Pinot Noir, seductive Merlot (Red Willow vineyard), and ripe Cabernet (Otis vineyard). Very good whites include Semillon, Gewürztraminer.

COLUMBIA CREST ★★★(★) (Washington) Highly drinkable wines, not expensive: Cabernet, Merlot, Chardonnay.

CUVAISON ★★★ (Napa) Delicious Merlot, Pinot Noir and Cabernet: elegant, understated, with unexpected complexity.

DEHLINGER ★★★★ (Sonoma) One of the best Pinots in North America; also good Cabernets including a good value Young Vine Cabernet.

DOMAINE CARNEROS ★★★(★) (Napa) This Taittinger-owned sparkling wine house makes remarkable vintage Brut and silky, powerful Blanc de Blancs.

DOMAINE CHANDON ★★★ (Napa) Owned by Champagne house Moët & Chandon, and making consistently good non-vintage bubblies, plus rich and creamy Reserve and Carneros Blanc de Blancs.

DOMAINE MUMM ★★★★ (Napa) Outstanding fizz, better than that made by the parent company in Champagne. Look for the Brut and impressive Blanc de Noirs.

DROUHIN ★★★★ (Oregon) The Pinot Noir we were all waiting for Oregon to make, from a Burgundian-owned company. There's a little Chardonnay, too.

DUCKHORN ★★★(★) (Napa) Intensely flavoured, deep and rich Three Palms Vineyard Merlot, and a weighty Cabernet.

ELK COVE VINEYARDS ★★★(★) (Oregon) One of Oregon's best Pinot Noirs, and very good Pinot Gris.

EYRIE ★★★ (Oregon) David Lett is Oregon's Pinot pioneer, and still makes some of the best: supple, flavoursome and characterful.

FLORA SPRINGS ★★★(★) (Napa) Excellent Chardonnay and a fair Bordeaux blend called Trilogy. Soliloquy is a creamy, rich, floral white that belies its Sauvignon Blanc base.

FRANCISCAN ★★★★ (Napa) The estate-bottled Chardonnays, especially the Cuvée Sauvage, are outstanding. Sleek Quintessa Bordeaux blend.

GRGICH HILLS★★★★ (Sonoma) Look for ageworthy Cabernet and rich Zinfandel.

HANDLEY CELLARS ★★★★ (Mendocino) Excellent fizz, especially Brut and rosé. Very good Chardonnay and Sauvignon, promising Pinot Noir.

HEITZ ★★★ (Napa) Martha's Vineyard Cabernet is a California blue chip, dark, uncompromising and expensive.

HESS COLLECTION ★★★★ (Napa) Chardonnay and Cabernet with balance and finesse.

IRON HORSE ★★★★ (Sonoma) Terrific racy, incisive fizz, very good Pinot Noir and Chardonnay. Cabernet is also well worth trying.

JORDAN ★★★★(★) (Sonoma) The rich, ripe Cabernet Sauvignon ages well, and there's a classic, biscuity fizz called 'J'.

KENDALL-JACKSON ★★★ (Lake) Makes massive amounts of smooth, rich, off-dry Chardonnay.

KENWOOD ★★★(★) (Sonoma) Consistent quality. Jack London and Artist Series Cabernets are outstanding, as is the Zinfandel and Sauvignon Blanc.

KUNDE ESTATE WINERY ★★★ (Sonoma) The powerful, buttery Reserve Chardonnay and the Sauvignon Blanc are the best; also rich old vine Zinfandel.

LAMOREAUX LANDING ★★★ (New York) Chardonnay is rather good; the Pinot Noir improves with each vintage.

LAUREL GLEN ★★★★ (Sonoma) Intense, black cherry Cabernet Sauvignon is the only wine here, very good at its best.

LENZ VINEYARDS ★★★ (New York) Merlot is elegant and quite powerful wine, and dry Gewürztraminer is tasty.

LOUIS MARTINI ★★★ (Napa) Quality is somewhat patchy these days. Highlights are Monte Rosso Cabernet, and Zinfandel, Chardonnay and Carneros Pinot Noir.

MAYACAMAS ★★★ (Napa) Firm Cabernet and rich Chardonnay are the stars here; there's some Pinot Noir as well.

ROBERT MONDAVI ★★★★(★) (Napa) Superb straight and Reserve Cabernets; Opus One reds seem to lack the Reserve's intensity. Improving Carneros Pinot Noir. Newest is a line of French wines under the Vichon Mediterranean label.

NEWTON ★★★★ (Napa) Excellent, unfiltered Chardonnay; cedary, cinnamon-spiced Cabernet and succulent Merlot.

PECONIC BAY VINEYARDS ★★★ (New York) Light, unoaked Chardonnay and a barrel-fermented Reserve.

PHELPS ★★★(★) (Napa) Best here is the Insignia Bordeaux blend. Mistral label is for interesting Rhône varieties.

RAVENSWOOD ★★★★ (Sonoma) Zinfandel is the only grape here. Dickerson Vineyard, Old Hill and Old Vines have ripe, concentrated fruit that is bold and stylish.

RIDGE ★★★★(★) (Santa Clara) Benchmark Zinfandel, probably California's best. The Monte Bello Cabernets are also remarkable, with great balance and long-lasting, perfumed fruit. Petite Sirah from York Creek is brilliant.

ROEDERER ESTATE ★★★★ (Mendocino County) Excellent Champagne-style sparklers from a company owned by Roederer Champagne. Brut and rosé are both very good, top of the range l'Ermitage rich and concentrated.

SAINTSBURY ★★★★ (Napa) Stylish, supple, elegant Pinot Noir and Chardonnay. Lovely Garnet, from young Pinot Noir vines.

SANFORD WINERY ★★★(★) (Santa Barbara) At its best, Sanford Pinot Noir can be a real treat, with spicy, lush, intense fruit. Good Sauvignon and Chardonnay.

SCHRAMSBERG ★★★★ (Napa) Big, lush fizz. Reserve Brut is best, often world class. Blanc de Noirs is big and bold.

SHAFER ★★★★ (Napa) Very good, very long-lived Cabernet Sauvignon and Merlot.

SIMI ★★★(★) (Sonoma) Rich, sometimes voluptuous, always reliable Chardonnay, concentrated Cabernets. Reserves are excellent, as is Sauvignon Blanc.

SONOMA-CUTRER ★★★★ (Sonoma) Out-and-out Chardonnay specialist. Les Pierres is made to age. Russian River Ranches is more forward, Cutrer is rich, archetypal California.

INSTANT CELLAR: US ZINFANDEL

• **1997 Clos du Val, Stags Leap District, £12.80, Averys** This is Zinfandel made in a Bordeaux style, if you can imagine that.
• **1996 Geyserville, Ridge, £18.90, Bennetts** I couldn't have a list of Zins without Ridge. It's simply the best: rich, spicy and very, very long.
• **1994 Ravenswood, £12.50 Croque-en-Bouche** Brambly fruit with good depth.
• **1995 Topolos, £8.99** Topolos does single vineyard Zins as well, but they're pricier. All are organic, and they're big, muscular wines.
• **1996 Nalle, £14.98, Domaine Direct** Concentrated, firm, blackberry flavours.
• **1995 Sebastiani Old Vines, Sonoma, £8.49, Bottoms Up, Thresher, Wine Rack, Victoria Wine** Old Vines should mean greater depth, and here it does.
• **1996 Mother Clone, Pedroncelli, £10.45, Lay & Wheeler** Sonoma Zin full of chocolate and blackberry fruit.
• **1995 Rocking Horse Howell Mountain, Napa, £13.99, Oddbins** Elegance and structure.

STAG'S LEAP WINE CELLARS ★★★★ (Napa) After a few years unaccountably adrift, the estate-bottled Cabernet Sauvignon is focused and back on track, especially the Cask 23 and the SLV Vineyard. Elegant Chardonnay, too.

STATON HILLS VINEYARD ★★★(★) (Washington) Silky Bordeaux-style Merlot; Cabernet with staying power.

STEELE WINES ★★★(★) (Lake County) Expensive, vivid Chardonnays. Shooting Star is a second, budget label.

ROD STRONG VINEYARDS ★★★(★) (Sonoma) Fine single-vineyard Cabernet Sauvignon, Pinot Noir, Chardonnay.

ZD WINES ★★★ (Napa) Excellent Cabernet Sauvignon, Pinot Noir and Chardonnay with lovely intensity and depth.

UNITED STATES PRICES

CALIFORNIA RED

Under £5.00

Cabernet Sauvignon E&J Gallo 1998 £4.99 (ASD)

Cabernet Sauvignon E&J Gallo 1997 £4.99 (MORR)

Cabernet Sauvignon E&J Gallo 1995 £4.99 (SAF)

Cabernet Sauvignon Sutter Home 1995 £4.99 (MORR) £5.29 (UN)

Californian Red Paul Masson **Non-vintage** £3.99 (ASD)

Dry Reserve E&J Gallo **Non-vintage** £4.49 (THR) £4.49 (WR) £4.49 (BOT)

Zinfandel E&J Gallo 1995 £4.49 (UN)

Zinfandel Sutter Home 1996 £4.91 (STE) £4.99 (MORR) £5.09 (JON) £5.45 (NA)

£5.00 → £5.99

★ Black Muscat Quady Elysium ½ bottle 1997 £5.99 (AV) £6.49 (MAJ) £6.50 (WS) £6.79 (JON) £6.95 (STA) £7.24 (PLAY) £7.99 (PHI)

Black Muscat Quady Elysium ½ bottle 1996 £5.98 (PEN) £6.39 (YOU) £6.99 (UN)

Cabernet Sauvignon Fetzer Bel Arbors 1994 £5.95 (JU)

Cabernet Sauvignon Glen Ellen 1996 £5.49 (SAF)

Cabernet Sauvignon Robert Mondavi Woodbridge 1993 £5.25 (NI)

Cabernet Sauvignon Pedroncelli 1994 £5.99 (DI)

Cabernet Sauvignon Sutter Home 1996 £5.09 (JON)

Pinot Noir Redwood Trail 1997 £5.90 (CRO) £5.99 (CO)

Pinot Noir Redwood Trail 1996 £5.49 (THR) £5.49 (WR) £5.99 (OD) £5.99 (SAF)

£6.00 → £7.99

Altaire Simi 1993 £7.99 (BAL) £9.30 (UB)

Barbera Monteviña 1994 £6.40 (CRO) £7.99 (VA) £8.17 (PLA)

Big House Red Ca' del Solo, Bonny Doon 1997 £7.99 (YOU) £8.20 (TAN) £8.40 (BEN)

Big House Red Ca' del Solo, Bonny Doon 1996 £7.85 (RAE) £8.23 (REI) £8.40 (MV) £8.64 (GW) £8.99 (UB) £8.99 (VA)

Big House Red Ca' del Solo, Bonny Doon 1995 £6.75 (SOM) £6.99 (NI) £7.99 (CON)

Black Muscat Quady Elysium ½ bottle 1995 £6.75 (CON) £6.95 (LEA)

Cabernet Sauvignon Fetzer Valley Oaks 1995 £6.99 (CO) £6.99 (VIC) £6.99 (THR) £6.99 (WR) £6.99 (BOT) £7.99 (JON)

Cabernet Sauvignon Robert Mondavi Woodbridge 1994 £6.50 (CRO) £7.05 (ROS) £8.39 (JON)

Cabernet Sauvignon Seven Peaks 1996 £7.35 (BAN) £12.99 (VA)

Côtes d'Oakley Cline Cellars 1996 £6.99 (GW) £6.99 (YOU) £7.60 (WT)

Grenache Bonny Doon Clos de Gilroy 1995 £7.99 (NI)

Pinot Noir Beaulieu Vineyard 1997 £7.99 (POR)

Pinot Noir Saintsbury ½ bottle 1996 £7.75 (FORT) £8.38 (PLAY)

Zinfandel Beringer 1996 £6.49 (NEZ)

Zinfandel Cline Cellars 1996 £7.99 (POR) £8.53 (GW) £12.25 (FORT)

Zinfandel Fetzer 1996 £6.25 (SOM) £6.49 (OD) £6.49 (SAF)

Zinfandel Fetzer 1995 £6.49 (VIC) £6.49 (THR) £6.49 (WR) £6.49 (BOT) £7.65 (JU)

Zinfandel Robert Mondavi Woodbridge 1996 £6.99 (THR) £6.99 (WR) £6.99 (BOT) £7.74 (STE) £7.85 (WRI) £8.60 (NA)

Zinfandel Robert Mondavi Woodbridge 1995 £6.20 (ROS)

MERCHANTS SPECIALIZING IN UNITED STATES
see Merchant Directory (page 413) for details

Adnams (AD), Averys (AV), Bennetts (BEN), Berry Bros (BER), Bibendum (BIB), Cave Cru Classé (CAV), Croque-en-Bouche (CRO), Lay & Wheeler (LAY), Majestic (MAJ), Morris & Verdin (MV), Oddbins (OD), James Nicholson (NI), Nobody Inn (NO), Reid (REI), Savage Selection (SAV), T&W Wines (TW), The Ubiquitous Chip (UB), Wine Treasury (WT).

Zinfandel Pedroncelli **1995** £7.79 (YOU)
£8.95 (RES)
Zinfandel Ravenswood North Coast
Vintners Blend **1996** £7.95 (WS) £11.99
(VA)

£8.00 → £9.99

Barbera Ca' del Solo **1995** £8.50 (CRO)
Barbera Monteviña **1995** £8.55 (PIP)
Black Muscat Quady Elysium ½ bottle
Non-vintage £8.25 (FORT)
Cabernet Durney Cachagua **1993** £8.95
(BU)
Cabernet Sauvignon Beaulieu Rutherford
1994 £9.25 (COC)
Cabernet Sauvignon Beringer **1996** £8.99
(NEZ) £11.99 (MAJ)
Cabernet Sauvignon Fetzer Bonterra
1996 £8.99 (TES) £8.99 (SAI)
Cabernet Sauvignon Hawk Crest **1997**
£8.21 (DOM)
Cabernet Sauvignon Kendall-Jackson
Vintner's Reserve **1994** £9.99 (DI)
Cabernet Sauvignon Laurel Glen Terra
Rosa **1995** £9.69 (REI) £13.41 (NO)
Cabernet Sauvignon Robert Mondavi
Woodbridge **1996** £8.06 (STE) £8.95 (NA)
Cardinal Zin Bonny Doon **1996** £8.99 (OD)
Merlot Pine Ridge **1986** £9.69 (REI)
Petite Sirah Foppiano Reserve **1995**
£9.93 (WT)
Pinot Noir Saintsbury Garnet **1997** £8.20
(SOM) £9.99 (CON)
Pinot Noir Saintsbury Garnet **1995** £9.50
(CRO) £9.95 (JU) £10.25 (BEN)
Sangiovese Rabbit Ridge **1995** £9.66 (NO)
Starboard Batch 88 Quady **Non-vintage**
£9.50 (STA)
Starboard Batch 88 Quady **1988** £8.12 (NO)
Zinfandel Dry Creek **1996** £9.99 (DI)
Zinfandel Kendall-Jackson Vintner's
Reserve **1996** £9.62 (NO)
Zinfandel Mount Eden **1996** £8.49 (YOU)
£8.99 (LIB)
★ Zinfandel Peachy Canyon Incredible Red
£9.95 (BER)
Zinfandel Ravenswood **1996** £9.99 (OD)
£23.35 (NO)

£10.00 → £11.99

Barbera Louis Martini **1993** £11.16 (WT)
Cabernet Sauvignon Fetzer Barrel Select
1994 £11.49 (JON)
Cabernet Sauvignon Firestone **1996**
£11.95 (PIP)

Cabernet Sauvignon Rutherford Hill **1994**
£11.00 (AV) £11.90 (UB)
Cabernet Sauvignon St-Supéry **1994**
£10.49 (WR) £10.49 (BOT)
Cotes du Soleil Jade Mountain **1996**
£10.99 (NI) £12.50 (BEN) £12.63 (PLA)
£13.00 (MV)
Mataro Ridge Bridgehead **1995** £11.99 (NI)
£12.94 (NO) £13.25 (FORT) £14.95 (LEA)
Mourvèdre Cline Cellars **1990** £10.95
(ROB)
Pinot Noir La Crema **1997** £11.95 (DI)
Pinot Noir Saintsbury **1996** £11.25 (SOM)
£13.30 (TAN) £13.49 (YOU) £13.50 (CON)
£13.50 (WS) £13.99 (WR) £14.95 (FORT)
Sangiovese Noceto **1996** £10.99 (YOU)
Syrah Qupé Bien Nacido Reserve **1995**
£11.63 (PLA)
★ Zinfandel Boeger **1995** £10.99 (GW)
Zinfandel Louis Martini **1993** £11.16 (WT)
Zinfandel Rochioli Sodini **1995** £11.95
(NI) £13.99 (YOU)

£12.00 → £13.99

Barbera Ca' del Solo **1996** £12.00 (BEN)
£12.21 (PLA) £12.99 (VA) £13.09 (NO)
Cabernet Carmenet Dynamite **1997**
£12.34 (BIB)
Cabernet Sauvignon Beringer **1994**
£13.95 (RES)
Cabernet Sauvignon Chalk Hill **1993**
£12.95 (JU)
Cabernet Sauvignon Matanzas Creek
1994 £13.75 (BEN)
Cabernet Sauvignon Robert Mondavi
1988 £13.80 (NI)
Cabernet Sauvignon Mount Eden **1992**
£12.95 (RAE)
Cabernet Sauvignon Renaissance **1993**
£12.95 (BU)
Cabernet Sauvignon Ridge Santa Cruz
Mountain **1995** £13.95 (NI) £16.49 (YOU)
£16.50 (BU) £17.49 (LAY) £17.50 (FORT)
£17.50 (MV) £17.95 (RES) £21.76 (NO)
Cabernet Sauvignon Simi **1995** £12.49
(YOU) £17.50 (FORT) £18.95 (RES)
Geyserville Ridge **1995** £13.95 (NI)
£16.61 (NO) £17.20 (PIP) £17.95 (ROB)

*Stars (★) indicate wines
selected by Oz Clarke in the
Best Buys section which begins
on page 9.*

Il Fiasco Ca' del Solo 1996 £12.21 (PLA)
La Provençale Jade Mountain 1996
£12.99 (NI) £14.49 (YOU) £14.95 (FORT)
£15.00 (MV) £15.50 (BEN)
Le Cigare Volant Bonny Doon 1992
£12.95 (RAE) £12.99 (NI)
Mataro Ridge 1996 £12.50 (SOM) £14.99
(YOU)
Merlot Clos du Bois 1995 £13.95 (WR)
Merlot Havens 1996 £13.51 (DOM)
Nebbiolo Il Podere dell'Olivos 1995
£13.00 (MV) £14.99 (VA)
Petite Sirah Ridge York Creek 1994
£12.94 (NO) £12.99 (NI) £13.51 (REI)
Pinot Noir Au Bon Climat 1997 £13.95
(BEN) £14.29 (YOU) £15.00 (MV)
Pinot Noir Byron 1995 £13.51 (PEN)
£16.99 (WR) £16.99 (BOT)
Pinot Noir Saintsbury 1997 £13.95 (FLE)
£15.30 (BEN) £15.95 (AD)
Sangiovese Atlas Peak 1994 £12.37 (HA)
Syrah Duxoup 1997 £12.93 (BIB)
Zinfandel Clos du Val 1995 £12.10 (AV)
£12.95 (STA)
Zinfandel Frog's Leap 1996 £13.89 (FLE)
£14.00 (MV) £14.94 (LAY) £15.00 (UB)
Zinfandel Lytton Springs 1995 £13.99 (NI)
Zinfandel Ravenswood 1994 £12.30 (CRO)

£14.00 → £15.99

Cabernet Sauvignon Clos du Bois 1987
£14.50 (BU)
Cabernet Sauvignon Matanzas Creek
1995 £14.25 (BEN)
Cabernet Sauvignon Ridge Santa Cruz
Mountain 1996 £14.75 (SOM) £17.60
(TAN) £18.50 (MV) £18.99 (PHI) £19.15
(PIP) £19.50 (LEA) £19.58 (FLE)
Cabernet Sauvignon Ridge Santa Cruz
Mountain 1994 £15.49 (CON)
Cabernet Sauvignon Ridge Santa Cruz
Mountain 1993 £15.86 (REI) £17.50 (MV)
£19.09 (JER)
Cabernet Sauvignon St-Supéry 1995
£14.95 (LIB)
Cabernet Sauvignon Shafer Stags Leap
1992 £14.99 (YOU)
Cabernet Sauvignon Stag's Leap Wine
Cellars 1994 £15.99 (BEN) £16.99 (GW)
£19.95 (ROB)
Geyserville Ridge 1996 £14.75 (SOM)
£17.60 (TAN) £17.70 (FLE) £17.99 (YOU)
£18.50 (WS) £18.50 (ELL) £18.50 (MV)
£18.90 (BEN) £18.95 (STA) £18.99 (PHI)
£19.39 (DOM) £19.50 (LEA) £19.95 (RES)

La Provençale Jade Mountain 1995
£14.86 (REI) £15.43 (GW) £17.94 (NO)
Le Cigare Volant Bonny Doon 1995
£14.95 (RAE) £14.99 (GW) £17.00 (PLA)
£17.04 (REI) £18.95 (ROB)
Le Mistral Joseph Phelps 1995 £14.29
(YOU) £15.56 (WT) £16.95 (RES)
Mataro Ridge Bridgehead 1996 £14.50 (BU)
£14.95 (RES) £15.40 (TAN) £15.50 (MV)
£15.95 (PHI) £16.10 (BEN) £16.50 (WS)
Mourvèdre Jade Mountain 1990 £15.50
(CRO)

Petite Sirah Ridge York Creek 1996
£14.95 (PHI) £15.00 (CON) £15.95 (BEN)
Petite Sirah Ridge York Creek 1995
£14.95 (RES) £15.50 (TAN) £15.50 (BU)
£15.99 (YOU) £16.50 (WS) £16.50 (LEA)
Pinot Noir Au Bon Climat 1996 £15.35 (BU)
£15.57 (REI) £15.75 (FORT) £16.95 (RES)
Pinot Noir Clos du Val 1995 £14.95 (AV)
Pinot Noir Robert Mondavi 1996 £15.80
(STE) £17.55 (NA)
Pinot Noir Robert Mondavi 1994 £15.86
(REI) £19.99 (SAI)
Pinot Noir Saintsbury 1991 £14.50 (CRO)
Zinfandel Nalle 1996 £14.98 (DOM)

£16.00 → £17.99

Cabernet Sauvignon Clos du Val 1994
£16.95 (AV)
Cabernet Sauvignon Frog's Leap 1994
£16.50 (CON)
Cabernet Sauvignon La Jota 1987 £16.95
(RAE)
Cabernet Sauvignon Robert Mondavi
1995 £16.50 (WS) £18.75 (WRI)
Cabernet Sauvignon Sequoia Grove 1995
£16.75 (WT)
Cabernet Sauvignon Shafer Stags Leap
1993 £17.88 (WT)
Cabernet Sauvignon Simi 1985 £16.00
(CRO)
Cabernet Sauvignon Stag's Leap Wine
Cellars 1996 £17.63 (DOM)
Le Cigare Volant Bonny Doon 1996
£16.99 (YOU) £17.00 (MV) £17.03 (GW)

Mataro Ridge Bridgehead 1997 £16.95 (VA)
Merlot Frog's Leap 1994 £17.84 (NO)
£18.00 (CON)
Merlot Shafer 1995 £17.95 (AD) £20.79
(YOU) £22.34 (WT)
Mourvèdre Jade Mountain 1995 £16.99
(YOU) £17.20 (TAN) £17.57 (GW) £18.04
(REI) £21.26 (NO)
Pinot Noir Monticello Corley Family
Vineyards 1996 £17.49 (LAY)
Pinot Noir Marimar Torres Estate Don
Miguel 1995 £16.95 (POR)
Syrah Cambria Tepesquet Vineyard 1994
£16.97 (WT) £18.95 (ROB)
Zinfandel Cline Cellars Bridgehead 1995
£16.59 (YOU) £18.20 (WT)
Zinfandel Frog's Leap 1993 £16.00 (CRO)
Zinfandel Ridge Lytton Springs 1996
£16.25 (BU) £17.50 (FORT) £17.60 (TAN)
£17.95 (CON) £17.95 (RES) £17.99 (YOU)
£18.50 (MV) £19.50 (LEA)
Zinfandel Ridge Lytton Springs 1995
£16.61 (NO) £16.85 (PIP) £17.95 (ROB)
Zinfandel Joseph Swan Frati Ranch 1995
£17.99 (RAE) £22.90 (GAU)
Zinfandel Topolos Rossi Ranch 1993
£16.95 (DI)

£18.00 → £19.99

Cabernet Sauvignon Beaulieu Vineyard
Georges de Latour Private Reserve
1989 £19.95 (JU)
Cabernet Sauvignon Frog's Leap 1996
£19.70 (LAY)
Cabernet Sauvignon Shafer 1994 £19.25
(FORT) £19.92 (REI) £20.95 (RES)
Cabernet Sauvignon Stag's Leap Wine
Cellars 1995 £18.21 (REI) £18.53 (GW)
£19.21 (WT) £20.95 (RES)
Cabernet Sauvignon Stag's Leap Wine
Cellars 1985 £19.00 (CRO)
Firebreak Shafer 1995 £19.59 (YOU)
£22.03 (REI) £22.19 (WT)
Merlot Clos du Val 1995 £19.80 (AV)
Merlot Frog's Leap 1995 £18.25 (FORT)
£19.95 (RES)
Merlot Havens Reserve 1995 £18.21 (DOM)
Mourvèdre Jade Mountain 1996 £18.00
(MV) £18.02 (GW) £18.20 (BEN)
Old Telegram Bonny Doon 1995 £19.99
(RAE)
Pinot Noir Robert Mondavi Reserve
1994 £19.40 (NI)
Syrah Alban Vineyards Reva 1996 £19.77
(WT)

Syrah Jade Mountain 1995 £18.95 (BU)
£19.30 (BEN) £19.50 (FORT) £19.95 (RES)
Syrah Qupé Bien Nacido Reserve 1996
£18.00 (MV) £19.60 (TAN)
Zinfandel Murrieta's Well 1994 £19.60
(PEN)

£20.00 → £29.99

Cabernet Sauvignon Carmenet Moon
Mountain Estate 1995 £24.00 (WS)
Cabernet Sauvignon Clos du Val 1979
£20.00 (CRO)
Cabernet Sauvignon Conn Creek 1977
£20.00 (BU)
Cabernet Sauvignon Cuvaison 1984
£22.00 (CRO)
Cabernet Sauvignon Grgich Hills 1994
£24.95 (RES)
Cabernet Sauvignon Kenwood Jack
London 1994 £27.30 (UB)
Cabernet Sauvignon Laurel Glen 1994
£22.50 (NI) £35.91 (NO)
Cabernet Sauvignon Peter Michael Les
Pavots 1989 £27.95 (RES)
Cabernet Sauvignon Robert Mondavi
Oakville 1995 £21.99 (WR) £21.99
(BOT)
Cabernet Sauvignon Robert Mondavi
Oakville 1992 £21.97 (PEN)
Cabernet Sauvignon Ravenswood 1994
£22.21 (NO)
Cabernet Sauvignon Shafer Stags Leap
1994 £20.33 (WT)
Cabernet Sauvignon Simi Reserve 1994
£28.00 (PEN) £33.00 (FORT)
Cabernet Sauvignon Viader 1996 £23.50
(DOM)
Counterpoint Laurel Glen 1994 £20.14
(NO)
Merlot Cuvaison 1995 £21.95 (TAN)
Merlot Duckhorn 1995 £25.75 (FORT)
£26.95 (RES)
Merlot Matanzas Creek 1995 £29.95
(BEN) £29.96 (REI)
Merlot Ridge Santa Cruz 1996 £28.50
(BEN) £29.95 (VA)

Please remember that
Oz Clarke's Wine Guide
*is a price **guide** and not a*
price list. It is not meant to
replace up-to-date
merchants' lists.

Merlot Ridge Santa Cruz **1995** £22.50
(NI) £25.50 (BU) £27.18 (NO) £27.50
(FORT) £28.00 (MV) £29.50 (RES) £29.50
(LEA)

Merlot Ridge Santa Cruz **1994** £27.80 (PIP)

Merlot Shafer **1996** £25.02 (WT)

Old Telegram Bonny Doon **1993** £22.00
(NO)

Pinot Noir Calera Jensen **1995** £27.20
(PIP) £30.50 (BEN) £34.10 (NO)

Pinot Noir Calera Jensen **1994** £24.50
(DI) £34.66 (REI)

Pinot Noir Clos du Val **1984** £20.00 (BU)

Pinot Noir Robert Mondavi Reserve
1996 £23.99 (MAJ)

Pinot Noir Robert Mondavi Reserve
1995 £22.99 (WR) £22.99 (BOT)

Pinot Noir Robert Mondavi Reserve
1993 £25.50 (WRI) £25.95 (BEN)

Pinot Noir Saintsbury Reserve **1996**
£24.95 (BEN) £26.50 (AD)

Pinot Noir Saintsbury Reserve **1995**
£22.50 (CON) £23.20 (BEN) £23.44 (NO)

Rubicon Niebaum-Coppola **1986** £21.74
(REI) £22.00 (CRO)

Syrah Jade Mountain **1990** £28.00 (CRO)

Syrah Joseph Phelps **1995** £23.95 (WT)

Zinfandel Cline Cellars Bridgehead **1994**
£24.72 (NO)

Zinfandel Lytton Springs **1997** £20.95 (VA)

Zinfandel Ravenswood Wood Road **1993**
£24.75 (NO)

£30.00 → £39.99

Cabernet Sauvignon Freemark Abbey
Sycamore **1986** £31.67 (REI)

Cabernet Sauvignon Jekel Private Reserve
1978 £30.00 (CRO)

Cabernet Sauvignon Robert Mondavi
Reserve **1989** £32.50 (NI) £41.13 (REI)

Cabernet Sauvignon Silver Oak Alexander
Valley **1993** £32.31 (TW) £44.95 (RES)

Cabernet Sauvignon Stag's Leap Wine
Cellars Cask 23 **1979** £34.00 (CRO)

Merlot Matanzas Creek **1994** £30.00 (BU)
£33.95 (ROB)

Syrah Jade Mountain **1996** £32.00 (MV)

£40.00 → £49.99

Cabernet Sauvignon Beringer Private
Reserve **1993** £41.95 (ROB)

Cabernet Sauvignon Diamond Creek
Volcanic Hill **1992** £42.00 (CRO)

Cabernet Sauvignon Far Niente **1995**
£42.95 (TW)

Cabernet Sauvignon Robert Mondavi
Reserve **1978** £48.00 (CRO)

Cabernet Sauvignon Ridge Monte Bello
1995 £45.50 (NI)

Cabernet Sauvignon Silver Oak Alexander
Valley **1989** £47.00 (TW)

Dominus Christian Moueix **1994** £40.00
(JU) £68.54 (CB)

Dominus Christian Moueix **1992** £47.98
(CB) £83.62 (FA)

£50.00 → £59.99

Cabernet Sauvignon Diamond Creek
Volcanic Hill **1995** £52.95 (RES)

Cabernet Sauvignon Robert Mondavi
Reserve **1990** £50.00 (BU)

Cabernet Sauvignon Ridge Monte Bello
1994 £56.20 (FA) £61.80 (TAN) £65.00
(CON) £65.00 (MV) £65.90 (BEN) £69.00
(LEA) £69.95 (RES)

Cabernet Sauvignon Ridge Monte Bello
1993 £56.30 (ELL) £57.00 (BEN) £65.00
(ROB)

Cabernet Sauvignon Ridge Monte Bello
1989 £52.00 (AD)

£60.00 → £69.99

Cabernet Sauvignon Dunn Howell
Mountain **1994** £67.95 (FA)

Cabernet Sauvignon Heitz Martha's
Vineyard **1982** £61.00 (CRO)

Cabernet Sauvignon Shafer Hillside Select
1994 £69.33 (WT)

Dominus Christian Moueix **1984** £63.06
(FA)

Opus One Mondavi/Rothschild **1995**
£66.90 (TAN) £90.22 (NO)

Opus One Mondavi/Rothschild **1994**
£63.00 (CRO) £70.00 (CON) £74.81 (FA)
£75.00 (FORT) £85.00 (ROB) £87.60 (NO)

£70.00 → £99.99

Cabernet Sauvignon Heitz Bella Oaks
1976 £92.24 (REI)

Insignia Joseph Phelps **1995** £72.80 (WT)

Opus One Mondavi/Rothschild **1996**
£72.00 (UN)

Over £100.00

Cabernet Sauvignon Caymus Vineyards
Special Selection **1987** £143.35 (FA)

Cabernet Sauvignon La Jota **1991** £111.63
(CAV)

Dominus Christian Moueix **1990** £141.00
(CAV)

CALIFORNIA WHITE

Under £4.00

Blossom Hill White **Non-vintage** £3.99
(MORR) £3.99 (CO)

Chenin Blanc E&J Gallo **Non-vintage**
£3.99 (UN) £3.99 (CO) £3.99 (VIC) £3.99
(THR) £3.99 (WR) £3.99 (BOT)

French Colombard E&J Gallo **Non-
vintage** £3.99 (SO) £3.99 (UN) £3.99
(SAF) £3.99 (THR) £3.99 (WR) £4.99 (ASD)

£4.00 → £5.99

Chardonnay Fetzer Sundial 1997 £5.99
(UN) £6.49 (SAI)

Chardonnay E&J Gallo **Non-vintage**
£4.99 (CO)

Chardonnay E&J Gallo 1998 £4.99 (ASD)

Chardonnay E&J Gallo 1997 £4.99 (SAF)

Chardonnay E&J Gallo 1996 £4.99 (MORR)
£4.99 (VIC) £4.99 (THR) £4.99 (WR)

Chardonnay Glen Ellen 1996 £4.99 (MORR)

Chardonnay Pedroncelli 1994 £4.49 (DI)

Chardonnay Redwood Trail 1996 £5.99
(WAI)

Chardonnay Sutter Home 1997 £4.91
(STE) £4.99 (MORR) £4.99 (UN)

Chardonnay William Wheeler Sonoma
1996 £5.95 (HED)

Fumé Blanc Fetzer 1997 £5.76 (FLE)

Riesling Firestone 1998 £5.99 (MAJ)

Sauvignon Blanc E&J Gallo **Non-vintage**
£4.39 (BO) £4.49 (VIC) £4.49 (THR)

Sauvignon Blanc E&J Gallo 1997 £4.49
(MORR) £4.49 (SAF)

Sauvignon Blanc Robert Mondavi
Woodbridge 1993 £5.39 (NI)

Sauvignon Blanc Sutter Home 1998 £4.91
(STE) £5.45 (NA)

£6.00 → £7.99

Big House White Ca' del Solo Bonny
Doon 1996 £6.99 (RAE)

Chardonnay Bel Arbors 1996 £6.60 (JU)

Chardonnay Edna Valley ½ bottle 1997
£6.80 (BEN)

Chardonnay Fetzer Bonterra 1996 £7.99
(TES) £7.99 (WAI) £7.99 (SAI) £7.99 (WR)

Chardonnay Fetzer Sundial 1996 £6.45
(SOM) £6.49 (THR) £6.49 (BOT) £6.99 (JON)

Chardonnay Jekel 1997 £7.49 (VIC) £7.49
(THR) £7.49 (WR) £7.49 (BOT)

Chardonnay Seven Peaks 1997 £7.35
(BAN) £12.99 (VA)

Chardonnay Villa Mt Eden 1996 £7.99
(UN) £8.35 (LIB)

Chardonnay Wente Riva Ranch 1997
£7.99 (MORR)

Chenin Blanc Dry Creek 1996 £6.75 (DI)
£8.95 (FORT)

Fumé Blanc Beringer 1997 £7.99 (MAJ)

Malvasia Ca' del Solo Bianca 1996 £7.99
(CON) £7.99 (POR) £7.99 (GW) £8.40
(CRO) £8.52 (REI) £8.95 (ROB)

Moscato Ca' del Solo Bonny Doon 1991
£6.95 (RAE)

Orange Muscat Quady Essensia ½ bottle
1997 £6.49 (MAJ) £6.50 (WS) £6.95 (WRI)
£7.24 (PLAY) £7.99 (PHI)

Orange Muscat Quady Essensia ½ bottle
1996 £6.39 (YOU) £6.40 (AV) £6.75
(CON) £6.95 (LEA)

Riesling Bonny Doon Pacific Rim 1997
£7.99 (POR) £8.25 (BU) £8.40 (BEN) £8.40
(MV)

Riesling Firestone Selected Harvest
Johannisberg 1996 £7.90 (PIP)

Sauvignon Blanc Clos du Bois 1996 £7.62
(HA)

Sauvignon Blanc Peter Michael l'Après
Midi 1992 £7.64 (REI)

Sauvignon Blanc Robert Mondavi
Woodbridge 1997 £6.99 (THR) £6.99
(WR) £6.99 (BOT) £7.16 (STE) £7.95 (NA)

Sauvignon Blanc St-Supéry 1997 £7.99
(THR) £7.99 (BOT) £8.95 (BER) £9.49 (LIB)

Viognier Fetzer 1997 £7.99 (OD) £7.99
(SAF) £7.99 (THR) £7.99 (WR) £7.99 (BOT)

£8.00 → £9.99

Chardonnay Beringer 1997 £8.99 (NEZ)
£10.99 (MAJ)

Chardonnay Fetzer Barrel-Select 1996
£9.99 (JON)

Chardonnay Hawk Crest 1996 £8.17 (DOM)

Chardonnay Kendall-Jackson Vintner's
Reserve 1997 £9.99 (VIC) £9.99 (THR)

Chardonnay Kendall-Jackson Vintner's
Reserve 1996 £9.99 (DI)

- *Wines are listed in A–Z
  order within each price
  band.*
- *For each wine, vintages are
  listed in descending order.*
- *Each vintage of any wine
  appears only once.*

Chardonnay Robert Mondavi **1995** £9.95
(ROS) £11.99 (NI)
Chardonnay Murphy-Goode **1997** £9.95
(AD)
Chardonnay Seven Peaks Reserve **1997**
£9.99 (BAN)
Fumé Blanc Murphy-Goode **1997** £8.50
(AD)
Il Pescatore Ca' del Solo **1995** £8.95 (NI)
£12.40 (GW) £12.63 (PLA)
Malvasia Ca' del Solo Bianca **1997** £8.15
(WRI) £8.20 (TAN) £8.40 (BEN) £8.53
(GW) £8.99 (VA) £10.50 (UB)
Riesling Bonny Doon Pacific Rim **1992**
£8.99 (UB)
Riesling Renaissance Select Late-Harvest
½ bottle **1993** £9.95 (BEN) £9.95 (BU)
Sauvignon Blanc Chalk Hill **1993** £9.95 (JU)
Sauvignon Blanc Clos du Bois **1990** £8.50
(BU)
Sauvignon Blanc Rochioli **1997** £9.50
(RAE) £9.99 (YOU) £11.90 (CRO)
Sauvignon Blanc Rochioli **1996** £8.79 (NI)
£9.50 (RAE) £11.10 (UB)
Sauvignon Blanc St-Supéry **1996** £8.80
(NO) £9.34 (REI)

£10.00 → £11.99

Chardonnay Beaulieu Vineyard **1994**
£11.95 (BU)
Chardonnay Rochioli **1995** £10.99 (NI)
£10.99 (RAE)
Chardonnay Rutherford Hill **1995** £10.80
(AV)
Chardonnay St-Supéry **1995** £11.25 (LIB)
£11.95 (TAN)
Chardonnay Saintsbury **1996** £10.35
(SOM) £12.00 (WS) £12.63 (NO) £12.90
(CRO) £12.99 (YOU) £13.20 (BEN)
Chardonnay Villa Mt Eden Cellar Select
1996 £10.20 (PIP)
Chardonnay Wente Riva Ranch **1994**
£10.89 (PEN)
Folle Blanche Louis Martini **1996** £11.16
(WT)
Fumé Blanc Robert Mondavi **1997** £11.07
(STE) £11.49 (MAJ) £11.50 (WRI) £11.50
(TAN) £12.30 (NA)
Il Pescatore Ca' del Solo **1996** £11.99
(VA) £12.28 (REI) £12.53 (GW)
Meritage White Carmenet **1996** £11.50
(WS)
Riesling Joseph Phelps Johannisberg
Selected Late-Harvest ½ bottle **1986**
£11.00 (CRO)

Riesling Mark West Johannisberg Late-
Harvest ½ bottle **1983** £10.00 (CRO)
Sauvignon Blanc Frog's Leap **1997** £11.50
(MV) £12.00 (ELL) £12.32 (NO) £13.99 (FLE)
Sauvignon Blanc Simi **1992** £10.21 (PLA)
£11.25 (CON)

£12.00 → £14.99

Chardonnay Acacia **1995** £12.95 (WAI)
Chardonnay Au Bon Climat **1997** £14.49
(YOU) £15.00 (MV) £15.50 (BEN)
Chardonnay Au Bon Climat **1996** £14.60
(TAN) £15.95 (FORT) £16.00 (WS)
Chardonnay Chalk Hill **1994** £12.90 (JU)
Chardonnay Clos du Val **1995** £12.63
(DOM) £13.50 (PIP) £13.95 (STA)
Chardonnay Cuvaison **1996** £13.99 (JON)
£14.00 (PIP) £14.29 (YOU) £14.69 (AME)
★ Chardonnay Landmark Overlook **1996**
£12.99 (OD)
Chardonnay Robert Mondavi **1994**
£14.70 (TAN)
Chardonnay Qupé **1996** £14.50 (MV)
£15.50 (RES)
Chardonnay Ridge **1995** £13.95 (NI)
£16.15 (BU) £16.49 (YOU) £16.61 (NO)
Chardonnay Rochioli **1996** £12.99 (YOU)
Chardonnay Saintsbury **1997** £13.20
(BEN) £13.95 (FLE) £14.50 (AD)
Chardonnay Saintsbury Reserve **1996**
£13.25 (FORT) £19.90 (TAN) £20.00 (WS)
£21.00 (CRO) £21.00 (BEN) £21.95 (AD)
Chardonnay Sanford **1996** £13.50 (WS)
£15.85 (WT)
Chardonnay Simi **1993** £13.04 (PEN)
Chardonnay Sonoma-Cutrer **1996**
£12.85 (AV) £14.95 (LEA)
Chardonnay Marimar Torres Estate Don
Miguel Vineyard **1995** £14.50 (POR)
£21.00 (CRO)
Chardonnay Marimar Torres Estate Don
Miguel Vineyard **1993** £14.64 (NO)
Gewürztraminer Joseph Phelps **1996**
£13.88 (WT)
Riesling Joseph Phelps Johannisberg
Selected Late-Harvest ½ bottle **1995**
£14.95 (BEN)
Riesling Stag's Leap Wine Cellars **1997**
£13.62 (WT)
Sauvignon Blanc Duckhorn **1996** £14.95
(RES) £14.95 (FORT)
Sauvignon Blanc Matanzas Creek **1995**
£14.50 (BAL) £14.95 (RES)
Sauvignon Blanc Sanford **1997** £12.70
(PIP) £12.72 (WT)

£15.00 → £19.99

Chardonnay Au Bon Climat 1995 £16.50 (ROB)
Chardonnay Beringer Private Reserve 1994 £18.47 (NO)
Chardonnay Far Niente 1988 £18.71 (NO)
Chardonnay Fritz Dutton Ranch 1996 £16.99 (YOU) £18.76 (WT) £19.95 (RES)
Chardonnay Frog's Leap 1995 £15.39 (CON)
Chardonnay Monticello Corley Select Reserve 1995 £16.95 (LAY)
Chardonnay Joseph Phelps 1994 £15.50 (BEN)
Chardonnay Ridge 1996 £16.00 (CRO) £16.99 (PHI) £18.75 (BEN) £19.50 (LEA) £19.95 (RES)
Chardonnay Ridge 1991 £16.39 (REI)
Chardonnay Saintsbury Reserve 1993 £18.50 (CON)
Chardonnay Sanford 1995 £15.99 (GW)
Chardonnay Shafer 1995 £18.49 (NO)
Chardonnay Simi 1996 £15.94 (CB)
Chardonnay Simi Reserve 1992 £17.99 (YOU)
Chardonnay Stag's Leap Wine Cellars 1996 £15.28 (DOM) £18.09 (WT)
Chardonnay Stag's Leap Wine Cellars 1995 £16.75 (GW) £19.95 (RES) £19.95 (ROB)
Chardonnay Stonestreet 1995 £17.95 (ROB) £20.10 (WT)
Chardonnay Swanson 1996 £16.60 (AV)
Marsanne Joseph Phelps 1995 £17.35 (BEN) £19.39 (REI)
Marsanne/Viognier Jade Mountain 1996 £17.50 (ROB)
Riesling Joseph Phelps Johannisberg Selected Late-Harvest ½ bottle 1985 £19.27 (NO)

£20.00 → £29.99

Chardonnay Au Bon Climat le Bouge d'à Côté 1996 £20.00 (MV) £21.75 (RES)
Chardonnay Au Bon Climat le Bouge d'à Côté 1995 £20.00 (BEN) £23.39 (NO)
Chardonnay Chalk Hill Estate Vineyard Selection 1994 £24.00 (JU)
Chardonnay Chalone 1996 £21.50 (FORT)
Chardonnay Far Niente 1996 £28.90 (AV) £30.32 (TW) £38.95 (RES)
Chardonnay Grgich Hills 1995 £26.50 (RES)
Chardonnay Matanzas Creek 1995 £21.75 (BEN) £22.50 (BAL) £23.95 (RES)

Chardonnay Patz & Hall Rutherglen 1993 £24.21 (NO)
Chardonnay Sonoma-Cutrer les Pierres 1994 £21.74 (PEN) £21.90 (UB)
Riesling Joseph Phelps Johannisberg Selected Late-Harvest ½ bottle 1997 £29.31 (WT)
Semillon Chalk Hill Botrytized Estate Vineyard Selection ½ bottle 1994 £25.00 (JU)
Viognier Alban Vineyards 1996 £23.68 (WT)
Viognier Joseph Phelps 1996 £21.73 (REI) £21.99 (WT) £23.95 (RES)
Viognier Sanford & Benedict Cold Heaven 1997 £23.00 (MV) £23.50 (BEN)

Over £30.00

Chardonnay Beringer Private Reserve 1996 £34.27 (CAV)
Riesling Chateau St Jean Belle Terre Johannisberg ½ bottle 1978 £32.42 (NO)
Sauvignon Blanc Robert Mondavi Botrytis 1983 £32.00 (CRO) £35.25 (REI)

CALIFORNIA ROSÉ

Under £4.50

White Grenache E&J Gallo **Non-vintage** £4.49 (THR) £4.49 (WR) £4.49 (ASD)
White Grenache E&J Gallo 1997 £4.49 (UN) £4.49 (SAF)
White Zinfandel E&J Gallo 1997 £4.49 (MORR)
White Zinfandel Sebastiani 1997 £4.49 (CO)
White Zinfandel Sutter Home 1997 £4.49 (MORR) £5.09 (JON)

£4.50 → £5.99

White Zinfandel Robert Mondavi 1994 £4.85 (NI) £7.50 (ROB)
White Zinfandel Sutter Home **Non-vintage** £4.69 (SAF)
White Zinfandel Sutter Home 1998 £4.69 (UN)

Over £6.00

Vin Gris de Cigare, Bonny Doon 1997 £7.99 (YOU) £8.00 (MV)
Vin Gris de Cigare, Bonny Doon 1996 £6.49 (NI) £7.65 (RAE)
White Zinfandel Robert Mondavi 1997 £6.75 (STA) £6.98 (STE) £7.75 (NA)
White Zinfandel Wente (Blush) 1994 £7.05 (PEN)

CALIFORNIA SPARKLING

Under £5.00

Gallo Brut **Non-vintage** £4.99 (MORR) £4.99 (SAF)

£9.00 → £9.99

Mumm Cuvée Napa Brut **Non-vintage** £9.29 (PHI) £9.99 (MORR) £9.99 (WAI) £9.99 (MAJ) £9.99 (CO) £9.99 (OD) £9.99 (SAF) £9.99 (VIC) £9.99 (THR) £9.99 (BOT) £9.99 (ASD) £10.50 (CRO) £10.99 (POR)
Mumm Cuvée Napa Rosé **Non-vintage** £9.99 (VIC) £9.99 (THR) £9.99 (WR) £9.99 (BOT) £10.99 (MAJ) £11.50 (CRO)

£10.00 → £15.99

Iron Horse Brut **1986** £14.00 (CRO)
Mumm Cuvée Napa Brut Blanc de Blancs **Non-vintage** £11.99 (VIC) £11.99 (THR) £11.99 (WR) £11.99 (BOT) £12.49 (OD)
Roederer Estate Quartet **Non-vintage** £13.46 (STE) £13.51 (REI) £13.90 (CRO) £13.90 (JU) £14.00 (NO) £14.95 (WAI) £14.95 (WS) £14.95 (NA) £14.99 (MAJ) £14.99 (JON) £14.99 (POR) £15.50 (STA)
Schramsberg Blanc de Blancs **1990** £15.50 (ROB)

OREGON/WASHINGTON RED

£8.00 → £9.99

Cabernet Sauvignon Chateau Ste Michelle **1993** £9.99 (YOU) £10.49 (LIB) £10.75 (WRI) £13.00 (PIP)
Cabernet Sauvignon Columbia Crest **1993** £8.49 (LIB) £11.00 (CRO)
Lemberger Covey Run **1995** £8.80 (PIP)
Merlot Covey Run **1994** £8.78 (PEN) £9.39 (PLA) £9.50 (BAL)
Pinot Noir Columbia **1995** £8.17 (PEN)

£10.00 → £14.99

Cabernet Sauvignon Chateau Ste Michelle **1988** £14.00 (CRO)
Cabernet Sauvignon Staton Hills **1993** £11.69 (CB) £15.50 (CRO)
Merlot Columbia Crest **1995** £10.75 (LIB) £12.99 (VA) £13.95 (ROB)
Pinot Noir Broadley Vineyards **1996** £14.65 (CON) £14.95 (BAL)
Pinot Noir Elk Cove Vineyards **1993** £13.75 (PEN)

£15.00 → £19.99

Cabernet Sauvignon Columbia Otis Vineyard **1985** £15.06 (PEN)
Merlot Chateau Ste Michelle **1993** £16.35 (PIP)
Pinot Noir Domaine Drouhin **1995** £17.95 (SOM) £20.99 (YOU) £22.21 (PEN)
Pinot Noir Domaine Drouhin **1993** £19.99 (NI)
Pinot Noir Rex Hill **1995** £15.99 (MOR)

Over £20.00

Pinot Noir Domaine Drouhin **1996** £21.99 (JON) £22.95 (LEA) £23.50 (FORT) £23.80 (BEN) £23.95 (STA)
Pinot Noir Domaine Drouhin Laurène **1994** £21.40 (SOM)
Pinot Noir Domaine Drouhin Laurène **1993** £25.85 (PEN)

WHITE

Under £7.00

Sauvignon Blanc Columbia Crest **1996** £6.49 (LIB) £7.99 (VA)
Sémillon Chateau Ste Michelle **1996** £6.99 (LIB) £7.29 (YOU)

£7.00 → £9.99

Chardonnay Chateau Ste Michelle **1994** £8.99 (LIB) £9.59 (YOU)
Chardonnay Salishan **1992** £9.91 (WT)
Riesling Argyle Petaluma Late Picked **1992** £8.44 (NO)

Over £10.00

Chardonnay Elk Cove Vineyards **1996** £11.50 (PIP)
Chardonnay Salishan **1991** £10.14 (WT)
Pinot Gris Elk Cove Vineyards **1995** £10.00 (PEN) £10.25 (CON) £10.95 (STA)

OTHER USA RED

Over £8.00

Merlot Palmer Vineyards **1991** £9.18 (NO)
Pinot Meunier Eyrie Vineyard **1988** £30.00 (CRO)
Pinot Noir Firesteed **1997** £9.95 (WRI) £9.95 (LIB) £9.99 (VA)
Pinot Noir Firesteed **1996** £8.25 (WS) £9.25 (CON) £12.95 (ROB)

OTHER REGIONS

The rest of the world is increasingly filling the gap left by price hikes in starrier regions. Take a look at Greek wines, as well as Argentine and Uruguayan

ARGENTINA

Do you remember the rich, smooth reds that so seduced us when Australian wines first started appearing here? Remember their luscious fruit, the softness of their tannins? Well, Aussie wines have moved in in a dozen new directions since, but that rich smoothness is still around. These days it's called Argentine Malbec.

This is undoubtedly Argentina's finest red grape. Even French oenologists have been known to agree that it does far better here than in its French homeland. And while there are lots of everyday versions around at good prices, there are some more serious Malbecs to be had, too – wines that bear out the claims that everyone is now making about Argentina's enormous potential for quality.

For whites, the aromatic Torrontés is tops. A good Torrontés knocks spots off most of the over-hyped Viogniers we see from France and elsewhere. High-altitude spots like Salta are producing the best Torrontes, while Mendoza seems to be Malbec's natural home. You haven't tasted them yet? You must, you must.

Try *Bodegas Norton, Humberto Canale, Catena* (and second label *Alamos Ridge*), *Cavas de Weinart, Esmeralda, Etchart, La Agrícola, La Rural, Lurton, Navarro Correa, San Telmo, Santa Isabel, Santa Julia, Trapiche, Valle de Vistalba, Viejo Surco*.

AUSTRIA

It's interesting to see the steady inroads that Austrian wines are making here, because they're the antithesis of everything that one might think of as being the modern international style. They're not remotely tropical-tasting, they're not (usually) oaky, and they're (generally) made from grape varieties other than Chardonnay. Yes, they've got plenty of fruit, but it tends to be the lean, minerally kind. Austria turned to this style over ten years ago, and whereas at first some of the wines seemed lean for the sake of leanness, now they have lovely structure and style. Rieslings are often the best, but Grüner Veltliners from the best producers are surprisingly serious (normally it's a grape to glug down without too much thought) and good Chardonnays (yes, they grow some – who doesn't?) are a delight, all elegant complexity. Sauvignon Blanc is less gooseberryish than New Zealand and often minerally. Zweigelt reds have nice blueberry fruit. Best producers include *Paul Achs, Bründlmayer, Feiler-Artinger, Heinrich, Franz Hirtzberger, Alois Kracher, Krutzler, Lenz Moser, Malat, Nekowitsch, Willi Opitz, Josef Pöckl, Prager, Prieler, Erich Salomon, Heidi Schröck, Georg Stiegelmar, Erwin Tinhof, Umathum, Dr Wolfgang Unger, Robert Wenzel* and *Fritz Wieninger*.

CANADA

Cool-climate wines that are mostly sound rather than exciting, though the Icewines (sweet wines made from grapes frozen on the vine in winter) can rise above that level. Grape varieties include Chardonnay (of course), Pinot Blanc, Pinot Gris, Riesling, Gewürztraminer and sometimes Merlot. The best Icewines are often made from the hybrid grape Vidal, but don't tell the Eurocrats that, because they're convinced as an article of faith that no hybrid grape can make anything worth having. The Canadians like hybrids because their winters are so cold that it can be a struggle getting vinifera grapes to stay alive until spring. Best names include *Calona Vineyards, Cedar Creek, Chateau des Charmes, Gray Monk,*

Hainle, Henry of Pelham, Hillbrand, Inniskillin, Mission Hill, Sumac Ridge and *Summerhill.*

CYPRUS

Commandaria can be reasonable, if you want a slightly dull sweet, raisiny fortified. The table wines are still best avoided. We keep being told that Cyprus is changing, and is going to start producing quantities of light, crisp wines any day. Well, okay, I've tasted *one*, but don't hold your breath.

GREECE

This is where a revolution really has taken place. Now, I don't want to suggest that everything Greek is going to be delicious, because it will take only one visit to your local Greek restaurant to prove me wrong. But there really are some nice fresh dry whites emerging. Reds have been good for longer; red wine always survives difficult cellar conditions better than white.

The native grape varieties are what make Greek wines special: there are vines like Agiortítiko (principally from the Nemea region), Mavrodaphne (especially from Patras), Xynomavro and Limnió; for whites, Assyrtiko, Moscophilero, Savatiano and others. Some supermarkets seem determined to make Greek wines taste as international as everything else, which is a shame; let's hope they don't all succumb.

Best bets include *Achaia-Clauss, Boutari, Chateau Carras, Chateau Harlaftis, Domaine Mercouri, Kourtakis, Semeli, Tsantalis* and sweet Muscat from Samos.

INDIA

Bordeaux oenologist Michel Rolland is the consultant winemaker for *Grover,* which is turning out respectable whites and reds, and of course there's *Omar Khayyam*, the sparkling wine made with Champagne know-how, but sadly not much Champagne style. But India was never intended by Mother Nature to be a winemaking country, and with so many terrific wines available from countries that were, I can't help thinking, why bother?

ISRAEL

Israel's top vineyard area, the Golan Heights, has in the past been earmarked for handing over to Syria as part of the peace process. Well, that was stalled for years, but at the time of writing things seem to be moving again, so who knows? The *Golan Heights* winery is the best producer. *Carmel* is bigger, and has recently improved its act, but the emphasis on producing Kosher wine means that the supervision of a rabbi can take precedence over the ideas of the winemaker. The idea that Kosher wine might also be nice to drink is of fairly recent date.

LEBANON

Chateau Musar is still the star here, making gutsy, spicy reds that will live 30 years. Serge Hochar, whose baby Musar is, reckons it's at its peak at 15 years, which still means you have to stash it away for quite a while after buying it. It's worth the wait, though it's temptingly good young, as well.

LUXEMBOURG

Difficult to find outside the Grand Duchy itself, and not frankly that exciting when you do find them. I mean, don't make a journey specially. Most are light and made from Müller-Thurgau, alias Rivaner. The vineyards are on the banks of the Mosel (or Moselle if you prefer), but don't start expecting the thrills of German Mosel – because you won't get them.

MEXICO

LA Cetto is the main player in Baja California, which is where most of Mexico's vineyards are. It's not a wine-drinking country, however, and so attention in the cellars tends to focus on export markets – which is good news for us. The range of wines is wide and could usefully be narrowed: grapes like Riesling just don't work in this hot climate – but Petite Sirah, Cabernet, Zinfandel and Nebbiolo can be terrific. *Santo Tomas* has a joint venture with Wente of California, which is producing some decent stuff. *Domecq* also has an operation there, but seems to have been less active lately.

NORTH AFRICA

This had a ready market for its wines in colonial days, but it's been steadily downhill ever since. And since those people who bought the stuff never bought it for its finesse or quality, the producers haven't had much to fall back on.

In any case, not only has the market turned against the sort of rustic, cooked flavours that characterize North African wines even at their best, but, under the influence of Islam, these countries tend not to look kindly on their indigenous wine industries. Algeria's Coteaux de Mascara is traditionally one of the better areas, and Tunisian Muscat can be reasonable. Other names to conjure with include *Domaine Cigogne, Domaine Mellil* and *Prestige du Menara* from Morocco.

SWITZERLAND

There's a distinct style to Swiss wines – as indeed you might expect of an industry that persists in making wines on a small scale in incredibly difficult terrain (all those mountains) when they could probably make more money by selling the land for building. The style (in the French-speaking cantons, which produce most of it) is elegant and subtle, based on the Chasselas grape for whites and the Pinot Noir and Gamay for reds. Italian-speaking wines are mostly Merlot and range, as befits Italian individuality, from pale rosés to substantial oak-aged reds, though most are on the pale, light and overcropped side. The German-speaking cantons concentrate on Müller-Thurgau, although out of what seems like perversity they call it Riesling-Sylvaner. It wouldn't set the world alight.

Can you get them over here? Yes, sometimes. A few are imported. Can you afford them? Well, yes. They're simple wines at relatively serious prices, that's all. And anyone who's ever even tried to have a cup of coffee in Switzerland knows that it's no bargain basement.

TURKEY

Not a serious wine-producing country: only a tiny proportion of the grape harvest, some two or three per cent, is turned into wine. Turkish restaurants (the better kind, at least) in Britain seem to be able to find perfectly decent house wines from Turkey, though.

URUGUAY

Tannat is the great discovery here: an obscure grape from South-West France is suddenly blossoming into lovely spicy reds. It wasn't all that long ago that you only had to mention Uruguayan wine to get an instant laugh: just goes to show how things can change. The whites, when they're made in a modern style, are also perfectly nice, but it's the reds that are leading the way to international recognition.

MERCHANTS SPECIALIZING IN THESE COUNTRIES
see Merchant Directory (page 413) for details

Good merchants often stock a scattering of wines from these countries. The following merchants have a slightly better choice: **Argentina** Oddbins (OD), Sommelier Wine Co (SOM); **Austria** Adnams (AD), Lay & Wheeler (LAY), Christopher Piper Wines (PIP), T & W Wines (TW), Noel Young (YOU); **Canada** Averys of Bristol (AV), Corney & Barrow (CB), Nadder Wine Co. (NA), Terry Platt (PLA), Stevens Garnier (STE); **Greece** Oddbins (OD), Tanners (TAN); **Israel** no actual specialists but Averys of Bristol (AV), Corney & Barrow (CB), and Safeway (SAF) have some; **Lebanon** Chateau Musar is widely available. For older vintages try Roberson (ROB)

OTHER REGIONS PRICES

ARGENTINA

Under £4.00

Argentine Dry Red Peñaflor Bright Bros
  1997 £2.99 (FUL)
Bonarda Bodegas Lurton **1997** £3.95 (WS)
Chardonnay Etchart Rio de Plata **1998**
  £3.99 (ASD)
Chardonnay La Rural 1885 **Non-vintage**
  £3.99 (CO)
Chenin Blanc La Rural Libertad **1998**
  £3.75 (FUL)
Malbec Balbi **1998** £3.99 (MORR) £4.49 (SAF)
Malbec Balbi **1997** £3.99 (CO) £4.49 (OD)
Malbec Bodegas Lurton **1997** £3.99 (FUL)
  £4.99 (JON) £5.39 (JER) £5.49 (POR)
Malbec/Sangiovese La Rural Libertad **1998**
  £3.79 (THR) £3.79 (WR) £3.79 (BOT)
Mission Peak Red **Non-vintage** £3.29 (BO)
★ Tempranillo La Agricola Santa Julia **1998**
  £3.99 (SOM)

£4.00 → £4.99

Barbera Vistalba **1997** £4.69 (YOU) £4.79
  (BO) £4.85 (ROS) £5.15 (CON)
Barbera Vistalba **1996** £4.50 (WS) £4.58
  (GW) £4.95 (PHI)
Cabernet Sauvignon Bodegas Esmeralda
  Alamos Ridge **1996** £4.99 (FUL) £5.99
  (SAF) £5.99 (YOU)
Cabernet Sauvignon Etchart Rio de Plata
  1997 £4.49 (ASD)
Cabernet Sauvignon Norton **1997** £4.95
  (WS) £4.99 (OD)
Cabernet Sauvignon Trapiche Oak Cask
  Reserve **1994** £4.69 (PLA) £5.95 (JU)
  £6.49 (DI)
Chardonnay Bodegas Esmeralda Alamos
  Ridge **1996** £4.99 (FUL) £5.95 (WS)
  £5.99 (SAF) £5.99 (YOU)
Chardonnay La Agricola Magdalena River
  1997 £4.99 (UN)
Chardonnay La Rural 1885 **1998** £4.70 (BIB)
Chardonnay/Semillon Santa Ana **1997**
  £4.49 (SAF)
Malbec La Rural 1885 **1997** £4.69 (BO)
Malbec/Cabernet Sauvignon La Agricola
  Magdalena River **1997** £4.99 (UN)
Malbec/Sangiovese Trapiche Parral **1998**
  £4.01 (STE) £4.50 (NA)
Merlot Goyenechea **1995** £4.83 (PEN)

Merlot La Rural 1885 **1998** £4.50 (PIP)
Merlot Norton **1996** £4.99 (NI) £4.99 (OD)
Pinot Noir Trapiche **1995** £4.69 (PLA)
Sangiovese Norton **1996** £4.99 (NI)
Syrah Goyenechea **1995** £4.32 (PEN)
Syrah Vistalba **1996** £4.99 (YOU) £5.71
  (ROS) £5.99 (CON) £6.10 (PHI)
Torrontés Etchart **1997** £4.69 (JON)
  £4.95 (UB)
Torrontés Norton **1998** £4.49 (NEZ) £4.49
  (OD) £5.95 (TAN)
Torrontés Norton **1997** £4.49 (THR) £4.49
  (WR) £4.49 (BOT) £4.59 (NI) £5.49 (YOU)
Torrontés/Chardonnay Navarro Correas
  Correas **1997** £4.52 (GW)

£5.00 → £5.99

Barbera Simonassi **1998** £5.49 (SAF)
Cabernet Sauvignon Etchart **1996** £5.69
  (JON)
Cabernet Sauvignon Finca El Retiro **1998**
  £5.99 (LIB) £5.99 (VA)
Cabernet Sauvignon La Agricola Santa
  Julia Oak Reserve **1996** £5.99 (TES)
Cabernet Sauvignon Navarro Correas
  Correas **1997** £5.49 (MOR)
Cabernet Sauvignon Vistalba **1995** £5.29
  (YOU) £5.50 (WS)
Carrascal Weinert **1996** £5.99 (STE)
Chardonnay Bodegas Esmeralda Alamos
  Ridge **1997** £5.97 (BIB) £6.70 (PIP)
Chardonnay Bodegas Lurton **1997** £5.99
  (CB)
Chardonnay La Agricola Santa Julia Oak
  Reserve **1997** £5.99 (UN)
Chardonnay Trapiche Oak Cask Reserve
  1995 £5.65 (WHI)
Malbec Bodegas Esmeralda Alamos Ridge
  1996 £5.95 (WS) £5.99 (YOU) £6.70 (PIP)
Malbec Finca El Retiro **1998** £5.99 (LIB)
  £5.99 (VA)
Malbec Humberto Canale **1996** £5.29
  (NO) £6.50 (HED)
Malbec La Agricola Santa Julia Oak
  Reserve **1997** £5.99 (UN)

> *Stars (★) indicate wines*
> *selected by Oz Clarke in the*
> *Best Buys section which begins*
> *on page 9.*

Malbec Navarro Correas Correas **1997** £5.49 (MOR)

Malbec Norton **1995** £5.95 (WS) £5.99 (YOU)

Malbec Viña Patagonia Isla Negra **1997** £5.49 (VIC) £5.49 (THR) £5.49 (WR)

Merlot Norton **1995** £5.99 (NEZ)

Shiraz Peñaflor Condor Peak Reserve San Juan **1997** £5.49 (YOU)

Syrah Navarro Correas **1996** £5.03 (GW)

Syrah Viña Morandé Vista Andes **1997** £5.81 (NO)

Tempranillo Finca El Retiro **1998** £5.49 (WAI)

Tempranillo La Agricola Santa Julia Oak Reserve **1997** £5.99 (UN)

£6.00 → £6.99

Cabernet Sauvignon Trapiche Andean **1995** £6.15 (PLAY)

Carrascal Weinert **1995** £6.75 (NA) £6.78 (ROS) £7.65 (CON) £7.95 (LEA) £8.00 (PIP)

Chardonnay La Rural Rutini **1997** £6.99 (YOU)

Chardonnay Norton Reserve **1997** £6.99 (NEZ)

Malbec Norton Reserve **1997** £6.99 (NEZ)

Malbec Trapiche **1994** £6.78 (HA) £7.65 (UB)

Merlot La Rural Rutini **1995** £6.76 (BIB)

Pinot Noir Humberto Canale **1998** £6.25 (ELL) £6.95 (HED)

Riesling Leoncio Arizu Luigi Bosca **1997** £6.90 (CRO)

Syrah Bodegas Lurton Oak Aged **1997** £6.99 (WR) £6.99 (BOT)

£7.00 → £9.99

Barbaro Balbi **1997** £7.99 (MORR)

Cabernet Sauvignon Bodegas Esmeralda Catena Agrelo **1995** £7.99 (FUL) £8.95 (WS)

Cabernet Sauvignon Bodegas Lurton Gran Lurton **1996** £7.99 (FUL) £9.99 (POR)

Cabernet Sauvignon Navarro Correas Colección Privada **1991** £8.99 (MOR)

Cabernet Sauvignon Weinert **1995** £8.64 (STE) £9.60 (NA)

Carrascal Weinert **1994** £7.50 (BAL) £7.59 (JON) £7.69 (MOR) £7.90 (TAN)

Caves de Weinert Weinert **1993** £9.95 (WS) £11.59 (YOU) £11.89 (JON) £11.95 (BU) £11.95 (LEA)

Chardonnay Bodegas Esmeralda Catena Agrelo **1997** £8.95 (WS)

Chardonnay Bodegas Esmeralda Catena Agrelo **1996** £7.99 (FUL) £8.81 (BIB) £9.29 (YOU)

Chardonnay Bodegas Lurton **1995** £7.90 (CRO)

Chardonnay Leoncio Arizu Luigi Bosca **1995** £8.74 (NO)

Malbec Bodegas Esmeralda Catena Agrelo **1996** £8.81 (BIB)

Malbec Luigi Bosca **1996** £7.45 (PHI)

Malbec Weinert **1994** £8.25 (WS) £9.50 (BAL) £9.59 (JON) £9.60 (TAN) £9.75 (LEA) £9.95 (BU) £10.09 (PIP)

Merlot Weinert **1996** £7.52 (STE)

Merlot Weinert **1994** £10.25 (PLAY)

Miscelánea Weinert **1997** £9.50 (BU)

Privada Norton **1996** £7.95 (WS) £7.99 (NEZ)

Syrah Navarro Correas **1993** £8.99 (MOR)

Over £10.00

Cabernet Sauvignon Weinert **1994** £11.50 (BU) £11.95 (LEA) £12.38 (PLAY) £12.98 (CB)

Cabernet Sauvignon Weinert **1992** £11.50 (BAL) £11.55 (JON)

Cabernet Sauvignon Weinert **1991** £10.49 (MOR) £10.95 (JU) £11.00 (CON)

Caves de Weinert Weinert **1990** £10.25 (NO)

Chardonnay Bodegas Esmeralda Catena Alta **1995** £19.99 (YOU)

AUSTRIA

£7.50 → £17.00

Beerenauslese Grand Cuvée, Alois Kracher **1995** £10.95 (JU)

Blauer Zweigelt, Weinbau Krutszler **1995** £8.95 (JU)

Bouvier/Neuburger Trockenbeerenauslese, Lenz Moser ½ bottle **1995** £13.20 (NO)

Grüner Veltliner Kabinett Langenloiser Steinhaus, Bründlmayer **1996** £7.69 (YOU)

★ Ruster Ausbruch Neusiedlersee Hügelland, Heidi Schröck 50cl **1995** £16.60 (SAV)

Over £26.00

Muscat Ottonel Schilfmandl, Willi Opitz **1990** £53.96 (NO)

Welschriesling Trockenbeerenauslese No 1, Alois Kracher **1995** £26.00 (JU)

CANADA

Under £11.00

Chateau des Charmes Paul Bosc
  Chardonnay **1994** £10.04 (STE) £11.15
  (NA)
Inniskillin Chardonnay **1996** £7.20 (AV)
Inniskillin Maréchal Foch Red **1996** £5.70
  (AV) £5.99 (DI)

CYPRUS

Under £9.00

Aphrodite Keo White **Non-vintage**
  £4.89 (UN)
Othello Keo Red **Non-vintage** £4.89 (UN)
St-Panteleimon Keo White **Non-vintage**
  £4.89 (UN)
Commandaria St-John **Non-vintage**
  £8.99 (VA)

GREECE RED

Under £9.00

Château Carras **1996** £7.80 (TAN)
Château Carras **1995** £8.74 (PLAY)
Château Carras **1994** £7.95 (POR)
Mavrodaphne Patras **Non-vintage** £5.22
  (NO)
Nemea Boutari **1994** £4.79 (OD)
Nemea Kouros **1993** £4.69 (UN)
VdP de Crète Kourtakis **1997** £3.45 (WAI)

GREECE WHITE

Under £9.00

Demestica Achaia Clauss **Non-vintage**
  £4.89 (DI)
Domaine Carras **1995** £5.99 (JON)
Patras Kouros **1996** £3.99 (WAI)
Retsina Kourtakis **Non-vintage** £3.29 (SAF)
  £3.35 (MORR) £3.59 (THR) £3.59 (BOT)
Retsina Tsantalis **Non-vintage** £3.95 (TAN)
Samos Nectar, Vinicoles de Samos **Non-
  vintage** £8.90 (TAN)

INDIA

c. £9.50

Omar Khayyam **1990** £9.02 (NO)

ISRAEL

Under £8.50

Carmel Cabernet Sauvignon **1995** £6.19
  (SAF)
Palwin No. 4 **Non-vintage** £4.99 (SAF)
Yarden Chardonnay **1995** £8.15 (AV)

LEBANON RED

Under £9.00

Château Musar **1995** £6.99 (MAJ)
Château Musar **1991** £9.39 (PEN) £9.45
  (ROS) £9.93 (REI) £9.99 (MORR) £9.99 (JON)
  £10.13 (STE) £10.95 (TAN) £10.95 (FORT)
  £10.95 (VIN) £10.95 (BALL) £11.08 (CHA)

£9.00 → £9.99

Château Musar **1993** £9.20 (FA) £9.79
  (POR) £9.99 (NI) £9.99 (BO) £10.33 (PLAY)
  £10.70 (WRI) £10.95 (NA) £10.99 (PLA)
  £10.99 (PHI) £10.99 (BEN) £11.50 (AD)
Château Musar **1990** £9.59 (WHI) £9.75
  (CON) £9.99 (YOU) £11.52 (FLE)
Château Musar **1989** £9.60 (GAU) £12.49
  (YOU) £13.70 (WRI) £14.50 (ROB)

Over £20.00

Château Musar **1981** £22.42 (FA) £24.50
  (ROB) £28.47 (PLAY)
Château Musar **1977** £34.50 (BEN)
Château Musar **1969** £55.22 (FA)

LEBANON WHITE

Under £9.50

Château Musar Blanc **1996** £6.95 (POR)
  £7.07 (ROS)
Château Musar Blanc **1995** £7.19 (BO)
  £8.45 (ROB)
Château Musar Blanc **1994** £7.45 (CON)
  £7.70 (WRI)

MEXICO

Under £10.00

L A Cetto Nebbiolo **1994** £9.90 (TAN)
L A Cetto Nebbiolo **1993** £5.95 (DI)
L A Cetto Petite Sirah **1996** £4.79 (SAF)
L A Cetto Petite Sirah **1994** £4.92 (PLA)
L A Cetto Petite Sirah **1993** £9.00 (CRO)

MERCHANT DIRECTORY

All these merchants have been chosen on the basis of the quality and interest of their lists. We feature wines from almost all of them in our Price Guides. The abbreviations used for these merchants in the Price Guides are shown in brackets after their names.

If you want to find local suppliers, merchants are listed by region in the Who's Where directory on page 450; if you're looking for a specialist in a particular country's wines, you'll find a list at the start of that country's Price Guides.

The following services are available where indicated: **C** = cellarage, **G** = glass hire/loan, **M** = mail order, **T** = tastings and talks. There is a key to name abbreviations on page 8.

ADNAMS (AD)

Head office & mail order The Crown, High Street, Southwold, Suffolk IP18 6DP, (01502) 727220, fax (01502) 727273; mail order (01502) 727222 • The Cellar & Kitchen Store, Victoria St, Southwold, Suffolk IP18 6JW • The Wine Shop, Pinkney's Lane, Southwold, Suffolk IP18 6EW • The Grapevine 109 Unthank Rd, Norwich NR2 2PE, (01603) 613998
E-MAIL wines@adnams.co.uk
HOURS Mail order: Mon–Fri 9–6.30, Sat 9–12; Cellar & Kitchen Store and Wine Shop: Mon–Sat 10–6.30; The Grapevine: Mon–Sat 10–8 **CARDS** MasterCard, Switch, Visa **DISCOUNTS** 5% for 5 cases or more **DELIVERY** Free for complete cases, £5 part cases **MINIMUM ORDER** (mail order) 1 mixed case **EN PRIMEUR** Australia, Bordeaux, Burgundy, California, Douro, Loire, Rhône. **C G M T**
There's a Fine & Rare list, aimed at fine and rare salaries, but if you have that kind of money to spend I'm not sure that you need this book. (I do, however, offer a Personal Shopping service to the stinking rich. No fee, just an open and ongoing invitation to dinner.) But if you're not stinking rich you certainly need Adnams. The under-£5.50 wines have been collected into a separate list, to save you

slavering over wines you can't afford, but there are stars everywhere. France is good pretty well all over, but especially in the Rhône and the South; Spain looks very good, as does Portugal. Germany contains lots of treats, and Australia shows that there is far more in this country than everlasting Chardonnay and Cabernet.
1998 Viña Godeval, Bodegas Godeval, Valdeorras, £6.95 Greengages and nuts in a complex white.
1996 Semillon/Sauvignon, Cullen, Margaret River, £12.75 Great complexity and finesse.
1997 Pinot Noir, Martinborough Vineyards, Wairarapa, £14.50 Lovely supple fruit – probably the best New Zealand Pinot around.
1998 Marsanne, Domaine Montmarin, Vin de Pays des Côtes de Thongue, £4.95 Lovely lime-flower fruit: Marsanne at its best.

AMEY'S WINES (AME)

83 Melford Road, Sudbury, Suffolk CO10 1JT, (01787) 377144
HOURS Tue–Sat 9.30–6 **CARDS** Amex, MasterCard, Switch, Visa **DISCOUNTS** 50p per bottle for a mixed dozen or 6 unmixed bottles, further discounts for an unmixed case or 5 or more mixed cases **DELIVERY** Free within 20 miles of Sudbury for orders over £120. **G T**
The focus here is shared between France and the New World, with a handful of good Germans and rather more good Spanish and Italians to round it out. It's a good place to look for lesser clarets, though Bordeaux being what it is, there's better value for money to be had elsewhere. Rhônes are excellent here, and if it came to a choice between Alain Paret's St-Joseph at £9.49 and almost anything from Bordeaux at the same price, I know which I would have.
1996 Château Lousteau-Vieil, Sainte-Croix-du-Mont, £9.95 I'm always looking for good-quality, good-value botrytized wines, and this fits the bill. Real botrytis character and nice weight.
1994 St-Joseph, Les Larmes du Père, Alain Paret, £9.49 Bursting with blackberries and smoke. Pretty well irresistible.

ASDA (ASD)

Head office Asda House, Southbank, Great Wilson Street, Leeds LS11 5AD, 0113-243 5435, fax 0113-241 8666. 229 stores
WEB SITE www.asda.co.uk
HOURS Mon–Fri 9–8, Sat 8.30–8; open most bank hols; selected stores open Sunday **CARDS** MasterCard, Switch, Visa **DISCOUNTS** £1 off any 4 bottles **DELIVERY** South London only. **G T**
No thrills here, but then not a lot over a fiver either. Asda is good at doing good-value basics – and that applies to the rest of the store just as much as the wine. Once you get away from the own-label wines you have a better chance of finding something with some character: why does Asda think we want wines without excitement? But choose carefully and you'll find some sound everyday bottles.
Baga, Bright Brothers, £3.99 Portuguese red with some character.

ASHLEY SCOTT (AS)

PO Box 28, The Highway, Hawarden, Flintshire CH5 3RY, tel & fax (01244) 520655
HOURS 24-hr answerphone **DISCOUNTS** 5%

unmixed case **DELIVERY** Free in North Wales, Cheshire, Merseyside; elsewhere at cost **MINIMUM ORDER** 1 mixed case. **G M T**
Some good producers appear in a short list of mixed quality. There's Alsace Willm, Corbans from New Zealand and Grant Burge from Australia.
Grant Burge Fine Old Tawny (12 Years Old), £10.50 This is how port-style wines from Australia are described these days: as 'tawny'. Grant Burge's is good – nutty and fairly light.

AUSTRALIAN WINE CLUB (AUS)

Kershaw House, Great Western Road, Hounslow, Middx TW5 0BU, freephone orderline (0800) 856 2004, freefax (0800) 856 2114, enquiries tel 0208-538 0718
E-MAIL sales@austwine.demon.co.uk
WEB SITE www.australian-wine.co.uk
HOURS Mon–Fri 9–6, Sat 9–2 **CARDS** Amex, MasterCard, Visa **DELIVERY** Free anywhere in UK orders over £75 **EN PRIMEUR** Australia. **M T**
As lower-priced European wines seem to dedicate themselves more and more to fruit-driven sameness, Australian wines are becoming ever more characterful and (dare I say it?) more terroir-driven. Admittedly this is not happening at the lower level, so it's not an exact comparison. But nevertheless…. If you want a guide to the further reaches of Aussie wine (plus Chardonnay and Cabernet, okay) this is the place to go. A lot of the most famous names aren't here because they're exclusive to other shippers, but there are plenty of exciting ones to replace them.
1997 Riesling, St Hallett, Eden Valley, £7.99 Glorious scents of lemon and apple blossom and tingling ripe freshness.
1997 Cabernet Franc, Buckleys, Clare Valley, £6.99 Lovely raspberry fruit. You don't often see Cabernet Franc bottled by itself.

AVERYS OF BRISTOL (AV)

Orchard House, Southfield Road, Nailsea, Bristol BS48 1JN (01275) 811100, fax (01275) 811101
HOURS Shop: 8 Park St, Bristol: Mon–Sat 10–6; Wine Cellar: Culver St: Mon–Sat 10–7 **CARDS** Amex, MasterCard, Switch, Visa **DISCOUNTS** Monthly mail order offers, Bin Club 10% off most list prices **DELIVERY** Free 2 or more cases,

otherwise £5.50 per consignment (£2 in Bristol area) **EN PRIMEUR** Bordeaux, Burgundy, Port. **C G M T**

Averys focuses on mail order, and there are regular special offers. An Averys director once explained to me that the non-special offer prices – the list prices, in other words – were set at a level to allow for price cutting, so it might be sensible to get on the list and wait for the offers rather than buy at full price. However you do it, this is a go-ahead list that manages to be strong in France, Italy (lovely Soaves from Tedeschi) and Germany as well as South Africa, New Zealand, Australia, California and Canada. Yes, Canada.

1996 Ulysse, Etna Rosso, £6.70 Nerello Mascalese and Nerello Cappuccio grapes: rich and intense but well balanced.

1994 Graacher Himmelreich Riesling Spätlese, Freidrich Wilhelm Gymnasium, £10.30 Glorious balance of steel and fruit; cheap at the price. You can hardly do better than this from Germany.

BALLANTYNES OF COWBRIDGE (BAL)

3 Westgate, Cowbridge, Vale of Glamorgan CF71 7AQ, (01446) 774840, fax (01446) 775253 **HOURS** Mon–Sat 9–5.30 **CARDS** MasterCard, Switch, Visa **DISCOUNTS** 8% on mixed/unmixed cases in shop **DELIVERY** Free 1 case or more, £6 for smaller orders **EN PRIMEUR** Bordeaux, Burgundy, Italy. **C G M T**

Suddenly there are lots of new wines here, with the South of France particularly strong. If you've got money burning a hole in your pocket the Bordeaux list is very good, as is Burgundy, at somewhat lower prices. Not low, you understand; just lower. Italy is full of interest and so is Australia: Ballantynes have decided to go in for Australia in a big way. But they're concentrating on better quality wines, not the standard blends, so you'll find producers like Mount Langi Ghiran, Bannockburn and Bass Philip. If you're feeling rich try Mount Mary's Triolet at £28.50 – it's a top-class blend of Sauvignon Blanc, Semillon and Muscadelle made on the Graves pattern. Altogether a terrific list, full of unexpected goodies.

1994 Bergerac Cuvée Non-Filtrée, Château Richard, £5.99 Just to show that the French can make splendid 100% Sémillon too: this is lovely and limy.

1994 Chassagne-Montrachet, Vieilles Vignes, Domaine Guy Amiot, £10.95 A fair price for a light but well-structured red Burgundy with real style.

1996 Anjou Les Gelinettes, Domaine de la Sansonnière, Marc Angeli, £9.95 A beautifully structured blend of Malbec, Gamay and Cabernet Franc. I just love these Loire reds.

BALLS BROTHERS (BALL)

313 Cambridge Heath Road, London E2 9LQ, 0207-739 6466, fax 0207-729 0258, direct sales tel 0207-739 1642 **E-MAIL** sales@ballsbrothers.co.uk **WEB SITE** www.ballsbrothers.co.uk **HOURS** Mon–Fri 9–5.30 **CARDS** Amex, Diners, MasterCard, Switch, Visa **DISCOUNTS** Still wines 5% off 5 or more cases, 10% off 10 or more;

C = cellarage   **G** = glass loan/hire   **M** = mail order   **T** = tastings and talks

sparkling 2.5% of 5 or more, 5% off 10 or more
DELIVERY Free 1 case or more locally; £6 1 case,
free 2 cases or more, England, Wales and
Scottish Lowlands; islands and Scottish Highlands
phone for details **EN PRIMEUR** Bordeaux,
Burgundy. **C M T**

*An extremely good Burgundy list, with growers like
Daniel-Étienne Defaix in Chablis, Étienne Grivot
and Drouhin. Bordeaux is impressive too, and Balls
Bros. have got heavily into French country wines –
hooray. Outside France, Italy looks good, as does
Australia, and there are some good Spanish and
South African wines.*

1996 Minervois, Château Maris Prestige, £6.95
Classy, spicy red from a newish estate in the
South of France. This one seems set to become
something of a cult wine.

1997 Viognier, Heggies, Eden Valley, £11.95
One of the best Viogniers around. What's more,
it ages for years, reaching a rich waxiness. Superb
wine.

**1997 Alsace Riesling Rosenbourg, Domaine
Blanck, £9.50** Intense smoky flavours from a
meticulous winemaker.

ADAM BANCROFT (BAN)

East Bridge Office North, New Covent Garden
Market, London SW5 5JB, 0207-627 8700, fax
0207-627 8766

HOURS Mon–Fri 9–6 **CARDS** MasterCard, Visa
DISCOUNTS Negotiable **DELIVERY** Free in
London; elsewhere, £7.65 1 case, £10 2 cases,
free 3 cases or more **MINIMUM ORDER** 1 mixed
case **EN PRIMEUR** Burgundy in top years.
C M T

*There are extremely well chosen wines from France
here, especially from the Rhône and the South, and
Burgundy. Italy is excellent too, with the wines of
Drius and Mario Schiopetto from Friuli.*

**1997 Bourgogne Cuvée des Forgets, Patrick
Javillier, £12.50** Basic Burgundy from a
perfectionist producer: plenty of character and
ripe fruit.

**1998 Dolcetto d'Alba, Vigneto del Fiasc,
Castiglione Faletto, £9.46** Not a Dolcetto to be
taken lightly: bags of structure and weight.

**1997 Côtes du Rhône Bouquet des Garrigues,
Domaine du Caillou, £7.63** It is what it says:
perfumed, herby red.

BENEDICT'S

28 Holyrood St, Newport, Isle of Wight PO30 5AU, (01983) 529596

HOURS Mon–Sat 9–5.30 **CARDS** Amex, MasterCard, Switch, Visa **DISCOUNTS** 5% on a case **DELIVERY** Free on island. **C G M T**

An attractive list with carefully chosen wines from most places. You could drink very well here from the Loire, Rhône, Alsace, Bordeaux, Burgundy…. The Italian selection is short but interesting, with Masi's Amarone and a Barolo from Ceretto; Spain and Portugal are in the same mould, and there are no fewer than eight wines from the Isle of Wight. There's lots from South Africa but just one from the US, though it is Opus One.

1995 Sancerre le Chêne Marchand, Pascal Jolivet, £13.40 Pascal Jolivet's wines have subtlety as well as pungency, which makes them (just about) worth the price.

1995 Bright Brothers Old Vines, Estremadura, £5.35 Good gutsy Portuguese red.

BENNETTS (BEN)

High Street, Chipping Campden, Glos GL55 6AG, (01386) 840392, fax (01386) 840974

HOURS Mon–Fri 10–1 & 2–6, Sat 9–6 **CARDS** MasterCard, Switch, Visa **DISCOUNTS** On collected orders **DELIVERY** Free 1 case locally. Elsewhere £6 1 case, £12 2 cases, free 3 cases or more (£1 per case surcharge Scotland) **EN PRIMEUR** Alsace, Australia, Burgundy, California, New Zealand, Rhône. **G M T**

Bennetts is increasingly sourcing and shipping its own wines, a policy that means more work but, unless the buyers have terrible palates, a much better list. The palates of Bennetts' buyers are clearly exceedingly good, because this list is one to be drooled over. There are some seriously serious wines here – 1967 Château d'Yquem at, ahem, £495 a bottle – and some lovely Burgundies. But for the rest of us there are some good Rhônes and masses of excellent Italians, Australians and Californians.

1997 Pacherenc de Vic Bilh sec, Château de Viella, £6.95 Dry, rich, spicy white from one of Bennetts' new finds. There's also a late-harvest version at £8.50, which sounds amazing value.

1996 Solalto, Le Pupille, £8.50 (half bottle) An Italian dessert wine made from Sauvignon, Traminer and Semillon – fascinating and unusual.

1998 Casa Gualda, Bodegas Nuestra Señora de la Cabeza, £5.75 Nice soft La Mancha red with quite a bit of style.

1997 Frascati Superiore Vigna dei Preti, Villa Simone, £6.95 Copybook Frascati: terrifically attractive, with a nice sour-milk tang.

BERRY BROS. & RUDD (BER)

3 St James's St, London SW1A 1EG, 0207-396 9600, order number 0207-396 9669, fax 0207-396 9611 • Berry's Wine Warehouse, Hamilton Close, Houndmills, Basingstoke, Hants RG21 6YB, (01256) 323566, fax (01256) 340106 • Terminal 3 departures, Heathrow Airport, TW6 1JH, 0208-564 8361/3, fax 0208-564 8379 • Terminal 4 departures, Heathrow, TW6 3XA 0208-754 1961/1970, fax 0208-754 1984

E-MAIL telesales@bbr.co.uk

WEB SITE www.bbr.co.uk

HOURS Orders office daily 8–8; St James's St: Mon–Fri 9–5.30, Sat 10–4; Berry's Wine Warehouse: Mon–Thurs 10–6, Fri 10–8, Sat 10–4; Heathrow: Daily 6am–10pm **CARDS** Amex, Diners, MasterCard, Switch, Visa **DISCOUNTS** 3–7.5% according to quantity **DELIVERY** Free for orders of £100 or more, otherwise £7.50 **EN PRIMEUR** Bordeaux, Burgundy, Port, Rhône. **C G M T**

If you feel intimidated about going through Berry Bros' rather grand portals in St James's, just repeat the word 'Basingstoke' to yourself. Basingstoke is, you see, where Berrys has its warehouse, and both geographically and spiritually, it's a long way from St James's. Likewise, Berrys' list is predictably strong in classic areas like Bordeaux and Germany, but it has its unexpected side too. The Rhône and Alsace are excellent, there's a good list of French regional wines, a short but good Austrian list and even some good Portuguese wines. California looks terrific.

1996 Almaviva, Maipo Valley, £37.50 Is this Chilean red, the result of a joint venture between Philippe de Rothschild of Bordeaux and Concha y Toro of Chile, actually worth its exalted price? Personally I have my doubts.

C = cellarage   **G** = glass loan/hire   **M** = mail order   **T** = tastings and talks

BORDEAUX INDEX ltd
The only
fine wine traders
worth ringing.

Tel: +44 (0) 171 278 9495
fax: +44 (0) 171 278 9707
E-Mail zk85@dial.pipex.com

BIBENDUM (BIB)

113 Regents Park Rd, London NW1 8UR, 0207-916 7706, fax 0207-916 7705
E-MAIL sales@bibendum-wine.co.uk
WEB SITE www.bibendum-wine.co.uk
HOURS Mon–Fri 9–6 **CARDS** Amex, MasterCard, Switch, Visa **DELIVERY** Free mainland England and Wales; elsewhere £10, 5 or more cases free **MINIMUM ORDER** 1 case (minimum 6 bottles of any one wine) **EN PRIMEUR** Bordeaux, Burgundy, New World, Rhône. **C G M T**

The shop is now closed, and Bibendum does internet and mail order sales only. But it's still an excellent list, whether you go for the fine wines or the common-or-garden stuff. (For 'common-or-garden', read Nicolas Joly and Domaine Huet from the Loire, Bernard Legland from Chablis, Weingut Nikolaihof from Austria, Basedow from Australia – that sort of thing.) As always, the list is excellently well chosen. In fact it's probably a good thing the shop is gone: the temptation to fill a carrier bag there was always rather strong.

1990 Anjou Rouge, Château de la Roche aux Moines, Nicolas Joly, £12.73 Loire red wine of great depth from a leader of bio-dynamic viticulture.
1997 Côtes du Rhône, Perrin Réserve, £7.05 Stylish red with good herby, earthy flavours.
NV Champagne Louis Roederer Brut Premier, £24.47 Wine of perfect elegance and finesse.
1998 Primitivo di Puglia, Allora, £5.20 Rich, figgy fruit from the southern Italian version of Zinfandel. Excellent value.

BOOTHS (BO)

4 Fishergate, Preston PR1 3LJ, (01772) 251701, fax (01772) 204316. 24 stores
HOURS Office: Mon–Fri 9–5; shop hours vary
CARDS MasterCard, Switch, Visa **DISCOUNTS** 5% any 6 bottles; 15% on orders of £150 or more. **G T**

A remarkably good list for any merchant, never mind a supermarket. That being said, you won't find Schlumberger's 1989 Pinot Gris, Cuvée Clarisse at £39 in every branch. But it's fair to expect good southern Portuguese reds at much the same price as Bulgarian reds, and they're far more interesting. There's also a very good list of proper sherries – I mean the authentically tangy stuff – from Lustau.

1996 Chablis Vieilles Vignes, Daniel Defaix, £10.99 This may seem a lot to pay for basic Chablis, but there's nothing basic about Defaix, nor about his Vieilles Vignes cuvée. Stunning, smoky, steely stuff.
San Emilio Pedro Ximenez, Emilio Lustau, £10.99 Dark, sticky sherry of rich, grapy intensity. Pour it over vanilla ice-cream.

BORDEAUX DIRECT

New Aquitaine House, Exeter Way, Theale, Reading, Berks RG7 4PL, 0118-903 0903, fax 0118-903 1073, order line tel 0118-903 0303, fax 0118-903 0313
E-MAIL orders@bordeaux-direct.co.uk
HOURS Mon–Fri 9–9, Sat–Sun 9–6 **CARDS** Amex, Diners, MasterCard, Switch, Visa
DISCOUNTS Special offers **DELIVERY** £4.99 per order **EN PRIMEUR** Australia, Bordeaux, Burgundy, Rhône. **C M T**

This company has sometimes seemed to suffer from a lack of direction in the past. It's currently on good form, with a good Bordeaux list and cheaper, interesting wines from all over. There's Chablis from Domaine Dampt, for example.

1997 La Forza, Rosso del Salento, £4.29 Easy going juicy red from the South of Italy.
1996 Rioja, Familia Martínez Bujanda, £6.29 Creamy, oaky white Rioja, quite delicious.

BOTTOMS UP (BOT)

See First Quench.

C = cellarage   **G** = glass loan/hire   **M** = mail order   **T** = tastings and talks

BUDGENS

Head office PO Box 9, Stonefield Way, Ruislip, Middx HA4 0JR, 0208-422 9511, fax 0208-864 2800, for nearest store call 0800 56002. 115 stores in South-East

HOURS Usually Mon–Sat 8–8, Sun 10–4 **CARDS** MasterCard, Switch, Visa **DISCOUNTS** 5% for 6 or more bottles. **G T**

If you happen to have one of the biggest Budgen stores near you it could be quite a good source, with good clarets (no vintages listed) up to La Fleur Pétrus at £32.99. Lesser stores presumably stick to safe everyday choices. The list puts Gallo's White Zinfandel under German wines, incidentally: does Budgens know something we don't?

Petite Sirah, L A Cetto, £4.39 Earthy, spicy stuff from Mexico.

BUTLERS WINE CELLAR (BU)

247 Queens Park Rd, Brighton BN2 2XJ, (01273) 698724, fax (01273) 622761

HOURS Tue–Wed 10–6, Thu–Sat 10–7 **CARDS** Amex, MasterCard, Switch, Visa **DELIVERY** Free locally 1 case or more, free mainland England, Wales and Scotland 3 or more cases. **G M T**

The two Butler gentlemen have taken to putting faintly alarming photographs of themselves on the front covers of their lists. Most wine merchants smile in their photographs. You feel you wouldn't dare crack a joke with these two. Which is odd, because the list is so quirky and interesting. One of its specialities is wines from anniversary years, but there's lots of well-priced standard stuff from Bordeaux as well. The Loire, the South of France – all these look good, as does Germany, and Italy is very good. The point of the list is its ever-changing nature: some of the wines are available in quantities of less than a case, so it's best to be on the mailing list, and then move quickly.

1977 Cabernet Sauvignon, Conn Creek, California, £20 Just the sort of rarity you can expect to find here.

1990 Kaseler Nies'chen Riesling Spätlese Trocken, Deinhard, £6.95 Petrol and lemon.

ANTHONY BYRNE (BY)

Ramsey Business Park, Stocking Fen Rd, Ramsey, Cambs PE17 1UR, (01487) 814555, fax (01487) 814962

E-MAIL Anthony.Byrne@dial.pipex.com
HOURS Mon–Fri 9–5.30 **CARDS** None **DISCOUNTS** available on cases **DELIVERY** Free 5 cases or more, or orders of £250 or more; otherwise £6 **MINIMUM ORDER** 1 case **EN PRIMEUR** Madiran. **C M T**

One of Anthony Byrne's many specialities is the South of France: for some years now he's proved himself adept at winkling out good wines from lesser-known appellations. Burgundy is also very strong, with growers like Sauzet and Michelot, and from Alsace he has probably every wine made by Zind-Humbrecht. And that's a lot of wines. Australia relies mostly on well-known names like Penfolds: France is clearly Byrne's first and main love. And why not?

1997 Tannat, Alain Brumont, Gascony, £3.98 A surprisingly seductive red from a very good grower.

CAPE PROVINCE WINES (CAP)

77 Laleham Rd, Staines, Middx TW18 2EA, (01784) 451860, fax (01784) 469267

E-MAIL capewines@msn.com
WEB SITE www.cape-wines.co.uk
HOURS Mon–Sat 9–5.30 **CARDS** MasterCard, Visa **DELIVERY** £6.50 1 case mainland UK, case rate reduces with quantity **MINIMUM ORDER** 6 bottles. **G M T**

A no-frills list of purely South African wines that doesn't give vintages. But it looks higher quality than ever before, with good names like Saxenburg and Backsberg.

Marlbrook, Klein Constantia, £8.83 A Merlot-based Bordeaux blend, nicely plummy.

Cabernet Sauvignon, Plaisir de Merle, £11.28 Supple, ripe and round.

CAVE CRU CLASSÉ (CAV)

Unit 13, Leathermarket, Weston Street, London SE1 3ER, 0207-378 8579, fax 0207-378 8544 and 403 0607

E-MAIL enquiries@ccc.co.uk
WEB SITE www.cave-cru-classe.com
HOURS Mon–Fri 9–5.30 **CARDS** Amex, MasterCard, Visa **DELIVERY** £15 per order in London and the South-East; price according to distance for other addresses **MINIMUM ORDER** 1 mixed case **EN PRIMEUR** Bordeaux. **M T**

Very much a fine wine specialist. There are top clarets here in vintages back to 1869 (Gruaud-Larose at £750 the bottle): that's pre-phylloxera. Among the Burgundies the Domaine de la Romanée-Conti is present in strength, as is Domaine Étienne Sauzet, and there is a sprinkling from the likes of Michel Niellon, Domaine Leroy and Hubert de Montille. There are Rhônes from Guigal, Jaboulet-Aîné and other top producers, and California includes Dominus, Caymus Special Selection, Ridge Monte Bello and others of that ilk. The list itself costs £5, so it's rather a shame that mine fell apart when I opened it.

1995 Bourgogne Aligoté, Domaine Coche-Dury, £17.63 This must be one of the cheapest wines on this list. It's also rather good: lemony and nutty.

CHÂTEAUX WINES (CHA)

Paddock House, Upper Tockington Rd, Tockington, Bristol BS32 4LQ, tel & fax (01454) 613959
E-MAIL cheryl.miller@bris.ac.uk
WEB SITE www.btinternet.com/~chateaux-wines
HOURS Mon–Fri 9–5.30, Sat 9–12.30 **CARDS** MasterCard, Switch, Visa **DISCOUNTS** Negotiable **DELIVERY** Free UK mainland 2 cases or £128 (inc VAT) in value **MINIMUM ORDER** 1 case (unmixed). **C M T**
The wines are mostly French on this short mail-order list; in fact the only ones that aren't are various vintages of Chateau Musar from Lebanon. It all looks a bit haphazard, but we've tasted some nice wines from here in the past.

1996 Chateau Listran, Cru Bourgeois Médoc, £8.70 Decent basic claret with good fruit.

Cave Cru Classé
it's in the bottle

Unit 13 The Leathermarket,
Weston Street, London SE1 3ER
Tel: +44 171 378 8579
Fax: +44 171 378 8544
www.cave-cru-classe.com
e-mail: enquiries@ccc.co.uk
contact: Sales Team

COCKBURNS OF LEITH INCORPORATING J E HOGG (COC)

The Wine Emporium, 7 Devon Place, Haymarket, Edinburgh EH12 5HJ, 0131-346 1113 and 337 6005, fax 0131-313 2607
HOURS Mon–Fri 9–6; Sat 10–5 **CARDS** Switch **DELIVERY** Free 12 or more bottles within Edinburgh; elsewhere £5 1–2 cases, free 3 cases or more **EN PRIMEUR** Bordeaux, Burgundy. **G T**
This list is less vast than some, but everything on it looks extremely tasty. And isn't that what one wants from wine? There are good Alsace wines from Kuentz Bas and Trimbach, and Burgundies from the greatly improved firm of Bouchard Père. The listed clarets are at the cheaper end – i.e. under a tenner – although there is also a changing range of fine wines. Tell them your preferences and they'll tell you what they've got. Or take a look at the web site they are developing: www.winelist.co.uk aims to pool information on thousands of different wines, any of which can be delivered within two weeks of ordering.

1995 Amarone delle Valpolicella Classico, Tedeschi, £14.41 Wonderful bitter-sweet red from northern Italy.

CONNOLLY'S WINE MERCHANTS (CON)

Arch 13, 220 Livery Street, Birmingham B3 1EU, 0121-236 9269/3837, fax 0121-233 2339
E-MAIL connowine@aol.com
HOURS Mon–Fri 9–5.30, Sat 10–variable closing times; ring to check **CARDS** Amex, MasterCard, Switch, Visa **DELIVERY** Surcharge outside Birmingham area **DISCOUNTS** 10% for cash & carry **EN PRIMEUR** Bordeaux, Burgundy, Port. **G M T**
Bordeaux, Burgundy and the Rhône all look very good, and there is an interesting German list, too. Italy has names like Isole e Olena and Allegrini (La Poja at £24.75) and from Spain there are Riojas from Faustino and Artadi. Top Aussies include Grant Burge, Yarra Yering and Shaw & Smith.

1996 Côtes du Rhône Rouge, Belleruche, Chapoutier, £6.49 Good smoky, spicy fruit, but supple with it.

1996 Quinta da Bacalhoa, Terras do Sado, Portugal, £7.69 This wine has been around for donkeys' years, but it's still chocolatey and rich.

CORNEY & BARROW (CB)

Head office 12 Helmet Row, London EC1V
3QJ, 0207-251 4051, fax 0207-608 1373/1142
• 194 Kensington Park Rd, London W11 2ES,
0207-221 5122 • 26 Rutland Sq, Edinburgh
EH1 2BW, 0131-228 2233 • Belvoir House,
High St, Newmarket CB8 8OH, (01638) 662068
• Corney & Barrow (Scotland) with Whighams
of Ayr, 8 Academy Street, Ayr KA7 1HT,
(01292) 267000

WEB SITE www.corbar1.demon.co.uk
HOURS Mon–Fri 9–6 (24-hr answerphone);
Kensington Mon–Sat 10.30–8, Sun 11–2;
Edinburgh Mon–Fri 9–6; Newmarket Mon–Sat
9–6; Ayr Mon–Sat 9.30–5.30 **CARDS** Amex,
MasterCard, Visa **DELIVERY** Free 2 or more
cases within M25 boundary, elsewhere free 3 or
more cases. Otherwise £8 plus VAT per delivery.
EN PRIMEUR Bordeaux, Burgundy, Port. **C M T**

*A great place to go if you want some really serious
claret – I mean Pétrus-type serious. C&B is the
agent for Pétrus – a useful wine to have on one's
list, no doubt. There are stacks of other good
clarets, as well as lots of Sauternes, and Burgundy
kicks off with the Domaine de la Romanée-Conti –
another useful exclusivity. But it's not all classic
wines here. There are some interesting-looking
bottles from Switzerland, and some goodies from
Italy; the German selection is good but smaller than
you might expect from a merchant still perceived
as being traditional, and the New World is well-
chosen. Definitely a merchant worth investigating,
even if you don't want to buy fine claret.*

**1996 Abbaye de Mont Grand Cru Blanc,
Réserve de la Ville de Lausanne, Switzerland,
£10.93** Part of a small allocation which C&B
managed to charm out of the city of Lausanne –
the only foreigners to have done so, it says.
Deeply flavoured with good backbone.
1993 Notre Dame de Landiras, £7.27 Pure
Sémillon from Bordeaux, waxy and tropical.
**1996 Bourgogne Blanc les Sétilles, Olivier
Leflaive, £8.75** If you want less expensive white
Burgundy you're far better off buying a
Bourgogne Blanc from a top producer like
Leflaive than a supposedly grander wine from
somebody less good. This is remarkably stylish.

CROQUE-EN-BOUCHE (CRO)

221 Wells Road, Malvern Wells, Worcestershire
WR14 4HF, (01684) 565612
E-MAIL croque@globalnet.co.uk
HOURS No fixed hours; open by telephone
appointment 7 days a week **CARDS** MasterCard,
Switch, Visa **DISCOUNTS** 4% on orders of £500
or more, if cash and collected; 2.5% if paid by
credit card **DELIVERY** Free locally 2 or more
cases elsewhere for orders over £300; otherwise
£8.50 **MINIMUM ORDER** 1 mixed case. **M**

*I simply don't know how you choose wine from a list
like this. I mean, I can see how you might narrow it
down to a top 50. You could then refine this to a
top 30, and even a top 20. Choosing a top ten
would be more arbitrary. And it must be terrible to
go to the restaurant and have to choose just one.
The waiters must be accustomed to long delays. I
mean, suppose you've settled on Rhône –
something of a speciality here – there are two-and-
a-half closely printed pages to choose from. That's
13 Gigondas, 57 Châteauneufs, and so on. Perhaps
it's better to avoid the Rhônes and settle on, say,
Russian sparkling: there's only one of those. ('More
interesting than exciting,' says the list.)*

1985 Ghemme Riserva, Brugo, £12 Sturdy
Nebbiolo with a good tarry nose.
1993 Rioja, Marqués de Griñon, £9.50 Subtlety
and finesse as well as power.
**1989 Late-Harvest Semillon, Lindemans, £7.50
(half bottle)** Sweet, rich and deeply fruity.

CWS (CO)

Head office New Century House, Manchester
M60 4ES, freephone 0800 317827 for stock
details, fax 0161-827 5117. 1377 licensed stores
WEB SITE www.co-op.co.uk
HOURS Variable **CARDS** Variable **EN PRIMEUR**
Bordeaux. **M T**

*They're keen on Argentinian red at the Co-op –
well, very sensible too. They also have Brazilian red
and white, which seems to me to be rather
misguided. (It doesn't take many days in Brazil
before you lose all interest in tasting the local wine
and start knocking back caipirinhas instead.)
Generally the own-label wines here are far behind
the rest of the selection, so look in areas like*

C = cellarage   **G** = glass loan/hire   **M** = mail order   **T** = tastings and talks

Portugal, where there are some good flavours at low prices. Or Spain. One of the hardest-to-find wines on this list must be Torres Gran Coronas Cabernet Sauvignon, in just 26 stores. By contrast, Jacob's Creek Shiraz Cabernet is in 1050 stores.

Petite Sirah, L A Cetto, £4.49 Good earthy, spicy red from Mexico, but only in 144 stores.

Primitivo del Salento, Le Trulle, £4.49 Juicy and ripe, and in 490 stores.

Ramada Branco, Estremadura, £2.99 Dirt-cheap fresh, light white from Portugal. In 740 stores.

DIRECT WINE SHIPMENTS (DI)

5/7 Corporation Square, Belfast, Northern Ireland BT1 3AJ, 028-9024 3906/9023 8700, fax 028-9024 0202

E-MAIL enquiry@directwine.co.uk
WEB SITE www.directwine.co.uk
HOURS Mon–Fri 9–6.30 (Thurs till 8), Sat 9.30–5
CARDS MasterCard, Switch, Visa **DISCOUNTS** 10% in the form of complimentary wine with each case **DELIVERY** Free Northern Ireland 1 case or more, £10 per case mainland UK **EN PRIMEUR** Bordeaux, Burgundy, Loire, Rhône.
C G M T

The thing about this list is that it's so interesting: there are lots of quirky corners, with some good growers tucked into them. There are lovely Calera Pinot Noirs from California, and Nebbiolo from top Mexican producer L A Cetto, the wonderfully complex Henschke wines from Australia, Mezzacorona Teroldega Rotaliano from northern Italy and Lustau Manzanilla Pasada sherry.

1997 Pouilly-Fuissé Sélection Vincent, J J Vincent, £13.50 Yes, it's expensive, but if you're going to splash out on Pouilly-Fuissé you might as well have a taste of what the top producer is doing. This is his cheaper wine: Château Fuissé is £18.50 upwards.

1996 Chinon Terroir, Charles Joguet, £7.95 A raspberry-fruited Loire red with excellent depth.

1995 Topolos Zinfandel, Russian River Valley, £8.99 Big, muscular California Zinfandel. It's organic, too.

1995 Vega Sicilia Alion, £17.95 Rich and refined red from a new estate owned by Vega Sicilia.

DOMAINE DIRECT (DOM)

10 Hardwick Street, London EC1R 4RB, 0207-837 1142, fax 0207-837 8605

E-MAIL domaine.direct@ndirect.co.uk
HOURS 8.30–5.30; or answering machine
CARDS Mastercard, Switch, Visa **DELIVERY** Free London; elsewhere in UK mainland 1 case £8.81, 2 cases £11.75, 3 or more free **MINIMUM ORDER** 1 mixed case **EN PRIMEUR** Burgundy, but not every year. **M T**

Domaine Direct has discovered the New World, which is very good news given that it has applied the same high standards as it does to its Burgundy list. So from Australia you'll find names like Grosset and St Hallett and Leeuwin Estate; from California producers like Ridge, Viader (expensive but beautifully structured) and Spottswoode. But Burgundy is still the main focus and it's still terrifically good, with a sensational selection.

1996 Zinfandel, Nalle, Dry Creek, £14.98 Concentrated, firm, blackberry flavours.

1994 Mercurey Blanc, Michel Juillot, £6.46 (half bottle) Good hazelnut fruit and correct oak.

BEN ELLIS WINES (ELL)

Brockham Wine Cellars, Wheelers Lane, Brockham, Surrey RH3 7BE, (01737) 842160, fax (01737) 843210

HOURS Mon–Fri 9–6 **CARDS** MasterCard, Visa
DELIVERY Free 1 case local area and Central London, elsewhere free 5 cases or orders over £400; other orders £10 **MINIMUM ORDER** 1 mixed case **EN PRIMEUR** Bordeaux, Burgundy, Rhône. **C G M T**

It's good to see some interesting Austrian wines here, including some from Styria, which can be hard to love, and from Schloss Gobelsburg in Kamptal, which are both refined and ripe. Look for the wines of Franz Hirtzberger from the Wachau, too. There's lots from France, with relatively inexpensive clarets for die-hards and nice Rhônes for when they decide to be adventurous. Alsace looks good, too, as does Spain, and New Zealand is a cut above the average, with names like Martinborough, Neudorf, Kumeu River and Vavasour. There's also a separate fine wine supplement to the list; here you'll find Cloudy Bay and top names from classic regions.

C = cellarage   **G** = glass loan/hire   **M** = mail order   **T** = tastings and talks

1995 Côtes du Rhône-Villages Rasteau,
Domaine la Soumade, £7.95 Good rich
southern Rhône flavours.
1994 Valdepusa Petit Verdot, Marqués de
Griñon, £12.25 A rare chance to taste this grape
alone.

FARR VINTNERS (FA)

19 Sussex St, London SW1V 4RR, 0207-821
2000, fax 0207-821 2020
E-MAIL sales@farr-vintners.com
HOURS Mon–Fri 10–6 **CARDS** None
DISCOUNTS Orders over £2000 **DELIVERY** Free
on wines sold at 'standard' price, otherwise
London £1 per case (min £10), elsewhere £4
per case (min £12) **MINIMUM ORDER** £500 plus
VAT **EN PRIMEUR** Bordeaux, Burgundy, Rhône.
C M T
*Farr Vintners is 21; doesn't seem possible. It sells, it
says, 'twice as much as all the auction houses
combined,' and that's a lot of wine. All of it is top-
class, investment-level stuff, but they put in new
finds as well. If you want to spend a lot of money,
this list is a must.*
1994 Monbazillac, Tirecul Gravière, £180 per
case Robert Parker loves this, and it's being
much hyped. Buy now?

FIRST QUENCH GROUP:
BOTTOMS UP (BOT), THRESHER
(THR), VICTORIA WINE (VIC), WINE
RACK (WR)

Head office Sefton House, 42 Church Street,
Welwyn Garden City, Herts AL8 6PJ, (01707)
385000, fax (01707) 385004; national delivery
via Drinks Direct, 0800 232221. 88 Bottoms Up
stores, 767 Thresher Wine Shops, 1016 Victoria
Wine stores, 236 Wine Rack stores
HOURS Mon–Sat 9–10 (some 10.30), Sun 12–3,
7–10; Scotland 12.30–10.30 **CARDS** MasterCard,
Switch, Visa **DISCOUNTS** Various offers
DELIVERY Free locally, some branches. **G T**
*First Quench sounds such a daft name, but there
you are. I wonder how they came up with it? Have
they read the excellent novel by Rupert Thomson
called Soft, which features a sinister soft drink
called Kwench!? Almost certainly not, I'd say. It's a
mega list with a fair number of wines available in all
the chains, but more in Bottoms Up and even more*

*in Wine Rack; but since your local branch of any of
them won't necessarily have the wine you want, and
probably will never even have heard of it, I
suggest you arm yourself with a copy of the list,
show them the wine you want and insist they get it.
It's worth the effort because there are masses of
good wines here. Just about everywhere is quite
strong: Australia, Spain, Chile, the Rhône, Italy…
Germany, though, is not. Victoria Wine used to be
excellent for German wines; will the new
dispensation change all that? I do hope not.*
1993 Vin Sec de Château Coutet, Graves,
£8.99, Bottoms Up, Wine Rack I have never
succeeded in finding this in these shops, but it's
listed. Clean, quince and wax fruit, from a top
Barsac château – this is the dry wine.
1995 Old Vines Zinfandel, Sebastiani,
California, £8.49, all chains Old Vines should
mean greater depth, and here it does.
1996 'O' Ormond Estate Chardonnay, Montana,
Gisborne, £10.99, all chains Complex New
Zealand wine.

LE FLEMING WINES (FLE)

9 Longcroft Avenue, Harpenden, Hertfordshire
AL5 2RB, (01582) 760125
E-MAIL CJEN101984@aol.com
HOURS 24-hour answering machine **DISCOUNTS**
5% on large orders **DELIVERY** Free locally
MINIMUM ORDER 1 case **EN PRIMEUR** Bordeaux,
Burgundy, Rhône. **G M T**
*A well-priced list of well-picked wines. It would be
hard to go wrong here, though personally I'd avoid
the Mouton-Cadet (which is most certainly not
what the list says it is: 'The well-known everyday
label for the first class growth Mouton Rothschild').
Alsace looks interesting, Portugal is pretty dire, but*

Australia is first class, with wines from Cullen, Charles Melton, Hollick, Rockford and Henschke.

1997 Jurançon Vendanges Tardives, Domaine Cauhapé, £14.26 Lovely sweet flavours of quince and nuts.

1995 Chardonnay, Cullen, Margaret River, £11.30 Excellent complex Chardonnay.

FORTNUM & MASON (FORT)

181 Piccadilly, London W1A 1ER, 0207-734 8040, fax 0207-437 3278

E-MAIL info@fortnumandmason.co.uk **WEB SITE** www.fortnumandmason.co.uk **HOURS** Mon–Sat 9.30–6 **CARDS** Amex, Diners, MasterCard, Switch, Visa **DISCOUNTS** 1 free bottle per dozen **DELIVERY** £5 per order **EN PRIMEUR** Bordeaux. **C M T**

Fortnum's staff still boasts an 'envious depth of knowledge,' and the list recommends drinking Muscat de Beaumes-de-Venise on 'wet Sundays when you read extracts from that well thumbed Austin [sic] novel'. Never mind. Peculiarities apart, this is an excellent list of excellent wines – as one would expect from Fortnum & Mason. Classic regions are well served; more surprisingly, so is the South of France, Australia and Italy.

Dry Oloroso Viejo de Jerez, Almacenista Viuda de Antonio Borrego, Lustau, £8.95 (half bottle) Glorious dry oloroso full of nuts and prunes.

FRIARWOOD (FRI)

26 New King's Road, London SW6 4ST, 0207-736 2628, fax 0207-731 0411

E-MAIL sales@friarwood.com **WEB SITE** www.friarwood.com **HOURS** Mon–Sat 10–7 **CARDS** Amex, Diners, MasterCard, Switch, Visa **DISCOUNTS** 5% on mixed cases, 12% unmixed **DELIVERY** Free locally, £5 1 or 2 cases in London, elswhere at cost **EN PRIMEUR** Bordeaux. **C G M T**

A list that is strongest in Bordeaux – good châteaux, good vintages – less strong in Burgundy, and has a sprinkling of wines from Italy and the New World. But Bordeaux is why you'd come here.

1995 Château Franc Grace Dieu, St-Émilion Grand Cru, £11.26 Nice modern claret at a nice modern claret price.

FULLER'S (FUL)

Head office Griffin Brewery, Chiswick Lane South, London W4 2QB, 0208-996 2000, fax 0208-996 2087. 65 branches in London and the South-East

HOURS Mon–Sat 10–10, Sun 11–10 **CARDS** MasterCard, Switch, Visa **DISCOUNTS** 1 bottle free with every case and 10% on selected unmixed cases **DELIVERY** Free locally. **G T**

It's funny how every chain and most supermarkets have to have a trophy wine or two – the sort of wine that you would never go to a high street chain specifically to buy, and are unlikely to see sitting around on the shelves of your local branch. In the case of Fuller's the trophy wine is Chateau d'Yquem 1990 at £145 a bottle. Why? Who buys it? Why is it there? You can buy some pretty serious wine at Fuller's – Pomerols like Château Gazin 1995 for £37.99, Burgundies like Henri Clerc's Bienvenues-Bâtard-Montrachet 1994 at £46 – but the only other Sauternes on the list is Château les Quints 1996 (I don't know it, but it's probably perfectly nice) at £8.99 for 50cl. Baffling. Anyway, on with the rest of the list. It's pretty impressive, strong in Bordeaux and Burgundy (as noted) but also in Chile, Australia and most of the New World. Southern France is good too: you know those wines with laddish names like Stonking Syrah and Utter Bastard? They're all here.

1996 Riesling, Rockford, Eden Valley, £8.99 Rocky Rockford makes superb wines, complex and subtle. This needs further age yet.

1995 Quinta do Crasto Reserva, Douro £7.99 The standard version of this Douro red is £5.95, but the Reserva is worth the extra.

GAUNTLEYS (GAU)

4 High St, Exchange Arcade, Nottingham NG1 2ET, 0115-911 0555, fax 0115-911 0557

E-MAIL rhone@innotts.co.uk **HOURS** Mon–Sat 9–5.30 **CARDS** Amex, MasterCard, Switch, Visa **DELIVERY** Free within Nottingham area, otherwise 1–2 cases £8 plus VAT, 3–5 cases £13 plus VAT **MINIMUM ORDER** 1 case **EN PRIMEUR** Burgundy, Rhône. **M T**

How refreshing: a merchant that isn't particularly interested in Bordeaux or the New World. Instead

---

C = cellarage   **G** = glass loan/hire   **M** = mail order   **T** = tastings and talks

the focus is on the Rhône, Loire, Alsace, Burgundy and the South of France – all areas that produce immensely interesting flavours. Gauntleys rhapsodizes about Bandol – quite right too. What's missing? Italy, do I hear you say? Coincidentally (or perhaps not) Gauntleys is moving into Italy even as I write this. Germany is next on the list, and Spain and Portugal are looking interesting.

1996 Teofilo Reyes, Ribera del Duero, £14.20 Luscious violets and blackcurrants backed up by big tannins.

1997 Côtes du Rhône-Villages Rasteau les Adres, Domaine Trapadise, £11.65 Lots of extraction and plenty of juicy fruit.

GELSTON CASTLE FINE WINES

Gelston, Castle Douglas, Scotland DG7 1QE, (01556) 503012, fax (01556) 504183
• 45 Warwick Square, London SW1V 2AJ, 0207-821 6841, fax 0207-821 6350
E-MAIL wines@gelstoncastle.co.uk
HOURS Mon–Fri 9–6 **CARDS** MasterCard, Switch, Visa **DISCOUNTS** For orders over 3 cases: within M25 £4 per case, elsewhere £2 per case **DELIVERY** Within M25 £10 1 case, £5 2 cases, free 3 or more; England and Wales £12.50 1 case, £7.50 2 cases, free 3 or more; higher charges apply in Scotland **MINIMUM ORDER** 1 case, £3 surcharge for mixed cases **EN PRIMEUR** Bordeaux, Burgundy, southern France, many others occasionally. **C G M T**
This mail-order-only outfit has found its niche: individual, high-quality wines of character and interest, not necessarily very commercial in flavour, and not much below £6. Sounds fair enough to me. If you want wines with Parker points or bargain basement prices you go elsewhere. If you opt for Gelston Castle you'll find an excellent range from France, especially Burgundy and the South, and Germany.

1983 Wallufer Walkenberg Riesling Spätlese, Becker, £15 Gloriously mature Rheingau Riesling with some weight.

GOEDHUIS & CO

6 Rudolf Place, Miles Street, London SW8 1RP, 0207-793 7900, fax 0207-793 7170
E-MAIL goedhuis@btinternet.com
HOURS Mon–Fri 9–6.30 **CARDS** MasterCard,

Visa **DELIVERY** Free 3 or more, otherwise £10 England, elsewhere at cost **MINIMUM ORDER** 1 unmixed case **EN PRIMEUR** Bordeaux, Burgundy. **C G M T**
Goedhuis is one of the places you go if you want top Burgundy and Bordeaux. There's some other stuff as well – Loire wines from Henri Pellé, Château de Beaucastel from the Rhône, a few Italians – but Bordeaux and Burgundy is where the Goedhuis heart lies. And it's a very impressive list. Bordeaux vintages go back to 1959 and run the gamut of the classed growths; Burgundy has lots of top names.

1996 Meursault, Domaine Matrot, £16.55 Textbook stuff, elegant and vegetal.

THE GREAT NORTHERN WINE COMPANY

The Old Bank, 342 Kirkstall Road, Leeds, W. Yorks LS4 2DS, 0113-230 4455, fax 0113-230 4488 • The Warehouse, Blossomgate, Ripon, N. Yorks HG4 2AJ, tel & fax (01765) 606767
E-MAIL gnw.leeds@onyxnet.co.uk
HOURS Mon–Fri 9–6, Sat 9.30–5 **CARDS** Amex,

MasterCard, Switch, Visa **DISCOUNTS** 5% for orders over £100 **DELIVERY** Free local area, elsewhere at cost, free 5 cases or more **MINIMUM ORDER** for deliveries £25 ex VAT **EN PRIMEUR** Bordeaux, Port. **G**

There's good wine from just about everywhere on this list, even a red from Franken in Germany. Now, anyone who stocks that sort of thing cannot be accused of being over-commercial. There are also wines from Chateau des Charmes in Canada, a producer which has come on enormously in the last couple of years, plus Tannat Viejo from Uruguay. Classic regions are equally well served, with Bordeaux and Burgundy fielding some very nice wines indeed. Agencies are De Gyffarde in New Zealand and F Baur et Fils in Alsace.

1996 Sancerre Rouge les Cailleries, Domaine Vacheron, £9.88 Terroir-driven red from a first-class producer.

GREAT WESTERN WINE (GW)

The Wine Warehouse, Wells Road, Bath BA2 3AP, (01225) 322800, fax (01225) 442139 **E-MAIL** post@greatwesternwine.co.uk **WEB SITE** www.greatwesternwine.co.uk **HOURS** Mon–Fri 10–7, Sat 10–6 **CARDS** Amex, MasterCard, Switch, Visa **DISCOUNTS** Negotiable **DELIVERY** Free 3 or more cases, otherwise £6.50 **MINIMUM ORDER** 1 mixed case **EN PRIMEUR** Bordeaux, Burgundy, Rhône. **C G M T**

This company showed tremendously well in our Best Buys tasting this year; its offerings were not just terrifically good quality, but they had character as well. And that is not as common as you might suppose. Somebody's been doing a lot of legwork to find interesting wines from the South of France, and Burgundy looks strong. The Rhône Valley has names like Alain Voge, and among the Loires is the St-Nicolas-de-Bourgueil of Domaine Taluau, which is easier to drink than to pronounce. Other parts of the world are at the same level.

1996 St-Nicolas-de-Bourgueil Cuvée du Domaine, Domaine Taluau, £8.99 Sturdy and rich, with good fruit.

PETER GREEN & CO

37a/b Warrender Park Road, Edinburgh EH9 1HJ, tel & fax 0131-229 5925 **HOURS** Mon–Thur 9.30–6.30, Fri 9.30–7.30, Sat 9.30–7 **CARDS** MasterCard, Switch, Visa **DISCOUNTS** 5% on a case or two unmixed half-dozens **DELIVERY** 1 case £6; extra cases £4 each. **G M T**

Classic regions are strong, with plenty of affordable claret and some affordable Burgundy. Italy is excellent, with names like Antinori, as is Spain, with Pesquera. Australia and NZ look classy. Peter Green has a good way of helping customers distinguish between German wines from Grosslagen (collections of sites) and German wines from Einzellagen (single sites). It's quite simple: you put a little 'e' in your list against Einzellagen wines and a 'g' against Grosslagen ones. Any other wine merchants want to pinch the idea?

1997 Bardolino Classico Superiore, Rizzardi, £5.95 Lovely light cherryish red.

1995 Barco Reale, Tenuta di Capezzana, £7.25 Excellent red Italian, with good depth and complexity.

ROGER HARRIS WINES (HAW)

Loke Farm, Weston Longville, Norfolk NR9 5LG, (01603) 880171, fax (01603) 880291 **E-MAIL** sales@rhwine.co.uk **WEB SITE** www.rhwine.co.uk **HOURS** Mon–Fri 9–5 **CARDS** Amex, MasterCard, Visa **DELIVERY** UK mainland, £3 for orders up to £100, £2 up to £150, free over £150 **MINIMUM ORDER** 1 mixed case. **M**

A Beaujolais specialist (indeed, I think the only Beaujolais specialist) with a passion for the wine and the region. And I love good Beaujolais – serious Beaujolais, I mean – though I don't think I could claim I love it more than many other wines. But finding serious Beaujolais is difficult, and I'm extremely glad that Roger Harris is prepared to do it for me. He stresses that too much can be made of Beaujolais' aging capacity, and that the majority of wines are made to be drunk young. I wonder what he'd think of the 1929 Moulin-à-Vent currently on Reid Wines' list? Roger Harris's list extends into the Mâconnais and Champagne, as well, but no 1929s there either, oddly enough.

1997 Juliénas, Jean Benon, £7.25 Firm and full, with good fruit. Juliénas is happily not one of the hopelessly overpriced crus.

1997 Morgon, Noël Aucoeur, £8.20 An oak-aged cuvée of considerable depth.

JOHN HARVEY & SONS (HA)

12 Denmark St, Bristol BS1 5DQ, 0117-927 5010, fax 0117-927 5002

HOURS Mon–Fri 10–6, Sat 10–5 **CARDS** Amex, Diners, MasterCard, Switch, Visa **DELIVERY** Free 4 cases or more UK mainland **EN PRIMEUR** Bordeaux. **C G M T**

A good list of Bordeaux and workmanlike elsewhere. Harveys seems to specialize in offering a good if pretty safe selection across the board; it's not one of those quirky merchants where you'll find wines you've never come across before. But you won't go far wrong here.

1995 Chardonnay Calcaire, Clos du Bois, Sonoma County £13.44 Elegant, French-influenced Chardonnay from California.

1996 Château la Tour-de-By, Cru Bourgeois Médoc, £8.79 Well-priced, reliable Médoc.

HAYNES HANSON & CLARK (HAH)

Sheep St, Stow-on-the-Wold, Glos GL54 1AA, (01451) 870808, fax (01451) 870508
• 25 Eccleston St, London SW1W 9NP, 0207-259 0102, fax 0207-259 0103

E-MAIL stow@hhandc.co.uk or london@hhandc.co.uk

HOURS Stow: Mon–Fri 9–6, Sat 9–5.30; London: Mon–Fri 9–7, Sat 10–4 **CARDS** Amex, MasterCard, Switch, Visa **DISCOUNTS** 10% unsplit case **DELIVERY** Free central London and Glos; elsewhere (per case) 1 case £6.80, 2 cases £4.90, 3–4 cases £4.20, free 5 or more cases or orders over £450 **MINIMUM ORDER** 1 case (mail order) **EN PRIMEUR** Bordeaux, Burgundy, Rhône. **G M T**

You'll get first-rate advice on Burgundy here, but it's also a place to come for Bordeaux, the Loire and the Rhône. Alsace comes from Domaine Charles Koehly, who makes some of the most elegant dry Muscat around, and there's good stuff from Australia and Italy.

1995 Vosne-Romanée Aux Réas, Domaine Anne-Françoise Gros, £20.85 The sort of red Burgundy it's worth splashing out for: great elegance and finesse.

1997 Muscat d'Alsace Charles Koehly et Fils, £8.85 The perfect match for asparagus.

Peter Green & Co
Independent Wine Merchants

1000 Wines
100 Malt Whiskies

Call or write for our list.
37a-b Warrender Park Road
Edinburgh EH9 1HJ
Tel/Fax:0131-229 5925

1996 Viura Jardin, Guelbenzu, Navarra, £4.80 Unusual spicy dry white.

1997 Barco Reale, Tenuta di Capezzana, £8.40 A beautifully balanced red that can be overlooked in the rush to find new fashions.

HEDLEY WRIGHT (HED)

11 Twyford Centre, London Road, Bishop's Stortford, Herts CM23 3YT, (01279) 506512, fax (01279) 657462

E-MAIL wine@hedleywright.com

HOURS Mon–Tue 9–6, Wed 9–5, Thu–Fri 9–7, Sat 10–6 **CARDS** MasterCard, Switch, Visa **DELIVERY** Free local area, 1 case £5, 2 or more cases £3 per case (max £12) **MINIMUM ORDER** 1 mixed case. **C G T**

Hedley Wright, a pioneering importer of South American wines, has absorbed Smedley Vintners and taken Derek Smedley's interesting selection of English wines from Warden Vineyards under its wing along the way. The list is a good all-rounder. Ports here are from Churchill, Alsace from Charles Koehly, and there's lovely Quinta do Fojo from the Douro Valley. Spain looks interesting, as does Italy. Agencies include Montes in Chile, source of the very good Montes Alpha Merlot and the very overpriced Montes Alpha M. You won't confuse them; the latter is three times the price of the former.

1996 Quinta do Fojo, Douro £10.95 Rich, supple red that's drinking beautifully now, but will go on improving.

1996 Merlot Montes Alpha, Montes, Curicó, £9.95 Vanilla plums – delicious.

C = cellarage   **G** = glass loan/hire   **M** = mail order   **T** = tastings and talks

DOUGLAS HENN-MACRAE

61 Downs View, Burham, Rochester, Kent ME1 3RR, (01634) 669394, fax (01634) 683096, mobile 07970 883785
E-MAIL drhm@clara.co.uk
HOURS Mail order & tel only, Mon–Sat to 10pm
CARDS None **DELIVERY** Free locally, otherwise £8 plus VAT per order **MINIMUM ORDER** 1 mixed case. **M T**

Douglas Henn-Macrae has one of the whackiest lists in the country. It's resolutely uncommercial, focusing as it does on the odder wines to emerge from Germany, and wines from the Pacific Northwest of the US. A lot of them are actually perfectly nice and would sit happily on a mainstream list – Columbia Crest Grenache or Chardonnay, for example, or Rheingau wines from the State Domaine. It's just that a lot wouldn't. Well, good for him.

1988 Chardonnay, Llano Estacado, Texas, £6.99 Just exactly how often does anyone you know offer round 11-year-old Texan Chardonnay? Henn-Macrae says this wine is 'now fully mature', so this is your chance.

HIGH BRECK VINTNERS (HIG)

Bentworth House, Bentworth, Nr Alton, Hants GU34 5RB, (01420) 562218, fax (01420) 563827
HOURS Mon–Fri 9.30–5.30, or by arrangement
DELIVERY Free locally, 2 or more cases; South-East, £6 for 1 case, £4 for 2, 3 free; rest of England and Wales £9 for 1, £6 for 2, £4 for 3, 4 or more free **MINIMUM ORDER** 1 mixed case
EN PRIMEUR Bordeaux. **G M T**

There are lots of exclusivities here: this is a merchant prepared to put effort into finding wines no-one else has, and the result is a most interesting list. Daniel Wiederhim in Alsace is just one example; or there's Gitton Père et Fils from the Loire (with a range of Sancerres and Pouilly-Fumés grown on different types of soil) and Roger Cuillerat in the southern Rhône. It's a list that anyone interested in wine should have. Get yourself a copy.

1995 Alsace Riesling Grand Cru Schoenenbourg, Daniel Wiederhirn, £9.99 Not a high price for an Alsace Grand Cru Riesling of great depth and finesse.

1993 Quarts de Chaume, Château de Bellevue, £6.99 High Breck is sick of the sight of this and a few other similar wines languishing on the list. And yet sweet Loire wines are wonderful: why won't you buy them?

JEROBOAMS (INCORPORATING LAYTONS) (JER)

Head office Jeroboams: 8–12 Brook Street, London W1Y 2BH, 0207-629 7916, fax 0207-495 3314 **Mail order** Laytons: 20 Midland Road, London NW1 2AD, 0207-388 4567, fax 0207-383 7419 • 50–52 Elizabeth Street, London SW1W 9PB, 0207-730 8108, fax 0207-730 9284 • 51 Elizabeth Street, London SW1W 9PP, 0207-823 5623, fax 0207-823 5722 • 25 Elystan Street, London SW3 3NT, 0207-581 2660, fax 0207-581 1203 • 20 Davies Street, London W1Y 1LH, 0207-499 1015, fax 0207-491 3052 • 77–78 Chancery Lane, London WC2A 1AB, 0207-405 0552, fax 0207-405 0553 • 96 Holland Park Avenue, London W11 3RB, 0207-727 9359, fax 0207-792 3672 • 6 Pont Street, London SW1X 9EL, 0207-235 1612, fax 0207-235 7246 • The Market Place, Cirencester, Glos GL7 2PE, (01285) 655842, fax (01285) 644101
E-MAIL sales@laytons.co.uk
WEB SITES www.jeroboams.co.uk *and* www.laytons.co.uk
HOURS Offices Mon–Fri 9–6, shops Mon–Sat 9–7 (may vary) **CARDS** Amex, MasterCard, Switch, Visa **DELIVERY** Shops: free for orders of £50 or over in central London; mail order: free for orders over £150, otherwise £10 **EN PRIMEUR** Bordeaux, Burgundy, Germany, Rhône. **C G M T**

Jeroboams (which used to be more cheese and stuff like that, with some wines) has now bought a controlling interest in Laytons, and the Laytons shops have been renamed. The erstwhile excellent-value Laytons Champagne seems to have kept its own name so far, but has shot up in price: at £17.63 it is no longer a good buy. This is a good list; not cheap, but good. There's an emphasis on subtlety of flavour that encompasses the choice from all regions, from Alsace to Australia.

C = cellarage   **G** = glass loan/hire   **M** = mail order   **T** = tastings and talks

1996 Soave Classico Superiore, Inama, £8.23
Proper Soave, from low-yielding vines. Clean, leafy and nutty.
1997 Riesling, Alkoomi, Western Australia, £7.44 Well-structured, crisp, pungent fruit.

S H JONES (JON)

27 High Street, Banbury, Oxfordshire OX16 8EW, (01295) 251179, fax (01295) 272352 • 9 Market Square, Bicester, Oxfordshire OX6 7AA (01869) 322448, fax (01869) 244588 • 121 Regent Street, Leamington Spa. Warwickshire CV32 4NU, (01926) 315609
HOURS Mon–Sat 8.30–6 **CARDS** Amex, MasterCard, Switch, Visa **DELIVERY** Free within van delivery area for 1 case or more; 'small delivery charge' otherwise. Elsewhere £7.50, free for orders over £150 **EN PRIMEUR** Bordeaux, Port. **C G M T**
You can drink exceptionally well here without breaking the bank – that's the whole aim of the company. So there are wines of great subtlety that are not hugely expensive: even these days, it can be done. From Bordeaux come lots and lots of petits châteaux, and Burgundy, too, tends to focus on the less expensive end, with wines from less central spots like St-Aubin or Montagny. The Loire, Alsace, the Rhône and the New World are all good, and Germany is especially fine.
1995 Graacher Himmelreich Riesling Kabinett, F W Gymnasium, £7.95 A perfect apéritif.

JUSTERINI & BROOKS (JU)

61 St James's Street, London SW1A 1LZ, 0207-493 8721, fax 0207-499 4653 • 45 George Street, Edinburgh EH2 2HT, 0131-226 4202, fax 0131-225 2351
E-MAIL j-b.retail@dial.pipex.com
HOURS London, Mon–Fri 9–5.30; Edinburgh, Mon–Sat 9.30–6 **CARDS** Amex, MasterCard, Switch, Visa **DISCOUNTS** £1 per case 2–4 cases, £2 per case 5–7 cases, £3 per case 8 cases and over **DELIVERY** Up to 2 cases, £9 UK mainland and N Ireland; free 2 cases and over; offshore UK £15 per case **EN PRIMEUR** Bordeaux, Burgundy, Rhône. **C G M T**
J&B celebrated its 250th anniversary in 1999, having opened its doors as a 'Foreign Cordial Merchant' in 1749. Not that it lingers behind the times. It was J&B who launched Le Dôme on an unsuspecting world – Le Dôme being a micro-cru from St-Émilion, made with enormous care and a great deal of new oak, which J&B snapped up at a high price in its first vintage. 'Will corks continue to be pulled if prices continue to be pushed higher and higher?' asks the list, of Bordeaux in general. Ask Le Dôme, say I. Bordeaux generally is very strong here: the oldest wine on the list is Haut-Brion 1895 at £2990 for a magnum (it's drinking now, apparently). Burgundy is pretty amazing too, with names like Marquis d'Angerville, Bruno Clair, Domaine Leroy and Jayer-Gilles. The Rhône and the Loire look terrific, and Alsace wines come from the extraordinary Domaine Weinbach. Outside France everything looks good, too – particularly Germany, Australia and Italy.
1996 Château La Louvière, Pessac-Léognan, £16 Quite rich white that will age well.
1989 Forster Kirchenstück Riesling Kabinett, Dr von Bassermann-Jordan, £7.95 Mature Riesling from the Pfalz.

KWIKSAVE

See Somerfield

LAY & WHEELER (LAY)

The Wine Centre, Gosbecks Park, Colchester CO2 9JT, (01206) 764446, fax (01206) 560002
E-MAIL layandwheeler@ndirect.co.uk
WEB SITE www.layandwheeler.co.uk
HOURS Mon–Sat 9–6.30, Sun 10–4; telephone orders Mon–Fri 8–6, Sat 8.30–4 **CARDS** Amex, MasterCard, Switch, Visa **DISCOUNTS** 5% 5 or more mixed cases, £3 per case if collected **DELIVERY** £6.95, free for orders over £150 **EN PRIMEUR** Bordeaux, Burgundy, Rhône. **C G M T**
A first-class list that's a joy to browse through, as well as to buy from. Classic regions like Bordeaux and Burgundy could hardly be better, and the Rhône, too (almost a classic region these days, I suppose) is excellent. Ditto the rest of France, and Australia. The many agencies include Henschke from Australia, Jean-Luc Colombo from the Rhône and Gaja in Piedmont.
1998 Château Nicot, Bordeaux Blanc, £5.98 A delicious blend of Sauvignon Blanc, Sémillon and Muscadelle.

1996 Zinfandel, Pedroncelli Mother Clone, Sonoma, £10.45 Full of chocolate and blackberry fruit. It comes from vines taken as cuttings in 1927.

LAYMONT & SHAW

The Old Chapel, Millpool, Truro, Cornwall TR1 1EX (01872) 270545, fax (01872) 223005 **E-MAIL** info@laymont-shaw.co.uk **WEB SITE** www.laymont-shaw.co.uk **HOURS** Mon–Fri 9–5 **CARDS** MasterCard, Visa **DISCOUNTS** £2.50 per case if wines collected, also £1 per case for 2 cases, £1.50 for 3–5, £2 for 6 or more **DELIVERY** UK mainland delivery included in wine price **MINIMUM ORDER** 1 mixed case. **G M T**
It's Iberia all the way with this enthusiastic list that points us towards all sorts of interesting corners of Spain and Portugal. If you want to be guided between traditional and modern bodegas, between light, juicy wines and oaky old ones, or you simply want to know which of the newer regions you might find interesting, Laymont & Shaw is your place. Highly recommended.

1995 Rioja Reserva, Muga, £8.75 Old-style Rioja, all vanilla and blackcurrants.
1996 Barbaldos, Bodegas Frutos Villar, £4.98 Youthful, fruit-first Tempranillo from Cigales.
1997 Quinta de Saes, Dão, £8.25 Lovely complex, spicy red from Portugal.

LAYTONS

See Jeroboams.

LEA & SANDEMAN (LEA)

170 Fulham Road, London SW10 9PR, 0207-244 0522, fax 0207-244 0533 • 211 Kensington Church Street, London W8 7LX, 0207-221 1982 • 51 Barnes High Street, London SW13 9LN, 0208-878 8643
HOURS Mon–Fri 9–8, Sat 10–8.30 **CARDS** Amex, MasterCard, Switch, Visa **DISCOUNTS** 5–15% depending on quantity **DELIVERY** £5 for 1 case; free 1 case or more London, and to UK mainland south of Perth on orders over £200 **EN PRIMEUR** Bordeaux, Burgundy, Cahors. **C G M T**
There are lots of terrific wines here that you won't find elsewhere; it's clear that Lea & Sandeman puts

a lot of legwork into its buying. A merchant that takes the trouble to find its own wines rather than just buying casefuls from another merchant is worth its weight in gold – and far more likely to turn up a bargain. France rules the list, with lots of Burgundy, Bordeaux and southern stuff; Italy is also excellent. Lea & Sandeman has masses of agencies, including Deiss in Alsace.

NV Champagne Laurent Perrier Brut 'Extra Aged' £19.95 Lea & Sandeman's stock of Laurent Perrier has an extra year of landed age compared to that on sale elsewhere, apparently. That's worth having for the richer flavour it gives.

1995 Kallista, Vriesenhof, Stellenbosch £8.95 Fine Bordeaux blend from South Africa. Very long finish.

1993 Vino Nobile di Montepulciano, Poliziano, Vigneto Caggiole, £14.95 Terrifically concentrated, with lots of sweet blackberry fruit balanced by ripe tannins.

1996 Cabernet Sauvignon, Pikes Polish Hill River Estate, Clare £9.95 Beautifully minty, raspberry fruit with great depth and elegance. One of Australia's most interesting producers.

LIBERTY WINES (LIB)

Unit A53, New Covent Garden Food Market, London SW8 5EE, 0207-720 5350, fax 0207-720 6158

E-MAIL order@libertywine.co.uk
HOURS 7.30–5.30 **CARDS** Mastercard, Switch, Visa **DELIVERY** Free 1 mixed case or more **MINIMUM ORDER** 1 mixed case. **M**

David Gleave has always had a passion for Italy, and the knack of getting hold of the best wines of that country. Accordingly he has names like Franz Haas, Fontodi, Isole e Olena, Selvapiana, Capezzana, Sassicaia, La Parrina, Villa Matilde…the list goes on and on, with wines at all price levels from the everyday to the very grand. From Australia there's Charles Melton, Mount Langi Ghiran, Plantagenet and others, and there are good wines from South Africa, Spain and the US as well as parts of France. But Italy is the main thing.

1997 Gavi di Gavi, La Giustiniana, Vigneti Centurionetta, £11.49 One of the best Gavis around, rich and perfumed.

1997 Chianti Classico, Isole e Olena, £13.95 Superb Chianti from a superb vintage. It's expensive because quantities were right down.

1997 Vigna Caracci, Fattoria Villa Matilde, £11.25 Barrel-fermented, single-vineyard white from Campania, with huge character and style.

LLOYD TAYLOR WINES LTD

Bute House, Arran Road, Perth PH1 3DZ, (01738) 444994, fax (01738) 447979
E-MAIL sales@lloyd-taylor-wines.com
WEB SITE www.lloyd-taylor-wines.com
HOURS Mon–Wed 9–5, Thur–Fri 9–5.30, Sat 12–3 **CARDS** MasterCard, Switch, Visa
DELIVERY Free UK mainland **MINIMUM ORDER** 1 mixed case **EN PRIMEUR** Bordeaux, Port.
G M T

There are well-chosen wines here from most parts of the world: not an enormous range from any one place, but every region boasts something interesting. Sherries are from Barbadillo, for example, and Alsace wines are from Schlumberger. The best Burgundies are those from Faiveley, and they're not overpriced. There's a good list of affordable clarets, too. The New World is interesting.

1997 Monica di Sardegna, Antigua, £6.79 Cherryish red with good weight.

MAJESTIC (MAJ)

Head office Odhams Trading Estate, St Albans Road, Watford, Herts WD2 5RE, (01923) 298200, fax (01923) 819105. 71 stores nationwide
E-MAIL info@majestic.co.uk
WEB SITE www.majestic.co.uk
HOURS Mon–Sat 10–8, Sun 10–6 (may vary)
CARDS Amex, Diners, MasterCard, Switch, Visa
DELIVERY Free mainland UK 1 case or more
MINIMUM ORDER 1 mixed case **EN PRIMEUR** Bordeaux. **G M T**

Bordeaux and Burgundy are good here, though not uniformly so; the Loire and the Rhône look better, as does Italy. The range is a complete mixture, from everyday commercial wines at low prices to good and interesting bottles; there seems to be little overall direction. But who cares, when the goodies are so very good?

C = cellarage   **G** = glass loan/hire   **M** = mail order   **T** = tastings and talks

1995 Capitel San Rocco Ripasso, Tedeschi, £6.99 Rich, bitter-cherry red at a good price.
1994 Marqués de Murrieta Reserva Especial, Rioja, £7.99 Classic oak-aged white Rioja with waxy flavours and good fruit.
1997 Trittenheimer Apotheke Riesling Auslese, Grans-Fassian, £8.99 Glorious Mosel Auslese with ripe fruit and taut acidity.

MARKS & SPENCER (MAR)

Head office Michael House, 47–67 Baker Street, London W1A 1DN, 0207-935 4422; 293 licensed stores nationwide
HOURS Variable **DISCOUNTS** 12 bottles for the price of 11. **T**
Good, well-made wines with attractive, commercial flavours. You're unlikely to buy anything here that you actively dislike. But the nature of the beast means that M&S goes to the largest producers for its wines, and anything too quirky or individual is out of the question. Expect clean, fruit-driven flavours that are typical of their grape, with no surprises. Prices are fair.
1998 Sauvignon Blanc, Kaituna Hills, Marlborough £5.99 Clean, gooseberry-tasting NZ Sauvignon.

MILLÉSIMA (MI)

87 Quai de Paludate, BP 89, 33038 Bordeaux Cedex, France, 0033 557 808813, fax 0033 557 808819, Freephone 00800 267 33289
E-MAIL millesima@millesima.com
WEB SITE www.millesima.com
HOURS Mon–Fri 8–5.30 **CARDS** MasterCard, Switch, Visa **DELIVERY** Free for orders over £500. Otherwise £20 **EN PRIMEUR** Bordeaux.
C M

Bordeaux-based merchant with no shop, but the prices are no-nonsense duty-paid, delivered to your door prices and the list is designed with UK customers in mind. These people really are trying to make it easy for you. Bordeaux is the main focus, of course, and vintages go back to 1970, which is pretty good for a nation that likes its red Bordeaux a great deal younger than that. Perhaps it's a sop to British customers. There are loads of magnums, double magnums and jeroboams, too. The rest of the world (which in Millésima's terms consists of the Rhône, Loire, Alsace, Provence, Italy, Portugal, Champagne and some spirits like Cognac) gets less of a look in, though the producers are good: Guigal in the Rhône, Nicolas Joly in the Loire, Gaja in Piedmont. Oddly, the Douro selection is rather good. Should you happen to be in Bordeaux, they will happily show you round their cellar. There are two million bottles there, apparently, but presumably you won't want to look at each one. Will you?
1996 Les Tourelles de Longueville, £16.67 The second wine of Château Pichon-Longueville. Rich fruit and good winemaking.
1996 Quinta Vale Dona Maria, Douro, £15 Well-made Portuguese red, all spices and figs and plums.

MONTRACHET (MON)

59 Kennington Road, London SE1 7PZ, 0207-928 1990, fax 0207-928 3415
E-MAIL charles.taylor.wines@dial.pipex.com
HOURS Office/mail order Mon–Fri 8.30–6,
CARDS MasterCard, Visa **DELIVERY** England and Wales £4 plus VAT 1 case, free 2 or more cases; Scotland ring for details **MINIMUM ORDER**

I unmixed case **EN PRIMEUR** Bordeaux, Burgundy. **M T**

An impressive range, with Chablis featuring William Fèvre, leading exponent of the oaky style, and Jean Brocard, a leading exponent of non-oaked. In the Côte d'Or there are wines from Domaine Jacques Gagnard-Delagrange, Louis Carillon, Marquis d'Angerville, Lucien Boillot, Comte de Vogüé and others; the Rhône has Domaine Marc Sorrel, Bernard Gripa and others. Bordeaux is also excellent at all price levels. So is Germany, which is very much a speciality. So you'll find a big range from Lingenfelder in the Pfalz, which is an agency. Rainer Lingenfelder is a slightly batty character with, apparently, an obsession with the letter Y. He's named a Silvaner Ypsilon, and declassified it to table wine so as to be able to spell the grape the French way, Sylvaner. He makes a Dornfelder called Onyx. And every car registration number has to have a Y in it. Why? (Ho ho.)

1996 Scheurebe Spätlese Old Vines, Lingenfelder, £9.79 Lingenfelder is one of the top producers of this somewhat difficult grape, which needs good ripeness and low yields – like this – if it is to succeed.

MORENO WINES (MOR)

11 Marylands Road, London W9 2DU, 0207-286 0678, fax 0207-286 0513
E-MAIL sales@moreno-wines.co.uk
HOURS Mon–Wed 4–10, Thurs–Fri 4–10.30, Sat 10-10.30, Sun 12–8 **CARDS** Amex, MasterCard, Switch, Visa **DISCOUNTS** 5% 1 or 2 cases, 10% 3 or more cases **DELIVERY** Free locally. **C G M T**
Spanish specialist with an all-embracing approach to its favoured country. There may be some Spanish regions not represented here, but I can't think of any. There's Clos Mogador from Gratallops in Priorato (a mere £32 a bottle); there's Pesquera and Alion from Ribera del Duero, and Vega Sicilia itself. Outside Spain Moreno is agent for Rex Hill Vineyards in Oregon and La Concepción in Bolivia.

1994 Tinto Reserva, Bodegas Muga, £8.60 Red Rioja from the most traditional of all bodegas.

1994 Con Class Barrel-Fermented Verdejo, Rueda, £6.99 Dry Verdejo with ripe lemony flavours.

1998 Txomín Etxaniz, Chacolí de Guetaria, £10.95 No, somebody hasn't been hitting all the wrong keys: this wine really is spelled like this. It comes from the Basque country and once you get past the name it's a nice crisp white with lemony and greengagy fruit, and high acidity.

MORRIS & VERDIN (MV)

10 The Leathermarket, Weston Street, London SE1 3ER, 0207-357 8866, fax 0207-357 8877
e-mail info@m-v.co.uk
HOURS Mon–Fri 8–6 **DISCOUNTS** 10% unmixed cases; further discounts 10 or more cases
DELIVERY Free central London and Oxford; elsewhere £10 up to 5 cases, free 6 or more
MINIMUM ORDER 1 mixed case **EN PRIMEUR** Bordeaux. **C G M T**
A real enthusiast's list that focuses on France but also has the wines of such agencies as Ridge in California, Vega Sicilia in Spain, Lustau in Jerez and Isabel Estate in New Zealand. The wines here have character: there's nothing conformist about them. Burgundy is excellent; so are the Loire, Alsace (from Domaine Ostertag), Germany (Weingut Selbach Oster among others) and California (Au Bon Climat, Il Podere dell' Olivos, Qupé, Bonny Doon and so on).

1996 Jurançon VT Symphonie de Novembre, Domaine Cauhapé, £14 Rich but delicate sweet wine from South-West France, all quince and orange peel. It will improve with aging, too.

1995 Hautes-Côtes de Beaune Champs Perdrix, Devevey, £10 Morris & Verdin reckons this wine is one of the stars of their list. I'm not about to argue.

C = cellarage   **G** = glass loan/hire   **M** = mail order   **T** = tastings and talks

WILLIAM MORRISON SUPERMARKETS (MORR)

Head office Wakefield 41 Industrial Estate, Wakefield, West Yorkshire WF2 0XF, (01924) 870000, fax (01924) 875300. 100 licensed branches

HOURS Variable, generally 8–8 **CARDS** MasterCard, Switch, Visa. **G T**

A good place to find inexpensive tasty wines: most of the range is under a fiver. As with all supermarkets, you won't find all the wines in all the stores, but if you're near a branch with a wide range, it's worth a visit.

Viña Albali Gran Reserva, £5 Vanilla and plum fruit from Spain, soft and attractive.

NADDER WINES LTD (NA)

Hussars House, 2 Netherhampton Road, Harnham, Salisbury, Wiltshire SP2 8HE, (01722) 325418, fax (01722) 421617

E-MAIL nadderwines@btinternet.com

HOURS Mon–Fri 9–5.30, Sat 9–1 **CARDS** Amex, MasterCard, Switch, Visa **DISCOUNTS** 5% on orders £100–£249, 7.5% on £250–£499, 10% on £500 plus. 7.5% discount card for regular customers **DELIVERY** Free Salisbury area; elsewhere at cost. 10 cases or over free **MINIMUM ORDER** 1 case. **G M T**

A useful list of tasty-looking wines from pretty well all over. The Rhône is Chapoutier and Max Aubert; the Loire has Vacheron, Château Moncontour and others; Italy is slightly sketchy but has some nice stuff from Avignonesi; Spain has names like El Coto, Campo Viejo, Torres, CVNE and Marqués de Murrieta, and Portugal is looking good with Sogrape. New Zealand has Selaks and Matua Valley, which are both good, and Australia has interesting names like Vasse Felix and Petaluma. From South Africa there are the African Sky wines of Drostdy Wine Cellars, which 'express the warmth, romance and beauty of the African sky at night.' Gosh. Nadder now operates in close association with Stevens Garnier (see entry), which offers a similar range of wines.

1998 Apremont de Savoie, Pierre Boniface, £6.43 Ski bums might feel nostalgic for this – and it's difficult to find here. Like ski-ing, I suppose…

1996 Douro Esteva Tinto, Ferreira, £5.50 Light, juicy red from Portugal.

NEW LONDON WINE (NLW)

1e Broughton Street, London SW8 3QJ, 0207-622 3000, fax 0207-622 2220

E-MAIL orders@newlondonwine.demon.co.uk

HOURS Mon–Fri 9–6 **CARDS** Amex, MasterCard, Switch, Visa **DELIVERY** Free locally, elsewhere at cost **MINIMUM ORDER** 1 case **EN PRIMEUR** Bordeaux. **G M T**

A curious list – there's a separate list of fine wines, with some serious clarets and ports, but the standard list, while it has one or two interesting wines, just doesn't have a lot to tempt you out of your way.

1995 Château Respide, Graves, £6.49 This is a red from the owner of Château Gilette in Sauternes – the latter being the estate where the wines are kept for decades in concrete vats before release. It's good, well-made red Graves.

NEW ZEALAND WINES DIRECT (NZW)

PO Box 476, London NW5 2NZ, 0207-482 0093, fax 0207-267 8400

E-MAIL margaret.harvey@btinternet.com

WEB SITE www.fwnz.co.uk

HOURS Mon–Sat 9–5 **CARDS** MasterCard, Visa **DISCOUNTS** 2 or more cases **DELIVERY** free 1 case or over mainland UK, £15 per case N Ireland **MINIMUM ORDER** 1 mixed case. **M T**

A small but perfectly formed list of – surprise, surprise – New Zealand wines. New Zealander Margaret Harvey MW was importing the wines of her homeland long before most people got in on the act, and it was she who introduced many of its top names. Look here for Redwood Valley, Ata Rangi, Hunters, Vidal and others, including Harvey's own label, Aotea.

1997 Cabernet Sauvignon, Redwood Valley Estate, Nelson, £8.70 Mulberry and blackcurrant flavours from the northern corner of South Island.

LE NEZ ROUGE (NEZ)

Berkmann Wine Cellars, 12 Brewery Rd, London N7 9NH, 0207-609 4711, fax 0207-607 0018

• Pagendam Pratt, Unit 456, Thorpe Arch Trading Estate, Wetherby, Yorkshire LS23 7BJ, (01937) 844711, fax (01973) 541058

• T M Robertson, 10 Gilmore Place, Edinburgh EH3 9PA, 0131-229 4522

E-MAIL emmad@berkmann.co.uk
WEB SITE www.berkmann.co.uk
HOURS Mon–Fri 9–5.30 **CARDS** MasterCard,
Switch, Visa **DISCOUNTS** £3.60 per case
collected. Other quantity discounts as well
DELIVERY Included in price for mainland UK
MINIMUM ORDER I mixed case. **C G M**
Italy is a great strength here, as is Australia, and as
is – most of all, in fact – France. The philosophy of
the list is that wine is to be drunk with food, rather
than overwhelm it, so this is a place to look if you
value subtlety in your wine rather than blockbusting
upfront power. Agencies include Antinori, Beringer
Vineyards in California, Georges Duboeuf in
Beaujolais and Norton in Argentina.
1996 Cervaro della Sala, Antinori, £16.50
I know it's expensive, but I'd love to buy a case
of this and lay it down for a few years. And
perhaps buy another case to drink right away.
Lovely subtle fruit.
1998 Muscadet les Ormeaux, Sauvion et Fils,
£4.70 Exemplary Muscadet, very carefully made.
1996 Le Arenarie Alghero Villamarina, Sella &
Mosca, Sardinia, £9.65 Classy herb-and-
greengage white.

JAMES NICHOLSON (NI)

27A Killyeagh St, Crossgar, Co. Down, Northern
Ireland BT30 9DG, 028-4483 0091, fax 028-
4483 0028
E-MAIL info@jnwine.co.uk
WEB SITE www.jnwine.co.uk
HOURS Mon–Sat 10–7 **CARDS** MasterCard,
Switch, Visa **DISCOUNTS** 8% mixed case
DELIVERY Free Northern Ireland for orders of
£50 or I case, otherwise at cost **EN PRIMEUR**
Bordeaux, Burgundy, California, Port.
G M T
One of those lists that make you wonder why all
wine merchants can't be this good: James Nicholson
makes it all look so easy. The South of France,
Bordeaux, Burgundy, the Loire, the Rhône (names
like René Rostaing and Château de Beaucastel)
and Alsace are all excellent; outside France, look for
Spain, some good Italians, adventurous Germans,
the cream of Australia and New Zealand and
terrific stuff from the Americas. Deeply impressive.

1997 Mas Collet, Capcanes, £6.25 Silky young
red from Tarragona.
1998 Basa, Rueda, £4.99 Ultra-modern white
from Spain, made from Verdejo, Viura and
Sauvignon Blanc. Stylish and crisp.

THE NOBODY INN (NO)

Doddiscombsleigh, Nr Exeter, Devon EX6 7PS,
(01647) 252394, fax (01647) 252978
E-MAIL inn.nobody@virgin.net
HOURS Mon–Sat 12–2.30 & 6–11 (summer),
6–11 (winter), Sun 12–3 & 7–10.30; or by
appointment **CARDS** Amex, MasterCard,
Switch, Visa **DISCOUNTS** 5% per case
DELIVERY £7.20 for I case, 2 or more cases
£3.20 per case. **G M T**
If you want 1935 Bonnezeaux this is your place;
but it's also your place if you want the best (and
not always the most expensive) from all over
France, Europe and the New World. You can pay
£154.47 (well, that's what it says) for a bottle of
L'Ermita from Priorato if you want to, but you might
prefer to stick to, say, a bottle of Castel de Pujol
Tannat from Uruguay at a more comforting £5.26.
You see? The Nobody Inn has it all.
Stanton & Killeen 25-year-old Rutherglen
Muscat, £9.71 Astonishingly luscious and
astonishingly old. Well, not quite as old (or as
luscious) as me.

ODDBINS (OD)

Head office 31–33 Weir Road, London SW19
8UG, 0208-944 4400, fax 0208-944 4411 **Mail**
order Oddbins Delivers, 0870-601 0015, fax
0870-601 0069. 245 shops
WEB SITE www.oddbins.co.uk
HOURS Generally Mon–Sat 10–10, Sun 10–8 in
England & Wales, 12.30–8 Scotland **CARDS**
Amex, MasterCard, Switch, Visa **DISCOUNTS**
5% split case wine; 10% split case tasting wines
on day of tasting. 7 bottles of Champagne and
sparkling wine for the price of 6 **DELIVERY** Free
locally from most shops. **G M T**
Oddbins never ceases to be inventive and
innovative. Its latest passion is for Greek wine, and
it's busy proving that Greece can and does make
some serious wines. Don't be alarmed by the

C = cellarage   **G** = glass loan/hire   **M** = mail order   **T** = tastings and talks

concept of the fine wine shops – not everything here is expensive, but everything is interesting and often unusual. So, yes, you'll find serious clarets and Burgundies, but great Australians as well, plus lots of stuff from all over. The standard shops are far from standard, too, with lots of curiosities. Obviously, the bigger the branch the bigger the selection.

1996 Olivares Monastrell Dulce, Jumilla, £16.99 Sweet red made from the Mourvèdre grape (alias Monastrell) in Spain. Rich, raspberryish, and unusual.

1995 Skouras Megas Oenos, Peloponnese, £8.99 Rich, unfiltered blend of Agiorgitiko and Cabernet Sauvignon.

1996 Bourgogne Blanc, Pascal, £6.99 (Fine Wine shops) Oddbins is billing this as 'declassified Puligny' – steely, elegant, lean.

THOS. PEATLING

Head office Westgate Brewery, Bury St Edmunds, Suffolk IP33 1QT, (01284) 763222, fax (01284) 706502; wine shop tel (01284) 714285, fax (01284) 714483 • The Causeway, Great Horkesley, Colchester, Essex CO6 4BH, (01206) 271236, fax (01206) 272026 • 37–39 Little London, Long Sutton, Lincs PE12 9LE, (01406) 363233, fax (01406) 365654

HOURS Variable **CARDS** Amex, MasterCard, Switch, Visa **DISCOUNTS** 5% mixed case **DELIVERY** Free UK mainland 2 or more cases. **C G M T**

Peatlings is very strong at the cheaper end; and yet, perversely, it specializes in regions (Bordeaux, for example) where try how you will you simply don't get good value at the cheaper end. From Portugal, for example, where there is sensational value to be had, Peatlings lists just two wines. A bit more lateral thinking would make this a more interesting list.

1995 Château Haut-Sociondo, £5.73 Well-made simple claret from a good year.

PENISTONE COURT WINE CELLARS (PEN)

The Railway Station, Penistone, Sheffield, South Yorkshire S36 6HP, (01226) 766037, fax (01226) 767310

E-MAIL pcwc@dircon.co.uk

HOURS Mon–Fri 10–6, Sat 10–3 **DELIVERY** Free locally, rest of UK mainland charged at cost 1 case or more. **G M**

There's slightly patchy quality here – the pasteurized red Burgundies of Louis Latour as well as Latour's very good white Burgundies, for example. Each area seems to rely on one or perhaps two famous producers, which are not necessarily the most interesting. The Rhône is good, with Chapoutier. Italy and the USA are probably the most interesting areas.

1996 Chardonnay, Sonoma-Cutrer, Russian River Valley, £13 Good rich, nutty Chardonnay from a top California name.

PHILGLAS & SWIGGOT (PHI)

21 Northcote Road, London SW11 1NG, 0207-924 4494, fax 0207-642 1308

HOURS Mon–Sat 10–7.30, Sun 12–6 **CARDS** Amex, Diners, MasterCard, Switch, Visa

DISCOUNTS 5% per case **DELIVERY** Free 1 case West End, Wandsworth and other South London boroughs, elsewhere £6.99. **G M T**

I love this shop and I'm deeply envious of all those lucky residents of SW11, who can stroll in anytime for a browse and a chat. There's a terrific selection of really interesting Australian wines – eight different Rieslings, including Henschke and Grosset, for example. The southern French wines have character and style rather than just masses of new oak; Italy is fascinating, Spain varied and the rest of the New World very well chosen. There's also a proper respect for pudding wines here – everything from sweet Jurançon through Monbazillac and Tokaji to Victoria Muscat. Prices are fair, but the shop doesn't specialize in the cheapest wines.

1997 Viognier, Heggies Family Reserve, Eden Valley, £10.99 Lovely orange-blossom scented wine.

1996 Vin de Pays d'Oc Aramon, Terrasses de Landoc, £4.59 Juicy, rich red from a grape variety (Aramon) that used to be thought fit only for vinegar. This is made by the owner of Mas de Daumas Gassac.

1997 Jurançon Moelleux, Clos Lapeyre, £14.99 P&S suggests this sweetie with wild salmon. I think I'd be just as happy with it on its own.

C = cellarage   **G** = glass loan/hire   **M** = mail order   **T** = tastings and talks

CHRISTOPHER PIPER WINES (PIP)

1 Silver St, Ottery St Mary, Devon EX11 1DB, (01404) 814139, fax (01404) 812100
HOURS Mon–Sat 9–6 **CARDS** MasterCard, Switch, Visa **DISCOUNTS** 5% mixed case, 10% 3 or more cases **DELIVERY** Free in South-West England for 4 cases, elsewhere free for 6 cases, otherwise £7.05 **MINIMUM ORDER** 1 mixed case **EN PRIMEUR** Bordeaux, Burgundy, Rhône.
C G M T

A huge, wide-ranging list that covers everywhere in great detail. Bordeaux is good, Burgundy a speciality and even better (Christopher Piper is agent for lots of Burgundy domaines, including Gérard Chavy, Gérard Thomas and Chantal Lescure). The Loire is impressive, and Australia and South Africa are also very strong.

1996 Savigny-lès-Beaune les Liards, Domaine Rossignol-Trapet, £13.40 Savigny is lovely young, all smoky raspberry fruit, and this is beautifully made.
1997 Riesling, Rockford Wines, Eden Valley, £8.85 A Riesling from Australia that will last for years yet, and really needs time to allow its lime and toast flavours to develop.

TERRY PLATT (PLA)

Ferndale Road, Llandudno Junction LL31 9NT, (01492) 592971, fax (01492) 592196 • World of Wine, 29 Mostyn Ave, Craig Y Don, (01492) 872997
E-MAIL plattwines@clara.co.uk
HOURS Ferndale Rd: Mon–Fri 8.30–5.30; Mostyn Ave: Mon–Sat 10–8, Sun 12–5 **CARDS** Amex, MasterCard, Switch, Visa **DELIVERY** Free locally and mainland UK 5 cases or more **MINIMUM ORDER** 1 mixed case. **G M T**

Full, ripe fruit seems to be the keynote of this list. South Africa and Chile are strong, and so are Alsace, the Rhône, the Loire and Bordeaux. Burgundy has some excellent growers and Spain is particularly good. There are plenty of wines under £5, too.

1996 Givry Rouge, Champ Lalot, Joseph Faiveley, £11.03 A fair price for a ripe, balanced Burgundy from a good producer: it's all cherries and smoke.
1996 Alsace Riesling, Trimbach, £9.40 Expensive, yes, but very good quality, with firm structure and steely, ripe fruit. Alsace at its best.

PLAYFORD ROS (PLAY)

Middle Park House, Sowerby, Thirsk, Yorkshire YO7 3AH, (01845) 526777, fax (01845) 526888
E-MAIL playford@bigfoot.com
HOURS Mon–Fri 8–5 **CARDS** MasterCard, Visa
DISCOUNTS 2.5% on orders over 6 cases
DELIVERY Free Yorkshire, Derbyshire, Durham, Newcastle, elsewhere on UK mainland (per case), £8.50 1 case, £5.50 2 cases, £4.50 3 cases, £3.50 4 cases, free 5 cases **MINIMUM ORDER** 1 mixed case **EN PRIMEUR** Bordeaux. **C G M T**

France is the main focus here: the South looks good, and from Burgundy there are the Chablis of Daniel Dampt as well as various offerings from Olivier Leflaive, Jacques Parent, Michel Noëllat et Fils, Lamy Pillot and others. The range of Beaujolais looks interesting, too. There are some nice white Rhônes, and Bordeaux is pretty well covered. There's a good range of crus bourgeois at prices which are not too horrifying, considering. (To pick out Château Potensac 1988 at £20.48 as being a shocking example of the prices Bordeaux now fetches is not intended as a criticism of Playford Ros. I think it just shows that the word 'value' has no meaning anymore when applied to Bordeaux.) Spain is good too; so is Australia.

1996 Loupiac, Domaine du Noble, £11.36 Quite rich sweet white Bordeaux from a good year. The price of Sauternes has now got so high that the only affordable sweet white Bordeaux come from regions like Loupiac and Monbazillac.
1997 Old Vines Semillon, Grant Burge, Barossa, £9.18 Lovely, beautifully made Aussie Semillon, at a most affordable price.
1995 Cabernet Sauvignon, Petaluma, Coonawarra, £16.16. This is quite expensive for

an Aussie red, isn't it? But compared to a Bordeaux it's positively cheap. And the ridiculous thing is that it could knock spots off claret of a similar price.

PORTLAND WINE CO (POR)

16 North Parade, off Norris Road, Sale, Cheshire M33 3JS, 0161-962 8752, fax 0161-905 1291 • 152a Ashley Road, Hale WA15 9SA, 0161-928 0357 • 82 Chester Road, Macclesfield SK11 8DL, (01625) 616147
E-MAIL portwineco@aol.com
WEB SITE www.portlandwine.co.uk
HOURS Mon–Sat 10–10, Sun 12–3 & 7–9.30
CARDS Amex, MasterCard, Switch, Visa
DISCOUNTS 10% off 1 mixed case, 5% off 6 bottles **DELIVERY** Free locally 1 case or more
EN PRIMEUR Bordeaux. **G M T**

There's a promising-looking list of lesser clarets here (I think I'm going to stop using the word 'affordable') – with some around a tenner. The southern Rhône selection looks good, and Italy is interesting – classy wines from the Veneto like Tedeschi's Amarone Classico and Pra's Soave Classico Superiore Montegrande. Portugal looks good too – and Portugal, you may have noticed, is my current benchmark for good-value, interesting flavours. Any merchant that claims to seek such wines and ignores Portugal is, I think, missing a trick. Spain has interesting stuff from Valdepeñas and Priorato. The New World looks equally well chosen.
1994 Château des Annereaux, Lalande-de-Pomerol, £8.99 Nice soft, well-balanced lesser claret.
1996 Valpolicella Capitel San Rocco Ripasso, Tedeschi, £7.99 Why does anyone buy overpriced claret when you can get rich reds with a sour-cherry twist like this?

RAEBURN FINE WINES (RAE)

21/23 Comely Bank Rd, Edinburgh EH4 1DS, 0131-343 1159, fax 0131-332 5166
E-MAIL raeburn@netcomuk.co.uk
WEB SITE raeburnfinewines.com
HOURS Mon–Sat 9.30–6, Sun 12.30–5 **CARDS** Amex, MasterCard, Switch, Visa **DISCOUNTS** 5% unsplit case, 2.5% mixed **DELIVERY** Free

local area 1 or more cases (usually); elsewhere £7.50 1–3 cases, free 4 or more **EN PRIMEUR** Alsace, Austria, Bordeaux, Burgundy, California, Germany, Italy, Loire, New Zealand, Rhône. **G M T**

Oh, what a lovely list. Burgundy has some of the best producers possible, Bordeaux is very good, and from Austria there are the gloriously elegant wines of Nikolaihof and Franz-Xaver Pichler. Zinfandel star Joseph Swan of California is an agency, as are Fritz Haag and Maximin Grünhaus of Germany. From the Loire there is Huet, and Paul Avril and Château de Beaucastel from the Rhône. And these are only some of the highlights.
1991 St-Joseph, Clos de l'Arbalestrier, £13.95 This looks to me like a terrific buy: mature St-Joseph from a tip-top estate.
NV Champagne Blanc de Blancs, Le Mesnil, £14.65 Elegant 100%-Chardonnay Champagne from a Côte de Blancs village where the wines are always slow to mature, but worth the wait.

REID WINES (1992) LTD (REI)

The Mill, Marsh Lane, Hallatrow, Nr Bristol BS39 6EB, (01761) 452645, fax (01761) 453642
HOURS Mon–Fri 9–5.30 **CARDS** MasterCard, Visa (3% charge) **DELIVERY** Free within 25 miles of Hallatrow (Bristol), and in central London **EN PRIMEUR** Burgundy, Italy, Rhône. **C G M T**

My treat of the year is going through this list (I live a quiet life normally.) So here are some of the star comments: 'Not so bad that you would refuse to drink them' (1960 clarets); 'Frankly, a disgrace. We suppose we should try to say something less damning but we cannot tell a lie' (1963 Sauternes, before listing Yquem at £115); 'Almost certainly worse than the previous bottle – very rare' (Château de Fargues 1965; the previous bottle in question being the Yquem '63). As you might have gathered, the Bordeaux list is extensive, honest and exceedingly good; Burgundy is equally quirky (La Tâche DRC 1975: 'Ho hum'). Rhône wines date back to 1961 (of a more recent vintage: 'The Lys de Volan Condrieu is back on form after the unfortunate 1995 which threw a huge sediment and eventually had to be sent to a Cusenier who put it into his sausages'). Coppola in California and

---

C = cellarage   **G** = glass loan/hire   **M** = mail order   **T** = tastings and talks

Wairau River in New Zealand are among the agencies here. The Loire, Alsace, Germany, Italy, Spain, Australia, port, Madeira: in all these areas Reid has one of the longest and most varied lists you'll find, and don't get me wrong, it does like the majority of the wines it sells – as should you. It's the sort of list that's stuffed full of wines you simply can't live without.

1995 Valpolicella Classico, Palazzo della Torre, Allegrini, £8.95 Reid describes this red from the Veneto as 'wonderful kit', and I'd agree.

1988 Champagne Pol Roger, £27.50 Reid prefers this to the fatter 1990 vintage; it's glorious stuff.

LA RÉSERVE (RES)

Knightsbridge: 56 Walton St, London SW3 1RB, 0207-589 2020, fax 0207-581 0250 • Battersea: 7 Grant Road, London SW11 2NU, 0207-978 5601, fax 0207-978 4934 • Hampstead: 29 Heath Street, Hampstead, London NW3 6TR, 0207-435 6845, fax 0207-431 9301 • Marble Arch: 47 Kendal Street, London W2 2BU, 0207-402 6920, fax 0207-402 5066 • Fulham: 203 Munster Road, London SW6 6BX, 0207-381 6930, fax 0207-385 5513
E-MAIL realwine@la-reserve.co.uk
WEB SITE www.netkonect.co.uk/lareserve/
HOURS Vary from shop to shop **CARDS** Amex, MasterCard, Switch, Visa **DISCOUNTS** 5% per case except accounts **DELIVERY** Free 1 case or more central London and orders over £200 UK mainland. Otherwise £7.50 **EN PRIMEUR** Bordeaux, Burgundy, Italy, Rhône.
C G T
My kind of list – varied, intelligent and without a trace of pomposity. 'The Bordelais continue to be the most irritating of people to deal with', it says, and I couldn't agree more. Bordeaux, Burgundy, the Loire, Spain, Italy, North America and Australia are all excellent, with well-chosen wines. There's nothing run-of-the-mill here, nothing boring. Well done, La Réserve. Agencies include Domaine des Baumard in the Loire.

1995 House Claret, Anthony Barton, £6.95 One of the few names you can really trust in Bordeaux for both quality and value.

1995 Morellino Riserva, Le Pulille, £14.95 Lovely ripe cherry fruit with serious depth.

HOWARD RIPLEY (RIP)

35 Eversley Crescent, London N21 1EL, 0208-360 8904, fax 0208-351 6564
HOURS Mon–Fri 9–10, Sat 9–1 **DELIVERY** London free 5 cases or more, otherwise £10.50 plus VAT, elsewhere at cost **MINIMUM ORDER** 1 mixed case **EN PRIMEUR** Burgundy. **G M T**
New to this sensational list are the wines of Colin-Deléger, Étienne Sauzet and Vincent Girardin; as you might gather, Howard Ripley specializes in Burgundy, and does it supremely well. (He used to be a dentist, which probably explains how he could afford to get to know Burgundy in the first place.) There are wines from over 40 producers, and they're all tip-top.

1996 Bourgogne Chardonnay, Domaine Guy Amiot, £10.46 Howard Ripley reports that 'in a recent blind tasting this blew away six Pulignys and Chassagne-Montrachets, three premier crus and one grand cru.' Sounds good, then.

ROBERSON (ROB)

348 Kensington High St, London W14 8NS, 0207-371 2121, fax 0207-371 4010
E-MAIL wines@roberson.co.uk
WEB SITE www.roberson.co.uk
HOURS Mon–Sat 10–8 **CARDS** Amex, Diners, MasterCard, Switch, Visa **DISCOUNTS** Mail order 5% on unmixed cases; shop 10% unmixed cases, 5% mixed **DELIVERY** Free locally 1 case or more, free mainland UK for orders over £150, otherwise £5 per case **EN PRIMEUR** Bordeaux, Burgundy, Italy. **C G M T**
A first-class list that covers everywhere in the world with great thoroughness. Quality is very high, and the buyers are clearly very enterprising, but prices have always seemed a little higher than those of other merchants. Bordeaux, Burgundy and Italy are specialities, and agencies include Châteaux Clarke in Listrac-Médoc and Haut-Caplane in Sauternes, Henri de Villamont in Burgundy, Viña San Pedro in Chile and Bodega Santa Celina in Argentina.

1993 Fumé Seyval Blanc, Breaky Bottom, £7.95 I don't know where else you can get the superb English wines of Breaky Bottom except at the vineyard.

1996 Frascati Superiore, Grillo, £5.25 Nice taste of nuts and sour cream: just what Frascati should taste of.

1997 Louis Semillon, Henschke, Eden Valley, £12.50 Refined, intense Aussie Semillon that will age and age.

ROSE TREE WINE COMPANY (ROS)

15 Suffolk Parade, Cheltenham, Gloucestershire GL50 2AE, (01242) 583732, fax (01242) 222159 **HOURS** Mon–Fri 9–7, Sat 9–6 **CARDS** MasterCard, Switch, Visa **DELIVERY** Free locally, elsewhere by arrangement **MINIMUM ORDER** 1 mixed case **EN PRIMEUR** Bordeaux. **C G M T**
A fairly short list of well-chosen wines. Italy looks interesting, with Pieropan's Soave and Terruzi's Vernaccia di San Gimignano; there's a nice sprinkling from most other places, too.
1997 Malbec, Vistalba, Lujan de Cuyo £5.24 Argentine red with good ripe pungent fruit.

THE RSJ WINE COMPANY (RSJ)

115 Wootton Street, London SE1 8LY, 0207-633 0881 fax 0207-401 2455
HOURS Mon–Fri 9–5, answering machine at other times **CARDS** MasterCard, Visa **DELIVERY** Free central London, minimum 1 case. England and Wales (per case), £8.25 1 case, £5.50 2 cases, £4.60 3–5 cases. **G M T**
This Loire specialist makes the very good point that few sweet Loire wines go well with puddings. Fruit-based puds work, but lots of other desserts are pretty horrid with sweet Chenin Blanc. 'Much better to enjoy a Loire moelleux as an apéritif with blue cheese, a rich pâté or a very rich fish dish – sauced lobster, for instance,' it says. Absolutely right. RSJ not only knows its wines, it knows its growers, too. It can (and does) talk in detail about the style favoured by each producer, the soil and the type of aging used. If you've dismissed the Loire until now, this list will show you what you've been missing. Prices are remarkably good value, too, for wines of such character.
1996 Anjou-Villages Croix de Mission, LeBreton, £8.05 Ripe Cabernet of great depth.
1992 Savennières Roche-aux-Moines, Domaine aux Moines, £9.85 Savennières can be the most fascinating of white wines, a wonderful balance of fruit and minerally acidity. It takes ages to mature, but this is drinking now.

SAFEWAY (SAF)

Head office 6 Millington Road, Hayes, Middlesex UB3 4AY, 0208-848 8744, fax 0208-573 1865. 474 stores nationwide
HOURS Mon–Sat 8–10, Sun 11–5 (most stores) **CARDS** Amex, MasterCard, Switch, Visa **DISCOUNTS** 5% on six or more bottles (not fortified wines). **G**
A mix of safe supermarket standby flavours and some more interesting wines – Tedeschi's Amarone, for example. My limited experience of Safeway, for what it's worth, is that you have to go to a bigger branch than I've ever been in to see the interesting parts of the list. But then I suppose that's true of most supermarkets these days. Anyway, Safeway's list is looking better this year than it has done for quite a while.
1996 Vila Regia, Sogrape, Douro, £3.99 Good-value Portuguese red, with bags of fruit and flavour.

SAINSBURY'S (SAI)

Head office Stamford House, Stamford St, London SE1 9LL, 0207-695 6000. 406 stores nationwide (including Savacentres)
WEB SITE www.j-sainsbury.co.uk
HOURS Variable, many open late **CARDS** Amex, MasterCard, Switch, Visa. **G**
A much-improved list, though it's difficult to know just what sort of a selection one would find in one's local branch, unless it happens to be one of those out-of-town superstores which bring ruin to villages and market towns up and down the land. Not, of course, that Sainsbury's is the only guilty party here. They've all been at it. Italy looks good, as does Chile and Bordeaux.
1995 Chianti Classico, Castello di San Polo in Rosso, £8.49 Rich, elegant Chianti. In 115 stores.
1996 Château Fourcas-Hosten, Listrac £9.99 A good price for well-made claret in a good year.

SATCHELLS (SAT)

North St, Burnham Market, Norfolk PE31 8HG, (01328) 738272, fax (01328) 730727
HOURS Mon, Tues, Thurs, Fri 9.30–1 & 2–6; Wed 9.30–1; Sat 9.30–7 **CARDS** MasterCard,

---

C = cellarage   **G** = glass loan/hire   **M** = mail order   **T** = tastings and talks

Switch, Visa **DISCOUNTS** 5% cases, larger orders negotiable **DELIVERY** Free locally, at cost nationally. **G M T**

Quite a nice list of mainly familiar names: Burgundies from Roland Thévenin and Albert Bichot; lots of Listel from the South of France.... Look beyond these, however, and you can find some more interesting bottles.

1995 Côtes du Rhône, Valvigneyre, Alain Paret, £6.95 Good supple, ripe red from the Rhône.

SAVAGE SELECTION (SAV)

The Ox House, Market Place, Northleach, Cheltenham, Glos GL54 3EG, (01451) 860896, fax (01451) 860996. Country Wine Merchant shop at same address, tel (01451) 860680, fax (01451) 861166

E-MAIL savage.selection@virgin.net **HOURS** Shop: Mon 10–5; shop & wine bar: Tues–Sat 10am–11pm **CARDS** Amex, MasterCard, Switch, Visa **DELIVERY** Free locally 1 case, elsewhere on UK mainland free 3 cases, otherwise £10 per consignment **EN PRIMEUR** Bordeaux, Burgundy, others occasionally. **C G M T**

I don't think Mark Savage could buy a dull wine if he tried. Not that he tries: the whole point of these wines is that they are not necessarily commercial, but that they have character and quality. There are lots of good Burgundies and Bordeaux, and excellent stuff from the South of France and the Rhône, but look too at Italy (100 per cent Garganega Soave from Stefano Inama), Spain (tremendous old sherry) and the fascinating wines from South Africa and the United States.

1986 Tokay Szamorodne, Doux, £7.50 (50cl) Tokaji from Slovakia, where the Tokaj vineyards extend over the border from Hungary. This wine is actually dry, despite the label, and ideal, says Savage, as an 'unusual and fascinating apéritif'.

1997 Nebbiolo, Aldo Vajra, Piedmont, £12.44 The 1997 vintage was excellent in Piedmont, and Vajra is a great producer of Barolo. This is his younger, lighter Nebbiolo.

1996 Pinot Noir, The Eyrie Vineyard, Oregon, £12.73 I seem to remember that Mark Savage was importing Eyrie Pinot Noir before anyone else thought of Oregon wines here. It's extremely good, subtle and complex.

SOMERFIELD (SO)

Head office Somerfield House, Hawkfield Business Park, Whitchurch Lane, Bristol BS14 0TJ, 0117-935 9359. 533 Somerfield stores and 793 Kwiksave stores nationwide **HOURS** Mon–Sat 9–8, variable late opening Friday all stores **CARDS** MasterCard, Switch, Visa **DISCOUNTS** £1.50 off 6 bottles **DELIVERY** Small selection available via Somerfield Direct. **M T**

There are lots of perfectly respectable everyday wines here, and some more interesting bottles. Nothing to frighten the horses, though.

1996 Corbières, Château de Caraguilhes, £4.75 Earthy raspberry fruit from the South of France.

SOMMELIER WINE CO (SOM)

23 St George's Esplanade, St Peter Port, Guernsey, Channel Islands, GY1 2BG (01481) 721677, fax (01481) 716818 **HOURS** Mon–Thu 10–5.30, Fri 10–6, Sat 9.30–5.30; 24-hour answerphone **CARDS** MasterCard, Switch, Visa **DISCOUNTS** 5% 1 case or more **DELIVERY** Free 1 unmixed case. **G T**

'When you can't tell if a Chardonnay has come from Chile, Australia or Mâcon, things can become pretty boring,' says Sommelier. I couldn't agree more. This is a tremendous selection of characterful wines from all over the world: the only gap I can find is Germany, where Sommelier gave up because of lack of interest on the part of their customers (shame on you) and are now trying again with just one Riesling. Prices throughout the list are rather good thanks to the lack of duty and VAT in Guernsey, so drop in if you're visiting – they'll explain what you can buy without being stung by UK customs.

1996 Côtes du Rhône Blanc, Clos Cuminaille, Pierre Gaillard, £13.05 White Côtes du Rhône with a high proportion of Viognier in it: lots of peachy fruit, but more complexity than straight . Viognier from round here.

1994 Durif, Mick Morris of Rutherglen, £9.65 Inky black, brooding Australian red that needs a couple more years in bottle yet. There's a lot of tannin there.

1996 Santadi Monica di Sardegna, Antigua, £5.20 Lightish red full of peppery, earthy fruit, quite supple. It's made from the Carignano grape.

FRANK STAINTON WINES (STA)

3 Berry's Yard, Finkle Street, Kendal, Cumbria LA9 4AB, (01539) 731886, fax (01539) 730396 **HOURS** Mon–Sat 9–5.30 **CARDS** MasterCard, Visa **DISCOUNTS** 5% mixed case **DELIVERY** Free Cumbria and North Lancashire; elsewhere (per case) £9 1 case, £6 2–4 cases, £4 5–9 cases, 10 cases free. **C G M T**

Bordeaux is on the whole better than Burgundy here, and elsewhere there are interesting wines from lots of places, but most notably from Germany and Italy. The New World is far from run-of-the-mill, too: there's Cuvaison and Clos du Val from California, and Neudorf and Redwood Valley from New Zealand.

1997 Crozes-Hermitage, la Mule Blanche, Paul Jaboulet Aîné, £10.60 Herby dry white from the Rhône.

1997 Shiraz, 60-year-old vines, Grant Burge, Barossa, £11.50 Classic Barossa Shiraz, all smoke and berries and leather. I suppose this would make rather a good 60th birthday present for

somebody, since 1939 and 1940 were remarkable for lots of things, but none of them was wine. There's also an 85-year-old vine version from the same producer. It's called Meshach, and it costs £34.95. Take your pick.

STEVENS GARNIER WINE MERCHANTS (STE)

47 West Way, Botley, Oxford OX2 OJF, (01865) 263303, fax (01865) 791594 **E-MAIL** stevensgarnier@claranet.co.uk **HOURS** Mon–Wed 10–6, Thu–Fri 10–7, Sat 9.30–6 **CARDS** Amex, MasterCard, Switch, Visa **DISCOUNTS** 10% on an unmixed case **DELIVERY** Usually free locally; 'competitive rates' elsewhere. **G T**

A good, but not outstanding list. Stevens Garnier is big brother to Nadder Wines, and the companies list pretty much the same wines – everything looks tasty, and some things look rather interesting. There are appealing French country wines for around a fiver and some interesting Loires from producers like Saget, Vacheron and Château Moncontour; Burgundies range from the not-too-expensive to the hugely expensive; Italy looks good, too. Sogrape from Portugal is an agency, as are Selaks in New Zealand and La Chablisienne in Chablis, among others.

1998 Nobilis Dry Rosé, Sogrape, Bairrada, £4.19 Lovely toasty strawberry stuff from Portugal.

SUNDAY TIMES WINE CLUB

New Aquitaine House, Exeter Way, Theale, Reading, Berks RG7 4PL, 0118-903 0903, fax 0118-903 1073; order line tel 0118-903 0405, fax 0118-903 0401 **E-MAIL** orders@wine-club.co.uk **HOURS** Mail order, 24-hr answerphone **CARDS** Amex, Diners, MasterCard, Switch, Visa **DISCOUNTS** On special offers **DELIVERY** £3.99 per order **EN PRIMEUR** Australia, Bordeaux, Burgundy, Rhône. **C M T**

The associate mail order company of Bordeaux Direct, with essentially the same list. The membership fee is £10 per annum. The club also runs tours and tastings and an annual festival in London, and does monthly promotions to its members. See Bordeaux Direct for more details.

T & W WINES (TW)

51 King St, Thetford, Norfolk IP24 2AU, (01842) 765646, fax (01842) 766407

WEB SITE www.tw-wines.co.uk
HOURS Mon–Fri 9.30–5.30, Sat 9.30–1.00
CARDS Amex, Diners, MasterCard, Visa
DELIVERY (most areas) 7–47 bottles £9.95 plus VAT, 4 or more cases free **EN PRIMEUR** Burgundy. **C G M T**

The list T&W sent us has one of the least appealing covers I've ever seen: captioned 'braised pheasant with truffle and cranberry jelly', it looks more like a road accident. Once one's got over that, however, the list is as good as ever. Burgundy is excellent, as is Alsace, Germany, California (Howell Mountain, Patz & Hall, Silver Oak Cellars), Italy (Villa Vistarenni, Bava, Le Terrazze) – I could go on. Be warned, though: T&W is not cheap.
1995 Pinot Noir, Benton-Lane, Oregon, £14.04 *Oregon Pinot made by a couple of refugees from California. It's supple, ripe and very good.*

TANNERS (TAN)

26 Wyle Cop, Shrewsbury, Shropshire SY1 1XD, (01743) 234500, fax (01743) 234501 • 4 St Peter's Square, Hereford HR1 2PG, (01432) 272044, fax (01432) 263316 • 36 High Street, Bridgnorth WV16 4DB, (01746) 763148 • The Old Brewery, Brook St, Welshpool SY21 7LF, (01938) 552542, fax (01938) 556565

E-MAIL sales@tanners-wines.co.uk
WEB SITE www.tanners-wines.co.uk
HOURS Shrewsbury Mon–Sat 9–6, branches 9–5.30 **CARDS** Amex, MasterCard, Switch, Visa
DISCOUNTS 5% 1 mixed case (cash & collection); 2.5% for 3 mixed cases, 5% for 5, 7.5% for 10 (mail order) **DELIVERY** Free 1 mixed case or more locally, or nationally over £80, otherwise £6 **EN PRIMEUR** Bordeaux, Burgundy, Rhône. **G M T**

A great list by any standards, with both depth and breadth in all areas, but strongest in the over-£5 range. The Loire is fascinating – lots of sweet Chenins at rather reasonable-looking prices – and in Bordeaux, too, Tanners has found some well-priced wines. The Rhône looks excellent, and while prices are certainly rising here, there's lots of good
value still to be had. Spain and Italy are both good, and Germany is outstanding. Austria has some excellent wines, and so does Switzerland (yes, they're expensive, but they really can be awfully good: subtle and complex). Try the Petite Arvine du Valais from Charles Bonvin: it's wonderfully greengagy and herby. California (not a region that ever believes in underpricing itself) is well worth looking at if you're feeling rich. There's also an extremely good list of half bottles from pretty well everywhere.
1998 Tavel Rosé, Canto Perdrix, Domaine Méjan-Taulier, £7.50 *I love good rosé; this has more substance than many.*
1997 Traisener Bastei Riesling Kabinett, State Domaine Nahe, £6.95 *Wonderfully concentrated, fiery stuff.*
1993 Tokaji Aszú 5 Puttonyos, Royal Tokaji Wine Company Blue Label, £6.90 (25 cl) *Note the size of the bottle: keep it in your pocket or handbag for those moments when you just have to have a glass of Tokaji.*

TESCO (TES)

Head office Delamare Road, Cheshunt, Herts EN8 9SL, (01992) 632222, fax (01992) 630794, Customer Service (0800) 505555. 566 licensed branches

HOURS Variable (open Sunday) **CARDS** MasterCard, Switch, Visa **DISCOUNT** 5% on 6 bottles or more. **G M T**

Australia is currently looking far more interesting in the over-£5 price range than in the under-£5 range, and that's reflected in Tesco's selection. There are wines like Lindemans Pyrus and St George Cabernet Sauvignon at £13.99 and £12.99 respectively, and Pipers Brook Pellion Pinot Noir at £13.99. This, as you will have spotted, is well over £5. There's also Penfolds Grange at £90 a bottle, which is even more over £5. This doesn't mean you have to spend fourteen quid at Tesco these days; just that Tesco seems to have abandoned the cheapest end of the market. And that's no bad thing: as we all know, the cheaper the wine, the greater the percentage of the price that is tax and the less the percentage that is wine. Some Tesco own-label is still at rock-bottom prices (and plenty

---

C = cellarage   **G** = glass loan/hire   **M** = mail order   **T** = tastings and talks

carries a silly name like Great With Indian Red), but the selection is better elsewhere on the shelves. Look particularly at the Rhône and Spain.

1996 St-Joseph, Cave de Tain, £6.99 Good smoky Rhône Syrah, but supple with it.

THRESHER (THR)
See First Quench.

THE UBIQUITOUS CHIP (UB)
8 Ashton Lane, Glasgow G12 8SJ, 0141-334 5007, fax 0141-337 1302
HOURS Mon–Fri 12–10, Sat 11–10 **CARDS** Amex, Diners, MasterCard, Switch, Visa
DISCOUNTS 5% cash or cheque purchases of cases **DELIVERY** Free Glasgow 3 cases or more, otherwise negotiable. **C G M T**

An extensive and often excellent list that covers most parts of the world. The Loire is very good, with all sorts of hopelessly unfashionable but utterly delicious wines like Vouvray (sec and demi-sec) from Huet and Prince Poniatowski, and sweet Anjou from 1928 at £48.50 a bottle. There's also Vin Jaune from Jean Bourdy at £43, and rather less expensively, dry Muscat from Domaine Gauby at £9.60. Australia looks pretty good, as do New Zealand and South Africa. Germany looks very good indeed – how brave of the Chip to list not just good German wines but some rather expensive ones, too.

1993 Vin de Pays des Côtes Catalanes Muscat Sec, Domaine Gauby, £9.60 I've just seen what vintage this is. Can dry Muscat keep and improve over six years? Hmmm.

1995 Graacher Dompropst Riesling Kabinett, Friedrich Wilhelm Gymnasium, £8.20 Lovely Mosel, all slate and honey.

UNWINS (UN)
Head office Birchwood House, Victoria Road, Dartford, Kent DA1 5AJ, (01322) 272711, fax (01322) 294469; 391 branches in South-East England
E-MAIL brouse@unwins.co.uk
WEB SITE www.unwins.co.uk
HOURS Variable, usually Mon–Sat 10–10, Sun 11–10 **CARDS** Amex, Diners, MasterCard,

Switch, Visa **DISCOUNTS** 10% mixed case, 5% on six bottles **DELIVERY** Free locally **EN PRIMEUR** Bordeaux, Burgundy. **C G M T**

This list seems rather better than of late. There's more variety than there was – Unwins clearly isn't aiming to be quirky, but you do begin to get the feeling that the buyers are being a little less routine in what they choose. Or perhaps it's just that they're being allowed a freer hand – who knows? Unwins still isn't going to set the world on fire, but it's improved.

1993 Madiran, Château de Crouseilles, £8.99 Herby, sweet fruit from South-West France.

VALVONA & CROLLA (VA)
19 Elm Row, Edinburgh EH7 4AA, 0131-556 6066, fax 0131-556 1668
E-MAIL sales@valvonacrolla.co.uk
HOURS Mon–Wed 8–6, Thu–Fri 8–7.30, Sat 8–6
CARDS Amex, MasterCard, Switch, Visa
DISCOUNTS 5% mixed case, 10% unmixed case
DELIVERY Free locally for orders over £30. Mail order £7.90 per case, £4.50 4 cases or more, free 10 or more. **G M T**

There's a nice list of Australian wines here (names like Mount Langi Ghiran and Cape Mentelle), some quirky Californians (Qupé, Ridge, Ravenswood), some good Spanish wines and the odd bottle from the South of France or Germany, but they are not what Valvona & Crolla is about. It's an Italian shop, run by Italians for, I suppose, Scots – plus anyone else who wants to avail themselves of mail order. And you know, if you're fond of Italian wines you should be shopping here. The list has three closely-printed pages of wines from Piedmont, and three-and-a-half from Tuscany; that's not to mention the wines from Lombardy, Basilicata, the Marche, Sicily, the Veneto, and the page of dessert wines. It's a simply fabulous selection, and at all prices. Valvona & Crolla demonstrates very successfully that if you want interesting flavours on a budget Italy should be at the top of your list. Yes, the names are often unfamiliar, but that's what wine merchants are for, isn't it?

1997 Vitiano, Falesco, Vino da Tavola, £6.99 V&C reckons that this wine from Lazio is one of central Italy's finest reds.

C = cellarage **G** = glass loan/hire **M** = mail order **T** = tastings and talks

1997 Teroldego Rotaliano, La Vis, £4.99
Blacker-than-black wine with juicy, jammy fruit.

VICTORIA WINE (VIC)
See First Quench.

LA VIGNERONNE
105 Old Brompton Rd, London SW7 3LE,
0171-589 6113, fax 0171-581 2983
E-MAIL lavig@aol.com
HOURS Mon–Fri 10–8, Sat 10–6 **CARDS** Amex,
Diners, MasterCard, Switch, Visa **DISCOUNTS**
5% mixed case (collected) **DELIVERY** Free
locally, £7.50 mainland England and Wales for
orders under £250; mainland Scotland at cost
EN PRIMEUR Bordeaux, Rhône. **M T**
*A shop where the owners must spend most of their
time trudging along dirt tracks in the more remote
parts of the wine world looking for small, high-
quality producers that everyone else has missed.
And they find them, again and again. Come to La
Vigneronne if you want characterful wines and are
prepared to snap them up when they're available;
this is not a place where particular wines are likely
to hang around on the shelves. Stock changes
constantly, and you'll find wines here that nobody
else has – and in fact the wines that other people
have are the wines that La Vigneronne is unlikely to
bother with. Agencies include Marc Kreydenweiss of
Alsace and Domaine Tempier of Bandol.*
1997 Mas Jullien Vin Blanc La Mejanne, £11.66
Rich, dry white from Languedoc-Roussillon

VINTAGE WINES LTD (VIN)
116 Derby Rd, Nottingham NG1 5FB, 0115-947
6565/941 9614, fax 0115-950 5276
HOURS Mon–Fri 9–5.15, Sat 9–1 **CARDS**
MasterCard, Switch, Visa **DISCOUNTS** 10% for
6 or more bottles collected, other discounts
negotiable **DELIVERY** Free within 60 miles
EN PRIMEUR Bordeaux. **C G M T**
*A nice list that covers the world quite effectively
without specializing in any one region or style. There
is lots of good drinking, like Guy Saget's Pouilly-
Fumé and Simon Hackett's Old Vine Grenache
from McLaren Vale. There are also some surprises,
for example a couple of rather startling Spanish
wines – 1976 Vina Bosconia Cosecha from Vina*

Tondonia, a very old Rioja at £49.95, and an even older Rioja, 1968 Castillo Ygay Gran Reserva from Marqués de Murrieta at £99.99.

1997 Old Vine Grenache, Simon Hacket, McLaren Vale, £10.79 Concentrated, supple red from South Australia.

WAITROSE (WAI)

Head office Doncastle Rd, Southern Industrial Area, Bracknell, Berks RG12 8YA (01344) 424680. (Mail order) freephone 0800 188881, freefax 0800 188888. 118 licensed stores
E-MAIL joe-wadsack@waitrose.co.uk
WEB SITE www.waitrose.co.uk
HOURS Mon–Tue 8.30–6, Wed–Thurs 8.30–8, Fri 8.30–9, Sat 8.30–6 **CARDS** Amex, MasterCard, Visa **DISCOUNTS** 5% 6 bottles or more **DELIVERY** (From Waitrose Direct/ Findlater Mackie Todd) Free for orders of £75 or more throughout mainland UK or Isle of Wight, otherwise £3.95 **EN PRIMEUR** Bordeaux, Port. **G M T**

Far and away the most interesting of the supermarkets. It's not absolutely the cheapest, but you get what you pay for: the quality is consistently good, and there is far less of the blandness that afflicts most supermarkets. Waitrose has for years been a good place to look for bargain sweet whites from Bordeaux, and it's excellent in less fashionable areas like Alsace and Germany. Waitrose own-label Champagne is one to look for, as well. It also sells Manzanilla in half bottles which actually tastes fresh: I'd almost given up buying Manzanilla because it is so hard to find anything that tastes remotely as it should. Waitrose is beginning to re-convert me. I just hope it keeps the standard up.

1996 Monbazillac, Château Vignal Labrie, £8.99 Good marzipan and peaches sweetie from a decent year.

1994 Marqués de Murrieta Reserva Blanco, £7.95 Lovely waxy white Rioja, fresher than it used to be but still nicely traditional in style.

WATERLOO WINE CO (WAT)

6 Vine Yard, London SE1 1QL, 0207-403 7967, fax 0207-357 6976; shop at 59–61 Lant Street, London SE1 1QN
HOURS Mon–Fri 10–6.30, Sat 10–5 **CARDS** Amex, MasterCard, Switch, Visa **DELIVERY** Free

5 cases in central London (otherwise £5); elsewhere (per case), 1 case £8.23, 2 cases £5.88, 3 cases £5.29, 4 cases £4.99, further reductions according to quantity. **G T**
An enterprising merchant that stocks wines it loves, rather than just what will sell easily. So you'll find lots of German wines here, including parcels of old bottles picked up at auction; umpteen different cuvées of Alsace from Seltz (which is an agency) and lots of Loires. Waterloo is the agent for Lamé-Delisle-Boucard, which sounds like an ad agency but is actually a terrifically good Bourgueil grower. Waterloo also has its own New Zealand vineyard, Waipara West; and you'll find Mark Rattray wines here as well.

1997 Corbières, Château Hélène, £4.75 Spicy red Corbières that manages to combine tradition with modernity.

1995 Bourgueil Cuvée Vieilles Vignes, Lamé-Delisle-Boucard, £5.65 Really needs a couple more years, but then it will last for years more. Rich but grassy fruit.

WHITESIDES OF CLITHEROE (WHI)

Shawbridge St, Clitheroe, Lancs BB7 1NA, (01200) 422281, fax (01200) 427129
E-MAIL brianh@anterprise.net
HOURS Mon–Fri 9–6, Sat 9–5.30 **CARDS** MasterCard, Switch, Visa **DISCOUNTS** 5% per case. **G M T**
A nice list that covers the world pretty effectively, without going into any single region in much depth. Australia looks interesting, with Rosemount's Cabernet Sauvignon from its Orange Vineyard in New South Wales; agencies include Viña Ijalba and Bodegas Los Tinos, both from Spain.

1993 Muscadet sur lie, Chateau de Chasseloir, £8.99 Muscadet that breaks the rules: not only is it not the youngest possible vintage (you probably spotted that), but it's been aged in oak. Rich and nutty.

WINE RACK (WR)

See First Quench.

WINE SOCIETY (WS)

Gunnels Wood Rd, Stevenage, Herts SG1 2BG, (01438) 741177, fax (01438) 761167; order line tel (01438) 740222

E-MAIL winesociety@dial.pipex.com
HOURS Mon–Fri 8.30–9, Sat 9–2; showroom:
Mon–Fri 9–5.30, Sat 9–4 **CARDS** MasterCard,
Switch, Visa **DISCOUNTS** (per case) £1 for 5–9,
£2 for 10 or more, £3 for collection **DELIVERY**
Free 1 case or more UK mainland and Northern
Ireland. Collection facility at Hesdin, France at
French rates of duty and VAT **EN PRIMEUR**
Bordeaux, Burgundy, Germany, Port, Rhône.
C G M T

*I seem to spend my life recommending The Wine
Society to people. And when I do, they always
sound surprised: why? Does the Wine Society have
a staid reputation? It shouldn't do. It has exactly the
sort of list that should appeal to anyone with a
serious interest in drinking interesting, varied wines
at good prices. In fact, in those terms it's extremely
hard to beat. This is quite simply one of the best
lists in the country. Pretty well every region is
covered in depth, from Beaujolais through the rest
of France; Tuscany and the rest of Italy; Spain;
Portugal (yippee); Australia, South America….
There's not a great deal from Eastern Europe (one
Bulgarian red, to be precise); I thought there'd been
more in previous years, but I can't be certain.*
**1997 Albis, Vinho Regional Terras do Sado,
£4.65** Aromatic, crisp, white and Portuguese.
**1993 Weinert, Cavas de Weinert, Argentina
£9.95** The Wine Society describes this red blend
as 'the cat's pyjamas'. I wouldn't dream of
arguing. Big, rich and luscious.
1996 Chardonnay, Heggies, Eden Valley, £9.95
This Aussie Chardonnay is all honey and cream,
and would knock spots of most white
Burgundies at the same price.

WINE TREASURY (WT)

69–71 Bondway, London SW8 1SQ, 0207-793
9999, fax 0207-793 8080
E-MAIL quality@winetreasury.com
WEB SITE www.winetreasury.com
HOURS Mon–Fri 9.30–5.30 **CARDS** MasterCard,
Visa **DISCOUNTS** 5% for unmixed cases; £60
per year Syndicate membership gives 25%
discount **DELIVERY** £6 1 case, free 2 or more
cases, England and Wales; Scotland phone for
details **MINIMUM ORDER** 1 mixed case. **M T**

*If you buy wine here you can join the Wine Treasury
Syndicate, which gives you a 25 per cent discount
on normal prices; there's an annual membership
fee of £60, however, so you've got to spend a fair
bit to make it worthwhile. Normal prices don't look
exactly cheap. There are lots of good agencies,
however: Phelps, Shafer, Stag's Leap Wine Cellars,
Cline, Sequoia Grove, Sanford, Alban and J Fritz in
California, and Penley Estate, Virgin Hills and Prince
Albert Vineyard in Australia among them. California
is a speciality, and the selection is excellent – but
California is expensive, and there's no way round
that. The Italian list is also strong, with wines from
Roberto Voerzio, Luciano Sandrone and others;
France is equally well covered.*
**1995 Mourvèdre Ancient Vines, Cline Cellars,
California, £10.26** Intensity and fruit, from the
grandson of the inventor of the Jacuzzi. I thought
you'd want to know that.

WINES OF WESTHORPE LTD (WIW)

Marchington, Staffs ST14 8NX, (01283) 820285,
fax (01283) 820631
E-MAIL wines@westhorpe.demon.co.uk
HOURS Mon–Sat 8.30–6 **CARDS** MasterCard,
Switch, Visa **DISCOUNTS** (per case) £2 for
6–15, £4 for 16–25; further discounts if wines
collected **DELIVERY** Free UK mainland 2 or
more cases **MINIMUM ORDER** 1 mixed case. **M**
*An Eastern European specialist with a long list from
Bulgaria and Hungary interspersed with Chileans
and Australians. The Tokajis look the best wines.*
**1988 Tokaji Aszú 5 Puttonyos Chateau
Messzelato, £7.28 (50cl)** Intense and unctuous.

C = cellarage   **G** = glass loan/hire   **M** = mail order   **T** = tastings and talks

WRIGHT WINE CO (WRI)

The Old Smithy, Raikes Rd, Skipton, N. Yorks
BD23 1NP, (01756) 700886, 24-hour
answerphone (01756) 794175, fax (01756)
798580
E-MAIL Bob@wineandwhisky.co.uk
WEB SITE www.wineandwhisky.co.uk
HOURS Mon–Sat 9–6 **CARDS** MasterCard,
Switch, Visa **DISCOUNTS** Wholesale price unsplit
case, 5% mixed case **DELIVERY** Free within 30
miles, elsewhere at cost. **G**

*There are masses of unusual wines here, and most
of them won't break the bank. Somebody has an
eye for good flavours and good value, and is also
taking the trouble to go off the beaten track in the
search for wines. When people do that it always
shows. In fact I'd say it's the difference between a
serious and exciting wine merchant and and a dull,
workaday one – who merely buys caseloads from
half a dozen wholesalers, and puts them on the
shelf. At Wright Wine you'll find good Bordeaux,
Rhône, Alsace, southern French, South African,
Australian, Spanish and Italian. Agencies include
Vidal-Fleury in the Rhône and Julian Chivite in
Navarra.*

**1997 Vin de Pays d'Oc Syrah, Cuvée de la
Couthiat, Domaine Alain Paret, £5.50** Berried
fruit with some smoke; good value.

PETER WYLIE FINE WINES (WY)

Plymtree Manor, Plymtree, Cullompton, Devon
EX15 2LE, (01884) 277555, fax (01884) 277557
E-MAIL peter@wylie-fine-wines.demon.co.uk
WEB SITE www.wyliefinewines.co.uk
HOURS Mon–Fri 9–6 **CARDS** None
DISCOUNTS Unsplit cases **DELIVERY** (per case)
1 case £15, 2 cases £7.50, 3–4 £6, 5 or more
£4.50 **EN PRIMEUR** Bordeaux. **C M**

*A serious list of seriously fine wines, focusing on
Bordeaux. Anniversary wines are a speciality: a half
bottle of Mouton Rothschild 1909, for example, for
£250 (and a half bottle is quite enough for anyone
coming up to their ninetieth birthday. Give them a
full bottle and anything could happen). I notice it
was £141 last year. You can buy le Pin here, and any
number of other fashionable and hugely expensive
clarets, plus double magnums and imperials.*

1900 Verdelho, d'Oliveira Reserve, £290
Madeira for the Millennium?

YAPP BROTHERS (YAP)

The Old Brewery, Mere, Wilts BA12 6DY,
(01747) 860423, fax (01747) 860929
E-MAIL sales@yapp.co.uk
WEB SITE www.yapp.co.uk
HOURS Mon–Fri 9–5, Sat 9–1 **CARDS**
MasterCard, Switch, Visa **DISCOUNTS** £3 per
case on collection, quantity discount on 6 or
more cases **DELIVERY** £3 single case, 2 or more
cases free. **C G M T**

*The Yapps have now been in business for 30 years
and have developed a superlative list from the
Rhône and Loire, with informed comment and
quirky wines from top producers. The list meanders
through the South of France, too, from Banyuls and
Jurançon to Bellet and the Coteaux d'Aix, most of
these being regions that are neglected by more
mainstream lists.*

**1997 Tavel Rosé la Forcadière, Armand &
Roger Maby, £7.75** Top-flight Tavel, all herbs
and strawberries.

1994 Alsace Riesling, Charles Schléret, £7.95
Superlative Alsace Riesling, meticulously made
and cheap at the price.

**1995 Irouléguy, Cuvée Bixintxo, Peio Espil,
£12.75** Pure Tannat from old vines; this wine
needs cellaring for several years. Apparently the
'x's are pronounced 'shush'. Try it: it sounds as
though your jaws have been wired together.

NOEL YOUNG WINES (YOU)

56 High Street, Trumpington, Cambridge CB2
2LS, (01223) 844744, fax (01223) 844736
E-MAIL admin@nywines.co.uk
WEB SITE www.nywines.co.uk
HOURS Mon–Sat 10–9, Sun 12–2 **CARDS**
MasterCard, Switch, Visa **DISCOUNTS** 5% for
orders over £500 **DELIVERY** £7.50 on orders up
to £50, £6 on orders up to £100, £5 on orders
up to £500, free over £500 **MINIMUM ORDER** 1
mixed case **EN PRIMEUR** Australia, Burgundy,
California, Rhône. **G M T**

*I think the wine world needs an official definition of
Fine Wines. Lots of merchants have Fine Wine lists,
kept hygienically separate from their main lists, and
no doubt useful as a place to keep the classed-
growth clarets. But when you look at them you
sometimes can't work out just where the
boundaries lie: why one wine is considered Fine*

while another, at much the same price, is considered Common or Garden. The problem is particularly acute at Noel Young because everything's so good. Most of the sherries, for example, don't make it to the Fine Wine list. Well, okay, I can understand why Croft Original doesn't – but Lustau's almacenista sherries don't, either. Not, of course, that it really matters. The point is that there is a terrific list of wines from all over the world here; Noel Young doesn't focus on the cheapest end of the market, though. Perhaps he should change the name to Noel Young Fine Wines. Then he could have a separate Even Finer Wines list.

1997 Fleurie les Garants, Domaine de Vissoux, Unfiltered, £9.79 Yes, I know it's a shocking price for Beaujolais, but it really is good: rich and plummy and well structured.

1994 Pago de Carraovejas, Bodegas Del Carraovejas, Ribera del Duero, £9.99 Rich red from Spain with a touch of Cabernet Sauvignon to it. It needs a bit more time in bottle.

1997 Riesling Select, Weingut Wieninger, Austria, £10.99 Dry Riesling from Vienna. Great power and body.

WHO'S WHERE

Name codes are shown for merchants whose wines appear in the Price Guides. All merchants are listed in the Merchant Directory.

LONDON

Balls Brothers	BALL
Adam Bancroft	BAN
Berry Bros. & Rudd	BER
Bibendum	BIB
Cave Cru Classé	CAV
Corney & Barrow	CB
Domaine Direct	DOM
Farr Vintners	FA
Fortnum & Mason	FORT
Friarwood	FRI
Fuller's	FUL
Gelston Castle Fine Wines	
Goedhuis & Co	
Haynes Hanson & Clark	HAH
Jeroboams	JER
Justerini & Brooks	JU
Lea & Sandeman	LEA
Liberty Wines	LIB
Montrachet	MON
Moreno Wines	MOR
Morris & Verdin	MV
New London Wine	NLW
NZ Wines Direct	NZW
Le Nez Rouge	NEZ
Philglas & Swiggot	PHI
La Réserve	RES
Howard Ripley	RIP
Roberson	ROB
RSJ Wine Company	RSJ
Unwins	UN
La Vigneronne	
Waterloo Wine Co	WAT
Wine Treasury	WT

SOUTH-EAST AND HOME COUNTIES

Australian Wine Club	AUS
Benedict's	
Berry Bros. & Rudd	BER
Butlers Wine Cellar	BU
Cape Province Wines	CAP
Ben Ellis Wines	ELL
Le Fleming Wines	FLE
Fuller's	FUL

Douglas Henn-Macrae	
High Breck Vintners	HIG
Unwins	UN

WEST AND SOUTH-WEST

Averys of Bristol	AV
Bennetts	BEN
Châteaux Wines	CHA
Croque-en-Bouche	CRO
Great Western Wine	GW
John Harvey & Sons	HA
Haynes Hanson & Clark	HAH
Laymont & Shaw	
Nadder Wines Ltd	NA
The Nobody Inn	NO
Christopher Piper Wines	PIP
Reid Wines (1992) Ltd	REI
Rose Tree Wine Co	ROS
Savage Selection	SAV
Peter Wylie Fine Wines	WY
Yapp Brothers	YAP

EAST ANGLIA

Adnams	AD
Amey's Wines	AME
Anthony Byrne	BY
Corney & Barrow	CB
Roger Harris Wines	HAW
Lay & Wheeler	LAY
Thos. Peatling	
Satchells	SAT
T & W Wines	TW
Noel Young Wines	YOU

MIDLANDS

Connolly's	CON
Gauntleys	GAU
Hedley Wright	HED
SH Jones	JON
William Morrison	MORR
Portland Wine Co	POR
Stevens Garnier	STE
Tanners	TAN
Vintage Wines Ltd	VIN
Wines of Westhorpe	WIW

NORTH

Booths	BO
Great Northern Wine Co	
Le Nez Rouge	NEZ

William Morrison	MORR
Penistone Court	PEN
Playford Ros	PLAY
Frank Stainton Wines	STA
Whitesides of Clitheroe	WHI
Wright Wine Co	WRI

WALES

Ashley Scott	AS
Ballantynes of Cowbridge	BAL
Terry Platt	PLA
Tanners	TAN

SCOTLAND

Corney & Barrow	CB
Gelston Castle Fine Wines	
Peter Green & Co	
Cockburns of Leith	COC
Justerini & Brooks	JU
Le Nez Rouge	NEZ
Lloyd Taylor Wines	
Raeburn Fine Wines	RAE
The Ubiquitous Chip	UB
Valvona & Crolla	VA

CHANNEL ISLANDS

Sommelier Wine Co	SOM

NORTHERN IRELAND

Direct Wine Shipments	DI
James Nicholson	NI

COUNTRYWIDE

ASDA	ASD
Bordeaux Direct	
Bottoms Up	BOT
CWS (Co-op)	CO
Majestic	MAJ
Marks & Spencer	MAR
Millésima	MI
Oddbins	OD
Safeway	SAF
Sainsbury's	SAI
Somerfield	SO
Sunday Times Wine Club	
Tesco	TES
Thresher	THR
Victoria Wine	VIC
Waitrose	WAI
Wine Rack	WR
Wine Society	WS

INDEX